TUTORIAL:

PRINCIPLES OF COMMUNICATION AND NETWORKING PROTOCOLS

Simon S. Lam

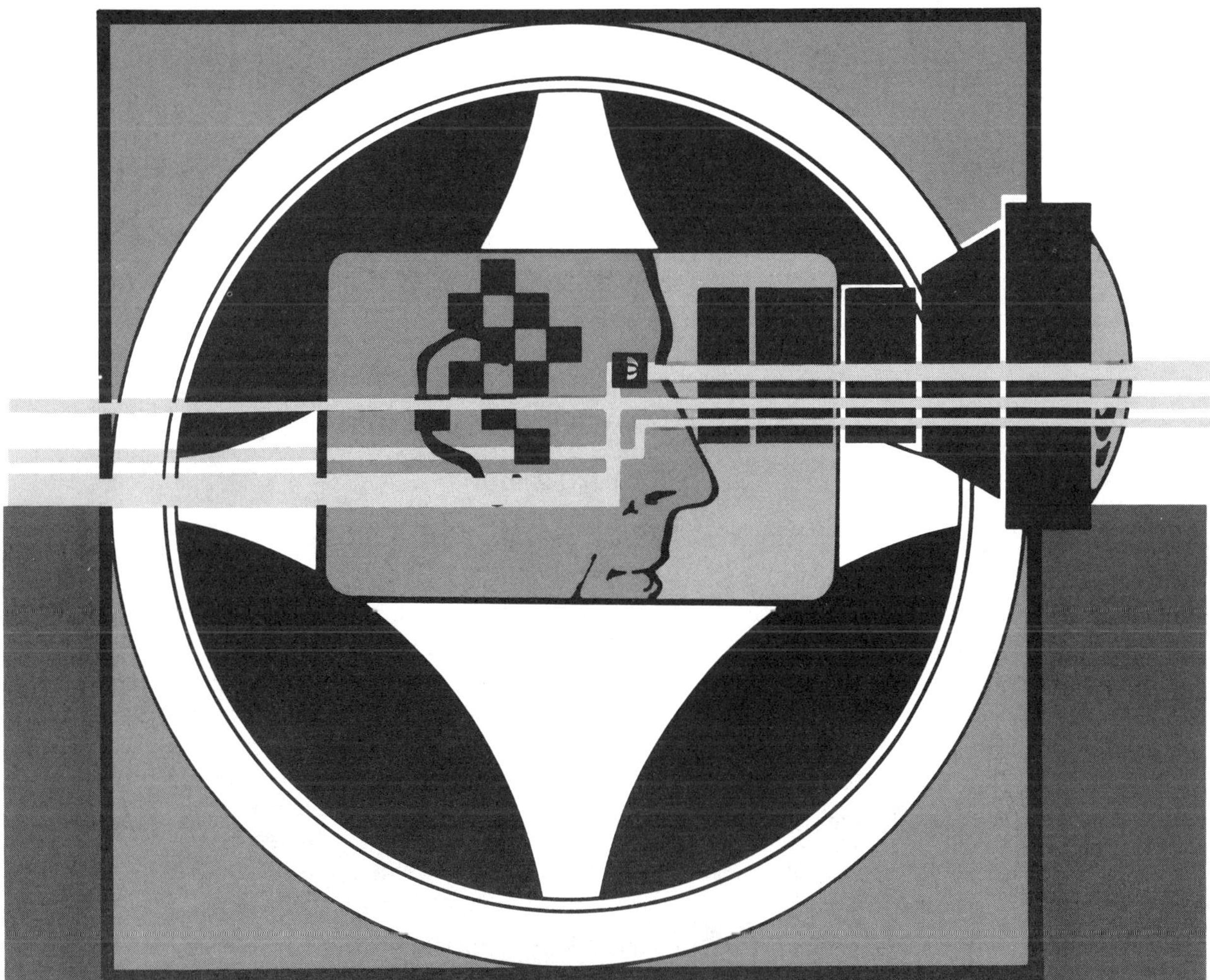

IEEE CATALOG NUMBER EHO216-2
LIBRARY OF CONGRESS NUMBER 84-81318
IEEE COMPUTER SOCIETY ORDER NUMBER 582
ISBN 0-8186-0582-0

COMPUTER SOCIETY PRESS

1884 1984 THE INSTITUTE OF ELECTRICAL AND ELECTRONICS ENGINEERS, INC.

IEEE COMPUTER SOCIETY

Published by IEEE Computer Society Press
1109 Spring Street
Suite 300
Silver Spring, MD 20910

IEEE CATALOG NUMBER EH0216-2
LIBRARY OF CONGRESS NUMBER 84-81318
IEEE COMPUTER SOCIETY ORDER NUMBER 582
ISBN 0-8186-0582-0 (Paper)
ISBN 0-8186-4582-2 (Microfiche)

Order from: IEEE Computer Society
Post Office Box 80452
Worldway Postal Center
Los Angeles, CA 90080

IEEE Service Center
445 Hoes Lane
Piscataway, NJ 08854

1884 · 1984 A CENTURY OF ELECTRICAL PROGRESS THE INSTITUTE OF ELECTRICAL AND ELECTRONICS ENGINEERS, INC.

PREFACE

For a computer communication network to provide communication services with desirable characteristics to its users and to utilize its resources efficiently, many protocols are needed. Such protocols are implemented as collections of parallel programs. Like any large programming system, the development of the protocols of a large network will benefit from a structured approach. Technical issues in the design and construction of protocols for computer communication networks constitute the subject matter of this tutorial. Protocols for most categories of packet-switching networks (local area nets, wide area nets and internets) are considered. This book is, however, different from the two other IEEE Computer Society tutorials in the general area of networking (*Local Computer Networks* by Thurber and Freeman and *Computer Networks* by Abrams and Cotton). Our emphasis is on the technical problems encountered in the design and construction of protocols and on solutions to these problems. We strive to illustrate fundamental principles for understanding protocols. For example, we do not present the open systems interconnection (OSI) model as *the* architectural model. Instead, we discuss protocol structuring principles (in Chapter 1). The OSI model is then presented as one of many models that can be derived from an application of such principles.

This book is organized into seven chapters. Chapter 1 presents fundamentals of computer communication networks. Chapter 2 covers data link control protocols. Chapter 3 covers multiple access protocols. Chapter 4 discusses local area networks. Chapter 5 addresses resource allocation problems and solution techniques in store-and-forward networks with point-to-point links. Chapter 6 covers communication protocols for wide area networks and internetworks. Chapter 7 presents some models and methods for protocol verification and construction. Each chapter begins with several sections of original text, followed by a list of references and a set of reprinted articles. We attempt to point out in the original text how the referenced articles and the reprinted articles in each chapter fit into some general framework and how different ideas and techniques relate to each other.

Most of the reprinted articles have been used in graduate courses on data communications and on network protocols that I have taught at the University of Texas at Austin over the past seven years. This book is intended to be a tutorial text and *not* a reprint collection of seminal articles and articles describing important developments for the first time. Although some of the reprinted articles are indeed seminal papers, many of the reprinted articles were chosen on the basis of their subject coverage, their depth of coverage, and writing style. For example, the Shoch-Dalal-Redell-Crane article on Ethernet is reprinted rather than the seminal paper by Metcalfe and Boggs. The reference lists also tend to be representative rather than bibliographical in nature. We believe that they provide an adequate starting set for newcomers to this field. But there is no doubt that we have left out numerous important articles in the literature.

This book should be appropriate as the text or a source of supplemental readings for a graduate-level course on computer communication networks. It should be valuable also as a reference for systems engineers and analysts who desire an understanding of the technical principles that underlie the design of communication network software and the performance tradeoffs involved in its design.

All of the original text and the majority of the reprinted articles can be read without any special background in mathematics. However, some experience with computer programming (in any high-level language) is helpful. Many of the reprinted articles in Chapters 3 and 7 and some in Chapter 5 do require a certain amount of background in calculus and basic probability theory. These articles are placed at the end of those chapters and can be skipped by the reader if so desired.

I wish to express my appreciation to the authors and publishers of the articles we have reprinted. I would also like to thank the Computer Society Press editor, Professor Chuan-Lin Wu, and the reviewers for their valuable inputs.

The final packaging of this tutorial was done by Margaret Brown of the Computer Society Press. The original text was typed by K. F. Carbone of the University of Texas at Austin. Both of them should be congratulated for a job well done.

Simon S. Lam

Table of Contents

Chapter 1
Fundamentals of Computer Communication Networks

1.1. WHY DO WE NEED PROTOCOLS?

First we attempt to answer a more fundamental question: What is a protocol? According to McQuillan and Cerf [MCQU 78], "the word protocol has been borrowed from the parlance of conventional social behavior to describe the orderly exchange of information between separate pieces of equipment." We shall, however, use the word *protocol* with a more concrete meaning. A protocol in this text is a set of parallel programs that provides one or more functions within a computer communication network environment, as defined by the protocol's service specification. There is a wide variety of such functions. They include, for examples, the management of logical channels, the opening/closing of logical channels, reliable data transfers at different levels (data link, host-to-host, etc.), routing, flow and congestion controls, deadlock avoidance, multiple access in broadcast channels, and concurrency control of distributed databases, among many others. Most of these functions fall into two broad categories: (1) communication functions, and (2) network resource allocation functions. Protocols that implement these functions will be referred to as *communication protocols* and *resource allocation protocols*, respectively.

The ultimate objective of a computer communication network is to allow *user processes* located in different computing equipment to exchange data reliably. This is really the same objective as interprocess communication within a multiprogramming or a multiprocessor environment. However, we must do without the reliability and speed of computer buses. As the geographical distance between communicating user processes increases, the general trend is that the speeds of the available communication channels decrease, their error rates go up, their propagation delays go up, and their costs go up drastically.

For examples, long-distance telephone lines at 56 Kbps with a bit error rate of 1 in 10^7 are considered to be of very high quality. Satellite channels can provide transmission rates of several to tens of Mbps over long distances, but they have a propagation delay of about 0.27 seconds. Earth stations for satellite communications at the 4 and 6 GHz frequencies are large and expensive. Satellite communications at higher frequencies, such as 12 and 14 GHz, permit the use of smaller, less expensive earth stations suitable for installation on user sites [BARN 77]. Using forward error correction coding (at a rate of approximately two-thirds), a bit error rate of 1 in 10^7 is achievable. However, transmissions at such high frequencies suffer from the problem of rain attenuation which decreases availability. On the other hand, local area networks which span only hundreds to thousands of feet have relatively good transmission characteristics. Presently, transmission speeds range from a few hundred Kbps for some to Ethernet's 10 Mbps and to Hyperchannel's 50 Mbps. Error rates ranging from 1 packet in 6,000 to 1 packet in 2,000,000 were reported for Ethernet [SHOC 80].

In Figure 1-1, we illustrate a set of computing equipment to be referred to as *user* (or *host*) nodes. A network of communication facilities provides the physical interconnection of these user nodes. Logical communication paths between processes residing in user nodes are provided by protocols. Because of the relatively high cost of the communication facilities, resource allocation protocols are often employed to dynamically share these facilities in some fashion. Because of errors and relatively large and unpredictable transit

EHO216-2/84/0000/0001$01.00

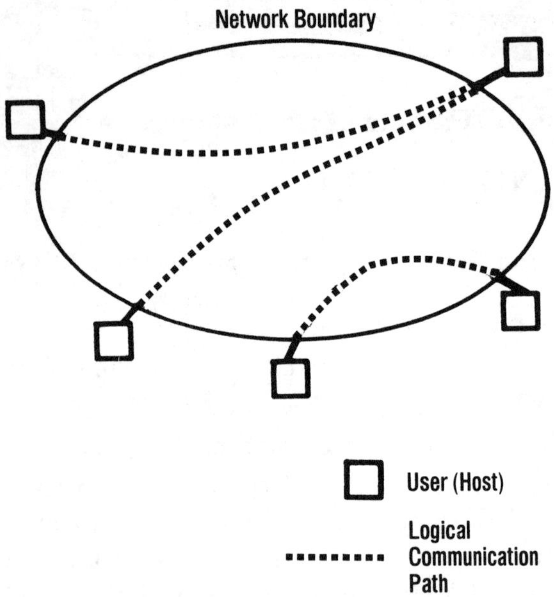

Figure 1-1. Logical communication paths between users.

delays, protocols are usually needed to provide the functions of error control and in-sequence delivery. For the same reasons, protocols are usually needed to reach various agreements between users, e.g., opening/closing of a dialog and security keys to be used. These are referred to as communication protocols.

1.2. SYNCHRONIZATION FUNCTIONS TO ACHIEVE COMMUNICATION

Network users correspond to various kinds of terminals and computers, large or small, which are generally referred to as data terminating equipment in the protocol standards literature. Each user node typically has a separate device, which we shall call a *transceiver*, with the the functional capability of sending and receiving bits serially over a communication link (or path). Examples of transceivers are modems for broadband channels or line driver-receiver units for baseband channels.

For this section, we shall ignore the complicating issues of network topologies and switching techniques. These will be addressed in Sections 1.3 and 1.4. Let us identify the basic functions for achieving communication between two processes residing in user nodes connected by a single communication link (Figure 1-2). These functions are referred to as *synchronization functions* and they can be structured into a hierarchy of five levels [LAM 83]. Figure 1-3 illustrates the levels as well as the concept of increasing time granularity which can be explained as follows. Consider the time points of event occurrences at the two communicating user nodes. Level *n* has a larger time granularity than that of level *n*-1 because the time points at which "synchronism" is achieved for level *n* are embedded in the time points at which "synchronism" is achieved for level *n*-1. This concept will become clear as we describe what the synchronization functions are. A discussion of the five levels of functions will proceed from the bottom of the hierarchy upwards.

Bit synchronization

This level deals with the receiver's ability to retrieve bits serially from an incoming signal. The users must agree upon the encoding and modulation techniques. The receiver must also be able to retrieve bit-timing information from the incoming signal. The subject of bit synchronization is beyond the scope of this text. The reader is referred to books by Schwartz [SCHW 80] and Viterbi [VITE 66] that cover this subject.

Frame synchronization

A frame is defined here to be a serial block of bits containing both data and control information. It is the basic unit of communication between two user nodes connected by a physical link. (This is consistent with the meaning of "frame" in the class of data link protocols exemplified by HDLC [LAM 83].) This level establishes conventions to delimit within a continuous stream of bits the beginning bit and the ending bit of a frame. Another function at this level is to detect errors in frames received and to filter out corrupted frames. With frame synchronization, uncorrupted blocks of bits containing data and/or control information can be sent from one user node to

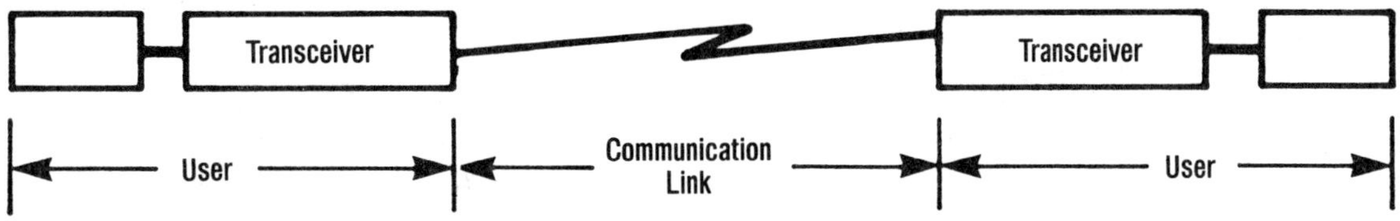

Figure 1-2. Two communicating users.

another via a dedicated physical link, although losses may occur.

Multiple access synchronization

This level of function is needed if a physical communication channel is shared by multiple sender-receiver pairs. Since frames transmitted by different senders are interleaved in time, an addressing scheme is needed to identify the sender and receiver of each frame. In addition, control messages and algorithms are needed to synchronize the actions of senders to avoid (or resolve) channel-access conflicts efficiently. With multiple access synchronization, uncorrupted frames can be sent from one user node to another via a *shared communication* link. Again, losses may occur.

Content synchronization

Given that user nodes can send frames to each other, this level of function is concerned with the information content of each frame, in particular: (1) how to differentiate between data and control information within a frame, (2) how to encode control messages, and (3) how to use control messages to perform error control and to achieve in-sequence delivery of frames, if these functions are desired by the user processes.

Dialog synchronization

The basic function at this level is the initiation and subsequent termination of a dialog between two user processes during which the transfer of frames containing data can take place. (Instead of a dialog between two processes, one can also think of a broadcast from one to many or a conference call involving multiple user processes.) In addition to reaching agreement on the status (up or down) of a logical connection between user nodes, other possible synchronization functions at this level are:

1. agreement on the relationship between the user nodes, e.g., balanced, and master-slave;
2. agreement on the mode of interaction suitable for a particular application, e.g., file transfer, database inquiry/response, and digital speech traffic;
3. agreement on flow control parameters; and
4. agreement on encryption/decryption keys for secure data transfer.

Recovery actions are needed when a disagreement is detected or when a connection is deemed to be lost (for instance, lack of response to a previous inquiry). This level of function also includes the responsibility of reporting errors and disagreements that cannot be recovered to the user processes.

In summary, we observe that bit and frame

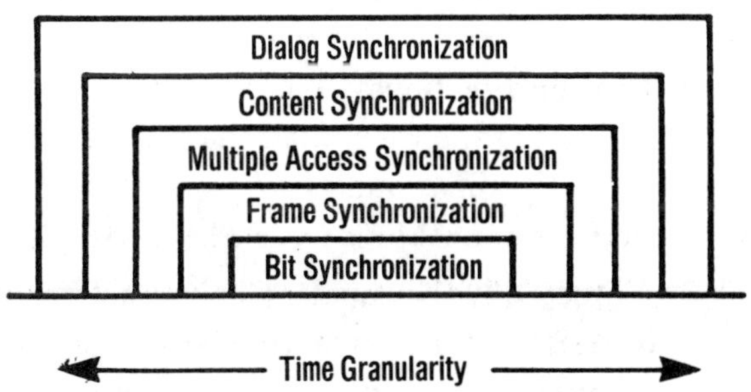

Figure 1-3. A hierarchy of synchronization functions.

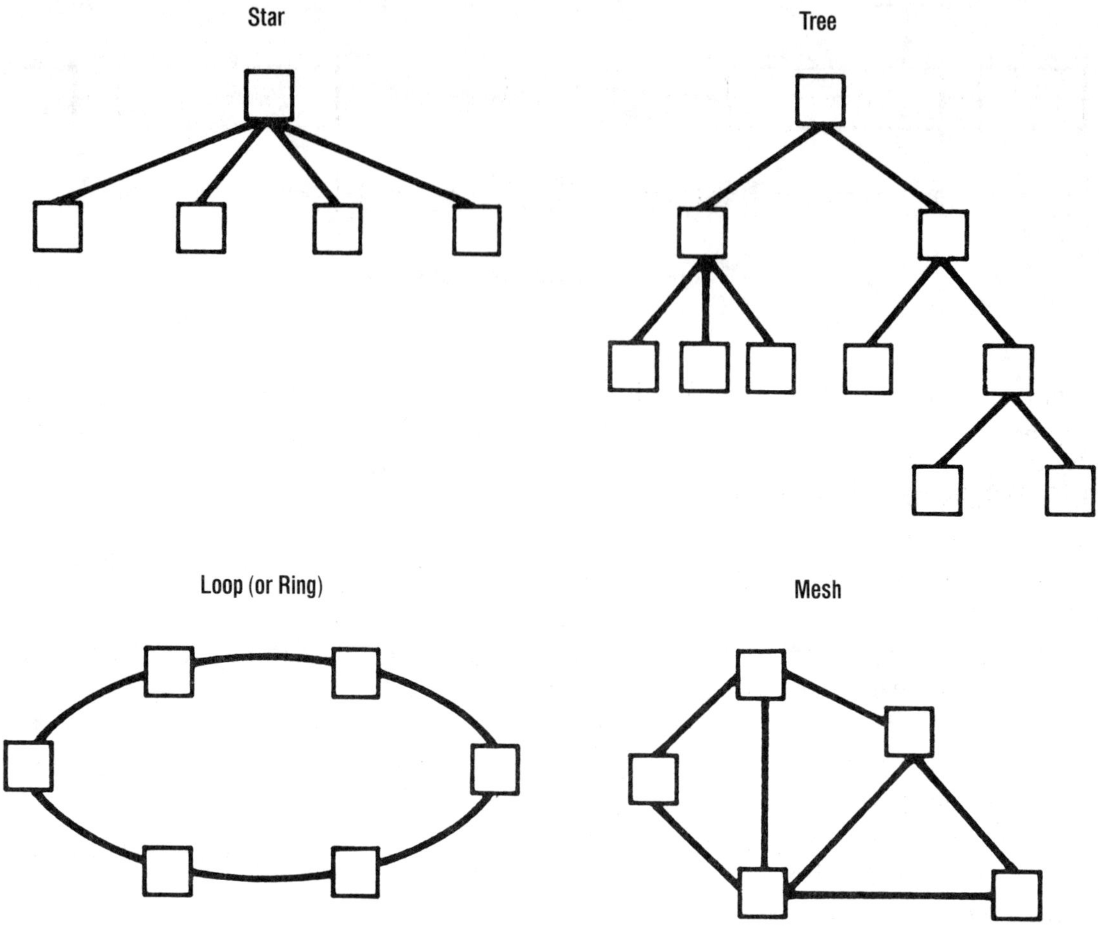

Figure 1-4. Topologies of networks with point-to-point links.

synchronizations are necessary for the most rudimentary form of communication between two different machines. Functions at the top three levels are not absolutely necessary, but they are useful for improving the efficient utilization of the communication link (in the case of multiple access synchronization functions) or for improving the quality and characteristics of the logical connection (in the case of content and dialog synchronization functions).

1.3. NETWORK TOPOLOGY

In Figure 1-1, the topology of the network of communication facilities is not shown. The topology of a network depends on the communication media involved. With point-to-point links, some common topologies are shown in Figure 1-4: star, loop (or ring), tree, and mesh. We define a mesh topology to be one that has at least two disjoint paths between any pair of nodes. Note that this definition is also satisfied by a loop. The loop is a limiting case of our definition and will be considered separately.

Broadcast networks are those that employ a broadcast channel for interconnection. Figure 1-5 illustrates three broadcast networks employing a coaxial cable, a radio channel and a satellite channel. Broadcast networks have the property that any node can transmit into the broadcast channel, and each transmission in the channel can be received by all nodes in the network.

The topology of a network may be organized into several levels. Typically, there are two levels,

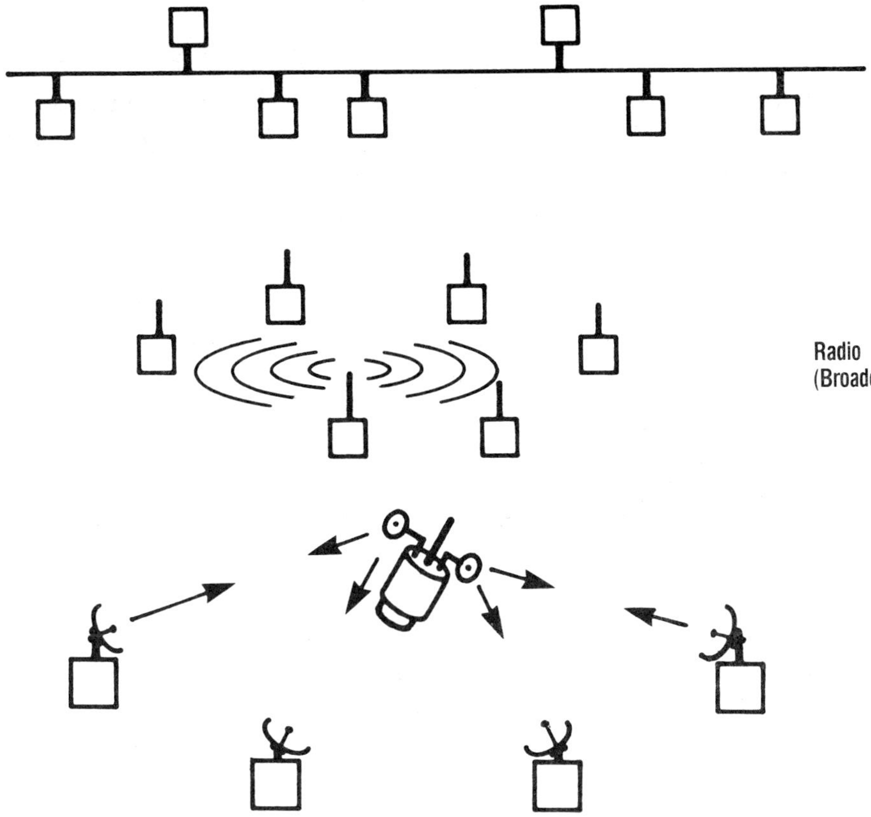

Figure 1-5. Broadcast networks.

i.e., a wide area network (WAN) serving as the backbone at the upper level, with access to it provided by many local area networks (LANs) at the lower level. Any one of the above topologies can be used for a WAN or a LAN. However, the topologies typically used for a LAN are: star, multipoint, loop, tree, and radio. The topologies typically used for a WAN are: mesh (for reliability), and satellite (for high capacity or for complete connectivity). A WAN may also be constructed with a combination of point-to-point links and satellite broadcast channels. LANs that access the WAN may have different topologies at different locations. (An example of a two-level topology is shown in Figure 1-6.)

A hierarchy of more than two levels may be used for several reasons. First, the topology of a very large network may be organized into several levels for efficiency considerations (e.g., to reduce the size of routing tables). The telephone network is a prime example [MART 76]. Second, the interconnection of autonomous WANs will immediately give rise to a three-level topology, as shown in Figure 1-7. (The interconnection of networks is addressed in Chapter 6.)

1.4. SWITCHING TECHNIQUES

The transmission channels of a communication network constitute the network's primary resource. This resource may be in the form of a single point-to-point communication channel, a network of point-to-point channels (any topology), a broadcast channel, or some combination of the above. Probably the first and most important choice in designing a network's resource allocation mechanisms is the network's *switching technique*.

1.4.1. Sharing a Point-to-Point Channel

Consider a point-to-point communication link between two clusters of users, such as that shown in Figure 1-8. Assume the link to be full-duplex, i.e., there are two communication channels for independent transmission in each of the two directions. (A half-duplex link is one in which transmission can take place in either direction but not simultaneously.)

Multiplexing technology

Each communication channel can be multiplexed into a number of subchannels. There are two different kinds of multiplexing: frequency division multiplexing (FDM) and time division multiplexing (TDM). Figure 1-9 illustrates FDM. The channel bandwidth is subdivided, and a subchannel corresponds to a segment of the bandwidth for all time. Figure 1-10 illustrates TDM. Time is divided into slots which are organized into frames. The entire bandwidth is available to a subchannel, but only during a designated time slot in consecutive frames. The term space division multiplexing is sometimes used to refer to a collection of subchannels, each of which is a separate physical link (e.g., a bundle of wires).

Fixed assignment of channels

This is the simplest resource allocation method. The communication channel to be shared is multiplexed into a number of subchannels, sufficient to allocate one to each sender-receiver pair present. Note that the subchannels do not have to be the same "size," but in practice a subchannel must be large enough to satisfy the response time requirement of the sender-receiver pair using it. For data communication, fixed-assigned subchannels are likely to be very poorly utilized for two reasons. First, user pairs with fixed-assigned subchannels may not be engaged in a dialog most of the time. This problem can be remedied by the demand assignment strategy to be discussed below. Second, even if a user pair is engaging in a dialog, a subchannel will still be lightly utilized if the sender generates data in a bursty manner, i.e., bursts of traffic in between long periods of silence. Highly bursty traffic is typical of most interactive computer applications [LAM 78].

Demand assignment of channels

The utilization of subchannels can be improved by having fewer subchannels than sender-receiver pairs, with the assumption that only some of the user pairs present are engaging in a dialog at any time. A subchannel is allocated only when there is a request to initiate a new dialog and is deallocated at the termination of the dialog. Demand-assigned subchannels will have higher utilization than fixed-assigned subchannels. The price to pay is some processing capability in the

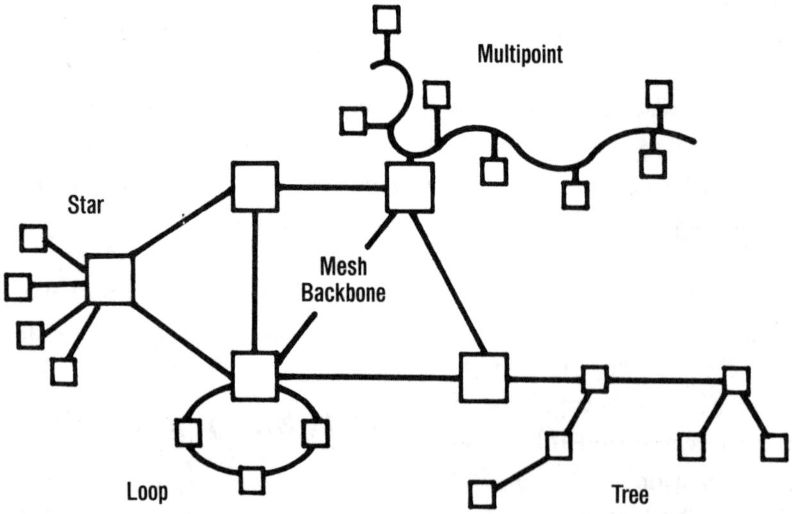

Figure 1-6. An example of a two-level topology.

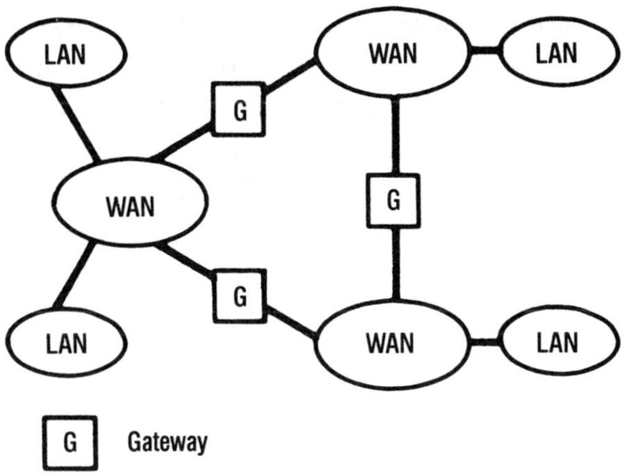

Figure 1-7. WANs interconnected by gateway nodes.

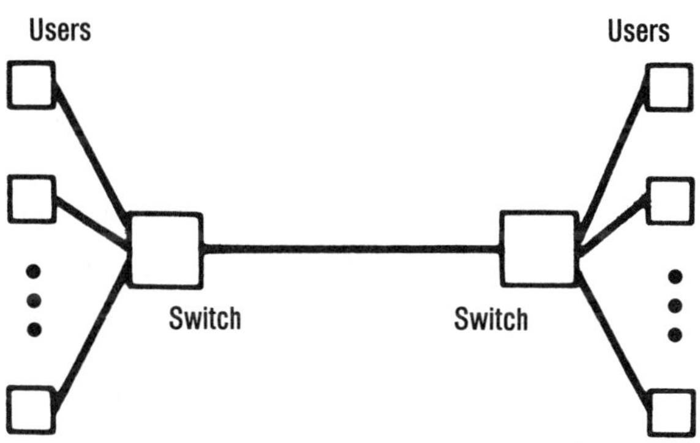

Figure 1-8. A shared point-to-point link.

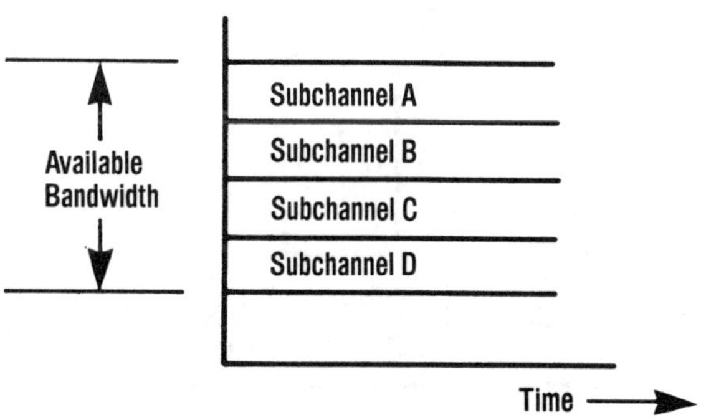

Figure 1-9. An illustration of Frequency Division Multiplexing (FDM).

switching nodes, as shown in Figure 1-8, as well as some delay that will be incurred whenever a request cannot be granted because no free subchannel is available. Note that a subchannel is allocated to a user for the entire duration of a dialog. If the user generates bursty traffic, there will still be long periods of silence during which the subchannel will not be utilized.

Statistical multiplexing

This technique is also called asynchronous time division multiplexing (ATDM). It is intended to allocate transmission bandwidth to a sender, one data unit at a time; in particular, allocation is made only when a data unit is waiting to be sent [CHU 69]. The switching node in this case is sometimes referred to as a data concentrator. Logically, it corresponds to simply a single-server queue (Figure 1-11). The communication channel is the server and the queue is formed of the data units generated by the user nodes that share the channel. This method will allow the communication channel to be utilized very efficiently even if each user node generates bursty traffic individually. What price do we pay for this improved efficiency? First, since data units belonging to different sender-receiver pairs are interleaved in the queue and in the communication channel, they must contain some form of identification (e.g., sender and receiver addresses, or logical channel number). Second, buffers are needed for the queue. And third, some processing capability is needed in the switching node to manage the queue and its scheduling.

The superiority of statistical multiplexing is based upon the phenomenon of scaling in queueing theory. The average delay-throughput performance of a single high-speed channel is better than that of multiple low-speed channels, even though the total amount of bandwidth is the same in each case [KLEI 76].

1.4.2. Sharing a Network of Point-to-Point Links

For user nodes interconnected by a network of communication channels and switching nodes, a routing algorithm is needed to establish a path, statically or dynamically, between each pair of user nodes. (Routing algorithms are covered in Chapter 5.) For this section, it suffices for us to consider a single path between a pair of communicating user nodes as shown in Figure 1-12. The switching techniques can again be divided into two categories: (1) allocation of channels to form end-to-end paths between pairs of users, and (2) allocation of bandwidth to data units (belonging to different source-destination user pairs) waiting in queues.

Channel-based techniques

Each link between two nodes in Figure 1-12 is a collection of channels or circuits. (We follow the common usage that a channel is a means for one-way transmission and a circuit is a means for two-way transmission. Also, we no longer care whether these channels are obtained by time, frequency, or space division multiplexing.) The path determined by a routing algorithm consists of a sequence of communication channels (circuits). As before, these channels (circuits) may be fixed-assigned indefinitely or *demand-assigned* only when there is a request to initiate a dialog between two user nodes and then deallocated at the termination of the dialog. These techniques are known as *circuit switching* (CS) and have been used for a long time in telephone networks.

Circuit switching has worked well as a resource allocation mechanism for networks that handle voice traffic. Channel-based techniques, in general, are appropriate if the users tend to communicate at a fairly constant rate for a long period of time (relative to the time necessary to set up the end-to-end path). Note that with circuit switching, the communicating user nodes must have compatible equipment; the network provides none of the functions mentioned in Section 1.2. In particular, the communicating user nodes must use the same code and operate at the same speed etc.

Figure 1-13(a) illustrates the timing of events along a path between two user nodes when circuit switching is used. Suppose that a user makes a request to set up a connection between itself and another user. A call-request signal then travels through the network according to some routing algorithm, seizing available channels along the way to form an end-to-end path. A call-accept signal travelling back informs the requesting user that the communication path has been set up and that communication may begin. It is obvious from Figure 1-13(a) that, if the connection time is short relative to the setup time or if there are long periods of silence during a connection, the circuits will be poorly utilized.

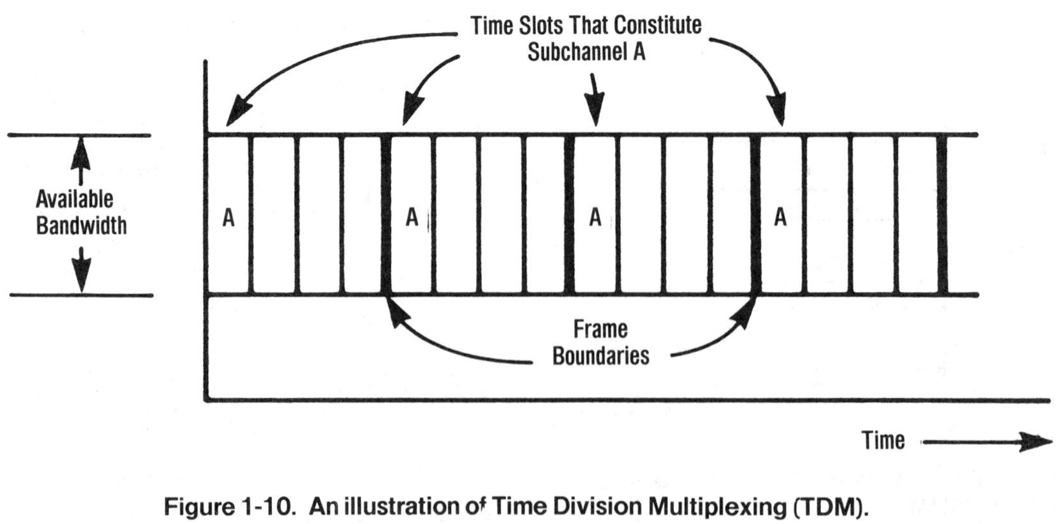

Figure 1-10. An illustration of Time Division Multiplexing (TDM).

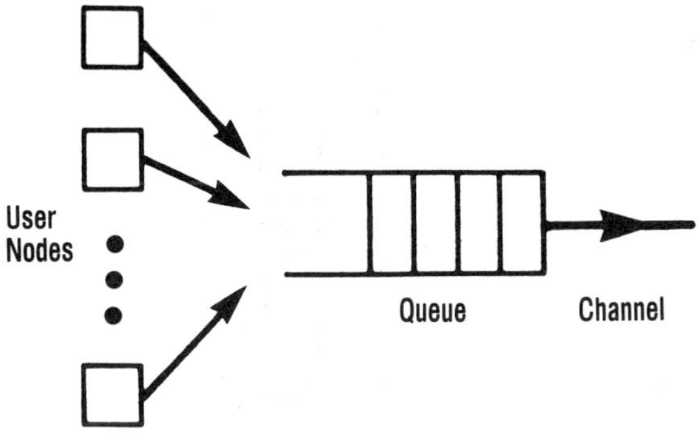

Figure 1-11. A single-server queue.

Queueing-based techniques

The use of queueing to share a communication channel can be extended to a network of channels that interconnect geographically distributed users. As before, the entire bandwidth of each communication channel is allocated to waiting data units, one at a time.

Each data unit travels from its source user node to its destination user node via a sequence of switching nodes along a path determined by some routing algorithm. Upon the receipt of a data unit, each switching node stores a copy of it and forwards the data unit to the next node in its path. Some queueing delay is encountered if the outgoing channel selected is busy. (The stored copy will be discarded when a positive acknowledgement is received from the next node. See discussions on error control in Chapter 2.)

A network operating in this fashion is called a ***store-and-forward*** (SF) network. There are two subcategories: message-switching (MS) networks and packet-switching (PS) networks. The distinction is made by considering what happens to the blocks of data bits that are exchanged between communicating processes residing in user nodes. Such a data block together with any necessary control information will be referred to as a *data message*. A network is said to be a message-switching network if data messages constitute the data units that travel through the network in a store-and-forward manner. A packet-switching network is one in which the data units that travel through the network have a maximum size, so that data blocks to be exchanged between communicating user processes may have to be split into smaller segments; these segments together with any necessary control information, referred to as *data packets*, constitute the data units that traverse the network in a store-and-forward manner. The maximum size of packets ranges from a few hundred bits to about 10,000 bits in most operational networks. The splitting may be done either in the source user node or by the network. (It may be done in the network layer or some

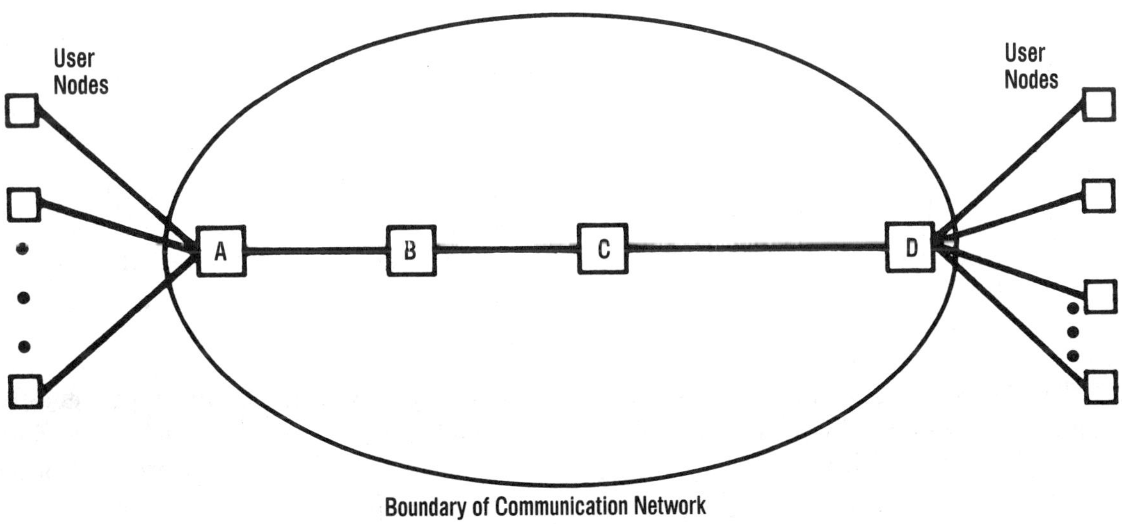

Figure 1-12. Switching nodes in a path between communicating user nodes.

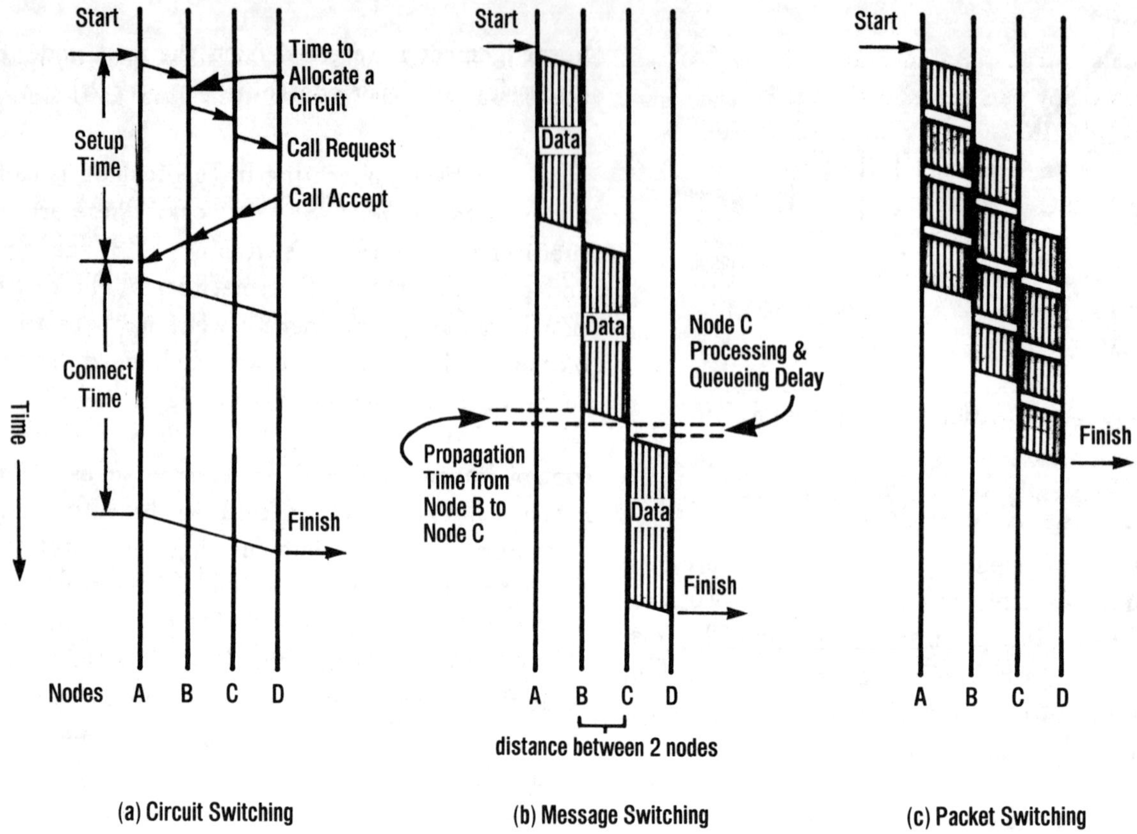

Figure 1-13. Timing of events in circuit, message, and packet switching.

protocol layer above it. Protocol layers will be addressed in Section 1.5.)

Note that both the end-to-end throughput available from a circuit-switched connection and its delay are constant for all practical purposes. However, logical connections offered by SF networks are characterized by time variations in both throughput and delay as the network load fluctuates. In general, communication channels are utilized more efficiently in an SF network than in a circuit-switching network if network users generate bursty traffic.

The switching nodes in an SF network must have significant processing capabilities and buffering capacities. As a result, speed and code conversion as well as a variety of other functions can be incorporated into an SF network to improve the quality and characteristics of its logical connections.

Packet switching vs. message switching

Examples of message-switching networks include the Telex network, the AUTODIN I network, and the SITA airline system. Most of the more recently developed networks and network architectures however are based upon packet switching, e.g., ARPANET, Telenet, Transpac and IBM's Systems Network Architecture (SNA), to name just a few. Packet switching offers many advantages over message switching but it also requires the network to take on additional responsibilities (functions). The following are the advantages:

1. Packet switching reduces the end-to-end delay required to deliver a data message from one user node to another user node. Three factors contribute to a reduction in delay. First, when several data packets are sent instead of

a single, large data message, the end-to-end delay can be reduced due to the effect of pipelining. Compare Figure 1-13(b) and Figure 1-13(c) and recall that in an SF network, each switching node must have received a data unit completely before forwarding it to the next node. Second, packets constituting the same message may travel in parallel paths to the destination. Third, according to queueing theory, a reduction in the variance of data unit sizes generally gives rise to a smaller average queueing delay.

2. Data packets having a bounded maximum size facilitate the management of buffers in switching nodes.

3. For a fixed number of error detection bits, the probability of undetected errors is greater for data messages than it is for the smaller data packets.

To implement packet switching instead of message switching, additional functional capabilities are required either of the user nodes or of network switching nodes: (1) the splitting of a data block to form data packets, and (2) the reassembling of a data block from its constituent data packets before delivery to the destination user process.

Header switching

In any node within an SF network, each data unit (message or packet) must be received in its entirety and checked to be error-free before it is forwarded to the next node on its path. Figures 1-13(b) and 1-13(c) show that pipelining reduces end-to-end delays when long data blocks are transported in smaller data packets. The degree of pipelining can be further increased if a data unit can be forwarded as soon as its control information header is received and the outgoing channel becomes available. Such a method was proposed and studied by Kermani and Kleinrock [KERM 79] and was referred to as "virtual cut-through." We have adopted the term "header switching" coined by this author [LAM 80] because it is more suggestive of what goes on and in the same vein as packet switching and message switching (Figure 1-14).

Each data unit typically consists of two parts: a control header followed by a data field. The header contains the data unit's identification (source-destination addresses or logical channel number) so that receipt of the header at an intermediate node is sufficient to determine the outgoing channel for the data unit. To implement header switching, the header should be protected by an error-detection code and checked at each intermediate node. On the other hand, no error checking is performed for the data field of a data unit. Hence there is no error control for data across each communication link. This is a price to pay for the increased pipelining. Error control is thus the responsibility of the entry and exit nodes of the network or of the source-destination user nodes. Note that the error rate of the entire path is the cumulative raw error rate of the links in the path. Thus header switching is appropriate for networks in which communication links have very low error rates and/or paths are not too long (in number of links). The use of header switching was suggested by this author for the environment of local area networks [LAM 80].

It is interesting to note that pipelining is

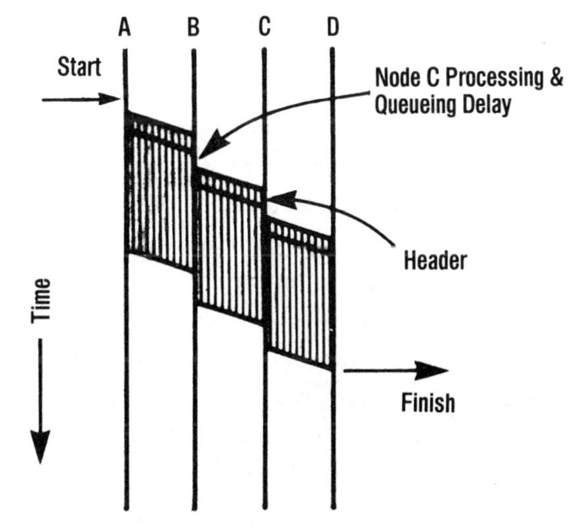

Figure 1-14. Timing of events in header switching.

achieved to an even greater extent in ring (or loop) networks than it is in header switching. In a ring topology, intermediate nodes need not make routing decisions. Also, error checking of the header of a data unit is usually not done in ring networks, assuming an environment of very low link error rates. Hence, in ring networks, each bit can be repeated downstream by a node as soon as the bit is received from upstream.

1.4.3. Sharing a Broadcast Channel

A broadcast channel is one that interconnects a population of geographically distributed users such that any user can transmit into the channel and any transmission in the channel can be received by all users. Broadcast channels can be realized using a variety of communication media: coaxial cable, radio, and satellite, to name the obvious. Techniques for sharing use of a broadcast channel are called *multiple access* techniques. They fall into two categories.

Channel-switching techniques

As in the sharing of a point-to-point communication channel, FDM or TDM can be used to multiplex the channel into subchannels. For a broadcast channel, these techniques take on the new names of frequency division multiple access (FDMA) and time division multiple access (TDMA), respectively. As before, a fixed assignment or a demand assignment strategy can be employed. Due to the broadcast nature of the transmission, the same subchannel can be used by a sender for all of its intended receivers. (With point-to-point channels, each sender-receiver pair requires the assignment of a subchannel.) In this case, transmissions must be identified with destination addresses and potential receivers of transmissions from a particular sender must monitor all transmissions in the subchannel allocated to that sender.

With FDMA, multiple modems that operate at different frequencies are needed for the different subchannels. In the sharing of a point-to-point communication link (Figure 1-8), all of these modems can be located in the switching node and shared by traffic from all user nodes. But with a broadcast channel and geographically distributed users, FDMA techniques would require either the deployment of multiple modems or a modem that is "frequency agile" for each user.

Packet-switching techniques

Data packets from geographically distributed users who access the same broadcast channel cannot be lined up to form a queue as in the sharing of a point-to-point link. The allocation of bandwidth on a per-packet basis will have to be achieved by two strategies: (1) by allowing conflicts to occur and employing a distributed algorithm to resolve conflicts and (2) by devising a protocol to coordinate the users so that a logical queue, one that is physically distributed, is formed. Packet switching techniques for the multiple access of a broadcast channel constitute the subject of Chapter 3 in this text.

1.4.4. Hybrid Networks

A network is sometimes described as "hybrid" because it handles a variety of traffic types (computer data, voice, facsimile, video etc.) or because it incorporates a mixture of switching techniques (packet switching, circuit switching, etc.) or because it employs a mixture of communication media (point-to-point circuits, satellites etc.). Quite often, to handle different traffic types in a network implies that it is desirable for the network to have multiple switching techniques and different communication media. Conventional wisdom seems to indicate that circuit switching is suitable for voice traffic and nonbursty data traffic, whereas packet switching is suitable for interactive computer applications that typically generate bursty traffic. The use of packet switching for digital voice traffic has been of interest to some researchers in recent years [FORG 77, GONS 83]. For the transmission of very large data and facsimile files as well as video, a satellite channel may be needed to provide the large bandwidths that are difficult to come by in terrestrial networks over long distances.

Integrated circuit and packet switching

Circuit and packet switching can be integrated in the sharing of a channel, point-to-point or broadcast, by partitioning the channel into two subchannels: one for circuit switching and one for packet switching. The subchannel allocated to circuit switching is further divided into smaller subchannels. The packet-switching subchannel is allocated on a per-packet basis, as described before.

A novel feature that can be incorporated into an integrated circuit and packet switching system is to make the partition between the CS and PS subchannels dynamically movable. Specifically, it means that any currently unallocated CS subchannel capacity is used to transmit packets waiting for the PS subchannel. Integrated CS/PS with a movable partition is conceptually feasible whether the multiplexing is done by frequency or time division. However, the movable-partition strategy is easiest to illustrate (and probably easiest to implement) assuming the use of TDM. We illustrate the integration of CS and PS based upon TDM in Figure 1-15. As in Figure 1-10 (illustrating a TDM channel), time is divided into consecutive frames. Each frame is partitioned into two subframes, one for CS traffic and one for PS traffic. The CS subframe is further divided into time slots. The number of CS subchannels available for fixed or demand assignment is equal to the maximum number of time slots in a CS subframe.

We have shown two slightly different versions of a dynamically movable partition in Figures 1-16(a) and 1-16(b), depending upon whether a slotted system is used for PS traffic or not. In Figure 1-16(a), a slotted system is used for PS traffic. In this case, the entire frame is slotted. End-to-end circuits are allocated time slots designated by their positions within the CS subframe. Any unallocated time slots within the CS subframe can be used for the transmission of waiting PS traffic.

Figure 1-16(b) illustrates an unslotted system for PS traffic. In such a system, the PS subframe is not slotted. Furthermore, CS traffic is "packed" at the beginning of the CS subframe, so that the remaining time in the frame is available to PS traffic in a contiguous piece. As a result, variable-length packets or messages can be packed inside it efficiently. The price to pay is the need to identify each block of CS transmission (with, say, a logical channel number that identifies the end-to-end circuit).

1.5. ARCHITECTURAL MODELS

Suppose we have a network of communication channels and switching nodes. The collection of programs (in hardware or software) to implement functions to achieve communication between processes in user nodes is extremely complex. The design and development of these parallel programs require adherence to sound structured programming principles. We shall begin by enunciating

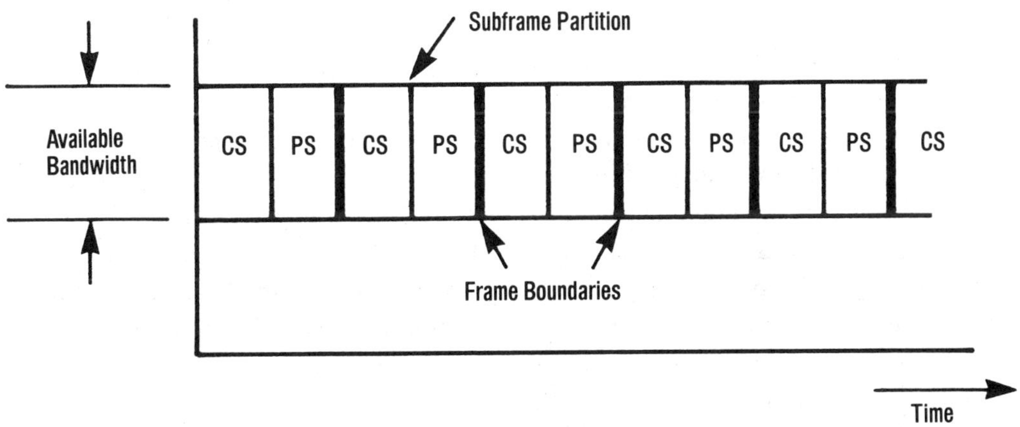

Figure 1-15. Integrated CS/PS based upon TDM.

three principles that we consider to be fundamental to a well-structured architectural model. This is the subject of Section 1.5.1. Some design and implementation issues are discussed in Section 1.5.2. Examples of architectural models are shown in Section 1.5.3 for both networking and internetworking (interconnection of autonomous networks).

1.5.1. Three Structuring Principles

Consider a protocol system in which an abstract "communication process" provides the ability for a population of user processes to send data to each other (Figure 1-17(a)). A line joining two processes in our figures is used to denote a two-way communication path. The path is internal to a machine if the processes reside in the same machine; it represents a communication link if the processes reside in different machines. Two processes connected by a line in our illustrations of architectural models are said to be *adjacent*. For the following discussions, a process is either a sequential process or a concurrent process. A sequential process is resident in a single machine. A concurrent process consists of several subprocesses resident in the same machine or different machines; each subprocess may in turn be either a sequential or concurrent process.

Stepwise refinement

We consider architectural models that can be obtained by a stepwise refinement procedure, as illustrated by the example shown in Figure 1-17. In performing stepwise refinement, a process with multiple functions in the current version of an architectural model is replaced by a set of interconnected processes (any topology) that provides the same functions. The communication process 1 in Figure 1-17(a) has multiple functions including the establishment and management of logical connections between pairs of user processes. This function is peeled off for implementation in separate processes which are labelled 1.1 in Figure 1-17(b). (Identical processes are labelled with the same number.) Next, the communication process 1.2 is refined to reveal its internal structure, which is a set of geographically distributed processes interconnected by point-to-point communication links (Figure 1-17(c)).

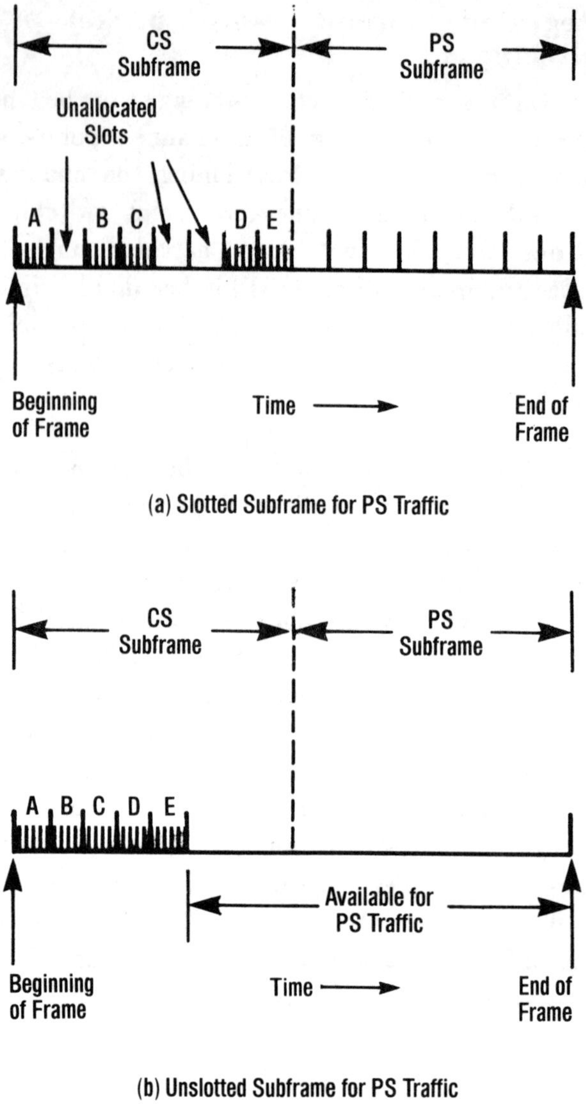

Figure 1-16. Two variants of an integrated CS/PS system.

We now make the observation that all of the 1.1 and 1.3 processes in Figure 1-17(c) are interconnected by physical links. Thus each must have the data link management and error control functions for every one of its physical links. Each such process is then split into two or more processes, one for the network management functions and the other(s) for the data link functions (one process for each separate data link). Thus, we ar-

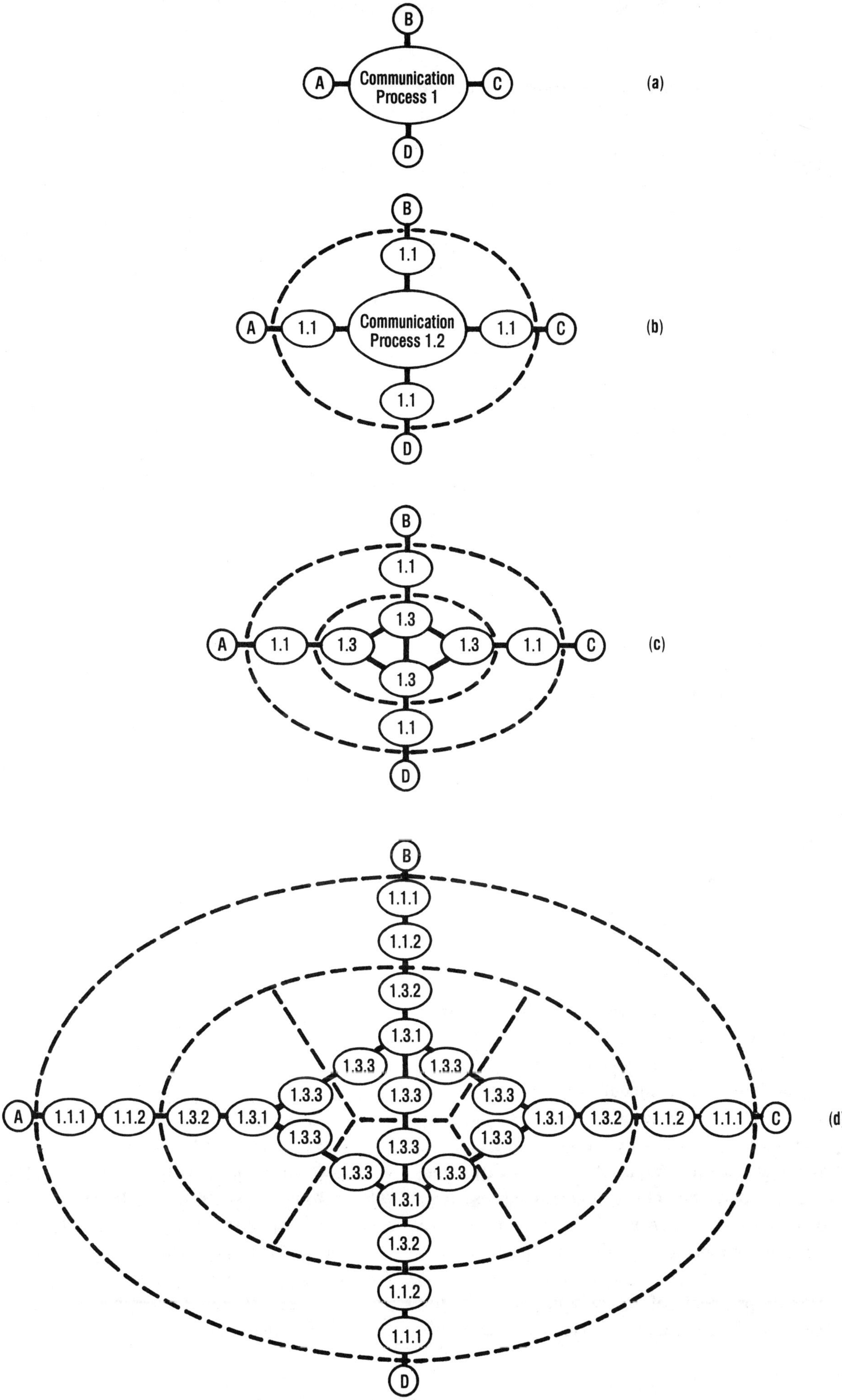

Figure 1-17. An illustration of stepwise refinement.

rive at the architectural model shown in Figure 1-17(d).

Hierarchy

At the time that new processes are created by stepwise refinement, they are classified into different levels of a process hierarchy. The user processes are at the top level of the process hierarchy. New processes created by stepwise refinement may reside at the same level or at one of the lower levels. The processes in Figure 1-17 are hierarchically ordered in Figures 1-18(a) to 1-18(d). To avoid drawing three-dimensional pictures, we have shown only the processes along a single path between user process A and user process C in Figure 1-17. We have further partitioned each data link process in Figure 1-18(d) into two processes, one for the physical data link and one for the logical data link functions, as shown in Figure 1-18(e). The graph in Figure 1-18(e) is also partitioned vertically to show the physical location of processes in different nodes. There are two types of nodes: user (or host) nodes and network switching nodes. Although not shown in Figure 1-18, two adjacent processes residing in the same node can be more than one level apart, i.e., one or more levels can be bypassed by a direct communication path.

Interprocess communication restriction: Two processes in the process hierarchy can communicate only if either they are within the same node and are adjacent to each other or they are at the same level of the process hierarchy.

The interaction between two processes residing in the same node can be handled by any of the interprocess communication techniques for a multiprogramming environment [BRIN 73]. Two processes at the same level of the process hierarchy can interact via the exchange of messages. If the processes are not adjacent to each other, messages are relayed by intermediate processes along a path between them. A routing protocol needs to be implemented when more than one path exists.

Most protocols of interest in the literature are concerned with communications among a subset of processes at the same hierarchical level but located in different nodes. Such communications are known as peer-to-peer communications and such protocols are referred to as *peer protocols*. The processes at each level of the process hierarchy together with their peer protocols are said to constitute a *protocol layer* of the architectural model. The simplified picture in Figure 1-19 is often shown in the literature instead of the process hierarchy in Figure 1-18(e). Conceptually, processes in each layer of the hierarchy (except layer 1) are provided with some communication services by the immediately next lower layer; these processes contribute some additional functions of their own and provide improved communication services to processes in the next higher layer of the hierarchy.

Peer protocols are defined for subsets of processes in each layer. Each peer protocol can provide a communication service to other processes in the same layer as well as to adjacent processes in a higher layer. (A process is adjacent to a subset of processes if it is adjacent to any process within the subset.) We shall refer to processes that use the communication service provided by a peer protocol as the *protocol users*. Several examples can be found in Figure 1-18(d). A data link protocol can be defined for processes 1.1.2 and 1.3.2 to provide a communication service to processes 1.1.1 and 1.3.1 in the next higher layer. A networking protocol can be defined for all the 1.3.1 processes in the subnetwork of switching nodes to provide a communication service to all the 1.1.1 processes in the same layer and located in user nodes. A network access protocol can be defined for each pair of 1.1.1 and 1.3.1 processes. The entire network layer also provides a communication service to user processes.

Data transparency

The issue of data transparency at the interface between a protocol and its users needs to be considered for both send operations by a protocol user and receive operations by a protocol process. We define *send transparency* to mean that a protocol user can give any sequence of bits to the protocol for delivery to another user. We define

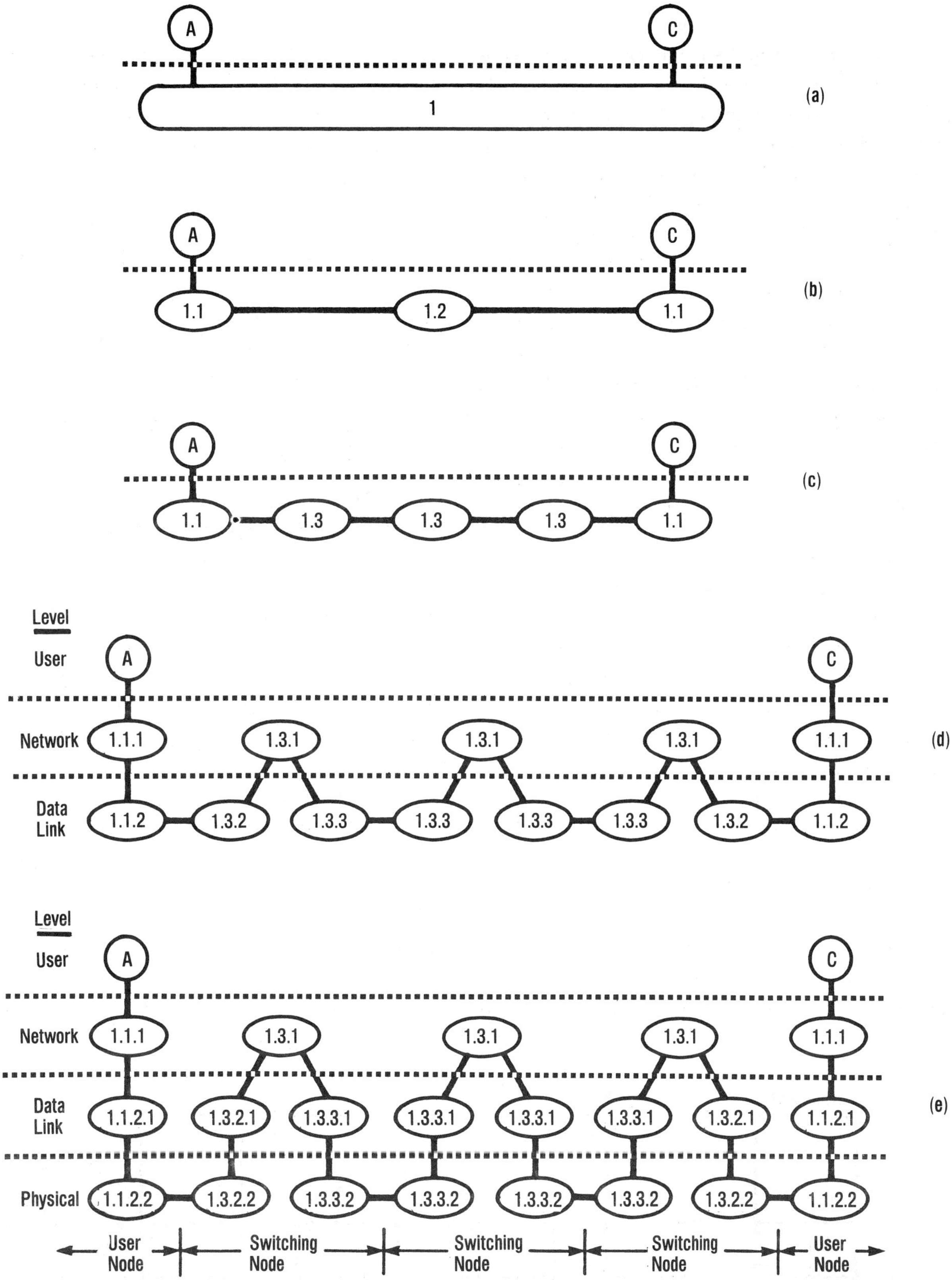

Figure 1-18. An illustration of hierarchy.

receive transparency to mean that any sequence of bits given by a protocol user to the protocol for delivery need not be interpreted by the protocol. Both send and receive transparency across an interface are required for the protocol interface to be called a *transparent interface*. The arbitrary bit sequences that are sent across a transparent protocol interface are referred to as *transparent data*. Typically, data transparency cannot be achieved at a protocol interface because of restrictions imposed by communication services utilized by the protocol itself. In this case, whether send transparency or receive transparency is affected depends upon whether the protocol processes or the protocol's users undertake the responsibility for satisfying those restrictions.

Data transparency is usually enforced in the design of all protocols in an architectural model, with the exception of the bottom layer(s) that must deal with the functions of bit synchronization and frame synchronization. In order to achieve bit synchronization (or phase synchronization), the sending node needs to guarantee that the signal, encoding a bit stream, has adequate transitions; if not, some bits may have to be inserted into the bit stream or the bit stream will have to be scrambled to create transitions [DAVE 72]. The receiving node then performs an inverse operation of deleting inserted bits or unscrambling to restore the original bit stream. To achieve frame synchronization, it is necessary to examine the stream of data bits and to insert/delete bits so that the "marker" of frame boundaries, in the form of a special sequence of bits, can be made unique. (Such frame synchronization techniques are described in Chapter 2.)

In practice, the operations of bit insertion/deletion and scrambling/unscrambling are typically done in hardware. Given such hardware, protocols of interest in this text (at the data link level and above) will be considered to have transparent interfaces.

1.5.2. Implementation and Design Issues

Data units given to a peer protocol for delivery will be referred to as the protocol's *service data units* (SDUs). A service data unit contains control information of upper layer protocols and possibly some actual data from an end-user process. To have a transparent interface, the protocol must regard the entire SDU as "pure data." The method of *encapsulation* is generally used to implement a transparent interface. In this method each SDU received from a protocol user is wrapped with a header and a trailer. (A trailer is necessary only in a data link protocol for marking the end of a frame.) We refer to a wrapped SDU as a *protocol data unit* (PDU). If the protocol utilizes a communication service offered by a protocol in a lower layer, the PDU is then given to the lower layer protocol which will in turn regard it as "pure data." The header-trailer of a

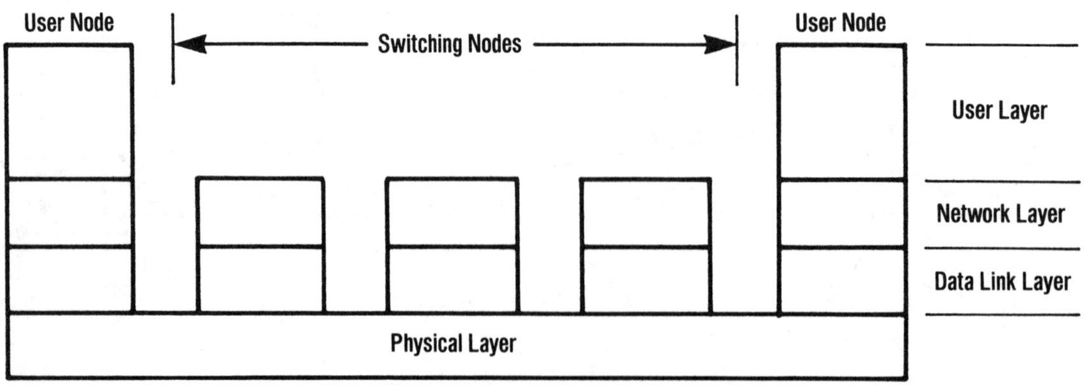

Figure 1-19. An illustration of protocol layers.

PDU provides the vehicle for processes that participate in this protocol for sending control messages to each other. Furthermore, if a process wants to send a control message, it can generate a PDU consisting of a header-trailer only, with nothing wrapped inside.

The header-trailer of a PDU is stripped away before the encapsulated SDU is delivered to an external process (Figure 1-20). Note that the interprocess communication restriction in the previous section dictates that external processes that utilize this protocol for the exchange of SDUs must reside in the same layer. These user processes can be at the same level as the protocol processes or at a higher level in the process hierarchy.

Figure 1-21 is an illustration of the series of wrappings and unwrappings that occur when a piece of data travels from user process A to user process C, as shown in Figure 1-18(d). Network-access protocols are defined between pairs of 1.1.1 and 1.3.1 processes. A network protocol is defined for all the 1.3.1 processes. Data link protocols are defined for pairs of 1.1.2 and 1.3.2 processes and for pairs of 1.3.3 processes.

In Figure 1-21, network access protocol headers are identified by the number 3. Network protocol headers are identified by 3'. Data link protocol header-trailers are identified by the number 2.

Note that the 1.3.1 processes participate not only in the network protocol but also in the network-access protocols. Each SDU for the network protocol is wrapped in the header of a network-access protocol when it arrives. For each data unit received, a 1.3.1 process unwraps the network-access protocol header, delivers the SDU to itself, and then rewraps it with a network protocol header.

The method of encapsulation implicitly assumes the *positional significance* approach for separating control and data information. A special bit pattern serves as a marker of frame boundaries. (A frame is a data unit transmitted across a physical link.) Data and control information are physically separated into different fields according to offsets from the beginning and end of each frame. A process participating in a protocol receives protocol data units either directly from another protocol process or indirectly from a lower layer protocol. Because of the interprocess communication restriction stated in Section 1.5.1, the unwrapping of the protocol's header-trailer is always performed at the beginning and the end of the data unit received (by simply peeling away fixed numbers of bits from the beginning and the end of the data unit received.)

Note that several peer protocols are usually present within a protocol layer, and a process can participate in more than one such protocol. As a

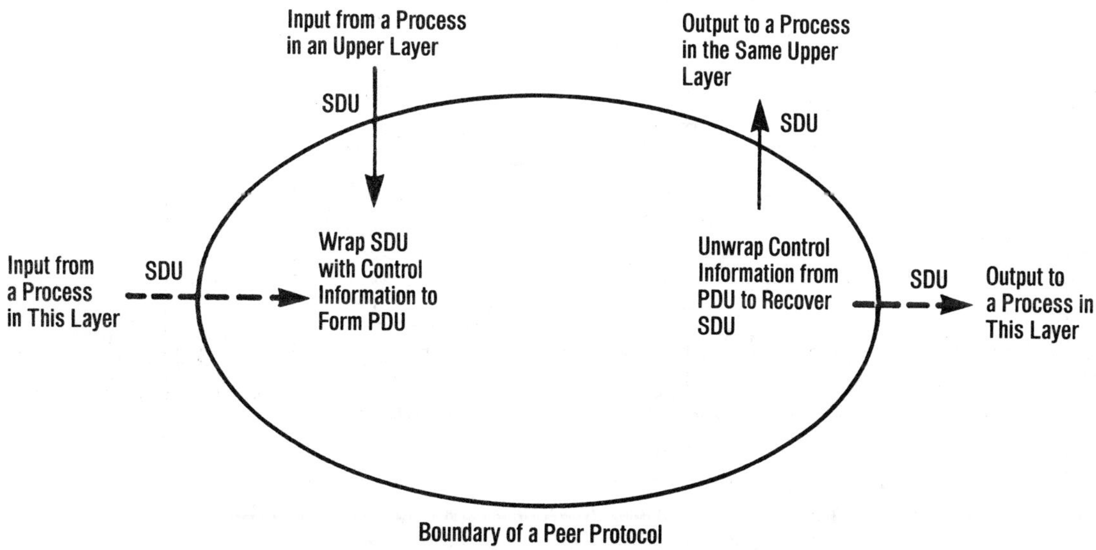

Figure 1-20. Wrapping and unwrapping in a peer protocol.

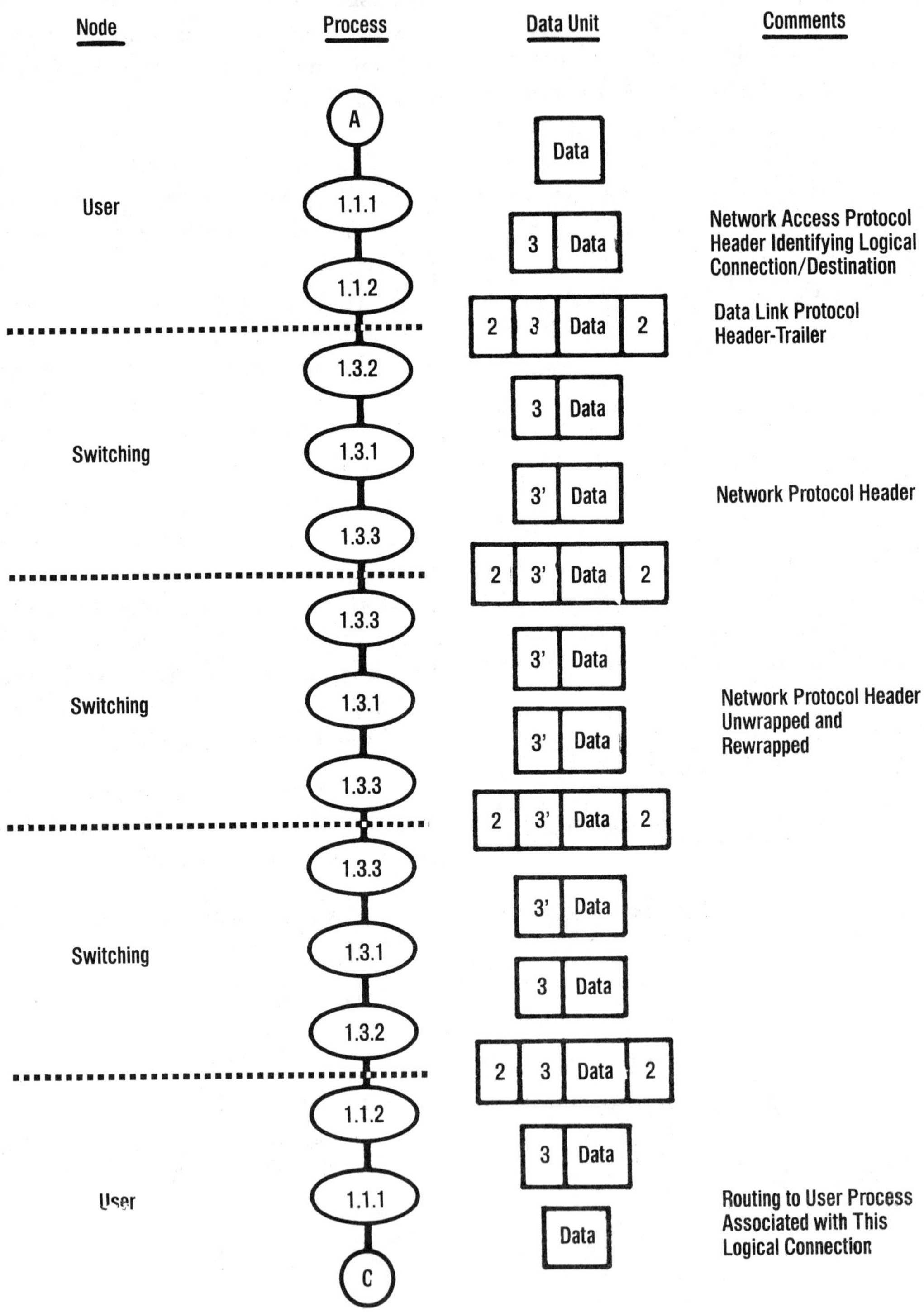

Figure 1-21. Wrappings and unwrappings along an end-to-end path.

result, data units and their header-trailers will sometimes have to be identified by both the layer to which they belong and the specific protocol within the layer for which they are used.

The properties of the communication service provided by a peer protocol depend upon the functions implemented by the protocol as well as the properties of the communication services utilized by the protocol processes. Two common types of services are described below.

1. *Datagram service:* Service data units are called datagrams. Each datagram is treated independently by the protocol. The protocol does not provide end-to-end error control. Losses may occur. (However, losses may be minimal if error-control functions are implemented in lower layer protocols.) Out-of-sequence delivery may occur; i.e., the protocol may deliver datagrams in a different order from the one in which they are given to the protocol (due to retransmissions or the use of parallel paths in a network).

2. *Virtual circuit service:* The protocol provides end-to-end error control as well as in-sequence delivery of service data units. Thus the communication service provided is a reliable FIFO logical pipe.

The provision of a datagram or virtual circuit service, or something in between, by protocols in different layers of a communications architecture is a design decision rather than an architectural consideration. Such decisions are concerned with the partitioning and placement of networking functions in a fashion that is optimal for a particular network environment.

There are several other design and implementation issues that impact the communication service provided by a peer protocol, regardless of whether it provides a datagram or virtual circuit service, namely: input control, maximum data unit sizes, segmenting, and blocking. We address these issues next.

Input control

The communication service provided by a protocol may not be available at all times for input. Controlling the input of service data units is necessary to deal with temporary overloads for protocols that implement statistical multiplexing of communication facilities. Input control of a source user is also necessary if the corresponding destination user is not accepting delivery of service data units from the protocol fast enough [GERL 80].

Maximum data unit sizes

For implementation purposes, a maximum size needs to be specified for the protocol data units of each protocol in an architectural model. The determination of the protocol data unit size is based upon some fundamental design and implementation considerations such as the size of buffers in switching nodes, the maximum number of data bits for which an error-detection code will work reliably, the maximum size of a data unit for which an error-control scheme is efficient (the probability of having errors in a block increases with the block length), and the reduction of end-to-end delay because of pipelining in a store-and-forward network (as discussed earlier). The maximum size of protocol data units may vary among the different protocols in the same architecture. Also, the maximum size of the service data units and protocol data units of the same protocol may differ. Such differences in an architectural model are handled by incorporating the functions of segmenting and blocking in its implementation.

Segmenting

A peer protocol providing a communication service can have a segmenting function such that a service data unit given to the protocol for delivery may be split into several segments (Figure 1-22). Each segment is wrapped individually with the protocol header-trailer to form an individual protocol data unit. When a service data unit is segmented, each segment is given a sequence number. The protocol data unit header includes the sequence number of the segment that it wraps as well as an indication of whether the segment is the last in a sequence.

The protocol may or may not reassemble segments before their delivery to a destination user. If a protocol implements a segmenting function but not a reassembly function, then it provides a communication service that handles transparent data although it may fragment units of such data. Note that these fragments of transparent data cannot be reassembled by another protocol in the same layer or in a higher layer. (The fragments have no sequence number information.)

Protocols providing either a datagram or virtual circuit service can implement segmenting and reassembly functions. Segmenting without reassembly, however, seems inconsistent with the objective of a virtual circuit service.

There are several reasons for a protocol to implement segmenting. An obvious reason is that the maximum protocol data unit size is smaller than the maximum service data unit size (or the service data unit size of a lower layer protocol utilized by it is too small).

Blocking

A peer protocol may also combine several of its protocol data units, each of which encapsulates a separate service data unit, into a single block. If given to another protocol for delivery, the entire block constitutes a single service data unit of the other protocol. This is known as blocking (Figure 1-23). One reason for blocking is to improve the efficiency of error control in a data link protocol [CHU 74]. Blocking is seldom implemented in practice.

When a protocol combines several of its protocol data units into a block, then the header of each protocol data unit must contain a count of its length, so that separate protocol data units can later be recovered from the block prior to delivery of their contents to destination users. Instead of a count, the trailer of each protocol data unit may contain a unique marker which serves to separate different protocol units within the block. However, to implement unique markers, the principle of data transparency may have to be compromised. Of course, if the protocol in question is a data link protocol, a unique marker has already been implemented for the purpose of frame synchronization.

Relationships between types of data units

Note that the wrapping of transparent data with a protocol's header-trailer must be done *after* segmenting, but *before* blocking, in order for each piece of transparent data to be uniquely identified. The following relationships exist between protocol data units and service data units in an architectural model. For a given protocol, a protocol data unit contains either an entire service data unit, a segment of a service data unit, or no service data unit. A service data unit of a protocol consists of one or *more* of the protocol data units of some protocol that utilizes this protocol.

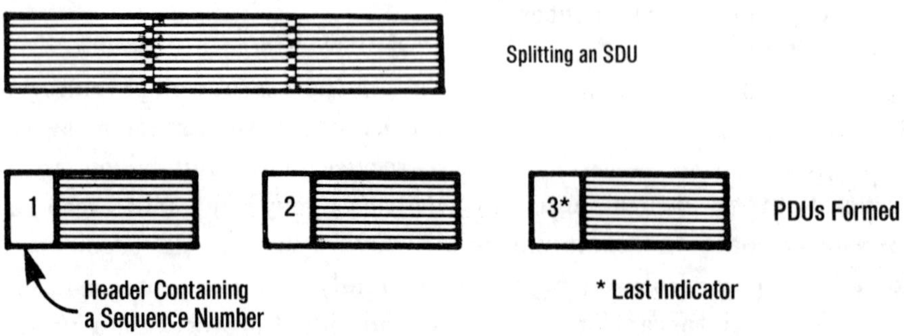

Figure 1-22. Segmenting an SDU to form multiple PDUs.

Let us reconcile our use of the terms protocol data units and service data units with the terms data packet and data message as used earlier in Section 1.4 in conjunction with our discussions of switching techniques. The conceptual message-switching network described in Section 1.4 had no segmenting or blocking function in any layer. *Data message* was a general term referring to any data unit in any layer. The conceptual packet-switching network described in Section 1.4 had no blocking function in any layer but had a segmenting function in one layer. Segmenting was done once in the network layer (or a higher layer) of a user node or in the network layer of a switching node, and the term *data packet* referred generally to data units in any layer after segmentation had occurred.

The term *frame* was used to refer to the protocol data units of a data link protocol. The term *datagram* was used to refer to the service data units of a peer protocol (typically a network layer protocol) that provides a datagram service.

Transparency and service characteristics

For a protocol with a limitation on the size of its service data units, one might argue that the protocol's interface is not transparent in an absolute sense. A protocol user does not need to examine the contents of a service data unit, but the user does have to determine its length and break it up if necessary.

For a protocol with possible delivery of fragmented service data units, the principle of data transparency as stated earlier is not violated. But fragmentation, together with the service characteristics of loss and reordering of service data units, is obviously undesirable for an end-to-end communication service. However, they may be acceptable characteristics of communication services provided by lower layer protocols in a communications architecture.

1.5.3. Models for Networking and Internetworking

Practically, every network that has been built has its own architectural model. There are numerous possibilities in the choice of communication facilities and switching techniques. The quality, characteristics, and type of communication services desired by user processes determine the network functions required, and there are numerous ways of allocating these functions to different protocol layers and dividing them between user nodes and switching nodes. Many of the successful networks in existence however, seem to conform to a great extent the three structuring principles described in Section 1.5.1. For examples, protocol layers in Ethernet, ARPANET and TYMNET architectures are shown in [CERF 78]. Protocol layers in SNA are shown in [CYPS 78]. A comparison of the functions in SNA and the Open Systems Interconnection (OSI) protocol layers is given in [RUTL 82].

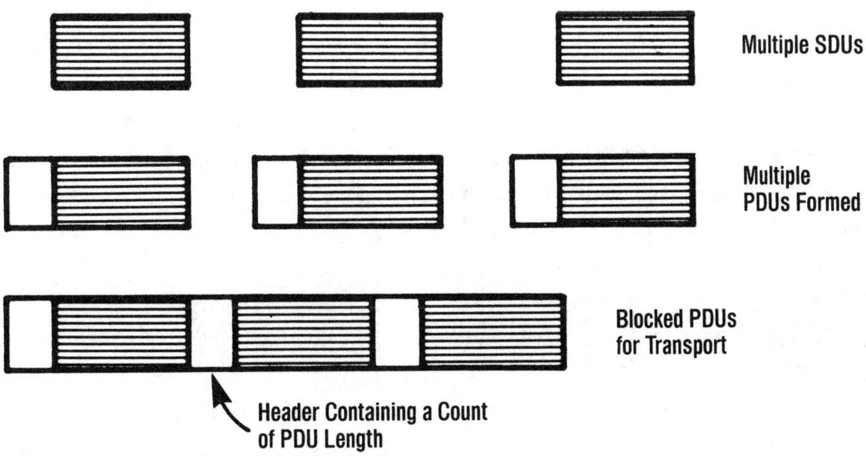

Figure 1-23. Blocking of PDUs.

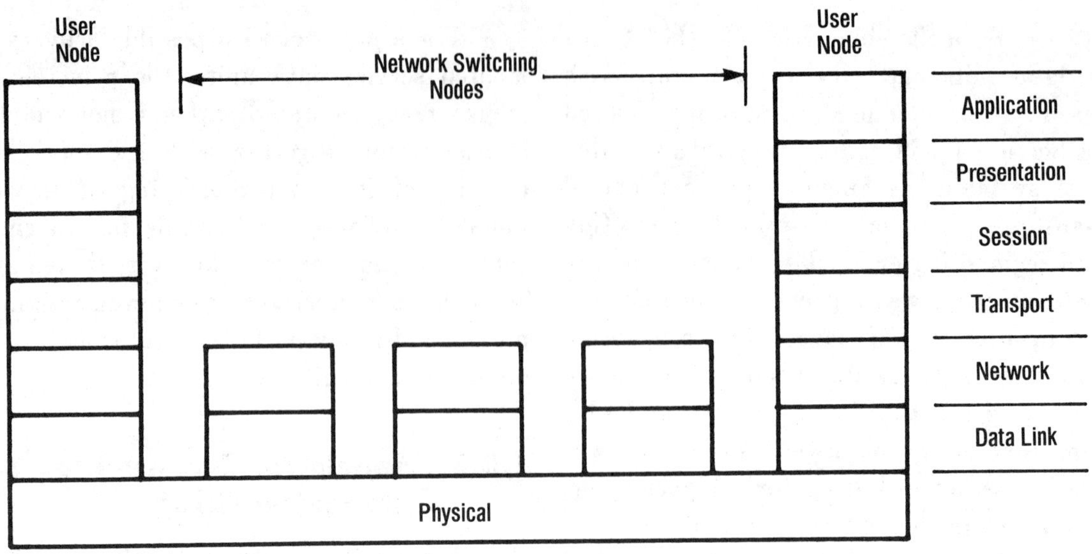

Figure 1-24. The seven layers of the OSI model.

The OSI reference model

The International Organization for Standardization (ISO) has been developing a reference model to guide standards development in networking. This model is known as the basic reference model for Open Systems Interconnection (OSI). The OSI model partitions the communication and networking functions into seven layers, as shown in Figure 1-24. Again, to avoid drawing a three-dimensional picture, we illustrate the OSI layers for a communication path consisting of three switching nodes between two user nodes (the same as Figures 1-18 and 1-19).

A brief description of the main functions of the OSI layers follows. The reader is referred to [OSI 81] for details. Note that not all functions allocated to a layer must be included in an implementation.

A *physical layer* protocol provides the function of bit synchronization, i.e., the delivery of a stream of bits between processes that utilize the physical layer protocol.

A *data link layer* protocol provides the functions of frame synchronization, and error control, as well as the sharing and management of a physical communication link.

Network layer protocols provide the ability for user nodes that are not connected by a dedicated physical link to send data units to each other. Specific network layer protocols depend upon the network topology, communication facilities, and switching techniques. Functions of routing, flow control, and congestion control are included in this layer for networks of point-to-point links. The function of multiple access is the responsibility of this layer for nodes interconnected by a broadcast channel. Protocols for network access by user nodes are also included in this layer.

A *transport layer* protocol provides the transportation of data units between processes residing in different user nodes. It is concerned with the establishment and management of end-to-end logical connections between user nodes as well as with improving the quality and characteristics of the communication service provided by the network layer (e.g., functions of end-to-end error control, in-sequence delivery, and reassembly).

A *session layer* protocol provides the means for binding two presentation layer processes into a relationship and then unbinding them, for synchronizing their dialog, and for managing their data exchange. (Note that many sessions may be multiplexed onto a transport layer connection.)

A *presentation layer* protocol represents information to communicating application processes in such a way that preserves meaning while resolving syntax differences (e.g., different codes, formats, and data compression techniques).

Application layer protocols provide services to the external users of the OSI environment. User specifiable parameters are made known to the OSI environment via the application layer.

The objective of the OSI model is to provide a framework to guide the development of protocol standards in the future and to foster compatibility in general. Functions described in [OSI 81] and their partitioning into the seven layers obviously do not constitute the only feasible architectural model. In the architectures of several existing networks [CERF 78, CYPS 78] many functions and some layers in the OSI model are missing. Some of the functions that are present are allocated to protocol layers in these architectures differently from the way they are allocated in the OSI model. Nevertheless, it is important to note that the relative positions of most functions within the hierarchy of functions are roughly the same in these architectures as in the OSI model. Of the architectural models shown in [CERF 78, CYPS 78], the SNA model is the only one that also has seven layers and appears to be closest to the OSI model. (There are some significant differences, as discussed in [RUTL 82].) This is probably no accident because both OSI and SNA are relatively new developments compared to the other architectures. Their evolutionary developments during the past few years must have influenced each other to some extent.

Synchronization functions revisited

It is instructional to reexamine the five basic synchronization functions described in Section 1.2 for achieving communication between two parties and to consider the presence or absence of these functions in peer protocols within each layer of the OSI model.

Bit synchronization is provided by a physical layer protocol between any two end points of a communication link (the link may be point-to-point or multipoint). This function is present only in the physical layer.

Frame synchronization is provided by a data link layer protocol between any two end points of a communication link. This function is present only in the data link layer. Methods for frame synchronization are described in Chapter 2.

Note that within the same architecture, different protocols can be specified within the physical layer and within the data link layer for different communication links.

Multiple access synchronization was described in Section 1.2 in the context of sharing a point-to-point communication channel. By expanding its definition to mean the sharing of communication facilities in general (physical or logical), the multiple access function is present in most layers; e.g., it is present in the sharing of a broadcast channel by a data link layer protocol or by a network layer protocol, in the form of routing and flow control functions in the network layer of a store-and-forward network, and in a session layer protocol that multiplexes a logical connection provided by a transport layer protocol into multiple logical connections.

The *content synchronization* function concerned with the separation and encoding of data and control information in protocol data units is present in protocols within all layers. The method of encapsulation to achieve transparency, as described in Section 1.5.2, implicitly assumes a positional significance approach for separating data and control information. Content synchronization also encompasses the functions of error control and in-sequence delivery. These functions may be present in protocols within all layers; e.g., a data link layer protocol at the two end points of a physical link, a network layer protocol at the two end points of a network path, or a transport layer protocol between two user nodes. In practice, the error-control function is most important in the data link layer where error rates are high. The in-sequence delivery function is most important in the transport layer.

Dialog synchronization is present in some form in all protocols within all layers. Note that not all processes within a layer will communicate with each other. The subset of processes within a layer that provides a service must interact so that the necessary logical connections will be made. Such start-up interactions must be an integral part of every protocol. For example, a data link protocol needs to establish and maintain the up/down status of a physical link, a routing protocol needs to establish and maintain the up/down status of all switching nodes that execute the routing algorithm and participate in the storing and forwarding of data units, and a transport protocol needs to establish and maintain the up/down status of an end-to-end logical path.

Models for internetworking

There are numerous difficult technical issues (in addition to political and administrative ones) in the interconnection of separate autonomous networks. The technical issues are discussed in Chapter 6.

The architectural model for the interconnection of networks depends upon the level at which interconnection occurs, the extent to which these networks are compatible with each other, and issues such as whether the interconnection gateways are located in host nodes or in switching nodes (in the form of gateway halves).

Two possible architectural models are shown in Figures 1-25 and 1-26. They appear here primarily as interesting examples of structured architectural models. They give the flavors of two approaches to internetworking, each of which has its advocates. For other approaches and details, the reader is referred to Chapter 6. In both Figures 1-25 and 1-26 we use the names of protocols to identify processes that participate in those protocols. The names A and B refer to protocols of networks A and B, respectively.

Figure 1-25 shows a model for interconnecting networks that have the same interface for network access by a packet-mode user node: in this example, the X.25 interface of the International Telegraph and Telephone Consultative Committee (CCITT). The X.25 interface embodies three protocols between a user node and a network switching node, one each for the network layer,

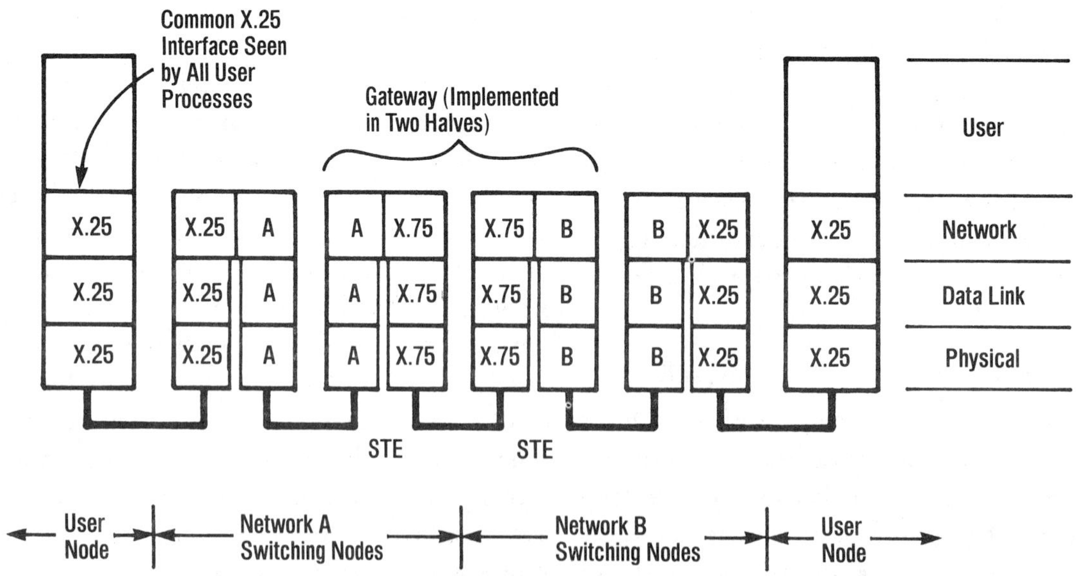

Figure 1-25. An internetworking model with a common network access interface.

the data link layer, and the physical layer. The network layer is referred to as the packet level in X.25. The initial X.25 protocol defined only virtual circuit services. Subsequent revisions have added a datagram service and a fast-select facility for virtual calls [RYBC 80, FOLT 80].

In addition to assuming a common network access interface that offers the same service(s), the model in Figure 1-25 also assumes a common physical address space for all user processes in all the networks interconnected. The interconnection of networks in this model may be accomplished with gateways located in user nodes or gateway halves located in switching nodes. The latter scenario is shown in Figure 1-25. The CCITT Recommendation X.75 specifies the protocols at the physical, data link, and network levels between two switching nodes implementing gateway halves. These switching nodes are called Signalling Terminal Equipments (STEs). The X.75 protocol is compatible with the X.25 protocol for virtual circuit services, but they have additional functions, called network utilities, that handle the signalling of internetwork administrative information. With this approach, an end-to-end virtual circuit is provided as a concatenation of virtual circuits in the networks being interconnected.

CCITT Recommendation X.121 defines an international numbering plan for public network addresses. Each public packet-switching network is assigned a data network identification code (DNIC). A DNIC is a four digit number; the first three digits identify the country and the fourth digit identifies the particular public packet-switching network in that country. For example, Telenet's DNIC is 3110 while Datapac's is 3020. Following the DNIC, an international address contains a network terminal number (NTN) which specifies the address of the terminal within the public data network. The NTN is a one- to ten-digit number and is assigned to a particular terminal by the public data network's administration. Generally, the routing of calls between public data networks is based on DNICs, while the routing of calls within a public data network is based on NTNs.

In summary, referring back to Figure 1-25, we see that protocol layers in user nodes are oblivious to the internals of the networks and gateways (with the exception of a common physical address space for all users in all networks). User processes in different networks can communicate because they see the same X.25 interface and service. The X.75 protocols provide the necessary interconnection functions. An application of this model is described in [UNSO 81] which is reprinted in Chapter 6.

Figure 1-26 shows an internetworking model that employs the method of encapsulation [CERF 78, POUZ 78]. In this model, a gateway intercon-

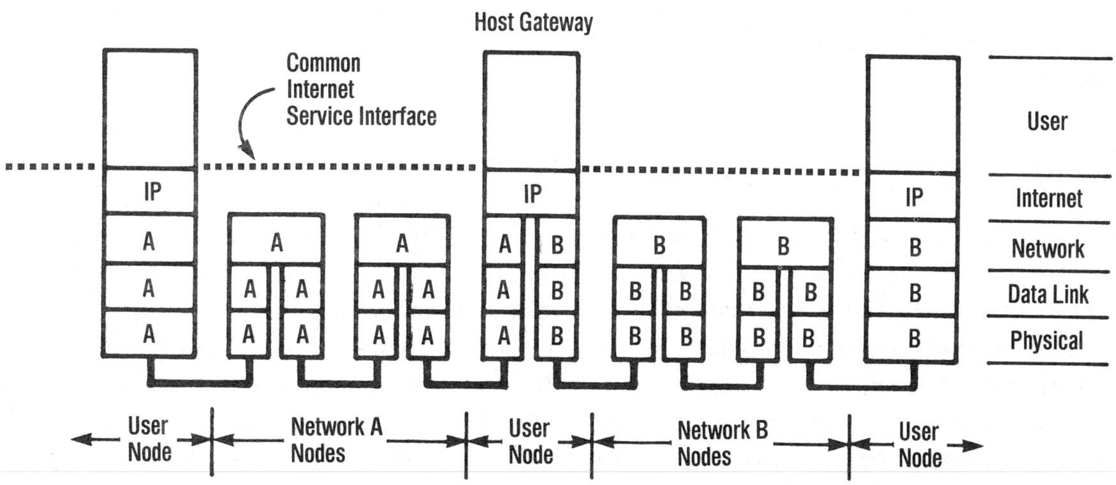

Figure 1-26. An internetworking model based upon encapsulation.

necting two networks resides in a user node that is indistinguishable from any other user node. Such a gateway is called a *host gateway.* The host gateway implements the unique network/data link/physical layer protocols for each network that it connects to. An extra layer is inserted into the process hierarchy (between the network layer and the transport layer in the OSI model). This layer is the same in all user nodes including the host gateways. What we have just described is the internetworking approach of the Defense Advanced Research Projects Agency (DARPA), and the protocol in this extra layer in DARPA's model is called the internet protocol (IP). This layer provides a datagram service to the user processes shown in Figure 1-26. Datagrams given by user processes to the IP layer for delivery are wrapped or encapsulated within the data units of individual network layer protocols. Additional protocols in layers above IP can be implemented to provide communication services having a higher quality and with better characteristics than those of the datagram service of IP.

In summary, referring to Figure 1-26, we see that user processes can communicate because they see the same IP layer interface. The interconnection functions (encapsulation, address translation, routing, segmentation, and reassembly) are provided by the IP layer and its interfaces with the different network layers. The basic advantage of this approach is that almost any sort of network can participate, which is especially useful for connecting networks with new architectures to older networks.

1.6. PROTOCOL STANDARDS

There are some boundaries in an architectural model where standardization of protocols between processes across those boundaries is extremely useful. A most natural boundary is the one that surrounds a packet-switching network. We have already encountered in Section 1.5.3 the X.25 protocol standard at the boundary between a user node, called a DTE (data terminal equipment), and a network switching node, called a DCE (data circuit-terminating equipment). We have also encountered the X.75 protocol standard at the boundary between switching nodes in two different networks, called STEs. DARPA's IP protocol is one that is situated at a different kind of boundary i.e. one that separates the network layer and user layer in Figure 1-26. It is not a protocol standard but it can conceivably become a de facto standard if its popularity grows.

Organizations involved in the development of standards for use in public data networks include CCITT, ISO, ANSI and EIA among others. These are briefly introduced below. The center of public data network standardization activities is Study Group VII of the International Telegraph and Telephone Consultative Committee (CCITT). CCITT is one of two committees of the International Telecommunications Union (ITU), an agency of the United Nations headquartered in Geneva, Switzerland. Over 100 countries make up the membership of the ITU. CCITT deals with technical issues and standards development associated with international telecommunications. Study Group VII is responsible for data communications over public data networks. Its work is contained in the X-series recommendations. Study Group XVII is responsible for data communications over telephone facilities. Its work is contained in the V-series recommendations.

The International Organization for Standardization (ISO) exists to develop standards to facilitate the international exchange of goods and services. It is a voluntary, nontreaty group. The members of ISO are representative standards organizations from more than 80 countries. The member organization from the United States is the American National Standards Institute (ANSI). The ISO work on data communications is focused in two subcommittees of Technical Committee 97 (computers and information processing): subcommittee SC6 is responsible for data communications, and subcommittee SC16 is responsible for open systems interconnection. The OSI model described earlier is the work of subcommittee SC16.

EIA stands for Electronics Industries Association, a national body that represents manufacturers in the U.S. electronics industry. The EIA work on data communications is carried out by Technical Committee TR30. EIA standards on data communication are published in their RS-series.

1.6.1. CCITT and Related Protocol Standards

Figure 1-27 illustrates the CCITT terminology for various user nodes and network switching nodes. It also illustrates the boundaries across which protocol standards are defined. Figure 1-28 gives an overview of the prominent CCITT protocol standards and their relationships to each other. A line joining two groupings in Figure 1-28 means that the protocol standards in the two groups are closely related. An arrow from one group to another means that the protocol standards at the arrow's head are incorporated as part of the protocol standards at its tail. CCITT protocol standards illustrated in Figure 1-27 are described below:

X.25 defines protocols across the boundary between a user node (a DTE), and a network switching node (a DCE);

X.75 defines protocols across the boundary between switching nodes (STEs) in two different networks;

X.3 defines a packet assembly/disassembly facility (PAD) in a public data network;

X.28 defines the protocols between a start-stop mode DTE and a PAD in a public data network within the same country; and

X.29 defines the protocols between a PAD and a packet-mode DTE.

In the initial version of X.25 approved in 1976, the network layer protocol (called the X.25 packet level) was defined to provide virtual circuit services. With a virtual call (VC) service, call establishment and clearing procedures are necessary to provide and to release a logical connection between two DTEs. With a permanent virtual circuit (PVC) service, the public data network provides an end-to-end logical connection between two DTEs for an indefinite period. (There are no call establishment and clearing procedures.) A DTE can have up to 4,096 logical connections across an X.25 interface (due to the use of a 12-bit logical channel number).

Various applications such as telemetry and inquiry-response systems (reservation systems, electronic funds transfer, etc.) require the sending or exchange of just a few small data units each time a logical connection is made. To accommodate such applications, a later version of X.25 adopted in 1980 contains two additional services:

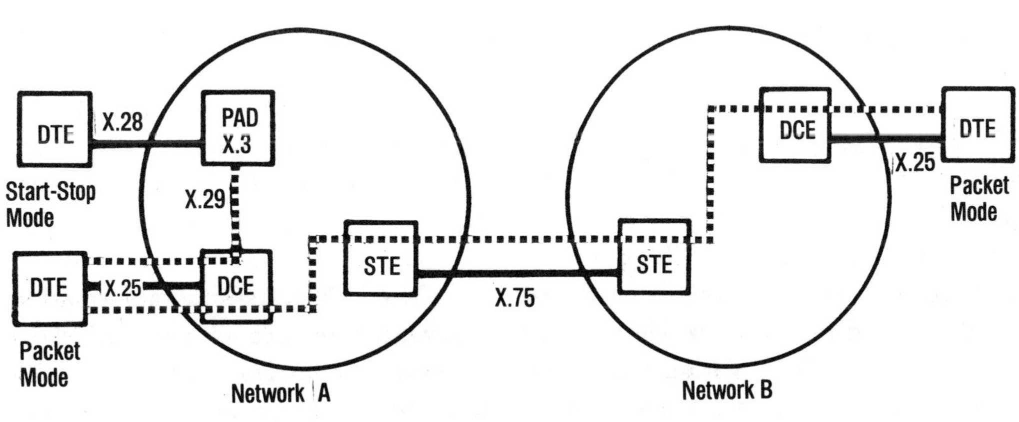

Figure 1-27. An illustration of CCITT terminology.

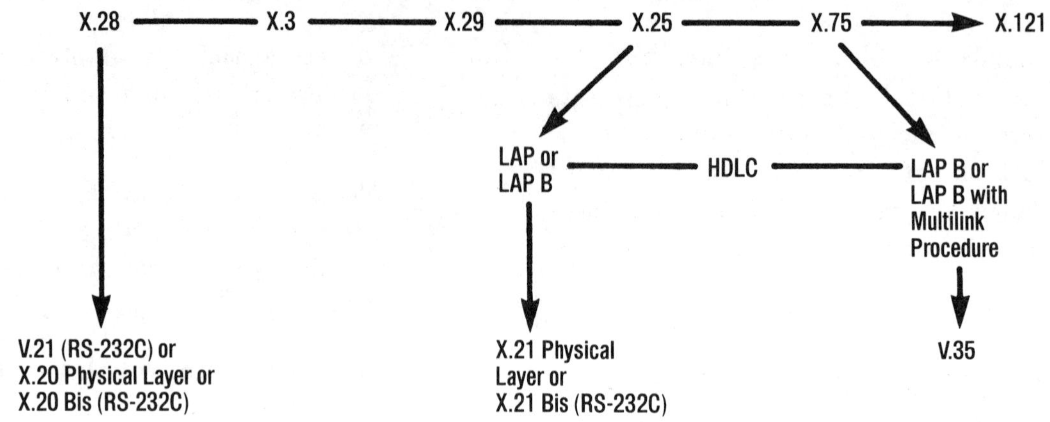

Figure 1-28. Relationships between various protocol standards.

a datagram service and a fast-select service. The fast-select service is an extension of the virtual call service such that the Call Request packet can contain up to 128 octets of user data and the destination DTE's response, in the form of a Call Accepted packet or a Clear Request packet, can contain up to 128 octets of user data.

The data link layer protocol of X.25 has two versions: LAP and LAP B. Both were based on the ISO data link protocol standard, HDLC. LAP was developed first and is not quite compatible with HDLC. LAP B was subsequently specified and is compatible with the Asynchronous Balanced Mode (ABM) of HDLC. Both LAP and LAP B are specified, but LAP B is the preferred specification.

The physical layer specification of X.25 is defined to be the same as the physical layer specification of X.21 (or X.21 bis). Note: physical layer interfaces are summarized in Table 1-1 and will be introduced below.

STEs implementing X.75 provide a gateway function between two different networks. Like X.25, X.75 specifies protocols for the network/data link/physical layers. The network layer protocol (called the X.75 packet level) establishes, maintains, and clears virtual calls across the interface between STEs. Various network utilities are defined so that network administrative information may be signalled in the Call Request, Call Connected, and Clear Request packets. An X.75 interface provides a virtual circuit that joins together virtual circuits in the interconnected networks. As in X.25, up to 4,096 logical connections can be multiplexed across an X.75 interface. The data link layer protocol for X.75 is LAP B in X.25. (LAP is not specified.) In addition, a multilink protocol is also specified that allows the interface to operate over multiple lines, thus achieving greater throughput and reliability. The multilink protocol is unique to X.75 at this time.

The X.75 physical layer is defined to be the CCITT V.35 interface to accommodate modems for higher speed circuits than the speeds of modems intended for use with X.25 (e.g., 48 Kbps). There is no corresponding EIA standard, but this interface is used in the United States.

Note that a DTE and a DCE across an X.25 interface are likely to be located at the same place (possibly even in the same room), whereas two STEs across an X.75 interface are likely to be geographically apart; modems are required, and a reliable connection would require the use of multiple links.

The X.3/X.28/X.29 protocols were defined to enable start-stop character-mode terminals to communicate with remote packet-mode DTEs that implement X.25 (i.e., host computers). The functions performed by a PAD and its operational

Table 1-1. Functional, electrical, and mechanical characteristics of four physical layer interface standards.

	Public Data Network Interfaces		Modem Interfaces	
	X.20 (physical layer)	X.21 (physical layer)	RS-449	RS-232C
Functional (interchange circuits)	X.24		compatible with V.24	
Electrical	X.26/V.10 compatible with RS-422A (unbalanced) X.27/V.11 compatible with RS-423A (balanced)			compatible with V.28
Mechanical	ISO DIS 4903 15-pin connector		compatible with ISO DIS 4902 37-pin connector	compatible with ISO DIS 2110 25-pin connector

characteristics depend upon the values of some internal variables called PAD parameters. A set of PAD parameters exists for each start-stop mode DTE independently. (The use of different parameter values gives rise to different interfaces for a variety of terminals.) Either the start-stop mode DTE or the packet-mode DTE or both can configure the PAD (by using the X.28 and X.29 protocols to set its parameters) so that the PAD's operation is adapted to the start-stop mode DTE's characteristics and possibly to the application program in the host computer as well.

Start-stop terminals and their PADs are assumed to be physically apart, and X.28 includes the specification of a physical layer protocol. For a start-stop terminal accessing the PAD via a public switched telephone network or a leased line, the physical layer specification is in accordance with CCITT Recommendation V.21 for an asynchronous modem at rates of up to 300 bps; this is compatible with the EIA RS-232C interface. For a start-stop terminal accessing the PAD via a public switched data network or leased line, the X.20 (or X.20 bis) interface is specified. In addition to a physical layer protocol, X.28 also defines device control functions as well as data link and network layer functions. The character code set of International Alphabet No. 5 (Recommendation V.3) is specified for X.28 data link protocols.

X.29 specifies a protocol between a PAD and a packet-mode DTE to perform network layer functions (establishing, clearing, and resetting of calls), as well as to perform flow control and data transfer functions. X.29 employs the user data field of the X.25 protocol data units to exchange control information and data between a PAD and a packet-mode DTE.

In addition to participating in X.28 and X.29 protocols to handle interactions with start-stop mode and packet-mode DTEs, respectively, a PAD assembles characters into packets destined for packet-mode DTEs and disassembles packets into characters going to start-stop mode DTEs. Like terminal interface processors (TIPs) in the ARPANET, a PAD provides the function of data concentration and the function of terminal handling. Architecturally, however, PADs and TIPs are very different. TIPs are host nodes in the ARPANET; PADs are part of the public data network [DAY 79]. Figure 1-29 illustrates how one would place the X.3/X.28/X.29 functions in relation to the bottom three layers of the OSI model. We have shown them to be straddling the boundary between the network layer and the upper layers. Processes identified by "NET" in Figure 1-29 implement protocols that are internal to the public data network for the physical, data link and network layers.

1.6.2. Data Link Protocol Standards

Data link protocols provide important functions for computer equipment connected by a physical link to communicate with each other (see Section 1.5.2). Their development started prior to the current activities on standards for public data networks. We have already encountered ISO's HDLC protocol standard in the above discussions. HDLC is closely related to ANSI's ADCCP protocol standard and IBM's SDLC protocol. All are essentially compatible. These data link protocols are said to be bit-oriented. An earlier generation of data link protocols, including the ANSI X3.28 protocol standard and IBM's BSC protocol, are character-oriented. (These character-oriented protocols are still widely used in practice.) The HDLC and BSC protocols will be described in Chapter 2 as prominent examples of the classes of bit-oriented and character-oriented protocols.

1.6.3. Physical Layer Interfaces

To define a physical layer interface requires specification of the following characteristics:

1. mechanical
2. electrical
3. functional (interchange circuits and their functions)
4. procedural (the subset of interchange circuits and the protocol using them for connection establishment and clearing)

Four interface standards are shown in Table 1-1: X.21, X.20, RS-232C, and RS-449. All four are serial-data DTE/DCE interfaces. X.21 and X.20 are for accessing a (digital) public data network. RS-232C and RS-449 are for the use of modems. Table 1-1 shows their functional, electrical, and mechanical specifications; these are given in terms

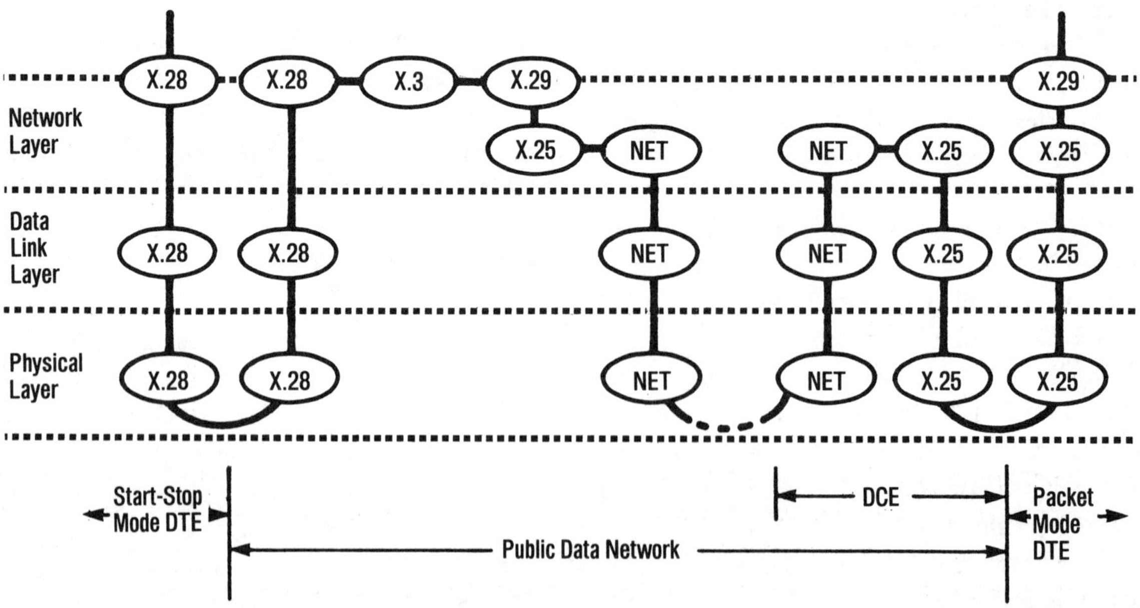

Figure 1-29. Placement of X.3, X.28, and X.29 functions in a structured architectural model.

of CCITT or ISO standards either adopted for the specific characteristics or compatible with the characteristics of these interfaces. (The X.21 and X.20 standards also define data link and network level functions. In this subsection, we are referring to their physical layer specifications only.)

First we look at the modem interfaces. The RS-232C interface is probably the most well known. It was developed by EIA in cooperation with the Bell System, various independent modem manufacturers, and computer manufacturers [MCNA 77]. It can be used with both asynchronous modems and synchronous modems (up to 19.2 Kbps). RS-449 was developed to replace RS-232C for improved performance, such as longer interface cables and a higher maximum data rate (to be achieved with the new electrical characteristics), additional interface functions, and a more precise and better mechanical specification.

Note that RS-449 has the same electrical characteristics as X.21. Why wasn't the X.21 interface adopted instead of developing a new interface to replace RS-232C? One reason is that the X.21 interface was designed for accessing a public data network, and it therefore defines only a small number of interchange circuits. There are both technical and performance problems in trying to adopt X.21 for use with a wideband modem [BERT 80]. Furthermore, interoperability of RS-449 with RS-232C may be accomplished by means of a simple passive adapter and some additional design criteria for the RS-449 interchange circuits; no modifications are needed for the RS-232C equipment.

In addition to the specifications of functional, electrical and mechanical characteristics shown in Table 1-1, a physical layer interface also requires the specification of a protocol for the establishment/clearing of a DTE/DCE connection, using a subset of interchange circuits. When modems are used, the protocols for using these interchange circuits are specific to different types of modems. Additional interchange circuits are required for a switched-network connection compared to a leased-line connection. CCITT defines various modem-specific procedures for the use of interchange circuits in V-series recommendations. For example, the V.21 recommendation is a procedure for low-speed, asynchronous switched network modems compatible with the functional specification of RS-232C. Obviously, different modem-specific procedures can be defined for the R-232C (or RS-449) characteristics in Table 1-1. Two pieces of equipment are often said to be "RS-232C compatible" if their mechanical, electrical, and functional characteristics are compatible. In fact, for them to be able to communicate they need to implement the same procedural specification as well.

We next consider the public data network interfaces. Recommendation X.20 defines a DTE/DCE interface for start-stop (asynchronous) transmission up to 300 bps on public data networks. (Bit synchronism is actually maintained during the transmission of each character but the time between characters may be arbitrary.) Recommendation X.21 defines a DTE/DCE interface for synchronous transmission on public data networks for a data rate of 600, 2400, 4800, 9600, or 48,000 bps. Both X.21 and X.20 specify circuit-switched and leased-circuit services. The provisions to acquire circuits on demand from a public data network correspond to network layer functions. Thus in their entirety, X.21 and X.20 are more than just a physical layer protocol.

We next briefly describe the X.21 interface. In addition to the specifications in Table 1-1, the procedural specification within the physical layer is given by a state transition diagram of quiescent states; each such state is defined by the conditions on four interchange circuits. One of the states corresponds to both DCE and DTE being ready. X.21 also defines a protocol for the use of a circuit-switched public data network [FOLT 80]. This is a protocol between DTE processes and DCE processes residing in the network layer of the OSI model. Addresses of DTEs are assigned in accordance with recommendation X.121. The protocol is said to be character-oriented because control information for call-establishment is exchanged using control characters from the International Alphabet No. 5 (on the R circuit from DCE to DTE and on the T circuit from DTE to DCE). Two data link layer functions are also defined. The first is byte timing (the determination of octet boundaries). This is accomplished by placing two or more contiguous SYN characters before each control sequence of characters. In addition, byte timing may also be provided by a circuit from DCE to DTE. Simple odd parity is applied to each character for error detection (also a data link layer function).

Let us now return to Figure 1-28. Note that X.25 and X.28 incorporate the physical layer specifications of X.21 and X.20, respectively (but without the data link and network layer functions). Also, X.21 bis and X.20 bis were specified as interim protocols that describe how a public data network should interface with existing DTEs designed for using modems. They simply mean the use of CCITT V-series modem-specific procedures in the physical layer that are compatible with RS-232C (or RS-449). Figure 1-30 illustrates the difference between X.21 and X.21 bis, as well as the fact that X.21 has network layer functions. Note that X.21 specifies the interface between a DTE and a DCE which are physically close. The DCE is considered as part of the public data network although it is located on the premises of the DTE. For a switched, public data network, the network layer protocol of X.21 acquires from the network a circuit to a distant DTE/DCE pair. An X.21 bis interface is intended to be an interim measure for DTEs that access the network via modems. In this case, the network layer functions of X.21 are implemented on top of a modem-specific physical layer interface. (See lower part of diagram in Figure 1-30.)

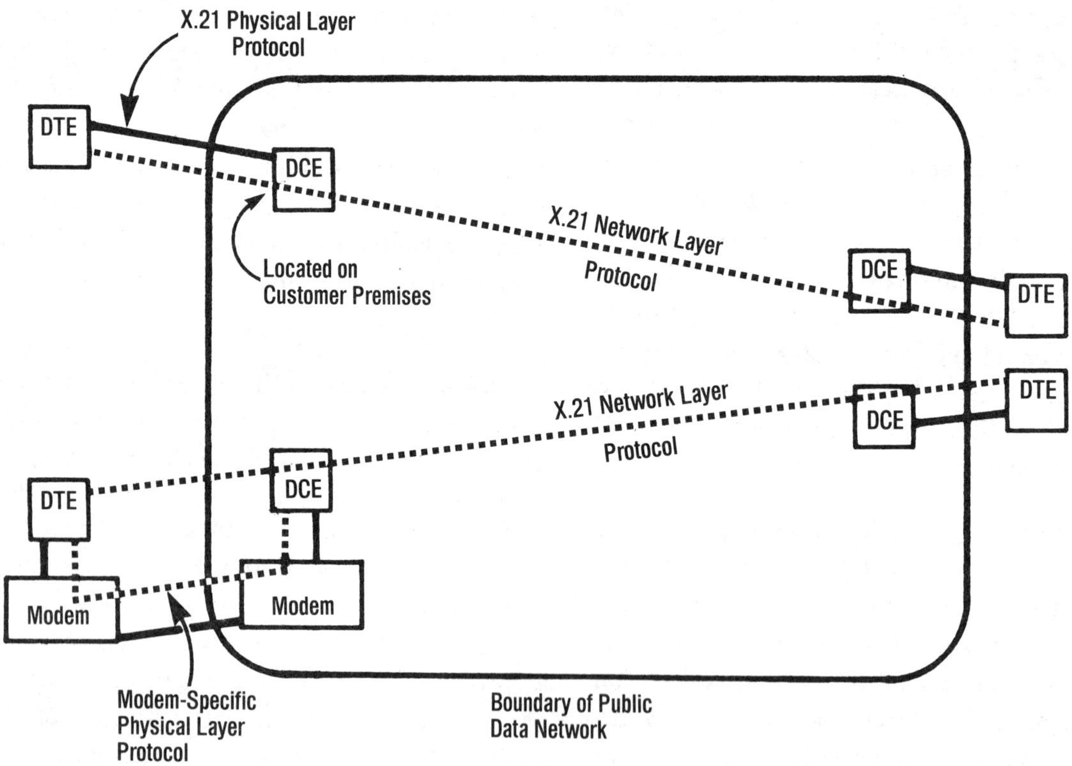

Figure 1-30. An illustration of X.21 and X.21 bis.

1.6.4. IEEE Local Area Network Standards

IEEE Standard 802 is a family of standards for local area networks. Protocols corresponding to the physical and data link layers of the OSI model are specified. In particular the data link layer is split into two sublayers: a logical link control layer, which implements functions of content and dialog synchronizations, and a multiple access control sublayer, which implements the functions of multiple access and frame synchronizations. As before, the physical layer implements the function of bit synchronization.

A peer protocol is specified for the logical link control sublayer. Two types of link operation are defined: a connectionless service and a connection-oriented service similar to that of HDLC. The interface between this sublayer and the network layer above and the interface between this sublayer and the multiple access control sublayer below are also defined. Several standards are specified for the multiple access control sublayer for different communication media: CSMA/CD for a bus, token-passing for a bus, and token-passing for a ring. The reader is referred to the standards documents for details [IEEE 82] and to Chapters 3 and 4 for discussions on multiple access protocols and local area networks respectively.

1.7. TRENDS AND APPLICATIONS

1.7.1. A Historical Perspective

In a 1978 article, Roberts gave an excellent historical perspective of the development of packet switching up to that time [ROBE 78]. He talked about pioneers and pioneering networks, the development of X.25 and public data networks, and the application of packet switching to satellite and radio communication networks. He observed that packet switching was not an invention. It was simply an application of the dynamic resource allocation principle and was introduced when digital electronics became inexpensive enough to render packet switching cost effective. He said, "In 1978 virtually all new data networks being built throughout the world are based upon packet switching." He also conjectured, "An open question at this time is how long will it take for voice communications to be revolutionized as well by the packet switching technology?" In fact, several researchers have studied the performance of sending digital voice traffic through packet switching networks [FORG 77, GONS 83]. It remains to be seen whether packet switching will displace circuit switching as the communication technology for voice traffic.

In his keynote speech at the 7th Data Communications Symposium, Kleinrock reviewed the fundamental principles that had evolved from a decade of network development. He described some of the successes, some of the technical problems to be addressed, some of the exciting applications, and the telecommunications revolution that had already begun. The 1982 article in the *Journal of Telecommunication Networks*, based on his speech, is reprinted below [KLEI 82].

1.7.2. Future Directions

Nowadays, data and text can be easily and conveniently stored, edited, retrieved, and communicated. The ease and convenience of handling such coded information behooves us to strive for networks and systems that will handle normally uncoded information like voice, image, and video in the same manner (after first digitizing and coding them). Currently, such uncoded information is handled separately, e.g., the use of telephone facilities and PBXs for voice and facsimile, and satellite and other wideband facilities for video. Filing, retrieving, and editing of voice messages, graphics displays etc. can be done but not conveniently. In fact it will be desirable to handle all information, data, text, voice, image, and perhaps also video, in the same communication networks (both local area and wide area networks) and in the same systems for office automation, home automation etc. Glimpses into such a scenario are given in Lewis Branscomb's keynote address at INFOCOM'83 [BRAN 83]. The scenario is also consistent with the CCITT activity on establishing the Integrated Services Digital Network (ISDN) concept for multiservice digital networks [DECI 82].

The biggest impact of office automation has been probably the ease with which documents are handled (created, filed, retrieved, perused, modified, deleted, distributed etc.). In his address, Branscomb envisioned the integration of voice, and data for creating compound documents with voice annotation and playback through a telephone headset. He conjectured that eventually, office systems will have to merge data, text, voice and image information into integrated electronic documents. The user will not be conscious of their form when stored. The transmission system will not care what form--words, voice, or pictures--the information was in originally. (This is of course consistent with the principle of data transparency as discussed earlier.)

Is such a scenario supported by the current PBX and LAN technologies? The basic function of a PBX is to support interactive human-to-human voice conversations. PBXs that support only 64-Kbps voice channels cannot meet the requirements of some future office applications. Hundreds of Kbps are needed for browsing through a document of coded information, and Mbps are needed for facsimile information. Packet-switched LANs do have such high bandwidths available on demand. On the other hand, it is doubtful that some of the current packet-switched LANs utilizing a baseband technology are suited to supporting large numbers of concurrent voice conversations between people in addition to data communications. Branscomb concluded that both a PBX and a LAN would be required to satisfy the needs of office applications in the foreseeable future. It seems that the "electronic paper clip," as referred to by Branscomb, that is needed to bind together documents integrating all kinds of information will have to be realized from one or more of the advanced technologies being developed for the LAN environment: broadband systems, frequency-agile modems, optical fibers, etc.

Let us now move away from the office automation environment to consider wide-area communication services. The ISDN concept is being established for an integration of telephone and data communication services in an evolutionary manner. CCITT Study Group XVIII is coordinating the ISDN activities within CCITT and the recommendation of standard interfaces. ISDNs are envisioned to evolve from the basic digital telephone networks founded on 64 Kbps PCM circuit switching. They will provide end-to-end connectivity (in digital form) to support a wide range of services including voice, data, sound and video transmissions. An ISDN provides a limited set of user interfaces and is recognized by the service characteristics of its interfaces rather than by its internal architecture, configuration, or technology. This concept provides the basis for permitting an evolutionary migration from the current generation of circuit-switched ISDNs. To accommodate services ranging from alarms and telemetry to voice, interactive and bulk data, electronic mail, videotex, and video, a variety of services are provided: leased lines, circuit-switched services, and virtual circuit and datagram services based upon packet switching etc. Internally, an ISDN may have separate communication facilities that constitute separate packet-switching and circuit-switching networks, or it may use a hybrid circuit-switching/packet-switching technology such as the one described earlier in Section 1.4.4. Networks that provide a wideband service may have to incorporate separate wideband facilities such as satellite channels.

1.7.3. Applications

Before we plunge into the technical details of communication and networking protocols in the following chapters, it is helpful to have in the back of our minds an overall view of the different kinds of computer networks together with their present and anticipated applications. We begin by mentioning a few of the pioneering networks.

Some early networks

The ARPANET was developed in the late 1960s with the original intention of sharing special resources, software and hardware, at different research sites. It turned out that this network demonstrated very convincingly the power of electronic mail and document creation and distribution. By linking various research groups together in the United States, it fostered the exchange of ideas and collaboration by researchers far away from each other. At about the same time, Tymnet was developed by Tymshare Corporation in 1970 to connect asynchronous terminals to its timesharing central computers. Airline reservation networks had been in operation since the early 1960s. But these networks, such as SABRE and PARS, were primarily centralized and terminal-oriented networks [SIWI 77]. An exception was the SITA network. SITA is a cooperative company of international air carriers organized to provide its members a world-wide data communication capability via a message switching network. In 1969 SITA began updating its design by replacing the major nodes of its message switching network with high-level network nodes organized to act like a packet-switching network. Incoming messages are subdivided into 240-byte packets and are stored and forwarded along predetermined routes to their destinations. Prestored distributed tables provide for alternate routes in the event of line failures [SCHW 77, ROBE 78].

Private networks

Many private networks exist to handle various general information processing functions of large corporations (information retrieval, file transfers, and document distribution) as well as to handle special applications (order processing, inventory control, etc.). Private networks are either homegrown or supplied by computer manufacturers, such as SNA networks by IBM and networks by DEC in accordance with its Digital Network Architecture (DNA). Private networks for a long time have been mostly centralized and terminal-oriented, meaning that they have a tree topology. The root node of the tree is made up of one or more host computers. The other nodes are either data concentrators or terminals. This approach is exemplified by the pre-SNA networks of IBM as well as SNA networks circa 1974. But the situation has been rapidly changing. The SNA multihost Advanced Communication Function (ACF) announced in 1976 permits "cross-domain" sessions. The SNA Network Interconnection technique was announced in 1983 [IBM 83]. DNA as described in [WECK 80] also permits multiple hosts as well as a mesh network topology.

Industry-wide networks

Various industry-wide networks have been in existence for some time. Aside from the airline reservations networks mentioned above, many financial services networks are in operation [WEIN 82]:

- networks for interbank transfers (electronic funds transfer systems),
- automatic tellermachine (ATM) networks,
- networks for securities trading, and
- networks for credit authorization, etc.

Some new developments are on the horizon. Extending credit authorization networks to include point-of-sale systems (electronic cash registers) is one example. Another development is the use of smart credit cards (containing microprocessors) for both automatic teller machines and point-of-sale systems. It is interesting to note that human operators are sometimes needed in credit authorization systems. In this respect the ISDN concept of integrating both voice and data traffic is quite appropriate here.

Local area networks

Local area networks have been developed and built within the local environments of college campuses and research laboratories. Their most important application, however, will probably be in office automation. The requirements of office automation are many and varied. We review some of them below:

- electronic mail, image mail, and voice mail
- document preparation, filing, perusal, retrieval, and printing
- data entry
- other personal computing functions
    - spread sheets
    - database access
    - graphics
    - calendar support

There are various other special applications for local area networks such as process control in manufacturing and energy management for a local environment.

Public data networks

The success of the packet-switching technology as demonstrated by the ARPANET and the extensive activities in the development of private networks in the early 1970s encouraged the development of public data networks. The most well known of them are Telenet in the U.S. (operational in 1975), Datapac in Canada (operational in 1977) and Transpac in France (operational in 1978). All of these are based upon the packet-switching technology and the use of the X.25 interface for customer access and the X.75 interface for internetworking. Numerous public data networks based upon X.25 have since become operational world-wide.

In the U.S., Tymnet was also approved as a carrier and began supplying public data services in the late 1970s.

These public data networks are often referred to as value added networks (VANs) because they are built on top of common carrier facilities.

Home and small business applications

Networking services to homes and small businesses have aroused a lot of interest. Such services constitute one of the main objectives of ISDNs. While ISDN is a solution that will slowly evolve from the current digital telephone networks, another possible solution is that of metropolitan area networks (MANs) based upon CATV systems. The IEEE 802 Standards documents contain a provision for such networks (IEEE 802.6 yet to be defined). If it is anything like the LAN network standards, the metropolitan area networks will be packet-switched systems that interconnect to packet-switched public data networks via gateways. Thus the ISDN and MAN concepts represent two solutions coming from different directions.

Various home applications that have been talked about include

- electronic mail,
- telebanking,
- teleshopping, and
- electronic publishing (database information services, news, etc.).

These home applications will involve personal computers. In the case of teleshopping that requires graphics and pictures with colors, videotex systems based upon consumer TV technology and the use of videodiscs are being investigated.

Various telemetry applications have also been mentioned in conjunction with ISDN. They include alarms, meter reading, energy management, and opinion polls, among others.

Some of the above-mentioned applications for homes and small businesses are already available, although the technologies of ISDN and MAN will not appear for some time.

CSNET provides an electronic mail service

Table 1-2. Some generic traffic models.

Communicating entities	Specific application examples	Traffic model	Special characteristics
terminal & terminal	electronic mail	data messages	short; not necessarily bursty
terminal & database	information retrieval	inquiry/response	interactive; asymmetric traffic
	reservation systems; financial services	transaction processing	interactive; typically bursty; database updates
terminal & program	time-sharing; A.I. applications such as medical diagnosis	remote job entry	may be interactive or batch
	data entry; telemetry	data messages	asymmetric traffic
program/database & program/database	file transfers	bulk data	could be bursty

to computer science researchers in the United States and Canada. It is a high-level logical network that spans several physical networks: Phonenet, ARPANET, and Telenet [DENN 83]. Plans are underway to develop both domestic and international gateways to connect to other networks as well.

Several systems--ITT, MCI Mail, Western Union's EasyLink and Graphnet's Freedom Network--provide a store-and-forward Telex service for people with personal computers. These vendors maintain store-and-forward computers and offer local or toll-free numbers for customers to call. To send a message, a customer dials up a store-and-forward computer using a modem and his telephone. He is assigned an electronic mailbox in the store-and-forward computer from which he can retrieve messages sent to him by others.

Numerous information databases are also available to people with personal computers. Access is again via a modem and dial-up telephone service.

Sears, IBM, and CBS announced a videotex service in February 1984 for shopping, financial and information services. It is also based upon the use of personal computers and the existing telephone system.

Traffic models

The applications and potential applications of communication networks are only limited by one's imagination. From the point of view of the designers of communication and networking protocols, it will be convenient to classify the myriad of applications into a small number of generic traffic models. We make an attempt at such a classification below by considering the different ways of pairing up the data traffic sources and sinks: terminals, databases, and programs (Table 1-2).

An important decision to make in the design of communication networks is whether to allocate communication bandwidth in small units for a relatively long duration (allocation of channels) or in large units for a relatively short duration (allocation to waiting packets). Such a decision is dependent upon the burstiness of traffic sources. Packet switching is suitable for applications with bursty traffic sources whereas circuit switching is not. A measure defined in [LAM 78] suggests that the burstiness of a traffic source is determined by the ratio of its mean response time requirement and the mean interarrival time of its data units. In particular *the smaller is this ratio for a particular traffic source, the more bursty it is.* Thus, an electronic mail system that specifies a mean delivery time of one day would be non-bursty and can probably be efficiently handled by some form of circuit switching (e.g., Telex). On the other hand, file transfers for a distributed database system with short response time requirements of say a few seconds would be bursty, and a packet-switching network would be required. Thus, burstiness is not necessarily associated with short units of data.

Lastly, with the anticipated integration of data, voice, image and video traffic into the same networks, additional traffic models will have to be characterized and understood.

References

[BARN 77] Barnla, J. D. and F. R. Zitzmann, "Digital Communications Satellite System of SBS," IEEE Electron. and Aerosp. Syst. Conv., Sept. 1977; reprinted in *Satellite* Communications, H. L. Van Trees (Ed.), IEEE Press, 1979.

[BERT 80] Bertine, H. V., "Physical Level Protocols," *IEEE Trans. on Commun.*, Vol. COM-28, No. 4, April 1980, pp. 443-444.

*[BRAN 83] Branscomb, L. M., "Networks for the Nineties," Keynote address, IEEE INFOCOM'83; in *IEEE Communications Magazine*, October 1983, pp. 38-43.

[BRIN 73] Brinch Hansen, P., *Operating System Principles*, Prentice-Hall, Englewood Cliffs, N.J., 1973.

[CCIT 78] CCITT Grey Book, *Provisional Recommendations X.3, X.25, X.28 and X.29 on packet-switched data transmission services*, Geneva, 1978.

[CERF 78] Cerf, V. G. and P. T. Kirstein. "Issues in Packet-Network Interconnection," *Proc. IEEE* 66, 11, November 1978, pp. 1386-1408.

[CHU 69] Chu, W. W., "A Study of Asynchronous Time Division Multiplexing for Time-sharing Computers," *AFIPS Proceedings*, Vol. 35, FJCC, 1969, pp. 669-678.

[CHU 74] Chu, W. W., "Optimal Message Block Size for Computer Communications with Error Detection and Retransmission Strategies," *IEEE Trans. on Commun.*, Vol. COM-20, No. 10, October 1974.

[CYPS 78] Cypser, R. J., *Communications Architecture for Distributed Systems*, Addison-Wesley, Reading, Mass., 1978.

[DAVE 72] Davey, J. R., "Modems," *Proc. IEEE*, November 1972, pp. 1284-1292.

[DAY 79] Day, J. D., "Resource Sharing Protocols," *Computer*, Vol. 12, No. 9, September 1979, pp. 47-56.

[DECI 82] Decina, M., "Progress Towards User Access Arrangements in Integrated Services Digital Networks," *IEEE Trans. on Commun.*, Vol. COM-30, No. 9, Sept. 1982, pp. 2117-2130.

[DENN 83] Denning, P. J., A. Hearn, and C. W. Kern, "History and Overview of CSNET," *Proc. ACM SIGCOMM'83 Symp. on Comm. Architectures and Protocols*, University of Texas at Austin, March 1983, pp. 138-145.

[FOLT 80] Folts, H. C., "X.25 Transaction-Oriented Features--Datagram and Fast Select." *IEEE Trans. Commun.*, Vol. COM-28, April 1980, pp. 496-500.

[FORG 77] Forgie, J. W. and A. G. Nemeth, "An Efficient Packetized Voice/Data Network using Statistical Flow Control," *Conf. Rec. ICCC'77*, Chicago, pp. 38.2-44 to 38.2-48, 1977.

[GERL 80] Gerla, M. and L. Kleinrock, "Flow Control: A Comparative Survey," *IEEE Trans. Comm.*, COM-28 (1980), pp. 553-574.

[GONS 83] Gonsalves, T. A., "Packet-voice Communication on an Ethernet Local Computer Network: An Experimental Study," *Proc. SIGCOMM'83 Symp. on Comm. Architectures and Protocols*, University of Texas at Austin, pp. 178-185, March 1983.

[IBM 83] Systems Network Architecture Special Issue, *IBM Systems Journal*, Vol. 22, No. 4, 1983.

[IEEE 82] IEEE Project 802 Local Area Network Standards, Draft IEEE Standard 802.2, Logical Link Control, Draft D, Nov. 1982; Draft IEEE Standard 802.3, CSMA/CD Access Method and Physical Layer Specifications, Revision D, Dec. 1982; Draft IEEE Standard 802.4, Token-Passing Bus Access Method and Physical Layer Specifications, Draft D, Dec. 1982. (Available from IEEE Computer Society.)

[KERM 79] Kermani, P. and L. Kleinrock, "Virtual Cut-Through: A New Computer Communication Switching Technique," *Comput. Networks*, Vol. 3, 1979, pp. 267-286.

[KLEI 76] Kleinrock, L., *Queueing Systems, Vol. 2: Computer Applications*, Wiley-Interscience, New York, 1976.

*[KLEI 82] Kleinrock, L., "A Decade of Network Development," *Journal of Telecommunication Networks*, Spring 1982, pp. 1-11.

[LAM 78] Lam, S. S., "A New Measure for Characterizing Data Traffic," *IEEE Trans. Commun.*, Vol. COM-26, January 1978.

[LAM 80] Lam, S. S., "A Packet Network Architecture for Local Interconnection," *Conf. Rec. Int. Conf. Commun.*, Seattle, June 1980.

[LAM 83] Lam, S. S., "Data Link Control Procedures," Chapter 3 in *Computer Communications, Vol. 1: Principles*. W. Chou (Ed.), Prentice-Hall, Englewood Cliffs, N.J., 1983.

[MART 76] Martin, J., *Telecommunications and the Computer*, Second Edition, Prentice-Hall, Englewood Cliffs, N.J., 1976.

[MCNA 77] McNamara, J. E., *Technical Aspects of Data Communication*, Digital Equipment Corp., Maynard, Mass., 1977.

[MCQU 78] McQuillan, J. M. and V. G. Cerf, *A Practical View of Computer Communications Protocols*, IEEE Computer Society Press, Silver Springs, Md., 1978.

[OSI 81] "Data Processing--Open Systems Interconnection--Basic Reference Model." Document ISO/TC97/SC16, American National Standards Institute, 1430 Broadway, New York, N.Y.; *Computer Networks*, Vol. 5, No. 2, 1981, pp. 81-118.

[POUZ 78] Pouzin, L. and H. Zimmerman, "A Tutorial on Protocols," *Proc. IEEE*, 66, 11, November 1978, pp. 1346-1370.

*[ROBE 78] Roberts, L., "The Evolution of Packet Switching," *Proc. IEEE*, Vol. 66, November 1978.

[RUTL 82] Rutledge, J. H., "OSI and SNA: A Perspective," *Journal of Telecommunication Networks*, Vol. 1, No. 1, 1982, pp. 13-27.

[RYBC 80] Rybczynski, A., "X.25 Interface and End-to-End Virtual Circuit Service Characteristics," *IEEE Trans. Commun.*, Vol. COM-28, April 1980, pp. 500-510.

[SCHW 77] Schwartz, M., *Computer-Communication Network Design and Analysis*, Prentice-Hall, Englewood Cliffs, N.J., 1977.

[SCHW 80] Schwartz, M., *Information Transmission, Modulation, and Noise*, Third Edition, McGraw-Hill, New York, 1980.

[SHOC 80] Shoch, J. F., and J. A. Hupp, "Measured Performance of an Ethernet Local Network," *Communications of the ACM*, 23 (12), December 1980.

[SIWI 77] Siwiec, J. E., "A High-performance DB/DC System," IBM Systems Journal, Vol. 16, No. 2, 1977, pp. 169-195.

[UNSO 81] Unsoy, M. S. and T. Shanahan, "X.75 Internetworking of Datapac and Telenet." *Proc. 7th Data Communication Symp.*, Mexico City, October 1981, pp. 232-239.

[VITE 66] Viterbi, A. J., *Principles of Coherent Communication*, McGraw-Hill, New York, 1966.

[WECK 80] Wecker, S., "DNA: The Digital Network Architecture," *IEEE Trans. on Commun.*, Vol. COM-28, No. 4, April 1980.

[WEIN 82] Weinstein, S. B., "A Perspective on Financial Industry Networking," *Journal of Telecomm. Networks*, Vol. 1, No. 4, 1982, pp. 317-332.

(* article reprinted below.)

The Evolution of Packet Switching

LAWRENCE G. ROBERTS, MEMBER, IEEE

Invited Paper

Abstract—Over the past decade data communications has been revolutionized by a radically new technology called packet switching. In 1968 virtually all interactive data communication networks were circuit switched, the same as the telephone network. Circuit switching networks preallocate transmission bandwidth for an entire call or session. However, since interactive data traffic occurs in short bursts 90 percent or more of this bandwidth is wasted. Thus, as digital electronics became inexpensive enough, it became dramatically more cost-effective to completely redesign communications networks, introducing the concept of packet switching where the transmission bandwidth is dynamically allocated, permitting many users to share the same transmission line previously required for one user. Packet switching has been so successful, not only in improving the economics of data communications but in enhancing reliability and functional flexibility as well, that in 1978 virtually all new data networks being built throughout the world are based on packet switching. An open question at this time is how long will it take for voice communications to be revolutionized as well by packet switching technology. In order to better understand both the past and future evolution of this fast moving technology, this paper examines in detail the history and trends of packet switching.

THERE HAVE ALWAYS been two fundamental and competing approaches to communications: pre-allocation and dynamic-allocation of transmission bandwidth. The telephone, telex, and TWX networks are circuit-switched systems, where a fixed bandwidth is preallocated for the duration of a call. Most radio usage also involves preallocation of the spectrum, either permanently or for single call. On the other hand, message, telegraph, and mail systems have historically operated by dynamically allocating bandwidths or space after a message is received, one link at a time, never attempting to schedule bandwidth over the whole source-to-destination path. Before the advent of computers, dynamic-allocation systems were necessarily limited to nonreal time communications, since many manual sorting and routing decisions were required along the path of each message. However, the rapid advances in computer technology over the last two decades have not only removed this limitation but have even made feasible dynamic-allocation communications systems that are superior to preallocation systems in connect time, reliability, economy and flexibility. This new communications technology, called "packet switching," divides the input flow of information into small segments, or packets, of data which move through the network in a manner similar to the handling of mail but at immensely higher speeds. Although the first packet-switching network was developed and tested less than ten years ago, packet systems already offer substantial economic and performance advantages over conventional systems. This has resulted in rapid worldwide acceptance of packet switching for low-speed interactive data communications networks, both public and private.

Manuscript received May 11, 1978; revised May 22, 1978.
The author is with Telenet Communications Corporation, Washington, DC 20036.

A question remains, however. Will dynamic-allocation techniques like packet switching generally replace circuit switching and other preallocation techniques for high-speed data and voice communication? The history of packet switching so far indicates that further applications are inevitable. The following examination of the primary technological and economic trade-offs involved in the growth of the packet switching communications industry should help to trace the development of the technology toward these further applications.

EARLY HISTORY

Packet switching technology was not really an invention, but a reapplication of the basic dynamic-allocation techniques used for over a century by the mail, telegraph, and torn paper tape switching systems. A packet switched network only allocates bandwidth when a block of data is ready to be sent, and only enough for that one block to travel over one network link at a time. Depending on the nature of the data traffic being transferred, the packet-switching approach is 3–100 times more efficient than preallocation techniques in reducing the wastage of available transmission bandwidth resources. To do this, packet systems require both processing power and buffer storage resources at each switch in the network for each packet sent. The resulting economic tradeoff is simple: if lines are cheap, use circuit switching; if computing is cheap, use packet switching. Although today this seems obvious, before packet switching had been demonstrated technically and proven economical, the tradeoff was never recognized, let along analyzed.

In the early 1960's, preallocation was so clearly the proven and accepted technique that no communications engineer ever seriously considered reverting to what was considered an obsolete technique, dynamic-allocation. Such techniques had been proven both uneconomic and unresponsive 20–80 years previously, so why reconsider them? The very fact that no great technological breakthrough was required to implement packet switching was another factor weighing against its acceptance by the engineering community.

What was required was the total reevaluation of the performance and economics of dynamic-allocation systems, and their application to an entirely different task. Thus, it remained for outsiders to the communications industry, computer professionals, to develop packet switching in response to a problem for which they needed a better answer: communicating data to and from computers.

THE PIONEERS

Rand

The first published description of what we now call packet switching was an 11-volume analysis, *On Distributed Communications*, prepared by Paul Baran of the Rand Corporation

Reprinted from *Proceedings of the IEEE*, Volume 66, Number 11, November 1978, pages 1307-1313.

in August 1964 [1]. This study was conducted for the Air Force, and it proposed a fully distributed packet switching system to provide for all military communications, data, and voice. The study also included a totally digital microwave system and integrated encryption capability. The Air Force's primary goal was to produce a totally survivable system that contained no critical central components. Not only was this goal achieved by Rand's proposed packet switching system, but even the economics projected were superior, for both voice and data transmissions. Unfortunately, the Air Force took no follow-up action, and the report sat largely ignored for many years until packet switching was rediscovered and applied by others.

ARPA I

Also in the 1962–1964 period, the Advanced Research Projects Agency (ARPA), under the direction of J. C. R. Licklider (currently at M.I.T.), sponsored and substantially furthered the development of time-sharing computer systems. One of Licklider's strong interests was to link these time-shared computers together through a widespread computer network. Although no actual work was done on the communication system at that time, the discussions and interest Licklider spawned had an important motivating impact on the initiators of the two first actual network projects: Donald Davies and me.

As previously indicated, the development of packet switching was primarily the result of identifying the need for a radically new communications system. Licklider's strong interest in and perception of the importance of the problem encouraged many people in the computer field to consider it seriously for the first time. It was in good part due to this influence that I decided, in November 1964, that computer networks were an important problem for which a new communications system was required [2]. Evidently Donald Davies of the National Physical Laboratory (NPL) in the United Kingdom had been seized by the same conviction, partially as a result of a seminar he sponsored in autumn 1965, which I attended with many M.I.T. Project MAC people. Thus, the interest in creating a new communications system grew out of the development of time-sharing and Licklider's special interest in the 1964–1965 period.

National Physical Laboratory

Almost immediately after the 1965 meeting, Donald Davies conceived of the details of a store-and-forward packet switching system, and in a June 1966 description of his proposal coined the term "packet" to describe the 128-byte blocks being moved around inside the network. Davies circulated his proposed network design throughout the U.K. in late 1965 and 1966. It was only after this distribution that he discovered Paul Baran's 1964 report.

The first open publication of the NPL proposal was in October 1967 at the A.C.M. Symposium in Gatlinburg, TN [3]. In nearly all respects, Davies' original proposal, developed in late 1965, was similar to the actual networks being built today. His cost analysis showed strong economic advantages for the packet approach, and by all rights, the proposal should have led quickly to a U.K. project. However, the communications world was hard to convince, and for several years, nothing happened in the U.K. on the development of a multinode packet switching network.

Donald Davies was able, however, to initiate a local network with a single packet switch at the NPL. By 1973 this local network was providing an important distribution service within the laboratory [4], [5]. This project, plus the strong conviction and continued effort by those at NPL (Davies, Barber, Scantlebury, Wilkinson, and Bartlett), did gradually have an effect on the U.K. and much of Europe.

ARPA II

In January 1967, I joined ARPA and assumed the management of the computer research programs under its sponsorship. ARPA was sponsoring computer research at leading universities and research labs in the U.S. These projects and their computers provided an ideal environment for a pilot network project; consequently, during 1967 the ARPANET was planned to link these computers together.

The plan was published in June 1967. The design consisted of a packet switching network, using minicomputers at each computer site as the packet switches and interfacing device, interconnected by leased lines. By coincidence, the first published document on the ARPANET was also presented at the A.C.M. Symposium in Gatlinburg, TN, in October 1967 [6] along with the NPL plan. The major differences between the designs were the porposed net line speeds, with NPL suggesting 1.5 Mbit/s lines. The resulting discussions were one factor leading to the ARPANET using 50-kbit/s lines, rather than the lower speed lines previously planned [7].

During 1968, a request for proposal was let for the ARPANET packet switching equipment and the operation of the network. The RFP was awarded to Bolt Beranek and Newman, Inc. (BBN) in Cambridge, MA, in January 1969. Significant aspects of the network's internal operation, such as routing, flow control, software design, and network control were developed by a BBN team consisting of Frank Heart, Robert Kahn, Severo Ornstein, William Crowther, and David Walden [8], [9], [10]. By December 1969. four nodes of the net had been installed and were operating effectively. The network was expanded rapidly thereafter to support 23-host computers by April 1971, 62 hosts by June 1974, and 111 hosts by March 1977.

The ARPANET utilized minicomputers at every node to be served by the network, interconnected in a fully distributed fashion by 50-kbit/s leased lines. Each minicomputer took blocks of data from the computers and terminals connected to it, subdivided them into 128 byte packets, and added a header specifying destination and source addresses; then, based on a dynamically updated routing table, the minicomputer sent the packet over whichever free line was currently the fastest route toward the destination. Upon receiving a packet, the next minicomputer would acknowledge it and repeat the routing process independently. Thus, one important characteristic of the ARPANET was its completely distributed, dynamic routing algorithm on a packet-by-packet basis, based on a continuous evaluation within the network of the least-delay paths, considering both line availability and queue lengths.

The technical and operational success of the ARPANET quickly demonstrated to a generally skeptical world that dynamic-allocation techniques–and packet switching in particular–could be organized to provide an efficient and highly responsive interactive data communications facility. Fears that packets would loop forever and that very large buffer pools would be required were quickly allayed. Since the ARPANET was a public project connecting many major universities and research institutions, the implementation and performance details were widely published [11], [12], [13],

[14], [15]. The work of Leonard Kleinrock and associates at UCLA on the theory and measurement of the ARPANET has been of particular importance in providing a firm theoretical and practical understanding of the performance of packet networks. (See "Principles and Lessons in Packet Communications" by L. Kleinrock, in this issue pp. 1320–1329.)

Packet switching was first demonstrated publicly at the first International Conference on Computer Communications (ICCC) in Washington, DC, in October 1972. Robert Kahn of BBN organized the demonstration. He installed a complete ARPANET node at the conference hotel, with about 40 active terminals permitting access to dozens of computers all over the U.S. This public demonstration was for many, if not most, of the ICCC attendees proof that packet switching really worked. It was difficult for many experienced professionals at that time to accept the fact that a collection of computers, wide-band circuits, and minicomputer switching nodes—pieces of equipment totaling well over a hundred—could all function together reliably, but the ARPANET demonstration lasted for three days and clearly displayed its reliable operation in public. The network provided ultra-reliable service to thousands of attendees during the entire length of the conference.

The widespread publicity the ARPANET demonstration earned contributed greatly to the task of introducing modern dynamic-allocation technology to a preallocation trained world. However, during the same period in the early 1970's many other dynamic-allocation techniques were being developed and tested in private networks throughout the world. Hopefully, the extensive publications on the ARPANET have not *oversold* the particular variety of packet switching used in this first major network experiment.

SITA

The Societe Internationale de Telecommunications Aeronautiques (SITA) provides telecommunications for the international air carriers. In 1969 SITA began updating its design by replacing the major nodes of its message switching network with High Level Network nodes interconnected with voice-grade lines—organized to act like a packet switching network. Incoming messages are subdivided into 240-byte packets and are stored and forwarded along predetermined routes to the destination. Prestored distributed tables provide for alternate routes in the event of line failures [16].

TYMNET

Also in 1969, a time sharing service bureau, Tymshare Corporation, started installing a network based on minicomputers to connect asynchronous timesharing terminals to its central computers. The network switches, which are interconnected by voice-grade lines, store and forward from node to node data characters for up to 20 calls packaged in 66-byte blocks. The data is repackaged at each node into new blocks for the next hop. Routing is not distributed, but is accomplished by a central supervisor on a call-by-call basis [17].

CYCLADES/CIGALE

In France the interest in packet switching networks grew quickly during the early 1970's. In 1973 the first hosts were connected to the CYCLADES network, which links several major computing centers throughout France. The name CYCLADES refers to both the communications subnet and the host computers. The communications subnetwork, called CIGALE, only moves disconnected packets and delivers them in whatever order they arrive without any knowledge or concept of messages, connections or flow control. Called a "datagram" packet facility, this concept has been widely promoted by Louis Pouzin, the designer and organizer of CYCLADES. Since a major part of the organization and control of the network is imbedded in the CYCLADES computers, the subnetwork, CIGALE, is not sufficient by itself. In fact, Pouzin himself speaks of the network as "including" portions of the host computers. The packet assembly and disassembly, sequence numbering, flow control, and virtual connection processing are all done by the host. The CYCLADES structure provides a good testbed for trying out various protocols, as was its intent; but it requires a more cooperative and coordinated set of hosts than is likely to exist in a public environment [18].

RCP

Another packet network experiment was started in France at about the same time by the French PTT Administration. This network, called RCP (Reseau a Commutation par Paquets), first became operational in 1974. By this time the French PTT had already decided to build the public packet network, TRANSPAC, and RCP was utilized primarily as testbed for TRANSPAC. The design of RCP, directed by Remi Despres, differed sharply from that of the other contemporary French network, CYCLADES. Despres' design was organized around the concept of virtual connections rather than datagrams. RCP's character as a prototype public network may have been a strong factor in this difference, since a virtual circuit service is more directly marketable, not requiring substantial modifications to customers' host computers. In any case, the RCP design pioneered the incorporation of individually flow-controlled virtual circuits into the basic packet switching network organization [19].

EIN

Organized in 1971 and originally known as the COST II Project and later as the European Informatics Network (EIN) is a multination-funded European research network. The project director is Derek Barber of NPL, one of the original investigators of packet switching in the U.K. Given freedom from the red tape of multinational funding, this project would have been one of the earliest pace-setters in packet networks in the world. As it happened, however, EIN was not operational until 1976 [20], [21].

Public Data Networks

The early packet networks were all private networks built to demonstrate the technology and to serve a restricted population of users. Besides those early networks already mentioned, which were the most public projects, many private corporations and service bureaus built their own private networks. Generally these private networks did not make provision for host computers at more than one location, and thus their organization usually developed into a star network.

All these networks were the result of a basic economic transition, which occurred in 1969 [22] when the cost of dynamic-allocation switching fell below that of transmission lines. This change made it economically advantageous to build a network of some kind rather than to continue to use direct lines or the circuit switched telephone network for interactive data communications. Universal regulatory conditions in all countries restricted "common carriage" to the government or government-approved carriers, and thereby led to the development of many private networks instead of a competitive market of public networks.

However, the extensive private network activity in the early 1970's encouraged some of these public carriers to make plans for building their own packet networks, although all public networks and plans for future networks were based on preallocation techniques until about 1973. Many plans to provide public data service arose; some were even under way, like the German EDS system; but all were based on circuit switching until that time. The shift in economics in the late 1960's that made packet switching more cost-effective, instigated more rapid change in communications technology than had ever before occurred.

The established carriers and PTT's took their time reacting to this new technology. The United Kingdom was the first country to announce a public packet network through the British Post Office's planned Experimental Packet Switched Service (EPSS) [23]. Donald Davies' 1966 briefings with the BPO on packet switching clearly played a strong role in the U.K.'s early commitment to this new technology.

In the United States the dominant carrier, American Telephone and Telegraph (AT&T), evidenced even less interest in packet switching than many of the PTT's in other countries. AT&T and its research organization, Bell Laboratories, have never to my knowledge published any research on packet switching. ARPA approached AT&T in the early 1970's to see if AT&T would be interested in taking over the ARPANET and offering a public packet switched service, but AT&T declined. However, the Federal Communications Commission (FCC), which regulates all communications carriers in the U.S., was in the process of opening up portions of the communications market to competition. Bolt Beranek and Newman, the primary contractor for the ARPANET, felt strongly that a public packet switched data communications was needed. The FCC's new policies encouraged competition, so BBN formed Telenet Communications Corporation in late 1972. In October 1973 Telenet filed its request with the FCC for approval to become a carrier and to construct a public packet switched network; six months later the FCC approved Telenet's request. (See "Legal, Commercial, and International Aspects of Packet Communications," by S. L. Mathison in this issue, pp. 1527–1539.)

In France in November 1973, the French PTT announced its plans to build TRANSPAC, a major domestic packet network patterned after RCP [24]. The next year, in October 1974, the Trans-Canada Telephone System announced DATAPAC, a public packet network in Canada [25]. Also during this period, the Nippon Telegraph and Telephone Corporation announced its plans to build a public packet switched data network in Japan [26].

Thus, only four years after the building of the first experimental networks, the concept of data communications networks began to move into the public arena. Still, the networks were only planned and had yet to be built; most PTT's and carriers adopted a wait and watch attitude toward these first public networks.

International Standardization and Acceptance

CCITT X.25

With five independent public packet networks under construction in the 1974–1975 period, there was strong incentive for the nations to agree on a standard user interface to the networks so that host computers would not have unique interfacing jobs in each country. Unlike most standards activities, where there is almost no incentive to compromise and agree, carriers in separate countries can only benefit from the adoption of a standard since it facilitates network interconnection and permits easier user attachment. To this end the parties concerned undertook a major effort, to agree on the host–network interface during 1975. The result was an agreed protocol, CCITT Recommendation X.25, adopted in March 1976.

The X.25 protocol provides for the interleaving of data blocks for up to 4095 virtual circuits (VC's) on a single full-duplex leased line interface to the network, including all procedures for call setup and disconnection. A significant feature of this interface, from the carriers' point of view, is the inclusion of independent flow control on each VC; the flow control enables the network (and the user) to protect itself from congestion and overflow under all circumstances without having to slow down or stop more than one call at a time. In networks like the ARPANET and CYCLADES which do not have this capability, the network must depend on the host (or other networks in interconnect cases) to insure that no user submits more data to the network than the network can handle or deliver. The only defense the network has without individual VC flow control is to shut off the entire host (or internet) interface. This, of course, can be disastrous to the other users communicating with the offending host or network.

Another critical aspect of X.25, not present in the proposals for a datagram interface, is that X.25 defines interface standards for both the host-to-network block transfer and the control of individual VC's. In datagram networks the VC interface is situated in the host computer; there can be, therefore, no network-enforced standard for labeling, sequencing, and flow controlling VC's. These networks are in the author's opinion, not salable as a public service since they must offer individual terminal interfaces, as well as host interfaces, to provide complete host–terminal communications; to sell these interfaces requires knowing how to interface to one VC as well as to a host.

The March 1976 agreement on X.25 and on virtual circuits as the agreed technique for public packet networks marked the beginning of the second phase of packet switching: large interconnected public service networks. In the two years since X.25 was adopted, many additional standards have been agreed on as well, all patterned around X.25. For example, X.28 has been adopted as the standard asynchronous terminal interface; X.29, a protocol used with X.25 to specify the packetizing rules for the terminal handler, will be the host control protocol. More recently X.75, the standard protocol for connecting international networks has been defined.

Public Data Network Services

Capitalizing on BBN's ARPANET experience, TELENET introduced the first public packet network service in August 1975. Initially TELENET consisted of seven multiply interconnected nodes. By April 1978 the network had grown to 187 network nodes which used 79 packet switches to provide 156 U.S. cities with local dial service to 180 host computers across the country, with interconnections to 14 other countries. Originally TELENET supported a virtual connection host interface similar to X.25. However, shortly after the specification was adopted, X.25 was introduced into TELENET as the preferred host interface protocol.

In early 1977 both EPSS in the U.K. and DATAPAC in Canada were declared operational. Also, in the U.S., TYMNET was approved as a carrier and began supplying public data services. EPSS, having been designed long before X.25 was specified, is not X.25 compatible, but the U.K. intends to provide X.25 based packet service within the next year.

DATAPAC was X.25 based from the start of commercial service since the development was held until X.25 was approved. Using X.25 lines, DATAPAC and TELENET were interconnected in early 1978. This connection demonstrated the ease of international network linking, once a common standard had been established.

In France, TRANSPAC is due to become operational later this year (1978); in Japan, the NTT packet network, DX-2, should become operational in 1978 or 1979. A semipublic network, EURONET, sponsored by nine European Common Market Countries, is due to become operational in late 1978 or 1979. Many other European countries, like Germany and Belgium, are making plans for public packet networks to start in 1979. These networks are all X.25 based and therefore should be similar and compatible.

Datagrams versus VC's

As part of the continuing evolution of packet switching, controversial issues are sure to arise. Even with universal adoption of X.25 and the virtual circuit approach by public networks throughout the world, there is currently a vocal group of users requesting a datagram standard. The two major benefits claimed for datagrams are reliability and efficiency for transaction-type applications.

Reliability: It is claimed that datagrams provide more reliable access to a host when two or more access lines are used, since any packet could take either route if a line were to fail. This reflects a true deficiency in X.25 as currently defined—the absence of a reconnect facility on the call request packet. If, when a call is initiated, a code number for the call is placed in the call request packet, the X.25 network (or host) can save the code number. If the line over which the call is placed fails, the network simply places a new call request, marked as a reconnect, over another line and supplies the original code number to insure reconnection to the correct VC. Since packets on each VC are sequence numbered, this reconnection can be accomplished with no data loss and usually just as quickly as rerouting of the packets in a datagram interface. If the network uses VC's internally, the same reconnect capability is used to insure against connection failures.

Cost: It is often assumed that datagrams would be cheaper for networks to provide than packets on VC's. However, the cost of memory and switching have fallen by a factor of 30 compared to transmission costs over the last nine years resulting in the overhead of datagram headers becoming a major cost factor. A datagram packet or end-to-end acknowledgment requires about 25 bytes of packet header in addition to the actual data (0–128 bytes) whereas only 8 bytes of overhead are required for similar packets on a virtual circuit. In the unique case of a single packet call, the overheads are the same. For all longer calls, datagram overhead adds 13–94 percent to the cost of all transmission costs, both long haul and local. Originally, this increase in transmission cost was more than offset by increased switch costs but with modern microprocessor switches very little of the increase is offset. Thus, with this radical shift in economics, datagram packets are now more expensive than VC packets.

Continuing Technological Change

A decade ago computers had barely become inexpensive enough to make packet switching economically feasible; computers were still slow and small, forcing implementers to invent all sorts of techniques to save buffers and minimize CPU time. Computer technology has progressed to the point where microcomputer systems have now been especially designed for packet switching, and there is no shortage of memory or CPU power. This development has been partially responsible for the shift from datagrams to virtual connections and has also eliminated buffer allocation techniques (which cost transmission bandwidth to save memory). The modularity and computational power of today's microprocessors has made it economical and practical to provide protocol conversion from X.25 to any existing terminal protocol, polled or not.

As a result of these improvements, packet networks are rapidly becoming universal translators, connecting everything to everything else and supplying the speed, code, and protocol conversions wherever necessary. As this trend continues, it is almost certain that the techniques in use today will have to be continually changed to respond to the changing economics and usage patterns.

For example, one major change that will be required in the next few years is an increase in the backbone trunk speed from 56 kbit/s to 1.544 Mbit/s (the speed of "T1" digital trunks). Both Paul Baran and Donald Davies in their original papers anticipated the use of T1 trunks, but present traffic demand has not yet justified their use. As the traffic does justify T1 trunks, many aspects of network design will change by a corresponding order of magnitude. Packet networks have always incorporated a delay in the 100–200 ms range. This delay has so strongly affected both the system design and the choice of applications that it is hard to remember which decisions depended on this delay factor.

With T1 carrier trunks, the transit delay in the net will drop to around 10 ms plus propagation time requiring a complete reexamination of network topology and processor design issues. The number of outstanding packets on a 2500 mile trunk will increase from around 3 to 75, requiring extended numbering, and perhaps, new acknowledgment techniques. The user will be most strongly affected by a 10–30 ms net delay; his whole strategy of job organization may change.

Of course, there will be a significant price decrease accompanying this change. This, combined with the short delay, will make many new applications attractive; remote job entry (RJE) and bulk data transfer applications through public packet networks will probably be economically and technically feasible, even before T1 trunks are introduced; but if not before, certainly afterwards, when the packet price reflects the new trunk speed. Dynamic-allocation permits savings over pre-allocation by a factor of four in line costs for RJE, and by a factor of two for bulk data transfer. As the switch cost continues to fall far more rapidly than the line cost, dynamic-allocation techniques will be used for RJE, batch transfer and even voice applications.

Future

Packet Satellite

One change which will clearly occur in packet networks in the next decade is the incorporation of broadcast satellite facilities. ARPA has sponsored extensive research into packet satellite techniques and, over the past few years, has tested these techniques between the U.S. and England. (See "General Purpose Packet Satellite Networks" by I. M. Jacobs, R. Binder, and E. Hoversten in this issue, pp. 1448–1467.) Fundamentally, a satellite provides a broadcast media which, if properly used, can provide considerable gains in the full statistical utilization of the satellite's capacity. Using ARPA's techniques, a single wideband channel (1.5 Mbit/s–60 Mbit/s) on a satellite provides an extremely economical way to interconnect high bandwidth nodes within a packet network.

With the current cost of ground stations ($150K–$300K), it appears to be marginally economic to install separate private ground stations at major nodes of a domestic packet network rather than to lease portions of commercial ground stations and trunk the data to the packet network nodes. However, either way, the cost of ground station facilities are such that the use of satellites only becomes economic compared to land lines when the aggregate data flow exceeds about 100 packets/s (100 kbit/s) to and from a node or city. Furthermore, satellite transmission has an inherent one-way delay of 270 ms; therefore, the packet traffic must logically be divided between two priority groups—interactive and batch. Only batch traffic can presently be considered for satellites, since the 270 ms delay is unacceptable for interactive applications, at least if any other options are available, even at a somewhat higher price. With current economics, the long-haul land line facilities only add about $0.50/hr to the price of interactive data calls, which is far too little a cost to encourage the acceptance of slower service. Therefore, interactive service will almost always require ground line facilities in addition to satellite facilities at all network nodes.

This introduces another factor that limits the potential satellite traffic: land lines can easily carry 10–25 percent batch traffic at a lower priority, using a dual queue, without any significant increase in cost. Further, if ground lines are required and satellite facilities are optional, the full cost for the satellite capability, must be compared with the incremental cost of simply expanding the land line facilities. All these factors considered, it is probable that satellites will be used by public data networks within the next five years for transmissions between major nodal points, but that ground facilities will be used exclusively for transmissions between smaller nodes.

Packet Radio

Since local distribution is by far the most expensive portion of a communications network, ground radio techniques are of considerable interest to the extent that they can replace wire for local distribution. Packet radio is another area where ARPA has been sponsoring research in applying dynamic-allocation techniques. The basic concept in packet radio is to share one wide bandwidth channel among many stations, each of which only transmits in short bursts when it has real data to send. (See "Advances in Packet Radio Technology" by R. E. Kahn *et al.*, in this issue, pp. 1468–1496.) This technique appears to be extremely promising for both fixed and mobile local distribution, once the cost of the transceivers has been reduced by, perhaps, a factor of ten. Considering the historical trend of the cost of electronics, this should take about five years; from that point onward packet radio should become increasingly competitive with wire, cable, and even light fibers for low to moderate volume local distribution requirements.

One important consequence would be the use of a simple packet radio system inside buildings to permit wireless communication for all sorts of devices. Clearly, as electronic devices multiply throughout the home and office, low-power packet radio would permit all these devices to communicate among themselves and with similar devices throughout the world via a master station tied into a public data network.

Voice

The economic advantage of dynamic-allocation over pre-allocation will soon become so fundamental and clear in all areas of communications, including voice, that it is not hard to project the same radical transition of technology will occur in voice communications as has occurred in data communications.

Digitized voice, no matter what the digitization rate, can be compressed by a factor of three or more by packet switching since in normal conversation each speaker is only speaking one third of the time. Since interactive data traffic typically can be compressed by a factor of 15, voice clearly benefits far less from packet switching than interactive data. This is the reason why packet switching was first applied to data communications. However, modern electronics is quickly eliminating any cost difference between packet switches and circuit switches, and thus packet switching can clearly provide a factor of three cost reduction in the transmission costs associated with switched voice service.

Probably there will be many proposals, and even systems built, using some form of dynamic-allocation other than packet switching during the period of transition. The most likely variant design would be a packetized voice system that does not utilize sum checks or flow control. Of course, this would be just a packet switch with those options disabled. If the similarity to present packet switching were not recognized, the packetized voice system might be built without providing these essential capabilities and would be useless for data traffic. However, the obvious solution would be an integrated packet switching network that provides both voice and data services.

On further consideration, it becomes apparent that the flow control feature of packet switching networks can provide a substantial cost reduction for voice systems. Flow control feedback, applied to the voice digitizers decreases their output rate when the network line becomes momentarily overloaded; as a result, peak channel capacity required by users can be significantly reduced.

In short, packet switching seems ideally suited to both voice and data transmissions. The transition to packet switching for the public data network has taken a decade, and still is not complete; many PTT's and carriers have not accepted its viability. Given the huge fixed investment in voice equipment in place today, the transition to voice switching may be considerably slower and more difficult. There is no way, however, to stop it from happening.

References

[1] P. Baran *et al.*, "On distributed communications, vols. I–XI," RAND Corporation Research Documents, Aug. 1964.

[2] T. Marill and L. G. Roberts, "Toward a cooperative network of time-shared computers," *Proc. FJCC* pp. 425–431, 1966.

[3] D. W. Davies, K. A. Bartlett, R. A. Scantlebury, and P. T. Wilkinson, "A digital communications network for computers giving rapid response at remote terminals," ACM Symp. Operating Systems Problems, Oct. 1967.

[4] R. A. Scantlebury, P. T. Wilkinson, and K. A. Bartlett, "The de-

sign of a message switching centre for a digital communication network," in *Proc. IFIP Congress 1968, vol. 2–Hardware Applications*," pp. 723–733.

[5] R. A. Scantlebury, "A model for the local area of a data communication network–Objectives and hardware organization," ACM Symp. Data Communication, Pine Mountain, Oct. 1969.

[6] L. G. Roberts, "Multiple computer networks and intercomputer communication," ACM Symp. Operating System Principles, Oct. 1967.

[7] L. G. Roberts and B. D. Wessler, "Computer network development to achieve resource sharing," *Proc. SJCC 1970*, pp. 543–549.

[8] F. E. Heart, R. E. Kahn, S. M. Ornstein, W. R. Crowther, and D. C. Walden, "The interface message processor for the ARPA computer network," in *AFIPS Conf. Proc. 36*, pp. 551-567, June 1970.

[9] R. E. Kahn and W. R. Crowther, "Flow control in a resource-sharing computer network," in Proc. Second ACM/IEEE Symp. Problems, Palo Alto, CA, pp. 108–116, Oct. 1971.

[10] S. M. Ornstein, F. E. Heart, W. R. Crowther, S. B. Russell, H. K. Rising, and A. Michel, "The terminal IMP for the ARPA computer network," in *AFIPS Conf. Proc. 40*, pp. 243–254, June 1972.

[11] H. Frank, R. E. Kahn, and L. Kleinrock, "Computer communications network design–Experience with theory and practice," in *AFIPS Conf. Proc.*, vol. 40, pp. 255–270, June 1972.

[12] L. Kleinrock, "Performance models and measurement of the ARPA computer networks," in *Proc. Int. Symp. Design and Application of Interactive Computer Systems*, Brunel University, Uxbridge, England, May 1972.

[13] L. Kleinrock and W. Naylor, "On measured behavior of the ARPA network," in *AFIPS Conf. Proc.*, vol. 43, NCC, Chicago, IL, pp. 767–780, May 1974.

[14] L. Kleinrock and H. Opderbeck, "Throughput in the ARPANET–Protocols and measurement," in *Proc. 4th Data Communications Symp.*, Quebec City, Canada, pp. 6-1–6-11, Oct. 1975.

[15] H. Frank and W. Chou, "Topological optimization of computer networks," *Proc. IEEE*, vol. 60, no. 11, pp. 1385–1397, Nov. 1972.

[16] G. J. Chretien, W. M. Konig, J. H. Rech, "The SITA network," in *Computer Communication Networks*, R. L. Grimsdale, F. F. Kuo, Eds. Noordhoff: NATO Advanced Study Institute Series, pp. 373–396, 1975.

[17] L. R. Tymes, "TYMNET–A terminal oriented communication network," *Proc. AFIPS, SJCC*, pp. 211–216, May 1971.

[18] L. Pouzin, "Presentation and major design aspects of the CYCLADES network," in *Third Data Communications Symp.*, Tampa, FL, pp. 80–85, Nov. 1973.

[19] R. F. Despres, "A packet network with graceful saturated operation," in *Proc. ICCC*, Washington, DC, pp. 345–351, Oct, 1972.

[20] D. L. A. Barber, "The European computer network project,"*Proc. ICCC*, Washington, DC, pp. 192–200, Oct. 1972.

[21] ——, "A European informatics network: Achievement and prospects," *Proc. ICCC*, Toronto, Canada, pp. 44–50, Aug. 1976.

[22] L. G. Roberts, "Data by the packet," *IEEE Spectrum*, Feb. 1974.

[23] R. C. Belton, J. R. Thomas, "The UKPO packet switching experiment," *ISS Munich*, 1974.

[24] A. Danet, R. Depres, A. LesRest, G. Pichon, S. Ritzenthaler, "The French public packet switching service: The TRANSPAC network," *Proc. ICCC*, Toronto, Canada, pp. 251–260, Aug. 1976.

[25] W. W. Clipsham, F. E. Glave, M. L. Narraway, "DATAPAC network overview," *Proc. ICCC*, Toronto, Canada, pp. 131–136, Aug. 1976.

[26] R. Nakamura, F. Ishino, M. Sasakoka, M. Nakamura, "Some design aspects of a public packet switched network," *Proc ICCC*, Toronto, Canada, pp. 317–322, Aug. 1976.

Reprinted with permission from *Journal of Telecommunication Networks*, Spring 1982, pages 1-11. Copyright © 1982 by Computer Science Press, Inc.

A Decade of Network Development

Leonard Kleinrock *

University of California

ABSTRACT The network technologies developed over the past decade, due largely to incredible advances in integrated chip production, have set the stage for an enormous DP revolution the impact of which will soon be felt in the business community and in the home and consumer markets. We have been able to identify those fundamental principles which render this new technology so cost effective. End-to-end communication services are now coming into place which will pass data, voice, video, fax, graphics, etc. from an individual terminal in an office or a living room across vast distances to remote processing facilities. The technological issues have been addressed, and in this paper we describe some of the successes and some of the remaining problems to be solved. As engineers, we cannot restrict our efforts to the purely technical (and "nice") problems, but rather we must accept the further responsibility of familiarizing ourselves with the overall environment in which our "products" must perform; if we fail in this regard, the world of commerce, trade and business will ignore our best efforts as irrelevant to its needs.

1. The Big Picture and the Real Issues

The age of modern telecommunications began more than a decade ago with the rise of the large-scale packet-switching networks. The first such network was the U.S. Defense Department's ARPANET which became operational late in 1969 as a four-node network [10]. In the decade following that event, we have seen enormous progress in packet communications in a world where data is beginning to dominate.

However, in all this time we have gained little real understanding of these systems. Sure, we know how to move data and we even know how to design "reasonably good" systems. But we really don't understand what distributed communications is all about; we have no idea what the issues of concurrency in processing and in communications actually involve; and we have precious few measures which provide us a meaningful metric of real system performance.

Moreover, in these ten years, as a technology we have made relatively little impact on the real world. Fortunately, that will not remain the case for long. The stage is now set for an enormous penetration in the world of business, commerce, government, education, home services, etc. This creates a challenge, an opportunity and a burden upon us, the system designers, in terms of providing systems which not only perform well according to *our* measures but also which perform well according to the needs of industry and the complex world of the end user.

*Leonard Kleinrock, Computer Science Department, University of California, Los Angeles, California 90024. Material based on a keynote speech at 7th Data Communications Symposium, Oct. 27, 1981, Mexico City, Mexico. This research was supported by the Advanced Research Projects Agency of the Department of Defense under Contract MDA 903-77-C-0272.

0276-0037/82/0101-11$3.85/0

Most of us recognize what has been the single most significant development which has acted as the prime mover for this revolution in telecommunications. It is simply the fantastic *microchip technology* and the continued phenomenal improvement in the price-to-performance ratio of these silicon devices. In Figure 1 we see a view of the interplay among technology, processing, communications, systems, end user tools, and the revolution (which has already begun). At the top of this chain we see the *integrated chip* from which we branch off and show its impact in two areas: processing and communications. In the field of *processing*, the rise of personal computers is due mostly to the large scale integrated (LSI) technology which has produced computers on a chip and highly efficient memory systems to go along with them. This also includes printing peripherals whose costs have begun to drop (but which still form a sizable investment for small machines). Following that, in increasing size of processors, we come to the pervasive small business machines which have been based on the eight-bit chips (Z80A, INTEL 8080, etc.) many of which are evolving to systems using 16-bit chips (Z8000, INTEL 8086, Motorola 68000) and soon we will likely see 32-bit small business machines. A number of competing operating systems have already entered the foray including CP/M, UNIX, OASIS, etc. From there we encounter the minicomputers which have grown in power enough to compete with the maxis (next on the list) and then on to the giant supercomputers. All these systems have enjoyed a decreasing price-to-performance ratio due largely to the integrated chip revolution.

The other branch leading from the chip technology is that in *communications* (the subject near and dear to the readers of this journal). Here we have seen a large variety of significant developments over the last decade, most of them concentrated in the last three to five years. The list in Figure 1 is organized in increasing order of the physical distances over which the communications is required to operate. We begin with the problem of providing communications on the tiny integrated chip itself. This turns out be a growing problem as the dimensions of the logical elements on a chip grow smaller and smaller (now challenging sub-micron dimensions) leading to chips with millions of logical elements. Following this we see the recent proliferation of a large number of local network systems providing communications among terminals, computers, peripherals, etc. within the environs of, say, a single office building. A large number of network architectures (perhaps too many) have been implemented including loops and rings, buses, stars, etc. (the most common of the bus architectures is perhaps the well-known ETHERNET). In addition we have seen the private automatic branch exchange (PABX) evolve into a computerized branch exchange (CBX) which has come to compete with the ETHERNET-like systems for in-building communication. Beyond that we have seen very significant improvements in modems (on a chip), modem-sharing units, and smart multiplexers (notably the statistical multiplexer); all these developments are, again, principally based upon the advancement in chip technology. In providing building-to-building and within-city communications, we encounter the problem known as local data distribution networks which tend to be based on some form of radio communication. In the case of mobile terminals, an entire technology of packet radio communications has arisen with its attendant and difficult problems to be described below. The ARPANET spawned a worldwide development of terrestrially-based networks whose backbone communications typically have been broadband telephone channels forming inter-city distributed networks across nationwide dimensions. Beyond that we have seen the emergence of satellite services (both point-to-point and broadcast) to provide cost-effective communications over long distances at wide bandwidths and typically crossing hostile terrain such as oceans. All these communication developments are due largely to the advancement in chip technology. (And chips are made of silicon. And silicon is made from the sand of the desert. And wouldn't you know who owns most of the sand!)

The communication components just described have been lashed together to provide a variety of large scale communication *systems* in the last decade. For example, a large number of value added networks (VANs)

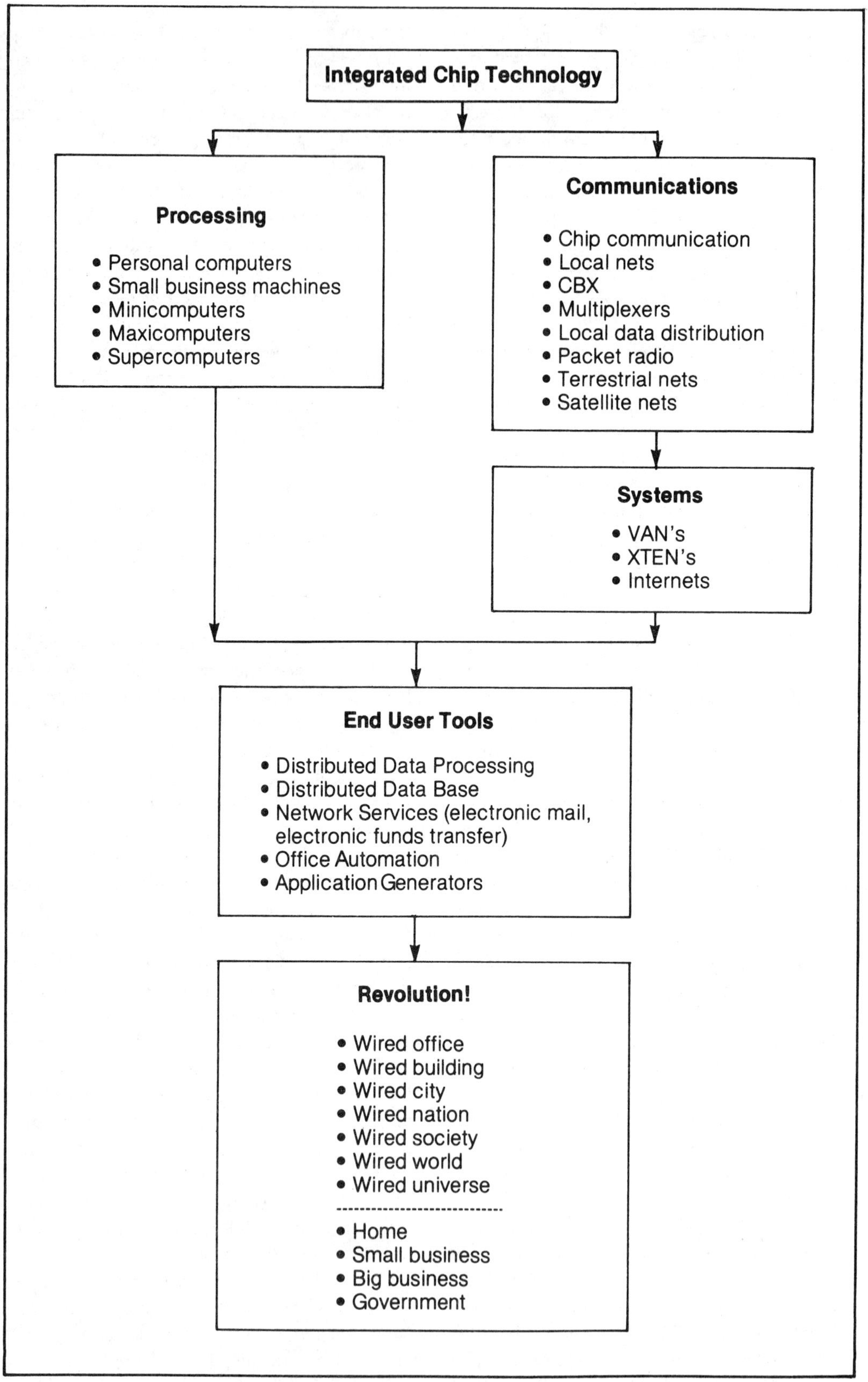

Fig. 1. The Structure of the Revolution.

have come into being across the world (TELENET, TYMNET, TRANSPAC, DATAPAC, PSS, EURONET, etc.). Moreover, a number of end-to-end specialized communication systems services have been described (such as Xerox's XTEN system, which, to our great misfortune, was never brought to the marketplace due to economic considerations). Systems similar to XTEN which provide end-to-end services from a terminal in an office, through an in-building local network, to a rooftop antenna, via a local data distribution system across the city, to an earth station feeding a satellite network and back down again through the hierarchy into a remote processing device are sure to emerge in the near future (for example, Isacomm's network and MACOMNET are already discussing such systems which are basically a kind of reincarnation of the XTEN concept). All of this implies the network interconnection of the various components we have described above and this leads to an entire new set of considerations involving internetting.

Referring once again to Figure 1, we see that the processing branch and the communications branch merge once again to provide a collection of irresistible *end user tools*. Among these we list: distributed data processing, distributed data bases, network services (including things such as electronic mail and electronic funds transfer), office automation, application generators, etc.

These end user tools will be packaged together to bring about the *revolution* which is already underway. We will progress from the wired office to the wired building to the wired city to the wired nation to the wired society to the wired world and to the wired universe (if we allow it) [16]. The impact here will extend from the individual personal computer in the home (which will be connected via a communication service to the rest of the world) on to the small business machines (an enormous market) to big business systems to government information systems, etc. The world of telecommunications is upon us! Few people within the world of technology and most people outside that world have any idea of the magnitude of the revolution which is underway. A decade from now when we look back to the early 80's, we will wonder why it was that so few people recognized that the revolution had already begun! It is bound to change almost everything we do in the world of science, commerce, education, business, government, management, work style, recreation, etc. The key is the ability to provide telecommunication networks which tie together all the processing elements, thereby providing a large variety of important services to the end user.

We, as technicians and experts in the field of telecommunications, run a serious danger of losing sight of the big picture in which our technology participates. This is a critical point. The end user really has very little interest in whether an arrival process is Poisson or some other complex stochastic process. He cares not if independence assumptions make sense or if algorithms are known to be optimum. Why should he worry if routing tables in a packet network are updated every half second or every half minute? These are issues with which you and I are concerned. But we are concerned with them in order to provide a product—a product which is useful out there in the real world (a world which understands nothing about our specialities). Their concerns revolve around measures which we seldom incorporate in our analysis and design. Among these measures we might include some which we have thought about but for which we have been able to give little advice, namely: reliability, availability, maintainability, security, privacy, expandability, single vendor lock-in, backup procedures, terminals supported, protocols supported, safety, interconnectability, transparency, software availability, documentation, etc. In fact, were you or I to go out and purchase a computer tomorrow, I suspect that if the application were at all worthwhile, our biggest concern would be *backup* of our important records, followed perhaps by cost, then by the details of the maintenance contract, etc. Way down the list we would finally find those measures with which all of us are so enamored, namely, throughput, response time, queue lengths, efficiency, stability, optimality, etc. This is not to say that our measures are not important (for indeed they are very important); but we must recognize that these other issues are the ones with which the end user is concerned, and too often we forget that these issues must be addressed in our technological evaluations. It is not enough for us to become excellent analysts—we must understand the environment in which our systems are to function, and it is too often that our technical experts fail in that regard. How many of us really understand the key characteristics of floppy disks and of the recent Winchester cartridges? What is the real market for 56 kilobit per second access from one's terminals and hosts? Of what use is a 500 millisecond response time if the CPU overheats and fails? Do you have any idea how distributed processing and distributed data bases really fit into the practical world of data processing and telecommunications? These broader issues come with experience and exposure, and it is up to you as experts to gain that experience and exposure in addition to developing the expertise of your trade.

2. State of the Art in Modeling and Design

In this section we will briefly review some of the key developments which have taken place over the past decade in our area of expertise (not withstanding the warnings at the end of the previous section) and discuss where further work must be done.

A. Resource Sharing. In the field of modeling and design we continually seek efficient ways to allocate processing and communication resources to a collection of demands which require access to these resources. The difficulty in this allocation procedure comes from the fact that these demands almost never tell you ahead of time when they want the resource, they seldom tell you how long they will need the resource, most of the time they never want the darned thing anyway, but when they do occasionally want it, they want it immediately! Such demands are extremely difficult to handle when the resources they want are scarce and precious. This, then, is the underlying problem in many of our considerations [8].

Indeed the problem involves a tradeoff whereby on the one hand we wish to give good service to the demands, but on the other hand we would like efficient use of the resources. At one extreme we could make a permanent assignment of resources to demands (i.e., let the demands permanently own a given resource). This provides terrific service but leads to inefficient resource use when the demands are bursty (in the sense that they only need the occasional use of the resource). In a heavy traffic situation where the demands do need the resource an overwhelming fraction of the time, then a permanent assignment is not especially bad and we may be willing to accept it. At the other extreme, we might choose to give no permanent assignments at all and allow the demands to grab the resources as they need them. In a light traffic situation where there are plenty of resources and few demands, this seems to be an acceptable procedure since it would be foolish to impose access restrictions in a plentiful environment. However, as the demand load begins to increase, this uncoordinated access scheme leads to conflict situations whereby more than one demand is attempting to access the same resource at the same time. This is known as the problem of *multiaccess*. The question is—how can we resolve such conflicts?

Conflict resolution is a key concept in telecommunications. More than one demand requires the same resource at the same time. What are the possible ways of resolving this conflict? Let us list a few of the more common ones:

1. *Queueing:* In this situation, *exactly* one demand gets access to the resource and the others are forced to join a queue and wait their turn. It matters not if we introduce priority queueing or preemption or some other interesting wrinkle on the queueing structure; the key idea here is that exactly *one gets service while all the others wait*. This is a civilized way to proceed and hopefully one which is commonly seen in the real world.
2. *Splitting:* In this case, the capacity of the resource is partitioned into a number of pieces, one piece given to each of the active demands. That is, *all get served simultaneously at some fractional rate*. The splitting need not be equal although it usually is and one well-known implementa-

tion is frequency division multiplexing (FDM).

3. *Blocking:* In blocking, *exactly one demand gets served and the others are refused service* and asked to leave (i.e., they are "blocked" or "lost"). The only demands which get served are those which arrive when the resource is idle.
4. *Smashing:* In this case, *when more than one demand requests the use of a resource then no one gets served.* This is the most disastrous of all the resolution schemes, and yet it does occur in such technologies as packet radio and local bus architectures using contention.

Of course it is possible to form hybrid mixtures of the above schemes. For example, one could invent an access scheme in which the first two customers were allowed to split the resource and the next 15 would be allowed to queue up and wait for the resource, and all the rest would be blocked from any use at all.

The first and second conflict resolution schemes mentioned above (queueing and splitting) are the more civilized. Let us discuss the gains to be had from these two schemes a bit further. The most important observation regarding queueing and/or splitting is that the resource being shared is not permanently assigned to a demand, but rather its full capacity is *dynamically shared* among those demands currently requiring access to the resource; this is a great improvement over the permanent assignment mentioned above and provides the key to the solution of our problem of satisfying unpredictable bursty demands.

We have two important resource sharing principles at work here. The first principle is the *law of large numbers* which simply states that a large population of demands will present a total load to a system of resources which is equal to the sum of the *average* requirements of each individual demand, and further this total load is a highly predictable quantity. This should be compared to the requirement in a permanently assigned environment in which the total resource capacity required is equal to the sum of the individual *peak* demands rather than the sum of the *average* demands. This smoothing effect of the law of large numbers is key to the resolution of resource assignment in a bursty demand environment. The second resource sharing principle has to do with *scaling*. The scaling result simply says that if we start with a certain demand for throughput and a certain total resource capacity, and if we then increase that throughput by a factor and increase the capacity by the same factor, then the response time in satisfying these demands will be reduced by that same factor. This scaling effect is rather important and can be stated in a number of ways [8]. The net result of these two resource sharing principles says that, if possible, we should take large capacity resources and allow large demand populations to share these resources dynamically. In so doing we get the gains from the smoothing effect of the law of large numbers and the gains from the scaling effect as well.

Now how can we apply these ideas to our telecommunications problem? The answer is, in principle, quite straightforward, namely, to gather together a large collection of demands for communication requirements and offer this population a wideband channel which they must share dynamically on a demand basis. Perhaps the best example of such an implementation is that of statistical multiplexing whereby a collection of terminals generates data to be transmitted over a shared wideband channel; their data requests are placed in a queue of other requests waiting for use of the channel in a first-come-first-served fashion. Indeed a queue is a wonderful device (it is a demand multiplexer) which provides the full bandwidth of the resource to one demand at a time. Each terminal transmits its data quickly at the full channel speed and then immediately releases the channel for use by some other terminal. This provides a "burst" communications mode, and it takes advantage of both of our resource sharing principles.

There are four major technologies which have arisen over this past decade of telecommunications progress and they form the components of our overall communications system. Properly designed, they can be made to operate in the burst mode just described. Chronologically, we first saw terrestrial networks rise in the form of packet-switching systems (e.g., ARPANET, TELENET, TYMNET, DATAPAC, TRANSPAC, etc.); the service here tended to be over nationwide distances.

Following that, satellite communications developed as a technology for data communications and was used to span long distances at wide bandwidths, thereby serving the role of connecting different terrestrial networks and also acting as support for the backbone communications of a single terrestrial network. Next we saw the introduction of packet radio technology to serve as local access to networks. Lastly we have seen an enormous rise in the use of local network systems to provide communications over distances typically less than a few miles and usually serving office buildings, universities, etc.; this tends to be communications on a cable or on a fiberoptic channel which connects directly to the terminals and devices of our networks. Each of these four technologies (terrestrial nets, satellite nets, packet radio systems, and local network systems) takes advantage of our two resource sharing principles in a variety of ways. In the following portions of this section we shall discuss these developments and point out where the open problems are from an analytic and design point of view.

B. Terrestrial Nets. Using networks such as the ARPANET as typical examples of implementations of a packet-switching network, we are all aware that progress in modeling, analyzing and designing these networks has been quite successful over this past decade. We have an excellent model for delay in these networks as given by $T = \Sigma_i (\lambda_i/\gamma) T_i$ [10]. Here T is the mean response time of the network, λ_i is the message traffic on the ith channel in the network, T_i is the mean response time of the ith channel (queueing plus transmission), and γ is the total network throughput. This equation is exact and quite general, requiring essentially no statistical assumptions. The particular form for T_i does depend upon the statistical assumptions made [9], and it is here where the analysis bogs down; however, there are excellent approximations which yield results for T which are quite acceptable for the state of the art. (Some particular network configurations do admit an exact solution, but they are quite limited in scope and will not be discussed further.)

So far as the more difficult areas of routing and flow control are concerned, we find that the situation here is not quite as good. First, in the area of routing procedures, we find that there have been a fair number of implementations as, for example, in the ARPANET (using flooding), in TYMNET (using centralized path setups), in TELENET (using call-by-call routing) and in SNA (using explicit path routing from table lookup). The analysis here has been poor to fair in the sense that dynamic routing procedures are difficult to analyze, but static analysis has been possible and provides a good approximation. The issues of looping, stability, transient response, etc. have not really yielded very well to analysis, although progress is being made continually on this front [3]. Static analysis using methods such as the flow deviation method in a centralized fashion [2], or attempts to implement flow deviation in a distributed environment [4] have been fairly effective. We still do find problems with routing procedures as, for example, in the recent article [17] which described yet another system crash due to a malfunction in procedures related to the routing function.

Flow control is perhaps one of the least understood control procedures in terrestrial networks (and in fact in all networks). Here again, a number of implementations may be found in the industry using various throttles such as stop-start procedures, buffer classes, window limitations, isarithmic schemes, etc. The analysis here is abysmal, and very little has been done which is of much use. This is an open area for investigation. Some high level models, however, have yielded to analysis including the work on power [14] and on certain other schemes [7]. The difficulty is that the dynamic nature of flow control is extremely difficult to analyze. In fact, it seems fair to say that flow control has the following cantankerous properties: you need it, it's tough to design, it's nearly impossible to analyze, and it's almost sure to cause you trouble (i.e., create deadlocks, degradations, and other lovely castastrophes). There is great opportunity here for further creative research!

As far as topological design of networks is concerned, here again some satisfactory heuristic design procedures have been in use for many years. The exact solution to the topological design problem is likely never to be found due to its inherent computational and probabilistic complexity, but this is no real impediment at this point since our current design procedures really seem to be quite efficient. However, a breakthrough here would be most welcome.

C. Satellite Networks. Packet switching over a satellite communication channel represents a perfect example of a multiaccess broadcast distributed communication channel. (It is multiaccess in the sense that more than one user may wish to access it at the same time. It is broadcast in the sense that many users hear the transmission in progress. It is distributed in the sense that users are not located in one centralized control facility.) In this case a number of earth stations distributed over a large geographical region attempt to share the common capacity of the satellite channel; the satellite simply transponds back to earth all that it receives in a broad beam covering a large portion of the earth. The question here is how one should access the channel in an efficient way. A number of such access schemes have been suggested [11], and experiments have been conducted as well [6, 12]. The principle feature of these channels is the enormous propagation delay (on the order of a quarter of a second roundtrip for geosynchronous satellites), and this strongly affects the class of access algorithms which make sense. Experiments have shown that packet broadcasting on a satellite channel can be effective not only for data but also for voice communications and for teleconferencing. Commercial offerings of point-to-point satellite channels for data are already available through the commercial organizations (e.g., SBS). The analysis of the access schemes here has progressed reasonably well. The concerns are ones of throughput, response time and stability. The stability question is quite important in these distributed channels and has been addressed at some length in the literature [5]. There is room for further research in this area, and we have seen a number of papers appearing in the recent literature on this subject.

D. Packet Radio. Here we provide the use of a common radio channel to a collection of communicating devices in a relatively small geographical area (on the order of a few tens of miles). The problem is similar to that of satellites, namely, we have a multiaccess broadcast distributed communication channel which places a burden on the access scheme, but in this case the propagation delay is tiny (tens of microseconds) and we can take advantage of this in our channel access protocols. In addition to the access scheme, however, a new class of extremely difficult problems arises, namely, that of routing, path finding, control and management of packet radio networks. In the case of mobile radio terminals, the problems are enormous and have so far met with little analytic success. Even in the stationary case, the problem of multi-hop communications (whereby one does not communicate with one's final destination in a single transmission but rather uses a relay of other packet radios to cross the distance between the source and the destination) is unmanageable. Only very approximate analyses for the multi-hop packet radio systems have been documented [13] and considerable work must yet be done in this area. The Department of Defense Advanced Research Projects Agency has experimented here as well as in the satellite case. A number of testbeds are already in place and experiments are currently going on. Most of the design difficulty focuses around the particular protocols to be used at the access level, at the routing level, at the flow control level and at the management level. A number of extremely difficult problems remain to be handled in this area. As mentioned earlier, a large number of access protocols have been documented and more are appearing every month. Here is a great opportunity for creative work in protocols, analysis and control.

E. Local Networks. Local networks, which provide communications among devices within a building or within a collection of buildings, is one of the newest of the various telecommunications areas. We have seen a veritable explosion in numbers of implementations and products being offered to satisfy the needs of in-building communications. Two access schemes have emerged as the most serious contenders for the Institute of Electrical and Electronics Engineers (IEEE) standard for local network access. These are: Carrier Sense Multiple Access with Collision Detection

(CSMA/CD) and the Token Ring. Analysis and simulation of these schemes are available in the literature [1], and the behavior is relatively well understood. New schemes appear each month in the literature of the field, and one wonders if the standard is not being forced upon us too early in this rapidly evolving technology. However, the access scheme is not the only issue of concern. There are a number of other critical issues which must be addressed. In Table 1, a list is given of considerations one must make in evaluating any local network. The list is divided into two parts, the left half of which describes those technical features which are typically amenable to analysis and to quantitative comparison. These are the measures we often see discussed in the technical literature. The right half of the list represents other (softer) issues and measures which one seldom sees addressed in the technical literature but which are of major concern in the commercial trade literature. It is this set of other issues which tends to determine which architecture is adopted by a given corporation or institution. Most of the readers of this journal are probably far more interested in the left half of the list rather than the right half; this is unfortunate. It is unfortunate because we find ourselves at a kind of dichotomy with the industry; they are concerned with the soft issues, and we keep feeding them results about the technical issues. At some point we will have to cross each other's boundaries and address each other's issues in a serious way if we are to make a significant impact.

Table 1: Local Network Issues

Technical	Other
Speed/Capacity	Cost
Topology	Reliability
Response Time	Installation
Efficiency	Expansion/Contraction
Channel Access	Standards
Length/Spacing	Protocol Interface
Number of Stations	Taps
Addressing	Voice/Data/Fax/Video
Acknowledgements	Security/Privacy
Medium for Transmission	Noise Immunity
	Safety
	Qualified Maintenance
	Transparency
	User Migration
	Vendor Lock-in
	Back-up Facilities
	Can Stations work if net is down
	Availability of Electronic Mail, File Servers, and Print Servers
	Error Checking
	Simple Access to Files
	Regulation
	Charging Policy
	Operations Staff
	Non-technical User Environment Needs

One of the interesting technical issues to discuss is the choice of medium for communication itself. Originally local network access was handled by twisted copper pairs through the use of telephone-supplied equipment, often using private automatic branch exchanges (PABX). More recently we have seen the PABX develop into a computerized branch exchange (CBX) still using twisted pairs. However the use of coaxial cable has recently emerged as a very attractive alternative to twisted pairs [15]. After all, the single half-inch diameter coaxial cable can replace more than 1500 twisted pairs. Baseband coaxial cables can provide data rates up to a few tens of megabits/second (MBPS) in half-duplex mode. Broadband can provide over 100 MBPS in full-duplex mode and it can be implemented using commercially available CATV components. Beyond coaxial cables we are looking at the remarkable technology of fiberoptic channels. These channels are made up of bundles of glass fibers, each a few thousandths of an inch thick and 100 times lighter than copper wire or coaxial cable. They can run four miles without a repeater, and have bandwidths measured in thousands of MBPS. Here we have a technology in which semiconductor lasers convert electronic signals into pulses of infrared light which are sent down the glass fiber and then converted back to electronic signals by photodetectors. Once again silicon (in the form of silica to make very pure glass) has come to the rescue! The fiberoptic channel, in fact, represents an enormous opportunity in providing huge bandwidths in an electonically secure environment (secure from simple tapping, from electromagnetic interference and from crosstalk).

A large number of firms are currently implementing various versions of the ETHERNET protocol (CSMA/CD), and these are already available in the market. For less than $1000 per interface one can connect a terminal to a local network and provide wideband communications among the devices within a given building.

The major question here seems to be one not so much of access protocols for data (these are reasonably well understood) but rather the need for integrated services which permit voice, data, facsimile, video and graphics all to be served by the same communication system. The needs of this integrated service have introduced some serious problems of access and control. Broadband coax using CATV components is being considered as one solution to this problem. The CBX also appears attractive for integrated services. Much research needs to be done in this area.

In all of the systems discussed above (ranging from terrestrial networks to satellite nets to packet radio nets and to local network architectures) we have seen that there is an opportunity whereby we can take advantage of our resource sharing principles in dynamically providing wideband communications among a large number of demands. A number of technical issues remain to be resolved as mentioned above (principally in the areas of routing, flow control, and access control), but some of the major problems lie beyond the analytic area and enter into the softer areas described earlier. Elevating our sights to much higher-level issues, we mention simply the enormously complex issues of tariffs, standards, politics, sociology, trade barriers, etc. Issues such as those will determine the direction in which telecommunications makes its real progress. Political considerations could easily strangle the effective use of telecommunications on a worldwide basis, and we must be wary of such tendencies. Of course, these are issues with which the technician is seldom concerned but issues of which he must be aware even if he contributes little to their solution.

3. The Real World and the Coming Revolution

As mentioned earlier, the telecommunication engineers and analysts must not close their eyes to the nontechnical telecommunications issues. One must be concerned with markets and market penetration. For example, which products should be developed at this point in time, and can they be appropriately marketed? What are the needs of the commercial community, and how can they best be met with our wonderful collection of telecommunication services? Indeed, what should those services be, and how should they be charged for? Should they be regulated, or should they be open to free competition? Who should be concerned with security and safety of the data? What agency or organization should be concerned with tying this collection of heterogeneous networks which span the world into a global network which functions in a cooperative fashion?

Answers to these questions will be forthcoming in one fashion or another. The demand is clearly here. Home services will be the first place where we will feel the impact. Television sets will become two-way terminals to the world's databases and information resources. Children will likely receive significant fractions of their education at a computer terminal in a highly interactive mode. Electronic funds transfer is a virtual certainty as is electronic mail. These are the services that one is likely to see in the home and also moving out into the business sector. At the moment the impact on business is being felt more strongly and has come in the form of software packages for finance, order entry, word processing, etc. These are real business needs which have been well served by the rapid expansion of data processing capabilites. Future systems are likely to include speech input/output word-processing machines (which implies speech recognition, understanding, editing, ect.), nearly paperless offices, large screen executive work stations, fourth generation languages for rapid application development, etc. Meanwhile, the software is abysmal and usually poorly supported and rapidly changing and poorly documented and slow! (The recent growth of the nonprocedural languages appears to be one way out of the software stranglehold; these languages include FOCUS, RAMIS, MAPPER, etc.) Such is the price of passing through a rapid transition into a new era. But that era is upon us, and few people are really aware of its enormity. As technicians we have a clear responsibility to provide the technical support for the telecommunications revolution (or, if you will, information revolution), but we have a second responsibility to keep aware of the real needs and demands as they exist out there in the commercial world and to fold that understanding into our own designs so as to provide a service which is both technically and functionally responsive to those needs.

References

1. Bux, Werner, "Local-Area Subnetworks: A Performance Comparison," *IEEE Transactions on Communications*, Vol. COM-29, No. 10, October 1981, pp. 1465-1473.

2. Fratta, L., M. Gerla and L. Kleinrock, "The Flow Deviation Method: An Approach to Store-and-Forward Communication Network Design," *Networks*, Vol. 3, No. 2, 1973, pp. 97-133.

3. Gafni, E. M. and D. P. Bertsekas, "Distributed Algorithms for Generating Loop-Free Routes in Networks with Frequently Changing Topology," *IEEE Transactions on Communications*, Vol. COM-29, No. 1, January 1981, pp. 11-17.

4. Gallager, R. G., "A Minimum Delay Routing Algorithm Using Distributed Computation," *IEEE Transactions on Communications*, Vol. COM-25, No. 1, January 1977, pp. 73-84.

5. Gerla, M. and L. Kleinrock, "Closed Loop Stability Controls for S-ALOHA Satellite Communications," *Proceedings of the Fifth Data Communications Symposium*, Snowbird, Utah, September 1977, pp. 2-10 to 2-19.

6. Gerla, M., L. Nelson and L. Kleinrock, "Packet Satellite Multiple Access: Models and Measurements," *Conference Record, National Telecommunications Conference*, Los Angeles, California, December 1977, pp. 12.2-1 to 12.2-8.

7. Gerla, M. and L. Kleinrock, "Flow Control: A Comparative Survey," *IEEE Transactions on Communications*, Vol. COM-28, April 1980, pp. 553-574.

8. Kleinrock, L., "Resource Allocation in Computer Systems and Computer Communications Networks," *Information Processing 74*, Proceedings of IFIP Congress 74, Stockholm, Sweden, August 1974, North Holland Publishing Company, Amsterdam, 1974, pp. 11-18.

9. Kleinrock, L., *Queueing Systems, Volume I: Theory*, Wiley Interscience, New York, 1975.

10. Kleinrock, L., *Queueing Systems, Volume II: Computer Applications*, Wiley Interscience, New York, 1976.

11. Kleinrock, L., "Performance of Distributed Multi-Access Computer-Communication Systems, *Information Processing 77*, Proceedings of IFIP Congress 77, Toronto, Canada, August 1977, North Holland, Amsterdam, 1977, pp. 547-552.

12. Kleinrock, L. and M. Gerla, "On the Measured Performance of Packet Satellite Access Schemes," *Proceedings of the Fourth International Conference on Computer Communication*, Kyoto, Japan, September 1978, pp. 535-542.

13. Kleinrock, L. and J. Silvester, "Optimum Transmission Radii for Packet Radio Networks or Why Six is a Magic Number," *Conference Record, National Telecommunications Conference*, Birmingham, Alabama, December 1978, pp. 4.3.2 to 4.3.5.

14. Kleinrock, L., "Power and Deterministic Rules of Thumb for Probabilistic Problems in Computer Communications," *Conference Record, International Conference on Communications*, Boston, Massachusetts, June 1979, pp. 43.1.1 to 43.1.10.

15. Levy, W. E. and M. Rothberg, "Coaxial Cable Finds a Home," *Mini-Micro Systems*, Vol. 14, No. 3, March 1981, pp. 99-108.

16. Martin, J. *The Wired Society*, Prentice-Hall, Inc., Englewood Cliffs, New Jersey, 1978.

17. Rosen, E. "Vulnerabilities of Network Control Protocols: An Example," *Computer Communication Review*, Vol. 11, No. 3, July 1981, pp. 10-16.

About the Author

Leonard Kleinrock received his B.E.E. degree from City College of New York in 1957 and the M.S.E.E. and Ph.D.E.E. degrees from Massachusetts Institute of Technology in 1959 and 1963, respectively.

In 1963 he joined the faculty of the School of Engineering and Applied Science, University of California, Los Angeles, where he is now Professor of Computer Science. His research spans the fields of computer networks, computer systems modeling and analysis, queueing theory, and resource sharing and allocation in general. At UCLA, he directs a group in advanced teleprocessing systems and computer networks. He is the author of three major books in the field of computer networks: *Communication Nets: Stochastic Message Flow and Delay*. New York, McGraw Hill, 1964; also New York, Dover, 1972. *Queueing Systems Vol. I: Theory*. New York, Wiley-Interscience, 1975, and *Queueing Systems, Vol. II: Computer Applications*. New York, Wiley-Interscience, 1976. He has published over 120 articles and contributed to several books. He serves as consultant for many domestic and foreign corporations and governments and he is a referee for numerous scholarly publications and a book reviewer for several publishers.

He is a Guggenheim Fellow, an IEEE Fellow, and has received various outstanding teacher and best paper awards, including the 1976 Lanchester prize for the outstanding paper in operations research, and the ICC '78 prize-winning paper award. He was recently elected to the National Academy of Engineering in recognition of his pioneering research contributions and educational leadership in the field of computer communications networks.

Networks for the Nineties

LEWIS M. BRANSCOMB

Keynote address—IEEE INFOCOM '83—San Diego, CA, April 17–22.

IT'S A PLEASURE to join you this morning, and I appreciate the chance to help launch this second IEEE INFOCOM . . . obviously bigger—and, by all indications, even better—than the first edition, a year ago in Las Vegas.

This group is fortunate in having the opportunity to help provide *access* to the productivity engine of our time—the computer. In his book, *The Wired Society*, James Martin recalls how "Max Lerner—on completing his massive two-volume work, *America as a Civilization*—was asked by a group of foreign professors if he could select any one word that epitomized what was special about America as a civilization. After some thought, the word he selected was 'access.' It is a country in which people have *access* to information . . . to management . . . to education . . . to opportunity . . . to politicians . . . [to media].

"It is perhaps pertinent," Martin added, "that America [and the free world] has generally had the world's best telecommunications. Totalitarian countries have generally had the worst."

The Computer as a Productivity Engine

Barely thirty years old, the information industry continues to grow at close to 15% a year, creating tens of thousands of new jobs annually. More importantly, this industry introduces new technology so rapidly that each year its products do about 25% more for the user, at constant cost.

Thus, looking at the value of these products (in this case, the computing power of the newer machines), productivity is increasing at an astounding 25% a year. That 25% increase in computing power per dollar is, of course, a measure of the *user's* opportunity for increasing his own productivity if he uses it well; it is a real benefit to the economy.

Finally, if you add those two numbers—the 15% growth and 25% productivity improvement—together, it's apparent that, allowing for inflation, available computing capacity is increasing at about 35% a year. At that rate, ten years from now the computer capability in place in the United States will be twenty times what it is today.

Will all that computing power be needed? I think so, because one must not think of the computer of the future as just a calculating device, as it was when it was invented. Now the computer is a device that handles all forms of information that people can perceive. I often refer to it as a "motor for the mind." Making this "motor" more accessible is especially significant right now, when, for the first time in American history, many parents no longer expect their children to grow up to a better life than their parents enjoyed. For, unless the growth of American productivity is rekindled, a decline in our standard of living can be expected.

Advances in Computer Communications

Computer communications has come a long way since the 1940's, when IBM first provided transceiver equipment for directly transmitting punched card data over telephone lines and reproducing it on cards at the other end.

Who, in those days, could have seriously predicted communicating personal computers . . . intelligent office terminals . . . multicomputer networks . . . satellite and fiber optic communications? Anyone who did would have been way ahead of British physicist Lord Ernest Rutherford, who pioneered the study of the atomic nucleus and discovered the alpha particle. He maintained—as late as 1933—that, "He who expects a source of power from the transformation of these atoms is talking moonshine."

Drawing lessons from the past can be risky, if we are to believe Shakespeare's Othello when he intoned, "To mourn a mischief which is past and gone, is the next way to draw new mischief on."

Still, since a keynote speech is expected to provide some perspective . . . return with me (for just a moment) to those not-so-thrilling days of yesteryear.

By the 1960's, there had already been great strides in reducing the cost of computing hardware, but it was still too expensive—and programming performance and reliability were insufficient—to justify on-line communications-based systems except in a few selected applications such as military ones. The carriers continued to focus on their voice networks, and most users remained batch-oriented at the end of the decade.

The 1970's brought further, significant reductions in data processing costs—both in the CPU environment and in remote, distributed processors—plus great strides in programming and, in particular, communications support. Carriers generally completed their voice network modernization, and began to condition their analog circuits for data and to introduce new features specifically oriented toward

Reprinted from *IEEE Communications Magazine*, October 1983, pages 38-43.

data—notably, packet switching networks, many employing various versions of the emerging X.25 standard.

The ARPA research network—introduced in 1970—demonstrated to everyone what some little computers, plus a little communications and a lot of imagination, could do. As a result of all this, those ten years saw on-line systems grow from a handful to the point where 60% of all central CPU's supported some kind of communications-based application, in many cases with distributed intelligence (that is, with application compute power distributed out from the central electronics complex to include the system periphery). Large, even huge, networks emerged, starting at the research level with ARPA, and then, as we in IBM like to think, strongly accelerated by the introduction for business use of Systems Network Architecture in 1974.

Need for Evolution and Planning

One important facet of SNA was the evolutionary nature of its capabilities. At the outset, it was clear that SNA would have to evolve; we had neither the number of programmers nor the technical skills in those early days to create overnight the full system capabilities that would eventually be required. Even today, getting there all at once just isn't possible, because, as our Communication Products Division President, Victor Goldberg, has pointed out, network architectures are different from building architectures.

"When you put up a building, you design it first, and then build it to those specifications. But by the time the industry began developing network architectures, we—and our customers—were already living in the building.

"Rarely do we have the luxury of starting with a clean slate; there is a lot of history to accommodate. One has to be constantly concerned with what customers have installed, and what they are trying to connect with."

One can see this in the way SNA gradually evolved from a single star topology with one host at the center to today's systems involving many cooperating, peer-connected hosts, serving tens of thousands of terminals. The important thing is not only to have a plan—to be implemented over time, but also to respond quickly when you see that customer needs don't match your plan as well as you thought. That goes for users, too.

In the growing trend toward personal computing in the office, for example, we see a phenomenon which parallels the one which took place with general-purpose minicomputers in the mid-seventies. The so-called "mini revolution" helped provide much-needed productivity in a hurry, but eventually resulted in information bottlenecks throughout many enterprises. Because there was no commonality or central planning, information collected or produced on local processors was not compatible with that of the rest of the organization. The way to avoid a repetition of that difficulty is to give serious thought to how *all* the organization's information handling systems—whether word processors, host-attached terminals, or personal computers—mesh with each other and with current host systems.

1980's: Decade of Office Automation

If the 1970's were the decade of common carrier-based, on-line systems and network growth through new architectures, the 1980's are clearly the decade of office automation and other intra-establishment networks.

The average factory worker today has his productivity backed up with $25,000 worth of machinery—and that's before full automation. In today's offices, on the other hand, there are still very few machines. The elementary office systems in use today are aimed largely at helping secretaries. Support per worker is one-tenth that of factory workers. Surprisingly little of the communication and other activity in today's offices is assisted by computer.

For example, one consultant estimates that there are eight file drawers containing 18,000 documents for every white-collar worker in the United States. Together, these workers produce 72-billion documents annually, and file and maintain another 300-billion. The information explosion, it seems, is proceeding at a rate of two file drawers per office worker per year. Yet, in the offices of most principals, or white-collar information workers, the only technology items to be found are a clock, telephone, pocket calculator, and some dictation equipment.

During the 1980's, support of the world's thirty million or so office principals will become a major focus of effort, for there are about nine times as many of these principals as there are secretaries. With typically higher salaries for principals, the incentive to improve their productivity is greater.

One implication of principal support is that the networks of the eighties will have to carry many more bits of information. This is virtually guaranteed by the use of facsimile and other image equipment, including full-screen, all-points-addressable terminals, along with vast numbers of more conventional text terminals. The need will arise to integrate voice and data for the purpose of creating compound documents with voice annotation and playback through a telephone handset.

Merging Forms of Information

Eventually, office systems will have to be able to merge most of today's separately handled data, text, voice, and image information into integrated electronic documents that can be communicated, retrieved, and otherwise dealt with, without the user being conscious of their form when stored.

Artificial distinctions between data, word, and image processing will gradually disappear as document distribution, filing, and retrieval systems for all kinds of documents are evolved. And when that day comes, how will we tie all this information together? We can't expect the transmission system to care which form—words, voice, or pictures—the information was in.

Obviously, an "electronic paper clip" will have to be invented, something to tie these disparate media together. This is a capability some people expect to emerge from work on the Integrated Services Digital Network concept.

Whatever you call it, that is a complicated system architecture problem that must be addressed at all interconnect levels, including the application level. It won't be as easy as bending a piece of wire.

Changing Telecommunications Services

For communications between establishments, computers and their users are already starting to benefit from the many public digital communications services and data networks now offered or planned, and from communications satellites, through which data can flow at the same speed at which the computers themselves operate.

This external telecommunications environment will, no doubt, continue to evolve, and agreement on and development of new standard interfaces for voice and data by common carriers around the world is another virtual certainty. More on these regulatory and standards matters later.

The main technical thrust of the eighties lies elsewhere, within the establishment, where local area networks, or LAN's; and the private branch exchange, or PBX, are the key elements in this rapidly changing environment.

Local Area Networks . . .

A local area network, by my definition, is any information transportation system that provides for high-speed connection between users within a single building or a campus complex—through a common wiring system, common communications adapter, common access protocol to allow connection between users, and common shared resources such as the largest files and the most powerful printers.

In designing such a system, a number of factors are paramount. The system must have a 15-20-year life. It must be responsive to current, future, and as yet undefined system requirements; recognize the growth of personal workstations; be compatible with a variety of types of workstations; be consistent with local area networking standards; and provide an economical and orderly migration path from today's networks.

As most of you know, several LAN approaches are in contention, including the token ring architecture which IBM submitted to the IEEE Project 802 Standards Committee about a year ago. Along with a token-passing approach, we favor using baseband transmission and a hierarchical wiring structure with star configurations going from wiring concentrators to offices, used in a logical ring configuration.

Sorting out the technical merits and application domains of the token ring, contention bus, and competing LAN approaches will be a major activity of the eighties. However that debate turns out, clearly, local area networks must be integrated into existing network architectures. That is driving the further evolution of SNA from its original hierarchical, large-host orientation toward one that increasingly fosters peer-to-peer communications, embracing intelligent workstations and both large and small hosts.

. . . vs. the Private Branch Exchange

The other facility that will have a significant and growing role in establishment and office systems of the future is, of course, the PBX.

The typical 1980's PBX can be expected to provide not only traditional PBX functions—attachment and control of conventional telephones, and data devices using modems—but advanced voice capabilities like speech messaging akin to that done by IBM's Audio Distribution System. And in addition to attachment of analog telephones and data devices with modems, we are likely to see digital telephone attachments and direct digital attachment of terminals to PBX's.

Will Both Be Needed?

The obvious question is, will either the LAN or PBX be sufficient to satisfy the needs of most users, or will both be required?

The basic function of a PBX is to support interactive, human-to-human voice conversations. Consequently, PBX's are optimized to support that application in a cost-effective manner, implying a full duplex data rate of, say, 64 kb/s over point-to-point connections. While this capability can clearly support a variety of data requirements, it is probably not sufficient to support the high speed and connectivity requirements of some future office applications. In fact, one analysis of an office application involving browsing through a document concluded that the demand placed on the link between the user terminal and the document file will approach hundreds of kb/s for coded information, and mb/s for noncoded or facsimile information.

This type of application is where the LAN packet-based approach, with high bandwidth available immediately on demand, excels. In addition, LAN's can support simultaneous sessions between workstations and *multiple* processors and their files.

Because of the point-to-point nature of PBX connections, this capability is not easily provided. Nor can the PBX so quickly terminate one session and initiate another, as can the LAN, because of the telephony protocols that even digital PBX's will follow. On the other hand, the LAN approach leaves it poorly suited to support large numbers of concurrent voice conversations between people.

Thus, *both* a PBX and LAN will be required to support the full range of applications that will evolve in future establishment systems. And furthermore, I suspect that most users will demand the functional capabilities that can be provided only by having both.

Testing New Ideas on Campus

One prototypical testbed for both LAN ideas and high-performance workstations is beginning to emerge at Carnegie-Mellon University in Pittsburgh. There, IBM and the university have just begun the joint development of a unique personal computing network.

One of CMU's goals, like that of most universities, is the full integration of computing into undergraduate and graduate education. Indeed, most of the following remarks apply not just to universities, but to any large organization that prefers to operate in a heavily decentralized and highly creative mode. That is the nature of a good university, and I believe it will become the nature of many commercial and public institutions in the future.

Eventually, it is expected that all CMU students, faculty, researchers, and professional staff will have access to personal computer workstations that are effectively twenty to one-hundred times more powerful than today's home computers. Each will also have access to shared, central databases, through a high-speed LAN. The planned configuration will consist of four system elements: the workstations, local area networks or clusters, a backbone communications network with gateways and bridges to the other elements, and a central computing and database facility. A mail system and electronic bulletin boards will allow users to communicate with each other. They will also be able to access files from any workstation and to access the system from home—or far beyond the campus—through cable television or telephone lines.

Wave of the Future: Networked Workstations

What the universities are exploring may become the wave of the future for the commercial world, too: easy-to-program workstations—a more powerful version of a personal computer—networked to similar workstations, to shared input/output devices, and to shared data on larger host systems.

One reason for this trend is that networked, intelligent workstations take advantage of both the negative economies of scale in logic, and the positive economies of scale in storage, printing, and other specialized I/O devices. These economy of scale numbers tend to favor distributed logic and data, but in DASD and printers, the opposite is true—you get more for your money in a larger, shared, higher-performance unit.

Bigger Mainframes and Distributed Workstations

Accompanying this trend toward large numbers of distributed, powerful workstations is the need for large processors of ever-increasing power. Our large commercial customers find their requirement for compute power in each of their computer centers growing very rapidly.

The amount of information stored in electronic form is increasing at some 40% a year. The management of massive databases, to which many people need quick access, requires a lot of compute power. Once big databases with high activity are online, the user's business growth typically drives the demand for workstation access to shared data even higher.

If the computer power of a typical center is growing at 40-50% a year, and most of this processing is to support terminal-based applications, it is not difficult to imagine that a huge increase in communications performance will have to occur, too, or this growth will be stifled. It is important to note that even a network comparable to CMU's ambitious plan will not necessarily change the way an enterprise is run, but a new range of possibilities is opened up; conventional views of organizational behavior will be challenged.

What such a network does is create a different set of relationships between people, giving them the flexibility to adapt their organization dynamically to the needs of the enterprise. I can envision in such organizations a much more open environment in which people can find others with common interests and establish relationships that lead to personal contact.

How Networks Foster Communities of Interest

I believe experience with computer networking already bears out that promise. The Defense Department, for example, made a greater contribution than it knew in establishing ARPANET, linking research groups in United States universities in the early 1970's.

The original idea was to permit sharing of computers that were not equally loaded. It turned out that this network was really used to discover the power of electronic mail, and document creation and distribution. This led to a new capability: remote collaboration by scientists thousands of miles apart.

IBM has also had this experience on a much larger scale with an open-ended, peer-connected network, called "VNET," which recently celebrated the 1,000th host processor node in hundreds of cities in 29 countries. VNET grew "bottom-up," so to speak, when two laboratories working on a joint project needed to exchange data. Soon, other related sites were added, and the network grew until virtually all our scientific and engineering locations worldwide are part of it. It is still growing. About fifty university computers are also hooked up, using this capability under the name BITNET. The acronym means, "Because It's Time."

Such networks have an almost unique ability, not only to improve the effectiveness of working groups, but to foster sub-communities of interest that the host organization isn't even aware of. And I'm equally convinced that, as this kind of network capability becomes generally available to everyone, the information habits and, indeed, the organizational and social habits of all Americans will be affected by the emergence of new electronic information services.

Emerging New Information Services

Consider videotex, for example, which to me means a database inquiry capability based on consumer TV technology, featuring extreme ease of use, color, and—of increasing importance—graphics.

One study suggests that worldwide expenditures on videotex systems service in 1992 will be 25 billion dollars, with another 50 billion spent on information content by enterprises using videotex systems to distribute information within the enterprise. So far, of course, there are only about 5,000 (non-paying) videotex users in the United States, and there are few serious projections that more than 10-20% of American households will have some form of videotex service by the year 1990.

Two things are missing: One is agreement on a single technical standard for videotex transmission and presentation, which is a challenge for the computer/communications community. The second is a *reason* for average citizens to want videotex systems, and that is a challenge for potential information providers.

From a technical perspective, the new electronic media do provide capabilities which go far beyond the printed page, television images, or motion pictures. And there are, at last count, 1,350 databases commercially available through electronic access in the United States. Clearly, the potential is there for genuinely new and unique media, and potentially new forms and types of information services.

But, as that great philosopher, Linus, once reminded Charlie Brown, "There is no heavier burden than a great potential."

Will videotex, the videodisc, and the personal computer, for example, live up to their potentials? Or are they merely new ways to shuttle about old information? The answer lies in how creatively people use them.

My own prediction is that video storage technology will eventually emerge as the powerful partner of the personal computer and videotex information services to form the basis for a truly powerful information system with all needed attributes.

The quality of the user interface will, of course, also strongly influence the growth rate for electronic information services. The key here is software. Much more research in both cognitive and computer science will be required to learn how to build information systems that are that easy to use and will provide user satisfaction. As jazz musician Charles Mingus put it, "Anybody can play weird; that's easy. What's hard is to be as simple as Bach. Making the simple complicated is commonplace; making the complicated simple, awesomely simple—that's creativity."

Influence of Governmental Controls

Besides technical inventions and the packaging of useful information to satisfy users' needs, other factors influencing the growth of telecommunications include the degree to which the implementation of new technologies is promoted or restricted by governmental regulatory policy. A fundamental requirement for the encouragement of innovation is the availability of reliable, low-cost basic transmission, that is, the movement of a user's information without change in its form or content. Such universally available services should be as transparent and flexible as they can be, so that competitive enhanced services can easily be built upon them.

Users Need Menu of Basic Services

Data users require the continued availability of a menu of basic telecommunications services from which to choose. For applications involving a heavy load of batch transmissions, for example, or constant interactive communication requiring very short response times, a dedicated circuit is most desirable. For applications involving relatively infrequent long transmissions, circuit switching may be best; and for short, bursty, interactive communications not keyed to short response times, packet switching might be most effective.

The point is, since application requirements vary greatly in terms of information volume, traffic pattern, response time, and type of processing required, users are best served by a large menu of basic offerings.

ISDN Must Not Limit User Choices

The natural next step is to extend switched digital services to the user premises and provide a single interface for all services. Indeed, this is the basis of the Integrated Services Digital Network (or ISDN) concept, the standardization of which is being attempted by the CCITT. ISDN will be all-digital, which is desirable for reliability and economy. It will be switched, and it may well be packet-switched.

What concerns me—and should concern all users, as well—is that the possible focus on *just* packet-switched digital service within the ISDN concept (which is supposed to solve almost everybody's total communications needs) could mean the end of existing digital leased services, and no further development of digital circuit-switched services. That packet-switched digital might become the *only* service available is our fear, regardless of what is said now about the eventual implementation of other services under ISDN. The problem is that users would then have to tailor their systems to one kind of service which, in many cases, might not be the most efficient for them.

BOC's Must Keep "Pipelines" Transparent

In the post-AT&T-settlement era, the divested Bell Operating Companies and the independent local telephone companies will link the user with AT&T and all the other long line providers. These exchange carriers can be either a pipeline or a bottleneck.

Traditionally, each transmission service has required a separate line to the customer's premises. But in the ISDN concept, all available services are swept together into a single pipeline that can take on the coloration of a packet-switched, circuit-switched, or whatever service the user calls for. For this to work in the United States with multiple service-suppliers, it is essential that the exchange carriers provide a *transparent* pipeline—with minimal constraints in the form of protocols—between the user and the central office, right up to the point where it fans out into various services.

One can and should debate whether a packet-switched interface (with legislated packet size, for example) is really transparent. A very important principle has been achieved in the work of the last 10 years of regulatory debate and legal settlement, the most important feature of which is agreement on the idea that there are basic transmission services that are the common base upon which competitive, unregulated services are built. However, this approach will work only if the definitions of the interfaces to those basic services are clean and technologically meaningful.

Don't Neglect International Standards

Another challenge I consider underrated by many people in this country is the influence of international recommendations and standards on United States developments. The information industry is, almost by definition, a global industry, and the FCC should take a more active role in CCITT and ISO, together with broad representation from the users of communications services as well as suppliers and manufacturers.

If I learned one thing from my experience as director of the National Bureau of Standards, it is that success in the voluntary standards process is critically dependent upon the participation of technically sophisticated and economically knowledgeable users. Most of the shortcomings in voluntary standards arise when the *users* are not active participants.

Questions of Public Policy

That brings me to the long-term question, which is: If the information industry is really going to be the lever on our national productivity, what does the United States have to do to make that possible?

This industry has a great potential for growth that could boost the productivity of our entire economy. But there are some obstacles—matters of public policy—to realizing these contributions. I am concerned, for example, that in our zeal to match or beat the Japanese in productivity, quality, and cost, we might lose sight of some American strengths: research and invention, not to mention entrepreneurship, individual initiative, and the generation of creative ideas.

Is America a Scientific Nation?

By most measures, America is still the most scientific nation the world has ever seen. We usually win so many Nobel Prizes that it embarrasses those who plead for more support by claiming our science has become second-rate. Historically, however, America has not always enjoyed a high level of basic science, except in the last 50 years.

Our science owes an enormous debt to Jewish, Oriental, and other scientists fleeing despotism and poverty. Most especially, we owe a debt to the absolutely unique period of economic dominance in the wake of World War II. In truth, science was the beneficiary of the economic boom of the fifties and sixties, not its cause. The public's extraordinary generosity to science in that golden period was, at least in part, a response to a perceived challenge to our security from the Soviet Union. This time, the challenge is not so much military as it is economic.

But it would be a mistake to assume that research is so deeply ingrained in our own culture that we can take our excellence and dedication for granted. Over the next few years, the achievements of our university and industrial laboratories alike will be vitally important to this country, and we should be nurturing them as never before. Yet, after a period of severely constrained growth, our universities find themselves with embarrassingly obsolete research equipment and facilities. How, then, *do* we foster the three interrelated elements of our national economic dilemma: the vitality of the nation's research enterprise, the competitiveness of the technology in our commercial enterprises, and the quality of education in our schools and universities?

There seems to be an emerging consensus that our national preoccupation with "band aids" for industries in trouble should be exchanged for a national commitment to success in "high technology," whatever that is. The true importance to our economy of the high-tech information industry is not just its own growth; it is the productivity-transforming power of its products and services in every walk of life. After all, high-technology industry is rarely an end in itself. Its main contribution is providing the tools and capabilities throughout our society to increase productivity in all segments of the economy, without exception.

Too few of the political advocates of "high tech" understand this. From a technical point of view, practically anything one wants to do can be done. The only question is, what do we want to do? What is the user requirement? The only limit is our imagination.

Lewis M. Branscomb, Vice-President and Chief Scientist of International Business Machines Corporation, is responsible for guiding the Corporation's scientific and technical programs to ensure that they meet long-term needs. He joined IBM in May, 1972.

A research physicist, Dr. Branscomb was appointed director of the National Bureau of Standards by the President in 1969 after a career at the Bureau since 1951. Dr. Branscomb was graduated from Duke University *summa cum laude* in 1945. He was awarded M.S. and Ph.D. degrees in physics by Harvard University in 1947 and 1949.

Among his affiliations, Dr. Branscomb is a member of the National Academy of Engineering, the National Academy of Sciences, and the National Academy of Public Administration. In 1979, he was appointed by President Carter to the National Science Board, and, in May 1980, was elected chairman. He is also a member of the President's National Productivity Advisory Committee and chairs its Subcommittee on Research, Development, and Technological Innovation.

Dr. Branscomb is a director of the Mobil and General Foods Corporations, and a trustee of Vanderbilt University. ■

Chapter 2
Data Link Control Protocols

2.1. OVERVIEW

Data Link Control (DLC) protocols provide functions of frame, multiple access, content, and dialog synchronization for communication using a physical link. Except for start-stop protocols, bit synchronism is assumed to be provided separately by hardware devices (modems, transceivers, etc.) that implement the physical layer function.

DLC protocols fall into two main categories: character-oriented protocols and bit-oriented protocols. In character-oriented protocols, all control and data information are exchanged in the form of characters chosen from a character code set (e.g., ASCII and EBCDIC). A popular example is IBM's BSC [IBM 70] which is akin to the ANSI X3.28 protocol standard [ANSI 75]. Bit-oriented protocols do not depend upon the use of any character code set. Bit-oriented protocols include HDLC which is a standard of ISO [ISO 78, ISO 79a, ISO 79b, ISO 80a, ISO 80b], ADCCP which is a standard of ANSI [ANSI 79] and IBM's SDLC [IBM 75]. All three protocols are essentially the same with only minor differences among them. The two protocol standards evolved out of IBM's submissions to the respective standards organizations. Some additional functions have been defined for HDLC and ADCCP, which were not available in the version of SDLC described in [IBM 75].

In [LAM 83], reprinted below, a brief introduction to start-stop protocols is first given. The BSC and SDLC protocols are then described in some detail; additional functional capabilities in HDLC and ADCCP are summarized. (SDLC was described instead of one of the protocol standards because this article was first written in 1979 when the protocol standards documents were not generally available.) Various computer manufacturers have also proposed similar bit-oriented DLC protocols, including DDCMP of Digital Equipment Corporation. An excellent description of DDCMP may be found in [MCNA 77].

We give some additional comments on the functions of frame, multiple access, content, and dialog synchronization and how they are implemented in different protocols.

2.2. FRAME SYNCHRONIZATION

There are two basic techniques for identifying frame boundaries. Character-oriented protocols use special control characters to do so. However, sending transparent data in such protocols requires character insertion/deletion operations. Bit-oriented protocols use a special sequence of 8 bits, 01111110 (called a flag), for marking frame boundaries. To render flags unique, bit insertion/deletion operations have to be performed (by hardware). The reader is referred to [LAM 83] for more details. The DDCMP protocol is a bit-oriented protocol, but it uses a third approach. The beginning of a frame is marked by two or more SYN characters (like character-oriented protocols), while the end of a frame is indicated by a byte count in the frame header.

Most DLC protocols use the cyclic redundancy check (CRC) method for error detection, except for start-stop protocols and some implementations of character-oriented protocols. A description of algorithms for CRC code generation and error detection can be found in Chapter 13 of [MCNA 77]. Note that a modified version of these algorithms is specified for HDLC (see the appendix of [ISO 79a]). The modification is intended to detect flags missing from between two consecutive frames.

2.3. MULTIPLE ACCESS SYNCHRONIZATION

For both classes of protocols considered above, very simple protocols (such as polling) are used for multiple access, or no protocol is necessary because each sender has its own dedicated channel. Much more sophisticated protocols are employed when the data link is actually a local area network (see Chapter 4). The subject of multiple access protocols is covered in Chapter 3.

2.4. CONTENT AND DIALOG SYNCHRONIZATION

In character-oriented protocols, the separation of control and data information is done by the use of different subsets of characters in the character code set. In bit-oriented protocols, the separation is done by positional significance; i.e., they reside in different fields within a frame.

Error control is provided by an automatic repeat request (ARQ) technique in all protocols mentioned above. In an ARQ protocol, the sender keeps a copy of a transmitted data unit. The copy is discarded upon receipt of an acknowledgement from the receiver. If no acknowledgement has been received within a timeout period, the data unit is retransmitted. There are two main categories of ARQ protocols: (1) stop-and-wait protocols, in which only one data unit can be in transit and awaiting acknowledgement at any time and (2) window protocols, in which up to N data units can be in transit and be awaiting acknowledgement. Two retransmission strategies can be used for window protocols. First, when the timer of a specific data unit awaiting acknowledgement has expired, only that particular data unit is retransmitted (selective repeat strategy). Second, the data unit whose timer has expired and all data units transmitted subsequent to it are retransmitted (sometimes referred to as the go-back-N strategy). Both classes of ARQ protocols, if implemented correctly, can also provide in-sequence delivery of data units, given certain assumptions about the behavior of the communication channels (such as finite lifetimes for data units in transit).

Window protocols that permit multiple data units to be in transit are necessary for the efficient utilization of data links that have either relatively long transit delays or high transmission rates, or both [BURT 72].

The protocol standards manuals describe protocol architectures, not their implementations. They typically define precisely low-level functions such as error detection and frame synchronization, frame formats, and the encoding of control messages. The meanings of control messages are given only informal descriptions and are illustrated with example sequences of message exchanges. Such specifications leave many options to be decided by protocol implementors. In particular, one can choose from a variety of data link configurations and operational modes and from different subsets of control messages instead of the entire set defined. Thus it is not easy for independent implementations of such DLC protocols to be compatible. Even if they assume the same configuration and message subset, the exact procedures for implementing the functions of data transfer and connection management may be different.

Lastly, like any distributed program, it is very hard to verify a DLC protocol to be correct. The subject of protocol specification and verification is covered in Chapter 7. In [SHAN 83a], reprinted below, a version of the HDLC protocol with the Asynchronous Balanced Mode is shown. This particular protocol has been verified to have desirable correctness properties for both data transfer and connection management [SHAN 83b]. A simple version of the BSC protocol implementing data transfer and connection management functions can be found in [CHOW 83]. This protocol is guaranteed to have certain correctness properties (freedom from deadlocks and unspecified receptions, and boundedness) by the construction methodology employed therein.

References

[ANSI 75] American National Standards Institute, "Procedures for the Use of the Communication Control Characters of American National Standard Code for Information Interchange in Specified Data Communication Links," ANSI X3.28-1976, December 1975.

[ANSI 79] American National Standards Institute, "American National Standard for Advanced Data Communication Control Procedures (ADCCP)," ANSI X3.66-1979, January 1979.

[BURT 72] Burton, H. O. and D. D. Sullivan, "Errors and Error Control," *Proc. IEEE,* November 1972.

[CHOW 83] Chow, C. H., M. G. Gouda, and S. S. Lam, "A Discipline for Constructing Multi-Phase Communication Protocols," Technical Report TR-233, Dept. of Computer Sciences, University of Texas at Austin, June 1983 (revised, October 1983), submitted for publication.

[IBM 70] IBM Corp., *General Information--Binary Synchronous* Communications, Manual No. GA27-3004-2, 3rd ed., October 1970.

[IBM 75] IBM Corp., *Synchronous Data Link Control--General Information,* Manual No. GA27-3093-1, May 1975.

[ISO 78] International Standards Organization, "Data Communication--HDLC Balanced Class of Procedures," Draft International Standard ISO/DIS 6256, 1978.

[ISO 79a] International Standards Organization, "Data Communication--High-level Data Link Control Procedures--Frame Structure," Ref. No. ISO 3309, Second Edition, 1979.

[ISO 79b] International Standards Organization, "Data Communications--HDLC Procedures--Elements of Procedures," Ref. No. ISO 4335, First Edition, 1979.

[ISO 80a] International Standards Organization, "Data Communication--High Level Data Link Control Procedures--Elements of Procedures (tertiary station) ADDENDUM 2," Draft Addendum ISO 4335/DAD2, 1980.

[ISO 80b] International Standards Organization, "Data Communication--HDLC Unbalanced Classes of Procedures," Ref. No. ISO 6159, First Edition, 1980.

*[LAM 83] Lam, S. S., "Data Link Control Procedures," Chapter 3 in *Computer Communications, Vol. 1: Principles.* W. Chou (ed.), Prentice-Hall, Englewood Cliffs, N.J., 1983.

[MCNA 77] McNamara, J. E., *Technical Aspects of Data Communication,* Digital Equipment Corp., Maynard, Mass., 1977.

*[SHAN 83a] Shankar, A. U. and S. S. Lam, "Specification and Verification of an HDLC Protocol with ARM Connection Management and Full-Duplex Data Transfer," ACM SIGCOMM '83 Symposium, University of Texas at Austin, March 1983; in *Computer Communication Review,* Vol. 13, No. 2, 1983, pp. 38-48.

[SHAN 83b] Shankar, A. U. and S. S. Lam, "An HDLC Protocol Specification and its Verification using Image Protocols., *ACM Trans. on Computer* Systems, Vol. 1, No. 4, November 1983, pp. 331-368.

(* article reprinted below.)

Reprinted with permission from *Computer Communications, Vol. 1: Principles*, W. Chou (editor), 1983, pages 81-113.

Data Link Control Procedures

SIMON S. LAM
The University of Texas at Austin
Austin, Texas

3.1 INTRODUCTION

Data link control (DLC) protocols are concerned with the communication of data between different machines. Communication is considered to be accomplished if the intended receiver of a data message acquires access to the same serial stream of bits as that of the sender within some acceptable time delay. Thus "communication" is used throughout this chapter to mean *synchronization* of data.

Communication between "processes" within the same machine is easily accomplished with shared memory and an operating system that coordinates the communicating processes. When the communicating processes reside in different machines, however, several problems arise:

1. Communications facilities are needed to transport data from one machine to the other.
2. Coordination of the communicating processes can no longer rely on an operating system but needs to be done by the processes exchanging control messages directly between themselves.
3. The error rates of communications channels are such that comprehensive error detection and recovery techniques are needed to handle (1) and (2) properly.
4. The communications channel, especially over a long distance, is expensive and may need to be shared among concurrent "dialogues."

We next define some terminology. Machines that communicate include various kinds of terminals and computers. They are known as *data terminal equipment* (DTEs) in the protocol literature. Each DTE has a mechanism, which we shall call a *transceiver*, with the functional capability of sending and receiving bits serially over a communications channel. Examples of transceivers are modems in common-carrier communications facilities, line driver/receivers in in-house cable networks, and so on. Together, a DTE and its transceiver will be referred to as a *station*; see Fig. 3.1 for

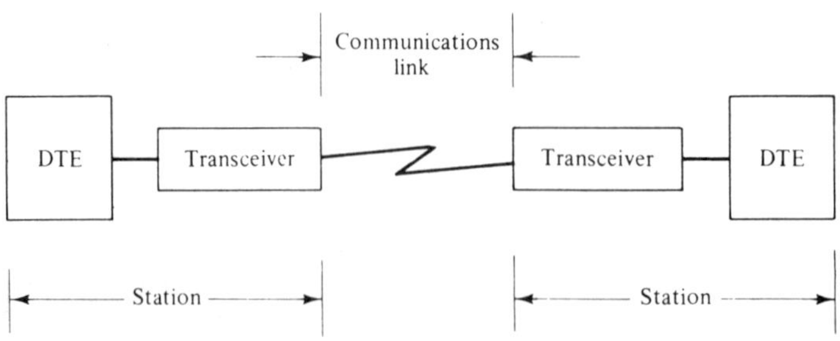

Figure 3.1. Two communicating stations.

illustration. A station is both a sender and a receiver of data messages (although not necessarily at the same time).

Although more than two stations may be involved in a "conference call" or "broadcast" mode of communication, present DLC protocols (of interest herein) deal mainly with dialogues between station pairs. To achieve communication between two stations, the synchronization functions required can be structured into a hierarchy of five levels of functions, to be referred to as the *hierarchical model* (see Fig. 3.2). Each level in the hierarchy depends on synchronism at the level below achieved over *finer grains of time*. Thus each level is offered a virtual (or real) communications channel by the level below, and in turn provides the level above with a virtual communications channel having improved characteristics. Together, the hierarchy of functions supplies the functional capabilities to bridge the gap between what is provided by communications channels and what is required for process-to-process communication.

The synchronization functions shown in Fig. 3.2 are defined in Sec. 3.2 and discussed in detail in Sec. 3.3 for the three major classes of DLC protocols: start–stop, character-oriented, and bit-oriented. Specifically, the hierarchical model is used as a framework for describing IBM's character-oriented BSC (Binary Synchronous Communication) protocol and bit-oriented SDLC (Synchronous Data Link Control) protocol. In Sec. 3.4 the different classes of DLC protocols are compared. For bit-oriented protocols, additional functional capabilities available in the protocol standards, HDLC (High-Level Data Link Control) and ADCCP (Advanced Data Communication Control Procedure), are discussed.

The objective of this chapter is to present DLC functional requirements using the hierarchical model as a framework and various existing protocols to illustrate solution techniques. For a detailed and complete description of these protocols, the reader should consult the latest manuals for up-to-date information.

Finally, we note that the hierarchical model introduced herein provides a structured representation of functional requirements for communication between two remote processes. Thus in addition to being a useful model for DLC protocols, it can be used to model higher-level communication protocol layers as well.

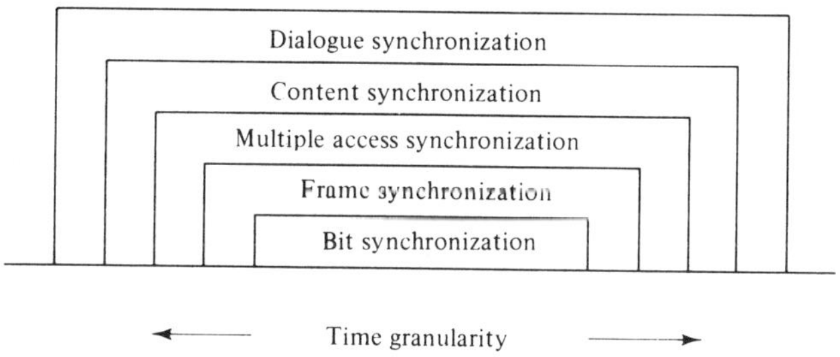

Figure 3.2. Hierarchy of communication functions.

3.2 SYNCHRONIZATION FUNCTIONS

We shall proceed from the bottom of the hierarchy shown in Fig. 3.2 upward.

Bit Synchronization

This level of functions deals with a receiver's ability to retrieve a stream of bits from an incoming analog signal by sampling for the bits at the proper times. The receiver needs to know (1) when to start sampling the first bit, and (2) the period (bit duration) between sampling consecutive bits.

Frame Synchronization

A frame is defined herein to be a stream of bits which is the basic unit of transfer of data and/or control information from a sender to a receiver. The frame synchronization level of functions establishes the conventions for a sender and receiver to delimit within a continuous stream of bits the beginning and the end of a frame. (We note that if the frame size is an integer multiple of the character size of a character-oriented system, character synchronization is also established.)

Another function at this level is error detection. Typically, to detect communication errors, redundancy is built into the bit stream to be transmitted using one of several coding techniques.

Multiple Access Synchronization

It is often necessary to share a physical communications channel among different concurrent sender–receiver pairs. In this case frames transmitted by different senders are interleaved in time. The multiple access synchronization level of functions is concerned with (1) control signals and protocols necessary to synchronize senders so as to avoid (or resolve) access conflicts, and (2) an addressing scheme for identifying senders and receivers. With multiple access synchronization, the higher-level protocol can then behave as if a dedicated (virtual) channel is provided for each sender–receiver pair.

The reader is referred to Chap. 4 for a tutorial treatment of multiple access protocols for channel sharing.

Content Synchronization

This level of functions is concerned with the information content of a frame transmitted from a sender to a receiver, in particular (1) how to differentiate between data and control information within the frame; (2) how to encode and decode control messages; (3) error control to ensure that a single error-free copy of each frame to be sent will arrive at the receiver within some acceptable duration of time; and (4) sequence control to ensure that when a data message is segmented and transported in multiple frames, the message segments are reassembled in the correct sequence.

Dialogue Synchronization

This level of functions is concerned with the initiation and subsequent termination of a dialogue between two stations during which the transfer of frames containing data can take place. Each station is both a sender and a receiver so that there are usually two sender–receiver pairs involved in a dialogue. Dialogue synchronization functions are also needed (1) to coordinate each station pair so that a sender transmits a frame only when it is in a state with the right to transmit and the receiver is in a state that can accept a new frame; and (2) to detect "nonsynchronous" conditions, attempt recovery upon detection of such conditions, and report unrecoverable conditions to higher-level protocols.

Examples of nonsynchronous conditions at the dialogue level are (1) incomplete protocol specification—a data or control message received is not among those expected by the receiver in its present state, and (2) deadlocks—mutual wait conditions between two stations.

In summary, we observe that bit and frame synchronization are necessary for the most rudimentary form of communication between two machines. Multiple access synchronization provides for the sharing of a communications channel by multiple sender–receiver pairs. Content synchronization provides for improved error characteristics, and the encoding of data and control information. Dialogue synchronization provides for data transfer in a mode of operation with desirable characteristics (flow control, interrupts, etc.)

3.3 ASYNCHRONOUS AND SYNCHRONOUS PROTOCOLS

The method for achieving bit synchronism between sender and receiver determines two basic forms of transmission: asynchronous and synchronous. In an asynchronous transmission system, bit synchronism is (in fact) maintained but only when data transmission is taking place and not during idle periods. The amount of data transmitted at a time is one character (5 to 8 bits). In a synchronous transmission system, bit synchronism is maintained at all times. DLC protocols normally used with

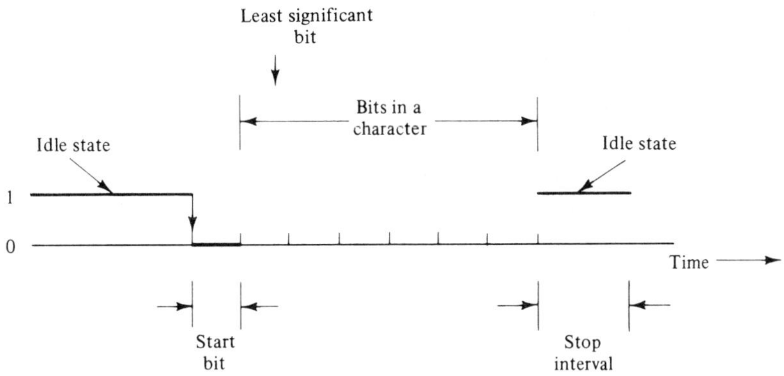

Figure 3.3. Asynchronous transmission.

a synchronous transmission system are said to be synchronous protocols, while DLC protocols normally used with an asynchronous transmission system are said to be asynchronous or start-stop protocols. We note that it is possible to use character-oriented protocols for both synchronous and asynchronous transmission systems. An example is the ANSI (American National Standards Institute) X3.28 protocol standard [ANSI 75], which is akin to the character-oriented BSC protocol to be described. However, both are much more sophisticated than early start-stop DLC protocols and will be classified as synchronous protocols in our discussions below.

3.3.1 Asynchronous Protocols [MCNA 77]

The history of start–stop protocols lies in early teleprinter systems. Consider a communications line connecting a sender to a receiver. By convention, the line is idle when current is flowing in it, which is called the 1 state or MARK condition. The no-current state is called the 0 state or SPACE condition. To start transmitting, the line is brought to the 0 state for one bit time; this is called the *start bit*. For the next 5 to 8 bits (the number depending on the character code being used) the line is brought to the 1 or 0 state as necessary to represent the character being sent. After each character, the line is maintained at the 1 state for a minimum duration of time (equal to 1, 1.5, or 2 bit times) before the transmission of another character can begin; this is the *stop interval* (see Fig. 3.3). Thus transmission is one character at a time, with the bits representing each character preceded by a start bit and succeeded by a stop interval. The stop interval ensures that a transition occurs at the beginning of each start bit, which is used by the receiver to acquire bit synchronization.

Start–stop protocols are said to be asynchronous because a new character can be transmitted at any time (thus asynchronously) following the stop interval of the previous character. Bit synchronism, however, is maintained during the transmission of each character. The receiver determines the initial sampling time from the 1-to-0 transition of the start bit. (This can be accomplished, for example, by a "16 x clock" which samples the incoming signal at 16 times the transmission bit rate.) The sampling period between bits is known from the transmission bit rate. However, since clocks in different machines may differ slightly, the sampling of the last bit in a character may be somewhat off center. This can be corrected in the reception of the next character by retiming the 1-to-0 transition of its start bit.

Start–stop protocols are based upon the use of a character code (Baudot, ASCII, etc.) for representing control messages and data. The start bit and stop interval, in addition to providing bit synchronization, also provides character synchronization (i.e., how to partition a stream of bits into characters). Most character codes provide for some control characters which are used for various DLC control functions (mentioned above) as well as necessary device control functions.

Typically, start–stop protocols are used for terminal devices with a keyboard, with no message buffer, and little intelligence; characters are sent one at a time as keys are struck. The terminal device is controlled remotely by its "host" computer. Start–stop protocols were mostly developed in the past in conjunction with the development of terminal devices. Each terminal type would have its own protocol. Such protocols are often incompatible between terminal types.

Although a significant portion of terminal devices currently in use are nonintelligent start–stop devices, we shall not dwell on start–stop protocols much more. First, for pedagogic reasons; start–stop protocols do not provide a good illustration of the hierarchy of DLC functions discussed in Sec. 3.2. Second, the technological trend is toward more intelligent terminals which can accommodate synchronous protocols having more sophisticated functions.

3.3.2 Synchronous Protocols

The proliferation of start–stop protocols associated with numerous terminal types is a problem. Another disadvantage of asychronous transmission is the overhead of a start bit and a stop interval associated with each character transmitted. With synchronous transmission the overhead above is eliminated by keeping bit synchronism between receiver and sender at all times, including idle periods. Most synchronous protocols are intended for terminal devices which have more buffering and processing capability than start–stop devices and therefore can implement more functions.

Bit Synchronization

When the receiver and transmitter are in proximity, bit synchronism can be maintained by a single shared clock for both the transmitter and the receiver. In other cases, bit timing will have to be recovered from the data signal at the receiver. To do so necessitates some provisions to ensure transitions in the data signal. Specifically, when a transmitter is first connected to a receiver, some number of initial transitions are necessary to establish bit synchronization. The sampling period between bits is known approximately from the data transmission rate but needs to be checked and adjusted periodically with the help of transitions in the data signal. This implies that certain bit streams may not be acceptable or that additional bits may have to be inserted to ensure an adequate number of transitions for reliable clock recovery. In most systems, the transceiver is a synchronous modem, which will recover symbol timing and provide bit timing to the DTE in a received data timing lead. (The transmit data timing may be provided by either the DTE or modem. Some synchronous modems do not need data link control to provide transitions in the data signal; for example, some have scrambler–descrambler circuits that create transitions in the data signal.)

The subject of modulation–demodulation and clock recovery are classical communication problems at a lower level of detail and are beyond the scope of this chapter. The reader is referred to [DAVE 72]. We shall only discuss bit synchronism in terms of certain DLC functions provided for preventing the transmission of transitionless data.

Two Classes of Synchronous Protocols

There are two main classes of synchronous protocols: character-oriented and bit-oriented. A main distinction between them, as suggested by the names, is the technique for accomplishing frame synchronization. But as we shall see, they differ in their methods for multiple access synchronization, content synchronization, and dialogue synchronization as well.

Character-oriented protocols include the X3.28 standard of ANSI and IBM's BSC protocol. They are very similar and the latter is used widely by industry. In Sec. 3.3.2.1, we shall describe the main features of BSC as documented in [IBM 70] to illustrate this class of protocols.

Bit-oriented protocols include ADCCP, which is a standard of ANSI; HDLC, which is a standard of ISO (International Standards Organization); and IBM's SDLC protocol. In Sec. 3.3.2.2 we describe the version of SDLC as documented in [IBM 75] to illustrate this class of protocols.[1] We note that SDLC, HDLC, and ADCCP are basically of the same genre; the two protocol standards have evolved out of IBM's submissions to the respective standards organizations. However, additional functions have been defined (or proposed) for HDLC and ADCCP, which are not present in the current version of SDLC [IBM 75]. These functions are discussed in Sec. 3.4.

Other computer manufacturers have also proposed similar DLC protocols, including BDLC of Burroughs, UDLC of Sperry-Univac, and DDCMP of Digital Equipment Corporation. DDCMP is byte-count oriented. An excellent discussion of DDCMP may be found in [MCNA 77].

3.3.2.1 Description of a Character-Oriented Protocol—BSC [IBM 70]

Suppose that bit synchronism is maintained between a receiver and a transmitter. Since both data and control must be encoded and transported in packages of bits called frames,[2] the synchronization problem at the next level involves the following:

		Bit positions 0, 1, 2, 3															
Bit positions 4, 5, 6, 7		0000	0001	0010	0011	0100	0101	0110	0111	1000	1001	1010	1011	1100	1101	1110	1111
	Hex	0	1	2	3	4	5	6	7	8	9	A	B	C	D	E	F
0000	0	NUL	DLE	DS		SP	&	—						{	}	\	0
0001	1	SOH	DC1	SOS						a	j	~		A	J		1
0010	2	STX	DC2	FS	SYN					b	k	s		B	K	S	2
0011	3	ETX	DC3							c	l	t		C	L	T	3
0100	4	PF	RES	BYP	PN					d	m	u		D	M	U	4
0101	5	HT	NL	LF	RS					e	n	v		E	N	V	5
0110	6	LC	BS	EOB / ETB	UC					f	o	w		F	O	W	6
0111	7	DEL	IL	PRE / ESC	EOT					g	p	x		G	P	X	7
1000	8		CAN							h	q	y		H	Q	Y	8
1001	9	RLF	EM							i	r	z		I	R	Z	9
1010	A	SMM	CC	SM		¢	!	¦	:								
1011	B	VT				.	$	,	#								
1100	C	FF	IFS		DC4	<	*	%	@								
1101	D	CR	IGS	ENQ	NAK	(	)	_	'								
1110	E	SO	IRS	ACK		+	;	>	=								
1111	F	SI	IUS	BEL	SUB	|	¬	?	"								

◸ Duplicate assignment

Figure 3.4. EBCDIC character assignments.

[1]Excellent discussions of SDLC concepts may be found in [CYPS 78, DONN 74].

[2]The term "frame" has been defined in this chapter but is not defined in [IBM 70].

(1) upon reception of a sequence of bits, to determine which bit is the beginning and which bit is the end of a frame; and (2) error detection.

In character-oriented protocols, all data and control information are encoded as characters. The IBM manual lists three character-code sets that can be used for BSC. They are EBCDIC with 8 bits per character for 256 assignments, USASCII with 7 bits plus a parity bit per character for 128 assignments, and 6-bit Transcode with 64 assignments. As an example the EBCDIC assignments are illustrated in Fig. 3.4.

Frame Synchronization

With a character-code set, BSC data and control characters are represented by unique bit sequences. (We discuss below how transparent data, i.e., an arbitrary stream of bits, can be transmitted.) In particular, the bit sequence representing the character SYN is unique. Because of the serial-by-character nature of transmission, frame synchronization and character synchronization are accomplished at the same time. Each frame transmitted is always preceded by two or more SYN characters. The receiver will hunt for the bit pattern of SYN SYN. (We use the shorthand notation of ∅ for SYN SYN as in [IBM 70].) When the receiver detects a sequence of two or more SYN characters in an incoming signal, the bits immediately following (6 or 8 bits, depending on the code set) will form the first character of the frame.[3] The receiver may detect more than two SYN characters in a row because SYN is also used to fill any idle time in between frames. If the frame contains data characters, it ends with either one of the following control characters: ITB, ETB, or ETX followed by two BCC characters for error detection. (See below for further explanation of these control characters.) If the frame contains only control information, one or more control characters may be present, representing one of a well-defined set of control messages.

We said earlier that bit synchronism may be maintained by the transceiver or DTE in a station. If it is done by the DTE, a special bit synchronization pattern needs to precede the frame synchronization pattern ∅. (This bit synchronization pattern can be the hex '55' '55' or the SYN SYN SYN SYN pattern that provides for the 16 transitions necessary for bit synchronization.) Bit synchronism will be assumed from now on.

To ensure that the first and last characters of a frame are properly transmitted by the transceiver, which may turn on and off abruptly, BSC requires the addition of a pad character immediately before the synchronization characters of a frame and immediately afterward. [The leading pad character may consist of alternating 0 and 1 bits (hex '55') or a SYN character. The trailing pad character consists of all 1 bits (hex 'FF').] With the frame synchronization method, BSC frames containing data and/or control information from a sender to a receiver will be in one of the following two formats:

PAD ∅ [heading and/or data] BCC BCC PAD
PAD ∅ [control] PAD

The two BCC characters are for error detection. The exact nature of the heading, control, and data fields in the frame formats above will be clarified in our discussions below on multiple access synchronization and content synchronization. For simplicity, we drop the leading and trailing PAD characters in our notation from now on.

Another function at the frame synchronization level is to detect the presence of errors within transmitted frames. Depending on the character-code set selected, one or more of the following three error-checking methods may be used for BSC:

VRC	Vertical redundancy checking
LRC	Longitudinal redundancy checking
CRC	Cyclic redundancy checking

[3]Note that this procedure is subject to errors. First, the ∅ sequence may be missed because of bit errors in it. On the other hand, the two-character bit pattern of ∅ is not unique and may appear in the middle of certain three-character sequences.

With each method, two BCC characters are generated at the sender and are included at the end of each data frame. They are used for error detection at the receiver. Note from the frame formats above that BSC control messages are not protected by error checking.

CRC is a much more powerful technique for error detection than VRC or LRC and can detect many types of multiple errors. It is to be preferred since errors in communications transmission systems tend to occur in bursts [BURT 72]. CRC is available with all three BSC character-code sets. For a detailed description of LRC, VRC, and the CRC coding algorithm, the reader is referred to [MART 70, MCNA 77].

Multiple Access Synchronization

The multiple access synchronization function determines which of a population of transmitters may access a shared communications channel. If the communications channel is dedicated to a single sender–receiver pair, the problem is trivially solved. Otherwise, some multiple access protocol is required.

The method for multiple access depends on the communications link configuration. BSC permits two types of communications link configurations between stations: point to point and multipoint. We consider first a point-to-point communications link between two stations. Remember that each station is both a sender and a receiver. BSC requires a *half-duplex* mode of operation such that only one station can be transmitting at a time. Half-duplex operation is required even if the communications link consists of two separate communications channels, one for each of the two directions of transmission. Note that whenever the line "turns around," reversing the direction of transmission, character synchronization (and possibly bit synchronization) need to be reestablished.

A point-to-point communications link is shared via a *contention* protocol. If a station wants to acquire control of the line, it sends the initialization sequence

ø ENQ

The other station replies with

ø ACK0	if ready to receive
ø NAK	if not ready to receive
ø WACK	if temporarily not ready to receive (try again later!)

Since it is possible that both stations bid for the line at about the same time, to avoid

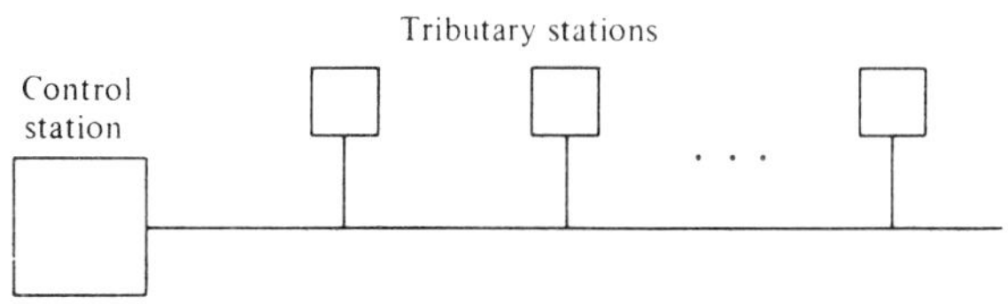

Figure 3.5. Multipoint link configuration.

any deadlock each station is designated to be primary or secondary. The primary station has high priority. When bidding for the line, the primary, but not the secondary, can continue to retry (up to a certain limit) until it gets an affirmative response.

The station with control of the line is the *transmitting station* and can transmit frames containing data to the *receiving station*. Following each such frame transmitted, the line may turn around for the receiving station to send a reply. The reply is a control message (ACK, NAK, etc.) and may not contain any data, except in the limited conversational mode (see below). A station relinquishes control of the line with the control message ø EOT. For 3 seconds the other station can bid for the line without competition. After 3 seconds, both stations may bid for control of the line.

BSC also permits a multipoint communications link configuration (see Fig.

3.5), with a control station and many tributary stations sharing the same line. Data flow is always between the control station and one of the tributary stations. The communications method is again half-duplex, so that transmission of data can take place in only one direction at a time, either from the control station to a tributary or from a tributary to the control station. There are two additional functions required: (1) sharing of the line among the tributary stations; and (2) addresses for identifying the tributary stations.

The communications link is shared among the tributary stations via *polling* and *selection* protocols under the supervision of the control station. The control station directs its incoming traffic by sequentially polling each tributary station. When polled, a tributary station has control of the line and assumes the role of the transmitting station with the control station acting as the receiving station, such as previously described for a point-to-point line. The control station directs its outgoing traffic by first selecting a tributary station as the receiving station. The control station then acts as the transmitting station. In both cases, the transmitting–receiving relationship is ended when the transmitting station sends the message ∅ EOT. If the transmitting station is a tributary station, control of the line is passed back to the control station.

The following sequence is used by the control station to poll or select a tributary station:

∅ EOT PAD ∅ [polling or selection address] ENQ

The polling or selection address sequence consists of one to seven characters. It gives the tributary station address (and also a specific device address if the station has several available). The possible replies from a polled tributary station are:

1. A frame containing data
2. ∅ EOT: negative reply when the station has nothing to send
3. ∅ STX ENQ: temporary text delay (TTD) when the station is unable to transmit its initial data within 2 seconds; this permits the polled station to retain control of the line and avoid being timed out by the control station

The possible replies from a selected tributary station are:

1. ∅ ACK0: affirmative, ready to receive
2. ∅ NAK: negative, not ready to receive
3. ∅ WACK: temporarily not ready to receive

Content Synchronization

With multiple access synchronization, two processes can send frames of bits to each other. The next level of functions is to enable a receiver to interpret correctly the content of a frame. There are three functions involved here:

1. To differentiate between control and data information within a frame; for control information, the receiver and sender must also agree on the encoding of a set of control messages.
2. To distinguish an arbitrary bit stream of data (transparent data), although some of the bits may be the same as control characters.
3. To remedy errors so as to ensure that a single error-free copy of each frame at the sender will arrive in sequence at the receiver within a reasonable amount of time.

Encoding of Data and Control. The separation of data and control is solved in BSC with the use of a character-code set. Data transfer is always in the form of a serial stream of characters. Characters in the code set are reserved to represent either data or control. BSC control characters are for DLC control functions as well as other high-level control functions, such as device control. (The mixing of control functions at different levels is one of the frequent criticisms of BSC.) Specifically, control of the data link is achieved through use of the following control characters and two-character sequences:

SYN	Synchronous Idle
SOH	Start of Heading
STX	Start of Text
ITB	End of Intermediate Transmission Block
ETB	End of Transmission Block
ETX	End of Text
EOT	End of Transmission
ENQ	Enquiry
ACK0/ACK1	Alternating Affirmative Acknowledgments
WACK	Wait-Before-Transmit Positive Acknowledgment
NAK	Negative Acknowledgment
DLE	Data-Link Escape
RVI	Reverse Interrupt
TTD	Temporary Text Delay
DLE EOT	Disconnect Sequence for a Switched Line

Several of the above are not defined in the character code sets but are represented as two-character control sequences. They are ACK0, ACK1, WACK, RVI, and TTD. Some minor variations in the designation of the characters and compositions of the character sequences exist among the different code sets. For example, ACK0 and ACK1 correspond to the two-character sequences DLE 0 and DLE 1 in USASCII but are coded as DLE '70' and DLE / in EBCDIC. On the other hand, TTD is represented by STX ENQ in all code sets.

BSC frames have the following formats:

∅ SOH [heading] STX [data] ETX BCC BCC

∅ [control character sequence]

Frames containing data or heading are sent only by a transmitting station to a receiving station. In these frames, SOH marks the beginning of a heading containing control information for high-level (non-DLC) functions such as message identification, routing, device control, and priority. STX marks the beginning of the data section. Either SOH [heading] or STX [data] may be absent in a frame. Each frame is terminated by one of the control characters ETX, ETB, or ITB. In all cases it is followed by two BCC characters for error detection.

Both ETX and ETB terminate frames started by STX or SOH and cause the communications channel to turn around and require a reply from the receiving station. ETX terminates a data message at the data processing level. At the DLC level, a data message may be segmented into *transmission blocks* for ease of processing and more efficient error control. Each transmission block begins with STX and ends with ETB, except for the last block of a data message, which ends with ETX.

The "SOH [heading] STX [data]" portion, where [data] can be either a complete data message or a transmission block, can be further segmented into *intermediate blocks* for increased reliability in error detection. When an intermediate block is sent in a frame, the frame is terminated by ITB, again followed by two BCC characters. The last intermediate block in a sequence is terminated by ETB or ETX as appropriate. After the first intermediate block, succeeding ones need not be preceded by STX or SOH in a frame (except in the case of transparent data to be discussed below). Frames terminated by ITB do not cause a line turnaround or require a reply from the receiver. Each sequence of intermediate blocks, comprising a data message or a transmission block, is treated as a whole by the receiving station. All BSC stations must have the ability to receive intermediate blocks. The ability to send intermediate blocks is an option.

Frames containing control information only have the format

∅ [control character sequence]

We have seen the use of some of these control messages for multiple access synchronization. We shall encounter some others in the following discussions.

Transparent Data. So far in our description of BSC, the characters that can be sent in the data portion of a frame have been assumed to be limited to a subset of the characters in the character-code set. To send an arbitrary stream of characters (transparent data) without some of the characters taking on any control meaning, BSC provides the *transparent text mode* of operation within a frame. During the transparent text mode, any control characters transmitted must be preceded by DLE to be recognized as denoting a control function. In particular, the transparent text mode is initiated by DLE STX and is terminated by any of DLE ETX, DLE ETB, or DLE ITB. (In the last case, if the succeeding intermediate block is also transparent, that intermediate block must begin with DLE STX. Recall that a beginning STX is not required of intermediate blocks in the nontransparent mode of operation if that intermediate block is not the first one.) Thus a frame in a transparent text mode may look like

∅ DLE STX [transparent data] DLE ETX BCC BCC

If a control character is needed within the transparent data, a DLE character is inserted in front of it. Also, if a DLE character appears in the transparent data (with no control meaning), an additional DLE must also be inserted in front of it lest it be misinterpreted as preceding a control character. The inserted DLC characters need to be stripped off at the receiver. The following procedure may be used by the receiver:

Step 1. Hunt for a DLE character in the input stream. When a DLE is received, discard it and go to Step 2.

Step 2. *If* the next character is a DLE *then* accept it as a data character and go to Step 1,

else accept the next character as a control character and go to Step 1.

Error Control. One of the content synchronization functions is to recover from transmission errors. BSC does so with an automatic-repeat-request (ARQ) technique. When a transmitting station ends a frame containing data with ETB or ETX, a reply is required of the receiving station. It can reply with ∅ ACK0 or ∅ ACK1, indicating "data accepted, ready for more," or ∅ NAK, indicating "data not accepted, retransmission necessary." The line then turns around again for the transmitting station to send a frame. If necessary, retransmission of a frame of data is attempted a number of times following the initial NAK, after which recovery action is required. If the transmitting station receives no reply after sending a frame of data, due to either the frame or the reply being garbled, the transmitting station can request a reply from the receiving station by sending the control message ∅ ENQ. The receiving station repeats the previous response: NAK, ACK0, or ACK1, as appropriate.

Two positive acknowledgment responses are used for the following reason. ACK0 is used as an affirmative response to the transmitting station's initial ENQ and for an affirmative response to all even-number transmission blocks. ACK1 is used for all odd-number transmission blocks. The odd or even count of a block does not change even when it is retransmitted. As a result the alternating affirmative replies enable the sender to detect the loss of a transmission block. Also, since transmission blocks are sent one at a time until successfully received and acknowledged, the original sequence of transmission blocks at the sender is preserved at the receiver. However, a transmission block does not actually contain a bit indicating it to be even or odd. It is thus not possible for the receiver to detect a duplicate transmission block. (A duplicate would be sent if, for instance, an ACK was garbled and turned into a NAK.)

Recall that only frames containing heading/data are protected by error detection. Control messages are not checked. The BSC manual mentions some provisions for using trailing pad characters for format checking which serves as a limited means of error detection.

The "accumulation" for the BCC characters begins right after the first STX or SOH character following either a line turnaround or a previous ITB termination of an intermediate block. All characters following that, including control characters, are used in the accumulation, with the exception of SYN idle characters inserted for bit and character synchronization considerations (see below).

Dialogue Synchronization

With content synchronization, it is now possible to send frames containing data from one station to another. There also exists a set of control messages which can be used for coordinating the actions and responses of two communicating stations in a dialogue fashion. The dialogue level functions consist of:

1. Initial dialogue synchronization
2. Recovery methods in the event of loss of synchronism and
3. Dialogue termination

Initial dialogue synchronization in BSC is trivially accomplished once multiple access synchronization has been established, with one station being in the "transmit" state and the other in the "receive" state.

In the case of switched-network (dial-up) operation, additional initial synchronization procedures are needed immediately following the establishment of a communications circuit. The calling station sends either one of the following messages:

∅ ENQ	Who are you?
∅ α. . . ENQ	I am α. . . . Who are you?

The called station replies positively with

∅ α. . . ACK0

where the called station identity α. . . is optional. The called station replies negatively with

∅ NAK
∅ WACK

The identity sequences α. . . may be 2 to 15 characters long. The minimum two-character sequence must consist of the same character transmitted twice (for reliability).

A dial-up call between two stations can be terminated by either one of the stations transmitting the disconnect message

∅ DLE EOT

A call may also be disconnected by the disconnect timeout to be described below.

Apart from the transmit and receive states, the stations may transit to other states as a result of the following control messages.

TTD (Temporary Text Delay). The TTD control sequence is sent by a transmitting station when it wishes to retain control of the line but is not ready to transmit data. It is sent after approximately 2 seconds to avoid the 3-second receive timeout at the receiving station. The receiving station responds NAK and waits for transmission to begin again. TTD can be repeated one or more times. TTD can also be used to abort a transmission. If following the receiving station's reply of NAK, the transmitting station sends EOT, the transmit–receive relationship is terminated. (This is called the forward abort sequence.)

RVI (Reverse Interrupt). RVI is a positive acknowledgment used in place of

ACK0 or ACK1 (depending on the current odd–even count). RVI is transmitted by a receiving station to request termination of the current transmit–receive relationship. The transmitting station treats RVI as a positive acknowledgment (0 to 1 as appropriate) and proceeds to transmit all data that might prevent it from becoming a receiving station. The ability to receive RVI is mandatory, but the ability to transmit RVI is optional.

WACK (Wait-Before-Transmit Positive Acknowledgment). WACK allows a receiving station to indicate a "temporarily not ready to receive" condition to the transmitting station. The normal transmitting station response to WACK is ENQ. The receiving station may continue to respond with WACK. The transmitting station has the option of terminating the dialogue by EOT or disconnecting a circuit with DLE EOT. The ability to receive WACK is mandatory. The ability to send WACK is optional.

Timeouts. Timeouts are used to attempt recovery from possible nonsynchronous conditions. There are four specific timeouts used in BSC:

1. *Transmit timeout.* This is a nominal 1-second timeout that establishes the rate at which synchronous idles are automatically inserted into frames containing heading and data. Ordinarily, SYN SYN is inserted every second. For transparent data, DLE SYN is inserted instead. These insertions permit character synchronization to be checked and in the case of SYN SYN, reestablished. If bit synchronism is maintained by the DTE, insertion of DLE SYN is required at least every 84 characters to ensure bit synchronism amid transitionless data. The inserted synchronous idle characters are not included in BCC accumulation for error detection.
2. *Receive timeout.* This is a nominal 3-second timeout and is used to limit the waiting time tolerated by a station to receive a reply as well as for other functions.
3. *Disconnect timeout.* This timeout is used optionally on switched network connections. It is used to prevent a station from holding on to a connection for a prolonged period of inactivity. After 20 seconds of inactivity, the station will disconnect from the switched network.
4. *Continue timeout.* This is a nominal 2-second timeout associated with the control messages TTD and WACK.

Additional BSC Features

1. A frame containing heading/data can be terminated prematurely by using an ENQ character which signals the receiving station to disregard the current frame. NAK is always the reply from the receiving station.
2. BSC permits a "limited conversational mode" whereby a frame containing heading/data can be sent in place of a positive acknowledgment by the receiving station as a reply to a frame that ended with ETX or DLE ETX. The transmitting station must then reply with a control message and not with another conversational reply.

Comments on the Structure of BSC

We have given a description of the BSC protocol using the hierarchical functional levels in Fig. 3.2 as a framework for elaboration. Ideally, a well-structured protocol should have minimal interfaces defined between adjacent functional levels so that functions and implementation techniques at one level can be changed without affecting adjacent levels if the interfaces are maintained to be the same. Since BSC was not originally designed with the hierarchical functional levels in mind, the decomposition of BSC functions into different levels such as we have done is somewhat awkward at places. We illustrate this observation by pointing out some dependencies between the BSC functional levels described earlier in this section.

1. The half-duplex mode of operation facilitates the logical design of dialogue

interactions between two communicating stations. Its effect pervades all functional levels. For instance, bit and character synchronization need to be reestablished whenever a line turns around. The stop-and-wait form of ARQ technique is used for error control.

2. The transmit–receive coordination of two communicating stations at the dialogue level is directly coupled to the transmit–receive coordination at the multiple access level of all stations sharing a multipoint link. The dialogue-level control messages WACK and TTD are used as an integral part of the multiple access protocol.

3.3.2.2 Description of a Bit-Oriented Protocol —SDLC [IBM 75]

The SDLC protocol will also be described in terms of the hierarchy of synchronization functional levels in Fig. 3.2; however, techniques used in SDLC for solving these synchronization problems are different from BSC and other character-oriented protocols.

Again, we begin on the premise that bit synchronism is maintained by the transceivers or the DTE. In either case, our description of data link control will be concerned only with avoiding the transmission of transitionless data.

Frame Synchronization

A bit-oriented protocol, as its name suggests, deals with a stream of bits rather than a stream of characters. A character-code set is therefore not required. To delimit the beginning and end of a frame, a unique sequence of 8 bits 01111110 called a flag, denoted by F, is used. So each frame looks like

F [control and data] FCS F

where FCS consists of 16 CRC bits for error detection. The ending F may be followed by a frame, by another F, or by an idle condition. A series of contiguous F's may be transmitted to maintain bit synchronism and to maintain the data link in an active state. An idle state is perceived by the receiver when he receives a succession of 15 or more consecutive binary ones.

The F bit sequence 01111110 is made unique by zero insertion at the transmitting station and zero deletion at the receiving station, performed as part of the DLC protocol. The transmitter inserts a binary zero after any succession of five consecutive 1's inside a frame following the beginning F. The receiver removes a zero that follows a received sequence of five continuous 1's. We shall see below that with unique flags, the transmission of transparent data is always possible rather than handled as a special case.

The contents of every SDLC frame, with the exception of the beginning and ending flags, are protected by cyclic redundancy checking. Specifically, the generating polynomial, $x^{16} + x^{12} + x^5 + 1$, which is a CCITT standard, is used for generating the error detection bits [MCNA 77]. These bits are put into the FCS field immediately preceding the ending flag of a frame. Note, however, that the computation of the FCS bits at the sender is done before the zero insertion operation. Therefore, the inserted zeros are not protected by FCS. At the receiver, the deletion of inserted zeros is performed before the FCS computation.

When data signal transitions are needed by the DTE or transceiver for bit synchronism considerations, SDLC specifies the zero complementing NRZI (Non-Return-to-Zero-Inverted) coding method, with which, to send a binary 1 in the data, the signal on the line remains in the same state. The signal switches to the opposite state to send a binary 0 in the data. Thus an extended period of binary zeros in the data is transmitted as continuous transitions in the channel. A long period of binary 1's in the data will have transitions in the channel as a result of the zero insertion requirement to make the flags unique. If NRZI is used, it must be used by all DTEs on the data link.

Multiple Access Synchronization

The basic data link configurations that are currently supported by the SDLC protocol are:

1. Point-to-point half-duplex line, switched or nonswitched
2. Point-to-point duplex line, nonswitched
3. Multipoint duplex line, nonswitched
4. Unidirectional loop consisting of point-to-point simplex line segments

where

- Simplex means data-carrying ability in one direction only
- Half-duplex means data-carrying ability in both directions but not at the same time
- Duplex means simultaneous bidirectional data-carrying ability

In any of the SDLC data link configurations, exactly one of the stations is designated to be the primary station of the data link. Thus each data link has a primary station and one or more secondary stations. Communication of data always takes place between the primary station and a secondary station. Secondary stations, if more than one is present, cannot communicate with each other. We remind the reader that sometimes a station has the capability to implement only half-duplex protocols, even if a full-duplex line is available. In a multipoint configuration, it is often the case that only the primary station operates duplex, while secondary stations operate half-duplex. Thus the primary may be transmitting to one secondary while simultaneously receiving from another secondary station.

With a point-to-point duplex line, both transmitter–receiver pairs have their own dedicated channels. In this case, multiple access synchronization is not necessary.

For all other configurations, sharing of a channel by multiple transmitter–receiver pairs is involved and multiple access synchronization is needed for conflict resolution. In SDLC, the encoding of control messages used for multiple access, content, and dialogue synchronization levels is integrated. Therefore, it is necessary for us to consider now the format of an SDLC frame.

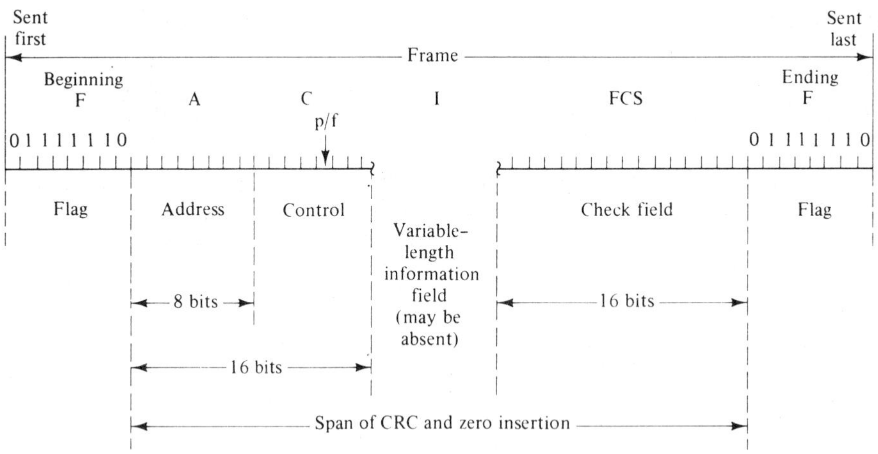

Figure 3.6. Fields of an SDLC frame.

With character-oriented DLC protocols, the character-code set usually provides for control characters. A sequence of one or more such control characters forms a control message. This approach necessitates special handling of transparent data.

Bit-oriented protocols separate control and data information by putting them in different parts of a frame. This approach, called *positional significance*, is possible because the beginning and ending flags can be uniquely identified (through zero insertion and deletion at the frame synchronization level) and thus provide reference points for locating data and control fields. Specifically, a frame consists of the fields shown in Fig. 3.6. For multiple-access synchronization we are presently interested only in the address field and the p/f-bit in the control field.[4]

In each of the SDLC data link configurations, there is a primary station and one or more secondary stations. The primary station acts as a central controller for data link access. It carries out this function using the address (A) field and the poll/final (p/f) bit in the control field. Since there is only one primary station, it never needs to be identified. The address of the secondary station in communication with the primary is always indicated in the address field (see Fig. 3.6). If the frame is from secondary to primary, the A field identifies the sender. If the frame is from primary to secondary, the A field identifies the intended receiver. In frames from the primary, a common address may be used for a group of secondary stations. In particular, an all-1's address field is often used as a broadcast or all-stations address.

In frames sent by the primary, the p/f-bit is a *poll bit*. In frames sent by a secondary station, the p/f-bit is a *final bit*. When the primary sends a frame to a secondary station with the poll bit turned on, it demands a response from the secondary station. Access right is also automatically granted to that secondary station for using the data link. The secondary station can then send a sequence of frames on the data link; the number of frames is limited only by error and sequence control

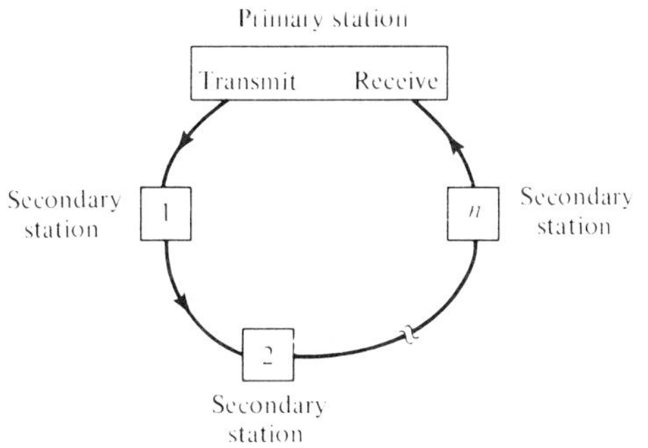

Figure 3.7. Loop configuration.

considerations to be addressed later. The secondary station relinquishes its access right when it sends a frame with the final bit turned on.

This use of the poll/final bit is adhered to for all primary-secondary dialogues even for a point-to-point full-duplex data link configuration where each transmitter–receiver pair has its own dedicated channel (see the discussion of the normal response mode in the dialogue synchronization section below).

In a point-to-point half-duplex line, the primary and secondary stations alternate use of the shared data link. In a multipoint full-duplex line, the primary-to-secondary channel is dedicated to the primary transmitter, which can send frames to any one of the secondary stations by identifying it in the address field. The secondary-to-primary channel is shared by the secondary stations and access right to the shared channel is controlled by the primary station via polling using the poll bit.

An SDLC loop consists of a series of point-to-point simplex lines. Each secondary station ordinarily acts as a repeater. Bits sent out of the primary station are relayed from one secondary station to the next one downstream until they return to the primary station (see Fig. 3.7). Such a loop is therefore unidirectional and half-duplex procedures between the primary and a secondary are used. The primary transmits a frame to any one of the secondary stations by identifying it in the address field. Or it may command a response from a secondary station by polling it.

The poll may be specific, as in point-to-point and multipoint configurations, with the poll bit turned on in a primary-to-secondary frame. Or the poll may be for a

[4]We use lowercase letters p and f to avoid confusion with F, which denotes a flag.

group of secondary stations with a common address. In the latter case the primary station polls by first sending an NSP (nonsequenced poll) control message with a common address in the address field (see below for the encoding of NSP and other control messages). After the NSP, the primary sends a binary zero followed by continuous 1's, which starts a *polling cycle*. If the poll bit in the NSP frame is also turned on, the addressed secondary stations are required to respond. If the poll bit is off, the addressed secondary stations are only invited to transmit. The response to an NSP control message requires turning on the final bit only if the command had the poll bit turned on.

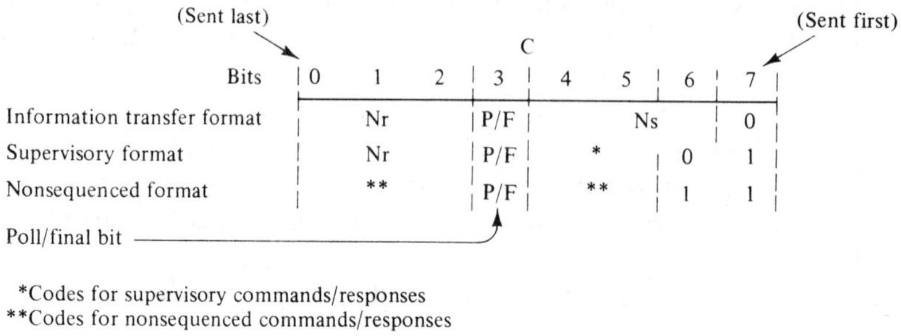

Figure 3.8. SDLC control field formats.

Thus a polling cycle begins with the transmission of an NSP control frame by the primary, followed by a "go-ahead" pattern consisting of a binary zero followed by continuous 1's. The first down-loop secondary station that has been polled receives the go-ahead when it has counted a zero and seven consecutive 1's in its input signal. It repeats the first six 1's and changes the seventh one to a binary zero. Thus an SDLC flag is generated. That secondary station then suspends the repeater function and transmits from itself to the primary station one or more frames. When it is finished, it resumes the repeater function. The ending binary zero in the ending flag of the last frame followed by continuous 1's now creates a go-ahead pattern again. The access right to the shared channel is then passed on to the next downstream secondary station that has been polled. Finally, when the primary station receives seven or more continuous 1's, the polling cycle is complete and the primary station is back in control of the data link.

Content Synchronization

As before, the functions included in this functional layer are: the separation of data and control, the encoding of control messages, error control, and the sequencing of frames.

The first function is provided using the positional significance approach discussed earlier: control and data are transmitted in different fields of a frame. The positions of these fields are measured from the beginning and end of the frame marked by unique flags. Unlike character-oriented protocols, the data transmitted are always considered to be transparent data and no special handling is required.

Depending on the values of bits 6 and 7 in the control field of a frame, SDLC defines three different kinds of frames with different formats:

Information transfer (I) frames
Supervisory (S) frames
Nonsequenced (NS) frames

The control field formats of these three kinds of frames are shown in Fig. 3.8, where bit 7 differentiates between I-frames and the others; bit 6 differentiates between S- and NS-frames. The p/f-bit in the control field has been encountered earlier for multiple-access synchronization. It is also used for some dialogue synchronization functions. The bit sequences N_r and N_S are for error and sequence control of I-frames. The remaining bits (marked * and ** in Fig. 3.8) are used to encode various control

Format (note 1)	Binary configuration (Sent last → Sent first)	Acronym	Command	Response	I-Field prohibited	Resets Nr and Ns	Confirms frames through Nr-1	Defining characteristics
NS	000 P/F 0011	NSI	X	X				Command or response that requires nonsequenced information
	000 F 0111	RQI		X	X			Initialization needed; expect SIM
	000 P 0111	SIM	X		X	X		Set initialization mode; the using system prescribes the procedures
	100 P 0011	SNRM	X		X	X		Set normal response mode; transmit on command
	000 F 1111	ROL		X	X			This station is off line
	010 P 0011	DISC	X		X			Do not transmit or receive information
	011 F 0011	NSA		X	X			Acknowledge NS commands
	100 F 0111	CMDR		X				Nonvalid command received; must receive SNRM, DISC, or SIM
	101 P/F 1111	XID	X	X				System identification in I field
	001 0/1 0011	NSP	X		X			Response optional if no P-bit
	111 P/F 0011	TEST	X	X				Check pattern in I field
S	Nr P/F 0001	RR	X	X	X		X	Ready to receive
	Nr P/F 0101	RNR	X	X	X		X	Not ready to receive
	Nr P/F 1001	REJ	X	X	X		X	Transmit or retransmit, starting with frame Nr
I	Nr P/F Ns 0	I	X	X			X	Sequenced I-frame

Note 1: NS = nonsequenced, S = supervisory, I = information

Figure 3.9. Summary of SDLC commands and responses

messages. The rest of the frame for all three formats are identical except for the I-field (see Fig. 3.6). In I-frames, the I-field can accommodate an arbitrarily long sequence of data bits, which must be a multiple of 8 bits. Otherwise, its length is subject only to error detection performance considerations. The I-field is not permitted in S-frames, while the I-field may be used to transmit link management data in NS-frames.

A listing of the encoding of SDLC control messages defined in [IBM 75] is shown in Fig. 3.9. We note that not all the bit sequences have been assigned. Hence additional control messages may be defined in the future as it becomes necessary.

A significant advantage of bit-oriented protocols over character-oriented protocols is the ease with which the set of control messages can be expanded. Recall that in BSC, the character-code set determines the available control characters. To define additional control messages one must employ longer and longer sequences of control characters. Character-oriented protocols are inefficient since only a very small number of the 8-bit sequences in a character is used for encoding control information. While with the positional significance approach in bit-oriented protocols, theoretically all 2^8 possible bit sequences can be used to encode control information.

We talk next about the error and sequence control functions of SDLC. Recall that error detection is performed for all frames. In addition, all I-frames are numbered in sequence. Sequence numbering is used to detect lost (garbled) frames or duplicated frames so as to guarantee that I-frames are delivered in their original order.

Recall that in BSC, data frames must be transmitted and acknowledged one at a time. Hence their order is preserved. Furthermore, the use of ACK0 and ACK1 for odd- and even-numbered transmission blocks ensures that a missing frame will be detected.

In SDLC, a transmitter can transmit up to seven I-frames before receiving positive acknowledgment. This is possible because the sequence numbering fields N_S and N_r are 3-bit sequences and have a counting capacity of 8.

Each station sequentially numbers every I-frame it transmits. This count is known as N_S, which is the sequence number (modulo 8) of the transmitted frame. The same station also keeps track, sequentially, of error-free I-frames it has received. N_r is the sequence number (modulo 8) of the next I-frame that it expects.

Consider two communicating stations, 1 and 2, with transmit and receive counts $V_s(1)$ and $V_r(1)$ at station 1, $V_s(2)$ and $V_r(2)$ at station 2. Suppose that an I-frame is sent from station 1 to station 2. It contains $N_s(1) = V_s(1)$, which is the sequence number of that particular I-frame. $V_s(1)$ is then incremented by 1. At station 2, if an error is detected in the frame, that frame is simply rejected. Suppose that it is error free. $N_s(1)$ is then compared to $V_r(2)$, which is the sequence number expected by station 2. If they agree, the frame is accepted and $V_r(2)$ is incremented by 1. If $N_s(1) \neq V_r(2)$, the received frame is rejected. [There are two possible cases. $N_s(1) < V_r(2)$ means that the received frame is a duplicate. On the other hand, $N_s(1) > V_r(2)$ means that the received frame is out of sequence and some I-frames are missing. Since $N_s(1)$ and $V_r(2)$ are modulo 8 numbers, the two cases cannot really be distinguished. However, the ability to distinguish the two cases is not necessary to achieve the objective of error and sequence control.]

Next consider the $N_r(1)$ field in the I-frame from station 1 to station 2. $N_r(1)$ is set equal to $V_r(1)$ and is a positive acknowledgment from station 1 to station 2 confirming correct reception of previously sent I-frames, from station 2 to station 1, with contiguous sequence numbers (modulo 8) up to and including $N_r(1) - 1$. The positive acknowledgment indicated by $N_r(1)$ is accepted as long as the I-frame is error free, even though it may be out of sequence. Buffers containing acknowledged frames may then be released.

We note several things regarding error and sequence control:

1. On a duplex data link, a transmitter can transmit I-frames continuously as long as it receives positive acknowledgments from incoming I-frames so that it does not have seven outstanding unacknowledged I-frames. On a half-duplex data link, at most seven I-frames can be transmitted at a time before the line turns around for an acknowledgment.
2. A single positive acknowledgment can acknowledge up to seven frames at the same time. This is unlike BSC, in which data frames must be acknowledged individually.
3. If an error is detected in any I-frame, all I-frames following it need to be retransmitted even if they have been correctly received. This protocol ensures that the original order of the I-frames is preserved at the receiver.
4. Supervisory and nonsequenced frames are not numbered. They are not therefore protected by sequence numbering against loss, duplication, or out-of-order reception. All frames, however, have CRC error detection.
5. Supervisory frames have the N_r field and can therefore be used to provide positive acknowledgments.
6. In the discussion above, the $N_r(1)$ count received by station 2 acknowledges correct reception of I-frames up to and including $N_r(1) - 1$. Note that this serves as a positive acknowledgment. Alternatively, the supervisory frame REJ can be used by station 1 to demand station 2 to transmit or retransmit starting with frame $N_r(1)$. In this respect, REJ is like a negative acknowledgment.

Dialogue Synchronization

In both multipoint and loop configurations, there are multiple secondary stations which may be engaging in concurrent dialogues with a single primary station. However, having achieved multiple access synchronization, we can consider each dialogue individually. A dialogue involves only two stations: a primary and a secondary. Control messages from primary to secondary are called *commands.* Control messages from secondary to primary are called *responses.* The primary always transmits first to initiate a dialogue, although on a switched data link either one may call the other first to make the physical connection. We note that in a network environment, a station may be attached to more than one data link; it can be a primary on one data link but a secondary on another data link.

The responses of a secondary depend on its "mode" status. The primary station of a dialogue can command one of three modes at the secondary station:

Normal disconnected mode (NDM)
Initialization mode
Normal response mode (NRM)

A secondary station that receives a DISC command assumes NDM; it also assumes NDM when power is turned on or when a switched connection is initially made.

Valid commands with the p-bit turned on cause a disconnected secondary station to respond with a request for on-line status (ROL) or, if needed, a request for initialization (RQI). In the latter case, the command SIM is expected, which causes the secondary to enter initialization mode and starts predefined initialization procedures stored at the secondary. The command SNRM puts the secondary in the NRM and subordinates the secondary to the primary; a secondary cannot transmit unless it has been polled by the primary. The primary and secondary transmit–receive counts V_r and V_s are reset to 0. The secondary station remains in NRM until it receives a DISC or SIM command. NSA is the affirmative response to the mode-setting commands SNRM, DISC, or SIM.

In SDLC, data transfer between primary and secondary takes place when the secondary is in NRM. In this mode, the secondary has access right to transmit only after it has received a frame from the primary with the p-bit turned on. It can then transmit one or more frames and relinquishes its access right when it turns the f-bit on in its last frame. (An exception to this procedure using the p/f-bit is the polling of secondary stations on a loop with the NSP command.) For the sequence control considerations discussed earlier, each station can have only up to seven unacknowledged I-frames outstanding. In a half-duplex link, to get a positive acknowledgment, the line must turn around. Therefore, the p- and f-bits also serve to turn the line around, thus alternating control of the line between primary and secondary. In a full-duplex link, the p- and f-bits serve only to assign and relinquish the access right of the secondary.

We have so far encountered one control message encoded in supervisory frames, REJ. There are two other control messages encoded in supervisory frames, which are used for flow control. They are RR (receive ready) and RNR (receive not ready). They can be sent by a receiver, either primary or secondary, to control the flow from the sender.

A dialogue may get out of synchronization when one or both stations become uncertain of the status of the other. Nonsynchronous conditions could occur because of lost frames, and frames received out of sequence. Timeouts and retries are the means for recovering synchronization. Some of the SDLC conditions for timeouts and retries are:

1. When the primary station transmits a frame with the p-bit turned on, response is expected within a certain time. The absence of a response may be due to no transmission from the secondary ("idle detect" condition) or garbled transmissions from the secondary ("nonproductive receive" condition). Timeouts are needed for both conditions to initiate recovery action at the primary. We note that a secondary cannot retry if there is no acknowledgment to its last frame with the f-bit turned on, since it has just given up its access right. In a loop, however, the secondary can retry following an NSP polling command.
2. Retries are made to obtain acknowledgment of a command. For example, NSA is the expected acknowledgment for SNRM, DISC, and SIM.
3. Retries are made to resume communication with a busy station following reception of RNR. Retries may be attempted by a primary or a secondary station.
4. Retries are made to achieve initial on-line status at a secondary station (ROL response).
5. Retries are made to initiate active communication at a secondary station (RQI response).
6. For a switched data link, an inactivity timeout of 20 seconds is used to alert stations of link disuse. If the timeout expires at either station, that station may

attempt to alert the other station. After a user-specified number of unsuccessful attempts, the station disconnects the switched circuit.

If a nonsynchronous condition cannot be recovered by the specified number of retries, help from protocols at a level above data link control will be necessary. The type of intervention required depends on the decision-making power available beyond that of data link control. At a terminal, for example, operator intervention may be needed. Some other conditions also require help from protocols at a level above data link control:

1. If a primary station transmits a command that is not valid for the receiving secondary station, the secondary responds with a CMDR frame. The I-field of the frame contains secondary station status data that the primary needs for appropriate recovery action. Intervention from a higher level is required to analyze and act on the secondary status report. The secondary then expects a mode-setting command from the primary station.
2. If a secondary station's response, XID, to the exchange of station identification contains the wrong identification, intervention from a higher level is required to analyze and act on the situation.

Additional SDLC Features

1. Apart from I-frames, SDLC provides another vehicle for either primary or secondary to send data to each other. These are the NSI frames of the nonsequenced format. NSI frames are not sequenced nor are they acknowledged at the DLC level.
2. A transmitter, primary or secondary, may abort the transmission of a frame by sending eight consecutive binary 1's with no zero insertion. This abort pattern terminates a frame without an FCS field or ending flag. The abort pattern may be followed by seven additional binary 1's, which will idle the data link, or it may be followed by a flag. An aborting secondary station may not start another frame until it receives a command from the primary. In the case of a loop, a loop secondary station may abort by first transmitting the abort pattern or by simply resuming the repeater function (thus propagating continuous 1's).

Comments on the Structure of SDLC

We found that the SDLC protocol can be decomposed to fit into the hierarchical functional levels in Fig. 3.2 very well with one obvious exception. That is the shared use of the p/f–bit by different levels. At the multiple-access level, the p/f–bit is used to effect the sharing of a data link by multiple secondary stations. At the dialogue level, the p/f–bit is used to effect the NRM dialogue interactions. The p/f–bit may also be used to provide a check point for error recovery action.

3.4 THE EVOLUTION OF DLC PROTOCOLS

In this chapter we have examined the main classes of data link control protocols in the chronological order of their development; first asynchronous or start–stop protocols, then synchronous character–oriented protocols, and finally synchronous bit-oriented protocols. Generally, synchronous protocols have a lot more functional capability than asynchronous protocols and are intended for computers and terminal devices that are intelligent and have memory for buffering relatively long messages.

Start–stop protocols were originally designed for nonintelligent unbuffered terminal devices. A significant percentage of terminals in use today are still of this type and start–stop protocols are still the only protocols that they are capable of using. However, both technological and marketing trends are pointing toward the use of more and more intelligent buffered terminal devices. Furthermore, the development of packet-switching networks poses new DLC requirements for communication between computers as equals (in addition to the traditional master–slave mode of operation). Bit-oriented synchronous protocols have been developed to meet these requirements and to take advantage of hardware capabilities not heretofore available. The importance of such protocols is emphasized by the emergence of the protocol standards.

In this section we first provide a critical review of the different classes of protocols described earlier. We then summarize functional capabilities in HDLC and ADCCP that are not available in the current version of SDLC described above.

Recall that communication has been defined herein as synchronization of data between different machines. We found that the synchronization problem can be structured into a hierarchy of functional levels, each level in the hierarchy depending on synchronism at the level below achieved over finer grains of time. The synchronization functional levels in the hierarchy are (in decreasing granularity of time):

Dialogue synchronization
Content synchronization
Multiple access synchronization
Frame synchronization
Bit synchronization

The most basic requirements are bit and frame synchronization, so that bits of data and control information can be transported as a package (frame) from one machine to another.

Start–stop protocols generally rely on a character-code set which defines data characters and some control characters. Both control and data are transmitted one character at a time. The start bit and stop interval accomplish both bit and character synchronization. The latter can be regarded as the equivalent of frame synchronization since characters are transmitted one at a time. Start–stop protocols have limited functions in the higher levels of the hierarchy and are typically specific to terminal device types. There has been a proliferation of start–stop protocols designed for different code sets and different terminal devices, resulting in a serious compatability problem. Nonintelligent terminals often have to be remotely controlled by the computers they are communicating with. As a result, device control in addition to data link control characters and sequences are intermixed with data in dialogue exchanges. Data link configurations are typically point-to-point half-duplex. Not only is there little sharing of communications facilities, but often an operator needs multiple terminals to interact with different application programs even though they reside within the same host computer. Finally, the irreducible overhead of a start bit and a stop interval associated with the transmission of every character is another decided disadvantage. These are some of the reasons that prompted the development of synchronous protocols for communication between computers and sophisticated data terminals or other computers.

Synchronous protocols, both character- and bit-oriented, avoid many of the deficiencies of asynchronous protocols, and provide essentially the complete hierarchy of functions identified earlier. Character-oriented protocols, such as BSC described earlier, still depend on a character–code set. Some of the frequent criticisms of BSC (and similar character-oriented protocols) are:

1. The character–code set contains both data link control and device control characters. There is no clear separation between data link control, device control, and various high-level source–destination control functions, which need to be decoded at the data link control level.
2. Control frames with control and address information are not protected by error checking. (Some format checking is done using pad characters as a rudimentary form of error detection. For example, the control characters EOT and NAK must be followed by a trailing pad character of all 1 bits. This is done to reduce the probability of a transmission line error converting a positive acknowledgment response into an EOT or NAK response.)

3. New control messages need to be defined as sequences of existing control characters. Upward compatibility is difficult as new functions are defined.
4. Also as a result of using a character–code set, transparent data are handled as a special case, using the transparent text mode described earlier.
5. Communication is always half-duplex even if a full-duplex communications line is used. Only one unacknowledged data frame can be outstanding at a time; each such data frame is individually acknowledged. As a result, frequent turnarounds of the communications line are necessary for data transfer, giving rise to inefficient utilization of the communications line, especially when the application calls for short transmission blocks.
6. A transmitting station, with control of the line, can continue to transmit indefinitely, thus monopolizing it; the receiving station can send only control messages in reply. Some partial remedies, however, are provided; such as the limited conversational mode and the reverse interrupt (RVI) control message.

Bit-oriented protocols, such as SDLC described above, provide improvements over character-oriented protocols with more functional capabilities and better solution techniques to the synchronization problems. The positional significance approach provides not only separation of control and data but also facilitates a clean separation of DLC from high-level communications protocol layers. This is consistent with the layering approach in communications network architecture, in which each protocol layer is associated with a positionally significant header and trailer of a frame [ZIMM 80]. Data link control, being the lowest protocol layer[5] in the communications network architecture, provides the outermost header and trailer of a frame. High-level functions (such as device control and session control) are encoded in headers and trailers which are treated as part of the "information field" of a frame by data link control protocols and are thus invisible to data link control facilities.

With positionally significant control and data fields within a frame, growth in functional requirements can be accommodated by expanding the size of the control field. (See the discussion of HDLC and ADCCP below.) Transparent data are also handled as a rule rather than an exception. All control and data information are contained within frames all of which are error checked.

Communication between SDLC stations can be full or half duplex. SDLC link configurations consist of loops, in addition to point-to-point and multipoint lines (available with BSC). Up to seven information frames can be transmitted before a positive acknowledgment is required. The considerations described above all contribute toward more efficient utilization of the communications facilities than do start–stop and BSC techniques. In a half-duplex configuration, the maximum of seven outstanding unacknowledged information frames also prevents a station from monopolizing the communications line.

Additional Functional Capabilities in HDLC and ADCCP [ANSI 79, ISO 79, CYPS 78]

SDLC, as described above, and the protocol standards HDLC and ADCCP are compatible protocols with the current version of SDLC [IBM 75] having only a subset of the repertoire of commands and capabilities adopted for HDLC and ADCCP. We discuss some of these extended capabilities in this section.[6] First we note that some of the control messages are called by different names in the protocol standards. In particular, the terminology "unnumbered" is used throughout in place of "nonsequenced"; thus NSI becomes UI (unnumbered information), NSA becomes UA (unnumbered acknowledgment), and NSP becomes UP (unnumbered poll). Also, the term FRMR (frame reject) is used instead of the SDLC term of CMDR (command reject).

HDLC and ADCCP provide for the use of an extended control field of 16 bits. Additional bits are available in supervisory and nonsequenced formats for encoding

[5]According to the OSI Reference Model [ZIMM 80], physical control, which is concerned with electrical characteristics, is actually the lowest functional layer.

[6]Since many of these extended capabilities were proposed by IBM to the standards organizations, it seems reasonable to expect that SDLC will be upgraded in the future to include them.

new control messages. Seven-bit fields are used for N_s and N_r counts, thus permitting the transmission of up to 127 information frames before positive acknowledgment. This is desirable for efficient utilization of very high speed communications channels and satellite links which have a large propagation delay (since the mean number of frames that can be enroute from a sender to a receiver is equal to the throughput rate times the average delay from the sender to the receiver). HDLC and ADCCP also include provisions for an extended address field.

An additional supervisory frame, SREJ (selective reject), is defined in the protocol standards. SREJ is a negative acknowledgment that indicates rejection of the information frame with the sequence number contained in the N_r field (but acceptance of frames numbered up to and including $N_r - 1$). However, unlike REJ, SREJ demands retransmission of only the specific information frame numbered N_r, and not subsequent frames that have also been sent. We note that this provision may alter the sequence ordering of information frames delivered from the transmitting station to the receiving station. If the original sequence of the information frames needs to be reestablished, it will have to be performed by protocols at a level higher than that of DLC. We note that in packet-switching networks, the frames exchanged by two packet-switching nodes typically belong to different "virtual circuits" and preservation of ordering is not important at the data link control level.

In the current version of SDLC, data transfer can take place only with the secondary station in the normal response mode. HDLC and ADCCP provide two additional secondary station modes for the transfer of information frames. An SARM (set asynchronous response mode) command places a secondary station in a mode in which it can initiate transmissions without having been polled first; otherwise the primary–secondary relationship between the stations is essentially the same as in NRM. The SABM (set asynchronous balanced mode) command is used to make stations into equals with identical command and response capabilities. The stations are called *combined stations* rather than primary and secondary stations. Each combined station is, in effect, a combination of a primary and a secondary station. The asynchronous balanced mode is intended primarily for point-to-point full-duplex links; note that in a packet network environment, a true full-duplex communications capability is important.

High-Level Communications Protocols

We have attempted to present data link control protocols as a structured set of functions. The hierarchical model introduced herein provides a structured representation of functional requirements for remote processes to communicate. Thus it can be used to model high-level communications protocol layers as well. In most network architectures (see, e.g., [ZIMM 80]) data link control constitutes just the lowest layer of a larger hierarchy of communications protocol layers. If we examine the functions in the hierarchy, we find that those functions within the high-level protocol layers can also be structured into functions for multiple-access synchronization, content synchronization, and dialogue synchronization, similar to what we have encountered at the data link control layer.

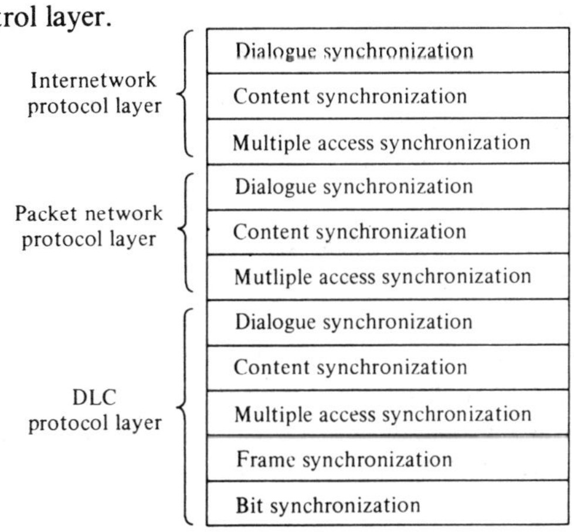

Figure 3.10. Communications protocol layers and their functional requirements.

We illustrate this idea in Fig. 3.10 by considering a somewhat simplified communications architecture for internetworking with three protocol layers. Note that the functional levels of dialogue, content, and multiple-access synchronization are reiterated three times: once in the DLC protocol layer, then in the packet network protocol layer, and finally in the internetwork protocol layer. Although the functional requirements are the same in the three protocol layers, the end points and the characteristics of the communications channel (virtual or real) assumed by different protocol layers are different. Consequently, the degrees of importance associated with various synchronization functions will not be the same in different protocol layers and the solution techniques will thus be different. Consider the end-to-end transport protocol layer of a packet-switching network. The multiple-access synchronization functional level again deals with the sharing of communications facilities by multiple sender–receiver pairs. But with a mesh topology and store-and-forward nodes, the multiple-access synchronization problems are: routing and the synchronization of routing information, congestion control, and so on, which are not the same as before for DLC. The dialogue and content synchronization levels still deal with flow control, error and sequence control, and so on, as described earlier for DLC. The specific protocols for solving these problems, however, are somewhat different because the characteristics of a packet network are different from those of a data link (at a lower level in the network). For example, flow control is probably more important for dialogue synchronization at the network level than at the DLC level, while error control is probably more important at the DLC level than at the network level (because the network transport protocols can count on reliable data links provided by DLC at the lower level). Finally, when different packet-switching networks are interconnected via gateways, it is not hard to see that the multiple access synchronization, content synchronization, and dialogue synchronization functions are needed again in internetworking protocols [CERF 78] for the network of gateways.

ACKNOWLEDGMENTS

This work was supported by the National Science Foundation under Grant ECS78-01803. The author would like to thank Wushow Chou of North Carolina State University and Vint Cerf of the Defense Advanced Research Projects Agency for their helpful comments. He is particularly indebted to an anonymous reviewer who painstakingly read an early draft, pointed out many errors, and made numerous valuable suggestions for improvement.

REFERENCES

ANSI 75 American National Standards Institute, "Procedures for the Use of the Communication Control Characters of American National Standard Code for Information Interchange in Specified Data Communication Links," ANSI X3.28-1976, December 1975.

ANSI 79 American National Standards Institute, "American National Standard for Advanced Data Communication Control Procedures (ADCCP)," ANSI X3.66-1979, January 1979.

BURT 72 Burton, H. O., and D. D. Sullivan, "Errors and Error Control," *Proc. IEEE*, November 1972.

CERF 78 Cerf, V. G., and P. T. Kirstein, "Issues in Packet-Network Interconnection," *Proc. IEEE*, Vol. 66, November 1978.

CYPS 78 Cypser, R. J., *Communications Architecture for Distributed Systems*, Addison-Wesley, Reading, Mass., 1978.

DAVE 72 Davey, J. R., "Modems," *Proc. IEEE*, November 1972.

DONN 74 Donnan, R. A., and J. R. Kersey, "Synchronous Data Link Control: A Perspective," *IBM Syst. J.*, May 1974.

IBM 70 IBM Corp., *General Information — Binary Synchronous Communications*, Manual No. GA27-3004-2, 3rd. ed., October 1970.

IBM 75 IBM Corp., *Synchronous Data Link Control — General Information*, Manual No. GA27-3093-1, May 1975.

ISO 79 International Standards Organization, "Data Communication — High-Level Data Link Control Procedures — Frame Structure," Ref. No. ISO 3309-1979; "Data Communication — High-Level Data Link Control Procedures — Elements of Procedures," Ref. No. ISO 4335-1979, 1979.

MART 70 Martin, J., *Teleprocessing Network Organization*, Prentice-Hall, Englewood Cliffs, N.J., 1970.

MCNA 77 McNamara, J. E., *Technical Aspects of Data Communication*, Digital Equipment Corp., Maynard, Mass., 1977.

ZIMM 80 Zimmermann, H., "OSI Reference Model — The ISO Model of Architecture for Open Systems Interconnection," *IEEE Trans. Commun.*, April 1980.

"Specification and Verification of an HDLC Protocol with ARM Connection Management and Full-Duplex Data Transfer" by A.U. Shankar and S.S. Lam from *Proceedings of the ACM SIGCOMM'83 Symposium*, March 1983, pages 38-48. Copyright 1983, Association for Computing Machinery, Inc., reprinted by permission.

SPECIFICATION AND VERIFICATION OF AN HDLC PROTOCOL WITH ARM CONNECTION MANAGEMENT AND FULL-DUPLEX DATA TRANSFER*

A. Udaya Shankar and Simon S. Lam

Department of Computer Sciences
University of Texas at Austin
Austin, TX 78712

ABSTRACT

We use an event-driven process model to specify a version of the High-level Data Link Control (HDLC) protocol between two communicating protocol entities. The HDLC protocol is based upon the Asynchronous Response Mode (ARM) of operation, and uses the basic repertoire of HDLC commands and responses (with the exception of the CMDR response). It includes the features of poll/final cycles for connection management and checkpointing, sliding windows for data transfer, and ready/not ready messages for flow control. HDLC has three distinguishable functions: connection management, and one-way data transfers in opposite directions between the protocol entities. Various logical safety properties of the HDLC protocol concerning these functions have been verified using the method of projections.

1. INTRODUCTION

The High-Level Data Link Control (HDLC) protocol corresponds to a layer 2 protocol within the OSI reference model [ISO 79a, ISO 79b, ISO 80, ZIMM 80]. It is intended to provide reliable full-duplex data transfer between layer 3 protocol entities, using error-prone physical communication channels of layer 1. The specification of HDLC in the ISO documents defines precisely low-level protocol functions, such as error detection and frame synchronization. Formats of three types of frames specifying the encoding of control and data messages are also clearly defined. Aside from these basic definitions, however, the HDLC documents leave many options to be decided by the protocol implementor. In particular, one can choose from a variety of data link configurations and three operational modes that specify balanced or unequal relationships between the communicating entities. Also, various subsets of the messages can be used, instead of the entire set defined. Further, some aspects of HDLC are described informally in English and are not rigorously specified.

*This work was supported by National Science Foundation Grant No. ECS78-01803

In this paper, we use an event-driven process model [SHAN 82a] to specify a version of the HDLC protocol. (Refer to Figure 1.)

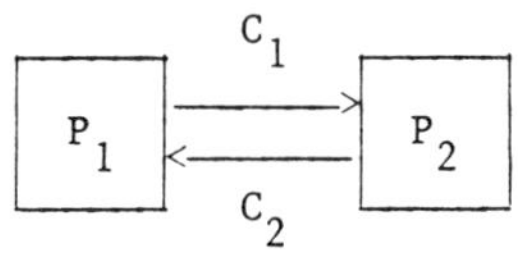

Figure 1. The protocol system model

Let P_1 denote the primary HDLC entity and P_2 the secondary HDLC entity operating in the Asynchronous Response Mode (ARM). C_1 and C_2 are (unreliable) communication channels. Our protocol uses the basic repertoire of HDLC commands and responses (with the exception of the CMDR response). It includes the use of poll/final cycles for checkpointing and connection management, timers for timeouts, sliding windows of size N for data transfers, and ready/not ready messages for flow control [ISO 79b]. Our protocol incorporates all of the principal HDLC functions.

HDLC has at least three distinguishable functions: connection management, and one-way data transfers in opposite directions. We state assertions that specify logical safety properties of the HDLC protocol concerning each function. These assertions have been verified to hold for the HDLC protocol specified herein [SHAN 82a, SHAN 82b].

1.1 The Method of Projections

A multi-function protocol such as HDLC is very complex and cannot be easily analyzed. Our analysis of the HDLC protocol has been achieved through an application of the method of projections [LAM 81, LAM 82a, LAM 82b, SHAN 82a] which breaks up the protocol analysis problem into smaller problems. The method of projections is described in detail in [LAM 82b, SHAN 82a]. Briefly, it constructs from a given multi-function protocol an <u>image protocol</u> for each of the functions that are of interest to us. An image protocol is specified just like any real protocol, and is obtained by retaining only those aspects of the multi-function protocol that are "relevant" to the function being projected. Single-function image protocols are smaller than the original multi-function protocol and are thus easier to analyze. For example, the image protocol for HDLC connection management is similar to a handshake protocol [BOCH 78]. The image protocol for HDLC one-way data transfer is similar to other one-way data transfer protocols based on a sliding window mechanism [STEN 76], but augmented with initialization and checkpointing features.

An image protocol obtained by our construction procedure satisfies the following: any safety property that holds for the image protocol also holds for the original protocol. Additionally, if an image protocol satisfies a well-formed property then it is faithful. Informally, an image protocol is faithful if the following is true: any logical property, safety or liveness, concerning the projected function holds in the image protocol if and only if it also holds in the original protocol (see [LAM 82b, SHAN 82a] for a precise definition). The construction of well-formed image protocols involves an examination of protocol entities individually. There is no need to examine the global reachability space of the protocol interaction. Herein lies a significant advantage of the method of projections.

1.2 Summary of our Results

In Section 2 of this paper, we first describe an event-driven process model of a protocol system. Each component (entity or channel) of the protocol system is modeled as an event-driven process that manipulates a set of variables local to itself and interacts with adjacent components by message passing. The model includes several realistic protocol features such as as multi-field messages and the use of timers. This model is then used to specify the HDLC protocol.

In Section 3 of this paper, we state invariant safety assertions concerning the logical behavior of each of the functions. These assertions have been verified to hold for the HDLC protocol specified herein [SHAN 82a, SHAN 82b]. Due to lack of space, we have not included their proofs in this paper.

Proofs of the assertions as well as an exposition of the work presented in this paper can be found in [SHAN 82b]. Image protocols for the three HDLC functions are also presented there. In addition, inductively complete assertions stating the logical safety properties are shown and proved for each of the image protocols. (Assertions are inductively complete if (a) they are true at initialization of the protocol system, and (b) for each event in the protocol system, given that the assertions hold before the event occurrence, the specification of the event is sufficient to show that the assertions hold after the event occurrence.) From the properties of image protocols, it follows that these safety properties proved for the image protocols are also satisfied by the HDLC protocol.

Of the three image protocols presented in [SHAN 82b], only the image protocol for connection management is well-formed (hence faithful to the HDLC protocol for all safety and liveness properties concerning connection management), while the image protocols for the one-way data transfers are not well-formed (hence may not be faithful to the HDLC protocol for all safety and liveness properties concerning data transfer). In order for the data transfer image protocols to be well-formed, they have to be made substantially larger to account for dependencies in the HDLC protocol between the two one-way data transfer functions. For this reason, the HDLC protocol cannot be considered as well-structured. We then suggest a minor modification to HDLC that makes it well-structured, i.e., small well-formed image protocols can be constructed for each of its three functions.

The reader is referred to [LAM 82b, SHAN 82a] for a detailed treatment of the theory of projections and the method to construct image protocols.

2. AN HDLC/ARM PROTOCOL

In this section, we describe the HDLC/ARM protocol for two protocol entities. ARM denotes the Asynchronous Response Mode of operation. Let P_1 be the primary HDLC entity, and let P_2 be the secondary HDLC entity. P_1 sends messages to P_2 using channel C_1, and P_2 sends messages to P_1 using channel C_2 (see Figure 1). There is a user at entity P_1 and a user at entity P_2. The HDLC protocol system offers to the users a reliable connection that (a) can be opened/closed by the user at P_1, and (b) when open, allows each user to send data blocks to the other user in sequence (without loss, duplication or reordering). The HDLC protocol system offers three functions to the users: connection management, and one-way data transfers in two directions.

2.1 Assumptions about the Environment

To obtain assertions about the logical behavior of the protocol system, a few assumptions are needed about the environment in which HDLC operates. At any time, channel C_i contains a (possibly empty) sequence of messages sent by P_i, for i=1 and 2. Messages in the channels may be corrupted by noise, but not reordered or duplicated. When P_i sends a message, that message is appended to the tail of the message sequence in C_i. When the channel C_i is not empty, the first message (at the head of the message sequence) can be removed and passed on to P_j ($j \neq i$), provided that the message is not corrupted. If the message is corrupted, it is deleted and not passed on to P_j (we assume a perfect error-detection mechanism). The frame-level functions of HDLC [ISO 79a] such as the frame formatting of HDLC messages, bit insertion/deletion to make flags unique, error detection, etc., are not considered as part of the entities P_1 and P_2, but have been included in the channel model. Finally, messages in the channels have a bounded lifetime. The first message in channel C_i is deleted if it has been in the channel for a specified time, denoted by $MaxDelay_i$.

2.2 Event-driven Process Model

Each component of the protocol system (i.e., protocol entity or channel) is modeled as an event-driven process that manipulates a set of variables local to itself and interacts with adjacent components by message passing. An event-driven process consists of events. The events of an entity consist of message sends, message receptions and changes internal to the entity. The events of a channel correspond to transformations on the channel message sequence. An event can occur only if variables of the protocol system satisfy certain conditions, referred to as the enabling condition of the event. When an enabled event occurs, variables of the protocol system are affected. Whenever an event-driven process has enabled events, any one of them can occur. We assume fairness in the choice of the event to occur.

2.2.1 Time variables and time events

For HDLC to function correctly, it is neccessary that each HDLC protocol entity guarantees certain constraints on the time intervals between occurrences of events involving that entity. Also, recall that messages in channels have bounded lifetimes. Because (physical) time elapses at the same rate everywhere, these time constraints give rise to precedence relations between remote events in different components. Furthermore, these precedence relations are vital to the proper functioning of the HDLC protocol. We cannot adequately model such a time-dependent system by using only entity and channel events [SHAN 82c, SHAN 82a]. It is neccessary to relate the elapsed times measured at different components. We do this by introducing time variables in the components to measure elapsed time in integer ticks, and time events to age the time variables.

Each time variable takes its values from N_t = {Off,0,1,2,...}. A time variable is termed inactive if its value is Off, else it is termed active. The value of a time variable can be changed in only two ways. First, it can be aged by a time event. When an active time variable is aged, its value is incremented by 1; when an inactive time variable is aged, its value is not affected. Second, a time variable in a component can be reset to any value in N_t by a system event involving that component. Thus, for an active time variable, the difference between its current value and the value it was last reset to, indicates the time elapsed since the last reset.

We will use two types of time variables in our model: global time variables and local time variables. All global time variables in a system model are aged by the same time event, referred to as the global time event. Thus, all active global time variables are coupled. The global time event models the elapse of physical time in the protocol system model. Global time variables are typically used to model time constraints that are satisfied by components without the use of timers.

Local time variables are used to model the timers that are implemented in system components. To each local time variable t there is a unique local time event that ages t (and t alone). Thus, t is not directly coupled to any other time variable. To specify its accuracy, we associate with t a global time variable t* and a reset value t_0. Whenever t is reset, both t* and t_0 are reset to the same value. t* is affected by the global time event just like any other global time variable. The accuracy of local time variable t is specified by its accuracy axiom which bounds t-t* at any time. For example, the accuracy axiom $|t-t^*| \leq 1 + a(t^*-t_0)$ can specify a timer with maximum relative error a in its clock frequency (Off-Off is treated as 0).

In this model, neither the local time event of t nor the global time event can occur, if such an occurrence would violate the accuracy axiom. By placing additional constraints on the set of allowed values for time variables, other types of time constraints satisfied by a component can be modeled. For example, let t be a time variable that is reset to 0 by event e_1 and reset to Off by event e_2. Let D be a specified delay. Then, to model the time constraint that e_2 occurs no later than D time units since the occurrence of e_1, we include (t<D) in the enabling condition of the time event of t. Such constraints on time events are known as time axioms. (For a more detailed presentation, the reader is referred to [SHAN 82c, SHAN 82a].)

2.2.2 Messages of the protocol model

The messages of the protocol system have multiple fields, and are specified in terms of message types. A message type M is specified by a tuple of the form $(M,F_1,F_2,\ldots,F_n)$, where $n \geq 0$. The first component contains the name of the message type and is a constant. The other components (if any) are the fields of the message type. Each field is a parameter that can take values from a specified set. We shall refer to $(M,F_1,F_2,\ldots,F_n)$ as the format of message type M. The messages sent by each entity are specified by a list of such message types.

2.2.3 Variables of the entities and channels

Each protocol entity has a set of variables, each with a specified domain of values. Some of these variables can be auxiliary variables that are not implemented, but which are useful in the specification/verification of the protocol system. Also, some of these variables can be time variables used in modeling time constraints satisfied by the entity.

In channel C_i, we associate with every message in transit a global time value that indicates the time spent by that message in the channel. This time value is referred to as the age of the message. For channel C_i, we define $Channel_i$ as the variable that represents, at any time, the sequence of (message,age) pairs in C_i.

2.2.4 Events of the protocol model

The events of the protocol system model can be categorized into entity events, channel events, and time events. We will describe them in that order.

There are three types of entity events. We describe these events for entity P_i.

1. For each message type M with format $(M,F_1,\ldots,F_n)$ sent by P_i, there is a Send_M event. This event is enabled if the values of the variables of P_i satisfy a specified enabling condition predicate. Its occurrence appends an M-type message $(M,f_1,\ldots,f_n)$ to the tail of $Channel_i$, and updates the values of variables of P_i (f_k is an allowed value of F_k).

2. For each message type M with format $(M,F_1,\ldots,F_n)$ sent by $P_j(j\neq i)$, there is a Rec_M event. This event is enabled if the entity variables of P_i satisfy a specified predicate, and the first message in $Channel_j$ is any M-type message $(M,f_1,\ldots,f_n)$. Its occurrence removes the message $(M,f_1,\ldots,f_n)$ from $Channel_j$, and updates the values of variables of P_i.

3. An internal event of P_i involves no messages. It is enabled if the entity variables of P_i satisfy a specified predicate. Its occurrence updates the values of the entity variables. Internal events are used to model interactions of the entity with its local user, channel controller, as well as timeouts and other internal transitions of the entity.

Note that both send and receive events affect the state of a channel, as well as the state of the entity.

We now describe the channel events. For i=1 and 2, the channel loss event for channel C_i is enabled whenever $Channel_i$ is not empty. Its occurrence deletes the first (message,age) pair in $Channel_i$. (Recall that the channel behavior in Section 2.1 assumes that only the first message in each channel may be lost.)

We now define the local time events and the global time event for the protocol model. For each local time variable t in P_i, there is a local time event whose occurrence ages t; this event is enabled if its occurrence does not cause t to violate its accuracy axiom or any time axiom involving t. There is one global time event whose occurrence ages all global time variables, including the age values in $Channel_1$ and $Channel_2$. This time event is enabled if its action does not cause any of the time or accuracy axioms to be violated, or result in an age value in $Channel_i$ that exceeds $MaxDelay_i$ for i=1 and 2.

For each entity, it is assumed that its implementation enforces mutual exclusion between the occurrences of events of that entity. Furthermore, we assume that simultaneous occurrences of events in different components of the protocol system can be represented as an arbitrary sequence of occurrences of the same events. This latter assumption is reasonable because events in communication protocol systems can usually be defined in such a way that their occurrences are instantaneous.

2.3 HDLC Messages

We shall now describe the HDLC messages that are sent by P_1 and P_2. Recall that messages are specified in terms of message types, and that the format of each message type is a tuple in which the first component is the name, and the other components are the fields. The interested reader should compare our message types with the three HDLC frame formats in [ISO 79a] and note the similarities.

Messages sent by P_1

We now list the message types sent by P_1. Each of these message types has a Poll_bit field (abbreviated as P field) that can take the value 0 or 1. Any message with the P field set to 1 is referred to as a Poll.

1. (U,P,Command) This U message type represents the Unnumbered frames sent by P_1 for connection management. The Command field can take the value SARM or DISC. SARM stands for Set Asynchronous Response Mode, and requests P_2 to go on-line. DISC stands for Disconnect, and requests P_2 to go off-line.

2. (I,P,Data,NS,NR) This I message type represents the Information frames sent by P_1 for transporting data blocks to P_2. Let DATABLOCKS denote the set of data blocks that can be transported by the HDLC protocol. The Data field contains a user data block, and can take any value from DATABLOCKS. NS and NR are sequence numbers that take values from $\{0,1,\ldots,N-1\}$. (N is 8 for normal HDLC operation and 128 for extended HDLC operation.) NS is referred to as the send sequence number, and is used to identify the position of the data block in the sequence of user data blocks. Successive user data blocks are sent with increasing send sequence numbers (modulo N). NR is referred to as the receive sequence number, and indicates the send sequence number of the I frame from P_2 next expected at P_1. NR is an acknowledgement for data flowing in the reverse direction (i.e., from P_2 to P_1), and acknowledges all data blocks with send sequence numbers up to NR-1. Finally, an I frame with P field set to 1 indicates that P_1 is ready to receive data from P_2.

3. (S,P,RStatus,NR) This S message type represents the Supervisory frames sent by P_1 for flow control and acknowledgement. The RStatus field can take the value RR or RNR, indicating that P_1 is respectively Ready or Not Ready to receive data from P_2. The NR field is the receive sequence number and has been described above.

Messages sent by P_2

We now list the message types sent by P_2. Each of these message types has a Final-bit field (abbreviated as F field) that can take the value 0 or 1. Any message with the F field set to 1 is referred to as a Final. P_2 responds to a received Poll by sending a Final at the earliest opportunity.

1. (U,F,Response) This U message type represents the Unnumbered frames sent by P_2. The Response field can take the value UA or DM. UA stands for Unnumbered Acknowledgement, and is sent to acknowledge reception of, and compliance with a U command received from P_1. DM stands for Disconnected Mode, and is sent when P_2 is off-line as a response to any message (except for SARM) received from P_1.

2. (I,F,Data,NS,NR) This I message type represents Information frames sent by P_2. The Data. NS and NR fields are similar to those in the I frames sent by P_1 (except that the roles of P_1 and P_2 are interchanged). Also, an I frame with the F field set to 1 indicates that P_2 is ready to receive data from P_1.

3. (S,F,RStatus,NR) This S message type represents Supervisory frames sent by P_2. The RStatus and NR fields are similar to those in the S frames sent by P_1 (except that the roles of P_1 and P_2 are interchanged).

Note that message types sent by P_1 and P_2 have similar names. This should however cause no confusion. (The P and F fields actually occupy the same bit position in HDLC frames. That bit is referred to as the P/F bit [ISO 79a].)

2.4 Variables of the HDLC Protocol Entities

We now list the variables of the protocol entities.

Variables of P_1

P_1, the primary HDLC entity, has the following variables (the domain of each variable is also listed using a Pascal-like notation):

```
{The following variables are primarily used
 in the Poll/Final cycle}

Poll_bit          : (0,1);
Poll_Timer        : (Off,0,1,2,...,PollTimeoutValue);
                    {local time variable}
$Poll_Timer       : (Off,0,1,2,....);
                    {global time variable
                     associated with Poll_Timer}
Poll_Retry_Count  : (0,1,...,MaxRetryCount);

{The following variable is primarily used
 in connection management}
Mode              : (Open, Opening, Closed,
                     Closing, LinkFailure);

{The following variables are primarily used
 in sending data blocks to P2}
Source : array[0.. ] of DATABLOCKS;
         {history variable of data blocks}
  User_in, S, A, : 0.. ;  {pointers to Source}
  VS, VA, VCS : 0..N-1;
                  {pointer variables modulo N}
  Checkpoint_Cycle : Boolean;
  Remote_RStatus : (RR,RNR);

{The following variables are primarily used
 in receiving data blocks from P2}

Sink : array[0.. ] of DATABLOCKS;
       {history variable of data blocks}
  User_out, R : 0.. ;  {pointers to Sink}
  VR : 0..N-1;  {pointer variable modulo N}
  Local_RStatus : (RR,RNR);
```

Variables of P_2

P_2, the secondary HDLC entity, has the following variables (along with their domains):

```
{The following variables are primarily used
 in the Poll/Final cycle}

Final_bit : (0,1);
$Response_Time : (Off,0,1,2,...,MaxResponseTime);
                 {auxiliary global time variable}

{The following variables are primarily used
 in connection management}

Mode       : (Open, Opening, Closed, Closing);
U_Response : (UA, DM, None);

{The following variables are primarily used
 in sending data blocks to P1}

Source : array[0.. ] of DATABLOCKS;
         {history variable of data blocks}
  User_in, S, A : 0.. ;  {pointers to Source}
  VS, VA, VCS : 0..N-1;
                 {pointer variables modulo N}
  Checkpoint_Cycle : Boolean;
  Remote_RStatus : (RR,RNR);

{The following variables are primarily used in
 receiving data blocks from P1}

Sink : array[0.. ] of DATABLOCKS;
       {history variable of data blocks}
  User_out, R : 0.. ;  {pointers to sink}
  VR : 0..N-1;  {pointer variable modulo N}
  Local_RStatus : (RR,RNR);
```

(Note that many variables in P_1 and P_2 have the same names. Whenever this can cause ambiguity, we will qualify the variable names with 1 or 2; e.g., $Mode_1$, $Mode_2$.)

2.5 Events of the HDLC Protocol

The events of the HDLC protocol system are formally specified in Tables 1-4. An informal description follows in the succeeding subsections. The events of the entities are shown in Tables 1 and 2. The program statements in upper case (POLL_SENT, FINAL_RECEIVED, INITIALIZE_SEND_VARIABLES, etc.) stand for code segments that are shown in Table 3. When used in an entity event, the variables they refer to are the variables of that entity. We use the notation $\oplus$ and $\ominus$ to refer to addition modulo N and subtraction modulo N respectively. The time events of the HDLC protocol are specified in Table 4. The initial state of this protocol is given by the following value assignments to the protocol system variables: Poll_bit=0, Poll_Timer=$Poll_Timer=Off, Poll_Retry_Count=0 and Mode=Closed in P_1; Final_bit=0, $Response_Time=Off, Mode=Closed and U_Response=None in P_2; both $Channel_1$ and $Channel_2$ are empty. We now describe the operation of the HDLC protocol informally.

2.5.1 Poll/Final cycle events

We first describe the P/F cycle involving the Poll and Final messages. Recall that P_2 responds to a received Poll by sending a Final at the earliest opportunity. A Poll is said to be outstanding (at P_1) if it has been sent and its acknowledging Final is being awaited. At any time, at most one Poll may be outstanding. Poll_bit set to 1 indicates that the next message sent by P_1 must be a Poll message. Final_bit set to 1 indicates that the next message sent by P_2 must be a Final message. Poll_Timer is used to measure the time elapsed since the last Poll was sent. When Poll_Timer is Off, there is no Poll that is outstanding and P_1 can send a Poll. Poll_Timer is started (reset to 0) when the Poll is sent. Poll_Timer is stopped (reset to Off) either when the acknowledging Final is received, or when a time duration PollTimeoutValue has elapsed. In the latter case, referred to as a Timeout event (see Table 1), P_1 presumes that either the Poll or the Final was lost.

Poll_Timer is treated as a local time variable, and $Poll_Timer is its associated global time variable. We shall consider its accuracy axiom to be $|\text{Poll\_Timer} - \text{\$Poll\_Timer}| \leq 1 + a(\text{\$Poll\_Timer})$, where a is the maximum relative error in Poll_Timer's clock frequency. (Since any reset to Poll_Timer leaves it either Off or 0, there is no need to specify an associated reset value for Poll_Timer.)

$Response_Time is an auxiliary global time variable that is active if (and only if) a Poll has been received and its Final has not yet been sent; it then indicates the (global) time elapsed since the reception of the Poll. MaxResponseTime denotes the maximum time needed by P_2 to respond to a Poll. This time constraint is modeled by assuming that P_2 satisfies the following local time axiom: $\text{\$Response\_Time} \leq \text{MaxResponseTime}$. By having PollTimeoutValue > $(1+a)(\text{MaxDelay}_1 + \text{PollResponseTime} + \text{MaxDelay}_2)$, P_1 ensures that the following P/F cycle properties hold:

(i) A Final received at P_1 is the response to the last Poll sent by P_1.

(ii) A Poll received at P_2 was sent after the last Final sent by P_2 left channel C_2 (the Final may not have been received by P_1).

Poll_Retry_Count indicates the number of Timeouts that have occurred since the last Final was received. If this exceeds MaxRetryCount, P_1 assumes that the data link (either C_1, P_2 or C_2) has broken down, and enters a LinkFailure mode, which can be exited only by user intervention.

2.5.2 Connection management events

Mode in entity P_1 indicates the status of the data link as perceived by P_1. Open/Closed are stable states indicating that P_1 is on-line/off-line. The user sets Mode to Opening/Closing to request P_1 to open/close the data link with the remote user. P_1 then polls P_2 with appropriate U commands (SARM/DISC), and upon receiving acknowledgement sets Mode to Open/Closed. LinkFailure indicates that P_1 perceives the data link to have broken down (in our model, this is due to Poll_Retry_Count exceeding MaxRetryCount).

Mode in entity P_2 is similar to that in P_1, except that LinkFailure is not one of its allowed values. Open/Closed are stable states. Opening/Closing indicate that P_2 has received a SARM/DISC command and has not yet sent the UA acknowledgement. Once the acknowledgement is sent, Mode is set to Open/Closed. U_Response indicates the kind of U message to be sent by P_2.

2.5.3 Data transfer and flow control events

Next we describe the data transfer variables at P_1. Source is a history variable that records the data blocks given by the local user to P_1 to send to the remote user. User_in, S and A are three pointers to Source. User_in points to the location in Source into which the local user places his next data block. S points to the data block in Source to be next sent to P_1. A points to the data block in Source to be next acknowledged by P_2. (See Figure 2(a)). VS is referred to as the <u>send state variable</u>, and indicates the send sequence number of the next data block to be sent. VA is referred to as the <u>acknowledgement state variable</u>, and indicates the send sequence number of the data block to be next acknowledged. VS (VA) points to the same data block in Source as S (A). Checkpoint_Cycle and VCS are explained later. Remote_RStatus is RR (RNR) if the latest flow control information from P_2 indicates that P_2 is Ready (not Ready) to receive data. Note that data blocks Source[A], Source[A+1], ..., Source[User_in-1] have to be saved in a local <u>send buffer</u> of P_1. Let SBuffSize be the size of this buffer.

Sink is a history variable that records the data blocks received from P_2, and accepted for delivery to the local user. R and User_out are pointers to Sink. R points to the location in Sink in which to place the next data block received in sequence from P_2. User_out points to the data block in Sink to be next delivered to the local user. VR is referred to as the <u>receive state variable</u>, and indicates the sequence number of the data block next expected. (See Figure 2(b).) VR points to the same data block as R. Local_RStatus is RR (RNR) if P_1 is Ready (Not Ready) to receive data blocks from P_2. Note that data blocks Sink[User_out], Sink[User_out+1],...,Sink[R-1] have to be saved in a local <u>receive buffer</u>. Let RBuffSize denote the size of this buffer. Local_RStatus reflects whether this buffer is full or not.

The data transfer variables of P_2 are similar to those of P_1 (except that the roles of P_1 and P_2 are interchanged).

At each entity, data can be sent and received only when Mode is Open. At each entity, each time that Mode is set to Open, the data transfer variables are initialized as follows: User_in=S=A=0, VS=VA=VCS=0, Checkpoint_Cycle=False, Remote_RStatus=RR, User_out=R=0, VR=0, and Local_RStatus=RR.

We will now describe informally the data transfer from P_1 to P_2. (Let Figure 2(a) represent the Source in P_1, and Figure 2(b) represent the Sink in P_2.) When the user at P_1 wants to send a data block, he places it in Source[User_in], and increments User_in by 1. When P_1 sends an I frame, the Data field contains Source[S], the NS and NR fields contain the current values of VS and VR. S is incremented by 1 and VS by 1 (modulo N). When an I frame arrives at P_2, if its NS equals the current value of VR, and Local_RStatus equals RR, then P_2 accepts the data block in the data field and places it in Sink[R]. R is then incremented by 1, and VR by 1 (modulo N). When the user at P_2 extracts the data block from Sink[User_out], User_out is incremented by 1. When P_1 receives an NR, that NR points to some data block in Source[A], Source[A+1],...,Source[S]. VA is updated to equal NR, and A is updated to point to the data block now outstanding.

Because the sequence numbers are cyclic, the number of outstanding blocks must never exceed N-1 (i.e., S-A should always equal (VS-VA) mod N); otherwise, a received sequence number will not point to a unique outstanding data block. Whenever a Poll is sent when data blocks are outstanding, Checkpoint_Cycle is set to True, and VCS is set to (VS-1 mod N) the NS of the most recently sent data block. Checkpoint_Cycle is set to False either when an NR equalling or exceeding VCS is received, or when a Final is received. In the latter case, if the NR with the Final does not acknowledge VCS, P_1 concludes that I frames were lost (because of the P/F cycle properties). VS and VA are then set to equal the received NR. S and A are adjusted accordingly. This method of checking data transfer progress (and initiating retransmission if necessary) is referred to as checkpointing.

In addition, P_2 sends flow control information indicating its current Local_RStatus to P_1. This information is sent in S frames, as well as in I frames that have their P field set to 1.

The data transfer from P_2 to P_1, and its flow control is similar, except that the roles of the Polls and Finals are interchanged in checkpointing. However, note that P_1 can initiate a Checkpoint_Cycle whereas P_2 cannot.

2.5.4 Time events

The time events of the protocol system are shown in Table 4. Poll_Timer_Tick is the local time event for Poll_Timer. Global_Tick is the global time event of the system. The procedure Age (in the actions of the time events) ages all its argument time variables by one tick. Note that the global time event cannot age $Response_Time beyond MaxResponseTime, nor can it cause a message to stay in $Channel_i$ for longer than $MaxDelay_i$, nor can it cause Poll_Timer to be more inaccurate than as specified by its accuracy axiom. Similarly Poll_Timer_Tick cannot cause Poll_Timer to be more inaccurate than as specified by its accuracy axiom.

3. SAFETY PROPERTIES OF THE HDLC PROTOCOL

The HDLC protocol described has three distinguishable functions offered to its users: connection management, and one-way data transfers in opposite directions. We will now state assertions that specify logical safety behavior of the HDLC protocol concerning each of these functions. Our analysis of the HDLC protocol was done through the use of protocol projections. An image protocol was constructed from the HDLC protocol for each of the three functions of interest. These image protocols were then verified to satisfy the safety properties described below. From the properties of image protocols, these assertions also hold for the HDLC protocol [LAM 82b, SHAN 82a]. It was easier to obtain the assertions from the image protocols than from the HDLC protocol, because each image protocol is smaller, both in the number of variables and in the complexity of event descriptions. The image protocols and proofs are given in [SHAN 82a, SHAN 82b].

We note that the Poll/Final cycle displays a time-dependent behavior. The essence of this time-dependent behavior is captured by the following assertion:

Poll_Timer = Off => No Poll in $Channel_1$
and Final_bit = 0
and no Final in $Channel_2$

This says that when Poll_Timer is Off (e.g., immediately after a Poll_Timeout occurrence), sufficient time has elapsed since the last Poll was sent so that the following hold: (a) the Poll is no longer in $Channel_1$, (b) if the Poll was received by P_2, then the acknowledging Final has already been sent, and (c) the acknowledging Final is no longer in $Channel_2$. This assertion allows us to deduce the P/F cycle properties described in Section 2.5.1. The HDLC protocol has been verified to satisfy the above assertion [SHAN 82b]. (We note that our event-driven process model includes measures of time which have been incorporated expressly for verifying assertions of time-dependent behavior.)

We will now state the logical safety properties satisfied by the HDLC protocol concerning each of the three functions.

3.1 Safety Properties for Connection Management

For this HDLC protocol, the following assertions concerning connection management is invariant (proof in [SHAN 82b]):

1. $Mode_1$ = Open => $Mode_2$ = Open
and no U frame in $Channel_1$
and no U frame in $Channel_2$
and U_Response = None

2. $Mode_1$ = Closed => $Mode_2$ = Closed
and $Channel_1$ is empty
and $Channel_2$ is empty
and U_Response = None

These assertions specify that the offline/online states of P_1 and P_2 are synchronized, and that the channels are not utilized when the two entities are offline.

3.2 Safety Properties for P_1 to P_2 Data Transfer

For the function of one-way data transfer from P_1 to P_2, the following two desirable properties have been verified to hold for the HDLC protocol (proof in [SHAN 82b]):

If $Mode_1 = Mode_2$ = Open then
1. $Sink_2[i] = Source_1[i]$ for $0 \leq i < User\_out_2$
2. $0 \leq A_1 \leq S_1 < A_1 + N$

The first says that while the data link is open, data is transferred in sequence from P_1 to P_2. The second says that the maximum number of outstanding data blocks (hence the minimum storage requirement) at P_1 is N-1.

3.3 Safety Properties for P_2 to P_1 Data Transfer

For the function of one-way data transfer from P_2 to P_1 the following two desirable properties have been verified for the HDLC protocol (proof in [SHAN 82b]):

If $Mode_2 = Mode_1$ = Open then
1. $Sink_1[i] = Source_2[i]$ for $0 \leq i < User\_out_1$
2. $0 \leq A_2 \leq S_2 \leq A_2 + N$

The first says that while the data link is open, data is transferred in sequence from P_2 to P_1. The second says that the maximum number of outstanding data blocks (hence the minimum storage requirement) at P_2 is N-1.

4. CONCLUSION

We have used an event-driven process model to specify and verify a version of the HDLC protocol between two communicating protocol entities. The HDLC protocol specified is based upon the Asynchronous Response Mode (ARM) of operation, and includes all of its important features. It uses the basic repertoire of HDLC commands and responses (with the exception of the CMDR response), and includes the use of poll/final messages for checkpointing and connection management, timers for timeouts, sliding windows of size N for data transfers, and ready/not ready messages for flow control.

The HDLC protocol has three distinguishable functions: connection management, and one-way data transfers between the two protocol entities. We stated assertions that specify desired logical safety properties of the HDLC protocol concerning the three functions. These assertions have been verified to hold for the HDLC protocol specified. The verification was done through an application of the method of projections. The image protocols of HDLC and proofs of the assertions can be found in [SHAN 82b]. The theory of projections and the method to construct image protocols are presented in [LAM 82b, SHAN 82a].

REFERENCES

[BOCH 78] Bochmann, G. V., "Finite State Description of Communication Protocols," Computer Networks, Vol. 2, 1978.

[ISO 79a] International Standards Organization, "Data Communications--HDLC Procedures--Frame Structure," Ref. No. ISO 3309, 1979.

[ISO 79b] International Standards Organization, "Data Communications--HDLC Procedures--Elements of Procedures," Ref. No. ISO 4335, 1979.

[ISO 80] International Standards Organization, "Data Communications--HDLC Unbalanced Classes of Procedures," Ref. No. ISO 6159, 1980.

[LAM 81] Lam, S. S. and A. U. Shankar, "Protocol Projections: A Method for Analyzing Communication Protocols," Conf. Rec. Nat. Telecomm. Conf., November 1981, New Orleans.

[LAM 82a] Lam, S. S. and A. U. Shankar, "Verification of Communication Protocols via Protocol Projections," Proc INFOCOM'82, April 1982, Las Vegas.

[LAM 82b] Lam, S. S. and A. U. Shankar, "Protocol Verification via Projections," Tech. Rep. 207, Dept. of Computer Sciences, Univ. of Texas at Austin, August 1982.

[SHAN 82a] Shankar, A. U., "Analysis of Communication Protocols via Protocol Projections," PhD thesis, Dept. of Elec. Eng., Univ. of Texas at Austin, December 1982.

[SHAN 82b] Shankar, A. U. and S. S. Lam, "An HDLC Protocol Specification and its Verification using Image Protocols," Tech. Rep. 212, Dept. of Computer Sciences, Univ. of Texas at Austin, September 1982.

[SHAN 82c] Shankar, A. U. and S. S. Lam, "On Time-Dependent Communication Protocols and their Projections," Proc. 2nd Int. Workshop on Protocol Spec., Test. and Verif., May 1982, Idyllwild, CA.

[STEN 76] Stenning, N. V., "A Data Transfer Protocol," Computer Networks, September 1976.

[ZIMM 80] Zimmermann, H., "OSI Reference Model--The ISO Model of Architecture for Open Systems Interconnection," IEEE Trans. on Commun. COM-28(4), April 1980.

TABLE 1. EVENTS OF PRIMARY HDLC ENTITY P_1

Event Name	Enabling Condition	Action
1. User_req_conn	Mode ≠ Opening or Closing	Mode := Opening
2. User_req_disc	Mode = Open	Mode := Closing
3. User_puts_data	Mode = Open and (User_in-A<SbuffSize)	{User places data in Source[User_in]} User_in := User_in + 1
4. User_gets_data	Mode = Open and (R-User_out > 0)	{User extracts data block from Sink[User_out]} User_out := User_out + 1; if Local_RStatus = RNR then Local_RStatus := RR

5. Send_U	Mode = Opening
	or Mode = Closing
	and Poll_bit = 1
		if Mode = Opening then Command:=SARM;
		if Mode = Closing then Command:= DISC;
		put(Channel$_1$, (U,1,Command));
		POLL_SENT

6. Rec_U	first(Channel$_2$) = U	get(Channel$_2$, (U,F,Response));
		if Response = DM then Mode := Closed;
		if (Response = UA) and (Mode = Closing)
		then Mode := Closed;
		if (Response = UA) and (Mode = Opening)
		then begin Mode := Open;
		INITIALIZE_SEND_VARIABLES;
		INITIALIZE_REC_VARIABLES
		end;
		if F = 1 then FINAL_RECEIVED

7. Poll_Timeout	Poll_Timer≥PollTimeoutValue	Reset(Poll_Timer, Off); if Poll_Retry_Count < MaxRetryCount then Poll_Retry_Count := Poll_Retry_Count + 1 else Mode := LinkFailure
8. Request_Poll	Poll_Timer = Off	Poll_bit := 1
9. Send_I	Mode = Open and VS⊕VA < N-1 and S < User_in and Remote_RStatus = RR and not(Poll_bit = 1 and Local_RStatus = RNR)	put(Channel$_1$, (I,Poll_bit,Source[S],VS,VR)); VS := VS ⊕ 1; S := S + 1; if Poll_bit = 1 then begin CHECKPOINT_SENT; POLL_SENT end
10. Send_S	Mode = Open	put(Channel$_1$, (S,Poll_bit,Local_RStatus,VR)); if Poll_bit = 1 then begin CHECKPOINT_SENT; POLL_SENT end

11. Rec_I	Mode = Open
	and first(Channel$_2$) = I
		get(Channel$_2$, (I,F,Data,NS,NR));
		DATA_NS_RECEIVED; NR_RECEIVED;
		if F = 1 then begin CHECKPOINT_RECEIVED;
		FINAL_RECEIVED;
		Remote_RStatus := RR
		end

12. Rec_S	Mode = Open
	and first(Channel$_2$) = S
		get(Channel$_2$,(S,F,RStatus,NR));
		Remote_RStatus := RStatus; NR_RECEIVED;
		if F = 1 then begin CHECKPOINT_RECEIVED;
		FINAL_RECEIVED;
		end

TABLE 2. EVENTS OF SECONDARY HDLC ENTITY P_2

Event Name	Enabling Condition	Action
1. User_puts_data	Mode = Open and (User_in-A<SbuffSize)	{User places data block in Source[User_in]} User_in := User_in + 1
2. User_gets_data	Mode = Open and (R - User_out > 0)	{User extracts data block from Sink[User_out]} User_out := User_out + 1; if Local_RStatus = RNR then Local_RStatus := RR

3. Rec_U	first(Channel$_1$) = U
	and U_Response ≠ UA
		get(Channel$_1$, (U,P,Command));
		if command = SARM begin Mode := Opening;
		U_Response := UA
		end;
		if (Command = DISC) and (Mode = Open)
		then begin Mode := Closing;
		U_Response := UA
		end;
		if (Command = DISC) and (Mode = Closed)
		then U_Response := DM;
		if P = 1 then POLL_RECEIVED

4. Send_U	U_Response ≠ None	put(Channel$_2$, (U,Final_bit,U_Response));
		U_Response := None;
		if Mode = Closing then Mode := Closed;
		if Mode = Opening
		then begin Mode := Open;
		INITIALIZE_SEND_VARIABLES;
		INITIALIZE_REC_VARIABLES
		end
		if Final_bit = 1 then FINAL_SENT

5. Send_I	Mode = Open and VS⊖VA < N-1 and S < User_in and Remote_RStatus = RR and not(Final_bit = 1 and Local_RSTATUS = RNR)	put(Channel$_2$, (I,Final_bit,Source[S],VS,VR)); VS := VS ⊖ 1; S := S + 1; if Final_bit = 1 then begin CHECKPOINT_SENT; FINAL_SENT; end
6. Send_S	Mode = Open	put(Channel$_2$, (S,Final_bit,Local_RStatus,VR)); if Final_bit = 1 then begin CHECKPOINT_SENT; FINAL_SENT end

7. Rec_I	first(Channel$_1$) = I
	and U_Response ≠ UA
		get(Channel$_1$, (I,P,Data,NS,NR));
		if Mode = Closed then U_Response := DM;
		if Mode = Open
		then begin
		DATA_NS_RECEIVED; NR_RECEIVED;
		if P = 1
		then begin CHECKPOINT_RECEIVED;
		POLL_RECEIVED;
		end
		end

8. Rec_S	first(Channel$_1$) = S
	and U_Response ≠ UA
		get(Channel$_1$, (S,P,RStatus, NR));
		if Mode = Closed then U_Response := DM;
		if Mode = Open then begin
		Remote_RStatus := RStatus;
		NR_RECEIVED;
		if P = 1
		then begin
		CHECKPOINT_RECEIVED;
		POLL_RECEIVED
		end
		end

TABLE 3. DETAILS OF CODE SEGMENTS USED IN TABLES 1-2

```
POLL_SENT::
    Reset(Poll_Timer, 0); Poll_bit := 0;

FINAL_RECEIVED::
    Reset(Poll_Timer, Off); Poll_Retry_Count := 0;

POLL_RECEIVED::
    Final_bit := 1; Reset($Response_Time, 0);

FINAL_SENT::
    Final_bit := 0; Reset($Response_Time, Off);

INITIALIZE_SEND_VARIABLES::
    User_in := 0; S := 0; A := 0; VS := 0; VA := 0;
    Checkpoint_Cycle := False;
    Remote_RStatus := RR;

INITIALIZE_REC_VARIABLES::
    User_out := 0; R := 0; VR := 0;
    Local_RStatus := RR;

DATA_NS_RECEIVED::
    if VR = VS and Local_RStatus = RR
       then begin Sink[R] := Data;
                  R := R + 1; VR := VR ⊖ 1;
                  if (R - User_out) = Rbuffsize
                     then Local_RStatus := RNR;
            end;

CHECKPOINT_SENT::
    if VS ≠ AS
       then begin Checkpoint_Cycle := True;
                  VCS := VS ⊕ 1
            end;

NR_RECEIVED::
    if Checkpoint_Cycle and NR ⊕ VA > VCS ⊕ VA
       then Checkpoint_Cycle := False;
    A := A + (NR ⊕ VA); VA := NR;

CHECKPOINT_RECEIVED::
    if Checkpoint_Cycle
       then begin Checkpoint_Cycle := False;
                  VS := VA; S := A
            end;
```

TABLE 4. TIME EVENTS FOR THE PROTOCOL SYSTEM

Event Name	Enabling Condition	Action
1. Poll_Timer_Tick	(Poll_Timer - \$Poll_Timer) $\leq$ a(\$Poll_Timer)	Age(Poll_Timer)
2. Global_Tick	(\$Poll_Timer - Poll_Timer) $\leq$ a(\$Poll_Timer) and (\$Response_Time < MaxResponseTime) and (all ages in $Channel_1$ < $MaxDelay_1$) and (all ages in $Channel_2$ < $MaxDelay_2$)	Age(\$Poll_Timer); Age(\$Response_Time); Age(all ages in $Channel_1$); Age(all ages in $Channel_2$);

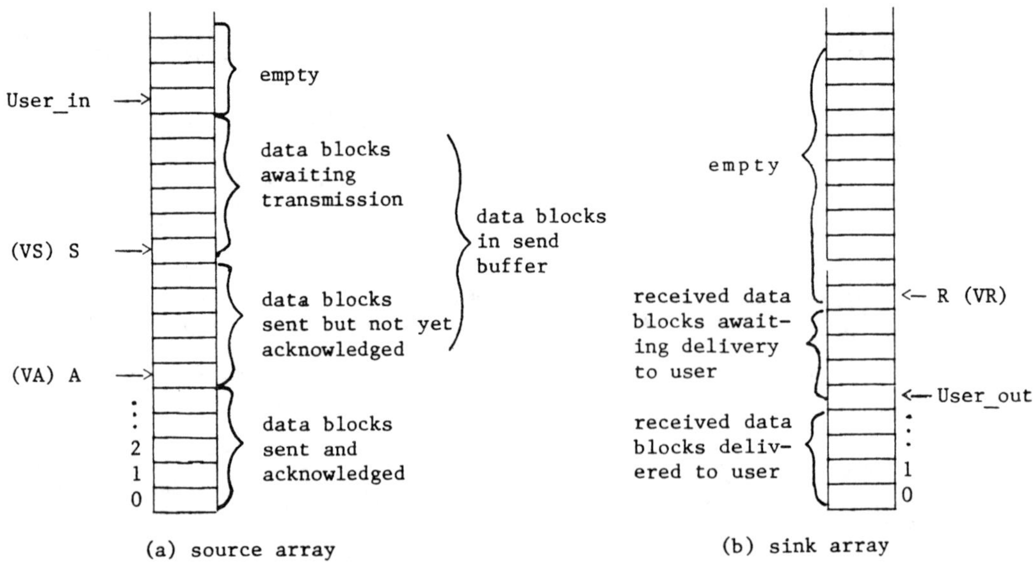

Figure 2. Pictorial representation of pointer positions for source and sink history arrays

Chapter 3
Multiple Access Protocols

3.1. INTRODUCTION

Consider the sharing of a single broadcast channel by a population of N distributed users. The set of rules and algorithms that define the method of sharing is referred to as the multiple access protocol. When we compare different multiple access protocols, we should bear in mind that the performance of a multiple access protocol depends on various parameter values that can differ greatly in different networks. Also, certain protocols assume specific hardware capabilities that are available in one network but that cannot be easily implemented in another network.

Let us begin by assuming only that the transmission of any user in the broadcast channel (if it is the only transmission present) is observable and can be received by all other network users after a small propagation delay. If the transmissions of two different users overlap in time in the channel, the "collision" is observable to all network users after a small propagation delay, but none of the transmissions can be received correctly (i.e., no spread spectrum capability). Several tutorial articles on multiple access techniques are available in the literature [LAM 79, TOBA 80a, LAM 83]. One of them [LAM 83] is reprinted below.

Traditional techniques for solving the multiple access problem are based upon dividing the broadcast channel into a pool of subchannels, using either frequency division or time division. These subchannels may be fixed-assigned to the population of users; in this case, N subchannels are needed. The subchannels may also be demand-assigned to the population of users; in this case, fewer than N subchannels are needed. Demand assignment may be achieved with either a central controller or a distributed control algorithm. These techniques are said to be *channel-oriented* since each unit of allocation is one subchannel for a relatively long time duration.

It is well known in queueing theory that a single, high-speed server is often preferable to multiple servers whose aggregate service capacity is the same as that of the single server. This is particularly true in data communications where traffic sources are typically very bursty [LAM 78]. Multiple access protocols of recent interest are primarily *packet-oriented*, i.e., packets from different users are scheduled in some fashion to use the entire broadcast channel.

The multiple access problem is thus simply the problem of forming a queue among a population of distributed users. To form such a *distributed queue*, there are two subproblems. (As shown below, these subproblems can be solved with either a central controller or a distributed control algorithm.)

1. Identify those users with data to send and who desire channel access (the *ready users*).
2. Assign the channel to a ready user according to some scheduling discipline.

Instead of identifying all ready users present in the population and employing an *explicit* scheduling discipline, the following variation may be employed. If the channel is idle, it is next assigned to the first ready user identified. In this case, the scheduling discipline is *implicit* in the algorithm for finding a ready user.

In Section 3.2, we give a taxonomy of multiple access protocols. We assert that most multiple access protocols that have been proposed are based upon one or a hybrid of these techniques. (Note: This taxonomy is different from the one in [LAM 83].) In Section 3.3, we provide two simple performance criteria for comparing different protocols. We also discuss techniques for enhancing the throughput-delay performance characteristics of the basic protocols described in Section 3.2. Section 3.4 gives an overview of protocols based on the availability of some advanced capabilities in the broadcast channel.

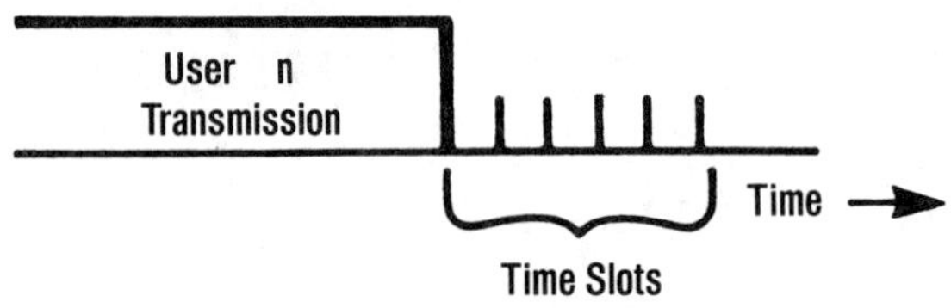

Figure 3-1. A time-slotted channel.

3.2. A TAXONOMY

Multiple access protocols employ one of three basic techniques for finding ready users: linear search, tree search, and contention.

Linear search

A prime example of a multiple access protocol based upon linear search is roll-call polling. A central controller is employed, and the population of users is queried according to some sequential ordering of the users.

Distributed control may also be used. In hub polling, a special message, called a *token*, is passed among the users according to some sequential order. When the token reaches a user who is ready, he is assigned access to the channel.

An alternative method to implement distributed control is as follows: Suppose that the users are time synchronized so that the channel is divided into time slots following the end of a transmission (Figure 3-1). A linear search of the users can be performed by assigning one user to each time slot according to a predefined sequential order. A user can indicate in his time slot whether or not he is ready. The time slot duration must be long enough so that at the end of a time slot the outcome of the slot is globally known.

Suppose that following the end of a transmission, the channel is next assigned to the first ready user found. The scheduling discipline can be implicitly defined by specifying the user sequence following a user n transmission (Figure 3-1). If the sequence is always 1, 2, 3, ..., then we have a priority discipline with user 1 having the highest priority and user N, the lowest priority. If the sequence is $n+1$, $n+2$, $n+3$, ..., (modulo N) then we have a round-robin discipline.

For example, both MSAP [KLEI 77] and BRAM [CHLA 79] are linear search techniques based on the use of time slots as described above.

Tree search

Protocols that find ready users by a tree search can also be implemented with either a central controller or by means of time slots and distributed control similar to what has been described earlier. Suppose that the network users correspond to the leaves of a tree. Without loss of generality, consider a binary tree. The tree is traversed starting from the root node, and the ready users are identified using a divide-and-conquer type of algorithm.

A central controller, if used, can "probe" a group of users simultaneously instead of polling them one after another. When probed, all ready users in the group will respond. The central controller can distinguish between two outcomes: (1) no response, or (2) some response (at least one ready user in the group). In the tree traversal, when a node is visited, the central controller probes the entire group of users that are the descendants of the visited node. If there is no response, the entire subtree is "pruned." On the other hand, if there is a response, then each of the two sons of the node will have to be visited subsequently in the tree traversal [HAYE 78].

The tree traversal can also be carried out using time slots (see Figure 3-1). If all users exercise the same tree traversal algorithm and observe the same outcomes in the time slots, they will arrive at the same conclusion about the status of each user. In this case, the node to be visited next in the tree traversal is assigned the next time slot. It is assumed that when a node is visited, all ready users who are descendants of that node will transmit into the assigned time slot. Suppose that three possible outcomes can be distinguished in a time slot: (1) no one ready, (2) a single user ready with his identity indicated, and (3) a collision (two or more users ready). When a node is visited, the occurrence of either of the first two outcomes will provide information on the status of all its descendants [CAPE 77, CAPE 79]. Hence, the subtree may be pruned. It should be clear that the ability to distinguish three outcomes in a time slot instead of the two outcomes from a probe will give rise to a more efficient search. In practice, the ability to recognize these and, perhaps, other outcomes will depend upon the communication technology being used. As before, if the channel is assigned to the first ready user found in each tree traversal, then the scheduling discipline is implicitly specified by the tree traversal order. We reprint [CAPE 79] below.

We note that the MLMA protocol in [ROTH 77] and the binary elimination protocol in [MOK 79] are also based on a tree search as described above.

As discussed below, tree search protocols have poor performance whenever the population of users contains many ready users. Both Hayes [HAYE 78] and Capetanakis [CAPE 77] investigated traffic conditions and techniques for adaptively switching their protocols between tree search and linear search. (See also Section 4.2.2 of [LAM 83] reprinted below.)

Contention

The third basic technique for finding ready users is based solely upon distributed control. In its purest form, called the ALOHA protocol, each user simply transmits a newly generated packet into the channel immediately, hoping that it will be successfully received without colliding with someone else's transmission [ABRA 70, ABRA 73]. A packet that has unfortunately collided with another packet is retransmitted after a random delay. A random delay is necessary to minimize the probability of collision with the same packet again [KLEI 73, KLEI 75]. This random delay determines the throughput-delay performance of the system and affects its stability behavior. It was found that the user population size is another important parameter that affects system stability. The stability, throughput, and delay of a slotted ALOHA system can be evaluated using a Markov chain model [LAM 74, KLEI 74, KLEI 75a]. Protocols based on contention should always be implemented in conjunction with some adaptive control algorithm to avoid unstable behavior. A variety of techniques is described in [LAM 75a, LAM 75b, GERL 77, LAM 80a]. The URN protocol described in [KLEI 78] is based on the use of asymmetric control policies instead of symmetric control policies considered in the above references. Two articles, one on the stability behavior and delay performance of ALOHA channels [KLEI 75a] and one on adaptive control schemes [LAM 75b], are reprinted below. The Exponential Binary Backoff algorithm employed in Ethernet [METC 76] is a specific instance of the class of Heuristic Retransmission Control procedures studied and described in [LAM 75b]. The article by Kleinrock and Yemini on the URN protocol [KLEI 78] is also reprinted below.

Contention protocols, in general, give rise to a random order of service. However, it is possible to favor some users over others by specifying different retransmission delays for them [LAM 80b].

3.3. PERFORMANCE CONSIDERATIONS

3.3.1. Two Simple Criteria for Comparing Protocols

Let us compare some multiple access techniques based on the three methods described in Section 3.2 for identifying ready users.

Consider two extreme traffic conditions: (1) exactly one of the N users is ready (light traffic condition) and (2) all of the N users are ready (heavy traffic condition). In Table 3-1, adapted

Table 3-1. Mean delays to find a ready user under two extreme traffic conditions.

	Light Traffic Condition One out of N users ready	**Heavy Traffic Condition** All N users ready
Linear search via		
polling	$(N+1)/2$ queries (mean value)	1 query
time slots	$(N+1)/2$ time slots (mean value)	1 time slot
Binary tree search via		
polling/probing	$1 + 3/2 \log_2 N$ queries (mean value)	$1 + \log_2 N$ queries
time slots	1 time slot	$1 + \log_2 N$ time slots
Contention in time slots	1 time slot	2.72 time slots (mean value given optimal symmetric controls)

from [LAM 80a], we show the mean assignment delay (amount of channel time wasted) for each of the techniques to identify a ready user under the two extreme traffic conditions. Under the light traffic condition, the ready user is assumed to be chosen randomly.

In Table 3-1, the linear search techniques are self-explanatory. The tree search techniques assume a balanced binary tree with users at all leaf nodes. For the contention technique we assume a time-slotted channel. At the end of a time slot, it is globally known whether it is empty, contains a single user's transmission, or contains a collision. It is assumed that a user who has a new packet will transmit it in the next time slot with a probability of 1. A packet that has had a collision is retransmitted in the next time slot with a probability (<1) that is adaptively controlled. The mean delay of 2.72 time slots shown in Table 3-1 corresponds to a slotted ALOHA protocol that is optimally controlled (with a maximum channel throughput of 0.368). With nonoptimal controls, the mean assignment delay under the heavy traffic condition would be somewhat larger than 2.72 time slots (3-4 time slots would be quite realistic).

Given a large N, Table 3-1 shows that linear search performs well under the heavy traffic condition but performs poorly under the light traffic condition. The opposite is true for tree search and contention techniques.

Note that the actual performance of each technique in a specific system depends upon system parameters which determine the time slot size or the time duration to conduct a query. Whether one technique is better than another (over a wide range of channel utilization) depends on the specific parameter values of a particular network. Adaptive control is necessary for the contention technique to handle heavy traffic (no matter how infrequently it occurs). It is also desirable for a protocol based on tree search to adaptively switch to linear search whenever the channel traffic becomes heavy.

In Figure 3-2, the general behavior of the mean delay versus throughput characteristic of a multiple access protocol is shown. Note that the maximum throughput S_{max} and the minimum delay D_{min} (at zero throughput) in Figure 3-2 can be predicted from the entries in Table 3-1 for each multiple access protocol. Specifically, the mean assignment delay d_1 of a multiple access technique under the light traffic condition determines D_{min} as follows

$$D_{min} = P + d_1$$

where P is the mean transmision time of a user data unit. The mean assignment delay d_2 under the heavy traffic condition determines S_{max} as follows

$$S_{max} = \frac{P}{P + d_2}$$

(Note: The above formulas may need to be adjusted slightly to account for channel propagation and carrier detection times.)

The D_{min} and S_{max} values that can be calculated from the entries in Table 3-1 indicate that generally the delay-throughput curves of a linear search technique and a contention technique cross each other as shown in Figure 3-3. (The comparison between linear search and tree search is similar.) The exact crossover point which determines which technique is better over a wider range of channel utilization depends on specific network parameters. A protocol that switches between contention and linear search (or between tree search and linear search) at the crossover point will get close to optimum performance.

To obtain the complete throughput-delay performance curve of a multiple access protocol requires a detailed mathematical analysis using queueing-theoretic or Markovian models. However, the D_{min} and S_{max} values of a protocol

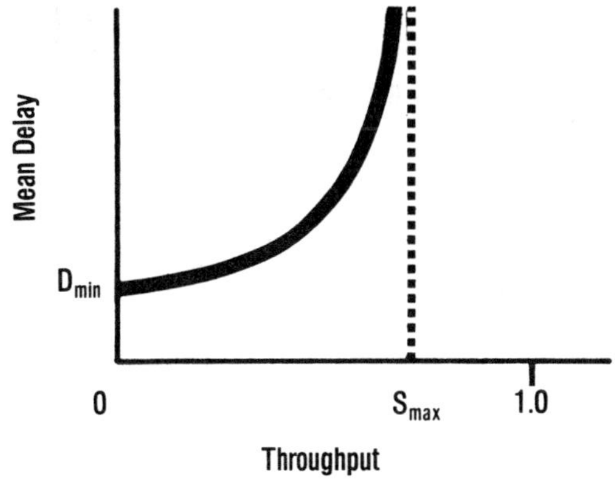

Figure 3-2. General delay-throughput performance characteristic of a multiple access protocol.

as calculated above are often adequate as an indication of a protocol's performance for many practical purposes.

3.3.2. Techniques to Enhance Performance

Suppose that data units offered by users for transmission in the broadcast channel are much longer than the duration of a time slot or a query used in the methods for identifying ready users. In this case, the throughput of the broadcast channel can be substantially increased with either the incorporation of a *reservation* protocol [ROBE 73, TOBA 76, CHU 78, JACO 78] or a *deference* protocol [CROW 73, KLEI 75b, METC 76, LAM 80c].

Reservation

Roberts [ROBE 73] described the first reservation protocol. In his protocol, the broadcast channel is time-multiplexed into two subchannels: a subchannel for reservation requests and a subchannel for data units. The request subchannel is accessed using a contention protocol. Data units belonging to successfully broadcasted requests join a (logical) queue to await transmission in the data subchannel. The maximum throughput of this protocol is high because the maximum throughput of the data subchannel is unity. Robert's protocol inspired the class of PODA protocols for satellite packet switching described in [CHU 78, JACO 78, CHU 79].

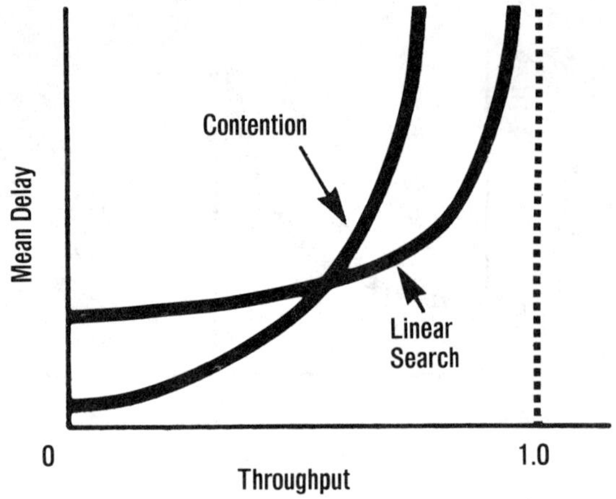

Figure 3-3. Linear search versus contention.

Deference

In deference protocols, the broadcast channel alternates between *search periods* and *transmission periods*. A search period corresponds to the time taken by a multiple access protocol to find a ready user. It is terminated as soon as a ready user is identified; transmission of the ready user's data unit(s) immediately follows. During this transmission period, all other users are required to keep quiet, i.e., to defer to the ongoing transmission. It is clear that the channel throughput is given by the ratio

$$\frac{\text{mean transmission period}}{\text{mean search period} + \text{mean transmission period}}$$

and can be made arbitrarily close to unity by having very long transmission periods (i.e. very large data units or maintaining very long queues at the users).

Deference can be easily implemented in a local area network environment with short propagation delays. Users are required to sense the presence of any ongoing transmission in the channel (carrier sensing) and to keep quiet until the transmission terminates. Any of the multiple access techniques can be used in search periods. However the CSMA protocol [TOBA 74, KLEI 75b, HANS 79] and the CSMA/CD protocol [METC 76], both based upon the use of contention in search periods, are the most well known. The use of collision detection in CSMA/CD improves channel throughput relative to CSMA by shortening the mean search period. It is interesting to note that if every transmission period in a CSMA/CD channel is shrunk to zero, then the CSMA/CD channel becomes an ALOHA channel.

The idea of deference actually first appeared in the R-ALOHA protocol proposed by Crowther et al. [CROW 73]. R-ALOHA was intended for a satellite channel with long propagation delays. A description of it can also be found in [LAM 83].

Adaptive hybrids

We have already encountered one other method to improve the delay-throughput performance of a broadcast channel, and that is to use a multiple access protocol that adaptively changes from one basic method to another for identifying the ready users. We refer to these protocols as adaptive hybrids. We have seen tree-search protocols that adaptively change to the use of linear search when traffic becomes heavy. The URN protocol changes from contention to linear search when traffic becomes heavy. On the other hand, the access protocol of Hyperchannel [THOR 75] uses a linear search initially (upon the termination of a transmission period). If a linear search of all users did not turn up a ready user, then the protocol switches to the use of contention (i.e., it switches to contention when traffic becomes light).

A local network access protocol described in [LAM 80b] also uses a combination of linear search and contention (but not adaptively). In this protocol, users belong to different priority classes. Upon the termination of a transmission period, the protocol performs a linear search of the classes (from high to low priority) to determine the highest priority class with ready users. If there are more than one ready user in this priority class, they compete for channel access by contention.

3.3.3. Performance Analyses

The delay-throughput performance of an

FDMA channel (fixed assigned) can be calculated using classical queueing theory results (e.g., the P-K formula for an M/G/1 queue). For a fixed-assigned TDMA channel, some slight modifications to the classical results are necessary owing to the need to observe time-slot boundaries. (See [LAM 77].)

The model of Konheim and Meister [KOHN 74] was developed for a polling system. Conceptually, their model can be used for any protocol employing a linear-search technique and round-robin scheduling. Equal traffic rates are assumed for all users.

For contention protocols, the Markov chain model developed in [LAM 74, KLEI 75a] for a slotted ALOHA system can predict not only the system's throughput-delay performance but also its stability behavior. A performance analysis of R-ALOHA was given by this author in [LAM 80c]. Performance analyses of CSMA/CD were given by Tobagi and Hunt [TOBA 80b] and this author [LAM 80a] using different analytic methods. Bux [BUX 81] presented a performance comparison of local area networks utilizing the multiple access methods described above. For their throughput-delay performance, he employed the model in [KOHN 74] for linear search, the model in [LAM 80a] for CSMA/CD, and a model of his own for the MLMA tree search technique. Both [BUX 81] and [LAM 80a] are reprinted below.

3.4. PROTOCOLS BASED ON ADVANCED NETWORKING CAPABILITIES

In recent years, many multiple access protocols have been proposed for local area networks based on the implementation of various advanced capabilities in broadcast channels.

In [MOK 79, MARK 80, ESWA 81, FRAT 83], the interconnection bus is made up of separate control wires in addition to a data channel. These control wires provide the capability to resolve access conflicts by a priority mechanism. User priorities are determined either by their addresses [MOK 79, MARK 80] or by their positions on the interconnection bus [ESWA 81, FRAT 83].

In [LI 81, LI 82], an improved protocol is proposed for token-passing on a bus. Each data unit contains a "token direction code" which enables users to detect the direction of the current token scan in the bus. This capability reduces the token-passing delays.

In the EXPRESS-NET proposal [TOBA 80c, FRAT 81], users are connected to directional inbound and outbound channels for receiving and transmitting, respectively. The channels are connected so that all signals in the outbound channel are duplicated in the inbound channel to achieve broadcast communication. The protocol provides a conflict-free, round-robin scheduling. It can guarantee users minimum bandwidth requirements and maximum packet delay constraints (which are essential for voice traffic).

References

[ABRA 70] Abramson, N., "THE ALOHA SYSTEM--Another Alternative for Computer Communications," *AFIPS Conf. Proc.*, Vol. 37, AFIPS Press, Montvale, N. J., 1970, pp. 281-285.

[ABRA 73] Abramson, N., "Packet Switching with Satellites," *AFIPS Conf. Proc.*, Vol. 42, AFIPS Press, Montvale, N. J., 1973, pp. 695-702.

*[BUX 81] Bux, W., "Local Area Subnetworks: A Performance Comparison," *IEEE Trans. on Commun.*, Vol. COM-29, October 1981, pp. 1465-1473.

[CAPE 77] Capetanakis, J. I., "The Multiple Access Broadcast Channel: Protocol and Capacity Considerations," Ph.D. dissertation, Department of Electrical Engineering and Computer Science, MIT, August 1977.

*[CAPE 79] Capetanakis, J. I., "Generalized TDMA: The Multi-Accessing Tree Protocol," *IEEE Trans. Commun.*, October 1979.

[CHLA 79] Chlamtac, I., W. R. Franta, and D. Levin, "BRAM: The Broadcast Recognizing Access Method," *IEEE Trans. Commun.*, Vol. COM-27, August 1979, pp. 1183-1190.

[CHU 78] Chu, W. W. and W. E. Naylor, "Measurement and Simulation Results of C-PODA Protocol Performance," *NTC 78 Conf. Rec. Natl. Telecommun. Conf.*, Birmingham, Ala., December 1978.

[CHU 79] Chu, W. W., et al., "Experimental Results on the Packet Satellite Network," *Conf. Rec. National Telecommunications Conference*, Nov. 1979.

[CROW 73] Crowther, W., et al., "A System for Broadcast Communication: Reservation-ALOHA," *Proc. 6th HICCS*, University of Hawaii, Honolulu, January 1973.

[ESWA 81] Eswaran, K. P., G. S. Shedler, and U. C. Hamacher, "Collision-Free Access Control for Computer Communication Bus Networks," *IEEE Trans. on Software Eng.*, November 1981.

[FRAT 81] Fratta, L., F. Borgonovo, and F. A. Tobagi, "The EXPRESS-NET: A Local Area Communication Network Integrating Voice and Data," International Conference on Performance of Data Communication Systems and their Applications, Paris, September 1981.

[FRAT 83] Fratta, L., "An Improved Access Protocol for Data Communication Bus Networks with Control Wire," *Proc. ACM SIGCOMM '83 Symposium*, Univ. of Texas at Austin, March 1983, pp. 219-225.

[GERL 77] Gerla, M., and L. Kleinrock, "Closed Loop Stability Controls for S-ALOHA Satellite Communication," *Proc. 5th Data Commun. Symp.*, Snowbird, Utah, September 1977.

[HANS 79] Hansen, L. W. and M. Schwartz, "An Assigned-Slot Listen-Before-Transmission Protocol for a Multiaccess Data Channel," *IEEE Trans. on Commun.*, Vol. COM-27, No. 6, June 1979.

[HAYE 78] Hayes, J. F., "An Adaptive Technique for Local Distribution," *IEEE Trans. Commun.*, Vol. COM-26, August 1978.

[JACO 78] Jacobs, I. M., R. Binder, and E. V. Hoverstern, "General Purpose Packet Satellite Networks," *Proc. IEEE*, Vol. 66, November 1978.

[KLEI 73] Kleinrock, L., and S. S. Lam, "Packet-Switching in a Slotted Satellite Channel," *AFIPS Conf. Proc.*, Vol. 42, AFIPS Press, Montvale, N.J., 1973, pp. 703-710.

[KLEI 74] Kleinrock, L., and S. S. Lam, "On Stability of Packet Switching in a Random Multi-access Broadcast Channel," 7th Hawaii Int. Conf. Syst. Sci., Honolulu, January 1974; *Proc. Spec. Subconf. on Comput. Nets*, 1974.

*[KLEI 75a] Kleinrock, L., and S. S. Lam, "Packet Switching in a Multiaccess Broadcast Channel: Performance Evaluation," *IEEE Trans. Commun.*, Vol. COM-23, April 1975, pp. 410-423.

[KLEI 75b] Kleinrock, L., and F. A. Tobagi, "Packet Switching in Radio Channels, Part 1: Carrier Sense Multiple Access Models and their Throughput-Delay Characteristics," *IEEE Trans. Commun.*, Vol. COM-23, No. 12, December 1975, pp. 1400-1416.

[KLEI 77] Kleinrock, L., and M. Scholl, "Packet Switching in Radio Channels: New Conflict-Free Multiple Access Schemes for a Small Number of Data Users," *Conf. Rec. Int. Conf. Commun.*, Chicago, June 1977.

*[KLEI 78] Kleinrock L., and Y. Yemini, "An Optimal Adaptive Scheme for Multiple Access Broadcast Communication," *Conf. Rec. ICC '78*, Toronto, June 1978.

[KONH 74] Konheim, A. G., and B. Meister, "Waiting Lines and Times in a System with Polling," *J. ACM*, Vol. 21, July 1974.

[LAM 74] Lam, S. S., "Packet Switching in a Multi-Access Broadcast Channel with Application to Satellite Communication in a Computer Network," Ph.D. dissertation, Computer Science Department, University of California, Los Angeles, March 1974.

[LAM 75a] Lam, S. S., and L. Kleinrock, "Packet Switching in a Multi-Access Broadcast Channel: Dynamic Control Procedures," *IEEE Trans. Commun.*, Vol. COM-23, September 1975, pp. 891-904.

*[LAM 75b] Lam, S. S., and L. Kleinrock, "Dynamic Control Schemes for a Packet Switched Multi-Access Broadcast Channel," *AFIPS Conf. Proc.*, Vol. 44, AFIPS Press, Montvale, N.J., 1975, pp. 143-153.

[LAM 77] Lam, S. S., "Delay Analysis of a Time Division Multiple Access (TDMA) Channel," *IEEE Trans. Commun.*, Vol. COM-25, December 1977, pp. 1489-1494.

[LAM 78] Lam, S. S., "A New Measure for Characterizing Data Traffic," *IEEE Trans. Commun.*, Vol. COM-26, January 1978.

[LAM 79] Lam, S. S., "Satellite Packet Communication--Multiple Access Protocols and Performance," *IEEE Trans. Commun.*, October 1979.

*[LAM 80a] Lam, S. S., "A Carrier Sense Multiple Access Protocol for Local Networks," *Comput. Networks*, Vol. 4, No. 1, February 1980, pp. 21-32.

[LAM 80b] Lam, S. S., "A Packet Network Architecture for Local Interconnection," *Conf. Rec. Int. Conf. Commun.*, Seattle, June 1980.

[LAM 80c] Lam, S. S., "Packet Broadcast Networks--A Performance Analysis of the R-ALOHA Protocol," *IEEE Trans. Comput.*, July 1980.

*[LAM 83] Lam, S. S., "Multiple Access Protocols," Chapter 4 in *Computer Communications, Vol. I:* Principles, W. Chou (ed.), Prentice-Hall, Englewood Cliffs N.J., 1983.

[LI 81] Li, L., and H. D. Hughes, "Definition and Analysis of a New Protocol," *Proc. 6th Conf. on Local Computer Networks*, Minneapolis, October 1981, pp. 21-29.

[LI 82] Li, L., H. D. Hughes, and L. H. Greenberg, "Performance Analysis of a Shortest-Delay Protocol," *Proc. 6th Berkeley Workshop on Distributed Data Management and Computer Networks*, February 1982, pp. 259-282.

[MARK 80] Mark, J. W., "Distributed Scheduling Conflict-Free Multiple Access for Local Area Communication Networks," *IEEE Trans. on Commun.*, Vol. COM-28, December 1980, pp. 1968-1976.

[MOK 79] Mok, A. K. and S. A. Ward, "Distributed Broadcast Channel Access," *Computer Networks*, Vol. 3, 1979, pp. 327-335.

[METC 76] Metcalfe, R. M., and D. R. Boggs, "Ethernet: Distributed Packet Switching for Local Computer Networks," *Commun. ACM,* Vol. 19, No. 7, July 1976.

[ROBE 73] Roberts, L., "Dynamic Allocation of Satellite Capacity through Packet Reservation," *AFIPS Conf. Proc.*, Vol. 42, AFIPS Press, Montvale, N.J., 1973, pp. 711-716.

[ROBE 75] Roberts, L. G., "ALOHA Packet System with and without Slots and Capture," ARPANET Satellite System Note 8, (NIC 11290), June 1972; reprinted in *Comput. Commun. Rev.*, Vol. 5, April 1975.

[ROTH 77] Rothauser, E. H., and D. Wild, "MLMA--A Collision-Free Multi-Access Method," *Proc. IFIP Congr. 77*, 1977, pp. 431-436.

[THOR 75] Thornton, J. E., et al., "A New Approach to Network Storage Management," *Computer Design*, November 1975.

[TOBA 74] Tobagi, F. A., "Random Access Techniques for Data Transmission over Packet Switched Radio Networks," Ph.D. Dissertation, Department of Comp. Sci., UCLA, December 1974.

[TOBA 76] Tobagi, F. A., and L. Kleinrock, "Packet Switching in Radio Channels: Part III. Polling and (Dynamic) Split-Channel Reservation Multiple Access," *IEEE Trans. Commun.*, Vol. COM-24, No. 8, August 1976, pp. 832-845.

[TOBA 80a] Tobagi, F. A., "Multiaccess Protocols in Packet Communication Systems," *IEEE Trans. Comm.* Vol. COM-28, No. 4, April 1980, pp. 468-488.

[TOBA 80b] Tobagi, F. A., and V. B. Hunt, "Performance Analysis of Carrier Sense Multiple Access with Collision Detection." *Computer Networks*, Vol. 4, No. 5, 1980, pp. 245-259.

[TOBA 80c] Tobagi, F. A., F. Borgonovo, and L. Fratta, "The EXPRESS-NET: A Local Area Communication Network Integrating Voice and Data," Technical Report No. 220, Computer Systems Lab., Stanford University, December 1980.

(* article reprinted below.)

Multiple Access Protocols

SIMON S. LAM
The University of Texas at Austin
Austin, Texas

4.1 INTRODUCTION

Packet-broadcasting networks may be defined as packet-switching networks in which the connectivity requirements of the network users are furnished by a broadcast medium (channel). Two examples of broadcast media are satellite and terrestrial radio channels. A less obvious example is that of a multipoint cable. Although multipoint networks have been in use for many years as broadcast networks, it was the ALOHANET using radio channels and a novel contention protocol [ABRA 70, BIND 75a] that first called attention to the concept of packet broadcasting as we know it now. This concept clearly emerged with the packet satellite project [ABRA 73, KLEI 73, ROBE 73, CROW 73, BUTT 74, JACO 77, JACO 78, WEIS 78] and the packet radio project [KAHN 77, KAHN 78] of the Advanced Research Projects Agency. Currently, packet broadcasting networks appear to be important in two areas. The first is satellite data networks. The rapid pace of development of commercial satellite systems in recent years has enabled substantial reductions in satellite system costs [ABRA 75]. Meanwhile, another marketplace is expanding rapidly: local area networks, which although outside the computer room, are confined to local environments (e.g., office complex, manufacturing plant, etc.). Such networks, based on CATV technology, are said to offer real advantages to computing facilities which serve many terminals and/or employ distributed processing [WILL 74, THOR 75, DEMA 76, METC 76, WEST 78]. An extensive bibliography of local computer networks can be found in [CLAR 78, THUR 79].

Of interest in this chapter are protocols for sharing a single broadcast channel by a population of users. The users have random traffic requirements as well as delay constraints. The central problem is that of *conflict resolution* among users desiring channel access. The methods for conflict resolution will be referred to as *multiple access protocols*. We present a classification of such protocols, illustrate each class with description of specific protocols, and compare their performance under various traffic and channel assumptions. To delimit the scope of this chapter, we consider only networks in which everyone in the population of users can "hear" everyone else over the broadcast channel (i.e., we have a one-hop broadcast network). Multi-hop networks with packet repeaters such as those described in [KAHN 78, LAM 80b] are not considered.

The key measure of performance of a multiple access (MA) protocol is its channel throughput versus average delay trade-off characteristic. The throughput of a channel is defined as follows. Let C be the channel transmission rate in bits per second (bps) and let there be on the average P bits in a transmitted block of data. The *channel throughput* S is defined to be the ratio of the rate of successfully transmitted data blocks to the rate C/P. Thus channel throughput is a normalized quantity between 0 and 1. It includes as useful throughput overhead bits contained in data blocks for bit synchronization, addressing, error control, and other network control functions; these overheads are not, however, directly attributable to the MA protocol. Other overheads that are directly attributable to the implementation of an MA protocol are accounted for in the calculation of channel throughput; the maximum achievable channel throughput is thus less than 1 and is of interest as a gross measure of performance.

We next discuss briefly traditional multiple access protocols which are channel-oriented rather than packet-oriented (of interest here). A model for characterizing traffic sources is then presented. Following that, the characteristics of different categories of multiple access protocols are surveyed. Specific protocols and their performance are examined in some detail in Secs. 4.2, 4.3, and 4.4.

4.1.1 Traditional Techniques

The problem of multiple access in the design of satellite systems, for example, has been solved in the past with voice communications in mind. The design objective is to maximize the number of (voice-grade) channels for given constraints of power and bandwidth. The common satellite multiple access techniques are frequency-division multiple access (FDMA), time-division multiple access (TDMA), and code-division multiple access (CDMA) [SCHW 73]. CDMA is also called spread-spectrum multiple access. It is by far the least efficient and has been used mainly for military systems with antijam and security requirements. TDMA is generally more efficient than FDMA; the price paid is an increase in the cost and complexity of the equipment of each user [PRIT 77].

Multiple access protocols have traditionally been channel-oriented. The transmission capacity available is subdivided into separate channels (with FDMA or TDMA). The basic unit for allocation is thus a channel. Channels can be either (1) fixed assigned, or (2) demand assigned to users. With demand assignment, a channel needs to be set aside for signaling among users. (Access to the signaling channel is another multiple access problem! A typical solution for this is TDMA with fixed assignment.) Demand assignment can then be accomplished with either a central controller or a distributed control algorithm [PRIT 77, PUEN 71].

The channel-oriented MA protocols are suitable for voice traffic and may also be suitable for some data traffic. Data communications in general, however, have very diverse requirements, ranging from inquiry–response systems with intermittent traffic to file transfers with large volumes of data. In this chapter we are interested mainly in the class of new packet-oriented MA protocols for time sharing a single broadcast channel. The broadcast channel under consideration for the shared use of a population of users may possibly have been derived at a higher level of resource allocation via FDMA, TDMA, or CDMA. (The allocation scheme at this level will be of no concern to us.) We concentrate on the conflict resolution aspect of the multiple access problem and its performance in terms of throughput and delay. Other aspects of the multiple access problem (such as modulation, coding, and clock synchronization) are classical problems and are beyond the scope of this chapter; see, for example, [ELLI 73, JACO 74, GARD 80].

4.1.2 Traffic Model

The following model will be used to represent the traffic characteristics and transmission requirements of users of a message (or packet)-oriented communication network. Examples of users are human operators of computer terminals, computer programs interacting with such human operators or with other programs/data bases in other machines, and data concentrators for a multiplicity of such traffic sources. We view a user simply as a traffic source that can be modeled as a random point process with instants of message arrivals being the points of interest. A message is defined to be a block of data that has a time-delay constraint associated with it for delivery to a destination user. (In a packet-oriented network, a message may be transported in one or more packets.) The definition above is quite general. For example, a message may be a computer data file that needs to be delivered within a period of hours. It may be a line of characters in an inquiry–response system that needs to be delivered in a fraction of a second. It may be a digital voice sample (8 bits) that has a delay constraint dictated by the real-time voice sampling rate (e.g., 8000 samples per second).

Computer data traffic sources are often described as "bursty." Traffic burstiness is an important characteristic that influences the design of packet communication systems. This concept is briefly reviewed and a quantitative measure of burstiness, called the *bursty factor*, as defined in [LAM 78A], is presented below.

The bursty nature of a data traffic source stems from more than just randomness in message generation time and size. The user-specified message delay constraints to be met for these traffic sources are actually the single most important factor in determining if data traffic sources behave in a bursty manner. Suppose that we are given a traffic source with

$$T = \text{average interarrival time between messages}$$

and

$$\delta = \text{average message delay constraint}$$

where δ can be estimated in practice from the performance specifications of the intended network users. Generally, a user-specified source–destination delay constraint can be broken up into several parts, each part becoming a constraint for a segment of the communication path. δ is defined here to be the constraint for the message transmission time plus any necessary conflict resolution and queueing delays; it excludes, however, propagation delays through the network as well as message-processing delays at the source and destination.

The bursty factor β of the traffic source is defined to be

$$\beta = \frac{\delta}{T} \tag{4.1}$$

Note that β depends only on δ and T, which are inherent user characteristics. (The delay constraint δ is indeed an inherent source characteristic in the eyes of the network designer. Failing to satisfy it means that the user will take his business elsewhere!) Next consider a traffic source that is formed by merging together N sources with different statistics and delay constraints. The bursty factor of the aggregate source is defined to be the sum of the bursty factors of the individual sources:

$$\beta = \beta_1 + \beta_2 + \ldots + \beta_N \tag{4.2}$$

The usefulness of β is due to the following observation [LAM 78A]. Suppose that a communication channel is dedicated to a traffic source with bursty factor β and that all delay constraints are met. Then the resulting ratio of peak to average channel data rates (PAR) satisfies

$$\text{PAR} \geq \frac{1}{\beta} \tag{4.3}$$

and the channel throughput S satisfies

$$S \leq \beta \tag{4.4}$$

In other words, β gives an upper bound on the duty cycle of a traffic source. This information is useful to the network designer and is available independent of the communication system eventually provided. A traffic source with a small β ($\ll 1$) is said to be *bursty*.

The result above also says that for bursty users, channel-oriented MA protocols using either fixed assignment or demand assignment (over a period of time $\gg \delta$) are going to be very inefficient ($S \ll 1$). To improve the throughput of a broadcast channel shared by users with random bursty traffic, it is desirable to dynamically allocate transmission capacity on a per message (or packet) basis. This benefits from the multiplexing effect of Eq. (4.2) as well as the scaling effect of large systems discussed in [KLEI 76, sec. 5.1]. The key to realizing these gains is to design MA protocols for resolving channel-access conflicts without excessive overhead.

We note that the definition of bursty factor in Eq. (4.1) does not involve the

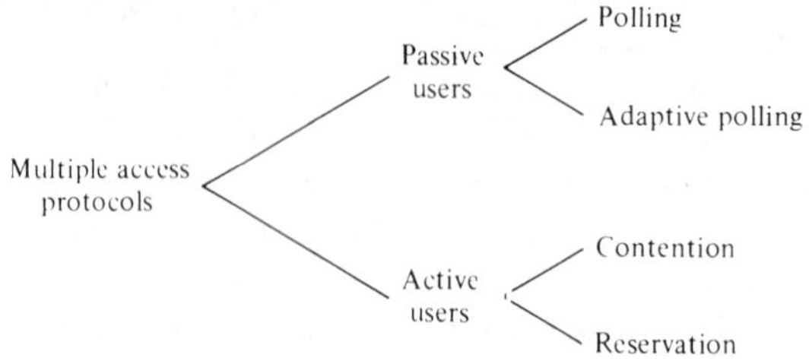

Figure 4.1. Classification of multiple access protocols.

average length of messages generated by a traffic source. Thus it is possible for a traffic source to generate very long messages but is still considered to be very bursty by definition. This average-message-length parameter, we shall see, also strongly affects the performance of MA protocols.

4.1.3 Network Assumptions

We consider a population of N users sharing use of a single broadcast channel. The ith user has a message generation rate of λ_i messages per second. Each message may give rise to one or more fixed-length packets with a mean number of L. Each packet carries a destination address so that when the packet is transmitted over the channel, with no interference from another user, it will be received by the proper addressee(s). Errors due to channel noise will be ignored. Such errors affect MA protocols equally and their effect can be evaluated separately. Notice that the specific connectivity requirements of the population of users are relevant only indirectly through the resulting set of message rates. Given the set of λ_i, it does not matter, for example, whether users want to communicate with each other or they all want to talk to a specific central site. Thus our only concern is the access problem of the broadcast channel.

Each user is capable of sending and receiving data at the channel transmission rate of C bps. In a number of MA protocols, the users are time synchronized so that the channel can be viewed as a sequence of time slots (just as in TDMA). Each time slot can accommodate one data packet. Minislots may also be interleaved with the data slots to accommodate small control packets.

When given access to the broadcast channel, a user can send data to any other user. Thus the MA protocol is simply an algorithm (possibly distributed as well as nondeterministic) for determining the channel-access rights of the users. In some protocols, the access right is not uniquely determined and it is possible for packet transmissions from different users to "collide" in the channel. It is assumed that the collisions are always destructive and that none of the packets involved in a collision can be correctly received. Each packet contains parity bits for error detection.

Suppose that it takes R seconds following a packet transmission for a user to find out whether it suffered a collision. R will be referred to as the *collision detection time*. In many systems [ABRA 73, METC 76], the user can find out the outcome of a transmission for himself by monitoring the broadcast channel. In this case, R is approximately equal to the propagation delay of the channel. (The propagation delay is always taken to be the maximum value between any pair of sender and receiver in the network.) If this collision detection mechanism is not possible, then R corresponds to the timeout period of a positive acknowledgment protocol [ABRA 70, BIND 75A].

4.1.4 A Classification of Protocols

The gamut of packet-oriented MA protocols can be classified as shown in Fig. 4.1 and may be illustrated by the following analogy.* Consider a group of students in a

*Another way to classify MA protocols, discussed in [LAM 80A] is to think of users desiring channel access as customers forming a distributed queue. The objective of a MA protocol is to identify such customers.

classroom who want to say something. Assume that if two or more students talk at the same time, the resulting speech will be unintelligible.

Passive versus Active Talkers

The students may be "passive." A student will talk only when specifically asked to do so by a teacher acting as a central controller. The teacher determines who wants to talk by polling the students one by one. Or the students may be "active." Whoever has something to say will try to do something about getting the opportunity to talk. Among protocols for active talkers, we further differentiate between two categories as follows.

Contention versus Reservation Protocols

Under a contention protocol, there is no attempt to coordinate the talkers. Each student tries to talk whenever he has something to say. In doing so, he might exercise some caution to try to minimize interference with other talkers by observing past activities in the room. The alternative is to use reservation protocols which may use one of the following two types of control.

Centralized versus Distributed Control

Under a reservation protocol, each student who wants to talk raises his hand to signal a request to talk. A teacher may be present to serve as a central controller to determine who should talk next. Alternatively, each student monitors the requests of all students and exercises a distributed algorithm to determine who should talk next.

In the next three sections we illustrate each class of protocols introduced above with descriptions of specific protocols. Performance implications of various channel and traffic parameters are discussed. In particular, a number of the protocols rely upon a short channel propagation delay for their efficiency and are thus not suitable for satellite channels.

4.2 PROTOCOLS FOR PASSIVE USERS

This class of protocols is commonly known as *polling protocols*. The presence of a central controller is required. Users are passive in the sense that they may access the channel only when specifically polled by the central controller. The controller has two functions: (1) to identify users with data to send (the *ready users*), and (2) to schedule use of the channel by these users.

4.2.1 Conventional Polling Protocols

In conventional polling protocols, the central controller performs the foregoing two functions by polling the population of users one after the other. Upon the arrival of a polling message, the user polled transmits all messages accumulated in his buffer. The time needed to poll every user once and transmit their accumulated data is said to be the polling cycle time t_c. This is just the time between successive polls of a specific user.

A very important parameter determining the efficiency of polling protocols is the total "walk time" in a polling cycle. This is the portion of cycle time attributable to necessary overheads such as channel propagation delay, transmission time of polling and response messages, modem synchronization time, and so on. A detailed breakdown of time elements in a polling cycle can be found in [MART 72].

Minor implementation variations of the foregoing description exist, such as, prioritized polling list, some users polled more than once in a cycle, the amount of data that a user can transmit at a time is limited, and others [MART 72]. These will not be considered.

The two conventional polling protocols most widely used are: roll-call polling and hub polling [SCHW 77, chap. 12]. In *roll-call polling*, the central controller sends a polling message to the user polled. The user transmits his waiting data (if any) and passes control back to the central controller before the next user is polled. In *hub polling*, the central controller initiates a polling cycle by polling the user at the top of its polling list. The user transmits his waiting data (if any) and passes the polling message on to the next user directly. The user at the bottom of the list passes control back to the central controller to complete a polling cycle. The obvious advantage of hub polling over roll-call polling is that the average walk time $\bar{w}$ between users is typically less. However, the individual users need to be more intelligent and reliable than those of roll-call polling.

To illustrate the key performance trade-offs in the design of polling protocols, we consider here some results from a queueing model of N identical users [KONH 74]. The same model applies to both roll-call and hub polling. (A detailed analysis of polling that takes into account various system features and response-time elements can be found in [CHOU 78].)

Suppose that each user has an arrival rate of λ messages per second and an average message transmission time of $1/\mu$ sec.

Define

$$\rho = \frac{\lambda}{\mu}$$

Let $\bar{w}$ be the average walk time between users and $\bar{t}_c$ be the average cycle time. Then it can be shown that [KONH 74]

$$\bar{t}_c = \frac{N\bar{w}}{1 - N\rho} \tag{4.5}$$

The waiting time of a message is defined here to be the interval from its time of arrival to the start of its transmission. An expression for the average waiting time W is derived in [KONH 74]. It can be easily shown that

$$W \geq \frac{\bar{t}_c}{2}(1 - \rho)$$

Thus the simple expression in Eq. (4.5) can be used as an indirect measure of the average delay of a message, which is

$$D = W + \frac{1}{\mu}$$

Equation (4.5) has the usual queueing theory form, with $N\rho$ being the traffic intensity of the broadcast channel. We have in the limit $\bar{t}_c \uparrow \infty$ as $N\rho \uparrow 1$. Observe that $\bar{t}_c$ is also directly proportional to the total walk time $N\bar{w}$ in a polling cycle. Consequently, the delay performance may be greatly degraded if $\bar{w}$ is large (e.g., satellite channel) or N is large.

We next consider a performance booby trap of polling protocols. Suppose that N is increased but a higher-speed channel is used such that the channel utilization $N\rho$ remains the same. This change will in general tend to decrease the average delay D as a result of the scaling effect [KLEI 76, sec. 5.1]. However, with a conventional polling protocol, the same change will affect D adversely as well as follows. Increasing N while keeping $N\rho$ constant increases the $\bar{t}_c/2$ portion of the average delay due to the increased polling overhead $N\bar{w}$!

So far we have assumed users with plenty of buffer capacity (i.e., infinite waiting room for queues). Under this assumption the maximum channel throughput of polling is 1 in the limit of infinite queues.

Consider now users that have limited buffering capacity, so that each user can transmit at most one message at a time. One consequence is that $\bar{t}_c$ is always finite. In addition, the channel throughput S can be easily shown to be bounded as follows:

$$S \leq \frac{1/\mu}{\bar{w} + (1/\mu)} \tag{4.6}$$

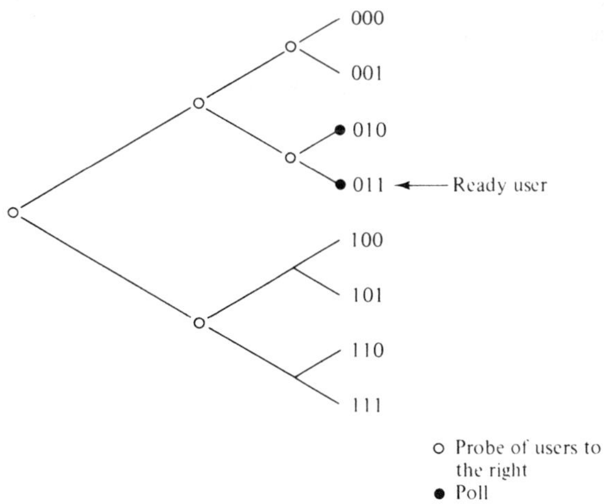

Figure 4.2. Inquiries (probe or poll) needed in an example of eight users.

The upper bound in Eq. (4.6) is the maximum channel throughput of polling for such users. In this case polling becomes extremely inefficient when the traffic consists of very short messages (e.g., terminals doing character-at-a-time transmission [WEST 72]).

4.2.2 Adaptive Polling

With conventional polling, when the network is lightly loaded, it is still necessary to poll every one of the users, although few users are *ready* (have data to send). The mean delay D in this situation is mainly determined by the polling overhead and not by the channel traffic intensity!

For a lightly loaded network, an adaptive polling protocol has been proposed by Hayes [HAYE 78] which significantly reduces the polling overhead. The key idea introduced is called *probing*. When a group of (two or more) users are probed, a polling message is sent by the central controller to all users in the group. Any users with data to send respond by transmitting some signal in the channel. To avoid cancellation by interference, the signal can be some noise energy. Note that if a group of users is probed and none responds, the whole group can be ignored until the next polling cycle. Thus when the network is lightly loaded, significant polling overhead reduction results through probing groups of users. The following implementation is suggested [HAYE 78].

Assume a total of $N = 2^n$ users. Each user is addressed by an n-bit binary number. The central controller can probe a group of users by sending the common prefix of the addresses of the users. At the beginning of each polling cycle, the central controller divides the users into 2^{n-j} groups of 2^j users each. The determination of j will be discussed later. Each of the 2^{n-j} groups is probed separately. If probing a group produces a positive response, each group is divided into two groups, which are then probed separately. This process is repeated until all ready users are identified and serviced.

A poll (of a single user) or a probe (of two or more users) will both be referred to as an *inquiry*. An example is illustrated in Fig. 4.2 with a group of eight users. Only one of them (address 011) is ready. Starting with probing all users ($j = 0$), a total of seven inquiries (five probes and two polls) are needed to complete the polling cycle.

Returning to our general problem, let us consider the following special cases.

Case 1. Pure polling, $j = 0$. The number of inquiries required is 2^n, which is independent of the number of ready users.

Case 2. Pure probing, $j = n$. Pure probing is excellent under very light loading. For instance, if there is exactly one ready user, the number of inquiries is $2n + 1$.

However, pure probing is penalized under heavy loading. If all users are ready, the number of inquiries will be $2^{n+1} - 1$.

From these extreme cases, we see that the group size 2^j to be selected at the beginning of each polling cycle is crucial to the performance of the protocol. It should be chosen to minimize the expected number of inquiries in the current polling cycle. Let

$$p = \text{Prob [a user has data to send in the current polling cycle]}$$

and

$$\bar{I}(j) = E[\text{number of inquiries}/j]$$

We want to determine j^* such that

$$\bar{I}(j^*) = \min_{0 \leq j \leq n} \bar{I}(j)$$

Let us compare the probing of a group of 2^j users and probing two groups of 2^{j-1} users. If we probe 2^j users, the probability that none will respond to the probe is

$$\text{Prob[no response}/j] = (1 - p)^{2^j}$$

In this event, the choice of j instead of $j - 1$ saves one inquiry. On the other hand, in the event that there is a positive response from the group of 2^j users, the choice of j instead of $j - 1$ spends one more inquiry. Thus we have

$$\begin{aligned} \Delta\bar{I}(j) &= \bar{I}(j) - \bar{I}(j - 1) \\ &= 2^{n-j}[(-1)(1 - p)^{2^j} + (1 - (1 - p)^{2^j})] \\ &= 2^{n-j}[1 - 2(1 - p)^{2^j}] \end{aligned}$$

for $j = 1, \ldots, n$. Note that the term $1 - 2(1 - p)^{2^j}$ increases monotonically with j. Thus $\bar{I}(j)$ is minimized by the largest j such that[1]

$$1 - 2(1 - p)^{2^j} < 0$$

or

$$(1 - p)^{2^j} > \frac{1}{2} \tag{4.7}$$

Equation (4.7) tells the central controller how to determine j at the beginning of each polling cycle as a function of p. An estimate of p is

$$p = 1 - e^{-\lambda t_c} \tag{4.8}$$

where λ is the Poisson rate of message arrivals to a user, and t_c is the duration of the last polling cycle. Equation (4.8) assumes that messages arriving during one polling cycle do not respond positively to an inquiry until the next polling cycle. (This gives a pessimistic view of the operation of the system.) From Eqs. (4.7) and (4.8), we have

$$2^j < \frac{\ln 2}{\lambda t_c} \tag{4.9}$$

At the beginning of each polling cycle, the central controller can determine j^* as a function of λ and t_c using Eq. (4.9)

Performance Summary

The mean cycle time for the adaptive polling protocol is still basically Eq. (4.5) but with the polling overhead term $N\overline{w}$ considerably reduced, especially under light loading. For instance, if there is only one ready user in a polling cycle, the number of inquiries is $2(\log_2 N) + 1$ instead of N. The adaptivity in the protocol assures that there

[1]This is a simpler proof than the one found in [HAYE 78]. It is interesting to note that in general if addresses use base m numbers so that each node of the tree in Fig. 4.2 has m branches, the optimality condition is $(1 - p)^{m^j} > 1/m$.

is no penalty during periods of heavy load. These above observations are illustrated in Fig. 4.3, which compares the mean number of inquiries per polling cycle as a function of p for pure polling, pure probing, and the optimum adaptive strategy using Eq. (4.7).

4.3 PROTOCOLS FOR ACTIVE USERS

We consider next two classes of protocols that require ready users to seek channel access actively instead of waiting to be polled. These are called contention and reservation protocols. Under *contention protocols*, there is no attempt to coordinate the ready users to avoid collisions entirely. Instead, each ready user makes his own decision regarding when to access the channel: he exercises caution, however, to minimize interference with other ready users as much as possible. Under *reservation protocols*, a reservation channel is provided for ready users to communicate among themselves such that only one ready user is scheduled for channel access at a time. Since users are geographically distributed, the multiple access problem has not really disappeared; it now exists in the access of the reservation channel for the transmission of small reservation requests.

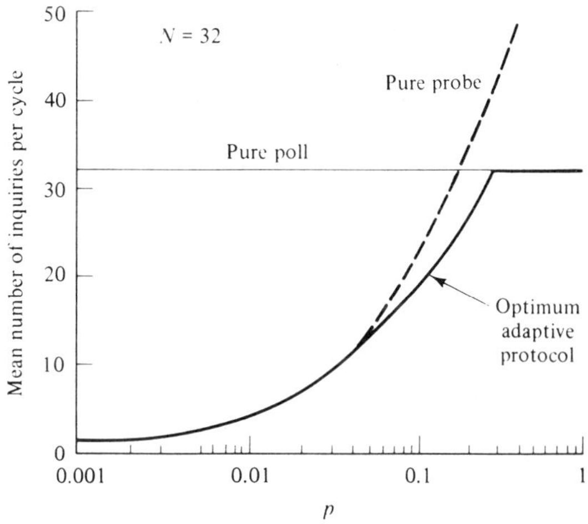

Figure 4.3. Performance of adaptive polling.

4.3.1 Contention Protocols

Unlike polling protocols, the overhead incurred by contention protocols for assigning channel access to ready users is independent of N but instead is dependent on the level of channel traffic. Thus pure contention protocols are suitable for a large population of bursty users (i.e., $N \uparrow \infty$ as $\beta \downarrow 0$ for each user but $N\beta$ remains constant). For a lightly loaded network, the delay performance of contention protocols can be far superior to polling protocols. Below we describe two pure contention protocols (ALOHA and slotted ALOHA), two contention protocols which include elements of reservation (R-ALOHA and CSMA), and an adaptive protocol (URN). We discuss, in the context of slotted ALOHA, the stability problem of contention protocols and the need for adaptive control in these protocols. We then describe a tree algorithm for resolving contention which guarantees channel stability. The algorithm is based on essentially the same idea as that of the adaptive polling algorithm described earlier.

4.3.1.1 The ALOHA Protocol [ABRA 70, BIND 75A]

Under the ALOHA protocol, users are not synchronized in any way. Each user transmits a data packet whenever one is ready. In the event that two or more packets collide (i.e., overlap in time), each user involved realizes this after R seconds (the collision detection time) and retransmits his packet after a randomized delay. As we discuss below, this randomized delay turns out to be crucial to the stability behavior and thus the throughput-delay performance of all contention-based protocols.

In [ABRA 70], Abramson first derived the maximum channel throughput of the ALOHA protocol in the limit of an infinite user population ($N \uparrow \infty$ and for each user $\beta \downarrow 0$). All messages consist of single packets. Hence the aggregate packet "birth process" is a Poisson process at a rate of S packets per packet transmission time.

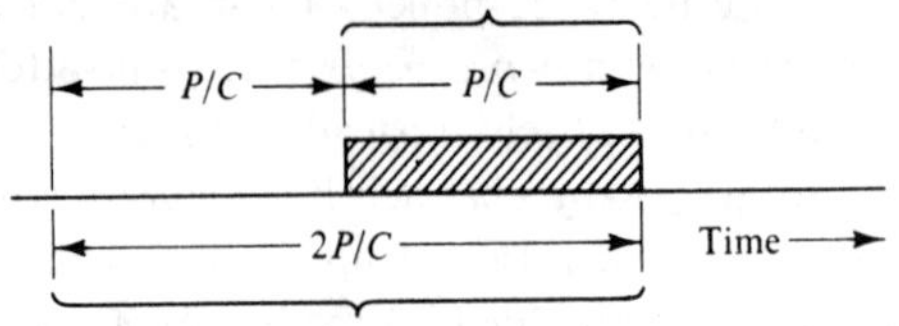

Figure 4.4. ALOHA and slotted ALOHA vulnerable periods of a transmitted packet.

Abramson also made the assumption that the sum of new transmissions and retransmissions in the channel (called *channel traffic*) can be approximated as a Poisson process at a rate of G packets per packet time. Furthermore, statistical equilibrium is assumed. The probability that a transmitted packet is successful is

$$\frac{S}{G} = e^{-2G} \tag{4.10}$$

which is obtained from consideration of Fig. 4.4; each transmitted packet has a vulnerable period of two packet time durations. It will be successful only if no other packet begins transmission within the vulnerable period.

From Eq. (4.10) the maximum possible ALOHA channel throughput is obtained at $G = 0.5$ and for an infinite-user population model (under the foregoing assumptions) is

$$C_A = \frac{1}{2e} \simeq 0.184 \tag{4.11}$$

4.3.1.2 The Slotted ALOHA Protocol [ROBE 72, ABRA 73, KLEI 73]

The slotted ALOHA protocol is just like ALOHA with the additional requirement that the channel is slotted in time. Users are required to synchronize their packet transmissions into fixed-length channel time slots. By requiring synchronization of packet start times, packet collisions due to partial overlaps are avoided and the vulnerable period of a transmitted packet is just the duration of a time slot (see Fig. 4.4). Under the same assumptions given above for ALOHA, we have

$$\frac{S}{G} = e^{-G} \tag{4.12}$$

where S is maximized at $G = 1$. The resulting slotted ALOHA maximum channel throughput for an infinite-user population model is twice that of the unslotted case:

$$C_{SA} = \frac{1}{e} \simeq 0.368 \tag{4.13}$$

Equations (4.10) and (4.12) are plotted in Fig. 4.5.

Two methods of scheduling retransmissions following the detection of a collision have been considered [METC 73, LAM 74]:

1. *Geometrically distributed delay.* A collided packet is retransmitted in a time slot with probability $p < 1$. With probability $1 - p$, the packet is delayed and the

Bernoulli trial is repeated in the next time slot.

2. *Uniformly distributed delay.* A time slot is selected for retransmitting a collided packet from the next K time slots chosen equally likely.

For purposes of performance modeling, simulation studies indicate that in many cases the mean value $\bar{k}$ (instead of the exact probability distribution) of the retransmission delay is sufficient for predicting the behavior of a slotted ALOHA channel [LAM 74].

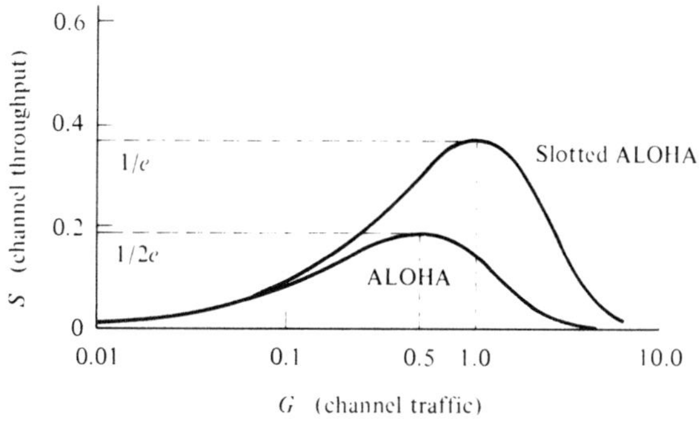

Figure 4.5. ALOHA and slotted ALOHA throughout curves.

4.3.1.3 Performance Considerations

The analysis of ALOHA and slotted ALOHA given above was based upon three assumptions: (A1) statistical independence of channel traffic, (A2) infinite user population, and (A3) statistical equilibrium. More detailed studies of slotted ALOHA investigated the validity of these assumptions. In particular, it was shown that a necessary condition for (A1) is that the mean randomized delay $\bar{k}$ for retransmissions must be large ($\bar{k} \to \infty$). However, simulations showed that the maximum channel throughput results given by Eqs. (4.11) and (4.13) are robust; they are already quite accurate if $N \geq 10$ and $\bar{k} \geq 5$ [KLEI 73, LAM 74]. In these same references, the delay performance of slotted ALOHA was first studied for finite values of $\bar{k}$. When the traffic distribution is unbalanced with a mixture of high-rate as well as low-rate users, it was shown that the slotted ALOHA maximum channel throughput of $1/e$ can be considerably improved [ABRA 73].

The validity of assumption (A3) was also examined. It was shown that the slotted ALOHA protocol, without adaptive control, is potentially unstable [METC 73, LAM 74, KLEI 74, KLEI 75A]. (We might have deduced this from the curves in Fig. 4.5, which show two equilibrium values of G for each value of S!) Statistical fluctuations may cause the channel to drift into a saturation state—the channel is filled up with collisions resulting in zero throughput. For an unstable channel, equilibrium conditions assumed earlier exist only for a finite period of time before channel saturation occurs. A Markov chain formulation of the infinite population slotted ALOHA model shows that it is always unstable, in the sense that a stationary probability distribution does not exist [LAM 74, KLEI 75A, FAYO 77].

Fortunately, N must be finite in a real network. In this case slotted ALOHA channels may exhibit stable or unstable behavior, depending upon the parameters N, $\bar{k}$, and S (channel input rate). In [LAM 74, KLEI 74, KLEI 75A], a theory of channel stability behavior is formulated. Specifically, a method for characterizing stable and unstable channels and a quantitative measure of instability for unstable channels are introduced. A theoretical treatment of the adaptive control of unstable channels using a Markov decision model can be found in [LAM 75A]. Various heuristic control algorithms and their performance are presented in [LAM 75B, LAM 79A, LAM 80A]. Several effective feedback control algorithms are proposed in [GERL 77A]. Simulations showed that these techniques are effective means of achieving stability, for initially unstable channels, at the expense of a small amount of delay-throughput performance degradation relative to lower-bound values.

Control algorithms for preventing channel saturation are based upon one or both of the following mechanisms: (1) reducing the probability of retransmitting a collided packet in a time slot (thus increasing the effective $\bar{k}$), and (2) revoking the access right of some users for a period of time (thus reducing the effective N). These two mechanisms have been referred to as retransmission control and input control, respectively [LAM 74, LAM 75A]. Recall that the slotted ALOHA channel throughput S is maximized when the channel traffic rate is 1. The goal of most adaptive control algorithms is to achieve the $G = 1$ condition in the channel. The main difficulty is the acquisition of global network status information by individual users. If, for example, the total number n of ready users can be made known to individual users instantaneously, then an adaptive strategy for realizing the $G = 1$ condition is to have each ready user transmit into the next time slot with probability $1/n$ (provided that $n \geq 1$).

Next we observe that the delay-throughput performance of contention protocols is not entirely independent of N, as we said earlier. When N is increased (accompanied by a decrease in β), slotted ALOHA channels tend to be less stable [LAM 74, KLEI 75A], which affects the delay-throughput performance. However, this is only a second-order effect.

We have discussed the stability problem and adaptive control techniques within the context of slotted ALOHA, which is a pure contention protocol. However, the stability problem is present in all contention-based protocols (many to be described in this section as well as the next section on reservation protocols) and must not be forgotten.

4.3.1.4 The R-ALOHA Protocol [CROW 73, LAM 78B, LAM 80C]

The traffic environment suitable for ALOHA and slotted ALOHA is that of a large population of low-rate bursty users with short messages (one packet per message). The R-ALOHA protocol was originally proposed by Crowther et al. [CROW 73] and is suitable for users who generate long multipacket messages or users with steady input traffic and queueing capability.

The R-ALOHA protocol requires, in addition to time slotting, that time slots are organized into frames. Time slots are identified by their positions in the frame. The duration of a frame must be greater than the maximum channel propagation time between any two users in the network. (This is of concern in practice only for a satellite channel.) Consequently, each user is aware of the usage status of time slots in the previous frame. The network operates without any central control but requires each user to execute the same set of rules for transmitting packets into a time slot depending on the outcome in the same time slot of the previous frame.

A time slot in the previous frame is *unused* if it was empty or contained a collision. Slots unused in the previous frame are available for contention by ready users in exactly the same manner as slotted ALOHA. A slot that had a successful transmission by a user in the previous frame is *used* and is reserved for the same user in the current frame. As a result, such a user now has the equivalent of an assigned TDMA channel for as long as he has traffic to send in it.

We further differentiate between two slightly different protocols depending on whether an end-of-use flag is included in the header of the last packet before a user gives up his reserved slot:

(P1) end-of-use flag not included

(P2) end-of-use flag included

Under (P1), a time slot is always wasted when a user gives up his reserved slot. The trade-off for adopting (P2) is some additional packet processing overhead by each user.

Under the assumption of equilibrium conditions, the channel throughput S_{RA} of R-ALOHA can be expressed in terms of the slotted ALOHA throughput S_{SA} for the contention portion of the channel [LAM 80C]:

$$S_{RA} = \frac{S_{SA}}{S_{SA} + 1/\bar{v}} \qquad \text{under (P1)}$$

or

$$S_{RA} = \frac{S_{SA}}{S_{SA} + [(1 - S_{SA})/\bar{v}]} \qquad \text{under (P2)} \tag{4.14}$$

where $\bar{v}$ is the average number of packets that a user transmits before he gives up a

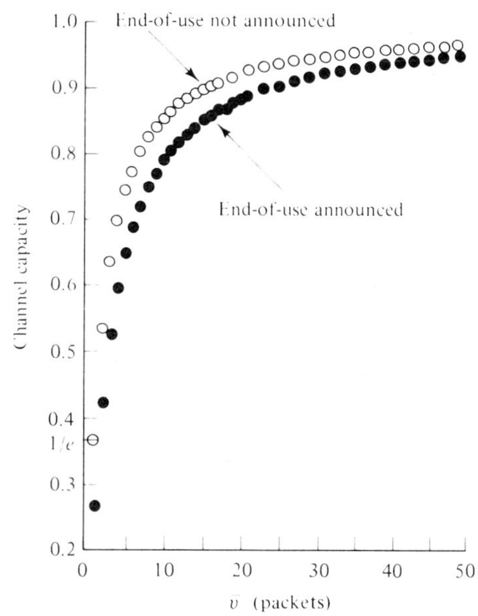

Figure 4.6. Maximum channel throughput versus v for R-ALOHA.

reserved slot. Note that S_{RA} is a monotonic function of S_{SA}, so that the maximum channel throughput of R-ALOHA is

$$C_{RA} = \frac{C_{SA}}{C_{SA} + 1/\bar{v}} \qquad \text{under (P1)}$$

or

$$C_{RA} = \frac{C_{SA}}{C_{SA} + [(1 - C_{SA})/\bar{v}]} \qquad \text{under (P2)}$$

Assuming that $C_{SA} = 1/e$, C_{RA} is plotted in Fig. 4.6 as a function of $\bar{v}$. Note that $\bar{v}$ range from 1 to infinity; thus we have

$$\frac{1}{1+e} \leq C_{RA} \leq 1 \qquad \text{under (P1)}$$

or

$$\frac{1}{e} \leq C_{RA} \leq 1 \qquad \text{under (P2)}$$

Notice that the R-ALOHA protocol adapts itself to the nature of the traffic. At one extreme, it behaves like slotted ALOHA when the users are bursty ($\bar{v} = 1$). At the other extreme, the channel throughput of R-ALOHA approaches 1 in the $\bar{v} \to \infty$ limit; this is the case for high-rate users who can accommodate very long queues. The reader is referred to [LAM 78B, LAM 79A, LAM 80C] for a queueing and message delay analysis of R-ALOHA as well as simulation results.

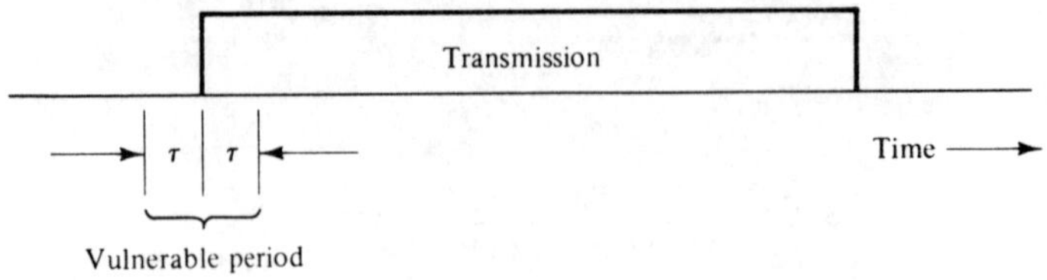

Figure 4.7. Unslotted CSMA vulnerable period.

4.3.1.5 CSMA Protocols [TOBA 74, KLEI 75B, METC 76, HANS 77, LAM 79B, LAM 80A, TOBA 79]

For broadcast channels with a *short propagation delay*, collisions in the channel can be significantly reduced by requiring each user to sense the channel for the presence of any ongoing transmission before accessing it, hence the name Carrier-Sense Multiple Access (CSMA). A ready user (user with data to send) transmits his data into the channel only if the channel has been sensed idle. Let τ seconds be the amount of time from the start of transmission by one user to when all users sense the presence of this transmission. It is equal to the maximum propagation delay between two users in the network plus carrier detection time. (The latter depends on the modulation technique and channel bandwidth. It was found to be negligible relative to the propagation delay in some cases [KLEI 75B].)

Given that a user sensed the channel to be idle and began a transmission, the vulnerable period of that transmission to collisions is 2τ seconds (see Fig. 4.7). In a short propagation delay environment, this vulnerable period is significantly smaller that those of ALOHA and slotted ALOHA. The channel may also be slotted into minislots of duration τ seconds each, thereby reducing the vulnerable period further to just τ seconds. (Note, however, that τ is the absolute minimum time-slot duration. A larger value is necessary in practice. The reader is referred to [ELLI 73, GARD 80] for a discussion of some techniques for time-synchronizing distributed users.)

Suppose that $\bar{x}$ is the average duration of a successful transmission. The maximum channel throughput of a CSMA protocol depends strongly upon the ratio

$$\alpha = \tau/\bar{x}$$

Specifically, we find out below that C_{CSMA} goes up to 1 if α is decreased to zero (by either letting $\tau \downarrow 0$ or $\bar{x} \uparrow \infty$; see below).

CSMA protocols have been studied extensively in the past within a packet radio network environment by Kleinrock and Tobagi [KLEI 75B, TOBA 74] and later by Hansen and Schwartz [HANS 77]. CSMA protocols were also implemented and analyzed within a multipoint cable network environment [METC 76, WEST 78,

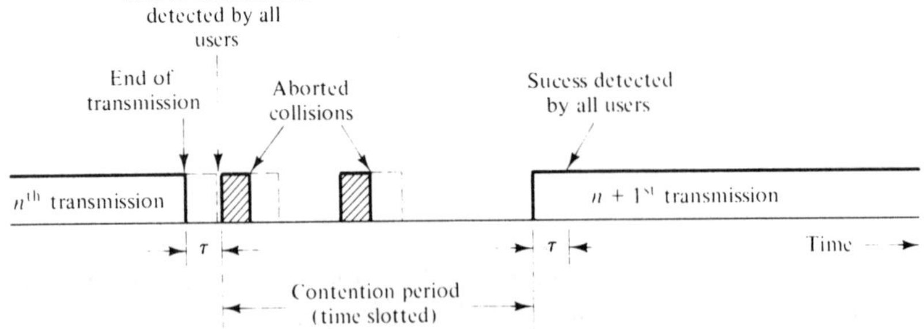

Figure 4.8. Illustration of the CSMA protocol.

LAM 79B, LAM 80A, TOBA 79]. The main difference between the two environments is as follows. In cable networks, collisions in the broadcast channel can be detected easily. Thus users involved in a collision can abort their transmissions immediately upon detecting the collision. Mechanisms for detecting collisions and aborting transmissions have been implemented in at least two networks [METC 76, WEST 78]. It appears, however, that this "collision abort" capability is not easily implementable in packet radio networks of interest in [TOBA 74, KLEI 75B].

We present next the CSMA protocol defined and analyzed in [LAM 80A] This particular version of CSMA clearly shows the relationship of CSMA to the slotted ALOHA protocol (in pretty much the same manner as R-ALOHA is related to slotted ALOHA). The analysis of this CSMA protocol is fairly complete. In addition to maximum channel throughput, explicit formulas for average message delay as well as the moment generating function of the number of ready users are available.

A description of the protocol follows; (see also Fig. 4.8). Network users are time synchronized so that following each successful transmission, the channel is slotted in time. To implement the collision abort capability discussed above, the minimum duration of a time slot is 2τ, so that within a time slot if a collision is detected and the collided transmissions are aborted immediately, the channel will be clear of any transmission at the beginning of the next time slot. (In practice, the duration of a time slot needs to be larger than 2τ. The slotted channel assumption is made mainly to facilitate the analysis. In a real network, either a slotted or unslotted channel may be implemented.) The protocol is defined by the two possible courses of action by ready users:

(C1) Following a successful transmission, each ready user transmits with probability 1 into the next time slot.

(C2) Upon detection of a collision, each ready user exercises an adaptive algorithm for selecting its transmission probability (less than 1) in the next time slot.

The adaptive algorithm in (C2) is not specified. Howevewever, it should be clear that the contention problem in the minislots is exactly the slotted ALOHA problem. An adaptive control algorithm (such as those considered for slotted ALOHA) is needed to guarantee that a successful transmission occurs within a finite number of slots following a collision. The first successful transmission terminates the contention period (see Fig. 4.8).

The maximum channel throughput of the CSMA protocol defined can be obtained as a function of the equilibrium slotted ALOHA throughput S_{SA}. Let C_{SA} be the maximum achievable value of S_{SA}. It is shown in [LAM 80A] that

$$C_{CSMA} = \frac{C_{SA}}{2\alpha + C_{SA}(1 + \alpha)} \tag{4.15}$$

We note that C_{CSMA} is equal to one in the $\alpha \downarrow 0$ limit. Recall that $\alpha = \tau/\bar{x}$. In both ground radio and cable environments, τ is typically very short, say 0.001 to 0.1 of a packet transmission time. Furthermore, if we consider users who are capable of accommodating long queues, so that $\bar{x}$ is now the average time to empty a user's queue instead of a single packet transmission time, the channel throughput will be one in the $\bar{x} \to \infty$ limit.

The CSMA protocol defined above has the desirable property that when the channel is lightly utilized, the delay in identifying and assigning channel access to a ready user is extremely short and is independent of N (unlike polling and probing, considered earlier also for a short-propagation-delay environment). In particular, when there is exactly one ready user, the delay is zero.

In Fig. 4.9 we plot the fraction of transmissions that incur zero delay in gaining channel access (given that the channel is free) as a function of α and channel throughput. These are analytic results obtained with $S_{SA} = 1/e$ in [LAM 80A], where a queueing and message delay analysis of the foregoing CSMA protocol can be found. A comparison of the delay-throughput performance of CSMA and polling is shown in Fig. 4.14 and discussed in Sec. 4.4. The stability problem and adaptive control of CSMA have also been addressed [TOBA 77, HANS 77]. An alternative method of solution to these problems is to view the contention periods as a slotted ALOHA channel; this is the approach taken here as well as in [METC 76].

4.3.1.6 *The URN Protocol* [KLEI 78, YEMI 78]

The slotted ALOHA protocol is an important component of both R-ALOHA and CSMA protocols. We also learned earlier that the slotted ALOHA protocol needs to be adaptively controlled. Furthermore, the goal of most adaptive control algorithms is to achieve the $G = 1$ condition in the channel. Let us assume for the moment that the number n of ready users at any time is in fact known to individual users instantaneously. (We discuss later how to estimate n.) Then an adaptive strategy for achieving the $G = 1$ condition is to have each ready user transmit into the next time slot with probability $1/n$, where $n \geq 1$.

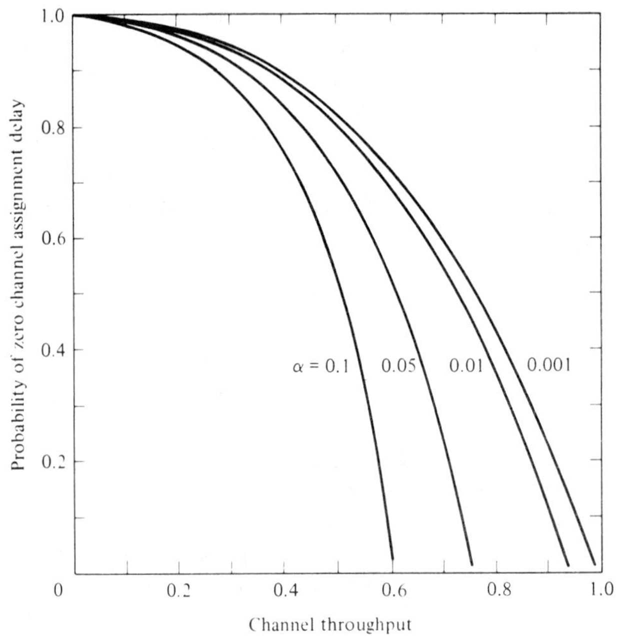

Figure 4.9. Probability of zero channel assignment delay versus throughput.

Kleinrock and Yemini [KLEI 78] proposed an alternative "pure" strategy for ready users to determine whether or not to transmit in the next time slot: the probability of transmission is either 1 or 0. In other words, some users have full channel-access rights, whereas others have none. (Consequently, the URN protocol is said to be *asymmetric*.) A user who has a channel-access right and is also ready transmits into the next time slot. It is possible to prove that optimal strategies are always pure strategies and therefore asymmetric [YEMI 78].

The URN protocol is described using the following URN model. Consider each user as a colored ball in an urn: black for ready, white for not ready. The access protocol is essentially a rule to sample balls from the urn. Let k be the number of balls drawn from the urn. The probability of a successful transmission (throughput) is that of getting exactly one black ball in the sample. The probability is

$$\text{Prob [throughput]} = \frac{\binom{n}{1}\binom{N-n}{k-1}}{\binom{N}{k}} \tag{4.16}$$

where N is the number of balls, and n is the number black balls. Equation (4.16) is maximized when $k = \lfloor N/n \rfloor$ where $\lfloor x \rfloor$ gives the integer part of x. Not only does this value of k maximize the probability of selecting exactly one black ball, but it also gives that the average number of black balls selected is equal to 1 (i.e., $G = 1$).

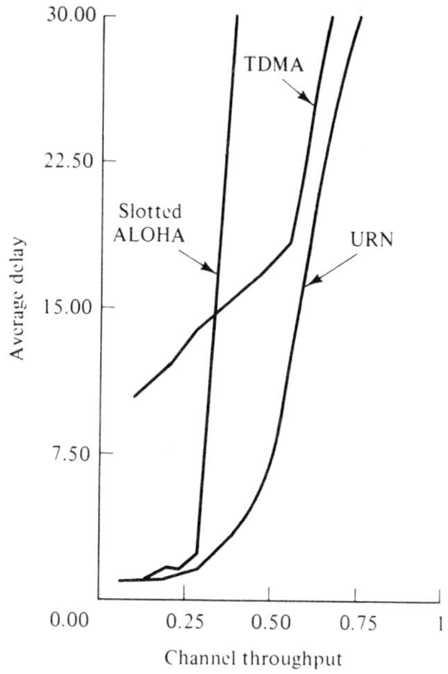

Figure 4.10. Simulated delay-throughput performance of URN.

The URN protocol adapts smoothly to network load fluctuations. When the network is lightly loaded, a large number of users get channel access rights. For instance, $n = 1$ gives risk to $k = N$; all users get access rights, but only one (the lone ready user) is going to make use of it. As the network load increases, n increases and the number k of users getting access rights is reduced. When $n > N/2$, then $k = 1$ and the URN protocol becomes effectively a TDMA protocol (which is most suitable for a heavy load). The maximum channel throughput of URN is thus unity. In Fig. 4.10 simulated delay-throughput results of URN obtained in [KLEI 78] are shown, illustrating the desirable traffic adaptivity of the protocol.

Two questions arise in the implementation of the URN protocol: How does an individual user obtain the up-to-date value of n? How does the protocol obtain coordination of the distributed decisions of individual users?

A solution for estimating n with high accuracy at the expense of a small overhead is proposed in the references. Briefly, it consists of a binary erasure reservation subchannel. An idle user who becomes ready (n increases by 1) sends a message of a few bits in the subchannel. When a ready user turns idle (n decreases by 1), the condition is detected by other users from examining his last packet or its positive acknowledgment in the broadcast channel. An erasure (collision) in the subchannel means that two or more users become ready in the same time slot. In this case, the increase in n is assumed to be 2 (an approximation). The resulting error in the estimate of n was found to be negligible since the probability of more than two users

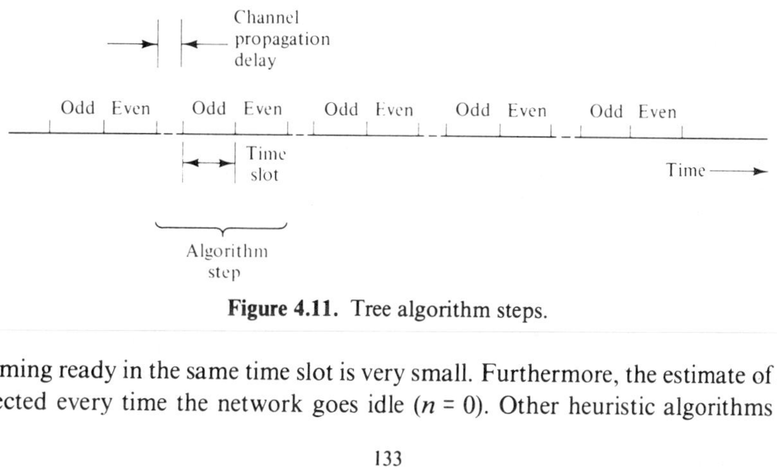

Figure 4.11. Tree algorithm steps.

becoming ready in the same time slot is very small. Furthermore, the estimate of n is corrected every time the network goes idle ($n = 0$). Other heuristic algorithms for estimating n can be found in [LAM 74, LAM 75A, LAM 75B].

Implementation of the URN protocol must also ensure that individual users agree on k, the number of users with access rights, as well as their identity. The optimal $k = \lfloor N/n \rfloor$ to be used is determined by each user from n estimated as described above. The selection of which k users should get access rights may be achieved via identical pseudo-random number generators at individual users, or via a window mechanism as well as other methods. The reader should consult the references for details.

4.3.1.7 A Tree Algorithm for Contention Resolution [CAPE 77, CAPE 79]

A tree algorithm for scheduling retransmission of packets involved in a collision was proposed by Capetanakis [CAPE 77]. A very desirable property of the algorithm is channel stability. The key idea of the algorithm is similar to that of adaptive polling considered earlier. The difference between the two is in implementation. Adaptive polling relies on a central controller probing passive users for status information. On the other hand, implementation of the tree algorithm is distributed, thus requiring users to be able to observe outcomes in the broadcast channel and make decisions. To do so, the channel needs to be time slotted. Furthermore, each algorithm step requires at least a channel propagation time plus two time slots to execute. The channel propagation time in each algorithm step is necessary to enable users to find out the outcomes of the previous algorithm step (see Fig. 4.11). For a satellite channel, some special technique is needed to avoid wasting the large propagation time interval between slot pairs. One method is to time multiplex the channel into subchannels that can be used independently by different user populations. For example, if P/C is the duration of a time slot, R is the channel propagation time, and m is an integer such that

$$\frac{2mP}{C} > R$$

then the satellite channel can be time multiplexed into $m + 1$ subchannels, each accessed by a population of users with the tree algorithm. For a high-speed satellite channel (m is large), much of the benefit from statistically averaging user demands discussed in Sec. 4.1.2 will be lost. Another idea suggested in the reference is to use a tree algorithm on $1/(m + 1)$ of the channel to make reservations for the other $m/(m + 1)$ of the channel (see Sec. 4.3.2).

The binary tree algorithm is described next. Suppose that each user corresponds to a leaf in a binary tree, such as that illustrated in Fig. 4.2 earlier (in the context of probing). Each user handles at most one packet at a time. The number of users can be finite or infinite. An infinite user population corresponds to a Poisson source of packet arrivals; in this case the binary tree extends to infinity. Time slots in the channel are paired into odd and even slots as shown in Fig. 4.11. To facilitate description of the algorithm, a last-in-first-out stack is assumed. (It is obviously not necessary.) Each algorithm step consists of the following three action steps. Initially, the stack is empty and step 3 is executed.

1. Remove the binary tree (or subtree) from top of stack and divide it into two subtrees. Users with access rights in the first subtree transmit in the odd slot; users with access rights in the second subtree transmit in the even slot.
2. Observe outcomes in the two slots. For each slot, discard the subtree if the slot is empty or contains a successful transmission; put the subtree back on the stack if the slot contains a collision.
3. If the stack is empty, give access rights to all new packets that have arrived in the meantime and put the entire tree on stack; go to step 1.

Note that new packet arrivals are only given access rights when the stack empties, which marks the end of one "epoch" and the beginning of the next. Arrivals during one epoch must wait to be served in the next epoch.

We make two observations. First, the objective of the algorithm is to divide the population of users into partitions, each containing at most one contending user. Therefore, the order of the tree search is not important. (In other words, the stack does not have to be last-in-first-out.) Second, the assignment of binary addresses to users does not have to be predetermined. Specifically, following a collision, a contending user may with equal probability join any one of the two resulting subtrees.

For the Poisson source model, Capetanakis [CAPE 77] showed that the tree that minimizes the number of time slots to process η packets, where η is a Poisson random variable, is binary everywhere except for the root node. The optimum degree d_0^* of the root node depends on the mean value of η.

An adaptive version of the tree algorithm (analogous to adaptive polling) can be designed to adjust dynamically the degree of the root node at the beginning of each epoch as a function of the mean number of accumulated packets λh where h is the number of time slots in the previous epoch and λ is the Poisson source rate. The optimum degree of the root node is

$$d_0^* = \begin{cases} 1 & \lambda h \leq 1.70 \\ n & 1.70 + 1.15(n-2) < h \leq 1.70 + 1.15(n-1) \end{cases}$$

The adaptive tree algorithm has a maximum channel throughput of 0.430 packet per slot and guarantees channel stability if $\lambda < 0.430$ packet per slot.

The tree algorithm can be used for contention resolution in CSMA instead of adaptively controlled random retransmission delays for ready users. The trade-off is the tree algorithm's requirement for time slotting; time-synchronizing distributed users to achieve small time slots is a nontrivial problem [ELLI 73, GARD 80].

4.3.1.8 Concluding Remarks

In this section we began with pure contention protocols (ALOHA, slotted ALOHA) and then moved on to more sophisticated contention-based protocols (R-ALOHA, CSMA, URN) with improved delay-throughput performance. A tree algorithm for contention resolution was also shown. These protocols all have distributed control. Each user makes his own decision regarding channel access based solely on observable outcomes in the broadcast channel. In the URN protocol implementation, however, a reservation subchannel is provided for users to communicate with each other in a limited fashion. In Sec. 4.3.2 we describe reservation protocols that require users to cooperate with each other to avoid collisions entirely through use of a reservation subchannel.

4.3.2 Reservation Protocols

The objective of reservation protocols is to avoid collisions entirely. Since users are distributed, a reservation subchannel is necessary for users to communicate with each other. There are two key problems to be solved for most reservation protocols: (1) implementation of the reservation subchannel, and (2) implementation of a queue for the entire population of distributed users (distributed global queue). We also examine some protocols for a short propagation delay environment which do not require a global queue.

4.3.2.1 The Reservation Channel

The original broadcast channel can be either time or frequency multiplexed into a reservation channel and a data channel. An advantage of time-multiplexed channels is that the partition may be variable. With a variable partition, the maximum throughput of data messages can be made very close to one under a heavy network load when users have long queues. With a fixed partition, the overhead lost to the reservation channel is a fixed fraction of the original channel capacity.

With a global queue, there is no conflict in the use of the data channel. However, the multiple access problem of the distributed users has not disappeared. It exists now in the access of the reservation channel. Any of the previously described multiple access protocols can be used. However, for simplicity, most proposed reservation protocols adopt either a fixed assigned TDMA protocol or some version of the slotted ALOHA protocol. We are faced with the same trade-off as before. A TDMA protocol performs poorly for a large population of bursty users. On the other hand, a slotted ALOHA protocol is independent of N but needs to be adaptively controlled for stable operation.

The high achievable channel throughput of reservation protocols (relative to pure contention) comes about from substantially reducing the volume of traffic requiring conflict resolution, and the concomitant overhead; the reduction is from the totality of data messages to just one short reservation packet per data message (or less). Note that R-ALOHA and CSMA derive their efficiency from essentially the same principle.

Part of the price that one pays for the gain in channel throughput of reservation protocols over contention protocols is an increase in message delay. The minimum delay incurred by a message, excluding message transmission time, is more than twice the channel propagation time. This consideration is important for satellite channels. The minimum delay can be reduced, however, if one can anticipate future arrivals and make reservations in advance! One possible example is packetized digital speech traffic.

4.3.2.2 The Distributed Global Queue

There are two approaches to implement a global queue of requests for a population of distributed users. One is to employ a central controller which tells the ready users when to access the channel; an additional subchannel for controller-to-user traffic is typically required. On the other hand, a distributed control implementation is more interesting and probably more desirable. In this approach each user maintains information on the status of the global queue and makes his own decision as to when is his turn to access the channel. An important problem here is the synchronization of queue status information of all users. This means that reservation packets broadcasted in the reservation channel need to be received correctly by *all* users. In the event of an error, an individual user must be able to detect the presence of error in his queue status information. Any such user who is out of synchronization, as well as new users who have just joined the network, must be able to acquire *queue synchronization* from observing the reservation and data channels within a reasonable duration of time.

Various queue disciplines may be used for the global queue [e.g., random selection, first-in-first-out (FIFO), round-robin, priority based upon type or delay constraint, etc.]. The processing requirement of a sophisticated scheduling algorithm may be quite substantial.

4.3.2.3 A Protocol with Distributed Control **[ROBE 73]**

The ideas of a reservation subchannel and a distributed global queue were first proposed by Roberts [ROBE 73]. A satellite channel was considered; the reservation protocol proposed, however, is applicable to other broadcast media. It is assumed that the channel is time slotted and that time slots are organized into frames. Each frame consists of a data subframe and a reservation subframe; each slot in the reservation subframe is further subdivided into V smaller slots. The small slots are for reservation packets as well as possibly positive acknowledgment packets and small data packets, to be used on a contention basis with the slotted ALOHA protocol.[2]

Roberts' protocol makes use of the broadcast capability of the channel; a reservation packet successfully transmitted with no interference is received by all users. Each reservation request is for a position in the global queue for a group of

[2]Our description varies slightly from the reference. In Roberts' original proposal, each reservation subframe is just one data slot long. He also considered a technique for adaptively changing the ratio of the subframe sizes as a function of traffic load. When the queue length is zero, the whole frame is used for making reservations.

packets. The queue discipline proposed by Roberts is FIFO according to the order reservation requests are received. We shall refer to this as the *FIFO protocol.* Each user maintains his copy of the queue status information. It is sufficient for each user to record only the queue length (in number of packets) as well as the queue positions of his own reservations.

It is necessary for a currently inactive user who wants to join the queue, to acquire queue synchronization. In this protocol the queue length information may be supplied in the header of each data packet transmitted. Alternatively, it may be announced periodically by a "master" controller. Note that such queue length information is one propagation delay old when received. To acquire queue synchronization, a user must update the queue length information so received with reservation requests received within a channel propagation time just prior to receiving the queue-length information.

To maintain synchronization among the users, it is necessary and sufficient that each reservation packet that is received correctly by any user be received correctly by all users. This condition may be assured by properly encoding the reservation requests. A simple strategy proposed by Roberts is to send parity-checked copies of requests in triplicate within a reservation packet.

As a result of the distributed nature of queue management, the impact of an error in a user's queue status is to cause some collisions in data slots and to delay some data packets momentarily. However, no catastrophic failure occurs. Users involved in such collisions must declare themselves to be out of synchronization. A user who receives a reservation packet with unrecoverable error must also do the same. Users who are out of synchronization discard their acquired reservations and reacquire queue synchronization in the same fashion as newly activated users described above.

4.3.2.4 Maximum Channel Throughput

The maximum channel throughput of a reservation protocol is $1 - \gamma$, where γ is the minimum fraction of the original channel capacity needed to accommodate the reservation request traffic. Consider the FIFO protocol above. Let L be the average number of data packets per reservation request. Since there are V small slots in a data slot, the ratio of data bits to reservation request bits transmitted is equal to

$$\bar{v} = VL$$

Suppose that the reservation channel is used by reservation packets only (excluding acknowledgment and small data packets mentioned above) and its maximum channel throughput is C_{SA} under the slotted ALOHA protocol. It can be easily shown that in this case

$$\gamma = \frac{1}{1 + C_{SA}\bar{v}} \tag{4.17}$$

The maximum channel throughput of the reservation protocol is $1 - \gamma$. We make several observations. First, the maximum throughput expression is the same as that for R-ALOHA, with just a slightly different interpretation for $\bar{v}$. Second, it is independent of N. Third, $\bar{v}$ is assumed to be a fixed parameter; thus the maximum channel throughput value is fixed and strictly less than 1.

Now suppose that the partition between data and reservation slots in a frame can be dynamically varied. Also, reservation requests can be piggybacked in the header of scheduled data packets. In this case, when the network is heavily loaded with long message queues at individual users, $\bar{v}$ will become very large; the maximum channel throughput becomes 1 in the $\bar{v} \to \infty$ limit.

Alternatively, if the frame is fixed partitioned and a fixed assignment TDMA protocol is used for the reservation subchannel, we have

$$\gamma = \frac{N}{MV} \tag{4.18}$$

where N is the number of users and M is the number of data slots in a frame.

A fixed assignment TDMA protocol is sometimes preferable to slotted ALOHA for the reservation subchannel since it is simple to implement; unlike slotted ALOHA, adaptive control is not needed. However, Eq. (4.18) shows that it is applicable only for a small user population. One can always increase M to increase channel throughput; a large M is undesirable, however, since the delay of reservation packets becomes large and hence the message delay as well.

The maximum throughput $1 - \gamma$ is plotted in Fig. 4.12 versus N for the two cases given by Eqs. (4.17) and (4.18).

4.3.2.5 Other Protocols with Distributed Control

Another reservation protocol with distributed control was proposed by Binder [BIND 75B]. The channel is divided into time slots which are organized into frames. Let M be the number of slots in a frame. The frame duration is required to be larger than the channel propagation time. Also, the number N of users is required to be less than or equal to M. Each user is fixed assigned a time slot within the frame and sends information concerning his current queue length in the header of each data packet

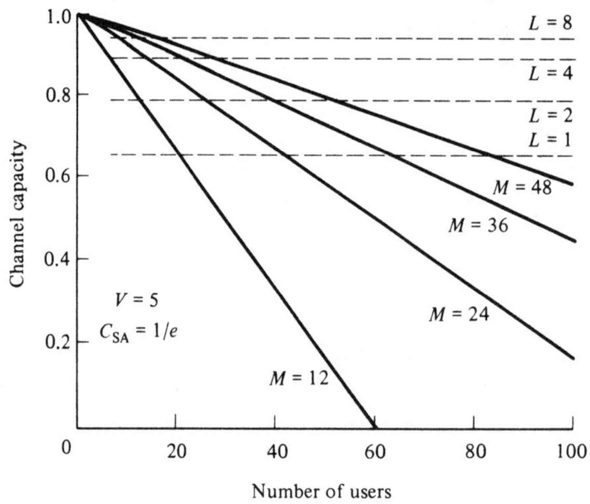

Figure 4.12. Maximum channel throughput versus number of users for reservation protocols.

that he transmits into his fixed assigned slot. Note that this is equivalent to a fixed assigned TDMA reservation subchannel.

The global queue is implemented via distributed control. The global queue status consists of the queue lengths of all ready users (those with nonempty queues). Each user exercises the following rules for channel access. A user may send data in his fixed assigned slot at any time. Any unassigned as well as unused slots (assigned to currently idle users) within a frame are used by the ready users in a round-robin fashion. A user who has been idle can transmit in his fixed assigned (owned) slot to deliberately generate a collision. Such a collision is noted by all users. Another rule dictates that following a collision, only the owner of the slot can use it in the next frame. Thus a special feature of this protocol is that even if a user is in the process of acquiring queue synchronization, he still has the use of a fixed assigned TDMA channel. A disadvantage is that the number of users N must be less than M. The problems of maintaining and acquiring queue synchronization are similar to those of the FIFO protocol above.

Recently, the PODA (Priority-Oriented Demand Assignment) protocol was proposed and implemented in SATNET, a prototype packet satellite network [JACO 77, JACO 78, WEIS 78]. Logically, PODA is an extension of Roberts' FIFO protocol with a much more sophisticated scheduling algorithm designed to handle the requirements of a general-purpose packet satellite network. These requirements include: multiple delay constraints, multiple priority levels, variable message length, fairness, efficient message acknowledgments, and the accommodation of "stream traffic." Stream traffic denotes a class of traffic sources typified by digital voice. Each such traffic source generates a stream of messages with a small interarrival-time variance. Also, the maximum acceptable delay for each message is only slightly larger than the channel propagation time. These characteristics are quite different from what we have considered so far. Thus stream traffic requires special handling apart from individual data messages (datagrams).

Like the FIFO protocol, PODA divides channel time into frames. Each frame consists of an information subframe and a reservation subframe. If slotted ALOHA is used for multiple access in the reservation subframe, the protocol is said to be contention-based and is called CPODA; if fixed assignment TDMA is used, the protocol is called FPODA. In addition to using the reservation subframe, a reservation request can also be piggybacked into the header of a scheduled message. While the total frame size is fixed, the reservation subframe is allowed to grow or shrink according to network loading. If the global queue is empty, the reservation subframe occupies the entire frame. The two types of traffic are distinguished when reservations are made. An explicit reservation is sent for each datagram while a reservation is sent only once for all messages of a particular stream. Each stream reservation contains information defining the stream repetition interval, desired maximum delay relative to this interval, and priority. Whenever the interval starting time is near, a reservation is automatically created and entered into the scheduling queue. The scheduling discipline of the global queue is very elaborate and depends on explicit priority, urgency, and fairness. Some measurement and simulation performance results of CPODA are reported in [GERL 77B, CHU 78]. Queue synchronization is addressed in [HSU 78, WEIS 78]. More on reservation protocols can be found in [BALA 79, BORG 77, BORG 78].

4.3.2.6 Short-Propagation-Delay Environment

The reservation protocols described above all maintain a global queue of reservations, one reservation for a group of packets, for channel access. Consider now networks with a very short propagation delay relative to the transmission time of a packet. Instead of a global queue, the following approach for conflict resolution has been proposed for a ground radio network environment by Kleinrock and Scholl [KLEI 77].

The broadcast channel is divided into minislots interleaved with data slots. Each data slot is preceded by N minislots, where N is the user population size. We shall refer to this class of protocols as the *minislotted protocols*. Before the start of every data slot, a priority ordering exists among the N users. Three priority disciplines were considered in [KLEI 77]: alternating priorities, round robin, and random order. The priority ordering determines the assignment of minislots: one per user. Ready users make their presence known by transmitting (carrier only) into their assigned minislots while idle users keep quiet. The first ready user appearing in a minislot gets the following data slot. Since there are N minislots associated with every data slot, the maximum channel throughput is

$$\frac{1}{1 + N\alpha}$$

where α is the ratio of minislot to data slot duration. Obviously, the performance of this class of protocols is acceptable only if $N\alpha \ll 1$. The delay-throughput-performance of minislotted protocols was found to be inferior to roll-call polling in many cases [KLEI 77].

To reduce the number of minislots needed for each data slot, the MSAP protocol was proposed. At the end of a packet transmission, the protocol operates as follows:

1. The user who transmitted the last packet is given priority.
2. The priority user can transmit immediately; other users defer via carrier sensing.
3. If the priority user is sensed idle, then one minislot later, access priority is passed on to the next user in sequence, and steps 2 and 3 are repeated.

The number of minislots in between contiguous packet transmissions ranges from 0 to $N - 1$. It should be clear that MSAP is analogous to conventional polling in its scheduling discipline but has distributed control and active users instead of centralized control and passive users. However, a minislot of duration τ (same as that in CSMA) in MSAP is typically much smaller than the corresponding average walk time $\bar{w}$ in polling. This is because the transmission time of a polling message needs to be included in $\bar{w}$ but no corresponding overhead is needed in τ. The delay-throughput performance of MSAP was found to be better than roll-call polling in all cases considered in [KLEI 77]. However, MSAP requires the nontrivial task of time synchronizing users to implement minislots.

Independently, a similar idea was explored by Rothhauser and Wild [ROTH 76] for a bit-synchronous broadcast channel (e.g., a data bus). As a result of bit synchronism, a single bit is sufficient for a user to indicate his status (ready or idle). With a population of N users, N bits are sufficient for identifying all ready users immediately preceding each data transfer phase using the "one-out-of-N" code. During the data transfer phase, ready users can transmit according to a priority sequence known to all users. A multilevel code structure was also proposed in [ROTH 76] that can substantially reduce the number of bits for identifying ready users [to a minimum of $\ln(N)$ bits when only one ready user is present]. This protocol is called *multilevel multiple access* (MLMA). A closer look shows that the multilevel code structure is based on the same "tree search" idea as Hayes' algorithm and the tree algorithm described earlier.

No provision for traffic adaptivity was mentioned in the MLMA proposal. Traffic adaptivity was found to be necessary for efficiency in times of heavy traffic in the other two algorithms.

4.3.2.7 Protocols with Centralized Control

The presence of a central controller eliminates the queue synchronization problem discussed earlier for distributed control protocols. Instead, the central controller manages the global queue, accepts reservations, and informs users when to access the channel. An additional subchannel is typically required for controller-to-user traffic. Since the multiple access problem of the reservation subchannel remains essentially the same as discussed above for distributed control protocols, we will not describe specific protocols.

Protocols with centralized control have been proposed and studied by Tobagi and Kleinrock for radio networks [TOBA 76], by Mark for a data bus [MARK 78], and by Ng and Mark for a satellite network with on-board processing that serves as the central controller [NG 77]. Recently, Mark and Ng proposed a coding scheme, called CMAP, that offers significant overhead reduction over the one-out-of-N code for identifying ready users [MARK 79].

4.4 PERFORMANCE COMPARISONS

Our focus in this chapter is mainly on the sharing and conflict resolution aspect of the multiple access problem. A broadcast channel of C bps is assumed. The performance criteria of interest are channel throughput and message delay. Engineering considerations such as modulation, clock synchronization, coding, and random-noise errors are not within the scope of this chapter. Different broadcast media are differentiated mainly by the effect of their channel propagation delay on an MA protocol's delay-throughput performance. (We note, however, that some protocols do have special requirements and can be implemented in some broadcast media but not others.)

Even within our limited scope of performance, it should be clear to the reader by now that there is no single protocol that is optimum. The performance of a multiple access protocol is strongly dependent on the traffic model and network loading. In general, some traffic characteristics do favor one class of protocols more than others. We list some of them below.

Traffic Model	Multiple Access Protocols Favored
Nonbursty users	Fixed assigned channels (TDMA, FDMA)
Bursty users, short messages	Pure contention
Bursty users, long messages, large N	Reservation protocols with contention reservation channel
Bursty users, long messages, small N	Reservation protocols with fixed TDMA reservation channel

For traffic models that are a fixed or time-varying combination of the models above, "mixed" protocols (such as R-ALOHA, CSMA) and adaptive protocols (such as URN, adaptive polling) may be suitable. To illustrate some of the observations above, we show the delay-throughput performance of representatives of the different classes of protocols under various specific traffic assumptions.

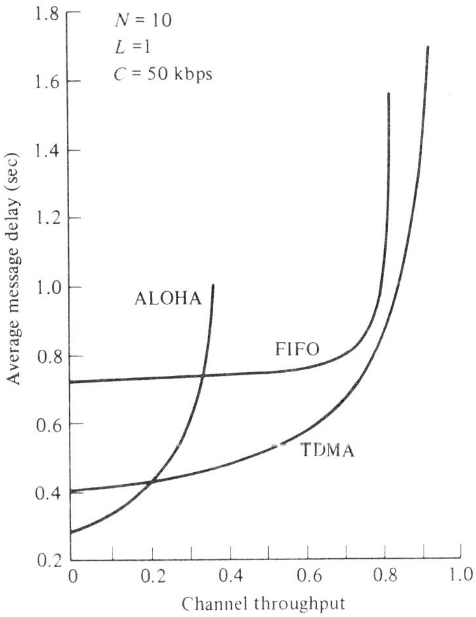

Figure 4.13. Delay-throughput trade-off for 10 users and short messages (one packet per message).

In Figs. 4.13, to 4.15, four protocols are considered: (1) fixed assigned TDMA channels, (2) slotted ALOHA, (3) FIFO modified to use a fixed TDMA reservation channel, and (4) FIFO with a slotted ALOHA reservation channel; they are labeled as TDMA, ALOHA, FIFO, and FIFO*, respectively, in the figures. Delay formulas for TDMA and slotted ALOHA from [LAM 77B, KLEI 73] are used. The expected delay of a message for the reservation protocols is taken to be the sum of the expected delay D_1 incurred by the reservation request and the expected delay D_2 incurred by the message itself after the reservation has been made. To calculate D_1 and D_2, we regard the original broadcast channel at C bps to be split up into two separate channels: a data channel at $(1 - \gamma)C$ bps and a reservation channel at γC bps. D_1 and D_2 are then calculated separately.

In Fig. 4.13 we show results obtained assuming 10 users sharing a 50-kbps satellite channel with a propagation delay of 0.27 second. All messages consist of

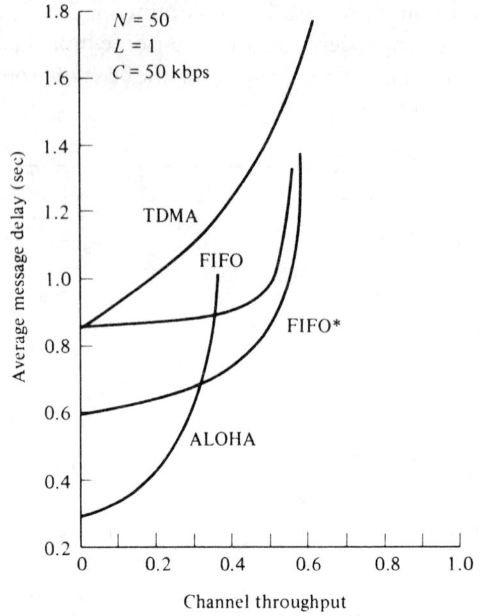

Figure 4.14. Delay-throughput trade-off for 50 users and short messages (one packet per message).

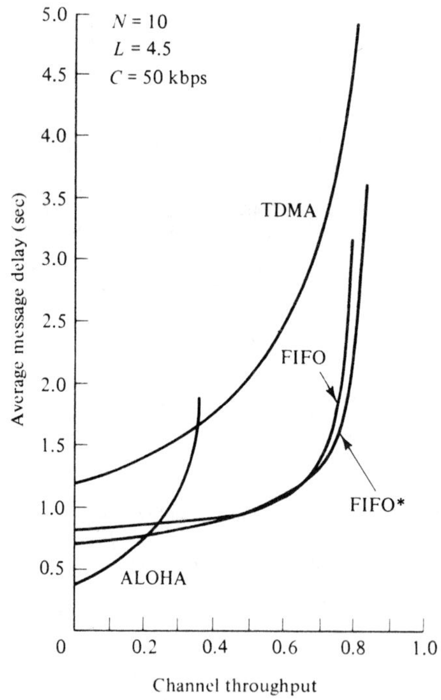

Figure 4.15. Delay-throughput trade-off for 10 users and multipacket messages.

single packets of 1125 bits each. In the case of FIFO, a frame size $M = 12$ is assumed with $V = 5$ and $\gamma = 1/6$. Observe that the performance of fixed assigned TDMA is the best for this traffic model except when the channel throughput is less than 0.2, where slotted ALOHA gives a smaller delay.

Now suppose that we consider a larger population of more bursty users than the traffic model above. Let N be increased from 10 to 50 (so that the bursty factor of each user is now 1/5 of that of the model above). Figure 4.14 shows that TDMA has the worst performance for this new traffic model. FIFO, with $M = 24$ and $\gamma = 5/12$, also has poor performance, due to the large reservation channel overhead needed for 50 users. FIFO*, with $\gamma = 0.4$ assuming $C_{SA} = 0.3$, has better performance than FIFO, but the reservation channel overhead is still quite large since each message consists of a single packet only. The delay-throughput performance of slotted ALOHA is independent of the change from the first to the second traffic model and appears to be the most suitable protocol for the second traffic model, provided that a channel throughput of about 0.3 or less is acceptable. If a channel throughput of more than 0.3 is desired, FIFO* should be employed.

Now suppose that we are back to having 10 users but that the data traffic consists of long messages (eight packets each) as well as short messages (one packet each) in equal number. The average message length L is increased from 1 to 4.5 packets. Delay-throughput results for the four protocols are shown in Fig. 4.15. The delay curve for slotted ALOHA is plotted using the delay formula for multipacket messages in [LAM 74]. For this traffic model, the reservation protocols have the best performance except at a channel throughput of less than 0.2, where slotted ALOHA is better. Slotted ALOHA, as we know, was not designed to take advantage of the presence of multipacket messages. Simulations also showed that when a large number of multipacket messages are present in the input traffic, the slotted ALOHA channel becomes more unstable [LAM 74].

Some protocols are designed to take advantage of a short-propagation-delay environment. They include CSMA protocols that are contention-based, the reservation protocols MSAP and MLMA, as well as polling protocols. Reservation protocols that are not contention-based and polling protocols have similar delay-throughput characteristics since the conflict resolution overhead in each case is proportional to N, the number of users. In particular, MSAP and polling are characterized by essentially the same delay formula; any difference in performance is just a consequence of different values for the minislot duration τ in MSAP and the corresponding average walk time $\bar{w}$ in polling [KLEI 77]. There are, of course, differences that do not show up explicitly in the delay-throughput performance, such as distributed control in MSAP versus centralized control in polling, and the need for time-synchronizing distributed users in MSAP but not in polling.

The delay-throughput performance of CSMA and roll-call polling are compared in Fig. 4.16 using the CSMA delay formula from [LAM 79B] and polling delay formula from [KONH 74]. The delay results shown for polling assume Poisson message arrivals and one packet per message. The ratio of propagation delay to the packet transmission time is $\alpha = 0.05$. The ratio of data to polling message length is $\bar{\nu} = 10$. Queueing of messages at indivdual users is assumed; hence the channel

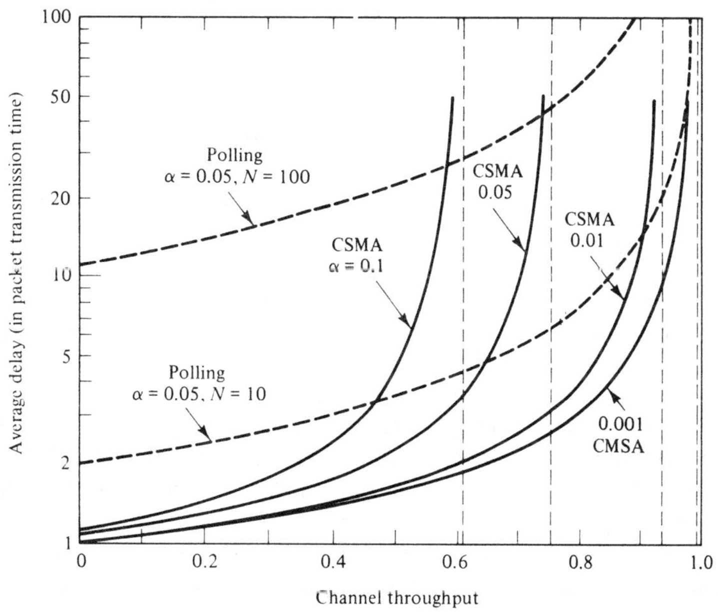

Figure 4.16. Comparison of CSMA and polling delay-throughout performance.

throughput approaches 1 when queues become very long under heavy traffic. Delay-throughput curves are shown for both 10 users and 100 users. The corresponding delay-throughput performance of CSMA at $\alpha = 0.05$ is independent of the number of users. Since the analysis in [LAM 79B] assumes that individual users handle one packet at a time, the maximum channel throughput is less than 1. As before, we observe that CSMA, being a contention-based protocol, is superior to polling when the channel throughput is low but becomes inferior when the channel throughput is increased to near 1. However, if queueing of messages is possible at individual users for CSMA, more than one message may be transmitted every time a user gains channel access; the amount of overhead per message is reduced. Hence as the network load is increased from 0 to 1, the delay performance of CSMA if first given by the $\alpha = 0.05$ curve at a small channel throughput but switches to the $\alpha = 0.01$ curve and then the $\alpha = 0.001$ curve and so on as the channel throughput increases and queues become long. The channel throughput of CSMA approaches 1 in the limit of infinitely long queues at individual users.

4.5 CONCLUSIONS

We considered the problem of interconnecting distributed users via a broadcast channel and surveyed a wide class of multiple access protocols. The throughput-delay performance characteristics of these protocols were examined and compared. Our emphasis has been on packet-oriented protocols. Channel-oriented protocols, however, are currently prevalent in existing systems and are in many cases more cost effective than packet protocols. Specifically, in broadcast networks with a large population of users, the total user interface cost, proportional to N, tends to dominate the network cost. Packet protocols become important only when the cost of user interface to a (shared) wideband broadcast medium is reduced to the point that a large population of users can be economically interconnected directly via the broadcast medium (i.e., without the user of a traffic multiplexor/concentrator to justify the cost of an interface). Trends in the costs of electronics and computing seem to be most encouraging toward packet protocols in the foreseeable future. Some specific observations follow.

With the current cost ($\geq$ \$100,000) and size (antenna size $\geq$ 5 m) of satellite earth stations*, it would not be economical to install a separate earth station at a packet network node unless it has a substantial amount of traffic (100 kbps or more [ROBE 78]). At such a traffic level, traditional channel-oriented multiple access protocols will perform very well; there will be no need for the more complex packet protocols. However, the advent of satellite systems at the higher frequencies (e.g., 14/12, 30/20 GHz) than are currently available will facilitate the development of small, inexpensive earth stations (say, 1-to-3-m antenna size) that can be sited almost anywhere for low-rate users. The packet protocols described herein will be very important in this new environment. Other developments in satellite communications that will affect the development of multiple access protocols include multibeam satellites (thus the broadcast network assumption in this paper needs to be modified) and the availability of on-board processing capability [PRIT 77, JACO 78].

In recent years, packet communication has made significant advances to reduce the cost of long-distance backbone networks. Local distribution and collection of data (between a central site and a population of terminals), however, remains by far the most expensive portion of many communication networks. We are addressing local area networks which, although outside the computer room, are confined to local environments, such as office complexes and manufacturing plants, without the use of common-carrier facilities. Local area networks serve several functions: for local interconnection, for access to local computing facilities, for access to a gateway into a backbone network, and so on. The broadcast media of interest here include CATV,

*These are 1978 figures when this chapter was first written [LAM 79C].

optical fiber, and radio. All of these are currently under intensive research and development. In this environment, packet protocols will again be important in networks that can economically interconnect a large population of users. With the availability of inexpensive microprocessors, the key to implementing such packet broadcast networks reduces to the development of inexpensive transceivers for the specific broadcast medium. The economic viability of packet broadcast networks using CATV-based technology has already been demonstrated at data rates of several Mbps [DEMA 76, METC 76, CLAR 78, WEST 78].

In conclusion, we have examined the basic principles and performance trade-offs of multiple access protocols for broadcast networks. For the sake of clarity, we have often omitted specific implementation details. Therefore, the protocols described herein form the basic elements of more sophisticated operational protocols. In the future, more flexible and reliable protocols will be needed to accommodate the increasing volume and diversity of data traffic, including digital voice, facsimile, and word processing systems, in addition to the present transaction-based terminal and file transfer traffic.

ACKNOWLEDGMENTS

The final manuscript has benefited tremendously from the comments and suggestions of the editor. This work was supported by the National Science Foundation under Grant ECS78-01803.

REFERENCES

ABRA 70 Abramson, N., "THE ALOHA SYSTEM—Another Alternative for Computer Communications," *AFIPS Conf. Proc.*, Vol. 37, AFIPS Press, Montvale, N.J., 1970, pp. 281–285.

ABRA 73 Abramson, N., "Packet Switching with Satellites," *AFIPS Conf. Proc.*, Vol. 42, AFIPS Press, Montvale, N.J., 1973, pp. 695–702.

ABRA 75 Abramson, N., and E. R. Cacciamani, "Satellites: Not Just a Big Cable in the Sky," *IEEE Spectrum*, Vol. 12, September 1975.

BALA 79 Balagangadhar, M. M., and R. L. Pickholtz, "Analysis of a Reservation Multiple Access Technique for Data Transmission via Satellites," *IEEE Trans. Commun.*, October 1979.

BIND 75A Binder, R., et al., "ALOHA Packet Broadcasting—A Retrospect," *Nat. Comput. Conf., AFIPS Conf. Proc.*, Vol. 44, 1975, pp. 201–215.

BIND 75B Binder, R., "A Dynamic Packet-Switching System for Satellite Broadcast Channels," *ICC '75 Conf. Rec.*, IEEE, New York, 1975, pp. 41-1 to 41-5.

BORG 77 Borgonovo, F., and L. Fratta, "A New Technique for Satellite Broadcast Communication," *Proc. 5th Data Commun. Symp.*, Snowbird, Utah, September 1977.

BORG 78 Borgonovo, F., and L. Fratta, "SRUC: A Technique for Packet Transmission on Multiple Access Channel," *Proc. ICCC*, Kyoto, Japan, September 1978.

BUTT 74 Butterfield, S. C., R. D. Rettberg, and D. C. Walden, "The Satellite IMP for the ARPA Network," *Proc. 7th Hawaii Int. Conf. Syst. Sci.*, Computer Nets Supplement, January 1974.

CAPE 77 Capetanakis, J. I., "The Multiple Access Broadcast Channel: Protocol and Capacity Considerations," Ph.D., dissertation, Department of Electrical Engineering and Computer Science, M.I.T., August 1977.

CAPE 79 Capetanakis, J. I., "Generalized TDMA: The Multi-accessing Tree Protocol," *IEEE Trans. Commun.*, October 1979.

CHOU 78 Chou, W., "Terminal Response Time on Polled Teleprocessing Networks," *Proc. Comput. Networking Symp.*, December 1978.

CHU 78 Chu, W. W., and W. E. Naylor, "Measurement and Simulation Results of C-PODA Protocol Performance," *NTC 78 Conf. Rec., Natl. Telecommun. Conf.*, Birmingham, Ala., December 1978.

CLAR 78 Clark, D. D., K. T. Pogram, and D. P. Reed, "An Introduction to Local Area Networks," *Proc. IEEE*, Vol. 66, November 1978.

CROW 73 Crowther, W., et al., "A System for Broadcast Communication: Reservation-ALOHA," *Proc. 6th HICSS*, University of Hawaii, Honolulu, January 1973.

DEMA 76 DeMarines, V. A., and L. W. Hill, "The Cable Bus in Data Communications," *Datamation*, August 1976.

ELLI 73 Ellingson, C., and R. Kulpinski, "Dissemination of System Time," *IEEE Trans. Commun.*, Vol. COM-21, May 1973.

FAYO 77 Fayolle, G., et al., "Stability and Optimal Control of the Packet Switching Broadcast Channel," *J. ACM*, Vol. 24, July 1977.

GARD 80 Gardner, F. M., and W. C. Lindsey, eds., *Special Issue on Synchronization, IEEE Trans. Commun.*, August 1980.

GERL 77A Gerla, M., and L. Kleinrock, "Closed Loop Stability Controls for S-ALOHA Satellite Communication," *Proc. 5th Data Commun. Symp.*, Snowbird, Utah, September 1977.

GERL 77B Gerla, M., L. Nelson, and L. Kleinrock, "Packet Satellite Multiple Access: Models and Measurements," *Conf. Rec. Natl. Telecommun. Conf.*, Los Angeles, December 1977.

HANS 77 Hansen, L. W., and M. Schwartz, "An Assigned-Slot Listen-before-Transmission Protocol for a Multiaccess Data Channel," *Conf. Rec. Int. Conf. Commun.*, Chicago, June 1977.

HAYE 78 Hayes, J. F., "An Adaptive Technique for Local Distribution," *IEEE Trans. Commun.*, Vol. COM-26, August 1978.

HSU 78 Hsu, N., and L. Lee, "Channel Scheduling Synchronization for the PODA Protocol," *Conf. Rec. ICC 78*, Toronto, June 1978.

JACO 74 Jacobs, I. M., "Practical Applications of Coding," *IEEE Trans. Inf. Theory*, Vol. IT-20, May 1974.

JACO 77 Jacobs, I., et al., "CPODA—A Demand Assignment Protocol for Satnet," *Proc. 5th Data Commun. Symp.*, Snowbird, Utah, September 27–29, 1977.

JACO 78 Jacobs, I. M., R. Binder, and E. V. Hoversten, "General Purpose Packet Satellite Networks," *Proc. IEEE*, Vol. 66, November 1978.

KAHN 77 Kahn, R. E., "The Organization of Computer Resources into a Packet Radio Network," *IEEE Trans. Commun.*, Vol. COM-25, January 1977.

KAHN 78 Kahn, R. E., et al., "Advances in Packet Radio Technology," *Proc. IEEE*, Vol. 66, November 1978.

KLEI 73 Kleinrock, L., and S. S. Lam, "Packet-Switching in a Slotted Satellite Channel," *AFIPS Conf. Proc.*, Vol. 42, AFIPS Press, Montvale, N.J., 1973, pp. 703–710.

KLEI 74 Kleinrock, L., and S. S. Lam, "On Stability of Packet Switching in a Random Multi-access Broadcast Channel," *7th Hawaii Int. Conf. Syst. Sci.*, Honolulu, January 1974; *Proc. Spec. Subconf. on Comput. Nets*, 1974.

KLEI 75A Kleinrock, L., and S. S. Lam, "Packet Switching in a Multiaccess Broadcast Channel: Performance Evaluation," *IEEE Trans. Commun.*, Vol. COM-23, April 1975, pp. 410–423.

KLEI 75B Kleinrock, L., and F. A. Tobagi, "Packet Switching in Radio Channels, Part 1: Carrier Sense Multiple Access Modes and Their Throughput-Delay Characteristics," *IEEE Trans. Commun.*, Vol. COM-23, No. 12, December 1975, pp. 1400–1416.

KLEI 76 Kleinrock, L., *Queueing Systems*, Vol. 2: *Computer Applications*, Wiley-Interscience, New York, 1976.

KLEI 77 Kleinrock, L., and M. Scholl, "Packet Switching in Radio Channels: New Conflict-Free Multiple Access Schemes for a Small Number of Data Users," *Conf. Rec. Int. Conf. Commun.*, Chicago, June 1977.

KLEI 78 Kleinrock, L., and Y. Yemini, "An Optimal Adaptive Scheme for Multiple Access Broadcast Communication," *Conf. Rec. ICC 78*, Toronto, June 1978.

KONH 74 Konheim, A. G., and B. Meister, "Waiting Lines and Times in a System with Polling," *J. ACM*, Vol. 21, July 1974.

LAM 74 Lam, S. S., "Packet Switching in a Multi-access Broadcast Channel with Application to Satellite Communication in a Computer Network," Ph.D. dissertation, Computer Science Department, University of California, Los Angeles, March 1974.

LAM 75A Lam, S. S., and L. Kleinrock, "Packet Switching in a Multiaccess Broadcast Channel: Dynamic Control Procedures," *IEEE Trans. Commun.*, Vol. COM-23, September 1975, pp. 891–904.

LAM 75B Lam, S. S., and L. Kleinrock, "Dynamic Control Schemes for a Packet Switched Multi-access Broadcast Channel," *AFIPS Conf. Proc.*, Vol. 44, AFIPS Press, Montvale, N.J., 1975, pp. 143–153.

LAM 77A Lam, S. S., "Satellite Multiaccess Schemes for Data Traffic," *Conf. Rec. Int. Conf. Commun.*, Chicago, June 1977, pp. 37.1-19 to 37.1-24.

LAM 77B Lam, S. S., "Delay Analysis of a Time Division Multiple Access (TDMA) Channel," *IEEE Trans. Commun.*, Vol. COM-25, December 1977, pp. 1489–1494.

LAM 78A Lam, S. S., "A New Measure for Characterizing Data Traffic," *IEEE Trans. Commun.*, Vol. COM-26, January 1978.

LAM 78B Lam, S. S., "An Analysis of the R-ALOHA Protocol for Satellite Packet Switching," *Conf. Rec. ICC 78, Int. Conf. Commun.*, Toronto, June 1978.

LAM 79A Lam, S. S., "On Protocols for Satellite Packet Switching," *Conf. Rec. Int. Conf. Commun.*, Boston, June 1979.

LAM 79B Lam, S. S., "A Study of the CSMA Protocol in Local Networks," *Proc. 4th Berkeley Conf. Distributed Data Manage. Comput. Networks*, San Francisco, August 1979.

LAM 79C Lam, S. S., "Satellite Packet Communication—Multiple Access Protocols and Performance," *IEEE Trans. Commun.*, October 1979.

LAM 80A Lam, S. S., "A Carrier Sense Multiple Access Protocol for Local Networks," *Comput. Networks*, February 1980.

LAM 80B Lam, S. S., "A Packet Network Architecture for Local Interconnection," *Conf. Rec. Int. Conf. Commun.*, Seattle, June 1980.

LAM 80C Lam, S. S., "Packet Broadcast Networks—A Performance Analysis of the R-ALOHA Protocol," *IEEE Trans. Comput.*, July 1980.

MARK 78 Mark, J. W., "Global Scheduling Approach to Conflict-Free Multiaccess via a Data Bus," *IEEE Trans. Commun.*, Vol. COM-26, September 1978.

MARK 79 Mark, J. W., and S. F. W. Ng, "A Coding Scheme for Conflict-Free Multiaccess Using Global Scheduling," *IEEE Trans. Commun.*, September 1979.

MART 72 Martin, J., *Systems Analysis for Data Transmission*, Prentice-Hall, Englewood Cliffs, N.J., 1972.

METC 73 Metcalfe, R. M., "Steady-State Analysis of a Slotted and Controlled ALOHA System with Blocking," *Proc. 6th Hawaii Int. Conf. Syst. Sci.*, Honolulu, January 1973.

METC 76 Metcalfe, R. M., and D. R. Boggs, "Ethernet: Distributed Packet Switching for Local Computer Networks," *Commun. ACM*, Vol. 19, No. 7, July 1976.

NG 77 Ng, S. F. W., and J. W. Mark, "A Multiaccess Model for Packet Switching with a Satellite Having Some Processing Capability," *IEEE Trans. Commun.*, Vol. COM-25, January 1977, pp. 128–135.

PRIT 77 Pritchard, W. L., "Satellite Communication—An Overview of the Problems and Programs," *Proc. IEEE*, Vol. 65, March 1977.

PUEN 71 Puente, J. G., W. G. Schmidt, and A. M. Werth, "Multiple-Access Techniques for Commercial Satellites," *Proc. IEEE*, Vol. 59, February 1971.

ROBE 72 Roberts, L. G., "ALOHA Packet System with and without Slots and Capture," ARPANET Satellite System Note 8, (NIC 11290), June 1972; reprinted in *Comput. Commun. Rev.*, Vol. 5, April 1975.

ROBE 73 Roberts, L., "Dynamic Allocation of Satellite Capacity through Packet Reservation," *AFIPS Conf. Proc.*, Vol. 42, AFIPS Press, Montvale, N.J., 1973, pp. 711–716.

ROBE 78 Roberts, L., "The Evolution of Packet Switching," *Proc. IEEE*, Vol. 66, November 1978.

ROTH 76 Rothhauser, E. H., and D. Wild, "MLMA: A Collision-Free Multi-access Method," IBM Research Report RZ802, November 1976.

SCHW 73 Schwartz, J. W., and M. Muntner, "Multiple-Access Communications for Computer Nets," *Computer-Communication Networks*, N. Abramson and F. Kuo, eds., Prentice-Hall, Englewood Cliffs, N.J., 1973.

SCHW 77 Schwartz, M., *Computer-Communication Network Design and Analysis*, Prentice-Hall, Englewood Cliffs, N.J., 1977.

THOR 75 Thornton, J. E., et al., "A New Approach to Network Storage Measurement," *Computer Design*, November 1975.

THUR 79 Thurber, K. J., and H. A. Freeman, "A Bibliography of Local Computer Network," *Comput. Commun. Rev.*, April 1979.

TOBA 74 Tobagi, F. A., "Random Access Techniques for Data Transmission over Packet Switched Radio Networks," Ph.D. dissertation, Computer Science Department, University of California, Los Angeles, Calif., December 1974.

TOBA 76 Tobagi, F. A., and L. Kleinrock, "Packet Switching in Radio Channels: Part III. Polling and (Dynamic) Split-Channel Reservation Multiple Access," *IEEE Trans. Commun.*, Vol. COM-24, No. 8, pp. 832–845, August 1976.

TOBA 77 Tobagi, F. A., and L. Kleinrock, "Packet Switching in Radio Channels: Part IV—Stability Considerations and Dynamic Control in Carrier Sense Multiple Access," *IEEE Trans. Commun.*, Vol. COM-25, October 1977.

TOBA 79 Tobagi, F. A., and V. B. Hunt, "Performance Analysis of Carrier Sense Multiple Access with Collision Detection," *Proc. Local Area Commun. Network Symp.*, Boston, May 1979.

WEIS 78 Weissler, R., et al., "Synchronization and Multiple Access Protocols in the Initial Satellite IMP," *Proc. Fall COMPCON '78*, Washington, D.C., September 1978.

WEST 72 West, L. P., "Loop-Transmission Control Structures," *IEEE Trans. Commun.*, Vol. COM-20, No. 3, Part II, June 1972, pp. 531–539.

WEST 78 West, A., and A. Davison, "CNET—A Cheap Network for Distributed Computing," Department of Computer Science and Statistics, Queen Mary College, University of London, Rep. TR120, March 1978.

WILL 74 Willard, D. G., "A Time Division Multiple Access System for Digital Communication," *Comput. Des.*, June 1974.

YEMI 78 Yemini, Y., "On Channel Sharing in Discrete-Time Packet Switched, Multi-access Broadcast Communication," Ph.D. dissertation, Computer Science Department, University of California, Los Angeles, Calif., 1978.

IEEE TRANSACTIONS ON COMMUNICATIONS, VOL. COM-29, NO. 10, OCTOBER 1981

Local-Area Subnetworks: A Performance Comparison

WERNER BUX

Abstract—This paper provides a comparative evaluation of the performance of ring and bus systems constituting subnetworks of local-area networks. Performance is measured in terms of the delay-throughput characteristics. Systems investigated include token-controlled and slotted rings as well as random-access buses (CSMA with collision detection) and ordered-access buses. The investigation is based on analytic models which describe the various topologies and access mechanisms to a sufficient level of detail. The paper includes a comprehensive discussion of how the performance of the different networks is affected by system parameters like transmission rate, cable length, packet lengths, and control overhead.

I. INTRODUCTION

LOCAL networks are intended to provide improved communication capabilities among terminals and computers within a limited geographical area like an establishment or a single building. In the local area, subnetworks like rings and buses which operate in a broadcast fashion represent attractive alternatives to store-and-forward and circuit-switching networks. Controversial arguments are used in the discussion about the attributes of the different systems, such as costs, ease of implementation, reliability, availability, serviceability, and performance. The objective of this paper is to shed more light onto the performance aspect which—probably more than the other issues—lends itself to an objective comparative evaluation. We consider four important candidates for local-area subnetworks: token ring; slotted ring (empty-slot technique); a random-access bus (carrier-sense multiple-access (CSMA) with collision detection); and an ordered-access bus (multilevel multiple-access (MLMA) scheme).

The investigation is based on analytic models which describe the various topologies and access mechanisms to a sufficient level of detail.

Our performance measure of prime interest is the delay-throughput characteristic of the systems. Delay is measured as the mean transfer time t_f of the packets which we define as the time interval from the generation of a packet at the source station until its reception at the destination. This means the transfer time includes the queueing and access delay at the sender, the transmission time of the packet, and the propagation delay.

II. MODELING OF SUBNETWORKS

In this section, the four subnetworks studied are described to the extent necessary for understanding their performance models. Explicit analytic results for the mean transfer time of all systems are given. To allow for direct comparison of the results, consistent assumptions with respect to traffic properties are used for all models: 1) Packets are generated at the S stations according to Poisson processes with rates λ_1 through λ_S. (We denote by λ the aggregate arrival rate $\lambda_1 + \cdots + \lambda_S$ of all stations.) 2) The packet lengths L_p can be generally distributed. In the subnetwork, a header of length L_h containing control and addressing information is added to every packet.

Furthermore, we denote by v the transmission rate (speed) and by τ the maximum end-to-end propagation delay in case of a bus, or the round-trip latency in case of a ring system (including possible delays of the signals caused within the stations). The propagation delay is assumed to be 5 μs/km cable length.

As pointed out above, the transfer time includes the propagation delay between source and destination of a packet. In what follows, we assume that the average distance between sender and receiver is half the maximum distance of the bus or ring. Finally, for this particular study, we exclude all effects related to transmission errors and their recovery.

A. Token Ring

In a token ring [1], [2], access to the transmission channel is controlled by passing a permission token around the ring. When the system is initialized, a designated station generates a free token which travels around the ring until a station ready to transmit changes it to busy and puts its packet onto the ring. The packet can, in principle, be of arbitrary length. The sending station is responsible for removing its own packet from the ring. At the end of its transmission, it passes the access permission to the next station by generating a new free token. Fig. 1 illustrates this operation for a ring with four stations. It shows how stations 1 and 3 and again station 1 subsequently access the ring to transmit their packets.

This operation is described by the performance model shown in Fig. 2 which is a single-server queueing model with as many queues as stations attached to the ring. The queues are serviced in a cyclical manner symbolized by the rotating switch which stands for the free token. The service time of a packet is given by $T_p = (L_h + L_p)/v$. The time needed for passing the free token from station i to station $i + 1$ (propagation delay plus additional latency within station i for token handling, etc.) is modeled by a constant switchover delay τ_i.

With respect to the order of service, several policies can be distinguished, e.g., that a queue is serviced until it is empty ("exhaustive service") or that only a limited number of packets (e.g., one) is serviced per access possibility ("nonexhaustive service"). Although, in principle, performance differences exist between these policies [3], it can be generally observed

Paper approved by the Editor for Computer Communication of the IEEE Communications Society for publication after presentation in part at the International Federation of Information Processing WG 6.4 International Workshop on Local-Area Networks, Zurich, Switzerland, August 1980. Manuscript received February 1, 1980; revised March 22, 1981.

The author is with the IBM Zurich Research Laboratory, 8803 Rüschlikon, Switzerland.

EHO216-2/84/0000/0149$01.00 © 1981 IEEE

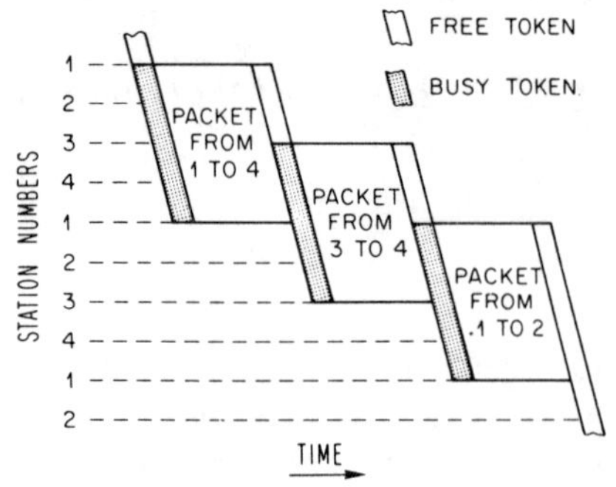

Fig. 1. Token ring: example of operation (4 stations).

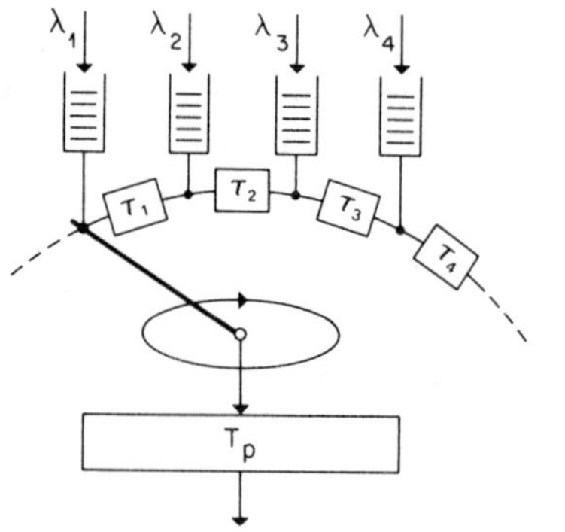

Fig. 2. Token-ring model (S = 4 stations; λ_i: packet arrival rates; T_p: packet service time; τ_i: latency of station i plus propagation delay from station i to station $i + 1$).

that for the parameters of interest in local networks, these differences are very small if the traffic is uniformly distributed among all stations. An intuitive explanation of this fact is that the total number of packets waiting simultaneously is distributed over a large number (e.g., 50 or more) of different queues, which means that the probability for more than one packet to be waiting within any queue is very low, unless the channel load is exceedingly high (e.g., >90 percent). A comparison of the results given below for the model of Fig. 1 with exhaustive service and the model in [4] provides additional confirmation of the above statement.

Using a discrete-time approach, an explicit solution for the mean queueing delay of the model described has been derived by Konheim and Meister [5] under the assumption of equal arrival rates λ_i and equal switchover delays τ_i. In order to eliminate the impact of the discrete time assumption for our comparison purposes, we subsequently consider the case of the discrete-time interval approaching zero. For this limiting case and Poisson arrival processes, we can deduce the following result for the mean transfer time t_f.

$$t_f = \frac{\rho E[T_p{}^2]}{2(1-\rho)E[T_p]} + E[T_p] + \frac{\tau\left(1 - \dfrac{\rho}{S}\right)}{2(1-\rho)} + \frac{\tau}{2} \qquad (1)$$

with

$$\rho = \lambda E[T_p], \quad T_p = (L_h + L_p)/v.$$

Equation (1) is also in consonance with a result given by Sykes [6] for the special case of $S = 2$ queues.

A necessary assumption underlying (1) is that all stations generate the same amount of traffic. If the traffic offered is unbalanced among the stations, no explicit analytic result is known; however, the following consideration provides some insight into the nature of this case. Let us consider a newly arriving packet. Under our exhaustive-service discipline, the token-passing overhead associated with the transmission of this and subsequent packets is maximum if the probability that the packet joins an empty queue is as high as possible. The latter probability is maximum if the arrival rates of all stations are equal. Although this consideration is obviously not a rigorous proof, it suggests that, with respect to the transfer delay averaged over all stations, (1) is not only exact for the balanced-traffic case but, moreover, represents an upper bound on the overall mean transfer delay, irrespective of the station-specific arrival rates.

Since token rings differ in the way their stations issue a new token, we subsequently discuss how these different possibilities can be analyzed.

In the basic model developed so far, a new free token was generated immediately after the last bit of a packet had left the sending station. This implies that, depending on packet length and physical length of the ring at any given time, multiple tokens can exist on the ring; at most one of them, however, is in the free state ("multiple-token" operation).

From a reliability and recovery point of view, it may be desirable never to have more than one token at a time on the ring. This can be achieved in two ways: 1) The conservative approach is that the sender of a packet issues the new token when he has completely erased his entire packet ("single-packet" operation). In our performance model, this can simply be taken into account by prolonging the packet service time T_p by the total ring round-trip delay τ. 2) A more efficient solution is that the sender of a packet does not issue a new token before he has received his own token ("single-token" operation). This rule becomes effective in cases when a packet is shorter than the ring latency. In our performance model, we can describe this mode by setting the service time T_p equal to the ring latency for all those packets shorter than the ring latency.

This means all three kinds of token-ring operation can be handled by the cyclical queueing model of Fig. 2 by appropriately adjusting the service-time distribution.

B. Slotted Ring

In the type of slotted rings [1], [2], [7] which we study, a constant number of fixed-length slots continuously circulates around the ring. A full/empty indicator within the slot header is used to signal the state of a slot. Any station ready to transmit occupies the first empty slot by setting the full/empty indicator to "full," and places its data into the slot. When the sender receives back the occupied slot, it changes the full/empty indicator to "empty." This operation prevents hogging of the ring and guarantees fair sharing of the bandwidth among all stations. Using a representation similar to the previous one, operation of the slotted ring is illustrated in Fig. 3. For simplicity, it is assumed that the ring carries a single slot only. Furthermore, it is assumed that both stations 1 and 2 have a packet ready to transmit. Usually, the slots in local

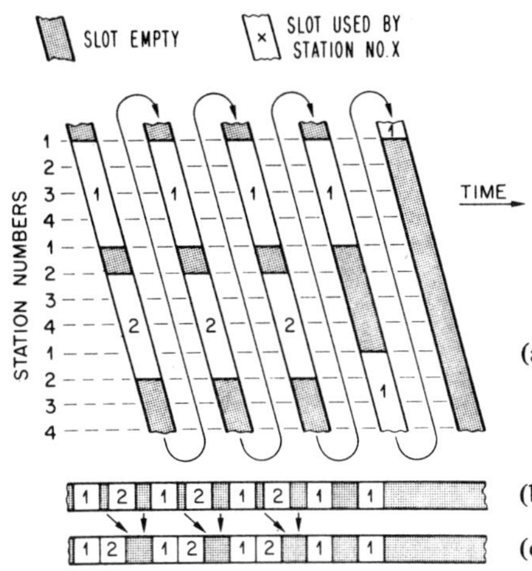

Fig. 3. Slotted ring: example of operation (4 stations, 1 slot).

rings are short, which means that a packet or message has to be transmitted within several slots. As the figure shows, both stations share the ring bandwidth in a fair way until they have completely transmitted their packets. Fig. 3(b), in a different representation, shows when and by which station the slot is occupied. What can be clearly observed from this representation is that between two subsequent access possibilities of a certain station, the slot travels exactly once around the ring in empty state. To simplify the modeling, we slightly modify the sequence of Fig. 3(b) as shown in Fig. 3(c). All time periods of one cycle during which the slot is empty are lumped together in one contiguous empty-slot interval. The inaccuracy in the transfer time introduced by this simplification is on the order of the slot length, which is negligible since we subsequently study the case of short slots.

The operation illustrated in Fig. 3(c) is described by the queueing model shown in Fig. 4 with $S + 1$ queues, where S is the number of stations attached to the ring. Packets waiting in one of the queues are served in sequence for a short time quantum Δt which corresponds to the slot length. Between two successive access possibilities of a station, the free slot has made exactly one complete cycle around the ring. Since the ring latency corresponds to one slot duration, it can be described exactly by the closed loop in Fig. 4 which constantly contains one fictitious customer.

For analytic convenience, we subsequently adopt the point of view that the service quantum Δt shrinks to zero. This concept was introduced by Kleinrock in the context of time-sharing systems [8]. It is well known that the resulting "processor-sharing" model yields very good approximations to the finite-quantum results if the quantum is sufficiently short compared to the mean service time [9]. Since in the local environment, on the average, packets are usually at least ten times longer than the slot, this condition is normally fulfilled.

If a ring operates with more than one slot, the exact description of the operation is less simple. However, if we again consider the limiting case of the slot size approaching zero, the processor-sharing model of Fig. 4 also applies for this case, as is subsequently explained. The concept for treating the case of $\sigma > 1$ slots is to fictitiously reorder the sequence of the slots such that always σ slots occupied by the same station can be conceived as lumped together forming one service quantum. The difference between the transfer time of the real scheme with the original slot sequence and the fictitious scheme with the reordered sequence is on the order of a slot, i.e., a service quantum. Hence, as the quanta shrink to zero, this reordering does not affect the transfer delay of the packets so that the processor-sharing model of Fig. 4 still applies.

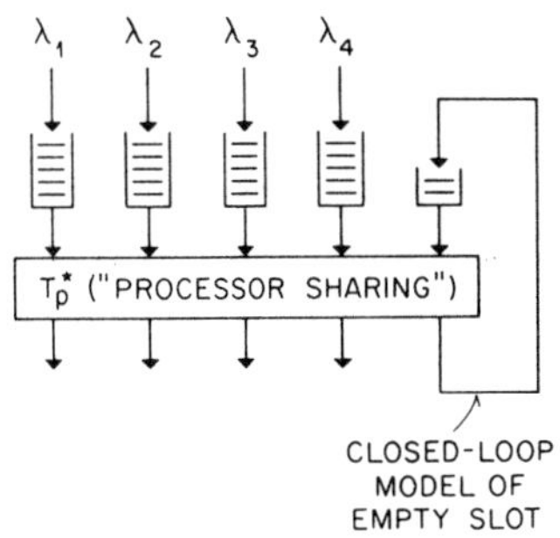

Fig. 4. Slotted-ring model ($S = 4$ stations; λ_i: packet arrival rates; T_P^*: packet service time).

In order to determine the mean transfer time, the model of Fig. 4 can be conceived as a simple mixed queueing network with $(S + 1)$ classes of customers [10]. If we denote by x_i the number of packets within queue Q_i, we can determine the steady-state probabilities of the model as

$$p(\vec{x}) = p(x_1, \cdots, x_S) = (1-\rho)^2 \binom{x_1 + \cdots + x_S + 1}{x_1, \cdots, x_S} \rho_1^{x_1} \cdots \rho_S^{x_S} \tag{2}$$

with

$$\rho_i = \lambda_i E[T_p^*]; \quad \rho = \sum_{i=1}^{S} \rho_i.$$

With respect to the average packet service time $E[T_p^*]$, we must note that every slot consists of a data field of length L_d and a header field of length L_h. We take this into account by prolonging the mean packet service time according to

$$E[T_p^*] = \frac{L_h + L_d}{L_d} \cdot \frac{E[L_p]}{v}. \tag{3}$$

It should be noted that in this way the impact of the overhead for control and addressing is correctly taken into account and that this must not be confused with the concept of considering the limiting case of the service quanta approaching zero length.

From (2), the expectation of the total number of packets in the system is simply derived; application of Little's theorem [9] leads directly to the following simple expression for the mean transfer time.

$$t_f = \frac{2}{1-\rho} E[T_p^*] + \frac{\tau}{2}. \tag{4}$$

Depending on the number of attached stations, a gap between the slots exists in a real system if the buffering capacity of the ring is not an integral multiple of the slot size. For the examples in Section III, we assume that the length of this gap is always zero, in other words, that the ring bandwidth can be fully utilized. This means we assume for simplicity that the following relation holds among ring latency τ, transmission rate v, slot length $L_h + L_d$, and the number of slots σ.

$$\tau \cdot v = \sigma(L_h + L_d). \tag{5}$$

The above analysis of a local-area slotted ring turns out to yield accurate results over a broad range of parameters as comparisons to simulation results show (see, e.g., Fig. 12).

C. CSMA Collision-Detection Bus

Among the numerous random-access schemes (see, for example, [9], [11]), carrier-sense multiple-access with collision detection (CSMA-CD) appears to be a very attractive solution for use on a bus system [2], [12]. Under a CSMA-CD protocol, every station wanting to transmit a packet must listen to the bus in order to find out whether any transmission is in progress. In this case, it defers its transmission until the end of the current transmission. In spite of carrier sensing, packet collisions cannot be completely avoided because of the nonzero propagation delay of the bus. Upon detection of a collision, transmission is aborted and the station reschedules its packet by selecting a random retransmission interval. Fig. 5 illustrates this operation. To avoid accumulation of retransmissions, in other words, to achieve stability, the retransmission interval is dynamically adjusted to the actual traffic load.

Performance analyses of CSMA-CD systems have been performed by Lam [13] and Tobagi and Hunt [14]. For our comparison, we adopt the solution given in [13] which has been derived under the assumption that the system is stabilized by using a suitable adaptive algorithm. For reasons of analytical tractability, a slotted channel with slot length 2τ was assumed in [13]. A consequence of this assumption is that even if the utilization approaches zero, packets have to wait for the time τ on the average before they are transmitted. Since this access delay does not occur in a nonslotted system, it may be the source of possible misinterpretations of our comparative results. Therefore, we heuristically modify the delay formula in [13] by reducing the mean delay by τ. This is further motivated by the consideration that the mean queueing delay of a normal $M/G/1$ queue and that of an $M/G/1$ queue with clocked service differs by half the clock interval. With this slight modification of the delay formula in [13], the mean transfer time of the bus with CSMA and collision detection is given by

$$t_f = \frac{\lambda\{E[T_p^2] + (4e+2)\tau E[T_p] + 5\tau^2 + 4e(2e-1)\tau^2\}}{2\{1 - \lambda(E[T_p] + \tau + 2e\tau)\}} + E[T_P] \tag{6}$$

$$+ 2\tau e - \frac{(1 - e^{-2\lambda\tau})\left(\frac{2}{\lambda} + \frac{2\tau}{e} - 6\tau\right)}{2\left\{F_p^*(\lambda)e^{-\lambda\tau}\frac{1}{e} - 1 + e^{-2\lambda\tau}\right\}} + \frac{\tau}{2}.$$

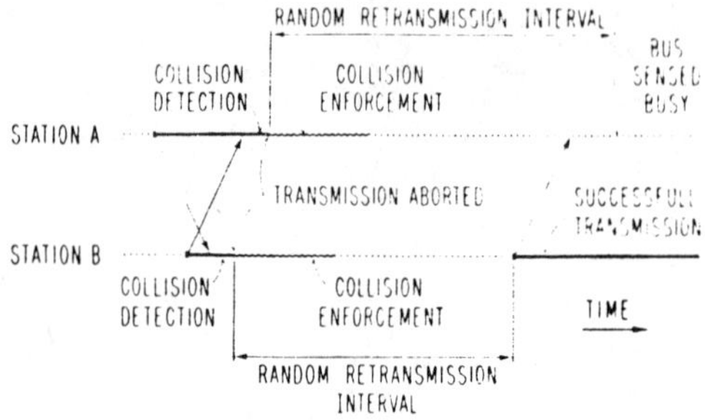

Fig. 5. CSMA collision-detection bus: example of operation.

The term $F_p{}^*$ in (6) stands for the Laplace transform of the probability density function of the packet service time $T_p = (L_h + L_p)/v$.

D. Ordered-Access Bus

As an example of a bus system employing ordered access, we consider the reservation-type scheme MLMA (multilevel multiple-access) proposed by Rothauser and Wild [15] which works as follows. Information transmission occurs in variable-length frames, the structure of which is shown in Fig. 6. A controller provides start flags at appropriate time intervals which signal the beginning of a frame. A frame is divided into two parts, a request slot and an arbitrary number of packets. In the version of MLMA considered here, every station attached to the bus owns one bit within the request slot. By setting its private bit, a station indicates that it wants to transmit a packet within this frame. At the end of the request cycle, all stations know which of the stations will make use of this frame. The transmission sequence is given by a priority assignment known to all stations.

The performance model to describe this kind of operation is shown in Fig. 7. The bus is modeled as a single-server facility. Packets from all stations, which have been newly generated and have not yet been scheduled, form the distributed queue Q_0. According to the above bus operation, these new packets cannot be transmitted within the current frame but have to wait until the new frame starts. At this point, all packets within Q_0 simultaneously obtain a first service phase of length T_S which represents the time needed for scheduling. To ensure that all stations know the entries made in the request slot, the scheduling time T_S may have to be significantly longer than the pure transmission time of the request slot. In our examples, we set T_S equal to twice the time needed to transmit S bits plus twice the propagation delay τ. Following the batch service of length T_S, the packets are put into queues Q_1-Q_S, where Q_1 contains the scheduled packets of the station with highest priority and, accordingly, Q_S those with lowest priority. When all packets in queues Q_1-Q_S have been transmitted, a new frame is started.

The version of the MLMA method described above is similar in concept to a bus access method which has been described and approximately analyzed by Mark [16], and to a contention resolution method for computer-interrupt systems suggested by Taub [17].

In the Appendix, the mean transfer time of this ordered-

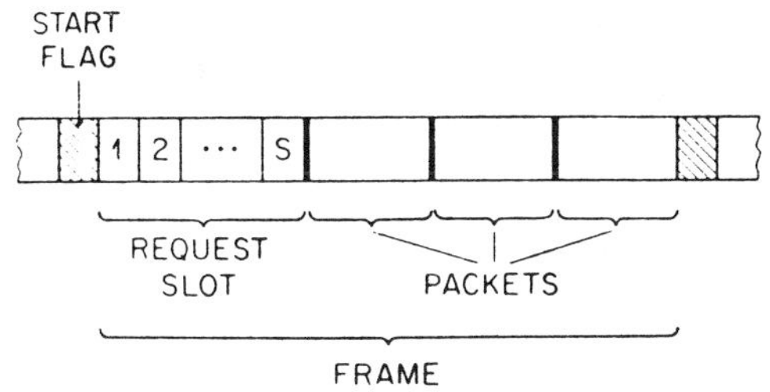

Fig. 6. Frame structure of the ordered-access bus.

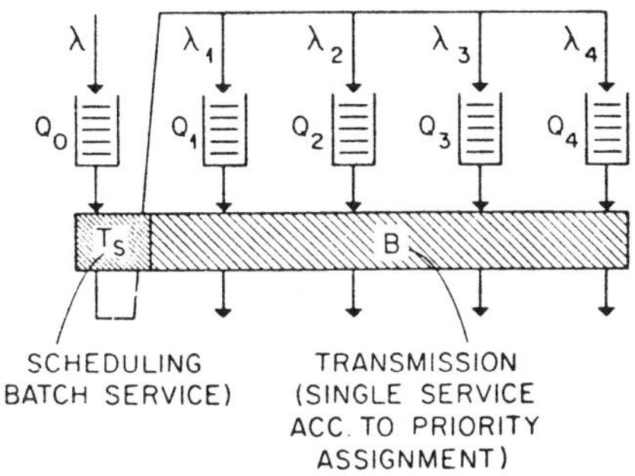

Fig. 7. Ordered-access bus model (S = 4 stations; λ_i: packet arrival rates; λ: total packet arrival rate; B: packet service time; T_S: scheduling time).

access bus is derived as

$$t_f = \frac{\rho' \left\{ E[T_p{}^2] + \tau E[T_p] + \dfrac{\tau^2}{3} \right\}}{2(1-\rho') \left\{ E\,[T_p] + \dfrac{\tau}{2} \right\}} + E[T_p] + \frac{3-\rho'}{1-\rho'} \frac{T_S}{2} + \frac{\tau}{2} \tag{7}$$

with

$$\rho' = \lambda \left\{ E[T_p] + \frac{\tau}{2} \right\}, \qquad T_p = (L_h + L_p)/v.$$

The underlying assumption of (7) is that the distance between two stations transmitting in succession is uniformly distributed between zero and the maximum bus length.

III. RESULTS

In this section, we present typical performance results for the four subnetworks. All subsequent figures show on the ordinate the mean transfer time t_f relative to the mean packet transmission time $E[L_p]/v$. (Note that packet transmission time is defined here as the time required to transmit a packet without header.) In Figs. 8-12, the abscissa represents the ratio of throughput rate $\lambda E[L_p]$ (bits/s) and transmission rate (speed) v.

Fig. 8 compares the delay-throughput characteristic of the four systems at a transmission rate of 1 Mbit/s. The figure shows that under these assumptions the token ring and the two buses perform almost equally well, because the overhead for the various access mechanisms is almost negligible. (Note that in this and the next two figures, the "single-token" kind of operation has been assumed for the token ring.) The slotted ring (one slot) exhibits considerably worse performance than the other systems because of the following two effects: 1) The buffering capability and, hence, slot length of the ring is small (60 bits in this example). This leads to an unfavorable ratio of the header length (24 bits assumed here) to the data field per slot. 2) The time needed for passing around access permission—in the form of an empty slot—is significant, as already discussed in the context of Fig. 3. An additional discussion of the delay behavior of slotted rings is provided below in the context of Fig. 12.

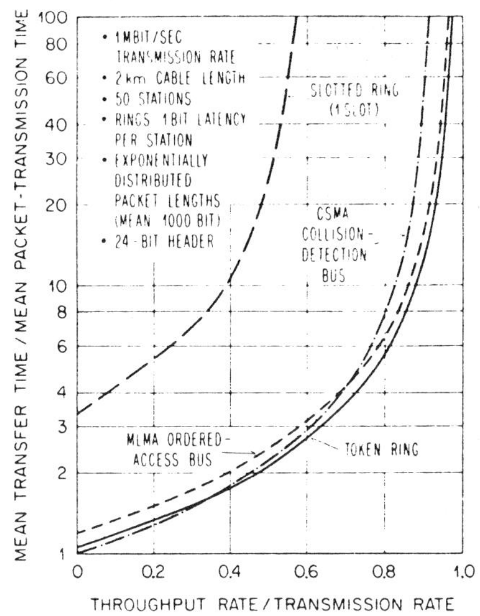

Fig. 8. Transfer delay-throughput characteristics of the four subnetworks at 1 Mbit/s.

In Fig. 9, only one parameter has been changed as compared to the previous example, namely, the transmission rate, which is now 10 Mbits/s. The most remarkable difference is observed for the CSMA-CD bus: whereas for loads less than 0.2 it shows the best performance, the transfer delay increases rather rapidly for loads greater than 0.4 and has a vertical asymptote at about 0.6. The obvious reason for this behavior is that for higher throughput values, the frequency of transmission attempts during the vulnerable period of the propagation delay is such that a significant portion of transmission attempts ends in collision. Thus, the transfer delay increases due to the need for retransmissions.

Investigations of other policies indicate that the maximum achievable throughput can be slightly increased by using a different CSMA-CD protocol [14]. Nevertheless, the general conclusion drawn from this figure remains true, namely, that even a sophisticated random-access scheme like CSMA-CD leads to inefficient operation if the ratio of propagation delay to packet transmission time is too high. It should be noted that our assumption of only 5 μs propagation delay per km cable represents an optimistic view, since other delay components such as signal rise times or repeater delays may significantly increase the total end-to-end propagation delay.

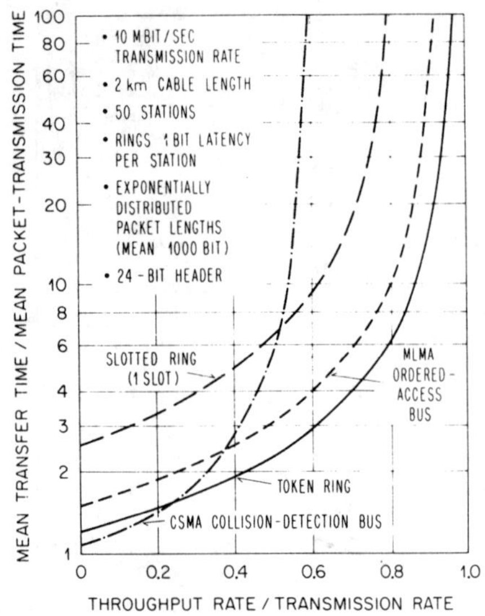

Fig. 9. Transfer delay-throughput characteristics of the four subnetworks at 10 Mbits/s.

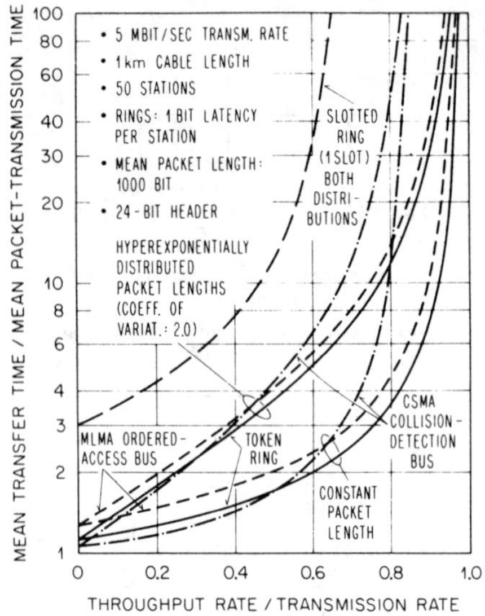

Fig. 10. Transfer delay-throughput characteristics of the four subnetworks for constant and hyperexponentially distributed packet lengths.

In contrast to the CSMA-CD bus, the token ring performs almost ideally also for higher speeds. Its slightly higher delay for low throughput is due to the access delay of the ring until a free token arrives. The transfer time of the MLMA ordered-access bus is slightly longer than that of the token ring over the whole range of throughput values. This is mainly due to the bus-scheduling overhead. As can be seen from comparison of Figs. 8 and 9, performance of the slotted ring improves considerably if the transmission rate is increased: since the slots become longer, the relative overhead for control and addressing decreases.

The examples considered so far have been gained under the assumption of exponentially distributed packet lengths. Fig. 10 shows the delay-throughput characteristics for two other types of packet-length distributions: constant length and hyperexponential distribution of order two with a coefficient of variation equal to two. According to (4), the mean transfer time of the slotted ring is independent of the type of packet-length distribution. This is a consequence of the processor-sharing type of operation. The other three subnetworks show growing transfer delay if the variance of the packet-length distribution increases. It can be seen, however, that the general relation among the transfer delay of the three systems is robust with respect to packet-length distribution.

The following figures show results for the individual subnetworks to demonstrate the impact of certain parameters especially critical for the different systems.

Fig. 11 visualizes that in a token ring the latency caused within the stations by actions like token handling or altering of control information represents a critical quantity. It shows, in particular, how the three different operational modes of the token ring described in Section II-A, "multiple-token," "single-token," and "single-packet," perform for different values of the station latency. Two conclusions can be drawn from this result: 1) In general, the station latency should be kept as low as possible, at least if a great number of stations is attached or short packets are used. 2) If the ring latency is low, no significant benefits can be drawn from allowing multiple concurrent tokens on the ring, whereas for greater latency, multiple-token operation appears necessary to achieve reasonable performance.

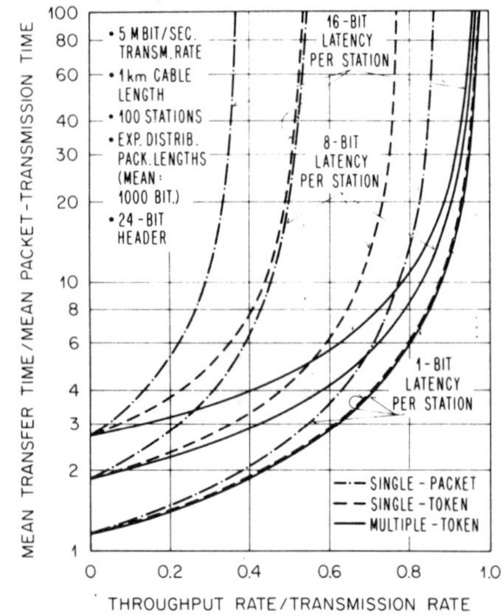

Fig. 11. Transfer delay-throughput characteristic of token rings. Impact of station latency and operational mode.

Fig. 12 shows that, from an efficiency point of view, for a slotted ring in the local environment, the use of one slot is usually preferable to using two or more slots. This insight is in accordance with results gained from a simulation study of slotted rings [18]. The relation of header length to data per slot can be improved by inserting artificial latency in the ring. As shown in Fig. 12 for the case of four-bit latency per station as compared to one bit, this can actually result in shorter transfer times. However, as becomes clear from (4), the mean transfer time of the slotted ring is roughly twice that of an $M/M/1$ queue even if the header length is zero. One can consider this as the price paid for the advantages of the processor-sharing kind of operation. Also shown in Fig. 12 are results obtained with a simulation model in which the ring operation was modeled in full detail. This and other examples indicate the

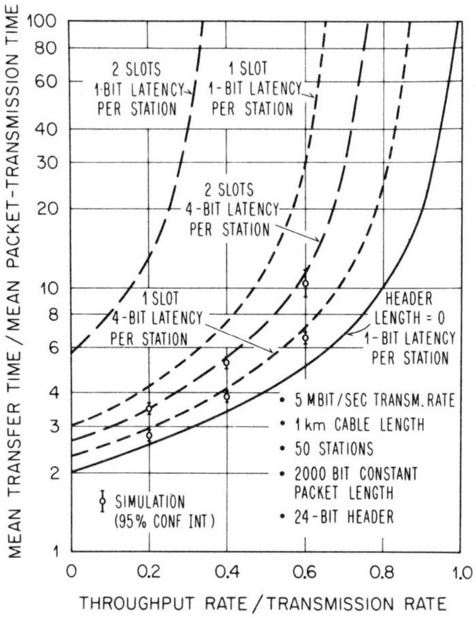

Fig. 12. Transfer delay-throughput characteristic of slotted rings. Impact of slot number and latency per station.

validity of the model developed in Section II-B over a broad range of slot numbers and sizes.

Fig. 13 shows for a CSMA-CD bus the mean transfer time relative to the mean packet-transmission time as a function of the propagation delay relative to the packet-transmission time. For simplicity, the header length has been set to zero in this example. The figure indicates that the CSMA-CD bus behaves ideally as long as the ratio of propagation delay to mean packet transmission time is sufficiently low. If for reasonable traffic loads this ratio exceeds 2-5 percent (as a rule of thumb), the increasing collision frequency causes significant performance degradation.

IV. SUMMARY

In this paper, we considered the performance of four local-area subnetworks: token ring, slotted ring, CSMA-CD bus, and an ordered-access bus. To guarantee a fair comparison, a prime objective was to study the systems based on consistent assumptions. Although the considered transfer delay-throughput behavior does not completely characterize all performance aspects of local-area networks, the analysis of this measure leads to basic insight into the performance properties of the different approaches.

APPENDIX

DERIVATION OF THE MEAN TRANSFER DELAY FOR THE ORDERED-ACCESS BUS

In this Appendix, we derive delay formula (7). We denote by $b(t)$ and $s(t)$ the probability density functions of the packet service time B and the scheduling interval T_S (assumed to be a random variable here). The service time B of a packet, i.e., the time it occupies the bus, has two components: 1) its transmission time, and 2) the propagation delay between subsequently transmitting stations. The assumption made for (7) is that the second component is uniformly distributed between zero and the maximum bus propagation delay.

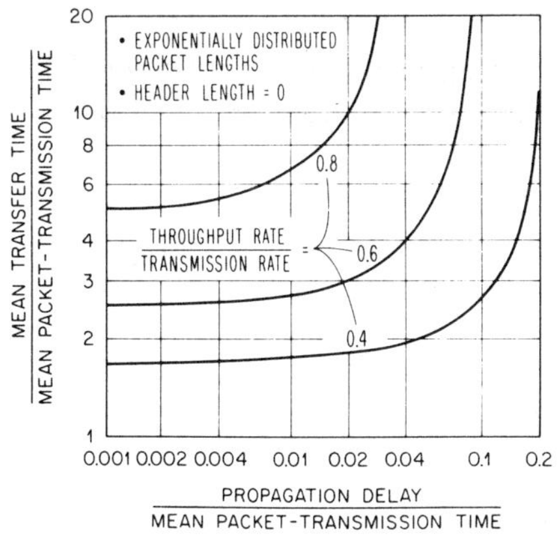

Fig. 13. Normalized mean transfer delay versus propagation delay relative to mean packet-transmission time for the CSMA-CD bus.

We derive the mean transfer time $t_f(k)$ of the packets from queue Q_k by tracing a "tagged" packet of this queue on its way through the system. The transfer delay of the tagged packet consists of the following parts: 1) the time until the start of the next frame, subsequently denoted as residual frame length F_r; 2) the scheduling delay T_S; 3) the delay $D_1(k)$ due to packets in the higher priority queues $Q_1, \cdots, Q_{k-1}$; 4) the delay $D_2(k)$ due to those packets in queue Q_k which are transmitted before the tagged packet; and 5) its own service time B.

Taking expectations of these times we obtain

$$t_f(k) = E[F_r] + E[T_S] + E[D_1(k)] + E[D_2(k)] + E[B]. \tag{A1}$$

We subsequently show how the unknown terms $E[F_r]$, $E[D_1(k)]$, and $E[D_2(k)]$ can be determined.

Residual Frame Length: If we denote by F the total random frame length, then the following relation is known from renewal theory (see, e.g., [9]).

$$E[F_r] = \frac{E[F^2]}{2E[F]}. \tag{A2}$$

We denote by $f_j(t)$ the probability density function of the length of the jth frame. Furthermore, let $F_j^*(p)$, $S^*(p)$, and $B^*(p)$ be the Laplace-Stieltjes transforms of $f_j(t)$, $s(t)$, and $b(t)$, respectively.

The length of the jth frame is given by the scheduling delay plus the sum of the transmission times of all packets which arrived during frame $(j-1)$. Hence, the following recursive relation holds.

$$f_j(t) = \sum_{n=0}^{\infty} \{b^{(n)}(t) * s(t)\} \int_0^{\infty} e^{-\lambda t} \frac{(\lambda t)^n}{n!} f_{j-1}(t)\, dt \tag{A3}$$

where $b^{(n)}(t)$ denotes the nth convolution of $b(t)$.

Transforming (A3) yields

$$F_j^*(p) = \sum_{n=0}^{\infty} B^*(p)^n S^*(p) \int_0^{\infty} e^{-\lambda t} \frac{(\lambda t)^n}{n!} f_{j-1}(t)\, dt$$

$$= S^*(p) F_{j-1}^*(\lambda\{1 - B^*(p)\}). \tag{A4}$$

Under stationary assumptions, we obtain the following functional equation for the limit of F_j^* as j approaches infinity.

$$F^*(p) = S^*(p)F^*(\lambda\{1 - B^*(p)\}). \tag{A5}$$

By differentiating (A5) and taking values for $p = 0$, we finally obtain

$$E[F] = \frac{E[T_S]}{1-\rho} \tag{A6}$$

$$E[F^2] = E[F]^2 + \frac{E[T_s^2] - E[T_S]^2 + \lambda E[F]E[B^2]}{1-\rho^2} \tag{A7}$$

with $\rho = \lambda E[B]$.

We remark that an alternative though less direct way to derive (A6) and (A7) is to make use of a result for the number of customers served during one cycle of a multiqueue system [19].

Delay Component $D_1(k)$: The mean number of packets in queue Q_ν which are generated after the start of the last frame but before the tagged packet is given by

$$\psi_b(\nu) = \lambda_\nu E[F_e] \tag{A8}$$

where F_e is defined as the elapsed frame length until the arrival of the tagged customer. Again, it is known from renewal theory that the distribution of the elapsed frame length is equal to the distribution of the residual frame length:

$$E[F_e] = E[F_r] = \frac{E[F^2]}{2E[F]}. \tag{A9}$$

The mean number of packets in queue Q_ν which are generated after the tagged packet but before the start of the next frame is given by

$$\psi_a(\nu) = \lambda_\nu E[F_r]. \tag{A10}$$

Therefore, the expectation of $D_1(k)$ is given by

$$E[D_1(k)] = \sum_{\nu=1}^{k=1} \{\psi_b(\nu) + \psi_a(\nu)\}E[B] \tag{A11}$$

$$= \sum_{\nu=1}^{k-1} \rho_\nu \frac{E[F^2]}{E[F]}.$$

Delay Component $D_2(k)$: Since we assume first-come/first-served within each queue, the delay $D_2(k)$ is due to packets in queue Q_k which arrived after the beginning of the last frame but before the tagged packet. Its expectation is therefore given by

$$E[D_2(k)] = \lambda_k E[F_e]E[B]$$

$$= \rho_k \frac{E[F^2]}{2E[F]}. \tag{A12}$$

Mean Transfer Time $t_f(k)$: We have now determined all components of the mean transfer time in (A1). By substituting (A2), (A6), (A7), (A11), and (A12) into (A1), we obtain

$$t_f(k) = \frac{1}{2}\left(1 + 2\sum_{\nu=1}^{k-1} \rho_\nu + \rho_k\right)\left\{\frac{E[T_S]}{1-\rho}\left(1 + C_s^2 \frac{1-\rho}{1+\rho}\right) + \frac{\rho E[B^2]}{(1-\rho^2)E[B]}\right\} + E[B] + E[T_S] \tag{A13}$$

with

$$C_s^2 = \frac{E[T_S^2] - E[T_S]^2}{E[T_S]^2}. \tag{A14}$$

For the case of a constant scheduling interval T_S and the particular definition of the packet service time given above, we finally obtain (7) from (A13) by averaging over all stations.

ACKNOWLEDGMENT

The author would like to thank K. Kümmerle for reviewing the manuscript, and H. L. Truong for his help in producing the simulation results.

REFERENCES

[1] B. K. Penney and A. A. Baghdadi, "Survey of computer communications loop networks: Parts 1 and 2," *Comput. Commun.*, vol. 2, pp. 165–180, 244–241, 1979.

[2] D. D. Clark, K. T. Pogran, and D. P. Reed, "An introduction to local area networks," *Proc. IEEE*, vol. 66, pp. 1497–1517, 1978.

[3] P. J. Kuehn, "Multiqueue systems with nonexhaustive cyclic service," *Bell Syst. Tech. J.*, vol 58, pp. 671–698, 1979.

[4] A. R. Kaye, "Analysis of a distributed control loop for data transmission," in *Proc. Comput. Commun. Networks and Teletraffic Symp.* Brooklyn, NY: Polytechnic, 1972, pp. 47–58.

[5] A. G. Konheim and B. Meister, "Waiting lines and times in a system with polling," *J. Ass. Comput. Mach.*, vol. 21, pp 470–490, 1974.

[6] J. S. Sykes, "Simplified analysis of an alternating-priority queueing model with setup times," *Oper. Res.*, vol. 18, pp. 1182–1192, 1970.

[7] A. Hopper, "Data ring at computer laboratory, University of Cambridge," in *Computer Science and Technology: Local Area Networking*. Washington, DC: Nat. Bur. Stand., NBS Special Pub. 500-31, 1977, pp. 11–16.

[8] L. Kleinrock, "Time-shared systems: A theoretical treatment," *J. Ass. Comput. Mach.*, vol. 14, pp. 242–261, 1967.

[9] ——, *Queueing Systems*, Vols. I and II. New York: Wiley, 1975, 1976.

[10] F. Baskett, K. M. Chandy, R. R. Muntz, and F. G. Palacios, "Open, closed, and mixed networks of queues with different classes of customer," *J. Ass. Comput. Mach.*, vol. 22, pp. 248–260, 1975.

[11] L. Kleinrock and F. A. Tobagi, "Packet switching in radio channels: Part I—Carrier sense multiple-access modes and their throughput-delay characteristics," *IEEE Trans. Commun.*, vol. COM-23, pp. 1400–1416, 1975.

[12] R. M. Metcalfe and D. R. Boggs, "Ethernet: Distributed packet

switching for local computer networks,'' *Commun. Ass. Comput. Mach.*, vol. 19, pp. 395–404, 1976.

[13] S. S. Lam, ''A carrier sense multiple access protocol for local networks,'' *Comput. Networks*, vol. 4, pp. 21–32, 1980.

[14] F. A. Tobagi and V. B. Hunt, ''Performance analysis of carrier sense multiple access with collision detection,'' *Comput. Networks*, vol 4, pp. 245–259, 1980.

[15] E. H. Rothauser and D. Wild, ''MLMA: A collision-free multi-access method,'' in *Proc. IFIP Congress 77*. Amsterdam, The Netherlands: North-Holland, 1977, pp. 431–436.

[16] J. W. Mark, ''Global scheduling approach to conflict-free multiaccess via a data bus,'' *IEEE Trans. Commun.*, vol COM-26, pp. 1342–1352, 1978.

[17] D. M. Taub, ''Contention-resolving circuits for computer interrupt systems,'' *Proc. Inst. Elec. Eng.*, vol 123, pp. 845–850, 1976.

[18] A. K. Agrawala, J. R. Agre, and K. D. Gordon, ''The slotted vs. the token-controlled ring: A comparative evaluation,'' in *Proc. COMPSAC 1978*. Chicago, IL: IEEE, 1978, pp. 674–679.

[19] M. A. Leibowitz, ''An approximate method for treating a class of multiqueue problems,'' *IBM J. Res. Develop.*, vol. 5, pp. 204–209, 1961.

★

Werner Bux received the M.S. and Ph.D. degrees in electrical engineering from the University of Stuttgart, Stuttgart, West Germany, in 1974 and 1980, respectively.

From 1974 to 1979 he was with the Institute of Switching and Data Techniques, University of Stuttgart, where he worked primarily in the field of performance analysis of data communication networks and computer systems. He joined the IBM Zurich Research Laboratory, Rüschlikon, Switzerland, in 1979, where he is currently working on the architecture and performance evaluation of local networks.

Reprinted with permission from *Computer Networks*, Volume 4, Number 1, February 1980, pages 21-32. Copyright © 1980 by North-Holland Publishing Company.

A Carrier Sense Multiple Access Protocol for Local Networks

Simon S. Lam
Department of Computer Sciences, University of Texas at Austin, Austin, Texas 78712, USA

A consequence of bursty traffic in computer communications is that among a large population of network users, at any one time only a small number of them have data to send (ready users). In this environment, the performance of an access protocol for a broadcast network depends mainly upon how quickly one of the ready users can be identified and given sole access to the shared channel. The relative merits of the access protocols of polling, probing and carrier sense multiple access (CSMA) with respect to this channel assignment delay in local networks are considered. A central controller is needed for polling and probing while CSMA employs distributed control. A specific CSMA protocol is defined which requires that "collisions" in the channel be detected and that the users involved in a collision abort their transmissions quickly. In addition, it is assumed that the contention algorithm is adaptive and gives rise to a stable channel. An analytic model is developed. Our main result is the moment generating function of the distributed queue size (number of ready users). Mean value formulas for message delay and channel assignment delay are also derived. These results on queue size and delay are the major contribution of this paper, since they are not available in prior CSMA models in closed analytical form. Numerical results are given to illustrate the performance of the CSMA protocol. When the channel utilization is light to moderate, the mean channel assignment delay of the CSMA protocol is significantly less than that of both polling and probing; consequently, the mean message delay is much smaller. It is also shown that when queueing of messages is permitted at individual users, the maximum channel throughput of CSMA approaches unity in the limit of very long queues. Finally, simulation results of several adaptive control algorithms are presented. The accuracy of our analytic formulas was carefully studied and found to be very good in all cases considered.

Keywords: Local Networks, broadcast channel, multiple access protocols, distributed queueing, performance analysis, queueing theory.

* This work was supported by National Science Foundation under Grant No. ENG78-01803.

Computer Networks 4 (1980) 21–32

1. Introduction

Multipoint networks have been widely used in local networking for the interconnection of terminals to a central site: either a central computing facility or a gateway to a resource sharing computer network. The terminals are typically unintelligent and access to the shared data path (channel) is managed by the central site using a polling protocol [1]. With increasing interest in local networking and the availability of inexpensive microprocessors, other interconnection topologies, transmission media and access protocols have been proposed and investigated. They include loop networks with centralized control [2] or distributed control [3], a digital cable network using time-division multiple access [4], the ALOHANET [5] and the Packet Radio Network [6]; the last two pioneered the use of radio channels and contention protocols for multiple access. Recently, considerable interest has been revived in multipoint cable networks

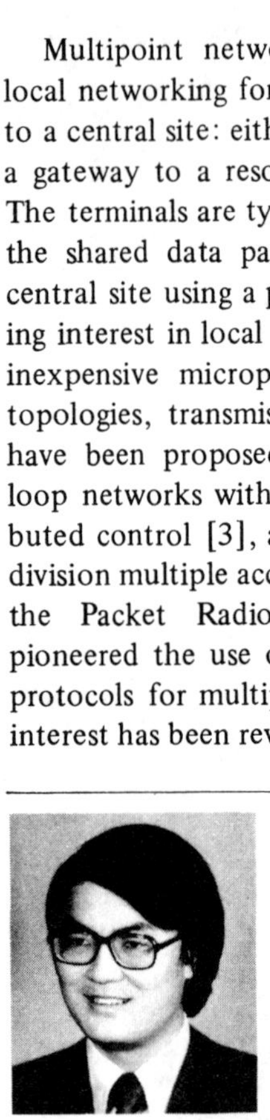

Simon S. Lam received the B.S.E.E. degree (with Distinction) from Washington State University, Pullman, Washington, in 1969, and the M.S. and Ph.D. degrees in engineering from the University of California at Los Angeles, in 1970 and 1974, respectively. From 1972 to 1974, he was with the ARPA Network project at UCLA and did research on satellite packet communication. From 1974 to 1977, he was a research staff member with the IBM Thomas J. Watson Research Center, Yorktown Heights, New York where he worked on performance analysis problems of packet switching networks, SNA and satellite networks. Since September 1977, he has been with the University of Texas at Austin where he is now Associate Professor of Computer Sciences. His current research interests include computer systems modeling and analysis, computer-communication networks and protocols. At the University of California at Los Angeles, he held a Phi Kappa Phi Fellowship from 1969 to 1970, and a Chancellor's Teaching Fellowship from 1969 to 1973. In 1975, he received the Leonard G. Abraham Award for the best paper of the year in the field of Communication Systems published in IEEE Transactions on Communications. Simon is a member of Tau Beta Pi, Sigma Tau, Phi Kappa Phi, Pi Mu Epsilon, the Association for Computing Machinery, and IEEE.

The author is pleased to acknowledge the programming assistance of Luke Lien. He is also indebted to an anonymous referee for his helpful comments.

(based upon CATV technology) employing a variety of multiple access protocols [7–12].

The multiple access problem in multipoint networks is addressed in this paper. A multipoint cable network such as those in [8–11] can be viewed upon as a broadcast channel shared by a population of distributed users. Suppose there are N users. There are two problems to be addressed by the access protocol: (1) among the N users, identify those with data who desire access to the channel, the *ready users*, and (2) assign channel access to exactly one of the ready users if at least one exists. We recognize the second problem to be a mutual exclusion problem with the broadcast channel being the shared resource [13]. The difficulty here is that the broadcast channel is also the only means of communication for coordinating the distributed users.

We can think of ready users as customers in a "distributed queue" waiting to use the broadcast channel. A consequence of the conservation law in queueing theory [14] is that the average message delay performance of an access protocol is independent of the order of service but depends mainly upon the amount of time wasted for assigning channel access. Thus, when access protocols are compared solely on the basis of average message delay performance for a given channel throughput level, the above two problems reduce to just the following. whenever the channel is free and there are one or more ready users, how quickly can channel access be assigned to a ready user? The amount of time needed will be referred to as the *channel assignment delay*.

Two major categories of multiple access protocols may be used: polling and contention protocols [15]. Polling protocols require a central controller. On the other hand, with contention protocols each network user makes his own decision according to an algorithm which is driven by observable outcomes in the broadcast channel. We shall consider multipoint networks that have short propagation delays between users relative to the transmission time of a message. In a short propagation delay environment, carrier sense multiple access (CSMA) protocols may be used. Under CSMA protocols, an individual user must sense the channel for the presence of any transmission in progress and is allowed to contend for the channel only if the channel is sensed idle. With carrier sensing, the probability of success of a transmitted message is much higher than that for pure random access i.e. ALOHA protocols [14–20]. However, "collisions" of transmissions by different users cannot be avoided entirely since the channel propagation delay between any two users is nonzero.

CSMA protocols have been studied extensively in the past within a packet radio network environment by Kleinrock and Tobagi [16,17] and later by Hansen and Schwartz [18]. Analytic results in these references are mainly concerned with the maximum channel "throughput" achievable by various protocols. Characterization of the number of ready users and message delay is limited to approximate numerical solutions or simulation results.

1.1. Summary of this paper

The main contribution of this paper is an accurate analytic model of a CSMA protocol. The protocol is defined in Section 2. In Section 3, the performance of various multiple access strategies under two extreme traffic conditions are compared. The figure of merit used is the mean value of channel assignment delay introduced earlier. The CSMA protocol is shown to possess some desirable performance characteristics. In Section 4, our CSMA analysis is presented. The moment generating function of the number of ready users is obtained. Formulas for the average message delay and average channel assignment delay are also derived. In Section 5, numerical results are plotted to illustrate the performance of the CSMA protocol, which is also compared with the performance of polling. A key assumption in our analysis is the presence of an effective adaptive control algorithm for contention. In section 6, several simple yet practical algorithms are given as well as simulation results of their performance. The accuracy of our analytic formulas is examined in detail. We conclude in the final section by discussing possible extensions and improvements of this work.

2. The CSMA Protocol

The main difference between the CSMA protocol studied in this paper and the p-persistent CSMA protocol of Kleinrock and Tobagi [16,17] is as follows. We assume here that collisions in the channel are detected and that users involved in a collision abort their transmissions immediately upon detecting the collision. Mechanisms for detecting collisions and aborting collided transmissions have been implemented in several multipoint cable networks [8,9, 11]. However, it appears to be much more difficult to

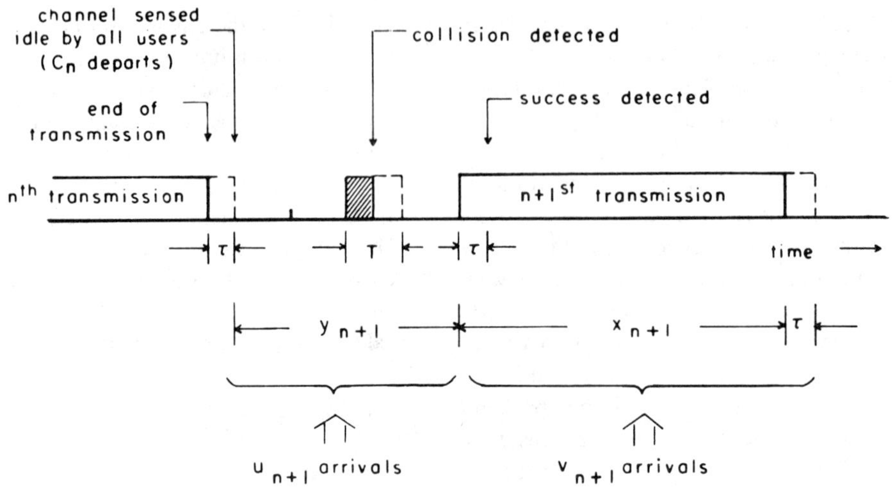

Fig. 1. A snapshot of the broadcast channel.

implement a "collision abort" capability in the radio environment of interest in [16,17].

Like the p-persistent protocol in [16,17], network users are assumed to be time synchronized so that following each successful transmission, the channel is slotted in time. (See Fig. 1.) Users can start transmissions only at the beginning of a time slot. Let τ be the amount of time from the start of transmission by one user to when all users sense the presence of this transmission. It is equal to the maximum propagation delay between two users in the network plus carrier detection time. (The latter depends upon the modulation technique and channel bandwidth. It was considered to be negligible relative to the propagation delay in [17].) In order to implement the collision abort capability described above, the minimum duration of a time slot is $T = 2\tau$, so that within a time slot if a collision is detected and the collided transmissions are aborted immediately, the channel will be free of any transmissions at the beginning of the next time slot.

The slotted channel assumption is made to simplify our analysis. The practical problem of time synchronizing all users in the network is a classical one and beyond the scope of this paper. (See [21].) It is reasonable to say that slotting can be accomplished fairly easily if the slot duration T is made much larger than 2τ; in other words, large guard times are used. In a real system, either a slotted or unslotted channel may be implemented.

Our CSMA protocol is defined by the following two possible courses of action for ready users:

(P1) Following a successful transmission, each ready user transmits with probability 1 into the next time slot.

(P2) Upon detection of a collision, each ready user uses an adaptive algorithm for selecting its transmission probability (<1) in the next time slot.

It should be clear at this point that we have effectively reduced the contention problem in CSMA to a slotted ALOHA problem. Slotted ALOHA has been studied extensively in the past [19,20,22–27], from which we learned that to prevent channel saturation (with zero probability of a successful transmission), the transmission probability of each ready user must be adaptively adjusted. Various control strategies have been proposed and studied. Experimental results have shown that a slotted ALOHA channel can be adaptively controlled to yield an equilibrium throughput rate S close to the theoretical limit of 1/e (=0.368) for a large population of users [23–26]. With an asymmetric strategy, the achievable S will be even higher [27].

3. A Comparison of Multiple Access Strategies

Using the mean value of channel assignment delay as a figure of merit, we shall examine in this section the performance of various multiple access strategies under two extreme traffic conditions. We shall first consider strategies using a central controller for "passive" users, and then strategies using distributed control for "active" users.

When a central controller is used, users are passive in the sense that they transmit only in response to a query from the central controller. In conventional polling protocols, the users are queried one by one, which is just a linear search procedure for identifying the ready users. To find out the status of all users (ready or not) in the population, the number of queries needed is N, which is just the number of users. This overhead is independent of the number of ready users actually present. Consider now two extreme traffic cnditions. First, suppose only one of the N users is ready (traffic condition 1). The mean number of queries needed to find the ready user is $(N + 1)/2$, assuming all users equally likely to be the ready user. The other extreme case is when all N users are ready (traffic condition 2). In this case, the number of queries needed to find a ready user (anyone) is 1.

The method of probing i.e. polling a group of users all at once, was recently proposed and studied by Hayes [28]. Each ready user responds to a probe by transmitting some noise energy in the channel. The central controller can only determine whether or not there is a response. He cannot tell, however, the exact number of ready users in the group probed. The key idea is as follows. If a group of users is probed and none responds because no one is ready, the whole group can be eliminated. If probing a group produces a positive response, it is subdivided into two (or more) groups which are then probed separately. When the network is lightly loaded, with few ready users, significant overhead reduction results through probing and eliminating groups of non-ready users all at once. Probing can be used in a tree search procedure for identifying ready users. For ease of exposition, suppose $N = 2^n$ for some positive integer n so that each user corresponds to a leaf in a binary tree. Suppose also that the search procedure begins with probing the whole tree. Again we consider the two extreme traffic conditions. First, if only one out of N users is ready, then it takes $2(\log_2 N) + 1$ queries to find out the status of all users; the mean number of queries needed to find the ready user is $\frac{3}{2}(\log_2 N) + 1$, assuming all users equally likely to be the ready user. On the other hand, if all N users are ready, then it takes $N^2 - 1$ queries to find out the status of all users and $(\log_2 N) + 1$ queries to find a ready user (anyone).

We next consider multiple access strategies based upon distributed control. Each ready user must actively seek channel access and make his own decisions according to an algorithm driven by observable outcomes in the broadcast channel. The contention protocol defined by (P1) and (P2) in the previous section is such a strategy. Under this protocol, when there is exactly one ready user and the channel is free, the channel assignment delay is 0. On the other hand, if all users are ready, then the mean channel assignment delay is 2.72 time slots. This last result is obtained under the assumption of an optimal algorithm for controlling the transmission probability in (P2) [19,20,22–27].

A linear search procedure can also be implemented using time slots and distributed control. An example is the MSAP protocol of Kleinrock and Scholl [29]. A time slot can be used to find out the status of a user by giving him sole access right to use the time slot. A user who is ready and has the access right to transmit in a time slot must do so. Suppose a sequential ordering of all users is known to individual users and synchronized in advance among all users. Each user can determine for himself the identity of the one with the access right to use the next time slot. With a linear search procedure, the mean channel assignment delay is $(N - 1)/2$ time slots for traffic condition 1 and is zero for traffic condition 2.

Similarly, a tree search procedure can be implemented using time slots and distributed control. An example is Capetanekis' algorithm [30]. Since his algorithm was originally designed for a satellite channel, we shall consider a variation of it suitable for our short propagation delay environment here. Suppose, as before, each user corresponds to a leaf in a binary tree. Also, a user who is ready and is given the access right to transmit in a time slot must do so. By assigning the access right to use a time slot to all users in a tree (or subtree), the time slot will have 3 possible outcomes (empty, success, collision) indicating the number of ready users in the tree (or subtree) to be 0, 1 or more than 1. Suppose, initially, all users are given the access right to use the next time slot. If exactly one user is ready (traffic condition 1), he transmits and the channel assignment delay is zero. If two or more users are ready, a collision results. The tree is then divided into two subtrees, which can be searched one after the other. It is easy to see that when all N users are ready (traffic condition 2), the channel assignment delay is $(\log_2 N) + 1$ time slots.

The above results are summarized in Table 1. For comparison between strategies for passive and active users, we need to compare the mean time $\overline{w}$ needed to complete a query and the duration T of a time slot. We learned earlier that $T \geqslant 2\tau$. How close T can be made to approach 2τ depends upon the amount of guard time needed by the time synchronization tech-

Table 1
Channel assignment delays of multiple access strategies under two extreme traffic conditions

	Traffic Condition 1: 1 out of N users ready	Traffic Condition 2: all N users ready
Linear search using polling	$\frac{N+1}{2}$ queries (mean value)	1 query
Binary tree search using probing	$\frac{3}{2}(\log_2 N) + 1$ queries (mean value)	$(\log_2 N) + 1$ queries
Contention using time slots	0	2.72 time slots (mean value assuming optimal symmetric adaptive control)
Linear search using time slots	$\frac{N-1}{2}$ time slots (mean value)	0
Binary tree search using time slots	0	$(\log_2 N) + 1$ time slots

nique. On the other hand, $\bar{w}$ must include the round-trip propagation delay between the central controller and the user queried, plus transmission times of the query message and response. Because of the transmission times, it is likely that in most cases $\bar{w} > T$ but they will probably be of the same order of magnitude.

Referring to Table 1, we shall next compare the strategies in terms of the number of steps (queries or time slots) needed by each strategy. The two traffic conditions represent a lightly utilized channel (condition 1) and a heavily utilized channel (condition 2). Under traffic condition 1, the linear search procedures have the worst performance. Binary tree search using probing is much better than linear search, especially when N is large. Contention and binary tree search using time slots have the best performance (zero channel assignment delay).

Under traffic condition 2, the linear search procedures have the best performance while both binary tree search procedures perform poorly. Thus binary tree search procedures need to adapt to the level of traffic and dynamically switch to a linear search procedure beyond a certain level of channel utilization. Some such adaptive algorithms are discussed in [28,30]. The contention protocol also requires adaptive control for stable operation in order to achieve the mean channel assignment delay of 2.72 time slots as discussed earlier.

To properly evaluate the relative merits of the different access strategies, we need to have a measure of how often the actual traffic condition approximates traffic condition 1 or traffic condition 2. One of the results of our analysis below shows that traffic condition 1 does in fact prevail a great deal of the time even when the channel utilization is moderately high. This demonstrates the superiority of the contention and tree search procedures (given adaptive control). The performance difference between these strategies and linear search increases as N becomes large.

Lastly, we note that either a slotted or an unslotted channel can be used with the contention protocol while time slotting is needed for the binary tree search procedure with distributed control.

4. Analysis of the CSMA Protocol

For our analysis of CSMA based upon the contention protocol defined by (P1) and (P2), we shall assume that in (P2) a suitable adaptive algorithm is used so that the probability of a successful transmission (slotted ALOHA throughput) in the next time slot is equal to a constant S. This assumption is an approximation but has been found to be a very good one in simulation studies [23–26].

We shall further assume that errors due to random noise are insignificant relative to errors due to collisions and can be neglected. The source of traffic to the broadcast channel consists of an infinite population of users who collectively form an independent. Poisson process with an aggregate mean message generation rate of λ messages per second. This approximates a large but finite population in which each user generates messages infrequently; each message can be transmitted in an interval much less than the average time between successive messages generated by a given user. Each user is allowed to store and attempt to transmit at most one message at a time. Thus the generation of a new message is equivalent to increasing the number of ready users by one. The effect of queueing messages at individual users is discussed later.

Finally, we assume that the transmission time of each message is an independent identically distributed (i.i.d.) random variable with the probability distribution function (PDF) $\beta(x)$, mean value b_1, second moment b_2 and Laplace transform $\beta^*(s)$.

The ready users can be considered to form a distributed queue with random order of service for the broadcast channel. We are interested in obtaining the equilibrium moment generating function of the distributed queue size. We shall use an imbedded Markov chain analysis. Under the assumptions of Poisson arrivals and that messages arrive and depart one at a time, the moment generating function of queue size obtained for the imbedded points is valid for all points in time.

A snapshot of the channel is illustrated in Fig. 1. We define the following random variables:

q_n = number of ready users left behind by the departure of the nth transmission, C_n,

y_{n+1} = time from the departure of C_n to the beginning of the next successful transmission,

u_{n+1} = number of new (Poisson) arrivals during y_{n+1},

x_{n+1} = transmission time of C_{n+1},

v_{n+1} = number of new (Poisson) arrivals during $x_{n+1} + \tau$.

We assumed earlier that x_{n+1} has the PDF $\beta(x)$. We shall let $B(x)$ be the PDF of $x_{n+1} + \tau$. The corresponding Laplace transform is thus

$$B^*(s) = \beta^*(s)\, e^{-s\tau} .$$

The random variable y_{n+1} is the sum of two independent random time intervals

$$y_{n+1} = (I_{n+1} + r_{n+1})\, T,$$

where T is the duration of a slot, I_{n+1} is the number of slots in an idle period immediately following the departure of C_n, and r_{n+1} is the number of slots in the contention period following a collision until the next successful transmission. The slot containing the initial collision is included in r_{n+1}. We note that I_{n+1} is nonzero only if $q_n = 0$. Also, if there has been no collision when C_{n+1} begins, $r_{n+1} = 0$.

Let p_j be the probability of j new arrivals (ready users) in a time slot.

$$p_j = \frac{(\lambda T)^j e^{-\lambda T}}{j!}, \quad j = 0, 1, 2, \ldots$$

At the start of the next time slot, each new arrival executes (P1) or (P2) in exactly the same manner as all other ready users.

Given our earlier assumption, we have

$$\mathrm{Prob}\,[I_{n+1} = k / q_n = 0] = (1 - p_0)\, p_0^{k-1}, \quad k = 1, 2, \ldots$$

Also,

$$\mathrm{Prob}\,[r_{n+1} = k/\text{collision occurred}] = S(1 - S)^{k-1} \quad k = 1, 2, \ldots$$

From this last result, the Laplace transform of the probability density function (pdf) of a contention period (given a collision occurred) is

$$C^*(s) = \frac{S e^{-sT}}{1 - (1 - S)\, e^{-sT}},$$

which has a mean of T/S and a second moment of

$$T^2 \left(1 + \frac{2(1 - S)}{S^2}\right).$$

The following important relationship is evident from Fig. 1.

$$q_{n+1} = q_n + u_{n+1} + v_{n+1} - 1, \tag{1}$$

where v_{n+1} is an independent random variable with the z-transform $B^*(\lambda - \lambda z)$, while u_{n+1} depends upon q_n in the following manner as a consequence of (P1) and (P2). Given

(1) $q_n = 0$,

$$u_{n+1} = \begin{cases} 1 & \text{with prob. } \dfrac{p_1}{1 - p_0} \\ j + \text{number of arrivals during a contention period} & \text{with prob. } \dfrac{p_j}{1 - p_0} \quad j = 2, 3, \ldots \end{cases}$$

(2) $q_n = 1$, $u_{n+1} = 0$

(3) $q_n \geqslant 2$, u_{n+1} = number of arrivals during a contention period. (2)

Given the occurrence of a collision, the number of new arrivals during a contention period is an independent random variable with the z-transform $C^*(\lambda - \lambda z)$.

The equilibrium queue length probabilities

$$Q_k = \lim_{n \to \infty} \mathrm{Prob}\,[q_n = k], \quad k = 0, 1, 2, \ldots$$

exist if $\lambda(b_1 + \tau + T/S) < 1$ (see [14]). Define the z-transform

$$Q(z) = \sum_{k=0}^{\infty} Q_k z^k .$$

By considering Eqs. (1) and (2) and taking the $n \to \infty$ limit, we obtain after some algebraic manipulations the following important result: *

$$Q(z) = B^*(\lambda - \lambda z)\Big\{Q_1 z[1 - C^*(\lambda - \lambda z)] + \frac{Q_0}{1 - p_0}[p_1 z(1 - C^*(\lambda - \lambda z)) - C^*(\lambda - \lambda z)(1 - e^{-\lambda T(1-z)})]\Big\} \times \Big(z - B^*(\lambda - \lambda z)\, C^*(\lambda - \lambda z)\Big)^{-1}, \tag{3}$$

where

$$Q_0 = \frac{1 - \lambda(b_1 + \tau + T/S)}{\lambda T\left(\dfrac{1}{1 - p_0} - \dfrac{1}{B^*(\lambda)\, S}\right)} \tag{4}$$

and

$$Q_1 = \left(\frac{1}{B^*(\lambda)} - \frac{p_1}{1 - p_0}\right) Q_0 \tag{5}$$

Using Eqs. (3)–(5), we can obtain the mean queue size. Application of Little's result [14] yields the mean message delay (time of arrival to time of departure) to be

$$D = \bar{x} + \frac{T}{S} + \frac{T}{2} - \frac{1 - p_0}{2[B^*(\lambda) S - (1 - p_0)]} \times \left(\frac{2}{\lambda} + ST - 3T\right) + \frac{\lambda[\overline{x^2} + 2\bar{x}(T/S) + T^2(1 + 2(1 - S)/S^2)]}{2[1 - \lambda(\bar{x} + T/S)]}, \tag{6}$$

where

$$\bar{x} = b_1 + \tau$$

and

$$\overline{x^2} = b_2 + 2b_1\tau + \tau^2 .$$

We next consider the channel assignment delay, that is, given that the channel is free and that there is at least one ready user, we want the pdf of the time from when the above conditions are satisfied to the start of the next successful transmission. Let d_n be a random variable representing the channel assignment delay immediately prior to the nth transmission and

$$d = \lim_{n \to \infty} d_n$$

* The derivation of $Q(z)$ does not depend upon the specific form of $C^*(s)$ as long as the contention period duration is an independent positive random variable.

It can be readily shown that

$$\text{Prob}[d = kT] = \begin{cases} Q_0 \dfrac{p_1}{1 - p_0} + Q_1, & k = 0 \\ \left\{Q_0\left(1 - \dfrac{p_1}{1 - p_0}\right) + \displaystyle\sum_{i=2}^{\infty} Q_i\right\} S(1 - S)^{k-1}, & k = 1, 2, \ldots \end{cases} \tag{7}$$

The mean channel assignment delay is thus

$$\bar{d} = \frac{1}{S}\left(1 - Q_0 \frac{p_1}{1 - p_0} - Q_1\right) T . \tag{8}$$

Note that $Q_0\, p_1/(1-p_0) + Q_1$ is the fraction of transmissions that incur zero assignment delay in gaining channel access (no collision).

5. Performance Observations

An important performance parameter is the ratio of the carrier sense time τ to the mean message transmission time b_1:

$$\alpha = \frac{\tau}{b_1} . \tag{9}$$

The *throughput* of the CSMA channel is defined to be the fraction of channel time utilized by data messages, which is

$$\rho = \lambda b_1$$

under equilibrium conditions. The requirement of $\lambda(\bar{x} + T/S) < 1$ gives rise to the following upper bound on the channel throughput

$$\rho < \frac{S}{2\alpha + (1 + \alpha) S} . \tag{10}$$

In Fig. 2, we show the delay performance of the CSMA channel as a function of α and ρ. The normalized delay D/b_1 is plotted and it is assumed that messages are of constant length. Observe that the delay performance of CSMA improves significantly as α becomes small. A small α may come about either by decreasing the carrier sense time τ or by increasing the duration b_1 of each user transmission.

In these numerical calculations, the probability S of a successful transmission during contention periods is assumed to be 1/e which is the optimum slotted ALOHA throughput rate for an infinite population model.

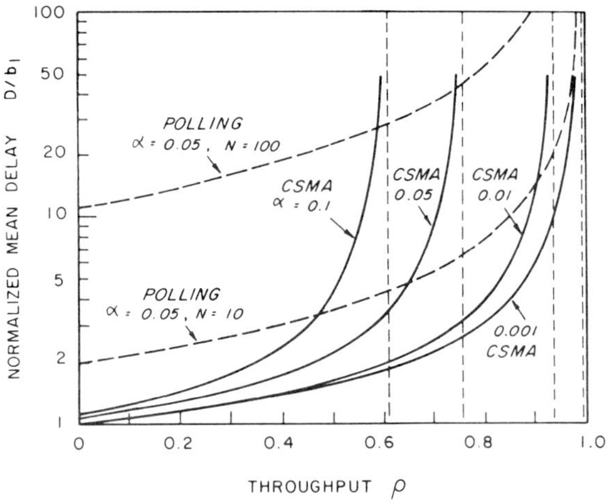

Fig. 2. Mean delay versus throughput.

The delay-throughput performance of roll-call polling is also shown using the delay formula in [31]. The delay results shown for polling assume Poisson message arrivals and constant message length. The ratio of propagation delay to message transmission time is $\alpha = 0.05$. The ratio of data to polling message length is 10. Queueing of messages at individual users is assumed; hence the maximum channel throughput is one. Delay-throughput curves for both 10 users and 100 users are shown. Note that the corresponding delay-throughput performance of CSMA at $\alpha = 0.05$ is independent of the number of users. It also permits no queueing of messages at individual users; hence the maximum throughput is less than 1. We observe that CSMA is superior to polling when the channel throughput is low but becomes inferior when the channel throughput is increased to one. However, if queueing of messages is possible at individual users for CSMA, more than one message may be transmitted every time a user gains channel access. Hence, as the network load ρ is increased from 0 to 1, the delay performance of CSMA is first given by the $\alpha = 0.05$ curve at a small channel throughput but switches to the $\alpha = 0.01$ curve and then the $\alpha = 0.001$ curve and so on as the channel throughput increases and queues become long. The channel throughput of CSMA is one in the limit of infinitely long queues at individual users.

In Fig. 3, we show the mean channel assignment delay $\bar{d}$ as a function of α and ρ. Note that $\bar{d}$ decreases to zero when ρ is small. This is because (P1) in the CSMA protocol permits a ready user to access the channel immediately. In Fig. 4 we plot the

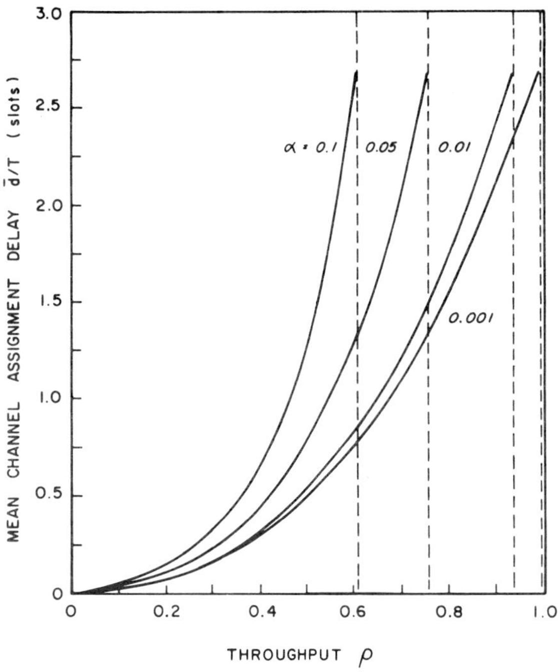

Fig. 3. Mean channel assignment dealy versus throughput.

fraction of transmissions that incur zero delay in gaining channel access given that the channel is free. For comparison, recall that when only one ready user is present, the mean channel assignment delay is

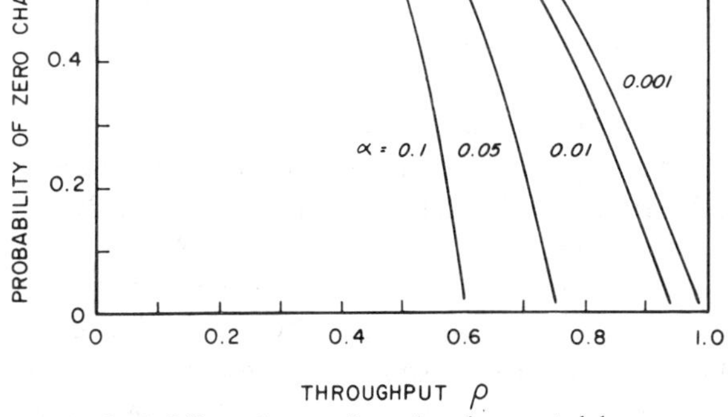

Fig. 4. Probability of zero channel assignment delay versus throughput.

$\frac{1}{2}(N+1)\ \bar{w}$ for conventional polling and $[\frac{3}{2}(\log_2 N) + 1]\ \bar{w}$ for probing.

Referring again to Figure 3, observe that as ρ is increased, $\bar{d}/T$ increases to the maximum value of $1/S$. This desirable property is a consequence of the presence of an adaptive algorithm that we assumed in (P2) which guarantees channel stability during contention periods.

6. Simulation Results

In this section, we compare the above analytic results with experimental results from simulation. We assume, as before, the aggregate arrival process of new messages to be a Poisson process. For simplicity, a deterministic message transmission time is used.

To carry out the simulation, it is now necessary to specify the adaptive algorithm in (P2) with which a ready user selects its transmission probability for the next time slot. Many adaptive algorithms have been proposed and studied in the past; see [8,23–27,30]. Since this is not the primary concern of this study, we limited ourselves to algorithms which are easy to implement, but may not be optimal. Specifically, the following class of algorithms that depend only upon locally available information was considered.

Each ready user transmit into a time slot with probability P_k where $k = 0, 1, 2, \ldots$ is the accumulated number of collisions incurred by the user. Each user determines his P_k according to one of the following algorithms:

(1) $P_k = (0.5)^k, \quad k = 0, 1, 2, \ldots$.
k is reset to 0 when the ready user has a successful transmission.

(2)
$$P_k = \begin{cases} 1, & k = 0 \\ p, & k = 1, 2, 3 \\ 0, & \text{otherwise} \end{cases}$$
k is reset to 0 following each successful transmission in the channel (by anyone). When k reaches 4, the ready user discards his message and becomes a nonready user.

We note that both algorithms (1) and (2) are not optimal. They also deviate slightly from the idealized properties of (P2) that we assumed in our analysis. Algorithm (1) was first proposed in [8]. Note that it does not reset k to 0 following every successful transmission in the channel as is expected by (P1). Algorithm (2) permits messages to be discarded occasionally in times of congestion. Algorithm (2) was first proposed and studied in [23–25].

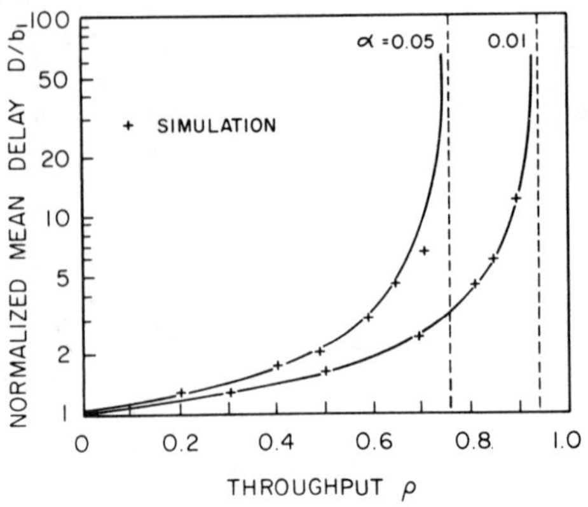

Fig. 5. Mean delay versus throughput for algorithm (1).

In Figures 5 and 6, we compare analysis and simulation results for mean message delay. We see from Figure 5 that the agreement between simulation and analysis is excellent for algorithm (1). Results for algorithm (2) are shown in Figure 6 for two values of p (0.1 and 0.2). We learned from our previous work that $p = 0.2$ is close to optimal while $p = 0.1$ is non-optimal [20,23]. We see from Figure 6, that $p = 0.1$ indeed gives rise to delay results slightly higher than the theoretical (optimum) values. Delay results for $p = 0.2$ are actually smaller than the theoretical values when the channel is heavily loaded. This is because the simulated mean delay values in Figure 6 are calculated only for successfully transmitted messages; the delays incurred by discarded messages are not accounted for. With $p = 0.2$, the collision probability is higher than that with $p = 0.1$ and will thus give rise to more discarded messages. The loss probability for the two cases is illustrated in Figure 7.

Comparing algorithms (1) and (2), note that while algorithm (2) discards some messages when the

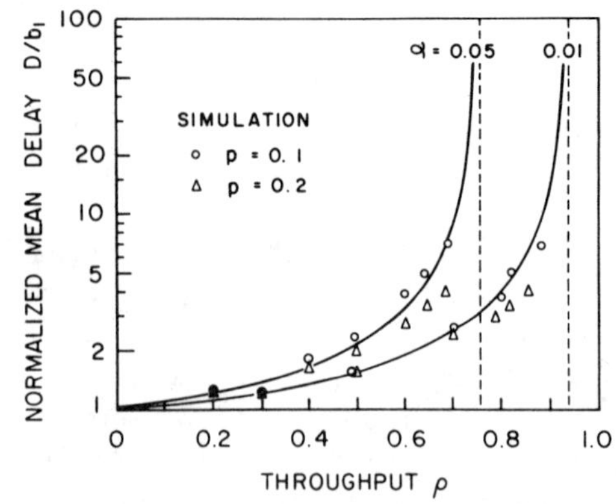

Fig. 6. Mean dealy versus throughput for algorithm (2).

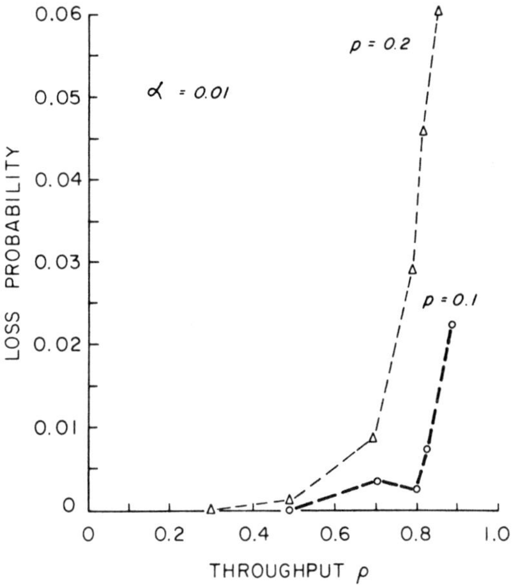

Fig. 7. Loss probability versus throughput for algorithm (2).

channel is heavily loaded, algorithm (1) does not. As a result, we observed that the variance in message delay of algorithm (1) is typically one or more orders of magnitude higher than that of algorithm (2) when the channel is moderately to heavily loaded.

In Figures 8 and 9, we plotted simulation and analysis results for the mean channel assignment delay. Here, the nonoptimality of algorithm (1) and

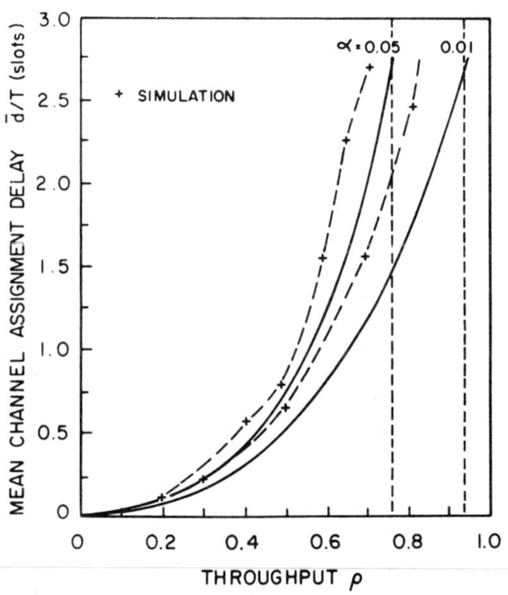

Fig. 8. Mean channel assignment delay versus throughput for algorithm (1).

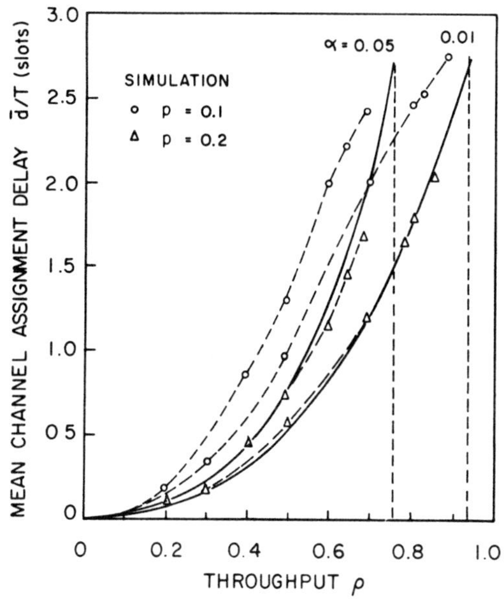

Fig. 9. Mean channel assignment dealy versus throughput for algorithm (2).

algorithm (2) with $p = 0.1$ is clearly shown. However, with a small α, the mean channel assignment delay is much smaller than the mean waiting time in the (distributed) queue. Hence, our main analytic results are robust; they are applicable for heuristic nonoptimal algorithms as long as they give rise to a stable channel.

In Figures 10 and 11, we plotted simulation and analysis results for the probability of zero delay in

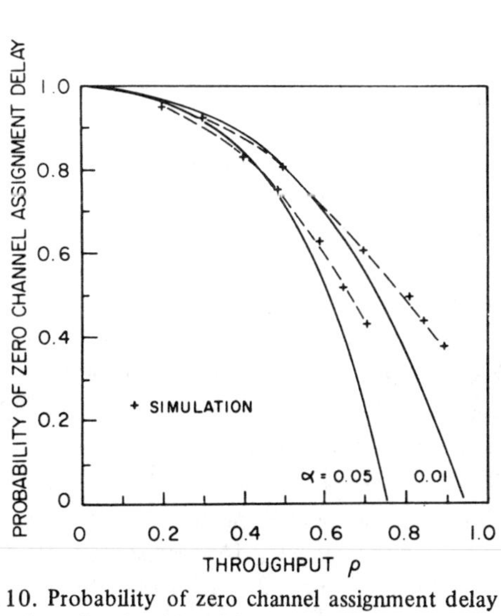

Fig. 10. Probability of zero channel assignment delay versus throughput for algorithm (1).

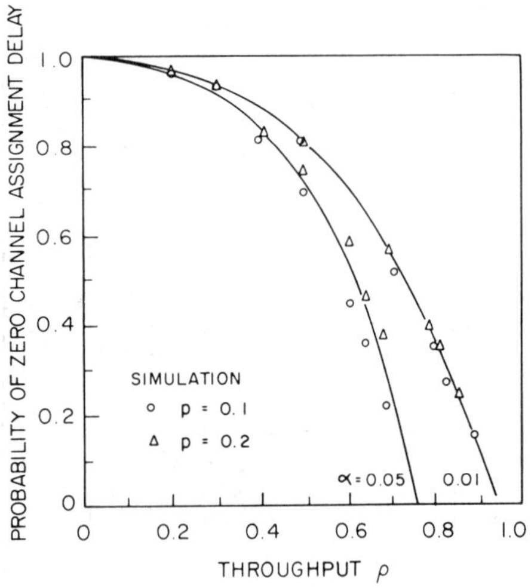

Fig. 11. Probability of zero channel assignment delay versus throughput for algorithm (2).

assigning channel access to a ready user. Note in Figure 11 that simulation and analysis agree very well for algorithm (2). In the case of Figure 10, the simulation results are actually better than the analysis results when the channel is heavily loaded. This is because algorithm (1) deviates from protocol (P2) by not requiring ready users to transmit into a time slot with probability 1 following each successful transmission in the channel. This requirement would produce a collision with a high probability when the channel is heavily loaded.

7. Conclusions

We proposed and analyzed a CSMA protocol as a distributed control technique for a population of users to share a broadcast channel. Specifically we considered local networks with short propagation delays. The capability of aborting collided transmissions is the main difference between our model and previous models of CSMA. It is also assumed that the channel is stable during contention periods (presence of an adaptive control algorithm). Our main results include the moment generating function of the number of ready users, as well as mean value formulas for message delay and channel assignment delay. These results are new. Characterization of the distributed queue size and message delay has previously been limited to numerical solutions or simulations.

We found that the CSMA protocol as defined in this paper has the desirable property that when the channel is lightly utilized, the channel assignment delay is extremely short. The performance of CSMA when the channel is heavily utilized depends upon the ratio α in Eq. (9). We make the following observation. If the number of users is finite and queueing of messages is permitted at individual users, then as $\rho \to 1$, we must have $\alpha \to 0$, since the transmission time of each user increases as a result of long queues. In this case, the maximum channel throughput of CSMA is one (the same as polling with queueing permitted at individual users).

In this paper, the performance measures of interest are average message delay and channel throughput. These are appropriate for a homogeneous population of users. We have neglected scheduling issues of fairness, discrimination, explicit and implicit priorities etc. These are important considerations in operational networks handling diverse traffic types with dissimilar performance goals (high throughput, low delay, real-time applications etc.) Some of these issues are addressed in [32].

References

[1] M. Schwartz, Computer-Communication Network Design and Analysis, Prentice-Hall, Englewood Cliffs, N.J., 1977.

[2] A. Fraser, "A Virtual Channel Network," Datamation, Vol. 21, Feb. 1975.

[3] D.J. Farber, and K.C. Larson, "The System Architecture of the Distributed Computer System – the Communications Systems," Proc. Symp. Computer-Communications Networks and Teletraffic, Polytechnic Institute of Brooklyn, April 1972.

[4] D.G. Willard, "Mitrix: A Sophisticated Digital Cable Communications System," Conf. Rec. National Telecommunications Conference, Nov. 1973.

[5] R. Binder, et al., "ALOHA Packet Broadcasting – A Retrospect," AFIPS Conf. Proc. Vol. 44, 1975.

[6] R.E. Kahn, "The Organization of Computer Resources into a Packet Radio Network," IEEE Trans. on Commun., Vol. COM-25, Jan. 1977.

[7] V.A. DeMarines, and L.W. Hill, "The Cable Bus in Data Communications," Datamation, August 1976.

[8] R.M. Metcalfe, and D.R. Boggs, "Ethernet: Distributed Packet Switching for Local Computer Networks," Communications of the ACM, 19, No. 7, July 1976.

[9] A. West, and A. Davison, "CNET – A Cheap Network for Distributed Computing," Department of Computer Science and Statistics, Queen Mary College, University of London, Report TR 120, March 1978.

[10] J.E. Thornton, et al., "A New Approach to Network Storage Management," Computer Design, Nov. 1975.

[11] K.J. Biba, and J.W. Yeh, "FordNet: A Front-End Approach to Local Computer Networks," Proc. Local Area Communications Network Symposium, Boston, May 1979.

[12] J. Yeh, P. Lehot and G. Steddum, "Hierarchical Design of a Family of Local Computer Networks," Proc. Pacific Telecommunications Conference, Honolulu, Jan. 1980.

[13] P. Brinch Hansen, Operating System Principles, Prentice-Hall, Englewood Cliffs, N.J., 1973.

[14] L. Kleinrock, Queueing Systems, Vol. I, 1975; Vol. II, 1976, Wiley-Interscience, N.Y.

[15] S.S. Lam, "Multiple Access Protocols," Dept. of Computer Sciences, University of Texas at Austin, Tech. Rep. TR-88, Jan. 1979; to appear in Computer Communication: State of the Art and Direction for the Future, edited by W. Chou, Prentice-Hall.

[16] F.A. Tobagi, "Random Access Techniques for Data Transmission over Packet Switched Radio Network," Ph.D. Dissertation, Computer Science Department, University of California at Los Angeles, Dec. 1974.

[17] L. Kleinrock, and F.A. Tobagi, "Packet Switching in Radio Channels: Part 1 – Carrier Sense Multiple Access Modes and their Throughput-Delay Characteristics," IEEE Trans. on Comm. Vol. COM-23, December 1975.

[18] L.W. Hansen and M. Schwartz, "An Assigned-Slot Listen-Before-Transmission Protocol for a Multiaccess Data Channel," Conf. Rec. International Conference on Communications, Chicago, June 1977.

[19] N. Abramson, "Packet Switching with Satellites," AFIPS Conf. Proc., Vol. 42, AFIPS Press, Montvale, New Jersey, 1973.

[20] L. Kleinrock, and S.S. Lam, "Packet-switching in A Slotted Satellite Channel," AFIPS Conf. Proc., Vol. 42, AFIPS Press, Montvale, N.J., 1973.

[21] C. Ellingson, and R. Kulpinski, "Dissemination of System Time," IEEE Trans. on Commun., Vol. COM-21, May 1973.

[22] L. Kleinrock and S.S. Lam, "Packet Switching in a Multiaccess Broadcast Channel: Performance Evaluation," IEEE Trans. on Commun., Vol. COM-23, April 1975.

[23] S.S. Lam, "Packet Switching in a Multi-Access Broadcast Channel with Application to Satellite Communication in a Computer Network," Ph.D. Dissertation, Computer Science Department, Univ. of California, Los Angeles, March 1974.

[24] S.S. Lam, and L. Kleinrock, "Dynamic Control Schemes for a Packet Switched Multi-access Broadcast Channel," AFIPS Conf. Proc., Vol. 44, AFIPS Press, Montvale, N.J., 1975.

[25] S.S. Lam, and L. Kleinrock, "Packet Switching in a Multiaccess Broadcast Channel: Dynamic Control Procedures," IEEE Trans. on Commun., Vol. COM-23, Sept. 1975.

[26] M. Gerla and L. Kleinrock, "Closed Loop Stability Controls for S-Aloha Satellite Communications," Proc. Fifth Data Communications Symposium, Snowbird, Utah, September 1977.

[27] L. Kleinrock, and Y. Yemini, "An Optimal Adaptive Scheme for Multiple Access Broadcast Communication," Conf. Rec. ICC'78, Toronto, June 1978.

[28] J.F. Hayes, "An Adaptive Technique for Local Distribution," IEEE Trans. on Commun., Vol. COM-26, August 1978.

[29] L. Kleinrock, and M. Scholl, "Packet Switching in Radio Channels: New Conflict-Free Multiple Accese Techniques for a Small Number of Data Users," Conf. Rec. Int. Conf. on Communications, Chicago, June 1977.

[30] J.I. Capetanekis, "The Multiple Access Broadcast Channel: Protocol and Capacity Considerations," Ph.D. Thesis, Dept. of Electrical Engineering and Computer Science, M.I.T., Aug. 1977.

[31] A.G. Konheim, and B. Meister, "Waiting Lines and Times in A System with Polling," J.ACM, Vol. 21, July 1974.

[32] S.S. Lam, "A Packet Network Architecture for Local Interconnection", Conf. Rec. Int. Conf. on Communications, Seattle, June 1980.

Corrigendum

"A Carrier Sense Multiple Access Protocol for Local Networks," *Computer Networks,* Vol. 4, February 1980, pp. 21-32.

The formula for the second moment of the contention period in this article should be

$$T^2(2-S)/S^2$$

instead of the expression on page 26. This mistake was brought to my attention by M. Niktash of Carleton University and also by Professor Mischa Schwartz of Columbia University. Since the average message delay formula in this article had been used by other authors (such as W. Bux) in performance comparisons of local area networks, Professor Schwartz wondered if those comparisons would be affected.

To answer his question, we performed numerical calculations of the average message delay for different values of α and b_1. (As in the numerical examples of the article, a constant message length was assumed.) We studied the error in the average message delay due to the incorrect expression for the second moment of the contention period. We found that the error increases with α and with the channel utilization but is independent of b_1. For $\alpha < 0.1$, the error is less than 1%. For $\alpha = 0.1$, the error is less than 1% in most cases but goes up to 3% for a heavily utilized channel. We conclude that previous performance comparisons utilizing the results of this article were not affected in any significant way.

I would like to thank C. H. Chow of the University of Texas at Austin who carried out the numerical calculations.

Reprinted from *IEEE Transactions on Communications*, Volume COM-23, Number 4, April 1975, pages 410-423.

Packet Switching in a Multiaccess Broadcast Channel: Performance Evaluation

LEONARD KLEINROCK, FELLOW, IEEE, AND SIMON S. LAM, MEMBER, IEEE

***Abstract*—In this paper, the rationale and some advantages for multiaccess broadcast packet communication using satellite and ground radio channels are discussed. A mathematical model is formulated for a "slotted ALOHA" random access system. Using this model, a theory is put forth which gives a coherent qualitative interpretation of the system stability behavior which leads to the definition of a stability measure. Quantitative estimates for the relative instability of unstable channels are obtained. Numerical results are shown illustrating the trading relations among channel stability, throughput, and delay. These results provide tools for the performance evaluation and design of an uncontrolled slotted ALOHA system. Adaptive channel control schemes are studied in a companion paper.**

INTRODUCTION

IN THIS and a forthcoming paper [1], a packet switching technique based upon the random access concept of the ALOHA System [2] will be studied in detail. This technique, referred to as slotted ALOHA random access, enables efficient sharing of a data communication channel by a large population of users, each with a bursty data stream. This packet switching technique may be applied to the use of satellite and ground radio channels for computer–computer and terminal–computer communications, respectively [3]–[10]. The multiaccess broadcast capabilities of these channels render them attractive solutions to two problems: 1) large computer–communication networks with nodes distributed over wide geographic areas, and 2) large terminal access networks with potentially mobile terminals.

The objective of this study is to develop analytic models and methods for the evaluation and optimization of the channel performance of a slotted ALOHA system. The problem of performance evaluation is addressed in this paper. In [1], we present dynamic channel control procedures as solutions to some of the issues considered herein.

In this paper, the rationale for multiaccess broadcast packet communication is first discussed. The mathematical model to be considered is then described. Following that, a theory is proposed which explains the dynamic and stochastic channel behavior. In particular, we display the delay-throughput performance curves obtained under the assumption of equilibrium conditions [6]. We then demonstrate that a slotted ALOHA channel often exhibits "unstable behavior." A stability definition is proposed which characterizes stable and unstable channels. A stability measure (FET) is then defined which quantifies the relative instability of unstable channels. An algorithm is given for the calculation of FET. Finally, numerical results are shown which illustrate the trading relations among channel stability, channel throughput, and average packet delay. Our main concern in this paper is the consideration of the stability issue and its effect on the channel throughput-delay performance.

MULTIACCESS BROADCAST PACKET COMMUNICATION

Rationale

For almost a century, circuit switching dominated the design of communication networks. Only with the higher speed and lower cost of modern computers did packet communication become competitive. It was not until approximately 1970 that the computer (switching) cost dropped below the communication (bandwidth) cost in a packet switching network [11]. This also marked the first appearance of packet switched computer–communication networks [2], [12].

Circuit switching is relatively inefficient for computer

Paper approved by the Associate Editor for Computer Communication of the IEEE Communications Society for publication after presentation at the 7th Hawaii International Conference on System Sciences, Honolulu, Hawaii, January 8–10, 1974. Manuscript received June 30, 1974; revised September 30, 1974. This research was supported by the Advanced Research Projects Agency of the Department of Defense under Contract DAHC 15-73-C-0368.

L. Kleinrock is with the Department of Computer Science, University of California, Los Angeles, Calif. 90024.

S. S. Lam is with the IBM Thomas J. Watson Research Center, Yorktown Heights, N. Y. 10598.

communications, especially over long distances. Measurement studies [13] conducted on time-sharing systems indicate that both computer and terminal data streams are *bursty*. Depending on the channel speed, the ratio between the peak and the average data rates may be as high as 2000 to 1 [5]. Consequently, if a high-speed point-to-point channel is used, the channel utilization may be extremely low since the channel is idle most of the time. On the other hand, if a low-speed channel is used, the transmission delay is large.

The above dilemma is caused by channel users imposing bursty random demands on their communication channels. By the law of large numbers in probability theory, the total demand at any instant from a large population of independent users is, with high probability, approximately equal to the sum of their average demands (i.e., a nearly deterministic quantity). Thus, if a channel is dynamically shared in some fashion among many users, the required channel bandwidth to satisfy a given delay constraint may be much less than if the users are given dedicated channels. This concept is known as *statistical load averaging* and has been applied in many computer–communication schemes to various degrees of success. These schemes include: polling systems [14], loop systems [15], asynchronous time division multiplexing (ATDM) [16], and the store-and-forward packet switching concepts [17]–[19] implemented in the ARPA network [12].

We are currently facing an enormous growth in computer networks [20]. To design cost-effective computer–communication networks for the future, new techniques are needed which are capable of providing efficient high-speed computer–computer and terminal–computer communications in a large network environment. The application of packet switching techniques to radio communication (both satellite and ground radio channels) appears to provide a solution.

Radio is a multiaccess broadcast medium. That is, a signal generated by a radio transmitter may be received over a wide area by any number of receivers. This is referred to as the *broadcast* capability. Furthermore, any number of users may transmit signals over the same channel. This is referred to as the *multiaccess* capability. (However, if two signals at the same carrier frequency overlap in time at a radio receiver[1], we assume that neither is received correctly. This destructive interference is the key issue in studying the multiaccess radio channel used in a packet switching mode.) Thus, a single ground radio channel provides a completely connected network topology for a large number of nodes within range of each other. Similarly, a satellite transponder in a geostationary orbit above the earth acts as a radio repeater. Any number of earth stations may transmit signals up to the satellite at one carrier frequency (the multiaccess channel). Any signal received by the satellite transponder is beamed back to earth at another frequency (the broadcast channel). This broadcasted signal may be received by all earth stations covered by the transponder beam. Thus, a satellite channel (consisting of both carrier frequencies) provides a completely connected network topology for all earth stations covered by the transponder beam.

Consider the use of packet communication in a computer–communication network environment to support large populatons of (bursty) users over a wide area. We can then identify and summarize the following advantages of satellite and ground radio channels over conventional wire communications.

1) Elimination of Complex Topological Design and Routing Problems: Topological design and routing problems are very complex in networks with a large population of users. Existing implementations suitable for a (say) 50 node network may become totally inappropriate for a 500 node network required to perform the same functions [21]. On the other hand, ground radio and satellite channels used in the multiaccess broadcast mode provide a completely connected network topology, since every user may access any other user covered by the broadcast.

2) Wide Geographical Areas: Wire communications become expensive over long distances (e.g., transcontinental, transoceanic). Even on a local level, the communication cost for an interactive user on an alphanumeric console over distances of over 100 miles may easily exceed the cost of computation [2]. On the other hand, satellite and radio communications are relatively distance independent, and are especially suitable for geographically scattered users.

3) Mobility of Users: Since radio is a multiaccess broadcast medium, it is possible for users to move around freely. This consideration will soon become important in the development of personal terminals in future telecommunication systems [22] as well as in aeronautical and maritime applications [23].

4) Large Population of Active and Inactive Users: In wire communications, the system overhead usually increases with the number of users (e.g., polling schemes). The maximum number of users is often bounded by some hardware limitation (e.g., the fan-in of a communications processor). In radio communication, since each user is merely represented by an ID number, the number of active users is bounded only by the channel capacity and there is no limitation to the number of inactive (but potentially active) users beyond that of a finite address space.

5) Flexibility in System Design: A radio packet communication system can become operational with two or three users. The size of the user population can be increased up to the channel capacity. More users can be accommodated by increasing the radio channel bandwidth. In other words, the communication system can be expanded or contracted without major changes in the basic system design and operational schemes.

6) Statistical Load Averaging: Wire communication links are more efficiently utilized in a store-and-forward packet switched network than in a circuit switched network. However, at any instant, there may be unused channel capacity in some parts while congestion exists in

[1] This event will be referred to as a *channel collision*.

other parts of the network. The application of packet switching techniques to a single high-speed satellite or radio channel permits the total demand of all user input sources to be statistically averaged at the channel. Note also that each user transmits data at the wide-band channel rate.

7) *Multiaccess Broadcast Capability:* This capability in radio communication may be useful for certain multipoint-to-multipoint communication applications.

The Multiaccess Channel Model

Consider a radio communication system such as a packet switched satellite system [5]-[10] or the ALOHA System [2]. In each case, there is a *broadcast* channel for point-to-multipoint communication and a *multiaccess* channel shared by a large number of users. Since the broadcast channel is used by a single transmitter, no transmission conflict will arise. All nodes covered by the radio broadcast can receive on the same frequency, picking out packets addressed to themselves and discarding packets addressed to others.

The problem we are faced with is how to effect time-sharing of the multiaccess channel among all users in a fashion which produces an acceptable level of performance. As soon as we introduce the notion of sharing in a packet switching mode, we must be prepared to resolve conflicts which arise when simultaneous demands are placed upon the channel. There are two obvious solutions to this problem: the first is to form a queue of conflicting demands and serve them in some order; the second is to "lose" any demands which are made while the channel is in use. The former approach is taken in ATDM and in store-and-forward networks assuming that storage may be provided economically at the point of conflict. The latter approach is adopted in the ALOHA System random access scheme; in this system, in fact, *all* simultaneous demands made on the radio channel are lost.

Let us define *channel throughput rate* S_{out} to be the average number of correctly received packet transmissions per packet transmission time (assuming stationary conditions). We also define *channel capacity* $S_{\max}$ to be the maximum possible channel throughput rate. The channel capacity of a pure ALOHA multiaccess channel was shown by Abramson to be $1/2e \simeq 18$ percent for a fixed packet size [2]. Under similar assumptions, Gaarder showed that a pure ALOHA channel with a fixed packet size is always superior (in terms of channel capacity) to one with different packet sizes [24].

Roberts suggested that the channel may be slotted by requiring all users to synchronize[2] the leading edges of their packet transmissions to coincide with an imaginary time slot boundary at the multiaccessed radio receiver [25]. The duration of a channel time slot is chosen to be equal to a packet transmission time. The resulting scheme will be referred to as "slotted ALOHA random access" or "slotted ALOHA." In this scheme, the users transmit newly generated packets into channel time slots independently. In the event of a channel collision, the collided packets are retransmitted after *random* retransmission delays. (See Fig. 1.) The channel capacity of a slotted ALOHA channel was shown to be $1/e \simeq 36$ percent [25].

To achieve a channel throughput rate larger than the 36 percent limitation, various other multiaccess broadcast packet swiching schemes have been proposed to take advantage of special system and traffic characteristics. The reader is referred to the references [3], [7], [26] for description of these schemes.

Consider a slotted ALOHA channel. The *channel input* in a time slot is defined to be a random variable representing the total number of *new* packets transmitted by all users in that time slot. Assuming stationary conditions, the channel input rate S is the average number of new packet transmissions per time slot. The *channel traffic* in a time slot is defined to be a random variable representing the total number of packet transmissions (both *new and previously collided* packets) by all users in that time slot. Assuming stationary conditions, the channel traffic rate G is the average number of packet transmissions per time slot. The *channel throughput* (or output) in a time slot is defined to be a random variable representing the number (0 or 1) of successful packet transmissions in that time slot. Assuming stationary conditions, the channel throughput (output) rate S_{out} is the probability of exactly one packet transmission in a channel time slot.

The retransmission delay (RD) incurred by an unsuccessful packet transmission may be regarded as the sum of a deterministic component (R) and a random component. The random component is necessary since if collided packets are retransmitted after the same deterministic delay, they will collide again for sure. In a ground radio system, RD corresponds to the positive acknowledgment time-out interval [2]. In a satellite system, since each channel user listens to the satellite broadcast, one round-trip propagation time after transmitting a packet he knows whether he was successful or if a channel collision occurred. In this case, the deterministic component corresponds to a round-trip satellite propagation delay. We shall assume a noise-free channel such that a packet is received incorrectly if and only if it suffered a channel collision. In [6], a uniform probability distribution is assumed for the random component of RD such that each user retransmits a previously collided packet at random during one of the next K slots (each such slot being chosen with probability $1/K$). Thus, retransmission will take place either $R+1, R+2, \cdots$ or $R+K$ slots after the previous transmission. This is said to be the uniform retransmission randomization scheme. Under this scheme, equilibrium throughput-delay tradeoffs have been obtained for a slotted ALOHA channel with a Poisson input source (the infinite population model). Such throughput-delay contours are shown here in Fig. 2 for different values of K. Note that the minimum envelope of these contours defines the optimum channel perform-

[2] The problem of synchronizing channel users is a nontrivial one. It will not be addressed in this paper.

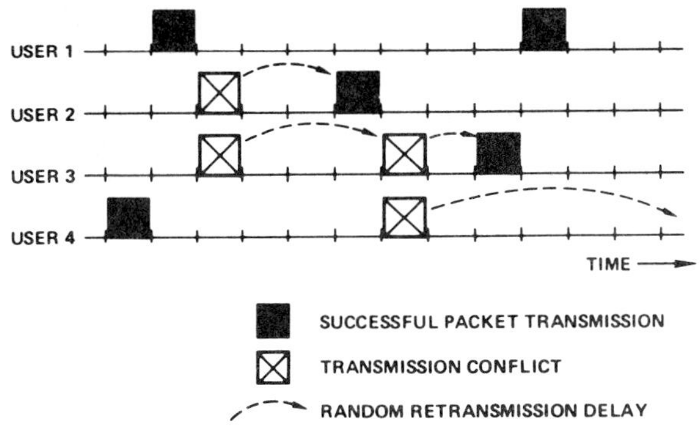

Fig. 1. Slotted ALOHA random access.

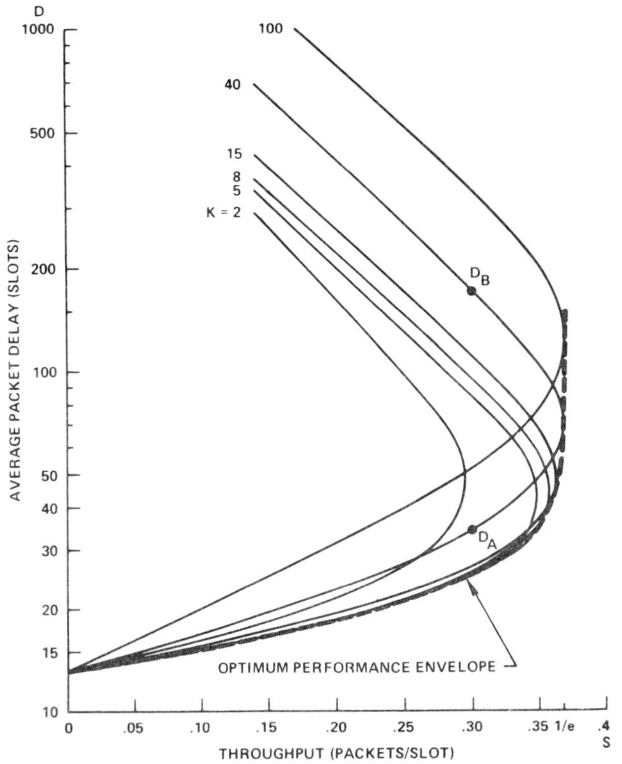

Fig. 2. Equilibrium throughput-delay tradeoff.

ance. These results correspond to the use of a 50 KPBS satellite channel, 1125 bits per packet, and a satellite round-trip propagation delay of 0.27 s for all users. Thus R is equal to 12 slots and there are 44.4 slots in one second. (These numbers will be assumed throughout this paper.) In Fig. 2, D represents the average packet delay in slots. Note that the channel input rate S is equal to the channel throughput rate S_{out} under the assumption of channel equilibrium. The channel capacity S_{max} approaches $1/e$ in the limit as $K \to \infty$. For $K = 15$, it is almost there. For values of K between 8 and 15, the equilibrium throughput-delay tradeoffs are very close to the optimum performance envelope over a wide range of S.

The analytic results presented so far are based upon the assumption that the channel is in equilibrium. Referring to Fig. 2, we see that given S and K (say $K = 40$), there are two possible equilibrium solutions for D! They correspond to a small delay value D_A and a much larger delay value D_B. (We shall refer to the equilibrium point given by S, K, and D_A as the *channel operating point*, since this is the desired channel performance given S and K.) This observation suggests that the assumption of equilibrium conditions adopted in most previous analytic models [4]–[7] may not be valid.

In order to study the dynamic behavior of these channels, simulations were performed for the infinite population model [10]. Each simulation run was observed to behave in the following manner. Starting from an initially empty system, the channel stays in equilibrium at the channel operating point for a finite period of time until stochastic fluctuations give rise to some high channel traffic rate which reduces the channel throughput rate which in turn further increases the channel traffic rate. As this vicious cycle continues, the channel becomes inundated with collisions and retransmissions. At the same time, the channel throughput rate vanishes rapidly to zero. This phenomenon will be referred to as *channel saturation*. Thus, we realize that the equilibrium throughput-delay tradeoffs are not sufficient to characterize the performance of the infinite population model. A more accurate measure of channel performance must reflect the trading relations among channel stability, throughput and delay. A mathematical model with a simpler structure than that used in [6] will be defined below. This model is similar to the one studied by Metcalfe [4]. Using this model, the concepts of channel saturation and stability in a slotted ALOHA random access channel have been characterized [8], [10].

STABILITY-THROUGHPUT-DELAY TRADEOFF PERFORMANCE

In this section, a Markovian model is first formulated for a population of M channel users. The variable M is assumed to be large and may be either finite or infinite. A theory is then proposed which characterizes the instability phenomenon in the following ways.

1) Stable and unstable channels are defined.

2) In a stable channel, equilibrium throughput-delay results (as shown in Fig. 2) are achievable over an infinite time horizon. In an unstable channel, such channel performance is achievable only for some finite time period before the channel goes into saturation.

3) For unstable channels, a stability measure is defined and an efficient computational procedure for its calculation is given.

4) Using the above stability measure, the stability-throughput-delay tradeoff for unstable channels is examined.

The Markovian Model

We consider a slotted ALOHA channel with a user population consisting of M users. Each such user can be in one of two states: *blocked* or *thinking*. In the thinking state, a user generates and transmits a new packet in a time slot with probability σ. A packet which had a channel collision and is waiting for retransmission is said to be *backlogged*. The retransmission delay RD of each backlogged packet is assumed to be geometrically distributed, i.e., each backlogged packet retransmits in the current time slot with probability p. Assuming bursty users, we must have $p \gg \sigma$. From the time a user generates a packet until that packet is successfully received, the user is blocked in the sense that he cannot generate (or accept from his input source) a new packet for transmission.

Let N^t be a random variable (called the *channel backlog*) representing the total number of backlogged packets at time t. The channel input rate at time t is $S^t = (M - N^t)\sigma$. Note that S^t decreases linearly as N^t increases. The vector (N^t, S^t) will be denoted as the *channel state vector*. In this context, both M and σ may be functions of time. We shall assume M and σ to be time-invariant unless stated otherwise. In this case, N^t is a Markov process (chain) with stationary transition probabilities and serves as the state description for the system. The discrete *state space* will now consist of the set of integers $\{0,1,2,\cdots,M\}$. The *one-step state transition probabilities* of N^t are, for $i = 0,1,2,\cdots,M$,

$$p_{ij} = \text{Prob}\,[N^{t+1} = j \mid N^t = i] = \begin{cases} 0 & j \le i-2 \\ ip(1-p)^{i-1}(1-\sigma)^{M-i} & j = i-1 \\ (1-p)^i(M-i)\sigma(1-\sigma)^{M-i-1} + [1 - ip(1-p)^{i-1}](1-\sigma)^{M-i} & j = i \\ (M-i)\sigma(1-\sigma)^{M-i-1}[1-(1-p)^i] & j = i+1 \\ \binom{M-i}{j-i}\sigma^{j-i}(1-\sigma)^{M-j} & j \ge i+2. \end{cases} \quad (1)$$

For the infinite population model in which $M \to \infty$ and $\sigma \to 0$ such that $M\sigma = S$ which is constant and finite, the above equation becomes

$$p_{ij} = \begin{cases} 0 & j \le i-2 \\ ip(1-p)^{i-1}\exp(-S) & j = i-1 \\ (1-p)^i S \exp(-S) + [1 - ip(1-p)^{i-1}]\exp(-S) & j = i \\ S\exp(-S)[1-(1-p)^i] & j = i+1 \\ \dfrac{S^{j-i}}{(j-i)!}\exp(-S) & j \ge i+2. \end{cases} \quad (2)$$

The assumption that RD has a memoryless geometric distribution permits a simple state description for the mathematical model. However, this assumption implies that RD has a zero deterministic component ($R = 0$). In a satellite channel this obviously represents an approximation. (However, it may be physically realizable in radio communications over short distances in which channel propagation delays are negligible compared to a packet transmission time.) A (geostationary) satellite channel has a round-trip propagation delay of 0.27 s, which necessitates a state description consisting of the channel history for at least R consecutive time slots. The difficulty in mathematical analysis using such a state description was illustrated in [10]. However, simulation results have shown that the slotted ALOHA channel performance (in terms of average throughput and delay) is dependent primarily upon the *average* retransmission delay ($\overline{\text{RD}}$) and quite insensitive to the exact probability distributions considered [10]. In order to use the analytic results of the Markovian model here to predict the throughput-delay performance of a slotted ALOHA channel with nonzero R, it is necessary to use a value of p in the Markovian model which gives the same $\overline{\text{RD}}$. For example, to approximate a slotted ALOHA channel with uniform retransmission randomization, we must let

$$p = \frac{1}{R + (K+1)/2} \quad (3)$$

such that $\overline{\text{RD}} = R + (K+1)/2$ in both cases.

We define the length of time for which a packet is backlogged to be the backlog time of the packet and denote the *average backlog time* by D_b. To obtain the average packet delay (as defined in [6]), we must add to D_b, $R + 1$ time slots, which represent the delay incurred by each successful transmission. Thus, we have

$$D = D_b + R + 1. \quad (4)$$

Numerical results in this paper will be expressed in terms of K (rather than p) through use of (3) and (4) for comparison with previous results for channel performance [6].

The Theory

Conditioning on $N^t = n$, the expected channel throughput $S_{out}(n,\sigma)$ is the probability of exactly one packet transmission in the tth time slot. Thus,

$$S_{out}(n,\sigma) = (1-p)^n(M-n)\sigma(1-\sigma)^{M-n-1} + np(1-p)^{n-1}(1-\sigma)^{M-n}. \quad (5)$$

For the infinite population model, i.e., in the limit as $M \uparrow \infty$ and $\sigma \downarrow 0$ such that $M\sigma = S$ is finite and the channel input is Poisson distributed at the constant rate S, the above equation reduces to

$$S_{out}(n,S) = (1-p)^n S \exp(-S) + np(1-p)^{n-1}\exp(-S). \quad (6)$$

This expression is very accurate even for finite M if $\sigma \ll 1$ and if we replace $S = M\sigma$ by $S = (M-n)\sigma$. We assume that the condition $\sigma \ll 1$ (which implies bursty users) is always satisfied in problems of interest to us.

In Fig. 3, for a fixed K we sketch $S_{out}(n,S)$ as a three-dimensional surface above the (n,S) plane. Note that there is an *equilibrium contour* in the (n,S) plane defined as the locus of points on which the channel input rate S is equal to the expected channel throughput $S_{out}(n,S)$ given by (6). In the crosshatched region enclosed by the equilibrium contour, $S_{out}(n,S)$ exceeds S; elsewhere, S is greater than $S_{out}(n,S)$. In Fig. 4, a family of equilibrium contours for various K are displayed. We see that if we increase the average retransmission delay (by increasing K or equivalently decreasing p), the equilibrium contour moves upwards. We show below that these equilibrium contours play a crucial role in determining the stability behavior of the channel.

Given an equilibrium contour in the (n,S) plane, we first consider the dynamic behavior of the channel subject to *time-varying* inputs using a *fluid approximation* interpretation. The following example serves to illustrate the underlying concepts.

Consider the case in which σ is constant while $M = M(t)$ is a function of time as shown in Fig. 5. We use the fluid approximation for the trajectory of the channel state vector (N^t,S^t) in the (n,S) plane as sketched in Fig. 6. Recall that $S^t = (M - N^t)\sigma$. The arrows indicate the "fluid" flow direction which depends on the relative magnitudes of the instantaneous channel throughput rate $S_{out}(n,S)$ and the channel input rate S. Two possible cases are shown corresponding to different values of the amplitude M_3, of the input pulse in Fig. 5. The solid line (Case 1) represents a trajectory which returns to the original state on the equilibrium contour despite the input pulse. The dashed line (Case 2) represents a less fortunate situation in which the decrease in the channel input rate at time t_2 is not sufficient to bring the trajectory back into the "safe" region (shown shaded) in which $S < S_{out}(n,S)$; eventually, the channel "fails" as a result of an increasing backlog and a vanishing channel throughput.

The above example demonstrates channel saturation due to a time-varying input. Let us now study the con-

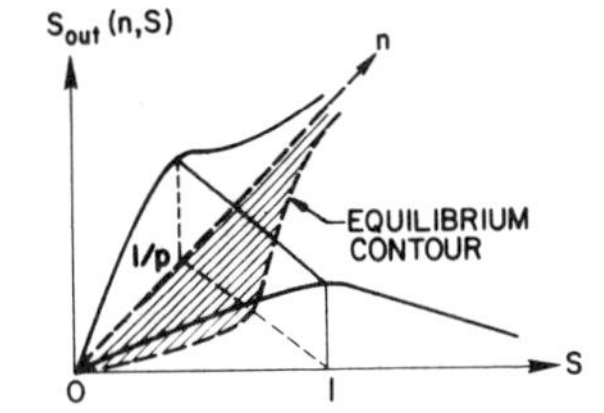

Fig. 3. Throughput surface above the (n,S) plane.

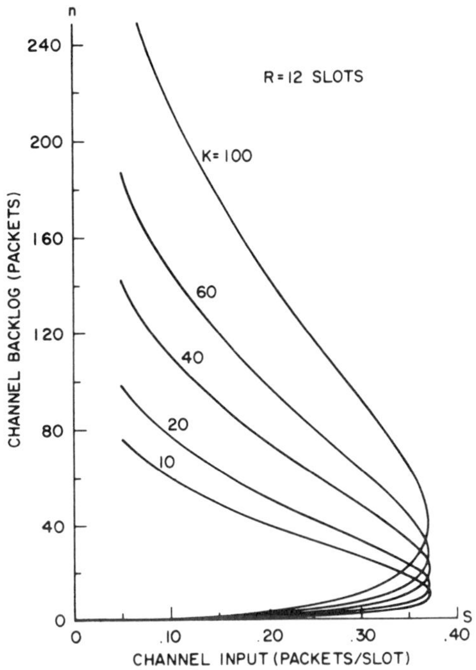

Fig. 4. Equilibrium contours in the (n,S) plane.

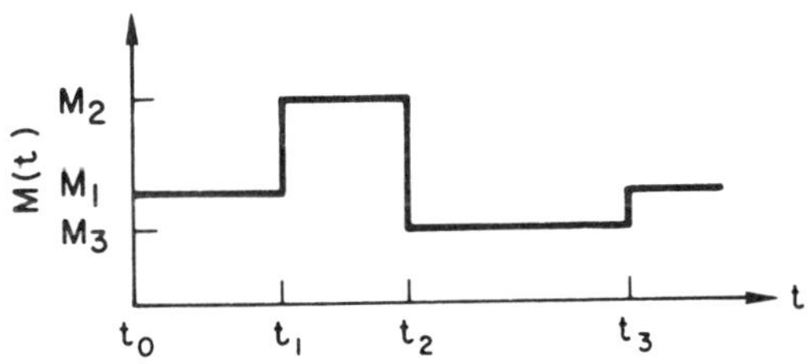

Fig. 5. $M(t)$.

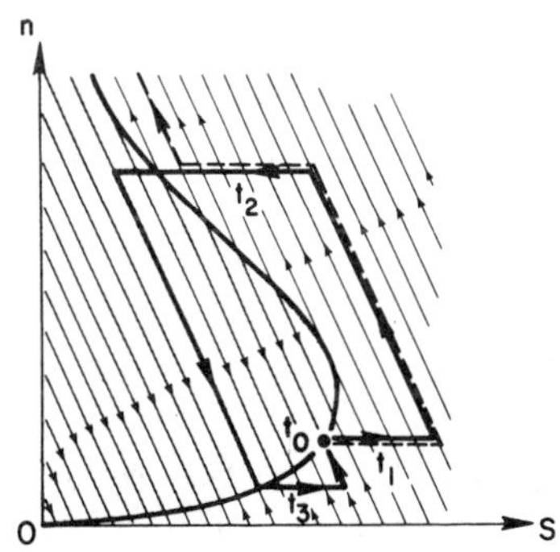

Fig. 6. Fluid approximation trajectories.

ditions under which the slotted ALOHA channel with a *stationary* input (constant M and σ) can go into saturation as a result of statistical fluctuations.

Assume that M and σ are constant. The trajectory of (N^t,S^t) is constrained to lie on the straight line $S = (M - n)\sigma$ called the *channel load line* which intercepts the n-axis at $n = M$ and has a slope equal to $-1/\sigma$. We now propose the following definition for characterizing stable and unstable channels.

The Stability Definition: A slotted ALOHA channel is said to be *stable* if its load line intersects (nontangentially) the equilibrium contour in exactly one place. Otherwise, the channel is said to be *unstable*.

Examples of stable and unstable channels are shown in Fig. 7. Arrows on the channel load lines indicate directions of fluid flow given by the fluid approximation. In other words, the arrows point in the direction of increasing backlog size if $S > S_{out}(n,S)$ and in the direction of decreasing backlog size if $S_{out}(n,S) > S$.

Each channel load line may have one or more equilibrium points. A point on the load line is said to be a *stable equilibrium point* if it acts as a "sink" with respect to fluid flow. It is a *globally stable equilibrium point* if it is the only stable equilibrium point on the channel load line. Otherwise, it is a *locally stable equilibrium point.* (Each stable equilibrium point is identified by a dot on channel load lines in Fig. 7 except in Fig. 7(c), where one of the stable equilibrium points is at $n = \infty$.) An equilibrium point is said to be an *unstable equilibrium point* if fluid flow emanates from it. Thus, the channel state N^t sitting on such a point will drift away from it given the slightest perturbation. The stability definition given above is equivalent to defining a stable channel to be one whose channel load line has a globally stable equilibrium point.

In Fig. 7(a), we show the channel load line of a stable channel. The globally stable equilibrium point on the load line, (n_o,S_o), will be referred to as the *channel operating point.* If M is finite, a stable channel can always be achieved by using a sufficiently large K (see Fig. 4). Of course, a large K implies that the equilibrium backlog size n_o is large; the corresponding average packet delay may be too large to be acceptable. Since the Markov chain N^t has a finite state space and is irreducible (assuming $p,\sigma > 0$), a stationary probability distribution always exists [27], [28]. The stationary probability distribution $\{P_n\}_{n=0}^M$ of N^t can be computed by solving the following set of linear simultaneous equations

$$P_j = \sum_{i=0}^{M} P_i p_{ij} \qquad j = 0,1,\cdots,M$$

and

$$\sum_{i=0}^{M} P_i = 1$$

where the state transition probabilities p_{ij} are given by (1). The steady-state channel throughput rate S_{out} and expected channel backlog $\bar{N}$ can then be obtained from

$$S_{out} = \sum_{n=0}^{M} S_{out}(n,\sigma)P_n \tag{7}$$

and

$$\bar{N} = \sum_{n=1}^{M} nP_n. \tag{8}$$

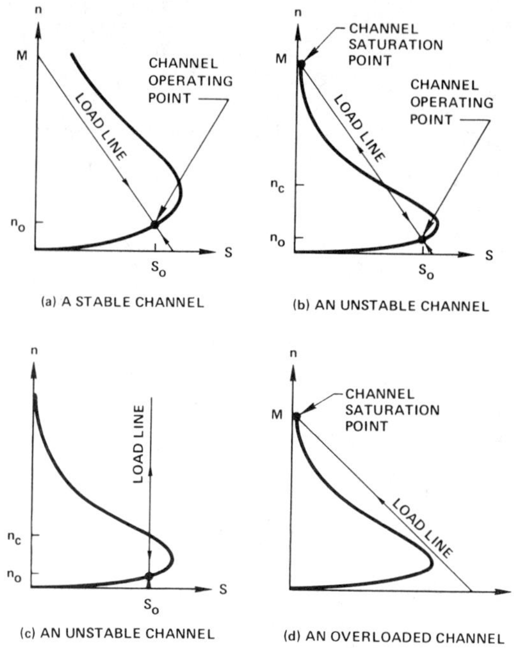

Fig. 7. Stable and unstable channels.

Numerical results have shown that these values of S_{out} and $\bar{N}$ for a stable channel are closely approximated by the equilibrium S_o and n_o at the channel operating point, and also by the equilibrium throughput-delay values in Fig. 2 for the infinite population model. For example, suppose $K = 60$, $M = 200$, and $1/\sigma = 536.1$; the equilibrium channel throughput rate at the channel operating point is $S_o = 0.346$. In Fig. 9 below (to be described later), we see that the steady-state channel throughput rate computed by using (7) is $S_{out} = 0.344$. For the same example, $\bar{N}$ is calculated to be 15.4 slots. By Little's result [27], the average backlog time is

$$D_b = \frac{\bar{N}}{S_{out}} = \frac{15.4}{0.344} = 44.8 \text{ slots.}$$

Applying (4), we get $D = 44.8 + 13 = 57.8$ slots. Now given $S_o = 0.346$, the $K = 60$ equilibrium throughput-delay contour for the infinite population model [6] gives $D = 56.5$ slots.

In Fig. 7(b), we show the channel load line of an unstable channel. The point (n_o,S_o) is again the desired channel operating point since it yields the larger channel throughput and smaller average packet delay between the two locally stable equilibrium points on the load line. In fact, the other locally stable equilibrium point, having a huge backlog and virtually zero throughput, corresponds to the channel saturation state; it will be referred to as the *channel saturation point.* Although it has a stationary probability distribution, N^t will "flip-flop" between the two locally stable equilibrium points in the following manner. Starting from an empty channel ($N^0 = 0$) quasi-stationary conditions will prevail at the operating point (n_o,S_o). The channel, however, cannot maintain equilibrium at this point indefinitely since N^t is a random process; that is, with probability one, the channel backlog N^t crosses the unstable equilibrium point n_c in a finite time, and as soon as it does, the channel input rate S exceeds $S_{\text{out}}(n,S)$. Under this condition, N^t will drift toward the saturation point. Although there is a nonzero probability that N^t may return below n_c, all our simulations show that the channel state N^t accelerates up the channel load line producing an increasing backlog and a vanishing throughput rate. Since the saturation point is a locally stable equilibrium point, quasi-stationary conditions will prevail there for some finite (but probably very long) time period. In this state, the communication channel can be regarded as having failed. (In a practical system, external control should be applied at this point to restore proper channel operation.) Thus, the two locally stable equilibrium points on the load line of an unstable channel correspond to the channel being "up" or "down". An unstable channel may be acceptable if the average channel up time is large and external control is available to bring the channel back up whenever it goes down.

In Figs. 8 and 9, we see how, as the number of channel users M increases, an originally stable channel becomes unstable although the channel input rate S_o at the operating point remains constant (by reducing σ). (These results are obtained by first solving for the stationary probability distribution of N^t and then applying (7) and (8).) For $S_o = 0.36$ and $K = 10$, we see that as M exceeds 80, the stationary channel throughput rate decreases and the average packet delay increases very rapidly with M. Using the $K = 10$ equilibrium contour in Fig. 4, the maximum value of M that is possible without making the channel load line intersect the equilibrium contour more than once is determined (graphically) to be $M_{\max} = 79$, which exactly gives the knees of the curves in Fig. 8. This excellent agreement provides the motivation for the stability definition proposed above. In Fig. 9, by using a larger value of K $(=60)$, a larger $M_{\max}$ is possible. Note, however, that the average packet delay ($\simeq$56 slots) for $K = 60$ is much larger than the average packet delay ($\simeq$36 slots) for $K = 10$.

Given K and S_o, $M_{\max}$ can be obtained graphically from the equilibrium contours such as shown in Fig. 4. In Fig. 10 we show $M_{\max}$ as a function of K with S_o fixed at the maximum possible value given K. Note the linear relationship between $M_{\max}$ and K for the values shown. In Fig. 11, we illustrate how an originally unstable channel can be rendered stable by using a sufficiently large K.

In Fig. 7(c), we show the channel load line of an infinite population model. This is an unstable channel since

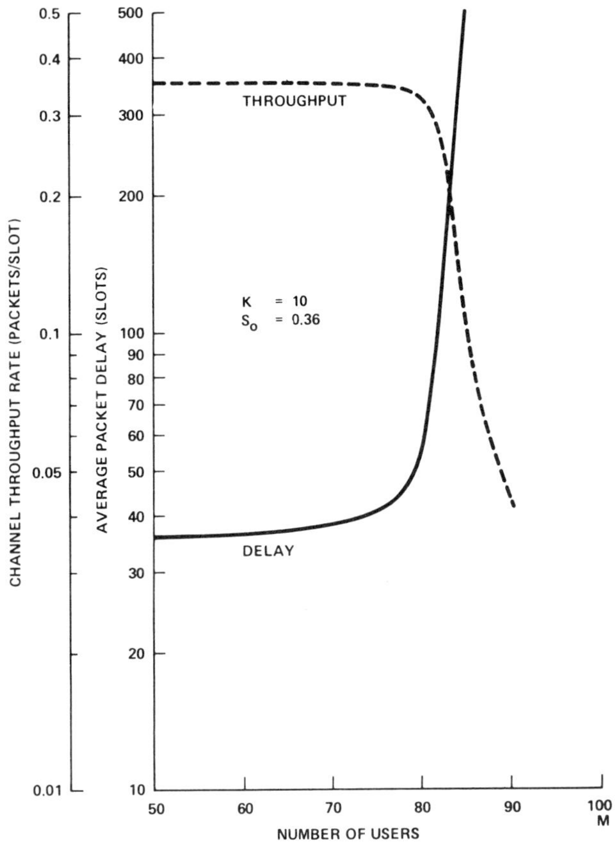

Fig. 8. Channel performance versus M at $K = 10$ and $S_o = 0.36$.

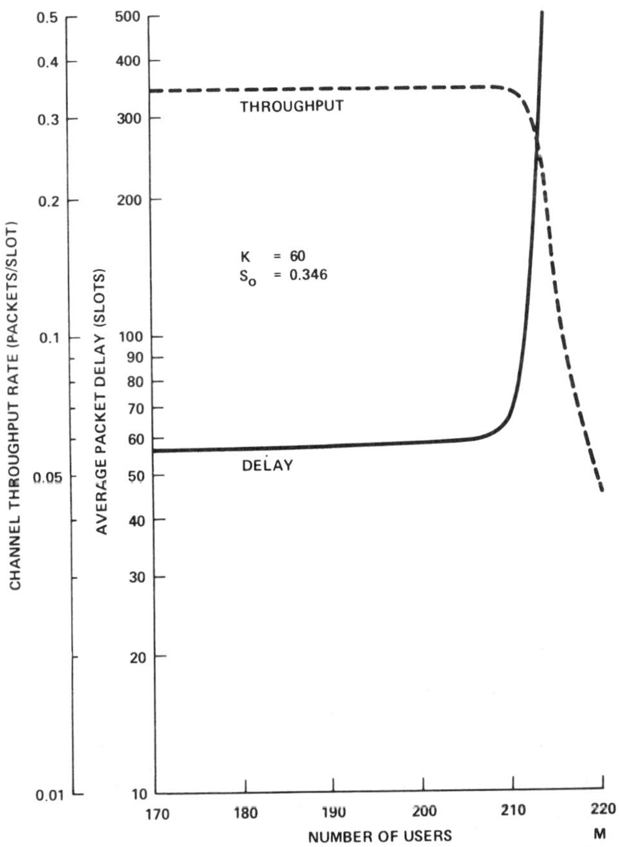

Fig. 9. Channel performance versus M at $K = 60$ and $S_o = 0.346$.

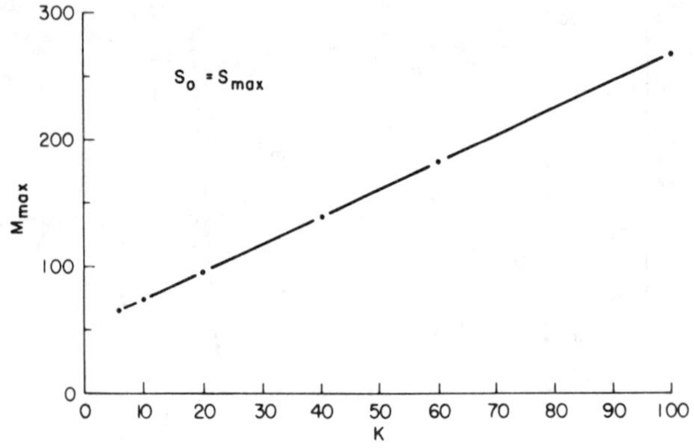

Fig. 10. M_{max} versus K.

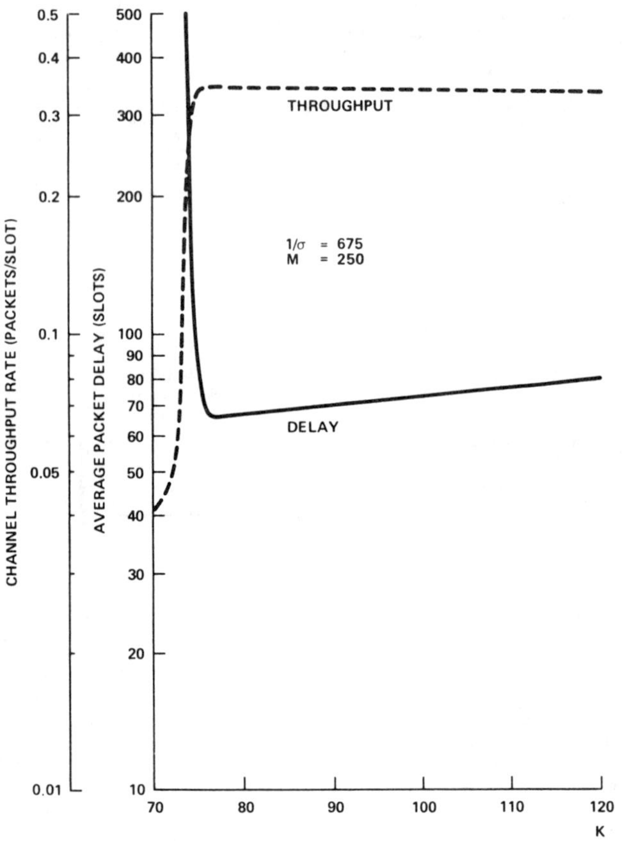

Fig. 11. Channel performance versus K at $M = 250$ and $1/\sigma = 675$.

stable equilibrium point in this case is the channel saturation point! Thus, this represents an "overloaded" channel as a result of bad system design. To correct this situation, the number of active users M supported by the channel should be reduced. From now on, a stable channel will always refer to the load line depicted in Fig. 7(a) instead of Fig. 7(d).

Let us summarize the major *conclusions* in the above discussion.

1) The steady-state throughput-delay performance of a stable channel is closely approximated by its globally stable equilibrium point and by the equilibrium throughput-delay results for the infinite population model.

2) In an unstable channel, the throughput-delay performance at a locally stable equilibrium point can be achieved only for some finite time period.

A Stability Measure

From the above discussion and referring to Fig. 7(b), the load line of an unstable channel can be partitioned into two regions. The *safe* region consisting of the channel states $\{0,1,2,\cdots,n_c\}$ and the *unsafe* region consisting of the channel states $\{n_c + 1,\cdots,M\}$. A good stability measure (for these unstable channels!) is the average time to exit into the unsafe region starting from a safe channel state. To be exact, we define FET to be the *average first exit time* into the unsafe region starting from an initially empty channel ($N^0 = 0$). Thus, FET gives an approximate measure of the average up time of an unstable channel. Below we derive the probability distributions and expected values of such first exit times. The derivations are based upon well-known results of first entrance times in the theory of Markov chains with stationary transition probabilities [28], [30].

Consider the Markovian model with constant M and σ, where M may be infinite. N^t is a Markov process (chain) with stationary transition probabilities $\{p_{ij}\}$ given by (1) or (2). Define the random variable T_{ij} to be the number of transitions which N^t goes through until it enters state j for the first time starting from state i. The probability distribution of T_{ij} (called the *first entrance probabilities* from state i to state j) may be defined as

$$f_{ij}(m) = \text{Prob}\,[T_{ij} = m] = \begin{cases} 0 & m = 0 \\ p_{ij} & m = 1 \\ \text{Prob}\,[N^{t+m} = j,\ N^{t+h} \neq j,\ h = 1,\cdots,m-1 \mid N^t = i] & m \geq 2. \end{cases} \tag{9}$$

$n = \infty$ is a stable equilibrium point. In fact, since N^t has an infinite state space and $S > S_{out}(n,S)$ for $n > n_c$, a stationary probability distribution does not exist for N^t. (See, for example, [29, pp. 543–546] for such a proof in a queueing context.)

The channel load line shown in Fig. 7(d) is stable according to the stability definition. However, the globally

The state space $\mathcal{S}$ for N^t consists of the set of nonnegative integers $\{0,1,2,\cdots,n_c,\ n_c + 1,\cdots,M\}$ which is partitioned into the safe region $\{0,1,2,\cdots,n_c\}$ and the unsafe region $\{n_c + 1,\cdots,M\}$. Now consider the modified state space $\mathcal{S}' = \{0,1,2,\cdots,n_c,n_u\}$ where n_u is an absorbing state such that N^t is now characterized by the transition probabilities

$$p_{ij}' = \begin{cases} p_{ij} & i, j = 0,1,\cdots,n_c \\ \sum_{l=n_c+1}^{M} p_{il} & i = 0,1,\cdots,n_c; j = n_u \\ 0 & i = n_u; j = 0,\cdots,n_c \\ 1 & i = j = n_u. \end{cases} \quad (10)$$

Define the random variable T_i to be the number of transitions which N^t goes through before it enters the unsafe region for the first time starting from state i in the safe region. T_i is called the *first exit time from state i*. The probability distribution of T_i is defined to be $\{f_i(m)\}_{m=1}^{\infty}$ which are called the *first exit probabilities*. It is trivial to show that starting from state i $(0 \leq i \leq n_c)$, the first entrance probabilities into the absorbing state n_u in the modified state space $\mathcal{S}'$ are the same as the first exit probabilities into the unsafe region of $\mathcal{S}$. Using (9), such probabilities are given by the following recursive equation [30],

$$f_{in_u}(m) = p_{in_u}'\delta(m-1) + \sum_{j=0}^{n_c} p_{ij}' f_{jn_u}(m-1) \qquad m \geq 1; i \neq n_u$$

where

$$\delta(m) = \begin{cases} 1 & m = 1 \\ 0 & \text{otherwise.} \end{cases}$$

The above equation can be rewritten in terms of the first exit probabilities as

$$f_i(m) = \sum_{j=n_c+1}^{M} p_{ij}\delta(m-1) + \sum_{j=0}^{n_c} p_{ij} f_j(m-1) \qquad m \geq 1; 0 \leq i \leq n_c \quad (11)$$

where $f_i(m)$ can be solved recursively for $m \geq 1$ starting with $f_i(0) = 0$ for all i.

The probability distribution $\{f_i(m)\}_{m=1}^{\infty}$ for the random variable T_i typically has a very long tail and cannot be easily computed. We had defined earlier FET as a stability measure for an unstable channel. By our definition, FET is the same as the expected value of the random variable T_0. Let $\bar{T}_i$ be the expected value and $\overline{T_i^2}$ be the second moment of T_i. These moments can be obtained by solving a set of linear simultaneous equations. It can easily be shown [30] that

$$T_i = \begin{cases} 1 & \text{with probability } p_{in_u}' \\ 1 + T_j & \text{with probability } p_{ij} \end{cases}$$

from which we obtain [28], [30]

$$\bar{T}_i = 1 + \sum_{j=0}^{n_c} p_{ij}\bar{T}_j \qquad i = 0, 1,\cdots,n_c \quad (12)$$

$$\overline{T_i^2} = 2\bar{T}_i - 1 + \sum_{j=0}^{n_c} p_{ij}\overline{T_j^2} \qquad i = 0, 1,\cdots,n_c. \quad (13)$$

Equation (12) forms a set of $n_c + 1$ linear simultaneous equations from which $\{\bar{T}_i\}_{i=0}^{n_c}$ can be solved and the stability measure FET $(=\bar{T}_0)$ determined. After $\{\bar{T}_i\}_{i=0}^{n_c}$ have been found, (13) can then be solved in a similar manner for $\{\overline{T_i^2}\}_{i=0}^{n_c}$.

Numerical Results

With the stability measure defined above, we are now in a position to examine quantitatively the tradeoff among channel stability, throughput and delay for *unstable* channels. Below we first give a computational procedure to solve for $\bar{T}_i$ and hence, FET. We then compute these quantities for various values of K, S_o, and M (corresponding to different channel load lines). The trading relations among channel stability, throughput, and delay are then illustrated.

The solution of the set of simultaneous equations in either (12) or (13) requires inverting the $(n_c + 1)$ by $(n_c + 1)$ matrix of p_{ij} for $i, j = 0, 1,\cdots,n_c$. When n_c is large, this becomes a nontrivial task because of the large number of computational steps and large computer storage requirement for the $[p_{ij}]$ matrix. The fact that $p_{ij} = 0$ for $j \leq i - 2$ in (1) and (2) enables us to use an algorithm given in the Appendix which is very efficient in terms of both computer time and space requirements. For our purposes, this algorithm is superior to conventional methods such as Gauss elimination [31] for solving linear simultaneous equations. In this algorithm, each p_{ij} is used exactly once and can be computed using (1) or (2) only when it is needed in the algorithm. This eliminates the need for storing the $[p_{ij}]$ matrix and practically eliminates any computer storage constraint on the dimensionality of the problem. The number of arithmetic operations $(+ - \times \div)$ required by the above algorithm is in the order of $2n_c^2$ which is comparable to that of Gauss elimination.

In Fig. 12, we show FET as a function of K for the infinite population model and for fixed values of the channel throughput rate S_o (at the channel operating point). We see that FET can be improved by either decreasing the channel throughput rate S_o or by increasing K (which in turn increases the average packet delay). The infinite population model results give the worst case estimates for channel stability as demonstrated in Fig. 13 in which we show FET as a function of M for $K = 10$ and four values of S_o. Note that FET increases as M decreases and there is a critical value of M below which the channel is always stable in the sense of Fig. 7(a). As M increases to infinity, FET reaches a limiting value corresponding to the infinite population model with a Poisson channel input. Fig. 14 is similar to Fig. 12 except now the number of users

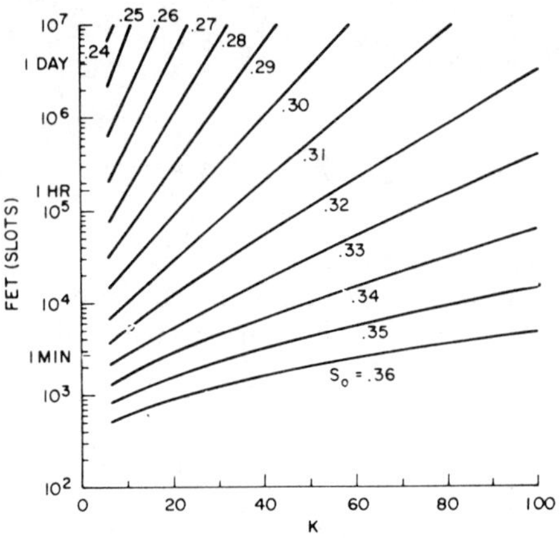

Fig. 12. FET values for the infinite population model.

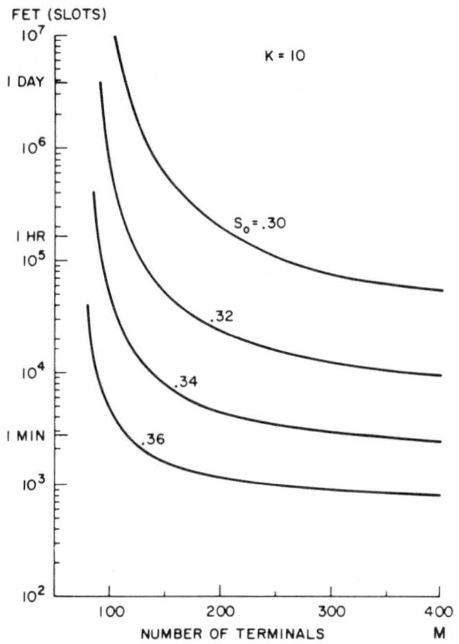

Fig. 13. FET versus M.

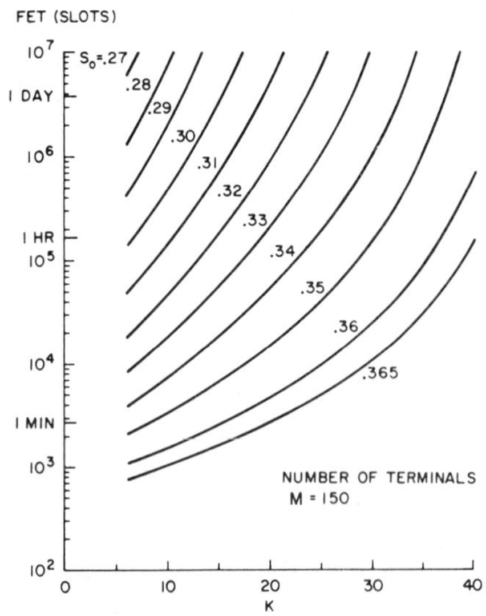

Fig. 14. FET values for a finite user population ($M = 150$).

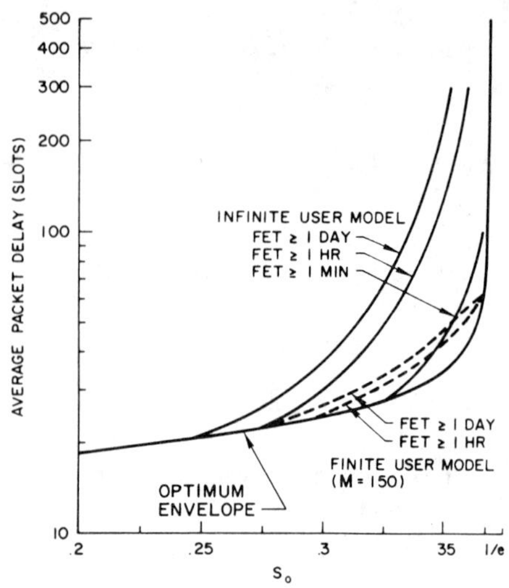

Fig. 15. Stability-throughput-delay tradeoff.

M is 150. Recall that if M is finite, the channel will become stable when K is sufficiently large.

As an example, we see that in Fig. 14 for $M = 150$, if the channel throughput rate S_o is kept at approximately 0.28 and $K = 10$ is used, the channel is estimated to fail once every two days on the average. If this is an acceptable level of channel reliability, then no other channel control procedure is necessary except to restart the channel whenever it goes into saturation. However, if absolute channel reliability is required at the same throughput-delay performance, then dynamic channel control strategies should be adopted. Channel control schemes have been studied [10] and the results will be published in a forthcoming paper [1].

In Fig. 15, we show the optimum performance envelope in Fig. 2 as a lower bound for the throughput-delay tradeoff of the infinite population model. This corresponds to the performance of the channel at the channel operating point. However, from Fig. 7, we see that *the channel operating point* (n_o,S_o) *provides no information regarding the stability behavior of the channel.* The equilibrium performance given by (n_o,S_o) is achievable in the long run if M is small enough such that the channel is stable; elsewhere it is achievable only for some random time period whose average is estimated by our stability measure FET.

In addition to the infinite population model optimum envelope, we also show in Fig. 15 two sets of equilibrium throughput-delay performance curves with guaranteed FET values. The first set consists of three solid curves corresponding to an infinite population model with the stability measure FET $\geq$ 1 day, 1 hour, and 1 minute. Again, these results represent worst case estimates if M is actually finite. The second set consists of two dashed curves corresponding to $M = 150$ with FET $\geq$ 1 day and 1 hour. These results were obtained by looking up the values of K and S_o in Fig. 12 or Fig. 14 corresponding to a fixed FET. The average packet delay was then obtained from Fig. 2. This figure illustrates the *fundamental tradeoff* among channel stability, throughput and delay. In [1], [10], control strategies are devised to dynamically regulate the channel usage to achieve truly stable throughput-delay performance close to the optimum performance envelope.

A Design Example

The designer of a slotted ALOHA channel is faced with the problem of deciding whether he wants 1) a stable channel by limiting its use to a small population of users and sacrificing channel utilization, or 2) an unstable channel which supports a large population of users operating at a certain level of reliability (some value of FET). For example, suppose K is chosen to be 10. (Note in Fig. 2 that $K = 10$ gives close to optimum equilibrium throughput-delay performance over a wide range of channel throughput rate.) Also, suppose that the channel users have an average think time of 20 s which, for our channel numerical constants, correspond to 888 time slots. Now if we draw channel load lines in Fig. 4 with a slope equal to -888, the channel is stable up to approximately 110 channel users. For $M = 110$, the channel throughput rate S_o is about 0.125 packet/slot. From Fig. 2, the average packet delay is roughly 16.5 time slots ($=0.37$ s). The same channel can be used (in an unstable mode) to support 220 users at a channel throughput rate of $S_o = 0.25$ packet/slot. The average packet delay is 21 time slots ($=0.47$ s). From Fig. 12, for $K = 10$ and $S_o = 0.25$, the average up time (FET) of the channel is approximately two days for the infinite population model. Note that this value represents a lower bound for the FET of $M = 220$. Thus, we see that if a channel failure rate of once every two days on the average is an acceptable level of reliability, the second channel design is much more attractive than the first since the number of channel users is more than doubled at a modest increase in delay.

CONCLUSIONS

In this paper, the rationale and some advantages for broadcast packet communication have been discussed. A mathematical model was then formulated for a slotted ALOHA random access system. Using this model, a theory was put forth which gives a coherent qualitative interpretation of the system stability behavior. Quantitative estimates for the relative instability of unstable channels were obtained through definition of the stability measure FET. Numerical results were shown illustrating the trading relations among channel stability, throughput and average packet delay. These results establish tools for the performance evaluation and design of an uncontrolled slotted ALOHA system. Further improvement in the system performance may be accomplished through adaptive control techniques studied in [1], [10].

APPENDIX

The algorithm below solves for the variables $\{t_i\}_{i=0}^{I}$ in the following set of $(I+1)$ linear simultaneous equations,

$$t_0 = h_0 + \sum_{j=0}^{I} p_{0j} t_j \tag{A1}$$

$$t_i = h_i + \sum_{j=i-1}^{I} p_{ij} t_j \qquad i = 1, 2, \cdots, I. \tag{A2}$$

The Algorithm

1) Define

$$e_I = 1$$

$$f_I = 0$$

$$e_{I-1} = \frac{1 - p_{II}}{p_{I,I-1}}$$

$$f_{I-1} = -\frac{h_I}{p_{I,I-1}}.$$

2) For $i = I-1, I-2, \cdots, 1$ solve recursively

$$e_{i-1} = \frac{1}{p_{i,i-1}} \left[e_i - \sum_{j=i}^{I} p_{ij} e_j \right]$$

$$f_{i-1} = \frac{1}{p_{i,i-1}} \left[f_i - h_i - \sum_{j=i}^{I} p_{ij} f_j \right].$$

3) Let

$$t_I = \frac{f_0 - h_0 - \sum_{j=0}^{I} p_{0j} f_j}{\sum_{j=0}^{I} p_{0j} e_j - e_0}$$

$$t_i = e_i t_I + f_i \qquad i = 0, 1, 2, \cdots, I-1.$$

Derivation of the Algorithm

Define

$$t_i = e_i t_I + f_i \qquad i = 0, 1, 2, \cdots, I-1 \tag{A3}$$

and

$$e_I = 1$$

$$f_I = 0. \tag{A4}$$

The last equation in (A2) is

$$t_I = h_I + p_{I,I-1} t_{I-1} + p_{II} t_I.$$

Substituting $t_{I-1} = e_{I-1} t_I + f_{I-1}$ into the above equation, we get

$$t_I = h_I + p_{I,I-1} e_{I-1} t_I + p_{I,I-1} f_{I-1} + p_{II} t_I.$$

Equating the coefficients of t_I and the constant terms, we have

$$e_{I-1} = \frac{1 - p_{II}}{p_{I,I-1}}$$

$$f_{I-1} = -\frac{h_I}{p_{I,I-1}}. \quad \text{(A5)}$$

Equation (A2) can be rewritten as follows,

$$t_{i-1} = \frac{1}{p_{i,i-1}} [t_i - h_i - \sum_{j=i}^{I} p_{ij}t_j]. \quad \text{(A6)}$$

In each of the above equations, use (A3) to substitute for t_i. We then have

$$e_{i-1}t_I + f_{i-1} = \frac{1}{p_{i,i-1}} [e_i t_I + f_i - h_i - (\sum_{j=i}^{I} p_{ij}e_j)t_I - \sum_{j=i}^{I} p_{ij}f_j].$$

Equating the coefficients of t_I and the constant terms, we get

$$e_{i-1} = \frac{1}{p_{i,i-1}} [e_i - \sum_{j=i}^{I} p_{ij}e_j]$$

$$f_{i-1} = \frac{1}{p_{i,i-1}} [f_i - h_i - \sum_{j=i}^{I} p_{ij}f_j]. \quad \text{(A7)}$$

From (A4), (A5), and (A7), e_i and f_i ($i = I - 2, I - 3, \cdots, 1, 0$) can then be determined recursively.

We next solve for t_I. Equation (A3) is used to substitute for t_i in (A1), which then becomes

$$e_0 t_I + f_0 = h_0 + (\sum_{j=0}^{I} p_{0j}e_j)t_I + \sum_{j=0}^{I} p_{0j}f_j.$$

Solving for t_I in the above equation, we have

$$t_I = \frac{f_0 - h_0 - \sum_{j=0}^{I} p_{0j}f_j}{\sum_{j=0}^{I} p_{0j}e_j - e_0}. \quad \text{(A8)}$$

Finally, t_i ($i = 0, 1, 2, \cdots, I - 1$) can be obtained from (A3), since e_i, f_i, and t_I are all known. The derivation of the algorithm is now complete.

REFERENCES

[1] S. S. Lam and L. Kleinrock, "Packet switching in a multiaccess broadcast channel: dynamic control procedures," *IEEE Trans. Commun.*, to be published; also in IBM Corp., Yorktown Heights, N. Y., Res. Rep. RC-5062, Oct. 1974.

[2] N. Abramson, "The ALOHA system—another alternative for computer communications," in *1970 Fall Joint Comput. Conf., AFIPS Conf. Proc.*, vol. 37. Montvale, N. J.: AFIPS Press, 1970, pp. 281–285.

[3] W. Crowther, R. Rettberg, D. Walden, S. Ornstein, and F. Heart, "A system for broadcast communication: reservation—ALOHA," in *Proc. 6th Hawaii Int. Conf. System Sciences*, Univ. Hawaii, Honolulu, Jan. 1973.

[4] R. M. Metcalfe, "Steady-state analysis of a slotted and controlled ALOHA system with blocking," in *Proc. 6th Hawaii Int. Conf. System Sciences*, Univ. Hawaii, Honolulu, Jan. 1973.

[5] N. Abramson, "Packet switching with satellites," in *1973 Nat. Comput. Conf., AFIPS Conf. Proc.*, vol. 42. New York: AFIPS Press, 1973, pp. 695–702.

[6] L. Kleinrock and S. S. Lam, "Packet-switching in a slotted satellite channel," in *1973 Nat. Comput. Conf., AFIPS Conf. Proc.*, vol. 42. New York: AFIPS Press, 1973, pp. 703–710.

[7] L. G. Roberts, "Dynamic allocation of satellite capacity through packet reservation," in *1973 Nat. Comput. Conf., AFIPS Conf. Proc.*, vol. 42. New York: AFIPS Press, 1973, pp. 711–716.

[8] L. Kleinrock and S. S. Lam, "On stability of packet switching in a random multi-access broadcast channel," in *Proc. 7th Hawaii Int. Conf. System Sciences (Special Subconf. Computer Nets)*, Univ. Hawaii, Honolulu, Jan. 8–10, 1974.

[9] S. Butterfield, R. Rettberg, and D. Walden, "The satellite IMP for the ARPA network," in *Proc. 7th Hawaii Int. Conf. System Sciences (Special Subconf. Computer Nets)*, Univ. Hawaii, Honolulu, Jan. 8–10, 1974.

[10] S. S. Lam, "Packet switching in a multi-access broadcast channel with application to satellite communication in a computer network," Ph.D. dissertation, Dep. Comput. Sci., Univ. Calif., Los Angeles, Mar. 1974; also in Univ. of Calif., Los Angeles, Tech. Rep. UCLA-ENG-7429, Apr. 1974.

[11] L. G. Roberts, "Data by the packet," *IEEE Spectrum*, vol. 11, pp. 46–51, Feb. 1974.

[12] L. G. Roberts and B. D. Wessler, "Computer network development to achieve resource sharing," in *1970 Spring Joint Comput. Conf., AFIPS Conf. Proc.*, vol. 36. Montvale, N. J.: AFIPS Press, 1970, pp. 543–549.

[13] P. E. Jackson and C. D. Stubbs, "A study of multiaccess computer communications," in *1969 Spring Joint Comput. Conf., AFIPS Conf. Proc.*, vol. 34. Montvale, N. J.: AFIPS Press, 1969, pp. 491–504.

[14] J. Martin, *Systems Analysis for Data Transmission.* Englewood Cliffs, N. J.: Prentice-Hall, 1972.

[15] J. R. Pierce, "Network for block switching of data," in *IEEE Conv. Rec.*, New York, Mar. 1971.

[16] W. W. Chu, "A study of asynchronous time division multiplexing for time-sharing computer systems," in *1969 Fall Joint Comput. Conf., AFIPS Conf. Proc.*, vol. 35. Montvale, N. J.: AFIPS Press, 1969, pp. 669–678.

[17] P. Baran, "On distributed communications XI. Summary overview," Rand Corp., Santa Monica, Calif., Memo. RM-3767-PR, Aug. 1964.

[18] L. Kleinrock, *Communication Nets: Stochastic Message Flow and Delay.* New York: McGraw-Hill, 1964 (out of print); reprinted by New York: Dover, 1972.

[19] D. W. Davies, "The principles of a data communication network for computers and remote peripherals," in *Proc. Int. Fed. Information Processing Congr.*, Edinburgh, Scotland, 1968, pp. D11–D15.

[20] P. Wright, "Facing a booming demand for networks," *Datamation*, vol. 19, pp. 138–139, Nov. 1973.

[21] H. Frank, M. Gerla, and W. Chou, "Issues in the design of large distributed computer communication networks," in *Proc. Nat. Telecommunications Conf.*, Atlanta, Ga., Nov. 26–28, 1973.

[22] L. G. Roberts, "Extensions of packet communication technology to a hand held personal terminal.," in *1972 Spring Joint Comput. Conf., AFIPS Conf. Proc.*, vol. 40. Montvale, N. J.: AFIPS Press, 1972, pp. 295–298.

[23] In *Inst. Elec. Eng. (London) Proc. Int. Conf. Satellite Systems for Mobile Communications and Surveillance*, Mar. 13–15, 1973.

[24] N. T. Gaarder, "ARPANET satellite system," ARPA Network Inform. Center, Stanford Res. Inst., Menlo Park, Calif., ASS Note 3 (NIC 11285), Apr. 1972.

[25] L. G. Roberts, "ALOHA packet system with and without slots and capture," ARPA Network Inform. Center, Stanford Res. Inst., Menlo Park, Calif., ASS Note 8 (NIC 11290), June 1972.

[26] L. Kleinrock and F. A. Tobagi, "Carrier-sense multiple access for packet switched radio channels," in *Proc. Int. Conf. Communications*, Minneapolis, Minn., June 1974.

[27] L. Kleinrock, *Queueing Systems, Vol. I, Theory, Vol. II, Computer Applications.* New York: Wiley-Interscience, 1975.

[28] E. Parzen, *Stochastic Processes.* San Francisco, Calif.: Holden-Day, 1962.

[29] J. W. Cohen, *The Single Server Queue.* New York: Wiley, 1969.

[30] R. Howard, *Dynamic Probabilistic Systems, Vol. 1: Markov Models and Vol. 2: Semi-Markov and Decision Processes.* New York: Wiley, 1971.

[31] E. J. Craig, *Laplace and Fourier Transforms for Electrical Engineers.* New York: Holt, Rinehart, and Winston, 1964.

Leonard Kleinrock (S'55–M'64–SM'71–F'73) was born in New York, N. Y., on June 13, 1934. He received the B.E.E. degree from the City College of New York, N. Y., in 1957, and the S.M.E.E. and Ph.D. degrees in electrical engineering from the Massachusetts Institute of Technology, Cambridge, in 1959 and 1963, respectively, while participating in the Lincoln Laboratory Staff Associate Program.

From 1951 to 1957, he was employed at the Photobell Company, Inc., New York, N. Y., an industrial electronics firm. He spent the summers from 1957 to 1961 at the M.I.T. Lincoln Laboratory, Lexington, Mass., first in the Digital Computer Group and later in the Systems Analysis Group. At M.I.T. he was a Research Assistant, initially with the Electronic Systems Laboratory, and later with the Research Laboratory for Electronics, where he worked on communication nets in the Information Processing and Transmission Group. After completing his graduate work at the end of 1962, he worked at Lincoln Laboratory on communication nets and on signal detection. In 1963 he accepted a position on the faculty at the University of California, Los Angeles, where he is now Professor of Computer Science. He is a referee for numerous scholarly publications, book reviewer for several publishers, and a consultant for various aerospace, research, and governmental organizations. He is principal investigator of a large contract with the Advanced Research Projects Agency (ARPA) of the Department of Defense. He has published over 60 papers and is the author of *Communication Nets; Stochastic Message Flow and Delay* (New York: McGraw-Hill, 1964), *Queueing Systems, Vol. 1: Theory* and *Vol. 2: Computer Applications* (New York: Wiley-Interscience, 1975). His main interests are in communication nets, computer nets, data compression, priority queueing theory, and theoretical studies of time-shared systems.

Dr. Kleinrock is a member of Tau Beta Pi, Eta Kappa Nu, Sigma Xi, the Operations Research Society of America, and the Association for Computing Machinery. He was awarded a Guggenheim Fellowship in 1971.

★

Simon S. Lam (S'69–M'74) was born in Macao on July 31, 1947. He received the B.S.E.E. degree in electrical engineering from Washington State University, Pullman, in 1969, and the M.S. and Ph.D. degrees in engineering from the University of California, Los Angeles, in 1970 and 1974, respectively.

At the University of California, Los Angeles, he held a Phi Kappa Phi Fellowship from 1969 to 1970, and a Chancellor's Teaching Fellowship from 1969 to 1973. He also participated in the ARPA Network project at UCLA as a postgraduate research engineer from 1972 to 1974 and did research on satellite packet communication. Since June 1974 he has been a research staff member with the IBM Thomas J. Watson Research Center, Yorktown Heights, N. Y. His current research interests include computer-communication networks and queueing theory.

Dr. Lam is a member of Tau Beta Pi, Sigma Tau, Phi Kappa Phi, Pi Mu Epsilon, and the Association for Computing Machinery.

"Dynamic Control Schemes for a Packet Switched Multi-Access Broadcast Channel" by S.S. Lam and L. Kleinrock from *AFIPS Conference Proceedings*, Volume 44, 1975 National Computer Conference, pages 143-153.

Dynamic control schemes for a packet switched multi-access broadcast channel*

by SIMON S. LAM
IBM Thomas J. Watson Research Center
Yorktown Heights, New York

and

LEONARD KLEINROCK
University of California
Los Angeles, California

INTRODUCTION

Domestic satellites are emerging as an exciting alternative to satisfying the communications requirements of data users, providing both flexibility and economy. Two attributes of satellites are especially advantageous for the transmission of data in large geographically distributed computer networks. They are (i) the availability of wide transmission bandwidths over long distances and (ii) the multi-access broadcast capability inherent in radio communications which permits transmission to, and reception from, all points in a satellite connected network. These considerations also apply (on a smaller geographical scale) to the use of ground radio channels in a terminal access computer-communication network exemplified by the ALOHA System at the University of Hawaii.[1]

The random access scheme of the ALOHA System has inspired a number of packet switching techniques which permit the sharing of a high-speed multi-access broadcast channel by a large population of channel users.[2–8] Such packet switched radio systems (both satellite and ground radio) have a number of advantages over conventional wire communication techniques for computer communications, such as: the elimination of complex topological design and routing problems in large networks, the possibility of mobile users, the cost reduction over long distances and the increased flexibility for system reconfiguration and upgrading. Another attractive feature is that in these systems each user is merely represented by an ID number. Thus, the number of active users is bounded only by the channel capacity and there is no limitation to the number of inactive (but potentially active) users beyond that of a finite address space. Moreover, measurement studies have shown that interactive computer data traffic tends to be bursty.[9] A single high-speed radio channel permits the total demand of a large population of bursty users to be statistically averaged at the channel. Furthermore, each user transmits data at the full wideband data rate of the radio channel. Such efficient sharing and wideband transmission are in general not possible in a geographically distributed computer-communication network using wire communications.

Of interest in this paper is the slotted ALOHA random access scheme.[3,4,7,10–13] A slotted ALOHA channel multi-accessed by a large number of users has been shown to exhibit unstable behavior, i.e., the system may drift into an undesirable saturation state with a virtually zero probability of transmission success as a result of repeated user conflicts.[4,7,10–12,14] In this paper, a model is first presented for a slotted ALOHA channel supporting input from a large population of bursty users; the data rate of each channel user is assumed to be much less than the channel transmission rate. The underlying concepts of channel stability are then introduced. A dynamic channel control model is next presented and four dynamic channel control algorithms are given. The performance of these algorithms are tested through simulation and compared to analytic results previously obtained.[7,13] We conclude that these algorithms are capable of preventing the occurrence of channel saturation under temporary channel overload conditions and at the same time achieving a level of channel performance close to the theoretical optimum.

The slotted ALOHA model here is similar to one previously studied by Metcalfe through a steady-state analysis.[10,14] He has also recognized the need for control of the channel and proposed a method for controlling the transmission probability of "ready" packets.

Other multi-access broadcast packet switching schemes have been proposed to take advantage of special system and traffic characteristics. A reservation scheme studied by Roberts[5] employs a slotted ALOHA subchannel for broadcasting block transfer reservation requests. Reservation-ALOHA[2] and carrier sense multi-access[8] are both interesting variants of the random access scheme. These systems seem to exhibit unstable behavior similar to that of slotted ALOHA and may be dynamically controlled by algorithms similar to those presented in this paper. Consider, for instance, the ALOHA System at the University of Hawaii which uses two 24 KBPS radio channels and which has been

* This research was supported in part by the Advanced Research Projects Agency of the Department of Defense under Contract No. DAHC-15-73-C-0368.

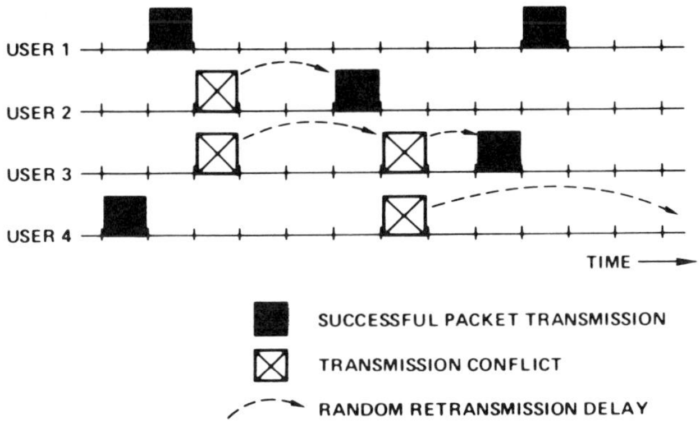

Figure 1—Slotted ALOHA random access

estimated to be able to support up to 500 interactive users.[1,3] We feel that this figure is unrealistic for an uncontrolled system, but may be achieved given some appropriate dynamic channel control.

THE RANDOM ACCESS CHANNEL MODEL

Consider a radio communication system such as a packet switching satellite system[3–7] or the ALOHA System.[1] In each case, there is a *broadcast* channel for point-to-multipoint communication and a *multi-access* channel shared by a large number of users. Since the broadcast channel is used by a single transmitter, no transmission conflict will arise. All nodes covered by the radio broadcast can receive on the same single frequency, picking out packet transmissions addressed to themselves and discarding packets addressed to others. The problem we are faced with is how to resolve conflicts which arise when "simultaneous" demands are placed upon the multi-access channel. If two or more packet transmissions overlap in time at the multi-accessed radio receiver (of the satellite transponder or the central computer), it is assumed that none is received correctly. This event will be referred to as a *channel collision.* The channel may be *slotted* by requiring all channel users to synchronize the leading edges of their packet transmissions at the multi-accessed radio receiver.[3–7] The duration of a channel time slot is set equal to a packet transmission time. In the slotted ALOHA random access scheme, all users transmit newly generated packets into channel time slots independently. In the event of a channel collision, each collided packet is retransmitted independently after a *retransmission delay* of RD slots. The above scheme is illustrated in Figure 1 for the case of a channel random-accessed by four users. (In a ground radio system, RD corresponds to the positive acknowledgment time-out interval.)

Consider a satellite multi-access broadcast system. Let R be the number of time slots in a round-trip satellite channel propagation time which is assumed to be the same for all earth stations. Thus, R time slots after transmitting a packet, a user will either hear that he was successful or know that he had a channel collision. (We have ignored the possibility of random noise errors assuming that the channel has a low error rate.) The retransmission delay RD for a collided packet must be greater than R. Randomization of RD is necessary to minimize the probability of repeated channel collisions for the same packets. Randomization schemes which have been considered include: (1) the uniform retransmission randomization scheme[4] in which the probability distribution of RD is given by

$$\text{Prob}\,[RD=i]=\begin{cases}0 & i\leq R\\ 1/K & R+1\leq i\leq R+K\\ 0 & i>R+K\end{cases} \tag{1}$$

and (2) the geometric retransmission randomization scheme[6,7,10–14] in which the probability distribution of RD is given by

$$\text{Prob}\,[RD=i]=\begin{cases}0 & i\leq R\\ p(1-p)^{i-R-1} & i>R\end{cases} \tag{2}$$

The uniform retransmission randomization scheme is adopted in Reference 4. In that reference, R is taken to be 12 and each time slot is 22.5 milliseconds long, giving 44.4 slots/second. These figures are computed from the assumptions of a 50 KBPS satellite voice channel, 1125 bits/packet and a roundtrip channel propagation time of 0.27 second for all channel users. These same numerical constants are adopted in this paper. However, to study the problems of stability and dynamic channel control, it is necessary to consider a simplified Markovian model in which $R=0$ and the geometric retransmission randomization scheme is assumed, such that RD has a memoryless geometric distribution.[7,10–14] Simulation results have shown that the slotted ALOHA channel performance (in terms of average throughput and delay) is dependent primarily upon the average retransmission delay $\overline{RD}$ and quite insensitive to the exact probability distributions considered.[7] In order to use the analytic results of the Markovian model to predict the throughput-delay performance of a real slotted ALOHA channel with nonzero R, it is necessary to use a value of p in the Markovian model which matches the value of $\overline{RD}$. For example, to approximate the slotted ALOHA channel with uniform retransmission randomization and for which $\overline{RD}=R+(K+1)/2$, we must let

$$p=\frac{1}{R+(K+1)/2} \tag{3}$$

such that $\overline{RD}$ is the same in both cases. Numerical results in this paper will always be expressed in terms of K (rather than p) through use of Equation (3).

Let us now introduce the Markovian model,[7,11–13] in which we consider a slotted ALOHA channel with a user population consisting of M users. Each such user can be in one of two states: *blocked* or *thinking*.[10,14] In the thinking state, a user generates (and transmits) a new packet in a time slot with probability σ. A packet which had a channel collision and is waiting for retransmission is said to be *backlogged.* The retransmission delay RD of each backlogged packet is assumed to be geometrically distributed, i.e., each backlogged packet retransmits in the current time slot with probability p. Assuming bursty users, we must have $p\gg\sigma$. From the time a user generates a packet until that packet is successfully received, the user is *blocked* in the sense that he cannot generate (or accept from his input source) a new packet for transmission.

Let N^t be a random variable (called the *channel backlog*) representing the total number of backlogged packets at time t. The "channel input" rate at time t is $S^t=(M-N^t)\sigma$. We shall assume M and σ to be time-invariant unless stated otherwise. In this case, N^t is a Markov process (chain) with stationary transition probabilities and serves as the state description for the system. The discrete *state space* consists of the set of integers $\{0, 1, 2, \ldots, M\}$.

CHANNEL STABILITY

In this section, we give a brief description of the stability behavior of an uncontrolled slotted ALOHA system studied earlier.[7,10–12,14] Consider the trajectory of (N^t, S^t) in the two-dimensional (n, S) plane. Assuming that M and σ are constant, (N^t, S^t) is constrained to lie on the straight line $S=(M-n)\sigma$ called the *channel load line*. Corresponding to a fixed value* of K, there is an *equilibrium contour* in the (n, S) plane defined as the locus of points for which the channel input rate S is exactly equal to the expected channel throughput (defined to be the probability of a successful packet transmission) $S_{out}(n, S)$ in a time slot. A family of such contours is illustrated in Figure 2. Let us focus upon an equilibrium contour corresponding to $K=K_o$ in Figure 3. In the shaded region enclosed by the equilibrium contour, $S_{out}(n, S)$ is greater than S; elsewhere, S exceeds $S_{out}(n, S)$. Arrows on the channel load lines point in the direction of "drift" of the channel backlog size N^t. Three channel load lines are also shown in Figure 3 corresponding to channel user population sizes M, M' and M'', and an average user think time of $1/\sigma$ slots.

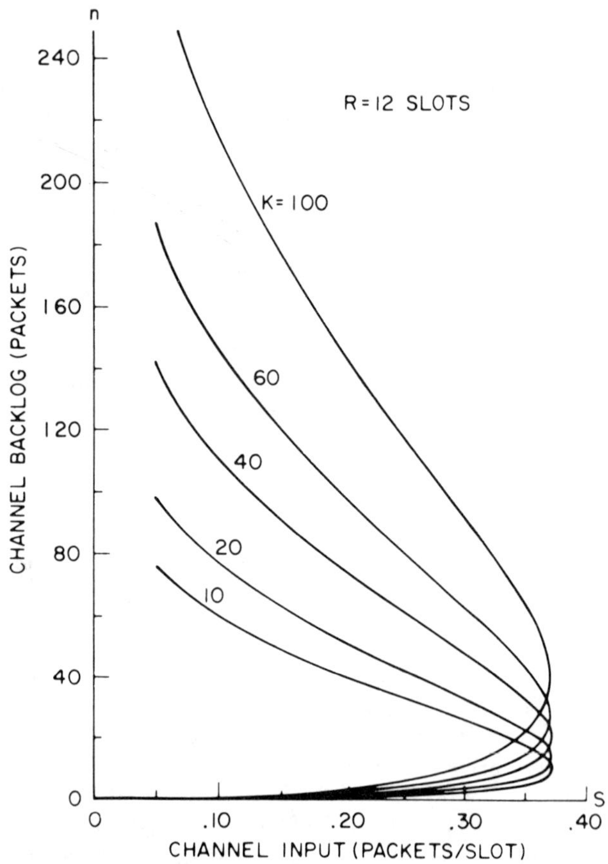

Figure 2—Equilibrium contours

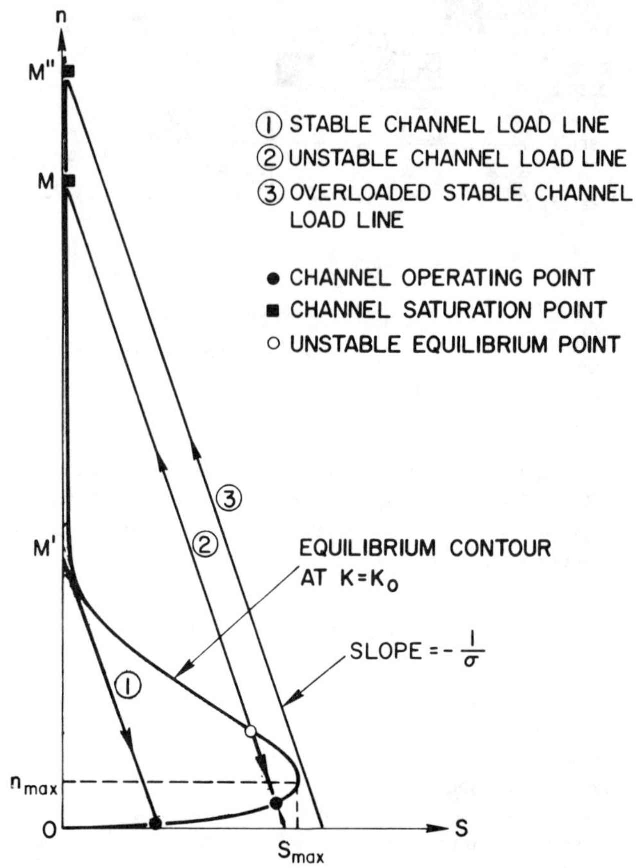

Figure 3—Stable and unstable channels

A channel load line may intersect the equilibrium contour one or more times, and we refer to these as equilibrium points which we denote by (n_e, S_e). An equilibrium point on a load line is said to be a *stable equilibrium point* if it acts as a "sink" with respect to the drift of N^t; an equilibrium point is said to be an *unstable equilibrium point* if it acts as a "source." A stable equilibrium point is said to be the *channel operating point* if $n_e \leq n_{max}$ as shown in Figure 3; it is said to be the *channel saturation point* if $n_e > n_{max}$. (We shall use (n_o, S_o) instead of (n_e, S_e) to distinguish the channel operating point from other equilibrium points.) A channel load line is defined to be *stable* if it has exactly one stable equilibrium point; otherwise it is defined to be *unstable*. Thus, the load lines 1 and 3 in Figure 3 are stable by definition; the load line 2 is unstable.

* Or equivalently a fixed value of p under Equation (3).

INPUT PARAMETERS => => =>
INPUT RATE = 0.350
PROPAGATION DELAY = 12
K = 15

AVERAGE VALUES IN 200 TIME SLOT PERIODS

TIME PERIOD	THROUGHPUT RATE- S	TRAFFIC RATE- G	PACKET DELAY- D	FRACTION EMPTY	AVERAGE BACKLOG
1 - 200	0.330	0.510	17.924	0.595	3.1
201 - 400	0.370	0.605	30.892	0.530	5.3
401 - 600	0.360	0.860	32.764	0.425	9.5
601 - 800	0.340	0.840	43.147	0.435	10.5
801 - 1000	0.315	1.415	58.889	0.250	21.5
1001 - 1200	0.380	1.260	72.066	0.260	16.0
1201 - 1400	0.325	0.455	37.215	0.610	3.0
1401 - 1600	0.355	0.480	20.803	0.590	2.5
1601 - 1800	0.275	0.405	20.600	0.665	2.6
1801 - 2000	0.360	0.560	27.528	0.550	4.5
2001 - 2200	0.330	0.430	18.561	0.620	1.8
2201 - 2400	0.310	0.545	22.065	0.580	4.3
2401 - 2600	0.335	0.840	44.866	0.455	9.9
2601 - 2800	0.320	0.705	34.703	0.500	7.5
2801 - 3000	0.325	1.085	43.815	0.350	14.1
3001 - 3200	0.310	1.715	67.161	0.180	26.9
3201 - 3400	0.105	3.255	147.143	0.050	61.6
3401 - 3600	0.015	5.910	220.333	0.000	113.4
3601 - 3800	0.000	9.155	0.000	0.000	179.3
3801 - 4000	0.000	12.400	0.000	0.000	243.8

Figure 4—An unstable channel drifting into saturation

If M is finite, a stationary probability distribution always exists for N^t. In a stable channel, the equilibrium point (n_e, S_e) gives (approximately) the steady-state throughput-delay performance of the channel over an infinite time horizon. On the other hand, an unstable channel exhibits "bi-stable" behavior; the throughput-delay performance given by the channel operating point is achievable only for a finite time period before the channel drifts toward the channel saturation point. When this happens, the channel performance degrades rapidly as the channel throughput rate decreases and the average packet delay increases. In this state, the communication channel can be regarded as having failed. (In a practical system, external control should be applied at this point to restore proper channel operation.) In Figure 4, we have shown a simulation of the above behavior. In this example, M is assumed to be so large that the channel input is Poisson distributed at a constant rate $S=0.35$.

The channel load line labelled 3 in Figure 3 has a channel saturation point as its only stable equilibrium point. It is overloaded in the sense that M'' is too big for the given σ and K. From now on, a stable channel load line will always refer to 1 instead of 3.

Given a channel load line, suppose K_{opt} is the optimum K which minimizes n_o and maximizes S_o at the channel operating point. For this value of K, the channel may be unstable in which case the optimum channel performance given by (n_o, S_o) is achievable only for a finite time period. In References 7, 11 and 12, the average "up" time of an unstable channel has been quantified as a stability measure of the channel. To render the channel stable, two obvious solutions are available: (1) use a larger value for K (see Figure 2), and (2) reduce the user population size M. The first solution gives rise to a smaller S_o and a larger n_o; the corresponding average packet delay may then be too large to be acceptable. In the second solution, a small M implies that $S_o \ll S_{max}$ (see Figure 3) since $\sigma \ll 1$ under the assumption of bursty users. This results in a waste of channel capacity.

The third solution is the use of dynamic channel control which constitutes the subject matter of the balance of this paper.

THE DYNAMIC CHANNEL CONTROL MODEL

To prevent the disastrous consequences of channel saturation, various dynamic control measures may be taken. In this section, we describe the dynamic channel control model studied in References 7 and 13, and outline some of the results obtained there under the assumption of *perfect channel state information*, i.e., each channel user knows the exact value of the channel backlog N^t at time t. In the next section, we shall consider practical control schemes which estimate the channel state and apply the theoretical optimal control policies using this estimate.

Consider the finite-state Markovian decision model obtained by injecting the following two classes of control actions into our earlier model for N^t:

(i) each packet arrival is accepted for transmission with probability β and rejected with probability $1-\beta$ where $0\leq\beta\leq 1$ and $\beta\in\{\beta_1, \beta_2, \ldots, \beta_m\}\triangleq\mathcal{A}_1$;
(ii) each backlogged packet is retransmitted with probability γ where $0<\gamma<1$ and $\gamma\in\{\gamma_1, \gamma_2, \ldots, \gamma_k\}\triangleq\mathcal{A}_2$.

$\mathcal{A}\triangleq\mathcal{A}_1\times\mathcal{A}_2$ is said to be the control action space. Three special cases have been studied extensively in References 7 and 13, namely,

(1) The Input Control Procedure (ICP) with $\mathcal{A}=\{0, 1\}\times\{p_o\}$,
(2) The Retransmission Control Procedure (RCP) with $\mathcal{A}=\{1\}\times\{p_o, p_c\}$, and
(3) The Input-Retransmission Control Procedure (IRCP) with $\mathcal{A}=\{0, 1\}\times\{p_o, p_c\}$.

In these control procedures, p_o corresponds to some K_o which optimizes the channel operating point of the given channel load line; p_c corresponds to some K_c which is sufficiently large to render the given channel load line stable.

A *control policy* f is defined to be any rule for choosing control actions in $\mathcal{A}$. The action α^t, at time t given by the policy f, specifies both the state transition probabilities and some predefined expected state transition cost for the tth time slot. Thus f determines both the evolution in time of N^t and the sequence of costs it incurs. Given a cost structure (denoted by δ), the *cost rate* $g_\delta(f)$ of N^t under a control policy f is defined to be the steady-state average cost per unit time incurred by N^t.

An important subclass of all policies is the class of stationary policies. A *stationary policy* is defined to be one which chooses an action at time t depending only upon the state of the process at that time. From well-known results in Markov decision theory, we know that (1) if f is a stationary policy, $g_\delta(f)$ is independent of the initial state of the process N^t, and (2) a stationary policy f^* exists, which minimizes $g_\delta(f)$ over the class of all policies. Thus in our search for an optimal control strategy, we can limit our attention to the class of stationary policies only.

As the process N^t evolves from one time slot to the next, various expected state transition costs may be incurred, such as

(1) the expected channel throughput in the tth time slot,
(2) the (delay) cost of holding backlogged packets, and
(3) the expected (delay) cost of rejecting packet arrivals.

Type 1 costs take on negative values since we want to maximize the channel throughput rate. Type 2 costs are chosen such that each backlogged packet incurs 1 unit of delay per time slot. In the references, the expected cost in units of delay per packet arrival rejected (type 3 costs) is assumed to be equal to an average user think time. This assumption is needed for our Markovian model formulation and may be justified in a terminal access communications environment as follows. A person sitting at a terminal generates a new packet with an average think time of $1/\sigma$ whenever his previous packet has been successfully transmitted. If, at the time of a packet arrival, the channel is in the reject state, this packet is lost in the sense that it is not transmitted over the channel immediately. In a practical situation, the user may be informed of the event and must enter some command character to "resend" the packet. Hence, the cost in terms of delay is probably in the order of an average think time $(=1/\sigma)$.

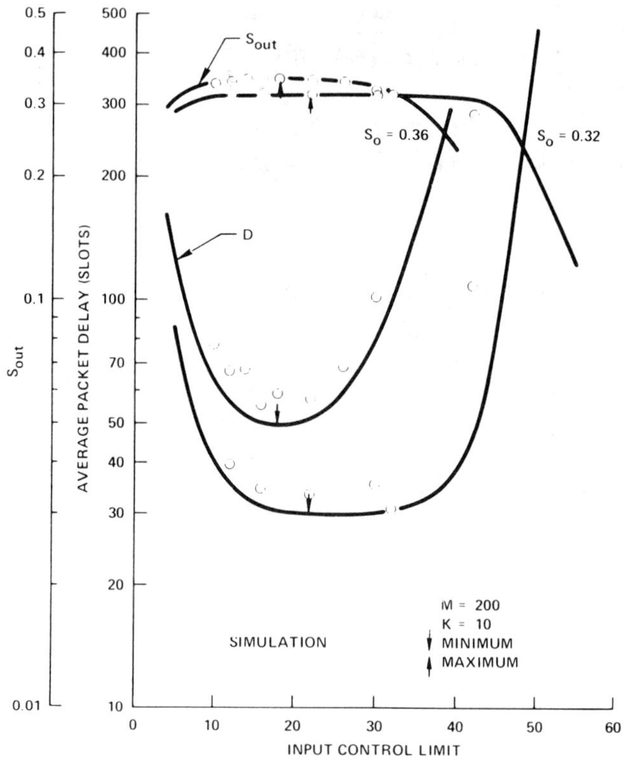

Figure 5—Channel performance versus ICP control limit for $M=200$

Let $g_s(f)$ denote the cost rate of N^t given by policy f and type 1 costs, and $g_d(f)$ denote the cost rate of N^t given by policy f and types 2 and 3 costs. The channel performance measures, namely, the *steady-state channel throughput rate* S_{out} and the *expected packet delay* D can then be calculated in terms of $g_s(f)$ and $g_d(f)$.

In the references, it is shown that for the given model an optimal stationary control policy maximizes S_{out} and minimizes D simultaneously. An efficient computational algorithm (POLITE) based upon Howard's policy-iteration method[15] is given for calculating the optimal policy. Given a channel load line and a dynamic control procedure ($\mathcal{A}$), this algorithm usually arrives at the optimal control policy and the optimum values of S_{out} and D in very few iterations. Furthermore, numerical results indicate that each optimal

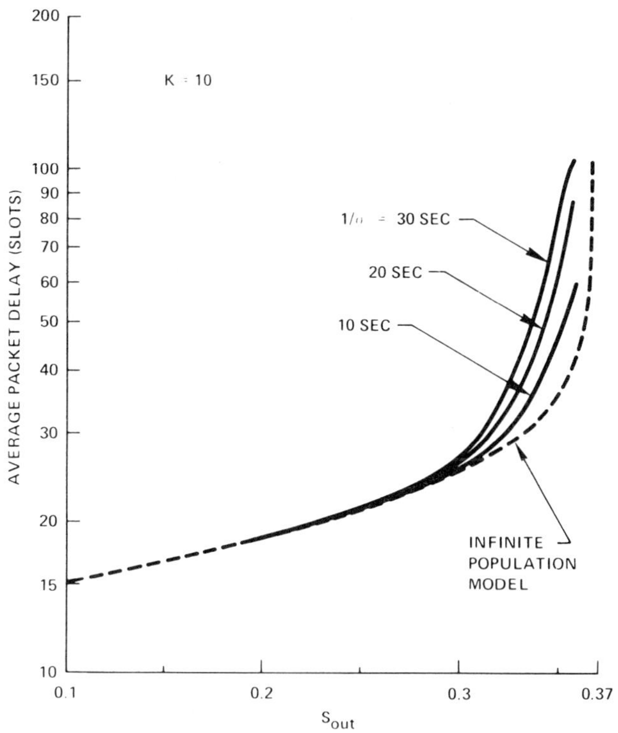

Figure 6—ICP optimum throughput-delay tradeoffs at fixed σ

control policy f for the control procedures ICP and RCP has the following structure:

$$f(i)=\begin{cases} a_o & 0\le i\le \hat{n} \\ a_c & \hat{n}<i\le M \end{cases} \quad (4)$$

where a_o corresponds to "accept" in ICP and "p_o" in RCP; a_c corresponds to "reject" in ICP and "p_c" in RCP. On the other hand, an optimal control policy f for IRCP has the following structure:

$$f(i)=\begin{cases} (\text{accept}, p_o) & 0\le i\le \hat{n}_1 \\ (\text{accept}, p_c) & \hat{n}_1<i\le \hat{n}_2 \\ (\text{reject}, p_c) & \hat{n}_2<i\le M \end{cases} \quad (5)$$

We shall refer to $\hat{n}$, $\hat{n}_1$ and $\hat{n}_2$ as control limits and the control policies in Equations (4) and (5) as *control limit policies.*

In Figure 5, we have shown the performance measures, S_{out} and D, for two channel load lines specified by $M=200$ and the channel operating point $(n_o, S_o)=(4,0.32)$ and $(7,0.36)$, over a range of ICP control limit policies. Observe that the same control limit minimizes D and maximizes S_{out} at the same time as predicted by the theory. Note the amazing flatness of S_{out} and D near the optimum point for the channel load line with $S_o=0.32$. The consequence is that even if a nonoptimal control policy is used (due, for example, to not knowing the exact current backlog size such as in most practical systems), it is still possible to achieve a throughput-delay performance close to the optimum.

In Figure 5, we have also shown simulation results for throughput and delay. In these simulations, channel control policies are applied assuming that the exact channel backlog size N^t is known to all channel users. However, contrary to the Markovian model, each collided packet is assumed to suffer the more realistic fixed delay R and its retransmission is randomized uniformly over the next K slots. The excellent agreement between the simulation and analytic results presented here demonstrates the accuracy of the approximation.

In Figure 6, we show optimum throughput-delay tradeoffs at fixed values of σ for ICP. ($1/\sigma$ is the average think time of a channel user.) In this case, increasing S_{out} corresponds to increasing M, that is, admitting more channel users. We see that the channel performance improves as the packet generation probability σ increases, since this implies that for the same S_{out}, the number of channel users M is smaller. In the latter case, the channel is "less unstable."[7,11,12]

PRACTICAL CONTROL SCHEMES

In a practical system, the channel users often have no means of communication among themselves other than the multi-access broadcast channel itself. Each channel user must individually estimate the channel state by observing the outcome in each channel slot. Moreover, whatever channel state information available to the channel users is at least one round-trip propagation delay (R) old and may introduce additional errors in the users' estimates if R is large (such as in a satellite channel). Thus, the control action applied based upon an estimate of the channel state may not necessarily be the optimal one at that time, which then will lead to some degradation in channel performance.

Below we first give a heuristic scheme for estimating the channel state assuming that the channel history (i.e., empty slots, successful transmissions or collisions) is available to all channel users. The optimal ICP, RCP and IRCP control policies will be applied based upon the above estimate. A heuristic control procedure is next proposed which circumvents the state estimation problem. These control procedures are then examined through simulation and compared with the optimum throughput-delay results in the previous section. The ability of these control procedures to handle time-varying inputs (with pulses) is also examined.

Channel control-estimation (CONTEST) algorithms

The *channel traffic* in a time slot is defined to be the number of packet transmissions (both new and previously collided packets) by all users in that time slot. Our heuristic procedure for estimating the channel state is based upon the observation that the channel traffic in a time slot is approximately Poisson distributed. (See Chapter 4 and Appendix A of Reference 7.) Below we present algorithms which implement channel control procedures studied in the previous sections using estimates of the channel state. These channel CONTrol-ESTimation algorithms will be referred to as CONTEST algorithms.

Here we give a procedure for implementing RCP. Suppose $\hat{n}$ is the RCP control limit such that the channel users switch their retransmission K value from K_o to K_c when the channel backlog size exceeds $\hat{n}$ and from K_c to K_o as soon as the channel backlog size drops below $\hat{n}$. We define

$$\hat{G}_o = \hat{n}p_o + (M - \hat{n})\sigma \tag{6}$$

and

$$\hat{G}_c = \hat{n}p_c + (M - \hat{n})\sigma \tag{7}$$

$\hat{G}_o$ and $\hat{G}_c$ represent the average channel traffic rates given that the channel backlog size is $\hat{n}$ packets with K equal to K_o and K_c respectively. Assuming that the channel traffic is approximately Poisson distributed, we define the following critical values (corresponding to the probability of zero channel traffic in a time slot),

$$\hat{f}_o = e^{-\hat{G}_o} \tag{8}$$

and

$$\hat{f}_c = e^{-\hat{G}_c} \tag{9}$$

Since $K_c > K_o$ we must have

$$\hat{f}_o < \hat{f}_c$$

Suppose each channel user keeps track of the channel history (one round-trip propagation delay ago) within a window frame of W slots. Let $\bar{f}^t$ be the measured fraction of empty slots in the W slots within the history window for the tth time slot. $\bar{f}^t$ will closely approximate the probability of zero channel traffic in the tth time slot provided that the channel traffic probability distribution does not change appreciably in $(W+R)$ time slots, that $W \gg 1$ and the Poisson traffic assumption holds. We give the following algorithm to be adopted by each channel user. d^t denotes the control decision at time t.

Algorithm 1 (RCP-CONTEST)—This algorithm generates the decision $d^t = K_o, K_c$ at each time point based upon the channel state estimate $\bar{f}^t$ and the RCP control limit $\hat{n}$. Start at step (1) or step (4).

(1) $t \leftarrow t + 1$
    $d^t = K_o$
(2) If $\bar{f}^t < \hat{f}_o$, go to (4)
(3) Go to (1)
(4) $t \leftarrow t+1$
    $d^t = K_c$
(5) If $\bar{f}^t > \hat{f}_c$, go to (1)
(6) Go to (4)

Next we consider a similar implementation for ICP. We define

$$\hat{G}_a = \hat{n}p + (M - \hat{n})\sigma \tag{10}$$

$$\hat{G}_r = \hat{n}p \tag{11}$$

$$\hat{f}_a = e^{-\hat{G}_a} \tag{12}$$

and

$$\hat{f}_r = e^{-\hat{G}_r} \tag{13}$$

Since $\hat{G}_a > \hat{G}_r$, we must have

$$\hat{f}_a < \hat{f}_r$$

TABLE I—Throughput-delay Results of a Controlled Channel ($M = 200$, $S_o = 0.32$)

CONTROL SCHEME	S_{out}	D
ICP (POLITE)	0.31778	29.857
RCP (POLITE)	0.31817	29.085
IRCP(POLITE)	0.31817	29.085
ICP (Simulation)	0.315	33.427
RCP (Simulation)	0.318	28.824
ICP-CONTEST W = 20	0.314	40.893
ICP-CONTEST W = 40	0.315	30.514
ICP-CONTEST W = 60	0.317	32.355
ICP-CONTEST W = 80	0.318	35.809
RCP-CONTEST W = 20	0.315	33.052
RCP-CONTEST W = 40	0.322	33.335
RCP-CONTEST W = 60	0.319	32.138
RCP-CONTEST W = 80	0.317	32.501
Heuristic RCP { K_1 = 10	0.316	33.720
Heuristic RCP { K_m = 60 $m \geq 2$	0.315	34.554
Heuristic RCP { K_1 = 10, K_2 = 60	0.310	35.425
Heuristic RCP { K_m = 120 $m \geq 3$	0.316	34.635

Algorithm 2 (ICP-CONTEST)—This algorithm generates the decision d^t = accept, reject at time t, based upon the channel state estimate $\bar{f}^t$ and ICP control limit $\hat{n}$. Start at step (1) or step (4).

(1) $t \leftarrow t+1$
    d^t = accept
(2) If $\bar{f}^t < \hat{f}_a$ go to (4)
(3) Go to (1)
(4) $t \leftarrow t+1$
    d^t = reject
(5) If $\bar{f}^t > \hat{f}_r$ go to (1)
(6) Go to (4)

Finally, to implement IRCP, we assume that the control policy is of the form given in Equation (5) such that it is uniquely specified by the control limits $\hat{n}_1$ and $\hat{n}_2$. We define $\hat{f}_o$ and $\hat{f}_c$ by using $\hat{n}_1$ in Equations (6)-(9), $\hat{f}_{ac}$ and $\hat{f}_{rc}$ by using $\hat{n}_2$ and p_c in Equations (10)-(13) and $\hat{f}_{ao}$ by using $\hat{n}_2$ and p_o in Equations (10) and (12). Since $p_o > p_c > \sigma$ and $\hat{n}_2 > \hat{n}_1$, we have $\hat{f}_{ao} < \hat{f}_o$ and $\hat{f}_{ac} < \hat{f}_c$.

Algorithm 3 (IRCP-CONTEST)—This algorithm generates the decision d^t = (accept, K_o), (accept, K_c), (reject, K_c)

TABLE II—Throughput-delay Results of a Controlled Channel ($M=400$, $S_o=0.32$)

CONTROL SCHEME	S_{out}	D
ICP (POLITE)	0.31807	33.096
RCP (POLITE)	0.31844	31.608
IRCP (POLITE)	0.31844	31.608
ICP (Simulation)	0.315	31.427
RCP (Simulation)	0.317	31.023
ICP-CONTEST W = 20	0.315	43.262
ICP-CONTEST W = 40	0.314	34.723
ICP-CONTEST W = 60	0.312	53.240
ICP-CONTEST W = 80	0.316	39.112
RCP-CONTEST W = 20	0.313	41.087
RCP-CONTEST W = 40	0.319	43.379
RCP-CONTEST W = 60	0.318	38.821
RCP-CONTEST W = 80	0.317	40.068
RCP-CONTEST W = 100	0.314	35.689
RCP-CONTEST W = 120	0.319	47.149
Heuristic RCP { $K_1 = 10$, $K_m = 150$ $m \geq 2$ }	0.316	45.150
	0.316	44.750
Heuristic RCP { $K_1 = 10$, $K_2 = 100$, $K_m = 200$ $m \geq 3$ }	0.312	42.040
	0.311	43.136

at time t based upon the channel state estimate $\hat{f}^t$ and IRCP control policy $(\hat{n}_1, \hat{n}_2)$. Start at step (1), (4), or (7).

(1) $t \leftarrow t+1$
   $d^t = (\text{accept}, K_o)$
(2) If $\hat{f}^t < \hat{f}_{ao}$ go to (7)
   otherwise, if $\hat{f}^t < \hat{f}_o$ go to (4)
(3) go to (1)
(4) $t \leftarrow t+1$
   $d^t = (\text{accept}, K_c)$
(5) If $\hat{f}^t > \hat{f}_c$ go to (1)
   otherwise, if $\hat{f}^t < \hat{f}_{ac}$ go to (7)
(6) go to (4)
(7) $t \leftarrow t+1$
   $d^t = (\text{reject}, K_c)$
(8) If $\hat{f}^t > \hat{f}_{rc}$ go to (4)
(9) go to (7)

The size W of the channel history window kept by each channel user is very important for successful channel state estimation. If W is too large, we may lose information on the dynamic behavior of the channel such that the necessary actions are taken too late. If W is too small, we may get large errors in approximating the probability of zero channel traffic by the fraction of empty slots in the history window. A good initial estimate is that W should be bigger than R and of the same order of magnitude. Below we compare simulation results on channel performance for different values of W.

Another retransmission control procedure

In this section we describe a simple heuristic control procedure which has the property that when the channel traffic increases the retransmission delays of backlogged packets will also increase. Hence, it will be referred to as the heuristic retransmission control procedure (*Heuristic RCP*). The advantage of such a control procedure is that it is simple and can be implemented easily without any need for monitoring the channel history and estimating the channel state.

Algorithm 4 (*Heuristic RCP*)—For a backlogged packet with m previous channel collisions, the uniform retransmission randomization* interval is taken to be $K=K_m$ where K_m is a monotone nondecreasing function in m.

When the channel traffic increases, the probability of channel collision increases. As a result, the "effective" value of K increases. If K_m is a steep enough function of m, we see that channel saturation will be prevented. An effective value of K can be defined only with respect to a specific performance measure (e.g., average packet delay). To illustrate the effect of the function K_m, we derive below the *average* value of K as a function of q (the probability of successful transmission) for two cases. Let

$$r_i = \text{Prob [a packet retransmits } i \text{ times before success]}$$
$$= (1-q)^i q \qquad i \geq 1$$

Case 1 $\quad K_m = K_2$ for $m \geq 2$ and $K_2 > K_1$

$\bar{K}$ = average value of K

$$= \frac{1}{1-q} \sum_{i=1}^{\infty} r_i \sum_{m=1}^{i} \frac{K_m}{i}$$

$$= \frac{1}{1-q} \sum_{i=1}^{\infty} (1-q)^i q \left(\frac{K_1}{i} + \frac{i-1}{i} K_2 \right)$$

$$= K_2 + \frac{q \ln q}{1-q} (K_2 - K_1) \tag{14}$$

which is equal to K_1 at $q=1$ and increases to K_2 as q decreases to zero; ln is the natural logarithm function.

Case 2 $\quad K_m = mK \qquad m \geq 1$

$$\bar{K} = \frac{1}{1-q} \sum_{i=1}^{\infty} r_i \sum_{m=1}^{i} \frac{K_m}{i}$$

$$= \frac{K}{1-q} \sum_{i=1}^{\infty} \frac{(1-q)^i q}{i} \sum_{m=1}^{i} m$$

$$= \frac{K}{2} \left(1 + \frac{1}{q} \right) \tag{15}$$

* Note that the same control scheme can be extended to geometric retransmission randomization by letting $p = p_m$ where p_m is a monotone nonincreasing function in m.

INPUT PARAMETERS:

NUMBER OF TERMINALS M = 400 , PROPAGATION DELAY R = 12
FOR THE TIME PERIOD 1-1000, INPUT RATE Mσ = 0.3232
FOR THE TIME PERIOD 1001-1200, INPUT RATE Mσ = 1.0
FOR THE TIME PERIOD 1201-6000, INPUT RATE Mσ = 0.3232
RETRANSMISSION CONTROL LIMIT = 23, INPUT CONTROL LIMIT = 116
K_o = 10 , K_c = 150 , WINDOW SIZE W = 60

AVERAGE VALUES IN 200 TIME SLOT PERIODS:

TIME PERIOD	THROUGHPUT RATE- S	TRAFFIC RATE- G	PACKET DELAY- D	FRACTION EMPTY	AVERAGE BACKLOG	PACKETS REJECTED
1 - 200	0.290	0.625	30.29	0.555	5.5	0
201 - 400	0.325	0.700	34.06	0.505	6.9	0
401 - 600	0.285	0.450	23.67	0.635	2.8	0
601 - 800	0.295	0.625	31.76	0.565	5.9	0
801 - 1000	0.325	0.850	42.57	0.455	9.3	0
1001 - 1200	0.205	2.345	524.32	0.190	50.0	49
1201 - 1400	0.345	1.330	389.68	0.325	75.2	13
1401 - 1600	0.355	0.880	188.11	0.435	51.5	0
1601 - 1800	0.375	0.735	179.37	0.460	34.9	0
1801 - 2000	0.225	1.295	297.85	0.385	33.7	5
2001 - 2200	0.325	1.005	530.77	0.415	35.3	21
2201 - 2400	0.380	0.905	127.32	0.365	16.7	0
2401 - 2600	0.305	0.485	27.64	0.605	3.1	0
2601 - 2800	0.290	0.430	20.86	0.640	2.3	0
2801 - 3000	0.345	0.745	35.38	0.485	7.2	0
3001 - 3200	0.300	0.455	17.62	0.635	2.4	0
3201 - 3400	0.280	0.615	28.48	0.575	5.6	0
3401 - 3600	0.390	0.810	37.90	0.425	7.9	0
3601 - 3800	0.330	0.655	30.65	0.520	5.6	0
3801 - 4000	0.300	0.390	19.30	0.655	1.7	0
4001 - 4200	0.315	0.615	29.24	0.560	5.1	0
4201 - 4400	0.335	0.600	24.51	0.545	4.5	0
4401 - 4600	0.300	0.450	24.32	0.630	2.6	0
4601 - 4800	0.280	0.480	25.29	0.625	3.7	0
4801 - 5000	0.285	0.585	32.07	0.580	5.3	0
5001 - 5200	0.330	0.570	26.41	0.555	4.3	0
5201 - 5400	0.335	0.550	23.67	0.560	3.7	0
5401 - 5600	0.335	0.640	28.81	0.530	5.2	0
5601 - 5800	0.275	0.410	21.56	0.660	2.4	0
5801 - 6000	0.285	0.445	22.35	0.645	2.7	0

Figure 7—Simulation run for IRCP-CONTEST subject to a channel input pulse

which is equal to K at $q=1$ and increases to infinity as q decreases to zero.

The above results indicate that the average value of K behaves in the desired manner, namely, $\bar{K}$ increases as q decreases due to an increasing channel traffic. Below we examine the CONTEST algorithms and Heuristic RCP through simulations.

Simulation results

We summarize in Tables I-II, throughput-delay results for channel load lines specified by

(1) $M=200$, $(n_o, S_o)=(4, 0.32)$
(2) $M=400$, $(n_o, S_o)=(4, 0.32)$

In both cases, we assume $K_o=10$ and $K_c=60$. Included in these tables are (a) optimum POLITE results for ICP, RCP and IRCP, (b) simulation results for ICP and RCP using optimal control policies and under the assumption of perfect channel state information, (c) simulation results for the CONTEST algorithm using ICP and RCP optimal control policies, and (d) simulation results for Heuristic RCP. The duration of each simulation run was taken to be 30,000 time slots. IRCP was not tested by simulation since the optimal value of $\hat{n}_2$ is in all cases so large that within the simulation duration, the channel state N^t (almost surely) will not exceed it; the control procedure becomes effectively RCP specified by $\hat{n}_1$.

The ICP-CONTEST algorithm was tested with channel history window sizes of 20, 40, 60, and 80 time slots. We see from Tables I and II that $W=40$ appears to give the best throughput-delay results. Note that for $R=12$ and $K=10$, $W=40$ is approximately twice $R+K$.

The RCP-CONTEST algorithm was also tested with various values of W. In this case, K takes on two values, K_o and K_c. There is no clear-cut optimal W. It appears that $W=60$ is a good choice.

There is no significant degradation in channel performance (from the theoretical optimum) given by the CONTEST algorithms and Heuristic RCP. The CONTEST algorithms, however, seem to have an edge over Heuristic RCP. The excellent performance of the CONTEST algorithms can be attributed to the flatness of S_{out} and D near the optimum as a function of the control limit (see Figure 5). We found that this flatness property is less pronounced for channel load lines with large values of S_o or M, such as $S_o=0.36$ or

INPUT PARAMETERS:

NUMBER OF TERMINALS M = 400 , PROPAGATION DELAY R = 12

FOR THE TIME PERIOD 1-1000, INPUT RATE $M\sigma$ = 0.3232

FOR THE TIME PERIOD 1001-1200, INPUT RATE $M\sigma$ = 1.0

FOR THE TIME PERIOD 1201-6000, INPUT RATE $M\sigma$ = 0.3232

$K_1 = 10$ $K_m = 150$ $(m \geq 2)$

AVERAGE VALUES IN 200 TIME SLOT PERIODS:

TIME PERIOD	THROUGHPUT RATE- S	TRAFFIC RATE- G	PACKET DELAY- D	FRACTION EMPTY	AVERAGE BACKLOG
1 - 200	0.285	0.395	19.877	0.665	2.1
201 - 400	0.320	0.390	16.328	0.650	1.2
401 - 600	0.255	0.425	22.824	0.660	2.8
601 - 800	0.290	0.475	26.172	0.630	4.0
801 - 1000	0.325	0.570	28.554	0.570	5.7
1001 - 1200	0.230	2.395	34.109	0.120	68.8
1201 - 1400	0.285	1.695	141.333	0.215	112.6
1401 - 1600	0.310	1.500	273.177	0.230	91.8
1601 - 1800	0.375	1.415	288.693	0.190	68.5
1801 - 2000	0.280	1.110	224.661	0.375	53.1
2001 - 2200	0.360	1.240	257.333	0.300	48.8
2201 - 2400	0.355	0.925	193.986	0.395	31.3
2401 - 2600	0.385	0.655	122.818	0.490	15.2
2601 - 2800	0.320	0.565	68.094	0.565	8.8
2801 - 3000	0.280	0.420	39.357	0.660	5.6
3001 - 3200	0.295	0.495	31.678	0.615	6.3
3201 - 3400	0.265	0.680	45.000	0.545	11.7
3401 - 3600	0.350	0.750	37.057	0.485	13.3
3601 - 3800	0.310	0.465	65.274	0.625	8.2
3801 - 4000	0.275	0.520	33.618	0.610	7.7
4001 - 4200	0.330	0.480	34.652	0.595	5.2
4201 - 4400	0.325	0.615	29.585	0.540	7.5
4401 - 4600	0.370	0.525	38.608	0.560	7.6
4601 - 4800	0.260	0.705	44.250	0.550	15.9
4801 - 5000	0.375	0.720	63.520	0.460	11.1
5001 - 5200	0.350	0.635	41.729	0.520	9.0
5201 - 5400	0.285	0.475	29.368	0.625	6.6
5401 - 5600	0.315	0.510	36.460	0.595	4.9
5601 - 5800	0.290	0.425	24.190	0.650	4.1
5801 - 6000	0.305	0.490	28.738	0.610	4.7

Figure 8—Simulation run for heuristic RCP subject to a channel input pulse

$M=400$. This explains the more significant degradation in channel performance given by the CONTEST algorithms shown in Table II for $M=400$ than in Table I for $M=200$.

In Figure 4, it was shown that in an uncontrolled slotted ALOHA channel, a channel input rate of 0.35 packet/slot was enough to cripple the channel indefinitely. In Figures 7 and 8, we show by simulation that under severe pulse overload circumstances both the IRCP-CONTEST algorithm and Heuristic RCP prevented the channel from going into saturation. In these simulations, the normal channel load line was given by $M=400$ and $(n_o, S_o)=(4, 0.32)$ both before and after the pulse. During a period of 200 slots (namely, the time period 1000-1200 in the figures), the packet generation probability σ was increased such that $M\sigma=1.0$ packet/slot. Observe that both algorithms handled the sudden influx of new packets with ease. In both cases, the channel throughput, instead of vanishing to zero as in an uncontrolled channel, maintained at a high rate and within less than 3000 slots, the channel returned to almost normal operation.

Further discussions of results

In a real system, the channel input source will typically vary slowly with time; for example, the number of users fluctuates during the day. We must emphasize the fact that the control policies considered have been optimized to control statistical channel fluctuations under the assumption of a stationary channel input. Although we have shown that they can temporarily handle very high channel input rates, additional control mechanisms should be designed into the system to make sure that channel overload conditions do not prevail for any long period of time (e.g., by limiting the maximum number of users who can "sign-on" and become active channel users).

The control action space of IRCP includes both control action spaces of ICP and RCP as subsets. Thus IRCP must give a channel performance at least as good as ICP and RCP. Next, comparing IRCP-CONTEST and Heuristic RCP, we see that the latter is easier to implement. However, under a normal load (say $S_o \leq 0.32$), IRCP-CONTEST is superior to Heuristic RCP. This is because Heuristic RCP introduces longer delays to collided packets even when these packets are merely unlucky in light channel traffic. On the other hand, with IRCP, control actions are not exerted until the channel traffic exceeds certain "dangerous" levels.

CONCLUSIONS

Packet switched satellite and ground radio systems have been proposed as new alternatives for computer communications. A multi-access broadcast packet switching technique that has attracted considerable interest is the slotted ALOHA random access scheme. A slotted ALOHA channel multi-accessed by a large population of users has been shown to exhibit unstable behavior. Dynamic control schemes are necessary to prevent the occurrence of channel saturation in unstable channels. The dynamic channel control problem has been studied using a finite-state Markovian decision model in References 7 and 13 under the assumption of perfect channel state information.

In this paper we have studied dynamic channel control algorithms (CONTEST algorithms) which implement the theoretical control policies by using a heuristic scheme to estimate the instantaneous channel state. A heuristic retransmission control algorithm has also been studied which circumvents the state estimation problem. Simulation results indicate that these control algorithms are capable of achieving a channel throughput-delay performance close to the theoretical optimum, as well as capable of preventing channel saturation under temporary overload conditions.

The problem of unstable behavior is very real in random access systems (e.g., ALOHA, slotted ALOHA, reservation-ALOHA, carrier sense multi-access, etc.). To guarantee an acceptable level of channel performance for such systems, some form of dynamic channel control is a must. The probabilistic model and dynamic channel control schemes introduced herein for a slotted ALOHA channel can probably be extended to solve stability and dynamic control problems of other random access systems.

REFERENCES

1. Abramson, N., "THE ALOHA SYSTEM—Another Alternative for Computer Communications," Fall Joint Computer Conference, *AFIPS Conference Proceedings*, 1970, Vol. 37, pp. 281-285.
2. Crowther, W., R. Rettberg, D. Walden, S. Ornstein and F. Heart, "A System for Broadcast Communication: Reservation-ALOHA," *Proceedings of the Sixth Hawaii International Conference on System Sciences*, University of Hawaii, Honolulu, January, 1973.
3. Abramson, N., "Packet Switching with Satellites," National Computer Conference, New York, June 4-8, 1973, *AFIPS Conference Proceedings*, 1973, Vol. 42, pp. 695-702.
4. Kleinrock, L. and S. S. Lam, "Packet-Switching in a Slotted Satellite Channel," National Computer Conference, New York, June 4-8, 1973, *AFIPS Conference Proceedings*, 1973, Vol. 42, pp 703-710.
5. Roberts, L. G., "Dynamic Allocation of Satellite Capacity Through Packet Reservation," National Computer Conference, New York, June 4-8, 1973, *AFIPS Conference Proceedings*, 1973, Vol. 42, pp. 711-716.
6. Butterfield, S., R. Rettberg and D. Walden, "The Satellite IMP for the ARPA Network," Seventh Hawaii International Conference on System Sciences, University of Hawaii, Honolulu, January 8-10, 1974, *Proceedings of the Special Subconference on Computer Nets*, 1974.
7. Lam, S. S., *Packet Switching in a Multi-Access Broadcast Channel with Application to Satellite Communication in a Computer Network*, Ph.D. Dissertation, Computer Science Department, University of California, Los Angeles, March 1974 (available as Technical Report UCLA-ENG-7429, April 1974).
8. Kleinrock, L. and F. A. Tobagi, "Carrier Sense Multiple Access for Packet Switched Radio Channels," *Proc. of the International Conference on Communications*, Minneapolis, Minn., June 1974.
9. Jackson, P. E. and C. D. Stubbs, "A Study of Multi-access Computer Communications," Spring Joint Computer Conference, *AFIPS Conference Proceedings*, 1969, Vol. 34, pp. 491-504.
10. Metcalfe, R. M., "Steady-State Analysis of a Slotted and Controlled ALOHA System with Blocking," *Proceedings of the Sixth Hawaii International Conference on System Sciences*, University of Hawaii, Honolulu, January 1973.
11. Kleinrock, L. and S. S. Lam, "On Stability of Packet Switching in a Random Multi-Access Broadcast Channel," Seventh Hawaii International Conference on System Sciences, University of Hawaii, Honolulu, January 8-10, 1974, *Proceedings of the Special Subconference on Computer Nets*, 1974.
12. Kleinrock, L. and S. S. Lam, "Packet Switching in a Multi-Access Broadcast Channel: Performance Evaluation," *IEEE Transactions on Communications*, Vol. COM-23, April 1975.
13. Lam, S. S. and L. Kleinrock, "Packet Switching in a Multi-Access Broadcast Channel: Dynamic Control Procedures," to appear in *IEEE Transactions on Communications*.
14. Metcalfe, R. M., *Packet Communications*, Ph.D. Dissertation, Harvard University, 1973 (available as MIT Project MAC Technical Report TR-114, December 1973).
15. Howard, R., *Dynamic Probabilistic Systems Vol. 1: Markov Models and Vol. 2: Semi-Markov and Decision Processes*, Wiley, New York, 1971.

AN OPTIMAL ADAPTIVE SCHEME FOR MULTIPLE ACCESS BROADCAST COMMUNICATION.

L. KLEINROCK
Y. YEMINI

Computer Science Department
University of California
Los Angeles.

0. SUMMARY.

The problem of multiple access to a broadcast channel is considered as a problem of real time distributed decision making. We assume that the decision makers are only aware of the total load on the channel when deciding access rights. This information is similar to that required by optimally controlled Slotted *ALOHA*. A new optimal access scheme under this assumption, the *urn scheme*, is described. This scheme is shown to perform better than optimally controlled Slotted *ALOHA* and Time Division Multiple Access (*TDMA*) for all ranges of traffic load. It smoothly adapts to the load on the channel, varying from Slotted *ALOHA* at light load, ranging through an asymmetric scheduling scheme, finally eliminating collisions as it converges to *TDMA* in the heavy traffic case; thus there is no limitation on the useful capacity. The scheme is robust w.r.t. errors in decisions or information used for decisions. The control overhead is negligible and does not depend upon the system size. A variety of possible implementations is presented together with the results of analysis and simulation.

1. THE ACCESS SCHEME PROBLEM.

In what follows we consider the problem of sharing a time slotted broadcast channel by a population of bursty Packet Radio Units (PRUs) [1]. Packets are generated at each PRU according to some random laws, stored in a buffer, transmitted (using some channel access scheme) over a broadcast channel during a time slot, and finally discarded upon acknowledgment (over an assumed free acknowledgment channel) of successful reception.

A simple model of the communication channel is assumed. Problems of modulation, synchronization, coding and the like are assumed to have been solved. It is also assumed that all PRUs are synchronized to slot boundaries. Therefore the channel is a mere succession of rectangular time slots. A slot may be empty, occupied by a single packet (a success), or contain more than one packet, i.e., a "collision". A collision of two or more packets in the same slot results in a total loss. A packet which does not collide is always successful. Our main concern is the mechanism responsible for sharing the channel resource.

The problem of channel sharing is essentially a problem of decision; i.e., which PRUs should have an access right at a given slot. An *access scheme* is defined to be an algorithm (possibly distributed and/or non deterministic) to determine access rights. A PRU which has both an access right and a packet ready for transmission, will transmit it.

The objective of an access scheme is to maximize the rate of successful packets (throughput). Once we specify the set of available strategies, the access scheme problem becomes that of controlling a queueing system through the service mechanism. Alas, the decision problem is non-classical, for both the observation of state and the decisions are distributed among the PRUs.

This research was supported by the Advanced Research Projects Agency of the Department of Defense under Contract MDA 903-77-C-0272.

At a given time slot t, a PRU may choose between having an access right or not. This binary choice is the set of his pure strategies. It is also possible to randomize the decision between the two pure strategies, i.e., by tossing a biased coin to create a mixed strategy. Thus a busy PRU may choose, at any slot, a probability of transmission $0 \le P \le 1$, reflecting his wish to achieve an harmonious set of decisions with other members of the PRU community.

The problem of distributed decision is distinguished from classical decision theories in two respects. First, each decision maker possesses only partial state information (usually distinct from his fellows) insufficient to estimate the state. Second, the different decision makers need to coordinate their policies. In the case of an access scheme, the optimal control rule a' la classical control theory is obvious; i.e., give access rights to any SINGLE busy PRU (a PRU is said to be *busy* if it has a packet ready for transmission). Our problem begins where control theory ends. That is, how would the different PRUs acquire information about the identity of the busy PRUs? How would they agree upon the identity of the lucky PRU to be selected for transmission?

One possible approach to the problem of access schemes is to consider the information used for decision as a point of departure. That is, for a given amount of information, what is the best decision rule to follow?

If no information is used, the PRUs cannot adapt to the instantaneous state of the communication demands. Therefore the allocation of transmission rights must be predetermined. In an environment where the demand for the communication channel is bursty, a scheme which is not adaptive results in a severe waste of the channel. Thus adaptivity is a very desirable property to incorporate in an access scheme.

An adaptive distributed decision mechanism requires that PRUs acquire information about the state of the community and coordinate their choice of strategy. However, the processes of information acquisition and coordination may prove to be expensive in terms of both the channel overhead and the delayed decision. Moreover, an algorithm which depends on detailed state information and coordination may be highly unreliable. Thus a real time decision process must use minimal information for adaptive and reliable decisions.

Let us consider the case where the information which is used to decide access rights consists simply of the knowledge of the total number of busy PRUs at the beginning of each given slot. (We use N to denote the total number of PRUs and n to denote the number of busy PRUs). This is a case of ***homogeneous*** and ***symmetric*** information. In other words, all PRUs are supposed to use the same information; moreover, the information used for adaptivity does not distinguish between the needs of different PRUs. As far as the decision making is concerned all PRUs look the same.

Symmetric homogeneous information is assumed by some schemes to control Slotted *ALOHA* [2,3,4,5,6]. We shall later describe an information acquisition mechanism to estimate the number of busy PRUs with a negligible error and at the expense of a minimal overhead. Information about the number of busy PRUs is less (much less in terms of overhead) than perfect information (which would give the identity of each of these busy PRUs); it is more (much more in terms of the ability to adapt) than no information. What is the best decision strategy to be employed given this information?

Reprinted from *Conference Record of the International Conference on Communications*, June 1978, pages 7.21-7.25. Copyright © 1978 by The Institute of Electrical and Electronics Engineers, Inc.

To develop insight into the solution let us consider the case of two PRUs (N=2). If both know that the number of busy PRUs is n=1, then the obvious solution is to give both of them full access rights; only one of them will actually transmit and succeed. In this case the optimal decision (i.e., transmit with probability 1) is symmetric; both PRUs are given the same pure access right.

Now consider the case N=2, n=2; i.e., both PRUs are busy and aware of it. What is the best selection of transmission probabilities? The expected throughput S describes a surface above the square of all possible transmission probability pairs. Figure (1) depicts the throughput surface as a function of the transmission probabilities. If we restrict ourselves to symmetric policies, i.e., the main diagonal, the optimal policy is (0.5,0.5). That is, each PRU should transmit with probability 1/2. This is precisely an "optimally controlled *ALOHA* policy". We shall use this term to denote a scheme where each PRU knows n and has an access right with probability 1/n (i.e., a mixed strategy).

However, the throughput obtained by the policy (0.5,0.5) is only 0.5. This is a saddle point of the throughput surface. A better solution would have been to choose either of the extreme policies (1,0) or (0,1). That is select an arbitrary PRU and give him full transmission rights; the other should be quiet. How can this be implemented? Here we use the homogeneity. If both PRUs use the same information for decision, then they can reach a coordinated decision through a preprogrammed set of rules. In this case it is only required to have some predetermined priority mechanism to select any one of them.

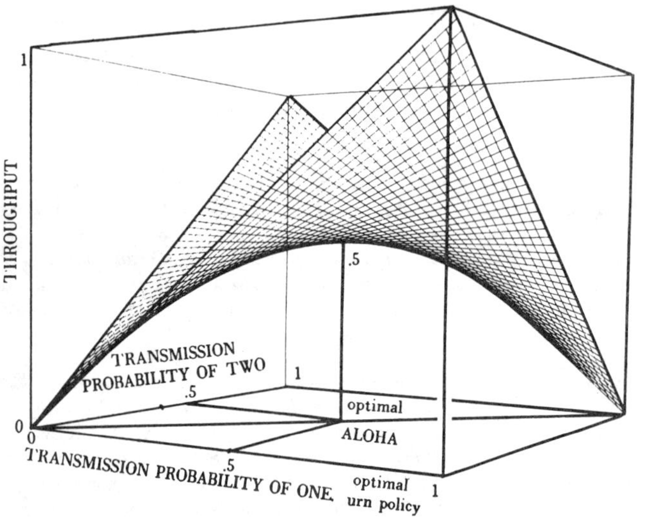

FIGURE (1): THROUGHPUT SURFACE

The optimal strategy is, therefore, ASYMMETRIC. It is possible to prove[7] that optimal strategies are always pure (extreme) strategies and therefore asymmetric. In other words some PRUs should get full transmission rights while others get none (i.e., the transmission probabilities P are 0 or 1). We shall not dwell upon the details of the proof. Rather, we describe an urn model of the problem which renders the solution intuitively clear.

Consider each PRU as a colored ball in an urn; black for busy, white for idle. The access scheme is essentially a rule to sample balls from the urn (those given full access rights). Let k be the number of balls drawn from the urn. The probability of successful transmission is that of getting a single black ball in the sample. This probability is given by an element of the Hypergeometric distribution

$$\frac{\binom{k}{1}\binom{N-k}{n-1}}{\binom{N}{n}}$$

The last expression assumes its maximum when $k=\lfloor N/n \rfloor$ ($\lfloor x \rfloor$ gives the integer part of x). Not only does this value of k maximize the probability of selecting exactly one black ball, but it also gives that the average number of black balls selected is equal to unity. (This result is not unlike Abramson's optimality condition [2], $1=G_1+G_2+...+G_N$ for Slotted *ALOHA* (where G_i is the transmission probability of the i-th PRU). Abramson's condition is such that the optimal choice of transmission probabilities for Slotted *ALOHA* gives an expected number of transmitted packets during a slot equal to unity. In fact, both optimality rules are shown[7] to be particular instances of a more general optimality condition for assigning access rights.) We call a scheme which allocates transmission rights to a sample of $k=\lfloor N/n \rfloor$ PRUs, an *URN SCHEME*.

Let us reconsider the example of two PRUs in terms of the urn model. When N=2 and n=1, the number of balls to be sampled is k=2, i.e., both PRUs should have access rights. When N=2 and n=2 then k=1, i.e., only one (any one) PRU should transmit. These numbers conform with the previous intuitive solution.

The urn scheme adapts smoothly to the load on the system. When the the system is lightly loaded, a large number of PRUs get the right to share channel slots. For instance n=1 implies k=N; all PRUs get transmission rights (as in Slotted *ALOHA*), however, only one is going to make use of it. As the load increases (i.e., as n grows), k decreases and sharing is gradually restricted. When the system is heavily loaded, sharing of slots is eliminated; indeed, when n>N/2 then k=1 and the urn scheme converges to Time Division Multiple Access (*TDMA*) which is the best scheme for a heavy load. If the sampling of k is random, the urn scheme converges to random *TDMA*; if the sampling of k is without repetitions from slot to slot (until all balls are sampled) the urn scheme converges to round robin *TDMA*.

Unlike optimally controlled *ALOHA* whose channel usage efficiency is 37%, and which uses the same information as the urn scheme, the channel usage efficiency of the urn scheme is 100%. When the traffic is light, the urn scheme permits some waste of the channel in the form of collisions and empty slots; this is the price of partial information. However, when the traffic increases, collisions are smoothly eliminated and the full channel capacity becomes available for actual service.

It is possible to show that the above properties (adaptivity and perfect efficiency) remain valid in the limit when N grows to infinity. Therefore the urn scheme is superior to optimally controlled *ALOHA* and *TDMA*, independent of the system size N. We now proceed to describe some possible implementations of the scheme and results of performance analysis and simulation.

2. *IMPLEMENTATION OF URN SCHEMES*.

The details of implementation may vary according to the particular environment considered. In what follows we consider a few versions of the urn scheme. Our main concern is to expose some issues that arise on the boundary between theoretical models and practical implementation. We do not give a detailed description of the implementation.

Two major issues arise in the implementation of a distributed adaptive access scheme: How does the decision algorithm acquire the information which it requires? How does the the algorithm obtain coordination of the distributed decisions?

2.1 *Information acquisition mechanisms.*

There are a few schemes to acquire information about the number of busy PRUs. For instance, it is possible to estimate n from the acknowledgment traffic. This requires a filter for a jump process. The problem has been solved in conjunction with the problem of controlled *ALOHA* [8]. The solution is general enough to be easily adapted to urn schemes. However, filtering n from the statistics of the acknowledgments is too slow an information acquisition mechanism; thus we shall not dwell upon filtering schemes to estimate n.

Also, it is possible to implement the urn scheme using the acknowledgment traffic directly [7]. This is a result of a general rule for optimal adaptivity, of which the urn scheme is a particular instance. There is no need to estimate n; it is enough to adjust k and monitor the statistics of the acknowledgment traffic. The scheme becomes quasi-static (in the sense of [9]). Quasi-static implementation (like the one suggested here, or in the previous paragraph) is to be preferred for systems with a limited ability to adapt.

Let us consider a possible scheme for estimating n with high accuracy, at the expense of a negligible overhead. All we need is a binary erasure shared reservation subchannel. The reservation channel may be implemented by means of a reservation mini-slot (whose size, unlike perfect reservation schemes[10,11,12], is independent of the total system size) at the beginning of each data slot. An idle PRU which turns busy sends a standard reservation message of few bits. If two or more PRUs send a reservation in the same minislot, the result is an erasure (i.e., a collision). We assume that the PRUs can detect three events over the reservation subchannel: no new busies, one new busy, or erasure. Figure (2) depicts a typical series of events over the channel.

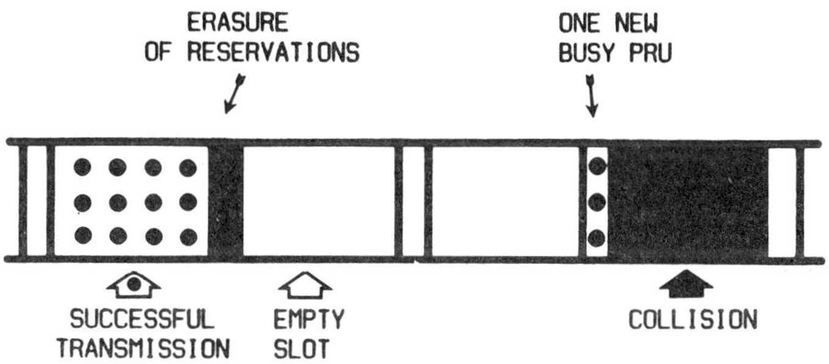

FIGURE (2): A SEQUENCE OF EVENTS OVER THE CHANNEL.

When a busy PRU turns idle the condition is detected by other PRUs from the acknowledgment of his last packet. Therefore the PRUs can follow the number of *newly idle* PRUs (with no error) and the number of *newly busy* PRUs (with some error due to erasures). Nevertheless, the information acquired by the PRUs is sufficient to determine the number of busy PRUs with a high accuracy. Consider a worst case analysis of the error. Let us consider an infinite system (i.e., $N=\infty$), and let all PRUs be idle, so that each arrival turns an idle PRU busy. Let us also assume that the overall number of new arrivals per slot is given by a Poisson distribution with a rate r ($0 \leq r \leq 1$ for stability).

The probability of at least two arrivals in the same slot (erasure over the reservation channel) is given by:

$$1-e^{-r}-re^{-r} \leq 0.26$$

The probability that more than two arrivals occurred, given an erasure over the reservation channel (i.e., at least two newly busy PRUs), is:

$$1 - r^2/2(e^r-1-r) \leq 0.3$$

This conditional error probability is depicted in figure (3) as a function of the input rate r. We note that the probability of more than two arrivals is less than 0.08. Thus estimation errors will occur in at most one out of 13 slots. We see that it is possible to develop a very accurate estimate of n which need only be corrected from time to time. For instance, every time the system goes idle, or every few hundred slots.

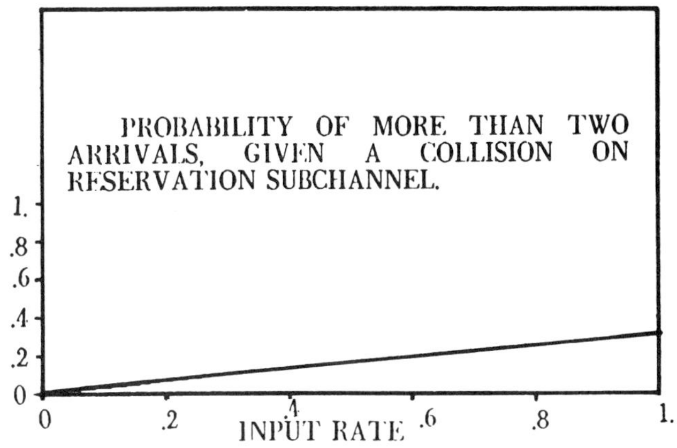

FIGURE (3): CONDITIONAL ERROR PROBABILITY.

Figure (4) illustrates an atypical sample path of the estimated n and its actual value, during a very long busy period, , as obtained from simulation. (Typical busy periods were shorter and the estimated n almost never diverged from the actual n; thus we had to use an atypical sample path to display the divergence of the estimate.) The estimation strategy which was simulated is to keep an underestimate of n i.e., an erasure is counted as two arrivals. Errors in estimation are detected when the estimated n becomes 1 and all PRUs have transmission rights. If the actual value of n is greater than 1, a collision occurs (indicating that our estimate n=1 was in error and was too small) and the estimated n is increased by one. The sample path in figure (4) was generated by a system with 10 PRUs for a total arrival rate of r=0.8 packets per slot. For lower traffic, simulated errors were very rare.

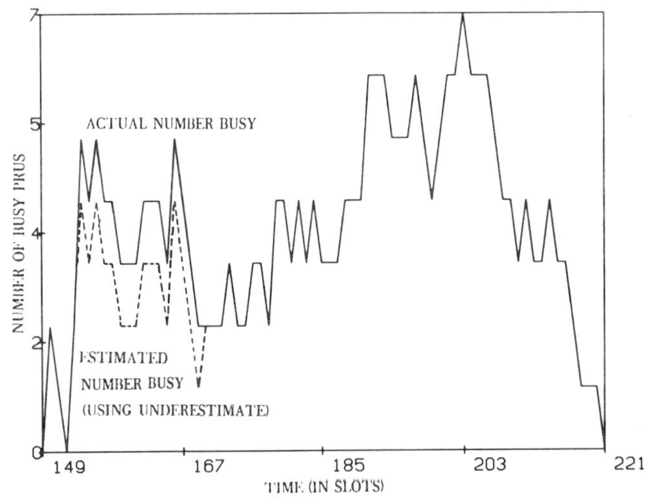

FIGURE (4): ERROR IN UNDERESTIMATION.

2.2 *Coordinated decision.*

The urn scheme requires that the PRUs agree upon k, the number of PRUs to be selected for access rights, and their identity. It is important to note that the scheme is robust w.r.t. errors in the two decisions. That is, the optimal $k=\lfloor N/n \rfloor$ is insensitive to small perturbations of n. Errors in k or failure to agree upon the identity of the k lucky PRUs do not lead to a complete breakdown. It is possible to build effective measures to restore normal operation every few hundred slots, to account for possible malfunctioning.

The selection of which k PRUs should get access rights may be obtained through a preprogrammed priority mechanism. For example, it is possible to employ a pseudo random number generator which uses the same seed at each PRU. Each PRU draws the same k numbers between 1 and N. Thus the lucky PRUs know who they are and know that they may transmit. This we shall call the random (or basic) urn scheme, to distinguish it from other implementations. The random urn scheme may be improved if we draw a permutation of the numbers from 1 to N and take k PRUs at a time, during each slot, avoiding repetitions during a cycle over the whole system. (The improvement is similar to that obtained by a round-robin *TDMA* over random *TDMA*).

An even more effective mechanism can make use of the asymmetric information which is acquired from the asymmetric sampling policy. We use a round-robin slot sharing *WINDOW* mechanism. The PRUs are ordered according to their numbers along an imaginary circle. The k lucky PRUs are selected by a window which rotates around the circle. When a collision occurs, the window stops and decreases in size (say to half its previous size); the process is repeated each slot until a success occurs. If there was no collision, the tail of the window is advanced along the circle to the head of the previous window and the window size is once again set equal to k (based on the current estimate of n). Window schemes offer an improvement over the basic urn scheme. The selection of PRUs to be given transmission rights, adapts to both the total load and the results of the selection of the previous slot. It is possible to design window schemes with memory span longer than one slot. Such algorithms may offer some improvement of the performance at the expense of higher complexity and lower reliability. We do not pursue that subject here.

3. *ANALYSIS AND SIMULATION.*

Access schemes are essentially service mechanisms of a queueing process. To analyze the performance of a scheme it is required that we model the arrival process and describe the queueing mechanism. We compare the performance of the basic (random) urn scheme to that of: optimally controlled Slotted *ALOHA* (i.e., with transmission probability 1/n); random *TDMA* (we use random *TDMA* to avoid the non-stationary behavior of the service mechanism from slot to slot); and perfect scheduling of the channel.

Arrivals are assumed to be independent from slot to slot and drawn from a time independent distribution. The service mechanism for the four different schemes (urn, optimal *ALOHA*, *TDMA* and perfect scheduling) is independent of the arrival process or the time. (The service depends, however, upon the number of busy PRUs). We assume that each PRU possesses a single buffer. Thus the number of busy PRUs is a finite Markov chain whose transition structure is depicted below

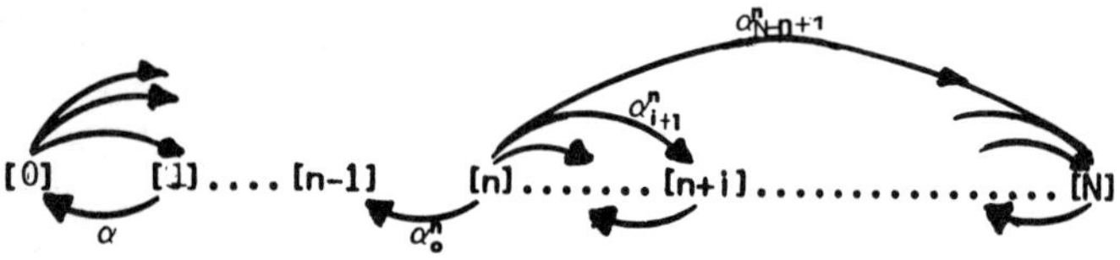

TRANSITION DIAGRAM FOR THE "NUMBER BUSY" PROCESS.

The transition matrix of the chain is given by an upper Hessenberg matrix. The steady state equation for the distribution of the number of busy PRUs has the form

$$(\pi_0,\pi_1,\ldots\pi_N)=(\pi_0,\pi_1,\ldots\pi_N)\begin{bmatrix} \alpha_1^0 & \alpha_2^0 & \cdots & \cdots & \alpha_{N+1}^0 \\ \alpha_0^1 & \alpha_1^1 & \cdots & \cdots & \alpha_N^1 \\ 0 & \alpha_0^2 & \cdots & \cdots & \cdot \\ & 0 & & & \cdot \\ & & \ddots & & \vdots \\ & & 0 & \alpha_0^N & \alpha_1^N \end{bmatrix}$$

Here π_n is the steady state probability of finding n busy PRUs in the system.

The steady state equations can be solved by a simple recursive routine. The solution may be used to compute the expected throughput and delay (using Little's result /3/). We applied this analytical method to the four different schemes. Figure (5) depicts typical delay-throughput curves for a system with N=10 PRUs. Figure (6) depicts the throughput as a function of the input rate for the four schemes. It may be seen that the random urn scheme adapts smoothly to the load; it is equivalent to optimally controlled Slotted *ALOHA* when the input load is light, but converges to *TDMA* when the load increases. In the medium range it is better than both. The difference between the performance of the urn scheme and perfect scheduling represents the price of imperfect information.

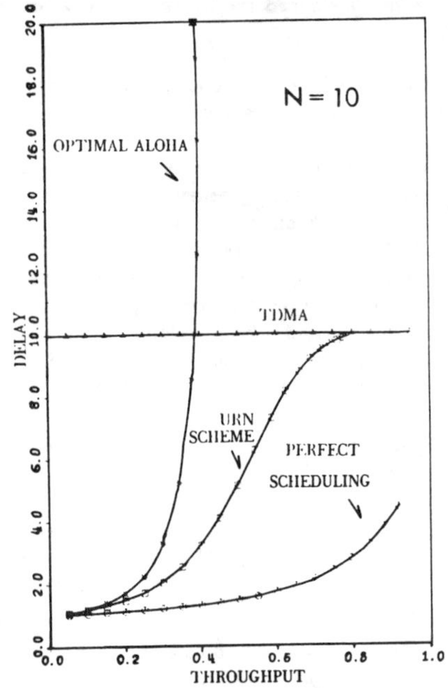

FIGURE (5): DELAY-THROUGHPUT COMPARATIVE ANALYSIS OF THE FOUR SCHEMES.

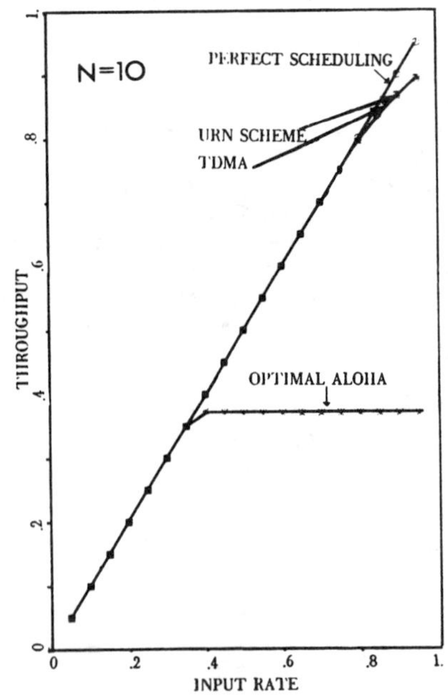

FIGURE (6): INPUT-THROUGHPUT ANALYSIS OF THE FOUR SCHEMES.

The random urn scheme and the window scheme were also simulated and compared with optimally controlled Slotted *ALOHA*, *TDMA* and perfect scheduling. Figures (7) and (8) compare the results of simulation and analysis. Figure (9) show the performance of the four schemes when each PRU has a buffer for 25 packets. Finally, figure (10) compares the delay-throughput performance of the random urn scheme and the window scheme of the previous section. It may be seen that the window scheme improves the performance significantly.

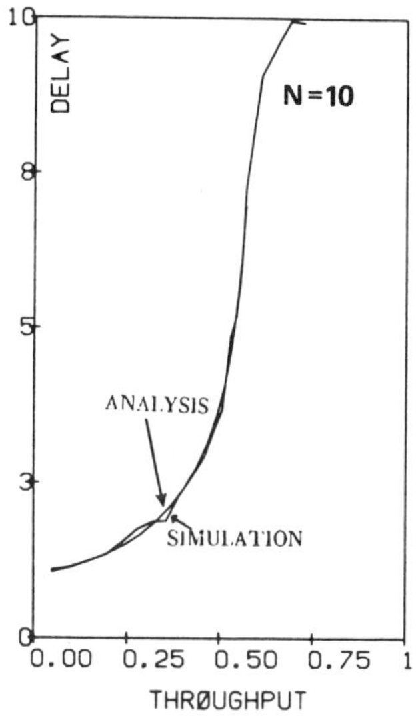

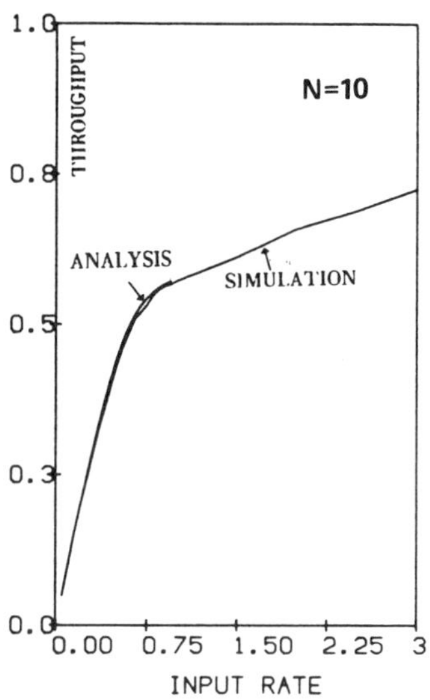

FIGURE (7): DELAY-THROUGHPUT FIGURE (8): INPUT-THROUGHPUT

ANALYSIS AND SIMULATION OF THE RANDOM URN SCHEME

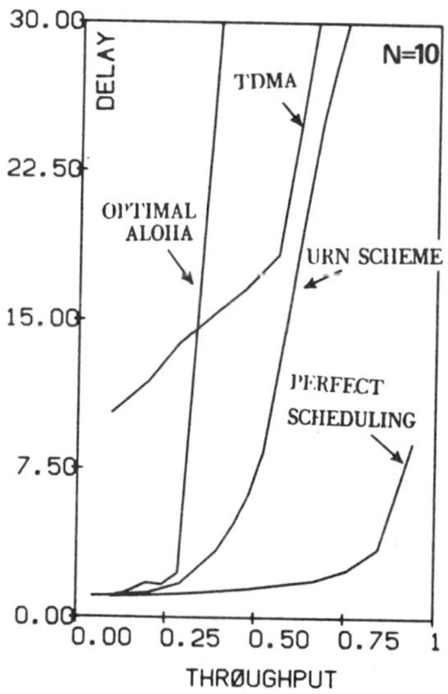

FIGURE (9): DELAY-THROUGHPUT OF THE FOUR SCHEMES. SIMULATION FOR BUFFERED PRUS.

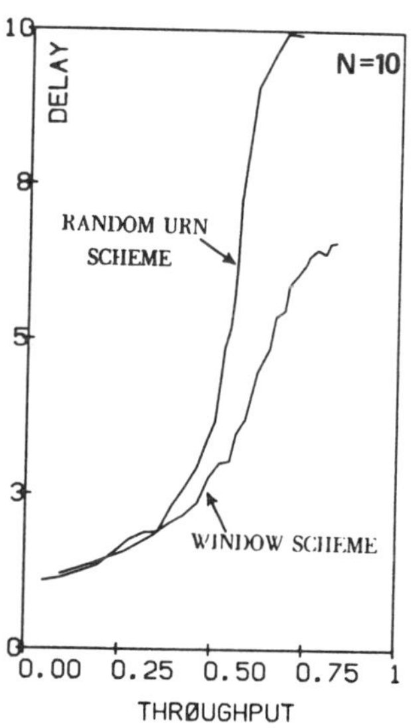

FIGURE (10): DELAY-THROUGHPUT OF THE SIMULATED RANDOM URN AND WINDOW SCHEME.

The question of robustness is currently under study. Also, urn schemes may be employed in a multi-hop environment [7]. The idea is simple. Each PRU may reside in two or more urns simultaneously. Access rights need to be resolved in all of those environments at the same time. It is possible to use a simple frequency division into three bands to localize the interaction between different environments. The network may be decomposed into local environments each of which looks almost similar to a one-hop system, and employs the urn scheme as a method to resolve the conflict over channel usage. These results will be published in a forthcoming paper.

4. *CONCLUSIONS.*

Urn schemes offer an attractive class of adaptive sharing policies for multiple access broadcast channels. The basic urn scheme performs better than optimally controlled Slotted *ALOHA*, which uses the same information for adaptivity. The urn scheme retains the simplicity and robustness of Slotted *ALOHA*; yet it does not limit the amount of available channel capacity. Adaptivity is obtained at the price of a negligible overhead. Versions of the scheme represent a feasible solution to the problem of access schemes in a multi-hop environment. Therefore the schemes offer a significant advancement from the practical point of view.

From a theoretical point of view, urn schemes demonstrate an optimal performance bound on adaptive access schemes which use symmetric state information only. Further research is required to develop a systematic attack on the problem of partial non-homogeneous information and the problem of coordination for real time distributed decision processes.

Acknowledgment:

We wish to thank Johanna Moore, Lou Nelson and Frank Heath for their help in simulating and plotting the results.

REFERENCES

[1] KAHN R.E *The Organization of Computer Resources into a Packet Radio Network.* IEEE Transactions on Communications Vol COM-25, 1, January 1977.

[2] ABRAMSON N., *Packet Switching with Satellites.* 1973 National Computer Conference, AFIPS Conference Proceeding 42, 695-702.

[3] KLEINROCK L., *Queueing Systems: Volume II, Computer Applications.* New York, Wiley Interscience, 1976.

[4] LAM S.S *Packet Switching in a Multiaccess Broadcast Channel.* Ph.D Dissertation Computer Science Department, School of Engineering and Applied Science UCLA, 1974.

[5] FERGUSON M.J *On the Control, Stability, and Waiting Time in a Slotted ALOHA Random-Access Systems.* IEEE Transaction Communication Vol. COM-23, November 1975.

[6] CARLEIAL A.B and HELLMAN M.E *Bistable Behavior of ALOHA-Type systems.* IEEE Transactions Communication Vol. COM 23, April 1975.

[7] YEMINI Y., *On Channel Sharing In Discrete-Time Packet Switched, Multiaccess Broadcast Communication.* Ph.D Dissertation Computer Science Department, School of Engineering and Applied Science UCLA, 1978.

[8] SEGALL A. *Recursive Estimation From Discrete-Time Point Processes.* IEEE Transaction on Information Theory Vol IT-22, July 1976.

[9] GALLAGER R. *A Minimun Delay Routing Algorithm Using Distributed Computation.* IEEE Transactions on Communications Vol COM-25, January 1977.

[10] Roberts L.G *Dynamic Allocation of Satellite Capacity Through Packet Reservation.* 1973 National Computer Conference, AFIPS Conference Proceeding 42, 695-702.

[11] KLEINROCK L., *Performance of Distributed Multi-Access Computer-Communication Systems.* Information Processing 77, Toronto, Canada, August 1977, pp. 547-552.

[12] SCHOLL M. *Multiplexing Techniques for Data Transmission Over Packet Switched Radio Systems.* Ph.D Dissertation Computer Science Department, School of Engineering and Applied Science UCLA, 1977.

Generalized TDMA: The Multi-Accessing Tree Protocol

JOHN I. CAPETANAKIS

Abstract—**The tree algorithm, a new basic protocol for accessing a satellite channel by a large number of independent users, is considered. Previous multi-accessing techniques suffered from long delays, low throughput and/or congestion instabilities. The ALOHA algorithm, for example, when applied to the Poisson source model, has a maximum throughput of .37 packets/slot and is unstable. The tree protocol, under similar conditions, is stable, has a maximum average throughput of .43 and has respectable delay properties. In this protocol, the sources are assigned to the leaves of a tree graph. Message contentions are resolved by systematically moving from node to node through the tree, trying to determine the branches containing the conflicting users.**

It is shown that the tree protocol is a generalization of TDMA and that an optimum dynamic tree adaptively changes from an essentially random access protocol in light traffic to TDMA in heavy traffic. A major result is that if q, the probability that a user has a packet to transmit, is greater than $1/\sqrt{2}$, then TDMA and the optimum tree protocol are the same. If, on the other hand, $q < 1/\sqrt{2}$, then the optimum tree protocol is more efficient than TDMA. The maximum average throughput of a system consisting of the optimum tree protocol and a finite number of users is one packet/slot.

The tree protocol may be applied either to a direct access system or to a demand assignment access system. Consequently, an example is presented comparing the average delay properties of tree and TDMA protocols when applied to direct access and to reservation access systems.

I. INTRODUCTION

THIS paper considers the tree algorithm, a time domain multi-accessing protocol that may be used by a set of independent users to access a satellite channel. Usually in such a system, the only means available to the users for communicating among themselves is through the satellite. Consequently, problems may arise since a fraction of the channel capacity must be used for accessing the channel itself. Depending on the multi-accessing algorithm that is used, these problems may manifest themselves as long message delays, low channel utilization (i.e., throughput), and congestion instabilities. The ALOHA algorithm [1], for example, when applied to the Poisson source model (i.e., an infinite number of sources that collectively generate traffic satisfying the Poisson statistic) has a maximum throughput of $1/e$ packets/slot and is unstable. (A multiple access system with sources satisfying the Poisson source model is defined to be stable if the average delay is finite.) Under similar source and channel conditions, the tree protocol presented here is stable, has maximum average throughput of .43 packets/slot, and exceptionally good delay properties.

Manuscript received January 18, 1979; revised July 6, 1979. This work was sponsored by the Department of the Air Force. The views and conclusions contained in this document are those of the contractor and should not be interpreted as necessarily representing the official policies, either expressed or implied, of the United States Government. This paper was presented at the International Conference on Communications, Boston, MA, June 1979.

The author is with M.I.T. Lincoln Laboratory, Lexington, MA 02173.

The system considered here consists of 2^N sources that independently generate packets to be transmitted over a slotted channel. A packet is a message of fixed length and may contain data to be transmitted, or reservation requests for channel capacity, along with source and destination addresses. The length of a channel slot equals that of a packet and a packet may be transmitted within only one slot. If a slot contains multiple packets, then a collision occurs and no one gets through. If, on the other hand, a collision does not occur, a packet is transmitted error-free. In addition, it is assumed that the sources have the means to determine whether there are zero, one, or multiple packets in any slot; and in a reservation access system, the sources have the means to determine the status of their requests.

When the tree protocol is applied to such a system, a user is essentially free to transmit a packet in any slot until a collision occurs. When a collision occurs, packet transmissions are controlled until it is resolved. The collision is resolved by dividing all the users into several groups and assigning a slot for retransmission to each group. Any one of these new groups may contain zero, one, or more than one of the contending packets. If, by chance, the subdivisions are such that each group contains at most one user with a packet, then the initial collision is resolved. If, on the other hand, multiple packets are assigned to any group, then a collision will reoccur. In such a case, the groups with conflicts are again subdivided into smaller groups and new slots are reassigned. This process of dividing and subdividing continues until all retransmissions result either in a packet being transmitted or in an empty slot. At worst, this process will continue until each user is assigned a unique slot.

In the following, this algorithm is formalized by assigning the sources to the leaves of a tree graph. Notice that, if a group with a conflict is divided into two equal subgroups, then the resulting algorithm is the basic binary tree protocol.

The tree algorithm may be used to access the satellite directly in a direct access system (DA) or to access the reservation channel in a reservation access system (RA). Thus, it is applicable to a very large class of satellite systems. [In RA, before a message is transmited, the user must reserve the channel, whereas in DA, reservations are not necessary. In DA, contention either is avoided by uniquely dedicating the channel to the various users, or it is allowed to occur and then resolved by appropriate conflict resolving algorithms.]

A useful measure of performance of a multi-accessing protocol is average message delay vs average throughput. As used here, average throughput and average delay have the following definitions:

Reprinted from *IEEE Transactions on Communications*, Volume COM-27, Number 10, October 1979, pages 1476-1484.

Average throughput—the ratio of the number of packets that are successfully transmitted in a very long interval to the maximum number of packets that could have been transmitted with continuous transmission on the channel.

Average delay—the ratio of the total delay of the packets in a very long interval to the number of packets in the interval. The delay is the time from the instant a packet is generated to the instant it is successfully received.

The tree algorithm, when applied to the Poisson source model, is considered in references [2] and [3]. This paper considers the tree algorithm when applied to certain finite source models (see Sections II and IV) and emphasizes its relationship to TDMA (i.e., the conventional time division multiple access protocol, where each user is sequentially allocated equal time segments).

More specifically, in Section II, the static binary tree algorithm is considered and an example is presented. In Section III, the optimum dynamic tree protocol is considered for a specific finite source model. This source model assumes that each of the 2^N sources generates messages according to (3.7). (A source can have at most two messages: one that has collided with messages from other sources and is in the process of being retransmitted, and one that has arrived since the collision.) The optimum dynamic tree protocol is a function of the message arrival rate and the transmission process. It is demonstrated that the tree algorithm is a generalization of TDMA and that the optimum dynamic algorithm adaptively varies from a binary tree protocol in light traffic to TDMA in heavy traffic. (In light traffic the tree protocol allows a user to transmit a packet in a slot immediately following the one it arrived in, whereas in TDMA a user may transmit only in its dedicated slot.) An interesting outcome of these considerations is that TDMA cannot be better than the optimum dynamic tree protocol. It is proved that if q, the probability that a source has a message to transmit, is greater than $1/\sqrt{2}$, then the optimum tree and TDMA are identical, whereas if $q < 1/\sqrt{2}$, then the optimum tree is more efficient than TDMA. The maximum average throughput of the optimum tree protocol is shown to be one packet/slot.

In Section IV, the tree and TDMA protocols are applied to direct access and reservations access satellite systems, and their performances are compared. Here, the tree protocol is optimized only with respect to the average message arrival rate. It is independent of the transmission process. The arrival process at each source is assumed to be Poisson, and each user is equipped with an infinite capacity buffer where messages that are not immediately transmitted are queued. Depending upon the particular tree used, the maximum average throughput for such a buffered system is greater than 1/2 packets/slot and less than or equal to one. The maximum average throughput of the optimized protocol, for this source model, is also one packet/slot. The average delay vs average throughput properties of these protocols are illustrated in Fig. 4.1 for DA and in Fig. 4.2 for RA. As can be seen, the tree protocol is considerably more efficient than TDMA.

In Section V, the concluding remarks are presented. In the Appendix, average conditional delay of the tree protocol and the average delay of the TDMA protocol are derived.

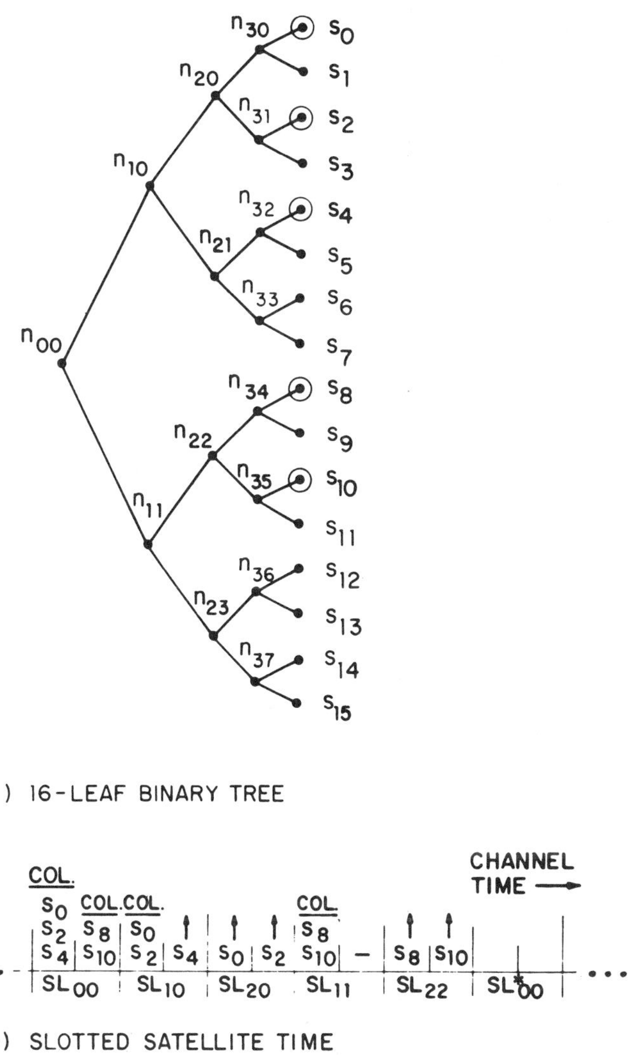

Fig. 2.1. An example of the binary tree algorithm.

II. STATIC BINARY TREE

In this section, the tree algorithm is stated and an example is presented. First, however, some definitions concerning the tree graph (see Fig. 2.1):

Depth of a node—the number of branches between the node and the root node. The root node is at depth zero.

Degree of node—the number of branches that emanate from a node.

Subtree T_{ij}—the binary rooted subtree whose root node is n_{ij}, where, in a binary rooted tree, j corresponds to the particular one of the 2^i nodes at depth i.

Algorithm Statement: Let each source correspond to a leaf on a binary tree as shown in Fig. 2.1(a). If the number of sources is infinite, then the tree extends to infinity. This representation of the sources may be considered to be a binary addressing scheme. For example, in Fig. 2.1(a) each source has a four-bit binary address. Also, let T_x and T_y be two binary rooted subtrees and assume that no collisions have occurred up to the beginning of the present pair of slots. Then, the binary tree algorithm is as follows:

1. Choose $T_x = T_{10}; T_y = T_{11}$.

2. Transmit all the packets in T_x in the first slot of the present pair of slots, and transmit all the packets in T_y in the second slot.

3. If any collisions occur in the preceding step, then

a. Until these collisions are resolved, do not transmit any new packets.†

b. Resolve the first collision (if any) before resolving the second (if any).

A collision in T_x (or T_y) is resolved by dividing T_x (or T_y) into two halves (say A and B), setting $T_x = A$, $T_y = B$, and then repeating steps 2 and 3.

This algorithm is equivalent to the following tree search. Beginning with the root node and at each succeeding node, ask whether there are zero, one, or more than one packets in the subtree stemming from each of the two emanating branches. If the answer at any of the branches is more than one, then proceed to the node at the end of this branch and repeat the question. Continue until all the leaves are separated into sets such that it is known that each set contains at most one packet. Note that the number of slots used in a conflict resolution interval equals twice the number of nodes visited.

Example: Let there be 16 sources $\{S_0, S_1, \cdots, S_{15}\}$ and let each correspond to a leaf on the 16-leaf binary tree as shown in Fig. 2.1(a). Figure 2.1(b) depicts the slotted satellite times. Note that the slots are paired and that a slot pair is designated by SL_{ij}. For convenience, the round-trip delay* τ is taken as zero. If $\tau > 0$, then the slot pairs would be separated by at least τ.

Now assume that no collisions have occurred until the beginning of SL_{00}, when sources S_0, S_2, S_4, S_8, and S_{10} each has a packet to transmit. Then beginning with SL_{00}, where the first contention arises, the tree algorithm takes the following steps in the indicated slot pairs:

SL_{00} All the sources in T_{10} that have packets to transmit (i.e., S_0, S_2 and S_4) do so in the first slot of SL_{00}, and the corresponding sources in T_{11} do so in the second slot. This results in two collisions, one among S_0, S_2, and S_4 and the other between S_8 and S_{10}. Since there was at least one collision in SL_{00}, any new packets that arrive are not transmitted until that contention is resolved.

SL_{10} Since there was a collision in T_{10}, the sources at T_{10} are divided in half and the packets in T_{20} and T_{21} are transmitted in the first and second slots of SL_{10}, respectively. This results in a collision between S_0 and S_2 and in a successful transmission by S_4.

† In Section IV, we consider a modified version of this algorithm. There, Step 3A is replaced by, "Until these collisions are resolved, do not transmit any new packets unless they arrive at sources which either did not have an opportunity to transmit or they did and the transmission resulted in a still unresolved conflict."

* In [4], it is suggested that if $\tau > 0$, several algorithms be interleaved together so that the results of one transmission are received before it is time to retransmit. In general, the number of algorithms that are interleaved is the smallest k satisfying $\tau \leqslant 2(k-1)$; τ is the round trip delay in message lengths.

SL_{20} Since there was a collision in T_{20}, T_{30} and T_{31} transmit their packets in the first and second slots of SL_{20}, respectively. This results in two successful transmissions by S_0 and S_2.

SL_{11} Since there was a collision in T_{11}, T_{22} and T_{23} transmit their packets in succession. This results in a collision between S_8 and S_{10} in the first slot and no transmission in the second.

SL_{22} Since there was a collision in T_{22}, T_{34} and T_{35} transmit. This results in two successful transmissions by S_8 and S_{10}.

SL^*_{00} Since each of the sources participated in at least one collision-free transmission we know that the original contention has been resolved. Any new packets that may have arrived at T_{10} during this conflict resolution interval are transmitted in the first slot of SL^*_{00}, and packets that arrived at T_{11} are transmitted in the second slot. The process continues, as described above.

In this example, 10 slots are used to transmit 5 packets.

The interval from the beginning of SL_{00} to the beginning of SL^*_{00} is one conflict resolution interval. This interval will also be called an epoch.

III. OPTIMUM DYNAMIC TREE PROTOCOL

Here, we first determine the optimum tree, and then combine it with a specific message arrival process to obtain the optimum dynamic tree protocol. The dynamic protocol optimally chooses the tree that is used to resolve a possible contention. The choice depends on observations of tne transmission process and the statistics of the arrival process. It also depends on the source model; consequently, the optimum dynamic protocol is presented at the end of this section after the source model is specified.

The optimum tree is defined to be that which minimizes the average number of slots needed to process the 2^N sources, given that the probability that any one has a packet to transmit is q. Here the tree is constrained to be binary everywhere except for the root node whose degree is a powei of two. More specifically, if we let $E\{l \mid q, N, K\}$ be the average number of algorithm steps needed to process 2^N sources when the root node degree is 2^K, then the problem is to choose $K = 1, 2, \cdots, N$ so that $E\{l \mid q, N, K\}$ is minimum. (An algorithm step consists of the transmissions in a pair of slots, the observation of the results of these transmissions, and the decision concerning what action to take in the following pair of slots. Also, note that $2l$ equals the number of slots used.)

The reason the initial degree is restricted to be a power of two is to allow easier implementation. Variations in the degree of the root node under this restriction are equivalent to starting the binary tree algorithm at different levels, thus not requiring a different tree each time the degree of the root node is changed. For example, an algorithm, whose tree has 2^N leaves and whose root node degree is 2^K, is equivalent to a binary tree algorithm that starts its search with the nodes of depth K.

Now, we will determine $\hat{K}$, the optimum K, as a function of q. More specifically, we will obtain an equation whose solution

$\hat{q}(K, N)$ is defined by

$$\hat{K} = K \quad \text{for} \quad \hat{q}(K, N) < q \leqslant \hat{q}(K+1, N). \tag{3.1}$$

Since a tree with 2^N leaves and root node degree 2^K is equivalent to 2^{K-1} binary trees, each containing 2^{N-K+1} leaves, it follows that

$$E\{l \mid q, N, K\} = 2^{K-1} E\{l \mid q, N-K+1, 1\} \tag{3.2}$$

Substituting (A.6) (see the Appendix) into this expression results in

$$E\{l \mid q, N, K\} = 2^{K-1}\{1 + 2D(q, N-K)\} \tag{3.3}$$

where $D(\cdot)$ is given in (A.7).

It can be shown** that $\hat{q}(N, K)$ is the solution to

$$E\{l \mid q, N, K-1\} = E\{l \mid q, N, K\}. \tag{3.4}$$

Substituting (3.3), (A.4) and (A.7) into (3.4) and rearranging results in

$$\psi(q, N-K+1) = 1/2 \tag{3.5}$$

where $\psi(q, m)$ is given by (A.4). Note that $\hat{q}$ is a function of $(N-K)$.

Equation (3.5) was solved for $N - K = 0, 1, 2, 3, 4, 5, 6$. The results are given in Table I.

From the table the following expression for $\hat{q}(N-K)$ is evident:

$$\hat{q}(N-K) = \begin{cases} 1/\sqrt{2} & \text{for } N-K = 0 \\ .38 & N-K = 1 \\ .8/2^{N-K} & N-K \geqslant 2. \end{cases} \tag{3.6}$$

TABLE I
OPTIMUM ROOT NODE DEGREE

$N-K$	$q(N-K)$
0	$1/\sqrt{2}$
1	.38
2	.20
3	.10
4	.05
5	.025
6	.0125

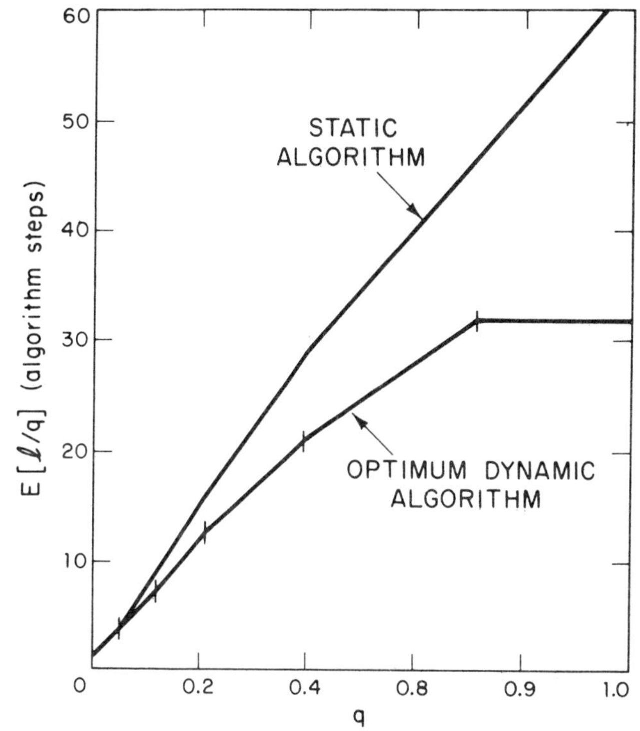

Fig. 3.1. $E\{l \mid q\}$ vs q for the binary and the optimum dynamic tree algorithm (64 users).

The optimum K for $N = 6$, which follows from (3.1) and (3.6), was substituted into (3.3) and the result is illustrated in Fig. 3.1. In that figure we also have $E\{l \mid q, N, 1\}$ for the binary tree. The optimum protocol is significantly superior for large values of q, suggesting that the optimum algorithm should be used when the traffic is heavy.

For $K = N$ the tree is a single node with 2^N branches emanating from it. This is recognized to be the conventional TDMA protocol, in which each user is sequentially allocated every 2^Nth slot. From (3.6) we see that for $q \geqslant 1/\sqrt{2}$, the optimum tree protocol and TDMA are identical, and from the definition of optimality we see that, for $q < 1/\sqrt{2}$, or tree algorithm exists that is superior to TDMA.

Optimum Tree Algorithm

Here we present an optimum tree algorithm for a specific source model. In this source model, a source may receive at most one new packet per epoch (i.e., a conflict resolution interval). The probability that a source will generate a packet in the next algorithm step, given that it has not yet generated one in the present epoch, is a constant*** and will be designated by ρ. It follows then, that q, the probability that a source will receive a packet in an epoch of length l, is given by

$$q - 1 - (1 - \rho)^l. \tag{3.7}$$

Note that, at any instant, a source can have at most two packets: one that has arrived in the previous epoch and which is in the process of being transmitted, and one that arrived in the present epoch and which will be processed in the following epoch.

From (3.6) and (3.7), it follows that the only observation of the transmission process that is required to obtain the optimum tree to be used in the following epoch is l, the length of

** That $\hat{q}$ is the solution to (3.4) follows by noting that (3.5) has a unique solution for each $(N-K)$ and that $E\{l \mid 0, N, K\}$ is an increasing function in K.

*** Here, ρ will be assumed to be a known system parameter. However, if ρ is unknown, its value may be estimated from a suitably long observation of the transmission process.

the preceding epoch. Consequently, an optimum dynamic tree protocol is possible, whereby the tree graph in one epoch depends optimally on ρ and the length of the preceding epoch. These observations may be formalized as follows:

Optimum Tree Algorithm Statement

1. Observe l, the length of the previous epoch.
2. Substitute l into (3.7) to obtain q.
3. Use the q, determined in Step 2, to obtain $\hat{K}$ from (3.6).
4. Use the tree, determined in Step 3, to resolve any contentions that may exist.

Notice that as ρ approaches zero (i.e., the message arrival rate decreases) the tree will tend to be binary, whereas as ρ approaches one, the tree becomes a single node with 2^N branches emanating from it (i.e., TDMA). Thus, the optimum protocol adaptively varies from an essentially random access protocol in light traffic to TDMA in heavy traffic. We find this to be an intuitively pleasing result.

The maximum average throughput for a binary tree protocol with 2^N users and 2^K root node degree is

$$E\{\text{throughput}\} = \frac{1}{2 - 2^{K-N}}. \tag{3.8}$$

To see this, note that for $q = 1$, all the users have a packet to transmit. In such a situation, $2(2^N - 2^K) + 2^K$ slots are needed to conduct one complete tree search. Equation (3.8) follows by dividing this result into 2^N, the number of packets that are processed by one tree search. Several observations are in order concerning (3.8). First, the maximum average throughput is a function of only $(N - K)$. Secondly, the tree with the greatest maximum average throughput is $N - K = 0$, i.e., TDMA, whereas, for a given N, the tree with smallest maximum average throughput is $K = 1$, i.e., binary rooted. In addition, note that the maximum average throughput of any tree is greater than 1/2 but less than or equal to one packet/slot; and that the maximum average throughput of the optimum tree protocol is one packet/slot.

From the preceding discussion it follows that the maximum average throughput is an increasing function of K. The advantage of small values of K is that, in light traffic, the average delay is also an increasing function of K. Therefore, an adaptive tree, where K varies optimally, has the minimum possible average delay while also having the greatest possible maximum average throughput (i.e., one packet/slot).

The delay analysis of the optimum tree protocol is carried out in [4] where an upper bound on the average delay versus a lower bound to the average throughput is obtained for $2^N = 64$. This result is illustrated in Fig. 3.2. Notice that the maximum average throughput is one.

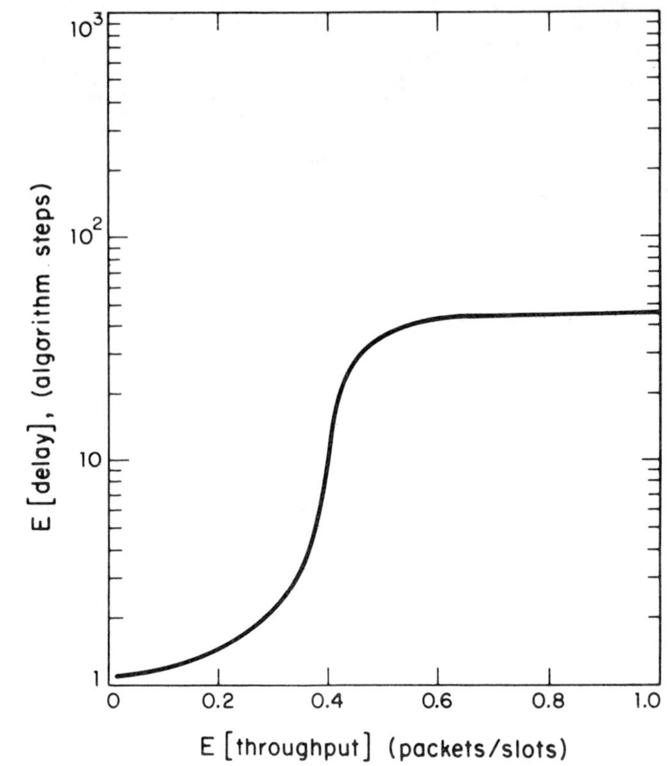

Fig. 3.2. An upper bound to the $E\{\text{delay}\}$ vs a lower bound to the $E\{\text{throughput}\}$ for the optimum dynamic tree algorithm (64 users).

IV. COMPARISON OF TDMA AND TREE PROTOCOLS

Two basic disciplines for accessing the satellite are direct access and reservation access. In DA, a message is directly transmitted. Contention among messages is either avoided by uniquely dedicating slots to users as in TDMA, or it is allowed to occur and then resolved by a suitable contention resolving algorithm, e.g., the tree or ALOHA algorithms. In RA, on the other hand, before transmitting a message, a user must reserve channel capacity. Reservations are carried out by transmitting reservations packets (usually much shorter than the message) over a portion of the uplink called the reservation channel. A protocol such as TDMA or the tree is required to access this reservation channel.

In this section, a specific system is considered, and the average delay as a function of average throughput is obtained for the following four protocols: DA with TDMA, DA with tree, RA with TDMA, and RA with tree. The tree protocol that is considered here is independent of the transmission process, but, as we will see, it optimally depends on the message arrival rate.

The system of interest here has 2^N independent users and U orthogonal (in frequency) uplink channels. Each user has a buffer of infinite capacity where messages, which are not successfully transmitted, are queued for retransmission. The length of a message is assumed to be s seconds, and the length of a reservation packet is assumed to be r seconds.

The message arrival process at each source is Poisson with normalized average arrival rate λ messages/message length/user. Since the buffers are infinite, it follows that, if the average delay exists, the average throughput equals the average arrival rate. Thus, in the following, the average delay is obtained as a function of μ, the average aggregate arrival rate per channel, where

$$\mu = \frac{2^N \lambda}{U} \text{ in messages/message length/channel.} \tag{4.1}$$

A. Direct Access

1. Direct Access with the Tree Protocol

The tree protocol considered here depends optimally on traffic conditions. However, it differs from the optimum protocol given in Section III in two aspects. First, a packet may be transmitted in the epoch of arrival if there are no other packets preceding it in the buffer and the corresponding user has already been assigned a slot. In Fig. 2.1, for example, if S_9 receives a packet after SL_{00} and before SL_{11}, it can join the on-going algorithm as if its packet arrived in SL_{00}, i.e., transmit in the first slot of SL_{11}. Secondly, the tree depends only on μ; it does not depend on the length of the preceding epoch. That is, given μ, 2^K the degree of the root node is chosen to minimize the average delay. Thus, if μ is constant, the tree is also constant. Allowing packets to be transmitted in the epoch of arrival results in a more efficient protocol, whereas allowing the tree to depend optimally only on μ results in a more convenient protocol.

It can be shown, by arguments similar to those that led to (3.8), that the maximum average throughput for this system is also given by

$$\text{Maximum } E\{\text{throughput}\} = \frac{1}{2 - 2^{K-N}}. \tag{4.2}$$

The average delay was obtained by computer simulation. In the simulation, $2^N = 1024$ and $U = 8$; thus, 128 sources are assigned to each uplink. Since the round trip delay τ to the satellite is nonzero, two optimum static tree algorithms (each with 64 users) are assigned to each uplink, and each algorithm uses every other pair of slots. Thus, if τ is less than 2 slots, a user will have received the results of the preceding transmission before it is time to retransmit. It should be noted that, in DA, a user is allowed to process at most one packet at a time even though there might be several packets in the buffer.

The average delay vs average throughput results of this simulation are illustrated in Fig. 4.1. The root node degree, 2^K, of the optimized (but static) 64 leaf tree is also indicated in Fig. 4.1. As can be seen, the maximum average throughput of DA-tree is one message/slot/channel.

2. Direct Access with TDMA

In DA-TDMA, if F users are assigned to an uplink channel, then each user is allowed to transmit sequentially in every F'th slot. The average delay in such a channel (see Appendix B) is given in message lengths by

$$E\{\text{delay}\} = \frac{F}{2} + 1 + \frac{\mu F}{2(1-\mu)}. \tag{4.3}$$

Equation (4.3) is illustrated in Fig. 4.1 for $F = 128$, where $F = 2^N/U$, $2^N = 1024$ and $U = 8$. The maximum average throughput of DA-TDMA is one message/slot/channel the same as that of DA-tree. However, as can be seen, the average delay of the DA-tree, for $\mu < .6$, is significantly better than the average delay of the DA-TDMA.

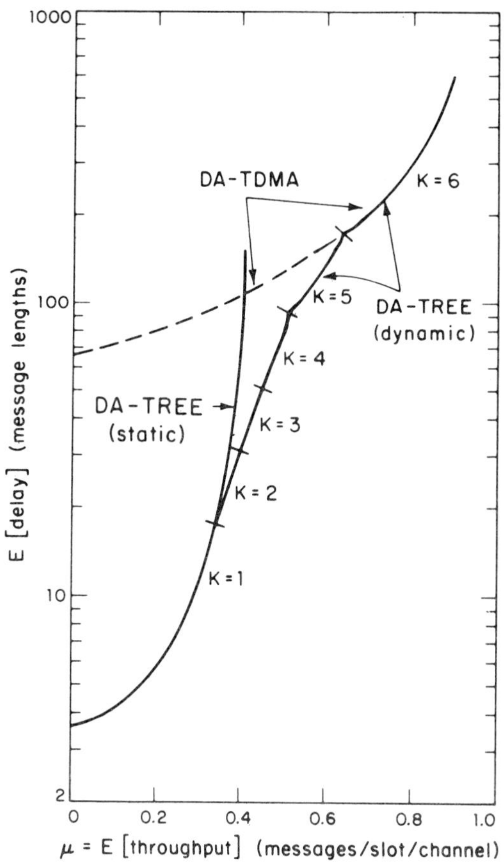

Fig. 4.1. $E\{\text{delay}\}$ vs $E\{\text{throughput}\}$ for direct access systems (1024 users, 8 uplinks).

B. Reservation Access

In RA, R of the uplink channels are used to reserve the other $U-R$ channels. There are two types of packets: reservation packets and data packets. The reservation packets are r seconds in length and are used to request channel capacity for the data packets that are s seconds in length.

The overall message delay may be broken up into two components D_r and D_m. D_r is the time from the instant a message is received to the instant the reservation is accomplished, and D_m is the time from the instant the reservation is accomplished to the instant the message is successfully transmitted. Thus,

$$E\{\text{delay}\} = E\{D_m\} + E\{D_r\}. \tag{4.4}$$

Three assumptions are made. First, a successfully transmitted request packet will reserve slots for all the messages that are in the source buffer immediately prior to its transmission. Secondly, the users are evenly assigned among the R channels and among the $U-R$ data channels, and they can transmit only in their assigned channels. Thirdly, the arrival process at a data channel is Poisson with average aggregate arrival rate $U\mu/(U-R)$.

It follows from these assumptions that $E\{D_m\}$ is the same for both the TDMA and the tree protocols. If, in addition, we recognize that a data channel is equivalent to the classic MD1 queue (see Appendix B) with the constraint that a busy period may begin only at integer multiples of the service time, we have

$$E\{D_m\} = \frac{3}{2} + \frac{U\mu}{2(U-R-U\mu)}. \tag{4.5}$$

$E\{D_r\}$ for TDMA in units of message lengths is given by

$$E\{D_r\}_{\text{TDMA}} = \left(\frac{2^N}{2R}\right)\left(\frac{r}{s}\right) + \frac{r}{s} + \tau. \tag{4.6}$$

The first term above is the average delay until transmission, the second is the transmission time, and the third is the round trip delay. Substituting (4.5) and (4.6) into (4.4), results in the following expression for the average delay of RA-TDMA.

$$E\{\text{delay}\} = \frac{3}{2} + \frac{U\mu}{2(U-R-U\mu)} + \left(\frac{2^N}{2R}+1\right)\frac{r}{s} + \tau. \tag{4.7}$$

Equation (4.7) is illustrated in Fig. 4.2 for $U = 8, N = 10$, $r/s = .2$, $R = 1, 2, 4$, and τ very small compared to the other terms in the $E\{\text{delay}\}$ expression.

Two observations are in order concerning (4.7). First, from Fig. 4.2, we see that the minimum $E\{\text{delay}\}$ is limited by the capacity of the reservation channel (i.e., R), whereas the maximum average throughput is limited by the capacity of the date channel (i.e., $U - R$). Secondly, the performance of RA-TDMA may be optimized with respect to R. In the example illustrated in Fig. 4.2, for instance,

$$R_{\text{opt}} = \begin{cases} 1, & \mu > .74 \\ 2, & .74 \geqslant \mu > .49 \\ 4, & \mu < .49. \end{cases} \tag{4.8}$$

In general, the range of optimality of R may be obtained directly from (4.7).

$E\{D_r\}$for the tree protocol was obtained by simulation, and combined with (4.4) and (4.5) to obtain the $E\{\text{delay}\}$ results that are also illustrated in Fig. 4.2. From this figure, we see that, for any R and all μ, the average delay of the RA-tree is less than or equal to the average delay of RA-TDMA. As a matter of fact, for small μ, the performance of the RA-tree is significantly better than that of RA-TDMA. For example, for $R = 2$ and $\mu \leqslant .5$, the average delay RA-tree is at least an order of magnitude smaller than that of the RA-TDMA.

V. CONCLUSION

We presented the tree protocol, a stable algorithm that may be used to access the satellite channel. The tree protocol may be considered to be a contention resolving algorithm and may be applied in accessing a communications channel directly, or in conducting reservations in a demand assignment multiple access system.

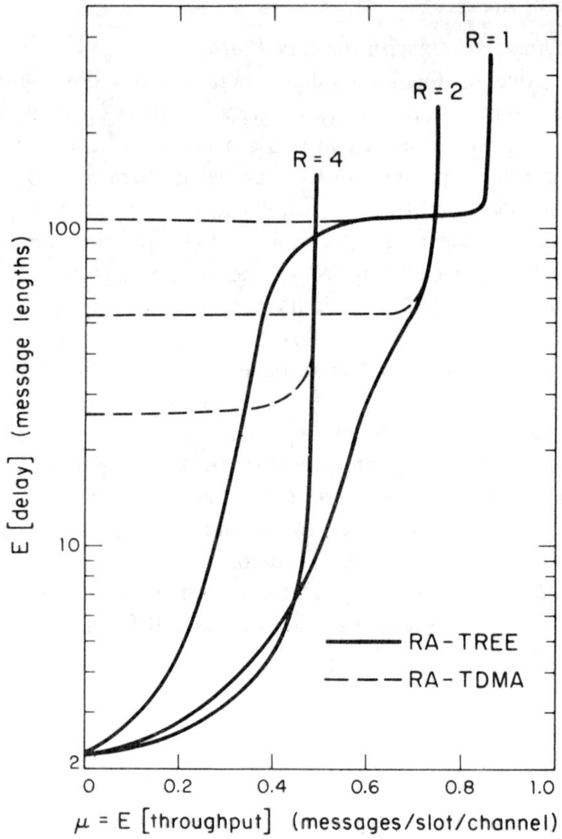

Fig. 4.2. $E\{\text{delay}\}$ vs $E\{\text{throughput}\}$ for reservation access systems (1024 users,8 uplinks, and reservation packet length to data packet length ratio equal to .2).

It was shown that the tree protocol is a generalization of TDMA, that the optimum dynamic tree is more efficient than TDMA, and that the optimum tree algorithm adaptively changes from an essentially random access protocol in light traffic to TDMA in heavy traffic. Specifically, it is shown that if q, the probability that a user has a packet to transmit, is greater than $1/\sqrt{2}$, then the optimum tree and TDMA are identical. If, on the other hand, $q < 1/\sqrt{2}$, then a tree exists which is more efficient than TDMA.

In addition, it is shown that a tree protocol servicing 2^N users (with a tree graph that has root node of degree 2^K and binary nodes elsewhere) has maximum average throughput $1/(2-2^{N-K})$ packets/slot. The maximum average throughput of the optimum tree protocol is one packet/slot.

The tree and TDMA protocols were applied to direct and reservation access satellite systems. The result is that both protocols have the same maximum throughput. However, for average throughput less than 1/2, the average delay for the tree is at least an order of magnitude smaller than that of TDMA (see Figs. 4.1 and 4.2).

The source models that were considered here consisted of a finite number of users. The Poisson source model (which assumes an infinite number of users that collectively generate message traffic that satisfies the Poisson statistic) is considered in [2] and [3]. It is shown there that a system consisting of the Poisson source model and the tree protocol has maximum average throughput of .43 packets/slot.†† In addition, such a system is stable in the sense that if the average arrival rate is less than .43 packets/slot, then all the moments of the delay are finite. Notice that the maximum average throughput of the tree protocol is one packet per slot for a finite number of sources (no matter how large that number might be), but it is only .43 packets/slot for an infinite number of sources.

This work is specifically applicable to the satellite channel. The results developed here, however, may be extended to any communications system that is accessable by a number of independent users. If, in such a system, the instantaneous maximum channel demand can exceed the system capacity, then the tree protocol may be applied to resolve the resulting contentions.

APPENDIX A

DERIVATION OF $E\{l \mid q, N, 1\}$

The number of nodes l visited by the algorithm may be written as follows:

$$l = 1 + \sum_{i=1}^{N-1} \sum_{j=0}^{2^i-1} x_{ij} \tag{A.1}$$

where

$$x_{ij} = \begin{cases} 1 & \text{if node } n_{ij} \text{ is visited} \\ 0 & \text{otherwise.} \end{cases} \tag{A.2}$$

Since a node n_{ij} is visited if there are at least two active sources in T_{ij} we have that

$$P(x_{ij} = 1/q) = \Psi(q, N-i) \tag{A.3}$$

where

$$\Psi(q,m) \equiv 1 - (1-q)^{2^m} - 2^m q(1-q)^{2^m-1} \tag{A.4}$$

and it follows that

$$E\{l \mid q\} = 1 + \sum_{i=1}^{N-1} 2^i \Psi(q, N-i) \tag{A.5}$$

or

$$E\{l \mid q\} = 1 + 2D(q, N-1) \tag{A.6}$$

where

$$D(q,m) = \sum_{i=0}^{m-1} 2^i \Psi(q, m-i). \tag{A.7}$$

Equations (A.4) through (A.7) are the desired results.

†† Modifications to the original tree algorithm by James Massey and Robert G. Gallager [5], and Jeannine Mosley [6] have increased the maximum average throughput to .487 packets/slot.

APPENDIX B

ON THE AVERAGE MESSAGE DELAY OF TDMA SYSTEMS

Define a synchronous MD1 queue (SMD1) to be the conventional MD1 queue (see eq. (5.67) in [7]) with the added restriction that busy periods may begin only at integer multiples of the service time. In this Appendix, first, a relationship is proved between the average waiting times of the conventional MD1 queue and the SMD1 queue. Secondly, this result is extended to the average message waiting time in a TDMA system. By waiting time, we mean the time spent by a customer in queue plus the time spent in the service facility.

Theorem: Let D_s and D_a be the average waiting times of the SMD1 and the conventional MD1 queues, respectively, and let X be the service time. Then,

$$D_s = D_a + \frac{X}{2}. \tag{B.1}$$

Proof: Choose a sample function from the Poisson arrival process and apply this particular function to an SMD1 queue and an MD1 queue. Next, choose any busy period in the MD1 queue, let $C = \{C_i; i = 1, 2, \cdots, k\}$ be the customers that were served in that busy period, and let $t_d = \{t_i; i = 1, 2, \cdots, k\}$ be the departure times of C.

Now, $\hat{t}_d$, the departure times of C in SMD1 are given by

$$\hat{t}_i = t_i + \Delta, \qquad \text{for } i = 1, 2, \cdots, k, \tag{B.2}$$

where Δ, in light of the Markovian property of the arrival process, is a random variable uniformly distributed between $[0, X]$. Taking expectations of both sides of (B.2) and noting that the arrival times of C in SMD1 are the same as in MD1, results in (B.1).

Q.E.D.

Corollary: Let $D_a(X)$ be the average waiting time in an MD1 queue with service time X. Also let D_{TDMA} be the average message delay (i.e., the waiting time in the buffer plus the transmission time of a randomly chosen packet) in a TDMA system with F users, each of which has infinite buffer capacity. In addition, assume that the message arrival process is Poisson, and that all messages have length s. Then,

$$D_{\mathrm{TDMA}} = D_a(Fs) + \frac{Fs}{2} - (F-1)s. \tag{B.3}$$

Proof: D_{TDMA} may be considered to be the delay of a randomly chosen customer in a SMD1 queue in which the randomly chosen customer has service time s but all others preceding it have service times Fs. Equation (B.3) follows from this observation and the preceding theorem.

Q.E.D.

REFERENCES

1. L. Kleinrock and S. Lam, "Packet Switching in a Multiaccess Broadcast Channel: Performance Evaluation," *IEEE Trans. on Communications,* April 1975.

2. J. I. Capetanakis, "The Multiple Access Broadcast Channel: Protocol and Capacity Considerations," Technical Report ESL-R-806, MIT, Cambridge, MA, March 1978.
3. J. I. Capetanakis, "Tree Algorithms for Packet Braodcast Channels," *IEEE Trans. on Information Theory,* September 1979.
4. J. I. Capetanakis, "Capacity Allocation Techniques for Multi-User Satellite Systems," Technical Note 1979-34, MIT Lincoln Laboratory, Lexington, MA, June 1979.
5. R. G. Gallager, Talk at Workshop on Communications Theory, Provincetown, MA, 17-20 September 1978.
6. J. Mosely, "An Efficient Contention Resolution Algorithm for Multiple Access Channels," Technical Report LIDS-TH-918, MIT Cambridge, MA, June 1979.
7. L. Kleinrock, *Queueing Systems Vol. I: Theory,* Wiley Interscience, New York, 1975.

John I. Capetanakis was born in Greece on December 5, 1944. He received the B.S. and M.S. degrees in 1970, the E.E. degree in 1971, and the Ph.D degree in 1977, all in electrical engineering from M.I.T. Cambridge, Massachusetts.

He joined M.I.T. Lincoln Laboratory, Lexington, Massachusetts, in 1972. He has been instrumental in the research, development, and implementation of modulation and coding techniques for the satellite channel. In addition, he has carried out research in satellite multiple accessing protocols, multiple acquisition techniques, and packet communications.

Dr. Capetanakis is a member of Eta Kappa Nu, Tau Beta Pi, and Sigma Xi.

Chapter 4
Local Area Networks

4.1. PACKET RADIO NETWORKS

The ALOHANET of the University of Hawaii was one of the first local area networks [ABRA 70, BIND 75]. It pioneered packet switching in broadcast radio channels. The random access protocol of the original ALOHANET was of seminal importance in the development of the class of contention techniques for multiple access (including CSMA/CD).

The Hawaii work also inspired the development of a multi-hop packet radio network (PRNET) under the sponsorship of DARPA. PRNET employs packet repeaters to cover a wide geographic area. Its network-level protocols are designed to handle network users that are highly mobile [KAHN 78].

4.2. MULTIPOINT NETWORKS (BASEBAND)

Multipoint networks have either a bus or a tree topology. They can be implemented with coaxial cables or twisted pairs. Ethernet is probably the most successful and well known of the baseband multipoint cable networks [METC 76], although various other multipoint cable networks had been developed earlier (e.g., [WILL 73]). The basic configuration of Ethernet consists of a coaxial cable which serves as a passive broadcast medium (Figure 4-1). Each user connects to the cable with a tap and a transceiver. Removing power from the transceiver causes it to disconnect from the cable. Thus, it is easy to ensure that failures in a transceiver (or user) do not affect the operation of the network. This approach gives Ethernet good reliability, extensibility, and reconfigurability. The other prominent feature of Ethernet is the use of a CSMA/CD protocol for multiple access (see Chapter 3). The topology of Ethernet can be extended to that of an unrooted tree by the use of active packet repeaters joining together separate Ethernet segments as shown in Figure 4-2. Ethernet has a maximum data rate of 2.94 Mbps (with segment length limited to 1 Km) or a maximum data rate of 10 Mbps (with segment length limited to 500 meters) [SHOC 82]. The article by Shoch et al. [SHOC 82] gives a detailed technical description of the second-generation Ethernet, and it is reprinted below. A version of the detailed Ethernet specification can be found in [ETHE 81].

Another highly successful cable bus network is the Hyperchannel [THOR 79]. It also uses non-directional taps and baseband signalling. Hyperchannel has a maximum data rate of 50 Mbps. It is intended for the interconnection of mainframe computers and storage devices.

4.3. MULTIPOINT NETWORKS (BROADBAND)

In baseband local area networks, data signals being transmitted are not modulated onto a carrier signal. They are transmitted in their (unmodulated) digital form. Broadband networks employ RF modems that make possible the utilization of the entire cable bandwidth (about 300-400 MHz). In fact, there is so much bandwidth that it is probably desirable to divide it into different bands (using FDM) and to assign each band to a different application (data, voice, video, etc.). Broadband networks are typically built using readily available, low-cost CATV equipment, e.g., 75-ohm cables. (In contrast, Ethernets use 50-ohm cables.)

The transmission in most broadband networks is directional. This means that a signal going from a tap into the cable in Figure 4-1 is constrained to propagate away from the tap in

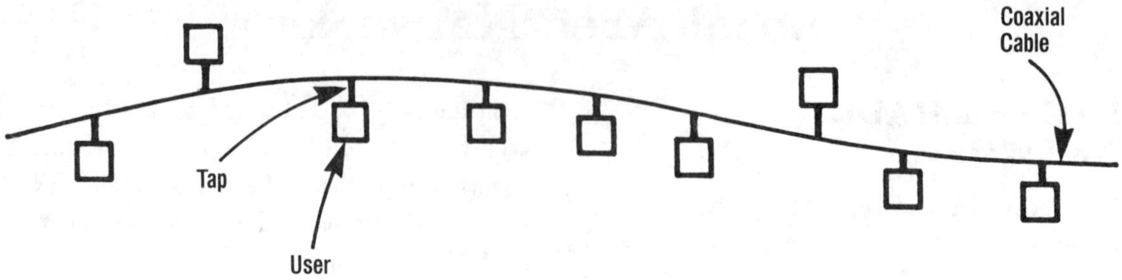

Figure 4-1. A multipoint bus network.

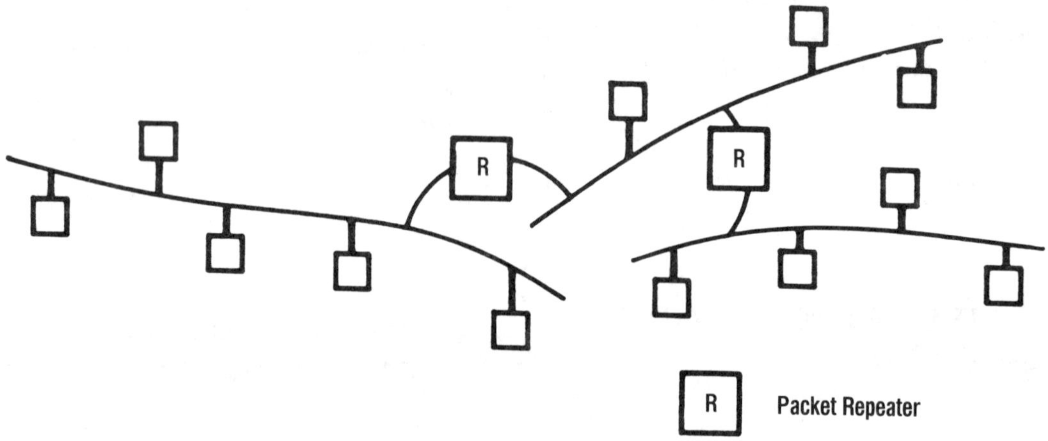

Figure 4-2. Multipoint cables joined by packet repeaters.

one direction only. (In a baseband bus network, a signal from a tap propagates in both directions away from the tap. Thus baseband networks are said to be bidirectional.)

Because of directional transmissions, the configuration of broadband networks are somewhat different from that shown in Figure 4-1. Three possible configurations are shown in Figure 4-3. In a single-cable system, the available frequency band is split into two, with one band for inbound transmission to the headend and the other band for the headend to retransmit anything that it has received outbound. A dual-cable system operates similarly but with two cables; thus the entire band is available in each transmission direction. In general, each cable, inbound or outbound, can be replaced by a tree configuration as shown in Figure 4-3(c). Appropriately spaced amplifiers powered from the center conductor of the cable (not shown in Figure 4-3(c)) can be used to maintain relatively constant receive signal strength for all users.

Each of the three configurations shown in Figure 4-3 is a broadcast channel as defined in Chapter 3. Previously described protocols, such as TDMA, CSMA/CD, and token passing, can be adapted for multiple access by users. For descriptions of some broadband networks, the reader is referred to [HOPK 79] and [BIBA 81].

4.4. RING NETWORKS

Ring networks constitute a major category of networks that are intrinsically different from packet radio and multipoint cable networks. For one thing, a ring is not a broadcast channel. Rather, it is a series of point-to-point channels. Each node on the ring is an active repeater joining two point-to-point segments.

There are three main protocols for sharing use of a ring network. An obvious one is token passing. This is the approach adopted in two recently developed ring networks [SALT 79, BUX 81] and in one of the IEEE Project 802 local area network standards. Farmer and Newhall probably wrote the first article describing a token ring [FARM 69]. An important consideration for token rings is how the network performs recovery when the control token is lost. A different approach, *slotted rings*, was proposed by several researchers in the early 1970s [PIER 72, FARB 72, WILK 79]. Think of a sequence of fixed-length slots traveling around the ring. Each slot is marked empty or busy. A node with a message to send will insert it into the first empty slot arriving from upstream

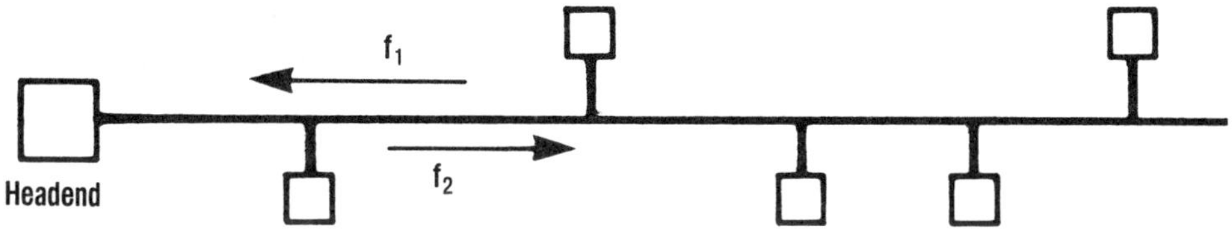

(a) Single-Cable System

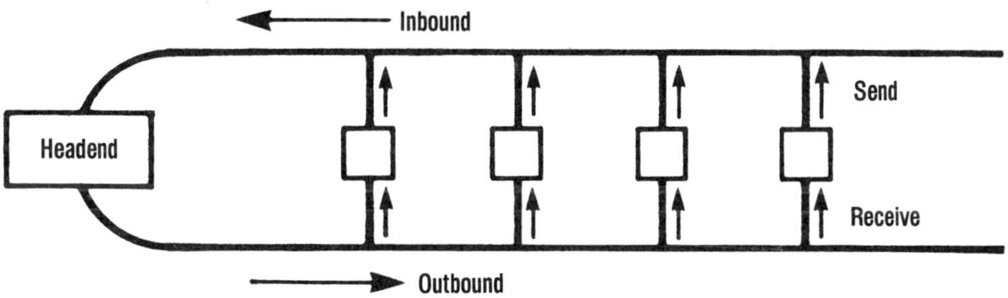

(b) Dual-Cable System

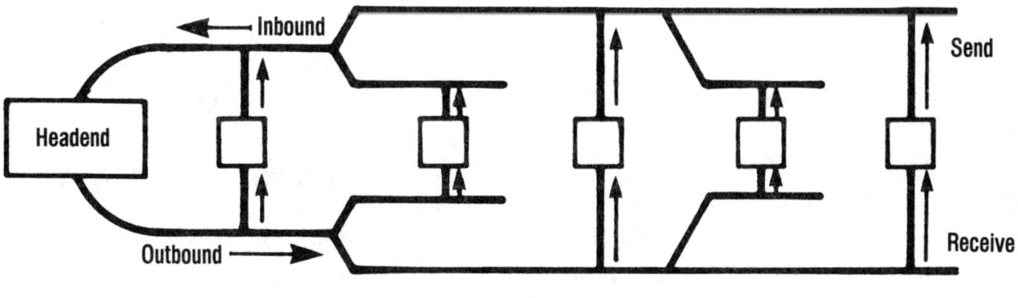

(c) Dual-Tree System

Figure 4-3. Broadband network configurations.

and will mark the slot busy as it is sent downstream. The subsequent removal of the message and the changing of the slot's status from busy to empty can be performed either by the receiver of the message or by the sender of the message (after the message has traveled all the way around the ring). The third approach, ***insertion rings,*** was also proposed by several people [BOUD 73, REAM 75]. In this approach, a ring interface has hardware buffering that enables it to buffer incoming data from upstream at the same time when it is transmitting a locally generated message downstream. Insertion rings have more complex ring interfaces than do the other two approaches but they can accommodate variable-length messages as well as simultaneous transmissions by different users.

We discuss here a few points of comparison between rings and multipoint cables which we find interesting. A major advantage of rings is that they are made up of point-to-point channels. It is much easier to engineer transceivers for point-to-point unidirectional channels than for a multipoint broadcast cable. Furthermore, fiber optics can be used for point-to-point segments in a ring network. It is currently impractical to implement a multipoint broadcast network using fiber optics [RAWS 79]. A major weakness of Ethernet-type networks is that the CSMA/CD protocol becomes inefficient at high data rates (say, tens of Mbps). This is because at high data rates the end-to-end cable propagation delay becomes comparable in duration to packet transmission times. As a result, the advantage of carrier sensing is diminished and a CSMA/CD channel becomes effectively an ALOHA channel (see Chapter 3).

The obvious weakness of ring networks is their reliability. A failure in any node on a ring can disrupt the entire network. Various methods have been considered to improve the reliability of ring networks. An obvious approach is to introduce more connectivity into a ring; i.e., each node in the ring is connected to several other nodes [RAGH 82]. Such networks however have poor extensibility and reconfigurability. Adding new nodes or changing the network configuration entail significant disruptions to the network's operation. A different approach proposed by Lee [LEE 79] and Goyal and Lipovski [GOYA 80] is to implement ring protocols on non-ring topologies. A Hamiltonian graph is considered in [LEE 79] and trees are considered in [GOYA 80]. In each case, network reconfiguration to accommodate new nodes or to bypass failures can be done without too much difficulty. But they are only logical ring networks.

The most promising approach is probably the idea of star-shaped rings as proposed and investigated by researchers at MIT [SALT 79] and IBM Research at Zurich [BUX 81]. This approach provides relative ease in bypassing failed nodes for reliability and in extending and reconfiguring an existing network. For a description of this approach, the reader is referred to the article by Andrews and Schultz [ANDR 82], reprinted below. This article describes IBM's proposal to the IEEE project 802 on local area network standards. Saltzer and Clark gave a careful comparison of rings versus Ethernet-like cable networks in [SALT 81]. This article is also reprinted below.

4.5. ADDITIONAL REFERENCES

Draft versions of some IEEE project 802 local area network standards were published by the IEEE Computer Society [IEEE 82a, IEEE 82b, IEEE 82c].

References

[ABRA 70] Abramson, N., "THE ALOHA SYSTEM--Another Alternative for Computer Communications," *AFIPS Conf. Proc.*, Vol. 37, AFIPS Press, Montvale, N. J., 1970, pp. 281-285.

*[ANDR 82] Andrews, D. W. and G. D. Schultz, "A Token-Ring Architecture for Local Area Networks: An Update," *Proc. Fall '82 COMPCON*, IEEE

Computer Society, 1982, pp. 615-624.

[BIBA 81] Biba, K. J., "Packet Networks for Broadband Coaxial Cable," *Local Networks and Distributed Office Systems,* Online Publications, Northwood, U.K., 1981.

[BIND 75] Binder, R., et al., "ALOHA Packet Broadcasting--A Retrospect," *Nat. Comput. Conf., AFIPS Conf. Proc.*, Vol. 44, 1975, pp. 201-215.

[BOUD 73] Boudreau, P. E., et al., "Terminal Interface for a Serial Loop Communications System having Store and Forward Capability," U.S. Patent 3,781,815, December 25, 1973.

[BUX 81] Bux, W., et al., "A Reliable Token-Ring System for Local-Area Communication," *Conf. Rec. NTC '81,* New Orleans, 1981, pp. A2.2.1-A2.2.6.

[ETHE 81] Ethernet, "A Local Area Network--Data Link Layer and Physical Layer Specifications," *Computer Communication Reviews,* Vol. 11, No. 3, ACM, July 1981, pp. 20-66.

[FARB 72] Farber, D. J. and K. C. Larson, "The System Architecture of the Distributed Computer System--the Communications Systems," *Proc. Symp. Computer-Communications Networks and Teletraffic,* Polytechnic Institute of Brooklyn, April 1972.

[FARM 69] Farmer, W. D. and E. E. Newhall, "An Experimental Distributed Switching System to Handle Computer Traffic," *Proc. ACM Symp. on Data Communications,* Pine Mountain, Ga., October 1969, pp. 1-33.

[GOYA 80] Goyal, A. and G. J. Lipovski, "Reconfigurable Hierarchical Rings," *Proc. Distributed Data Acquisition, Computing andd Control Symposium,* Miami Beach, Florida, December 1980.

[HOPK 79] Hopkins, G. T., "Multimode Communications on the MITRENET," *Computer Networks,* Vol. 4, No. 5, 1980, pp. 229-234.

[IEEE 82a] IEEE Project 802 Local Area Network Standards, "Logical Link Control," Draft IEEE Standard 802.2, Draft D, November 1982.

[IEEE 82b] IEEE Project 802 Local Area Network Standards, "CSMA/CD Access Method and Physical Layer Specifications," Draft IEEE Standard 802.3, Revision D, December 1982.

[IEEE 82c] IEEE Project 802 Local Area Network Standards, "Token-Passing Bus Access Method and Physical Layer Specifications," Draft IEEE Standard 802.4, Draft D, December 1982.

[KAHN 78] Kahn, R., et al., "Advances in Packet Radio Technology," *Proc. IEEE,* Vol. 66, November 1978.

[LEE 79] Lee, R. P., "The Architecture of a Dynamically Reconfiguragle Insertion-Ring Network," IBM Research Report RJ2485, San Jose, March 1979.

[METC 76] Metcalfe, R. M. and D. R. Boggs, "Ethernet: Distributed Packet Switching for Local Computer Networks," *Commun. ACM,* Vol. 19, No. 7, July 1976.

[PIER 72] Pierce, J. R., "Networks for Block Switching of Data," Bell System

Technical Journal, Vol. 51, No. 6, pp. 1133-1145, 1972.

[RAGH 82] Raghavendra, C. S., M. Gerla, and D. S. Parker, "Multi-Connected Loop Topologies for Local Computer Networks," *Proc. INFOCOM 82*, Las Vegas, 1982, pp. 184-190.

[RAWS 79] Rawson, E. G., "Application of Fiber Optics to Local Networks," *Proc. Local Area Networks* Symposium, Boston, May, 1979, pp. 155-167.

[REAM 75] Reames, C. C. and M. T. Liu, "A Loop Network for Simultaneous Transmission of Variable-Length Messages," *Proc. 2nd Annual Symposium on Computer Architecture*, Houston, Texas, January 1975.

[SALT 79] Saltzer, J. H. and K. Pogran, "A Star-Shaped Ring Network with High Maintainability," *Computer Network*, Vol. 4, No. 5, 1980, pp. 239-244.

*[SALT 81] Saltzer, J. H. and D. D. Clark, "Why a Ring?" *Proc. 7th Data Commun. Symp.*, Mexico City, October 1981, pp. 211-217.

*[SHOC 82] Shoch, J. F., Y. K. Dalal, D. D. Redell, and R. C. Crane, "Evolution of the Ethernet Local Computer Network," *Computer*, IEEE, August 1982, pp. 10-27.

[THOR 79] Thornton, J. E., "Overview of Hyperchannel," *COMPCON Spring*, San Francisco, Calif., February 1979, pp. 262-265.

[WILL 73] Willard, D. G., "Mitrix: A Sophisticated Digital Cable Communications System," *Conf. Rec. National Telecommunications Conference*, November 1973.

[WILK 79] Wilkes, M. V., and D. J. Wheeler, "The Cambridge Digital Communication Ring," *Proc. Local Area Comm. Network Symp.*, Boston, May 1979, pp. 47-61.

(* article reprinted below.)

Reprinted from *Computer*, August 1982, pages 10-26. Copyright © 1982 by
The Institute of Electrical and Electronics Engineers, Inc.

Evolution of the Ethernet Local Computer Network

As it evolved from a research prototype to the specification of a multi-company standard, Ethernet compelled designers to consider numerous trade-offs among alternative implementations and design strategies.

John F. Shoch, Yogen K. Dalal, and David D. Redell, Xerox
Ronald C. Crane, 3Com

Reprinted from *Computer*, August 1982, pages 1–27. Copyright © 1982 by
The Institute of Electrical and Electronics Engineers, Inc.

With the continuing decline in the cost of computing, we have witnessed a dramatic increase in the number of independent computer systems used for scientific computing, business, process control, word processing, and personal computing. These machines do not compute in isolation, and with their proliferation comes a need for suitable communication networks—particularly local computer networks that can interconnect locally distributed computing systems. While there is no single definition of a local computer network, there is a broad set of requirements:

- relatively high data rates (typically 1 to 10M bits per second);
- geographic distance spanning about one kilometer (typically within a building or a small set of buildings);
- ability to support several hundred independent devices;
- simplicity, or the ability "to provide the simplest possible mechanisms that have the required functionality and performance";[1]
- good error characteristics, good reliability, and minimal dependence upon any centralized components or control;
- efficient use of shared resources, particularly the communications network itself;
- stability under high load;
- fair access to the system by all devices;
- easy installation of a small system, with graceful growth as the system evolves;
- ease of reconfiguration and maintenance; and
- low cost.

One of the more successful designs for a system of this kind is the Ethernet local computer network.[2,3] Ethernet installations have been in use for many years. They support hundreds of stations and meet the requirements listed above.

In general terms, Ethernet is a multi-access, packet-switched communications system for carrying digital data among locally distributed computing systems. The shared communications channel in an Ethernet is a passive broadcast medium with no central control; packet address recognition in each station is used to take packets from the channel. Access to the channel by stations wishing to transmit is coordinated in a distributed fashion by the stations themselves, using a statistical arbitration scheme.

The Ethernet strategy can be used on many different broadcast media, but our major focus has been on the use of coaxial cable as the shared transmission medium. The Experimental Ethernet system was developed at the Xerox Palo Alto Research Center starting in 1972. Since then, numerous other organizations have developed and built "Ethernet-like" local networks.[4] More recently, a cooperative effort involving Digital Equipment Corporation, Intel, and Xerox has produced an updated version of the Ethernet design, generally known as the Ethernet Specification.[5]

One of the primary goals of the Ethernet Specification is compatibility—providing enough information for different manufacturers to build widely differing machines in such a way that they can directly communicate with one another. It might be tempting to view the Specification as simply a design handbook that will allow designers to develop their own Ethernet-like network, perhaps cus-

EHO216-2/84/0000/0215$01.00 © 1982 IEEE

tomized for some specific requirements or local constraints. But this would miss the major point: Successful interconnection of heterogeneous machines requires equipment that precisely matches a single specification.

Meeting the Specification is only one of the necessary conditions for intermachine communication at all levels of the network architecture. There are many levels of protocol, such as transport, name binding, and file transfer, that must also be agreed upon and implemented in order to provide useful services.[6-8] This is analogous to the telephone system: The common low-level specifications for telephony make it possible to dial from the US to France, but this is not of much use if the caller speaks only English while the person who answers the phone speaks only French. Specification of these additional protocols is an important area for further work.

The design of any local network must be considered in the context of a distributed system architecture. Although the Ethernet Specification does not directly address issues of high-level network architecture, we view the local network as one component in an *internetwork* system, providing communication services to many diverse devices connected to different networks.[6,9] The services provided by the Ethernet are influenced by these broader architectural considerations.

As we highlight important design considerations and trace the evolution of the Ethernet from research prototype to multicompany standard, we use the term Experimental Ethernet for the former and Ethernet or Ethernet Specification for the latter. The term Ethernet is also used to describe design principles common to both systems.

General description of Ethernet-class systems

Theory of operation. The general Ethernet approach uses a shared communications channel managed with a distributed control policy known as *carrier sense multiple access with collision detection*, or CSMA/CD. With this approach, there is no central controller managing access to the channel, and there is no preallocation of time slots or frequency bands. A station wishing to transmit is said to "contend" for use of the common shared communications channel (sometimes called the Ether) until it "acquires" the channel; once the channel is acquired the station uses it to transmit a packet.

To acquire the channel, stations check whether the network is busy (that is, use *carrier sense*) and defer transmission of their packet until the Ether is quiet (no other transmissions occurring). When quiet is detected, the deferring station immediately begins to transmit. During transmission, the transmitting station listens for a collision (other transmitters attempting to use the channel simultaneously). In a correctly functioning system, collisions occur only within a short time interval following the start of transmission, since after this interval all stations will detect carrier and defer transmission. This time interval is called the *collision window* or the *collision interval* and is a function of the end-to-end propagation delay. If no collisions occur during this time, a transmitter has acquired the Ether and continues transmission of the packet. If a station detects collision, the transmission of the rest of the packet is immediately aborted. To ensure that all parties to the collision have properly detected it, any station that detects a collision invokes a *collision consensus enforcement procedure* that briefly jams the channel. Each transmitter involved in the collision then schedules its packet for retransmission at some later time.

To minimize repeated collisions, each station involved in a collision tries to retransmit at a different time by scheduling the retransmission to take place after a random delay period. In order to achieve channel stability under overload conditions, a controlled retransmission strategy is used whereby the mean of the random retransmission delay is increased as a function of the channel load. An estimate of the channel load can be derived by monitoring the number of collisions experienced by any one packet. This has been shown to be the optimal strategy among the options available for decentralized decision and control problems of this class.[10]

Stations accept packets addressed to them and discard any that are found to be in error. Deference reduces the probability of collision, and collision detection allows the timely retransmission of a packet. It is impossible, however, to guarantee that all packets transmitted will be delivered successfully. For example, if a receiver is not enabled, an error-free packet addressed to it will not be delivered; higher levels of protocol must detect these situations and retransmit.

Under very high load, short periods of time on the channel may be lost due to collisions, but the collision resolution procedure operates quickly.[2,11-13] Channel utilization under these conditions will remain high, particularly if packets are large with respect to the collision interval. One of the fundamental parameters of any Ethernet implementation is the length of this collision interval, which is based on the round-trip propagation time between the farthest two points in the system.

Basic components. The CSMA/CD access procedure can use any broadcast multi-access channel, including radio, twisted pair, coaxial cable, diffuse infrared, and fiber optics.[14] Figure 1 illustrates a typical Ethernet system using coaxial cable. There are four components.

Station. A station makes use of the communication system and is the basic addressable device connected to an Ethernet; in general, it is a computer. We do not expect that "simple" terminals will be connected directly to an Ethernet. Terminals can be connected to some form of terminal controller, however, which provides access to the network. In the future, as the level of sophistication in terminals increases, many terminals will support direct connection to the network. Furthermore, specialized I/O devices, such as magnetic tapes or disk drives, may incorporate sufficient computing resources to function as stations on the network.

Within the station there is some interface between the operating system environment and the Ethernet controller. The nature of this interface (often in software) depends upon the particular implementation of the controller functions in the station.

Controller. A controller for a station is really the set of functions and algorithms needed to manage access to the channel. These include signaling conventions, encoding and decoding, serial-to-parallel conversion, address recognition, error detection, buffering, the basic CSMA/CD channel management, and packetization. These functions can be grouped into two logically independent sections of each controller: the transmitter and the receiver.

The controller functions are generally implemented using a combination of hardware, microcode, and software, depending on the nature of the station. It would be possible, for example, for a very capable station to have a minimal hardware connection to the transmission system and perform most of these functions in software. Alternatively, a station might implement all the controller functions in hardware, or perhaps in a controller-specific microprocessor. Most controller implementations fall somewhere in between. With the continuing advances in LSI development, many of these functions will be packaged in a single chip, and several semiconductor manufacturers have already announced plans to build Ethernet controllers. The precise boundary between functions performed on the chip and those in the station is implementation-dependent, but the nature of that interface is of great importance. As many of the functions as possible should be moved into the chip, provided that this preserves all of the flexibility needed in the construction and use of system interfaces and higher level software.

The description of the controller in this article is functional in nature and indicates how the controller must behave independent of particular implementations. There is some flexibility in implementing a correct controller, and we will make several recommendations concerning efficient operation of the system.

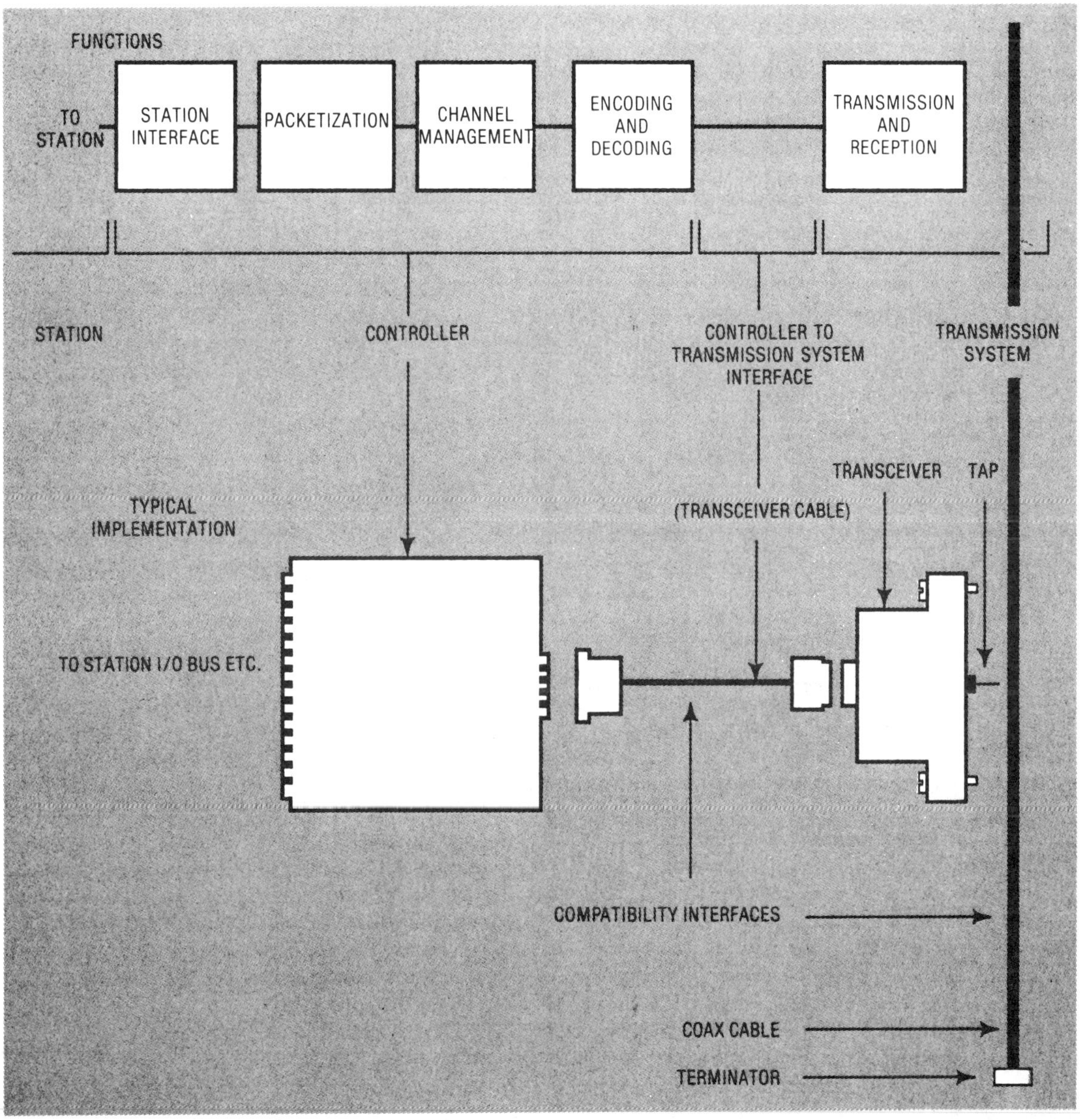

Figure 1. A general Ethernet implementation.

Ethernet 1.0 Technical Summary

Packet Format

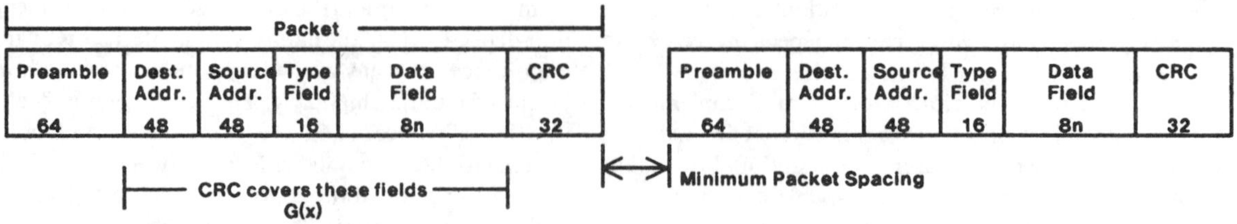

Stations must be able to transmit and receive packets on the common coaxial cable with the indicated packet format and spacing. Each packet should be viewed as a sequence of 8-bit bytes; the least significant bit of each byte (starting with the preamble) is transmitted first.

Maximum Packet Size: 1526 bytes (8 byte preamble + 14 byte header + 1500 data bytes + 4 byte CRC)

Minimum Packet Size: 72 bytes (8 byte preamble + 14 byte header + 46 data bytes + 4 byte CRC)

Preamble: This 64-bit synchronization pattern contains alternating 1's and 0's, ending with two consecutive 1's. The preamble is: 10101010 10101010 10101010 10101010 10101010 10101010 10101010 10101011.

Destination Address: This 48-bit field specifies the station(s) to which the packet is being transmitted. Each station examines this field to determine whether it should accept the packet. The first bit transmitted indicates the type of address. If it is a 0, the field contains the unique address of the one destination station. If it is a 1, the field specifies a logical group of recipients; a special case is the broadcast (all stations) address, which is all 1's.

Source Address: This 48-bit field contains the unique address of the station that is transmitting the packet.

Type Field: This 16-bit field is used to identify the higher-level protocol type associated with the packet. It determines how the data field is interpreted.

Data Field: This field contains an integral number of bytes ranging from 46 to 1500. (The minimum ensures that valid packets will be distinguishable from collision fragments.)

Packet Check Sequence: This 32-bit field contains a redundancy check (CRC) code, defined by the generating polynomial:

$$G(x) = x^{32} + x^{26} + x^{23} + x^{22} + x^{16} + x^{12} + x^{11} + x^{10} + x^{8} + x^{7} + x^{5} + x^{4} + x^{2} + x + 1$$

The CRC covers the address (destination/source), type, and data fields. The first transmitted bit of the destination field is the high-order term of the message polynomial to be divided by G(x) producing remainder R(x). The high-order term of R(x) is the first transmitted bit of the Packet Check Sequence field. The algorithm uses a linear feedback register which is initially preset to all 1's. After the last data bit is transmitted, the contents of this register (the remainder) are inverted and transmitted as the CRC field. After receiving a good packet, the receiver's shift register contains 11000111 00000100 11011101 01111011 ($x^{31}, \ldots, x^{0}$).

Minimum Packet Spacing: This spacing is 9.6 usec, the minimum time that must elapse after one transmission before another transmission may begin.

Round-trip Delay: The maximum end-to-end, round-trip delay for a bit is 51.2 usec.

Collision Filtering: Any received bit sequence smaller than the minimum valid packet (with minimum data field) is discarded as a collision fragment.

Control Procedure

The control procedure defines how and when a station may transmit packets into the common cable. The key purpose is fair resolution of occasional contention among transmitting stations.

Defer: A station must not transmit into the coaxial cable when carrier is present or within the minimum packet spacing time after carrier has ended.

Transmit: A station may transmit if it is not deferring. It may continue to transmit until either the end of the packet is reached or a collision is detected.

Abort: If a collision is detected, transmission of the packet must terminate, and a *jam* (4-6 bytes of arbitrary data) is transmitted to ensure that all other participants in the collision also recognize its occurrence.

Retransmit: After a station has detected a collision and aborted, it must wait for a random *retransmission delay*, defer as usual, and then attempt to retransmit the packet. The random time interval is computed using the backoff algorithm (below). After 16 transmission attempts, a higher level (e.g. software) decision is made to determine whether to continue or abandon the effort.

Backoff: Retransmission delays are computed using the *Truncated Binary Exponential Backoff* algorithm, with the aim of fairly resolving contention among up to 1024 stations. The delay (the number of time units) before the nth attempt is a uniformly distributed random number from [0 to 2^n-1] for $0 < n \leq 10$ (n = 0 is the original attempt). For attempts 11-15, the interval is *truncated* and remains at [0 to 1023]. The unit of time for the retransmission delay is 512 bit times (51.2 usec).

Channel Encoding

Manchester encoding is used on the coaxial cable. It has a 50% duty cycle, and insures a transition in the middle of every bit cell ("data transition"). The first half of the bit cell contains the complement of the bit value, and the second half contains the true value of the bit.

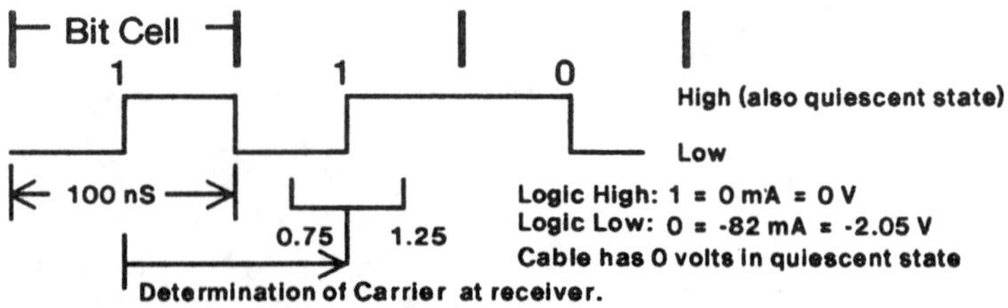

Data Rate

Data rate is 10 M bits/sec = 100 nsec bit cell ± 0.01%.

Carrier

The presence of data transitions indicates that carrier is present. If a transition is not seen between 0.75 and 1.25 bit times since the center of the last bit cell, then carrier has been lost, indicating the end of a packet. For purposes of deferring, carrier means any activity on the cable, independent of being properly formed. Specifically, it is any activity on either receive or collision detect signals in the last 160 nsec.

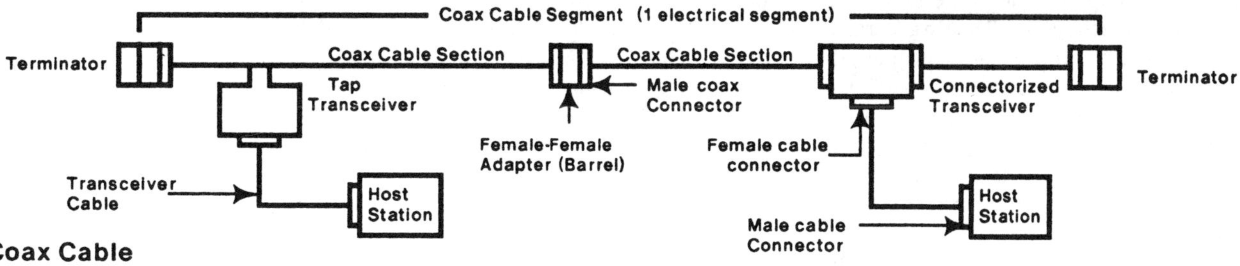

Coax Cable

Impedance: 50 ohms ± 2 ohms (Mil Std. C17-E). This impedance variation includes batch-to-batch variations. Periodic variations in impedance of up to ± 3 ohms are permitted along a single piece of cable.

Cable Loss: The maximum loss from one end of a cable segment to the other end is 8.5 db at 10 MHz (equivalent to ~500 meters of low loss cable).

Shielding: The physical channel hardware must operate in an ambient field of 2 volts per meter from 10 KHz to 30 MHz and 5 V/meter from 30 MHz to 1 GHz. The shield has a transfer impedance of less than 1 milliohm per meter over the frequency range of 0.1 MHz to 20 MHz (exact value is a function of frequency).

Ground Connections: The coax cable shield shall not be connected to any building or AC ground along its length. If for safety reasons a ground connection of the shield is necessary, it must be in only one place.

Physical Dimensions: This specifies the dimensions of a cable which can be used with the *standard tap*. Other cables may also be used, if they are not to be used with a tap-type transceiver (such as use with connectorized transceivers, or as a section between sections to which standard taps are connected).

Center Conductor:	0.0855" diameter solid tinned copper
Core Material:	Foam polyethylene or foam teflon FEP
Core O.D.:	0.242 " minimum
Shield:	0.326" maximum shield O.D. (>90% coverage for outer braid shield)
Jacket:	PVC or teflon FEP
Jacket O.D.:	0.405"

Coax Connectors and Terminators

Coax cables must be terminated with male N-series connectors, and cable sections will be joined with female-female adapters. Connector shells shall be insulated such that the coax shield is protected from contact to building grounds. A sleeve or boot is acceptable. Cable segments should be terminated with a female N-series connector (can be made up of a barrel connector and a male terminator) having an impedance of 50 ohms ± 1%, and able to dissipate 1 watt. The outside surface of the terminator should also be insulated.

Transceiver

CONNECTION RULES

Up to 100 transceivers may be placed on a cable segment no closer together than 2.5 meters. Following this placement rule reduces to a very low (but not zero) probability the chance that objectionable standing waves will result.

COAX CABLE INTERFACE

Input Impedance: The resistive component of the impedance must be greater then 50 Kohms. The total capacitance must be less than 4 picofarads.

Nominal Transmit Level: The important parameter is average DC level with 50% duty cycle waveform input. It must be -1.025 V (41 mA) nominal with a range of -0.9 V to -1.2 V (36 to 48 mA). The peak-to-peak AC waveform must be centered on the average DC level and its value can range from 1.4 V P-P to twice the average DC level. The voltage must never go positive on the coax. The quiescent state of the coax is logic high (0 V). Voltage measurements are made on the coax near the transceiver with the shield as reference. Positive current is current flowing out of the center conductor of the coax.

Rise and Fall Time: 25 nSec ± 5 nSec with a maximum of 1 nSec difference between rise time and fall time in a given unit. The intent is that dV/dt should not significantly exceed that present in a 10 MHz sine wave of same peak-to-peak amplitude.

Signal Symmetry: Asymmetry on output should not exceed 2 nSec for a 50-50 square wave input to either transmit or receive section of transceiver.

TRANSCEIVER CABLE INTERFACE

Signal Pairs: Both transceiver and station shall drive and present at the receiving end a 78 ohm balanced load. The differential signal voltage shall be 0.7 volts nominal peak with a common mode voltage between 0 and +5 volts using power return as reference. (This amounts to shifted ECL levels operating between Gnd and +5 volts. A 10116 with suitable pulldown resistor may be used). The quiescent state of a line corresponds to logic high, which occurs when the + line is more positive than the - line of a pair.

Collision Signal: The active state of this line is a 10 MHz waveform and its quiescent state is logic high. It is active if the transceiver is transmitting and another transmission is detected, or if two or more other stations are transmitting, independent of the state of the local transmit signal.

Power: +11.4 volts to +16 volts DC at controller. Maximum current available to transceiver is 0.5 ampere. Actual voltage at transceiver is determined by the interface cable resistance (max 4 ohms loop resistance) and current drain.

ISOLATION

The impedance between the coax connection and the transceiver cable connection must exceed 250 Kohms at 60 Hz and withstand 250 VRMS at 60 Hz.

Transceiver Cable and Connectors

Maximum signal loss = 3 db @ 10 MHz. (equivalent to ~50 meters of either 20 or 22 AWG twisted pair).

Transceiver Cable Connector Pin Assignment

Pin	Signal	Pin	Signal
1.	Shield*		
2.	Collision +	9.	Collision -
3.	Transmit +	10.	Transmit -
4.	Reserved	11.	Reserved
5.	Receive +	12.	Receive -
6.	Power Return	13.	+ Power
7.	Reserved	14.	Reserved
8.	Reserved	15.	Reserved

*Shield must be terminated to connector shell.

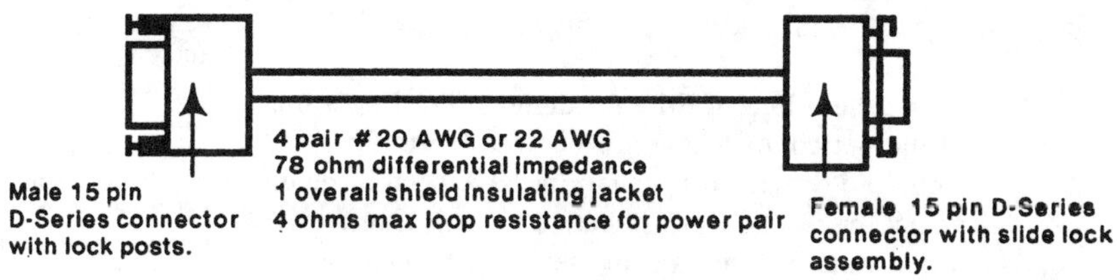

Transmission system. The transmission system includes all the components used to establish a communications path among the controllers. In general, this includes a suitable broadcast transmission medium, the appropriate transmitting and receiving devices—transceivers—and, optionally, repeaters to extend the range of the medium. The protocol for managing access to the transmission system is implemented in the controller; the transmission system does not attempt to interpret any of the bits transmitted on the channel.

The broadcast transmission medium contains those components that provide a physical communication path. In the case of coaxial cable, this includes the cable plus any essential hardware—connectors, terminators, and taps.

Transceivers contain the necessary electronics to transmit and receive signals on the channel and recognize the presence of a signal when another station transmits. They also recognize a collision that takes place when two or more stations transmit simultaneously.

Repeaters are used to extend the length of the transmission system beyond the physical limits imposed by the transmission medium. A repeater uses two transceivers to connect to two different Ethernet segments and combines them into one logical channel, amplifying and regenerating signals as they pass through in either direction.[15] Repeaters are transparent to the rest of the system, and stations on different segments can still collide. Thus, the repeater must propagate a collision detected on one segment through to the other segment, and it must do so without becoming unstable. A repeater makes an Ethernet channel longer and as a result increases the maximum propagation delay of the system, meaning delay through the repeater and propagation delay through the additional segments. To avoid multipath interference in an Ethernet installation, there must be only one path between any two stations through the network. (The higher level internetwork architecture can support alternate paths between stations through different communications channels.)

Controller-to-transmission-system interface. One of the major interfaces in an Ethernet system is the point at which the controller in a station connects to the transmission system. The controller does much of the work in managing the communications process, so this is a fairly simple interface. It includes paths for data going to and from the transmission system. The data received can be used by the controller to sense carrier, but the transmission system normally includes a medium-specific mechanism for detecting collisions on the channel; this must also be communicated through the interface to the controller. It is possible to power a transceiver from a separate power source, but power is usually taken from the controller interface. In most transmission systems, the connection from the controller is made to a transceiver, and this interface is called the transceiver cable interface.

Two generations of Ethernet designs. The Experimental Ethernet circa 1972 confirmed the feasibility of the design, and dozens of installations have been in regular use since then. A typical installation supports hundreds of stations and a wide-ranging set of applications: file transfer, mail distribution, document printing, terminal access to timesharing systems, data-base access, copying disks, multimachine programs, and more. Stations include the Alto workstation,[16] the Dorado (an internal research machine),[17] the Digital Equipment PDP-11, and the Data General Nova. The system has been the subject of extensive performance measurements confirming its predicted behavior.[12,13]

Based upon that experience, a second-generation system was designed at Xerox in the late 1970's. That effort subsequently led to the joint development of the Ethernet Specification. Stations built by Xerox for this network include the Xerox 860, the Xerox 8000 Network System Processor, and the Xerox 1100 Scientific Information Processor (the "Dolphin").

The two systems are very similar: they both use coaxial cable, Manchester signal encoding, and CSMA/CD with dynamic control. Some changes were made based on experience with the experimental system or in an effort to enhance the characteristics of the network. Some of the differences between the systems are summarized in Table 1.

An "Ethernet Technical Summary," which brings together the important features of Version 1 of the joint specification on two pages, is included for reference (pp. 14-15). (In building a compatible device or component, the full Ethernet Specification[5] remains the controlling document. In describing the Ethernet Specification, this article corresponds to Version 1.0; Version 2.0, including extensions and some minor revisions, will be completed later this year.)

Figure 2 is a photograph of some typical components from the Experimental Ethernet, including a transceiver and tap, transceiver cable, and an Alto controller board. Figure 3 is a photograph of similar components based on the Ethernet Specification. Note that both controller boards have been implemented with standard MSI circuits.

Transmission system design

A number of design issues and trade-offs emerged in the development of the Ethernet transmission system, and several lessons were learned from that experience.

Coaxial cable subsystem. In addition to having favorable signaling characteristics and the ability to handle multimegabit transmission rates, a single coaxial

Table 1.
Comparison of Ethernet systems.

	Experimental Ethernet	Ethernet Specification
Data rate	2.94M bps	10M bps
Maximum end-to-end length	1 km	2.5 km
Maximum segment length	1 km	500 m
Encoding	Manchester	Manchester
Coax cable impedance	75 ohms	50 ohms
Coax cable signal levels	0 to +3V	0 to −2V
Transceiver cable connectors	25- and 15-pin D series	15-pin D series
Length of preamble	1 bit	64 bits
Length of CRC	16 bits	32 bits
Length of address fields	8 bits	48 bits

cable can support communication among many different stations. The mechanical aspects of coaxial cable make it feasible to tap in at any point without severing the cable or producing excessive RF leakage; such considerations relating to installation, maintenance, and reconfigurability are important aspects in any local network design.

There are reflections and attenuation in a cable, however, and these combine to impose some limits on the system design. Engineering the shared channel entails trade-offs involving the data rate on the cable, the length of the cable, electrical characteristics of the transceiver, and the number of stations. For example, it is possible to operate at very high data rates over short distances, but the rate must be reduced to support a greater maximum length. Also, if each transceiver introduces significant reflections, it may be necessary to limit the placement and possibly the number of transceivers.

The characteristics of the coaxial cable fix the maximum data rate, but the actual clock is generated in the controller. Thus, the station interface and controller must be designed to match the data rates used over the cable. Selection of coaxial cable as the transmission medium has no other direct impact on either the station or the controller.

Cable. The Experimental Ethernet used 75-ohm, RG-11-type foam cable. The Ethernet Specification uses a 50-ohm, solid-center-conductor, double-shield, foam dielectric cable in order to provide some reduction in the magnitude of reflections from insertion capacitance (introduced by tapping into the cable) and to provide better immunity against environmental electromagnetic noise. Belden Number 9880 Ethernet Coax meets the Ethernet Specification.

Terminators and connectors. A small terminator is attached to the cable at each end to provide a termination impedance for the cable equal to its characteristic impedance, thereby eliminating reflection from the ends of the cable. For convenience, the cable can be divided into a number of sections using simple connectors between sections to produce one electrically continuous segment.

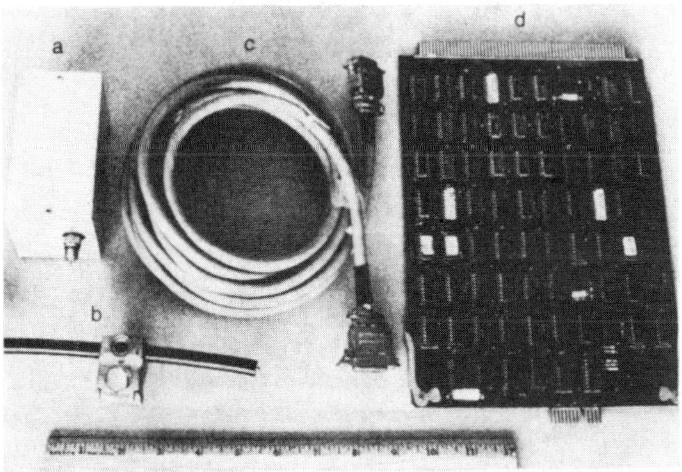

Figure 2. Experimental Ethernet components: (a) transceiver and tap, (b) tap-block, (c) transceiver cable, and (d) Alto controller board.

Segment length and the use of repeaters. The Experimental Ethernet was designed to accommodate a maximum end-to-end length of 1 km, implemented as a single electrically continuous segment. Active repeaters could be used with that system to create complex topologies that would cover a wider area in a building (or complex of buildings) within the end-to-end length limit. With the use of those repeaters, however, the maximum end-to-end length between any two stations was still meant to be approximately 1 km. Thus, the segment length and the maximum end-to-end length were the same, and repeaters were used to provide additional flexibility.

In developing the Ethernet Specification, the strong desire to support a 10M-bps data rate—with reasonable transceiver cost—led to a maximum segment length of 500 meters. We expect that this length will be sufficient to support many installations and applications with a single Ethernet segment. In some cases, however, we recognized a requirement for greater maximum end-to-end length in one network. In these cases, repeaters may now be used not just for additional flexibility but also to extend the overall length of an Ethernet. The Ethernet Specification permits the concatenation of up to three segments; the maximum end-to-end delay between two stations measured as a distance is 2.5 km, including the delay through repeaters containing a point-to-point link.[5]

Taps. Transceivers can connect to a coax cable with the use of a *pressure tap,* borrowed from CATV technology. Such a tap allows connection to the cable without cutting it to insert a connector and avoids the need to interrupt network service while installing a new station. One design uses a tap-block that is clamped on the cable and uses a special tool to penetrate the outer jacket and shield. The tool is removed and the separate tap is screwed into the block. Another design has the tap and tap-block integrated into one unit, with the tap puncturing the cable to make contact with the center conductor as the tap-block is being clamped on.

Alternatively, the cable can be cut and connectors fastened to each piece of cable. This unfortunately disrupts the network during the installation process. After the connectors are installed at the break in the cable, a T-connector can be inserted in between and then connected to a transceiver. Another option, a connectorized transceiver, has two connectors built into it for direct attachment to the cable ends without a T-connector.

Experimental Ethernet installations have used pressure taps where the tap and tap block are separate, as illustrated in Figure 2. Installations conforming to the Ethernet Specification have used all the options. Figure 3 illustrates a connectorized transceiver and a pressure tap with separate tap and tap-block.

Transceiver. The transceiver couples the station to the cable and is the most important part of the transmission system.

The controller-to-transmission-system interface is very simple, and functionally it has not changed between the two Ethernet designs. It performs four functions: (1) transferring transmit data from the controller to the transmission system, (2) transferring receive data from the transmission system to the controller, (3) indicating to the controller that a collision is taking place, and (4) providing power to the transmission system.

It is important that the two ground references in the system—the common coaxial cable shield and the local ground associated with each station—not be tied together, since one local ground typically may differ from another local ground by several volts. Connection of several local grounds to the common cable could cause a large current to flow through the cable's shield, introducing noise and creating a potential safety hazard. For this reason, the cable shield should be grounded in only one place.

It is the transceiver that provides this ground isolation between signals from the controller and signals on the cable. Several isolation techniques are possible: transformer isolation, optical isolation, and capacitive isolation. Transformer isolation provides both power and signal isolation; it has low differential impedance for signals and power, and a high common-mode impedance for isolation. It is also relatively inexpensive to implement. Optical isolators that preserve tight signal symmetry at a competitive price are not readily available. Capacitive coupling is inexpensive and preserves signal symmetry but has poor common-mode rejection. For these reasons transformer isolation is used in Ethernet Specification transceivers. In addition, the mechanical design and installation of the transceiver must preserve this isolation. For example, cable shield connections should not come in contact with a building ground (e.g., a cable tray, conduit, or ceiling hanger).

The transceiver provides a high-impedance connection to the cable in both the power-on and power-off states. In addition, it should protect the network from possible internal circuit failures that could cause it to disrupt the network as a whole. It is also important for the transceiver to withstand transient voltages on the coax between the center conductor and shield. While such voltages should not occur if the coax shield is grounded in only one place, such isolation may not exist during installation.[1]

Negative transmit levels were selected for the Ethernet Specification to permit use of fast and more easily integrated NPN transistors for the output current source. A current source output was chosen over the voltage source used in the Experimental Ethernet to facilitate collision detection.

The key factor affecting the maximum number of transceivers on a segment in the Ethernet Specification is the input bias current for the transceivers. With easily achievable bias currents and collision threshold tolerances, the maximum number was conservatively set at 100 per segment. If the only factors taken into consideration were signal attenuation and reflections, then the number would have been larger.

Controller design

The transmitter and receiver sections of the controller perform signal conversion, encoding and decoding, serial-to-parallel conversion, address recognition, error detection, CSMA/CD channel management, buffering, and packetization. Postponing for now a discussion of buffering and packetization, we will first deal with the various functions that the controller needs to perform and then show how they are coordinated into an effective CSMA/CD channel management policy.

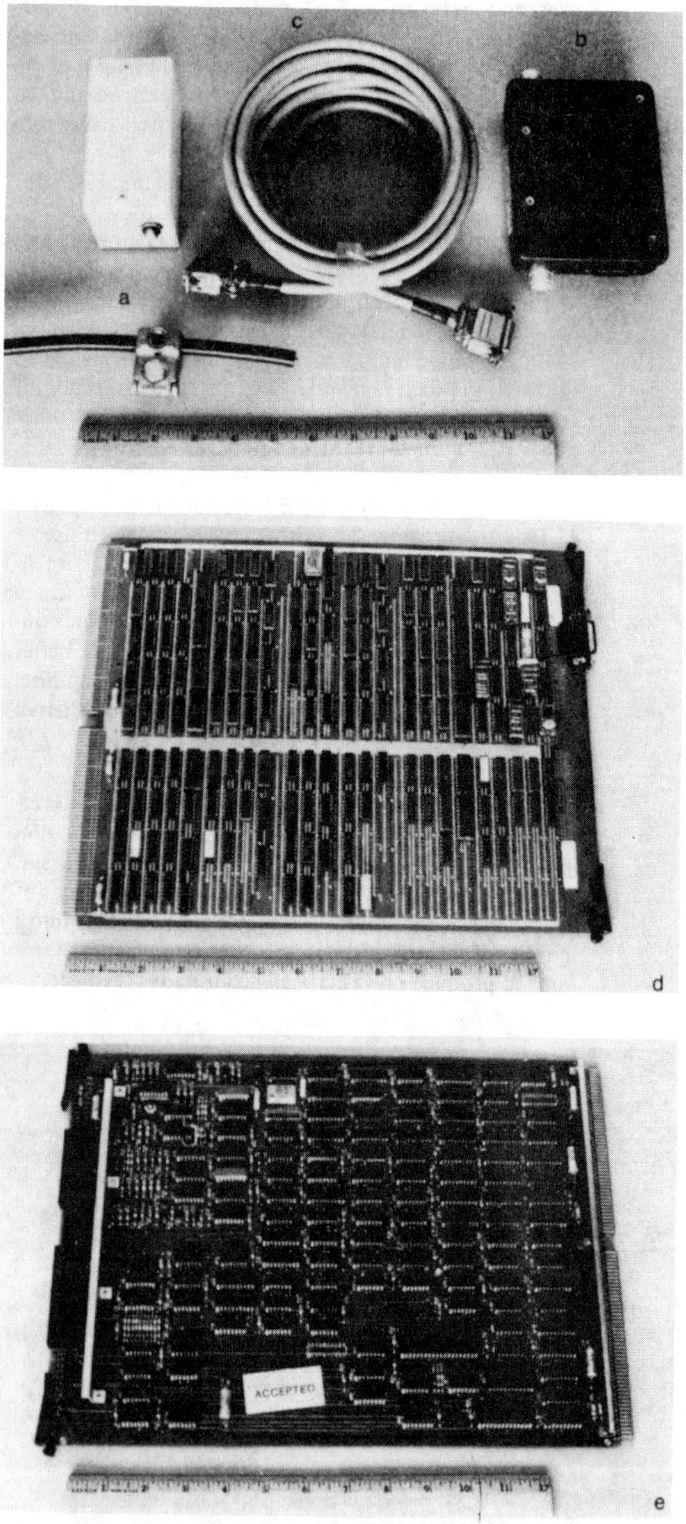

Figure 3. Ethernet Specification components: (a) transceiver, tap, and tap-block, (b) connectorized transceiver, (c) transceiver cable, (d) Dolphin controller board, and (e) Xerox 8000 controller board.

Signaling, data rate, and framing. The transmitter generates the serial bit stream inserted into the transmission system. Clock and data are combined into one signal using a suitable encoding scheme. Because of its simplicity, Manchester encoding was used in the Experimental Ethernet. In Manchester encoding, each bit cell has two parts: the first half of the cell is the complement of the bit value and the second half *is* the bit value. Thus, there is always a transition in the middle of every bit cell, and this is used by the receiver to extract the data.

For the Ethernet Specification, MFM encoding (used in double-density disk recording) was considered, but it was rejected because decoding was more sensitive to phase distortions from the transmission system and required more components to implement. Compensation is not as easy as in the disk situation because a station must receive signals from both nearby and distant stations. Thus, Manchester encoding is retained in the Ethernet Specification.

In the Experimental Ethernet, any data rate in the range of 1M to 5M bps might have been chosen. The particular rate of 2.94M bps was convenient for working with the first Altos. For the Ethernet Specification, we wanted a data rate as high as possible; very high data rates, however, limit the effective length of the system and require more precise electronics. The data rate of 10M bps represents a trade-off among these considerations.

Packet framing on the Ethernet is simple. The presence of a packet is indicated by the presence of carrier, or transitions. In addition, all packets begin with a known pattern of bits called the *preamble*. This is used by the receiver to establish bit synchronization and then to locate the first bit of the packet. The preamble is inserted by the controller at the sending station and stripped off by the controller at the receiving station. Packets may be of variable length, and absence of carrier marks the end of a packet. Hence, there is no need to have framing flags and "bit stuffing" in the packet as in other data-link protocols such as SDLC or HDLC.

The Experimental Ethernet used a one-bit preamble. While this worked very well, we have, on rare occasions, seen some receivers that could not synchronize with this very short preamble.[18] The Ethernet Specification uses a 64-bit preamble to ensure synchronization of phase-lock loop receivers often used at the higher data rate. It is necessary to specify 64 bits to allow for (1) worst-case tolerances on phase-lock loop components, (2) maximum times to reach steady-state conditions through transceivers, and (3) loss of preamble bits owing to squelch on input and output within the transceivers. Note that the presence of repeaters can add up to four extra transceivers between a source and destination.

Additional conventions can be imposed upon the frame structure. Requiring that all packets be a multiple of some particular byte or word size simplifies controller design and provides an additional consistency check. All packets on the Experimental Ethernet are viewed as a sequence of 16-bit words with the most significant bit of each word transmitted first. The Ethernet Specification requires all packets to be an integral number of eight-bit bytes (exclusive of the preamble, of course) with the least significant bit of each byte transmitted first. The order in which the bytes of an Ethernet packet are stored in the memory of a particular station is part of the controller-to-station interface.

Encoding and decoding. The transmitter is responsible for taking a serial bit stream from the station and encoding it into the Manchester format. The receiver is responsible for decoding an incoming signal and converting it into a serial bit stream for the station. The process of encoding is fairly straightforward, but decoding is more difficult and is realized in a *phase decoder*. The known preamble pattern can be used to help initialize the phase decoder, which can employ any of several techniques including an analog timing circuit, a phase-locked loop, or a digital phase decoder (which rapidly samples the input and performs a pattern match). The particular decoding technique selected can be a function of the data rate, since some decoder designs may not run as fast as others. Some phase decoding techniques—particularly the digital one—have the added advantage of being able to recognize certain phase violations as collisions on the transmission medium. This is one way to implement collision detection, although it does not work with all transmission systems.

During transmission a controller must recognize that another station is also transmitting.

The phase decoders used by stations on the Experimental Ethernet included an analog timing circuit in the form of a delay line on the PDP-11, an analog timing circuit in the form of a simple one-shot-based timer on the Alto, and a digital decoder on the Dorado. All stations built by Xerox for the Ethernet Specification use phase-locked loops.

Carrier sense. Recognizing packets passing by is one of the important requirements of the Ethernet access procedure. Although transmission is baseband, we have borrowed the term "sensing carrier" from radio terminology to describe the detection of signals on the channel. Carrier sense is used for two purposes: (1) in the receiver to delimit the beginning and end of the packet, and (2) in the transmitter to tell when it is permissible to send. With the use of Manchester phase encoding, carrier is conveniently indicated by the presence of transitions on the channel. Thus, the basic phase decoding mechanism can produce a signal indicating the presence of carrier independent of the data being extracted. The Ethernet Specification requires a slightly subtle carrier sense technique owing to the possibility of a saturated collision.

Collision detection. The ability to detect collisions and shut down the transmitter promptly is an important feature in minimizing the channel time lost to collisions. The general requirement is that during transmission a controller must recognize that another station is also transmitting. There are two approaches:

(1) *Collision detection in the transmission system.* It is usually possible for the transmission system itself to recognize a collision. This allows any medium-dependent technique to be used and is usually implemented by comparing the injected signal with the received signal. Comparing the transmitted and received signals is best done in the transceiver where there is a known relationship between the two signals. It is the controller, however, which needs to know that a collision is taking place.

(2) *Collision detection in the controller.* Alternatively, the controller itself can recognize a collision by comparing the transmitted signal with the received signal, or the receiver section can attempt to unilaterally recognize collisions, since they often appear as phase violations.

Both generations of Ethernet detect collisions within the transceiver and generate the collision signal in the controller-to-transmission-system interface. Where feasible, this can be supplemented with a collision detection facility in the controller. Collision detection may not be absolutely foolproof. Some transmission schemes can recognize all collisions, but other combinations of transmission scheme and collision detection may not provide 100-percent recognition. For example, the Experimental Ethernet system functions, in principle, as a wired OR. It is remotely possible for one station to transmit while another station sends a packet whose waveform, at the first station, exactly matches the signal sent by the first station; thus, no collision is recognized there. Unfortunately, the intended recipient might be located between the two stations, and the two signals would indeed interfere.

There is another possible scenario in which collision detection breaks down. One station begins transmitting and its signal propagates down the channel. Another station still senses the channel idle, begins to transmit, gets out a bit or two, and then detects a collision. If the colliding station shuts down immediately, it leaves a very small collision moving through the channel. In some approaches (e.g., DC threshold collision detection) this may be attenuated and simply not make it back to the transmitting station to trigger its collision detection circuitry.

The probability of such occurrences is small. Actual measurements in the Experimental Ethernet system indicate that the collision detection mechanism works very well. Yet it is important to remember that an Ethernet system delivers packets only with high probability—not certainty.

To help ensure proper detection of collisions, each transmitter adopts a *collision consensus enforcement* procedure. This makes sure that all other parties to the collision will recognize that a collision has taken place. In spite of its lengthy name, this is a simple procedure. After detecting a collision, a controller transmits a *jam* that every operating transmitter should detect as a collision. In the Experimental Ethernet the jam is a phase violation, while in the Ethernet Specification it is the transmission of four to six bytes of random data.

Another possible collision scenario arises in the context of the Ethernet Specification. It is possible for a collision to involve so many participants that a transceiver is incapable of injecting any more current into the cable. During such a collision, one cannot guarantee that the waveform on the cable will exhibit any transitions. (In the extreme case, it simply sits at a constant DC level equal to the saturation voltage.) This is called a *saturated collision.* In this situation, the simple notion of sensing carrier by detecting transitions would not work anymore. In particular, a station that deferred only when seeing transitions would think the Ether was idle and jump right in, becoming another participant in the collision. Of course, it would immediately detect the collision and back off, but in the extreme case (everyone wanting to transmit), such jumping-in could theoretically cause the saturated collision to snowball and go on for a very long time. While we recognized that this form of instability was highly unlikely to occur in practice, we included a simple enhancement to the carrier sense mechanism in the Ethernet Specification to prevent the problem.

We have focused on collision detection by the transmitter of a packet and have seen that the transmitter may depend on a collision detect signal generated unilaterally by its receiving phase decoder. Can this receiver-based collision detection be used just by a receiver (that is, a station that is not trying to transmit)? A receiver with this capability could immediately abort an input operation and could even generate a jam signal to help ensure that the collision came to a prompt termination. With a reasonable transmitter-based collision detection scheme, however, the collision is recognized by the transmitters and the damaged packet would come to an end very shortly. Receiver-based collision detection could provide an early warning of a collision for use by the receiver, but this is not a necessary function and we have not used it in either generation of Ethernet design.

CRC generation and checking. The transmitter generates a cyclic redundancy check, or CRC, of each transmitted packet and appends it to a packet before transmission. The receiver checks the CRC on packets it receives and strips it off before giving the packet to the station. If the CRC is incorrect, there are two options: either discard the packet or deliver the damaged packet with an appropriate status indicating a CRC error.

While most CRC algorithms are quite good, they are not infallible. There is a small probability that undetected errors may slip through. More importantly, the CRC only protects a packet from the point at which the CRC is generated to the point at which it is checked. Thus, the CRC cannot protect a packet from damage that occurs in parts of the controller, as, for example, in a FIFO in the parallel path to the memory of a station (the DMA), or in the memory itself. If error detection at a higher level is required, then an end-to-end software checksum can be added to the protocol architecture.

In measuring the Experimental Ethernet system, we have seen packets whose CRC was reported as correct but whose software checksum was incorrect.[18] These did not necessarily represent an undetected Ethernet error; they usually resulted from an external malfunction such as a broken interface, a bad CRC checker, or even an incorrect software checksum algorithm.

Selection of the CRC algorithm is guided by several concerns. It should have sufficient strength to properly detect virtually all packet errors. Unfortunately, only a limited set of CRC algorithms are currently implemented in LSI chips. The Experimental Ethernet used a 16-bit CRC, taking advantage of a single-chip CRC generator/checker. The Ethernet Specification provides better error detection by using a 32-bit CRC.[19,20] This function will be easily implemented in an Ethernet chip.

Addressing. The packet format includes both a source and destination address. A local network design can adopt either of two basic addressing structures: *network-specific* station addresses or *unique* station addresses.[21] In the first case, stations are assigned network addresses that must be unique on *their* network but may be the same as the address held by a station on another network. Such addresses are sometimes called *network relative* addresses, since they depend upon the particular network to which the station is attached. In the second case, each station is assigned an address that is unique over all space and time. Such addresses are also known as absolute or universal addresses, drawn from a flat address space.

To permit internetwork communication, the network-specific address of a station must usually be combined with a unique network number in order to produce an unambiguous address at the next level of protocol. On the other hand, there is no need to combine an absolute station address with a unique network number to produce an unambiguous address. However, it is possible that internetwork systems based on flat (internetwork and local network) absolute addresses will include a unique network number at the internetwork layer as a "very strong hint" for the routing machinery.

If network-specific addressing is adopted, Ethernet address fields need only be large enough to accommodate the maximum number of stations that will be connected to one local network. In addition, there must be a suitable administrative procedure for assigning addresses to stations. Some installations will have more than one Ethernet, and if a station is moved from one network to another it may be necessary to change its network-specific address, since its former address may be in use on the new network. This was the approach used on the Experimental Ethernet, with an eight-bit field for the source and the destination addresses.

We anticipate that there will be a large number of stations and many local networks in an internetwork. Thus, the management of network-specific station addresses can represent a severe problem. The use of a flat address space provides for reliable and manageable operation as a system grows, as machines move, and as the overall topology changes. A flat internet address space requires that the address space be large enough to ensure uniqueness while providing adequate room for growth. It is most convenient if the local network can directly support these fairly large address fields.

For these reasons the Ethernet Specification uses 48-bit addresses.[22] Note that these are station addresses and are not associated with a particular network interface or controller. In particular, we believe that higher level routing and addressing procedures are simplified if a station connected to multiple networks has only one identity which is unique over all networks. The address should not be hard-wired into a particular interface or controller but should be able to be set from the station. It may be very useful, however, to allow a station to read a unique station identifier from the controller. The station can then choose whether to return this identifier to the controller as its address.

In addition to single-station addressing, several enhanced addressing modes are also desirable. *Multicast* addressing is a mechanism by which packets may be targeted to more than one destination. This kind of service is particularly valuable in certain kinds of distributed applications, for instance the access and update of distributed data bases, teleconferencing, and the distributed algorithms that are used to manage the network and the internetwork. We believe that multicast should be supported by allowing the destination address to specify either a physical or logical address. A logical address is known as a *multicast ID. Broadcast* is a special case of multicast in which a packet is intended for all active stations. Both generations of Ethernet support broadcast, while only the Ethernet Specification directly supports multicast.

Stations supporting multicast must recognize multicast IDs of interest. Because of the anticipated growth in the use of multicast service, serious consideration should be given to aspects of the station and controller design that reduce the system load required to filter unwanted multicast packets. Broadcast should be used with discretion, since all nodes incur the overhead of processing every broadcast packet.

Controllers capable of accepting packets regardless of destination address provide *promiscuous* address recognition. On such stations one can develop software to observe all of the channel's traffic, construct traffic matrices, perform load analysis, (potentially) perform fault isolation, and debug protocol implementations. While such a station is able to read packets not addressed to it, we expect that sensitive data will be encrypted by higher levels of software.

CSMA/CD channel management

A major portion of the controller is devoted to Ethernet channel management. These conventions specify procedures by which packets are transmitted and received on the multi-access channel.

Transmitter. The transmitter is invoked when the station has a packet to send. If a collision occurs, the controller enforces the collision with a suitable jam, shuts down the transmitter, and schedules a retransmission.

Retransmission policies have two conflicting goals: (1) scheduling a retransmission quickly to get the packet out and maintain use of the channel, and (2) voluntarily backing off to reduce the station's load on a busy channel. Both generations of Ethernet use the *binary exponential back-off algorithm* described below. After some maximum number of collisions the transmitter gives up and reports a suitable error back to the station; both generations of Ethernet give up after 15 collisions.

The binary exponential back-off algorithm is used to calculate the delay before retransmission. After a collision takes place the objective is to obtain delay periods that will reschedule each station at times quantized in steps at least as large as a collision interval. This time quantization is called the *retransmission slot time.* To guarantee quick use of the channel, this slot time should be short; yet to avoid collisions it should be larger than a collision interval. Therefore, the slot time is usually set to be a little longer than the round-trip time of the channel. The real-time delay is the product of some retransmission delay (a positive integer) and the retransmission slot time.

Collisions on the channel can produce collision fragments, which can be eliminated with a fragment filter in the controller.

To minimize the probability of repeated collisions, each retransmission delay is selected as a random number from a particular retransmission interval between zero and some upper limit. In order to control the channel and keep it stable under high load, the interval is doubled with each successive collision, thus extending the range of possible retransmission delays. This algorithm has very short retransmission delays at the beginning but will back off quickly, preventing the channel from becoming overloaded. After some number of back-offs, the retransmission interval becomes large. To avoid undue delays and slow response to improved channel characteristics, the doubling can be stopped at some point, with additional retransmissions still being drawn from this interval, before the transmission is finally aborted. This is referred to as *truncated binary exponential back-off.*

The truncated binary exponential back-off algorithm approximates the ideal algorithm where the probability of transmission of a packet is 1/Q, with Q representing the number of stations attempting to transmit.[23] The retransmission interval is truncated when Q becomes equal to the maximum number of stations.

In the Experimental Ethernet, the very first transmission attempt proceeds with no delay (i.e., the retransmission interval is [0-0]). The retransmission interval is doubled after each of the first eight transmission attempts. Thus, the retransmission delays should be uniformly distributed between 0 and $2^{\min(\text{retransmission attempt, } 8)} - 1$. After the first transmission attempt, the next eight intervals will be [0-1], [0-3], [0-7], [0-15], [0-31], [0-63], [0-127], and [0-255]. The retransmission interval remains at [0-255] on any subsequent attempt, as the maximum number of stations is 256. The Ethernet Specification has the same algorithm with ten intervals, since the network permits up to 1024 stations; the maximum interval is therefore [0-1023]. The back-off algorithm restarts with a zero retransmission interval for the transmission of every new packet.

This particular algorithm was chosen because it has the proper basic behavior and because it allows a very simple implementation. The algorithm is now supported by empirical data verifying the stability of the system under heavy load.[12,13] Additional attempts to explore more sophisticated algorithms resulted in negligible performance improvement.

Receiver. The receiver section of the controller is activated when the carrier appears on the channel. The receiver processes the incoming bit stream in the following manner:

The remaining preamble is first removed. If the bit stream ends before the preamble completes, it is assumed to be the result of a short collision, and the receiver is restarted.

The receiver next determines whether the packet is addressed to it. The controller will accept a packet in any of the following circumstances:

(1) The destination address matches the specific address of the station.
(2) The destination address has the distinguished broadcast destination.
(3) The destination address is a multicast group of which the station is a member.
(4) The station has set the controller in promiscuous mode and receives all packets.

Some controller designs might choose to receive the entire packet before invoking the address recognition procedure. This is feasible but consumes both memory and processing resources in the controller. More typically, address recognition takes place at a fairly low level in the controller, and if the packet is not to be accepted the controller can ignore the rest of it.

Assuming that the address is recognized, the receiver now accepts the entire packet. Before the packet is actually delivered to the station, the CRC is verified and other consistency checks are performed. For example, the packet should end on an appropriate byte or word boundary and be of appropriate minimum length; a minimum packet would have to include at least a destination and source address, a packet type, and a CRC. Collisions on the channel, however, can produce short, damaged packets called collision fragments. It is generally unnecessary to report these errors to the station, since they can be eliminated with a fragment filter in the controller. It is important, however, for the receiver to be restarted promptly after a collision fragment is received, since the sender of the packet may be about to retransmit.

Packet length. One important goal of the Ethernet is data transparency. In principle, this means that the data field of a packet can contain any bit pattern and be of any length, from zero to arbitrarily large. In practice, while it is easy to allow any bit pattern to appear in the data field, there are some practical considerations that suggest imposing upper and lower bounds on its length.

At one extreme, an empty packet (one with a zero-length data field) would consist of just a preamble, source and destination addresses, a type field, and a CRC. The Experimental Ethernet permitted empty packets. However, in some situations it is desirable to enforce a minimum overall packet size by mandating a minimum-length data field, as in the Ethernet Specification. Higher level protocols wishing to transmit shorter packets must then pad out the data field to reach the minimum.

At the other extreme, one could imagine sending many thousands or even millions of bytes in a single packet. There are, however, several factors that tend to limit packet size, including (1) the desire to limit the size of the buffers in the station for sending and receiving packets, (2) similar considerations concerning the packet buffers that are sometimes built into the Ethernet controller itself, and (3) the need to avoid tying up the channel and increasing average channel latency for other stations. Buffer management tends to be the dominant consideration. The maximum requirement for buffers in the station is usually a parameter of higher level software determined by the overall network architecture; it is typically on the order of 500 to 2000 bytes. The size of any packet buffers in the controller, on the other hand, is usually a design parameter of the controller hardware and thus represents a more rigid limitation. To insure compatibility among buffered controllers, the Ethernet Specification mandates a maximum packet length of 1526 bytes (1500 data bytes plus overhead).

Note that the upper and lower bounds on packet length are of more than passing interest, since observed distributions are typically quite bimodal. Packets tend to be either very short (control packets or packets carrying a small amount of data) or maximum length (usually some form of bulk data transfer).[12,13]

The efficiency of an Ethernet system is largely dependent on the size of the packets being sent and can be very high when large packets are used. Measurements have shown total utilization as high as 98 percent. A small quantum of channel capacity is lost whenever there is a collision, but the carrier sense and collision detection mechanisms combine to minimize this loss. Carrier sense reduces the likelihood of a collision, since the acquisition effect renders a given transmission immune to collisions once it has continued for longer than a collision interval. Collision detection limits the duration of a collision to a single collision interval. If packets are long compared with the collision interval, then the network is vulnerable to collisions only a small fraction of the time and total utilization will remain high. If the average packet size is reduced, however, both carrier sense and collision detection become less effective. Ultimately, as the packet size approaches the collision interval, system performance degrades to that of a straight CSMA channel without collision detection. This condition only occurs under a heavy load consisting predominantly of very small packets; with a typical mix of applications this is not a practical problem.

If the packet size is reduced still further until it is less than the collision interval, some new problems appear. Of course, if an empty packet is already longer than the collision interval, as in the Experimental Ethernet, this case cannot arise. As the channel length and/or the data rate are increased, however, the length (in bits) of the collision interval also increases. When it becomes larger than an empty packet, one must decide whether stations are allowed to send tiny packets that are smaller than the collision interval. If so, two more problems arise, one affecting the transmitter and one the receiver.

The transmitter's problem is that it can complete the entire transmission of a tiny packet before network acquisition has occurred. If the packet subsequently experiences a collision farther down the channel, it is too late for the transmitter to detect the collision and promptly schedule a retransmission. In this situation, the probability of a collision has not increased, nor has any additional channel capacity been sacrificed; the problem is simply that the transmitter will occasionally fail to recognize and handle a collision. To deal with such failures, the sender of tiny packets must rely on retransmissions invoked by a higher level protocol and thus suffer reduced throughput and increased delay. This occasional performance reduction is generally not a serious problem, however. Note that only the sender of tiny packets encounters this behavior; there is no unusual impact on other stations sending larger packets.

While occasional collisions should be viewed as a normal part of the CSMA/CD access procedure, line errors should not. One would therefore like to accumulate information about the two classes of events separately.

The receiver's problem with tiny packets concerns its ability to recognize collision fragments by their small size and discard them. If the receiver can assume that packets smaller than the collision interval are collision fragments, it can use this to implement a simple and inexpensive fragment filter. It is important for the receiver to discard collision fragments, both to reduce the processing load at the station and to ensure that it is ready to receive the impending retransmission from the transmitter involved in the collision. The fragment filter approach is automatically valid in a network in which there are no tiny packets, such as the Experimental Ethernet. If tiny packets can occur, however, the receiver cannot reliably distinguish them from collision fragments purely on the basis of size. This means that at least the longer collision fragments must be rejected on the basis of some other error detection mechanism such as the CRC check or a byte or word alignment check. One disadvantage of this approach is that it increases the load on the CRC mechanism, which, while strong, is not infallible. Another problem is that the CRC error condition will now be indicating two kinds of faults: long collisions and genuine line errors. While occasional collisions should be viewed as a normal part of the CSMA/CD access procedure, line errors should not. One would therefore like to accumulate information about the two classes of events separately.

The problems caused by tiny packets are not insurmountable, but they do increase the attractiveness of simply legislating the problem out of existence by forbidding the sending of packets smaller than the collision interval. Thus, in a network whose collision interval is longer than an empty packet, the alternatives are

(1) *Allow tiny packets.* In this case, the transmitter will sometimes fail to detect collisions, requiring retransmis-

sion at a higher level and impacting performance. The receiver can use a partial fragment filter to discard collision fragments shorter than an empty packet, but longer collision fragments will make it through this filter and must be rejected on the basis of other error checks, such as the CRC check, with the resultant jumbling of the error statistics.

(2) *Forbid tiny packets.* In this case, the transmitter can always detect a collision and perform prompt retransmission. The receiver can use a fragment filter to automatically discard all packets shorter than the collision interval. The disadvantage is the imposition of a minimum packet size.

Unlike the Experimental Ethernet, the Ethernet Specification defines a collision interval longer than an empty packet and must therefore choose between these alternatives. The choice is to forbid tiny packets by requiring a minimum data field size of 46 bytes. Since we expect that Ethernet packets will typically contain internetwork packet headers and other overhead, this is not viewed as a significant disadvantage.

Controller-to-station interface design

The properties of the controller-to-station interface can dramatically affect the reliability and efficiency of systems based on Ethernet.

Turning the controller on and off. A well-designed controller must be able to (1) keep the receiver on in order to catch back-to-back packets (those separated by some minimum packet spacing), and (2) receive packets a station transmits to itself. We will now look in detail at these requirements and the techniques for satisfying them.

Keeping the receiver on. The most frequent cause of a lost packet has nothing to do with collision or bad CRCs. Packets are usually missed simply because the receiver was not listening. The Ethernet is an asynchronous device that can present a packet at any time, and it is important that higher level software keep the receiver enabled.

The problem is even more subtle, however, for even when operating normally there can be periods during which the receiver is not listening. There may, for instance, be turnaround times between certain operations when the receiver is left turned off. For example, a receive-to-receive turnaround takes place after one packet is received and before the receiver is again enabled. If the design of the interface, controller, or station software keeps the receiver off for too long, arriving packets can be lost during this turnaround. This occurs most frequently in servers on a network, which may be receiving packets from several sources in rapid succession. If back-to-back packets come down the wire, the second one will be lost in the receive-to-receive turnaround time. The same problem can occur within a normal workstation, for example, if a desired packet immediately follows a broadcast packet; the workstation gets the broadcast but misses the packet specifically addressed to it. Higher level protocol software will presumably recover from these situations, but the performance penalty may be severe.

Similarly, there may be a transmit-to-receive turnaround time when the receiver is deaf. This is determined by how long it takes to enable the receiver after sending a packet. If, for example, a workstation with a slow transmit-to-receive turnaround sends a packet to a well-tuned server, the answer may come back before the receiver is enabled again. No amount of retransmission by higher levels will ever solve this problem!

It is important to minimize the length of any turnaround times when the receiver might be off. There can also be receive-to-transmit and transmit-to-transmit turnaround times, but their impact on performance is not as critical.

Sending to itself. A good diagnostic tool for a network interface is the ability of a station to send packets to itself. While an internal loop-back in the controller provides a partial test, actual transmission and simultaneous reception provide more complete verification.

The Ethernet channel is, in some sense, half duplex: there is normally only one station transmitting at a time. There is a temptation, therefore, to also make the controller half duplex—that is, unable to send and receive at the same time. If possible, however, the design of the interface, controller, and station software should allow a station to send packets to itself.

Recommendations. The Ethernet Specification includes one specific requirement that helps to solve the first of these problems: There must be a minimal interpacket spacing on the cable of 9.6 microseconds. This requirement applies to a transmitter getting ready to send a packet and does not necessarily mean that all receivers conforming to the Specification must receive two adjacent packets. This requirement at least makes it possible to build a controller that can receive adjacent packets on the cable.

Satisfying the two requirements described earlier involves the use of two related features in the design of a controller: full-duplex interfaces and back-to-back receivers. A full-duplex interface allows the receiver and the transmitter to be started independently. A back-to-back receiver has facilities to automatically restart the receiver upon completion of a reception. Limited back-to-back reception can be done with two buffers; the first catches a packet and then the second catches the next without requiring the receiver to wait. Generalized back-to-back reception can be accomplished by using chained I/O commands; the receiver is driven by a list of free input buffers, taking one when needed. These two notions can be combined to build any of the following four interfaces: (1) half-duplex interface, (2) full-duplex interface, (3) half-duplex interface with back-to-back receive, and (4) full-duplex interface with back-to-back receive.

The Experimental Ethernet controller for the Alto is half duplex, runs only in a transmit or receive mode, and must be explicitly started in each mode. The need to explicitly start the receiver (there is no automatic hardware turnaround) means that there may be lengthy turnaround times in which packets may be missed. This approach allows sharing certain components, like the CRC function and the FIFO.

Experimental Ethernet controllers built for the PDP-11 and the Nova are full-duplex interfaces. The transmit-to-receive turnaround has been minimized, but there is no provision for back-to-back packets.

The Ethernet controller for the Xerox 8000 processor is a half-duplex interface with back-to-back receive. Although it cannot send to itself, the transmit-to-receive turnaround delay has been avoided by having the hardware automatically revert to the receive state when a transmission is completed.

The Experimental Ethernet and Ethernet Specification controllers for the Dolphin are full-duplex interfaces with back-to-back receivers. They are the ultimate in interface organization.

Our experience shows that any one of the four alternatives will work. However, we strongly recommend that all interface and controller designs support full-duplex operation and provide for reception of back-to-back packets (chained I/O).

The controller-to-station interface defines the manner in which data received from the cable is stored in memory and, conversely, how data stored in memory is transmitted on the cable.

Buffering. Depending upon the particular data rate of the channel and the characteristics of the station, the controller may have to provide suitable buffering of packets. If the station can keep up with the data rate of the channel, only a small FIFO may be needed to deal with station latency. If the station cannot sustain the channel data rate, it may be necessary to include a full-packet buffer as part of the controller. For this reason, full compatibility across different stations necessitates the specification of a maximum packet length.

If a single-packet buffer is provided in the controller (a buffer that has no marker mechanism to distinguish boundaries between packets), it will generally be impossible to catch back-to-back packets, and in such cases it is preferable to have at least two input buffers.

Packets in memory. The controller-to-station interface defines the manner in which data received from the cable is stored in memory and, conversely, how data stored in memory is transmitted on the cable. There are many ways in which this parallel-to-serial transformation can be defined.[24] The Ethernet Specification defines a packet on the cable to be a sequence of eight-bit bytes, with the least significant bit of each byte transmitted first. Higher level protocols will in most cases, however, define data types that are multiples of eight bits. The parallel-to-serial transformations will be influenced by the programming conventions of the station and by the higher level protocols. Stations with different parallel-to-serial transformations that use the same higher level protocol must make sure that all data types are viewed consistently.

Type field. An Ethernet packet can encapsulate many kinds of client-defined packets. Thus, the packet format includes only a data field, two addresses, and a type field. The type field identifies the special client-level protocol that will interpret the data encapsulated within the packet. The type field is never processed by the Ethernet system itself but can be thought of as an escape, providing a consistent way to specify the interpretation of the rest of the packet.

Low-level system services such as diagnostics, bootstrap, loading, or specialized network management functions can take advantage of the identification provided by this field. In fact, it is possible to use the type field to identify all the different packets in a protocol architecture. In general, however, we recommend that the Ethernet packet encapsulate higher level internetwork packets. Internetwork router stations might concurrently support a number of different internetwork protocols, and the use of the type field allows the internetwork router to encapsulate different kinds of internetwork packets for a local network transmission.[25] The use of a type field in the Ethernet packet is an instance of a principle we apply to all layers in a protocol architecture. A type field is used at each level of the hierarchy to identify the protocol used at the next higher level; it is the bridge between adjacent levels. This results in an architecture that defines a layered tree of protocols.

The Experimental Ethernet design uses a 16-bit type field. This has proved to be a very useful feature and has been carried over into the Ethernet Specification.

Summary and conclusions

We have highlighted a number of important considerations that affect the design of an Ethernet local computer network and have traced the evolution of the system from a research prototype to a multicompany standard by discussing strategies and trade-offs between alternative implementations.

The Ethernet is intended primarily for use in such areas as office automation, distributed data processing, terminal access, and other situations requiring economical connection to a local communication medium carrying bursts of traffic at high peak data rates. Experience with the Experimental Ethernet in building distributed systems that support electronic mail, distributed filing, calendar systems, and other applications has confirmed many of our design goals and decisions.[26-29]

Questions sometimes arise concerning the ways in which the Ethernet design addresses (or chooses not to address) the following considerations: reliability, addressing, priority, encryption, and compatibility. It is important to note that some functions are better left out of the Ethernet itself for implementation at higher levels in the architecture.

All systems should be reliable, and network-based systems are no exception. We believe that reliability must be addessed at each level in the protocol hierarchy; each level should provide only what it can guarantee at a reasonable price. Our model for internetworking is one in which reliability and sequencing are performed using end-to-end transport protocols. Thus, the Ethernet provides a "best effort" datagram service. The Ethernet has been designed to have very good error characteristics, and, without promising to deliver all packets, it will deliver a very large percentage of offered packets without error. It includes error detection procedures but provides no error correction.

We expect internetworks to be very large. Many of the problems in managing them can be simplified by using absolute station addresses that are directly supported within the local network. Thus, address fields in the Ethernet Specification seem to be very generous—well beyond the number of stations that might connect to one local network but meant to efficiently support large internetwork systems.

Our experience indicates that for practically all applications falling into the category "loosely coupled distributed system," the average utilization of the communications network is low. The Ethernet has been designed to have excess bandwidth, not all of which must be utilized. Systems should be engineered to run with a sustained load of no more than 50 percent. As a consequence, the network will generally provide high throughput of data with low delay, and there are no priority levels associated with particular packets. Designers of individual devices, network servers, and higher level protocols are free to develop priority schemes for accessing particular resources.

Protection, security, and access control are all system-wide functions that require a comprehensive strategy. The Ethernet system itself is not designed to provide encryption or other mechanisms for security, since these techniques by themselves do not provide the kind of protection most users require. Security in the form of encryption, where required, is the responsibility of the end-user processes.

Higher level protocols raise their own issues of compatibility over and above those addressed by the Ethernet and other link-level facilities. While the compatibility provided by the Ethernet does not guarantee solutions to higher level compatibility problems, it does provide a context within which such problems can be addressed by avoiding low-level incompatibilities that would make direct communication impossible. We expect to see standards for higher level protocols emerge during the next few years.

Within an overall distributed systems architecture, the two generations of Ethernet systems have proven to be very effective local computer networks. ■

Acknowledgments

Many people have contributed to the success and evolution of the Ethernet local computer network. Bob Metcalfe and David Boggs built the Experimental Ethernet at the Xerox Palo Alto Research Center, and Tat Lam built and supplied the many transceivers. Since then, Ed Taft, Hal Murray, Will Crowther, Roy Ogus, Bob Garner, Ed Markowski, Bob Printis, Bob Belleville, Bill Gunning, and Juan Bulnes have contributed to the design and implementation of the Ethernet. Cooperation among Digital Equipment Corporation, Intel, and Xerox also produced many important contributions to the Ethernet Specification.

References

1. R. C. Crane and E. A. Taft, "Practical Considerations in Ethernet Local Network Design," *Proc. 13th Hawaii Int'l Conf. Systems Sciences,* Jan. 1980, pp. 166-174.
2. R. M. Metcalfe and D. R. Boggs, "Ethernet: Distributed Packet Switching for Local Computer Networks," *Comm. ACM,* 19:7, July 1976, pp. 395-404.
3. R. M. Metcalfe, D. R. Boggs, C. P. Thacker, and B. W. Lampson, "Multipoint Data Communication System with Collision Detection," US Patent No. 4,063,220, Dec. 13, 1977.
4. J. F. Shoch, *"An Annotated Bibliography on Local Computer Networks"* (3rd ed.), Xerox Parc Technical Report SSL-80-2, and IFIP Working Group 6.4 Working Paper 80-12, Apr. 1980.
5. *The Ethernet, A Local Area Network: Data Link Layer and Physical Layer Specifications,* Version 1.0, Digital Equipment Corporation, Intel, Xerox, Sept. 30, 1980.
6. D. R. Boggs, J. F. Shoch, E. A. Taft, and R. M. Metcalfe, "PUP: An Internetwork Architecture," *IEEE Trans. Comm.,* Apr. 1980, pp. 612-624.
7. H. Zimmermann, "OSI Reference Model—The ISO Model of Architecture for Open Systems Interconnection," *IEEE Trans. Comm.,* Apr. 1980, pp. 425-432.
8. Y. K. Dalal, "The Information Outlet: A New Tool for Office Organization," *Proc. On-line Conf. Local Networks and Distributed Office Systems,* London, May 1981, pp. 11-19.
9. V. G. Cerf and P. K. Kirstein, "Issues in Packet-Network Interconnection," *Proc. IEEE,* Vol. 66, No. 11, Nov. 1978, pp. 1386-1408.
10. F. C. Shoute, "Decentralized Control in Computer Communication," Technical Report No. 667, Division of Engineering and Applied Physics, Harvard University, Apr. 1977.
11. R. M. Metcalfe, "Packet Communication," Thesis Harvard University, Project MAC Report MAC TR-114, Massachusetts Institute of Technology, Dec. 1973.
12. J. F. Shoch and J. A. Hupp, "Performance of an Ethernet Local Network—A Preliminary Report," *Local Area Comm. Network Symp.,* Boston, May 1979, pp. 113-125. Revised version *Proc. Compcon Spring 80,* San Francisco, pp. 318-322.
13. J. F. Shoch and J. A. Hupp, "Measured Performance of an Ethernet Local Network," *Comm. ACM,* Vol. 23, No. 12, Dec. 1980, pp. 711-721.
14. E. G. Rawson and R. M. Metcalfe, "Fibernet: Multimode Optical Fibers for Local Computer Networks," *IEEE Trans. Comm.,* July 1978, pp. 983-990.
15. D. R. Boggs and R. M. Metcalfe, Communications network repeater, US Patent No. 4,099,024, July 4, 1978.
16. C. P. Thacker et al., "Alto: A Personal Computer," Xerox Palo Alto Research Center Technical Report CSL-79-11, Aug. 1979.
17. "The Dorado: A High-Performance Personal Computer," Three Reports, Xerox Palo Alto Research Center, CSL-81-1, Jan. 1981.

18. J. F. Shoch, *Local Computer Networks,* McGraw-Hill, in press.

19. J. L. Hammond, J. E. Brown, and S. S. Liu, "Development of a Transmission Error Model and an Error Control Model," Technical Report RADC-TR-75-138, Rome Air Development Center, 1975.

20. R. Bittel, "On Frame Check Sequence (FCS) Generation and Checking," ANSI working paper X3-S34-77-43, 1977.

21. J. F. Shoch, "Internetwork Naming, Addressing, and Routing," *Proc. Compcon Fall 78,* pp. 430-437.

22. Y. K. Dalal and R. S. Printis, "48-bit Internet and Ethernet Host Numbers," *Proc. Seventh Data Comm. Symp.,* Oct. 1981.

23. R. M. Metcalfe, "Steady-State Analysis of a Slotted and Controlled Aloha System with Blocking," *Proc. Sixth Hawaii Conf. System Sciences,* Jan. 1973. Reprinted in *Sigcom Review,* Jan. 1975.

24. D. Cohen, "On Holy Wars and a Plea for Peace," *Computer,* Vol. 14, No. 10, Oct. 1981, pp. 48-54.

25. J. F. Shoch, D. Cohen, and E. A. Taft, "Mutual Encapsulation of Internetwork Protocols," *Computer Networks,* Vol. 5, No. 4, July 1981, pp. 287-301.

26. A. D. Birrell et al., "Grapevine: An Exercise in Distributed Computing," *Comm. ACM,* Vol. 25, No. 4, Apr. 1982, pp. 260-274.

27. H. Sturgis, J. Mitchell, and J. Israel, "Issues in the Design and Use of a Distributed File System," *ACM Operating Systems Rev.,* Vol. 14, No. 3, July 1980, pp. 55-69.

28. D. K. Gifford, "Violet, an Experimental Decentralized System," Xerox Palo Alto Research Center, CSL-79-12, Sept. 1979.

29. J. F. Shoch and J. A. Hupp, "Notes on the 'Worm' Programs—Some Early Experiences with a Distributed Computation," *Comm. ACM,* Vol. 25, No. 3, Mar. 1982, pp. 172-180.

Yogen K. Dalal is manager of services and architecture for office systems in the Office Products Division of Xerox Corporation. He has been with the company in Palo Alto since 1977. His research interests include local computer networks, internetwork protocols, distributed systems architecture, broadcast protocols, and operating systems. He is a member of the ACM and the IEEE. He received the B. Tech. degree in electrical engineering from the Indian Institute of Technology, Bombay, in 1972, and the MS and PhD degrees in electrical engineering and computer science from Stanford University in 1973 and 1977, respectively.

David D. Redell is a staff scientist in the Office Products Division of Xerox Corporation. He was previously on the faculty of the Massachusetts Institute of Technology. His research interests include computer networks, distributed systems, information security, and computer architecture. He received his BA, MS, and PhD degrees in computer science from the University of California at Berkeley.

John F. Shoch is deputy general manager for office systems in the Office Products Division of Xerox Corporation. From 1980 to 1982, he served as assistant to the president of Xerox and director of the corporate policy committee. He joined the research staff at the Xerox Palo Alto Research Center in 1971. His research interests have included local computer networks (such as the Ethernet), internetwork protocols, packet radio, and other aspects of distributed systems. In addition, he has taught at Stanford University, is a member of the ACM and the IEEE, and serves as vice-chairman (US) of IFIP Working Group 6.4 on local computer networks. Shoch received the BA degree in political science and the MS and PhD degrees in computer science from Stanford University.

Ronald C. Crane, a founder of 3Com Corporation in Mountain View, California, now heads advanced engineering for the firm. From 1977 to 1980 he served as a technical staff member and subsequently a consultant to Xerox's Office Products Division in Palo Alto where he was a principal designer of the Digital, Intel, Xerox Ethernet system. His research interests have included adaptive topology packet networks, digital broadcasting systems (Digicast), and baseband transmission systems. He is a member of the ACM and IEEE. He received the BS degree in electrical engineering from the Massachusetts Institute of Technology in 1972 and the MS degree in electrical engineering from Stanford University in 1974.

WHY A RING?*

Jerome H. Saltzer and David D. Clark

Massachusetts Institute of Technology
Laboratory for Computer Science
Cambridge, Massachusetts

Kenneth T. Pogran

Bolt Beranek and Newman Inc.
Cambridge, Massachusetts

Abstract

In a world increasingly populated with Ethernets and Ethernet-like nets a few sites continue to experiment with rings of active repeaters for local data communication. This paper explores some of the engineering problems involved in designing a ring that has no central control, and then compared the M.I.T.-designed ring with the Ethernet on a variety of operational and subtle technical grounds, on each of which the ring may possess important or interesting advantages.

Introduction

The M.I.T. Laboratory for Computer Science has, for more than two years, been operating a prototype one Mbit/sec. distributed control ring network of eight nodes. The laboratory is engaged in checkout of an improved, simpler, ten Mbit/sec. ring design, intended to link groups of up to 250 desktop computers. Since there are already several competing local network designs that use contention-controlled broadcast on passive coaxial cable rather than a repeater ring, we are often asked why one should bother to develop an alternative approach--the contention-controlled broadcast technology is field proven, its properties are well understood and adequate for the application. In addition, there are at least three difficult engineering problems involved in the design of a distributed control ring network: reliability of the repeater string, distributed initialization and recovery, and closed-loop clock coordination. Of course the ring approach has also been field-proven[1,2,3], but in no case in a form that settles all the questions. Upon analysis, it appears that an apparent preference for contention-controlled broadcast networks in the United States but for ring networks in Europe has been more determined by accidental historical precedents than by persuasive technical arguments.

This paper examines briefly nine technical differences between the contention-controlled broadcast approach and the ring, and argues that it seems interesting to pursue the ring technology. It assumes that the reader is familiar with the basic concepts involved in local networks and in ring networks as described in published papers[4,5]. There are a wide variety of possible designs both for rings and for passive proadcast networks, and these design choices have both gross and subtle differences that affect comparisons. To be specific, the kind of ring network assumed in this discussion is a token-controlled system in which the originator removes his own message and in which there is no central control or monitor station. Both the one and ten Mbit/sec. rings at M.I.T. mentioned earlier are of this design. For contrast, the Ethernet local communication network developed by the Xerox Palo Alto Research Center will be used, with the understanding that it is typical of a contention-controlled passive coaxial cable broadcast design[6,7,8]. The Mitre Corporation MITREBUS[9], another contention-controlled broadcast design, is mentioned for comparison also.

These specific designs are chosen because they reflect two distinct and important design choices:

- access control by contention (Ethernet) versus token (ring), and

- communication by broadcast (Ethernet) versus point-to-point (ring).

As shall be seen, the nine technical differences discussed all flow directly from these two choices. This point should be kept in mind when applying the observations to other local network designs that use a different combination of design choices, for example, a token-controlled broadcast net or a contention-controlled ring.

*Authors' addresses: J.H. Saltzer and D.D. Clark, M.I.T. Laboratory for Computer Science, 545 Technology Square, Cambridge, Mass. 02139. K.T. Pogran, Bolt Beranek and Newman Inc., 50 Moulton Street, Cambridge, Mass. 02138. Please address correspondence to J. H. Saltzer, telephone (617) 253-6016.

This research was supported by the Advanced Research Projects Agency of the Department of Defense and was monitored by the Office of Naval Research under contract number N00014-75-C-0661.

Reprinted from *The Proceedings of the Seventh Data Communications Symposium*, 1981, pages 211-217.

Ring design problems

The three difficult ring engineering problems referred to above appear to have elegant and straightforward solutions, and one of the reasons for trying out ring technology in the field is to verify that these solutions work well in practice. Other papers[5,10,11,12] explore these three engineering problems and considerations in their solution in some depth, so they are only summarized here:

1. Reliability of the repeater string. The basic problem here is that a failure in any one repeater can disrupt the entire local network and, if one strings together one hundred or more active repeaters, one would expect to end up with a very fragile system. Further, locating the troublesome repeater could require perambulation of the entire network. Very reliable repeaters and careful system engineering seem to be needed at first glance. However, a simpler solution to these problems is to arrange the transmission links between successive nodes so that each internode link loops through a central point, a wire center. At the wire center, bypass relays that are energized remotely by the network stations can do a majority of the reconfiguration operations automatically. The resulting configuration, a star-shaped ring, creates a centralized location for maintenance and reconfiguration and at the same time provides reliability, without compromising the distributed nature of the ring control. Further, clusters of nodes can be connected by nearby wire centers that are in turn connected hierarchically through more distant wire centers. This approach reduces the wiring cost that one might anticipate in a star topology.

2. Distributed initialization and recovery. To avoid designating some one ring node as special (and thereby making ring operation depend on that node's continued good health) some algorithm is required whereby all active repeaters can quickly and simply agree upon the need for initialization and recovery, and not fall all over one another trying to accomplish it. A suitable strategy can be devised using two ideas developed for passive broadcast networks: First, when any node detects ring trouble, it jams (as in Ethernet) the ring net with a characteristic signal that insures agreement among all participants. Second, after jamming, a virtual token, whose time of arrival is based on the station's address (as in the Chaosnet[13],) determines which single station actually performs network reinitialization.

3. Closed-loop clock coordination. A subtle problem of distributed agreement on data transmission rate arises in a ring. The issue is that not only must the collection of repeaters agree on a common clock rate, but that clock rate must result in an integral number of bit times of delay when traversing the closed ring. Fortunately, there appear to be at least three different, workable ways of achieving this agreement. The simplest of these ways is to open the ring when originating a message, and thereby allow all non-originating repeaters simply to track the originator. An intermediate approach based on inserting time wedges in the clock at repeaters that fall behind the fastest repeater was used in the prototype ring[5]. The most sophisticated approach is to have a phase-locked-loop in each repeater tracking its preceding neighbor, and design loop filters so that the resulting ring of PLL's is stable[12].

These three problems are, of course, problems only until they are solved. Since good solutions appear to be in hand, the following discussion assumes that the ring design being compared with the Ethernet includes the star topology, automatic decentralized reinitialization, and any one of the clock coordination techniques.

Nine points of comparison of rings with Ethernets

1. The contention-controlled broadcast net has a significant analog engineering component, while the ring net is almost entirely a digital design. This difference looks very interesting to explore, because of its possible ramifications in ability to exploit rapidly advancing progress in digital technology and VLSI. To understand this difference, consider that a broadcast net transmitter's signal must be receivable by all receivers on the cable. These receivers are at varying distances from the transmitter and therefore will experience different attenuations and echoes. Similarly each receiver must be able to hear every transmitter. In all, there are $N(N-1)$ such combinations that must work in an N-node network, and the transceiver system must be designed conservatively enough that the worst possible receiver-transmitter placement combination (in terms of echo buildup and attenuation) must deliver acceptable performance. The analog noise level contributed by idle transmitters grows with the number of nodes, though probably less than linearly. Finally, in order for a "listen-while-transmit" collision detection feature of an Ethernet to work, an active transceiver must be able to notice that it is not the only active one. Thus the receiver part must be capable of detecting the weakest other transmitter during its own transmissions and distinguishing that other transmitter from its own transmitter's echoes. This set of requirements is not impossible to meet, but very careful analog transmission system engineering is needed, and the resulting design has many analog components. In contrast, the analog part of a ring network repeater is more tractable. Any given transmitter sends a signal down a private line to only one receiver. The receiver has one echo environment and one received signal level to cope with. Thus, a relatively simple line driver/line receiver combination can suffice. For this reason, the passive broadcast technology is straining to reach a 10 Mbit/sec. signalling rate with a 200 node net, while the ring can operate at

that speed and scale with a fairly elementary analog system.

While engineering in the analog domain is substantially easier in the ring, in the digital domain the situation reverses. Note that two of the three difficult ring engineering problems discussed earlier (initialization and clock coordination) can be handled by techniques that are mostly digital. This difference in the character of the hard engineering problems of the two technologies offers an exploitation opportunity that may favor the ring network. The recent and projected waves of technology improvement have benefited the digital domain more than the analog, mostly because it is easy to see how to solve problems systematically by increasing digital component count; it often seems to be harder to take systematic advantage of increased numbers of components in the analog domain. A less compelling, but still interesting, argument is that because of the simple analog transmission system required by the ring, even the line drivers and receivers might be integrable into a future VLSI implementation; it is probably harder to do this integration for the more complex analog transceiver technology of the passive broadcast net.

2. A problem with the Ethernet that is closely related to its analog domain engineering emphasis lies in ground reference and power supply. It is important that a local network not impose a uniform ground reference on all attached hosts. If it did, the network risks carrying large ground currents or creating ground loops. In order to obtain maximum transceiver performance, all present Ethernet designs seem to require direct coupling of an active component (e.g., the base of a transistor) to the cable, with consequent need for a power supply whose ground reference is the cable shield. To avoid adding a central, shared component, a per-node, isolated power supply for the active part of the transceiver electronics seems to be a requirement of an Ethernet. The ring, on the other hand, can be designed to deliver enough energy that ground isolation can be achieved in the signal path ahead of the first active component of the receiver. (The prototype M.I.T. ring used optical isolators for this purpose; the ten Mbit/sec. ring uses pulse transformers.) Finally, because sensitive, active electronic components are directly attached to the Ethernet coaxial cable conductors, transient suppression (e.g., from lightning) requires that the coaxial cable ground shield system be grounded at no more than one point. To enforce this requirement and maintain the ability to divide a long cable into sections for trouble shooting, the Ethernet specification[8] requires that there be <u>no</u> ground for the cable. Such a floating conductive system becomes a severe personnel hazard in the case in which it accidentally becomes shorted to an electric power conductor.

3. Electromagnetic compatibility between the net and other physically adjacent electrical equipment is generally easier to engineer with a balanced transmission medium than with an unbalanced one. One of the attractions of the Ethernet is the ease of attaching to it at any point, which ease relies on the use of clamp-on connectors with coaxial cable, an unbalanced medium. If one tried to use a balanced transmission medium for the Ethernet, it would probably become necessary to install ordinary connectors every time a new node is added, and the easy attachment virtue would be compromised. In addition, the Ethernet strategy of listening for collisions depends on the transmitter being off half the time. Collision detection with balanced lines would probably become more complex, since in the most obvious balanced waveform modulation schemes the transmitter runs continuously rather than for half of each bit time. In contrast, the ring network can use shielded twisted pair and balanced waveform modulation, thereby reducing both radiation to other equipment and susceptibility of the network to noise spikes and electrical interference originating elsewhere. At the same time, the passive star arrangement for a ring captures much of the easy attachment property.

4. An attraction of the passive broadcast net is the intrinsic high reliability that comes from having a minimum number of active components whose failure can disrupt the net. The most important shared component--the coaxial cable--is completely passive. In contrast, the primary objection to a ring network is the operational fragility of a series string of 100 or more repeaters. However, this fragility appears to be easy to overcome by the passive star arrangement of the ring network.

5. Another attraction of the passive broadcast net is that it is exceptionally easy to install--a single cable is routed through the building, near every office or other location in which a network node might be needed. Actual attachment of nodes can be deferred until the node is required, at which time attachment can be accomplished by clamp-on connectors; attachment does not disrupt network operation. However, hand-in-hand with this convenience goes an associated inconvenience, namely that trouble isolation and first-aid repair cannot easily be centralized. Some kinds of failures will require foot-by-foot inspection of the network and each node attachment, involving access to offices and other spaces throughout the building. The passive star configuration of the ring network appears to completely overcome this potential problem. With a passive star, addition of a new station involves running a cable from the office to a nearby wire center, so one might consider wiring a building in advance by running one such cable per office. Then, installation of a station is done by attaching a connector and plugging it in. No extra disruption is associated with this kind of installation. Further, many buildings are already designed with cable trays and wire ducts in place that emanate from a wire center, because both telephone and electric power wiring practice also call for wire centers. Field experience with both kinds of networks is really required to determine which is more effective on day-to-day operational issues such as this and the previous two. Such experience is being reported for the Ethernet[7,14]; corresponding experience with a ring is not yet so extensive.

6. There is an intrinsic limitation in the contention-controlled broadcast net approach in its ability to make effective use of higher speed transmission media, such as optical fibers. In a contention network, at the beginning of each packet transmission there is a period when there is a risk of collision: this period is proportional to the length of the transmission medium, since the packet is exposed to collision until its first bit propagates to the farthest transceiver. The duration of this exposure is thus fixed by the physical configuration. As the transmission speed increases, the time required to transmit an average size packet decreases, until the packet transmission time becomes as short as the cable propagation time. At that point, most of the advantage of carrier sense is lost and the system becomes an ordinary Aloha channel, with an intrinsic data capacity limit of about 18% of the channel capacity[6,15]. For a 1 Km. coaxial cable, the end-to-end propagation time is typically 4500 nsec. This is comparable to the time required to transmit a 60-octet packet at 100 Mbit/sec. Thus an attempt to build a 100 Mbit/sec. passive broadcast net might result in an effective performance limit near 20 Mbit/sec. The ring, because it does not use a contention access scheme, does not have any corresponding limiting effect, and thus can be scaled up directly to a 100 Mbit/sec. configuration. (The importance of this limitation in contention-controlled nets depends critically on the distribution of packet sizes. If most packets are 6000, rather than 60, octets in length the limitation would be inconsequential at a 100 Mbit/sec. rate. One can make a good argument that any application that requires a 100 Mbit/sec. transmission rate for 100 nodes will not typically generate small packets because of per-packet software overhead, so there should be an opportunity to avoid the Aloha phenomenon. Until some more experience is gained with applications that really require this bandwidth, the questions will remain unanswered. Experience with the Hyperchannel[16] network, which is a contention-controlled net that runs at 50 Mbit/sec., may be useful in this regard.

7. A second limitation of the passive broadcast net approach that appears to require some considerable ingenuity to overcome is to take advantage of fiber optic technology. This technology offers the attraction of very high speed, excellent electromagnetic compatibility, avoidance of lightning and ground reference problems, and (predicted) low cost. However, the problems of turning optical fiber into a broadcast medium are formidable. One must invent a satisfactory technique for tapping an optical fiber and detecting a signal without diverting too much optical energy or else the system will not scale up very well in number of nodes. Yet the same tap must allow introducing a new signal without loss. (Some recent experiments with many-tailed star couplers are promising, but that approach gives up the single cable routed by every office that is one of the chief attractions of the Ethernet[17].) In contrast, since a ring network uses one-way, point-to-point transmission, replacing the wire links in a ring network with fiber optic links is quite straightforward. The Cambridge ring has operated for some time with one fiber optic link[1].

8. Because it uses repeaters, a ring network can with ease span much greater physical distances than can the passive broadcast net. The passive broadcast net can also be augmented with repeaters, as in the new Ethernet standard and the Mitrebus. However, use of contention control, which makes the propagation time between the two most widely separated stations a critical, performance-limiting parameter, limits the distance that one can extend a broadcast net even with repeaters. Since in order to arrange a ring to span a longer distance at least parts of it must be "stretched out" rather than fully looped back in a passive star, one trades away some maintenance ease to gain a greater geographical span. Thus the contention-controlled broadcast net trades both performance and maintenance ease with increased geographical coverage, while the ring trades only maintenance ease. The distance spanning effect is quite substantial, for two reasons. First, when using comparably expensive driver, receiver, and cable technology, a single ring link, being point-to-point rather than broadcast, can be slightly longer than a single broadcast cable segment. Second, when successive ring links are placed in tandem the maximum geographical span is multiplied by half the number of stations--perhaps a factor of 100. Thus for an area such as a campus of a hundred buildings and building wings, a ring may have a considerable advantage over a passive broadcast network.

9. A final, practical question to consider is whether or not there might be anything about a ring network that intrinsically requires either more or less complex logic than a contention-controlled broadcast network. Only examination of in-field designs can answer this question, but such examination is trickier than one might expect, because every local net designer seems to have chosen a different function packaging approach. Thus one design includes packet buffers, another doesn't but includes a direct memory access channel for some popular computer bus, the next assumes that part of the network control will be handled by software rather than hardware. To compare more carefully, implementations for the experimental Ethernet, the M.I.T. Artificial Intelligence Laboratory Chaosnet, and the ten Mbit/sec. ring network were compared by measuring the board area required to hold the implementation of the network control logic up to but not including speed-matching buffers. All three were found to require something less than 50 square inches of densely packed wire-wrap card. Casual observation of the implementation of a Mitrebus interface and a Prime Computer ring net controller suggested that these two network designs were similar in complexity to the others.

The conclusion is that there is no significant intrinsic difference in the complexity of implementation of the two approaches, and a straightforward TTL implementation of a ring network should require about the same amount of hardware as an equivalent function contention-controlled broadcast net operating at the same speed. (This comparison of hardware complexity is distinct from that of point one, earlier, which raised some questions about the ease of VLSI implementation of the analog components of the broadcast network.)

Non-determinism

A sometimes-mentioned point of difference between token control as used in the ring and contention control as used in the Ethernet is the ability to predict the maximum time one must wait to obtain access. Superficially, it appears that a carefully-designed token control net could have an advantage here. If one limits the maximum message length, and insists that the token must be passed along after sending one message, then every network user has a guarantee that the token makes steady progress, and one can calculate with confidence the maximum length of time one might have to wait for access. In contrast, in the case of the Ethernet, since every attempt to transmit could in principle produce a collision, there is a worrisome possibility that one could go on engaging in collisions indefinitely. Such a possibility would be of concern, for example, in a distributed real-time process control application in which a deadline might be missed. This property is sometimes summarized by saying that the Ethernet is "non-deterministic".

That analysis is, however, superficial, because it omits a real-world consideration that intervenes to make the contention network and the token network much more similar than one might expect. In any network, no matter how access is controlled, there is a finite probability of transmission error. In a token-controlled ring, an error may destroy the token at the worst possible time, or when a station nearing a deadline finally receives the token the message it sends may be damaged by an error, and retransmission may be needed. Thus the prospective recipient of the message can find that the deadline has been missed; the token ring is non-deterministic, too. One must accept the fact that the real-world provides no guarantees, only a probability of success. Once that principle is clear, one can specify a required success probability and choose system parameters accordingly. However, this approach applies equally well to the token and contention networks. Given a required probability of successfully meeting a deadline, one can calculate immediately a loading level for an Ethernet that meets the deadline with more than the required probability in the face of contention. The rest of the system must, of course, be designed to insure that the intended Ethernet load is not exceeded, either absolutely or else with a probability consistent with the system success goal.

The numbers that result can be quite practical. For example, in a 50-node ring, one must plan to wait for as many as 50 maximum length messages to be sent until the token arrives. The probability that an Ethernet is busy for n or more successive message intervals when it is loaded to a fraction of its capacity r (r<1, exponential message arrivals, fixed message length) is approximately r\n. For r = 0.5 (a 50% loaded network) the probability that a wait of more the 50 message intervals occurs is thus less than about 10\-16, probably 5 orders of magnitude smaller than the probability of a transmission error that calls for retry or reinitialization.

In practice there is one more level of subtlety to this line of argument. Suppose we have designed both an Ethernet and a ringnet for a time-critical application, and have determined the error rates on both nets and the maximum allowed load on the Ethernet so that the chance of missing the deadline is acceptably small. In the case of a token-controlled ring, if any host attempts to present an abnormal traffic load to the network, the token-control mechanism effectively throttles the runaway host, and other network participants still have their usual chance of meeting their deadlines. In the contention-controlled Ethernet, an abnormally active host can increase the probability of contention and perhaps thereby lower the chance of meeting deadlines. This difference represents a genuine advantage of the token ring. But if the system is correctly designed, this effect must be second order, when one considers that any single host is normally throttled internally by software overhead anyway. Although one might hypothesize a conspiracy of several runaway nodes, such a hypothesis takes us into the realm of predictably low-probability events. (One can also argue about whether incorrectly designed Ethernets fail more spectacularly than incorrectly designed token rings, but that somehow seems to be an uninteresting discussion.)

Thus it appears to us that the non-determinism of the contention system is an unimportant difference with the token approach.

Broadband

A related idea is that of using radio frequency broadcast signalling on coaxial cable ("Broadband") as, for example, the Mitre Corporation has done[9]. In these systems, both broadcast and contention control of access are used, so this scheme boils down to translating an Ethernet from baseband to some carrier frequency. It thus has most of the same attractions and disadvantages of the Ethernet, but with three extra appeals:

a) The same coaxial cable can also carry other radio frequency signals with different purposes, for example cable television. Thus bringing the data network into an office would automatically bring the CATV system there, too.

b) The coaxial cable is used in a frequency range where there is less dispersion (change of propagation velocity with frequency) so a greater bandwidth can be obtained.

c) The cable television industry has developed a useful collection of modestly priced components, including cable attachment hardware and radio frequency linear integrated circuits that one could exploit. In particular, high bandwidth, low delay analog repeaters are available at a modest price; this availability leads to more uniform, higher signal levels. Higher signal levels in turn allow simpler analog design and ground isolation techniques to be used.

The radio frequency signalling approach, however, ends up with the same kind of large analog engineering component as does the Ethernet-type broadcast net, this time in the form of wide-band linear amplifiers, voltage controlled oscillators, filters, modems, and phase-locked loops. Although there are available integrated circuits that help perform those functions, in real applications those circuits must be surrounded by additional analog components---capacitors, resistors, transformers, etc. In exploiting cable television industry developments, one misses the opportunity to exploit what may be even more potent (by reason of volume and potential total integration) economic forces in the digital logic area. Finally, if one tries to make use of the potential for higher bandwidth it turns out that one cannot so easily take advantage of the television industry chips. But if one uses discrete components, the cost climbs substantially.

Apart from these considerations, the broadband network is an example of a contention-controlled broadcast system, so the earlier technical comparisons with the token-controlled ring seem to apply to it also.

Conclusions

Considering these various technical arguments, it appears that one cannot make a clear case for either the contention-controlled broadcast net or the ring technologies. Both approaches have good arguments in their favor, and it is likely that operational issues such as ease of installation, maintenance, and administration will dominate the detailed technical issues. Thus practical experience with 100-node ring networks is really required to establish concrete comparisons of reliability and ease of maintenance and reconfiguration in the field. The answer to the question asked in the opening paragraph is that there seems to be substantial technical interest in continuing to develop ring technology.

A second conclusion concerns the interpretation of standards for local networks, such as the recently announced Ethernet standard of Xerox, Intel, and Digital Equipment Corporation[8]. With the current state of understanding and with substantial technical issues still to be resolved, such standards today can only provide guidance on how to implement a particular technology, not on choice of technology itself. A second standard may be required for ring technology, just as separate standards apply to phonograph records and magnetic tapes. It is possible that one could define a local network interconnection interface standard that is technology-independent although one may anticipate substantial technical arguments about what functions are desirable or feasible in a compatibility interface. (The IEEE Data Link Media Access Committee seems to have started some of these arguments rolling[18].)

Acknowledgements

This paper is a collection of conclusions and thoughts developed in conversations over several years with ring and Ethernet advocates too numerous to identify. Comments on drafts of this paper by Butler Lampson and David Reed sharpened up several of the observations.

References

1. Wilkes, M.V., and Wheeler, D.J., "The Cambridge Digital Communication Ring," Proc. Local Area Comm. Network Symposium, May, 1979, pp. 47-61.

2. Gordon, R.L., et al., "Ringnet: A packet switched local network with decentralized control," 4th Conf. on Local Networks, Minneapolis, October, 1979, pp. 13-19.

3. Okuda, N., Kunikyo, T., and Kaji, T., "Ring Century Bus-an Experimental High Speed Channel for Computer Communications," Proc. Fourth Int. Conf. on Computer Communications, September, 1978, pp. 161-166.

Clark, D.D., Pogran, K.T., and Reed, D.P., "An Introduction to Local Area Networks," Proc. IEEE 66, 11 (November, 1978), pp. 1497-1517.

5. Mockapetris, P.V., et al., "On the Design of Local Network Interfaces," 1977 IFIP Congress Proceedings, pp. 427-430.

6. Metcalfe, R.M., and Boggs, D.R., "Ethernet: Distributed Packet Switching for Local Computer Networks," CACM 19, 7 (July, 1976) pp. 395-404.

7. Crane, R.C., and Taft, E.A., "Practical Considerations in Ethernet Local Network Design," Hawaii Int. Conf. on System Sciences. January, 1980.

8. "The Ethernet," Version 1.0, Digital Equipment Corp., Intel Corp., and Xerox Corp., September, 1980.

9. Meisner, N.B., et al., "Time Division Digital Bus Techniques Implemented on Coaxial Cable," Proc. Comp. Network Symposium, National Bureau of Standards, Gaithersburg, Md., December 15, 1977, pp. 112-117.

10. Saltzer, J.H., and Pogran, K., "A Star-Shaped Ring Network with High Maintainability," Proc. Local Area Communications Network Symposium, Mitre Corp., May, 1979, pp. 179-190.

11. Saltzer, J.H., "Communication ring initialization without central control," M.I.T. Laboratory for Computer Science

Technical Memorandum TM-202, July, 1981.

12. Leslie, I.M., "Frequency Stability in a Unidirectional Ring of Phase Locked Loops," unpublished working paper of University of Cambridge Computer Laboratory, ca. 1979.

13. Moon, D.A., "Chaosnet," Massachusetts Institute of Technology Artificial Intelligence Laboratory Memorandum 628, (June, 1981).

14. Shoch, J.E., and Hupp, J.A., "Performance of an Ethernet Local Network: A Preliminary Report," Proc. of Local Area Comm. Network Symposium, May, 1980, pp. 113-125.

15. Abramson, N., "Packet switching with satellites," AFIPS Conf. Proc. (NCC 1973), New York, June 1973, pp. 695-702.

16. Thornton, J.E., "Overview of Hyperchannel," COMPCON Spring 1676, San Francisco, CA., February 1979, pp. 262-265.

17. Rawson, E.G., "Application of Fiber Optics to Local Networks," Proc. Local Area Networks Symposium, Mitre Corp., May, 1979, pp. 155-167.

18. IEEE Data Link Media Access Committee draft standard, in preparation.

Reprinted from *The Proceedings of COMPCON F82*, 1982, pages 615-624.

A TOKEN-RING ARCHITECTURE FOR LOCAL-AREA NETWORKS: AN UPDATE

by Don W. Andrews and Gary D. Schultz

IBM Corporation
Communication Products Division
Research Triangle Park, North Carolina, USA

Abstract

The increasing automation of today's office environment has led to new requirements for local-area networks. These requirements include a long-range wiring strategy for interconnecting large numbers of terminals within office complexes, an integrated approach to handling diverse applications (data, voice, facsimile), and a flexible means to exploit technological advances in transmission media.

In this paper, we discuss a system design that meets these requirements. Our primary focus is on a token-ring architecture upon which such a system could be based.

Introduction

The ideas presented here were originally proposed to the IEEE Project 802 in a technical paper[1] submitted by IBM. This is an update of that original paper that reflects changes (primarily in formats) adopted by the 802 committee in its draft standard.[2]

Basic Token-Ring Concepts

A local-area network employing a high-speed transmission ring configuration is shown in Figure 1.

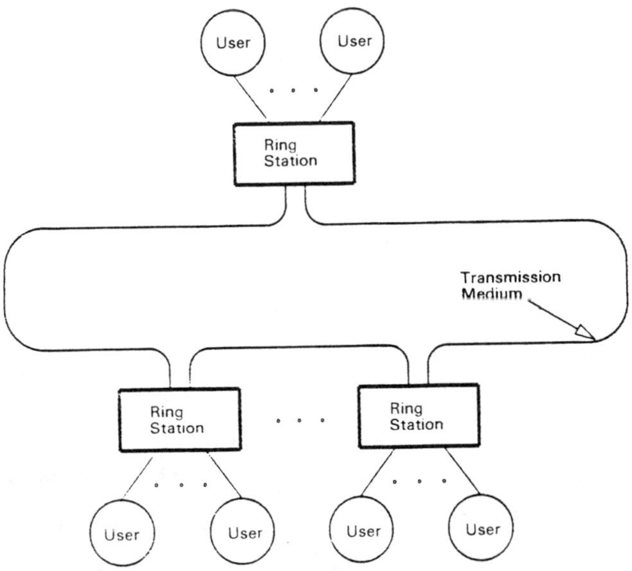

Figure 1. Basic Ring Structure

The ring consists of a set of ring stations serially connected by a transmission medium. Data is transferred sequentially, bit by bit, from station to station. Each station contains an adapter through which one or more attached ring users (terminals, computers) communicate with other users on the ring. A station transfers data from one of its users to the ring, where the data circulates from station to station. Each station on the ring introduces about a one-bit delay, during which it regenerates and repeats a received bit. The total delay consists of the sum of the station delays plus the propagation delay introduced by the transmission medium. A destination station along the way copies the data for one of its users while passing the data on. Upon arriving back at its originating station, the data is overwritten with more data or with idles (0's).

Ring configurations are not new: the basic circular data path was originally used in loops.[3] The difference between a loop and a ring is that a loop generally uses centralized control (with one station acting as a polling primary and the others as secondaries), while a ring uses distributed control (with all stations sharing control as peers). On a loop, generally the secondaries do not communicate with each other: traffic is exchanged only between the primary and secondaries. On a ring, any station can communicate directly with any other station.

Various rings have been described in the technical literature over the last decade. The main distinction between them lies in the control strategy used for inserting data onto the ring. Among the schemes used in the past have been slotted insertion, "train and caboose," and register insertion.[4,5]

Free-Token Capture

In this paper, we discuss a ring control strategy that uses a free-token capture technique, which derives from work on rings performed at the IBM Zurich Research Laboratory over several years.[6,7,8]

On a token ring, a station gains the right to transmit data when it captures a free token--a control signal that circulates on the ring between data transfers. A ring station capturing a free token changes it to a busy token and passes it on, followed by the data for a destination station to copy. After the busy token eventually returns to its origin, having traversed the ring, the originating station (if it has finished sending the data frame) releases a new free token for another station to capture and carry on the process.

Using a single-token protocol, at most one token circulates on the ring at any time. A station that transforms a free token to a busy token waits until the busy token returns (and it has completed sending all associated data) before releasing a free token. This differs from single-frame and multiple-token protocols. Using a single-frame strategy, an originating station waits until it has purged all the data from the ring before releasing a free token. This causes the ring to be idle between the end of a data frame and the next free token for a time equal to the ring delay. Using a multiple-token strategy, an originating station releases a free token as soon as it has finished sending data, even if the leading

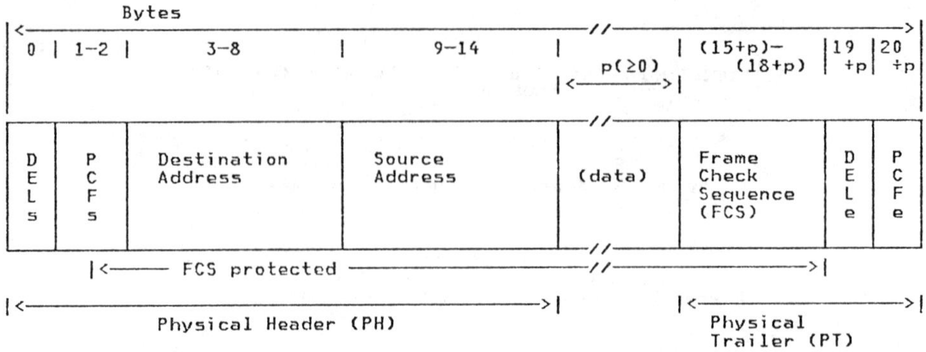

Figure 2. Frame Format

busy token has not yet returned. This reduces the idle time on the ring compared to that for the single-token strategy when the length of a data frame is less than the ring delay. When the ring delay is small, the performance of single- and multiple-token protocols is about the same, except when the ring traffic consists primarily of very small data frames.[6]

The primary advantage of the single-token strategy is that its efficiency is comparable to that of the multiple-token approach, but its complexity is considerably less--particularly in designing a robust priority scheme and in recovering from errors. In the remainder of this paper, we assume that the ring uses the single-token strategy.

Frame and Free Token Formats

The basic transmission unit on the ring is the frame, which has the format shown in Figure 2.

Starting Delimiter (DELs): The starting delimiter, DELs, for a frame consists of one octet having the format:

Bits 0 – 7							
V	V	0	V	V	0	0	0

Starting Delimiter

The value VV in bits 0-1 and 3-4 uses a code violation technique exploiting the underlying differential Manchester coding system (see Appendix), which uses two contiguous signaling elements to indicate a single bit value. Because only two of the four possible values of each pair of signaling elements are used for binary data, the other two values violate normal usage. This technique avoids using a special pattern of normally-encoded bits for delimiters and consequently does not require bit insertion and deletion, as in HDLC and SDLC.

Starting Physical Control Field (PCFs): The starting physical control field (PCFs), shown below, consists of two octets and carries information needed for managing access to the ring.

Bits 0-2	3	4	5-7	Bits 0-1	2-7
PPP	T	M	RRR	FF	CCCCCC
PCFs(0)				PCFs(1) (<- Start of FCS)	

PPP = Priority Mode
T = Token
M = Monitor Count
RRR = Priority Reservation
FF = Frame Format
CCCCCC = Control Indicators

Starting Physical Control Field (PCFs)

The priority mode indicates the priority of a free token, and therefore which stations are allowed to use the free token (change it to busy). In a multiple-priority system, different stations can be authorized to use different priorities. In a basic ring, only the lowest priority (000) need be defined.

The token indication is set to 0 (free) or 1 (busy). When a station detects a free token with its priority or lower, it can generally change it to busy (on the fly) and transmit any data it has to send in the frame format shown in Figure 2. The format of the free token is shown in Figure 3.

Byte 0	1	2
DELs	PCFs(0)	DELe

Figure 3. Free Token Format

The monitor count in PCFs(0) is used for error recovery and is discussed in a later section. The priority reservation indicators exist for extension of the basic ring protocols and allow a high priority station to request in a busy token that the next free token be issued at its priority.

The frame format in PCFs(1) indicates whether the data field contains ring signaling information (FF=00) or a data link control header and data (FF=01). The values 10 and 11 are reserved for future use.

The control indicators contain information related to ring status. In signaling frames, these indicators contain information that all stations "read" to determine the ring status. Signaling frames that carry no urgent messages set CCCCCC = 000000. Signaling frames with CCCCCC ≠ 000000 carry urgent ring management information and so indicate that the frame must be copied. (The nonzero CCCCCC value may also indicate the specific urgent signal type.)

There may be situations in which a ring station cannot copy frames normally because of some malfunction; in this case, it continues to participate in ring error recovery procedures. The control indicators can be used to indicate to ring stations in such a state that the frame must be serviced. For example, the beacon signaling frame contains information about the ring station that is beaconing. The ring station responsible for ring recovery must be able to copy the beacon frame to do its job. Therefore the beacon frame contains a nonzero control indicator (CCCCCC = 000010).

Some urgent signals are of interest only to a specific ring station (identified by the destination address). Others may carry status (beaconing, monitor contention, etc.) of interest to all ring stations. To conserve code points in the control indicators field, urgent signals of interest only to the destination share use of CCCCCC = 000001. Those of more general interest use higher values.

In frames containing higher-layer data, these indicators are set to 000000 and are reserved for future use.

Destination/Source Addresses: The destination and source addresses are each six octets in length. The source address identifies the station that generated the data frame, while the destination address identifies the station that is to copy the frame.

Data: The variable-length data field contains information exchanged between higher-level layers (using the ring) or ring management information.

Frame Check Sequence (FCS): The frame check sequence is a 32-bit cyclic redundancy check (CRC) applied to the second octet of the PCFs, the address fields, and the data field. The first octet of the PCFs has bits that can be changed on the fly by intermediate stations, and so are not checked by the CRC. The frame check sequence is calculated in accordance with the latest revision of HDLC.[11]

Ending Delimiter (DELe): The ending delimiter, DELe, consists of an octet having the following format:

<— Bits 0-6							7 —>
V	V	1	V	V	1	0	EDI

Ending Delimiter

As in the case of the starting delimiter, bits 0-1 and 3-4 contain a code violation pair to indicate a delimiter; however, the delimiter used in DELe is different from that used in the starting delimiter by having bits 2 and 5 set to 1 (see Appendix). Using different delimiting patterns simplifies the detection of each and reduces the likelihood of ring noise changing one delimiter into another.

Bit 7 is the error-detected indicator (EDI). The originating station sets it to 0; the first station on the ring to detect a transmission error sets it to 1. Each station on a ring checks the FCS for all frames; each one also checks for "spurious" (as opposed to delimiting) code violations within frames. The first station to detect an error counts the error for problem determination and fault localization; by setting the EDI bit to 1, it prevents other stations from also logging the error.

Ending Physical Control Field (PCFe): The ending PCF has the following format:

<— Bits 0-7 —>							
ARI	FCI	0	0	ARI	FCI	0	SEI

Ending PCF

The address-recognized indicator (ARI) is used by the originating ring station to determine if any other ring station recognized the address in the destination address field. (It is duplicated in the octet to provide a redundancy check, since the PCFe is not otherwise checked.) The originating ring station sets the bit to 0; any other station on the ring sets it to 1 if it recognizes the address as its own. (There is no dependence on the frame actually being copied.) Also, a destination station detecting that a frame's address has already been recognized can log a possible duplicate address problem.

The frame-copied indicator (FCI) is used to monitor congestion on the ring. (It is duplicated in the octet for the reason described for ARI.) The originating station sets it to 0. If the destination station copies the frame (into a read buffer), it sets the FCI to 1. This allows the originating station to log the instances when congestion has prevented a destination station from copying a frame. It depends on the application type (voice, data) whether a ring station copies a frame with a frame check sequence error.

The soft error indicator (SEI) is normally set to 0. When a ring station's error counter exceeds a threshold, the ring station sends a signaling frame with the soft error indicator set to 1. This informs all stations on the ring that an error condition has been detected on the ring.

Abort Delimiter: An originating station can abort a frame that it is transmitting at any time by transmitting an abort delimiter:

<— Bits 0-7								8-15 —>							
V	V	0	V	V	0	0	0	V	V	1	V	V	1	0	0

Abort Delimiter

This indicates either a transient or a "hard" error at the originating ring station itself. For a transient error, the ring station transmits idles until the abort delimiter returns, whereupon it releases a free token and enters "repeat" state. For a hard error, the ring station enters the "repeat" state immediately.

Relationship to Data Link Control

In this paper we view the token-ring architecture as corresponding to the lowest level of a network architecture. This is called the physical layer in the Open Systems Interconnection (OSI) Reference Model,[9] as defined by the International Organization for Standardization (ISO), and in IBM's Systems Network Architecture (SNA).[10] The physical layer is just below the data link control layer. Views on mapping the token-ring architecture to the traditional layers of OSI or SNA may vary. More important is agreement on relative placement of functions and sublayers.

The token-ring design provides a means of sharing physical layer resources (the ring) among a large community of data link control (DLC) stations. Any two DLC stations, connected by ring stations to the ring, can interact using their customary DLC protocols as though they had dedicated use of the ring.

In the past, physical layer resources have been shared using various protocols. Using multipoint protocols, link controls such as BSC, HDLC, and SDLC allow a primary DLC station and multiple secondary DLC stations to share a link connection; the primary station multiplexes traffic between the various secondary stations and itself using polling/selection protocols. In X.25 protocols, level 3 provides a virtual circuit appearance at one node that represents a connection to some other node attached to the X.25 network. Level 2 provides DLC-level assurance (e.g., frame checking) across the interface between a node and the inner network, while level 1 provides a physical layer interface such as RS-232-C or X.21. Within the X.25 network, physical resources are shared transparently to the attached outer nodes.

A token-ring system may be defined to allow any DLC station to connect to a ring adapter and use its regular DLC protocols on top of the physical layer interface for which it was designed. This would allow the vast population of existing terminals to attach without modification to existing DLC conventions. Each DLC station (or a set of them) is associated with a unique ring station address. (A leading identifier in the data field can distinguish among logical connections between multiple DLC stations at the ring station and DLC stations at other ring stations.) Any point-to-point DLC protocols would be suitable, with either primary-secondary or peer relationships allowed. (Multipoint DLC could also be used, but is redundant with the any-station to any-station support on the ring.) The ring effectively can support as many "logical links" as there are pairs of DLC stations wishing to communicate. A ring station may support DLC in either of two ways: by encapsulating the DLC transmission (DLC frame) within the data field of the ring frame, or by "native" DLC attachment--one optimized for the ring. The former is convenient for migration of existing terminals to a token-ring approach, while the latter takes advantage of the existing addressing and checking functions defined in the token-ring architecture.

The ring addressing functions are needed so that communication between any two DLC stations connected to the ring can be uniquely identified, with address handling and assignment transparent to the independent DLC stations. Checking is necessary so that the ring can preserve the integrity of its own transmissions that control access to, and management of, the ring. These requirements overlap with the customary DLC functions of addressing and of checking physical connection integrity. Addressing of another DLC station can be independent of the underlying physical configuration; association of a DLC station identifier with a ring station can be dynamic, and transparent to the DLC layer. A native DLC station could eliminate checking and DLC frame delimiting from its own protocols.

The error recovery protocols related to frame sequence numbering, acknowledgments, and retransmission remain a DLC responsibility, as the token ring does not supply this level of recovery.

The Token-Ring System

The previous section described the basic concepts of a token-ring. The emphasis was on the basic ring station in normal operation and on the logical topology of the ring. In this section we examine the token-ring system in terms of its physical components and configuration, its functional sublayering, and its ring management responsibilities.

Physical Components and Configuration

The topological view of a ring shown in Figure 1 is an idealization. In practice, a wiring configuration that physically implemented that topology would be impractical to install, operate, service, and maintain in a typical office environment. The simple view of a ring is that it consists of a set of ring stations connected serially by some transmission medium, such as twisted pairs or optical fibers. Each ring station contains a <u>repeater</u> for regenerating and retransmitting a signal received from one neighboring ring station to another. Thus, transmission is point to point between stations; this allows simpler technology to be employed at

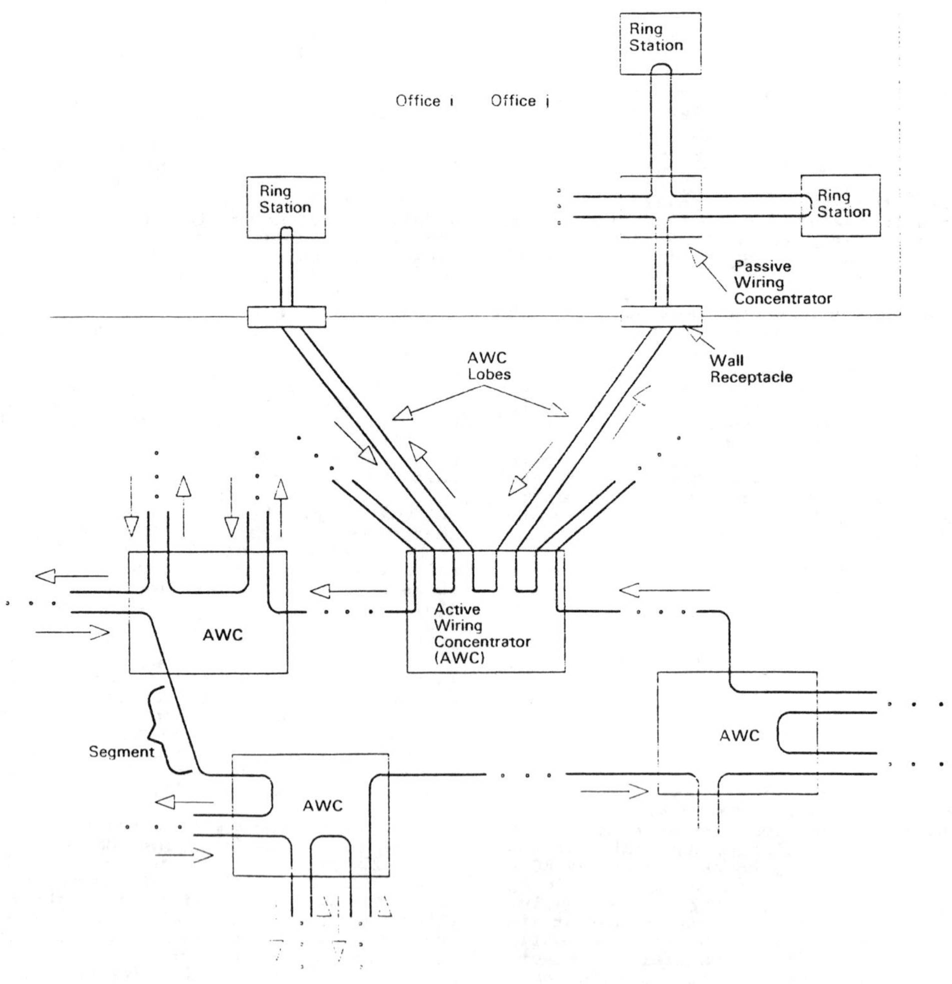

Figure 4. Radial Hierarchy for a Ring

each station than would be needed if each station had to listen reliably to all transmitting stations. On the other hand, Saltzer and Pogran,[12] who have implemented a ring at MIT, cite some of the problems in the simple ring configuration:

- The entire ring can be disrupted by the failure of a single repeater or by a cable breakage.
- Fault localization requires manual traversal of the ring and access to all offices and wire runs that house the ring components.
- Installation of new stations and cabling, adapting to changes in cable lengths between stations after removal of old stations (to retune transmission circuitry), and abandonment of old cable all lead to complications in maintaining an up-to-date record of the ring configuration, in site maintenance, and in problem determination.

The configuration approach described here is similar to that employed in the MIT ring, as well as in older, loop systems:[13,14] wiring is radial and hierarchical as shown in Figure 4.

In this configuration, ring stations in offices are radially connected to active wiring concentrators, which provide points of wiring concentration strategically located in wire cabinets, for easy trouble shooting, servicing, and reconfiguration. The hierarchical relationship of active wiring concentrator (AWC) and AWC lobe (the radial connection between an AWC and one or more office ring stations) can be imbedded within the physical address assignment on a ring, to aid in automatic localization of faults.

Active wiring concentrators themselves act as ring stations on a ring; in a later section, we shall see that they can act as address servers where dynamic address assignment is used.

An active wiring concentrator has its own power supply and contains relays or digital switches for inserting an AWC lobe into the ring, or bypassing it. Multiple active wiring concentrators can also be connected together (say, one on each floor of an office building) in the prime ring, with a backup ring also connecting them. (The backup ring is discussed in section 4, "RAS Aspects," and is not shown in Figure 4.)

A passive wiring concentrator (PWC) can also be deployed to connect multiple office ring stations to an active wiring concentrator lobe; it derives power from the attached ring station and contains relays (driven by the office ring stations) for connecting them to the lobe. Passive wiring concentrators are not functionally ring stations; their capability is limited to recognizing powering up/down states (to open and close relays). In the simplest ring, all wiring concentrators may be passive.

Various concerns, related to signal quality ("jitter" and distortion) and to manageability, may limit the number of ring stations (repeaters) attached to a single ring. A token-ring architecture could allow interconnection of multiple rings, using bridges, as shown in Figure 5. (Assume each ring has the configuration shown in Figure 4.) Each bridge is connected through an active wiring concentrator to a given ring and acts as a ring station on each ring to which it is attached. Acting as a digital switch, it can buffer frames and perform transmission speed changes in switching data from one ring to another.

The bridge acts only as a repeating ring station except in handling the ARI, FCI, and SEI bits. On a ring from which it copies a frame, the bridge sets the ARI and FCI to 1. (In the case of congestion, the bridge may be unable to copy the frame, thereby setting only ARI to 1.) The bridge sets ARI and FCI to 0 on the destination ring or bridge backbone. The bridge also changes an SEI from 1 to 0, since this indicator has relevance only on a ring basis, not from one ring to another. Because this indicator is in the PCFe it is not checked and can be modified by the bridge without affecting the computed FCS value.

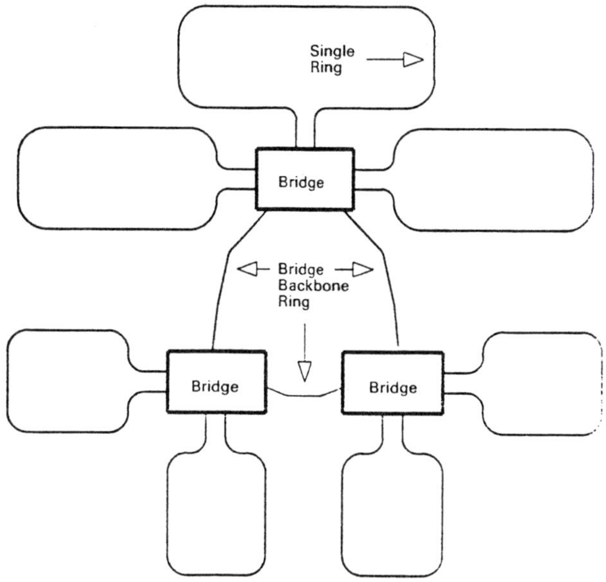

Figure 5. Rings Connected by Bridges

The composite ring is characterized by parallel operation of the individual rings. The composite ring address space is partitioned using ring numbers. (These ring numbers are used by a bridge to ignore a frame or to switch it to another ring attached to the bridge. In the case of an all-rings ring number, the bridge switches the frame to all other rings attached to it.) Thus, a ring address consists of a ring number (two octets) and a ring element (four octets). Later we discuss the distinction between routing and physical addresses.

Functional Sublayering within the Token-Ring Architecture

The token-ring architecture comprises the physical layer of a network architecture, but can be further divided into functional sublayers. Figure 6 shows the sublayering of the physical layer at a single ring station.

Ring Connection: The lowest sublayer is the ring connection, consisting of the transmission medium (or mixture of media) and associated circuit switches used to dynamically reconfigure the various physical components of the ring. This sublayer performs encoding of electrical signals and generation of timing information.

Ring Access: The ring access sublayer has the following functions:

- Address recognition
- Frame processing: repeating, inserting new frames, purging old frames, formatting, checking (CRC processing)
- Token generation
- Error logging
- Buffering of frames transmitted or copied
- Time-out controls

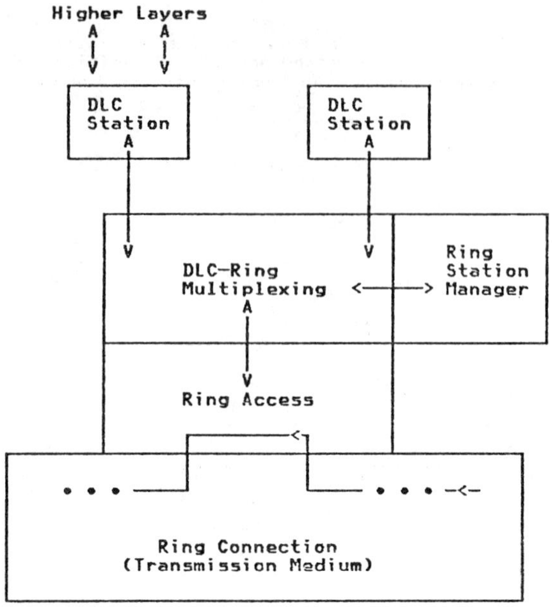

Figure 6. Functional Sublayering within a Ring Station

Besides these basic, access-control functions, one station on each ring takes responsibility for token monitoring. Monitoring functions can exist at any station, but only one station acts as active monitor on a ring at any time. The other stations may do passive monitoring, waiting for possible failure of the active monitor; if it fails, or is disconnected, one of the passive monitors becomes the new active monitor.

Ring operation depends on the reliability of the token mechanism. The monitor supervises proper token operation and performs rapid recovery when errors disrupt the token flow, such as in the following cases.

- Lost token: No token--busy or free--is circulating on the ring. This occurs at ring initialization or when noise disturbs a starting or ending delimiter. The monitor uses a time-out, having a period exceeding that required for the longest possible frame allowed to completely traverse the ring, to detect this condition. To recover, the monitor purges the ring of any residual data (by transmitting a signal frame) and generates a free token.

- Circulating busy token: A busy token persists on the ring, thereby preventing stations awaiting a free token from transmitting. This condition arises when a station generating the busy token fails before removing the busy token, or when noise transforms a circulating free token into a busy token. To safeguard against this problem, the monitor sets the monitor count bit to 1 in any busy token that passes it; thus, a busy token arriving at the monitor with the monitor count already set to 1 has not been properly removed. The monitor purges the ring and generates a free token. (This technique also applies to extensions of the basic ring protocols allowing priority tokens--priority free tokens are not allowed to persist.)

Other errors can also occur. For example, noise can create a free token, resulting in multiple tokens on the ring. If two stations transmit concurrently, typically each will detect disruption from the other (by receipt of a busy token with the wrong source address, or by disruption of the ending delimiter). Neither station releases a new free token, resulting in a lost-token condition as described above.

Besides error recovery, the monitor is responsible for introducing a minimum delay (24 bits) into the ring to handle the case when few stations are connected. This guarantees that the starting delimiter and the first (token) octet of the PCFs can be completely transmitted before arriving back (overlapping) at a station.

Each passive monitor uses a free-token time-out control to detect loss of the active monitor. (The time-out periods differ so that an active monitor responds to a regular lost-token condition before the stand-by monitors do.) An alerted passive monitor attempts to take on the active role by generating a busy token (with the signaling indicator set to 0) followed by a monitor-active signal in the data field. Because contention can occur, a monitor persists in sending the signal until receiving one with a source address value greater than its own (in which case it yields to the other) or equal to it (in which case it has succeeded in assuming the active role). The new active monitor restores the ring to normal operation and continues to preserve the ring integrity.

DLC-Ring Multiplexing: This sublayer multiplexes traffic from the attached DLC stations onto the ring. It maintains the association of DLC stations with the identifiers carried in the data field, and routes data received from the ring to the appropriate DLC station. The multiplexing sublayer passes frame error indications received from the ring access sublayer to the DLC station for DLC-level error recovery. In the simplest configuration--one DLC station, static (strapped-in) address assignment--the DLC-ring multiplexing sublayer may not exist: DLC and the ring access sublayer may interact directly.

Ring and Ring-Station Management: Ring stations can contain optional management functions related to ring or station control:

- Dynamic reconfiguration of the ring involves insertion of new DLC and ring stations, and requires routing identification of destination DLC stations.

- Problem determination and error localization require that statistics be recorded and reported.

The multiplexing sublayer routes information from DLC stations and the ring access sublayer to the management components for processing; the management components drive certain ring protocols and initialize sublayer tables in accordance with ring operation.

Specific management responsibilities are discussed in the next section.

Management Functions

A ring typically can have a very dynamic existence. The configuration is subject to on-going changes, with DLC stations and ring stations being regularly added to, moved around, or removed from the ring. Stations can be powered-up or disconnected from a ring at any time. Reliability, availability, and serviceability (RAS) considerations require that effective problem determination and error statistics gathering be built into ring operation. In this section we consider the management functions required in the ring environment.

Address Servers: Attachment of DLC stations and ring stations to a ring can involve a mixture of static and dynamic address-assignment and address-resolution actions. Each ring station has a routing address (used as a source or destination address in a frame header). As discussed earlier, a ring address consists of a two-octet ring number and a four-octet ring element. The ring element uniquely identifies a ring station within an establishment, which may consist of multiple rings connected by bridges.

Upon powering up, a ring station transmits an address assignment request, which is copied by an address server somewhere on the ring. The assignment request has the frame format in the PCFs(1) octet set to 00 and includes an address-requested signal in the data field. The destination address is set to a special element address--one of the well-known addresses defined for ring management--indicating an address server. The source address consists of an all-zeros ring number and the station's unique ring element. One or more ring stations on a ring can implement an address server. The first one seeing the request, and able to comply (not congested), sets the frame-copied bit so that other servers will ignore the request.

The address server sends a responding frame in which the destination address is the same as the source address in the request and the source address is the address server's own unique ring station address; the frame format in PCFs(1) is set to 00 and the data field contains an address-granted signal and a routing address. This routing address consists of the statically assigned element address and the dynamically assigned ring number. The requesting station thereafter uses this routing address in generating a source address and in recognizing a destination address in a frame.

For ring management purposes, it is convenient to introduce a physical address, which identifies the particular location of a station on a ring. For simple configurations, this may not be needed; for more complex configurations with high RAS requirements, physical addresses are useful in localizing outages and recovering from them. In a later section, we discuss some of these uses.

To avoid address-server contention situations (in assigning a physical address to a ring station), dynamic assignment of the routing ring number and the physical address can be done off-ring by an active wiring concentrator (AWC), prior to inserting an initialized ring station onto the ring. In this process, the concentrator assigns a routing ring number and a physical address to the ring station as the station powers up. The ring number is assigned as described for the on-ring process. The physical address identifies the station's ring number, AWC, and AWC lobe. (Passive wiring concentrators are not identified.) The routing address is used in frame headers, while the physical address is used only in the data field in ring management contexts.

Address Resolution: To locate another ring station (and its associated DLC stations) on the set of connected rings (the composite ring), a ring station transmits an address-resolution request. The resolution request carries a destination address consisting of an all-rings number and the element address for which a specific ring number is requested. The request is disseminated to all rings in the system and copied by the ring station identified by the element address, which returns a response carrying its full routing address, including the specific ring number that it has been assigned.

This address resolution process is followed by any two stations for which a logical connection is desired, and allows easy resumption of communication despite relocation of stations within an establishment. This means a terminal can be moved, as required, to any office having a receptacle connecting to the ring.

Other Management Functions: Ring stations can include additional management functions for ring outage control, problem determination, and statistics gathering. These functions exploit the existence of physical addresses and are concerned generally with RAS aspects of ring operation. We consider these in the next section.

Reliability, Availability, and Serviceability

Because a ring is a serial system, it relies on the health of its constituent parts, or on some means of bypassing unhealthy ones, for unimpaired operation. To foster robust operation in the presence of errors, a ring employs self-diagnosis of components, a RAS-oriented wiring strategy, and integrated ring monitoring and management techniques. Environmental, or medium, noise is handled by the transient-error functions previously discussed (frame checking, DLC-level recovery, token monitoring). In this section, we consider hard failures of ring components, and the overall RAS management services for the ring.

The basic ring preserves its integrity by inclusion of self-diagnostic tests in each ring station adapter. Self-diagnosis determines whether the station is a danger to ring operation. A station can remove itself from the ring when it diagnoses an abnormality in its own operation. Ring operation continues unimpeded because of the bypass logic in each adapter. For ring systems connecting large numbers of stations and concentrators, other techniques come to the fore; these exploit the use of physical addresses.

In a configuration having active wiring concentrators and physical address protocols, lobe bypass can isolate an aberrant ring station or lobe. On detecting loss of input signal, a station generates a beacon signal to inform downstream stations of the outage. The beacon frame includes the station's physical address to identify the physical locale of the error. Each ring station on the ring repeats the frame. Within any active wiring concentrator (AWC) subsystem (an AWC and its attached lobes), the AWC ring station itself is the last ring station in the downstream direction of the signal flow to the next AWC. This enables the AWC ring station to receive a beacon signal from any of its attached stations. The AWC can then identify the failed lobe and remove it from the ring by closing the appropriate bypass switch.

The failure of a ring segment connecting two concentrators is handled in a similar, but somewhat more involved, fashion. We illustrate an example of the outage and recovery process in Figure 7. The circled numbers in the figure indicate the separate events that occur:

1. A ring segment fails.

2. Ring station 1 detects input-signal loss and (repetitively) transmits a beacon frame; each consecutive downstream station repeats the beacon.

3. The ring station in AWC1 receives the beacon and recognizes its source by the physical address in the data field.

4. The concentrator attempts to solve the problem by removing the beaconing station's lobe from the ring.

5. Because the outage is upstream from the suspect lobe, the condition persists; ring station 2 now sends a beacon frame with its physical address.

6. This time, the ring station in AWC1 recognizes that the ring outage is probably upstream from the lobe it previously bypassed.

7. It therefore reinserts the originally suspect lobe back onto the ring, and connects the back-up segment from AWC3 to the reinserted lobe. This action isolates the failed (prime-ring) segment from the AWC1 subsystem and also breaks the flow of timing signals normally carried on the back-up ring from AWC1 to AWC2.

8. AWC2 recognizes the failure of the flow on the back-up segment from AWC1 and switches the prime-ring flow from its own AWC ring station to the back-up segment leading to AWC3. This restores the ring integrity by completely isolating the failed prime-ring segment; the AWC2-AWC3 and AWC3-AWC1 back-up segments replace it.

Notice the reason for the opposite flows on the prime and back-up segments: one AWC detecting an outage on its upstream prime segment can alert the upstream AWC to the outage through forcing the same condition on the back-up ring, on which that AWC (AWC2 in the example) is downstream. The price of this simple back-up strategy is a lengthening of the

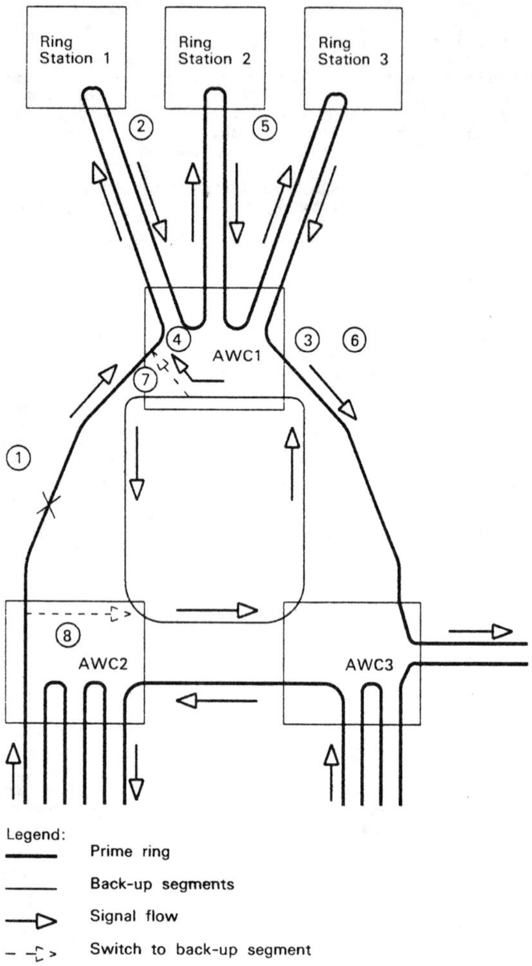

Figure 7. Example of Segment Outage and Reconfiguration

ring. The ring, if it started with n segments, has 2(n-1) segments after completion of the back-up procedure.

Hard failures, while readily recovered from as discussed above, are not the only RAS concerns in a system. Slow degradation of a system can also occur, resulting in unsatisfactory performance. For any system, techniques for isolating errors, collecting reliability data, and correcting degradation through problem determination and reconfiguration are desirable. The larger the system and the more an enterprise relies on it, the more critical such techniques become.

In a ring system, fault isolation is relatively simple. Because the ring uses serial, rather than broadcast, transmission, degradation can be pinpointed by checking error data collected at each ring station. Earlier we noted that each station does error checking on frames. The first station detecting an error logs it and turns on the error-detected indicator in the ending delimiter of the frame; this prevents other stations from also logging the error, resulting in an increase in the logged error statistics only at the faulty component's nearest downstream station. Separate statistics on token errors can be maintained by the active monitor on each ring.

The token-ring architecture also allows additional RAS management services to be integrated into the ring operation. These services are collectively referred to as ring network management, or RNM. RNM services are conceptually patterned after the counterpart communication network management (CNM) services[15] integrated into IBM's multiple-layer network architecture, SNA.

RNM allows RAS management to be centrally controlled from a particular ring station, or to be coordinated through distributed control at multiple stations. A specially assigned ring-element address identifies an RNM ring station.

An RNM station is the focus of RAS management:

- Any ring station can transmit an error-threshold frame, which is copied by an RNM station. The error-threshold signal indicates that the error count at a station has exceeded a predetermined threshold.
- An RNM station can solicit error statistics from any ring station in order to monitor ring performance.
- An RNM station can request a ring reconfiguration action (e.g., at an active wiring concentrator) as a result of problem determination, or in response to a command from a person interfacing with the RNM services. A ring station notifies the RNM station of the completion of a reconfiguration action, whether the RNM initiated it or not.

The RNM services allow timely monitoring and control of the ring condition to identify and correct outages and degradation. The integration of these services into a local-area network is especially useful for environments where high-RAS performance is critical.

Extendibility of the System

The provision of priority and reservation bits in the PCFs allows extension of a basic ring system to accommodate applications that demand more timely access to the ring than usual, and require higher priorities. The lowest priority is suitable (because of the high bandwidth of the ring) for most applications involving data or nonconversational digitized voice (filed speech or voice annotation). For other applications, higher priorities are useful in a mixed-application environment. Priority usage can also be used to enhance ring operational efficiency when bridges are used.

Because bridges are a shared resource used to exchange frames between multiple rings, ring efficiency is enhanced if the bridges are relatively free to open their (limited) buffering to cross-ring flows. To diminish bridge congestion, one priority class, asynchronous priority, could be allocated for bridge access to rings. This priority could be just higher than that used for single-ring data and nonconversational voice, which would use the lowest priority.

Conversational voice and facsimile applications demand an even higher priority, for different reasons. Conversational voice, to be viable on a ring, requires real-time servicing of exchanges. This means that ring servicing must be synchronous with human exchanges; otherwise, the human factors of the (telephone) conversation between two people conversing in ring-connected offices would be severely degraded, to the point that another connection alternative would be sought. Thus, a synchronous priority, higher than the asynchronous priority, is needed.

Another application, facsimile, may also require synchronous priority. In this application, the objective is to ship large volumes of data while simplifying connection protocols. Facsimile data is typically highly redundant, as is voice. There is little need to correct transmitted data (through retransmission) if errors occur. To avoid large buffering requirements at a facsimile station, it would be desirable for the station to ship the facsimile data in a timely way consonant with its buffering capability. This is a synchronous priority, allowing the station to transmit data as its buffer fills. The facsimile device itself can then transmit large amounts of data without interruption. By ignoring frame check errors, it can also accept erroneous data without requiring data-link-control recovery, thereby simplifying the logic in the facsimile device.

Priorities are used as follows. A station of a given priority class can set the reservations bits in a busy token to indicate its priority, if its priority is higher than the current reservation already indicated. When the busy-token originator releases a new free token, it sets the priority indicators in accordance with the highest priority set in the reservation bits of its busy token. Only a station in that priority class or higher can capture the released free token, except that synchronous (highest) priority stations capture only the tokens carrying synchronous priority. Also, for fairness, a station capturing a free token is always the generator of the next free token in its priority class (even if higher priority free tokens intervene). This allows the free token within each priority class to be passed fairly around the ring.

Summary

The advent of the wired office has been widely heralded in the industry and the press. The wired office translates to a need to interconnect large numbers of terminals and processors, concentrated in a small geographical area, in a flexible and reliable fashion.

In this paper, we have described the features of a token-ring architecture that can be applied to the local-area network requirements. These features address the following aspects of the automated office environment:

- Basic Interconnection: A ring topology and token-capture technique characterize transmission-medium sharing, allowing any-station to any-station interaction.
- Long-Range Configuration Strategy: For long-range planning for site wiring and configuration management, a hierarchical, radial wiring strategy is employed, easing site maintenance and RAS concerns.
- Extendibility to Mixed Applications: The token protocols allow priority demands on ring access to accommodate distinctions between real-time and as-available use of the facilities. Redundant-data applications can simplify device logic through relaxation of error processing.
- Flexibility of Attachment: Dynamic address assignment and address resolution allow easy reconfiguration of the system. This means new terminals can be readily introduced into the system, old ones deleted, and existing ones moved around the composite ring, without disturbing the normal operation of the system.
- RAS Aspects: Ring services include provision for localizing and correcting outages. Dynamic rerouting on the ring, to enhance reliability and availability, is another aspect of the attention given to reconfiguration in the token-ring architecture. Serviceability is enhanced through integration of statistics gathering and problem determination techniques into ring management.

The token-ring architecture presented here, like SNA, is intended to suit an evolutionary system. Today it represents the best response to the known environment; in the future, it can adapt to new requirements and technologies, and the realities of practice.

Appendix: Manchester Encoding

The token-ring architecture uses a differential Manchester code to convert binary data (bits) into signal elements. Manchester encoded signals have the desirable properties of:

- containing no direct-current (DC) components, thereby avoiding plating or other deterioration at attachment contacts.
- allowing the receiver to derive clocking pulses from the encoded signal.

The code consists of two signal elements of opposite polarity for each bit of data. This maintains the DC balance in each bit and guarantees a transition for clocking. The value of 1 or 0 assigned to each bit is determined by comparing the first signal element of the bit with the last signal element of the previous bit: if the signal elements have the opposite polarity (i.e., a transition occurred at the bit boundary), the bit is a 0; otherwise, it's a 1. This is illustrated in Figure 8.

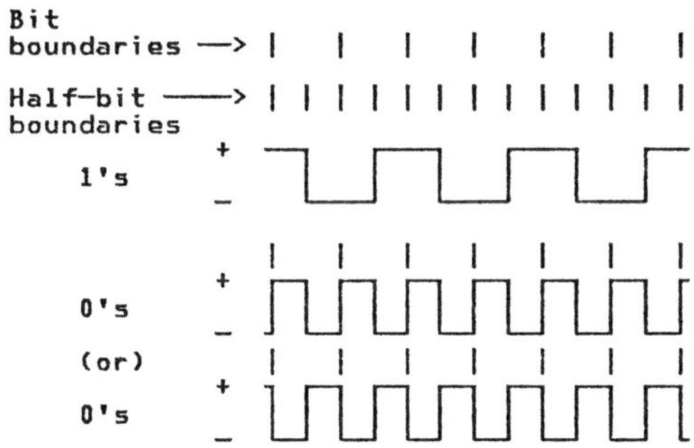

Figure 8. Differential Manchester Code

The polarity (positive or negative) of the signal element does not affect the decoding of the 1's and 0's; only the transition--or lack of one--at the bit boundary is used in decoding.

A code violation is said to occur if there is no transition (from + to -, or vice versa) at the bit midpoint. The frame delimiters use four code violations (two positive, two negative, to maintain DC balance) to guarantee uniqueness from the data stream. This delimiting violation constitutes the first six bit-times of any delimiter as shown in Figures 9 and 10.

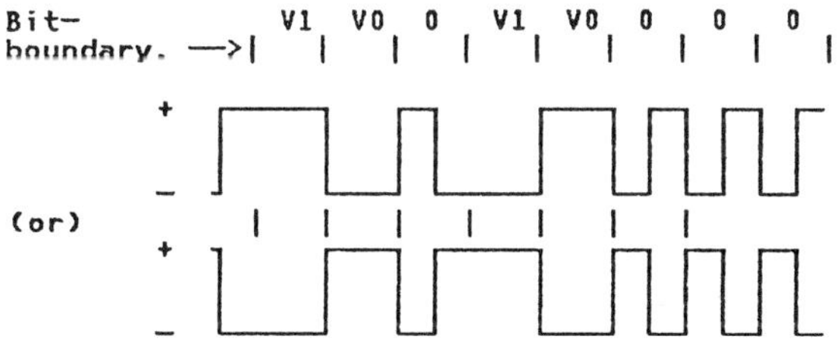

Figure 9. Starting Delimiter

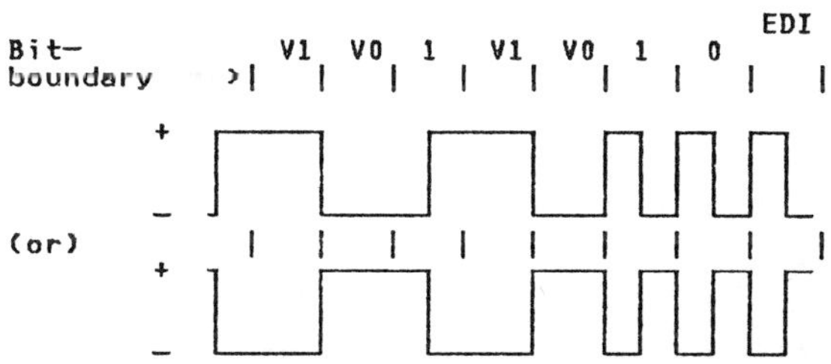

Figure 10. Ending Delimiter

We use the bit pattern "VV0VV0" to denote the delimiting violation in the start delimiter and "VV1VV1" for the delimiting violation in the ending delimiter--the "V" indicating that the bit is not DC balanced. The delimiting violations use the form illustrated, i.e., the first violation in the delimiter is a "1" bit (denoted by "V1" in Figure 9) and the second violation is a "0" bit (denoted by "V0"). Any code violation that is not the delimiting violation pattern is called a spurious violation. The ending delimiter is shown as it is transmitted by the originating ring station, with the EDI set to 0.

References

1. Andrews, D.W., and Schultz, G.D., "A Token-Ring Architecture for Local-Area Networks," submission to IEEE Project 802, March 1982.

2. Local Network Standards, Draft C, IEEE Project 802, May 1982.

3. West, L.P., "Loop Transmission Control Structures," IEEE Transactions on Communications, Vol. COM-20, No. 2, June 1972, pp. 531-539.

4. Cotton, I.W., "Technologies for Local-Area Computer Networks," Computer Networks, 4 (1980), pp. 197-208.

5. Dixon, R.C., "Ring Network Topology for Local Data Communications," Proc. of IEEE COMPCON 82 Fall, September 1982, this proceedings.

6. Bux, W., "Local-Area Subnetworks: A Performance Comparison," IEEE Transactions on Communications, Vol. COM-29, No. 10, October 1981, pp. 1465-1473.

7. Bux, W., Closs, F., Janson, P.A., Kummerle, K., Muller, H.R., and Rothauser, E.H., "A Local-Area Communication Network Based on a Reliable Token-Ring System," IFIP International Symposium on Local-Computer Networks, April 1982.

8. Muller, H.R., Keller, H., and Meyr, H., "Transmission in a Synchronous Token Ring," IFIP International Symposium on Local-Computer Networks, April 1982.

9. Zimmerman, H., "OSI Reference Model--The ISO Model of Architecture for Open Systems Interconnection," IEEE Transactions on Communications, Vol. COM-28, No. 4, April 1980, pp. 425-432.

10. IBM Corp., SNA Concepts and Products, IBM Form No. GC30-3072.

11. Data Communication -- High-Level Data Link Control Procedures -- Frame Structure, ISO Draft Proposal ISO/DP 3309 (Revision of ISO Standard ISO/3309-1976), October 1981.

12. Saltzer, J.H., and Pogran, K.T., "A Star-Shaped Ring Network with High Maintainability," Computer Networks, 4 (1980), pp. 239-244.

13. Hippert, R.O., "IBM 2790 Transmission Loop," IBM J. of Research and Development, 14, 6, November 1970, pp. 662-667.

14. IBM Corp., Multi-use Communications Loop Planning Guide, IBM Form No. GA23-0038.

15. Weingarten, R.A., "An Integrated Approach to Centralized Communications Network Management," IBM Systems Journal, Vol. 18, No. 4, 1979, pp. 484-506.

Chapter 5
Resource Allocation in Store-and-Forward Networks with Point-to-Point Links

5.1. NETWORK ROUTING

There are two major classes of distributed routing algorithms, depending on where routing decisions for individual packets are made.

In the class of algorithms exemplified by the ARPANET algorithm, routing decisions are made by network switching nodes. Once packets are handed over to a network node, the source has no control over the routes to be selected for its packets. A description and an assessment of the original ARPANET algorithm was given by McQuillan et al. [MCQU 78b]. A description of the second-generation ARPANET algorithm appears in [MCQU 80, ROSE 80]. We reprint [MCQU 80] below. The design of this class of distributed routing algorithms that possess various correctness properties (e.g., loop-free, failsafe) has been addressed by Tajibnapis [TAJI 77], Merlin and Segall [MERL 79, SEGA 81], and Jaffe and Moss [JAFF 82], among others.

In the second major class of distributed routing algorithms, proposed by some IBM researchers and others, routing decisions for packets are made at the source nodes where the packets enter the network. Algorithms in this class are called *explicit path routing* or source routing. We reprint the article by Jueneman and Kerr [JUEN 76] below. A more detailed exposition of this approach can be found in the paper by Maruyama and Markowsky [MARU 80].

The problem of rerouting traffic flows to optimize network delay was addressed by Fratta, Gerla, and Kleinrock [FRAT 73] and Gallager [GALL 77]. They presented algorithms to reroute flows to achieve certain optimality conditions. See also [KLEI 76, GERL 77]. Various enhanced message-addressing modes in network routing (e.g., broadcast routing) were discussed by Dalal and Metcalfe [DALA 78] and McQuillan [MCQU 78a]. A good survey of routing algorithms as used in some existing networks can be found in [SCHW 80] which is reprinted below. Hierarchical routing was studied by Kamoun and Kleinrock [KAMO 79] and also by Chu and Shen [CHU 80].

5.2. FLOW AND CONGESTION CONTROLS

Early simulation work to study congestion problems and the performance of the isarithmic method for congestion control was described by Price [PRIC 77]. An analysis of the performance of a two-level isarithmic scheme was presented by Wong and Unsoy [WONG 77].

The buffer requirements of store-and-forward networks was studied by this author in [LAM 76]. An analysis of buffer-sharing schemes was given by Kamoun and Kleinrock [KAMO 80].

Extensive simulations were conducted by Giessler et al. to study the performance of flow controls, congestion controls, and deadlock-avoidance buffer management schemes [GIES 78]. Deadlock-avoidance schemes were proposed and studied by Gunther [GUNT 81], and independently by Merlin and Schweitzer [MERL 80].

The input buffer limit (IBL) scheme for congestion control was proposed and analyzed in [LAM 79]. Extensive simulations reported in [LAM 81a] showed that IBL schemes are very effective in controlling network congestions due to temporary network overloads. This article also provides a comprehensive treatment of network performance characteristics as functions of input buffer limits for congestion control, virtual channel window sizes, and nodal buffer capacities. It is reprinted below.

A description of routing and flow control in IBM's SNA networks can be found in [AHUJ 79].

An excellent tutorial on the topic of flow and congestion controls was given by Gerla and Kleinrock in [GERL 80], which is reprinted below.

5.3. MODELING AND ANALYSIS

Available analytic tools and methods for network design and analysis are mostly based on an open-chain queueing network model first formulated by Kleinrock in 1964 [KLEI 64, KLEI 76]. It has the advantage of having an explicit formula for the mean network delay in terms of the parameters of link (and processor) capacities and traffic flows, and is thus useful for optimal routing and channel capacity assignment studies [FRAT 73, GERL 77]. However this model is an abstraction of a network in which the mechanisms of flow and congestion controls are ignored. The conditions under which Kleinrock's model is accurate were investigated in [LAM 81b]. It was found that the interplay between routing and flow control has little effect on the accuracy of Kleinrock's model for networks that are lightly utilized. The accuracy of Kleinrock's model suffers significantly, however, when some of the links in the network are moderately or heavily utilized.

Queueing networks with closed chains and other population size constraints permit the modeling of a network's flow and congestion control constraints as well as its routing behavior [PENN 75, LAM 77, LAM 79, REIS 79, LAM 81b, LAM 82a, LAM 82b]. A serious drawback of closed-chain models is that they require algorithmic solutions for network performance measures (virtual channel throughputs and their mean delays). The computational time and space requirements of such algorithms grow exponentially with the number of closed chains (virtual channels). Existing algorithms have been designed primarily for models of multiprogramming systems and can only solve closed-chain models of networks with just a few virtual channels [SAUE 81]. To get around this difficulty, the tree convolution algorithm [LAM 83] was developed. It exploits the routing information of a given network which had not been utilized by previous algorithms. It provides an exact solution to networks with tens of closed chains having time and space requirements that are manageable on current computers.

The tutorials in [WONG 82, LAM 82b] on the modeling and analysis of packet-switching networks are reprinted below.

References

[AHUJ 79] Ahuja, V., "Routing and Flow Control in Systems Network Architecture," *IBM Syst. J.*, Vol. 18, No. 2, 1979.

[CHU 80] Chu, W. W. and M. Shen, "A Hierarchical Routing and Flow Control Policy for Packet Switching Networks," *IEEE Transactions on Computers*, May 1980.

[DALA 78] Dalal, Y. K. and R. M. Metcalfe, "Reverse Path Forwarding of Broadcast Packets," *Comm. ACM,* Vol. 21, December 1978, pp. 1040-1048.

[FRAT 73] Fratta, L., M. Gerla and L. Kleinrock, "The Flow Deviation Method: An Approach to Store-and-forward Network Design," Networks 3 (1973), 97-113.

[GALL 77] Gallager, R. G., "A Minimum Delay Algorithm using Distributed Computation," *IEEE Trans. Commun.*, Vol. COM-25, pp. 73-85, January 1977.

[GERL 77] Gerla, M. and L. Kleinrock, "On the Topological Design of Distributed Computer Networks," *IEEE Trans. on Communications*, COM-25 (1977), pp. 48-60.

*[GERL 80] Gerla, M. and L. Kleinrock, "Flow Control: A Comparative Survey," *IEEE Trans. Comm.*, COM-28 (1980), pp. 553-574.

[GIES 78] Giessler, A., J. Haenle, A. Koenig and E. Pade, "Packet Networks with Deadlock-free Buffer Allocation--An Investigation by Simulation," *Comput. Networks* 2 (1978), pp. 191-208.

[GUNT 81] Gunther, K. D., "Prevention of Deadlocks in Packet Switched Data Transport Systems," *IEEE Trans. on Commun.*, Vol. COM-29, April 1981, pp. 512-524.

[JAFF 82] Jaffe, J. M. and F. H. Moss, "A Responsive Distributed Routing Algorithm for Computer Networks," *IEEE Trans. on Commun.*, Vol. COM-30, July 1982, pp. 1758-1762.

*[JUEN 76] Jueneman, R. R. and G. S. Kerr, "Explicit Path Routing in Communications Networks," *Proc. Internat. Conf. on Computer* Communication, 1976, pp. 340-342.

[KAMO 79] Kamoun, F. and L. Kleinrock, "Stochastic Performance Evaluation of Hierarchical Routing for Large Networks," *Computer Networks*, Vol. 3, No. 5, November 1979, pp. 337-353.

[KAMO 80] Kamoun, F. and L. Kleinrock, "Analysis of Shared Finite Storage in a Computer Network Environment under General Traffic Conditions," *IEEE Trans. Comm.*, COM-28, 1980, pp. 992-1003.

[KLEI 64] Kleinrock, L., *Communication Nets--Stochastic Message Flow and Delays*, McGraw-Hill, New York, 1964.

[KLEI 76] Kleinrock, L., *Queueing Systems, Volume 2: Computer Applications*, Wiley-Interscience, New York, 1976.

[LAM 76] Lam, S. S., "Store-and-Forward Buffer Requirements in a Packet Switching Network," *IEEE Trans. on Communications*, COM-24 (1976) pp. 394-403.

[LAM 77] Lam, S. S., "Queueing Networks with Population Size Constraints," *IBM J. Res. Develop.* 21, 1977, pp. 370-378.

[LAM 79] Lam, S. S. and M. Reiser, "Congestion Control of Store-and-Forward Networks by Input Buffer Limits--An Analysis," *IEEE Trans. on Commun.*, January 1979.

*[LAM 81a] Lam, S. S. and Y. L. Lien, "Congestion Control of Packet Communication Networks by Input Buffer Limits--A Simulation Study," *IEEE Trans. on Comput.* Vol. C-30, 1981, pp. 733-742.

[LAM 81b] Lam, S. S. and Y. L. Lien, "Modeling and Analysis of Flow Controlled Packet Switching Networks," *Proc. 7th Data Communication Symposium*, Mexico City, October 1981, pp. 98-107.

[LAM 82a] Lam, S. S. and Y. L. Lien, "Optimal Routing in Networks with Flow Controlled Virtual Channels," *ACM Performance Evaluation Rev.* 11 (1), 1982, pp. 38-46.

*[LAM 82b] Lam, S. S. and J. W. Wong, "Queueing Network Models of Packet Switching Networks, Part 2:

Networks with Population Size Constraints," *Performance Evaluation*, Vol. 2, No. 3, 1982, pp. 161-180.

[LAM 83] Lam, S. S. and Y. L. Lien, "A Tree Convolution Algorithm for the Solution of Queueing Networks," *Comm. ACM*, Vol. 26, No. 3, March 1983, pp. 203-215.

[MARU 80] Maruyama, K. and G. Markowsky, "On the Generation of Explicit Path Routing Tables," *Proc. ICCC*, Atlanta, October 1980, pp. 90-95.

[MCQU 78a] McQuillan, J. M., "Enhanced Message Addressing Modes for Computer Networks," *Proc. IEEE* (Special Issue on Packet Communication Networks), November 1978.

[MCQU 78b] McQuillan, J. M., G. Falk, and I. Richer, "A Review of the Development and Performance of the ARPANET Routing Algorithm," *IEEE Trans. on Comm.*, COM-26, 12, December 1978, pp. 1802-1811.

*[MCQU 80] McQuillan, J. M., I. Richer, and E. C. Rosen, "The New Routing Algorithm for the ARPANET," *IEEE Trans. on Comm.*, COM-25, 5, May 1980.

[MERL 79] Merlin, P. M. and A. Segall, "A Failsafe Distributed Routing Protocol," *IEEE Trans. Comm.*, Vol. COM-27, No. 9, September 1979, pp. 1280-1287.

[MERL 80] Merlin, P. M. and P. J. Schweitzer, "Deadlock Avoidance in Store-and-Forward Networks I: Store-and-Forward Deadlock, and II: Other Deadlock Types," *IEEE Trans. on Commun.*, March 1980.

[PENN 75] Pennotti, M. and M. Schwartz, "Congestion Control in Store and Forward Tandem Links," *IEEE Trans. on Commun.*, Vol. COM-23, 1975, pp. 1434-1443.

[PRIC 77] Price, W. L., "Data Network Simulation Experiments at the National Physical Laboratory 1968-76," *Computer Networks*, Vol. 1, 1977.

[REIS 70] Reiser, M., "A Queueing Network Analysis of Computer Communication Networks with Window Flow Control," *IEEE Trans. on Communications* COM-27 (1979) pp. 1199-1209.

[ROSE 80] Rosen, E. C., "The Updating Protocol of ARPANET's New Routing Algorithm," *Comput. Networks*, Vol. 4, February 1980, pp. 11-19.

[SAUE 81] Sauer, C. H. and K. M. Chandy, *Computer Systems Performance Modeling*, Prentice-Hall, 1981.

*[SCHW 80] Schwartz, M. and T. E. Stern, "Routing Techniques Used in Computer Communication Networks," *IEEE Trans. on Comm.*, COM-28, 4, April 1980, pp. 539-552.

[SEGA 81] Segall, A., "Advances in Verifiable Fail-Safe Routing Procedures," *IEEE Trans. on Commun.*, Vol. COM-29, April 1981, pp. 491-497.

[TAJI 77] Tajibnapis, W. D., "A Correctness Proof of a Topology Information Maintenance Protocol for Distributed Computer Networks," *CACM*, 20 (7), July 1977, pp 477-485.

[WONG 77] Wong, J. W. and M. S. Unsoy, "Analysis of Flow Control in Switched Data Networks," *Proc. IFIP Congress 77* (1977), pp. 315-320.

*[WONG 82] Wong, J. W. and S. S. Lam, "Queueing Network Models of Packet Switching Networks, Part 1: Open Networks," *Performance Evaluation*, Vol. 2, No. 1, 1982, pp. 8-20.

(* article reprinted below.)

The New Routing Algorithm for the ARPANET

JOHN M. McQUILLAN, MEMBER, IEEE, IRA RICHER, MEMBER, IEEE, AND ERIC C. ROSEN

Abstract—The new ARPANET routing algorithm is an improvement over the old procedure in that it uses fewer network resources, operates on more realistic estimates of network conditions, reacts faster to important network changes, and does not suffer from long-term loops or oscillations. In the new procedure, each node in the network maintains a database describing the complete network topology and the delays on all lines, and uses the database describing the network to generate a tree representing the minimum delay paths from a given root node to every other network node. Because the traffic in the network can be quite variable, each node periodically measures the delays along its outgoing lines and forwards this information to all other nodes. The delay information propagates quickly through the network so that all nodes can update their databases and continue to route traffic in a consistent and efficient manner.

An extensive series of tests were conducted on the ARPANET, showing that line overhead and CPU overhead are both less than two percent, most nodes learn of an update within 100 ms, and the algorithm detects congestion and routes packets around congested areas.

I. INTRODUCTION

THE last decade has seen the design, implementation, and operation of several routing algorithms for distributed networks of computers. The first such algorithm, the original routing algorithm for the ARPANET, has served remarkably well considering how long ago (in the history of packet switching) it was conceived. This paper describes the new routing algorithm we installed recently in the ARPANET. Readers not familiar with our earlier activities may consult [1] for a survey of the ARPANET design decisions, including the previous routing algorithm; readers interested in a survey of routing algorithms for other computer networks and current research in the area may consult [2].

A distributed, adaptive routing scheme typically has a number of separate components, including: 1) a *measurement process* for determining pertinent network characteristics, 2) a *protocol* for disseminating information about these characteristics, and 3) a *calculation* to determine how traffic should be routed. A routing "algorithm" or "procedure" is not specified until all these components are defined. In the present paper, we discuss these components of the new ARPANET algorithm. We begin with a brief outline of the shortcomings of the original algorithm; then, following an overview of the new procedure, we provide some greater detail on the individual components. The new algorithm has undergone extensive testing in the ARPANET under operational conditions, and the final section of the paper gives a summary of the test results. This paper is a summary of our conclusions only; for more complete descriptions of our research findings, see our internal reports on this project [3]-[5].

Paper approved by the Editor for Computer Communication of the IEEE Communications Society for publication without oral presentation. Manuscript received May 11, 1979; revised October 5, 1979. This work was supported by the Defense Advanced Research Projects Agency under ARPA Order 3941, and by the Defense Communications Agency (DoD) under Contract MDA903-78-C-0129, monitored by DSSW.

The authors are with Bolt Beranek and Newman Inc., Cambridge, MA 02138.

II. PROBLEMS WITH THE ORIGINAL ALGORITHM

The original ARPANET routing algorithm and the new version both attempt to route packets along paths of least delay. The total path is not determined in advance; rather, each node decides which line to use in forwarding the packet to the next node. In the original approach, each node maintained a table of estimated delay to each other node, and sent its table to all adjacent nodes every 128 ms. When node I received the table from adjacent node J, it would first measure the delay from itself to J. (We will shortly discuss the procedure used for measuring the delay.) Then it would compute its delay via J to all other nodes by adding to each entry in J's table its own delay to J. Once a table was received from all adjacent nodes, node I could easily determine which adjacent node would result in the shortest delay to each destination node in the network.

In recent years, we began to observe a number of problems with the original ARPANET routing algorithm [7] and came to the conclusion that a complete redesign was the only way to solve some of them. In particular, we decided that a new algorithm was necessary to solve the following problems.

1) Although the exchange of routing tables consumed only a small fraction of line bandwidth, the packets containing the tables were long, and the periodic transmission and processing of such long, high-priority packets can adversely affect the flow of network traffic. Moreover, as the ARPANET grows to 100 or more nodes, the routing packets would become correspondingly larger (or more frequent), exacerbating the problem.

2) The route calculation is performed in a distributed manner, with each node basing its calculation on local information together with calculations made at every other node. With such a scheme, it is difficult to ensure that routes used by different nodes are consistent.

3) The rate of exchange of routing tables and the distributed nature of the calculations causes a dilemma: the network is too slow in adapting to congestion and to important topology changes, yet it can respond too quickly (and, perhaps, inaccurately) to minor changes.

The delay measurement procedure of the old ARPANET routing algorithm is quite simple. Periodically, an IMP counts the number of packets queued for transmission on its lines and adds a constant to these counts; the resulting number is the "length" of the line for purposes of routing. This delay measurement procedure has three serious defects.

1) If two lines have different speeds, or different propagation delays, then the fact that the same number of packets is

queued for each line does not imply that packets can expect equal delays over the two lines. Even if two lines have the same speed and propagation delay, a difference in the size of the packets which are queued for each line may cause different delays on the two lines.

2) In the ARPANET, where the queues are constrained to have a (short) maximum length, queue length is a poor indicator of delay. The constraints on queue length are imposed by the software in order to fairly resolve contention for a limited amount of resources. There are a number of such resources which must be obtained before a packet can even be queued for an output line. If a packet must wait a significant amount of time to get these resources, it may experience a long delay, even though the queue for its output line is quite short.

3) An instantaneous measurement of queue length does not accurately predict average delay because there is a significant real-time fluctuation in queue lengths at any traffic level. Our measurements show that under a high constant offered load, the average delay is high, but many individual packets show low delays, and the queue length often falls to zero! This variation may be due to variation in the utilization of the CPU, or to other bottlenecks, the presence of which is not accurately reflected by measuring queue lengths.

These three defects are all reflections of a single point, namely, that the length of an output queue is only one of many factors that affect a packet's delay. A measurement procedure that takes into account only one such factor cannot give accurate results.

The new routing algorithm is an improvement over the old one in that it uses fewer network resources, operates on more realistic estimates of network conditions, reacts faster to important network changes, and does not suffer from long-term loops or oscillations.

III. OVERVIEW OF THE NEW ROUTING PROCEDURE

The routing procedure we have developed contains several basic components. Each node in the network maintains a database describing the network topology and the line delays. Using this database, each node independently calculates the best paths to all other nodes, routing outgoing packets accordingly. Because the traffic in the network can be quite variable, each node periodically measures the delays along its outgoing lines and forwards this information (as a "routing update") to all other nodes. A routing update generated by a particular node contains information only about the delays on the lines emanating from that node. Hence, an update packet is quite small (176 bits on the average), and its size is independent of the number of nodes in the network. An update generated by a particular node travels *unchanged* to all nodes in the network (not just to the immediate neighbors of the originating node, as in many other routing algorithms). Since the updates need not be processed before being forwarded because they are small, and since they are handled with the highest priority, they propagate very quickly through the network, so that all nodes can update their databases rapidly and continue to route traffic in a consistent and efficient manner.

Many algorithms have been devised for finding the shortest path through a network. Several of these are based on the concept of computing the entire tree of shortest paths from a given node, the root of the tree. A recent article [9] discusses some of these algorithms and references several survey articles. The algorithm we have implemented is based on one attributed to Dijkstra [10]; because of its search rule, we call it the shortest-path-first (SPF) algorithm.

The basic SPF algorithm uses a database describing the network to generate a tree representing the minimum delay paths from a given root node to every other network node. Fig. 1 shows a simplified flowchart of the algorithm. The database specifies which nodes are directly connected to which other nodes, and what the average delay per packet is on each network line. (Both types of data are updated dynamically, based on real-time measurements.) The tree initially consists of just the root node. The tree is then augmented to contain the node that is closest (in delay) to the root and that is adjacent to a node already on the tree. The process continues by repetition of this last step. LIST denotes a data structure containing nodes that have not yet been placed on the tree but are neighbors of nodes that are on the tree. The tree is built up shortest-paths-first—hence, the name of the algorithm. Eventually, the furthest node from the root is added to the tree, and the algorithm terminates. We have made important additions to this basic algorithm so that changes in network topology or characteristics require only an incremental calculation rather than a complete recalculation of all shortest paths.

Fig. 2 shows a six-node network and the corresponding shortest path tree for node 1. The figure also shows the routing directory which is produced by the algorithm and which would be used by node 1 to dispatch traffic. For example, traffic for node 4 is routed via node 2. Only the routing directory is used in forwarding packets; the tree is used only in creating the directory.

The two other important components of the routing procedure are the mechanism for measuring delay and the scheme for propagating information. The routing algorithm must have some way of measuring the delay of a packet at each hop. This aspect of the routing algorithm is quite crucial; an algorithm with poor delay measurement facilities will perform poorly, no matter how sophisticated its other features are.

Each node measures the actual delay of each packet flowing over each of its outgoing lines, and calculates the average delay every 10 s. If this delay is significantly different from the previous delay, it is reported to all other nodes. The choice of 10 s as the measurement period represents a significant departure from the old routing algorithm. Since it takes 10 s to produce a measurement, the delay estimate for a given line cannot change more often than once every 10 s. The old routing algorithm, on the other hand, would allow the delay estimate to change as often as once every 128 ms. We now believe, however, that there is no point in changing the estimate so often, since it is not possible to obtain an accurate estimate of delay in the ARPANET in less than several seconds. (See Section IV-B.)

The updating procedure for propagating delay information is of critical importance because it must ensure that each update is actually received at all nodes so that identical databases of routing information are maintained at all nodes. Each update is transmitted to all nodes by the simple but reliable

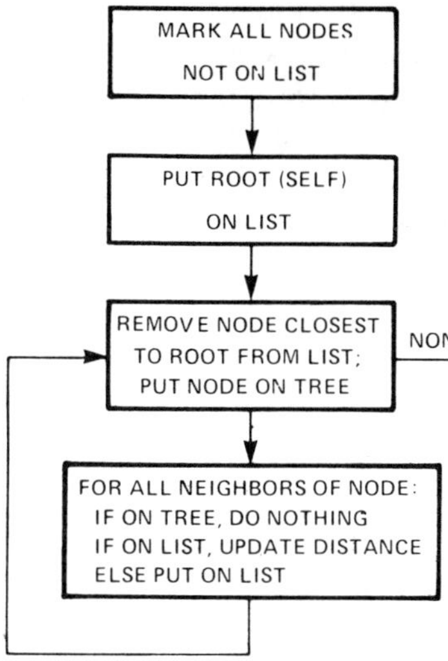

Fig. 1.

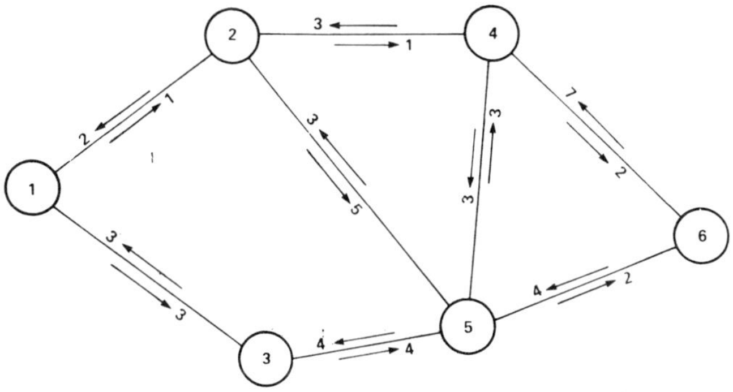

(a)

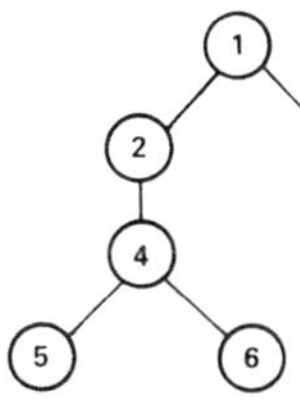

(b)

DESTINATION NODE	2	3	4	5	6
ROUTE TRAFFIC VIA NODE	2	3	2	2	2

(c)

Fig. 2. (a) Example network (line lengths indicated by the numbers beside the arrowheads). (b) Shortest path tree. (c) Routing directory.

method of transmitting it on all lines. When a node receives an update, it first checks to see if it has processed that update before. If so, the update is discarded. If not, it is immediately forwarded to all adjacent nodes. In this way, the update flows quickly (within 100 ms) to all other nodes. The fact that an update flows once in each direction over each network line is the basis for a reliable transmission procedure for the updates. Because the updates are short and are generated infrequently, this procedure uses little line or node bandwidth (less than two percent). We have augmented this basic procedure with a mechanism to ensure that databases at nodes are correctly updated when a new node or line is installed, or when a whole set of previously disconnected nodes joins the network. This is discussed in more detail in Section IV-C.

Since all nodes perform the same calculation on an identical database, there are no permanent routing loops. Of course, transient loops may form for a few packets when a change is being processed, but that is quite acceptable, since it has no significant impact on the average delay in the network.

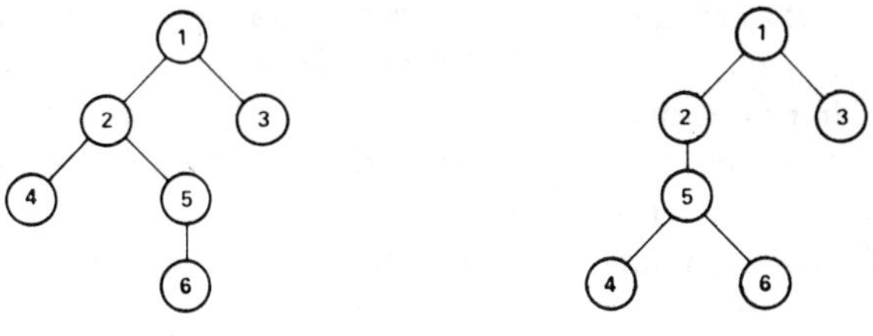

(a) (b)

Fig. 3. (a) Shortest path tree for network of Fig. 2(a) after the length of the line 2 → 4 increase to 6. (b) Modified tree after the length of line → 5 decrease to 2.

IV. DETAILED DESCRIPTION OF THE NEW ROUTING PROCEDURES

A. Routing Calculation–The SPF Algorithm

We now describe the additions to the basic algorithm of Fig. 1 which we have developed to handle various possible changes in network status without having to recalculate the whole tree. For each change described below, we assume that the shortest path tree rooted at node I prior to the change is known.

First, consider the case where the delay of the line AB from node A to node B increases. Clearly, if the line is not in the tree (i.e., not in the shortest path from that node to any other node), nothing need be done because if the line were not part of any shortest path prior to the change, then it will certainly not be used when its delay increases. If the line is in the tree, then the delay to B increases, as does the delay to each node whose route from I passes through B. Thus, the nodes in the subtree whose root is B are candidates for changed positions in the tree. Conversely, nodes not in this subtree will not be repositioned.

The first two steps for handling an increase of X in the delay from A to B are as follows.

1) Identify nodes in B's subtree and increase their delays from I by X.

2) For each subtree node S, examine S's neighbors which are not in the subtree to see if there is a shorter path from I to S via those neighbors. If such a path is found, put node S on LIST.

At the conclusion of these steps, LIST either will be empty or will contain some subtree nodes for which better paths have been found. In order to find the best paths to the nodes on LIST, a slightly modified version of SPF can be invoked. This will also find better paths, if any exist, for other subtree nodes. Fig. 3(a) shows the modification to the tree of Fig. 2 that results when the delay of the line from node 2 to node 4 increases to 6.

Now consider the case where the delay on AB decreases by X. If this line is in the tree, then paths to the nodes of the subtree which have B as its root will be unchanged because the subtree nodes were already at minimum delay, and hence the decreased delay will only shorten their distances from I. Moreover, any node whose delay from I is less than or equal to B's new distance from I will not be repositioned, since the node's path must reach B first in order to take advantage of the improved line. However, nodes which are not in the subtree and which are farther from I than B may have a shorter distance via one of the subtree nodes.

The algorithm must thus first perform the following steps.

1) Identify the nodes in the subtree and decrease their distances from I by X.

2) Try to find a shorter distance for each node K that is not in the subtree but is adjacent to a subtree node by identifying a path to K via an adjacent node which is in the subtree. If such a path is found, put node K on LIST.

At the conclusion of these steps, LIST will contain some (possibly zero) subtree adjacent nodes that have been repositioned. Nodes adjacent to these that are not in the subtree are also candidates for improved paths, and starting with the LIST generated in step 2) above, the basic SPF algorithm (with minor modifications) can be used to restructure the rest of the tree. Fig. 3(b) shows how the tree of Fig. 3(a) changes when the length of the link from node 2 to node 5 decreases to 2, while the length of the link from node 2 to 4 remains at 6.

If the delay on line AB improved, but AB was *not* originally in the shortest path tree, the algorithm first determines whether B can take advantage of this improvement. Since the delay from I to A cannot be improved, the delay to B using the line AB will be equal to the original distance to A plus the new delay of AB. If the new delay is greater than or equal to the former delay from I to node B, then the improved line does not help and no changes are made to the tree or to the routing table. If, on the other hand, the updated delay is less than the original delay, then the best route to B now includes AB. The first change to the shortest path tree is, therefore, to relocate B (and its subtree), attaching it to node A via line AB. Now the situation is identical to that of the previous paragraph in which the line from A to B was in the tree in the first place and its delay decreased.

Finally, a change in the status of a node—namely, the addition of a new node, the removal of a node, a node failure, or its recovery from a failure—is implicitly recognized by the change in the status of its lines. For example, if a node fails, its neighbors determine that the lines to that node have failed, and when other nodes receive this information, they calculate that the failed node is unreachable. (Of course, nodes can become unreachable even if their lines do not fail.) Thus, the algorithm need explicitly consider only line changes.

The basic SPF calculation and all of the above incremental cases are consolidated into the semiformal version of the algorithm given in the Appendix.

B. Delay Measurement

Measuring the delay of an individual packet is a simple matter. When the packet arrives at the IMP, it is time-stamped with its arrival time. When the first bit of the packet is transmitted to the next IMP, the packet is stamped with its "sent time." If the packet is retransmitted, the original sent time is overwritten with the new sent time. When the acknowledgment for the packet is received, the arrival time is subtracted from the sent time. To this difference are added the propagation delay of the line (a constant for each line) and the packet's transmission delay (found by looking it up in a table indexed by packet length and line speed). The result is the packet's total delay at that hop—the time it took the packet to get from one IMP to the next.

Every 10 s the average delay of all packets which have traversed a line in the previous 10 s is computed. Our measurements show that when we take an average over a period of less than 10 s, the average shows too much variation from measurement period to measurement period, even when the offered load is constant. There is a tradeoff here: a longer measurement period means less adaptive routing if conditions actually change; a shorter period means less optimal routing because of inaccurate measurements.

Another important aspect of the measurement technique is that the measurement periods are *not* synchronized across the network. Rather, the measurement periods in the different IMP's are randomly phased. This is an important property because synchronized measurement periods could, in theory, lead to instabilities [4], [11].

The new routing algorithm does not necessarily generate and transmit an update at the end of each measurement period; it does so only if the average delay just measured is "significantly" different from the average delay reported in the last update that was sent (which may or may not be the same as the delay measured in the previous measurement period). The delay is considered to have changed "by a significant amount" whenever the absolute value of the change exceeds a certain threshold. The threshold is not a constant but is a decreasing function of time because whenever there is a large change in delay, it is desirable to report the new delay as soon as possible, so that routing can adapt quickly; but when the delay changes by only a small amount, it is not important to report it quickly, since it is not likely to result in important routing changes. However, whenever a change in delay is long lasting, it is important that it be reported eventually, even if it is small; otherwise, additive effects can introduce large inaccuracies into routing. What is needed, then, is a scheme which reacts to large changes quickly and small changes slowly. A threshold value which is initially high but which decreases to zero over a period of time has this effect. In the scheme we have implemented, the threshold is initially set to 64 ms. After each measurement period, the newly measured average delay is compared with the previously reported delay. If the difference does not exceed the threshold, the threshold is decreased by 12.8 ms. Whenever a change in average delay equals or exceeds the threshold, an update is generated, and the threshold is reset to 64 ms. Since the threshold will eventually decay to zero, an update will always be sent after a minute, even if there is no change in delay. (This feature is needed to ensure reliability of the updating protocol under certain conditions. See Section IV-C.) It should be pointed out that when a line goes down or comes up, an update reporting that fact is generated immediately.

C. Updating Policy

We next discuss the policy for propagating the delay information needed in SPF calculations, which require identical data bases at all the nodes [12]. The updating technique must meet two basic criteria, high efficiency (i.e., low utilization of line and CPU bandwidth) and high reliability. Efficiency is important both under normal conditions and when a change is detected that requires immediate updating. Reliability means that updates must be processed in sequence, handled without loss during equipment failures, and treated correctly after failure recovery.

Rather than having separate updates for each line, each update contains information about all the lines at a particular IMP. That is, each update from a given node specifies all the neighbors of that node, as well as the delay on the direct line to each of the neighbors. This results in more efficiency (i.e., less overhead), and the simplicity of only one single serial number per node. The latter makes sequencing and other bookkeeping easier.

We considered different approaches for distributing the updates [8] and decided on "flooding," in which each node sends each new update it receives on all its lines except the line on which the update was received. An important advantage of flooding is that the node sends the same message on all its lines, as opposed to creating separate messages on the different lines. These messages are short (no addressing information is required), so that the total overhead due to routing updates is much less than one percent. A final consideration which favors flooding is that it is independent of the routing algorithm. This makes it a safe, reliable scheme.

We considered several different ways of augmenting the basic flooding scheme to ensure reliable transmission [4]. An important feature of all the schemes is that updates which need to be retransmitted can be reconstructed from the topology tables in each IMP. The protocol we have adopted uses an explicit acknowledgment which is a natural extension of the basic flooding scheme. Using flooding, there is no need to transmit an update back over the line on which it was received since the neighbor on that line already has the update. In our protocol, however, the updates are transmitted over *all* lines, including the input line. The "echo" over the input line serves as an acknowledgment to the sender; if the echo is not received in a given amount of time (measured by a retransmission timer for each line), the update is retransmitted. In order to cover the case of a missed echo, the retransmitted update is specially marked (with a "Retry" bit) to force an echo even if the update has been seen before. Note that acknowledging an update at each hop ensures that the update will be received by all nodes which have a path to the source.

One difficult problem in maintaining duplicate databases at all nodes is that some nodes may become disconnected from each other due to a network partition. For some period of time, certain nodes are unable to receive routing updates from certain other nodes. When the partition ends, the nodes in one segment of the network may remember the serial numbers of the last updates they received from nodes in the other segment. However, if the partition lasted a long enough time, the serial numbers used by the disconnected nodes may have *wrapped around* one or more times. If there has been wrap-around, it is meaningless to compare the serial numbers of new updates with the serial numbers of old updates. Some method must be developed to force all nodes to discard the prepartition updates in favor of the postpartition ones. The obvious approach of ignoring updates from unreachable nodes is not workable, since the SPF databases may temporarily be inconsistent, and different nodes may ignore different updates.

This problem is resolved by having the update packets carry around some indication of their age. There is a k-bit field in each packet, and each node has a clock which ticks once every t seconds. When an update is first generated, the "age field" is $2k - 1$. When an update is received, its age field is decremented once each tick of the clock. An update is considered "too old" when its age field has been decremented to zero. This scheme ensures that the age of an update as seen by a given node is determined by the time it has been held in the given node, plus the time it was held in any nodes from which it was retransmitted. The use of a time-out scheme like the one just described places several constraints on the parameters used by the routing scheme.

1) It should be impossible for the serial numbers of updates generated by any one node to wrap around (i.e., to get halfway through the sequence number space) before the time-out period expires.

2) The time-out period should be somewhat longer than the maximum period between updates from a single node. This means that good, recent updates from reachable nodes will not time out.

3) It should be impossible for a node to stop and be restarted within the time-out interval. This ensures that all of the node's old updates will time out before any new updates are sent.

There is one other important facet to the updating protocol. When a network line which has been down is determined to be in good operating condition, it is placed in a special "waiting" state for a period of one minute. The line is not "officially" considered to be up until the waiting period is over. While a line is in the waiting state, therefore, no data can be routed over it. However, routing updates *are* transmitted over lines in the waiting state. As we indicated in Section IV-B, each node is required to generate at least one update per minute, even if there is no change in delay. This means that while a line is in the waiting state, an update from every node in the network will traverse it; the line cannot come up until enough time has elapsed so that recent updates from all nodes have been transmitted over it. This feature is needed for three reasons.

1) In order to properly perform the routing computation, a node must have a copy of the network database which is identical to the copies in all the other nodes. Recall that the database specifies the topology of the network (i.e., which nodes are direct neighbors of which other nodes), as well as the delay on each network line. When a new node is ready to join the network, it has none of this information. It must somehow obtain the information before it can be permitted to join. Note, however, that the procedure described above ensures that a node cannot come up (because its lines cannot come up) until it has received an update from each other node. Since an update from a given node specifies the neighbors of that node, as well as the delay on the line to each neighbor, it follows that a node cannot come up until it has received enough information to construct a complete and up-to-date copy of the network database.

2) When the network is partitioned, the partition must not

be permitted to end until updates from each segment have flowed into the other. Otherwise, nodes in one segment may have copies of the database which are inconsistent with those in the other segment. Again, the procedure of having each node generate at least one update per minute, while holding a line in the waiting state before allowing it up, is sufficient to avoid this problem. Since a partition can only end when a line comes up, and a line cannot come up until updates from all nodes have traversed it, a partition cannot end until all nodes have complete, consistent, and up-to-date copies of the database.

3) There are certain peculiar cases in which flooding is not totally reliable, even when augmented by a retransmission strategy. For example, suppose a node has two lines, one of which comes up at the precise moment the other goes down. An update which is being flooded around the network might arrive at each line at a time when it is down. This means that the update may never reach that node, even though there is no instant when both of the node's lines are down. However, by ensuring that a line cannot come up until enough time has passed for updates from all nodes to have traversed it, this situation is prevented.

V. PERFORMANCE

We next describe some analytical and empirical results on the performance of the new routing algorithm. One important measure of the efficiency of the SPF algorithm is the average time required to process changes in the delays along network lines, since such changes comprise the bulk of the processing requirements. When a given node receives an update message indicating that the delay along some line has increased, the running time of the SPF algorithm is roughly proportional to the number of nodes in that line's subtree; that is, it is roughly proportional to the number of nodes to which the delay has become worse. When a given node receives an update message indicating that the delay along some line has decreased, the amount of time it takes to run the incremental SPF algorithm is roughly proportional to the number of nodes in that line's subtree *after* the algorithm is run; that is, it is roughly proportional to the number of nodes to which the delay got better. Thus, in either case, the SPF running time is directly related to the subtree size.

Since the average subtree size provides a measure of SPF performance, it is useful to understand how this quantity varies with the size of the network. Let N denote the number of network nodes, and let hi represent the number of hops on the path from the source node, $i = 1$, to node i; in other words, if the length of each line is 1, then hi is the length of the path to node i. Clearly, node i appears in i's subtree and in the subtrees of all the nodes along the path to i. Thus, hi is equal to the number of subtrees in which node i is present, so that

$$\text{total number of all subtree nodes} = \sum_{i=2}^{N} h_i$$

and since there are $N - 1$ subtrees (the complete tree from the source node is not considered to be a "subtree"), the average subtree size is given by

$$\text{average subtree size} = \frac{1}{N-1} \sum_{i=2}^{N} h_i.$$

But this expression is identical to the average hop length of all paths, and thus we have the remarkable result that in any tree, the average subtree size is equal to the average hop length from the root to all nodes. This result is significant because the average hop length generally increases quite slowly as the number of nodes increases. (For a network with uniform connectivity $c > 2$, the average hop length increases roughly as $\log N/\log (c - 1)$ [3].)

To establish some estimate of the running time of the algorithm, we programmed a stand-alone version for the ARPANET nodes. We randomly assigned each line in the ARPANET a length between 1 and 20. We ran the SPF algorithm to initialize the data structure in each node. Then we picked 50 lines at random and successively gave each a new random length. Every time we changed the length of a line, we changed it by at least 15 percent. Also, some lines were brought down by being assigned a length which represented infinity. Each time we did this, we ran the SPF algorithm with each node as the source node. We obtained the following results.

1) The average time per node to run the incremental SPF algorithm was about 2.2 ms.

2) The average time per subtree node to run the incremental SPF algorithm was about 1.1 ms.

Since we calculated that the average subtree size multiplied by the probability that a line is in the tree is about 2, these two results are in agreement. Note that these are average times; actual times varied from under 1 to 40 ms.

The figures given above are for the shortest path calculation only. Processing an update invokes a routine to maintain the topology database (including the ability to dynamically add or delete lines and nodes), and a routine to determine which nodes can be reached from the root node. These modules increase the running time by about a factor of two; and the total storage requirement, including these modules, the topology database, and the measurement and updating packages, is about 2000 16-bit words.

We designed and programmed the new routing procedure over a period of about six months. We than began an extensive series of tests on the ARPANET, at off-peak hours but under actual network conditions [5]. Our tests involved a great deal more than simply turning the new routing algorithm on to see whether it would run. The tests were specifically designed to stress the algorithm, by inducing those situations which would be most difficult for it to handle well. To stress its ability to react properly to topological changes, we induced line and node failures in as many different ways as we could think of, including multiple simultaneous failures. We also generated large amounts of test traffic in order to see how the algorithm performs under heavy load. (In this respect, it should be noted that the periods during which we were testing were "off-peak" only with respect to the amount of ordinary user traffic in the network. The amount of test traffic we generated far exceeds the amount of traffic generated by users, even during peak hours.) We experimented with many different traffic patterns, in order to test the algorithm under a wide variety of heavily loaded conditions. In particular, we tried to induce those situations which would be most likely to result in loops or in wild oscillations. We also designed and implemented a sophisticated set of measurement and instrumentation tools, so that we could evaluate the routing algorithm's performance. Some of these tools enabled us to monitor the utilization of resources used by the algorithm. Others enabled us to monitor changes in delay (as measured by the routing algorithm), as well as changes in the routing trees themselves at particular network nodes. One of our most important tools was the "tagged packet." A tagged packet is a packet which, as it travels through the network, receives an imprint from each node through which it travels. When such a packet reaches its destination, it contains a list of all the nodes it has traversed, as well as the delay it experienced at each node. These packets provided us with a very straightforward indication of the routing algorithm's performance. Of course, since the network was also in use by ordinary users during our tests, we cannot claim to have performed "controlled" experiments, in the strict scientific sense. However, all our experiments were repeated many times before being used to draw conclusions. Some of our main results are as follows.

1) Utilization of resources (line and processor bandwidth) by the new routing algorithm is as expected, and compares quite favorably with the old algorithm. Line overhead is less than one percent; CPU overhead is less than two percent. We have measured these quantities repeatedly since the new routing algorithm became operational in May 1979, and we have found this result to hold even during peak hours on the network.

2) The new algorithm responds quickly and correctly to topological changes; most nodes adapt to the change within 100 ms.

3) The new algorithm is capable of detecting congestion, and will route packets around a congested area.

4) The new algorithm tends to route traffic on minimum hop paths, unless there are special circumstances which make other paths more attractive.

5) The new algorithm does *not* show evidence of serious instability or oscillations due to feedback effects.

6) Routing loops occur only as transients, affecting only packets which are already in transit at the time when there is a routing change. The few packets that we have observed looping have not traversed any node more than twice. However, the loop can be many hops long. Although packets which loop may experience a longer delay than packets which do not, there is no significant impact on the average delay in the network.

7) Under heavy load, the new algorithm will seek out paths where there is excess bandwidth, in order to try to deliver as much traffic as possible to the destination.

Of course, the new routing algorithm does not generate optimal routing—no single-path algorithm with statistical input data could do that. It has performed well, and is successful in eliminating many of the problems associated with the old routing scheme. After several months of careful testing during which both old and new routing algorithms were resident in the network and used for experiments [5], we began to operate the ARPANET with the new routing scheme in May 1979, and removed the old routing program. Since that time, we have continued to monitor the performance of the algorithm. The results obtained during our test periods have continued to hold, even during peak hours, and no new or unforeseen problems have yet arisen.

Is the new routing algorithm really better than the old? We are convinced that it is for reasons that we will summarize shortly. We would like first to point out, though, that there is no general answer to the question, "What makes routing algorithm *A* better than routing algorithm *B*?" If one could claim that algorithm *A* performs better in every possible situation than algorithm *B* does, according to some well-defined metric of performance, then one would have a good reason for preferring *A*. However, such a claim could never be supported for it is untestable. One might try to claim that algorithm *A* performs better than algorithm *B* in "most" situations, but that would not necessarily show that *A* is a better algorithm than *B*. *A*'s performance in the minority of situations might be so much worse than *B*'s that *B* is to be preferred. Furthermore, it is difficult to define a performance metric which is equally applicable to every possible situation. For example, in some situations it may be desirable to minimize delay; in others to maximize throughput. Yet these two intuitively desirable performance metrics are in conflict. In attempting to decide which of two routing algorithms is the better one, one cannot appeal to any procedure simple enough to be followed by rote. Rather, one must first look at particular situations which are known to give rise to performance difficulties. Then one must decide what sort of performance one would like to see in those situations (a decision often akin to a value judgment). Only then can one compare the two algorithms to see which gives the more desirable performance.

Our purpose in designing and implementing a new routing algorithm for the ARPANET was to eliminate certain problems in the performance of the old algorithm, while at the same time maintaining the strengths of the old algorithm. We believe that one of the strengths of the old algorithm was that it was distributed, in the sense that the routing computation was performed by every node. In the ARPANET environment, this makes good sense from the point of view of reliability and efficiency. The new routing algorithm retains this feature by replicating the SPF computation at every node. There is a sense, however, in which the old routing computation was a distributed computation but the SPF computation is not. In the old algorithm, the inputs to the computation at one node were the outputs of the computation at the neighboring nodes. In this sense, then, the old routing computation was a global computation, with each node performing just a piece of it. Since the nodes performed the computation in an unsynchronized manner, the output of the global computation at any instant depended more on the history of events around the network than on the traffic in the network at that instant. The SPF computation, on the other hand, is a local computation. It does depend on measurements which have been made all around the network, but the updating protocol provides these measurements to all nodes unchanged and unprocessed; the SPF computation at one node never learns of the results of the SPF computation at any other node. In this way, we have kept the advantages of distributed routing while dispensing with the disadvantages of having a distributed computation.

Another good quality of the old algorithm was its attempt to adapt to changing delay conditions in the network. We realize that there may be certain applications, where network traffic can be accurately predicted and the network can be sized to handle exactly that traffic load and pattern, in which it may not be important for the routing to be adaptive. In the ARPANET, however, nodes and trunks are frequently added or removed. These changes are primarily made for administrative or economic reasons, rather than for the purpose of optimizing traffic flows. The traffic in the ARPANET is quite unpredictable, being largely determined by the behavior of a community of researchers. Furthermore, although there are sites on the ARPANET separated by as many as 11 hops, about one-third of the messages in the network travel no more than one hop; about half travel no more than three hops. This leads to situations in which the load in the network is very nonuniform, and these are the situations in which adaptive routing is likely to be of great utility. For reasons such as these, adaptive routing seems no less important to us now than it did to the original designers of the ARPANET many years ago. There were, however, several problems in the way the old algorithm responded to changes in network delay. Most of the problems stemmed from deficiencies in the delay measurement procedure of the old algorithm (see Section II). Because of these deficiencies, the old algorithm was often incapable of detecting congestion, and would sometimes send traffic directly into a congested area, thereby causing the congestion to spread. Our tests [5] show that we have eliminated this problem, and have done so without introducing any countervailing problems, such as instability or wild oscillation of the routing patterns. In its ability to adjust to changes in delay, the new algorithm appears to dominate the old completely.

An important deficiency of the old algorithm was its slow response to topological changes. The old algorithm would take many seconds to respond properly to a node or line failure. During this period, many nodes could be directing traffic towards a failed node. Having to buffer such traffic for seconds at a time was a significant cause of congestion in the network. With the new algorithm, however, the time for all nodes to respond to topological changes is on the order of 100 ms. Since the new algorithm was installed, we have not observed any congestion arising due to slow response to line or node failures.

The updates of the old routing algorithms were over 1200 bits long. There were often as many as seven such updates per second on each line. The new routing updates average 176 bits. Even during peak periods, it is rare to see more than two updates per second per line. One of the problems with the old algorithm was the increase in the delay of ordinary data packets due to the presence of the long, frequently sent routing updates. Clearly, the new routing updates interfere much less with ordinary network traffic than did the old.

The old routing algorithm took a fixed amount of time (15-20 ms) to process an update. The new algorithm, as we have pointed out, takes a variable amount of time, with the amount of time proportional to the size of the routing change necessitated by the update. This results in a much more efficient use of the CPU.

One of the major problems of the old algorithm was that it was prone to form loops which might persist for several seconds at a time. A given packet might be trapped in such a loop for a significant amount of time. Often a large number of packets would get "sucked in" to such loops, causing congestion which began at the locus of the loop and then spread throughout the network. While the new algorithm cannot be said to be loop-free, the loops that it forms occur only as transients while the network is adapting to a routing change. The loops which do form do not persist; a packet will sometimes loop once, but we have never seen packets traveling around and around in a loop, as would sometimes happen with the old algorithm. The small amount of looping which has been observed has *never* led to congestion, or even to a significant increase in average network delay. We conclude, therefore, that looping is not a problem with the new algorithm, as it was with the old.

Someone might object that any algorithm that permits loops is seriously deficient; this point is worth commenting on briefly. It is certainly true that, other things being equal, it is better not to have looping than to have it. But other things are never equal—we know of no pair of routing algorithms that perform exactly alike, except that one permits looping and the other does not. An algorithm which does not permit looping does not necessarily result in lower delay, less variable delay, higher throughput or less congestion than an algorithm which does. We simply do not believe that a small amount of transient looping should be regarded as a problem.

Are there any ways in which the old algorithm is better than the new one? The new algorithm does take about three times the memory as the old one, but conservation of memory is not generally considered to be an important desideratum for routing algorithms. From the point of view of performance, the new algorithm seems to dominate the old one in every respect. This is not to say that our approach is appropriate for every possible application, or even that it is the only possible approach for *our* application. We do believe, though, that we have met our goal of designing a new routing algorithm which kept the known strengths of the old one while eliminating many of its known weaknesses.

APPENDIX

This Appendix gives a semiformal description of the algorithm to calculate and update the shortest path tree. SOURCE denotes the node in which the algorithm is running. The algorithm's basic data structure, LIST, is a variable-length list whose elements are ordered triples. An ordered triple T is of the form ⟨SON, FATHER, DISTANCE⟩ where SON and FATHER are nodes and DISTANCE is a member. (We use the notation SON (T) in the obvious way to mean the first element of the triple T.) Each triple represents a particular path from SOURCE to SON. The penultimate hop on this path is FATHER, and the total length of this path is DISTANCE. The algorithm we describe here has been modified so that changes to the tree can be computed incrementally, without having to recalculate those parts of the tree that do not change. Hence, it does not correspond exactly to the flow chart in Fig. 1.

SPF Algorithm

0) If no tree exists, place ⟨SOURCE, SOURCE, 0⟩ on LIST, and go to Step 4).

1) If the change was to line *AB*, then perform one of the following steps.

a) If *AB* is in the tree, set DELTA equal to the change in distance along *AB*.

b) If *AB* is not in the tree, set DELTA equal to the distance to node *A* plus the distance along *AB* minus the distance to *B*; if DELTA is greater than or equal to 0, done.

2) Identify *B* and all of *B*'s descendants (both first generation and succeeding generations) as members of the subtree; increase the distances of all subtree members by DELTA.

3) For each subtree node *S*, perform one of the following steps.

a) If DELTA is positive, try to find a shorter path to *S* via each of *S*'s neighbors that is not in the subtree; if such an improved path is found, put the triple representing *S* on LIST.

b) If DELTA is negative, try to find a shorter path to each of *S*'s nonsubtree neighbors by attempting to route each neighbor via *S*; if such an improved path is found, put the triple for the neighbor node on LIST.

4) Search LIST for the triple *T* with the smallest DISTANCE. Remove *T* from LIST; place SON (*T*) on the shortest path tree so that its father on the tree is FATHER (*T*). (Exception: if SON (*T*) = SOURCE, place it in the tree as its root.)

5) For each neighbor *N* of SON (*T*), do *one* of the following steps.

a) If *N* is already in the shortest path tree, then

i) if its distance from SOURCE along the tree is less than or equal to DISTANCE (*T*) + LINE-LENGTH (SON (*T*),*N*), do nothing;

ii) if its distance from SOURCE along the tree is greater than DISTANCE (*T*) + LINE-LENGTH (SON (*T*), *N*), remove *N* from the tree and place ⟨*N*, SON (*T*), DISTANCE (*T*) + LINE-LENGTH (SON (*T*), *N*)⟩ on LIST.

b) If there is no triple *T'* on LIST such that SON (*T'*) = *N*, then place the triple ⟨*N*, SON (*T*), DISTANCE (*T*), + LINE-LENGTH (SON (*T*), *N*)⟩ on LIST.

c) If there is already a triple *T'* on LIST such that SON (*T'*) = *N*, and if DISTANCE (*T'*) ⩽ DISTANCE (*T*) + LINE-LENGTH (SON (*N*), do nothing.

d) If there is already a triple *T'* on LIST such that SON (*T'*) = *N*, and if DISTANCE (*T'*) > DISTANCE (*T*) + LINE-LENGTH (SON (*T'*)*N*), then

i) remove *T'* from LIST;

ii) place the triple ⟨*N*, SON (*T*), DISTANCE (*T*) + LINE-LENGTH (SON (*T*), *N*)⟩ ON LIST.

6) If LIST is nonempty, go to step 4). Otherwise, the algorithm is finished.

REFERENCES

[1] J. M. McQuillan and D. C. Walden, "The ARPANET design decisions," *Comput. Networks*, vol. 1, Aug. 1977.

[2] J. M. McQuillan, "Routing algorithms for computer networks—A survey," presented at the 1977 Nat. Telecommun. Conf., Dec. 1977.

[3] J. M. McQuillan, I. Richer, and E. C. Rosen, "ARPANET routing algorithm improvements—First semiannual technical report," BBN Rep. 3803, Apr. 1978.

[4] J. M. McQuillan, I. Richer, E. C. Rosen, and D. P. Bertsekas, "ARPANET routing algorithm improvements—Second semiannual technical report," BBN Rep. 3940, Oct. 1978.

[5] E. C. Rosen, J. Herman, I. Richer, and J. M. McQuillan, "ARPANET routing algorithm improvements—Third semiannual technical report," BBN Rep. 4088, Apr. 1979.

[6] J. M. McQuillan, G. Falk, and I. Richer, "A review of the development and performance of the ARPANET routing algorithm," *IEEE Trans. Commun.*, Dec. 1978.

[7] J. M. McQuillan, I. Richer, and E. Rosen, "ARPANET routing study—Final report," BBN Rep. 3641, Sept. 1977.

[8] J. M. McQuillan, "Enhanced message addressing modes for computer networks," *Proc. IEEE (Special Issue on Packet Communication Networks)*, Nov. 1978.

[9] D. B. Johnson, "Efficient algorithms for shortest paths in sparse networks," *J. Ass. Comput. Mach.*, vol. 24, pp. 1–13, Jan. 1977.

[10] E. Dijkstra, "A note on two problems in connection with graphs," *Numer. Math.*, vol. 1, pp. 269–271, 1959.

[11] D. P. Bertsekas, "Dynamic models of shortest path routing algorithms for communications networks with a ring topology," in preparation.

[12] E. C. Rosen, "The updating protocol of the ARPANET's new routing algorithm: A case study in maintaining identical copies of a changing distributed data base," in *Proc. 4th Berkeley Conf. Distributed Data Management and Comput. Networks*, Aug. 28–30, 1979, pp. 260–274.

★

John M. McQuillan (M'77) was born in New York, NY, on February 23, 1949. He received the A.B., S.M., and Ph.D. degrees in 1970, 1971, and 1974, respectively, from Harvard University, Cambridge, MA, all in applied mathematics.

Since 1971 he has been with Bolt Beranek and Newman (BBN) Inc., where he was a major contributor to the design and implementation of the ARPANET. He has investigated several types of advanced computer communications systems, directed BBN's consulting in this field, and published over 30 articles in this area.

★

Ira Richer (S'58–M'63) received the B.E.E. degree from Rensselaer Polytechnic Institute, Troy, NY, in 1959, and the M.S. and Ph.D. degrees in electrical engineering from the California Institute of Technology, Pasadena, in 1960 and 1964, respectively.

After holding postdoctoral positions at the Technical University of Denmark, Lyngby, and at Cal Tech, Pasadena, he joined M.I.T. Lincoln Laboratory, Lexington, MA, where he was involved in a number of advanced communications projects that spanned orders of magnitude in both the frequency and altitude domains (ELF to UHF and submarine to satellite). In 1977 he joined Bolt Beranek and Newman (BBN) Inc., Cambridge, MA. As a Senior Scientist at BBN, he consults to both commercial and government organizations on a variety of network and communications topics.

★

Eric C. Rosen received the S.B. degree in 1973 from the Massachusetts Institute of Technology, Cambridge, and the Ph.D. degree in philosophy in 1976 from Princeton University, Princeton, NJ.

He has worked for M.I.T.'s Laboratory for Computer Science, for Boeing Computer Services, and since 1977, for the Computer Systems Division of Bolt Beranek and Newman (BBN), Inc. While at BBN, he has been extensively involved in measuring the performance of the ARPANET, and in designing and testing the ARPANET's new routing algorithm. He is currently conducting research in routing and congestion control techniques for computer networks.

Explicit Path Routing in Communications Networks

R. R. Jueneman and G. S. Kerr
IBM Corporation, U.S.A.

ABSTRACT

An algorithm for Explicit Path Routing is introduced as a form of content guided routing. The algorithm allows an originating node to choose a unique path to any destination, from a set of one or more available paths. Each path is uniquely identified to the network by the origin ID, destination ID, and an n bit (n=8) routing field. Each message transmitted would contain these fields in the message header. The algorithm guarantees FIFO message ordering along any selected path, and hence loop-free transmission of packets. Routing tables are contained in each network node, requiring on the order of KN bytes, where K is the average number of alternate paths to a destination node in an N node network. Adaptive routing policies which react to network topology changes are supported without recourse to a centralized network routing center. Given a message reordering capability in each node, fully parallel transmission can be utilized for highest throughput. The algorithm is suitable for implementation in a network of non-homogenous links and nodes.

I. INTRODUCTION

In a store and forward or packet switching network there are typically multiple paths from a source node to a sink node, via different intermediate nodes and links. The steering of a message from a source to a sink is called routing. In general, the process involves routing tables in each node which are used to determine the next path segment a message should traverse.

The various types of routing algorithms that have been proposed or implemented in the past can be fitted into three categories:

1. Fixed Routing, Centralized Control. A consistent set of routing tables is determined at a central agency and is distributed to all of the affected nodes. At any one time there exists only one path a message can take from origin to destination.

2. Stochastic Routing, Distributed Control. Each node makes independent decisions as to the best way to route the message at hand, based upon whatever information about the network is available. Previous routing decisions need not influence current decisions. (The ARPA network is perhaps the best example.)[1].

3. Content Guided Routing, Message Control. Wherein information carried in the message helps to determine the message routing. Examples might include transaction routing, session ID routing, and explicit node-by-node routing.

The usual approach to the fixed routing solution is to have a centralized Networking Routing Center (NRC) which monitors the traffic in the network and the status of all the links and nodes. If the traffic or the topology changes, new routing tables are computed for all nodes and sent out via the network. If the traffic flow is reasonably stable, the fixed routing scheme can be optimized to produce excellent results. Fixed routing may include provisions for replacing a failed link with an alternate automatically but the procedure is predetermined and unique.

The major problems with this approach are the need to multiply-interconnect all nodes, in order to ensure that the NRC can communicate with a node in the event of a failure. In addition, the NRC must be replicated to protect against its failure. Replication can create problems of synchronization between the prime and backup control centers. Also, if the network traffic is not quiesced during the switchover, message looping or meandering may occur with possible loss of FIFO order and arbitrary delays.

Stochastic routing methods have the advantage of being adaptive to changes in traffic intensity or link availability. They also have significant disadvantages arising from the independent and often conflicting decisions made by individual nodes (e.g., optimizing node to node transmission at the expense of end-to-end traffic). Opderbeck recently cited as major research problems the need for (1) a method for preventing loops, (2) routing in large networks and (3) routing in non-homogenous networks[2].

It should be apparent that the stochastic algorithms are inherently non-FIFO. As conditions change in the network, elements of a message chain may be sent down different links. Depending upon the queues which exist downstream, the first message sent may be delayed longer than the second and thus arrive out of order. With a large buffer storage at the destination node, a natural FIFO ordering of packet arrivals may permit substantially increased throughput if chains of messages are considered, avoiding message reassembly lockup problems[3]. Conversely, minimizing buffer requirements may reduce hardware costs at the destination node and thereby improve the cost/performance ratio of the system.

In addition, a non-deterministic routing algorithm may cause operational problems. If a message is corrupted by the time it arrives at its destination and there is no way of knowing the links and nodes through which it passed, then the problems of diagnosing and maintaining the network can be considerably aggravated.

For these reasons, it is appropriate to seek a routing algorithm which:

a. Permits routing decisions to be made on a decentralized basis.

b. Guarantees FIFO message ordering along a single path.

c. Allows full parallel path ("spray") transmission for load balancing or high bandwidth applications.

d. Allows implementation of a network of heterogenous links and nodes, requiring modest amounts of storage for routing tables in each node, minimal space overhead in the packet header, and minimal processing overhead in each node.

The algorithm below meets these criteria.

II. EXPLICIT PATH ROUTING ALGORITHM

The Explicit Path Routing algorithm provides deterministic, end-to-end routing by a simple table lookup mechanism which references precomputed tables. A field is provided in the message header which is updated at each node along the path, thereby allowing node tables of size KN, where K is the number of alternate paths available and N is the number of possible destinations.

The method involves a message header which contains at least the identification of the destination node (and the origin node when error recovery is provided by the system), plus two routing fields. The first of these will be called the Path Indicator (PIN), which is set by the origin node to indicate the original path choice. The second field, called the Next Node Index (NNI), is used to steer the table-lookup routing algorithm and is updated at each node along the path.

Each node contains a set of pre-computed, static routing tables, one for every destination node in the network. In operation, the destination node address (DN) in the message header is used to select (1) the explicit path routing table associated with that DN. The NNI is then used to select (2) the particular adjacent link/ station to which the message should be routed, along with an updated NNI value for use (3) at that next node. The algorithm thus routes the message to and through the next node (4), until it arrives at the destination node. There are multiple paths stored for each DN but only the one indicated by the NNI in the message header is selected. By setting the PIN/NNI initially, the user determines which path will be used, thus establishing the routing criteria on a message by message basis.

A diagram may aid in understanding the sequence.

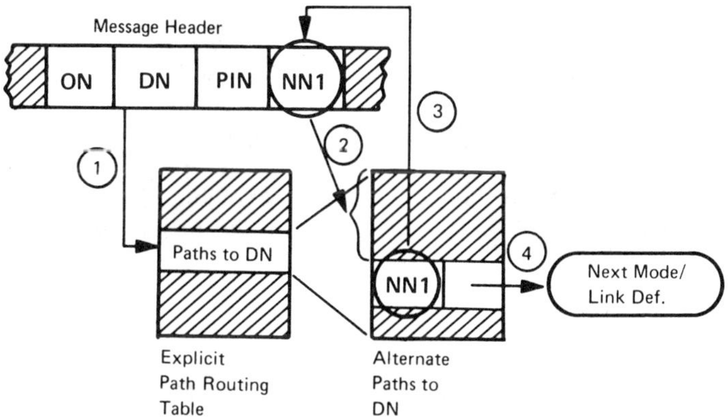

The path identified by selection of an initial NNI consists of a sequence of links and nodes which connect the origin to the destination. An alternate path may pass through different links and nodes entirely or for only a part of the path. The initial choice of a path at the origin node may be made according to many different criteria. For example, a simple strategy would be to use the best (cheapest, fastest, etc.) path from origin to destination for all messages. Only if a path failed would one of the alternates be used. (Note: non-FIFO arrival may occur after a path failure unless a consistent strategy for path error recovery is used.)

It is not immediately obvious why the NNI field must be updated by each node in the path. Indeed, for certain network configurations a fixed path number, or even the initial choice of the link to be used would suffice to uniquely determine the path. But this path is not sufficient for a generalized configuration, as the following illustrates.

Consider the following network:

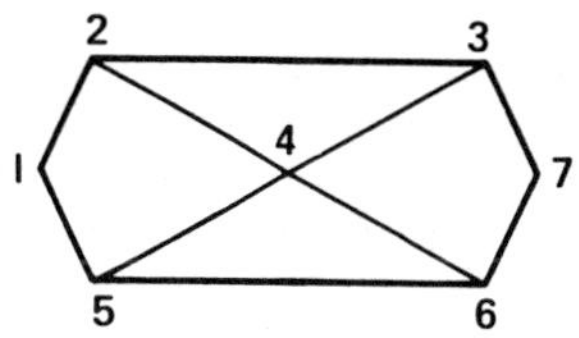

Between node 1 and node 7, there are exactly 12 non-looping paths, any one of which might be desirable under certain circumstances:

1237, 1567,
12437, 12467, 15437, 15467,
124567, 154237, 123467, 156437,
1234567, 1564237

It is instructive to examine the eight paths which involve node 2. They are 1237, 12437, 12467, 124567, 154237, 123467, 1234567, and 1564237. Once the message arrives at node 2, it can proceed to node 7 by means of six unique subpaths, via 237, 2437, 2467, 24567, 23467, and 234567.

Merely specifying the next node (or even the next several nodes) is not sufficient in general to specify the entire path. In the example, three paths all involve subpath 2-4 (2437, 2467, and 24567). Instead, it is necessary to have a consistent path numbering scheme and a way of conveying via the message the path that should be taken out of the next node, for each node in turn. The routing scheme has been described above. It remains to discuss the means by which a consistent set of routing tables can be generated.

III. ROUTING TABLE CONSTRUCTION

The algorithm for constructing the routing tables was inspired by the shortest path algorithm of Dijkstra[4]. Other references in the literature discuss various aspects of the problem[5].

The algorithm constructs the set of all possible non-looping paths to all other nodes. The set of paths from a node is "grown" a step at a time by examining the connectivity matrix and catenating any node not already in the path. If more than one node can be catenated, i.e., the path forks, then the existing path ID is retained for one of the new paths and new ID's assigned to the others. Assigning path ID's in this way ensures that each path can be unambiguously identified.

The catenation process stops when no path can be extended without including a node already in the path. At this point, all possible paths from the root node to the remaining network nodes are uniquely defined and labelled. Conversely, all paths to the root node have also been traced.

To allow the tracing and eventual selection of explicit paths between nodes, the algorithm takes advantage of the fact that in any tree there is exactly one path from any place in the tree to the root node. We need only record the path ID at each node and the corresponding path ID at the next higher node (toward the root of the tree).

In other words, if each node tells the node along the desired path what path ID to follow, the sequence of nodes in the path is unique. In effect, the paths were traced backwards.

Thus the construction process records the current node, the next node, the current path ID, and the next path ID for all the paths in the example network that lead to a given destination node. The process must then be repeated for the other nodes.

It remains to sort these entries for a given destination, first by origin node, then by some impedence value associated with the particular path to the destination. One possible impedence function is the number of nodes traversed, with ties being broken in favor of the path with the lowest path ID. Another is cost (or distance) of each path. The ordering decision thus becoming a part of the path selection criteria used by each origin node.

It is now necessary to step through each path and replace the arbitrary path IDs with the sequentially assigned Next Node Index (NNI) values, by retracing all paths starting with the nodes added last, and ending with the root node. The algorithm could utilize Next Path ID in operation, but this would require a hash table or similar lookup process to find the proper Path ID in each successive node in the path. Instead, the paths are traced and the index of the Next Path ID in the next node's table replaces the Path ID. There is no ambiguity in this procedure because the paths were numbered uniquely at each step in the generation process, and the sort quarantees that the paths are consistently ordered. Once this is done, the routing of a given destination node requires only a one level look up.

It should be noted that the first path listed for each pair of nodes is the shortest path, as would result from applying the conventional shortest path algorithm. If the number of paths allowed between nodes is restricted to one, this algorithm will produce the network of shortest paths; simply taking the first entry from each node table will also produce this network.

IV. IMPLEMENTATION CONSIDERATIONS

If the number of lines between interconnected network nodes is limited to a maximum of 8 per node, and a maximum of 16 paths are allowed between any pair of nodes, then the explicit path routing tables can be represented as a vector of up to 16 bytes per destination node (4 bits for NNI and 3 bits for the link number plus one bit for a path status indicator). A 50 node network would, therefore, require 800 bytes per node for routing tables at a maximum. The computations required to handle the actual routing are minimal.

It should be observed that 16 paths (or some smaller number) may not be sufficient to describe all possible paths, particularly if dial-up lines from almost any point to any point must be planned for. In this event, some scheme must be used to ensure that paths are discarded in a consistent manner, or the lack of a path at one intermediate node may preclude some path at a more distant node. (This is why the path ID was used as a third sort field, in order to break ties during the ordering process.)

In the case of a non-homogenous network, there may be some paths that are better suited to a particular session's characteristic than others would be. It may be desirable to implement a session specific Path Selection Mask, which would indicate which paths were allowable for this session. For example, a satellite path could be used for high volume batch data, while a land line network could be used for interactive traffic.

Within the paths permitted by the Path Selection Mask, a number of heuristic, load balancing routing policies could be supported. Since explicit paths are used, message transmit times for each path could feasibly piggy-back existing message and acknowledgement traffic. No information need be exchanged between nodes that are not presently communicating, thereby saving significant network overhead.

V. SUMMARY

A routing algorithm has been presented which will support a wide diversity of routing policies. By requiring only minimal processing and table storage in the intermediate nodes (which are insensitive to the routing policies implemented at the original node), the algorithm is particularly well suited for the routing of messages between disparate elements of a non-homogenous network.

For example, transmissions between two computers might take advantage of the buffers available, and make optimum use of a highly parallel, non-FIFO set of paths. On the other hand, communications between two low speed, limited storage devices might use a one-at-at-time alternate path algorithm to minimize the problems inherent in non-FIFO message arrival. Both of these environments could coexist in one common network, without change to any of the intermediate node functions.

VI. BIBLIOGRAPHY

1. Fultz, G. L., "Adpative Routing Techniques for Message Switching Computer Communication Networks", PhD Dissertation, Computer Science Department, University of California at Los Angeles, 1971. NTIS Accession Number AD 749678.

2. Opderbeck, H., "Problems in the Design of Control Procedures for Computer Networks", *Computer Communication Review*, (ACM SIGCOMM Newsletter) Vol. 5, No. 2, April 1975, pp 1-8.

3. Opderbeck, H., and Kleinrock, L., "The Influence of Control Procedures on the Performance of Packet-Switched Networks", National Telecommunications Conference, San Diego, California, December 1874, pp 810-817.

4. Dijkstra, E. W., "A Note on Two Problems in Connection with Graphs", *Numerische Mathematik 1* (1959), pp 269-271.

5. Fox, B. L., "More on kth Shortest Paths", *Comm. ACM* 18, 5 (May 1975), p. 279.

R. R. Jueneman

G. S. Kerr

Robert R. Jueneman: B.S. Physics, South Dakota School of Mines and Technology, 1963. After joining IBM in 1962, he helped Federal Systems Division install one of the first System/360's in support of the Apollo Space project. Later work included real-time systems in Thailand and Germany, and compiler development projects in Cambridge, Mass., and in Morris Plains, N.J. He is currently an Advisory Programmer in IBM's System Communications Division, wnere he has worked on networking architecture and communication satellite systems. He is a member of the ACM and holds a patent in the field of radiant energy conductors.

Gordon S. Kerr: B.S. Operations Research, Johns Hopkins University, 1966. He joined the Federal Systems Division of IBM in 1966 where he worked on real-time systems architecture and design, including sensor-based systems for the U.S. Air Force in Thailand and air traffic control systems for the FAA. His most recent assignments have been in real-time systems for oil refineries, advanced systems technology under Dr. Harlan Mills, and in 1975 in the United Kingdom providing teleprocessing marketing support to Rolls Royce Aeroengine and the British Steel Corporation. He is now a Marketing Representative for the IBM 5100 computer in the Washington, D.C., area.

Routing Techniques Used in Computer Communication Networks

MISCHA SCHWARTZ FELLOW, IEEE, AND THOMAS E. STERN, FELLOW, IEEE

(Invited Paper)

Abstract—**An overview is provided in this paper of the routing procedures used in a number of operating networks, as well as in two commercial network architectures. The networks include TYMNET, ARPANET, and TRANSPAC. The network architectures discussed are the IBM SNA and the DEC DNA. The routing algorithms all tend to fall in the shortest path class. In the introductory sections, routing procedures in general are discussed, with specialization to shortest path algorithms. Two shortest path algorithms, one appropriate for centralized computation, the other for distributed computation, are described. These algorithms, in somewhat modified form, provide the basis for the algorithms actually used in the networks discussed.**

INTRODUCTION

IN this paper, we provide an overview of routing techniques used in a variety of computer communication networks in current operation. These include the public data networks TYMNET and TRANSPAC (the former is a specialized common carrier network based in the United States, but with connections to Europe as well; the latter is the French government PTT data network), ARPANET, the U.S. Department of Defense Computer Network, and the commercial network architectures SNA (Systems Network Architecture) and DNA (Digital Network Architecture), developed by IBM and Digital Equipment Corporation, respectively. The networks are all examples of store-and-forward networks with data packets[1] moving from a source to a destination, buffered at intermediate nodes along a path. The path is defined simply as the collection of sequential communication links ultimately connecting source to destination.

The routing algorithms used in these networks all turn out to be variants, in one form or another, of shortest path algorithms that route packets from source to destination over a path of least cost. The specific cost criterion used differs among the networks. As will become apparent in the discussion following, some networks use a fixed cost for each link in the network, the cost being roughly inversely proportional to the link transmission capacity in bits per second. For a network with equal capacity links, minimization of the path cost generates a minimum hop path. Links with measured congestion and/or high error rates may be assigned higher costs, steering traffic away from them. Costs may also vary with the type of traffic transmitted—whether interactive, asynchronous terminal type, synchronous traffic, or file transfers between computers. Other networks attempt to estimate average packet time delay on each link and use this to assign a link cost. The resultant source-destination path chosen tends to provide the path of minimum average time delay.

Since a least cost routing algorithm is used in all cases, we provide in the next section a unifying discussion of least cost routing to further demonstrate the similarities in the network algorithms.

Although the basic routing procedures are similar, differing primarily in the choice of a link cost function used to establish the minimum cost path, the routing techniques used tend to differ in implementation and the place at which the algorithms are run. The routing algorithm may be run in centralized fashion by a central supervisory program or Network Control Center, or may be carried out in a decentralized or distributed way with individual nodes in the network running the routing algorithm separately. In the former (centralized) case, global information about the network required to run the algorithm (current topology, line capacity, estimated link delays if required, condition of links and nodes, etc.) need only be kept by the central supervisor. Path setup is then accomplished through routing messages sent to each node along the path selected. In the latter (distributed) case, the required information must be exchanged among nodes in the network. This implies some means of disseminating changes in topology (nodes and links coming up or going down), congestion, and estimated time delay information if used in the algorithms. In the next section, we discuss two least cost routing algorithms, which are the basis for routing procedures in many networks.

The routing procedures adopted also differ in how dynamic they are—how rapidly and in what manner they adapt, if at all, to changes in network topology and/or traffic information. In some cases, routes are fixed during the time of a user session. (This is the length of a call from sign-on or connect time to sign-off or disconnect time.) A node or link failure during a session will then abort the call or may, in some cases, cause a

Manuscript received September 28, 1979; revised December 7, 1979. This work was supported by the National Science Foundation under Grant ENG 78-08260.

The authors are with the Departments of Electrical Engineering and Computer Science, Columbia University, New York, NY 10027.

[1] We use the word packet here to represent a self-contained block of user data, of possibly varying size, that will traverse the network as one cohesive unit. In some networks, this is synonymous with a message. In others, a message may be broken at the source node, into several smaller packets. For this reason, we make no real distinction between the two, and we shall, in fact, sometimes use the words interchangeably.

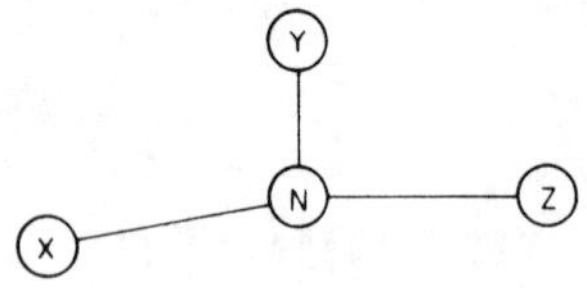

(a) CURRENT NODE AND NEIGHBORS

PACKET IDENTIFICATION	NEXT NODE ASSIGNMENT
(1,4)	X
(1,5)	Y
(2,4)	X
(2,5)	Z
(2,6)	Y
⋮	⋮

(b) ROUTING TABLE

Fig. 1. Routing at a node in a network.

new route to be selected, transparent to the user. In other cases, paths may be changed during a session (although unknown to the user and relatively slowly to avoid stability problems).

Once the path has been determined, routing tables, set at each node, are used to steer individual packets to the appropriate outgoing link. An example appears in Fig. 1. A typical node N in a network is shown, with three neighboring nodes X, Y, Z to which it is connected. In part (b) of the figure, a partial routing table is shown, associating individual user packets with an appropriate outgoing line leading to one of the neighboring nodes. The packet identification requires two numbers. The two numbers could be source and destination address, or they could be a mapping of these two fields into a corresponding pair given by the incoming link number and a number associated with that link. (This is variously called the logical record number, the logical link number, next node indicator etc.) The source-destination addresses could also be combined into one unique network-wide virtual circuit number, although this becomes difficult to monitor and assign with large networks. If all packets routed to a particular destination follow the same path, only a destination address is required to determine the proper outgoing link. (This would be the case, for example, if the paths chosen are independent of message class, type, etc.)

It is obvious that routing procedures play an important role in the design of data networks. Together with the techniques of flow and congestion control, they are implemented as part of the transport level or end-to-end protocols of networks. In layered protocols, this is the level just above the data link level that ensures correct transmission and reception of packets between any neighboring nodes in a network.

Because of their importance to the proper operation of data networks, routing techniques have received a great deal of attention in recent years. They have been variously classified as deterministic, stochastic, fixed, adaptive, centrally controlled, or locally controlled [1].

The fixed versus adaptive classification is particularly vague, since all networks provide some type of adaptivity to accommodate topological changes (links and/or nodes coming up or going down, new topologies being established). In the past, the distinction had been made primarily on the basis of individual packet handling. In the original ARPA routing algorithm, routing tables could be updated at intervals as short as 2/3 s [2]. Routing changes were made by individual nodes in a decentralized manner. As a result, individual packets in a message could follow diverse routing paths. The ARPA adaptive routing algorithm was adopted by a number of other networks as well [3], [4]. The French Cigale network used a related decentralized algorithm [5].

The hope was that by adapting on a packet-by-packet basis, the network could be made more responsive to changes in traffic characteristics and to topology, enabling packets to arrive at their destinations more rapidly, as well as avoiding failed links and/or nodes and regions of congestion. This was the case to some extent, yet the ARPA experience indicated some fundamental problems arising—there were problems with message reassembly at the destination, packet looping, adaptation problems ("too rapid a response to good news and too sluggish a response to bad news") [2], etc. As a result, the ARPA algorithm has been changed, making it less dynamic.

Although these routing techniques will be called adaptive in the sense of responding to network changes, the time constants are considerably longer. In the case of the new ARPA algorithm, changes may take place about every 10 s. Details appear in Section III.

If the algorithms used in most of these networks are adaptive and of the shortest path type, how then are they to be distinguished? We have already indicated that they may differ in the cost criterion used, and as to whether the computations are done centrally or on a distributed basis. The rate of adaptation is another distinguishing characteristic. This has also been noted already—the ARPA network, as an example, will change routes, if necessary, every 10 s. TYMNET makes changes from session to session only. DNA changes paths only when necessary.

Other differences arise due to the actual implementation: the size of routing tables, the routing overhead required, the time required to set up a path or change one if necessary; all of these will be found to differ in the networks to be described. Other differences will be noted during the discussion.

Interestingly, shortest path single routes turn out not to be optimum if the long-term average *network* time delay is to be minimized. In this case, multiple or bifurcated paths arise [6], [1]. Packets at a node are assigned to one of several outgoing links on a probabilistic basis. Bifurcated routing has not as yet been used in routing algorithms implemented in operating networks, although there are plans to incorporate this procedure in future routing mechanisms for the Canadian DATAPAC network [7].

In Section II, we provide a more detailed treatment of routing procedures in networks, focusing, as already noted, on shortest path (least cost) algorithms. In Section III, we then describe the routing implementation currently found in TYMNET, ARPANET, TRANSPAC, and the two commercial network architectures, IBM's SNA and Digital Equipment's DNA. In these last two cases, the routing procedures adopted are part of the overall protocol design and do not refer to a specific network implementation.

II. STRUCTURE OF ROUTING PROCEDURES IN PACKET-SWITCHED NETWORKS

Efficient utilization and sharing of the communications and nodal processing resources of a packet-switched communication network require various types of control, perhaps the most important of these being packet routing, that is, selecting paths along which packets are to be forwarded through the network. The objective of any routing procedure is to obtain good network performance while maintaining high throughput. "Good performance" usually means low average delay through the network, although many other performance criteria could be considered equally valid. Since poor routing algorithms often lead to congestion problems, and conversely, local congestion often requires at least temporary modification of routing rules, the routing problem cannot be completely divorced from that of congestion control [8]. Nevertheless, in this paper, we restrict ourselves to routing under the assumption that the better the routing algorithm, the less congestion is likely to occur.

While routing procedures can be set up within a network more or less independently of the protocols seen by the users (i.e., the devices external to the network), the choice of an appropriate routing procedure is influenced to some extent by the transport protocols operating at the network/user interface. It is convenient to classify these as either *virtual circuit-oriented* or *message-oriented.* In the former case, a device, or a process within a device (e.g., an application program within a computer), prepares to communicate with another device by exchanging a number of control messages with the network. The purpose of these messages is to determine whether the destination device is connected and ready to receive messages, to agree on certain aspects of the transmission protocol, and to set up a virtual circuit (VC) from source to destination.[2] Fig. 2 illustrates three VC's connecting terminals *T*1, *T*2, *T*3 to a host *H*. The VC appears to the external devices as if it were a dedicated line; under normal operation, individual data packets arrive at the destination essentially without loss or error and in the proper sequence. It is important to note, however, that *within* the network, packets from many different virtual circuits are generally sharing the same communication lines; errors, losses, and changes of packet order may occur. However, it is the function of the internal network protocols to correct for all of these effects. In the message-oriented case, communication is on a message-by-message basis. Each message or packet (often called a *datagram* in this case) must therefore contain its own destination address, but no preliminary control messages are required to set up a communication path.

A. Functions of Routing Procedures

In an idealized situation where all parameters of the network are assumed to be known and not changing, it is possible to determine a routing strategy which optimizes network performance, e.g., minimizes average network delay. The routing problem posed in this form is equivalent to the multicommodity flow problem well known in the operations research literature, and has been treated extensively in the communications network context [6], [8]-[11]. Changing situations in real networks, such as a line failure or a change in the traffic distribution, necessitate some degree of adaptivity. Any adaptive routing procedure must perform a number of functions.

1) Measurement of the network parameters pertinent to the routing strategy.

2) Forwarding of the measured information to the points(s) (Network Control Center (NCC) or nodes) at which routing computation takes place.

3) Computation of routing tables.

4) Conversion of routing table information to packet routing decisions. (This may include dissemination of a centrally computed routing table to each switching node as well as the conversion of this information to a form suitable for "dispatching" packets from node to node.)

Typical information that is measured and used in routing computation consists of states of communication lines, estimated traffic, link delays, available resources (line capacity, nodal buffers), etc. The pertinent information is forwarded to the NCC in a centralized system and to the various nodes in a distributed system. In the distributed case, two alternatives are possible: 1) forward only a limited amount of network information to each node (i.e., only that which is required for computing its local routing decisions), or 2) forward "global" network information to all nodes. (See Section III-A1) for a comparison of these two strategies in a specific network.) Based on the measured information, "costs" can be assigned to each possible source-destination path through the network. Routing assignments may be based on the principle of assigning a single path to all traffic between a given pair of source/destination nodes, or else traffic for a given source/destination pair might be distributed over several paths, resulting in the *multiple path*, or *bifurcated routing* procedure mentioned in Section I. In the latter case, single paths might still be maintained for each virtual circuit (if a VC-oriented protocol is used). This case is illustrated in Fig. 2, wherein VC_1 and VC_2 involve the same source/destination nodes, but take different paths. (Bifurcated routing on a packet basis is illustrated in Fig. 3.) While maintenance of single paths for each VC is not an optimal procedure, it has a number of practical advantages, an important one being the fact that packets always arrive at their destination in the proper order. It is therefore not surprising that most of the networks currently in operation use VC-oriented protocols with single-path routing per VC. These paths generally remain fixed for the duration of operation of the VC, unless a failure occurs.

Once one thinks in terms of single-path routing, it is natural to choose the "shortest" or, more generally, the *least cost* path whenever alternate paths exist. The path costs can, of course, be assigned using whatever cost functions seem appropriate (see above), the only essential property being that the *path* cost is computed as the sum of the costs of the *links* comprising that path. In such a case, the routing problem is equivalent to that of finding the shortest path through a graph, wherein link "length" is understood to have the more general

[2] VC's set up in this manner are termed "switched" VC's, in contrast to "permanent" VC's, which require no call setup procedure.

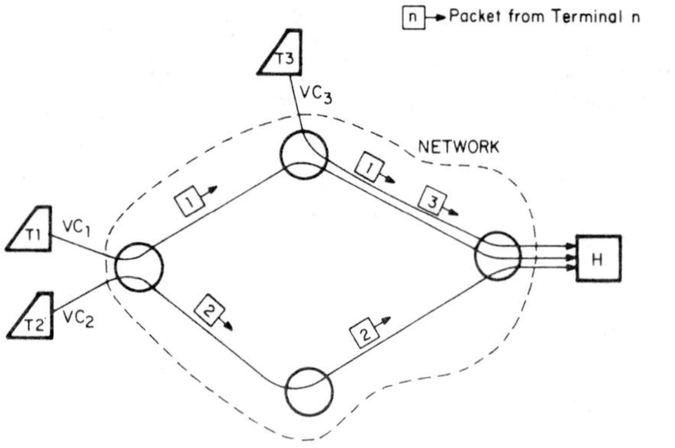

Fig. 2. Virtual circuits.

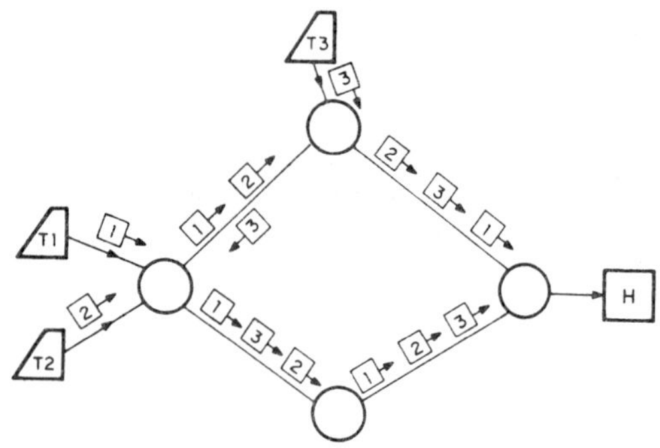

Fig. 3. Bifurcated routing.

meaning of link "cost." The set of shortest paths from all source nodes to a common destination node in a network forms a tree with the destination as root node. Thus, it is clear that if single-path routing on a source/destination basis is to be used, the path of a packet is uniquely determined by its destination alone. (Optimal bifurcated routing on a packet basis also only requires destination information.) On the other hand, single-path-per-VC routing requires either explicit or implicit VC identification for each packet; source/destination information alone is insufficient. This is because each time a new VC comes into operation, the costs determining the shortest path may be different since they generally change with time as network operating conditions change. Thus, VC's between the same source/destination pairs, established at different times, may take different paths as illustrated in Fig. 2.

B. Shortest Path Algorithms

The shortest path problem described above has received much attention in the literature. A variant of this problem, that of finding the k shortest paths between source and destination, is also applicable to the routing problem. (One is often interested in two or three alternate routes ranked in order of cost.) This too has been extensively treated. Since most operating networks use some version of shortest path routing, we discuss in this section the two algorithms most commonly used in communication network shortest path calculations. Algorithm A, due to Dijkstra [12], [13], is adapted to centralized computation, while B, a form of Ford and Fulkerson's algorithm [14], is particularly useful in distributed routing procedures. Since they are simple and intuitive, we present them informally, aided by an example.

Consider the network of Fig. 4(a) in which the numbers associated with the links are the link costs. (It is assumed for simplicity that each link is bidirectional with the same cost in each direction. However, both algorithms are applicable to the case of links with different costs in each direction.) We first use algorithm A to find shortest paths from a single source node to all other nodes. The algorithm is a step-by-step procedure where, by the kth step, the shortest paths to the k nodes closest to the source have been calculated; these nodes are contained in a set N. At the $(k + 1)$th step, a new node is added to N, whose distance to the source is the shortest of the remaining nodes outside of N. More precisely, let $l(i, j)$ be the length of the link from node i to node j, with $l(i, j)$ taken to be $+\infty$ when no link exists. Let $D(n)$ be the distance from the source to node n along the shortest path *restricted to nodes within* N. Let the nodes be indicated by positive integers with 1 representing the source.

1) Initialization. Set $N = \{1\}$, and for each node v not in N, set $D(v) = l(1, v)$.

2) At each subsequent step, find a node w not in N for which $D(w)$ is a minimum, and add w to N. Then update the distances $D(v)$ for the remaining nodes not in N by computing

$$D(v) \leftarrow \text{Min}\,[D(v), D(w) + l(w, v)].$$

Application of the algorithm to the network of Fig. 4(a) is shown in Table I, and the resultant tree of shortest paths appears in Fig. 4(b), together with a *routing table* for node 1, indicating which outbound link the traffic arriving at that node should take. (It should be clear that the same algorithm can be used to find shortest paths *from* all nodes to a common *destination.*)

Now consider algorithm B. This is an iterative procedure, which we will use in the same network to find shortest paths from all nodes to node 1, considered now as the common *destination*. To keep track of the shortest paths, we label each node v with a pair $(n, D(v))$ where $D(v)$ represents the current iterate for the shortest distance from the node to the destination and n is the number of the next node along the currently computed shortest path.

1) Initialization. Set $D(1) = 0$ and label all other nodes $(\cdot, +\infty)$.

2) Update $D(v)$ for each nondestination node v by examining the current value $D(w)$ for each adjacent node w and performing the operation

$$D(v) \leftarrow \underset{w}{\text{Min}}\,[D(w) + l(v, w)].$$

Update of node v's label is completed by replacing the first argument n by the number of the adjacent node which minimizes the above expression. Step 2) is repeated at each node until no further changes occur, at which time the algorithm terminates.

Table II illustrates the procedure for the network of Fig. 4(a). Two complete cycles of updates are required, after which

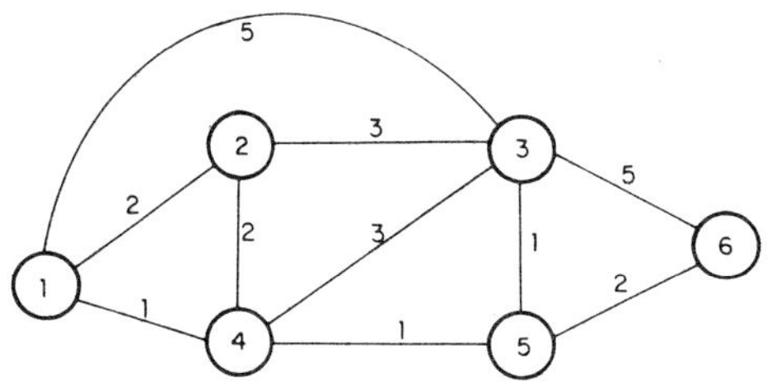

(a) NETWORK

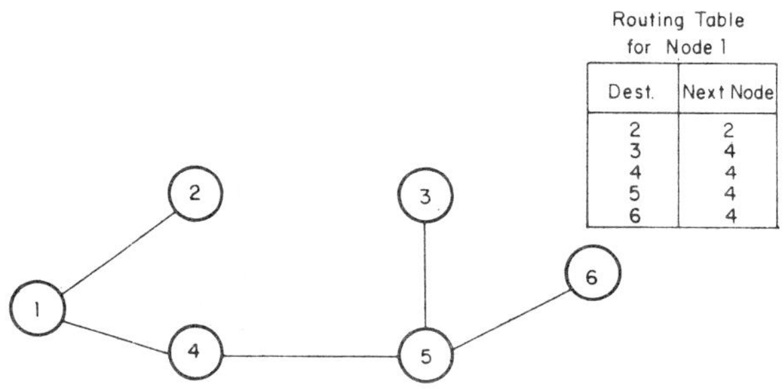

(b) TREE

Fig. 4. Example of shortest path routing.

TABLE I
ALGORITHM A

Step	N	D(2)	D(3)	D(4)	D(5)	D(6)
Initial	{1}	2	5	1	∞	∞
1	{1,4}	2	4	1	2	∞
2	{1,2,4}	2	4	1	2	∞
3	{1,2,4,5}	2	3	1	2	4
4	{1,2,3,4,5}	2	3	1	2	4
5	{1,2,3,4,5,6}	2	3	1	2	4

TABLE II
ALGORITHM B

Cycle	Node →	2	3	4	5	6
Initial		(·,∞)	(·,∞)	(·,∞)	(·,∞)	(·,∞)
1		(1,2)	(2,5)	(1,1)	(4,2)	(5,4)
2		(1,2)	(5,3)	(1,1)	(4,2)	(5,4)

no further changes occur and the iteration is complete. The tree of shortest paths generated is, of course, the same as that of Fig. 4(b). In this case, the nodes were updated in numerical order; however, any arbitrary order, cyclic or acyclic, will work. For each nondestination node, the first argument of its final label indicates the next node on the shortest path to the destination, and thus supplies the necessary routing information (for this destination *only*).

A word of comparison is now in order. Construction of routing tables based on algorithm A requires a shortest path tree calculation for each node in the manner described above. The tree is constructed with the particular node chosen as source (root) node, and the routing information that is generated is used to construct the table for that node as illustrated in Fig. 4(b). The tree can then be discarded. It should be noted that tree construction for each node requires *global* information about the network. Construction of a routing table using algorithm B requires repeated application of the algorithm for each *destination* node, resulting in a *set* of labels for each node, each label giving the routing information (next node) and distance to a particular destination. Note that in this case, the algorithm can be conveniently implemented in a *distributed* fashion, in which case each node requires only information from its neighbors.

Evaluation of the comparative merits of the two algorithms depends on a number of factors: amount of overhead required in passing measured information to the point (s) at which computation is performed, amount of data to be stored, complexity of the computation, speed with which the algorithm can respond to changes in link costs, etc. These comparisons can only be made meaningful in the context of a specific network. See Section III-A1), ARPANET, for an example.

Finally, it should be noted that the algorithms described here have been assumed to be operating under *static* conditions of topology and link costs. (Their convergence has been proved in the literature for this case only.) In some applications, the link costs are defined to depend in some fashion on link traffic, which in turn depends, through the routing algorithm, on link cost; the result is a feedback effect. By studying the dynamics of such situations, it has been shown [15] that poor choices of link cost functions can, in fact, produce instabilities in the resultant traffic patterns. Stability can, however, be ensured by making the link costs sufficiently insensitive to link flow.

C. Packet Routing Implementation

As indicated in Section II-A, computation of the routing tables does not complete the routing procedure. These tables must be converted to a form appropriate for dispatching packets from node to node. In this section, we describe a method which underlies a number of schemes used for implementing routing on a single-path-per-VC basis in some existing or proposed systems [16], [17]. The essence of the procedure is that each VC has a *path number* (PN) associated with each link it traverses; if two VC's share a link, they obtain different path numbers on that link. Each packet carries the appropriate PN, which is updated as the packet traverses the network. The updating procedure is determined by, and replaces the routing table, at each node. The PN contains all information necessary for routing; thus, the packet need not carry a VC number. To illustrate, consider a set of four active virtual circuits traversing the network of Fig. 5. The second column of Table III indicates the node sequence for the paths chosen for these VC's. (Note that VC_1 and VC_2 have the same source/destination node pair, but different paths.) Let PN (n) be a path number associated with a path on a link outbound from node n; each link will have as many path numbers as there are distinct active VC's sharing that link. The remaining columns of Table III show how a sequence of PN's is assigned at each node, serving to identify uniquely the path to be followed by a packet on each VC. When a packet is received on an inbound line at a node, its PN must be updated, and the packet must be placed

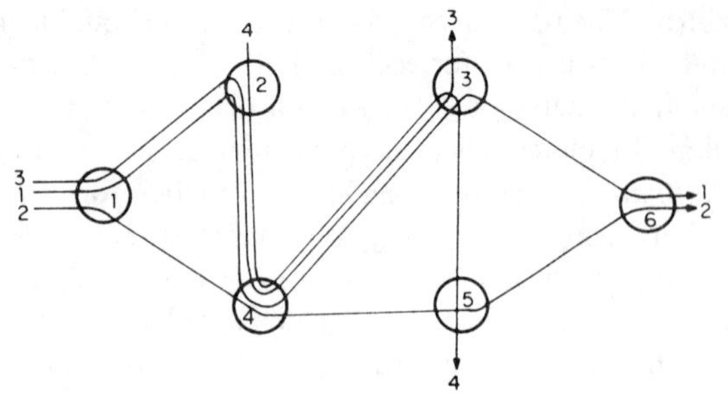

Fig. 5. Example of routing implementation.

TABLE III
PATH NUMBERS

VC#	Path	PN(1)	PN(2)	PN(3)	PN(4)	PN(5)
1	1-2-4-3-6	1	1	1	1	-
2	1-4-5-6	1	-	-	1	1
3	1-2-4-3	2	2	-	3	-
4	2-4-3-5	-	3	1	2	-

on the proper outbound line or released to its destination. At each node, a simple table lookup procedure can perform this function. In Table IV we show the necessary table for node 4. Note that it is derived directly from the routing information in Table III.

The PN used in this section is roughly equivalent to the *logical record number* used by TYMNET [16] [see Section III-A2)] and the *next node indicator* (NNI) proposed for explicit routing [17]. It might be thought that it would be simpler to tag each packet with a unique VC number rather than using the procedure outlined here. However, there will generally be far more active VC's in the network (perhaps thousands) than there are distinct VC's sharing a link (up to 256 in the case of TYMNET, for example). Thus, the PN approach is generally more efficient in memory requirement and table lookup time than any method using VC numbers.

III. EXAMPLES OF ROUTING PROCEDURES USED IN PRACTICE

A. Computer and Data Networks

1) ARPANET, A Computer Network:[3] ARPANET [18] was created in 1969 as an experiment in computer resource sharing. Beginning with four nodes in 1969, it now runs as an operational system with over 100 computers connected to 56 nodes throughout the continental United States, Hawaii, and Europe. It is a distributed network with at least two paths between any pair of nodes. Most of its lines are 50 kbit/s synchronous links. It is a store-and-forward packet-switched network in which the transport protocol is message-oriented. Messages longer than the maximum packet length are segmented into up to 8 packets at the source node and are reassembled at the destination node. This requires special

[3] The authors are indebted to Dr. John McQuillan of Bolt Beranek and Newman for providing information on ARPANET.

TABLE IV
ROUTING AT NODE 4

Arriving from node	Old PN	New PN	Next node
1	1	1	5
2	1	1	3
2	2	3	3
2	3	2	3

provision for buffer allocation at the nodes to prevent various types of lockups (a significant problem in the early stages of network development).

The network was originally operated with a distributed adaptive routing algorithm of the minimum cost, i.e., shortest path, type wherein link cost was evaluated in terms of measured link delay. Since the measured delays were determined by queue lengths encountered along a packet's transmission path, these quantities varied rapidly with time. Routing was on an individual packet basis where each packet was forwarded along the path that was perceived by the forwarding node to be the shortest in time to the packet's destination at the time of transmission. Since adaptivity was quite rapid, and different nodes could have different views of network conditions, perceptions of shortest paths could change during the period the packet traversed the network. The shortest path algorithm used was essentially our algorithm B (Section II-B), with information necessary for node updates passed among neighbors at 2/3 s intervals. Details of the algorithm can be found in [19]. A number of difficulties appeared in the algorithm, and it underwent several modifications [2] from the time it was implanted until May 1979 when it was replaced by a basically different procedure [20].

The new routing algorithm is distributed in the sense that each node independently computes its own routing tables using what is called a *shortest path first* algorithm (essentially our algorithm A with some modifications). That is, each node computes a shortest path tree with itself as the root node. Since algorithm A requires availability of global network information at the node doing the routing computation, this procedure can also be viewed as a "partially" centralized method.

Link costs are evaluated in terms of time delays on the links. Each node calculates an estimate of the delay on each of its outbound links by averaging the total packet delay (processing, queueing, transmission, retransmission, propagation time) over 10 s intervals. (One of the problems with the first algorithm was that delay estimates were obtained too frequently to be accurate.) Since all nodes must be informed of any changes in link time delays, a "flooding" technique is used for forwarding the measured delays throughout the network. Each node transmits to all its neighbors delay information for all of its outgoing links. It also acts as a repeater, broadcasting to all of its neighbors the link delay information it has received from other nodes. (Transmitting delay information back to the adjacent node from which it was received provides an automatic positive acknowledgment mechanism.) Duplicate delay information packets are dropped, so that while the information propagates to all nodes in the network, it does not circulate indefinitely. To reduce the amount of communication overhead involved in this information exchange, the 10 s average link delay measurements are not always transmitted. Only when the *change* in link delay since the last transmission exceeds a certain threshold does a new transmission take place. The threshold is reduced as time increases since the previous transmission. (However, a change in the status of a line is reported immediately.) The total communication overhead involved in delay update exchanges is less than 1 percent.

Since a complete execution of algorithm *A* at each update requires considerable computation, the algorithm has been modified so that "incremental" computation can be performed. When a single link delay changes (or if a link or node is added or deleted from the network), each node does a *partial* computation to restructure its shortest path tree. (This, of course, implies that each node must store the most recently updated tree as a basis for future updates, imposing an additional memory requirement.) Also, to take care of the case where link or node failures cause a complete partition of the network, an indication of "age" is inserted in each delay update packet. In this way, "out of date" delay information can be recognized and discarded when lines are reconnected and routing tables are recomputed. Operational results indicate that complete processing of a routing update at a node requires several milliseconds on the average.

A series of tests were performed with the algorithm under actual operating conditions, revealing a number of its features: it responds fairly rapidly (100 ms) to topological changes (one of the problems with the earlier algorithm was that it responded too slowly to line failures); it usually does minimum hop routing, but under heavy load conditions it spreads traffic over lines with excess capacity; it can respond to congestion by choosing paths to avoid congested nodes; and it seems to be stable and free of sustained looping.

Based on the information available at this time, the new algorithm seems to show some advantages over the old in terms of speed of response to changing topology, stability, and suppression of looping. These advantages are apparently attained without undue overhead. It must be kept in mind that in going from algorithm *B* to *A*, many other aspects of the routing scheme were also changed, most importantly, the procedure for estimating and forwarding link delay information. Many of the problems encountered using algorithm *B* were due to the extremely rapid updating that was used based on information whose accuracy did not warrant such rapid adaptivity.

2) TYMNET Routing Algorithm: TYMNET is a computer-communication network developed in 1970 by Tymshare, Inc. of Cupertino, CA. It has been in commercial operation since 1971 [1], [21], [22]. Originally developed for time-shared purposes, it has more recently taken on a network function as well, and is classified by the Federal Communications Commission as a valued-added specialized carrier. As of 1978, the network had 300 nodes in operation and was growing at the rate of 2 nodes/week [16]. Almost all nodes are connected to at least two other nodes in the network, giving rise to a distributed topology with alternate path capability. The network is designed primarily to handle interactive terminal users, although it does handle higher speed synchronous traffic as well. The lines connecting the nodes range in speed from 2400 to 9600 bits/s. The network covers the United States and Europe, with connections also made to the Canadian Datapac Network. Trans-Atlantic lines are cable with satellite backup. Satellites are avoided, where possible, for interactive users because of the substantial delay involved.

Individual user data packets or logical records, each preceded by a 16-bit header incorporating an 8-bit logical record number to be discussed below and an 8-bit packet character count, are concatenated to form a physical record of at most 66 8-bit characters, including 16 bits of header and 32 bits of checksum for error detection [1]. These data packets can range in length from a few characters to a maximum of 58 characters. (Physical records are transmitted as soon as available, without waiting for a specified size logical record to be assembled.)

TYMNET routing is set up centrally on a virtual circuit, fixed path, basis by a supervisory program running on one of four possible supervisory computers in the network.

A least cost algorithm [1], [16] is used to determine the appropriate path from source to destination node over which to route a given user's packets. The path is newly selected each time a user comes on the network, and is maintained unchanged during the period of the user connection or session. (In the event of an outage, the session is interrupted and a new routing path has to be computed. In TYMNET I, the version of TYMNET that has operated to the present, this could take up to 2.5 min as the supervisor learned of the incident and established the new topology. In the newer TYMNET II, which is gradually replacing the earlier version, rerouting in the event of an outage is carried out by the supervisor in a manner transparent to the user.) The algorithm used by the supervisor is a modification of Floyd's algorithm, a variation of our algorithm *B*.

Integer-valued costs are assigned to each link, and costs are then summed to find the path of least cost. The cost assignments depend on line speed and line utilization. Thus, the number 16 is assigned to a 2400 bit/s link, 12 to a 4800 bit/s link, and 10 to a 9600 bit/s link. A penalty of 16 is added to a satellite link for low-speed interactive users. This shifts such users to cable links, as noted above.

A penalty of 16 is added to a link if a node at one end complains of "overloading." The penalty is 32 if the nodes at both ends complain. Overload is experienced if the data for a specific virtual circuit have to wait more than 0.5 s before being serviced. This condition is then reported by the node to the supervisor. An overload condition may occur because of too many circuits requesting service over the same link, or it may be due to a noisy link with a high error rate, in which case the successive retransmissions which are necessary slow the effective service rate down as well. The penalty used in this case serves to steer additional circuits away from the link until the condition clears up.

Details of the specific algorithm used appear in [16]. In the absence of overloading, the algorithm tends to select the shortest path (least number of links) with highest transmission speed. As more users come on the network, the lower speed links begin to be used as well. In lightly loaded situations, users tend to have relatively shorter time delays through the network. The minimum hop paths, favored in the lightly loaded case, also tend to be more reliable than ones with more links. Users coming on in a busy period may experience higher time delays due both to congestion and to the use of lower speed lines. The use of the overload penalties tends to spread traffic around the network, deviating from the shortest path case, but attempting to reduce the time delay. In practice, the average response time for interactive users in 0.75 s [16].

It takes 12 ms for the supervisor to find the least cost path using this algorithm [23]. Once the path has been selected, the supervisor notifies each of the nodes along the path, assigning an 8-bit *logical record number* to each link on that path. (This allows up to 256 users or channels to share any one link. In practice, the maximum number ranges from 48 for a 2400 bit/s line to 192 for a 9600 bit/s line. In addition, one number or channel is reserved for a node to communicate with the supervisor and one channel is reserved for communications with the neighboring node.) The supervisor also associates a logical record number on an incoming link to a node with a number on the appropriate outgoing link setting entries in routing tables, called permuter tables in TYMNET terminology. This process, described in more detail later, is basically the same as the method of *path numbers* described in Section II-C. In the TYMNET II version of the network, the nodal computers themselves establish the routing table sizes and entries, as well as the buffers associated with them, relieving the supervisor of this burden.

Routing information is sent to a particular node in a 48-bit supervisory record with the usual 16 bits of logical record overhead as part of a normal physical record. The data transmission overhead due to the dissemination of this routing information is calculated, on a worst case basis, to be 1.6 percent [23]. This assumes that the circuit to be set up is 4 links long, with 5 nodes to be notified (the average path in TYMNET is 3.1 links) during a busy period in which an average of 1 user/s requests entry to the network. The supervisory overhead is taken as distributed equally over a minimum of 8 outgoing 2400 bit/s links from the supervisor. This calculation does not assign any physical record overhead to the supervisory logical record. The assumption is made that there are always data waiting to be transmitted and that the supervisory record is piggybacked onto a normal data record, as noted earlier.

Each node acknowledges receipt of the routing information, again doing this as part of a physical record. (Nodes, in addition, report any link outages to the supervisor as part of a 48-bit record transmitted every 16 s.)

The procedure at a node for forwarding an incoming data packet (logical record) to the appropriate outgoing link, or to either a host computer or terminal if at the destination node, proceeds as follows. As noted earlier, there is a routing or permuter table associated with each link at a node. Each logical record number in either direction on the link is associated with an entry in the table. That entry, in turn, corresponds to the address of a pair of buffers at the node, one for each direction of data flow (inbound and outbound). For L links at a node, L permuter tables are needed, each receiving up to 256 buffer addresses. An error-free physical record arriving at a node is disassembled into its component data packets (logical records). Each data packet is steered by the permuter table entry to its appropriate buffer. Data in buffers destined for terminals and/or computers associated with this node are then transferred to the appropriate device. This node thus represents the destination node for these logical records. Logical records waiting in transit buffers are handled differently. A physical record for a given outgoing link is created, under program control, by scanning sequentially the entries in the permuter table for that link. As each buffer address is read, a determination is made as to whether its *pair* has had data entered. If so, the data are then formed into a logical record with their corresponding new logical record number. This logical record is incorporated in the physical record and is transmitted out over the link.

A specific example appears in Fig. 6 [23]. Fig. 6(a) shows a typical two-link virtual circuit connecting nodes numbered 5, 7, and 10. In this example, terminal data enter the network via a terminal port at node 5, destined for a Host computer connected to node 10. The link connecting nodes 5 and 7 is labeled 1, as seen at the node 5 side, and 2 as seen at the node 7 side. Similarly, the link connecting nodes 7 and 10 is labeled 3 at the node 7 side and 1 at the node 10 side.

Fig 6(b) portrays the logical record number assignments and permuter table entries in detail, node by node. (Eight possible logical record numbers only have been assumed for simplicity.) The logical record numbers 4 and 6 have been assigned to this virtual circuit over the two links shown, respectively. At node 5, the entry node, the number 3 in entry 4 in the permuter table for link 1 indicates that data with logical record number 4 are to be found in buffer 2, the pair of buffer 3.

At node 7, data coming from link 2 are stored in buffers designated by the contents of the permuter table for link 2 at that node. Continuing with this example, data arriving at that link with logical record 4 are to be further transmitted over outgoing link 3 to node 10. Their outgoing logical record number is to be changed to 6. To accomplish this, note that the contents of entry 4 of permuter table 2 and entry 6 of permuter table 3 are paired together. Data arriving over incoming link 2 are stored in buffer 8. They are read out over link 3 when the entries for the permuter table for that link are scanned, entry 6 pointing to buffer 9, the pair of buffer 8. At node 10, the destination node for this virtual circuit, data arriving with logical record 6 are stored in buffer 100 of that node and are then transferred to the appropriate Host.

3) Routing in TRANSPAC:[4] TRANSPAC, the French public packet-switching service [24], began operation in December 1978 with ten nodes (soon to be expanded to twelve) in a distributed network configuration. As is the case with most public packet-switching services, the transport procedures for TRANSPAC follow the X.25 international standard protocol. Thus, this is a virtual-circuit-oriented system, and the routing procedures discussed below reflect this orientation. For pur-

[4] The authors are indebted to J. M. Simon of TRANSPAC for providing information used in preparing this section.

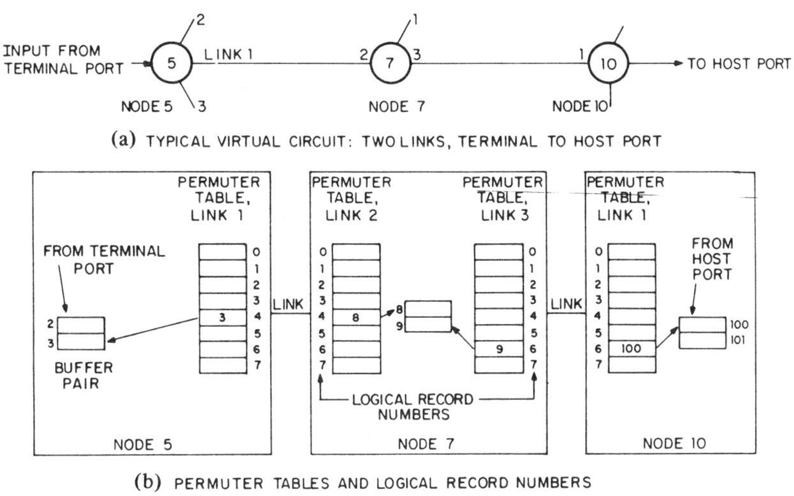

Fig. 6. Routing example, TYMNET.

poses of reliability, there are at least two 72 kbit/s lines, following different physical paths, connecting each node to the remainder of the network. Each node consists of a control unit (CU) (a CII Mitra 125 minicomputer) to which are attached a number of switching units (SU). Each incident link is controlled by an SU, which executes all data link procedures. The SU's also execute the access protocols for customers connected to the node. Routing is handled by the CU, using information from the Network Management Center (see below).

Network control is partially decentralized through six local control points which handle a certain amount of statistics gathering and perform test and reinitialization procedures in case of node or line failures. However, general network supervision, including the bulk of the routing computation, is exercised through a single Network Management Center (NMC).

Routes in TRANSPAC are assigned on a single-path-per VC basis. The algorithm of interest to us here is that which governs the assignment of a route to a switched virtual circuit, i.e., a VC which is established temporarily in response to a "call request." The call request takes the form of a *Call Packet*, emitted by equipment connected to the originating network node, and requesting connection to a specified destination. The path that eventually will be retained by the switched VC is identical to that taken by the Call Packet as it is forwarded through the network, Routing of the Call Packet is effected through routing tables stored at each node; as indicated in Section II, the tables associate a unique outbound link with each destination node. The network as currently configured has two classes of nodes. One class is connected in a distributed fashion, with alternate route capability. The second class consists of nodes homing in via a single link to a node of the first class. Node 5 in Fig. 7 is an example of a node of the first type; node 6 is a node of the second type. Messages destined to nodes of the second type are routed to the "target" node to which they are connected. In Fig. 7, messages destined for node 6 have node 5 as a target node.

The routing tables for the network are constructed in an essentially centralized fashion, using a minimum cost, i.e.,

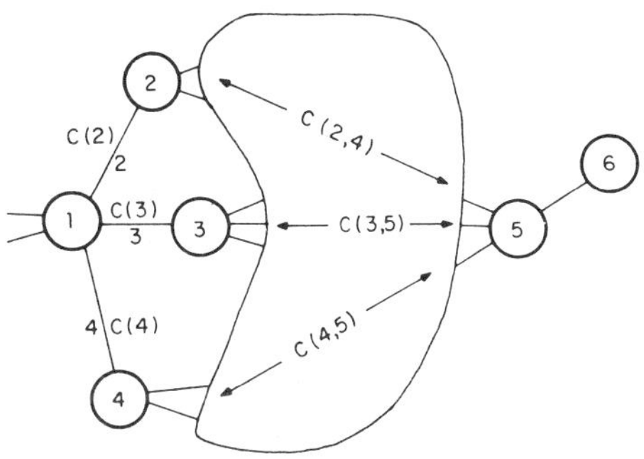

Fig. 7. Routing example, TRANSPAC.

shortest path criterion. Link costs are defined in terms of link resource utilization. Thus, the cost assigned to a link varies dynamically with network load. We shall first describe the method of evaluation of link cost and then the routing algorithm [25], [26]. Consider a full duplex link k connected to nodes m and n. Let $C_m(k)$, $C_n(k)$ be the cost assigned to link k as perceived by nodes m and n, respectively, and let $C(k) =$ Max $[C_m(k), C_n(k)]$ be the "combined" estimate of link cost. The quantities $C_i(k)$ are the basic data on which routing computation is based; they are determined locally by each node's CU which gathers estimated and measured data from its associated SU's. Link cost is defined as a function of the level of utilization of two types of resources: line capacity and link buffers. The utilization of these quantities is evaluated both by estimation (based on the parameters of the active VC's using the link) and by measurement. The cost $C_i(k)$ is set to infinity if either the link is carrying its maximum permissible number of VC's or it has exceeded a preset threshold of buffer occupancy. Otherwise, $C_i(k)$ is defined as a piecewise constant increasing function of average link flow, quantized to a small number of levels and including a "hysteresis" effect. A typical function is shown in Fig. 8, with the arrows indicating the way link cost changes as a function of changing utilization. The nodes' send updated values of their $C_i(k)$'s to the NMC whenever a change occurs; these events are infrequent due to the combined effect of coarse quantization and hysteresis. At the

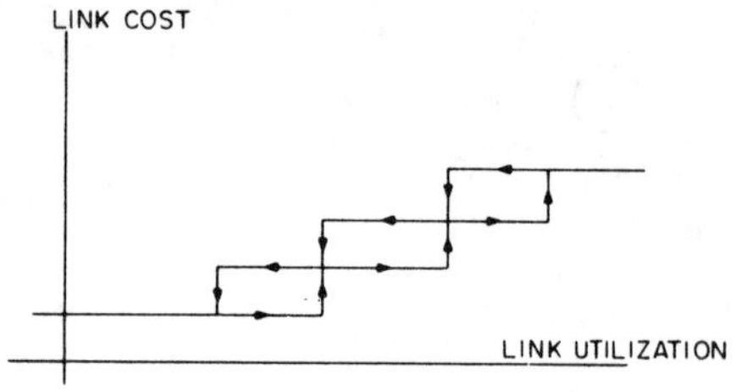

Fig. 8. A typical link cost relation, TRANSPAC.

NMC, the costs perceived by the nodes at both ends of each link are compared to form $C(k)$ as defined above.

The major part of the routing computation takes place at the NMC, but some local information is used at each node. The procedure is illustrated by an example in Fig. 7 in which a Call Packet arriving at node 1 (which may be either the originating node or an intermediate one) is to be forwarded through one of the adjacent nodes 2, 3, 4 to the target node 5, and finally to the destination node 6. Let $C(k, n)$ (computed by the NMC) be the total cost associated with the minimum cost path between nodes k and n. Node 1 determines the "shortest" route to node 5 by choosing the value of k which minimizes $C(k, 5) + \text{Max}\ [C(k), C_1(k)]$, $k = 2, 3, 4$. In this way, node 1 chooses the intermediate node that would have been chosen by the NMC, unless the value of $C_1(k)$ has changed recently. Ties are resolved by giving priority to the shortest hop path. Because of the way in which link costs are defined, the routing procedure becomes a minimum hop method upon which is superimposed a bias derived from the level of link resource utilization.

Although the TRANSPAC routing algorithm has many of the features of a typical centralized routing procedure, its operation departs from being purely centralized by allowing the final routing decision to be made locally, based on a combination of centrally and locally determined information. This is similar to the concept of "delta routing" suggested by Rudin [27].

By examining the current topology of the network [24], one can deduce the order of magnitude of the computational load at the NMC. The $C(k, n)$'s must be determined for all k and n belonging to the subset of all possible target nodes. Only six out of the twelve currently planned network nodes are in this category. Furthermore, rather than doing a complete shortest path computation to determine these quantities, the designers chose to limit the shortest path computation to a minimization over a prescribed subset of four or five paths joining each pair of nodes. Thus, the computation of all pertinent $C(k, n)$'s involves at most 75 path length evaluations.

At this writing, the network has recently entered its operational phase, with 300–400 subscribers as compared to an expected full load population of 1500. It is reported that the routing algorithms are operating satisfactorily, without undue overhead.

B. Commercial Network Architectures

The examples discussed thus far have all been operational networks. Specific physical implementations exist, although the networks have been steadily growing and changing their topologies. In the two examples discussed in this section, we focus on another type of distributed network architecture for which routing procedures become important. These are the network protocols introduced by most large computer system manufacturers during the past decade or so to enable private users to configure their own computer networks. Such networks are being increasingly developed to handle such diverse tasks as distributed processing, distributed database handling, and computer resource sharing. A computer manufacturer's protocol is designed to enable a user to interconnect a variety of computer systems and terminals in any desired configuration. All of these network protocols tend to follow a layered architecture, starting at the lowest level, that of setting up physical connections, continuing to the next, data link level, which controls the flow of data packets between neighboring nodes, then proceeding to the transmission or transport level, involved with end-to-end (source to destination) control of packet flow, routing, and congestion control, and finally concluding, at the highest levels, with several levels of "handshaking" between users or programs at the two ends. Other papers in this Special Issue discuss these network protocols in detail.

In this section, we describe the routing procedures defined for distributed versions of the IBM Systems Network Architecture (SNA) and the Digital Equipment Corporation's Digital Network Architecture (DNA). These are both relatively recent developments since earlier versions of both SNA and DNA were tailored primarily to star- or tree-type network configurations with no real need for routing. It will be noted that, unlike the network examples discussed previously, where networking is essentially transparent to the user, it is left to the user of either SNA on DNA to configure his own network. There is a certain flexibility in the routing procedures as well, with the user free to define his own link costs and paths to be taken. This is, of course, not the case in the earlier networks described.

1) IBM's Systems Network Architecture (SNA):[5] The early versions of SNA, appearing in 1974, were designed for single-computer system tree-type networks [28], [29]. In these networks, it is apparent that routing was not really a significant problem. Later versions of SNA allow two or more such single-system networks to be interconnected, leading to the concept of cross-domain networking [28]. Here, too, routing requirements were quite simple. IBM's latest SNA architecture, termed SNA 4.2 [30], envisions multiple computer systems interconnected to form a distributed network. Routing thus plays an important role in the architecture.

The routing procedure chosen for SNA incorporates predetermined fixed paths from source to destination. A multiplicity of possible routes is provided to increase the probability that a route will be available when needed to achieve load leveling, to provide alternate route capability in the event of node/link failures or congestion, and to provide different types of services for different classes of users [30], [31]. For example, batch traffic would normally be routed differently from interactive traffic. (Not only are the response time re-

[5] The authors are indebted to Dr. James P. Gray of IBM for help with this section.

quirements different calling usually for different capacity links, as noted earlier in discussing the TYMNET routing procedure, but one would not normally want to have batch traffic interfering with, and hence slowing down, interactive traffic. In SNA 4.2, this can be done by assigning a lower transmission priority to batch traffic.) Some traffic may require high security handling and will therefore be routed differently.

Multiple routing is provided at two levels: when first initiating a session, the user specifies a name corresponding to a particular class of service. Examples of classes of service include low response time, high capacity lines, more secure paths, etc. Associated with each class of service name is a list of possible virtual routes for use by sessions specifying that name. This list provides load balancing and backup capability. A particular session uses only one of these virtual routes at a time. This corresponds to the first level of multiple routing. Each virtual route provides a full-duplex connection between source and destination nodes, and can support multiple users or sessions. Each virtual route in turn maps into a so-called explicit route, the actual physical path from source to destination. It is this path that has been precalculated to provide the desired performance. Multiple explicit routes will exist, on a unidirectional basis, between any source-destination nodal pair. The multiple explicit routes provide the second level of multiple route control noted earlier. In the current SNA 4.2 release, up to eight explicit routes can be made available between any source-destination nodal pairs. Several virtual routes may use the same explicit route.

Although explicit routes are established by the source node on a unidirectional basis, explicit routes are used in pairs that are physically reversible. This simplifies user notification of route failure.

Up to 24 virtual routes are currently available between any pair of nodes. These are grouped into three levels of transmission priority, with eight possible virtual route numbers associated with each level. The entire set of virtual routes, each identified by a virtual route number and transmission priority, is stored in a virtual route identifier list. Class of service names are then associated with subsets of this list, in some preassigned order. A user setting up a session specifies his class of service name. He is then assigned to the first virtual route in the virtual route list that is available or can be activated. Multiple sessions may be assigned to the same virtual route. The virtual route is defined by four fields—the source and destination addresses, a virtual route number, and the transmission priority.

The explicit route corresponding to a specific virtual route is, in turn, defined by the source and destination addresses and an explicit route number. Each explicit route number represents one of the eight distinct routes possible between any source-destination nodal pair. A given explicit route is made up of a sequence of logical links connecting adjacent nodes along the path.

The term transmission group is used for logical link in the SNA terminology. Transmission groups may consist of multiple physical links. Thus, a set of parallel physical links between any two nodes can be divided into one or more transmission groups. This adds flexibility to the transmission function: physical links may be combined in parallel to provide higher capacity, links may be dynamically added or deleted without disruption, and scheduling of links is employed to optimize the composite bandwidth or capacity available. But the use of multiple-link transmission groups means that data packets or blocks may arrive out of sequence. Out-of-order blocks must thus be reordered at the receiving end of each transmission group along the composite path.

Routing of data packets is carried out by examining the destination address and explicit route number as a packet arrives at an intermediate node along the path. An explicit routing table at each node associates an appropriate outgoing transmission group with the destination address and explicit route number. An example of such a table at a particular node appears in Fig. 9. The letters represent the transmission groups to which packets with the corresponding address, route number pair are directed. By changing the explicit route number for a given destination, a new path will be followed. This introduces alternate route capability. If a link or node along the path becomes inoperative, any sessions using that path can be reestablished on an explicit route that bypasses the failed element. Explicit routes can also be assigned on the basis of type of traffic, types of physical media along the path (satellite or terrestrial, for example), or other criteria, as already noted. Routes could also be listed on the basis of cost, the smallest cost route being assigned first, then next smallest cost route, etc.

Note that the explicit routing concept is similar to that adopted by TYMNET in its virtual circuit approach. Here the path selected may be changed by the source node, however, by choosing a new explicit route number. In essence, a variety of alternate routes is laid out in advance. This introduces the alternate route capability noted above. In the current TYMNET approach, the central supervisor must set up a new path if one is desired.

The concept of explicit routing, as first enunciated and as noted in Section II earlier, is somewhat broader than the one described here [17]. There, rather than using a fixed explicit route number, a variable "next node index" (NNI) field was proposed for the packet header. The combination of the destination address and the NNI field then directs the packet to the appropriate outgoing transmission group. The NNI is changed at the same time as well. This allows more explicit routes to be defined than through the use of a fixed explicit route number. The idea is similar to the (variable) logical record number concept used by TYMNET. In addition, some form of intermediate or local node routing capability could be introduced through the use of the NNI. For by changing the NNI locally, a new path from that point on will be followed. This makes it possible to introduce alternate route capability along the initial path chosen in the event of localized congestion or some other delaying phenomenon. The British NPL, in a series of network simulation experiments, has shown the benefits of alternate route capability [32]. Rudin has proposed as well a routing strategy that combines centralized routing with a measure of local adaptability [27]. The general idea of explicit routing thus enables centralized, distributed, and local routing strategies (or some combination of them) to be introduced into the

DESTINATION ADDRESS ↓ \ EXPLICIT ROUTE NUMBER →	1	2	3	4	5 ···
1	A	–	B	–	–
2	A	–	–	C	–
3	–	–	B	C	–
4	B	–	–	–	–
⋮					

Fig. 9. Explicit routing table, SNA.

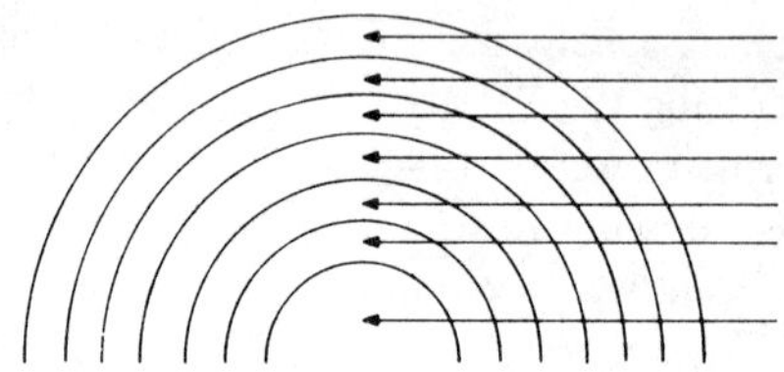

Fig. 10. DNA layered architecture.

network. In the current IBM implementation, however, only precalculated routes are used.

Three steps are required to activate a route. The individual links of the transmission groups forming the explicit route must be brought up. The explicit route is then activated. Finally, the virtual route to be used that maps into this explicit route must be activated. Special command packets are used for this purpose [31]. For example, an explicit route is activated by transmitting a specific activate command from node to node along the path. This packet verifies the routing tables of the nodes along the path. It ensures loop-free routes by checking the routing tables of nodes along the route. It verifies that there are no packets along the path with the same source-destination address pairs. It also measures the length of the explicit route in hops. Activation of the explicit route is considered completed when verified by a reply command from the destination. If the activation of the first-choice virtual route and its associated explicit route fails, the second-choice virtual route is tried, repeating with the third choice, and so on, if necessary.

The user is involved in setting the routing tables, and hence in route definition in the SNA architecture. Thus, the user can define the routes he desires, given his physical topology, by providing table entries at system definition time. The user can also ensure that a session is established on a desired route. For unique or specialized requirements, the user can write a user-exit routine that is invoked during session establishment. This exit can assign a session to a specific route.

2) Routing in Digital's DNA:[6] Digital Equipment Corporation's network architecture is called Digital Network Architecture, or DNA for short. It provides the interfaces and protocols that enable users to create their own networks using Digital Equipment Corporation Systems. The family of network products supporting DNA is generally called DECnet. DNA and DECnet were first introduced in 1973.

As does the IBM SNA, DNA employs a layered architecture. Six levels have been defined, as shown in Fig. 10 [33]. The Transport Layer shown in the figure was sufficiently simple in the Phase II DECnet implementations introduced in 1978 so as to be encompassed within the Network Services Layer. Phase II provides for point-to-point connections with no routing capability required. The next phase, Phase III DECnet, will have provision for store-and-forward distributed topologies requiring routing, flow and congestion control, and a network management capability. For this phase of DECnet, the Transport Layer has been defined and provides the necessary routing and congestion control features. In this section of the paper, we focus on routing in Phase III of DECnet.

[6] The authors are indebted to Anthony Lauck of the Digital Equipment Corporation for providing information used in preparing this portion of the paper.

The routing procedure adopted by Digital Equipment Corporation is based on a variant of the distributed shortest path algorithm (our algorithm *B*), with each node carrying out its own calculations. It is similar to the protocol analyzed by Tajibnapis [34] which has been implemented on the Michigan MERIT Computer Network. The routing algorithm adapts to changes in network topology (it does not use traffic flow information), and so needs to be invoked only when a link or node in the network comes up or fails. Unlike the IBM SNA approach, routing is done on a packet-by-packet or datagram basis, as contrasted to a virtual circuit service.

To carry out the least cost routing procedure, each link in the network is assigned a fixed cost. The specific cost is set by the user, but is approximately inversely proportional to link capacity. (Note that these assignments are then roughly similar to those used by TYMNET.) Paths with high capacity links are favored. These costs are used by each node to derive a routing database (or routing table) which lists the cost to each destination using each of the node's outgoing lines. An example appears in Fig. 11(a). (Each node in the network is assigned a unique address. Naming and addressing are carried out at a level higher than the Transport level.)

Packets going to a particular destination are routed to the output link with the smallest cost. In the example of Fig. 11(a), packets going to destination *C* would take output line 2 with a cost of 2 units. Those going to destination *B* would take output line 1. The listing of minimum cost outgoing lines, one for each destination, that is used in routing the packets is kept in a second database, called the forwarding database. An example appears in Fig. 11(b) for the routing table of Fig. 11(a). (A third, Boolean, database indicates whether each destination is reachable or not. This is discussed briefly later.)

As noted earlier, these tables are changed only on receipt of routing messages, triggered by a line (or node) coming up or going down. Specifically, a node, on learning that one of its links or a neighboring node has either been brought up or has failed, will update its tables. If the minimum cost to any destination has changed, the cost information is broadcast using a routing message to all the neighbors. These nodes, in turn, add to the cost forwarded for each destination the link cost for the link over which the message has arrived. The sum is then entered in the routing database. Minimization is then carried out row by row (i.e., for each destination), and the forwarding database is changed. If the resultant cost changes, this is, in turn, broadcast, using routing messages, to all neighbors. In this way, changes percolate throughout the network.

Routing messages contain 16 bits per destination, with a

OUTBOUND LINE →

DESTINATION NODE ↓	1	2	3
A	3	4	5
B	3	5	6
C	5	2	6
D	4	5	2
E	⋮	⋮	⋮
F			

a. ROUTING DATA BASE

DESTINATION ↓	MINIMUM COST OUTBOUND LINE
A	1
B	1
C	2
D	3
E	⋮
F	

b. FORWARDING DATA BASE

Fig. 11. Typical nodal routing tables, DNA routing protocol. (Similar tables are kept at each node.)

maximum of 128 nodes allowed at present. The routing message thus consists of a maximum of 256 bytes. Of the 16 bits, 11 are used to transmit total cost information and 5 bits represent a hop count that is transmitted as well. This hop count is incremented by 1 at each node, and is used for reachability analysis. To avoid indefinite ping-ponging, one node adding 1, its neighbor adding 1, back and forth, a destination is declared unreachable if the hop count reaches a specified maximum. This maximum could be one more than the maximum path length, it could be the diameter of the network, etc.

Packets going to an unreachable destination are discarded. However, there is an option of notifying the source that a particular destination is unreachable through the use of a "return to sender" packet. This would be used on setting up a connection or initializing the operation of the network.

If a link fails, packets queued on that link are discarded as well. To maintain end-to-end (source to destination) integrity, an acknowledgment and time-out procedure is carried out by the higher level Network Service layer of DNA. (The lower level digital data communications message protocol-DDCMP-provides link, or node-to-node, error control as well. This is, of course, similar to link error control carried out by HDLC, SDLC, and other data link control protocols [1].)

How does a node know if a link is down? This is based on the number of retransmissions of packets needed. If the number 7 is reached the link is declared down. In addition, provision is made for transmitting a low-priority "Hello" message to a neighboring node that has not been heard from for a while. If there is no acknowledgment, the node is declared down.

The actual software implementation of the routing procedure involves three processes: a *decision process* which receives routing messages; an *update process* which updates the routing tables; and a packet *forwarding process* which uses the forwarding database to route the packets. Normally, the third process only is used. The first two are run only when changes in the network topology dictate changes in the routing table. Provision is made to check the routing algorithm periodically, if desired, with the use of a timer. Such a check might be made once a minute, for example. Although the forwarding database (minimum cost paths) is normally used for routing, the entire routing database is retained as well at each node. This is required to run the distributed routing algorithm when needed. The routing database can also be used to provide alternate path capability as well, if desired, or if necessary.

Some additional factors provided by the DNA phase III Transport Layer in addition to routing include a packet lifetime control and a congestion control mechanism. The packet lifetime control is used to bound the time a packet spends in the network. A nodal visit count is kept in each data packet. If the number is too large, the packet is purged. The congestion control involved is the one analyzed by Irland [35]. The queues at each outbound link at a node are limited in size. Packets are discarded if the number queued will exceed this maximum value. Priority is, however, given to transit messages (those already in the network, as contrasted to packets originating at the node in question).

IV. CONCLUSIONS

After a brief discussion of routing in general, we have presented the basic features of routing procedures currently used in five representative packet-switched communication networks and network architectures. While the networks were chosen to represent a broad spectrum of operational characteristics, it is interesting to note that there are many similarities in their routing algorithms. At the same time, there is a great deal of diversity in the manner in which these algorithms are implemented. Most of the networks use some variation or approximation of a shortest path routing strategy. However, each network defines the "length" or "cost" of a communication link differently. Some use centralized computation, some decentralized, and some use a hybrid of the two. Adaptivity ranges from the bare minimum necessary to react to line failures to more sophisticated procedures sensing and responding to queueing delays, error rates, and line loading. Undoubtedly, a larger set of representative networks would have yielded a still richer set of alternative schemes for information gathering, routing computation, and packet forwarding. One can conclude from this survey that while the routing function is central to the smooth and efficient operation of packet-switched networks, no one scheme can be identified as "best." Many viable alternatives exist at all levels of the routing function.

REFERENCES

[1] M. Schwartz, *Computer Communication Network Design and Analysis.* Englewood Cliffs, NJ: Prentice-Hall, 1977.

[2] J. M. McQuillan, G. Falk, and I. Richer, "A review of the development and performance of the ARPANET routing algorithm," *IEEE Trans. Commun.*, vol. COM-26, pp. 1802–1811, Dec. 1978.

[3] T. Cegrell, "A routing procedure for the TIDAS message-switching network," *IEEE Trans. Commun.*, vol. COM-23, pp. 575–585, June 1975.

[4] F. Poncet and C. S. Repton, "The EIN communications sub-network: Principles and practice," in *Proc. 3rd ICCC*, Toronto, Ont., Canada, Aug. 1976, pp. 523–531.

[5] J. L. Grangé and M. I. Irland, "Thirty-nine steps to a computer network," in *Proc. 4th ICCC*, Kyoto, Japan, Sept. 1978, pp. 763–769.

[6] L. Fratta, M. Gerla, and L. Kleinrock, *The Flow Deviation Method: An Approach to Store-and-Forward Communication Network Design, Networks*, vol. 3. New York: Wiley, 1973, pp. 97–133.
[7] W. Older and D. A. Twyver, personal communication.
[8] J. M. McQuillan, "Interactions between routing and congestion control in computer networks," in *Proc. Int. Symp. Flow Contr. in Comput. Networks*, Versailles, France, Feb. 1979, J. L. Grangé and M. Gien, Eds., Amsterdam: North-Holland, pp. 63–75.
[9] M. Schwartz and C. Cheung, "The gradient projection algorithm for multiple routing in message-switched networks," *IEEE Trans. Commun.*, vol. COM-24, pp. 449–456, Apr. 1976.
[10] R. Gallager, "An optimal routing algorithm using distributed computation," *IEEE Trans. Commun.*, vol. COM-25, pp. 73–85, Jan. 1977.
[11] T. E. Stern, "A class of decentralized routing algorithms using relaxation," *IEEE Trans. Commun.*, vol. COM-25, pp. 1092–1102, Oct. 1977.
[12] E. W. Dijkstra, "A note on two problems in connection with graphs," *Numer. Math.*, vol. 1, pp. 269–271, 1959.
[13] A. V. Aho, J. E. Hopcroft, and J. D. Ullman, *The Design and Analysis of Computer Algorithms*. Reading, MA: Addison-Wesley, 1974.
[14] L. R. Ford, Jr. and D. R. Fulkerson, *Flows in Networks*. Princeton, NJ: Princeton Univ. Press, 1962.
[15] D. P. Bertsekas, "Dynamic behavior of a shortest path routing algorithm of the ARPANET type," presented at the Int. Symp. Inform. Theory, Grignano, Italy, June 1979.
[16] A. Rajaraman, "Routing in TYMNET," presented at the European Computing Conf., London, England, May 1978.
[17] R. R. Jueneman and G. S. Kerr, "Explicit routing in communications networks," in *Proc. 3rd ICCC*, Toronto, Ont., Canada, Aug. 1976, pp. 340–342.
[18] D. C. Walden, "Experiences in building, operating, and using the ARPA network," presented at the 2nd U.S.A–Japan Comput. Conf., Tokyo, Japan, Aug. 1975.
[19] J. M. McQuillan, "Adaptive routing algorithms for distributed computer networks," BBN Rep. 2831, May 1974.
[20] J. M. McQuillan *et al.*, "The new routing algorithm for the ARPANET," *IEEE Trans. Commun.*, vol. COM-28, pp. 711–719, May 1980.
[21] L. Tymes, "TYMNET—A terminal oriented communication network," in *1971 Spring Joint Comput. Conf.*, AFIPS Conf. Proc., vol. 38, 1971, pp. 211–216.
[22] J. Rinde, "Routing and control in a centrally-directed network," in *1977 Nat. Comput. Conf., AFIPS Conf. Proc.*, vol. 46, 1977, pp. 603–608.
[23] ——, "TYMNET I: An alternative to packet technology," in *Proc. 3rd ICCC*, Toronto, Ont., Canada, Aug. 1976, pp. 268–273.
[24] A. Danet, R. Despres, A. LaRest, G. Pichon, and S. Ritzenthaler, "The French public packet switching service: The Transpac network," in *Proc. 3rd ICCC*, Toronto, Ont, Canada, Aug. 1976, pp. 251–260.
[25] J. M. Simon and A. Danet, "Contrôle des ressources et principes du routage dans le réseau Transpac," in *Proc., Int. Symp. Flow Control in Comput. Networks*, Versailles, France, Feb. 1979, J. L. Grangé and M. Gien, Eds. Amsterdam: North-Holland, pp. 33–44.
[26] J. M. Simon, personal communication.
[27] H. Rudin, "On routing and "Delta-routing": A taxonomy and performance comparison of techniques for packet-switched networks," *IEEE Trans. Commun.*, vol. COM-24, pp. 43–59, Jan. 1976.
[28] R. J. Cypser, *Communications Architecture for Distributed Systems*, Reading, MA: Addison-Wesley, 1978.
[29] P. E. Green, "An introduction to network architectures and protocols," *IBM Syst. J.*, vol. 18, no. 2, pp. 202–222, 1979.
[30] J. P. Gray and T. B. McNeill, "SNA multiple-system networking," *IBM Syst. J.*, vol. 18, no. 2, pp. 263–297, 1979.
[31] V. Ahuja, "Routing and flow control in systems network architecture," *IBM Syst. J.*, vol. 18, no. 2, pp. 298–314, 1979.
[32] W. L. Price, "Data network simulation experiments at the National Physical Laboratory, 1968–1976," *Comput. Networks*, vol. 1, no. 4, pp. 199–210, 1977.
[33] Digital Network Architecture, General Description, AA-H202A-TK, Digital Equipment Corp., Maynard, MA, Nov. 1978.
[34] W. D. Tajibnapis, "A correctness proof of a topology information maintenance protocol for distributed computer networks," *Commun. Ass. Comput. Mach.*, vol. 20, pp. 477–485, July 1977.
[35] M. Irland, "Buffer management in a packet switch," *IEEE Trans. Commun.*, vol. COM-26, pp. 328–337, Mar. 1978.

★

Mischa Schwartz (S'46–A'49–M'54–SM'54–F'66) received the B.E.E. degree from Cooper Union, New York, NY, in 1947, the M.E.E. degree from the Polytechnic Institute of Brooklyn, Brooklyn, NY, in 1949, and the Ph,D. degree in applied physics from Harvard University, Cambridge, MA, in 1951.

From 1947 to 1952 he was a Project Engineer with the Sperry Gyroscope Company, working in the fields of statistical communication theory, radar detection, and radar design. From 1952 to 1974 he was Professor of Electrical Engineering at the Polytechnic Institute of Brooklyn, serving as Head of the Electrical Engineering Department from 1961 to 1965. During the year 1965–1966 he was an NSF Science Faculty Fellow at the Laboratoire de Physique, Ecole Normale Superieure, Paris, France. During the academic year 1973–1974 he was a Visiting Professor at Columbia University, New York, NY, joining that institution in September 1974 as Professor of Electrical Engineering and Computer Science.

Dr. Schwartz was a Director of the IEEE, formerly Chairman of the Information Theory Group and on the Board of Governors of the Communications Society. He is author or coauthor of five books on communications, signal processing, and computer-communication networks, and has published extensively in the technical literature. He is on the editorial boards of *Networks, Computer Networks*, and the German technical journal *AEU*. He has lectured extensively both in this country and abroad on various aspects of communication theory, communication systems, digital communications, and computer communications. He was a recipient of a Distinguished Visitor Award in 1975 from the Australian-American Education Foundation. He is a Fellow of the AAAS, and Chairman, Commission C, U.S. National Committee/URSI. He has been a consultant on communications, computer communications, signal processing, and radar to many companies.

★

Thomas E. Stern (S'54–M'57–SM'67–F'72) received his education at the Massachusetts Institute of Technology, Cambridge, receiving the B.S. and M.S. degrees in 1953 and the Sc.D. degree in 1956, all in electrical engineering.

He joined Columbia University, New York, NY in 1958 as Assistant Professor and is at present Professor of Electrical Engineering and Computer Science at that institution. He served as Department Chairman from 1972 to 1974. In addition to his activities at Columbia, he spent the academic year 1965–1966 as a Fulbright Research Scholar at the University of Paris, 1971–1972 at the IBM Research Center, La Gaude, France, under an IBM Fellowship, and 1974–1975 as a Visiting Professor at the University of Nice. He has published in the areas of information and system theory, and is the author of a textbook on the theory of nonlinear networks and systems.

Dr. Stern is a member of the IEEE Computer Communication Committee and has served on the IEEE Publications Board.

Congestion Control of Packet Communication Networks by Input Buffer Limits—A Simulation Study

SIMON S. LAM, SENIOR MEMBER, IEEE, AND Y. C. LUKE LIEN, STUDENT MEMBER, IEEE

Abstract—**An experimental study was conducted using a network simulator to investigate the performance of packet communication networks as a function of: the network resource capacities (channels, buffers), the network load (number of virtual channels, virtual channel loads), protocols (flow control, congestion control, routing), and protocol parameters (virtual channel window size, input buffer limits). Performance characteristics are shown and the design of input buffer limits for network congestion control, virtual channel window size, and nodal buffer capacity addressed. Network design strategies for the control of load fluctuations are proposed and discussed.**

Index Terms—**Buffer management, congestion control, flow control, input buffer limits, packet switching networks, performance analysis, resource allocation, store-and-forward networks.**

Manuscript received December 30, 1980; revised May 5, 1981. This work was supported by the National Science Foundation under Grant ECS78-01803. A short version of this paper was presented at the International Conference on Computer Communications, Atlanta, GA, October 1980.

S. S. Lam is with the Department of Computer Sciences, University of Texas, Austin, TX 78712.

Y. C. L. Lien was with the Department of Computer Sciences, University of Texas, Austin, TX 78712. He is now with the IBM T. J. Watson Research Center, Yorktown Heights, NY 10598.

I. Introduction

THE OBJECTIVE of a packet communication network is to reliably deliver packets from their sources to their destinations within acceptable time delays. Thus, an important performance measure of a packet network is its throughput rate in packets delivered per second.

Throughput is generated when individual packets progress through the network following finite (preferably acyclic) paths. Packets admitted into the network require the allocation of different types of resources to progress. The packet buffers at a network node form one type of resource. There are different types of buffer resources corresponding to different nodes in the network. The set of communication channels (usually just one) that transports packets from one node to another node is another type of resource. There are different types of channel resources corresponding to different communication links.

To generate a packet's worth of throughput, the network must first admit a packet and then allocate to it a set of resources consisting of the communication channels as well as one buffer at each node along its route from source to destination.[1] A complete allocation of resources needed by a packet before its admittance and subsequent journey is deemed wasteful. Almost all packet networks employ a store-and-forward protocol, whereby once a node has accepted a packet, it attempts to forward the packet to the succeeding node on the packet's route. It also buffers a copy of the packet. The buffer is released only after a positive acknowledgment has been received from the succeeding node indicating successful receipt and acceptance of the packet. With the store-and-forward protocol, a partial allocation of resources will enable packets to progress through the network; specifically, a packet residing in node i can proceed if it has acquired the resources of a buffer in node i, the channel (i, j) on its route, and a buffer in node j. (We assume that packets follow fixed routes.)

It is well known that partial allocation of resources to concurrent processes may result in a "circular wait" condition, under which none of the processes can satisfy its resource needs and progress [1]. The condition is known as a store-and-forward deadlock in packet networks [2]; the throughput rate of a deadlocked network is zero.

Buffer allocation algorithms have been proposed [3], [4] for the prevention of store-and-forward deadlocks. It has been proved that using these algorithms at least one packet in the network can satisfy its resource needs at any time. This ensures that the network throughput rate will never be zero.

The *objective of this experimental study* is to investigate conditions for packet networks to operate at a high throughput rate (instead of just ensuring that it will not become zero). The impact of network protocols for flow control, congestion control, and routing on the network throughput rate is investigated. The network performance as a function of resource capacities (channels and buffers), network load (number of virtual channels, virtual channel load), and protocol parameters (window sizes for virtual channel flow control, input buffer limits for network congestion control) is investigated.

The experimental performance results illustrate interactions and tradeoffs among input buffer limits, virtual channel window sizes, nodal buffer capacities, and offered load levels. Specifically, we found a good (heuristic) rule for the design of input buffer limits. We also found that a uniform assignment strategy for input buffer limits is significantly better than designing them proportional to nodal traffic levels.

II. The Network Congestion Phenomenon and Control Techniques

A packet in transit within a network is at any time either *enabled* (resource requirements for progress met) or *blocked* (resource requirements not met). The number $y(t)$ of enabled packets in the network at time t depends upon: nodal buffer capacities, the number of packets in transit within the network, and the distribution of these packets over queues for channels. The last two in turn depend upon the network load and the network's routing and flow and congestion control protocols.

The maximum possible value of $y(t)$ is equal to the number of communication channels in the network (given a nontrivial number of buffers at each node). There are two conditions under which $y(t)$ takes on small values. First, there are few packets in the network (due to a small network load). Second, there are many packets in the network competing for resources; however, their distribution over the channel queues are such that few packets can satisfy their resource requirements for progress (the network is *congested!*).

The network throughput rate is directly proportional to the expected number $\bar{y}$ of enabled packets under steady-state conditions.[2] Fig. 1 is a qualitative picture of the network throughput rate, given that the network has n packets in transit, plotted as a function of n.

Flow and Congestion Control Protocols

We shall consider networks that provide virtual channels between packet sources and sinks. The virtual channels are end-to-end flow controlled. Examples of end-to-end flow control protocols are SNA pacing [5], [6], RFNM in the Arpanet [7], and various window mechanisms [8], [9]. An important function of such end-to-end protocols is synchronization of the source input rate to the sink acceptance rate. All of them work by limiting the number of packets that a virtual channel can have in transit within the network. Suppose L_i is the maximum number of packets for virtual channel i (called its *window size*) and the network has K virtual channels. The maximum number of packets permitted to enter the network is thus

$$n_{\max} = L_1 + L_2 + \cdots + L_K.$$

The fact that $n_{\max}$ is bounded does not imply that a separate network congestion control protocol is not necessary. In fact, one of the motivations for packet networks in the first place is that data traffic sources are typically bursty [10]. In other words, virtual channels between source-sink pairs require network resources only intermittently with a small duty cycle. If, for example, a network is operated such that $n_{\max}$ is at point B in Fig. 1, it is obvious that a network congestion control protocol is not necessary. However, due to the bursty nature of resource demands from virtual channels, the average number of packets utilizing the network will be very low such as at point A. It is therefore desirable for packet networks to operate on the principle of overcommitment such that $n_{\max}$ is far to the right, such as at point C in Fig. 1; through averaging, the network utilization is at point B with a correspondingly high throughput rate. An immediate consequence is that a separate network congestion control protocol is now necessary to deal with temporary overloads (due to time and statistical fluctuations in network user demands).

Any network congestion control protocol must effectively reduce input into the network to alleviate temporary overloads

[1] With various high-level network protocols (not considered herein) other types of resources are needed, such as, logical channels, sockets, control blocks, sequence numbers, etc. Nodal processors are not considered because nodal processing delays are typically much smaller than communication channel delays.

[2] If the mean number of network links, denoted by $\bar{L}$, traversed by packets from source to destination is fixed and all channels have the same capacity c, then the network throughput rate is $(\bar{y}c)/\bar{L}$.

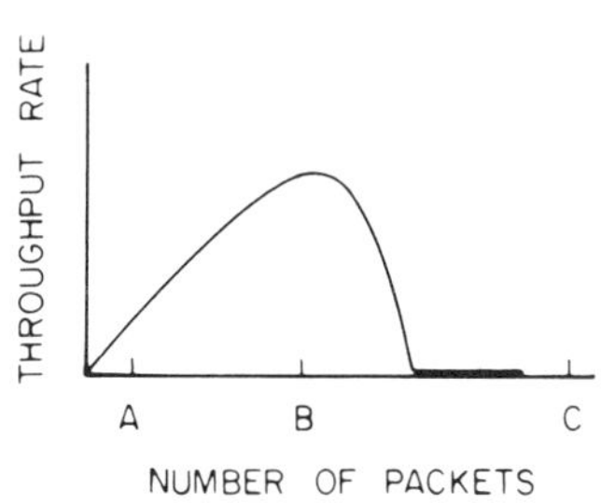

Fig. 1. Network throughput rate versus number of packets in transit.

on the network. The isarithmic principle proposed by Davis [11] and studied by Price [12] provides the above function by setting a limit on the number of packets permitted inside a network. This is accomplished by circulating a fixed number of "containers" in the network. A packet can be sent through the network only if its source can get hold of an empty container. The objective of limiting the admission of packets into a network can also be achieved by reducing the window sizes of virtual channels or by shutting down some virtual channels entirely. We have examined in our experiments the effect of window sizes and the number of virtual channels on the network throughput rate.

The control protocol that is of special interest in this paper is called input buffer limits. Network nodes are required to differentiate between "input packets" generated by local sources and "transit packets" routed to them by other nodes. A limit is imposed upon the fraction of buffers in the node that input packets can occupy. This fraction is called the *input buffer limit* (IB limit or IBL) of the node. No limit is placed on the number of buffers that transit packets can occupy.

The advantage of favoring transit packets over input packets was observed by Price [12]. A similar idea was discussed by Chou and Gerla [13]. The use of IB limits was explored in the GMD simulation study [4]. Our experimental study reported below covers different grounds from that of the GMD simulation study. Specifically, although the GMD study explored the use of IB limits for congestion control, it was not known how to design such limits nor were the conditions under which IB limits are effective demonstrated. Both our design rule for IB limits and our study of performance tradeoffs among protocol parameters, buffer capacities, and offered load levels are new.

In [14] the performance of packet networks employing IB limits for congestion control was analyzed by modeling them as an extended class of queueing networks [15]. Using the analytic model, the tradeoffs among network load, buffer capacity N_T, and IB limits were investigated. It was found that when the network load is large, there is a critical value for the IB limits beyond which the throughput capacity of the network is seriously impaired. This critical value we shall refer to as the *IB capacity*. The explanation for the drastic degradation in the network throughput rate when IB limits exceed the IB capacity turns out to be an intuitive one. For each new packet that the network admits into an input buffer, additional buffers are needed elsewhere for the packet's subsequent journey to its destination. Therefore, there is a natural ratio of the number of input buffers to the total number of buffers in the network that serves as an upper bound for IB limits. Suppose IB limits are designed to be larger than the IB capacity. It will occur that (almost) all input buffers are filled by input packets, a likely occurrence when the network is temporarily heavily loaded. The network will subsequently not have enough buffers to satisfy the demands of the resulting transit packets. The number of packets which are enabled becomes very small and the network throughput rate decreases to a small value (or zero if the network is not deadlock-free).

A significant observation in [14] is that IB limits can be made much smaller than the IB capacity without sacrificing much network throughput (from the maximum throughput rate assuming infinite buffers).

A homogeneous network consisting of nodes with identical channel configurations and traffic demands was considered in [14]. It was found that for homogeneous networks the IB capacity (identical for all nodes) is equal to $1/\overline{H}$, where $\overline{H}$ is the mean number of network nodes traversed by packets. Our experimental results below illustrate IB capacities for general nonhomogeneous networks.

III. The Network Simulator

Our experiments were performed with a simulation program written in the Pascal language using the discrete-event simulation methodology.

Several network and traffic configurations have been simulated. They are described in Section IV below in conjunction with their experimental results. For instance, the most frequently used configuration has 7 nodes, 9 full-duplex links, and 168 virtual channels. In some cases up to 336 virtual channels were simulated. Most experiments were run for 150 s of simulated time, so that each virtual channel delivered about 150–300 packets of throughput during a simulation run (except for those cases in which the network becomes congested or deadlocked). For the case of 168 virtual channels, the network throughput of each simulation run was about 25 000–45 000 packets. (For comparison, in [4] the number of virtual channels simulated was about 50, and the network throughput for each simulation run was 2000 packets.) We also observed the throughput rates of virtual channels as a function of time and found that they reached steady-state values in a few seconds. Hence, 150 s of simulation time is relatively a long time.

The class of networks that can be simulated is quite general and contains the following features.

1) Network Topology: An arbitrary topology of links and nodes can be specified.

2) Traffic Sources and Sinks: Each virtual channel has a traffic source and sink. Messages are generated by the source according to a message length probability distribution. Each message generated may be segmented into one or more packets. A packet is the basic unit of data transfer in the network.

In the experiments for this particular study, each message generated consisted of a single fixed-length packet. If the flow control window of the virtual channel is not full and the input buffer limit of the network node connected to the source has not been reached, then the source generates a new packet with rate λ (to be referred to as the *virtual channel load*); the time to packet birth was assumed to be an exponentially distributed random variable with mean $1/\lambda$ s.

For networks that are lightly loaded, λ can be interpreted as the packet generation rate of an external network user. For networks that are heavily loaded that are of interest in our experiments, the external user's packet queue for the virtual channel is almost never empty. Hence, λ models the reaction speed of the external user to a control message (or signal) from the network node authorizing input. The mean delay $1/\lambda$ may also be adjusted by a control mechanism in the external user's network interface protocol. We shall be concerned only with the effect of the parameter λ in this paper.

Sinks are modeled by queues and absorption time probability distributions. Note that a packet, at its destination node, is considered to be absorbed once it has been handed over to the sink interface protocol layer, although it may still be physically present in the node.

At a communication channel speed of say, 50 Kbit/s, both nodal processing times and sink absorption times of packets are negligible compared to channel delays. They were assumed to be zero in the present study. The problem of slow sinks is handled in practice by end-to-end control in the source-sink transport protocol. Assuming that such controls have been provided at the transport protocol level, slow sinks no longer pose a problem at the network level (of interest here).

3) *Routing:* Fixed routing using a table look-up procedure is implemented.

4) *Queueing:* In the present study all queues employ a FCFS discipline.

5) *Data Link Control:* The data link control protocol in the simulated networks is similar to that of Arpanet [16]. Each communication channel is multiplexed into 8 logical channels. A packet must acquire a logical channel to be transmitted; following the transmission it must be positively acknowledged before the logical channel is released. With 8 logical channels a node can transmit up to 8 packets over a communication channel before receiving any positive acknowledgment. Packets are individually acknowledged. A positive acknowledgment may be piggybacked in a data packet or sent as a stand-alone short packet (assumed to be 1/10 of the length of a data packet). Packets are retransmitted if not acknowledged within a time-out period. It is assumed that packet errors due to channel noise are negligible. Packets are not positively acknowledged only if they have not been accepted due to buffer, flow, or congestion control constraints. It is further assumed that positive acknowledgments are always accepted, even when the data packets containing those positive acknowledgments have been rejected.

6) *Buffer Management and Congestion Control:* Each node has a finite number of buffers. The buffers may be partitioned into classes to implement a deadlock-free buffer allocation algorithm [4]. In the present study IB limits are the only mechanism simulated for network congestion control. Additional buffer classes were not simulated to reduce the simulation cost. (In practice, although they may not be needed for congestion control they may be desirable for avoiding deadlocks.)

7) *End-to-End Flow Control:* Virtual channels are end-to-end flow controlled using windows. The window size of a virtual channel is the number of packets that it can have in transit within the network, and is specified separately for each virtual channel. Presently, end-to-end acknowledgments are not explicity modeled so that when a packet is delivered to the sink of a virtual channel this is known to the source right away. Or we can interpret the mean delay $1/\lambda$ considered earlier as consisting of the mean delay to return an end-to-end acknowledgment in addition to the mean reaction delay of the external user. End-to-end acknowledgments may be implemented in the simulator fairly easily but are deemed to add significantly and unnecessarily to the cost of simulation. Note that the buffer requirements of acknowledgments are small and also separate from those of data packets.

IV THE EXPERIMENTAL STUDY

The first network used in our study, shown in Fig. 2, consists of 7 nodes and 9 full-duplex links. Between each source-sink pair of nodes, the first and second shortest routes between them are selected. Routes of equal length (in number of links) are chosen randomly. (No attempt is made to optimize routing.) Altogether 84 different routes are used. When each route is used by k virtual channels, we shall say that the network load consists of $84 \times k$ virtual channels. Table I shows the number of virtual channels using each communication channel in the 7-node network; the number varies from 7 to 15 (assuming one virtual channel per route). The wide variation in channel utilizations was designed to depart from the homogeneous network assumption of [14].

The virtual channel load λ takes on values of 1, 2, or 10 packets/s.

The communication channel speed is assumed to be 50 packets/s; this corresponds to, for instance, a packet size of 1000 bits and a channel speed of 50 Kbit/s.

The number N_T of store-and-forward buffers is the same for each node.

The window size of a virtual channel is specified as an integer multiple of the *virtual channel path length* (in number of links). The motivation for this is to reduce the number of parameters that we need to consider. Its effect is to minimize the variation in the throughput rates of individual virtual channels. We have considered window sizes of 1, 2, or 3 $\times$ path length.

We next examine the results of a series of experiments to investigate contributions to the network load by the virtual channel load λ, the number of virtual channels, and the virtual channel window size, as well as their impact on network performance. For the moment, IB limits for network congestion control are not used.

The Effect of Increasing the Virtual Channel Load λ

In Fig. 3 the network throughput rate is plotted as a function of the number N_T of buffers at each node for λ = 1, 2, 10 packets/s. The network supports 84×2 virtual channels. Each virtual channel has a window size of $2 \times$ path length.

Note the drastic decrease in network throughput rate when

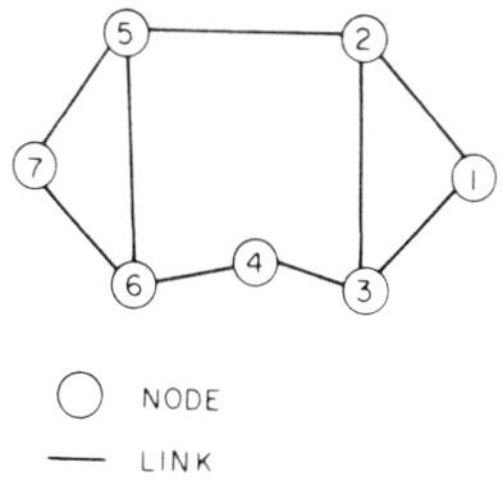

Fig. 2. A 7-node network.

TABLE I
UTILIZATION OF COMMUNICATION CHANNELS IN 7-NODE NETWORK

COMMUNICATION CHANNEL	NO. OF VIRTUAL CHANNELS	COMMUNICATION CHANNEL	NO. OF VIRTUAL CHANNELS
(1,2)	8	(4,6)	13
(1,3)	8	(5,2)	13
(2,1)	8	(5,6)	13
(2,3)	13	(5,7)	8
(2,5)	13	(6,4)	13
(3,1)	8	(6,5)	13
(3,2)	13	(6,7)	8
(3,4)	13	(7,5)	8
(4,3)	13	(7,6)	8

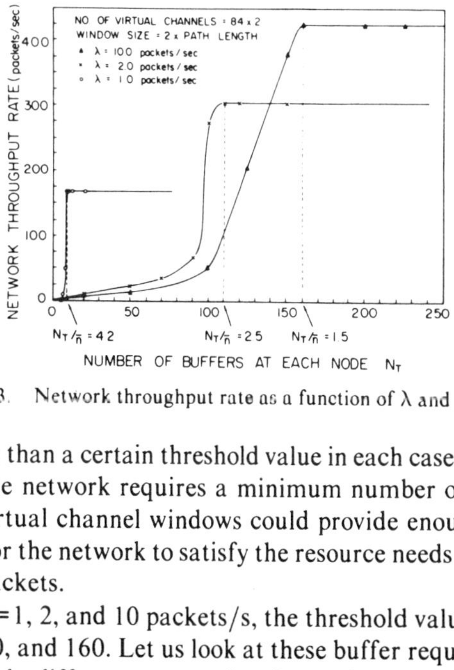

Fig. 3. Network throughput rate as a function of λ and N_T.

N_T is less than a certain threshold value in each case. In other words, the network requires a minimum number of buffers before virtual channel windows could provide enough input control for the network to satisfy the resource needs of its admitted packets.

For $\lambda = 1$, 2, and 10 packets/s, the threshold values of N_T are 9, 110, and 160. Let us look at these buffer requirements in a slightly different perspective. Let $\bar{n}$ denote the average number of packets in a node, assuming that the network nodes have infinitely many buffers; $\bar{n}$ can be either calculated using a queueing network model or obtained from simulation. Now consider the ratio of the threshold values of N_T to $\bar{n}$ for each λ. That ratio is 4.2, 2.5, and 1.7, respectively, for $\lambda = 1$, 2, and 10 (see Fig. 3). Note that the ratio actually decreases as $\bar{n}$ increases. A possible explanation is that the decrease is a consequence of the variance reduction effect of the law of large numbers.

λ is the rate at which packets are offered to a virtual channel. As λ becomes large, say $\lambda = 2$ packets/s, the number of packets that a virtual channel has in transit will be equal to the window size much of the time. As a result the rate at which packets are admitted by a virtual channel levels off very quickly as λ increases. Further increase in λ (say from 10 to ∞) will only have a marginal effect on the network loading; in this way, virtual channel windows provide an input control function for the network.

As expected, the maximum throughput rate of each curve in Fig. 3 increases as the virtual channel load λ increases, assuming the provision of sufficient buffers. Given a modest supply of buffers (say 20–100), Fig. 3 indicates that $\lambda = 1$ should be the expected load on the network in the long run, $\lambda = 2$ would be a moderate overload, while $\lambda = 10$ would be a heavy overload on the network. With no other network congestion control protocol to guard against a temporary overload of $\lambda = 2$, the network will require 110 buffers per node; to guard against a temporary overload of $\lambda = 10$, the network will require 160 buffers per node.

The Effect of Increasing the Number of Virtual Channels

In Fig. 4 the network throughput rate is plotted as a function of N_T for a network supporting 84×1, 84×2, and 84×4 virtual channels. The offered load to each virtual channel is $\lambda = 2$ packets/s. Each virtual channel has a window size equal to $2 \times$ path length.

Increasing the number of virtual channels increases the number of packets in transit within the network. The network requires a minimum number of buffers at each node to meet the resource needs of the admitted packets. Corresponding to the network load of 84×1, 84×2, and 84×4 virtual channels, the threshold values of N_T are 9, 110, and 300, respectively; the respective ratios of $N_T/\bar{n}$ are 4.3, 2.5, and 1.7. As expected, the maximum throughput rate of each curve in Fig. 4 increases as the network load increases, assuming the provision of sufficient buffers.

With a modest supply of buffers (say 20–100 per node), Fig. 4 indicates that 84×1 virtual channels correspond to the expected network load, while 84×2 virtual channels would be a moderate overload and 84×4 virtual channels would be a heavy overload on the network. Note that the buffer requirement here for the case of 84×4 virtual channels is much more severe than the case of $\lambda = 10$ in Fig. 3. The explanation is as follows. While virtual channel windows provide some form of input control for the network when λ becomes large, they provide little control when the network overloading is from an increase in the number of virtual channels. When network transit delays become large because of too many packets in the network, the virtual channel acceptance rate does decrease somewhat (in accordance with Little's formula [17]). However, it is an indirect means of control and Fig. 4 indicates that it is not very effective.

In real networks the number of virtual channels fluctuates in time depending upon network user demands. The number of possible virtual channels can be very large. For example, a single $X.25$ packet network interface [18] can potentially activate up to 4095 virtual channels.

Fig. 4 shows that with no other network congestion control protocol to guard against a temporary network overload due to an increase in the number of virtual channels, the network will require a tremendous amount of additional buffers.

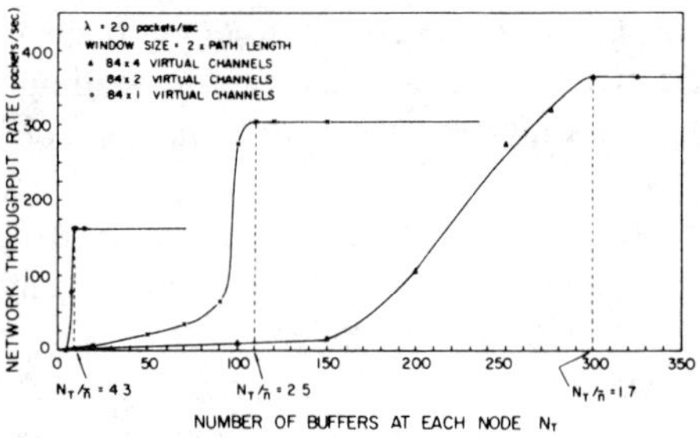

Fig. 4. Network throughput rate as a function of number of virtual channels and N_T.

The Effect of Increasing the Virtual Channel Window Size

In Fig. 5 the network throughput rate is plotted as a function of N_T for virtual channels with window sizes equal to 1 ×, 2 ×, and 3 × path length. The network supports 84 × 2 virtual channels. The virtual channel load is $\lambda = 2$ packets/s.

Note that increasing the virtual channel window sizes increases the number of packets in transit within the network and the network resource requirements. Corresponding to window sizes of 1 ×, 2 ×, and 3 × path length, the threshold values of N_T are 45, 110, and 175. It is interesting to note that the threshold ratios of $N_T/\bar{n}$ remain constant at 2.5 for all three cases. This may be due to the fact that the maximum throughput rate (assuming the provision of sufficient buffers) is almost the same for all three curves.

That the maximum network throughput rate does not change as the window sizes are increased is expected because the network load (λ and the number K of virtual channels) is the same for all three cases. If the network has sufficient buffers and if virtual channel window sizes are not too small relative to network transit delays, then almost all packets offered to the network are accepted and transported. The network throughput rate is thus close to $K\lambda$ in all three cases.

Fig. 5 shows that window sizes equal to 1 × path length give rise to as much network throughput as the other 2 cases of larger window sizes. But the threshold value of N_T required is the smallest. We should, however, keep in mind that from the point of view of individual virtual channels, each virtual channel must have a window size big enough to achieve its desired throughput rate.

In the above three sets of experiments no explicit network congestion control protocol was used, although the virtual channel windows did provide some amount of input control for the network. Each data point shown in Figs. 3–5 was obtained from a simulation run of 150 s. Store-and-forward buffer deadlock conditions were observed for those cases with $N_T = 5$.

We consider next the use of IB limits for congestion control and examine the resulting network performance characteristics. Various network design strategies for congestion control are discussed.

The Design of IB Limits for Congestion Control

In [14] it was discovered that for homogeneous networks consisting of nodes with the same channel configuration and traffic demands, the input buffer limit (IBL) of each node should be the same and satisfy

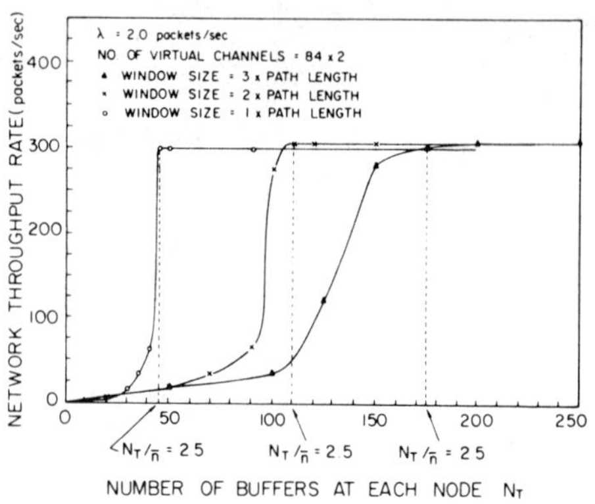

Fig. 5. Network throughput rate as a function of virtual channel window size and N_T.

$$\text{IBL} < 1/\overline{H}$$

where $\overline{H}$ is the mean number of network nodes traversed by packets. The above design rule was found to work well by both analysis and simulation.

When we first turned our attention to designing IB limits for general nonhomogeneous networks, we treated the problem as a capacity assignment problem. By considering a packet network as a queueing network and virtual channels as "closed subchains," various network statistics (virtual channel throughput rates, mean queue lengths, etc.) can be calculated under the assumption of infinite nodal buffer capacities [19]–[21]. We then attempted to invent heuristic algorithms for designing IB limits for individual nodes to match their traffic demands. We investigated several such heuristic algorithms and found that when networks with a small number of buffers were considered, none of these algorithms was *robust* (i.e., worked well for different network configurations, traffic patterns, and nodal buffer capacities).

We subsequently discovered that despite the consideration of nonhomogeneous networks, a very robust IB limit design strategy is still uniform assignment: using the same IB limit for each node given by

$$\text{IBL} = \alpha/\overline{H} \tag{1}$$

where α is a scaling factor less than 1 needed to account for the "traffic imbalance" in a nonhomogeneous network. In general, as to be shown below, the applicable α decreases as the network traffic imbalance increases (which will also be aggravated by an increase in the network load).

Given values of IBL and N_T, the maximum number N_I of buffers in a node that input packets can occupy is determined from

$$N_I = \lfloor \text{IBL} \cdot N_T \rfloor \tag{2}$$

where $\lfloor x \rfloor$ is the integer part of x.

In Fig. 6 the impact of uniformly assigned IB limits on the network's throughput rate performance is shown. The network has 84 × 2 virtual channels, $\lambda = 2$ packets/s, and virtual channel window sizes of 2 × path length. This network load was considered to be a moderate overload if individual nodes have 20–100 buffers each. Fig. 6 shows that IB limits with a properly designed α can provide a significant improvement in the network throughout rate despite the overload. There is no

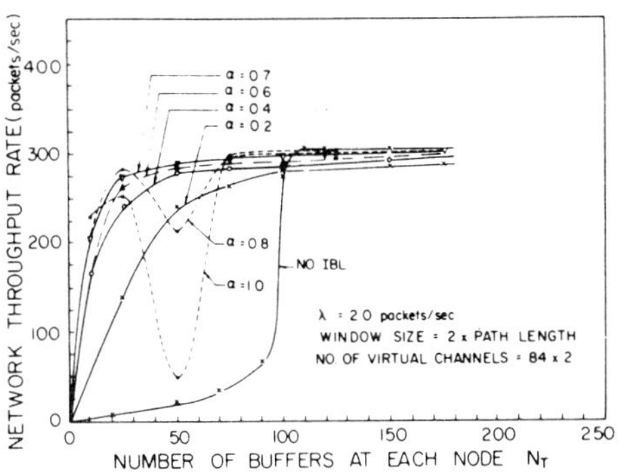

Fig. 6. The effectiveness of uniformly assigned input buffer limits.

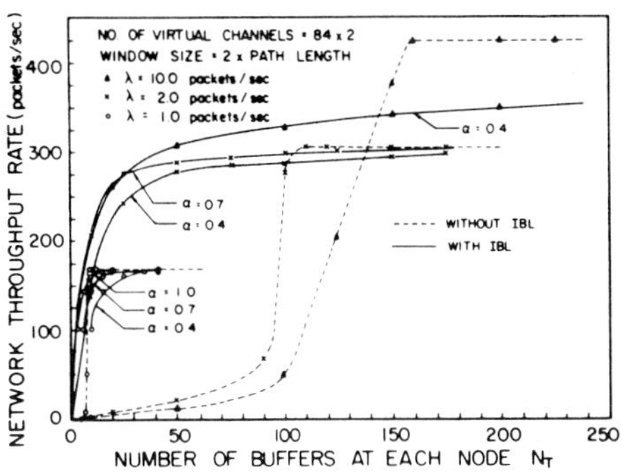

Fig. 7. Input buffer limits for overloads due to fluctuations in λ.

obvious explanation for the dip in the curves for $\alpha = 0.8$ and $\alpha = 1.0$ at $N_T = 50$. We conjecture that it occurs because loss probabilities of input and transit packets are not linear functions of N_I and N_T.

The experiments that we conducted for Fig. 6 lasted for about 150 s of simulated time each. For those cases in which the network throughput rate was not seriously degraded, each virtual channel transported close to 300 packets each (on the average).

Fig. 6 shows that the network using IB limits with $\alpha = 0.7$ can withstand the moderate overload for at least 150 s. (The exact duration depends upon the specific value of N_T.) If the network overload is infrequent and is not expected to persist for more than 150 s, we see that input buffer limits using $\alpha = 0.7$ will provide the best network throughput performance. If, however, a larger network overload or a longer overload duration is expected, then a smaller value of α may have to be used.

Design Strategies to Control Temporary Network Overloads

Let us reconsider the three different network loads first illustrated in Fig. 3 for a network with no explicit congestion control protocol. In Fig. 7 we have plotted the same network throughput curves together with new curves obtained using the same network loads, but with the network employing IB limits for congestion control.

Recall that with a modest supply of buffers (20–100), $\lambda = 1$ corresponds to the expected network load, $\lambda = 2$ is a moderate overload, while $\lambda = 10$ is a heavy overload on the network. The largest applicable value of α, for a simulation duration of 150 s, is 1 for $\lambda = 1$, 0.7 for $\lambda = 2$, and 0.4 for $\lambda = 10$. Note that as λ increases, α should be decreased.

Suppose N_T is 50. Without IB limits a substantial increase in λ, to say $\lambda = 2$, will cause the network throughput rate to degrade badly. However, with IB limits using $\alpha = 0.7$, then the network can withstand an overload of $\lambda = 2$ packets/s for at least 150 s. If IB limits corresponding to $\alpha = 0.4$ are used, then the network can withstand an overload of $\lambda = 10$ packets/s for at least 150 s.

An important observation here is that IB limits provide protection against large fluctuations in the virtual channel load λ. This protection is obtained with little or no degradation in the network throughput performance when the network is not congested even though the IB limits are fixed assigned (nonadaptive).

A network overload condition may also result from an increase in the number of virtual channels. This will happen because in most packet networks virtual channels are established by nodes without any central control. Fig. 4 shows that as the number of virtual channels increases, the network buffer requirement increases very rapidly. Throughput curves for the network loads of 84 × 1 and 84 × 2 virtual channels in Fig. 4 are reproduced in Fig. 8 together with the throughput curves corresponding to the same network loads, but with the addition of IB limits in the network.

Obviously, one way to control network congestion and prevent throughput degradation is by holding down the number of virtual channels permitted in the network. This can be accomplished by requiring the establishment of a new virtual channel to be authorized by a central controller. An alternative is to provide a network congestion control protocol, such as IB limits.

Fig. 8 shows that with N_T within the range of 20–100, input buffer limits using $\alpha = 0.7$ will enable the network to withstand an overload of 84 × 2 virtual channels for at least 150 s. This protection is achieved with a static assignment of input buffer limits. When the network is not congested (because of more buffers or a smaller load), there is little or no throughput degradation caused by the statically assigned input buffer limits.

The network loads considered in Fig. 5 for different virtual channel window sizes are reconsidered in Fig. 9, both with and without the use of IB limits for congestion control. The largest applicable values of α that can be used (for a simulation duration of 150 s) are 1, 0.7, and 0.6, respectively, for window sizes equal to 1 ×, 2 ×, and 3 × path length.

We make two observations. First, Fig. 9 shows that the strategy of reducing virtual channel window sizes when network congestion occurs will help; but Fig. 9 also shows that the use of IB limits is more effective. Second, the window size of a virtual channel is typically negotiated between the source–destination pair of nodes and not subject to any form of central control. As a result of such distributed, possibly uncoordinated, decisions and because network users will demand large virtual channel window sizes to achieve their desired throughput rates, the overload condition of having a large number of virtual channels with large window sizes will occur. Fig. 9 shows that a network overload due to all virtual channels having a window size equal to 3 times its path length can be taken care of by installing input buffer limits using $\alpha = 0.6$. Note again that

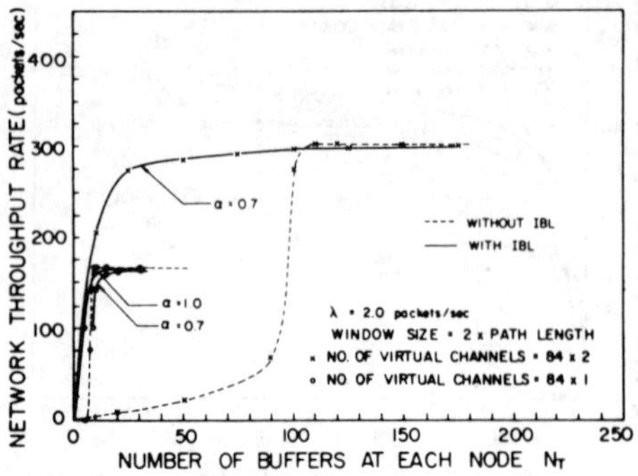

Fig. 8. Input buffer limits for overloads due to fluctuations in number of virtual channels.

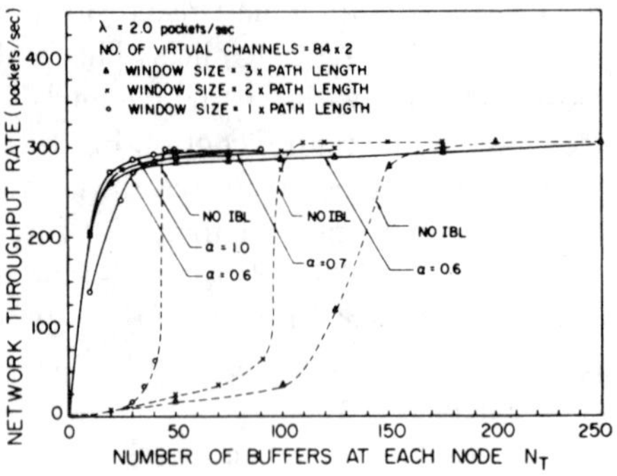

Fig. 9. Input buffer limits for overloads due to fluctuations in virtual channel window sizes.

the network throughput degradation due to statically assigned IB limits with $\alpha = 0.6$ is quite small when the network is not congested.

The Effect of Improving Routing

The design of IB limits using the uniform assignment strategy requires $\alpha < 1$ in (1) for general nonhomogeneous network with an "unbalanced" distribution of traffic over its nodes. The extent of the traffic imbalance in a network is magnified when the network load increases. The experimental results presented in Figs. 6–9 show that the applicable value of α for IB limits should be smaller if the network overload (being designed for) is more severe or prolonged.

The traffic imbalance in a network can be alleviated with improved routing. It was found in [14] that for homogeneous networks, $\alpha = 1$ can be used in (1) for the design of IB limits.

To further confirm this observation, we considered again the above 7-node network with 84 × 2 virtual channels, $\lambda = 2$ packets/s, and window sizes equal to 2 × path length. Previously, the 84 routes that we used were made up of the two shortest paths between each source–destination node pair, where ties in the selection of routes are broken by random selection. For our experiment here, we selected a somewhat different set of 84 routes. Again, shortest paths are selected, but when there is a tie between routes having the same path length we tried to select the route that provides a more balanced utilization of communication channels. Table II shows the number of virtual channels using each communication channel in the network. The traffic distribution in Table II is somewhat more balanced than the traffic distribution in Table I.

TABLE II
UTILIZATION OF COMMUNICATION CHANNELS IN 7-NODE NETWORK WITH IMPROVED ROUTES

COMMUNICATION CHANNEL	NO. OF VIRTUAL CHANNELS	COMMUNICATION CHANNEL	NO. OF VIRTUAL CHANNELS
(1,2)	7	(4,6)	13
(1,3)	7	(5,2)	15
(2,1)	7	(5,6)	14
(2,3)	14	(5,7)	7
(2,5)	15	(6,4)	13
(3,1)	7	(6,5)	14
(3,2)	14	(6,7)	7
(3,4)	13	(7,5)	7
(4,3)	13	(7,6)	7

The throughput rate versus N_T curves for the network using the original set of routes and the improved set of routes, both with and without the use of IB limits for congestion control are shown in Fig. 10. Observe from Fig. 10 that with improved routing the throughput performance is better for the network without the use of IB limits. If IB limits are used, the network throughput performance is also improved and the maximum applicable α is 1.0 (for 150 s of simulated time) instead of 0.7 before the routes were improved.

A Different Network Configuration

To illustrate that the performance characteristics and design strategies above are not unique to the network and traffic configurations of Fig. 2 and Table I, similar experiments were repeated for an 8 node network, shown in Fig. 11, with 11 full-duplex links. As before, the two shortest routes (ties broken by random selection) between each source–destination pair of nodes are used. There are 112 distinct routes altogether. Two cases have been considered corresponding to each route used by 1 virtual channel and 2 virtual channels. The number of virtual channels supported by a communication channel ranges from 8 to 16 (assuming 1 virtual channel per route), as shown in Table III. The simulation results for this network are similar to those shown in Figs. 3–9. (See [22].)

V. DISCUSSIONS

The aggregate network throughput rate has been our sole measure of network performance. Two other useful performance measures are the following:

1) the distribution of virtual channel throughput rates, and

2) the average delay of packets admitted into the network.

Although we have not shown them, both measures (and various others) are available from our simulator.

The average network delay should be interpreted differently for two different network operating conditions. First, if the network has sufficient channel and buffer resources for its load (i.e., N_T within the regions of high throughput rate in Figs. 3–5), then the average network delay increases as the network throughput rate increases, such as predicted by queueing theory under the assumption of infinite buffer capacity [17], [19]–[21].

Second, if the network does not have sufficient buffer capacities for its load, then the following behavior was observed.

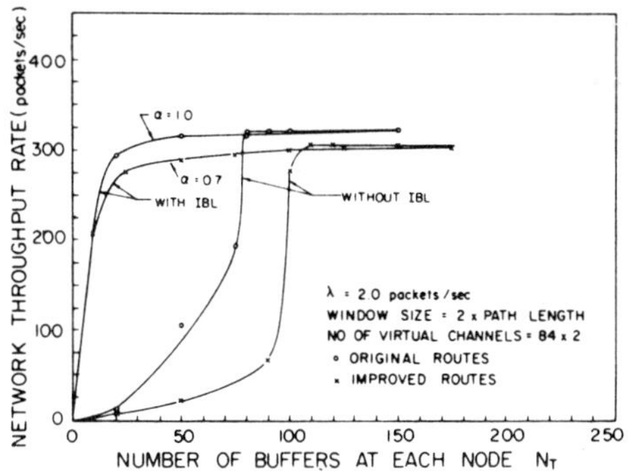

Fig. 10. The effect of improved routes on network performance.

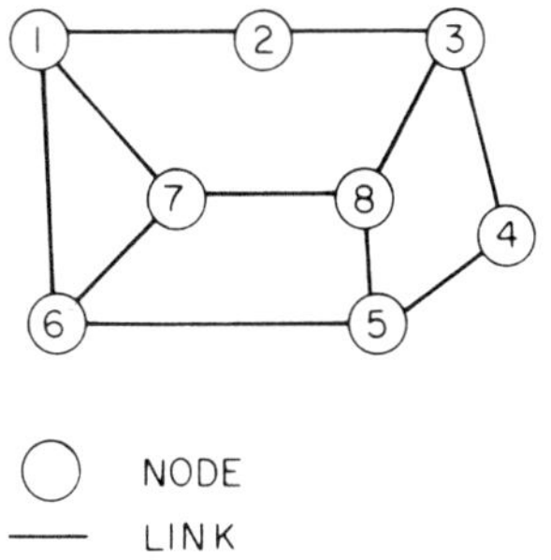

Fig. 11. An 8-node network.

TABLE III
UTILIZATION OF COMMUNICATION CHANNELS IN 8-NODE NETWORK

COMMUNICATION CHANNEL	NO. OF VIRTUAL CHANNELS	COMMUNICATION CHANNEL	NO. OF VIRTUAL CHANNELS
(1,2)	11	(5,6)	11
(1,6)	8	(5,8)	14
(1,7)	13	(6,1)	8
(2,1)	11	(6,5)	11
(2,3)	11	(6,7)	11
(3,2)	11	(7,1)	13
(3,4)	11	(7,6)	11
(3,8)	14	(7,8)	16
(4,3)	11	(8,3)	14
(4,5)	11	(8,5)	14
(5,4)	11	(8,7)	16

When N_T is decreased, the network throughput rate decreases due to more and more packets being rejected by the network. However, the average network delay for those packets admitted into the network may actually decrease. In this case the network throughput rate is a more meaningful measure of network performance than average delay.

Network Design Strategies

In general, the set of virtual channels constitutes the network load requiring the use of the network's channel and buffer resources. The routing, flow, and congestion control protocols allocate and regulate such demands on the network.

Let us review the key variables affecting the performance of packet networks.

The rate λ represents the load on a virtual channel. The effect of λ was considered in Fig. 3. λ may be controlled by the network access interface protocol for network users.

The number and distribution of virtual channels are not easily controlled for networks in which virtual channels are established and terminated by individual node pairs. If, however, a central controller is used to authorize the creation of new virtual channels, then overloads due to too many virtual channels can be prevented. (See Fig. 4.) However, a central controller may not be desirable for various reasons.

Virtual channel window sizes are useful for controlling the throughput rates of individual virtual channels. Fig. 5 shows that a means of network congestion control is to adaptively reduce virtual channel window sizes. The implementation of such a strategy requires either a central controller or a distributed algorithm that can effectively coordinate the actions of individual nodes. (Such an algorithm is not presently available. We encounter here the same difficulty as the one in the design of an effective algorithm for redistributing empty containers in an isarithmic protocol.)

We found that IB limits are effective for controlling short-term overloads on a network (due to time or statistical load fluctuations). We also found that the uniform assignment strategy of using the same IB limit at each node with

$$\text{IBL} = \alpha/\overline{H}$$

where $\overline{H}$ is the mean path length of packets and $\alpha < 1$ is an effective and robust method of network congestion control. Load fluctuations due to changes in the virtual channel loads, number of virtual channels, and virtual channel window sizes can be handled using IB limits designed with an appropriate choice of α. The value of α depends upon two considerations, namely, the severity and time duration of the overload being designed for. We found that networks using IB limits with $\alpha = 0.4$, for example, could withstand extremely severe overloads for a simulation duration of 150 s. (See Figs. 6–9.) If an overload persists, even smaller IB limits should then be adopted.

If the network load has changed, it is desirable to improve the routing to reduce the variance in communication channel utilizations. (This is the same objective as that of optimal routing to minimize average network delay [17].) We found that improved routes will enhance the effectiveness of IB limits for network congestion control. (See Fig. 10.)

We found that IB limits are effective and "inexpensive" for controlling occasional short-term overloads on a network. However, if increases in the network load are on a long-term basis, then instead of relying on IB limits the network should be equipped with more resources (channels, buffers) to handle the larger load.

ACKNOWLEDGMENT

The authors wish to thank the anonymous reviewers for their thoughtful and constructive comments.

REFERENCES

[1] E. Coffman, M. Elphick, and A. Shoshani, "System deadlocks," *Comput. Surveys*, vol. 2, pp. 67–78, June 1971.

[2] R. Kahn and W. Crowther, "Flow control in a resource-sharing computer network," *IEEE Trans. Commun.*, vol. COM-20, June 1972.

[3] K. D. Guenther, "Prevention of buffer deadlocks in packet-switching networks," presented at IFIP-IIASA Workshop Data Commun., Laxenburg, Austria, 1975.

[4] A. Giessler, J. Haenle, A. Konig, and E. Pade, "Free buffer allocation—An investigation by simulation," *Comput. Networks*, vol. 2, 1978.

[5] G. Deaton and D. Franse, "A computer network flow control study," in *Proc. 4th Int. Conf. Comput. Commun.*, Kyoto, Japan, Sept. 1978.
[6] IBM Corp., "Systems network architecture general information," GA27-3102-0, Jan. 1975.
[7] H. Opderbeck and L. Kleinrock, "The influence of control procedures on the performance of packet-switched networks," in *Proc. Nat. Telecommun. Conf.*, San Diego, CA, Dec. 1974.
[8] L. Pouzin, "Presentation and major design aspects of the Cyclades computer network," in *Data Networks: Analysis and Design, 3rd Data Commun. Symp.*, St. Petersburg, FL, Nov. 1973.
[9] V. Cerf and R. Kahn, "A protocol for packet network intercommunication," *IEEE Trans. Commun.*, vol. COM-22, pp. 637–648, May 1974.
[10] S. S. Lam, "A new measure for characterizing data traffic," *IEEE Trans. Commun.*, vol. COM-26, pp. 137–140, Jan. 1978.
[11] D. W. Davies, "The control of congestion in packet switching networks," *IEEE Trans. Commun.*, vol. COM-20, June 1972.
[12] W. L. Price, "Data network simulation experiments at the National Physical Laboratory 1968–1976," *Comput. Networks*, vol. 1, 1977.
[13] W. Chou and M. Gerla, "A unified flow and congestion control model for packet networks," in *Proc. 3rd Int. Conf. Comput. Commun.*, Toronto, Canada, Aug. 1976.
[14] S. S. Lam and M. Reiser, "Congestion control of store-and-forward networks by input buffer limits—An analysis," *IEEE Trans. Commun.*, vol. COM-27, pp. 127–134, Jan. 1979.
[15] S. S. Lam, "Queueing networks with population size constraints," *IBM J. Res. Develop.*, vol. 21, pp. 370–378, July 1977.
[16] J. McQuillan, W. Crowther, B. Cosell, D. Walden, and F. Heart, "Improvements in the design and performance of the ARPA network," in *AFIPS Conf. Proc., Fall Joint Comput. Conf.*, Dec. 1972.
[17] L. Kleinrock, *Queueing Systems, Vol. 1: Theory, Vol. 2: Computer Applications.* New York: Wiley-Interscience, 1975 and 1976.
[18] A. Rybczynski *et al.*, "A new communication protocol for accessing data networks—The international packet-mode interface," in *Nat. Comput. Conf., AFIPS Conf. Proc.*, vol. 45, 1976.
[19] M. Reiser, "A queueing network analysis of computer communication networks with window flow control," *IEEE Trans. Commun.*, vol. COM-27, pp. 1199–1209, Aug. 1979.
[20] S. S. Lam and J. W. Wong, "Queueing network models of packet switching networks," Dep. Comput. Sci., Univ. of Waterloo, Waterloo, Ont., Canada, Tech. Rep. CS-81-06, Feb. 1981.
[21] S. S. Lam and Y. L. Lien, "A tree convolution algorithm for the solution of queueing networks," Dep. Comput. Sci., Univ. of Texas, Austin, Tech. Rep. TR-165, Jan. 1981.
[22] ——, "An experimental study of the congestion control of packet communication networks," Dep. Comput. Sci., Univ. of Texas, Austin, Tech. Rep. TR-142, Mar. 1980.

Simon S. Lam (S'69–M'74–SM'80) was born in Macao, on July 31, 1947. He received the B.S.E.E. degree (with Distinction) from Washington State University, Pullman, in 1969, and the M.S. and Ph.D. degrees in engineering from the University of California, Los Angeles, in 1970 and 1974, respectively.

From 1972 to 1974 he was with the ARPA Network project at UCLA and did research on satellite packet communication. From 1974 to 1977 he was a Research Staff Member with the IBM T. J. Watson Research Center, Yorktown Heights, NY, where he worked on performance analysis problems of packet switching networks, SNA, and satellite networks. Since September 1977 he has been with the University of Texas at Austin, where he is Associate Professor of Computer Sciences. His current research interests include modeling and analysis of computer systems, communication networks, and protocols. At the University of California at Los Angeles he held a Phi Kappa Phi Fellowship from 1969 to 1970, and a Chancellor's Teaching Fellowship from 1969 to 1973. In 1975 he received the Leonard G. Abraham Award for the best paper in the field of Communications Systems published in IEEE TRANSACTIONS ON COMMUNICATIONS.

Dr. Lam is a member of Tau Beta Pi, Sigma Tau, Phi Kappa Phi, Pi Mu Epsilon, and the Association for Computing Machinery. He serves on the Editorial Board of the international journal *Performance Evaluation*.

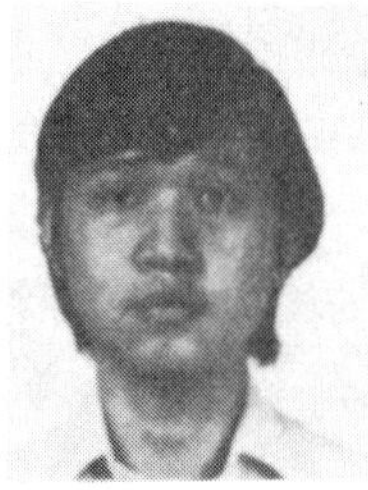

Y. C. Luke Lien (S'81) was born in Chia-I, Taiwan, on September 16, 1951. He received the B.S. degree from Fu-Jen Catholic University, Taiwan, in 1973, and the M.S. degree from the University of Kansas, Lawrence, in 1975, both in physics.

From 1977 to 1981 he was a graduate student and a Research Assistant in the Department of Computer Sciences, University of Texas, Austin, from which he is expecting to receive the Ph.D. degree in computer science in 1981. Recently, he joined the IBM T. J. Watson Research Center, Yorktown Heights, NY, as a Research Staff Member.

Mr. Lien is a member of the Association for Computing Machinery, Phi Kappa Phi, and the IEEE Communications Society.

Flow Control: A Comparative Survey

MARIO GERLA, MEMBER, IEEE, AND LEONARD KLEINROCK, FELLOW, IEEE

(Invited Paper)

Abstract—Packet switching offers attractive advantages over the more conventional circuit-switched scheme, namely, flexibility in setting up user connections and more efficient use of resources after the connection is established. However, if user demands are allowed to exceed the system capacity, unpleasant congestion effects occur which rapidly neutralize the delay and efficiency advantages. Congestion can be eliminated by using an appropriate set of traffic monitoring and control procedures called flow control procedures. Flow control can be exercised at various levels in a packet network. The following levels are identified and discussed in this paper: hop level, entry-to-exit level, network access level, and transport level. For each level, the most representative techniques are surveyed and compared. Furthermore, the interaction between the different levels is discussed.

I. INTRODUCTION

A packet-switched network may be thought of as a distributed pool of productive resources (channels, buffers, and switching processors) whose capacity must be shared dynamically by a community of competing users (or, more generally, processes) wishing to communicate with each other. Dynamic resource sharing is what distinguishes packet switching from the more traditional circuit switching approach, in which network resources are dedicated to each user for an entire session. The key advantages of dynamic sharing are greater speed and flexibility in setting up user connections across the network and more efficient use of network resources after the connection is established.

These advantages of dynamic sharing do not come without a certain danger, however. Indeed, unless careful control is exercised on the user demands, the users may seriously abuse the network. In fact, if the demands are allowed to exceed the system capacity, highly unpleasant congestion effects occur which rapidly neutralize the delay and efficiency advantages of a packet network. The type of congestion that occurs in an overloaded packet network is not unlike that observed in a highway network. During peak hours, the demands often exceed the highway capacity, creating large backlogs. Furthermore, the interference between transit traffic on the highway and on-ramp and off-ramp traffic reduces the effective throughput of the highway, thus causing an even more rapid increase in the backlog. If this positive feedback situation persists, traffic on the highway may come to a standstill. The typical relationship between effective throughput and offered load in a highway system (and, more generally, in many uncontrolled, distributed dynamic sharing systems) is shown in Fig. 1.

By properly monitoring and controlling the offered load many of these congestion problems may be eliminated. In a highway system, it is common to control the input by using access ramp traffic lights. The objective is to keep the interference between transit traffic and incoming traffic within acceptable limits, and to prevent the incoming traffic rate from exceeding the highway capacity.

Similar types of controls are used in packet switched networks, and are called *flow control* procedures. As in the highway system, the basic principle is to keep the excess load out of the network. The techniques, however, are much more sophisticated since the elements of the network (i.e., the switching processors) are intelligent, can communicate with each other, and therefore can coordinate their actions in a distributed control strategy.

Internal network congestion may also be relieved by rerouting some of the traffic from heavily loaded paths to underutilized paths. It is important to understand, however, that *routing* can reduce and, perhaps, delay network congestion; it cannot prevent it. We do not discuss the interactions between routing and flow control in this paper. The interested reader is referred to the routing protocol survey paper by Schwartz and Stern in this TRANSACTIONS [51].

The main functions of flow control in a packet network are:

1) prevention of throughput degradation and loss of efficiency due to overload,

2) deadlock avoidance,

3) fair allocation of resources among competing users, and

4) speed matching between the network and its attached users.

Throughput degradation and deadlocks occur because the traffic that has already been accepted into the network (i.e., traffic that has already been allocated network resources) exceeds the nominal capacity of the network. To prevent overallocation of resources, the flow control procedure includes a set of constraints (on buffers that can be allocated, on outstanding packets, on transmission rates, etc.) which can effectively limit the access of traffic into the network or, more precisely, to selected sections of the network. These constraints may be fixed, or may be dynamically adjusted based on traffic conditions.

Apart from the requirement of throughput efficiency, network resources must be fairly distributed among users.

Manuscript received December 15, 1979; revised Jaunary 8, 1980. This work was supported by the Advanced Research Projects Agency of the Department of Defense under Contract MDA 903-77-C-0272.

The authors are with the Department of Computer Science, University of California, Los Angeles, CA 90024.

Reprinted from *IEEE Transactions on Communications,* Volume COM-28, Number 4, April 1980, pages 553-574. Copyright © 1980 by The Institute of Electrical and Electronics Engineers, Inc.

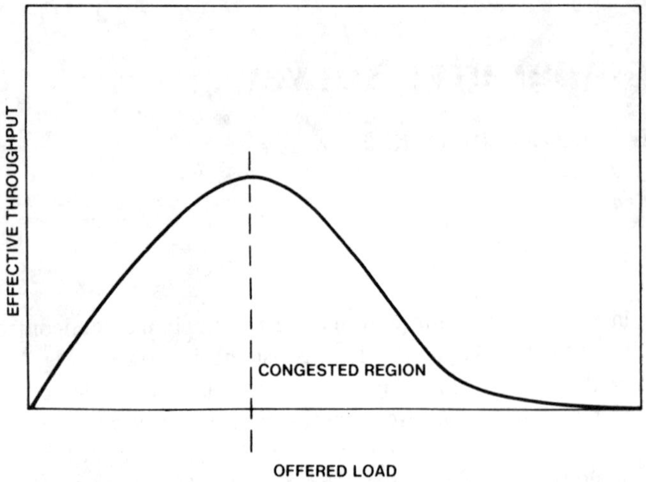

Fig. 1. Effective throughput versus offered load in an uncontrolled, distributed dynamic sharing system.

Unfortunately, efficiency and fairness objectives do not always coincide. For example, referring back to our highway traffic situation, the effective throughput of the Long Island Expressway could be maximized by opening all the lanes to traffic from the Island to New York City during the morning rush hour, and in the opposite direction during the evening rush hour. This solution, however, would also maximize the discontent of the reverse commuters (and we all know how dangerous it is to anger a New Yorker)! In packet networks, unfairness conditions can also arise (as we will show in the following sections); but they tend to be more subtle and less obvious than in highway networks because of the complexity of the communications protocols. One of the functions of flow control, therefore, is to prevent unfairness by placing *selective* restrictions on the amount of resources that each user (or user group) may acquire, in spite of the negative effect that these restrictions may have on dynamic resource sharing and, therefore, overall throughput efficiency.

Flow control can be exercised at various levels in a packet network. The following levels are identified and discussed in this paper.

1) *Hop Level*: This level of flow control attempts to maintain a smooth flow of traffic between two neighboring nodes in a computer network, avoiding local buffer congestion and deadlocks. (We shall devote Section II to the discussion of this form of flow control.)

2) *Entry-to-Exit Level*: This level of flow control is generally implemented as a protocol between the source and destination switch, and has the purpose of preventing buffer congestion at the exit switch (Section III).

3) *Network Access Level*: The objective of this level is to throttle external inputs based on measurements of internal (as opposed to destination) network congestion (Section IV).

4) *Transport Level*: This is the level of flow control associated with the transport protocol, i.e., the protocol which provides for the reliable delivery of packets on the "virtual" connection between two remote processes. Its main purpose is to prevent congestion of user buffers at the process level (i.e., outside of the network) (Section V).

Some authors reserve the term "flow control" for the transport level, and refer to the other three levels of control as *congestion control* [34]. This terminology is used to emphasize the physical distinction between the first three levels, which are realized in the communications subnet (and therefore are the responsibility of the network implementer) and the fourth level, which is realized in the user devices (and therefore is the responsiblity of the network customer). In this paper, we have chosen to use the term flow control for all four levels.

The design of an efficient flow control strategy for a packet network is a complex task in many ways. The most critical issue is the fact that flow control is a multilayer distributed protocol involving several different levels. At each level, the flow control implementation must be consistent and compatible with other protocol functions existing at the same level. Furthermore, the interactions between different levels must be carefully studied in order to avoid duplication of functions on one hand, and lack of coordination on the other.

The purpose of this paper is to provide a taxonomy of flow control mechanisms based on the above defined multilevel structure. First, we review problems, functions, and performance measures of flow control. Then, for each level we survey the most representative flow control techniques that have been proposed and/or implemented, providing a performance comparison among techniques at the same level, and discussing the interaction between techniques at different levels. Finally, we briefly mention some new flow control issues raised by novel computer network applications.

II. FLOW CONTROL: PROBLEMS, FUNCTIONS, AND MEASURES

Our overall problem is to identify mechanisms which permit efficient dynamic sharing of the pool of resources (channels, buffers, and switching processors) in a packet network. In this section, we first describe and illustrate the congestion problems caused by *lack* of control. Then we define the functions of flow control and the different levels at which these functions are implemented. Finally, we introduce performance measures for the evaluation and comparison of different flow control schemes.

A. Loss of Efficiency

The main cause of throughput degradation in a packet network is the *wastage* of resources. This may happen either because conflicting demands by two or more users make the resource unusable (e.g., collisions on a random access channel); or because a user acquires more resources than strictly needed, thus starving other users (e.g., a slow sink fed by a fast source may create a backlog of packets within the network which prevents other traffic from getting through). The two resources that are most commonly "wasted" in a packet network are *communications capacity* and *storage capacity*.

Buffer wastage is an indirect consequence of limited nodal storage: a given end-to-end packet stream may be blocked at an intermediate node along the path because all of the buffers have been "hogged" by other streams. This may happen even if channel bandwidth is plentiful along the blocked stream path, thus causing an unnecessary loss of throughput. The source of this throughput degradation is that some users unnecessarily monopolize (i.e., waste) the buffers at some congested node.

A simple example of throughput degradation caused by buffer interference is shown in Fig. 2. Two pairs of hosts, (A, A') and (B, B'), are engaged in data transmission through a single network node. Access line speeds (in arbitrary units) are given in Fig. 2. The traffic requirement from A to A' is constant and is equal to 0.8 (measured in the same units as the line speed). The requirement from B to B' is variable, and is denoted by λ. When λ approaches 1, the output queue from the switch to host B' grows indefinitely large filling up all the buffers in the switch. Packets arriving when all the buffers are full are discarded, and are later retransmitted by the source host (we refer to this model as the *retransmit model*). If we plot the total throughput, i.e., the sum of (A, A') and (B, B') delivered traffic as a function of λ (as in the solid curve of Fig. 3), we note that for $\lambda = 1$, the throughput experiences a sharp drop from 1.8 to 1.1. The drop is due to the fact that the switch can handle the entire user demand $= \lambda + 0.8$ for $\lambda < 1$; while for $\lambda \geqslant 1$, the switch buffers become full, causing overflow. Consequently, large queues build up in both the A and B hosts. With a heavy load, the rate of packet transmissions (and retransmissions) from B is 10 times the rate from A because of the difference in line access speeds. Thus, packets from B have a 10 times better chance of being accepted when a buffer becomes free than packets from A, leading to a 10 to 1 imbalance in effective throughput. Since the (B, B') throughput is limited to 1, the (A, A') throughput is reduced to 0.1 (i.e., one tenth of the AA' throughput), yielding a total throughput = 1.1 for $\lambda \geqslant 1$.

In this example, we have observed a *decrease in useful throughput* caused by an *increase of offered load* beyond the critical system capacity. This throughput degradation is typical of congested systems, and is often taken as a definition of congestion (i.e., a system is "congestion-prone" if an increment in offered load causes a reduction in throughput) [27].

In the previous example, we assumed that dropped packets would be retransmitted from the host. A similar analysis can be carried out assuming that dropped packets are lost (*loss model*). The throughput versus offered load performance is similar to that of the retransmit model, although the drop is somewhat smoother in this case (the dashed curve of Fig. 3).

Throughput degradation effects, caused by inefficient allocation (and therefore wastage) of buffers are found also in multinode networks as reported by several studies [27], [13], [18]. To prevent this type of degradation, proper buffer allocation rules are generally established at each node, as soon described.

Another cause of throughput degradation is channel wastage. This problem manifests itself very clearly in multi-access channels (e.g., packet satellite, or packet radio channels), when users transmit packets at random times without prior coordination (random access). A well-known example is offered by the ALOHA channel [23]. Packets that collide are lost, thus causing channel wastage and consequently, throughput degradation. Congestion prevention in multi-

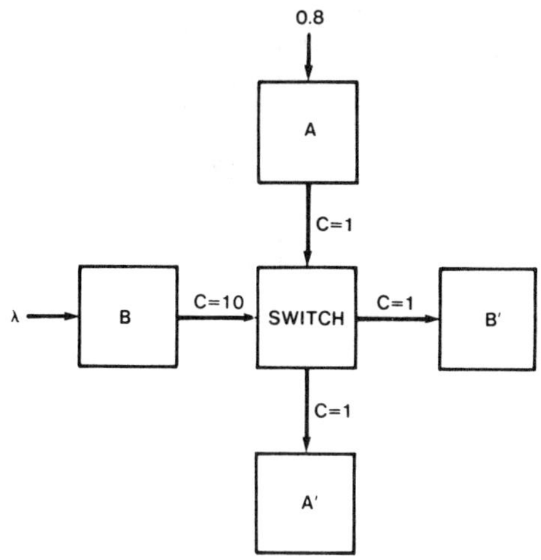

Fig. 2. Buffer interference example.

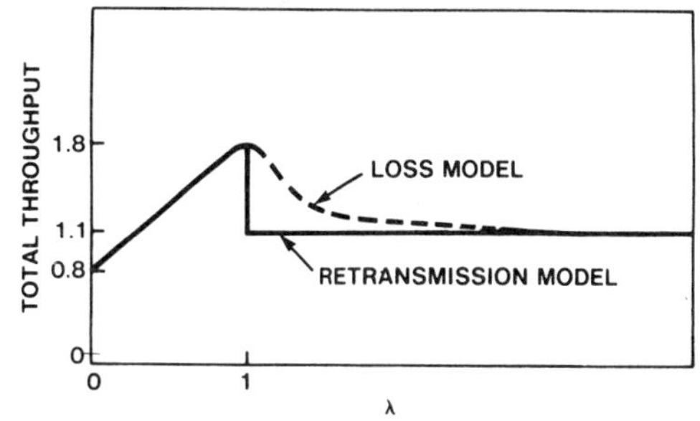

Fig. 3. Throughput degradation of system of Fig. 2 due to buffer interference.

access channels is discussed in [46] in this TRANSACTIONS. Also, it is clear that unnecessary retransmissions of a packet represent another form of channel wastage. Yet another manifestation is the use of unnecessarily long paths in a network (e.g., looping in routing algorithms).

B. Unfairness

Unfairness is a natural byproduct of uncontrolled competition. Some users, because of their relative position in the network or the particular selection of network and traffic parameters, may succeed in capturing a larger share of resources than others, and thus enjoy preferential treatment.

One example of unfairness has already been given in Figs. 2 and 3 where the $(B\text{-}B')$ flow is allowed to exceed the $(A\text{-}A')$ flow by a factor of ten. Another obvious example of unfairness is offered by the single switch loss model in Fig. 4. The speed of the output trunk is 1. Hosts A and B are injecting data into the switch with rates 0.5 and λ, respectively. For fairness, the output trunk should be equally shared by the two hosts. However, the *loss model* performance results shown in Fig. 5 indicate that for large values of λ, host B captures the entire output trunk bandwidth, reducing the A throughput to zero. As previously observed, for $\lambda \gg 0.5$ host B has a far better chance to seize free buffers in the switch than host A. Specifically, the ratio of A-packets to B-packets in the switch at heavy load is roughly equal to $0.5/\lambda$. Thus, the ratio of A-throughput to B-throughput is also $0.5/\lambda$, explaining the behavior in Fig. 5.

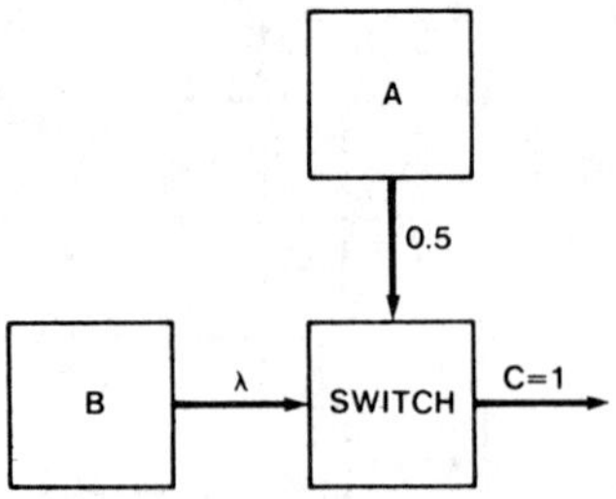

Fig. 4. Example of unfairness.

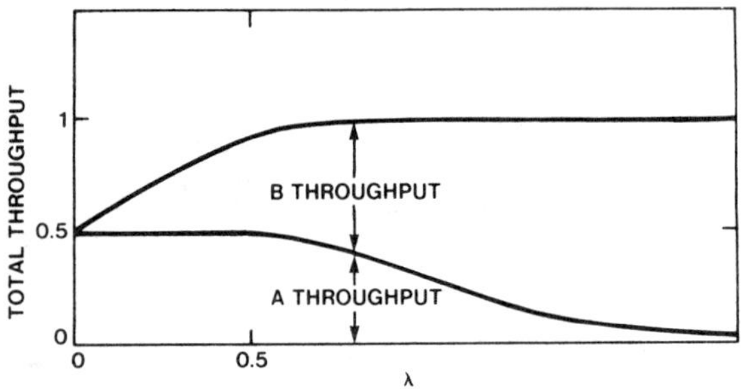

Fig. 5. Performance of system shown in Fig. 4.

Cases of unfairness have been reported in many multinode network studies, and several "fairness" techniques have been proposed. Unfortunately, the problem of fairness is considerably more difficult to deal with than the problem of total throughput degradation because a general, unambiguous definition of fairness is not always possible in a distributed resource sharing environment.

C. Deadlocks

A deadlock condition manifests itself by a (total or partial) network crash. Deadlocks often occur because of a cyclic wait of resources to become available. That is, one user is holding a portion of the resources that he currently needs and is waiting for another user to release the remaining resources necessary to complete his task and this user is waiting for yet a third user, etc., such that the sequence of "waiting" users closes into a cycle, and it is immediately seen that no user in the cycle can make any progress [3]. Thus, the throughput for this subset of users is reduced to zero.

Deadlocks are likely to occur in a network when the offered load exceeds network capacity. For a simple example of a deadlock, consider two switches, A and B, connected by a trunk carrying heavy traffic in both directions (see Fig. 6). Under the heavy traffic assumption, node A rapidly fills up with packets directed to B; and vice versa, B fills up with packets directed to A. If we assume that dropped packets are retransmitted, then each node must hold a copy of each packet (and therefore a buffer) until the packet is accepted by the other node. This may result in an endless wait in which a node holds all of its buffers to store packets being transmitted to the other node, and keeps retransmitting packets to the other node waiting for buffers to be freed there. Consequently, no useful data are transferred on the trunk. It turns out that this type of deadlock (known as direct store-and-forward deadlock [19]) is relatively easy to prevent by

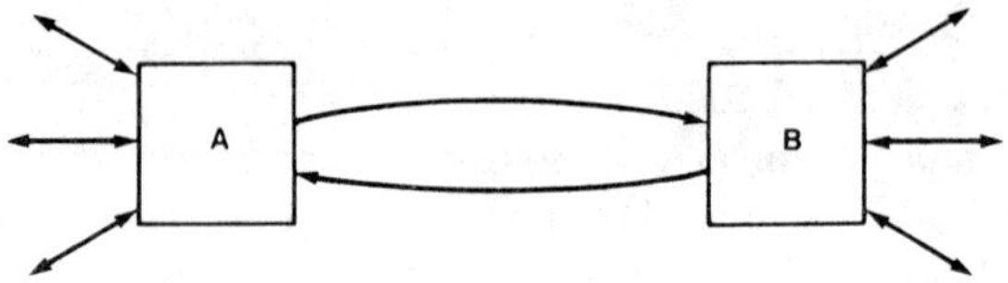

Fig. 6. Deadlock example.

setting simple restrictions on buffer usage at each node. A more extensive discussion of deadlocks will be given in Section II.

It is important to point out that buffer deadlocks are possible only in networks which retransmit dropped packets, i.e., which save a copy of a packet at each node while transmitting the packet to the next node on the path, and retransmit a copy of the packet in case of overflow (retransmit model). If dropped packets are not retransmitted (i.e., a loss model), the sending node is not required to save a copy of the packet until acceptance at the next node, thus removing a necessary condition for deadlocks. Thus, lossy networks are deadlock free; however, an additional recovery mechanism for lost packets must then be provided at the end-to-end level.

D. Flow Control Functions

Flow control may be defined as a protocol (or more generally, a set of protocols), designed to protect the network from problems related to overload and speed mismatches. Solutions to the three problems just discussed (maintaining efficiency, fairness and freedom from deadlock) are accomplished by setting rules for the allocation of buffers at each node and by properly regulating and (if necessary) blocking the flow of packets internally in the network as well as at network entry points. Actually, multiple levels of flow control are generally implemented in a network, as we shall see.

Efficiency and congestion prevention benefits of flow control do not come for free. In fact, flow control (as with any other form of control in a distributed network) may require some exchange of information between nodes to select the control strategy and possibly, some exchange of commands and parameter information to implement that strategy. This exchange translates into channel, processor, and storage overhead. Furthermore, flow control may require the dedication of resources (e.g., buffers, bandwidth) to individual users, or classes of users, thus reducing the statistical benefits of complete resource sharing. Clearly, the tradeoff between gain in efficiency (due to controls) and loss in efficiency (due to limited sharing and overhead) must be carefully considered in designing flow control strategies. This tradeoff is illustrated by the curves in Fig. 7, showing the effective throughput as a function of offered load. The ideal throughput curve corresponds to perfect control as it could be implemented by an ideal observer, with complete and instantaneous network status information. Ideal throughput follows the input and increases linearly until it reaches a horizontal asymptote corresponding to the maximum theoretical network throughput. The controlled throughput curve is a typical curve that can be obtained with an actual

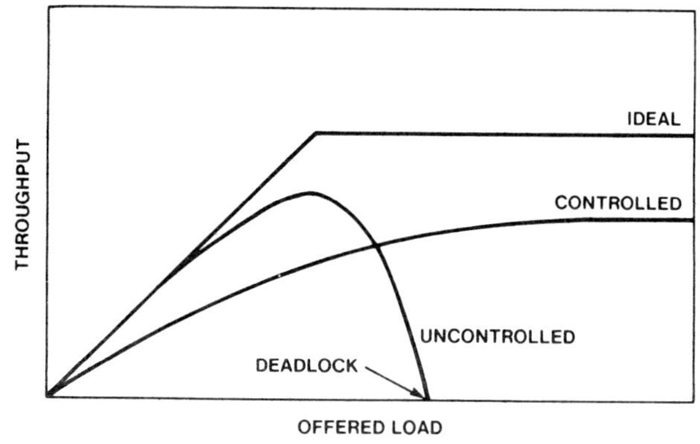

Fig. 7. Flow control performance tradeoffs.

control procedure. Throughput values are lower than with the ideal curve because of imperfect control and control overhead. The uncontrolled curve follows the ideal curve for low offered load; for higher load, it collapses to a very low value of throughput and, possibly, to a deadlock.

Clearly, controls buy safety at high offered loads at the expense of somewhat reduced efficiency. The reduction in efficiency is measured in terms of higher delays (for light load) and lower throughput (at saturation). Furthermore, experience shows that flow control procedures are quite difficult to design and ironically, can themselves be the source of deadlocks and degradations. In particular, when one controls flow, one places *constraints* on the flow. If one cannot meet a constraint, then the result is a deadlock. Or, if one is slow in meeting the constraint, the result is a throughput degradation.

E. Levels of Flow Control

Flow control in a packet network can be best described as a multilayered structure consisting of several mechanisms operating independently at different levels. Since flow control levels are closely related to (and sometimes imbedded in) protocol levels, it is helpful for us to begin by briefly reviewing the network protocol structure, pointing to the flow control provisions existing at each level [17]. The flow control level structure will then be defined following the protocol structure model.

Fig. 8 depicts the typical protocol layer architecture implemented in a packet network, using as a reference a network path connecting user devices called DTE's (data terminating equipment) through a number of intervening communications switches called DCE's (data communications equipment). For the user-to-network (i.e., DTE-to-DCE) interface, a standard set of protocol levels is now being defined by ISO and ANSI [9]. For the internode protocols within the communications subnetwork, there is less emphasis on standardization since different network manufacturers tend to select different solutions to best exploit their equipment capabilities. In spite of these differences, it is still possible to define a set of reference levels for internal network protocols which closely parallel the DTE-DCE interface protocol levels.

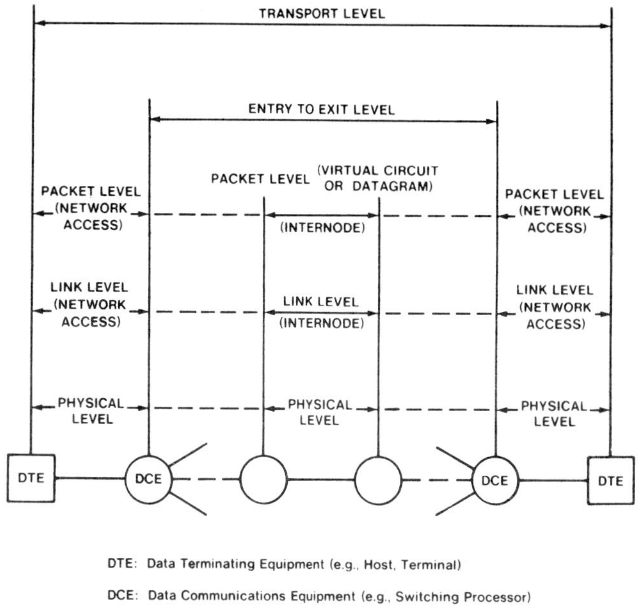

Fig. 8. Network protocol levels.

Starting from the bottom of the protocol hierarchy, we have the *physical level* which has the function of activating and deactivating the electrical connection between the nodes. No flow control functions are assigned to this level.

Above the physical level, we have the *link level* which serves the purpose of transporting packets reliably across individual physical links. One of the functions of this protocol is related to flow control, and consists of retransmitting packets that are dropped because of congestion at the receiving node. In some protocols, a congested receiver may stop the sender by using appropriate commands (e.g., RNR: receiver not ready, in HDLC and SDLC; or, XOFF in asynchronous terminal connections). As mentioned before, we find two different types of links in the network: the internal (or node-to-node) link and the network access link. Correspondingly, we have (at the same level in the protocol hierarchy) two types of link protocol: the *network access protocol* and the *node-to-node protocol.* Typical examples of link protocol implementation are HDLC, SDLC, and X.25 level 2 (which is a subset of HDLC).

Above the link level, we have the *packet level protocol,* which defines the procedures for establishing end-to-end user connections through the network, and specifies the format of the control information used to route packets to their destinations. Two different versions of packet protocol exist: the *virtual circuit* protocol and the *datagram* protocol.

When the virtual circuit (VC) implementation is used, a "virtual" circuit connection must be set up between a pair of users (or processes) wishing to communicate with each other *before* the data transfer can be started. The establishment of this circuit implies dedication of resources of one form or another along the network path. A typical virtual circuit implementation, used in Transpac [7], assigns a fixed path to each connection at setup time. A virtual circuit ID number, stamped in the packet header, uniquely identifies the packets belonging to a connection, and is used to route packets to the destination using routing maps implemented at each intermediate node at set up time. From the flow control point of view, the VC protocol has the distinguishing feature of permitting *selective* flow control on each individual user connection. This selective flow control can be applied at the internode level as well as at the network access level. Since a fixed path is maintained for the entire user session, the selective flow control can also be extended from entry to exit switch and if so desired, even from entry to exit DTE.

As opposed to the virtual circuit implementation, the datagram implementation does not require any circuit set-up before transmission. Each packet is independently submitted to the network, and explicitly carries in its header all the information required for its delivery to destination [34]. Selective flow control, on a connection by connection basis, is not available in the datagram implementation since the packet header does not contain specific connection information (it merely posts source and destination DTE addresses).

Above the packet protocol, we find (within the subnet only) the *entry-to-exit* (ETE) protocol. The objective of this protocol is the reliable transport of single and multipacket messages from network entry to network exit node. Important functions of this protocol which are related to flow control are the reassembly of multipacket messages at the exit node and the regulation of input traffic using buffer allocation and windowing techniques. Some network implementations do not have the ETE level of protocol. In this case, the ETE functions are relegated to higher level protocols.

The highest level of network protocol which has impact on flow control is the *transport protocol.* This protocol provides for the reliable delivery of packets on the "virtual" connection between two remote processes. One of the flow control related functions of this protocol is the protection of destination buffers. The goal is to regulate the flow so as to make the most efficient use of network resources, while avoiding buffer overflow at the destination. "Window" and "credit" schemes are generally used for this purpose.

The above network protocol review has identified various flow control functions and capabilities built into different levels of protocols, and has brought to our attention the fact that each protocol level has its own distinct flow control responsibilities. It is now clear that the classification into the four types of flow control procedures mentioned earlier parallels the classification of network protocols. Recall that there is:

1) hop (or node-to-node) level (Section II),
2) network access level (Section III),
3) entry-to-exit level (Section IV), and
4) transport level (Section V).

The diagram in Fig. 9 illustrates these levels of flow control for a typical network path. A comparison with Fig. 8 reveals the close relationship between flow control and protocol level structures.

Unfortunately, the true system behavior is far more complex than our models and classifications attempt (or can afford) to portray. Therefore, actual networks may not always mechanize all of the above four levels of flow control with distinct procedures. It is quite possible, for example, for a single flow control mechanism to combine two or more levels of flow control. On the other hand, it is possible that one or more levels of flow control may be missing in the network implementation. The matrix in Fig. 10 provides a synopsis of the main network implementations and flow control schemes that will be surveyed in this paper. It is seen that some of the schemes cover more than one level.

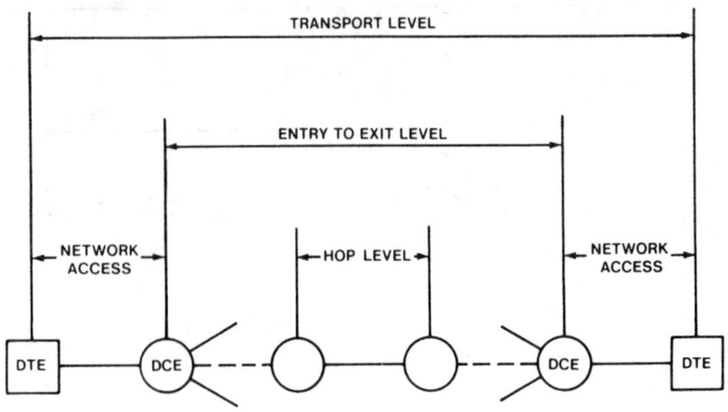

Fig. 9. Flow control levels.

F. Performance Measures

We wish to define a quantitative measure of flow control performance for various reasons. First, we wish to be able to "tune" the parameters of a given flow control scheme so as to optimize a well defined performance criterion. Second, we wish to carefully weigh performance benefits against overhead introduced by flow control. Third, we are interested in comparing the performance of alternative flow control schemes in quantitative terms.

Throughput efficiency (where throughput is expressed in packets/s) is probably the most common measure of flow control performance. Total effective throughput (sum of all the individual contributions) is evaluated as a function of offered load. This representation is particularly useful to determine the critical load in an uncontrolled system and to assess the throughput efficiency of a controlled network at heavy load.

Another common measure is the *combined delay and throughput performance*. The delay-throughput profile allows us to determine the delay overhead introduced by the controls (which the throughput versus offered load curve did not display). In general, it gives us a more complete picture of system performance than does throughput behavior alone. In fact, a system may be designed to deliver high throughput at heavy load, and yet it may experience intolerable delays at light load.

A more compact measure of combined throughput and delay performance is offered by the concept of "*power*" [13], [24]. The simplest definition of power is the ratio of throughput over delay; it is, therefore, a function of the offered load. In fact, it defines the "knee" of the throughput-delay profile as that point where power is maximized, and as shown in Fig. 11 this knee occurs where a ray out of the origin is tangent to the performance profile [24]. A very nice characterization of this maximum power point is such that it occurs when the average buffer occupancy at each

	ARPA			TRANSPAC	SNA			GMDNET	
	CQL	RFNM	NCP	X.25	SDLC	VR PACING	SESSION PACING	I-C	SBP
HOP LEVEL	•			•	•	•		•	•
NETW. ACC.				•			•	•	
ENTRY-EXIT		•		•		•	•		•
TRANSP.			•	NOT DEFINED			•	NOT DEFINED	

Fig. 10. Classification of actual flow control implementations.

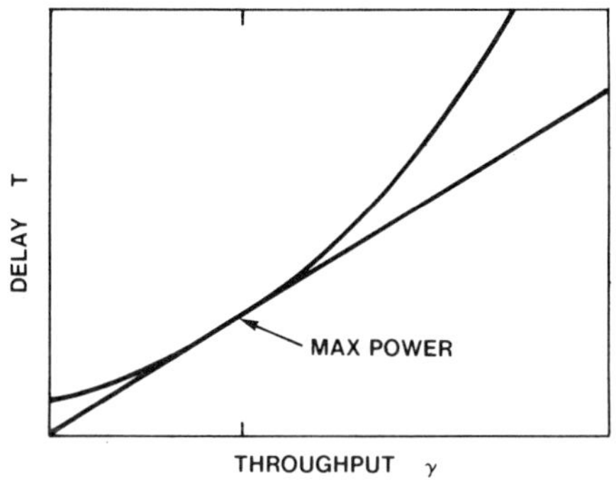

Fig. 11. Delay, throughput, and power.

intermediate node on the path is unity. In [25], it was shown that blocking due to loss systems could easily be included in a more general definition of power (by multiplying the simple definition by one minus the blocking probability); this leads to system designs whose optimum operating point is easily found and which corresponds to the operating point one would intuitively choose. Much more general definitions of power are also studied in [25].

In some important cases, power is maximized for a value of offered load which is approximately half of the saturation load [24]. The maximum power value reflects both delay performance (at light load) and throughput performance (at heavy load) and therefore, represents a good figure of merit of the flow control implementation.

III. HOP LEVEL FLOW CONTROL

A. Objective

The objective of hop level flow control is to prevent store-and-forward buffer congestion and its consequences, namely, throughput degradation and deadlocks. Hop level flow control operates in a local, "myopic" way in that it monitors local queues and buffer occupancies at each node and rejects store-and-forward (S/F) traffic arriving at the node when some predefined thresholds (e.g., maximum queue limits) are exceeded. The function of checking buffer thresholds and discarding (and later retransmitting) packets on a network link is often carried out by the data link control protocol.

This locality of the control does not preclude, however, possible end-to-end repercussions of hop level flow control due to the "backpressure" effect [i.e., the propagation of buffer threshold conditions from the congested node upstream to the traffic source(s)]. In fact, the backpressure property is efficiently exploited in several network implementations (as soon described).

Store-and-forward congestion has two unpleasant consequences: throughput degradation and deadlocks. These conditions were described in Sections II-A and II-C, respectively. In the remainder of this section, we survey and compare a number of hop level flow control procedures, specifically designed to eliminate these problems.

B. Classification of Hop Level Control Schemes

The hop level flow control scheme can play the role of arbitrator between various *classes of traffic* competing for a common buffer pool in each node. A fundamental distinction between different flow control schemes is based on the way the traffic entering a node is subdivided into classes.

One family of hop flow control schemes distinguishes incoming packets based on the output queue they must be placed into. Thus, the number of classes is equal to the number of the output queues; the flow control scheme supervises the allocation of store-and-forward buffers to the output queues. Some limit (fixed or dynamically adjustable) is defined for each queue; packets beyond this limit are discarded. Hence, the name *channel queue limit* schemes is generally given to such mechanisms (see Section III-C).

Another important family of hop flow control schemes distinguishes incoming packets based on the "hop count" (i.e., the number of network links that they have so far traversed). This implies that each node keeps track of $N-1$ classes of traffic, where $N-1$ = number of different hop counts, and N = the number of nodes in the network (note that if loopless routing is assumed, no network path can exceed $N-1$ loops in length), and allocates a (fixed or adjustable) number of buffers to each class. We will refer to this family of schemes as *buffer class* schemes (see Section III-D).

A third family distinguishes packets based on the virtual circuit (i.e., end-to-end session) they belong to. This type of scheme requires, of course, a virtual circuit network architecture; it assumes that each node can distinguish incoming packets based on the virtual circuit they belong to and keep track of a number of classes equal to the number of virtual circuits that currently traverse it. Note that the number of classes varies here with time (since virtual circuits are dynamically created and realeased), as distinct from the previously mentioned schemes where the number of classes is merely a function of the topology. Upon creation, a virtual circuit is allocated a set of buffers (fixed or variable) at each node. When this set is used up, no further traffic is accepted from that virtual circuit. We will refer to this family of schemes as *virtual circuit hop level* schemes (see Section III-E).

Many other traffic subdivisions are possible: for example, a traffic class may be associated with each traffic source; with each traffic destination; or with each source-destination node pair. Indeed, these are all legitimate and, in many respects, well justified choices for a link level flow control scheme. However, we will restrict our study to the three schemes just mentioned, since these are the only schemes which have been extensively analyzed in the published literature and implemented in real networks.

Apart from traffic class distinctions, another parameter that is often used to characterize and classify hop flow control schemes is the degree of dynamic sharing of the store-and-forward buffers. Here, several possibilities exist, namely:

1) fixed, uniform partitioning of buffers among buffer classes (no sharing);

2) buffer partitioning proportional to traffic in each class (no sharing);

3) overselling (i.e., the sum of the buffer limits, one for each class, is larger than the total buffer pool); and

4) dynamic adjustment of buffer limits based on relative traffic fluctuations.

The following sections discuss each hop flow control class in more detail.

C. Channel Queue Limit Flow Control

In the channel queue limit (CQL) scheme, the traffic classes correspond to the channel output queues, and there are restrictions on the number of buffers each class can seize. We may define the following versions of the CQL scheme [20].

1) Complete Partitioning (CP)—Letting N = number of output queues, and n_i = number of packets on the ith queue and B = buffer size, we have the following constraint:

$$0 \leqslant n_i \leqslant \frac{B}{N}, \qquad \forall i.$$

2) Sharing with Maximum Queues (SMXQ)—Let b_{max} be the maximum queue size allowed (where, $b_{max} > B/N$); we have the following constraints:

$$0 \leqslant n_i \leqslant b_{max}, \qquad \forall i$$

$$\sum_i n_i \leqslant B.$$

3) Sharing with Minimum Allocation (SMA)—Let b_{min} be the minimum buffer allocation which is guaranteed to each queue (typically, $b_{min} \leqslant B/N$). The constraint then becomes

$$\sum_i \max(0, n_i - b_{min}) \leqslant B - Nb_{min}.$$

4) Sharing with Minimum Allocation and Maximum Queue—This scheme combines 2) and 3) in that it provides for a minimum buffer guarantee and a maximum buffer allocation for each queue at the same time.

The above options assume that the buffer limit parameters are fixed in time and are the same for all queues. Additional flexibility may be introduced in these schemes by allowing the buffer parameters to change dynamically in time and from queue to queue based on traffic fluctuations.

Having defined a number of CQL flow control options, we now proceed to show that this form of flow control can eliminate the performance degradation and deadlock effects mentioned in Section II. Referring first to Fig. 2, we note that in the presence of CQL flow control, the traffic component (B, B') will no longer be permitted to seize all the buffers in the switch. Therefore, traffic can now flow freely from A to A', and the throughput degradation effect is removed. Similarly, the deadlock condition depicted in Figs. 6 and 7 cannot occur since the buffers in node A cannot be taken over completely by the channel (A, B) queue. Therefore, some buffers in A will always be available to receive packets from node B.

Some form or another of CQL flow control is found in every network implementation. The ARPANET IMP (interface message processor) has a shared buffer pool with minimum allocation and maximum limit for each queue, as shown in Fig. 12 [30]. Of the total buffer pool (typically, 40 buffers), two buffers for input and one buffer for output are permanently allocated to each internode channel. Similarly, ten buffers are permanently dedicated to the reassembly of messages directed to the hosts. The remaining buffers are shared among output queues and the reassembly function, with the following restrictions: reassembly buffers $\leqslant 20$, output queue $\leqslant 8$, the total store-and-forward buffers $\leqslant 20$.

Next we proceed to the evaluation and comparison of CQL implementations, and briefly review the main results available in the published literature [18], [20]. We first report on some throughput degradation conditions observed in absence of flow control. Fig. 13 from [18] shows throughput performance as a function of link load for a variety of buffer control policies. The curve labeled "unrestricted sharing" corresponds to a system without flow control. We notice that, for increasing input load, the throughput of the uncontrolled system reaches a peak and then degrades asymptotically to unity. This behavior confirms the throughput degradation predictions made in Section II.

Throughput degradation is easily corrected with the introduction of CQL flow control, as shown by the remaining curves in Fig. 13. The "no sharing" system (i.e., complete partitioning of the buffer pool among the outgoing queues) is, as expected, the most conservative and throughputwise least efficient scheme. The best scheme is the "optimal sharing" scheme, which corresponds to optimally reselecting a new buffer limit for each level of traffic (i.e., dynamic SMXQ). A heuristic approximation of the optimal scheme is offered by the "square root scheme," a load invariant scheme with fixed buffer limit $=B/N$, where B = total number of buffers and N = number of output channels. The square root scheme is simpler to implement than the optimal scheme since it does not depend on traffic load and, therefore, does not require the reoptimization of the buffer limit values as a function of traffic pattern changes, and yet, it was shown to be practically as efficient as the optimal sharing for a number of cases [18].

Kamoun [20] used a similar switch model to investigate the sharing with minimum allocation (SMA) scheme. The results, obtained in a balanced load environment, show no substantial difference between SMXQ and SMA; in fact, neither scheme is consistently better over the entire range of offered loads. We conjecture, however, that with strongly unbalanced traffic SMA would exhibit better "fairness" since SMA guarantees minimum throughput (with low delay) for each output channel even when the shared portion of the buffer pool is captured by a few heavily loaded queues.

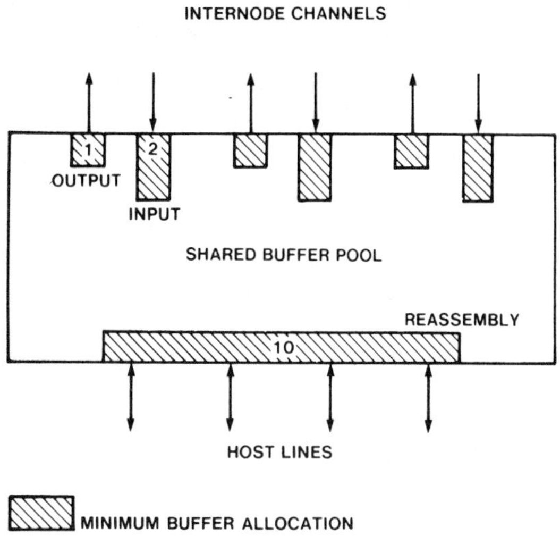

Total buffer pool = 40 buffers

	minimum allocation	maximum allocation
Reassembly	10	20
Internode input queue	2	
Internode output queue	1	8
Total internode queues (i.e., total S/F buffers)		20

Fig. 12. Buffer allocation in Arpanet IMP (1972 version).

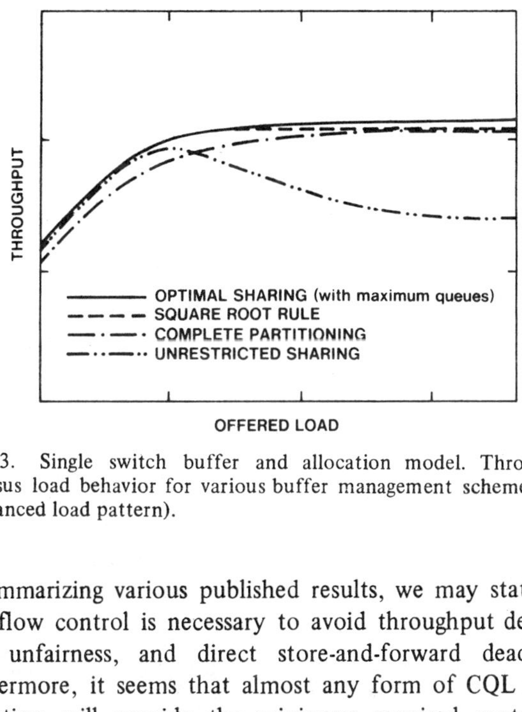

Fig. 13. Single switch buffer and allocation model. Throughput versus load behavior for various buffer management schemes (unbalanced load pattern).

Summarizing various published results, we may state that CQL flow control is necessary to avoid throughput degradation, unfairness, and direct store-and-forward deadlocks. Furthermore, it seems that almost any form of CQL implementation will provide the minimum required protection. The safest scheme (for fairness reasons) seems to be the combination of SMXQ and SMA, which imposes a maximum and minimum limit on each queue (incidentally, this was the scheme used in ARPANET).

D. Structured Buffer Pool (SBP) Flow Control

We have shown in the previous section that CQL flow control eliminates direct store-and-forward deadlocks. However, there is another, more general form of deadlock which can arise in packet networks, namely, *indirect store-and-forward deadlocks* [19]. Fig. 14 illustrates a typical indirect store-and-forward deadlock situation. Suppose that unfavorable traffic conditions in the ring topology shown in Fig. 14 cause each queue to be filled with Q_{max} packets, where Q_{max} is the limit imposed by the CQL strategy. Furthermore, assume that the packets at each node are directed to a node two or more hops away (e.g., all packets queued on link (A, B) are directed to C). In these conditions, no traffic can move in the network since all the queues are full. Thus, we have a deadlock even if the network is equipped with CQL flow control (which is known to prevent direct store-and-forward deadlocks)!

Prevention of indirect store-and-forward deadlocks is obtained with the "structured buffer pool" strategy proposed by Raubold *et al.* [37]. In this strategy, packets arriving at each node are divided into classes according to the number of hops they have covered. For example, packets entering a node from the host belong to class 0 of that node, since they have not yet covered any hops. The highest class H_{max} corresponds to packets that have traversed H_{max} hops, where H_{max} is the maximum path length in the network (a function of the topology and the routing algorithm). The highest class H_{max} also includes all the packets that have reached their destinations and are therefore being reassembled into messages before delivery to the hosts. The nodal buffer organization reflects this class structure as shown in Fig. 15. Each packet class has the right to use a well-defined set of buffers. Class 0 can access only the buffers available in set 0. Buffer set 0 is large enough to store the largest size message entering the network. Class $i + 1$ can use all the buffers available to class i, plus one additional buffer. Finally, class H_{max} can access all the buffers available to class $H_{max}-1$, plus a number of buffers sufficient to reassemble the largest message to be delivered to any destination (this provision is necessary, although not sufficient, to avoid "reassembly deadlocks," as will be shown in Section IV).

Under normal traffic conditions, only set 0 buffers are used. When the load increases beyond nominal levels, buffers fill up progressively from level 0 to level H_{max}. When at a given node the buffers at levels $\leqslant i$ are full, arriving packets which have covered $\leqslant i$ hops are discarded. Thus, in case of congestion, "junior" packets are dropped in the attempt to carry "senior" packets to their destination. This is a desirable property, since senior packets correspond to a higher network resource investment.

It can easily be shown that this strategy eliminates deadlocks of both the direct and indirect type [37]. To prove this, we consider the "resource graph" [3] associated with the packet switch network. In this graph, there is an arc associated with each packet in the network. The arc originates from the buffer currently occupied by the packet and terminates in the (currently unavailable, but awaited) buffer in the next node on the path. A deadlock occurs if and only if there is a cycle in the graph, i.e., there is a chain of arcs which starts from one buffer, and terminates at the same buffer. The existence of cycles can easily be recognized in the deadlock situations depicted in Figs. 6 and 14.

With the structured buffer pool, however, no cycle can occur in the resource graph since each arc starts from a buffer of class i and points to a buffer of class $i + 1$ (recall that a

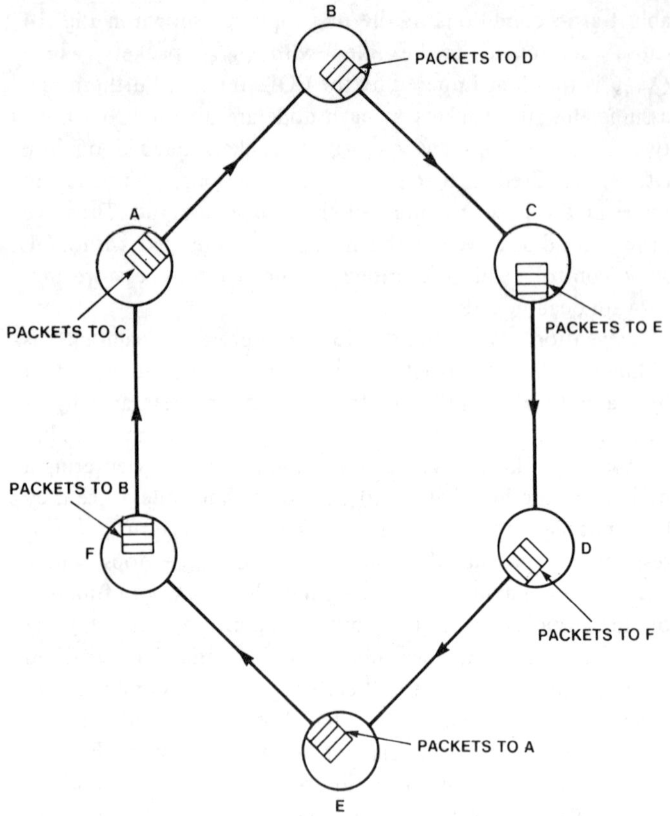

Fig. 14. Indirect store-and-forward deadlock.

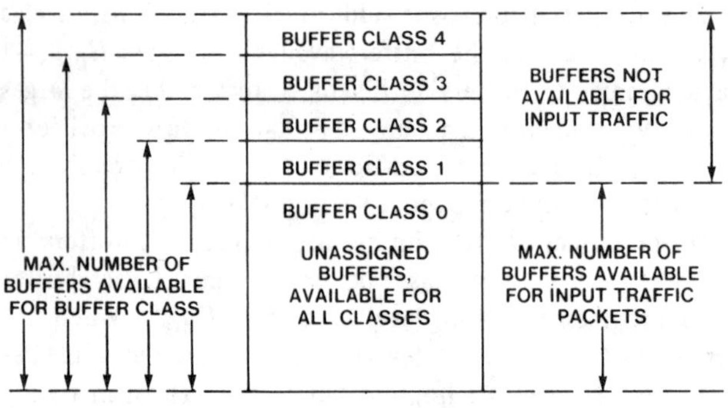

Fig. 15. Structured buffer pool.

packet gains seniority at each hop; an illustration of this property is shown in Fig. 16. Thus, both direct and indirect store-and-forward deadlocks are prevented.

The SBP method was developed by the GMD group in Darmstadt, Germany, for implementation in GMDNET, an experimental packet switch network [37]. Before implementation, an extensive simulation effort was carried out to verify and evaluate the performance of all the network protocols, and of the SBP procedure in particular [13]. Early simulation results showed that the proposed flow control scheme was effective in eliminating deadlocks, but was not successful in preventing throughput degradation when the offered load exceeded the critical threshold (some SBP simulation experiments with typical packet switch network topologies showed that the throughput in heavy load conditions was four to five times lower than the maximum throughput).

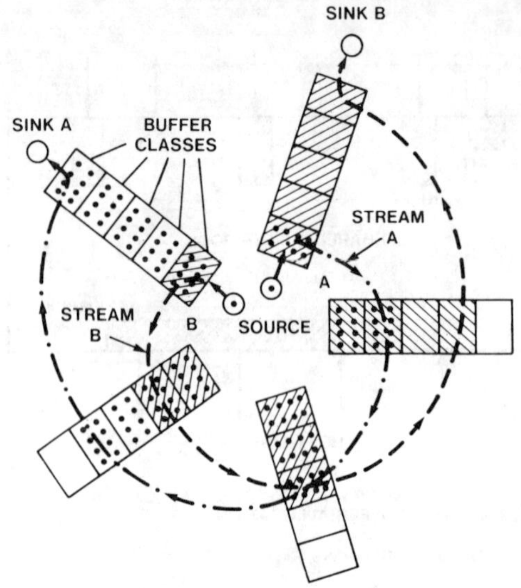

Fig. 16. Access to buffer classes. Example for two data streams. Dotted area: buffers available for stream A; hatched area: buffers available for stream B.

To correct the loss of throughput efficiency under heavy loads, additional constraints were imposed on the number of buffers that each traffic class could seize. The most dramatic improvement was obtained by limiting the number of class 0 buffers that could be seized by input packets (i.e., packets entering the network from external sources). In the absence of this constraint, input packets had the tendency to monopolize all class 0 buffers, leaving only a "thin" buffer layer for the transit traffic to circulate. The control of input traffic, known as "input flow control" in GMDNET is a form of network access flow control and will be discussed more extensively in Section V.

Additional improvements in the SBP scheme were obtained in the case of datagram networks, by setting a specific buffer size constraint $L(i)$ on each class i [13]. (In other words, instead of having a nested buffer pool in which class i can access all buffers available to class $i - 1$, plus one buffer, a different constraint is set on each class). The constraint $L(i)$ was dynamically adjusted to adapt to the relative demands of the various classes. It is interesting to note that the deadlock prevention property is *not* affected by dynamic changes in buffer class size (as long as at least one buffer is dedicated to each class at all times).

E. Virtual Circuit (Hop Level) Flow Control

We recall that packet switch networks can be subdivided into two broad classes: datagram (DG) networks and virtual circuit (VC) networks. In DG networks, each packet in a user session is carried through the network independently of the other packets in the same session; that is, packets in the same session may follow different routes, and may be delivered out of sequence to the destination. In VC networks, a physical network path is set up for each user session and is released when the session is terminated. Packets follow the preestablished path in sequence. Sequencing and error control are provided at each step along the path.

The previously mentioned flow control schemes, namely CQL and SBP, are applicable to both DG and VC nets. In addition, VC nets permit the application of *selective flow control* to each individual VC stream (VC flow control). There are two forms of VC flow control:

1) hop level (or stepwise) VC flow control, which controls VC flow at each hop along the path, and is designed to avoid S/F buffer congestion; and

2) source-sink (or end-to-end) VC flow control, whose function it is to adjust source rate to sink rate so as to maximize VC throughput, yet avoiding sink buffer congestion.

In this section we will mainly deal with VC hop level (VC-HL) flow control; we discuss end-to-end VC flow control in more detail in Section IV.

The basic principle of operation of the VC-HL scheme consists of setting a limit M on the maximum number of packets for each VC stream that can be in transit at each intermediate node. The limit M may be fixed at VC setup time, or may be dynamically adjusted, based on load fluctuations. The buffer limit M is enforced at each hop by the VC-HL protocol, which regulates the issue of transmission "permits" and discards packets based on buffer occupancy.

The advantage of VC-HL (over CQL and SBP) is to provide a more efficient and prompt recovery from congestion by selectively slowing down the VC's directly feeding into the congested area. By virtue of backpressure, the control then propagates to all the sources that are contributing to the congestion, and reduces (or stops) their inputs, leaving the other traffic sources undisturbed. Without VC-HL flow control, the congestion would spread gradually to a larger portion of the network, blocking traffic sources that were not directly responsible for the original congestion, and causing unnecessary throughput degradation and unfairness.

As in the case of CQL and SBP schemes, various buffer sharing policies can be proposed. At one extreme, M buffers can be dedicated to each VC at setup time; at the other extreme, buffers may be allocated, on demand, from a common pool (complete sharing). It is easily seen that buffer dedication can lead to extraordinary storage overhead, since there is, generally, no practical upper bound on the number of VC's that can simultaneously exist in a network; furthermore, the traffic on each VC is generally bursty, leading to low utilization of the reserved buffers. For these reasons, most of the implementations employ dynamic buffer sharing.

The shared versus dedicated buffer policy also has an impact on the deadlock prevention properties of the VC-HL scheme. With buffer dedication, the VC-HL scheme becomes deadlock free. This can easily be deduced by considering the resource graph and recognizing that the graph cannot contain loops, since virtual circuits are loopless by construction. (For deadlock freedom, it actually suffices that at least one buffer be reserved for each virtual circuit). If, on the other hand, no buffer reservations are made and buffers are allocated strictly on demand, deadlocks may occur unless additional protection (e.g., the SBP scheme) is implemented.

In the following, we briefly describe three different versions of VC-HL flow control implemented in existing networks, and report on some performance results.

Tymnet is probably the earliest VC network developed [39]. As distinct from most VC networks, Tymnet uses a "composite" packet internode protocol. This means that data from different VC's traveling on the same trunk can be packed in the same envelope, for the purpose of link overhead reduction. Tymnet is a character-oriented network in the sense that data flows on the virtual circuit in the form of characters, rather than packets (i.e., characters are assembled into packets at the entry node, and are then disassembled at the exit node). The character-oriented nature of Tymnet implies that VC-HL buffer allocation is based on character (rather than packet) counts.

In Tymnet [39], a throughput limit is computed for each VC at setup time according to terminal speed, and is enforced all along the network path. Throughput control is obtained by assigning a maximum buffer limit (per VC) at each intermediate node and by controlling the issue of transmission permits from node to node based on the current buffer allocation. Periodically (every half second), each node sends a backpressure vector to its neighbors, containing one bit for each virtual circuit that traverses it. If the number of currently buffered characters for a given VC exceeds the maximum allocation (e.g., for low speed terminals—10 to 30 cps—the allocation is 32 characters), the backpressure bit is set to zero; otherwise the bit is set to one. On the transmitting side, each VC is associated with a counter which is initialized to the maximum buffer limit and is decremented by one for each character transmitted. Transmission stops on a particular VC when the corresponding counter is reduced to zero. Upon reception of a backpressure bit = 1, the counter is reset to its initial value and transmission can resume.

The effect of backpressure from an individual hop back along the VC in Tymnet constitutes a good example of the "hybrid" character of many practical flow control implementations, since we see here a mixture of hop level and transport level flow control. This was pointed out earlier in connection with Fig. 10, and we shall encounter other examples as we proceed.

Transpac, the French public data network, is a VC network which uses X.25 as an internode protocol [42]. One of the distinguishing features of Transpac is the use of the throughput class concept in X.25 for internal flow and congestion control. Each VC call request carries a throughput class declaration which corresponds to the maximum (instantaneous) data rate that the user will ever attempt to present to that VC. Each node keeps track of the aggregate declared throughput (which represents the worst case situation), and at the same time, monitors actual throughput (typically, much lower than the declared throughput) and average buffer utilization. Based on the ratio of actual to declared throughput, the node may decide to *oversell* capacity, i.e., it will attempt to carry a declared throughput volume higher than trunk capacity. Clearly, overselling implies that input rates may temporarily exceed trunk capacities, so that the network must be prepared to exercise flow control. Packet buffers are dynamically allocated to VC's based on demand (complete sharing), but thresholds are set on individual VC allocations as well as on overall buffer pool utilization.

Of particular interest is the impact of overall buffer pool thresholds on VC-HL. Three threshold levels [S_0, S_1, and S_2 (where $S_0 < S_1 < S_2$)] are defined and are used in the following way:

1) S_0: do not accept new VC call requests;

2) S_1: slow down the flow on current VC's (by delaying the return of ACK's at the VC level); and

3) S_2: selectively disconnect existing VC's.

The threshold levels S_0, S_1, and S_2 are dynamically evaluated as a function of declared throughput, measured throughput and current buffer utilization.

Another example of a VC network is offered by GMDNET [13]. As we mentioned before, GMDNET applies SBP flow control. In addition, it applies I-control (individual control) on each virtual circuit. I-control consists of two components: end-to-end flow control and hop level flow control. End-to-end and hop level flow control are implemented using variable size windows PUL_E and PUL_L, respectively (PUL = packet underway limit). The window is defined as the maximum number of packets that a sender is allowed to transmit before receiving an ACK, or permit [5]. The windows PUL_E and PUL_L are dynamically adjusted based on sink congestion and intermediate node congestion, respectively; their values may vary within predefined ranges ($1 \leqslant PUL_E \leqslant W_E$; $1 \leqslant PUL_L \leqslant W_L$) [37], [13]. The buffer pool is completely shareable, without specific reservations for individual VC's.

Simulation results on the performance of the I-control scheme lead to the following important conclusions.

1) I-control alone cannot prevent throughput degradation, unfairness, and deadlocks. Experimental results clearly show that an I-controlled network without SBP becomes deadlocked immediately after the applied load exceeds the critical value (this confirms our prediction that VC flow control without specific buffer reservations for individual VC's cannot prevent deadlocks).

2) The end-to-end component of I-control is very effective in preventing network congestion in the case of source rates exceeding sink rates. Without I-control (i.e., the SBP control alone), a five-fold throughput degradation was observed in a typical network experiment.

IV. ENTRY-TO-EXIT FLOW CONTROL

The main objective of the entry-to-exit (ETE) flow control is to prevent buffer congestion at the exit node due to the fact that remote sources are sending traffic at a higher rate than can be accepted by the hosts (or terminals) fed by the exit node. The cause of the bottleneck could be either the overload of the local lines connecting the exit node to the hosts, or the slow acceptance rate of the hosts. The problem of congestion prevention at the exit node becomes more complex when this node must also reassemble packets into messages, and/or resequence messages before delivery to the host. In fact, reassembly and resequence deadlocks may occur, which require special prevention measures.

In order to understand how reassembly deadlocks can be generated, let us consider the network path shown in Fig. 17, where three store-and-forward nodes (node 1, node 2, and node 3, respectively) relay traffic directed to host 1. In the situation depicted in Fig. 17, three multipacket messages A, B, and C are in transit towards host 1. Without loss of generality we assume that the message size is $\leqslant 4$ packets and that 4 buffers are dedicated to messages being assembled at a node; furthermore, a channel queue limit $Q_{max} = 4$ is set on each trunk queue, for hop level flow control. We note from Figure 17 that message A (which has siezed all four reassembly buffers at node 3) cannot be delivered to the host since packet A_2 is missing. Packet A_2, on the other hand, cannot be forwarded to node 2 since the queue at node 2 is full. The node 2 queue, in turn, cannot advance until reassembly space becomes available in node 3 for B or C messages. Deadlock!

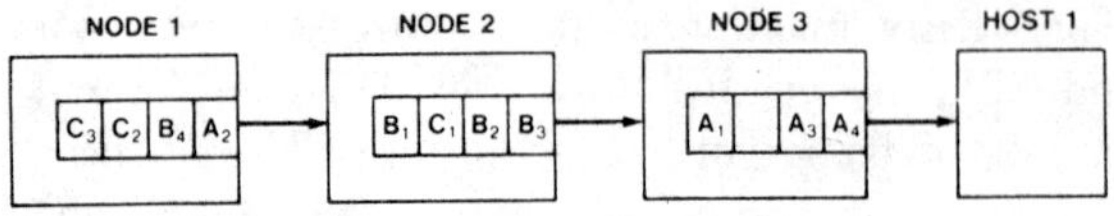

Fig. 17. Reassembly buffer deadlock.

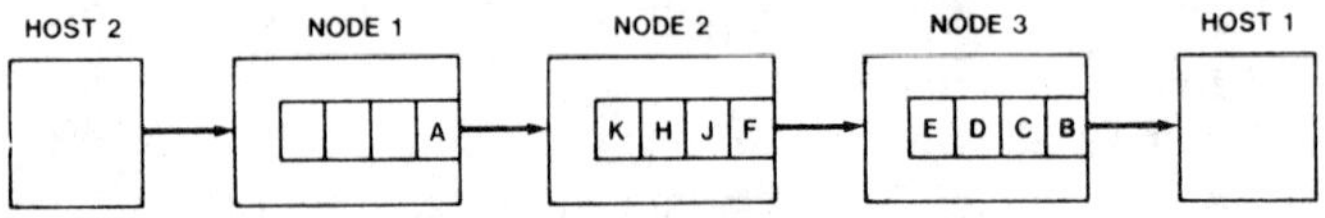

Fig. 18. Resequence deadlock.

A very similar order of events leads to resequence deadlocks as shown in Fig. 18. Assume that a sequence of single packet messages A, B, $\cdots$, K originating from host 2 and directed to host 1 is traveling through a three-node network. If messages must be delivered in sequence, messages B, C, D, E in node 3 cannot be transmitted to host 1 until message A is received at node 3. However, due to store-and-forward buffer unavailability in node 2, message A cannot reach node 3. Deadlock!

Various schemes can be used to prevent these types of deadlocks. In the ARPANET, for example, reassembly deadlocks are avoided by requiring a reassembly buffer reservation for each multipacket message entering the network; resequence deadlocks are avoided by discarding out-of-sequence messages at the destination. Other networks (e.g., Telenet) have sufficient nodal storage to permit out-of-sequence messages to be accepted at a destination node with the understanding that these may be discarded later if storage congestion occurs; again, the existence of a source copy saves the day. These and other schemes are discussed in more detail in the following sections.

While the main objective of ETE controls is to protect the exit node from congestion, an important byproduct is the prevention of global (i.e., internal) congestion. Virtually all ETE controls are based on a window scheme that allows only up to W sequential messages to be outstanding in the network before an end-to-end ACK is received. If the network becomes congested (this may occur independently of destination node congestion), messages and ACK's incur high end-to-end delays. These delays, combined with the restriction on the total number of outstanding messages, effectively contribute to reduce the input rate of new packets into the network.

Several varieties of ETE flow control schemes have been proposed and implemented. We first describe four representative examples, and then briefly review some analytical and simulation models for the performance evaluation and comparison of such schemes.

A. ARPANET RFNM and Reassembly Scheme

ETE flow control in ARPANET is exercised on a host-pair basis [30], [23]. Specifically, all messages traveling from the same source host to the same destination host are carried on the same logical "pipe." Each pipe is individually flow controlled by a window mechanism. An independent message number sequence is maintained for each pipe. Numbers are sequentially assigned to messages flowing on the pipe, and are checked at the destination for sequencing and duplicate detection purposes. Both the source and the destination keep a small window w (presently, $w = 8$) of currently valid message numbers. Messages arriving at the destination with out-of-range numbers are discarded. Messages arriving out of order are discarded since storing them (while waiting for the missing message) may lead to potential resequence deadlocks. Correctly received messages are acknowledged with short ETE control messages called RFNM's (ready for next message). Upon receipt of an RFNM, the sending end of the pipe advances its transmission window, accordingly.

RFNM's are also used for error control If an RFNM is not received after a specified time out (presently about 30 s), the source IMP sends a control message to the destination inquiring about the possiblity of an incomplete transmission. This technique is necessary to keep source and destination message numbers synchronized and also to request a retransmission from the host in the case of message loss.

The window and message numbering mechanisms described so far support ETE flow control, sequencing and error control functions in the ARPANET. A separate mechanism, known as reassembly buffer allocation [30], is used to prevent reassembly deadlocks. Each multipacket message must secure a reassembly buffer allocation at the destination node before transmission. This is accomplished by sending a reservation message called a REQALL (request for allocation) to the destination and waiting for an ALL (allocation) message from the destination before attempting transmission. To reduce delay (and, therefore, increase throughput) of steady multipacket message flow between the same source-destination pair, ALL messages are automatically piggybacked on RFNM's, thus eliminating the reservation delay for all messages after the first one. If a pending allocation at the source node is not claimed within a given time-out (250 ms), it is returned to the destination with a "giveback" message. Single packet messages are transmitted to their destinations without buffer reservation. However, if upon arrival at the destination, all the reassembly buffers are full, the single packet message is discarded and a copy is retransmitted from the source IMP after an explicit buffer reservation has been obtained. Some pitfalls inherent in such schemes are described in [23].

B. SNA Virtual Route Pacing Scheme

The IBM systems network architecture (SNA) is an architecture aimed at providing distributed communications and distributed processing capabilities between IBM systems [15], [16]. SNA was first announced in 1974. Since then, the original set of functions which supported single rooted networks (i.e., single host) have been enhanced to support multiple-domain (i.e., multiple host) networking. In this paper, we refer to SNA release 4.2 [16].

SNA devices can be subdivided into four main categories: host computers (e.g., system/370), communications controllers (e.g., 3704 and 3705), terminal cluster controllers, and terminal devices (e.g., TTY's, CRT's, readers, and printers). Distributed communications with full routing, flow control, and global addressing capabilities are provided only on store-and-forward networks interconnecting host computers and communication controllers. These nodes are called subarea nodes in SNA. Terminals and terminal cluster controllers are connected into this high level at these subarea nodes, which provide the necessary boundary functions (e.g., global/local address conversion, etc.). Thus, for purposes of this section, SNA can be viewed as the usual two-level network architecture, with terminals and terminal cluster controllers at the lower level, and hosts and communications controllers at the higher level.

SNA is essentially a virtual circuit network, in the sense that each user session is associated with a physical route at session setup time. The routing policy is a static, multipath policy which maintains up to eight distinct routes between each source-destination pair in the high-level network (i.e., between subarea nodes). These routes are called ER's (explicit routes), to distinguish them from VR's (virtual routes) defined below. ER's are defined as an ordered sequence of network trunks, and are uniquely identified by ER numbers. When a failure is detected on an ER currently being used, the next ER on the list is then "switched in." One difficulty here is that the list of ER's must be established by the network designer each time the network topology is changed.

Next, virtual routes (VR's) are defined between each source-destination node pair of the high level network. A VR is essentially a virtual pipe which is constructed on top of an ER and is subject to flow control. Three sets of VR's, each with a different level of priority are maintained between each subarea node pair. Each set may consist of up to eight VR's, thus allowing for up to 24 VR's between each high level network node pair. Active VR's are identified by VR numbers and are stored in lists at each node.

At setup time, the entry node scans the VR list and assigns the user session to the first available virtual route of desired priority. Several user sessions may be multiplexed on the same VR. In turn, several VR's may be multiplexed on the same ER. Finally, several ER's can be multiplexed on the same trunk.

The rationale for the distinction between virtual routes and explicit routes (a unique SNA feature among all VC networks, which typically associate a virtual route with a fixed path) is to "...insulate the virtual route layer from the physical configuration" [16]. As a consequence, user packets are driven through the network using the ER ID number, while the VR ID number needs to be checked only at the endpoints of the path. This feature considerably reduces storage and processing overhead with respect to conventional VC schemes, which typically require large maps at each intermediate node to store the information relative to all virtual circuits traversing that node.

In the high-level network, flow control is applied independently to each VR from entry to exit node. This scheme, known as *VR pacing* is actually a combination of ETE and hop level flow control. It is based on a window mechanism, in which the entry node must request (and obtain) permission from the exit node before sending a new group of k packets, where k = window size. The destination may grant (or delay) such permission depending on local buffer availability. The window size k varies from h to $3h$, where h is the path hop length. The value of k is dynamically adjusted not only by the exit node, but also by any intermediate node along the path on the basis of its buffer availability [1]. The fact that both the end node and the intermediate nodes can "modulate" the window size k makes VR pacing a hybrid ETE and hop flow control scheme.

In addition to VR-pacing control, which operates between subarea nodes, the SNA architecture provides also for *session level pacing* which, for terminals, extends beyond subarea nodes and individually flow controls each user session between terminal and host computer. Session pacing is discussed in Section VI.

C. GMD Individual Flow Control

In GMDNET, entry-to-exit flow control is exercised individually on each virtual circuit, hence the name of individual flow control assigned to the scheme [37]. We recall that GMDNET is a VC network in which a fixed route is assigned to each user session at session setup time.

The main purpose of entry-to-exit flow control in GMDNET is to protect the exit node from overflow caused by low sink rates. When the source host rate exceeds the sink host rate, the flow control mechanism intervenes to slow down inputs from the source host into the entry node. This is achieved by maintaining a window of outstanding packets between entry and exit node for each virtual circuit. The window must be large enough to permit each virtual circuit to efficiently utilize the bandwidth available on the path. GMD simulation experiments have shown that $w = h + 1$ (where h = hop length of the path) is a satisfactory choice under nominal load conditions. Window size can be reduced if the sink is slow in accepting packets. More precisely, when for a given VC the queue waiting to be transferred from exit node to sink reaches the value w, further arrivals to the exit node within that VC are discarded and a negative ACK is returned to the source node. Each negative ACK causes a window size reduction of 1 at the source node, until the minimum window size $w = 1$ is reached. Each positive ACK, on the other hand, increases window size by 1, until the maximum window size $w = h + 1$ is reached. In this way, window size is dynamically controlled in the range 1 to $h + 1$ by positive and negative acknowledgments [37].

In addition to the entry-to-exit flow control, each hop of the virtual circuit is also independently flow controlled (see Section III). The two layers of flow control, entry-to-exit and hop, are logically separated one from the other, in that the ETE window is controlled by exit buffer occupancy, while hop window is controlled by intermediate node congestion.

Packets within the same virtual circuit must be delivered to the host in sequence, and in case of multipacket messages, must be reassembled before delivery to the host. Fixed path routing and link level sequencing imply that packets arrive at their destination in sequence. This sequencing property, and the fact that a number of buffers sufficient to reassemble the largest size packet is permanently dedicated to traffic leaving the network, preclude the possibility of reassembly deadlocks and eliminate the need for reassembly buffer allocation schemes of the type implemented in ARPANET.

D. Datapac Virtual Circuit Flow Control

The Canadian public data network, Datapac, implemented with the Northern Telecom SL-10 Packet Switching System provides virtual circuit services using an internal transport protocol built on top of a datagram subnetwork [28]. Flow control is exercised from entry to exit node on a virtual circuit basis, although no physical path is actually assigned to each virtual circuit, as was the case with SNA and GMDNET. The absence of a fixed path leads to some complications in the resequencing and loss recovery procedures, which will soon be discussed.

In Datapac, a virtual circuit is provided between the two endpoints of each user session. The virtual circuit is implemented as the concatenation of three protocol segments: a packet level X.25 protocol from the source device (i.e., data terminating equipment or DTE) to entry node (i.e., data communications equipment or DCE), an internal protocol from entry DCE to exit DCE, and a packet level X.25 protocol from exit node (DCE) to destination node (DTE). Each one of these protocol segments is flow controlled by a window mechanism. Of particular interest to us is the fact that window controls on these three segments are synchronized so as to provide a means of matching source DTE transmission rate with destination DTE acceptance rate. Window control synchronization is achieved by withholding the return of ACK's on a window if the downstream window is full.

As an example, let us assume that all windows are of size $w = 3$, and that the window between entry and exit DCE is full (i.e., there are three outstanding packets). The next packet arriving from the source DTE to the entry DCE will be accepted (assuming buffer space is available), but will not be immediately acknowledged; rather, the ACK will be withheld until an ACK from the exit DCE is received, thus opening up the downstream window [28].

Within the concatenated window mechanism the entry-to-exit flow control serves the function of promptly reflecting back to the source an exit segment congestion situation by withholding ACK's. Recall that in GMDNET the entry-to-exit flow control provided a similar service by dynamically adjusting the window with positive or negative ACK's. In Datapac, things are complicated, however, by the fact that the window mechanism is used not only for flow control, but also for sequencing, packet loss recovery, and duplicate detection. These latter functions are not required in the GMDNET, since sequencing is enforced there by the fixed path routing policy, and packet loss could occur only if a node along the path failed, in which case the virtual circuit would be automatically reinitialized.

The use of window ACK's for loss recovery in Datapac leads to the following problem. If the exit DCE does not return to the entry DCE an ACK for a correctly received packet (because the exit segment is congested), the entry DCE will retransmit the packet after a time-out, under the assumption that the packet was lost (or was dropped by the exit DCE for lack of resequence space). If no ACK is received after a specified number of retransmissions, the entry DCE will clear the virtual circuit. In order to minimize the generation of duplicate packets, the value of time-out must be carefully selected as a function of window size and other network parameters.

E. Performance Models

The great majority of entry-to-exit flow control mechanisms are based on the window scheme. Critical parameters in the window implementation are the size of the window, and if error and loss recovery are to be provided, the retransmission time-out interval. Several analytic and simulation models have been developed recently to investigate the impact of these parameters on throughput and delay performance. This section briefly surveys some of the most significant contributions in this area.

We start with the Kleinrock and Kermani model of a single source-to-destination stream flow controlled by a window mechanism [26]. The network entry-to-exit delay is simplified as an $M/M/1$ queue delay, and the round trip delay therefore follows an Erlang-2 distribution. (This approximation is supported by simulation experiments showing that more accurate delay assumptions do not significantly change the nature of the results.) The exit node has finite storage and delivers packets to the destination host on a finite capacity channel. Consequently, the exit node may occasionally overflow and drop packets. To provide for transmission integrity, the entry node will retransmit an unacknowledged packet after a time-out interval. This simplified window model is solved analytically, yielding the optimal (i.e., minimum delay) window size and time-out interval for a given throughput requirement and destination buffer storage size.

In a subsequent paper [22], the same authors propose an adaptive policy (the "look-ahead" policy) for the dynamic adjustment of window size to time-varying traffic rate. In the proposed policy, the window size is dynamically controlled by the queue size at the exit node. Numerical results show that the delay versus throughput performance of the adaptively controlled scheme is somewhat superior to the performance of a scheme operated under static control, in which the window is adjusted in accordance with the traffic volume. These results are very encouraging, and are consistent with simulation experiments on dynamic window control carried out in multinode networks [1], [13].

The models in [26], [22] approximate the network as a single queue and therefore do not offer insight into the dependence of window size w on the number of intermediate hops. This issue is addressed by a simple multihop model developed by Kleinrock in [24]. In this model a packet stream from a single destination is transmitted across the network on a k-hop network path. Infinite buffer storage, and negligible error rates are assumed on each hop. The stream is flow controlled by a window mechanism. In this model, as the window size w increases, the end-to-end delay grows without limit while the throughput asymptotically reaches the path capacity. In order to find a meaningful criterion for the optimization of w, the concept of "power" as defined in Section II-F is used. We find that power is optimized by $w = k$. This implies that, at optimum, there should be on the average one packet in each intermediate queue. This result agrees with out intuition that the "entry-to-exit pipe should be kept full (in fact, *just* full)" for satisfactory performance. The general validity of this result is confirmed by actual window implementations. In fact, the SNA pacing scheme allows the window to dynamically vary from h to $3h$, where h = number of intermediate hops. Similarly, the GMD individual flow control scheme uses a maximum window of $h + 1$.

The main limitation of the two previous models is the single source, single destination traffic assumption which excludes interference at a given node by other traffic traversing it. The model by Pennotti and Schwartz [32] includes the effect of interference in an approximate fashion in that it represents a virtual link situation in which end-to-end link traffic flowing on a multihop path must compete at each hop with external traffic. This is essentially a "one hop" interference model in which some external traffic λ is injected into one node along the path and is transmitted to the next node on the path, where it then is removed from the network. The purpose of this study is to evaluate the possible path congestion caused by an increase in the virtual link rate λ_0, both with and without flow control. Congestion is defined as the relative average increase in time delay experienced by external users due to an increase in λ_0, taking $\lambda_0 = 0$ as a reference. Without flow control, congestion rapidly grows to infinity even for moderate values of λ_0. By introducing end-to-end window control which limits to w the number of packets outstanding on the virtual link at any one time, congestion can be bounded for any value of λ_0. The value of the upper bound varies with w, and decreases for decreasing w, as expected.

As an alternative to window flow control, hop flow control was also implemented in the Pennotti and Schwartz model by setting a limit on the number of link packets that would be stored at each intermediate node [32]. This scheme exhibited essentially the same performance as the window scheme. The above experiments show that flow control (either window or hop) can be used effectively to maintain fairness in a multiuser environment with conflicting requirements; that is, by adjusting the window parameter w, one can balance the relative user throughputs as desired.

The previously mentioned model offers some insight into multiuser flow control, but suffers from the limitation that only one virtual circuit can be flow controlled at a time, the remaining traffic components being kept constant. To remove this limitation, a number of multiple source, multiple destination models with selectively controlled user pairs have been developed. These models combine ETE flow control with network access flow control, and therefore may be regarded as hybrid models. Wong and Unsoy analyze a simple 5-node network to which individual entry-to-exit window control as well as isarithmic control are applied [41]. The isarithmic scheme is a network access flow control scheme which controls the total number of packets allowed in the entire network (see Section V for additional details). The major finding of this study is the fact that isarithmic control alone is not enough to guarantee efficient network operation. In fact, under some unfavorable traffic situations, one node pair may capture most of the permits, starving other pairs and leading to unfairness and to overall performance degradation. Similar results were found by Price in a series of simulation experiments [36]. The problem is corrected by introducing individual entry-to-exit flow controls in addition to isarithmic control.

The exact analysis of multinode networks with individually controlled node pairs becomes impractical for topologies with more than five to six nodes because of the rapidly increasing computational complexity of exact solution techniques [41]. To circumvent this problem, Reiser recently proposed an approximate solution technique based on a mean value analysis which is computationally affordable even for large networks, and which reaches a typical accuracy of 5 percent in throughput and 10 percent in delay [38]. With this technique it is now possible to analyze the interaction of various flow control schemes in a much more realistic environment (i.e., large networks; varied traffic patterns) than was possible with previous methods. Important design problems such as the optimization of window parameters for all source-destination pairs in order to maximize network throughput (within given fairness constraints), now become approachable.

In spite of the previously mentioned advances in computational solution techniques, some window flow control issues are still too complex to be attached analytically. For example, the dynamic control of window size in a multinode network is not amenable to a network-of-queues model even with the approximate solution methods. In these cases, simulation is still the leading performance evaluation tool [13], [1], [36].

V. NETWORK ACCESS FLOW CONTROL

A. Objective

The objective of network access (NA) flow control is to throttle external inputs based on measurements of internal network congestion. Congestion measures may be local (e.g., buffer occupancy in the entry mode), global (e.g., total number of buffers available in the entire network), or selective (e.g., congestion of the path(s) leading to a given destination). The congestion condition is determined at (or is reported to) the network access points and is used to regulate the access of external traffic into the network.

NA flow control differs from LL and ETE flow control in that it throttles external traffic to prevent *overall internal buffer congestion*, while LL flow control limits access to a specific store-and-forward node to prevent *local congestion and store-and-forward deadlocks*, and ETE flow control limits the flow between a specific source-destination pair to prevent *congestion and reassembly buffer deadlocks at the destination*. As we mentioned earlier, however, both LL and ETE schemes indirectly provide some form of NA flow control by reporting an internal network congestion condition back to the access point either via the backpressure mechanism (LL scheme), or via the credit slowdown caused by large internal delays (ETE scheme).

Three NA flow control implementations will be discussed: the isarithmic scheme, a global congestion prevention scheme based on the circulation of a fixed number of permits [8]; the input buffer limit scheme, a local congestion scheme which sets a limit on the number of input packets stored at each node [27], [13]; and the choke packet scheme, a selective congestion scheme based on the delivery of special control packets of that name from the congested node back to the traffic sources [29].

B. The Isarithmic Scheme

Since the primary cause of network congestion is the excessive number of packets stored in the network, an intuitively sound congestion prevention principle consists of setting a limit on the total number of packets that can circulate in the network at any one time. An implementation of this principle is offered by the Isarithmic scheme proposed for the National Physical Laboratories network [8], [35].

The isarithmic scheme is based on the concept of a "permit," i.e., a ticket that permits a packet to travel from the entry point to the desired destination. Under this concept, the network is initially provided with a number of permits, several held in store at each node. As traffic is offered by a host to the network, each packet must secure a permit before admission to the high level node is allowed. Each accepted packet causes a reduction of one in the store of permits available at the accepting node. The accepted data packet is able to traverse the network, under the control of node and link protocols, until its destination node is reached. When the packet is handed over to the destination subscriber, the permit which has accompanied it during its journey becomes free and an attempt is made to add it to the permit store of the node in which it now finds itself.

In order to achieve a viable system in which permits do not accumulate in certain parts of the network at the expense of other parts, it is necessary to place a limit on the number of permits that can be held in store by each node. If then, because of this limit, a newly freed permit cannot be accommodated at a node (overflow permit), it must be sent elsewhere. The normal method of carrying the permit in these circumstances is to "piggyback" it on other traffic, be this data or control. Only in the absence of other traffic need a special permit-carrying packet be generated.

A simulation program was developed by NPL to evaluate the performance of the isarithmic scheme in various network configurations and in the presence of different network protocols [35]. The main conclusion of these simulation studies was that the isarithmic scheme is a simple congestion prevention mechanism which performs well in uniform traffic pattern situations, but may lead to unnecessary throughput restrictions, and therefore, to poor performance in the case of nonuniform, time-varying traffic patterns. In particular, in the presence of high bandwidth data transfers, there is the possibility that permits are not returned to the traffic sources rapidly enough to fully utilize network capacity (the "permit starvation" problem). This would be the case when the destination node redistributes the overflow permits randomly in the network. If, on the other hand, the destination systematically returns all the permits to the source, the source-destination pair may end up capturing most of the network permits, thus causing unfairness. Tradeoffs between different permit distribution schemes are investigated with an analytical model in [41]. Finally, a delicate problem in isarithmic control is the bookkeeping of permits, to avoid unauthorized generation or disappearance of permits.

In spite of the above limitations, the isarithmic scheme proved to be very effective in *weakly controlled* networks (namely, networks without hop level flow control), eliminating congestion and deadlocks that had occurred without flow control. Some simulation experiments were also carried out on networks with hop level flow control (specifically CQL), and with a simple form of local access control (one buffer on each output queue was reserved for store-and-forward traffic). For this class of networks (called *strongly controlled* networks), it was found that the network performance did not show congestion tendencies even without isarithmic control in the case of a fixed routing discipline. When the fixed discipline was replaced with an adaptive routing discipline, it was found that the network would become easily congested since the simple form of network access control implemented would not prevent external traffic from flooding all the queues in the entry node. Again, the introduction of the isarithmic scheme was successful in eliminating the congestion problem for the adaptive routing case [36].

Critical parameters in the isarithmic scheme design are the total number of permits P in the network and the maximum number of permits L that can be accumulated at each node (permit queue). Experimental results show that optimal performance is achieved for $P = 3N$, where $N =$ total number of nodes, and $L = 3$. An excessive number of permits in the network would lead to congestion. An excessive value of L would lead to unfairness, accumulation of permits at a few nodes, and throughput starvation at the others.

C. Input Buffer Limit Scheme

The input buffer limit (IBL) scheme differentiates between input traffic (i.e., traffic from external sources) and transit traffic, and throttles the input traffic based on buffer occupancy at the entry node. IBL is a *local* network access method since it monitors local congestion at the entry node, rather than global congestion as does the isarithmic scheme. Entry node congestion, on the other hand, is often a good indicator of global congestion because the well known backpressure effect will have propagated internal congestion conditions back to the traffic sources.

The function of IBL controls is to block input traffic when certain buffer utilization thresholds are reached in the entry node. This flow control approach clearly favors transit traffic over input traffic. Intuitively, this is a desirable property since a number of network resources have already been invested in transit traffic. This intuitive argument is supported by a number of analytical and simulation experiments proving the effectiveness of the IBL scheme.

Many versions of IBL control can be proposed. Here, we describe and compare four different implementations that have been experimentally evaluated.

The term input buffer limit scheme refers to a scheme restricting the number of buffers made available to input traffic and was first introduced by the GMD research group [37], [13]. The scheme proposed for GMDNET is a by-product of the nested buffer class structure used to allocate buffers to different classes of traffic. We recall from Section III-D that the ith traffic class consists of all the packets that have already covered i hops. Input traffic is assigned to class zero (zero hops covered). Traffic class zero is entitled to use buffer class zero, which is a subset of the nodal buffer pool (in general, class i is entitled to use all buffer classes $\leqslant i$). Thus, input packets are discarded when class zero buffers are full. The size of buffer class zero (referred to as input buffer limit) was found to have a significant impact on throughput performance under heavy loads. Simulation experiments indicate that for a given topology and traffic pattern there is an optimal input buffer limit which maximizes throughput for heavy offered load. The use of lower or higher limits leads to a substantial drop in throughput [13].

A version of IBL control that is simpler than the GMD version was proposed by Lam [27] and analytically evaluated in an elegant model. Only two classes of traffic—input and transit—are considered in this proposal. Letting N_T be the total number of buffers in the node and N_I the input buffer limit (where $N_I \leqslant N_T$), the following constraints are imposed at each node:

1) number of input packets $\leqslant N_I$, and
2) number of transit packets $\leqslant N_T$

The analytical results confirm simulation results independently obtained by the GMD group. There is an optimal ratio N_I/N_T, which maximizes throughput for heavy offered load, as shown in Fig. 19. A good heuristic choice for N_I/N_T is the ratio between input message throughput and total message throughput at a node. As shown in the figure, throughput performance does not change significantly even for relatively large variations of the ratio N_I/N_T around the optimal value, thus implying that the IBL scheme is robust to external perturbations such as traffic fluctuations and topology changes. One shortcoming of this model is that all nodes in the net

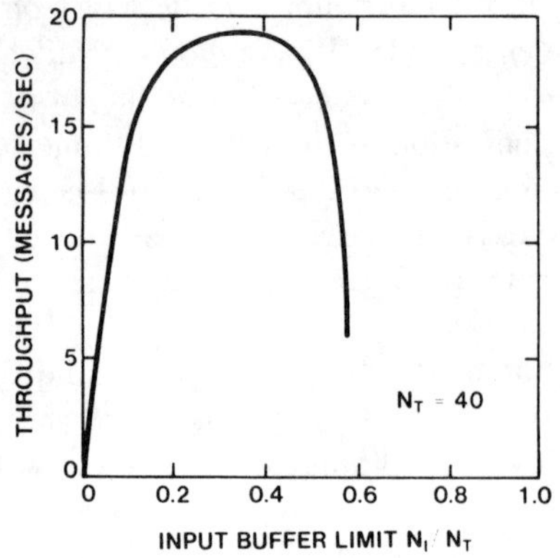

Fig. 19. Input buffer limit scheme: throughput versus buffer limitation for heavy offered load.

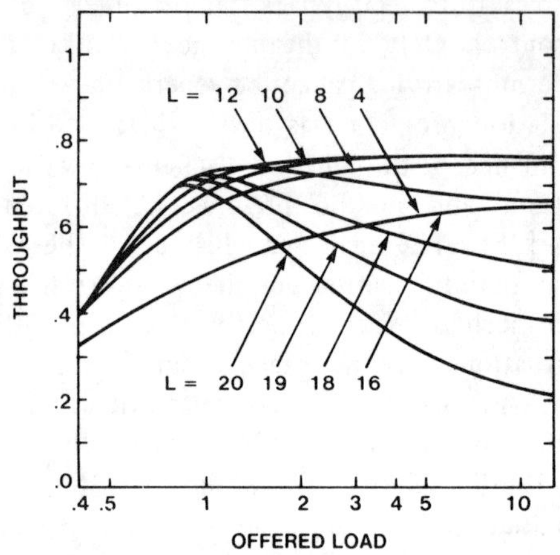

Fig. 20. Throughput versus load for a 121-node network for drop-and-throttle flow control.

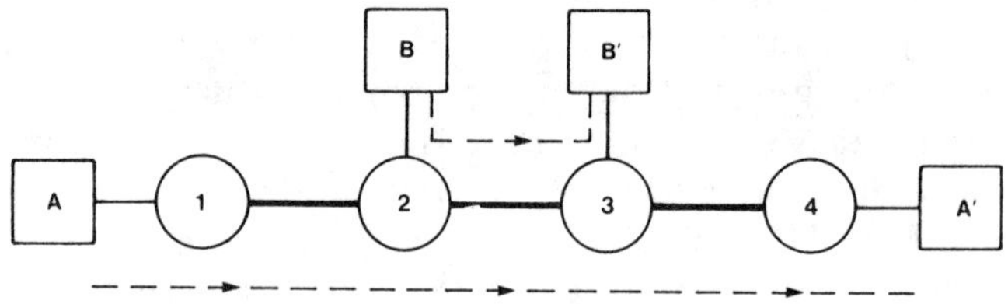

Fig. 21. Unfairness condition produced by input buffer limit and drop-and-throttle flow control schemes.

are assumed to have the same blocking probability, a somewhat unrealistic assumption.

A scheme similar to Lam's IBL scheme had been earlier proposed by Price [35]. In order to prevent input traffic from monopolizing the entire buffer pool, one buffer in each output queue was reserved for transit traffic. This is essentially equivalent to setting an input buffer limit $N_I = N_T - C$, where C = number of output channels. Simulation studies showed that this simple network access control based on source buffer utilization was quite successful in single level networks.

Kamoun [21] proposes yet another version of IBL control, in which an input packet is discarded if the *total* number of packets in the entry node exceeds a given threshold (whereas in Lam's scheme an input packet is discarded when the number of *input* packets exceeds a given threshold). Transit packets, instead, can freely claim all the buffers. The scheme is called drop-and-throttle flow control (DTFC) policy since a transit packet arriving at a full node is dropped and lost (loss model); while all previous schemes assumed link level retransmission of overflow packets (retransmit model). The DTFC scheme was analyzed using a network of queues model [21]. The results, shown in Fig. 20, clearly indicate that there is an optimal threshold value L which maximizes throughput for each value of offered load. Below the threshold, the network is "starved"; above the threshold, the network is congested. A similar scheme, referred to as the free flow scheme, is described and analyzed by Schwartz and Saad in [41]. Preliminary results indicate that, while free flow and IBL throughput performances are compatible, the free flow scheme offers substantial delay improvements.

We have pointed out that IBL control prevents congestion by favoring transit traffic over input traffic. In most cases (indeed, in all cases analyzed in the previously referenced studies), this favoritism leads to throughput improvements. In some cases, however, *unfairness* may result. Consider, for example, the 4-node network shown in Fig. 21. In this network, two file transfers, A to A' and B to B', respectively, are simultaneously competing for trunk (2, 3). Node 2 sees traffic A as transit traffic, so it gives it preferential treatment over traffic from B. Consequently, the A-A' packet stream can acquire more buffers in node 2, and thus achieve better throughput performance than the B-B' stream. The unfairness is particularly dramatic when DTFC is used. With the DTFC policy, if the A-packet queue in node 2 exceeds the buffer threshold (this could easily occur if $C_{23} < C_{12}$), B-packets cannot be accepted by node 2. Consequently B-traffic is completely shut off until the A-A' file transfer is completed.

D. Choke Packet Scheme

The choke packet (CP) scheme, proposed for the Cyclades network [29], is based on the notion of trunk and path congestion. A trunk (link) is defined to be congested if its utilization (measured over an appropriate history window with exponential averaging) exceeds a given threshold (e.g., 80 percent). A path is congested if any of its trunks are congested. Path congestion information is propagated in the network together with routing information and thus, each node knows hop distance and congestion status of the shortest path to each destination.

When a node receives a packet directed to a destination whose path is congested it takes the following actions.

1) If the packet is an *input* packet (i.e., it comes directly from a host), then the packet is dropped.

2) If the packet is a *transit* packet, it is forwarded on the path; but a "choke" packet (namely, a small control packet) is sent back to the source node informing it that the path to that destination is congested and instructing it to block any subsequent input packets to this destination. The path the to destination is gradually unblocked if no choke packets are received during a specified time interval.

This is a greatly simplified description of the CP scheme. Several other features (which are essential to make the scheme workable) are discussed in [29].

It is clear that the CP scheme attempts to favor transit traffic over input traffic, much in the same way as the IBL scheme did. The basic difference between the two schemes is the fact that IBL uses a local congestion measure, namely, the entry node buffer occupancy, to indiscriminately control all input traffic; whereas, CP uses a path congestion measure to exercise *selective* flow control on input traffic directed to different destinations.

Simulation experiments based on the Cigale network topology are given in Fig. 22 and show that the CP scheme can introduce substantial throughput improvements (with respect to the uncontrolled case) in sustained load conditions, asymptotically achieving the ideal performance for infinite load [29].

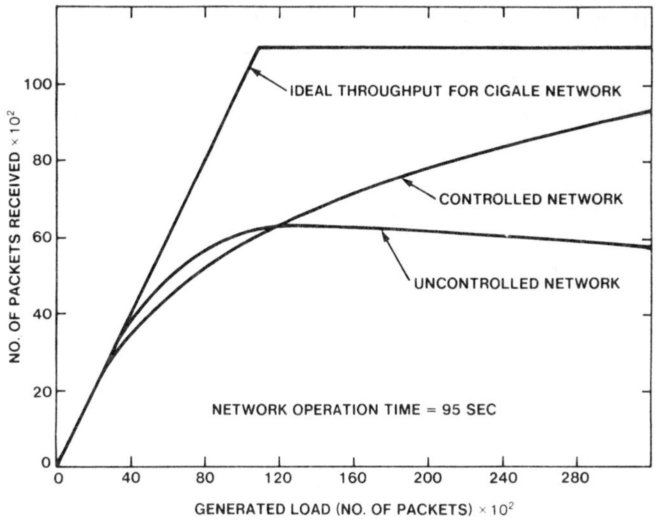

Fig. 22. Throughput performance in Cigale with and without flow control.

VI. TRANSPORT LEVEL FLOW CONTROL

A. Objectives

A transport protocol is a set of rules that govern the transfer of control and data between user processes across the network. The main functions of this protocol are the efficient and reliable transmission of messages within each user session (including packetization, reassembly, resequencing, recovery from loss, elimination of duplicates) and the efficient sharing of common network resources by several user sessions (obtained by multiplexing many user connections on the same physical path and by maintaining priorities between different sessions to reflect the relative urgency).

For efficient and reliable reassembly of messages at the destination host (or more generally, the DTE), the transport protocol must ensure that messages arriving at the destination DTE are provided adequate buffering. The transport protocol function which prevents destination buffer congestion and overflow is known as *transport level flow control.* Generally, this level of flow control is based on a "credit" (or window) mechanism as discussed earlier. Namely, the receiver grants transmission credits to the sender as soon as reassembly buffers become free. Upon receiving a credit, the sender is authorized to transmit a message of an agreed-upon length. When reassembly buffers become full, no credits are returned to the sender, thus temporarily stopping message transmissions [5].

The credit scheme described above is somewhat vulnerable to losses, since a lost credit may hang up a connection. In fact, a sender may wait indefinitely for a lost credit, while the receiver is waiting for a message. A more robust flow control scheme is obtained by numbering credits relative to the messages flowing in the opposite direction. In this case, each credit carries a message sequence number, say N, and a "window size" w. Upon receiving this credit, the sender is authorized to send all backlogged messages up to the $(N + w)$th message. With the numbered credit scheme, if a credit is lost then the subsequent credit will restore proper information to the sender [45].

Besides preventing destination buffer congestion, the credit scheme also indirectly provides global network congestion protection. In fact, store-and-forward buffer congestion at the intermediate nodes along the path may cause a large end-to-end credit delay, thus slowing down the return of credits to the sender, and consequently, reducing the rate of fresh messages input into the network.

B. Implementations

Several versions of the transport protocol are in existence, each incorporating its own form of transport level flow control. Here, we briefly describe four representative implementations.

The earliest example of transport protocol implementation is the original version of the ARPANET network control program (NCP) [4]. NCP flow control is provided by unnumbered credits called "allocate" control messages (see Section IV-D). Only one allocate could be outstanding at a time (i.e., window size $W = 1$).

The French research network Cyclades provided the environment for the development of the transport station (TS) protocol [50]. In the TS protocol, the flow control mechanism is based on numbered credits, each credit authorizing the transmission of a variable size message called a letter. Flow control is actually combined with error control in that credits are carried by acknowledgment messages.

The transmission control program (TCP) was a second generation transport protocol developed by the ARPANET research community in order to overcome the deficiencies of the original NCP protocol [5]. As in the TS protocol, flow and error control are combined in TCP. As a difference, however, error and flow control are on a byte (rather than letter) basis. This allows a more efficient utilization of reassembly buffers at the destination.

In SNA, the transport level flow control is provided by session pacing. The purpose of session-level pacing is to prevent one session end from sending data more quickly than the receiving session end can process the data [16]. As in TCP and TS, session-level pacing is based on a window concept, in which the receiving end grants "credits" to the sending end based on its buffer availability and processing capability. As a difference, however, subarea nodes in SNA can control the inbound flow from a cluster controller into the network by withholding the credits (called pacing responses in SNA) for a given session, if the subarea node buffers are congested or if the Virtual Route (VR) transmission queue for that session is congested. Specifically, session level pacing responses are intercepted at the entry node to exercise *network access* flow control from the terminal into the high-level network [16]. Thus, session pacing may be viewed as a hybrid form of transport level flow control, which is obtained by concatenating a network access level segment (from the terminal to the high-level network node) and an entry-to-exit level segment (controlled by virtual route pacing).

VII. CONCLUSIONS AND DIRECTIONS FOR FURTHER RESEARCH

In this paper we have proposed a taxonomy of flow control mechanisms based on a multilevel structure. We have defined four levels of flow control and have shown how these levels are actually embedded into corresponding levels of protocols. To the extent that these levels can be independently defined, the analysis, design evaluation and comparison of flow control schemes is greatly simplified, since any complex control structure can be decomposed into smaller modules, and each module individually analyzed. The overall performance is then obtained by studying the interaction of the various modules.

Recent advances in queueing theory have led to reasonable success in the modeling and analysis of individual levels of flow control. We have reported on several performance results, and have used such results to compare different schemes.

In real life, however, some control structures defy the simple, hierarchical representation here proposed, and seem to combine two or more levels into hybrid solutions (see Fig. 10). This is particularly common in homogeneous networks (e.g., SNA) in which a single manufacturer is responsible for the implementation of both DCE and DTE equipment and, therefore, has more freedom in the design of the various flow control levels.

The existence of multiple levels of flow control and the possible integration of some of these into hybrid arrangements immediately brings up a very critical issue in flow control which requires further study, namely, the *interaction between levels*. Given that we understand the throughput and delay implications of each specific level of flow control, we still have to study the combined effect when these levels are operating simultaneously in the network. For instance, network experience seems to indicate that a network equipped with a very conservative hop level flow control, such as the SBP scheme in GMDNET or the VC-HL scheme in Tymnet, does not require strong network access or ETE flow control schemes since network congestion situations are immediately reported back to the entry node by back pressure through the hop level [36]. This type of issue can be fully investigated only by developing models which include multiple levels of flow control. An interesting example in this direction was the combined isarithmic and entry to exit flow control model presented in [47]. More research is required in this area.

Hybrid packet and circuit networks are now emerging as a solution to multimode (voice and data; batch and interactive) user requirements [11]. These networks must be equipped with novel flow control mechanisms. In fact, if the network were to apply conventional flow control schemes to the packet switched (P/S) component only, leaving the circuit switch (C/S) component uncontrolled, then the C/S component would very likely capture the entire network bandwidth during peak hours. This may not cause congestion, since the C/S protocol is not as congestion prone as the P/S protocol, but it certainly creates unfairness. Some form of flow control on C/S traffic which is sensitive to the relative P/S load is therefore required.

The *integration of voice and data* requirements in packet switched networks has been vigorously advocated in recent years on grounds of improved efficiency and reduced cost [14]. Unfortunately, little attention has been given to the fact that integrated networks require a complete redesign of the conventional flow control schemes since voice traffic cannot be buffered and delayed in case of congestion. Priorities are of help only if the voice traffic is a small fraction of the total traffic. For the general case, new flow control techniques must be developed for voice. These techniques should be *preventive* in nature, i.e., they should block calls before congestion occurs, rather than *detecting* congestion and then attempting to *recover* from it, as is the case for most of the conventional flow control schemes for data [10], [31].

Routing and flow control procedures have traditionally been developed independently in packet networks, under the assumption that flow control must keep excess traffic out of the network, and routing must struggle to efficiently transport to destination whatever traffic was permitted into the network by the flow control scheme. It seems, however, that routing and flow control can be brought together into useful cooperation in virtual circuit networks, where a path must be selected before data transfer on a user connection begins [12]. In this case, the routing algorithm can be invoked first to determine whether a path of sufficient residual bandwidth is available. If no path is available, the virtual circuit connection is blocked immediately at the entry node by the network access flow control level, thus *preventing* congestion rather than allowing it to occur and then attempting to *recover* from it. A combined routing and flow control strategy is implemented in Tymnet [39].

Challenging flow control problems exist in *multiaccess broadcast networks*. In single hop multiaccess systems, congestion prevention and stability mechanisms are well understood, and are usually directly embedded in the channel access protocol [46]. In distributed, multihop, multiaccess systems (e.g., multihop ground radio networks), congestion prevention becomes a very hard problem because of the interaction between buffer and channel congestion. Conventional flow control schemes used in hardwired nets cannot be directly applied. In particular, the hop level flow control should be revised to combine the buffer allocation strategy with the retransmission control strategy. Some pioneering work in this direction is reported in [2], [48], [43].

Finally, growing user demands require the *interconnection* of networks which may implement different flow control policies and which may even be built on different media (e.g., satellite, radio, cable, or optical fiber). These networks are interconnected by gateways which provide for internet routing and flow control, as well as for protocol conversion between two adjacent networks [44], [6]. It appears that a new level of flow control must therefore be defined in our hierarchy, namely, the gateway-to-gateway level. This level should be designed to prevent the congestion of gateways along the path, and should be supported by explicit gateway-to-gateway protocols for the exchange of status information. The status information should include buffer occupancy at the gateway, and load conditions in the adjacent networks, and could probably be exploited also for gateway routing. Functionally, the gateway-to-gateway protocol is positioned between the entry-to-exit protocol and the transport protocol hierarchy in Fig. 9. All the other levels remain unchanged. The actual implementation of the gateway-to-gateway flow control will be dependent on the internet protocol used. If the CCITT X.75 Recommendation, which is an extension of the X.25 virtual circuit concept to internet connections [45] is adopted, the gateway-to-gateway flow control will be virtual-circuit oriented, and will be exercised on a connection-by-connection basis. Alternatively, datagram-oriented gateway level flow control schemes can also be implemented.

The design of efficient gateway flow control schemes is very challenging. It requires *vertical* consistency between the gateway level and all the other levels implemented in each individual network as well as *horizontal* consistency across the various networks on the internet path. Specifically, the gateway level flow control must be able to balance loads between extremely diverse network environments such as point-to-point, satellite, cable, and ground radio. These design requirements further emphasize the need for continuing research in *multilevel* flow control models in order to understand the vertical interactions between the various levels in the hierarchy, as well as the horizontal interactions between the various segments of a flow control chain along an internet path.

In summary, we have presented a framework for the study of flow control, showing that flow control mechanisms have advanced somewhat beyond simply being "a bag of tricks" [34], and indeed can be conceptually organized into a useful and well-structured system of controls. This structure is extremely helpful in the survey and comparison of existing flow control implementations, as well as in the development of flow control models. In particular, complex control systems can be (and should be) decomposed into smaller modules, thus simplifying the analysis of each module as well as the analysis of interactions between different modules. Furthermore, the proposed flow control structure is sufficiently flexible to permit extensions in response to new networking technologies and applications.

Although our focus has been on flow control models and performance criteria, we expect that the proposed structure will prove to be useful also for the actual implementation of flow control techniques. One must be aware, of course, of the fact that in actual networks, it is not always possible to develop and update flow controls in a well structured fashion. The designer, in fact, is usually confronted with a number of constraints imposed by the preexisting protocol structure (in which flow control mechanisms must be embedded) and by limited storage and processing resources. The designer must therefore avoid overburdening the switch with overly sophisticated flow control mechanisms, and creating inconsistencies and possibly deadlocks. These constraints, together with the fact that flow control is a distributed multilevel control function that cannot be confined to a well-defined modular "black box," make flow control design a very hard task. It is our strong opinion, however, that the only way to prevent flow control implementations from degrading to the state of an uncontrollable "bag of tricks" is to identify an underlying structure in the early stage of flow control design, and to continuously verify this structure during the various updates of protocols and flow control procedures.

Indeed, it is important that one be able to subject a proposed flow control algorithm to various tests of correctness, consistency and proper termination [33], [49]. This is, in general, a very difficult task whose solution requires advances in the frontier of computer science. Unfortunately, since it is relatively difficult to create efficient, deadlock-free, flow control algorithms, we cannot totally ignore this need for verification. Moreover, many difficulties with flow control procedures often arise due to errors in the detailed implementation of otherwise correct algorithms. Consequently, it is important that a modular approach to flow control design be taken, that the code itself be confined to isolated portions of the network operating system (rather than sprinkled through thousands of lines of code) and that the mechanisms be simple enough to be understood and tested via simple procedures.

REFERENCES

[1] V. Ahuja, "Routing and flow control in systems network architecture," *IBM Syst. J.*, vol. 18, no. 2, pp. 298–314, 1979.

[2] G. Akavia and L. Kleinrock, "Performance tradeoff distributed packet-switching communication networks," Dep. Comput. Sci., School of Eng. Appl. Sci., Univ. of California, Los Angeles, Tech. Rep. UCLA-ENG-7942, Sept. 1979.

[3] P. Brinch-Hansen, *Operating System Principles.* Englewood Cliffs, Prentice-Hall, 1973.

[4] S. Carr *et al.*, "Host/host protocol in the ARPA network," in *Proc. Spring Joint Comput. Conf.*, 1970, pp. 589–597.

[5] V. G. Cerf and R. Kahn, "A protocol for packet network intercommunication," *IEEE Trans. Commun.*, vol. COM-22, May 1974.

[6] V. G. Cerf, "DARPA activities in packet network interconnection," in *Interlinking of Computer Networks* (NATO Advanced Study Inst. Series). Reidel.

[7] A. Danet *et al.*, "The French public packet switching service: The Transpac network," in *Proc. Conf. Comp. Commun.*, Toronto, Ont., Canada, Aug. 1976.

[8] D. W. Davies, "The control of congestion in packet-switching networks," *IEEE Trans. Commun.*, vol. COM-20, June 1972.

[9] H. C. Folts, "International standards in computer communications," in *Proc. Nat. Telecommun. Conf.*, Nov. 1979, pp. 59.5.1–59.5.5.

[10] J. Forgie and A. Nemeth, "An efficient packetized voice/data network using statistical flow control," in *Proc. Int. Conf. Commun.* Chicago, IL, June 1977.

[11] M. Gerla and G. DeStasio, "Integration of packet and circuit transport protocols in the TRAN data network," in *Proc. Comput. Network Symp.*, Liege, Belgium, Feb. 1978.

[12] M. Gerla, "Routing and flow control in virtual circuit computer networks," in *Proc. INFO II Int. Conf.*, July 1979.

[13] A. Giessler *et al.*, "Free buffer allocation—An investigation by simulation," *Comput. Networks*, vol. 2, pp. 191–208, 1978.

[14] I. Gitman and H. Frank. "Economic analysis of integrated voice and data networks," *Proc. IEEE*, pp. 1549–1570, Nov. 1978.

[15] J. P. Gray, "Network services in systems network architecture," *IEEE Trans. Commun.*, vol. COM-25, pp. 104–116, Jan. 1977.
[16] J. P. Gray and T. B. McNeill, "SNA multiple-system networking," *IBM Syst. J.*, vol. 18, no. 2, 1979.
[17] P. E. Green, "An introduction to network architectures and protocols," *IBM Syst. J.* no. 2, 1979, reprinted in this issue, pp. 413–424.
[18] M. Irland, "Buffer management in a packet switch," *IEEE Trans. Commun.*, vol. COM-26, pp. 328–337, Mar. 1978.
[19] R. E. Kahn and W. R. Crowther, "A study of the ARPA computer network design and performance," Bolt Beranek and Newman, Inc., Tech. Rep. 2161, Aug. 1971.
[20] F. Kamoun, "Design considerations for large computer communications networks," Ph.D. dissertation, Univ. of California, Los Angeles, Eng. Rep. 7642, Apr. 1976.
[21] F. Kamoun, "A drop and throttle flow control (DTFC) policy for computer networks," presented at the 9th Int. Teletraffic Congr., Spain, Oct. 1979.
[22] P. Kermani and L. Kleinrock, "Dynamic flow control in store and forward computer networks," *IEEE Trans. Commun.*, vol. COM-27, Feb. 1979.
[23] L. Kleinrock, *Queueing Systems: Volume II, Computer Applications.* New York: Wiley-Interscience, 1976.
[24] ——, "On flow control in computer networks," in *Proc. Int. Conf. Commun.*, June 1978.
[25] ——, "Power and deterministic rules of thumb for probabilistic problems in computer communications," in *Proc. Int. Conf. Commun.*, June 1979.
[26] L. Kleinrock and P. Kermani, "Static flow control in store and forward computer networks," *IEEE Trans. Commun.*, vol. COM-27, Feb. 1979.
[27] S. Lam and M. Reiser, "Congestion control of store and forward networks by buffer input limits," in *Proc. Nat. Telecommun. Conf.*, Los Angeles, CA, Dec. 1977.
[28] R. Magoon and D. Twyer, "Flow and congestion control in SL-10 networks," in *Proc. Int. Symp. Flow Control Comput. Networks*, Versailles, France, Feb. 1979.
[29] J. C. Majithia *et al.*, "Experiments in congestion control techniques," in *Proc. Int. Symp. Flow Control Comput. Networks*, Versailles, France, Feb. 1979.
[30] J. M. McQuillan *et al.*, "Improvements in the design and performance of the ARPA network," in *Proc. Fall Joint Comput. Conf.*, 1972.
[31] W. E. Naylor, "Stream traffic communication in packet-switched networks," Ph.D. dissertation, Dep. Comput. Sci., School Eng. Appl. Sci., Univ. of California, Los Angeles, Sept. 1977.
[32] M. Pennotti and M. Schwartz, "Congestion control in store and forward tandem links," *IEEE Trans. Commun.*, Dec. 1975.
[33] J. Postel, "A graph model analysis of computer communications protocols," Ph.D. dissertation, Univ. of California, Los Angeles, Jan. 1974.
[34] L. Pouzin, "Flow control in data networks—Methods and tools," in *Proc. Int. Conf. Comp. Commun.*, Toronto, Ont. Canada, Aug. 1976.
[35] W. L. Price, "Data network simulation experiments at the National Physical Laboratory," *Comput. Networks*, vol. I, 1977.
[36] W. L. Price, "A review of the flow control aspects of the network simulation studies at the National Physical Laboratory," in *Proc. Int. Symp. Flow Control in Comput. Networks*, Versailles, France, Feb. 1979.
[37] E. Raubold, and J. Haenle, "A method of deadlock-free resource allocation and flow control in packet networks," in *Proc. Int. Conf. Comp. Commun.*, Toronto Ont., Canada, Aug. 1976.
[38] M. Reiser, "A queueing network analysis of computer communication networks with window flow control," *IEEE Trans. Commun.*, pp. 1199–1209, Aug. 1979.
[39] J. Rinde, "Routing and control in a centrally directed network," in *Proc. Nat. Comput. Conf.*, Dallas, TX, June 1977.
[40] J. Rinde and A. Caisse, "Passive flow control techniques for distributed networks," in *Proc. Int. Symp. Comput. Networks*, Versailles, France, Feb. 1979.
[41] M. Schwartz, and S. Saad, "Analysis of congestion control techniques in computer communications networks," in *Proc. Int. Symp. Comput. Networks*, Versailles, France, Feb. 1979.
[42] J. M. Simon and A. Danet, "Controle des ressources et principes du routage dans le reseau TRANSPAC," in *Proc. Int. Symp. Comput. Networks*, Versailles, France, Feb. 1979.
[43] J. Silvester "On spatial capacity of packet radio networks," Ph.D. dissertation, Dep. Comput. Sci., School Eng. Appl. Sci., Univ. of California, Los Angeles, Mar. 1980.
[44] A. C. Sunshine, "Interconnection of computer networks," *Comput. Networks*, vol. 1, 1977.
[45] A. C. Sunshine, "Transport protocols for computer networks," in *Protocols and Techniques for Data Communications Networks*, F. Kuo, Ed. Englewood Cliffs, NJ: Prentice-Hall, 1980.
[46] F. Tobagi, "Multiaccess protocols in packet communication systems," this issue, pp. 468–488.
[47] J. W. Wong, and M. S. Unsoy, "Analysis of flow control in switched data networks," in *Proc. Int. Fed. Inf. Processing Soc. Conf.*, Aug. 1977.
[48] Y. Yemini and L. Kleinrock, "On a general rule for access control or, silence is golden...," in *Proc. Int. Symp. Flow Control Comput. Networks*, Versailles, France, Feb. 1979.
[49] P. Zafiropulo, "A new approach to protocol validation," in *Proc. Int. Conf. Commun.* June, 1977.
[50] H. Zimmermann, "The Cyclades end-to-end protocol," in *Proc. 4th Data Commun. Symp.*, Quebec, P. Q., Canada, Oct. 1975, pp. 7:21–26.
[51] Schwartz and Stern, "Routing algorithms: A comparative survey," this issue, pp. 539–552.

★

Mario Gerla (M'75) received a graduate degree in electrical engineering from the Politecnico of Milan, Milan, Italy, in 1966, and the Ph.D. degree in engineering from the University of California, Los Angeles, in 1973.

He came to UCLA with a Fulbright scholarship in 1969, and worked on the ARPA network project as a Research Assistant. In January 1973, he joined Network Analysis Corporation, Glen Cove, NY, where as Manager of Computer Networking, he was involved in several computer network design projects for both government and industry. Since July 1977, he has been on the faculty of the Department of Computer Science at UCLA. His research interests are in the areas of design, control, and performance evaluation of data communications networks and distributed processing systems.

★

Leonard Kleinrock (S'55–M'64–SM'71–F'73) received the B.E.E. degree from the City College of New York, New York, NY, in 1957, and the M.S.E.E. and Ph.D.E.E. degrees from Massachusetts Institute of Technology, Cambridge, in 1959 and 1963, respectively.

In 1963, he joined the faculty of the School of Engineering and Applied Science, University of California, Los Angeles, where he is now Professor of Computer Science. His research spans the fields of computer networks, computer systems modeling and analysis, queueing theory, and resource sharing and allocation in general. At UCLA, he directs a large group in advanced teleprocessing systems and computer networks. He is the author of three major books in the field of computer networks: *Communication Nets: Stochastic Message Flow and Delay* (New York: McGraw-Hill, 1964; also New York: Dover, 1972); *Queueing Systems, Vol. I. Theory* (New York: Wiley-Interscience, 1975); and *Queueing Systems, Vol. II: Computer Applications* (New York: Wiley-Interscience, 1976). He has published over 100 articles and contributed to several books. He serves as consultant for many domestic and foreign corporations and governments, and he is a referee for numerous scholarly publications and a book reviewer for several publishers.

Dr. Kleinrock is a Guggenheim Fellow and has received various outstanding teacher and best paper awards, including the 1976 Lanchester prize for the outstanding paper in operations research, and the ICC 1978 prizewinning paper award.

Queuing Network Models of Packet Switching Networks Part 1: Open Networks *

J.W. Wong
Department of Computer Science, University of Waterloo, Waterloo, Ontario, Canada

and

S.S. Lam
Department of Computer Sciences, University of Texas at Austin, Austin, TX 78712, U.S.A.

Received 20 February 1981; revised version received 28 December 1981

An overview of the application of product-form queuing network models to the performance analysis of store-and-forward packet-switching networks is presented. Multiple routing chains are used to model the different routing behaviors of data packets. Queuing networks with open chains are considered in this paper. Kleinrock's formula for the mean end-to-end delay of packets is first derived. The application of this delay formula to optimal channel capacity assignment and optimal routing is discussed. Analytic results for the mean and distribution of the end-to-end delay of each chain are presented. The issue of fairness among chains is also addressed.

The application of queuing networks with closed chains and population size constraints to the performance analysis of store-and-forward packet-switching networks is illustrated in a companion paper [1].

Keywords: Queuing Network Models, Packet Switching Networks, End-to-End Delay, Delay Distribution, Capacity Assignment, Routing, Fairness.

* The work of J.W. Wong was supported by the Natural Sciences and Engineering Research Council of Canada. The work of S.S. Lam was supported by National Science Foundation Grant No. ECS78-01803.

North-Holland Publishing Company
Performance Evaluation 2 (1982) 9–21

1. Introduction

A store-and-forward packet-switching network consists of a set of switching nodes interconnected by communication channels. Host computers and terminals constitute sources and sinks of data messages to be transported by the network (see Fig. 1). The basic unit of data transfer within the network

J.W. Wong received the B.S. in engineering, the M.S. and Ph.D. degrees in computer science from the University of California at Los Angeles in 1970, 1971, and 1975, respectively. He is currently an Associate Professor of Computer Science at the University of Waterloo, Waterloo, Ontario, Canada.

Simon S. Lam received the B.S.E.E. degree (with Distinction) from Washington State University, Pullman, Washington, in 1969, and the M.S. and Ph.D. degrees in engineering from the University of California at Los Angeles, in 1970 and 1974, respectively.

From 1972 to 1974, he was with the ARPA Network project at UCLA and did research on satellite packet communication. From 1974 to 1977, he was a research staff member with the IBM Thomas J. Watson Research Center, Yorktown Heights, New York, where he worked on performance analysis problems of packet switching networks, SNA and satellite networks. Since September 1977, he has been with the University of Texas at Austin where he is now Associate Professor of Computer Sciences. His current research interests include modeling and analysis of computer systems, networks and communication protocols.

At the University of California at Los Angeles, he held a Phi Kappa Phi Fellowship from 1969 to 1970, and a Chancellor's Teaching Fellowship from 1969 to 1973. In 1975, he received the IEEE Leonard G. Abraham Award for the best paper in the field of Communications Systems. Simon is a member of Tau Beta Pi, Sigma Tau, Phi Kappa Phi, Pi Mu Epsilon and the Association for Computing Machinery, and a senior member of IEEE.

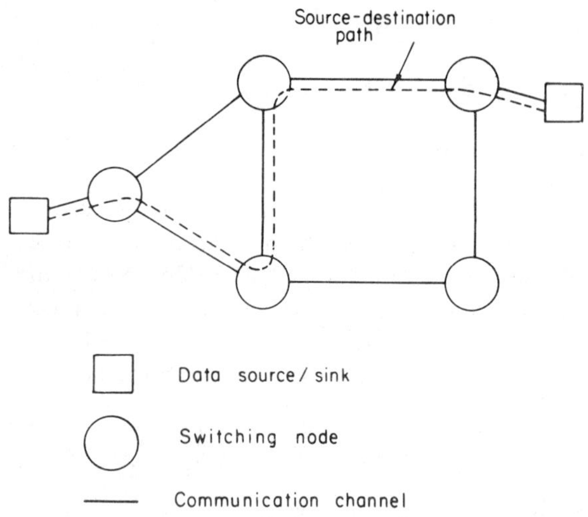

Fig. 1. Store-and-forward packet switching network.

is a packet. [1] Each packet traverses from its source node to its destination node through a series of nodes and communication channels along its path (route). Queues are formed for the communication channels inside the switching nodes. The progress of packets in the network is governed by certain communication protocols. The objective of this paper is to review recent efforts on the application of product-form open queuing networks [2–4] to model store-and-forward packet communication networks. The application of queuing networks with closed chains and population size constraints [2–5] is considered in a companion paper [1].

A store-and-forward network can be viewed as a collection of resources shared by data sources and sinks. There are three types of physical resources in the network: communication channels, packet buffers, and nodal processors. In modeling such a network, the nodal processors are often neglected because processor delays incurred by packets are typically substantially less than communication channel delays.

To transport a packet from one node to another in a store-and-forward network, the resources needed along the source–destination path are communication channels and one buffer in each node along the path. It is obvious that the set of communication channels and/or the set of nodal buffers can be preallocated. Preallocation is a 'safe' operational strategy. However, it is extremely wasteful because data sources are typically very bursty [6].

A store-and-forward protocol is a means for dynamically allocating network resources and thus sharing them statistically. In a store-and-forward network, a packet can progress from one node to the next along its route with the allocation of just a communication channel and two buffers (one at each side of the channel). If the packet is successfully received and accepted in the next node, a positive acknowledgement message will be returned to the previous node, either separately as a short packet or piggybacked in the header of a data packet traveling in the reverse direction. The packet buffer in the previous node can then be freed. If, however, no acknowledgement has been received at the end of a timeout period, the packet will be queued for retransmission.

Currently, there are two basic types of packet communication services: datagram and virtual channel [7]. We shall consider their differences from the modeling viewpoint only. In a datagram network, each data packet (datagram) traverses the network as an independent entity. In a virtual channel network, data packets belong to 'virtual channels' connecting data sources and sinks. The admittance of packets into a virtual channel is controlled. Also, packets in the same virtual channel are usually characterized by the same routing behavior.

Given a set of external traffice demands, the efficient utilization of a network's channel and buffer resources depends on the network's routing algorithm as well as its flow and congestion control techniques. Measurements of network performance typically include its throughput (in packets delivered per second) and some measure of the network transit delay. These performance measures may need to be characterized for all packets transported by the network or for individual classes of packets (e.g., packets between specific source–sink pairs).

Product-form queuing network models have been successfully applied to the performance analysis of store-and-forward network with some or all of the above features. To do so, several simplifying

[1] When a data message to be transported is longer than the size of a packet, it is segmented into several packets which need to be reassembled later to form the original message. The segmentation and reassembly functions may be either performed by the network nodes or by the data sources and sinks.

assumptions are necessary; they will be introduced in Section 2. Queuing network models also have a number of limitations. One such limitation is that adaptive routing [6] cannot be modeled. Analysis results are available for situations where a set of paths is provided between each source–destination node pair, and these paths may be either chosen deterministically or randomly, but not adaptively for packets.

The accuracy of queuing network models is affected by the presence of various communication protocols, which may impede the progress of packets through the network but which cannot be easily modeled (examples are segmentation and reassembly of messages, some of the data link control functions, etc.). Also, various network measurement and control traffic are often not accounted for in the models to be described below. Therefore queuing network models results should be viewed in most cases as a somewhat optimistic prediction of network performance.

2. Assumptions and definitions

The key assumption necessary for the application of queuing network models to analyze a store-and-forward network was originally introduced by Kleinrock [6,8].

The Independence Assumption. Each time a packet joins a queue in the network, its length is determined afresh from the probability density function

$$b(x) = \mu \exp(-\mu x), \quad x \geqslant 0,$$

where $1/\mu$ is the mean packet length (in number of bits).

The above assumption removes the statistical dependence of the transmission times of a packet at the various channels of its route. Without this assumption, the analysis of store-and-forward networks is not mathematically tractable.

In actual networks, packets usually have a maximum length. Also, measurement results indicate that packet lengths are not really exponentially distributed [6,9]. Therefore, analytic results provided by queuing network models are merely approximations. However, these approximate results are generally deemed to be adequate and valuable for the design and performance characterization of store-and-forward packet-switching networks [6].

We next define the class of queuing networks suitable for modeling store-and-forward networks. (This class of network models is only a subset of network models that have a product-form solution [2–5].) The notation to be used throughout this paper is also introduced.

Servers in the network model are indexed by $i = 1, 2, \ldots, M$. We shall only consider first-come first-served (FCFS) servers to model communication channels, and infinite-server (IS) servers to model random delays. Customers (i.e., packets) belong the different 'routing chains'; these chains are indexed by $k = 1, 2, \ldots, K$. Specifically, the routing behavior of chain k is modeled by a first-order Markov chain with transition probabilities

$$p_{ij}^{(k)} = \text{Prob}[\text{to server } j \mid \text{currently at server } i] \qquad i, j = 1, 2, \ldots, M. \quad (2.1)$$

We note that a first-order Markov chain is adequate for modeling both the case of a single route and the case of multiple routes between a given source and destination. Retransmission and rerouting due to random transmission errors can also be modeled by an appropriate definition of the transition probabilities [10].

Since the routing behavior of packets traveling between different source–destination node pairs are different, a queuing network model must specify at least one routing chain for each source–destination node pair. It is sometimes desirable to specify multiple chains between each source–destination node pair to correspond to virtual channels connecting several data sources in the same source node to several data sinks in the same destination node. For a datagram network, it is sufficient to define just one chain for each source–destination node pair.

It is assumed that chain k packets arrive to the first server of the chain according to a Poisson process with rate γ_k packets per second, where $k = 1, 2, \ldots, K$. Define

$$\gamma = \gamma_1 + \gamma_2 + \cdots + \gamma_K.$$

γ is the total external arrival rate to the network. Given γ_k and $p_{ij}^{(k)}$, the mean rate λ_{ik} of chain k packet arrivals to server i in the queuing network model is determined from:

$$\lambda_{ik} = \gamma_k \delta_{ik} + \sum_{j=1}^{M} \lambda_{jk} p_{ji}^{(k)}, \qquad (2.2)$$

where

$$\delta_{ik} = \begin{cases} 1 & \text{if } i \text{ is the first server of chain } k, \\ 0 & \text{otherwise.} \end{cases} \tag{2.3}$$

The arrival rate of packets from all chains to server i is

$$\lambda_i = \sum_{k=1}^{K} \lambda_{ik}. \tag{2.4}$$

It is assumed that if server i is FCFS, it works at a constant rate of C_i bits per second. If server i is IS, it works at a rate of C_{ik} bits per second for chain k packets. The traffic intensity of chain k packets at server i is defined to be

$$\rho_{ik} = \begin{cases} \dfrac{\lambda_{ik}}{\mu C_i}, & \text{server } i \text{ is FCFS,} \\ \dfrac{\lambda_{ik}}{\mu C_{ik}}, & \text{server } i \text{ is IS,} \end{cases} \tag{2.5}$$

and the overall traffic intensity of server i is

$$\rho_i = \sum_{k=1}^{K} \rho_{ik}. \tag{2.6}$$

Let the state of the queuing network be denoted by

$$S = (\boldsymbol{n}_1, \boldsymbol{n}_2, \ldots, \boldsymbol{n}_M),$$

where

$$\boldsymbol{n}_i = (n_{i1}, n_{i2}, \ldots, n_{iK}),$$

where n_{ik} is the total number of chain k packets at server i. Define

$$n_i = n_{i1} + n_{i2} + \cdots + n_{iK}$$

and

$$\boldsymbol{n} = (n_1, n_2, \ldots, n_M).$$

A chain is said to be *open* if it allows both external arrivals and departures to occur freely. As a result, the number of packets in a chain can range from 0 to ∞. For a network with open chains, the equilibrium probability of the network state S has the following-product form solution [3]:

$$P(S) = \prod_{i=1}^{M} \frac{p_i(\boldsymbol{n}_i)}{G_i}, \tag{2.7}$$

where

$$p_i(\boldsymbol{n}_i) = \begin{cases} n_i! \displaystyle\prod_{k=1}^{K} \frac{\rho_{ik}^{n_{ik}}}{n_{ik}!}, & \text{server } i \text{ is FCFS,} \\ \displaystyle\prod_{k=1}^{K} \frac{\rho_{ik}^{n_{ik}}}{n_{ik}!}, & \text{server } i \text{ is IS,} \end{cases} \tag{2.8}$$

and

$$G_i = \begin{cases} 1/(1-\rho_i), & \text{server } i \text{ if FCFS,} \\ \exp(\rho_i), & \text{server } i \text{ is IS.} \end{cases} \tag{2.9}$$

The equilibrium probability of $\boldsymbol{n}$ also has a product form [3]:

$$P(\boldsymbol{n}) = \prod_{i=1}^{M} \frac{p_i(n_i)}{G_i}, \tag{2.10}$$

where

$$p_i(n_i) = \begin{cases} \rho_i^{n_i}, & \text{server } i \text{ is FCFS,} \\ \dfrac{\rho_i^{n_i}}{n_i!}, & \text{server } i \text{ is IS.} \end{cases} \tag{2.11}$$

A routing chain is said to be *closed* if the number of packets in the chain is fixed. Queuing networks with closed chains as well as other forms of chain population size constraints are useful for modeling flow and congestion control in store-and-forward networks. These models are discussed in the companion paper [1].

Given a set of traffic demands modeled by the rates $\{\gamma_k, k = 1, 2, \ldots, K\}$, the basic performance measures of interest are the network throughput and mean end-to-end (or source-to-destination) delay. Define

γ^* = network throughput in packets per second,
T = mean end-to-end delay over all packets transported by the network.

These two measures may be adequate by themselves. In some cases, it may be necessary to characterize the performance of individual routing chains. We thus define

γ_k^* = throughput of chain k in packets per second,
T_k = mean end-to-end delay of chain k packets transported by the network.

If the network switching nodes have adequate buffers and channel capacities so that packets are never rejected (a situation modeled by queuing networks with open chains), the chain throughput is the same as the chain arrival rate, i.e.,

$$\gamma_k^* = \gamma_k, \quad k = 1, 2, \ldots, K. \tag{2.12}$$

Otherwise, some external arrivals are rejected due to buffer, flow or congestion control constraints and the throughput is smaller than the corresponding arrival rate, or

$$\gamma_k^* < \gamma_k, \quad k = 1, 2, \ldots, K. \tag{2.13}$$

The difference between γ_k and γ_k^* is the rate at which chain k arrivals are rejected. Since rejected packets are retransmitted later, the ratio γ_k/γ_k^* can be interpreted as the mean number of tries needed for a packet to gain admittance to the network. (See [1].)

The balance of this paper is organized as follows. An analytic formula for T, the mean end-to-end delay over all packets, is derived in Section 3. The application of this formula to channel capacity assignment and optimal routing is next discussed. In Section 4, the mean and distribution of the end-to-end delays of individual chains are considered. Finally, the issue of fairness among chains is discussed in Section 5.

3. Mean end-to-end delay over all chains

We consider in this section the efficient utilization of communication channels in a packet network via channel capacity assignment or routing assignment.

Queuing network models with open chains are employed. The number of buffers at each node is assumed to be very large (infinite). The effect of packet transmission errors is assumed to be negligible.

3.1. A formula for the mean end-to-end delay

The mean end-to-end delay T for an arbitrary packet transported by the network was first derived by Kleinrock [6,8]. It can be obtained as follows. By Little's formula [11], the mean number of packets in transit within the network is equal to γT. Let $E[n_i]$ be the mean number of packets at channel i. We have

$$\gamma T = \sum_{i=1}^{M} E[n_i]. \tag{3.1}$$

Since the communication channel delays typically dominate most other delays, we shall assume that the M servers are all communication channels modeled by FCFS queues. The marginal queue length distribution from (2.11) gives rise to the following mean queue lengths:

$$E[n_i] = \frac{\rho_i}{1-\rho_i}, \quad i = 1, 2, \ldots, M. \tag{3.2}$$

Thus

$$\gamma T = \sum_{i=1}^{M} \frac{\rho_i}{1-\rho_i}. \tag{3.3}$$

Since $\rho_i = \lambda_i/(\mu C_i)$ (see (2.4) to (2.6)), we have

$$T = \frac{1}{\gamma} \sum_{i=1}^{M} \frac{\lambda_i}{\mu C_i - \lambda_i}, \tag{3.4}$$

which is sometimes written as

$$T = \frac{1}{\gamma} \sum_{i=1}^{M} \frac{f_i}{C_i - f_i}, \tag{3.5}$$

where $f_i = \lambda_i/\mu$ (in bits per second) is called the channel i *flow* [12].

Recall that under our present assumption, $\gamma^* = \gamma$. Using T, as given by (3.5), as our performance measure, we shall consider next the problems of channel capacity assignment and optimal routing.

In practice, it may be advisable to refine the model considered above by including delays due to channel propagation times, nodal processing times, and any control message traffic. The reader is referred to [6] for more details. However, (3.5) is the basic formula used in the capacity assignment and optimal routing problems.

3.2. Capacity assignment

Suppose we are given the traffic requirement $\{\gamma_k, k = 1, 2, \ldots, K\}$. The network topology is fixed and routing has been specified in the form of (2.1). A meaningful question to ask is as follows: given a fixed budget for communication channels, how do we select the set of channel capacities $\{C_i, i = 1, 2, \ldots, M\}$? This problem was addressed by Kleinrock [6,8] and to keep the problem simple, he made the following assumptions:

(a) channel capacities can be selected from a continuum of values;

(b) the channel cost is a linear function of the channel capacity so that the network cost is

$$\sum_{i-1}^{M} d_i C_i + \text{a fixed cost}. \tag{3.6}$$

Let D be the available budget for channels after the fixed cost has been accounted for. One can then pose the following optimization problem:

$$\min_{\{C_i\}} T = \frac{1}{\gamma} \sum_{i=1}^{M} \frac{f_i}{C_i - f_i},$$

$$\text{subject to} \quad \sum_{i=1}^{M} d_i C_i \leq D. \tag{3.7}$$

Note that T is a convex function and the set of feasible channel capacities is a convex set. Hence, a unique optimal solution exists. The above constrained optimization problem can be converted to an unconstrained optimization problem by the Lagrange multiplier method which yields the following solution for optimal capacity assignment [6,8]:

$$C_i^* = f_i + \left(D_e \sqrt{f_i d_i}\right) / \left(d_i \sum_{j=1}^{M} \sqrt{f_j d_j} \right), \tag{3.8}$$

where

$$D_e = D - \sum_{j=1}^{M} f_j d_j > 0. \tag{3.9}$$

If $D_e \leq 0$, a feasible capacity assignment does not exist to achieve a finite T. The minimum mean delay corresponding to the above capacity assignment is:

$$T^* = \frac{1}{\gamma D_e} \left[\sum_{j=1}^{M} \sqrt{f_j d_j} \right]^2. \tag{3.10}$$

The dual of the optimization problem in (3.7) can also be formulated to minimize the network cost subject to a mean delay constraint as follows:

$$\min_{\{C_i\}} \sum_{i=1}^{M} d_i C_i,$$

$$\text{subject to} \quad \frac{1}{\gamma} \sum_{i=1}^{M} \frac{f_i}{C_i - f_i} \leq T_{\max}. \tag{3.11}$$

Again, applying the Lagrange multiplier method, the optimal capacity assignment is

$$C_i^* = f_i + \frac{\sum_{j=1}^{M} \sqrt{f_j d_j}}{\gamma T_{\max}} \sqrt{\frac{f_i}{d_i}}. \tag{3.12}$$

The minimum network cost for channels is then

$$D^* = \sum_{j=1}^{M} f_j d_j + \frac{1}{\gamma T_{\max}} \left[\sum_{j=1}^{M} \sqrt{f_j d_j} \right]^2. \tag{3.13}$$

The optimal capacity assignment given by (3.8) or (3.12) provides a network designer with some initial guidance for selecting channel capacities. In reality, channel capacities are limited to a set of discrete capacity values that are available from common-carriers. Also, as a result of economy of scale, the cost-function $d_i(C_i)$ of a channel with capacity C_i should be a concave function in C_i instead of a linear function assumed above. To incorporate the above considerations into the capacity assignment problem, one must then resort to numerical solution techniques [12]. Finally, we also note that most communication links available from the common-carriers are full-duplex with the same capacity for each of the channels in opposite directions. The usual assumption that enables us to apply the above optimal capacity assignment result is to consider a symmetric network traffic pattern. If, however, the network traffic pattern is highly asymmetric, then one must again resort to a numerical solution technique to account for this additional constraint.

3.3. Optimal routing

In the capacity assignment problem above, the routing was assumed to be pre-specified. Suppose the channel capacities have already been selected. We now consider the problem of assigning routes to satisfy a set of traffic requirements $\{\gamma_k, k = 1, 2, \ldots, K\}$ so that some performance criterion is optimized. This is known as the optimal routing problem.

Operationally, optimal routing is difficult to achieve. Due to the geographical distribution of network nodes, fresh information on the global status of a network is generally not available. In the ARPANET, for example, each node exchanges status information with its neighbors periodically. Considerable time delays, however, are needed for such information to propagate throughout the network [13].

With most performance objectives, optimal routing can be formulated as a shortest path problem with an appropriate distance metric for the communication channels within a path. In the ARPANET, the distance metric is simply the (estimated) mean delay of a communication channel. Each packet, regardless of its origin, is routed to an outgoing channel along the path with the shortest (estimated) mean delay to the packet's destination node. Note that this particular routing strategy minimizes the (estimated) mean delay of each individual packet. It has been shown that such an individual optimization strategy does not necessarily lead to a globally optimized situation; specifically, the mean transit delay T for all packets transported by the network is not optimized. In order to optimize T, the following result was obtained [12,14].

Given the traffic requirements $\{\gamma_k\}$ and a specific routing assignment $\{p_{ij}^{(k)}\}$, the channel arrival rates $\{\lambda_i\}$ can be determined using (2.2) and (2.4). Recall that the flow in channel i is $f_i = \lambda_i/\mu$ in bits per second. Denote the set of channel flows by the flow vector

$$\boldsymbol{f} = (f_1, f_2, \ldots, f_M).$$

A flow vector $\boldsymbol{f}$ is said to be feasible if

$$0 \leqslant f_i < C_i \quad \text{for } i = 1, 2, \ldots, M$$

and if it is the result of a routing assignment which satisfies the traffic requirements.

Necessary and sufficient conditions for $\boldsymbol{f}$ (hence, indirectly for the routing assignment) to minimize T are obtained as follows. Let $T(\boldsymbol{f})$ be the mean network delay corresponding to the feasible flow vector $\boldsymbol{f}$. Let $\boldsymbol{v}$ be another flow vector. Given $\boldsymbol{f}$, a feasible flow vector $\boldsymbol{f}'$ near $\boldsymbol{f}$ can be represented as a convex combination of $\boldsymbol{f}$ and $\boldsymbol{v}$, i.e.,

$$\boldsymbol{f}' = (1-\varepsilon)\boldsymbol{f} + \varepsilon\boldsymbol{v} = \boldsymbol{f} + \varepsilon(\boldsymbol{v} - \boldsymbol{f}), \quad 0 \leqslant \varepsilon \leqslant 1. \tag{3.14}$$

Note that the flow vector $\boldsymbol{v}$ can be chosen without satisfying $v_i < C_i$ for all i. In this case, a sufficiently small ε should be used in order for $\boldsymbol{f}'$ to be feasible. Suppose $\varepsilon \ll 1$ so that the change in the flow vector (in the $\boldsymbol{v}$ direction) is small and is given by:

$$\Delta \boldsymbol{f} = \varepsilon(\boldsymbol{v} - \boldsymbol{f}). \tag{3.15}$$

The resulting change in the mean network delay is

$$\Delta T(\boldsymbol{f}) = \sum_{i=1}^{M} \frac{\partial T(\boldsymbol{f})}{\partial f_i}(v_i - f_i)\varepsilon = \varepsilon \sum_{i=1}^{M} L_i(v_i - f_i), \tag{3.16}$$

where

$$L_i = \frac{\partial T(\boldsymbol{f})}{\partial f_i}. \tag{3.17}$$

Eq. (3.17) above requires that the function $T(\boldsymbol{f})$ be differentiable. If, moreover, the function $T(\boldsymbol{f})$ is also convex, then we know that a unique minimum exists among the set of feasible flow vectors (which is a convex set [12,14]). Thus, a necessary and sufficient condition for a feasible flow vector $\boldsymbol{f}$ to be optimal is

$$\Delta T(\boldsymbol{f}) \geqslant 0 \quad \text{for any } \boldsymbol{v}, \tag{3.18}$$

or

$$\sum_{i=1}^{M} L_i(v_i - f_i) \geqslant 0 \quad \text{for any } \boldsymbol{v}, \tag{3.19}$$

or

$$\min_{\boldsymbol{v}} \sum_{i=1}^{M} L_i v_i \geqslant \sum_{i=1}^{M} L_i f_i. \tag{3.20}$$

If the condition in (3.20) is not satisfied, then $\boldsymbol{f}$ (and the corresponding routing assignment) is not optimal. Moreover, (3.16) indicates that if a 'small' amount of source–destination traffic is to be rerouted (or if some new traffic is to be added to the network) then that traffic should follow a shortest path from its source node to its destination node using $\{L_i\}$ as the distance metric to minimize its impact on the mean network delay. Recall that with the open queuing network model, from (3.5),

$$T(\boldsymbol{f}) = \frac{1}{\gamma} \sum_{i=1}^{M} \frac{f_i}{C_i - f_i}. \tag{3.21}$$

Hence

$$L_i = \frac{\partial T(\boldsymbol{f})}{\partial f_i} = \frac{1}{\gamma} \frac{C_i}{(C_i - f_i)^2}. \tag{3.22}$$

Given the traffic requirements $\{\gamma_k\}$, the optimal flow vector $\boldsymbol{f}$ (and hence, route assignments) can be determined by a downhill search technique using any feasible flow vector as a starting point. The reader is referred to [12,14] for details.

Finally, we comment that in practice, instead of doing capacity assignment and optimal routing as separate problems, it is desirable to do both optimizations together. The resulting problem is much more difficult than each of the above, and one must resort to heuristic search techniques for optimal solutions. The reader should consult Gerla's thesis [12] for this and other network design problems.

4. End-to-end delay for each routing chain

Our discussion so far has been based on the mean end-to-end delay over all packets transported by the network. The key result, given by (3.4), provides a gross characterization of network delay. It is useful in the formulation of various optimization problems for network design. For various reasons, one might be interested in a more detailed characterization of network delay than the mean over all packets. For example, users sending packets from node A to node B will be interested in the end-to-end delay from A to B.

4.1. Mean end-to-end delay

We shall consider only networks which employ path-oriented routing. When multiple paths exist between a given source–destination node pair, the source node selects the complete path for each packet to follow in order to reach the destination. A notable example of path-oriented routing is the explicit path routing technique of Jueneman and Kerr [15] proposed for IBM's System Network Architecture [16]. The ARPANET, on the other hand, is a notable exception where routing decisions are made by intermediate store-and-forward nodes. Path-oriented routing has the advantages that (a) routing decisions are decentralized, (b) packets are guaranteed to arrive in FCFS order along each path, (c) loops can be avoided, and (d) the impact of bad decisions made by a source node is limited. A simple example of path-oriented routing is fixed routing where there is a unique path for each source–destination node pair. Another example is 'random routing' where one or more paths are set up for each source–destination node pair and the path of each packet is selected independently by the source node according to a probability distribution. In a virtual channel network, several virtual channels may be present between each source–destination node pair; either fixed or random routing may be employed for each virtual channel.

For path-oriented routing, each path can conveniently be modeled by a routing chain. In this section, we consider the mean end-to-end delay of each routing chain in the network. The results can then be used to obtain the mean end-to-end delay for any given source–destination node pair (or any virtual channel) which employs multiple paths. It is also possible to get the probability density function of the end-to-end delay for a class of routing algorithms. These results will be presented in Section 4.2.

Let π_k be the path (or ordered set of channels) over which chain k packets are routed. The transition probabilities of chain k take on values of 0 and 1 only, i.e.,

$$p_{ij}^{(k)} = \begin{cases} 1 & \text{if } i \text{ and } j \text{ are successive channels in } \pi_k, \\ 0 & \text{otherwise.} \end{cases} \tag{4.1}$$

With this definition for $p_{ij}^{(k)}$, it is easy to verify that the solution to (2.2) is

$$\lambda_{ik} = \begin{cases} \gamma_k & \text{if } i \in \pi_k, \\ 0 & \text{otherwise.} \end{cases} \tag{4.2}$$

Since each channel in the network model is a FCFS server and all routing chains are assumed to be open, the equilibrium states probability has the following product form [3] (see (2.7)):

$$P(S) = \prod_{i=1}^{M} (1-\rho_i) n_i! \prod_{k=1}^{K} \frac{\rho_{ik}^{n_{ik}}}{n_{ik}!}, \tag{4.3}$$

where ρ_{ik} and ρ_i are given by (2.5) and (2.6) respectively. From (4.3), we get the following expression for the marginal queue length distribution at channel i:

$$P(\boldsymbol{n}_i) = (1-\rho_i) n_i! \prod_{k=1}^{K} \frac{\rho_{ik}^{n_{ik}}}{n_{ik}!}. \tag{4.4}$$

The mean number of chain k packets at channel i can then be obtained from:

$$E[n_{ik}] = \sum_{j=0}^{\infty} j \sum_{\boldsymbol{n}_i \in R_j} P(\boldsymbol{n}_i), \tag{4.5}$$

where

$$R_j = \{\boldsymbol{n}_i : n_{ik} = j\}. \tag{4.6}$$

Substituting (4.4) into (4.5) and after some simplications, we get:

$$E[n_{ik}] = \frac{\rho_{ik}}{1-\rho_i}. \tag{4.7}$$

Applying Little's formula [11], the mean delay of chain k packets at channel i is

$$T_{ik} = E[n_{ik}]/\gamma_k = \frac{1}{\mu C_i (1-\rho_i)}. \tag{4.8}$$

It is of interest to note that the mean delay at

channel i is determined by the total utilization of channel i, and is the same for all chains that are routed through this channel. Finally, the mean end-to-end delay of chain k is:

$$T_k = \sum_{i \in \pi_k} \frac{1}{\mu C_i (1-\rho_i)}. \tag{4.9}$$

As a remark, the mean end-to-end delay over all packets can be obtained from:

$$T = \sum_{k=1}^{K} \frac{\gamma_k}{\gamma} T_k \tag{4.10}$$

and it can be verified that (3.4) and (4.10) are identical.

We now illustrate how the result in (4.9) can be used to obtain the mean end-to-end delay for each source–destination node pair. For convenience, we refer to packets sent from source node s to destination node d as (s,d) packets. Let $\gamma_{s,d}$ be the mean arrival rate of (s,d) packets and $A_{s,d}$ be the set of routing chains for these packets. Also let $\alpha_{s,d}^{(k)}$ be the probability that a (s,d) packet is sent along the path corresponding to chain k. $\alpha_{s,d}^{(k)}$ is zero if chain $k \notin A_{s,d}$; and for the case of fixed routing, there is only one chain in each $A_{s,d}$ and the $\alpha_{s,d}^{(k)}$ for this chain is one. From the above definitions, it is easy to see that the mean arrival rate of chain k is given by:

$$\gamma_k = \gamma_{s,d} \alpha_{s,d}^{(k)} \tag{4.11}$$

and the mean end-to-end delay of (s,d) packets is:

$$T_{s,d} = \sum_{k \in A_{s,d}} \alpha_{s,d}^{(k)} T_k. \tag{4.12}$$

Similar results can also be obtained for a virtual channel network (with no flow control) where fixed or random routing is used for each virtual channel.

4.2. Distribution of end-to-end delay

In this section, we consider the distribution of end-to-end delay given path-oriented routing. This is a detailed characterization of end-to-end delay and the results are useful for calculating statistics such as variance and 90-percentile.

Our discussion is based on the work reported in [17,18]. Let $t_k(x)$ be the probability density function (pdf) of the end-to-end delay of chain k and $T_k^*(\xi)$ be its Laplace transform, i.e.,

$$T_k^*(\xi) = \int_0^\infty \exp(-\xi x) t_k(x)\, \mathrm{d}x. \tag{4.13}$$

Let $N_k(z)$ be the generating function of the number of chain k packets in the network. As a result of the product form solution, $N_k(z)$ can be written as:

$$N_k(z) = \prod_{i \in \pi_k} N_{ik}(z), \tag{4.14}$$

where $N_{ik}(z)$ is the generating function of the number of chain k packets at channel i. $N_{ik}(z)$ is by definition, given by:

$$N_{ik}(z) = \sum_{j=0}^{\infty} \sum_{\boldsymbol{n}_i \in R_j} P(\boldsymbol{n}_i) z^j \tag{4.15}$$

where R_j is given by (4.6). Substituting (4.4) into (4.15), and after some simplifications, we get

$$N_{ik}(z) = \frac{1-\rho_i}{1-\rho_i+\rho_{ik}(1-z)}. \tag{4.16}$$

It then follows from (4.14) and (4.15) that

$$N_k(z) = \prod_{i \in \pi_k} \frac{1-\rho_i}{1-\rho_i+\rho_{ik}(1-z)}. \tag{4.17}$$

Since the arrival process of chain k packets is Poisson and the number of chain k packets in the network changes by unit steps, we also have [19,20]:

$$N_k(z) = D_k(z) \tag{4.18}$$

where $D_k(z)$ is the generating function of the number of chain k packets left behind in the network by a chain k departure.

Consider an arbitrary 'tagged' chain k packet. Let its end-to-end delay be t_k (Laplace transform of pdf is $T_k^*(\xi)$). With path-oriented routing and FCFS discipline at each channel, the number of chain k packets left behind when the tagged packet departs is equal to the number of chain k arrivals during t_k.

Suppose the tagged packet enters the network at time 0. Let $a_k(\tau)$ be the number of chain k arrivals in $[0,\tau]$. $D_k(z)$ is then the generating function of $a_k(t_k)$. For chain k arrivals following a Poisson process, $D_k(z)$ is given by [19]:

$$D_k(z) = T_k^*(\gamma_k - \gamma_k z) \tag{4.19}$$

provided that t_k and $a_k(\tau)$ are independent for all τ. Substituting ξ for $\gamma_k - \gamma_k z$, (4.19) is reduced to:

$$T_k^*(\xi) = D_k(1 - \xi/\gamma_k). \tag{4.20}$$

Finally, using (4.17) and (4.18) in (4.19), we get

$$T_k^*(\xi) = \prod_{i \in \pi_k} \frac{\mu C_i(1-\rho_i)}{\xi + \mu C_i(1-\rho_i)}. \tag{4.21}$$

Let $|\pi_k|$ be the number of channels in π_k. Eq. (4.21) indicates that the end-to-end delay of chain k is given by the sum of $|\pi_k|$ independent random variables; the i-th random variable is exponentially distributed with mean $1/[\mu C_i(1-\rho_i)]$. This observation allows us to write the following expression for the variance of chain k end-to-end delay [17]:

$$\sigma_k^2 = \sum_{i \in \pi_k} \frac{1}{[\mu C_i(1-\rho_i)]^2}. \tag{4.22}$$

To obtain statistics such as the 90-percentile of end-to-end delay, one must first obtain $t_k(x)$ by inverting $T_k^*(\xi)$. This can easily be done by the technique of partial fraction expansion [19].

It should be noted that (4.19) (and therefore (4.21)) is true only when t_k and $a_k(\tau)$ are independent for all τ. In an arbitrary network, these two random variables are not independent in general, as illustrated by the example shown in Fig. 2 [18,24]. Suppose a tagged chain 1 packet arrives at channel i at time 0, and is somewhere in the network (except at channel j) at time τ. If $a_1(\tau)$ is large, then most packets leaving channel i (after the tagged packet) are from chain 1 and the tagged packet is expected to find a small number of chain 2 packets when it arrives at channel j. On the other hand, if $a_1(\tau)$ is small, then most packets leaving channel i are from chain 2 and the tagged packet is expected to find a large number of chain 2 packets at channel j. The delay experienced by the tagged packet at channel j is therefore affected by $a_1(\tau)$. Consequently, t_1 and $a_1(\tau)$ are not independent. A similar argument also applies to t_2 and $a_2(\tau)$.

From the above discussion, we observed that t_k is dependent on $a_k(\tau)$ whenever it is possible for packets (belonging to other chains) arriving after a tagged chain k packet at one channel to overtake this tagged packet at another channel. This dependency would not be present if the paths in the network were such that no such overtaking is possible. We can therefore give the following sufficient condition for t_k and $a_k(\tau)$ to be independent for all τ [18].

Nonpassing Condition. For each pair of channels i, j in π_k, packet arriving after any tagged chain k packet at channel i never overtake this tagged packet at channel j.

The Laplace transform of chain k end-to-end delay is given by (4.21) if the above condition is satisfied.

Despite the fact that t_k and $a_k(\tau)$ are not independent in general, (4.21) is very useful in practice for characterizing in detail the end-to-end delays of routing chains. For a given network model, it is likely that the nonpassing condition is satisfied for a large fraction of routing chains. The result is then applicable to each of these chains. For those chains where the nonpassing condition is not satisfied, simulation experiments have shown that (4.21) gives accurate approximations to the variance as well as 90-percentiles of end-to-end delay [18]. Furthermore, in some networks, the network topology and path assignments are such that the overtaking phenomenon shown in Fig. 2 is not possible. Consequently, (4.21) is applicable to all chains in the network. Obvious examples of such networks are tree networks and ring networks. Another example is the class of networks where the routing algorithm does not use any path with more than three channels. One such network is the example shown in Fig. 1 under shortest path routing.

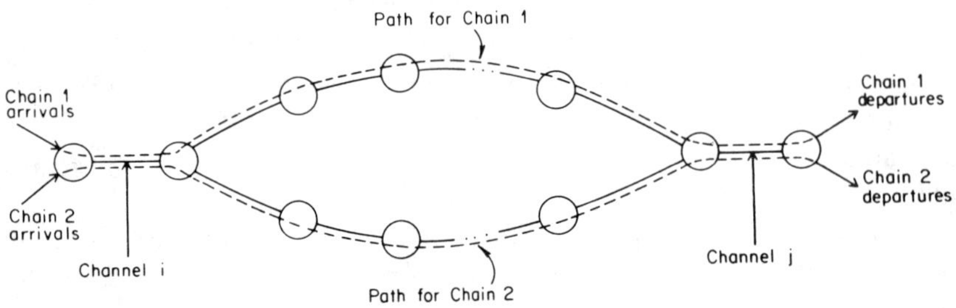

Fig. 2. Dependency between t_k and $a_k(\tau)$.

As a final remark, one can also obtain results for the pdf of end-to-end delay for a given source–destination node pair (or a given virtual channel). Following the developments which lead to $T_{s,d}$ in (4.12), the pdf of (s,d) end-to-end delay can be obtained by inverting

$$T^*_{s,d}(\xi) = \sum_{k \in A_{s,d}} \alpha^{(k)}_{s,d} \prod_{i \in \pi_k} \frac{\mu C_i(1-\rho_i)}{\xi + \mu C_i(1-\rho_i)} \quad (4.23)$$

and the corresponding variance is

$$\sigma^2_{s,d} = \sum_{k \in A_{s,d}} \alpha^{(k)}_{s,d} \times \left[\sum_{i \in \pi_k} \frac{1}{[\mu C_i(1-\rho_i)]^2} + T_k^2 \right] - T^2_{s,d} \quad (4.24)$$

where T_k and $T_{s,d}$ are given by (4.9) and (4.12) respectively.

5. Fairness among chains

The analysis of end-to-end delay presented in Section 4 is based on a FCFS discipline at each channel. One can easily observe from the result in (4.9) that the mean end-to-end delay of chain k is affected by the number of channels in π_k, and the utilization of these channels. As a result, there is a disparity of end-to-end delays experienced by different chains. A natural question to ask is whether a network with FCFS discipline at each channel is fair or not.

One approach to study the fairness of a network is to relate the mean end-to-end delay to network tariffs [21]. Some networks, e.g., Datapac [22], have an uneven tariff structure. For these networks, one can argue that subscribers who are paying more due to their physical locations should not be penalized with a longer end-to-end delay. A reasonable (or 'fair') strategy is then to make T_k the same for all k. In other networks, e.g., Telenet [23], a fixed tariff is applied regardless of location; and a reasonable strategy is to have T_k proportional to the number of channels in π_k.

It is easy to observe that FCFS may not be flexible enough to implement either one of the strategies mentioned above. One needs a parameterized queuing discipline which enables the chain delays to be adjustable by changing the parameter values. An example of such a discipline is Kleinrock's time-dependent priority discipline [6]. Under this discipline, a parameter β_k is associated with routing chain k, $k = 1, 2, \ldots, K$. Suppose a chain k packet arrives at channel i at time t_0, its instantaneous priority at time t $(t > t_0)$ is given by $(t - t_0)\beta_k$. When the channel is ready for the next packet, the instantaneous priorities of all packets in queue are evaluated, and the one with the highest value is served. This discipline thus favors chains with large values of β_k, and also those packets that have been waiting in queue for a long time.

The product-form solution for open queuing network models does not apply when Kleinrock's time-dependent priority discipline is used. However, the following assumption may be employed to get approximate results for the chain delays [21].

Poisson Assumption. For all i and k, the arrival process of chain k packets to channel i is Poisson regardless of the channel queuing discipline used.

Suppose the routing chains are ordered such that: $0 \leq \beta_1 \leq \beta_2 \leq \cdots \leq \beta_K$.

The mean delay of chain k packets at channel i (denoted by $T_{ik}(\mathrm{td})$ for Kleinrock's time-dependent discipline) can be expressed as:

$$T_{ik}(\mathrm{td}) = W_{ik} + \frac{1}{\mu C_i} \quad (5.1)$$

where W_{ik} is the mean waiting time in queue and is given recursively by [6]

$$W_{ik} = \left(\frac{\rho_i}{\mu C_i(1-\rho_i)} - \sum_{j=1}^{k-1} \rho_{ij} W_{ij} \left(1 - \frac{\beta_j}{\beta_k}\right) \right) \times \left(1 - \sum_{j=k+1}^{K} \rho_{ij} \left(1 - \frac{\beta_k}{\beta_j}\right)\right)^{-1} \quad (5.2)$$

where ρ_{ij} and ρ_i are given by (2.5) and (2.6) respectively. The mean end-to-end delay under Kleinrock's time-dependent discipline can then be obtained from:

$$T_k(\mathrm{td}) = \sum_{i \in \pi_k} T_{ik}(\mathrm{td}). \quad (5.3)$$

It is easy to see from (5.1) and (5.3) that the chain delays can be adjusted by manipulating the β_k's. Such manipulation, however, may affect the mean end-to-end delay over all packets; and adjusting the chain delays may become undesirable if the mean end-to-end delay is subtantially increased. In what follows, we shall first present a conservation theorem [21] which deals with the effect of channel scheduling on mean end-to-end delay, and then illustrate how this theorem and Kleinrock's time-dependent discipline can be used to improve the fairness of a network.

5.1. Conservation Theorem

The effect of channel scheduling on mean end-to-end delay can be characterized by the following theorem [21].

Conservation Theorem. For our open network model with the Poisson assumption, the mean end-to-end delay is identical for all work-conserving, non-preemptive disciplines, and is given by (3.4), i.e.,

$$T = \frac{1}{\gamma} \sum_{i=1}^{M} \frac{\lambda_i}{\mu C_i - \lambda_i}.$$

This theorem indicates that the sensitivity of mean end-to-end delay to channel scheduling is determined by the accuracy of the Poisson assumption. Simulation results reported in [21] have shown that the Poisson assumption is accurate for Kleinrock's time-dependent discipline, and that adjusting the chain delays by manipulating the β_k's would not have a significant effect on the mean end-to-end delay.

5.2. Improvement of fairness

We have mentioned earlier that a network can be considered as being 'fair' if the T_k's bear some desired relationship with respect to each other (e.g., T_k is the same for all k, or T_k is proportional to the number of channels in π_k). In general, suppose the objective is to have T_k proportional to α_k, where α_k is a parameter indicating the importance of chain k (chain k is more important than chain m if $\alpha_k < \alpha_m$). This objective implies that ideally, we would like to have $T_k = \alpha_k \cdot A$ for all k, where A is a constant. Under this ideal condition, the mean end-to-end delay over all chains is given by:

$$T = \sum_{k=1}^{K} \frac{\gamma_k}{\gamma} \alpha_k A. \tag{5.4}$$

Eq. (5.4) and the Conservation Theorem allow us to obtain the following expression for A:

$$A = \left(\sum_{i=1}^{M} \frac{\lambda_i}{\mu C_i - \lambda_i} \right) \Big/ \left(\sum_{k=1}^{K} \gamma_k \alpha_k \right). \tag{5.5}$$

It follows that the ideal (or 'target') T_k can be determined uniquely from:

$$T_k\ (\text{target}) = \alpha_k \left(\sum_{i=1}^{M} \frac{\lambda_i}{\mu C_i - \lambda_i} \right) \Big/ \left(\sum_{m=1}^{K} \gamma_m \alpha_m \right). \tag{5.6}$$

The original objective of having T_k proportional to α_k is thus equivalent to that of having the chain delay equal to the target delay for all chains. Due to the disparity in channel utilizations and in the number of channels visited by the various chains, this objective may not be achievable. As an example, consider a routing chain (say chain k) which visits only one channel. One might encounter a situation where the utilization of this channel is so low that $T_k(\text{td})$ is smaller than T_k (target) even if chain k is given the lowest priority (by setting β_k to zero). Under such situations, one would be interested in the deviation of the chain delays from the target delays. This deviation is used in [21] to define the following measure of fairness:

$$F = \frac{1}{T^2} \sum_{k=1}^{K} \frac{\gamma_k}{\gamma} \left(T_k(\text{td}) - T_k\ (\text{target}) \right)^2. \tag{5.7}$$

F has the same form as the squared coefficient of variation. In general, a smaller F means a fairer network, and a network is said to be ideally fair if $F = 0$.

We note from (5.1) and (5.3) that the chain delays under Kleinrock's time-dependent discipline are functions of the β_k's. Since the target delays can be uniquely determined, F is also a function of the β_k's. One can therefore formulate the following optimization problem to determine the best setting of the β_k's so that F is minimized:

Given:	topology, $\{\gamma_k\}$, routing algorithm.
Minimize:	F.
Constraints:	$\beta_k \geq 0$, $k = 1, 2, \ldots, K$.

The solution to this optimization problem for some example networks can be found in [21].

6. Concluding remarks

In this paper, we have discussed in detail the application of product-form open queuing networks to the performance analysis of store-and-forward packet-switching networks. The topics considered include channel capacity assignment, optimal routing, distribution of end-to-end delay, and fairness among routing chains. In a companion paper [1], the application of queuing networks with closed chains and other forms of population size constraints to the performance analysis of networks with window flow control, buffer management schemes, and permit-oriented network congestion control is discussed.

References

[1] S.S. Lam and J.W. Wong, Queuing network models of packet switching networks, Part 2: Networks with population size constraints, Performance Evaluation 2 (3) (1982) to appear.

[2] J.R. Jackson, Jobshop-like queuing systems, Management Sci. 10 (1963) 131–142.

[3] F. Baskett, K.M. Chandy, R.R. Muntz and F. Palacios, Open, closed, and mixed networks of queues with different classes of customers, J. ACM 22 (1975) 248–260.

[4] M. Reiser and H. Kobayashi, Queuing networks with multiple closed chains: Theory and computational algorithms, IBM J. Res. Develop. 19 (1975).

[5] S.S. Lam, Queuing networks with population size constraints, IBM J. Res. Develop. 21 (1977) 370 378.

[6] L. Kleinrock, Queuing Systems, Vol. 2: Computer Applications (Wiley-Interscience, New York, 1976).

[7] J.M. McQuillan and V. Cerf, A Practical View of Computer Communications Protocols (IEEE Press, 1978).

[8] L. Kleinrock, Communication Nets – Stochastic Message Flow and Delays (McGraw-Hill, New York, 1964).

[9] L. Kleinrock and W.E. Naylor, On measured behavior of the ARPA network, AFIPS Conf. Proc., National Computer Conference 43 (1974) pp. 767–780.

[10] S.S. Lam, Store-and-forward buffer requirements in a packet switching network, IEEE Trans. Comm. COM-24 (1976) 394–403.

[11] J.D.C. Little, A proof of the queuing formula: $L=\lambda W$, Oper. Res. 9 (1961) 383–387.

[12] M. Gerla, The design of store-and-forward networks for computer communications, Ph.D. dissertation, Department of Computer Science, UCLA (1973).

[13] J.M. McQuillan, I. Richer and E.C. Rosen, The new routing algorithm for the ARPANET, IEEE Trans. Comm. COM-28 (1980) 711–719.

[14] L. Fratta, M. Gerla and L. Kleinrock, The flow deviation method: An approach to store-and-forward network design, Networks 3 (1973) 97–133.

[15] R.R. Jueneman and G.S. Kerr, Explicit path routing in communications networks, Proc. Internat. Conf. on Computer Communication (1976) pp. 340–342.

[16] V. Ahuja, Routing and flow control in systems network architecture, IBM Systems J. 18 (1979) 298–314.

[17] J.W. Wong, Distribution of end-to-end delay in message-switched networks, Comput. Networks 2 (1978) 44–49.

[18] J.W. Wong, Distribution of end-to-end delay in packet switching networks – Exact and approximate results, CCNG Rept., University of Waterloo, to appear.

[19] L. Kleinrock, Queuing Systems, Vol. 1: Theory (Wiley-Interscience, New York, 1975).

[20] R. Cooper, Introduction to Queuing Theory (MacMillan, New York, 1972).

[21] J.W. Wong, J.P. Sauve and J.A. Field, A study of fairness in packet-switching networks, IEEE Trans. Comm. COM-30 (1982) 346–353.

[22] The Bell Telephone Company of Canada, General Tariff CTC (TP), No 6716, Item 4200, Datapac Service, Effective June 15, 1977.

[23] Logica Ltd., Packet Switching Report (London, 1978) p. 152.

[24] R. Foley, Virginia Polytechnic Institute and State University, private communication.

Reprinted with permission from *Performance Evaluation*, Volume 2, 1982, pages 161-180.

Queueing Network Models of Packet Switching Networks Part 2: Networks with Population Size Constraints *

S.S. Lam
Department of Computer Sciences, University of Texas at Austin, Austin, TX 78712, U.S.A.

J.W. Wong
Department of Computer Science, University of Waterloo, Waterloo, Ontario, Canada

Received 2 February 1981
Revised 2 April 1982

An overview of the application of product-form queueing networks to the performance analysis of store-and-forward packet communication networks is presented. Queueing network models with closed chains and other forms of population size constraints are considered. The modeling and analysis of networks with window flow controlled virtual channels are described first. Models for the performance analysis of strategies for nodal buffer management and permit-oriented network congestion control are then presented.

Keywords: Queueing Network Models, Packet Switching Networks, Flow Control, Congestion Control, Buffer Management, Resource Sharing, Computational Algorithms.

1. Introduction

Recent efforts on the application of product-form queueing network models [1–4] to the performance analysis of store-and-forward packet switching networks are reviewed in this paper and a companion paper [5]. Open queueing network models are covered in the companion paper. The class of open network models is characterized by

Simon S. Lam received the B.S.E.E. degree (with Distinction) from Washington State University, Pullman, Washington, in 1969, and the M.S. and Ph.D. degrees in engineering from the University of California at Los Angeles, in 1970 and 1974, respectively.

From 1972 to 1974, he was with the ARPA Network project at UCLA and did research on satellite packet communication. From 1974 to 1977, he was a research staff member with the IBM Thomas J. Watson Research Center, Yorktown Heights, New York, where he worked on performance analysis problems of packet switching networks, SNA and satellie networks. Since September 1977, he has been with the University of Texas at Austin where he is now Associate Professor of Computer Sciences. His current research interests include modeling and analysis of computer systems, networks and communication protocols.

At the University of California at Los Angeles, he held a Phi Kappa Phi Fellowship from 1969 to 1970, and a Chancellor's Teaching Fellowship from 1969 to 1973. In 1975, he received the IEEE Leonard G. Abraham Award for the best paper in the field of Communications Systems. Simon is a member of Tau Beta Pi, Sigma Tau, Phi Kappa Phi, Pi Mu Epsilon and the Association for Computing Machinery, and a senior member of IEEE.

J.W. Wong received the B.S. in engineering, the M.S. and Ph.D. degrees in computer science from the University of California at Los Angeles in 1970, 1971, and 1975, respectively. He is currently an Associate Professor of Computer Science at the University of Waterloo, Waterloo, Ontario, Canada.

* The work of S.S. Lam was supported by National Science Foundation Grant No. ECS78-01803. The work of J.W. Wong was supported by the Natural Sciences and Engineering Research Council of Canada.

North-Holland Publishing Company
Performance Evaluation 2 (1982) 161–180

0166-5316/82/0000–0000/$02.75

explicit formulas for the performance measures of mean delay and throughput that are of interest. Queueing networks with closed chains and other forms of chain population size constraints are useful as models for the analysis of various network flow and congestion control mechanisms and buffer management strategies. This class of queueing network models is characterized by algorithmic solutions for the mean delay and throughput performance measures. These models constitute the subject of this paper.

The key modeling assumptions, notation and definitions needed in this paper are presented next. The reader is referred to [5] for a more detailed treatment.

The basic unit of data transfer in the communication networks being modeled is a packet; it corresponds to a customer in the queueing network models. A store-and-forward packet switching network consists of a set of switching nodes interconnected by full-duplex communication channels (see Fig. 1). The function of the communication network is to transport packets from their sources to their sinks. Each packet traverses from its source node to its destination node through a series of intermediate nodes and communication channels along a selected path (or route). Queues of packets are formed inside the switching nodes. The key assumption necessary for the application of queueing network models was first stated by Kleinrock [6].

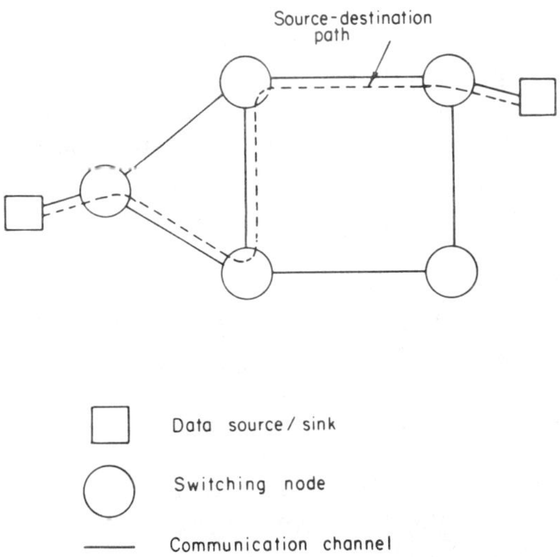

Fig. 1. A store-and-forward packet switching network.

The Independence Assumption. Each time a packet joins a queue in the network, its length is determined afresh from the probability density function

$$b(x)=\mu \exp\{-\mu x\}, \quad x \geqslant 0$$

where $1/\mu$ is the mean packet length (in number of bits).

In the queueing network models to be considered, first-come first-served (FCFS) servers are used to model communication channels and IS servers are used to model random delays associated with acknowledgements and timeouts. (An IS server is a service center with infinitely many servers in parallel [2].) Processing delays within switching nodes are often ignored since they are typically much smaller than channel delays. If included, nodal processors are also modeled as FCFS servers [7]. The servers in a network model are indexed by $i=1, 2,\ldots,M$. Customers (i.e., packets) belong to different (routing) chains, indexed by $k=1,2,\ldots,K$. Chains are characterized by different routing behaviors. The routing behavior of customers in chain k is specified by a first-order Markov chain with transition probabilities

$$p_{ij}^{(k)}=\mathrm{P}(\text{to server } j \mid \text{currently at server } i), \quad i,j=1,2,\ldots,M.$$

Such a representation is adequate for modeling both the case of a single fixed route between a source and a sink and the case of multiple routes. When multiple routes exist, the selection of a route for individual packets is done probabilistically. Retransmissions and rerouting due to random transmission errors can also be modeled by an appropriate definition of the transition probabilities [8]. (A limitation of the class of product-form queueing networks is that adaptive routing cannot be modeled.)

Since the routing behaviors of packets travelling between different source–destination node pairs must be different, at least one routing chain must be specified for each source–destination node pair for which there is nonzero traffic. Sometimes, multiple chains may be needed between the same source–destination node pair to correspond to different virtual channels connecting data sources in the same source node and data sinks in the same destination node.

It is assumed that the source of chain k generates new packets according to a Poisson process with rate γ_k packets per second where $k = 1, 2, \ldots, K$. Define

$$\gamma = \gamma_1 + \gamma_2 + \cdots + \gamma_K.$$

The corresponding throughput rates are denoted by γ^* and γ_k^* for $k = 1, 2, \ldots, K$. We must have

$$\gamma_k^* \leq \gamma_k, \quad k = 1, 2, \ldots, K,$$

since external arrivals to a virtual channel may not always be accepted due to buffer, flow or congestion control constraints.

Let the state of the queueing network be denoted by

$$S = (\boldsymbol{n}_1, \boldsymbol{n}_2, \ldots, \boldsymbol{n}_M)$$

where

$$\boldsymbol{n}_i = (n_{i1}, n_{i2}, \ldots, n_{iK})$$

where n_{ik} is the number of chain k packets at server i. Define

$$n_i = n_{i1} + n_{i2} + \cdots + n_{iK}$$

and

$$\boldsymbol{n} = (n_1, n_2, \ldots, n_M).$$

A chain in the queueing network model is said to be *open* if both external arrivals to the chain and departures from the chain can occur freely. A routing chain is said to be *closed* if the number of customers (circulating) in the chain is fixed. (The concept of closed chains will be explained further below.)

In Section 2 below we shall describe queueing network models with closed chains for the performance analysis of packet switching networks with flow controlled virtual channels. A communication network typically has many virtual channels. The main source of difficulty in the modeling of such networks is that the computational requirements of conventional solution techniques [3, 9, 10] increase exponentially with the number K of closed chains in a queueing network model. Some approximate models and approximate solution techniques have been proposed and found to be useful. They are described in Section 2. Also described is the tree convolution algorithm [11] which provides an exact solution and has been designed to exploit the sparseness property of chains that is typical of communication network models. The problem of optimally routing a small amount of incremental traffic is also considered.

In Section 3 queueing network models with various population size constraints for the analysis of congestion control and buffer management strategies are described. Approximate models and solution techniques for a network of finite-buffer nodes are also presented.

2. Queueing network models with closed chains

Most packet networks nowadays provide virtual channels that are end-to-end flow controlled. Flow controlled virtual channels may be maintained between data sources and sinks [12,13] or between pairs of source-destination nodes [14,15]. In some networks, both types of flow controlled virtual channels are maintained [14]. In the queueing network models to be considered, only one type of flow controlled virtual channel is assumed. Such virtual channels may be interpreted as being maintained either between packet sources and sinks or pairs of source–destination switching nodes.

An important function of end-to-end flow control protocols is the synchronization of the data source input rate to the data sink acceptance rate. All of them work by limiting the number of packets that a virtual channel can have in transit within the network. Hence, they also provide, to some extent, a congestion control capability for the network as a whole. (However, when the number of virtual channels supported by the network is very large, a separate congestion control mechanism for the network is often necessary. Some such congestion control mechanisms are considered in Section 3.)

In this section we consider the modeling of flow controlled virtual channels as closed chains. The chain population size corresponds to the maximum number of packets that can be in transit within the virtual channel. This number will be referred to as the *virtual channel window size.* The effect of virtual channel window sizes on the throughput-delay characteristics of the network can be studied using queueing network models with closed chains.

2.1. Modeling virtual channels with closed chains

Fig. 2 illustrates a queueing network model of a packet switching network with K virtual channels. Each virtual channel has a source and a sink both of which are also modeled as FIFO servers with

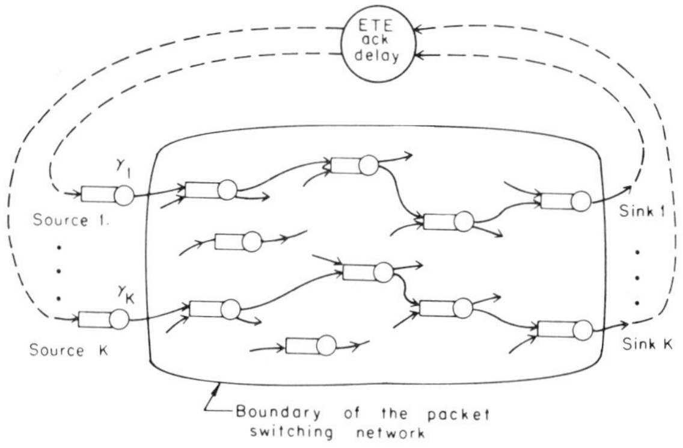

Fig. 2. Modeling flow controlled virtual channels in a packet switching network.

exponentially distributed service times. Packets in the same virtual channel follow a fixed route which may be chosen probabilistically from a finite set of routes between source and sink.

The delay for the return of an end-to-end (ETE) acknowledgement (ACK) from the sink to the source indicating receipt of a packet is modeled by an independent random variable, the distribution of which may be different for different virtual channels. This delay is modeled by an IS server that joins the sink to the source to yield a closed chain in the queueing network model. It is not really important to model the route of an ACK explicitly because ETE ACKs are typically either sent piggybacked in data packets, or, if sent separately, very short. Thus, they consume relatively small amounts of buffer and channel resources in the network, which may be acounted for separately. In [16] Reiser suggested that the ACK traffic may be accounted for by reducing the channel capacities by amounts equal to the throughputs of ACK packets.

The flow control window size of a virtual channel is the maximum number of packets that it can have in transit within the communication network at the same time. Let N_k denote the window size of virtual channel k for $k = 1,\ldots,K$. If the number of packets in transit within a virtual channel is equal to its window size, then the source server is 'blocked'. A blocked source server is later unblocked when an ETE ACK returns from the sink indicating receipt of a packet.

The blocking behavior is naturally modeled in a queueing network by a closed chain with a fixed number of circulating customers. Each customer corresponds to an 'access token'. Initially, N_k tokens are placed at the source server of virtual channel k. Each packet admitted into the network carries a token with it. When there is no more token at the source server, it is blocked. A packet arriving at the sink node of the virtual channel releases its token which is then carried back by the ETE ACK to the source server to be reused again. Thus, the N_k circulating tokens of a virtual channel correspond to the N_k circulating customers of a closed chain.

When the source server is not blocked, it generates a new packet for input into the network at the rate γ_k. The physical interpretation of the rate γ_k depends upon the loading on the virtual channels. For a lightly loaded network, γ_k may be interpreted as the external arrival rate of packets to the user of virtual channel k. (This corresponds to the assumption of packet generation according to a Poisson process.) For a heavily loaded network such that the queue of data packets at the source is nonempty most of the time, γ_k may be interpreted as the reaction speed of the user to a signal (or message) from the network interface of the virtual channel authorizing new input [17,18].

For Section 2 we shall make the assumption that the number of buffers at each switching node is very large (infinite). But, with flow control windows, a virtual channel does not always accept packets from its source. Thus the throughput γ_k^* of a virtual channel (modeled by chain k) is less than the rate γ_k; the latter is often referred to in the literature as the offered load of the virtual channel. With the above interpretation, the ratio γ_k^*/γ_k measures the fraction of time virtual channel k is not blocked. The above model assumptions enable us to focus our attention upon the network behavior only and ignore the behavior of queues external to the packet switching network.

2.2. The solution of closed queueing networks

A closed chain has a fixed number of circulating customers. However, it is sometimes physically meaningful to think of a closed chain as an open chain with the following two mechanisms in place at all times [1,4]:

(a) A loss mechanism whereby an external arrival to the chain is rejected and lost forever.

(b) A trigger mechanism whereby a departure from the network triggers an instantaneous injection of a new customer into the same chain as the departed customer (from an infinite source of customers).

For a closed chain (say k), its packet arrival rate to server i in the queueing network can only be determined to within a multiplicative constant, called the *scaling factor* of the chain, from

$$\lambda_{ik} = \sum_{j=1}^{M} \lambda_{jk} p_{ji}^{(k)}, \quad i = 1, 2, \ldots, M. \tag{2.1}$$

This is due to the fact that the matrix of transition probabilities of chain k is a stochastic matrix. The arrival rate of packets from all chains to server i is

$$\lambda_i = \sum_{k=1}^{K} \lambda_{ik}. \tag{2.2}$$

If server i is FCFS, it works at a constant rate of C_i bits per second. If server i is IS, it works at a rate of C_{ik} bits per second for chain k packets. The traffic intensity of chain k packets at server i is defined to be

$$\rho_{ik} = \begin{cases} \dfrac{\lambda_{ik}}{\mu C_i}, & \text{server } i \text{ is FCFS,} \\[2ex] \dfrac{\lambda_{ik}}{\mu C_{ik}}, & \text{server } i \text{ is IS,} \end{cases} \tag{2.3}$$

and the overall traffic intensity of server i is

$$\rho_i = \sum_{k=1}^{K} \rho_{ik}. \tag{2.4}$$

Consider a network consisting of closed chains only. Let N_k be the population size of chain k and define the *population vector*

$\boldsymbol{N} = (N_1, N_2, \ldots, N_K).$

The equilibrium network state probability has the following product form [2]:

$$\mathrm{P}(S) = \frac{1}{G(\boldsymbol{N})} \prod_{i=1}^{M} p_i(\boldsymbol{n}_i) \tag{2.5}$$

where

$$p_i(\boldsymbol{n}_i) = \begin{cases} n_i! \displaystyle\prod_{k=1}^{K} \frac{\rho_{ik}^{n_{ik}}}{n_{ik}!}, & \text{server } i \text{ is FCFS,} \\[2ex] \displaystyle\prod_{k=1}^{K} \frac{\rho_{ik}^{n_{ik}}}{n_{ik}!}, & \text{server } i \text{ is IS} \end{cases}$$

and $G(\boldsymbol{N})$ is the *normalization constant*. By definition,

$$G(\boldsymbol{N}) = \sum_{S \in \mathcal{S}(\boldsymbol{N})} \prod_{i=1}^{M} p_i(\boldsymbol{n}_i) \tag{2.6}$$

where the summation is done over the following set of feasible network states:

$$\mathcal{S}(\boldsymbol{N}) = \left\{ S: \sum_{i=1}^{M} \boldsymbol{n}_i = \boldsymbol{N} \right\}. \tag{2.7}$$

From (2.5) the following can be derived:

$$\mathrm{P}(\boldsymbol{n}) = \frac{1}{G(\boldsymbol{N})} \prod_{i=1}^{M} f_i(n_i) \tag{2.8}$$

where $f_i(n_i)$ is given by

$$f_i(n_i) = \begin{cases} \rho_i^{n_i}, & \text{server } i \text{ is FCFS,} \\[2ex] \dfrac{\rho_i^{n_i}}{n_i!}, & \text{server } i \text{ is IS.} \end{cases}$$

We mentioned earlier that the λ_{ik}'s can only be determined to within a multiplicative constant for each k. We note that, although $P(S)$ is independent of the scaling factors, they do affect the numerical value of the normalization constant [19]. Note that the normalization constant $G(\boldsymbol{N})$, defined by (2.6), is the sum of an extremely large number of product terms when K is large and also when the chain population sizes $\{N_k\}$ are large. There are two difficult problems in the evaluation of $G(\boldsymbol{N})$. First, depending on the scaling factors selected in the determination of $\{\lambda_{ik}\}$ in (2.1), $G(\boldsymbol{N})$ may become very large (causing a floating point overflow) or very small (causing a floating point underflow). This problem may be solved by a dynamic scaling technique [19]. The second problem is the extremely large computational time and space requirements to evaluate $G(\boldsymbol{N})$ for large values of K and $\{N_k\}$ using either the convolution algorithm [3,9], or the MVA algorithm [10]. The convolution algorithm is presented next. The MVA algorithm is introduced in Section 2.4.

Note that each of the functions p_i in (2.6) can be represented by a K-dimensional array indexed between $\boldsymbol{0}$ and $\boldsymbol{N}$, where $\boldsymbol{0}$ is a K-vector of all zeros. The convolution of two such functions, say p_1 and p_2, defines a real-valued function, say g_2, over the same domain, as follows [3,9]:

$$g_2(\boldsymbol{i}) = \sum_{j_1=0}^{i_1} \cdots \sum_{j_K=0}^{i_K} p_1(\boldsymbol{j})\, p_2(\boldsymbol{i}-\boldsymbol{j}) \quad \text{for } \boldsymbol{0} \leqslant \boldsymbol{i} \leqslant \boldsymbol{N}. \tag{2.9}$$

In shorthand notation, (2.9) will be written as

$$g_2 = p_1 \otimes p_2 = p_2 \otimes p_1. \tag{2.10}$$

We note that $G(\boldsymbol{N})$ is simply the element indexed by $\boldsymbol{N}$ in the following array:

$$g_{\{1,2,\ldots,M\}} = p_1 \otimes p_2 \otimes \ldots \otimes p_M. \tag{2.11}$$

The convolution algorithm solves for $G(\boldsymbol{N})$ by performing the convolutions in (2.11) sequentially as follows:

$$g_{\{1,2,\ldots,m\}} = g_{\{1,2,\ldots,m-1\}} \otimes p_m \quad \text{for } m = 2, 3, \ldots, M. \tag{2.12}$$

The time requirement to compute the array $g_{\{1,2,\ldots,M\}}$ and hence $G(\boldsymbol{N})$ is of the order of $(M-1)\prod_{k=1}^{K}(\frac{1}{2}(N_k+2)(N_k+1))$ while the space requirement is of the order $2\prod_{k=1}^{K}(N_k+1)$. Note that both requirements grow exponentially with K. Two observations can be made to reduce the time requirement in queueing network models considered herein [3]. First, for the purpose of evaluting $G(\boldsymbol{N})$, all IS servers can be lumped together into an equivalent IS server with a traffic intensity equal to the combined traffic intensities of the individual IS servers. Second, if server m is an FCFS server with a constant service rate, the convolution of (2.12) can be accomplished with the following recursion:

$$g_{\{1,2,\ldots,m\}}(\boldsymbol{0}) = 1, \tag{2.13}$$

$$g_{\{1,2,\ldots,m\}}(\boldsymbol{i}) = g_{\{1,2,\ldots,m-1\}}(\boldsymbol{i}) + \sum_{\text{all } k,\, i_k>0} \rho_{mk}\, g_{\{1,2,\ldots,m\}}(\boldsymbol{i} - \boldsymbol{1}_k)$$

where i_k is the kth component of $\boldsymbol{i}$ and $\boldsymbol{1}_k$ is a K-vector with its kth component equal to one and all others equal to zero. The time requirement of the convolution algorithm based on (2.13) is of the order $MK\prod_{k=1}^{K}(N_k+1)$ which is still exponential in K.

The performance measures of throughputs and mean ETE delays of individual routing chains can be obtained as follows. The throughput of chain k at server m for a network of closed chains with population vector $\boldsymbol{N}$ is [3, 20]

$$\lambda^*_{mk}(\boldsymbol{N}) = \lambda_{mk}\frac{G(\boldsymbol{N}-\boldsymbol{1}_k)}{G(\boldsymbol{N})} \quad \text{for } \boldsymbol{N} \geq \boldsymbol{1}_k \tag{2.14}$$

where $G(\boldsymbol{N}-\boldsymbol{1}_k)$ is the normalization constant of the same network but with population vector $\boldsymbol{N}-\boldsymbol{1}_k$, and λ_{mk} is the relative arrival rate of chain k customers to server m given by (2.1). The chain throughput γ^*_k is then equal to the throughput of chain k customers at the source server of the chain.

The mean number of chain k customers at a FCFS server, say m, is given by [3]

$$q_{mk}(\boldsymbol{N}) = \rho_{mk}\frac{G_{m+}(\boldsymbol{N}-\boldsymbol{1}_k)}{G(\boldsymbol{N})} \quad \text{for } \boldsymbol{N} \geq \boldsymbol{1}_k \tag{2.15}$$

where G_{m+} is the result of convolving p_m (again) with $g_{\{1,2,\ldots,M\}}$. The mean delay incurred by chain k customers at a FCFS server (m) is given by Little's formula [21] to be $q_{mk}(\boldsymbol{N})/\lambda^*_{mk}(\boldsymbol{N})$.

We also know that the mean number of chain k customers at an IS server (m) is ρ_{mk}. Finally, the mean ETE delay of a virtual channel is given by

$$T_k = \frac{1}{\gamma^*_k}\sum_{m\in Q(k)} q_{mk} \tag{2.16}$$

where $Q(k)$ is the set of servers within the boundary of the packet switching network that are visited by chain k (see Fig. 2). Note that the argument $\boldsymbol{N}$ is omitted from T_k, γ^*_k and q_{mk} in (2.16). We shall do so as long as there is no ambiguity.

In the rest of Section 2 we shall first discuss two approximate analysis approaches that avoid the large space-time computational requirements encountered when the number of virtual channels is large. The first approach, in Section 2.3, is to focus upon a single closed chain and replace all other closed chains by open chains having the same throughputs [22]. The second approach, in Section 2.4, is an approximate solution technique [16] that is a natural extension of the mean value analysis (MVA) algorithm of Reiser and Lavenberg [10]. The tree convolution algorithm [11] for an exact analysis is next introduced in Section 2.5. The algorithm makes use of routing information and is very efficient when routing chains have sparseness and locality properties that are typical of communication network models. Next, we examine in Section 2.6 the traffic conditions under which an open-chain model accurately predicts the mean ETE delays of a closed-chain model having the same chain throughputs [17,18]. Finally, in Section 2.7, we discuss the problem of optimally routing a small amount of incremental traffic [18].

2.3. Analysis of a single virtual channel

One approach to avoid the large computational requirements of analyzing a closed network is to approximate some of the closed chains by open chains having the same throughputs. (We discuss the accuracy of this approximation in Section 2.6.) We thus have a queueing network model where some routing chains are open while others are closed. This is referred to as a mixed network model [2]. In this section we first present analytic results for mixed networks and then illustrate how these results can be applied to a model which focuses on a single virtual channel.

For an open chain (say k) its packet arrival rates to servers in the queueing network are determined uniquely by

$$\lambda_{ik} = \gamma_k q_i^{(k)} + \sum_{j=1}^{M} \lambda_{jk} p_{ji}^{(k)}, \quad i = 1, 2, \ldots, M \tag{2.17}$$

where $q_i^{(k)}$ is the probability for a customer freshly generated by the source of chain k to be routed next to server i. For a closed chain these packet arrival rates to servers are given by (2.1) to within a multiplicative constant. The traffic intensities ρ_{ik} and ρ_i for all i and k are defined as before by (2.3) and (2.4) for both open and closed chains in a mixed network model.

The equilibrium state probability of a mixed network also has the product-form solution [2], i.e.,

$$\mathrm{P}(S) = \frac{1}{G} \prod_{i=1}^{M} p_i(\boldsymbol{n}_i) \tag{2.18}$$

where $p_i(\boldsymbol{n}_i)$ is the same as defined in (2.5). The normalization constant G can be written as [3]

$$G = G^{\mathrm{o}} G^{\mathrm{c}}(\boldsymbol{N}) \tag{2.19}$$

where G^{o} and $G^{\mathrm{c}}(\boldsymbol{N})$ are defined as follows. Let

$$\rho_i^{\mathrm{o}} = \sum_{\substack{\text{all open}\\ \text{chains, } k}} \rho_{ik} \quad \text{and} \quad \rho_i^{\mathrm{c}} = \sum_{\substack{\text{all closed}\\ \text{chains, } k}} \rho_{ik}$$

for $i = 1, 2, \ldots, M$.

G^{o} is given by

$$G^{\mathrm{o}} = \prod_{i=1}^{M} G_i^{\mathrm{o}} \tag{2.20}$$

where

$$G_i^{\mathrm{o}} = \begin{cases} 1/(1-\rho_i^{\mathrm{o}}), & \text{server } i \text{ is FCFS,} \\ \exp\{\rho_i^{\mathrm{o}}\}, & \text{server } i \text{ is IS.} \end{cases}$$

$G^{\mathrm{c}}(\boldsymbol{N})$ is equal to the normalization constant of a network model with closed chains only and with the following modification to the traffic intensities of the closed chains:

$$\rho'_{ik} = \begin{cases} \rho_{ik}/(1-\rho_i^{\mathrm{o}}), & \text{server } i \text{ is FCFS,} \\ \rho_{ik}, & \text{server } i \text{ is IS.} \end{cases} \tag{2.21}$$

We now apply the above results to the single virtual channel model shown in Fig. 3. This model is based on the abstraction of all other network traffic into a single open chain, an approach used by Pennotti and Schwartz [22]. Thus, there are two routing chains: Chain 1 is closed and models the virtual channel, and chain 2 is the open chain mentioned above. For notational convenience, the ETE ACK delay is assumed to be zero. (All servers in Fig. 3 are of the FCFS type. However, an IS server representing an ETE ACK delay can be included without much difficulty.) The service time at the source server is assumed to be exponentially distributed with mean $1/\gamma_1$. Without loss of generality, packets belonging to the open chain (chain 2) are assumed to arrive from an external source to server m, for $m = 2, 3, \ldots, M$, at rate λ_{m2} and depart from the network after receiving service from server m.

For chain 1, a solution to (2.1) is $\lambda_{i1} = 1$ for all i. The equilibrium state probability is then given by

$$\mathrm{P}(S) = \frac{1}{G} \prod_{i=1}^{M} n_i! \prod_{k=1}^{2} \frac{\rho_{ik}^{n_{ik}}}{n_{ik}!}$$

where

$$\rho_{i1} = \begin{cases} 1/\gamma_1, & i = 1, \\ 1/(\mu C_i), & i = 2, 3, \ldots, M \end{cases}$$

and

$$\rho_{i2} = \begin{cases} 0, & i = 1, \\ \lambda_{i2}/(\mu C_i), & i = 2, 3, \ldots, M. \end{cases}$$

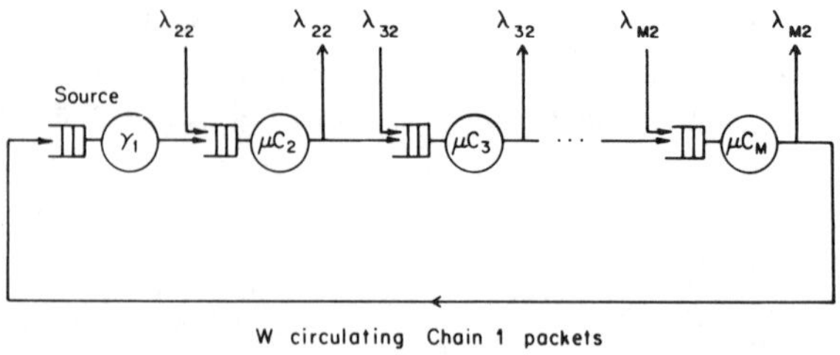

Fig. 3. A model of a single virtual channel.

Applying (2.19), G is given by

$$G=\left(\prod_{i=2}^{M}(1-\rho_{i2})\right)G^{c}(W)$$

where $G^c(W)$ is the normalization constant for a network with a single closed chain of W circulating customers and with traffic intensity $\rho'_{i1}=\rho_{i1}/(1-\rho_{i2})$ for $i=1,2,\ldots,M$.

From the equilibrium state probability, the marginal queue length distribution of chain 1 (the virtual channel being considered) can be shown to be given by [3, 22]

$$\mathrm{P}(\{n_{11},n_{21},\ldots,n_{M1}\})=\frac{1}{G^{c}(W)}\prod_{i=1}^{M}\left(\frac{\rho_{i1}}{1-\rho_{i2}}\right)^{n_{i1}}.$$

This is the same as the queue length distribution of a network model with only the closed chain but with the service rate of channel i reduced by the factor of $(1-\rho_{i2})$ for all i. The reduction factor accounts for the presence of open-chain packets in the network.

The mean number of chain 2 (open-chain) packets at channel i has the following simple form [22]:

$$\mathrm{E}[n_{i2}]=\frac{\rho_{i2}}{1-\rho_{i2}}(1+\mathrm{E}[n_{i1}]). \tag{2.22}$$

Note that the term $\rho_{i2}/(1-\rho_{i2})$ is the mean queue length in a network model with the open chain only. The expansion factor $(1+\mathrm{E}[n_{i1}])$ accounts for the presence of closed-chain packets in the network. $\mathrm{E}[n_{i1}]$ may be computed by any of the computational algorithms for closed networks using the set of modified traffic intensities $\{\rho'_{i1}\}$.

2.4. A heuristic solution technique based upon the MVA algorithm

The time and space complexity of the MVA algorithm [10] are of the same order as the convolution algorithm. However, it has an intuitively appealing extension to an efficient heuristic solution technique that is shown to be asymptotically valid as the chain population sizes become infinite [10].

Let $Q(k)$ be the set of servers visited by chain k and $C(i)$ be the set of chains that visit server i. Also define the following notation for a closed queueing network with population vector $\boldsymbol{N}$:

- $T_{ik}(\boldsymbol{N})$ – mean delay of a chain k packet at server i,
- $q_{ik}(\boldsymbol{N})$ – mean number of chain k packets at server i,
- $\gamma_k^*(\boldsymbol{N})$ – throughput of chain k in packets per second (this is equal to the throughput of the source server).

We first introduce the MVA algorithm which is based upon the following recursive equation,[1] for $i=1,2,\ldots,M$ and $k=1,2,\ldots,K$:

$$T_{ik}(\boldsymbol{N})=\begin{cases}\tau_{ik}\left(1+\sum_{c\in C(i)}q_{ic}(\boldsymbol{N}-\mathbf{1}_k)\right), & \text{server } i \text{ is FCFS},\\ \tau_{ik}, & \text{server } i \text{ is IS}\end{cases} \tag{2.23}$$

where τ_{ik} is the mean service time of server i. It is equal to $1/\mu C_i$ for any k if server i is a communication channel (FCFS server). $q_{ic}(\boldsymbol{N}-\mathbf{1}_k)$ is zero if N_k in $\boldsymbol{N}$ is zero.

Using Little's formula first for chain k, and then for chain k at server i, the following is also derived for the MVA algorithm:

$$\gamma_k^*(\boldsymbol{N})=\frac{N_k}{\sum_{i\in Q(k)}T_{ik}(\boldsymbol{N})}\quad\text{for } k=1,2,\ldots,K \tag{2.24}$$

and

$$q_{ik}(\boldsymbol{N})=\gamma_k^*(\boldsymbol{N})\,T_{ik}(\boldsymbol{N})\quad\text{for}\quad i=1,2,\ldots,M,\; k=1,2,\ldots,K. \tag{2.25}$$

Starting with $q_{ik}(\mathbf{0})=0$ for $i=1,2,\ldots,M$ and $k=1,2,\ldots,K$, $T_{ik}(\boldsymbol{N})$, $\gamma_k^*(\boldsymbol{N})$ and $q_{ik}(\boldsymbol{N})$ can be solved recursively using (2.23)–(2.25) for all i and k.

The computational time and space requirements of the above MVA algorithm grow exponentially with K. For communication network models characterized by a large K, a heuristic technique was proposed by Reiser [16] to solve the above set of equations iteratively. Suppose we can calculate the difference

$$\varepsilon_{ic}(k-)=q_{ic}(\boldsymbol{N})-q_{ic}(\boldsymbol{N}-\mathbf{1}_k)\quad\text{for } i=1,2,\ldots,M,\quad c=1,2,\ldots,K. \tag{2.26}$$

[1] It is shown in [23] that the MVA recursion in (2.23) can be derived very simply from the convolution algorithm's recursion in (2.13). Also, for simplicity, each chain is assumed to have a single fixed route.

Then the MVA equations above can be written as

$$T_{ik}=\begin{cases}\tau_{ik}\left\{1+\sum\limits_{c\in C(i)}\left(q_{ic}-\varepsilon_{ic}(k-)\right)\right\}, \\ \qquad \text{server } i \text{ is FCFS}, \\ \tau_{ik}, \quad \text{server } i \text{ is IS},\end{cases} \tag{2.27}$$

$$\gamma_k^*=\frac{N_k}{\sum\limits_{i\in Q(k)} T_{ik}} \tag{2.28}$$

and

$$q_{ik}=\gamma_k^* T_{ik} \tag{2.29}$$

where the argument N has been omitted from T_{ik}, γ_k^* and q_{ik}.

Eqs. (2.26)–(2.29) form a set of nonlinear simultaneous equations. A simple method for solving them is by a successive substitution technique starting with an initial set of mean queue lengths $\{q_{ik}\}$ and iterating sequentially through the four equations until convergence is observed.

The space requirement is now substantially less since we only need to keep a single set of values for T_{ik}, γ_k^*, q_{ik} and $\epsilon_{ic}(k-)$. The time requirement is also significantly reduced with the following heuristic method [16] for evaluating $\epsilon_{ic}(k-)$, $i=1,2,\ldots,M$, $c=1,2,\ldots,K$:

(a) Assuming that the chain with one less packet is affected the most, use the estimate

$$\epsilon_{ic}(k-)=0 \quad \text{for any } c\neq k. \tag{2.30}$$

(b) $\epsilon_{ik}(k-)$ is estimated by a single-chain network with suitably redefined parameters as follows. The mean service time for all FCFS servers in the single-chain network is

$$\tau_i=\frac{\tau_{ik}}{1-\sum\limits_{c\in C(i),\, c\neq k}\gamma_c^*\tau_{ic}} \tag{2.31}$$

where $\{\gamma_c^*\}$ is the set of chain throughputs at the current iteration step. Eq. (2.31) suggests that a chain k packet sees only a fraction of the channel capacity and it is consistent with the interference effect of the open-chain traffic on closed chains at a FCFS queue considered in the last section. Let $q_i(N_k)$ denote the mean queue size of server i in the single-chain network with service times given by (2.31). These mean queue lengths can be calculated quickly since $K=1$. The following estimate is used in conjunction with those in (2.30) for the heuristic method,

$$\epsilon_{ik}(k-)=q_i(N_k)-q_i(N_k-1). \tag{2.32}$$

The time complexity per iteration step in the heuristic solution is of the order $KM(N_1+N_2+\cdots+N_K)$ which is affordable even for large population sizes provided that convergence is achievable within a small number of iterations. It was observed empirically by Reiser [16] that the above iterative procedure converges rapidly from any set of initial values for $\{q_{ik}\}$ and $\{\gamma_k^*\}$. The only requirements to be satisfied by the initial condition are

$$q_{ik}\geqslant 0 \quad \text{for all } i,k$$

and

$$\sum_{i\in Q(k)} q_{ik}=N_k \quad \text{for all } k.$$

If was also argued that the iterative procedure is asymptotically valid as population sizes become infinite. This heuristic technique has also been generalized to queueing network models that do not have the product-form solution [16].

2.5. The tree convolution algorithm

A computational algorithm, called the tree convolution algorithm, was recently reported in [11]. It is intended for the solution of product-form queueing networks in which routing chains do not visit all servers (or service centers) in the network. In models of communication networks and distributed systems, it is often true that chains visit only a small faction of all queues in the network (*sparseness property*). Furthermore, chains are often clustered in certain parts of the network and their routes are constrained by the network topology (*locality property*). By making use of the routing information of chains, the time and space requirements of the tree convolution algorithm can be made substantially less than those of the (sequential) convolution and MVA algorithms presented earlier. The number of routing chains that can be handled varies depending upon the extent of sparseness and locality present in their routes. In [24], many numerical examples with 32–50 routing chains have been found to be solvable. In some cases, the solution of networks with up to 100 routing chains has been found to be possible.

The tree convolution algorithm provides an exact solution of normalization constants and performance measures for product-form queueing networks. It is based upon two ideas. First, we note that the convolution in (2.11) can be performed in any order to obtain $g_{\{1,2,\ldots,M\}}$. Specifically, in the tree convolution algorithm, the arrays $\{p_m\}$ are placed at the leaf nodes of a tree (see Fig. 4). Each node in the tree corresponds to a subset of service centers that are descendants of that node. To compute the array $g_{\{1,2,\ldots,M\}}$, visit all nodes in the tree according to some order of tree traversal. The root node is visited last. A branch node may be visited only after all its sons have been visited. When a branch node is visited, an array g_{SUBNET} is computed for the node from the arrays g_{SUBNET1} and g_{SUBNET2} of its (two) sons by

$$g_{\text{SUBNET}} = g_{\text{SUBNET1}} \otimes g_{\text{SUBNET2}} \tag{2.33}$$

where SUBNET = SUBNET1 ∪ SUBNET2. If the node has more than two sons, then convolutions are performed sequentially one after the other. Finally, when the root node is visited, the array $g_{\{1,2,\ldots,M\}}$ is obtained.

Both the tree convolution algorithm and the sequential convolution algorithm require $M-1$ convolutions. In fact, it is easy to see that the sequential convolution algorithm is just a special case of the tree algorithm. However, substantial time and space savings can be achieved by the general tree algorithm by making use of the following additional observation.

Consider routing chain k. Let CENTERS(k) be the set of service centers visited by chain k. Let SUBNET denote a subset of the M service centers. With respect to SUBNET, chain k is said to be *fully covered* if CENTERS(k) ⊆ SUBNET; chain k is said to be *noncovered* if the intersection of CENTERS(k) and SUBNET is null; otherwise, chain k is said to be *partially covered*.

Partition the set of K chains into the following 3 sets with respect to SUBNET:

$\sigma_{\text{pc}} = \{k \mid \text{chain } k \text{ is partially covered by SUBNET}\}$,

$\sigma_{\text{fc}} = \{k \mid \text{chain } k \text{ is fully covered by SUBNET}\}$,

$\sigma_{\text{nc}} = \{k \mid \text{chain } k \text{ is noncovered by SUBNET}\}$.

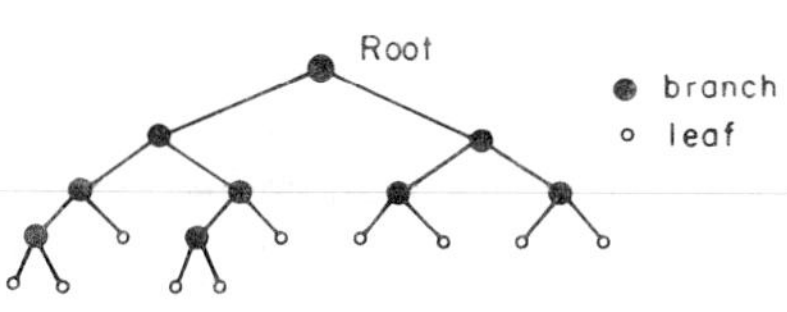

Fig. 4. A tree.

Now make the observation that only those elements of g_{SUBNET} corresponding to the following index values are needed for further convulsions to arrive at $G(\boldsymbol{N})$,

$$\{\boldsymbol{i} \mid i_k = 0, 1, 2, \ldots, N_k,\ k \in \sigma_{\text{pc}};\ i_k = N_k,\ k \in \sigma_{\text{fc}};\ i_k = 0,\ k \in \sigma_{\text{nc}}\}.$$

Let $|\sigma|$ denote the cardinality of set σ. For the purpose of computing $G(\boldsymbol{N})$ it is sufficient to store g_{SUBNET} in an array with dimensionality $|\sigma_{\text{pc}}|$ indexed by $\boldsymbol{i}_{\text{pc}} = \{i_k,\ k \in \sigma_{\text{pc}}\}$. Such an array is termed a *partially covered array*. The amount of space needed for a partially covered array is $\prod_{k \in \sigma_{\text{pc}}}(N_k + 1)$ locations. (Additionally, a small amount of space is also needed to store the set σ_{pc}.) The time requirement of the convolution in (2.33) using partially covered arrays is shown in [11]. Very large time and space savings are possible if $|\sigma_{\text{pc}}| << K$ at every node of the tree.

Given a subset of centers in a network that has many centers and sparse routing chains, it is highly likely that only a few chains will be partially covered by the subset. Thus, for queueing networks with properties of sparseness and locality, the time and space savings from the use of partially covered arrays instead of K-dimensional arrays will be very substantial.

The actual time and space needed for the tree convolution algorithm also depend upon the following 'tree planting' decisions: the tree configuration, the order of tree traversal and the placement of service centers at leaf nodes. The objective of tree planting is to minimize the overall space and time needed by the algorithm by minimizing the numbers of partially covered chains in subnets associated with branch nodes in the tree. Tree planting algorithms are discussed in [11, 24].

In addition to substantial space and time savings, the tree convolution algorithm has several additional significant advantages over the other algorithms. First, the tree of partially covered arrays employed by the algorithm provides a very flexible data structure for tailoring time-space tradeoffs to individual queueing networks in the calculation of network performance measures. It will also facilitate the solution of very large queueing networks with the help of storage management techniques or by means of parallel computation on a multiprocessor machine. Furthermore, the computation of the marginal distribution of queue lengths in a service center may be obtained with $(\log_2 M) - 1$ convolutions instead of $M - 1$ convolutions needed by a sequential convolution algorithm, where M is the total number of service centers and a balanced binary tree is assumed. Lastly, an analysis of the expected time and space requirements of the algorithm as a function of the sparseness of routing chains is presented in [25].

2.6. Network design using both closed-chain and open-chain models

With the tree convolution algorithm, communication network models with many queues and a relatively large number of sparse routing chains can be solved exactly. (Chains are said to be sparse if the average number of queues visited by a chain is much smaller than the number of queues in the network.) Both throughputs and mean transit delays for individual chains can be calculated exactly with time and space requirements within the limits of present computers. However, these time and space requirements are still fairly large. Hence, the tree algorithm is not very practical for use within network design procedures that require numerous applications of the algorithm.

Both Pennotti and Schwartz [22] and Gerla and Nilsson [26] suggested the use of open chains to approximately model flow controlled virtual channels. The difficulty encountered is that the throughputs of the flow controlled virtual channels needed as input parameters of an open-chain model are not known. Lam and Lien [17,18] proposed to use a combination of both open-chain and closed-chain models in design procedures for networks with flow controlled virtual channels. A closed-chain model is first employed and chain throughputs and mean delays are computed exactly using the tree convolution algorithm. An open-chain model with the same chain throughputs is then employed for a sequence of intermediate optimization steps in the network design procedure (e.g., the routing of incremental flows to be considered in Section 2.7). To avoid the accumulation of errors, the closed-chain model is employed at various checkpoints of the design procedure to recompute chain throughputs and mean delays. The question of interest then is: How accurate is such an approximation?

The above question was addressed by Lam and Lien [17,18] who considered a network model with 64 communication channels and 32 virtual channels. The throughputs and mean ETE delays of a closed-chain model are first computed using the tree convolution algorithm. An open-chain model having the same chain throughputs is then specified and its mean ETE delays calculated using the M/M/1 delay formula for individual queues as described in [5–7].

The service rate of each communication channel was assumed to be the same; $\mu C_m = 10$ packets/second for all m. The source input rate of each virtual channel was also assumed to be the same; $\gamma_k = \gamma$ for all k (see Fig. 2).

The effect of varying the relative source and communication channel speeds γ and μC was considered. γ was varied from 10 to 0.5 while keeping μC constant at 10 packets/second. The accuracy of the open-chain model was found to be very poor for $\gamma = 10$ (same value as μC) and it improved as γ was decreased. The average error in the mean ETE delays of the virtual channels was 40.3% for $\gamma = 10$, 2.02% for $\gamma = 1$ and 0.40% for $\gamma = 0.5$. There are two possible reasons for this behavior. First, when the utilization of a M/M/1 queue is high, its delay distribution has a long tail, which gives rise to a poor estimate of the delay in a closed network where the queue lengths are bounded. Note that when $\gamma = \mu C$, the bottleneck in a routing chain is at one of the communication channels within the packet switching network. On the other hand, when μC is much smaller than γ, the source server is the bottleneck in a routing chain and it behaves like a Poisson source at rate γ much of the time (i.e., like an open chain).

In general, the accuracy of the open-chain model suffers from the presence of bottlenecks within the network (either due to a large γ or due to poor routing).

The effect of varying the virtual channel window size was also investigated. Window sizes of 2, 3 and 4 were considered. It was found that as the window size increases, the accuracy of the open-chain model improves, despite increases in the channel utilizations.

Finally, another observation in [17,18] is that in almost all cases considered, the mean delay estimates are larger than the actual mean delays. There are two possible reasons for the open-chain model to overestimate mean delays. First, delay estimates are obtained from M/M/1 queue delay distributions that have long tails. Second, the mean-value analysis shows that the mean delay encountered by a closed-chain customer is determined by the mean queue lengths of a network with that customer removed [10]. The open-chain model as described above does not account for this behavior.

A consequence of the overestimation of delays is that the impact of bottlenecks on chain delays in an open-chain model is exaggerated compared to that in a closed-chain model. This means that if an open-chain model is used for the routing of incremental flows (see the following section), bottlenecks will be avoided more 'rigorously' than if a closed-chain model is employed.

2.7. Optimal routing of incremental flows

We consider the problem of introducing a small amount of incremental flow from a source node to a destination node into a network with existing flows. Several optimal routing problems may be formulated depending upon the nature of the incremental flow and the optimization objective.

The objective of the ARPANET routing algorithm [27] is to minimize the (estimated) delay of an individual packet from its source node to its destination node. However, it has been observed by several authors [28,29] that routing algorithms with the objective of individual-optimization do not necessarily lead to network-optimization, i.e., minimizing the mean delay of all packets in the network. The flow deviation method [7,30,31] considers an incremental flow that is infinitesimal relative to existing flows in the network. The network-optimization objective is pursued; specifically, the route for the incremental flow is chosen to minimize the (infinitesimal) increase ΔT in the mean network transit delay T of all packets.

A similar problem for networks with flow-controlled virtual channels was posed by Lam and Lien in [18]. The incremental flow corresponds to the addition of a new virtual channel with a window size of one (not necessarily an infinitesimal amount of flow). In this case, one method to evaluate ΔT is to calculate T using the tree convolution algorithm for the network both with and without the additional virtual channel (given a specific route for it). However, to determine the optimal route with this approach would require numerous applications of the tree convolution algorithm and would be very expensive in terms of computation time.

The solution approach described in Section 2.6 was proposed [18]. A closed-chain model is initially used to calculate the throughputs of the existing flow controlled virtual channels. These are then modeled as open chains. The new virtual channel to be added is modeled as a closed chain.

Let the aggregate arrival rate of the existing traffic in the network to communication channel m be denoted by λ_m packets/second. The service rate of channel m is μC_m packets/second where $1/\mu$ is the average length of a packet in bits and C_m is the channel speed in bits/second. Define $\rho_m = \lambda_m/(\mu C_m)$. The total throughput rate at which open-chain packets leave (or enter) the network is γ_o packets/second. The mean ETE delay of open-chain packets is T_o. The closed chain representing the virtual channel being added has a population size of one (i.e., window size is one), a source server work-rate of γ packets/second and a mean ETE ACK delay of τ seconds. The source and sink nodes of the virtual channel are known but its route is to be determined.

Let Q denote the set of communication channels constituting a route chosen for the new virtual channel. The increase in the mean network delay due to the incremental traffic was found to be

$$\Delta T = \frac{\sum_{m\in Q} \dfrac{\mu C_m}{(\mu C_m - \lambda_m)^2} - T_o}{\gamma_o\left(\dfrac{1}{\gamma} + \tau + \sum_{m\in Q} \dfrac{1}{\mu C_m - \lambda_m}\right) + 1}. \qquad (2.34)$$

Since the amount of incremental traffic is not infinitesimal, it makes sense to impose a maximum delay bound τ_{max} on the mean delay of the new virtual channel. (Most likely, the user requesting for the new virtual channel will want his mean delay to be bounded.) The following constrained optimization problem results:

$$\min_{Q} \quad \Delta T$$

$$\text{s. t.} \quad \sum_{m\in Q} \frac{1}{\mu C_m - \lambda_m} < \tau_{max}. \qquad (2.35)$$

A dual of the above problem is

$$\min_{Q} \quad \sum_{m\in Q} \frac{1}{\mu C_m - \lambda_m}$$

$$\text{s. t.} \quad \Delta T < \Delta_{max} \qquad (2.36)$$

where Δ_{max} is a bound on ΔT. The above problems were formulated by Lam and Lien [18] who also provided an algorithm to solve the problem in (2.35). We can interpret each of the above constrained problems as a compromise between the objectives of individual-optimization and network-optimization. Note that the individual-optimization objective of ARPANET routing does not consider the impact of the incremental flow on the network. On the other hand, the network-optimization objective of flow deviation ignores the performance of the incremental flow (since it is assumed to be infinitesimal). The above constrained problems take into account both considerations.

3. Queueing network models with population size constraints

In this section we shall consider the modeling of congestion control and buffer management strategies in packet networks. To do so, we need to introduce the class of queueing networks with population size constraints [4].

3.1. The model

Routing chains in queueing network models considered prior to now in this paper and in [5] are either open or closed. Recall our discussion in Section 2.2 that a closed chain can be viewed as an open chain with the loss and trigger mechanisms in place at all times. Suppose the loss and trigger mechanisms are invoked or revoked as a function of the network's population vector $\boldsymbol{N}=(N_1, N_2,\dots,N_K)$. Such queueing networks are said to have population size constraints. Given the loss and trigger mechanisms as functions of $\boldsymbol{N}$, let V be the set of feasible network population vectors. A sufficient condition for the equilibrium network state probability $\mathrm{P}(S)$ to have the product-form solution is stated in [4]:

> For any chain k and population vectors $\boldsymbol{N}$ and $\boldsymbol{N}+\mathbf{1}_k$ in V, the loss mechanism is invoked for a chain k external arrival in any network state with population vector $\boldsymbol{N}$ if and only if the trigger mechanism is invoked for a chain k external departure in any network state with population vector $\boldsymbol{N}+\mathbf{1}_k$.

This is equivalent to the condition that feasible transitions between population vectors in V are always paired.

By permitting V to be a singleton set as well as an infinite set, both networks of closed chains and networks of open chains are included here as special cases. The set of feasible network states is $\mathbb{S}=\bigcup_{\boldsymbol{N}\in V}\mathbb{S}(\boldsymbol{N})$ where $\mathbb{S}(\boldsymbol{N})$ is defined by (2.7). Thus, the (improper) equilibrium probability of the set of states $\mathbb{S}(\boldsymbol{N})$ is equal to the normalization constant $G(\boldsymbol{N})$ of an equivalent closed network with population vector $\boldsymbol{N}$; chain arrival rates to individual servers are given by (2.1) for closed chains and (2.17) for chains that permit external arrivals [4,19]. For constant external chain arrival rates, a queueing network model with population size constraints has the product-form solution given by (2.5) with the following expression for the normalization constant:

$$G=\sum_{\boldsymbol{N}\in V} G(\boldsymbol{N}). \tag{3.1}$$

In Sections 3.2–3.4 we discuss queueing network models with population size constraints for the analysis of strategies for buffer management and congestion control.

3.2. Finite-buffer single node model

When a packet is in transit in a packet switching network, it occupies buffer space in the intermediate store-and-forward nodes. When nodes with finite buffers are considered, the allocation of buffers to the various chains will affect the node's performance (and hence, the network's performance).

To model a packet switching network with finite buffer space, one must consider the situation when a packet forwarded to a node finds no available buffer in that node. The store-and-forward protocol requires the sending node to keep a copy of the packet until an ACK is returned from the receiving node. If an ACK is not received within a time-out interval, the packet is retransmitted. Buffer space in the sending node is therefore occupied by this packet until an ACK is received.

An exact analytic model of an entire network with finite buffers at each node is not presently available. Models of a single switching node, however, have been successfully analyzed [32–35]. In this section, buffer allocation strategies studied by

Kamoun and Kleinrock [35] are considered. Their model does not include ACKs. As soon as a packet has been transmitted on an outgoing channel, its buffer space is assumed to be released immediately. A single node model with provisions for ACK and timeout delays [8,32] will be discussed in Section 3.4. Approximate solution techniques to analyze a network of finite-buffer nodes will also be described in that section.

The single node model analyzed by Kamoun and Kleinrock [35] is shown in Fig. 5. It is a specialized queueing network model with M servers in parallel, one for each outgoing channel. There are M routing chains: packets routed to the same outgoing channel are in the same chain. The arrival process of chain i packets to the node is assumed to be Poisson with rate λ_i, $i = 1, 2, \ldots, M$. The population size constraints for the various routing chains are determined by the buffer management scheme used.

Packets belonging to the various chains share a total of B buffers. When an arriving packet is rejected from entering the node, it is assumed to be lost. (In a network of finite-buffer nodes, rejected packets are not really lost, but are retransmitted later; hence, the arrival process to each node is not likely to be Poisson. The Poisson arrival assumption mentioned above is therefore only an approximation in this context.)

We next present a general buffer allocation scheme that includes as special cases the four different buffer-sharing strategies studied in [35]. The general scheme is specified in terms of minimum allocations and maximum limits for the different classes of packets. Define

(i) the number of buffers dedicated to chain i to be b_i ($b_i \geq 0$), and

(ii) the maximum number of buffers that chain i packets can occupy to be B_i ($B_i \leq B$) for $i = 1, 2, \ldots, M$.

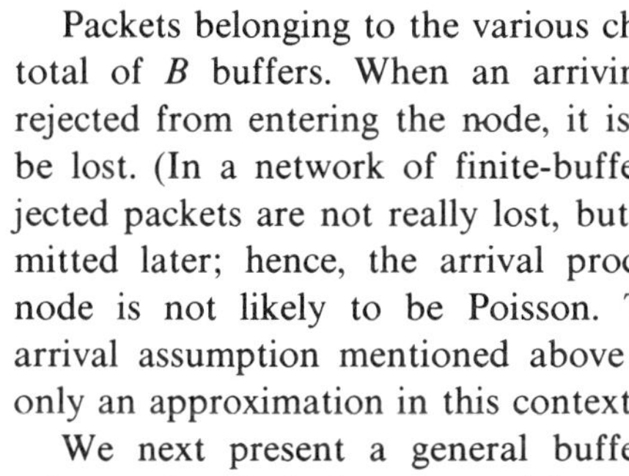

Fig. 5. A model of a switching node with a finite buffer pool.

We must have $b_i \leq B_i$ for all i, $\sum_{i=1}^{M} b_i \leq B$, and $\sum_{i=1}^{M} B_i \geq B$ to be physically meaningful.

It is often desirable to use an over-commitment strategy such that

$$\sum_{i=1}^{M} B_i > B.$$

Let a state of the single node model be

$$\boldsymbol{m} = (m_1, m_2, \ldots, m_M)$$

where m_i is the number of chain i packets in the node.[2]

The general buffer allocation scheme can be modeled by a queueing network model with population size constraints. The set of feasible states can be written as

$$V = \left\{ \boldsymbol{m}\colon m_i \leq B_i, \text{ for all } i, \text{ and } \sum_{i=1}^{M} \max\{0, m_i - b_i\} \leq B - \sum_{i=1}^{M} b_i \right\}. \tag{3.2}$$

Applying the product-form solution, the equilibrium network state probability is given by

$$\mathrm{P}(\boldsymbol{m}) = \frac{1}{G} \prod_{i=1}^{M} \rho_i^{m_i} \tag{3.3}$$

where $\rho_i = \lambda_i/(\mu C_i)$ and

$$G = \sum_{\boldsymbol{m} \in V} \prod_{i=1}^{M} \rho_i^{m_i}. \tag{3.4}$$

Special cases of the above scheme that have been studied by Kamoun and Kleinrock [35] are the following:

Case 1. Complete partitioning ($b_i > 0$ and $\sum_{i=1}^{M} b_i = B$) – The B buffers are partitioned into M groups, the ith group (with size b_i) is allocated to chain i. There is no sharing of buffers among chains. Hence, B_i is equal to b_i, and we also have $\sum_{i=1}^{M} B_i = B$.

[2] In a general network model, n_{ik} denotes the number of chain k packets at channel i. Since the current model has the simple behavior that chain i packets visit channel i only, n_{ii} is therefore the only non-zero element in the vector $\boldsymbol{n}_i$. We use m_i instead of $(0, \ldots, n_{ii}, \ldots, 0)$ for convenience. Furthermore, feasible states in this model correspond to feasible population vectors considered in Section 3.1.

Case 2. Complete sharing ($b_i = 0$ and $B_i = B$) – The B buffers are completely shared by the M chains. Buffers are allocated on a FCFS basis.

Case 3. Sharing with maximum allocations ($b_i = 0$ and $B_i < B$) – The B buffers are shared by all chains with the restriction that the number of buffers occupied by chain i cannot exceed B_i.

Case 4. Sharing with minimum allocations ($b_i > 0$ and $B_i = B$) – Chain i packets are guaranteed at least b_i buffers, and the remaining $B - \Sigma_{i=1}^{M} b_i$ buffers are shared by all chains.

We now illustrate how one can obtain analytic expressions for performance measures such as blocking probability, throughput and mean delay. Let $V_i \subset V$ be the set of states in which a chain i arrival is rejected. For the general buffer allocation scheme, V_i is given by

$$V_i = \left\{ \boldsymbol{m}: m_i = B_i \text{ or } \left(m_i \geq b_i \text{ and } \sum_{i=1}^{M} \max\{0, m_j - b_j\} = B - \sum_{j=1}^{M} b_j \right) \right\}. \tag{3.5}$$

Let β_i be the blocking probability of chain i packets,

$$\beta_i = \sum_{\boldsymbol{m} \in V_i} \mathrm{P}(\boldsymbol{m}). \tag{3.6}$$

The throughput of chain i packets is then given by

$$\gamma_i^* = \lambda_i(1 - \beta_i). \tag{3.7}$$

To get the mean delay experienced by chain i packets, we must first get the mean number of chain i packets in the node. This can be obtained from

$$\mathrm{E}[m_i] = \sum_{\boldsymbol{m} \in V} m_i \mathrm{P}(\boldsymbol{m}). \tag{3.8}$$

Little's formula [21] is then used to get the following expression for the mean delay of chain i:

$$T_i = \mathrm{E}[m_i]/\gamma_i^*. \tag{3.9}$$

It should be noted that the mean delay in (3.9) is for packets which are accepted into the node. It does not include those that are rejected.

Eqs. (3.6)–(3.9) are expressed in terms of a summation over a set of network states. In special cases, they can often be simplified and expressed in terms of the normalization constant G. The reader is referred to [35] for such simplifications. Numerical examples showing the relative merits of the four special cases are also provided in that reference. A general conclusion is that the best scheme and the best setting of parameters (b_i and B_i) depend upon the values of the ρ_i's.

3.3. Permit-oriented congestion control

A packet switching network can be viewed as a set of resources shared by a population of users. Such resources include channels and buffers. If the resources are not managed properly, an increased demand from a single user or a group of users may cause degradation in network performance. This degradation is usually in the form of substantially reduced throughput [36, 37]. When this happens, the network is said to be in a state of congestion. The objective of congestion control is then to prevent the network from going into the congestion state. Congestion control schemes usually involve some form of restriction on the amount of network resources allocated to each external user. The window flow control mechanism discussed in Section 2.1 provides a congestion control function because it places a limit on the number of packets belonging to a virtual channel in the network. However, if the number of virtual channels is large, the combined load on the network can still become excessive, and an additional network-wide congestion control scheme may be required.

A basic principle is to apply control at the point of entry to the network. An example of such a technique is the isarithmic control scheme suggested by Davies [38]. This scheme places a limit on the total number of packets in the network; no discrimination is made on the basis of routing chains. It can be implemented by circulating a number of 'permits' in the network, and requiring a packet to secure a permit before it can be admitted into the network. Another example is window flow control which specifies different types of permits for packets belonging to different virtual channels.

We observe that the principles of permit-oriented congestion control schemes for a network are basically the same as those of buffer allocation schemes for a switching node. Here, permits play the role of buffers considered earlier in Section 3.2. The general scheme, based upon the specification of maximum limits and minimum allocations, discussed there can be used to specify the allocation of permits for network congestion control as well. In this section we present the work reported in [39] which considers the special case of maximum limits only.

The routing chains in the network are assumed to be partitioned into disjoint groups, and the number of permits used by each group cannot exceed some pre-specified maximum. The notion of group allows the flexibility of imposing controls on selected sets of routing chains. The resulting congestion control scheme provides a two-level isarithmic control [39, 40]. At level 1, a limit is placed on the total number of packets in the network; and at level 2, separate limits are placed on each group. Let L be the total number of permits, D be the number of groups, and L_u be the limit for group u, $u = 1, 2, \ldots, D$. The general scheme can be implemented by two types of permits. Type 1 consists of L permits shared by all packets. Type 2 permits are also distinguished by a group number; the number of permits for group u is L_u. A packet must acquire *both* a type 1 permit and a type 2 permit for its group before it can be admitted into the network.

The two types of permits are not always needed in special cases. For example, the complete sharing scheme corresponds to the method of isarithmic control [38], which can be implemented by the L type 1 permits only. In the complete partitioning scheme, type 2 permits are required while type 1 permits are not used.

The implementation of permit-oriented congestion control for a network is substantially more complicated than buffer allocation schemes for a node, due to the need for decentralized control in a network. A packet acquires one or more permits when it enters the network and releases its permit(s) when it reaches its destination node. The distribution of free permits is an important but difficult implementation problem. One would like to minimize the probability that when a permit is needed at a particular node, all the free permits are somewhere else in the network. Davies [38] suggested that each node may keep up to a maximum number of free permits, and extra permits are sent to randomly-selected neighbors. (Note that this is a maximum allocation strategy applied to individual nodes.)

We now consider the use of a queueing network model with population size constraints to study permit-oriented congestion control. For mathematical tractability we need to assume that the buffer space at each node is unlimited. It is also necessary to assume that free permits circulate through the network with no delay so that an external packet arrival to the network receives a permit right away if a free one is present in the network. In reality, a packet's entry to the network may be delayed because the available free permits may be in other parts of the network. The last assumption therefore results in optimistic estimates of network performance.

Recall that the state of the network model is given by $S = (\boldsymbol{n}_1, \boldsymbol{n}_2, \ldots, \boldsymbol{n}_M)$ where $\boldsymbol{n}_i = (n_{i1}, n_{i2}, \ldots, n_{iK})$; n_{ik} is the number of chain k packets at server i. The K routing chains are partitioned into D groups, and a packet is said to belong to group u (denoted by Γ_u) if its routing chain is in group u. The equilibrium network state probability $\mathrm{P}(S)$ is given by the product term in (2.5). The appropriate normalization constant is defined below.

It is convenient to define a less detailed state description

$$S' = (y_1, y_2, \ldots, y_M)$$

where

$$y_i = (m_{i1}, m_{i2}, \ldots, m_{iD})$$

where m_{iu} is the number of group u packets at server i. Let

$$N_u = \sum_{i=1}^{M} m_{iu}$$

be the population size of group u packets when the network is in state S'. The set of feasible network states is

$$\mathcal{S}' = \bigcup_{N \in V} \mathcal{S}'(\boldsymbol{N})$$

where $\boldsymbol{N}$ denotes the population vector $(N_1, N_2, \ldots, N_D)$; the set of feasible population vectors is

$$V = \left\{ \boldsymbol{N}\colon \sum_{u=1}^{D} N_u \leq L \text{ and } N_u \leq L_u \text{ for all } u \right\} \quad (3.10)$$

and

$$\mathcal{S}'(\boldsymbol{N}) = \left\{ S'\colon \sum_{i=1}^{M} y_i = \boldsymbol{N} \right\}.$$

By adding all state probabilities $\mathrm{P}(S)$ such that $\sum_{k \in \Gamma_u} n_{ik} = m_{iu}$ for $i = 1, 2, \ldots, M$ and $u =$

$1, 2, \ldots, D$, we get [39]

$$P(S') = \frac{1}{G} \prod_{i=1}^{M} m_i! \prod_{u=1}^{D} \frac{\phi_{iu}^{m_{iu}}}{m_{iu}!}, \quad S' \in \mathbb{S}' \tag{3.11}$$

where

$$m_i = \sum_{u=1}^{D} m_{iu}, \qquad \phi_{iu} = \sum_{k \in \Gamma_u} \rho_{ik}$$

and

$$G = \sum_{N \in V} G(N)$$

where $G(N)$ is the normalization constant of a closed network with the same set of traffic intensities $\{\phi_{iu}\}$ and N as its population vector [19]. $G(N)$ may be evaluated using any of the computational algorithms described earlier in Section 2.

To obtain the network throughput of each group, we follow the developments which lead to (3.7) in Section 3.2. The blocking probability of group u packets is

$$\beta_u = \sum_{N \in V_u} G(N) \tag{3.12}$$

where

$$V_u = \left\{ N: \sum_{i=1}^{D} N_i = L \text{ or } N_u = L_u \right\}. \tag{3.13}$$

The throughput of group u is then given by

$$\gamma_u^* = \sum_{k \in \Gamma_u} \gamma_k (1 - \beta_u). \tag{3.14}$$

3.4. Finite-buffer network models

The peak throughput of a network is attained when all its communication channels are transmitting packets (assuming that the mean packet length and the mean path length of packets in the network are constant). The network throughput over a period of time is usually less than the peak value because of (i) the lack of input traffic, or (ii) some constraints or interference effects that force communication channels to be 'nonproductive' part of the time. In Sections 3.2 and 3.3 we considered models which were used to study the throughput degradation behavior arising from interference between different streams of traffic [34, 35, 39]. In this section we shall consider network throughput degradation behavior due to insufficient buffers at switching nodes.

In what follows we shall first describe an approximate analysis method for dealing with the problem of blocking arising from the assumption of finite nodal buffer pools. Two special applications of the analysis method are discussed: A model for determining nodal buffer requirements needed to achieve small nodal blocking probabilities, and a model for studying the performance of the 'input buffer limit' strategy for network congestion control [8, 41].

A packet received by a switching node for forwarding may be accepted or discarded in accordance with some buffer management strategy depending upon some attribute of the packet (such as its priority level, class, destination, etc.) and the utilization level(s) of the node's buffer pool(s). A packet, discarded in this fashion, is said to be *blocked*. The sending node, however, has a copy of the packet and will retransmit it later when a timeout occurs and no positive ACK has been received.

To get around the difficulty of modeling blocking in a queueing network, the following approximate solution technique was first proposed in [8]. The overall problem (network of switching nodes) is first decomposed into a set of analytically tractable problems, i.e., a queueing network model for each switching node. The single-node results are then combined by requiring conservation of the various packet flows within the network as described below.

The queueing network model of a switching node shown in Fig. 6 was proposed by Lam and Schweitzer [8, 32] to study buffer requirements for networks with completely shared buffer pools. It

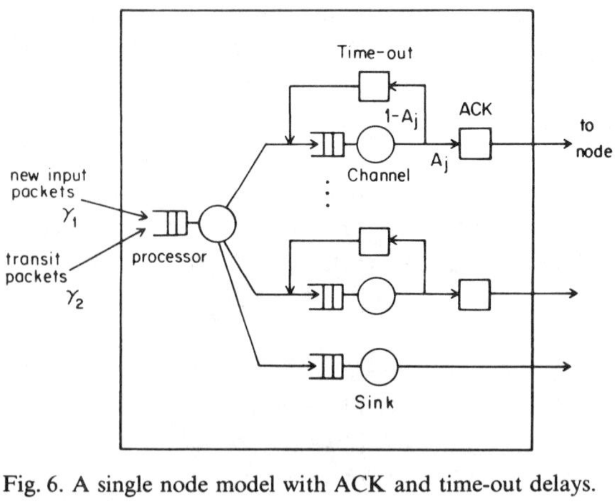

Fig. 6. A single node model with ACK and time-out delays.

was also employed later by Lam and Reiser [41] to study the input buffer limit strategy for network congestion control. FCFS servers are used to model the nodal processor, the communication channels and the sink for packets destined for this node. IS servers are used to model ACK delays and time-out delays.

Two types of packets are distinguished [3]: Transit packets forwarded by adjacent nodes and new input packets generated locally. They are represented by two routing chains with exernal arrival rates γ_2 and γ_1 respectively. The following buffer management strategy is considered. Suppose the node has N_T buffers. Transit packets are rejected only when all buffers are occupied. However, when there are N_I input packets in the node, any newly arrived input packet is rejected. We have $N_I \leqslant N_T$. The ratio N_I/N_T is said to be the *input buffer limit.*

For each routing chain, routing transition probabilities from the nodal processor to one of the communication channels or the sink are determined by the routing behavior of source-destination paths in the real network. The routing transition probability from a communication channel to either the ACK or the time-out IS server depends upon the rejection probability for transit packets of the neighboring node (say node j) at the other end of the communication channel. A packet is accepted by the neighboring node with probability A_j; it joins the ACK server and subsequently leaves the current node (when an ACK is received). A packet is rejected with probability $1-A_j$ by the neighboring node; no ACK will be returned. Conceptually, the packet joins the time-out server and subsequently rejoins the channel queue. Note that this routing behavior is consistent with the probabilistic routing behavior defined for product-form queueing network models. The acceptance probability A_j is assumed to be the product $(1-E)(1-\beta_j)$ where E is the probability of a transmission error in the packet and β_j is the blocking probability of node j.

Suppose that the set of nodal blocking probabilities $\{\beta_j\}$ for transit packets is known for each communication channel in Fig. 6. Then the node can be modeled by a product-form queueing network with two routing chains and the population size constraints

$$0 \leqslant N_1 + N_2 \leqslant N_T$$

and

$$0 \leqslant N_1 \leqslant N_I.$$

Let $P_m(N_1, N_2)$ be the equilibrium probability of having N_1 input packets and N_2 transit packets in node m. The equilibrium blocking probability for transit packets at this node is

$$\beta_m = \sum_{N_1=0}^{N_I} P_m(N_1, N_T - N_1), \quad m = 1, 2, \ldots, M. \tag{3.15}$$

Since the set $\{P_m(N_1, N_2)\}$ in turn depends upon the set $\{\beta_j\}$, we thus have a set of M nonlinear equations for the M unknowns in $\{\beta_j\}$, which can be solved numerically.

Note that in the calculation of $P_m(N_1, N_2)$ for node m, the arrival rate γ_2 of its transit packets should be set equal to the throughput rate of such transit packets multiplied by $1/A_m$ to account for retransmissions following rejections. Also, if γ_1 is the arrival rate of new input packets (offered load), then the throughput rate of such packets should be reduced by a fraction equal to the blocking probability of input packets at node m, which is

$$\beta_m + \sum_{N_2=0}^{N_T-N_I-1} P_m(N_I, N_2).$$

An iterative solution technique incorporating the Newton–Raphson method was developed [8] for the special case of $N_I = N_T$ at each node, i.e., no input buffer limit control and the buffer pool is completely shared. It was found that the model is accurate when switching nodes have adequate buffers (for given external input rates) so that $\{\beta_j\}$ takes on small values. The model is thus useful for predicting buffer requirements to achieve small nodal blocking probabilities. (Note that in a procedure to determine such buffer requirements, although the model results may not be very accurate at intermediate steps of the procedure, the results at the termination of the procedure would be accurate.) The model is also useful for comparing the performance of various buffer capacity assignment schemes.

The above model was also employed in [41] to

[3] The model can be used for many types of packets. Only two types of packets are considered to reduce the computational requirements of the model.

study the design of input buffer limits that can effectively prevent throughput degradation due to insufficient buffers when the network is under a heavy external load. Both the analytic results in [41] and a subsequent simulation study [42] showed that input buffer limits can be designed to provide a very effective congestion control mechanism for temporary network overloads. For a detailed treatment of input buffer limits as a congestion control mechanism, see [41, 42]. A slightly different input buffer limit strategy was later proposed and studied by Saad and Schwartz [43] and independently by Kamoun et al. [44].

In [41] the *homogeneous network model* was also proposed to reduce the computational complexity of solving numerically the set of nonlinear equations in (3.15). Instead of considering a specific network topology, it is assumed that the network is 'homogeneous' so that each node has identical behavior. Specifically, the blocking probability is the same at each node. As a result, the evaluation of a single queueing network model representing a single switching node is sufficient at each iteration step of the numerical solution. The homogeneous network model permits us to examine the influence of the input buffer limit strategy on the network's performance without the computational complexity that goes with an arbitrary network topology.

4. Conclusions

We have provided in this paper and in [5] a tutorial treatment of both exact and approximate models based upon product-form queueing networks, that have proved to be useful for analyzing the performance of packet communication networks. Some approximate solution techniques have also been described.

We have tried to provide a general framework for the various models presented. First we observed that the class of product-form queueing networks with population size constraints [4] include open networks, closed networks and mixed networks as special cases [2]. Open network models are considered in Part 1 [5]. The topics there include: channel capacity assignment, optimal routing, distributions of chain ETE delays and a study of fairness among routing chains. All these problems may be thought of as resource allocation problems related to the sharing of finite-capacity communication channels in a packet network. Problems related to the sharing of finite nodal buffer pools are considered herein (Part 2). Queueing networks with closed chains and other forms of population size constraints are employed to study the performance of window flow controlled virtual channels, and strategies for buffer management and permit-oriented network congestion control. We observed that all these strategies (including window flow control) fall within the *general resource allocation scheme of differentiating packets into classes, and providing each class with a minimum allocation and a maximum limit of the shared resource.*

We have restricted our discussions to the formulation and application of models based upon product-form queueing networks only. An earlier survey article on this subject appeared in [45]. For a comprehensive survey of network design problems using the basic model in Part 1, the reader is referred to [46]. For an in-depth treatment of the subject of network flow and congestion control strategies discussed in Part 2, the reader is referred to [47].

References

[1] J.R. Jackson, Jobshop-like queueing systems, Management Sci. 10 (1963) 131–142.

[2] F. Baskett, K.M. Chandy, R.R. Muntz and F. Palacios, Open, closed and mixed networks of queues with different classes of customers, J. Assoc. Comput. Mach. 22 (1975) 248–260.

[3] M. Reiser and H. Kobayashi, Queueing networks with multiple closed chains: Theory and computational algorithms, IBM J. Res. Develop. 19 (1975) 283–294.

[4] S.S. Lam, Queueing networks with population size constraints, IBM J. Res. Develop. 21 (1977) 370–378.

[5] J.W. Wong and S.S. Lam, Queueing network models of packet switching networks, Part 1: Open networks, Performance Evaluation 2(1) (1982) 8–20.

[6] L. Kleinrock, Communication Nets – Stochastic Message Flow and Delays (McGraw-Hill, New York, 1964).

[7] L. Kleinrock, Queueing Systems, Vol. 2: Computer Applications (Wiley-Interscience, New York, 1976).

[8] S.S. Lam, Store-and forward buffer requirements in a packet switching network, IEEE Trans. Comm. COM-24 (1976) 394–403.

[9] K.M. Chandy, U. Herzog and L.S. Woo, Parametric analysis of queueing networks, IBM J. Res. Develop. 19 (1975) 36–42.

[10] M. Reiser and S. Lavenberg, Mean value analysis of closed multichain queueing networks, J. Assoc. Comput. Mach. 27 (1980) 313–322.

[11] S.S. Lam and Y.L. Lien, A tree convolution algorithm for the solution of queueing networks, Tech. Rept. TR-165, Department of Computer Sciences, University of Texas at Austin, 1981; Comm. ACM, to appear.
[12] L. Pouzin, Presentation and major design aspects of the CYCLADES computer network, Proc. 3rd Data Communications Symposium, St. Petersburg, Florida, 1973.
[13] V. Cerf and R. Kahn, A protocol for packet network intercommunication, IEEE Trans. Comm. COM-22 (1974) 637–648.
[14] V. Ahuja, Routing and flow control in Systems Network Architecture, IBM Systems J. 18 (1979) 298–314.
[15] H. Opderbeck and L. Kleinrock, The influence of control procedures on the performance of packet-switched networks, Proc. Nat. Telecommunications Conference, San Diego, 1974.
[16] M. Reiser, A queueing network analysis of computer communication networks with window flow control. IEEE Trans. Comm. COM-27 (1979) 1199–1209.
[17] S.S. Lam and Y.L. Lien, Modeling and analysis of flow controlled packet switching networks, Proc. 7th Data Communications Symposium, Mexico City, 1981.
[18] S.S. Lam and Y.L. Lien, Optimal routing in networks with flow controlled virtual channels, Performance Evaluation Rev. 11 (1) (1982) 38–46.
[19] S.S. Lam, Dynamic scaling and growth behavior of queueing network normalization constants, Tech. Rept. TR-148, Department of Computer Science, University of Texas at Austin, 1980; J. Assoc. Comput. Mach. 29 (1982) 492–513.
[20] J.P. Buzen, Computational algorithms for closed queueing networks with exponential servers, Comm. ACM 16 (1973) 527–531.
[21] J.D.C. Little, A proof of the queueing formula: $L = \lambda W$, Oper. Res. 9 (1961) 383–387.
[22] M. Pennotti and M. Schwartz, Congestion control in store and forward tandem links, IEEE Trans. Comm. COM-23 (1975) 1434–1443.
[23] S.S. Lam, A simple derivation of the MVA and LBANC algorithms from the convolution algorithm, Tech. Rept. TR-184, Department of Computer Sciences, University of Texas at Austin, 1981.
[24] Y.L. Lien, Modeling and analysis of flow-controlled computer communication networks, Ph.D. Thesis, Department of Computer Sciences, University of Texas at Austin, 1981.
[25] S.S. Lam and Y.L. Lien, An analysis of the tree convolution algorithm for queueing networks, Tech. Rept. TR 166, Department of Computer Sciences, University of Texas at Austin, 1981.
[26] M. Gerla and P.O. Nilsson, Routing and flow control interplay in computer networks, Proc. 5th ICCC, Atlanta, 1980.
[27] J.M. McQuillan, G. Falk and I. Richer, A review of the development and performance of the ARPANET routing algorithm, IEEE Trans. Comm. COM-26 (1978) 1802–1811.
[28] C.E. Agnew, On quadrative adaptive routing algorithms, Comm. ACM 19 (1976) 18–22.
[29] R. Gallager, An optimal routing algorithm using distributed computation, IEEE Trans. Comm. COM-25 (1977) 73–85.
[30] L. Fratta, M. Gerla and L. Kleinrock, The flow deviation method: An approach to store-and-forward network design, Networks 3 (1973) 97–133.
[31] M. Gerla, The design of store-and-forward networks for computer communications, Ph.D. Dissertation, Department of Computer Sciences, UCLA, 1973.
[32] P.J. Schweitzer and S.S. Lam, Buffer overflow in a store-and-forward network node, IBM J. Res. Develop. 20 (1976) 542–550.
[33] M.A. Rich and M. Schwartz, Buffer sharing in computer-communication network nodes, IEEE Trans. Comm. COM-25 (1977) 958–970.
[34] M. Irland, Buffer management in a packet switch, IEEE Trans. Comm. COM-26 (1978) 328–337.
[35] F. Kamoun and L. Kleinrock, Analysis of shared finite storage in a computer network environment under general traffic conditions, IEEE Trans. Comm. COM-28 (1980) 992–1003.
[36] W.L. Price, Data network simulation experiments at the national physical laboratory, Comput. Networks 1 (1977).
[37] A. Giessler, J. Haenle, A. Koenig and E. Pade, Packet networks with deadlock-free buffer allocation – An investigation by simulation, Comput. Networks 2 (1978) 191–208.
[38] D. Davies, The control of congestion in packet switching networks, IEEE Trans. Comm. COM-23 (1975) 546–550.
[39] J.W. Wong and M.S. Unsoy, Analysis of flow control in switched data networks, proc. IFIP Congress 77 (1977) pp. 315–320.
[40] M.S. Unsoy, Credit-oriented congestion control in two-level hierarchical packet switching networks, Ph.D. Thesis, University of Waterloo, 1980.
[41] S.S. Lam and M. Reiser, Congestion control of store-and-forward networks by input buffer limits – An analysis, IEEE Trans. Comm. COM-27 (1979) 127–134.
[42] S.S. Lam and Y.L. Lien, Congestion control of packet communication networks by input buffer limits – A simulation study, IEEE Trans. Comput. C-30 (1981) 733–742.
[43] S. Saad and M. Schwartz, Input buffer limiting mechanisms for congestion control, ICC '80 Conf. Rec. (1980) 23.1.1–23.1.5.
[44] F. Kamoun, A. Belguith and J.L. Grange, Congestion control with a buffer management strategy based on traffic priorities, Proc. 5th Internat. Conf. Comp. Comm. (1980) pp. 845–850.
[45] J.W. Wong, Queueing network modeling of computer communication networks, ACM Comput. Surveys 10 (1978) 343–352.
[46] M. Gerla and L. Kleinrock, On the topological design of distributed computer networks, IEEE Trans. Comm. COM-25 (1977) 48–60.
[47] M. Gerla and L. Kleinrock, Flow control: A comparative survey, IEEE Trans. Comm. COM-28 (1980) 553–574.

Chapter 6
Network and Internetwork Communication Services

6.1. VIRTUAL CIRCUIT AND DATAGRAM SERVICES

We consider peer protocols in the network layer or internetwork layer that provide packet-transport services. (See Figures 1-24 to 1-26.) The end users may be attached to the same network or to different networks.

As discussed in Section 1.5.2, a packet-transport protocol may provide a virtual circuit or a datagram service. A virtual circuit service is provided by networks that support the X.25 network access protocol. For a description of X.25, see the articles by Rybczynski et al. [RYBC 76, RYBC 80a, RYBC 80b]; we reprint [RYBC 80a] below. Folts described a datagram service and a fast select capability for the X.25 virtual circuit service that were later added to the X.25 standard [FOLT 80]. A detailed X.25 specification appeared in [CCIT 80].

The DOD Internet Protocol (IP) standard is probably the most widely used protocol that provides a datagram service [POST 80a, POST 81]. Protocol software to implement an IP-to-X.25-interface for the CSNET was described in [COME 83].

6.2. INTERNETWORKING ISSUES

Sunshine [SUNS 77], and Cerf and Kirstein [CERF 78] provided excellent tutorials on the issues and problems of interconnecting different networks. ([CERF 78] is reprinted below.) The specific issue of fragmentation is covered in detail in an article by Shoch [SHOC 79]. The interrelated issues of naming, addressing and routing were also treated by Shoch [SHOC 78]. Both articles by Shoch are reprinted below. A specific implementation proposal to use 48-bit absolute addresses was made by Dalal and Printis [DALA 81]. Sunshine discussed some difficult problems in designing, naming and addressing techniques for multi-network systems [SUNS 82].

6.3. INTERNETWORKING APPROACHES

Excellent tutorials on internetworking approaches can be found in the article of Cerf and Kirstein [CERF 78], reprinted below, and one by Postel [POST 80c]. The two main internetworking approaches that have been implemented were introduced in Section 1.5.3. (See Figures 1-25 and 1-26.) The encapsulation approach was adopted in the DARPA Internet Protocol [POST 80a, POST 81], and in Xerox's Pup internetwork architecture [BOGG 80]. ([POST 81] is reprinted below.) See also the article of Shoch, Cohen and Taft [SHOC 81] on the concept of mutual encapsulation. A draft standard of the ISO Internetwork Protocol can be found in [ISO 84].

The common network access interface approach is the basis of public data networks that implement X.25/X.75 protocols. Descriptions of X.75 implementations can be found in [WEIR 80, RYBC 80c, BLEV 80, UNSO 81]. The article by Unsoy and Shanahan describing an implementation of the X.75 interface between Datapac and Transpac is reprinted below.

6.4. THE DESIGN OF HOST-TO-HOST PROTOCOLS

Host-to-host protocols that provide a reliable transport service between user processes in host computers were of significant interest dating back to the early days of ARPANET. DARPA's

Transmission Control Protocol (TCP) is probably the best known example around. Cerf and Kahn [CERF 74] described the early proposal that led to the current TCP [POST 80b]. Garlick et al. [GARL 77] described various issues and problems in the design and implementation of host-to-host protocols. Both [CERF 74] and [GARL 77] are reprinted below.

A specific problem that makes host-to-host protocols difficult to design is the many different types of errors that they must deal with. A packet-switching network not only will damage or lose packets, but it may also duplicate packets and deliver them out of order. What is worse is that a packet may reside in the network for a random and indefinite amount of time before getting to its destination. Such behavior makes the use of sequence numbers to uniquely identify packets a very difficult design problem. Discussions of these issues and some solutions can be found in the articles by Tomlinson [TOML 75], Dalal [DALA 75], and Sunshine and Dalal [SUNS 78]. This last article is reprinted below.

A slightly different approach to solve the above problem is to introduce mechanisms in the packet-switching network to enforce bounds on packet lifetimes [SLOA 83]. Given bounded packet lifetimes, the host-to-host protocols can be made simpler [WATS 81]. In fact, it is obvious from our work on protocol modeling and verification [SHAN 82, SHAN 83] that it is extremely difficult, if at all possible, to design a correct host-to-host protocol without bounded packet lifetimes.

6.5. SECURITY KEY DISTRIBUTION PROTOCOLS

Network security is a vast subject much of which is beyond the scope of this text. But protocols for key distribution and for obtaining current authentication of communicants are important constituents of any networking protocol hierarchy for secure communications (either one-way or interactive). Such protocols are needed whether conventional or public-key encryption algorithms are employed. We reprint below the article by Needham and Schroeder [NEED 78] on this topic. Improvements to the protocols of Needham and Schroeder were published by Denning and Sacco [DENN 81] and by Bauer et al. [BAUE 83]. See also the survey article by Denning [DENN 83]. Survey articles on the general subject of network security can be found in [POPE 79, VOYD 83].

References

[BAUE 83] Bauer, R. K., T. A. Berson and R. J. Feiertag, "A Key Distribution Protocol using Event Markers," *ACM Trans. on Computer* Systems, Vol. 1, No. 3, August 1983, pp. 249-255.

[BLEV 80] Blevanus, J. and G. Mitaut, "The Use of X.75 in the Transpac International Gateway," *Proc. of the 5th ICCC*, Atlanta, October 1980, pp. 723-728.

[BOGG 80] Boggs, D. R., J. F. Shoch, E. A. Taft, and R. M. Metcalfe, "Pup: An Internetwork Architecture," *IEEE Trans. on Commun.* 28, 4, April 1980, pp. 612-623.

[CCIT 80] CCITT, "Draft Revised Recommendation X.25," *Computer Communication Review*, Vol. 10, Nos. 1 & 2, ACM, 1980, pp. 56-129.

*[CERF 74] Cerf, V. and R. Kahn, "A Protocol for Packet Network Intercommunication," *IEEE Trans. on Comm.*, Vol. COM-22, No. 5, May 1974, pp. 637-648.

*[CERF 78] Cerf, V. G. and P. T. Kirstein, "Issues in Packet-Network Interconnection," *Proc. IEEE,* Vol. 66, November 1978, pp. 1386-1408.

[COME 83] Comer, D. and J. T. Korb, "CSNET Protocol Software: The IP-to-X.25 Interface," *Proc. SIGCOMM '83 Symposium*, University of Texas at Austin, March 1983, pp. 154-159.

[DALA 75] Dalal, Y. K., "More on Selecting Sequence Numbers," *Proceedings of the ACM SIGCOMM/SIGOPS Interprocess Communications Workshop*, March 24-25, pp. 25-33, 1975.

[DALA 81] Dalal, Y. K. and R. S. Printis, "48-bit Internet and Ethernet Host Numbers," *Proc. 7th Data Communications Symp.*, Mexico City, October 1981, pp. 240-245.

[DENN 81] Denning, D. E. and M. S. Sacco, "Timestamps in Key Distribution Protocols," *Commun. ACM*, Vol. 24, No. 8, August 1981, pp. 533-536.

[DENN 83] Denning, D. E., "Protecting Public Keys and Signature Keys," Computer, Vol. 16, No. 2, February 1983, pp. 27-35.

[FOLT 80] Folts, H. C., "X.25 Transaction-Oriented Features--Datagram and Fast Select," *IEEE Trans. Commun.*, Vol. COM-28, April 1980, pp. 496-500.

*[GARL 77] Garlick, L. L., R. Rom and J. Postel, "Issues in Reliable Host-to-Host Protocols," *Proc. 5th Data Comm. Symp.*, Snowbird, Utah, September 1977.

[ISO 84] ISO/TC97/SC6, "Information Processing Systems--Data Communications--Protocol for Providing the Connectionless Network Service," Draft Proposal ISO/DP8473; in *Computer Communication Review*, Vol. 14, No. 1, April 1984.

*[NEED 78] Needham, R. M. and M. D. Schroeder, "Using Encryption for Authentication in Large Networks of Computers," *Commun. ACM*, Vol. 21, No. 12, December 1978, pp. 993-999.

[POPE 79] Popek, G. J. and C. S. Kline, "Encryption and Secure Computer Networks," *ACM Comput. Surv.*, Vol. 11, No. 4, December 1979, pp. 331-335.

[POST 80a] Postel, J. (ed.), "DOD Standard Internet Protocol," Defense Advanced Research Projects Agency, Information Processing Techniques Office, RFC 760, IEN 128, January 1980; in *ACM Computer Communication Review*, Vol. 10, No. 4, October 1980, pp. 12-51.

[POST 80b] Postel, J. (ed.), "DOD Standard Transmission Control Protocol," Defense Advanced Research Projects Agency, Information Processing Techniques Office, RFC 761, IEN 129, January 1980; in *ACM Computer Communication Review*, Vol. 10, No. 4, October 1980, pp. 52-132.

[POST 80c] Postel, J., "Internetwork Protocol Approaches," *IEEE Trans. on Commun.* 28, (4) April 1980, pp. 604-611.

*[POST 81] Postel, J., C. A. Sunshine, and D. Cohen, "The ARPA Internet Protocol," *Computer Networks*, 5, (4) July 1981, pp. 261-271.

[RYBC 76] Rybczynski, A., et al., "A New Communication Protocol for Accessing Data Networks - The International Packet-Mode Interface," AFIPS National Computer Conference, N.Y., June 1976.

*[RYBC 80a] Rybczynski, A., "X.25 Interface and

End-to-End Virtual Circuit Service Characteristics," *IEEE Trans. Commun.*, Vol. COM-28, April 1980, pp. 500-510.

[RYBC 80b] Rybczynski, A. and J. Palframan, "A Common X.25 Interface to Public Data Networks," *Computer Networks* 4, 1980, pp. 97-110.

[RYBC 80c] Rybczynski, A., J. Palframan, and A. Thomas, "Design of the Datapac X.75 Internetworking Capability," *Proc. 5th Int. Conf. on Computer Communication*, October 1980, pp. 735-740.

[SHAN 82] Shankar, A. U. and S. S. Lam, "On Time-Dependent Communication Protocols and their Projections," *Proc. 2nd Int. Workshop on Protocol Specification, Testing and Verification*, Idyllwild, Calif., North-Holland Publishing Co., Amsterdam, 1982.

[SHAN 83] Shankar, A. U. and S. S. Lam, "An HDLC Protocol Specification and its Verification using Image Protocols," *ACM Trans. on Computer* Systems, November 1983.

*[SHOC 78] Shoch, J. F., "Inter-Network Naming, Addressing, and Routing," *Proc. 17th IEEE Computer Society Int. Conf.*, September 1978, pp. 72-79.

*[SHOC 79] Shoch, J., "Packet Fragmentation in Inter-Network Protocols," *Computer Networks*, Vol. 3, No. 1, February 1979.

[SHOC 81] Shoch, J. F., D. Cohen, and E. A. Taft, "Mutual Encapsulation of Internetwork Protocols," *Computer Networks* 5, (4), July 1981, pp. 287-301.

[SLOA 83] Sloan, Lansing, "Mechanisms that Enforce Bounds on Packet Lifetimes," ACM SIGCOMM '83 Symposium, University of Texas at Austin, March 1983; in *ACM Trans. on Computer Systems*, November 1983.

[SUNS 77] Sunshine, C. A., "Interconnection of Computer Networks," *Computer Networks* 1, (3), January 1977, pp. 175-195.

*[SUNS 78] Sunshine, C., and Y. Dalal, "Connection Management in Transport Protocols," *Computer* Networks, Vol. 2, No. 6, December 1978, pp. 454-473.

[SUNS 82] Sunshine, C. A., "Addressing Problems in Multi-Network Systems," *Proc. INFOCOM '82*, IEEE Computer Society Press, Silver Spring, Md., 1982, pp. 12-18.

[TOML 75] Tomlinson, R. S., "Selecting Sequence Numbers," *Proceedings of the ACM SIGCOMM/SIGOPS Interprocess Communications Workshop*, March 24-25, pp. 11-23, 1975.

*[UNSO 81] Unsoy, M. S. and T. Shanahan, "X.75 Internetworking of Datapac and Telenet," *Proc. 7th Data Communication Symp.*, Mexico City, October 1981, pp. 232-239.

[VOYD 83] Voydock, V. L. and S. T. Kent, "Security Mechanisms in High-level Network Protocols," *ACM Computing Surveys*, Vol. 15, No. 2, June 1983, pp. 135-171.

[WATS 81] Watson, R. W., "Timer-Based Mechanisms in Reliable Transport Protocol Connection," *Computer Networks*, Vol. 5, No. 1, February 1981, pp. 47-56.

[WEIR 80] Weir, D. F., J. B. Holmblad, and A. C. Rothberg, "An X.75 Based Network Architecture," *Proc. 5th Int. Conf. on Computer* Communication, October 1980, pp. 741-750.

(* article reprinted below.)

Reprinted from *IEEE Transactions on Communications,* Volume COM-28, Number 4, April 1980, pages 500-510.

X.25 Interface and End–to–End Virtual Circuit Service Characteristics

ANTONY RYBCZYNSKI, MEMBER, IEEE

(Invited Paper)

***Abstract*—Public packet switching networks around the world use CCITT Recommendation X.25, which is the standard device-independent interface between packet networks and user devices operating in the packet-mode. Since its development in 1976 and with four years of network operational experience, the X.25 interface specification has reached a high level of maturity. A revised version of X.25 has been approved by CCITT Study Group VII at its meeting in February 1980. The revised X.25 specification is more complete than its predecessor, eliminates a number of ambiguous areas which lead to network implementation differences, and has been enhanced by the addition of new capabilities both to the X.25 interface and to the end-to-end service.**

This paper presents a consolidated view of the end-to-end characteristics of the virtual-circuit-based services accessible through the X.25 interface. It then discusses the characteristics of the revised X.25 interface, with emphasis on areas that have been addressed in the revised Recommendation.

The revised Recommendation leads the way to greater commonality among network implementations. The increased functionality of the end-to-end virtual-circuit services has impact on the relationship of X.25 to system architectures being discussed by international standards bodies.

Manuscript received May 7, 1979; revised December 18, 1979.

The author is with the Computer Communications Group, Trans-Canada Telephone System, Ottawa, Ont., Canada.

I. INTRODUCTION AND GENERAL DESCRIPTION

A. Introduction

THE 1970's heralded the beginning of the development of public networks either in the form of experimental networks (France: RCP, U.K.: EPSS, Japan: DDX) or commercial networks (Canada: Datapac, U.S.A.: Telenet). The basis of all of these networks was the belief that packet-switching was an appropriate technology for public data networks (PDN's). However, in their embryonic stages, the designs of each of these networks incorporated substantially different terminal access procedures for both host computers and slow speed character terminals. It was recognized that the commercial viability of these networks hinged largely on the development and adoption of standard access protocols. These standards would facilitate the connection of varying types of data terminal equipments (DTE's) to the various public networks being developed, as well as facilitate international internetworking. Without these standards, users would almost definitely not be benefiting from the establishment of public data networks on a worldwide basis.

The International Telegraph and Telephone Consultative Committee (CCITT), a permanent organ of the International Telecommunications Union, is responsible for establishing "Recommendations" applicable to various aspects of international communications, including public data networks. A number of recommendations related to PDN services have been approved within the last four years, most notably X.25 [1]-[3].

The year 1980 finds us with PDN's offering packet-mode services being available in the U.S.A., Canada, the U.K., France, and Japan and on the verge of being established in a large number of other countries [4]. All of these networks are based on the support of the aforementioned CCITT Recommendations. Furthermore, international services have already been established among a number of these countries. In order to meet the market need of gaining access to X.25 services, a number of mainframe and terminal manufacturers have announced products supporting X.25.

CCITT Recommendation X.25 was first approved in March 1976. The last formal revision took place in 1977 with the addition of data link control procedures, which are compatible with the high-level data link control (HDLC) procedures standardized by the International Organization of Standardization (ISO). The next formal revision of X.25 will take place in the fall of 1980. This paper conveys the important enhancements to X.25 which have been agreed and are currently contained in the proposed text of the revised Recommendation [5].

B. General Description of the X.25 Interface

The X.25 interface between the DTE and the data circuit-terminating equipment (DCE) consists of three distinct levels of control procedures as illustrated in Fig. 1:

1) the physical level
2) the frame level, and
3) the packet level.

Each of these levels functions independently of the other levels, with the exception that failures at a level may affect the operation of higher levels.

The physical level specifies the use of a duplex, point-to-point synchronous circuit, thus providing a physical transmission path between the DTE and the network. It also specifies the use of the V.24 physical interface (i.e., the EIA RS-232-C standard) between the DTE and a data set or modem. Therefore, no changes to the interface hardware of the DTE are required. The physical level also specifies the use of Recommendation X.21 [6] although this capability is not yet widely available.

The frame level specifies the use of data link control procedures which are compatible with HDLC [7] and with the advanced data communications control procedure (ADCCP) standardized by the U.S. American National Standards Institute (ANSI). The frame level uses the principles of an ISO class of procedures for a point-to-point balanced system; in X.25, these procedures are referred to as the balanced link access procedures (LAPB). The use of this data link control procedure ensures that packets provided by the packet level and contained in HDLC information frames (see Fig. 2) are ac-

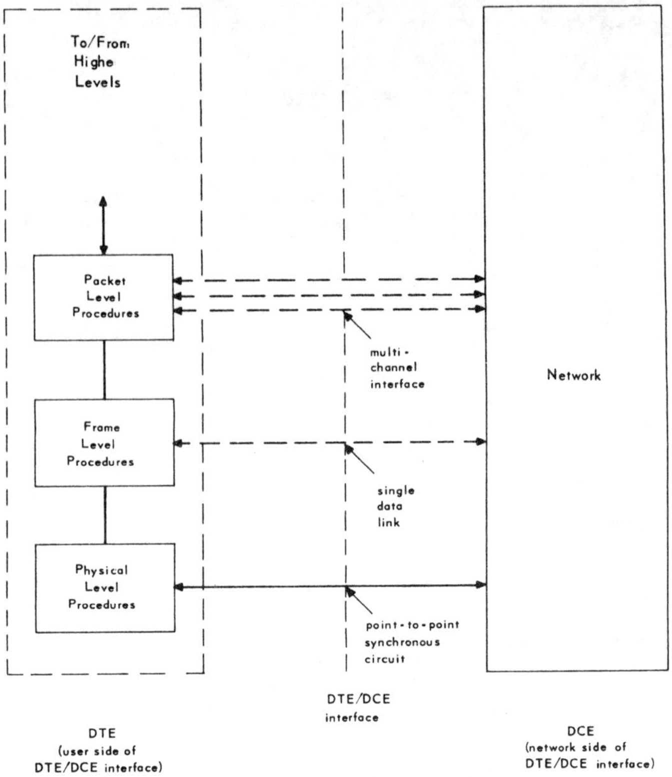

Fig. 1. Structure of the X.25 interface.

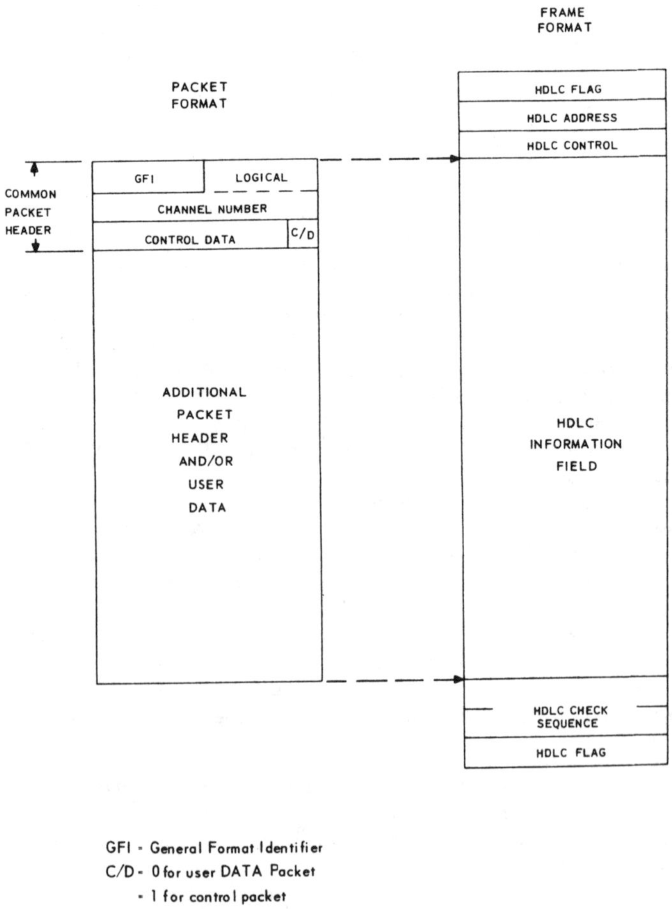

Fig. 2. General X.25 packet and frame formats.

curately exchanged between the DTE and the network. The functions performed by the frame level interface include:

1) the transfer of data in an efficient and timely fashion;

2) the synchronization of the link to ensure that the receiver is in step with the transmitter;

3) the detection of transmission errors and recovery from such errors; and

4) the identification and reporting of procedural errors to higher layers for recovery.

The major significance of the frame level is that it provides the packet level with an error-free, variable delay link between the DTE and the network.

The packet level is the highest level of the X.25 interface and specifies the manner in which control information and user data are structured into packets. The control information, including addressing information, is contained in the packet header field and allows the network to identify the DTE for which the packet is destined. It also allows a single physical circuit to support communications to numerous other DTE's concurrently.

The characteristics of the packet level are further described in Section III.

C. Network Services Available to X.25 DTE's

A distinction must be made between the X.25 interface and the services provided on a PDN operating in the packet-mode and accessed across this interface by the DTE. Recommendation X.25 defines procedures to be used across the interface between the packet-mode DTE and the common-carrier equipment, generally referred to as the DCE. The X.25 interface Recommendation provides access to the following services that may be provided on public data networks:

1) switched virtual circuits (SVC's), also called virtual calls;

2) permanent virtual circuits (PVC's); and

3) datagrams.

A virtual circuit (VC) is a bidirectional transparent, flow-controlled path between a pair of logical or physical ports. A switched virtual circuit is a temporary association between two DTE's and is initiated by a DTE signaling a call request to the network. A permanent virtual circuit is a permanent association existing between two DTE's, which is analogous to a point-to-point private line. Thus, it requires no call set-up or call clearing action by the DTE.

A datagram (DG) is a self-contained entity of data containing sufficient information to be routed to the destination DTE (independently of all other entities) without the need for a call to be established. At this time, the datagram service is not provided on any PDN's. This service is not within the scope of this paper (see, however, [8]).

The characteristics of virtual circuits are now presented.

II. X.25 END-TO-END VIRTUAL CIRCUIT SERVICE CHARACTERISTICS

A. Introduction

The virtual circuit service characteristics are currently specified in a nonsystematic way in various sections of Recommendation X.25. This section attempts to consolidate the specification of VC characteristics. The perspective for this discussion is a view of the DTE-to-DTE services provided by VC's rather than a view of the signaling at either of the two interfaces.

B. Establishment and Clearing of a Virtual Circuit

A switched virtual circuit is established when the call request issued by the calling DTE is accepted by the called DTE. A permanent virtual circuit is always established and therefore, no establishment procedures are required. The call request identifies the called and calling addresses and facilities requested for the call, and may include user data. The user data sent during the call establishment phase is available for use by the higher layers (e.g., system passwords).

During the call establishment phase, the calling DTE may request certain optional user facilities (e.g., reverse charging) to be associated with the VC. In some cases (e.g., throughput class) the called DTE may wish to alter the facility values requested by the caller. Thus, the VC service provides mechanisms for facility negotiations during call setup. Optional user facilities are discussed in Section IV.

If the call is refused by the called DTE, the DTE can signal the reason for call clearing to the calling DTE in a diagnostic code. If the call attempt fails for some other reason, a call progress signal is transmitted across the network indicating one of the causes specified in X.25 and given in Table I. As will be seen in the next section, the diagnostic code is also used by the network to provide extra information to the DTE when it has made a local interface procedure error. This latter use is a characteristic of the X.25 interface rather than of the virtual circuit itself.

Once the call has entered the data transfer phase, either DTE can clear the call using the diagnostic code to signal to the remote DTE the reason for the clearing. If the call is cleared by the network, it will signal this fact and indicate a call progress signal (Table I). When a call is cleared, data may be discarded by the network since the clear is not sequenced in respect to user data. All data generated by the DTE before initiation of a clear procedure will either be delivered to the remote DTE before completion of the clearing procedure at the remote DTE/DCE interface, or be discarded by the network. When a DTE initiates a clear, all data which were generated by the remote DTE before it has received the corresponding indication will be either delivered to the initiating DTE before the clear procedure is completed locally, or discarded by the network.

C. Data Transfer

In the data transfer phase, user data which are conveyed in DATA and INTERRUPT packets are passed transparently through the network. DTE's wishing universal operation on all networks should transmit all packets with data fields containing only an integral number of octets.

Virtual circuit flow control is a mechanism provided to ensure that the transmitting DTE does not generate data at a rate that is faster (on average) than that which the receiving

TABLE I
CLEARING CALL PROGRESS SIGNALS

Call Progress Signal	Explanation
DTE Originated	Called DTE has refused the call or remote DTE has cleared it.
Number busy	The called DTE is engaged in other calls and cannot accept the incoming call.
Out of order	The remote number is out of order. (X.25 Physical and/or Frame levels not in operation).
Remote procedure error	An X.25 procedure error has occurred at the remote DTE/DCE interface.
Reverse charging acceptance not subscribed*	Network has blocked the call because the called DTE does not accept reverse charged calls.
Incompatible destination	The remote DTE/DCE interface does not support a function used or facility requested.
Fast select acceptance not subscribed*	The network has blocked the call because the called DTE does not support fast select calls.
Invalid facility request	Facility request invalid (e.g., a request for a facility which has not been subscribed to or is not available in the local network).
Access barred	The calling DTE is not permitted the connection to the called DTE. (e.g., incompatible closed user group).
Local procedure error	A procedure error is detected at the local DTE/DCE interfaces. (e.g., incorrect format, expiration of a time-out).
Network congestion	Temporary network congestion or a temporary fault condition has occurred within the network.
Not obtainable	The called DTE address does not correspond to any assigned address.
RPOA Out of Order*	The RPOA nominated by the calling DTE is unable to forward the call.

* received only if the corresponding facility is requested by the caller.

DTE can accept. This is achieved by the receiving DTE controlling the rate at which it accepts DATA packets across the DTE/DCE interface, noting that there is an upper limit on the number of DATA packets which may be in the network on a virtual circuit. Thus, flow control has end-to-end significance in that back pressure exerted by a receiving DTE is reflected back to the sending DTE.

A considerable debate has taken place in the past on whether the DTE or the network should determine the maximum number of DATA packets which may be in the network on a virtual circuit. On the one hand, there is a need for the network to assign resources to the VC based on information available to it (e.g., call routing) and on performance, specifically throughput, characteristics associated with the service. In this case, the network determines the maximum number of DATA packets that can be on a VC and the DTE need not be concerned with this aspect. On the other hand, there is a need to allow DTE's to select the maximum number of DATA packets that can be on a VC and thus be able to ascertain whether certain DATA packets have been delivered to the remote DTE. This information can be used in conjunction with a higher level DTE-to-DTE error control protocol. With the addition of the delivery confirmation procedure in X.25, both objectives can be met simultaneously.

It has been agreed that DTE-to-DTE acknowledgment of delivery be available as a standard characteristic of X.25 virtual circuits. Specifically, if a DTE wishes to receive end-to-end acknowledgment for data it is transmitting across the X.25 interface, it uses an indicator called the delivery confirmation, or *D* bit, contained in the header of DATA packets. The *D* bit is always associated with the last octet in the DATA packet in which it is set by the DTE; this relationship is preserved by the network on an end-to-end basis even when the maximum packet lengths used at the DTE/DCE interfaces at each end of a VC are not the same. The acknowledgment is signaled via the packet receive sequence number $P(R)$, discussed in Section III.

Since the network may perform packet-length conversion, X.25 defines a "complete packet sequence" which is a sequence of DATA packets which may be combined by the network. The only DATA packets which can be combined with subsequent DATA packets are those that are full, have the *D* bit set to zero and have an indication set by the sending DTE that more data is to follow; the *D* bit has priority over the more data indication in packet combination so that a DATA packet with the *D* bit set to one is never combined with a subsequent packet. The more data indication may only be set by the DTE in full DATA packets or in partially full DATA packets which also have the *D* bit set to one. A sequence of DATA packets each carrying a more data indication except fo the last one will be delivered as an equivalent sequence of DATA packets.

Two independent mechanisms are provided to transfer user control information between a pair of DTE's outside the normal flow of data on a VC. The first mechanism transfers user control data within the normal flow control and sequencing procedures on a virtual circuit. This is called the data qualifier procedure and applies to "complete packet sequences."

The second mechanism bypasses the normal DATA packet transmission sequence and provides an out of band (non-sequenced) signaling channel on VC's. The INTERRUPT packet, which is used in this case, may contain one octet of user data and is always delivered at or before the point in the stream of DATA packets at which it was generated, even when DATA packets are being flow controlled.

The maximum attainable throughput on virtual circuits carried at the DTE/DCE interface may vary due to the statistical sharing of transmission and switch resources and is constrained by:

1) the access line speed, local flow control parameters, and traffic on other calls at the local DTE/DCE interface;

2) the access line speed, local flow control parameters, and traffic on other calls at the remote DTE/DCE interface; and

3) the maximum throughput achievable through the network independent of access line characteristics. This limit may differ for national and varying types of international calls.

The above throughput will generally not be reached unless a) the access data links of both ends of the VC are traffic engineered properly, b) the receiving DTE is not flow controlling the DCE, c) the transmitting DTE is sending DATA packets which have the maximum data field length, and d) use of the *D* bit does not constrain the throughput.

TABLE II
RESETTING CALL PROGRESS SIGNALS

Call Progress Signal	Explanation
DTE Originated	Remote DTE reset the VC
Out of order (PVC only)	The remote DTE is out of order (e.g., X.25 Physical and/or Frame levels not in operation).
Remote procedure error	The call is cleared because of a procedure error at the remote DTE/DCE interface.
Local procedure error	A procedure error is detected at the local DTE/DCE interfaces. (e.g., incorrect format, expiration of a time-out).
Network congestion	Temporary network congestion or temporary fault condition has occurred within the network.
Remote DTE operational (PVC only)	Remote DTE/DCE interface is ready to resume normal operation after a temporary failure or out of order condition.
Network operational (PVC only)	Network is ready to resume normal operation after a temporary failure or congestion.
Incompatible destination	The remote DTE/DCE interface does not support a function used.

D. Error Recovery

The reset procedure is used to reinitialize the virtual circuit and in so doing removes in each direction all user data which may be in the network. When the reset is initiated by the DTE, it may convey to the remote DTE the reason for the resetting via a diagnostic code. If it is a network-generated reset, the reason is conveyed to both DTE's. Table II lists call progress signals associated with resetting in X.25.

All data generated by a DTE before initiation of a reset will either be delivered to the remote DTE before the corresponding indicator, or discarded by the network; all data generated after completion of a reset procedure at the local interface will be delivered after completion of the corresponding reset procedure at the remote interface. When a DTE initiates a reset procedure, all data which was generated by the remote DTE before its receipt of the corresponding indication are either delivered to the initiating DTE before the procedure is completed locally, or discarded by the network. Multiple and simultaneous resets are handled at the local interface as defined by the procedures for single resets.

The maximum number of packets which may be discarded when the clearing or resetting procedure has been invoked is a function of network end-to-end delay and network resources assigned in conjunction with the provided throughput. The maximum number of packets with the *D* bit set is a parameter of an X.25 interface (i.e., the local DTE transmit window size discussed in Section III-D).

TABLE III
X.25 PACKET FORMATS

Packet Type	Common*	Cause	Diagnostic	Addresses and Address Length	Facilities and Facility Length	Data
CALL REQUEST	REQ	-	-	REQ	REQ	OPT (16)
CALL CONNECTED	REQ	-	-	OPT	OPT	-
DATA	REQ			-	-	OPT (120)
INTERRUPT	REQ	-	-	-	-	REQ(1)
RR/RNR	REQ	-	-	-	-	-
RESET/CLEAR RESTART REQUEST	REQ	REQ	OPT	-	-	-
INTERRUPT/ RESET/CLEAR/ RESTART CONFIRMATION	REQ	-	-	-	-	-

REQ: required
REQ (X): required, of maximum length X octets
OPT: optional (only if all subsequent optional fields are not present)
OPT (X): optional, of maximum length X octets
- : not applicable
* Three octet Common Packet Header Field

III. X. 25 PACKET LEVEL INTERFACE CHARACTERISTICS

A. Introduction

Recommendation X.25 specifies the procedures to be used by DTE's in establishing, maintaining and clearing virtual circuits. This section now discusses these packet level interface procedures (see, also, [9]).

Packet formats for the various types of packets are summarized in Table III.

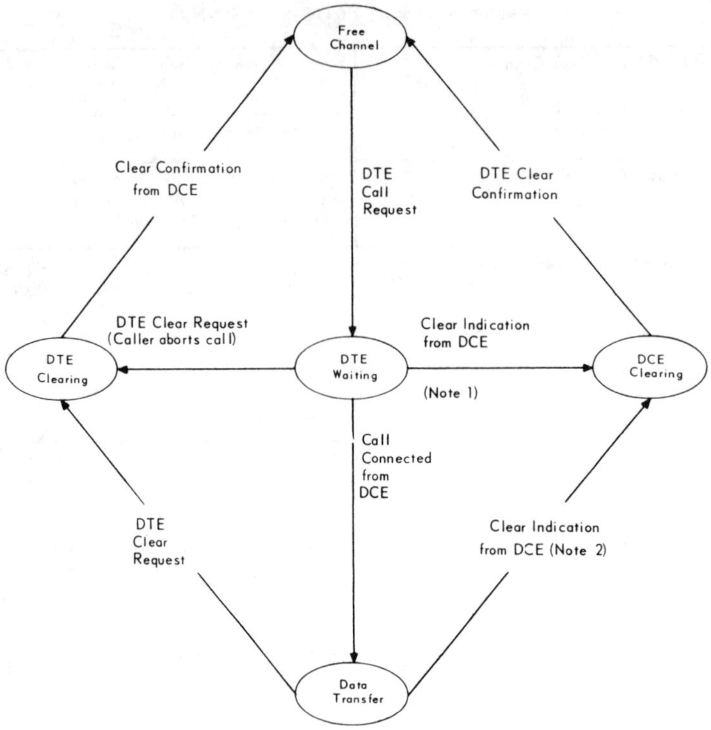

Note 1: Either called DTE refused call or call attempt has failed *

Note 2: Either called DTE cleared down call or call cleared due to network failure *

* : Reason signalled as call progress signal

Fig. 3. Illustration of call establishment and clearing at the calling DTE/DCE interface.

B. Multiplexing at the X.25 Interface

In order to allow a DTE to establish concurrent virtual circuits with a number of DTE's over a single physical access circuit, the X.25 packet level employs packet-interleaved statistical multiplexing. This multiplexing technique is used to exploit the fact that a typical virtual circuit to a remote DTE may actually be carrying data for only a small percentage of the time. Each packet contains a logical channel number which identifies the packet with a switched or permanent virtual circuit for both directions of transmission.

The range of logical channel numbers that can be used for virtual circuits is established at subscription time by agreement between the DTE and the network. If the DTE can only support a single VC, then logical channel number one will be used. If both PVC's and SVC's are used, then individual PVC's are statically assigned logical channel numbers in a range starting from number one, while logical channels for calls are assigned a range above this. Logical channel numbers for SVC's are dynamically assigned during call establishment and identify all packets (i.e., control and data) associated with the VC. The logical channel numbers are only significant at a particular DTE/DCE interface.

Every packet transferred across an X.25 DTE/DCE interface consists of a three-octet common packet header field as shown in Fig. 2.

C. Establishing and Clearing a Virtual Circuit

A signaling method is provided to allow a DTE to establish switched virtual circuits to other DTE's using logical channel numbers at each end to locally designate these switched virtual circuits.

A DTE initiates a call by sending a CALL REQUEST packet (Fig. 3) to the network. The CALL REQUEST packet includes the logical channel number chosen by the DTE to be used to identify all packets associated with the call. It also includes the network address of the called DTE. A facility field is present only when the DTE wishes to request an optional user facility requiring some indication at call setup. Reverse charging is an example of such a facility. User data may follow the facility field and may contain up to a maximum of 16 octets.

The calling DTE will receive a CALL CONNECTED packet as a response indicating that the called DTE has accepted the call. (Fig. 3.)

If the call is refused by the called DTE, or if the attempt fails, the calling DTE will receive a CLEAR INDICATION indicating the appropriate call progress signal, and a one-octet diagnostic field, generated by the DTE and by the network in the former and latter cases, respectively.

Call clearing, once the call enters the data phase, may be initiated by either DTE (or by the network in case of failure).

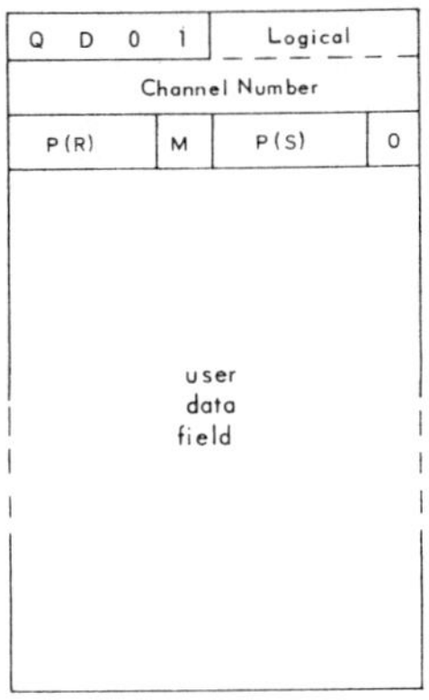

Q - Data Qualifier Bit
D - Delivery Confirmation Bit
M - More Data Bit
P(S) - Packet send sequence Number
P(R) - Packet receive sequence Number

Fig. 4. DATA packet format.

In any event, the logical channel number can be used again for another call when the clearing procedure is completed, normally by the transfer of a CLEAR CONFIRMATION packet.

D. Data Transfer

DATA packets, illustrated in Fig. 4, can only be transferred across a logical channel after the virtual circuit has been established and if flow control constraints are not violated.

P(S) is the packet send sequence number of the packet. Only DATA packets are numbered, the numbering normally being performed modulo 8. The maximum number of sequentially numbered DATA packets that the DTE (or DCE) may be authorized to transmit, without further authorization from the network (or DTE), may never exceed seven. The actual maximum value, called the window size *W*, is set for the logical channel either at subscription time or at call setup time [using the facility described in Section IV-B2)]. The default value for *W* is two.

Each DATA packet also carries a packet receive sequence number, *P(R)*, which authorizes the transmission of *W* DATA packets on this logical channel starting with a send sequence number equal to the value of *P(R)*. If the DTE or the network wishes to authorize the transmission of one or more DATA packets across the interface, but there is no data flow on a given logical channel in the reverse direction on which to piggy-back this information, it can transmit a RECEIVE READY (RR) packet, If, on the other hand, the DTE or the network wishes to confirm the acceptance of a DATA packet with the *D* bit set to one, but does not wish to authorize the transmission of any more data, it can transmit a RECEIVE NOT READY (RNR) packet. Flow control based on the conveyance of *P(R)* numbers across a logical channel ensures that a sending DTE does not transmit data at an average rate which is greater than that at which the receiving DTE can accept that data.

The data field of a DATA packet may be any length up to some maximum value. The latter may be established independently at each end of a virtual circuit. Every network will support a maximum value of 128 octets.

When the delivery confirmation or *D* bit is set to zero, the *P(R)* number is used to locally convey flow control information. When the *D* bit in Fig. 4 is used, the corresponding *P(R)* is used to convey delivery confirmation information and therefore has DTE-to-DTE significance.

In order to allow two communicating DTE's to each operate at their locally selected packet sizes, the user may indicate, in a full DATA packet, or any DATA packet with the *D* bit set to one, that there is a logical continuation of his data in the next DATA packet on a particular logical channel. This is done with the more data "*M*" bit contained in the DATA packet header as indicated in Fig. 4. Only a full DATA packet may have a more data indication since a partially full packet is treated as if it had the *M* bit off.

The procedures used in conjunction with the data qualifier procedure are identical to those that apply to DATA packets. The format used in this procedure is identical to that of the DATA transfer packet except that the "*Q*" bit is set in the DATA packet header (see Fig. 4).

INTERRUPT packets, on the other hand, may be transmitted across the DTE/DCE interface even when DATA packets are being flow controlled. They may contain neither send nor receive sequence numbers. Only one unconfirmed INTERRUPT may be outstanding at a given time.

E. Error Recovery

1) *Reset Procedure*: The reset procedure is used to reinitialize the flow control procedure on a given logical channel to the state it was in when the virtual circuit was established (i.e., all sequence numbers equal to zero and no data in transit). To reach this state, all DATA and INTERRUPT packets which may be in transit at the time of resetting are discarded. RESET REQUEST and CONFIRMATION packets are used in the reset procedure.

2) *Restart Procedure*: The restart procedure provides a mechanism to recover from major failures. The issuance of a RESTART REQUEST packet is equivalent to sending a CLEAR REQUEST on all logical channels for switched virtual circuits and a RESET REQUEST on all logical channels for permanent virtual circuits. Thus, the restarting procedure will bring the user/network interface to the state it was in when service was initiated.

3) *Error Handling*: Recommendation X.25 (1976) layed the groundwork for further study on how packet level errors were to be handled at the X.25 interface. The following principles were established:

a) procedural errors during call establishment and clearing are reported to the DTE by clearing the call;

b) procedural errors during the data transfer phase are reported to the DTE by resetting the VC;

c) a diagnostic field is included in the reset packet to provide additional information to the DTE;

d) timers are essential in resolving some deadlock conditions;

e) some DTE procedural errors are a result of the DTE and DCE not being aligned as to the subscription options provided at the interface; and

f) rudimentary error tables define the action of the

DCE on receiving various packet types in every various states of the interface.

Several important error conditions were still not covered. Consequently, a major effort was expended to expand the error tables in X.25, to reach agreement on time-out strategies, and to increase the amount of information provided to DTE's via diagnostic codes and via a newly defined DIAGNOSTIC packet mechanism. These will now be briefly discussed.

Error tables were enhanced in two ways. Firstly, the number of error conditions handled was increased significantly. Secondly, the information content was increased by indicating not only the action taken by the DCE on detecting an error condition but also the state which the DCE enters.

A number of special error cases (e.g., packet on unassigned logical channel) have been identified in X.25 for which it is inappropriate to inform a DTE of a procedural error by resetting or clearing the logical channel. In this case it has been agreed that a DIAGNOSTIC packet be used. The DIAGNOSTIC packet is nonprocedural in nature and solely for DTE logging. The DIAGNOSTIC packet identifies the logical channel number on which an error condition has been detected, and includes a diagnostic code.

Two areas associated with time-outs have been addressed. The first area relates to the length of time the DTE has to respond to an incoming call. On one hand, the network wishes to minimize its resources. On the other hand, short time-out values are not reasonable due to the interaction between calls on a single interface, and between the packet and frame levels, and due to user processing within higher layers. A minimum value of three minutes has been agreed.

The second area relates to the action of the DCE when no confirmation has been received to an indication packet (i.e., during resetting, clearing and restarting). In order to avoid long looping conditions, it has been agreed that the DCE will not retransmit indication packets. Instead, the DCE will take the following actions.

1) On expiry of a 60-second timer after issuing a RESET INDICATION, the DCE will clear the call, indicating the reason for clearing via the diagnostic code, and call progress signal. On a PVC, a DIAGNOSTIC packet is sent.

2) On expiry of a 60-second timer after issuing a CLEAR INDICATION, the DCE will issue a DIAGNOSTIC packet and should eventually assume the interface has entered the ready state. In this state, the DCE does not ignore any packets sent by the DTE.

3) On expiry of a 60-second timer after a RESTART INDICATION has been issued, the DCE will issue a DIAGNOSTIC packet. The DCE considers this condition serious and will stay in this state indefinitely.

Diagnostic codes have been defined for reset, clear, and restart packets. The contents of the diagnostic code field provide nonprocedural information which do not alter the meaning of the call progress signal also provided. A DTE is not required to undertake any action on the content of the diagnostic code field. However, the DTE is advised to log the diagnostic to facilitate the correction of the problem.

Network-generated diagnostic codes are hierarchical. That is, for any specific diagnostic code there is always a code which is of a more general nature. The specific codes provide information allowing the DTE implementor to quickly diagnose problems. The more general codes are used when relatively uncommon or unanticipated problems occur. To accelerate trouble resolution, the X.25 error tables have been further enhanced by indicating the diagnostic code generated under each error condition.

F. Interrelationship Between Levels

Changes of the operational states of the physical and frame levels of the DTE/DCE interface do not implicitly change the state of each logical channel at the packet level; such changes when they occur are explicitly indicated by the use of packet level restart, clear, or reset procedures as appropriate.

A failure at the physical and/or frame levels is defined as a condition in which the DCE cannot transmit and receive any frames because of abnormal conditions caused by, for instance, a line fault between the DTE and the DCE. When a failure is detected, the DCE will transmit to the remote end a reset indicating out of order for a permanent virtual circuit and a clear indicating out of order for an existing virtual call. During the failure, the DCE will clear any incoming virtual calls.

When the failure is recovered, the DCE will send a RESTART INDICATION packet indicating network operational to the local DTE; this will result in a reset indicating remote DTE operational to be transmitted to the remote end of each permanent virtual circuit.

IV. OPTIONAL USER FACILITIES

A. Introduction

CCITT Recommendation X.2 defines the availability of various optional user facilities as being universally available or only available in some countries. Recommendation X.25 defines the interface procedures associated with all optional user facilities, irrespective of their availability.

This section describes only those optional user facilities which are proposed to be universally available.

B. Optional User Facilities

1) *Closed User Group Facility*: Closed user group is an optional user facility agreed to for a period of time between the administration and a group of users. This facility permits the users of the group to communicate with each other, but precludes communication with all other users. A DTE may belong to more than one closed user group.

The calling DTE specifies the closed user group selected for a virtual call using the optional user facility parameters in the CALL REQUEST packet. The closed user group selected for a call is indicated to a called DTE using the optional user facility parameters in the INCOMING CALL packet.

2) *Flow Control Parameter Selection*: Flow control parameter selection is an optional user facility agreed to for a period of time which can be used by a DTE for its logical channels. The flow control parameters considered are the packet and window sizes for each logical channel at the DTE/DCE interface for each direction of data transmission.

When the DTE has subscribed to the facility, it may, in a CALL REQUEST packet, separately request packet sizes and window sizes for each direction of data transmission. The maximum packet sizes that may be supported on public data networks are 16, 32, 64, 128, 256, 512, and 1024 octets. If a particular packet or window size is not explicitly requested, the DCE assumes default requests of 128 octets and 2, respectively.

When the DCE transmits a CALL CONNECTED packet, it indicates in the facility field the flow control parameters to be used by the calling DTE. The only valid facility indications in the CALL CONNECTED packet as a function of the facility requests in the CALL REQUEST packet are specified by the following general negotiation rules:

a) window sizes can be changed in the direction of $W = 2$; and

b) packet sizes can be changed in the direction of 128 octets.

When the called DTE subscribes to the facility, the DCE transmits flow control parameter facility indications to be used by the called DTE in selecting the flow control parameters for the call. The called DTE can change the indicated values using the above negotiation rules.

The flow control parameters for logical channels used for PVC's are established at subscription time.

The network may have to constrain the available parameter ranges in order to allow the call to be established.

3) *Throughput Class Negotiation*: Throughput class negotiation is an optional user facility agreed for a period of time which can be used by a DTE for virtual circuits. This facility permits negotiation on a per call basis of the throughput classes. The throughput classes are considered independently for each direction of data transmission.

A throughput class for one direction of transmission is an inherent characteristic of a virtual circuit related to the amount of network resources allocated to it. This characteristic is meaningful when the D bit is set to 0 in DATA packets. It is a measure of the throughput that is not normally exceeded on the VC. However, due to the statistical sharing of transmission and switching resources, it is not guaranteed that the throughput class can be reached 100 percent of the time.

Default values are agreed between the DTE and the network. The default values correspond to the maximum throughput classes which may be associated with any virtual circuit at the DTE/DCE interface.

4) *One-way Outgoing Logical Channel*: The one-way outgoing logical channel is an optional user facility agreed for a period of time. This user facility restricts the use of a range of logical channels to outgoing calls. One-way logical channels retain their full-duplex nature with respect to data transfer.

5) *Incoming or Outgoing Calls Barred*: Incoming or outgoing calls barred are two optional user facilities agreed for a period of time. These facilities apply to all logical channels used at the DTE/DCE interface for switched virtual circuits.

Incoming calls barred prevents incoming calls from being presented to the DTE. The DTE may originate outgoing calls. Outgoing calls barred prevents the DCE from accepting outgoing calls from the DTE. The DTE may receive incoming calls.

V. CONCLUDING REMARKS

A. A Common X.25 DTE

Network implementations of X.25 have come under some criticism in technical papers, such as one from IBM [10], which question whether a sufficient degree of commonality exists in the various X.25 implementations. The revised CCITT Recommendation X.25, which has been approved by Study Group VII in February 1980, resolves a number of key areas which lead to network differences.

From a DTE implementation point of view, a common X.25 interface can be defined [11], which consists of the following universally available features:

1) an ISO-compatible frame level procedure (i.e., LAPB);

2) use of logical channel number one as the starting point for logical channel assignment;

3) modulo 8 packet level numbering;

4) dynamic $P(R)$ significance by use of the delivery confirmation bit;

5) a standard procedure for selecting packet and window sizes, with defaults of 128 octets and 2, respectively;

6) two mechanisms for user control data transfer (i.e., qualified DATA and INTERRUPT packets); and

7) a standard way of specifying required call throughput.

What remains is for various network implementors to announce their implementation plans of the above features.

B. Relationship of X.25 to the Open System Architecture

The set of commonly agreed standards, which make possible meaningful interworking between any combination of communication processing and data processing systems and the relationships among these standards, are collectively known as the Open Systems Architecture (OSA) [12]. The purpose of the OSA is to provide a complete reference structure of standards necessary to achieve system interworking. The reference structure will place existing standards in perspective and facilitate the identification of areas in existing standards requiring additional developments and of areas where standards should be developed.

The CCITT is developing a "layered model of public data network service applications" [13] for the purpose of facilitating DTE interworking or gaining access to network services (e.g., directory assistance, electronic mail). At the same time, ISO is defining a model for open system interconnection [14]. A high degree of compatibility between CCITT's and ISO's Models is desirable; this will be facilitated by the cooperation which already exists between the two organizations.

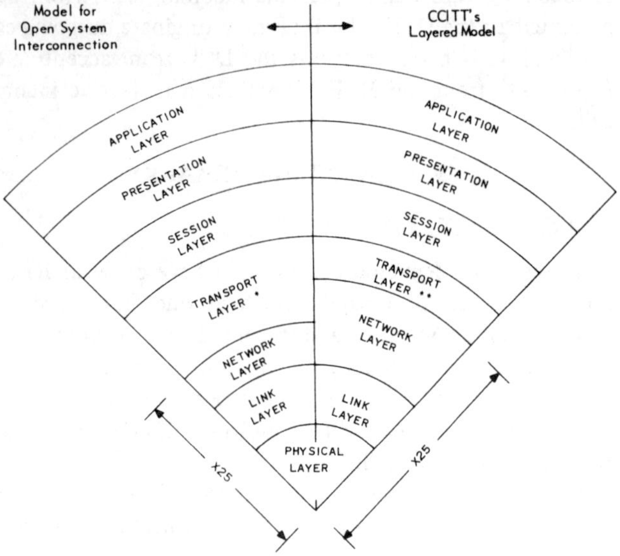

* The Transport Layer is required to provide functions not assumed to be available from X.25 VC's.
** The Transport Layer becomes a null layer if the quality of service provided by X.25 VC's is adequate.

Fig. 5. Relationship of X.25 to ISO and CCITT models.

It has been generally agreed within ISO and CCITT that the basic structuring technique in OSA is layering, whereby a network of cooperating systems is logically structured into layers. A number of criteria to be applied to the question of how many layers there should be and where layer boundaries should be placed have been defined.

Both ISO and CCITT agree on a seven-layer architecture, as illustrated in Fig. 5. A major difference is in the interpretation of the services provided by the network and transport layers and their relationship to X.25 virtual circuits.

The current view of the CCITT Rapporteur's Group studying OSA is that the services provided by the transport and network layers are identical except perhaps in the quality of service provided, and can be provided by X.25 virtual circuits; these can be provided by packet switching networks, or by using X.25 between DTE's in leased-line and circuit-switching networks. Quality of service becomes an issue since the network layer may vary in its success in reaching the performance level required by the transport layer (e.g., error rates, reliability, cost, throughput). When a transport connection of higher reliability than that provided by the network layer is required, this may be provided by the use of additional procedures within the transport layer. Since these procedures do not add service features, but only increase an aspect of the quality of service, these procedures may be contained in a sublayer within the transport layer.

The current ISO view appears to be that the services provided by the network layer are somewhat primitive, resulting in distinctly different services being provided by the network and transport layers. The services of the network layer can be provided by X.25 virtual circuits. However, in this model, many of the VC characteristics discussed in Section II are not used; instead, these functions are provided by the transport layer.

The above discussion reflects two views of the relationship of X.25 to OSA. Complete alignment between the two models may yet be achieved.

C. Future Developments

Future activity and further work are required in the following areas:

1) The characteristics of virtual circuits are defined in X.25, though much would be gained by having a separate CCITT Recommendation addressing them.

2) The X.25 interface has become functionally complete after nearly four years of network operational experience. Further work will concentrate on new optional user facilities, and the addition of multilink procedures defined for the frame level.

3) Presently, some networks require the data fields of DATA packets to contain an integral number of octets. The transmission by the DTE of data fields not containing an integral number of octets to the network may cause a loss of data integrity. Further considerations regarding the trends of future requirements and implementations toward either bit-orientation (any number of bits) or octet-orientation (an integral number of octets) for data fields in X.25 packets are under study in CCITT.

4) The evolving Open Systems Architecture provides a basic structure on which future work in ISO and CCITT can be built. The view that X.25 virtual circuits can provide the basic Transport layer services required by the Session layer in OSA must be studied further.

5) There is a real need to select meaningful performance criteria, bearing in mind that the meaningfulness of criteria is viewed differently by network users and by the network providers. Once these criteria have been defined, realistic performance objectives should be set based on user requirements as well as on operating experience. The costs associated with meeting these objectives must also be considered.

ACKNOWLEDGMENT

CCITT relies heavily on contributions submitted by numerous parties including ISO. It has not been practical to reference all of the relevant contributions of the over three hundred which have been submitted to SGVII in this study period. Many of these contributions made proposals, reported on operating experience or more generally discussed areas in X.25 which have been discussed in this paper. Their contribution is acknowledged.

REFERENCES

[1] CCITT Recommendations X.1, X.2, X.25, X.92 and X.96 "Public data networks," *CCITT Orange Book*, vol. VIII.2. Geneva, Switzerland: ITU, 1977.

[2] CCITT Provisional Recommendations X.3, X.25, X.28, and X.29, *CCITT Grey Book*. Geneva, Switzerland: Grey Book. 1978.

[3] CCITT Provisional Recommendations X.75 and X.121, *CCITT Grey Book*. Geneva, Switzerland: ITU, 1979.
[4] P. T. F. Kelly, "Public packet switched data networks, international plans, and standards," *Proc. IEEE*, vol. 66, pp. 1539–1549, Nov. 1978.
[5] CCITT Rapporteur on X.25—Level 3, "Draft revised recommendation X.25," CCITT COM VII-no. 439, as amended, Feb. 1980.
[6] H. Folts, "Procedures for circuit-switched service in synchronous public data networks," in this issue, pp. 489–496.
[7] HDLC, Documents IS3309 and IS4335 plus approved amendments (TC97/SC6/N1300 and 1445) and DP6256, ISO, Geneva, Switzerland.
[8] H. Folts, "X.25 transaction oriented features—Datagram and fast select," in this issue, pp. 496–500.
[9] R. Hovey, "Packet-switched networks agree on standard interface," *Data Commun*. pp. 25, 39, May/June 1976.
[10] M. L. Hess, *et al.*, "A comparison of four X.25 public data networks," in *Proc. Int. Conf. Commun.*, June 1979.
[11] A. M. Rybczynski and J. D. Palframan, "A common X.25 interface to public data networks," to be published, Spring of 1980.
[12] H. Zimmermann, "The ISO model of architecture for open systems interconnection," in this issue, pp. 425–432.
[13] "Report of the 3rd meeting of the CCITT rapporteur on layered models of public data network service applications," CCITT COM VII-no. 393, San Francisco, CA, Sept. 1979.
[14] "Reference model for open systems interconnection, version 4," ISO/TC97/SC16 N227, June 1979.

Antony Rybczynski (S'68–M'72) received the B.Eng. degree from McGill University, Montreal, P.Q., Canada, in 1970, and the M.Sc. degree from the University of Alberta, Edmonston, Alta., Canada, in 1972, both in electrical engineering.

He is Supervising Engineer in Computer Communications Planning, Bell Canada, Ottawa, Canada. After completing his formal education, he joined a multidisciplinary task group formed within Bell Canada to study the marketing, technical, and economic feasibility of a public packet-switching network in Canada. This activity resulted in the development of the Datapac network. He has acted as design authority representing the TransCanada Telephone System in the development of the X.25 interface specification, in close cooperation with members of the staff of the French PTT, the UKPO, the NTT of Japan, and GTE Telenet Corporation of the U.S.A. This activity culminated in the ratification of Recommendation X.25 by the CCITT Plenary in October 1976. He has also been involved in the revised X.25 specification approved by CCITT SG VII in February 1980. In 1978, he was responsible for the establishment of international services between Datapac and Telenet and Tymnet networks. At present, he is responsible for planning the interconnection of Datapac with a number of overseas packet networks, and for the development of the Datapac X.75 internetworking capability.

Mr. Rybczynski is a member of the Association of Professional Engineers of Ontario.

Issues in Packet-Network Interconnection

VINTON G. CERF AND PETER T. KIRSTEIN

Invited Paper

Abstract—This paper introduces the wide range of technical, legal, and political issues associated with the interconnection of packet-switched data communication networks. Motivations for interconnection are given, desired user services are described, and a range of technical choices for achieving interconnection are compared. Issues such as the level of interconnection, the role of gateways, naming and addressing, flow and congestion control, accounting and access control, and basic internet services are discussed in detail. The CCITT X.25/X.75 packet-network interface recommendations are evaluated in terms of their applicability to network interconnection. Alternatives such as datagram operation and general host gateways are compared with the virtual circuit methods. Some observations on the regulatory aspects of interconnection are offered and the paper concludes with a statement of open research problems and some tentative conclusions.

I. Introduction

It is the theme of many papers in this issue, that people need access to data resources. In many cases this access must be over large distances, in others it may be local to a building or a single site. Data networks have been set up to meet many user needs—often, but not necessarily, using packet-switching technology. For single organizations, these data networks are often private ones, built with a technology optimized to the specific application. For communication between organizations, these networks are being set up by licensed carriers. In North America, there are many such licensed carriers, e.g., TELENET [1], DATAPAC [2], and TYMNET [3]. In the rest of the world, the Post, Telegraph, and Telephone Authority (PTT) in each country has a near monopoly on such services; special public data networks being set up in these countries include TRANSPAC [5] in France, EURONET [6] for inter-European traffic, DDX [7] in Japan, EDS [8] in the Federal Republic of Germany, and the Nordic Public Data Network (NPDN, [9]) in Scandinavia. These public data networks are considered in greater detail in other references (e.g., [10]–[12]). Most of the above networks use packet-switching technology; some of them, e.g., EDS and the NPDN, do not do so yet, but may do so in the future. In some cases special data networks have been authorized for specific communities, e.g., SITA [13] for the airlines, and SWIFT [14] for the banks. In addition many private networks have been set up among individual organizations, and experimental networks of different technologies have been developed also, e.g., ARPANET [15], [16], CYCLADES [17], ETHERNET [18], SPYDER [19], PRNET [20], [21] and SATNET [22].

Manuscript received June 20, 1978; revised July 21, 1978.

V. G. Cerf is with the Advanced Research Projects Agency, U.S. Department of Defense, Arlington, VA 22209.

P. T. Kirstein is with the Department of Statistic and Computer Science, University College, London, England.

Reprinted from *Proceedings of the IEEE*, Volume 66, Number 11, November 1978, pages 180-202.

It is a common user requirement that a single terminal and access port should be able to access any computing resource the user may desire—even if the resource is on another data network. From this requirement, there is a clear user need to have data networks connected together. By the same token, the providers of data network services would like to have their networks used as intensively as possible; thus they also have a strong motivation to connect their data networks to others. As a result of these considerations, there has been a high recent interest in the issues arising in the connection of data networks [23]-[26], [32].

From the user viewpoint, the requirement for interconnection of data networks is independent of the network technology. From the implementation viewpoint, there can be some considerable complications in connecting networks of widely different technologies—such as circuit-switched and datagram packet-switched networks (these terms are explained below). On the whole we will consider only, in this paper, the interconnection of packet-switched data networks. In many cases, however, the arguments will be equally valid for the interconnection of packet-switched to circuit-switched networks.

Network interconnection raises a great many technical, legal, and political questions and issues. The technical issues generally revolve around mechanisms for achieving interconnection and their performance. How can networks be interconnected so that packets can flow in a controllable way from one net to another? Should all computer systems on all nets be able to communicate with each other? How can this be achieved? What kind of performance can be achieved with a set of interconnected networks of widely varying internal design and operating characteristics? How are terminals to be given access to resources in other networks? What protocols are required to achieve this? Should the protocols of one net be translated into those of another, or should common protocols be defined? What kinds of communication protocol standards are needed to support efficient and useful interconnection? Who should take responsibility for setting standards?

The legal and political issues are at least as complex as the technical ones. Can private networks interconnect to each other or must they do so through the mediation of a public network? How is privacy to be protected? Should there be control over the kinds of data which move from one net to another? Are there international agreements and conventions which might be affected by international interconnection of data networks? What kinds of charging and accounting policies should apply to multinetwork traffic? How can faults and errors be diagnosed in a multinet environment? Who should be responsible for correcting such faults? Who should be responsible for maintaining the gateways which connect nets together?

We cannot possibly answer all of these questions in this paper, but we deal with many of them in the sections below.

This paper is divided into eleven sections. In the next section we provide some definitions, and in Section III we explore some of the motivations for network interconnection. In Section IV we discuss the range of end-user service requirements and choices for providing multinetwork service. Section V reviews the concept of computer-communication protocol layering. Section VI reviews the basic interconnection choices and introduces the concept of gateways between nets, protocol translation and the impact of common protocols; it elaborates also on the function of gateways. Section VII discusses the CCITT recommendations X.25 and X.75 and their role in network interconnection. Section VIII describes some of the network interconnections achieved and some of the experiments in progress. Section IX outlines regulatory issues raised by network interconnection alternatives. Section X mentions some unresolved research questions, and the final section offers some tentative conclusions on network interconnection issues.

II. The Definition of Terms

The vocabulary of networking is extensive and not always consistent. We introduce some generic terms below which we will use in this paper for purposes of discussion. It is important for the reader not to make any *a priori* assumptions about the physical realization of the objects named or of the boundary of jurisdictions owning or managing them. For instance, a gateway (see below) might be implemented to share the hardware of a packet switch and be owned by a packet-switching service carrier; alternatively it might be embedded in a host computer which subscribes to service on two or more computer networks. Roughly speaking, we are assigning names to groups of functions which may or may not be realized as physically distinct entities.

Packet: A packet of information is a finite sequence of bits, divided into a control header part and a data part. The header will contain enough information for the packet to be routed to its destination. There will usually be some checks on each such packet, so that any switch through which the packet passes may exercise error control. Packets are generally associated with internal packet-network operation and are not necessarily visible to host computers attached to the network.

Datagram: A finite length packet of data together with destination host address information (and, usually, source address) which can be exchanged in its entirety between hosts, independent of all other datagrams sent through a packet switched network. Typically, the maximum length of a datagram lies between 1000 and 8000 bits.

Gateway: The collection of hardware and software required to effect the interconnection of two or more data networks, enabling the passage of user data from one to another.

Host: The collection of hardware and software which utilizes the basic packet-switching service to support end-to-end interprocess communication and user services.

Packet Switch: The collection of hardware and software resources which implements all intranetwork procedures such as routing, resource allocation, and error control and provides access to network packet-switching services through a host/network interface.

Protocol: A set of communication conventions, including formats and procedures which allow two or more end points to communicate. The end points may be packet switches, hosts, terminals, people, file systems, etc.

Protocol Translator: A collection of software, and possibly hardware, required to convert the high level protocols used in one network to those used in another.

Terminal: A collection of hardware and possibly software which may be as simple as a character-mode teletype or as complex as a full scale computer system. As terminals increase in capability, the distinction between "host" and "terminal" may become a matter of nomenclature without technical substance.

Virtual Circuit: A logical channel between source and destination packet switches in a packet-switched network. A virtual circuit requires some form of "setup" which may or may not be visible to the subscriber. Packets sent on a virtual circuit are delivered in the order sent, but with varying delay.

PTT: Technically PTT stands for Post, Telegraph, and Telephone Authority; this authority has a different form in different countries. In this paper, by PTT we mean merely the authority (or authorities) licensed in each country to offer public data transmission services.

We have attempted to make these definitions as noncontroversial as possible. For example, in the definition of packet switch, we alluded to a host/network interface. The reader should not assume that subscriber services are limited to those offered through the host/network interface. The packet-switching carrier might also offer host-based services and terminal access mechanisms as additional subscriber services.

III. The Motivating Forces in the Interconnection of Data Networks

In the introduction, we mentioned that there was a strong interest, among both the users and suppliers of data serivces, in the interconnection of data networks. However, the technical interests of the different parties are not identical. The end user would merely like to be able to access any resources from a single terminal, with a single access port, as economically as possible according to his own performance criteria. A Public Carrier, or PTT, has a strong motivation to connect its network to other PTT's. As in the telephone system, the concept of all subscribers being accessible through a single Public Data Service, is considered highly desirable; however the different PTT's may have restricted geographic coverage, or only a specific market penetration.

The motivation of the PTT's to interface to private networks is weaker and more complex. They always provide facilities to attach single terminals, where a terminal may be a complex computer system; they are often not interested, at present, in making any special arrangements when the "terminal" is a whole computer network. The operators of private networks often have a vital interest in connecting their networks to other private networks and to the public ones. Even though in many cases the bulk of its traffic is internal to the private network, which is why it was set up in the first place, there is usually a vital need to access resources not available on that network. The regulatory limitations often imposed on the method of interconnection of private networks are discussed in Section IX. In some countries, it is not permitted to build private networks using leased line services, but intrabuilding networks may be permitted. Interconnection of such local networks to public networks may play a crucial role in making the local network useful.

To date the PTT's have tried to standardize on access procedures for their Public-Packet Data Services. The standardization has taken place in the International Consultative Committee on Telegraphy and Telephony (called CCITT) in a set of recommendations called X.3, X.25, X.28, and X.29 ([27]-[29]). Not all PTT's have such forms of access yet, but most of the industrialized nations in the West are moving in this direction. This series of recommendations is discussed in much more detail in Section VI; it does not pay special attention to the attachment of private networks ([31], [32]), but the recommendations are themselves expected to change to meet this requirement. The PTT's are agreeing on a set of interface recommendations and procedures called X.75 [33], to connect their networks to each other; so far this interface procedure (and its corresponding hardware) is not intended to be provided to private networks.

While most PTT's have preferred to ignore the technical implications of the attachment of private networks to the public ones, most private network operators cannot ignore this requirement. They are often motivated to add some extra "Foreign Exchange" capability as an afterthought, with minimum change to their intranetwork procedures; this approach can be successful up to a point, but will usually be limited by the lack of high-level procedures between the different networks. These high-level procedures have not yet been considered by CCITT, but it has been proposed that CCITT Study Group VII investigate high-level procedures and architectural models, in cooperation with the investigation of "open system architectures" by Technical Committee 97, Sub-Committee 16 of the International Standards Organisation (ISO). This subject is also considered later in this paper, in Section VI.

An aim of these standardization exercises is to ensure that both manufacturer and user implementations of network resources can communicate with each other through single private or public data networks. A consequence should be that the resources are also compatibly accessible over connected data networks.

Depending on the applications and spatial distribution of subscribers, the preferred choice of packet-switching medium will vary. Intrabuilding applications such as electronic office services may be most economically provided through the use of a coaxial-packet cable system such as the Xerox ETHERNET [18] and LCSNET [64], or twisted pair rings such as DCS [34], coupled with a mix of self-contained user computers (e.g., intelligent terminals with substantial computing and memory capacity) and shared computing, storage, and input-output facilities. Larger area regional applications might best employ shared video cables [35] or packet radios [20], [21] for mobile use. National systems might be composed of a mixture of domestic satellite channels and conventional leased-line services. International systems might use point-to-point links plus a shared communication satellite channel and multiple ground stations to achieve the most cost-effective service.

A consequence of the wide range of technologies which are optimum for different packet-switching applications is that many different networks, both private and public, may co-exist. A network interconnection strategy, if properly designed, will permit local networks to be optimized without sacrificing the possibility of providing effective internetwork services. The potential economic and functional advantages of local networks such as ETHERNET or DCS will lead naturally to private user networks. Such private network developments are analogous to telephone network private automated branch exchanges (PABX) and represent a natural consequence of the marriage of computer and telecommunication technology.

Two further developments can be expected. First, organizations which are dispersed geographically, nationally, or internationally, will want to interconnect these private networks both to share centralized resources and to effect intraorganization electronic mail and other automated office services. Second, there will be an increasing interest in interorganization interconnections to allow automated procurement and financial transaction services, for example, to be applied to interorganization affairs.

In most countries where private networks are permitted, interorganization telecommunication requires the involvement of a PTT. Hence the most typical network interconnection scenarios will involve three or four networks. Within one national administration the private nets of different organizations will be interconnected through a public network. International interconnections will involve at least two public networks. We will return to this topic in Section VI.

In addition to permitting locally optimized networks to be interconnected, a network interconnection strategy should also support the gradual introduction of new networking technology into existing systems without requiring simultaneous global change throughout. This consideration leads to the conclusion that the public data networks should support the most important user requirements for internet service from the outset. If this were the case, then changes in network technology which require a multinetwork system during phased transition would not, *a priori*, have to affect user services.

IV. Provision of End-User Multinetwork Services

The ultimate choice of a network interconnection strategy will be strongly affected by the types of user services which must be supported. It is useful to consider the range of existing and foreseeable user service requirements without regard for the precise means by which these requirements are to be met. We will leave for discussion in subsequent sections the choice of supporting the various services within or external to the packet-switched network. The types of service discussed below are general requirements for network facilities. For this reason they also should be supported across interconnected networks.

Most of the currently prevalent computer-communication services fall into four categories:

1) terminal access to time-shared host computers;
2) remote job entry services (RJE);
3) bulk data transfer;
4) transaction processing.

The time-sharing and transaction services typically demand short network and host response times but modest bandwidth. The RJE and file transfer services more often require high amounts of data transfer, but can tolerate longer delay. Some networks were designed to support primarily terminal service, leaving RJE or file transfer services to be supported by dedicated leased lines. Packet-switching techniques permit both types of service to be supported with common network resources, leading to verifiable economies. However, bulk data transfer requires increasingly higher throughput rates if delivery delays are to be kept constant as the amount of data to be transferred increases.

As distributed operating systems become more prevalent, there will be an increased need for host-to-host transaction services. A prototypical example of such a system is found in the DARPA National Software Works [4], [36]. In such a system, small quantities of control information must be exchanged quickly to coordinate the activity of the distributed components. Broadcast or multidestination services will be needed to support distributed file systems in which information can be stored redundantly to improve the reliability of access and to protect against catastrophic failures.

Transaction services are also finding application in reservation systems, credit verification, point of sale, and electronic funds-transfer systems in which hundreds or thousands of terminals supply to, or request of, hosts small amounts of information at random intervals. Real-time data collection for

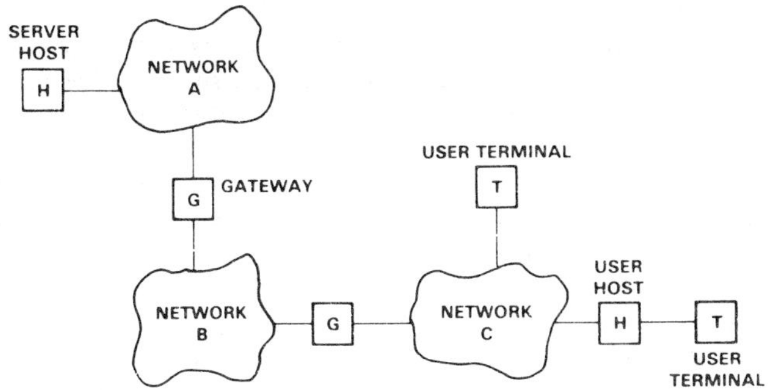

Fig. 1. Network concatenation.

weather analysis, ground and air traffic control, and meter reading, for example, also fall into this category.

More elaborate user requirements can be foreseen as electronic mail facilities propagate. Multiple destination addressing and end-to-end encryption for the protection of privacy as well as support for text, digitized voice, and facsimile message transmission are all likely requirements. Electronic teleconferencing using mixtures of compressed digital packet speech, videographics, real-time cursors (for pointing at video images under discussion), and text display will give rise to requirements for closed user groups and time-synchronized mixes of transaction-like (e.g., for cursor tracking and packet speech) and reliable circuit-like services (e.g., for display management).

Reliability and rapid response will be increasingly important as more and more computer-based applications requiring telecommunications are integrated into the business, government, military, and social fabric of the world economy. The more such systems are incorporated into their daily activities, the more vulnerable the subscribers are to failures. Reliability concerns lead to the requirement for redundant alternatives such as distributed file systems, richly connected networks, and substantial local processing and storage capability. These trends increase the need for networking to share common hardware and software resources (and thus reduce their marginal cost), to support remote software maintenance and debugging, and to support intra- and inter-organizational information exchange.

We have described the end-user services required across one or more data networks. We have carefully refrained from discussing which services should be provided in the data network, and which should be provided in the hosts. Here the choice in single networks will depend on the network technology and the application requirements. For example, in a network using a broadcast technology such as ETHERNET or the SATNET, multidestination facilities may well be incorporated in the data network itself. In typical store-and-forward networks, this feature might be provided at the host level by the transmission of multiple copies of packets. This example highlights immediately the difficulty of using sophisticated services at the data network level across concatenated networks. If A, B, and C are data networks connected as in Fig. 1, and A and C but not B support broadcast or real-time features, it is very difficult to provide them across the concatenation of A, B, and C.

The problem of achieving a useful set of internetwork services might be approached in several ways, as follows.

1) Require all networks to implement the entire range of desired services (e.g., datagram, virtual circuit, broadcast, real-

time, etc.), and then attempt to support these services across the gateways between the networks.

2) Require all networks to implement only the most basic services (e.g., datagram or virtual circuit), support these services across gateways, and rely on the subscriber to implement all other services end-to-end.

3) Allow the subscriber to identify the services which he desires and provide error indications if the networks involved, or the gateways between them, cannot provide the desired services.

4) Allow the subscriber to specify the internetwork route to be followed and depend on the subscriber to decide which concatenation of services are appropriate and what end-to-end protocols are needed to achieve the ultimately preferred class of service.

5) Provide one set of services for local use within each network and another, possibly different set for internetwork use.

The five choices above are by no means exhaustive, and, in fact, only scratch the surface of possibilities. Nothing has been said, thus far, about the compatibility of various levels of communication protocols which exist within each network, within subscriber equipments, and within the logical gateway between networks. To explore these issues further, it will be helpful to have a model of internetwork architecture, taking into account the common principle of protocol layering and the various possible choices of interconnection strategy which depend upon the protocol layer at which the networks are interfaced. We consider this in the next section.

V. Layered Protocol Concepts

Both to provide services in single networks, and to compare the capabilities of different networks, a very useful concept in networking is protocol layering. Various services of increasing capability can be built one on top of the other, each using the facilities of the service layer below and supporting the facilities of the layer above. A thorough tutorial on this concept can be found in the paper by Pouzin and Zimmermann in this issue [37]. We give some specific examples below of layering as a means of illustrating the scope of services and interfaces to be found in packet networks today—and some of the problems encountered in offering services across multiple networks.

Table I offers a very generic view of a typical protocol hierarchy in a store-and-forward computer network, including layers usually found outside of the communication network itself. There are several complications to the use of generic protocol layering to study network interconnection issues. Chief among these is that networks do not all contain the same elements of the generic hierarchy. A second complication is that some networks implement service functions at different protocol layers. For instance, virtual circuit networks implement an end/end subscriber virtual circuit in their intranet, end/end level protocol. Finally, the hierarchical ordering of functions is not always the same in all networks. For instance, TYMNET places a terminal handling protocol within the network access layer, so that hosts look to each other like one or more terminals. Figs. 2–7 illustrate the functional layering of some different networks. It is important to note how the functions vary with the choice of transmission medium.

TABLE I
Generic Protocol Layers

PROTOCOL LAYER	FUNCTIONS
6. APPLICATION	FUNDS TRANSFER, INFORMATION RETRIEVAL, ELECTRONIC MAIL, TEXT EDITING . . .
5. UTILITY	FILE TRANSFER, VIRTUAL TERMINAL SUPPORT
4. END/END SUBSCRIBER	INTERPROCESS COMMUNICATION (E.G. VIRTUAL CIRCUIT, DATAGRAM, REAL-TIME, BROADCAST)
3. NETWORK ACCESS	NETWORK ACCESS SERVICES (E.G. VIRTUAL CIRCUIT, DATAGRAM . . .)
2. INTRANET, END-TO-END	FLOW CONTROL, SEQUENCING
1. INTRANET, NODE-TO-NODE	CONGESTION CONTROL, ROUTING
0. LINK CONTROL	ERROR HANDLING, LINK FLOW CONTROL

<table>
<tr><td>APPLICATION</td><td colspan="3">------------</td></tr>
<tr><td>UTILITY</td><td>FILE TRANSFER</td><td>VIRTUAL TERMINAL</td><td rowspan="2">DIRECTORY LOOK-UP, FILE ACESS</td></tr>
<tr><td rowspan="2">END-TO-END SUBSCRIBER</td><td colspan="2">STREAM PROTOCOL</td></tr>
<tr><td colspan="3">RELIABLE PACKET PROTOCOL</td></tr>
<tr><td>NETWORK ACCESS</td><td colspan="3">BROADCAST DATAGRAM (UNRELIABLE)</td></tr>
<tr><td></td><td colspan="3"></td></tr>
<tr><td></td><td colspan="3"></td></tr>
<tr><td>LINK CONTROL</td><td colspan="3"></td></tr>
</table>

Fig. 2. ETHERNET protocol layering.

A. ETHERNET

In Fig. 2, we represent the Xerox ETHERNET protocol hierarchy. The basic link control mechanism is the ability of the interface device to detect conflict on a shared coaxial cable. If a transmitting interface detects that another interface is also transmitting, it immediately aborts the transmission. Hosts attached to the network interface present datagrams to be transmitted and are told if the datagram was aborted. Datagrams can be addressed to specific interfaces or to all of them. The end/end subscriber layer of protocol is split into two parts: a reliable datagram protocol in which each datagram is reliably delivered and separately acknowledged, and a stream protocol which can be thought of as a virtual circuit. This split is possible, in part, because there is a fairly large maximum datagram size (about 500 bytes) so that user applications can send datagrams without having to fragment and reassemble them. This makes the datagram service useful for many applications which might otherwise have to use the stream protocol. All higher level protocols, such as Virtual Terminal and File Transfer, are carried out in the hosts.

B. ARPANET

The ARPANET protocol hierarchy is shown in Fig. 3. The basic link control between packet switches treats the physical link as eight independent virtual links. This increases effective throughput, but does not necessarily preserve the order in which packets were originally introduced into the network. The intranet node-to-node protocols deal with adaptive routing decisions, store-and-forward service, and congestion control. Hosts have the option of either passing messages (up to

APPLICATION	RJE	ELECTRONIC MAIL	
UTILITY	TELNET	FTP	
END/END SUBSCRIBER	NCP	TCP	NVP/NVCP
NETWORK ACCESS	PERMANENT VIRTUAL CIRCUIT		DATAGRAM
INTRANET, END/END	FLOW CONTROL, SEQUENCING, MESSAGE REASSEMBLY		
INTRANET, NODE/NODE	ADAPTIVE ROUTING, STORE AND FORWARD, CONGESTION CONTROL		
LINK CONTROL	NON-SEQUENCED, MULTI-CHANNEL ERROR CONTROL		

Fig. 3. ARPANET protocol layering.

8063 bits of text) across the host/network interface, which will be delivered in sequence to the destination, or passing datagrams (up to 1008 bits of text) which are not necessarily delivered in sequence. The user's network access interface is datagram-like in the sense that no circuit setup exchange is needed even to activate the sequenced message service. In effect, this service acts like a permanent virtual circuit over which a sequence of discrete messages are sent. For the sequenced messages, there is exactly one virtual circuit maintained for each host/host pair. In fact, these virtual circuits are set up dynamically and terminated by the source/destination packet switches so as to improve resource utilization [38], [62].

The end/end subscriber layer of ARPANET contains two main protocols: Network Control Protocol (NCP, [39], [40]) and Transmission Control Protocol (TCP, [25]). NCP was the first interprocess communication protocol built for ARPANET. It relies on the sequenced message service provided by the network and derives multiple virtual circuits between pairs of hosts by multiplexing. The TCP can use either the sequenced message service or the datagram service. It does its own sequencing and end/end error control and derives multiple virtual circuits through extended addressing and multiplexing. TCP was designed for operation in a multinet environment in which the only service which reasonably could be expected was an unreliable, unsequenced datagram service.

To support experiments in packetized voice communication, two protocols were developed for use on the ARPANET. The Network Voice Protocol (NVP) and Network Voice Conferencing Protocol (NVCP) use the datagram service to achieve very low delay and interarrival time variance in support of digital, compressed packet speech (more on these protocols may be found in [41]). The NVP could be considered the basis for a generic protocol which could support a variety of real-time, end/end user applications.

The higher level utility protocols such as terminal/host protocol (TELNET, [40], [42]) and file transfer protocol (FTP, [40], [42]) use virtual circuits provided by NCP or TCP. The FTP requires one live interactive stream to control the data transfer, and a second for the data stream itself. Yet higher level applications such as electronic mail and remote job entry (RJE, [40], [42]) use mixtures of TELNET and FTP to effect the service desired. These protocols are usually put into the hosts. There is one anomaly, which occurs in many networks. Because terminal handling is required so frequently, a Terminal Interface Message Processor (TIP, [43]) was built. This device is physically integrated with the packet switch (IMP, [38]); it includes also the NCP and TELNET protocols.

END/END SUBSCRIBER	TERMINAL-TO-HOST
NETWORK ACCESS	VIRTUAL CIRCUIT
INTRANET END-END	
INTRANET NODE-NODE	FRAME DISASSEMBLY, REASSEMBLY, ROUTING, STORE/FORWARD, CONGESTION CONTROL
LINK CONTROL	FRAME-BASED ERROR CONTROL, RETRANSMISSION, SEQUENCING

Fig. 4. TYMNET protocol layering.

C. TYMNET

TYMNET (see Fig. 4) is one of the oldest of the networks in the collection described here [3]. Strictly speaking, it operates rather differently than other packet-switched networks, because the frames of data that move from switch to switch are disassembled and reassembled in each switch as an integral part of the store-and-forward operation. Nevertheless, the network benefits from the asynchronous sharing of the circuits between the switches in much the same way that more typical packet-switched networks do. The network was designed to support remote terminal access to time-shared computer resources. The basic service is the transmission of a stream of characters between the terminal and the serving host. A frame is made up of one or more blocks of characters, each block labeled with its source terminal identifier and length. The switch-to-switch layer of protocol disassembles each frame into its constituent blocks and uses a routing table to determine to which next switch the block should be sent. Blocks destined for the same next switch are batched together in a frame which is checksummed and sent via the link control procedure to the next switch. Batching the blocks reduces line overhead (the blocks share the frame checksum) at the expense of more CPU cycles in the switch for frame disassembly and reassembly.

The protocol between TYMNET switches also includes a flow control mechanism which, because of the fixed routes, can be used to apply back pressure all the way back to the traffic source. This is not precisely an end-to-end flow control mechanism, but a hop-by-hop back pressure strategy. Character blocks are kept in sequence along the fixed routes so that no resequencing is required as they exit from the network at their destinations. The network interface is basically a virtual circuit designed to transport character streams between a host and a terminal. The same virtual circuits can be used to transport character streams between hosts, which look to each other like a collection of terminals. Above the basic virtual circuit service, is a special echo-handling protocol which allows the host and the terminal handler in the "remote TYMSAT" to coordinate the echoing of the characters typed by a user.

D. PTT Networks

Many PTT networks, e.g., TELNET, TRANSPAC, DATAPAC, and EURONET use a particular network-access protocol, X.25 [28], [29] (see Fig. 5). This protocol has been recommended by the CCITT for public packet-switched data networks. X.25 is a three-part protocol consisting of a hardware electrical interface, X.21 [44], the digital equivalent of the usual V.24 or EIA-RS232C modem interface [45], a link control procedure, High Level Data Link Control (HDLC, [46]), and a packet-level protocol for effecting the setup, use, termination, flow, and error control of virtual circuits.

UTILITY	TERMINAL HANDLING X.28, X.29
END/END SUBSCRIBER	
NETWORK ACCESS	X.25, PERMANENT OR TEMPORARY VIRTUAL CIRCUITS
INTRANET, END-END	MULTIPLE VIRTUAL CIRCUITS, FLOW CONTROL
INTRANET NODE-NODE	ROUTING, STORE/FORWARD, CONGESTION CONTROL
LINK CONTROL	HDLC OR EQUIVALENT

Fig. 5. PTT protocol layering.

In all but the DATAPAC network, a fixed route for routing packets through the network is selected at the time the virtual circuit is created. "Permanent" virtual circuits are a customer option; if used, the setup phase is invoked only in the case of a network failure. Between source and destination packet switches, a virtual circuit protocol is operated which implements end-to-end flow control on multiple virtual circuits between pairs of packet switches. Up to 4096 virtual circuits between pairs of host ports can be maintained by each packet switch, as compared to the single virtual circuit provided by ARPANET (on which hosts can multiplex their own virtual circuits). This choice has a noticeable impact on the subscriber interface protocol which becomes complicated because the subscriber host and the packet switch to which it attaches must maintain a consistent view of the state of each virtual circuit in use.

To provide for echo control, user commands, code conversion, and other terminal-related services, these networks implement CCITT Recommendations X.28 [29] and X.29 [29] in a PAD (Packet Assembly and Disassembly unit). These protocols sit atop the virtual circuit X.25 protocol. In order to serve customers desiring a terminal-to-host service with character terminals, such as is provided by TYMNET or by the ARPANET (through the TIP), most of the PTT networks mentioned are developing a PAD unit. A matching X.29 (PAD control protocol) layer must be provided in hosts offering to service terminals connected to PAD's.

E. High Level Protocols

The X.25/X.28/X.29 protocol hierarchy does not include an end/end subscriber or high-level protocol layer. Some customers will, in fact, implement end-to-end protocols on top of the virtual circuit protocol, but others may not. Several attempts are being made to standardize protocols above the network access level. The ARPANET community has developed a Transmission Control Protocol [25] for internetwork operation to replace the Network Control Program (NCP) developed early in the ARPANET project. The International Federation of Information Processing (IFIP) has proposed a Transport Station through its Working Group 6.1 on Network Interconnection [47]; the proposal has been submitted to the International Standards Organisation (ISO) as a draft standard. In addition, other communities, e.g., the High Level Protocol Working Group in the UK, have devised protocols for Virtual Packet Terminals (VPT, [48]) and File Transport Protocol (FTP, [49]) which are intended to be network independent and which may be submitted to CCITT. The ISO study on "open systems architecture" and the proposed similar study by CCITT Study Group VII will attempt to evolve higher level protocol recommendations for existing and future data networks.

This brief summary of different network-protocol layerings is in no way comprehensive, but illustrates the diversity of protocol designs which can be found on nets providing different types of services to subscribers.

VI. Technical Interconnection Choices

A. The Issues

Beginning with the earliest papers dealing with strategies for packet-network interconnection [23]-[26], [32], the common objective of all the proposed methods is to provide the physical means to access the services of a host on one network to all subscribers (including hosts) of all the interconnected networks. Of course, limitations to this accessibility are envisaged, imposed either for administrative reasons or by the scarcity of resources. The achievement of this objective invariably requires that data produced at a source in one net be delivered and correctly interpreted at the destination(s) in another network. In an abstract sense, this boils down to providing interprocess communication across network boundaries. Even if a person is the ultimate source of the data, packet-switching networks must interpose some degree of software processing between the person and the destination service, even if only to assemble or disassemble packets produced by a computer terminal.

A fundamental aspect of interprocess communication is that no communication can take place without some agreed conventions. The communicating processes must share some physical transmission medium (wire, shared memory, radio spectrum, etc.), and they must use common conventions or agreed upon translation methods in order to successfully exchange and interpret the data they wish to communicate. One of the key elements in any network interconnection strategy is therefore how the required commonality is to be obtained. In some cases, it is enough to translate one protocol into another. In others, protocols can be held in common among the communicating parties.

In any real network interconnection, of course, a number of secondary objectives will affect the choice of interconnection strategy. For example achievable bandwidth, reliability, robustness (i.e., resistance to failures), security, flexibility, accountability, access control, resource allocation options, and the like can separately and jointly influence the choice of interconnection strategy. Combinations of strategies employing protocol standards and protocol translations at various levels of the layered protocol hierarchy are also likely possibilities.

There are a number of issues which must be resolved before a coherent network interconnection strategy can be defined. A list of some of these issues, which will be treated in more detail in succeeding sections, is:

1) level of interconnection;
2) naming, addressing, and routing;
3) flow and congestion control;
4) accounting;
5) access control;
6) internet services.

B. Gateways and Levels of Network Interconnection

The concept of a gateway is common to all network interconnection strategies. The fundamental role of the gateway is to terminate the internal protocols of each network to which it is attached while, at the same time, providing a common

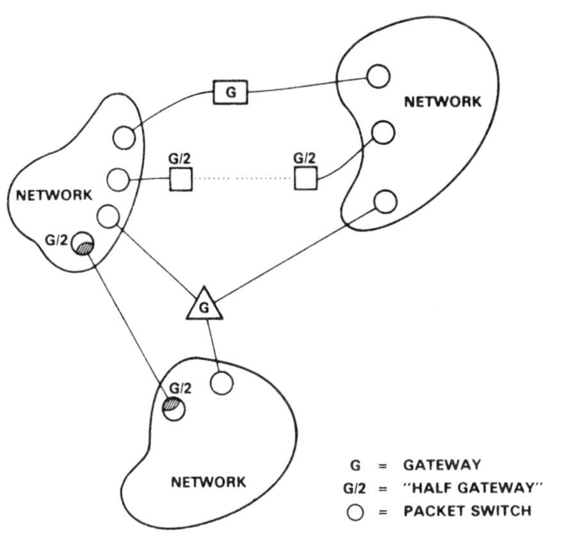

Fig. 6. Various gateway configurations.

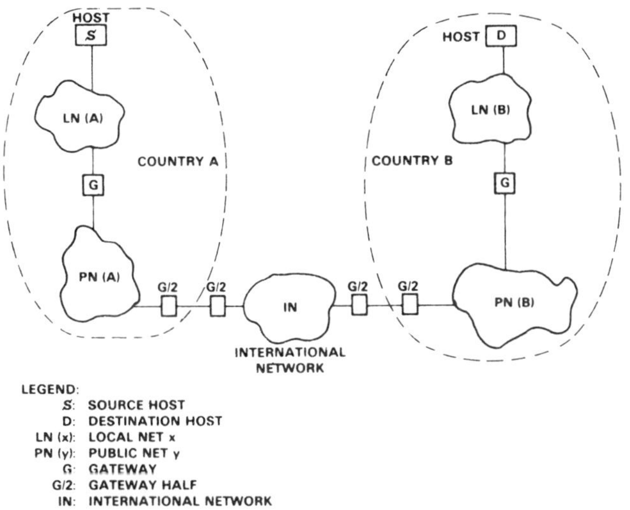

Fig. 7. International packet-networking model.

ground across which data from one network can pass into another. However, the choice of functions to be performed in the gateway varies considerably among different interconnection strategies (see Fig. 6). The term "gateway" need not imply a monolithic device which joins a pair of networks. Indeed, the gateway may merely be software in a pair of packet switches in different networks, or it may be made up of two parts, one in each network (a sort of "gateway half"). In the latter case, the two halves might be devices separate and distinct from the network packet switches or might be integrated with them. Furthermore, a gateway might interconnect more than two networks. In the material which follows, every attempt has been made to avoid any implicit choice of gateway implementation. It is worth pointing out, however, that the "half gateway" concept is highly attractive from both a technical and a purely administrative point of view. Technically, each half could terminate certain levels of protocol of the net to which it is attached. Administratively each half could be the responsibility of the network to which it belongs. Then the only matters for jurisdictional negotiation are the physical medium by which the half-gateways exchange data, and the format and protocol of the exchange.

It is important to realize that typical applications may involve three or more networks. Where local networks are used, they will usually need to be interconnected to realize the benefits of interorganizational data exchange. In most countries, such interconnections will only be permitted through a public network. Thus for a typical national situation, three networks and two gateways will be involved in providing the desired host-to-host communication.

The international picture is similar, except that more networks are likely to be involved. Shown in Fig. 7, the path from a host, S, on local network $LN(A)$ in country A, passes through a public network, $PN(A)$ in country A, through an international network IN, through a public network $PN(B)$ in country B, and finally through a local network, $LN(B)$, to the destination host, D. There are four internetwork gateways involved. It is this model involving multiple gateways that guides us away from network interconnection methods which rely on the source and destination hosts being in adjacent networks connected by the mediation of a single gateway.

1) Common Subnet Technology (Packet Level Interconnection): The level at which networks are interconnected can be determined by the protocol layers terminated by the gateway. For example, if a pair of identical networks were to be interconnected at the interpacket-switch level of protocol, we might illustrate the gateway placement as shown in Fig. 8. Here the "gateway" may consist only of software routines in the adjacent packet switches, e.g., $P(A)$ and $P(B)$, which provide accounting, and possibly readdressing functions. The contour model of protocol layer is useful here since it shows which levels are common to the two networks and which levels could be different. In essence, those layers which are terminated by the gateways could be different in each net, while those which are passed transparently through the gateway are assumed to be common in both networks. This network interconnection strategy requires that the internal address structure of all the interconnected networks be common. If, for example, addresses were composed of a network identifier, concatenated with a packet-switch identifier and a host identifier, then addressing of objects in each of the networks would be straightforward and routing could be performed on a regional basis with the network identifiers acting as the regional identifiers, if desired. Alternatively, two identical networks could adopt a common network name and assign nonduplicative addresses to each of the packet switches in both networks. This may require that addresses in one network be changed.

The strategy described above might be called the "common subnetwork strategy," since, in the end, subscribers of the newly formed joint network would essentially see a single network. This strategy does not rule out the provision of special access control mechanisms in the gateway nodes which could filter traffic flowing from one network into the other. Similarly, the gateway nodes could perform special internetwork traffic accounting which might not normally be performed in a subnet switching node. This network interconnection method is limited to those cases in which the nets to be connected are virtually identical, since the gateways must participate directly in all the subnet protocols. The end-to-end subnet protocols (e.g. source/destination packet-switch protocols) must pass transparently through the gateways to permit interactions between a source packet switch in one net and a destination packet switch in another. The resulting network presents the same network access interface to all

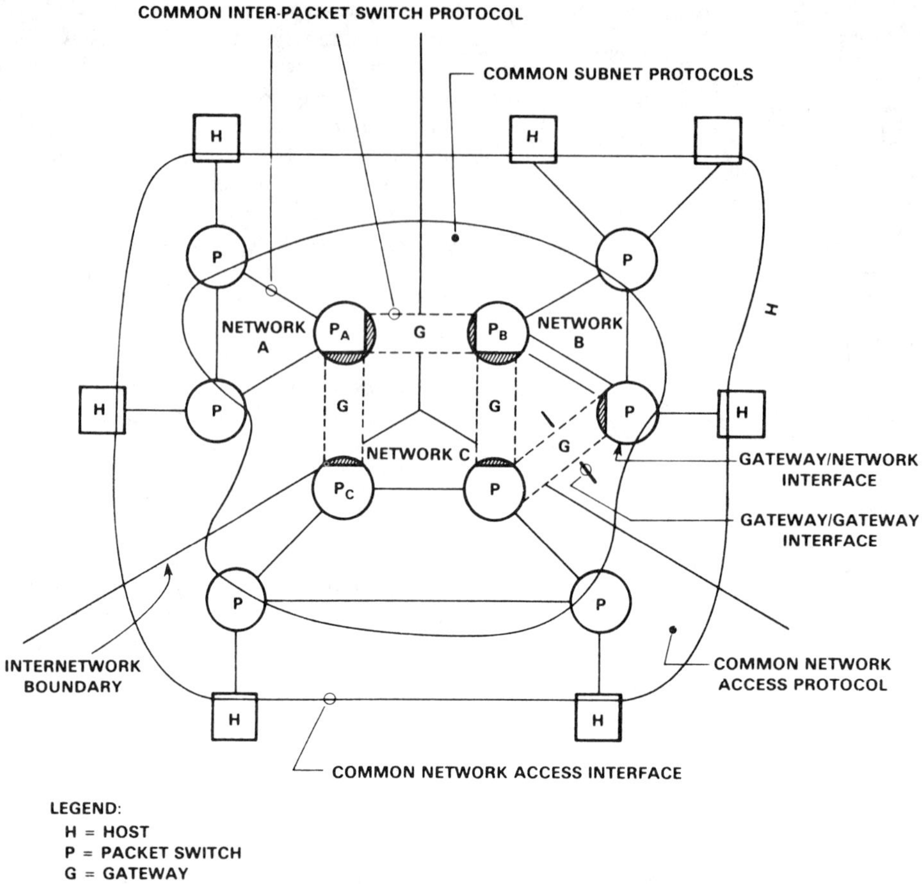

Fig. 8. Interconnection of common subnetworks.

subscribers, and this leads us to the next example which is based on the concept of a common network access interface.

2) Common Network Access Interfaces: If the subnetwork protocols are not identical, the next opportunity to establish internetwork commonality is at the network access interface. This is illustrated in Fig. 9. Each network is assumed to have its own intranet protocols. However, each network presents the same external interface to subscribers. This is illustrated by showing a common interface passing through all hosts, marked "common network access interface" in the figure.

Once again, the gateway could be thought of as software in adjacent packet switches. Each gateway is composed of two halves formed by linking the packet switches of two nets together. However, in this case, the subnetwork protocols are terminated at the gateway so that the intergateway exchange looks more like network access interaction than a node-to-node exchange. This is the approach taken by CCITT with its X.25 packet network interface recommendation and X.75 intergateway exchange recommendation.

It is important to note that the intergateway interface could be similar to the standard network access interface, but it need not necessarily be identical.

There are two basic types of network interface currently in use: 1) the datagram interface [31]; and 2) the virtual circuit interface [32]. The details of these generic interface types vary in different networks; some networks even offer both types of interface. In some, the interface to use may be chosen at subscription time; in others it may be possible for a subscriber to select the access method dynamically.

A datagram interface allows the subscriber to enter packets into the network independent of any other packets which have been or will be entered. Each packet is handled separately by the network. A virtual circuit interface requires an exchange of control information between the subscriber and the network for the purpose, for example, of setting up address translation tables, setting up routes or preallocating resources, before any data packets are carried to the destination. Some networks may implement a *fast select* virtual circuit interface in which a circuit setup request is sent together with the first (and possibly last) data packet. Other control exchanges would be used to close the resulting virtual circuits set up in this fashion.

It is essential to distinguish datagram and virtual circuit services from datagram and virtual circuit interfaces. A datagram service is one in which each packet is accepted and treated by the network independently of all others. Sequenced delivery is not guaranteed. Indeed, it may not be guaranteed that all datagrams will be delivered. Packets may be routed independently over alternate network paths. Duplicate copies of datagrams might be delivered.

Virtual circuit service tries to guarantee the sequenced delivery of the packets associated with the same virtual circuit. It typically provides to the host advice from the network on flow control per virtual circuit as opposed to the packet-by-packet acceptance or rejection typical of a datagram service. If the network operation might produce duplicate packets, these are filtered by the destination packet switch before delivery to the subscriber. Duplicate packet creation is a

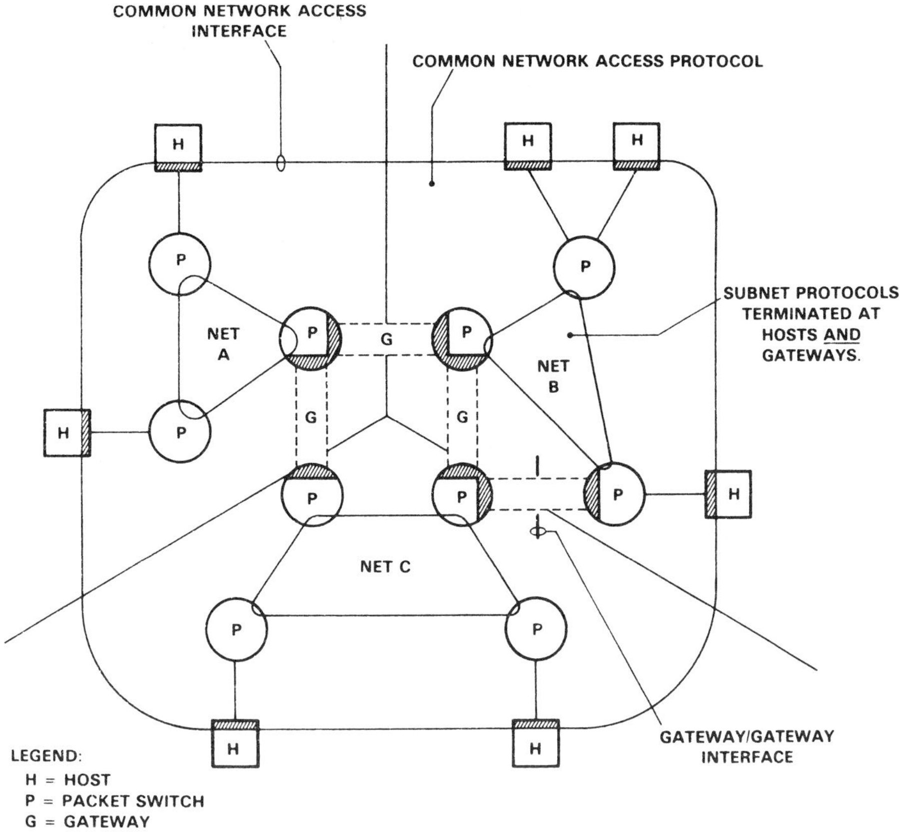

Fig. 9. Interconnection of networks with common network-access interfaces.

common phenomenon as in packet-switched store-and-forward systems. The basic mode of operation is to forward a packet to the next switch and await an acknowledgment. After a timeout, the packet is retransmitted. If an acknowledgment is lost due to line noise, for example, then two copies of the packet would have been transmitted. Even if the next switch is prepared to filter duplicates out, a network which uses adaptive routing can deliver a duplicate packet to the periphery of the network. For example, if a packet switch receives a packet successfully but the line to the sender breaks before the receiver can acknowledge, the sender may send another copy to a *different* packet switch. Both packet copies may be routed and delivered to the destination packet switch where final duplicate filtering would be needed if virtual circuit service is being provided.

Some networks offer both a datagram and a virtual circuit service; some offer a single interface, but different services. For example, the ARPANET has a basic datagram interface. However, the subnetwork will automatically provide a sequenced virtual circuit service (i.e., packets are kept in sequence when they are delivered to the destination) if the packet is marked appropriately. Otherwise, packets are not delivered in sequence nor are packet duplicates or losses, except for line by link correction, recovered within the network for nonsequenced types of traffic.

By contrast, TRANSPAC offers a virtual circuit interface and service. Subscribers transmit "call request" packets containing the full destination address to the packet switch. The request packet is forwarded to the destination, leaving behind a fixed route. The destination subscriber returns a "call accepted" packet which is delivered to the caller. As a result of this exchange, the source subscriber has associated a "logical channel number" or LCN, with the full source-destination addresses. Thus subsequent packets to be sent on the same logical channel are identified by the LCN and are kept in sequence when delivered to the destination.

Finally, it is possible to implement a datagram-like service using a virtual circuit interface. In this case, the exchange of *request* and *accept* packets might be terminated at the subscriber's local packet switch, so that even if packets were not delivered in sequence they might employ abbreviated addressing for local subscriber and packet-switch interaction.

If network interaction is to be based on a standard interface, then agreement must be reached both on the interface and an associated service or services. Furthermore, a common addressing system is needed so that a subscriber on one network can address a packet to a subscriber on any other network. A weaker assumption could be made but we are deliberately assuming a truly common service, interface, and addressing mechanism. We will return to this topic in a later section.

The choice of a standard network service through which to effect network interconnection has a primary impact on the flexibility of implementable network interconnection methods. We will consider two choices: datagram service and virtual circuit service.

a) Datagram service as a standard for network interconnection: For this case, it is assumed that every network offers a common datagram service. A uniform address space makes it possible for subscribers on any network to send packets addressed to any other subscriber on a connected network. Packets are routed between subscriber and gateway and between gateways based on the destination address. No attempt is made to keep the datagrams in any order in transit or upon delivery to the destination. Individual datagrams may be freely routed through different gateways to recover from failures or to allow load-splitting among parallel gateways joining a pair of networks.

The gateway/gateway interface may be different than the network access interface, if need be (see Fig. 9).

This strategy requires that all networks implement a common interface for subscribers. The simplicity and flexibility of the datagram interface strategy is offset somewhat by the need for all networks to implement the same interface. This is true for the pure virtual circuit interface strategy as well, as will be shown below.

One of the problems which has to be faced with any network interconnection strategy is congestion control at the gateways. If a gateway finds that it is unable to forward a datagram into the next network, it must have a way of rejecting it and quenching the flow of traffic entering the gateway en route into the next network. The quenching would typically take the form of an error or flow control signal passing from one gateway half to another on behalf of the associated network. Similar signals could be passed between subscribers and the packet network for similar reasons. Since datagram service does not undertake to guarantee end/end reliability, it is possible to relieve momentary congestion by discarding datagrams, as a last resort.

b) Virtual circuits for network interconnection: Another alternative standard network service which could be used for network interconnection is virtual circuit service (Fig. 10). Independent of the precise interface used to "set up" the virtual circuit, a number of implementation issues immediately arise if such a service is used as a basis for network interconnection.

Since it is intended that all packets on a virtual circuit be delivered to the destination subscriber in the same sequence as they were entered by the source subscriber, it is necessary that either: 1) all packets belonging to the same virtual circuit take the same path from source subscriber, through one or more gateways, to destination subscriber; or 2) all packets contain sequence numbers which are preserved end-to-end between the source DCE in the originating network and the destination DCE in the terminating network.

In the first case, virtual circuits are set up and anchored to specific gateways so that the sequencing of the virtual circuit service of each network can be used to preserve the packet sequence on delivery. This results in the concatenation of a series of virtual circuits through each gateway and, therefore, the knowledge of each virtual circuit at each gateway (since the next gateway to route the packet through must be fixed for each virtual circuit).

In the second case, there is no need to restrict the choice of gateway routing for each virtual circuit since the destination DCE will have sufficient information to resequence incoming packets prior to delivery to the destination subscriber.

In either case, the destination DCE will have to buffer and resequence packets arriving out of order due either to disordering within the last network or to alternate routing among networks, if this is permitted. Some networks may keep packets in sequence as they transit the network. This will only be advantageous at the destination DCE if the packets enter the network in the desired sequence. If such a service is relied upon in the internet environment, then each gateway must assure that on entry to such a net, the packets are in the desired order for delivery to a destination subscriber or another gateway.

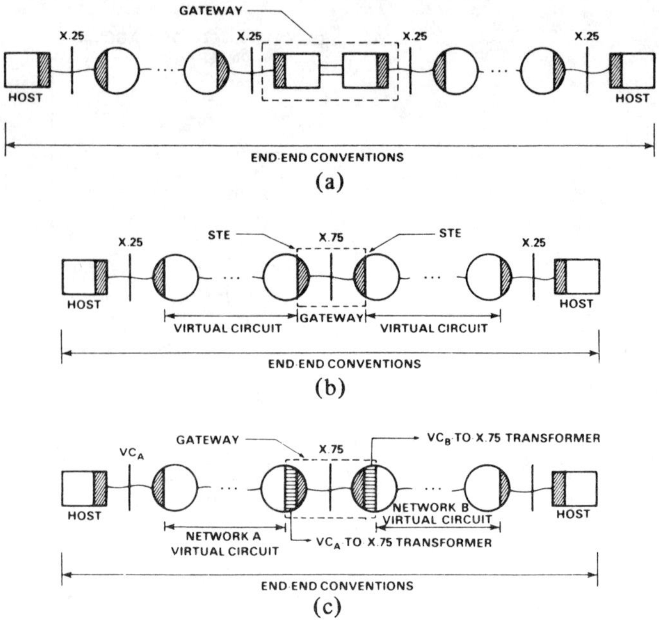

Fig. 10. Virtual circuit network interconnection strategies. (a) Subscriber-based gateway. Internet source and destination carried in user data field of X.25 call set-up packets. (b) X.75 based gateway. Note how much of the X.25 VC service is terminated at the STE. (c) X.75-based gateways with general virtual circuit networks.

The buffering and resequencing of packets within the networks or at gateways introduces substantial variation in buffer space requirements, packet transit delays, and the potential for buffer lockups to occur [50], [51], [61].

If packets for a specific virtual circuit are restricted to pass through a fixed series of gateways, and if a standard flow-control method is agreed upon as part of the virtual circuit service, then it is possible for each internet gateway to participate in end-to-end flow control by modifying the flow control information carried in packets carried end-to-end from the source DCE to the destination DCE. Consequently, a gateway may be able to adjust the amount of traffic passing through it and thereby achieve a kind of internet gateway congestion control. If this is done by allocating buffer space for "outstanding" packets, then either the gateways must guarantee the advertised buffer space or there must be a retransmission capability built into the internet virtual circuit implementation, perhaps between source DCE and destination DCE or between DCE's and gateways.

Such a mechanism does not, however, solve the problem of network congestion unless the gateway-flow control decisions take into account resources both in the gateway and in the rest of the network. Although it is tempting to assume that virtual circuit-flow control can achieve internetwork congestion control, this is by no means clear, and is still the subject of considerable research.

As a general rule, compared to the datagram method, the virtual circuit approach requires more state information in each gateway, since knowledge of each virtual circuit must be maintained along with flow control and routing information. The usual virtual circuit interface is somewhat more complex for subscribers to implement as well, because of the amount of state information which must be shared by the subscriber and the local DCE. For example, implementations of the X.25

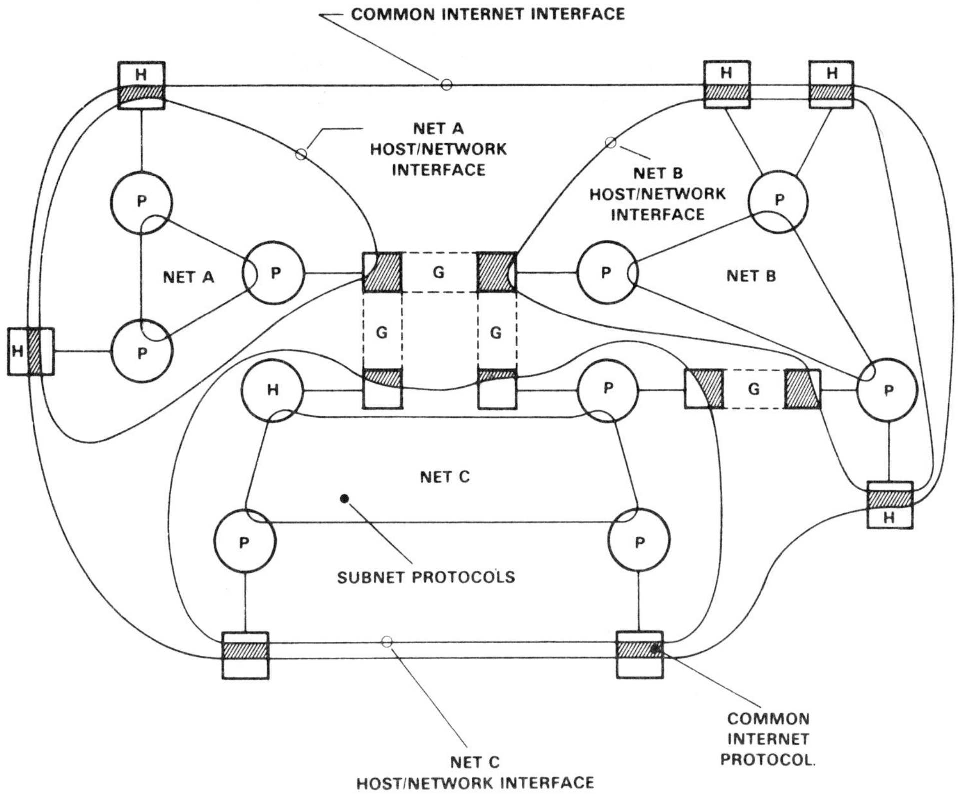

Fig. 11. Common internet interface.

interface protocol have been privately reported by Computer Corporation of America and University College London to require 4000–8000 words of memory on Digital Equipment Corporation PDP-11 computers. By contrast, the ARPANET and Packet Radio Network datagram interfaces require 500–1000 words of memory on the same machine. For internetwork operation, this may be even more burdensome, since any failure at a gateway may require a subscriber-level recovery through an end-to-end protocol, in addition to the virtual circuit interface software, as is shown in [52].

Nevertheless, it may be advantageous to consider internetworking standards which usefully employ both datagram and virtual circuit interfaces and services. For example, some special internet services such as multidestination delivery may be more efficient if they are first set up by control exchanges between the subscriber and the local network and perhaps gateways as well. Once set up, however, a datagram mode of operation may be far more efficient than maintaining virtual circuits for all destinations. Implicit virtual circuits which are activated by simple datagram-like interfaces are also attractive for very simple kinds of terminal equipment.

If it is not possible for all networks to implement a common network-access interface, then the next opportunity is to standardize only the objects which pass from one net to the next and to minimize any requirements for the sequencing of these objects as they move from net to net.

3) General Host Gateways: In this model, a gateway is indistinguishable from any other network host and will implement whatever host/network interface is required by the networks to which it is attached. For many networks, this may be X.25, but the strategy does not rely on this. The principle assumption is that packet networks are at least capable of carrying subscriber packets up to some maximum length, which may vary from network to network. It is specifically not assumed that these packets will be delivered in order through intermediate networks and gateways to the destination host. This minimal type of service is often termed "datagram" service to distinguish it from sequenced virtual circuit service. A detailed discussion of the tradeoff between datagram and virtual circuit types of networks is given elsewhere [52].

The basic model of network interconnection for the datagram host gateway is that internetwork datagrams will be carried to and from hosts and gateways and between gateways by encapsulation of the datagrams in local network packets. Pouzin describes this process generically as "wrapping" [37]. The basic internetwork service is therefore a datagram service rather than a virtual circuit service. The concept is illustrated in Fig. 11.

Datagram service does not offer the subscriber as many facilities as virtual circuit service. For example, not all datagrams are guaranteed to be delivered, nor do those that are delivered have to be delivered in the sequence they were sent. Virtual circuits, on the other hand, do attempt to deliver all packets entered by the source in sequence to the destination. These relaxations allow dynamic routing of datagrams among multiple, internetwork gateways without the need for subscriber intervention or alert.

The internet datagram concept gives subscribers access to a basic internet datagram service while allowing them to build more elaborate end-to-end protocols on top of it. Fig. 12 illustrates a possible protocol hierarchy which could be based on the internet datagram concept. The basic internet datagram service could be used to support transaction protocols or real-time protocols (RTP) such as packet-voice protocols (PVP) which do not require guaranteed or sequenced data

UTILITY	FTP	VTP	RTP	VP
END/END SUBSCRIBER	END/END VIRTUAL CIRCUIT		END/END DATAGRAM	
INTERNET ACCESS	INTERNET DATAGRAM			
NETWORK ACCESS	NETWORK SPECIFIC			
INTRANET, END-END	NETWORK SPECIFIC			
INTRANET, NODE-NODE	NETWORK SPECIFIC			
LINK CONTROL	NETWORK SPECIFIC			

Fig. 12. Protocol layering with internetwork datagrams.

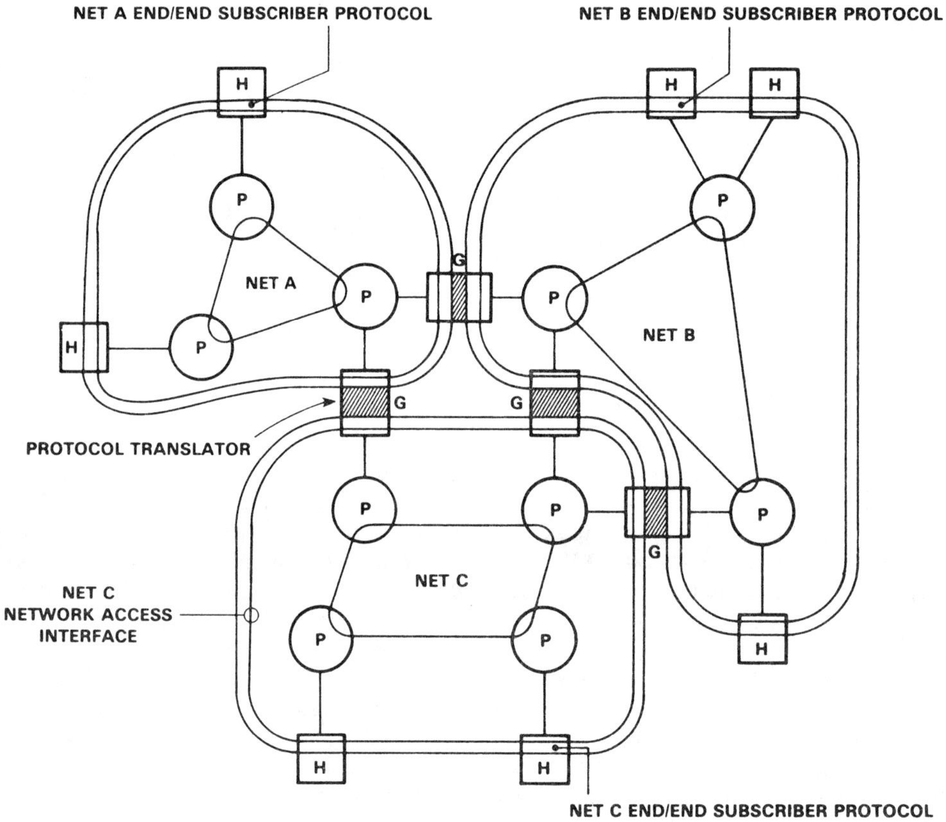

Fig. 13. Host protocol translation gateway.

delivery; reliable, sequenced protocols could be constructed above the basic internet datagram service to perform end/end sequencing and error handling. Applications such as virtual terminal protocols (VTP) [40], [42], [48] or file-transfer protocols [40], [42], [49] could be built above a reliable, point-to-point, end/end service which is itself built atop internet datagrams. Under this strategy, the basic gateway functions are the encapsulation and decapsulation of datagrams, mapping of internet source/destination addresses into local network addresses and datagram routing. Gateways need not have any knowledge of higher level protocols if it is assumed that protocols above the internet datagram layer are held in common by the communicating hosts. Datagrams can be routed freely among gateways and can be delivered out of sequence to the destination host.

The basic advantage of this strategy is that almost any sort of network can participate, whether its internal operation is datagram or virtual circuit oriented. Furthermore, the strategy offers an easy way for new networks to be made "backwards compatible," with older ones while allowing the new ones to employ new internal operations which are innovative or more efficient.

Every subscriber must implement the internet datagram concept for this strategy to work, of course. The same problem arises with the standard network interface strategy since all subscribers must implement the same network interface.

4) Protocol Translation Gateways: It would be misleading to claim that the concept of protocol translation has not played a role in the discussion thus far. In a sense, the encapsulation of internet datagrams in the packet format of each intermediate network is a form of protocol translation. The basic packet carrying service of one network is being translated into the next network's packet carrying service (see Fig. 13). This concept could be extended further. For example, if two networks have a virtual circuit concept, one implemented within the subnetwork and the other through common host/host protocols, it might be possible, at the gateway between the nets, to map one network's virtual circuit into the other's. This same idea could be applied to higher level protocol mappings as well; for instance, the virtual terminal protocol for one network might be transformed into that of another "on the fly."

The success of such a translation strategy depends in large part on the commonality of concept between the protocols to be translated. Mismatches in concept may require that the service obtained in the concatenated case be a subset of the services obtainable from either of the two services being translated. Extending such translations through several gateways can be difficult, particularly if the protocols being translated do not share a common address space for internetwork sources/destinations. In the extreme, this strategy can result in subscribers "logging in" to the gateway in order to activate the protocols of the next network. Indeed, front-end computers could be considered degenerate translation gateways since they transform host/front-end protocols into network protocols.

There are circumstances when translation cannot be avoided. For instance, when the protocols of one network cannot be modified, but internet service is desired, there may be no alternative but to implement protocol translations. The model typically used to guide protocol translation gateways is that the source/destination hosts lie on either side of the translation gateway. Concatenation of protocol translations through several networks and gateways is conceivable, but may be very difficult in practice and may produce very inefficient service.

C. Names, Addresses, and Routes

In order to manage, control, and support communication among computers on one or more networks, it is essential that conventions be established for identifying the communicators. For purposes of this discussion, we will use the term *host* to refer to all computers which attach to a network at the network-access level of protocol (see Table I). Subscribers to terminal-access services can be thought of as attaching to hosts, even if the host is embedded in the hardware and software of a packet switch as a layer of protocol. Consequently, we can say that the basic task of a packet-switching network is to transport data from a source host to one or more destination hosts.

To accomplish this task, each network needs to know to which destination packets are to be delivered. Even in broadcast nets such as the ETHERNET, this information is necessary so that the destination host can discriminate packets destined for itself from all others heard on the net. At the lowest-protocol levels it is typical to associate destinations with *addresses*. An address may be simply an integer or it may have more internal structure.

At higher levels of protocol, however, it is more common to find text strings such as "MULTICS" or "BBN-TENEX" used as *names* of destinations. Application software, such as electronic mail services, might employ such names along with more refined destination identifiers. For example, one of the authors has an electronic mailbox named "KIRSTEIN at ISI" located in a computer at the University of Southern California's Information Sciences Institute.

Typically, application programs transform names into addresses which can be understood by the packet-switching network. The networks must transform these addresses into *routes* to guide the packets to their destination. Some networks bind addresses to routes in a relatively rigid way (e.g., setting up virtual circuits with fixed routing) while others determine routes as the packets move from switch to switch, choosing alternate routes to bypass failed or congested areas of the network. Broadcast networks need not create routes at all (e.g., SATNET).

In simple terms, a *name* tells what an object is; an *address* tells where it is; and a *route* tells how to get there [54]. A simple model involving these three concepts is that hosts transform names into addresses and networks transform addresses into routes (if necessary). However, this basic model does leave a large number of loose ends. The subject is so filled with issues that it is not possible in this paper to explore them all in depth. In what follows, some of the major issues are raised and some partial resolutions are offered.

One major question is "Which objects in the network should have names? addresses?" Pouzin and Zimmermann offer a number of views on this question in their paper in this issue [37]. A generic answer might be that at least all objects which can be addressed by the network should have names as well so that high-level protocols can refer to them. For example, it might be reasonable for every host connection on the network to have an name and an address. There also may be objects internal to the network which also have addresses such as the statistics-gathering *fake hosts* in the ARPANET [38].

A related issue is whether objects should or can have multiple names, multiple addresses, and multiple routes by which they can be reached. The most general resolution of this issue is to permit multiple names, addresses, and routes to exist for the same object. An example taken from the multinetwork environment may serve to illustrate this notion. Fig. 6 shows three networks which are interconnected by a number of gateways. Each gateway (or pair of gateway halves) has two interfaces, one to each network to which it is attached. Plainly there is the possibility that several alternate routes passing through different gateways and networks could be used to carry packets from a source host in one net to a destination host in another net. This is just the analog of alternate routing within a single network.

Furthermore, each gateway has two addresses, typically one for each attached network. This is just the analog of a host on one network attached to two or more packet switches for reliability. The term *multihoming* is often used to refer to multiply attached hosts.

Finally, it may be useful to permit a gateway to have more than one name, for example, one for each network to which it is attached. This might allow high-level protocols to force packets to be routed in certain ways for diagnostic or other reasons. Multiple naming also allows the use of nicknames for user convenience. Many of these same comments would apply to hosts attached to multiple networks.

An interesting addressing and routing problem arises in mobile packet radio networks. Since hosts are free to move about, the network will need to dynamically change the routes used to reach each host. For robustness, it is also desirable that hosts be able to attach dynamically to different packet radios. Thus failure of a packet radio need not prevent hosts from accessing the network. This requires that host names and perhaps host addresses be decoupled from packet radio addresses. The network must be able to search for hosts or alternatively, hosts must "report-in" to the network so that their addresses can be associated with the attached packet radio to facilitate route selection based on host address. This is just a way of supporting *logical host addressing* rather than using the more common *physical host addressing* in which a host's address is an extension of the packet-switch address.

A crucial issue in network interconnection is the extent to which it should or must impact addressing procedures which are idiosyncratic to a particular network. It is advantageous not to require the subscribers on each network to have detailed knowledge of the network address *structure* of all interconnected networks. One possibility is to standardize an internetwork address structure which can be mapped into local network addresses as needed, either by subscribers, by gateways or by both. Subscribers would know how to map internetwork service names into addresses of the form NETWORK/SERVER. Subscribers need not know the fine structure of the SERVER field. Gateways would route packets on the basis of the NETWORK part of the address until reaching a gateway attached to the network identified by NETWORK. At this point, the gateway might interpret the SERVER part of the address, as necessary, to cause the packet to be delivered to the desired host.

The addressing strategy presently under consideration by CCITT (X.121, [30]) is based on the telephone network. Up to 14 digits can be used in an address. The first 4 digits are a "destination network identification code" or DNIC. Some countries are allocated more than one DNIC (the United States has 200). The remaining ten digits may be used to implement a hierarchical addressing structure, much like the one used in the existing telephone network.

Since the CCITT agreements are for international operation, it might be fair to assume that the United States will not need more than 200 public network identifiers. However, this scheme does not take into account the need for addressing private networks. The private networks, under this addressing procedure will most likely appear to be a collection of one or more terminals or host computers on one or more public networks. It is too early to tell how much this asymmetry in addressing between public and private networks will affect private multinetwork protocols.

A related problem which is not unique to network interconnection has to do with addressing (really multiplexing and demultiplexing) at higher protocol levels. The public carriers tend to offer services for terminal as well as host access to network facilities. This typically means that addresses must be assigned to terminals. The issue is whether the terminal address should be associated with or independent of the protocols used to support terminal-to-host communication.

The present numbering scheme would not distinguish between a host address and a terminal address. A host might have many addresses, each corresponding to a process waiting to service calling terminals.

There has been discussion within CCITT concerning "subaddressing" through the use of a user data field carried in virtual call "setup" packets. This notion would support the concept of a single host address with terminal or process level demultiplexing achieved through the use of the user data field subaddressing.

It seems reasonable to predict that, as terminals increase in complexity and capability, it will eventually be attractive to support multiple concurrent associations between the terminal and several remote service facilities. Applications requiring this capability will need terminal multiplexing conventions beyond those currently provided for in the CCITT recommendations.

To simplify implementations of internet protocol software, it is essential to place bounds on the maximum size of the NETWORK/SERVER address. Otherwise, subscribers may have to construct name-to-address mapping tables with arbitrarily large and complex entries.

Even if all these issues are resolved, there is still a question of "source routing" in which a subscriber defines the route to be taken by a particular packet or virtual circuit. Depending on the range of internetwork services available, a subscriber may want to control packet routes. It is not yet clear how such a capability will interact with access control conventions, but this may be a desirable capability if gateways are not able to automatically select routes which match user service requirements.

D. Flow and Congestion Control

For purposes of discussion, we distinguish between flow and congestion control. Flow control is a procedure through which a pair of communicators regulate traffic flowing from source to destination (each direction possibly being dealt with separately). Congestion control is a procedure whereby distributed network resources, such as channel bandwidth, buffer capacity, CPU capacity, and the like are protected from oversubscription by all sources of network traffic. In general, the successful operation of flow-control procedures for every pair of network communicants does not guarantee that the network resources will remain uncongested.

In a single network, the control of flow and congestion is a complex and not well understood problem. In a multinetwork environment it is even more complex, owing to the possible variations in flow and congestion control policies found in each constituent network. For example, some networks may rigidly control the input of packets into the network and explicitly rule out dropping packets as a means of congestion control. At the other extreme, some networks may drop packets as the sole means of congestion control.

At this stage of development, very little is known about the behavior of congestion in multiply interconnected networks. It is clear that some mechanisms will be required which permit gateways and networks to assert control over traffic influx especially when a gateway connects networks of widely varying capacity. This problem is likely to be most visible at gateways joining high speed local networks to long-haul public nets. The peak rates of the local nets might exceed that of the long-haul nets by factors of 30–100 or more. Generic procedures are needed for gateway/network and gateway/gateway flow and congestion control. Such problems also show up in single networks, but are amplified in the multinetwork case.

E. Accounting

Accounting for internetwork traffic is an important problem. The public networks need mechanisms for revenue sharing and subscribers need simple procedures for verifying the accuracy of network-provided accountings.

The public packet-switching networks appear to be converging on procedures which account for subscriber use on the basis of the number of virtual circuits created during the accounting period and the number of packets sent on each virtual circuit. Indeed, it has been argued that accounting on the basis of virtual circuits at gateways requires less overhead than accounting on a pure datagram basis [32]. Scenarios can be cited which support the opposite conclusion.

Suppose there is a choice between setting up virtual circuits for each transaction and sending a datagram for each transaction, and that virtual circuit accounting includes information on each virtual circuit setup (as in the present telephone network). If datagram accounting simply accumulates the number of datagrams sent between particular sources and destinations without regard to the time at which they are sent, then the amount of accounting information which is collected for the datagram case will be substantially less than for the virtual circuit case. In the limit (i.e., one packet per transaction), the virtual circuit accounting information is proportional to $2N$, where N is the number of transactions, while for the datagram case, it is proportional to log N (base 2). This is simply because the datagram case only sums counts for traffic between source/destination pairs while the virtual circuit accounting would identify start/stop times for each virtual circuit.

Alternatively, if the bulk of the traffic involves a large number of packets per transaction, then the two accounting procedures would accumulate more nearly the same information since each would predominantly involve accounting for packet flow.

If it is chosen not to account for virtual circuit duration, but merely to account independently for the number of virtual circuits and the number of packets sent between source/destination pairs, then the virtual circuit accounting would be closer to the datagram case.

The important conclusion to be drawn is that accounting for datagrams is generally less complex than accounting for virtual circuits, but that the two can be made arbitrarily similar by suitable choice of the details of the accounting information collected.

F. Access Control

In multinetwork environments, it may be necessary for each network to establish and enforce a policy for "out-of-network" routing. For example, a public network might conclude agreements with other networks regarding the type and quantity of traffic it will forward into other networks. This might even be a function of the time-of-day. Consequently, mechanisms are needed which will permit networks to prevent traffic from entering or leaving or to meter the type and rate of traffic passing into or out of the network.

Another example of the need for control arises with the possibility of third-party routing. That is, traffic destined from network A to network B is routed through network C. It cannot be assumed that all networks have gateways to all others. However, some nets may want to limit the amount of *transit* traffic they carry. There may be explicit agreements among a subset of the nets regarding revenue sharing for transit services. If a particular network does not have a revenue-sharing agreement with the particular source/destination networks of a given virtual circuit or datagram, then it must be able to reject the offending traffic if it so chooses.

There does not seem to be any technical barrier to separating the access control policy decision mechanism from the enforcement of the policy. For example, a gateway might simply enforce policy by sending traffic for which it has no known access rules to an *access controller*. If we adhere to the model that gateways have two *halves*, then each half deals with the network to which it is connected. The access controller can either dynamically enable the flow by causing table entries at the gateways which permit the flow to be created or it can tell the gateway to reject all further traffic of that type.

Clearly, access control policies will affect routing strategies, so this adds a complicating factor into any internetwork routing strategy implemented by the gateways. At present, very little experience has been accumulated with internet access control and routing policies. For the most part, agreements among public networks have been bilateral and transit routing has been treated as a very special case. When EURONET [6] becomes operational, this problem will be particularly important to solve.

G. Internet Services

It is by no means clear what set of services should be standardized and available from, at least, all public data networks. The current CCITT recommendations provide for virtual circuit service and terminal access service on all public packet-switching networks.

Although the recommendations (X.3, X.25) provide for *fragmentation* of packets being delivered to a subscriber on a virtual circuit, the current X.75 gateway draft recommendation uses an agreed maximum packet size of 128 octets of data, not including the header. This agreement avoids for the moment the need to fragment packets crossing a network boundary, as long as all subscribers recognize that the maximum length internetwork packet allowed is 128 octets. Bilateral exceptions to this rule may develop but neither a fixed size nor a collection of special cases represent a very general solution to this problem.

It has been argued [25] that a general scheme for dealing with fragmentation is desirable so that new network technologies supporting larger packet sizes can be easily integrated into the multinetwork environment.

Apart from fragmentation, there are a set of special services such as multidestination addressing and broadcasting which could be used to good advantage to support multinetwork applications such as teleconferencing, electronic mail distribution, distributed file systems, and real-time data collection. Other services such as low delay, high reliability, high bandwidth, and high priority are also candidates for standardization at the internet level.

As in the case of access control, selection of such services might constrain the choice of packet routing to networks capable of supporting the desired services. Once again, very little experience with standard internet services has been accumulated so this subject is still a topic for research. For the most part, terminal-to-host services have been successfully offered across network boundaries using nearly all of the network interconnection methods described in this paper. It remains to be seen whether more complex applications can be equally well supported.

VII. X.25/X.75–The CCITT Strategy for Network Interconnection

The common network access interface concept is favored by CCITT for network interconnection. In the CCITT model of packet networking, all networks offer the same interface to packet-mode subscribers and this is called X.25. X.25 is a virtual circuit interface protocol. However, gateways between networks employ an interface protocol called X.75 [33], which is much like X.25 but accommodates special network/network information exchange, such as routing information, accounting information, and so on.

Fig. 10(a) illustrates the basic network interconnection strategy proposed by CCITT. To appreciate the difference between this strategy and the "common subnetwork" strategy, it is necessary to have some understanding of the X.25 packet network interface. X.25 provides a virtual circuit interface for the setup, use, and termination of virtual circuits between subscribers of the networks. X.25 provides for flow control of packets per virtual circuit flowing into or out of the network. Subscribers may set up switched virtual circuits by sending "call request" packets into the network and receiving "call confirmation" packets in return. The standard also provides for permanent virtual circuits.

The public networks plan to employ X.25 interfaces; it can therefore be assumed that source and destination hosts in different networks will essentially want to exchange "call request" and "call accepted" packets through the mediation of one or more gateways. This strategy could result in a series of virtual circuits chaining source host to gateway, gateway to gateway, and gateway to destination host; alternately an end-to-end virtual circuit could be set up from source host to destination host, with the gateways acting as relays without any special knowledge of the virtual circuits passing across the network boundary.

The principle difference between the X.25 interface and X.75 interface is that virtual circuit setup and clearing packets are passed transparently by the X.75 gateway to the next gateway or destination. For reasons which are described below, it is necessary to maintain the sequence of packets belonging to a given X.25 virtual circuit as they pass through a gateway and enter the next network. Therefore, a virtual circuit is in fact created between the source host and intermediate gateway and between gateways. The X.75 gateway does not spontaneously generate any "call acceptance" packets in response to "call request" packets, but it does participate in the sequencing and flow control of packets on each virtual circuit passing through. Other differences between the X.25 and X.75 interface have to do with the nature of the internetwork accounting or routing information which might be exchanged over X.75 which would not be appropriate for a subscriber to exchange with the network over the X.25 interface.

The design of the X.75 type of gateway depends in principle upon all networks' use of the X.25 subscriber interface. Some networks, like the ETHERNET, cannot implement it without extensive modification, because there are no packet switches in the network to support the required packet reordering at the destination. The alternative is to insist that all internet applications rely on a sequenced data protocol built into the hosts or front-ends. For some services, such as packet speech, the potential overhead of resequencing packets before delivery to the destination may prevent the service from being viable. This problem could be amplified if packets are constrained to remain in sequence as they pass the X.75 boundary.

Fig. 10(b) and (c) shows variants of the CCITT interconnection strategy. In Fig. 10(b), we see an example in which only X.25 is used both as a network access method and as a means of passing traffic across network boundaries. A single subscriber or a pair of subscribers to two nets could interface to their networks via X.25 and to each other by means of some agreed and possibly private protocol.

Virtual circuits would be explicitly set up from source host to gateway, gateway to gateway, and gateway to destination host. The "internet" addresses of the source and destination hosts could be carried in the so-called "Call User Data Field" of an X.25 Call Request packet. This leaves the packet address field free to identify intermediate destinations (e.g., gateways), but preserves an ultimate internetwork source/destination address which the gateway can use to select the destination to which the next intermediate virtual circuit is to be set up.

An alternative to this is shown in Fig. 10(c) in which the subnets *A* and *B* use nonstandard virtual circuit interfaces, but agree to build gateway software employing X.75 signaling procedures across the gateway interface. This solution is substantially the same as that shown in Fig. 10(b), except there is now additional translation software in each gateway half to make each virtual circuit network-access protocol compatible with X.75 procedures.

There are some specific problems with the X.25/X.75 gateway strategy, which do not necessarily apply to other virtual call gateways [63]. The basic X.25 interface provides for the sequence numbering of subscriber packets mod. 8 or, optionally, mod. 128. Since X.25 is an interface specification, this numbering can only be relied upon to have local significance (i.e., host-to-packet switch). Some X.25 implementations use these host-assigned sequence numbers on an end-to-end basis. Others generate internal, network-supplied numbers to allow for repacking of subscriber packets into larger or smaller units for transport to the destination. If packet sequence numbers assigned by the source host were carried transparently to the destination without change, it might be possible to allow packets to flow out-of-order across the X.75 boundary to a gateway and thence into the next network. If the packet sequence numbers were still intact, they could be carried out-of-order to the next destination which might either be a gateway or an X.25 host. In the latter case, the original packet-sequence numbers could be used to resequence the packets before delivery. If the packets were being delivered to an intermediate gateway, they would not have to be sequenced there. However, the X.25 interface specification does not undertake to carry the host-supplied sequence numbers to the destination gateway or host in a transparent fashion, primarily so that the subnetwork can deal more freely with the physical packaging of the packet stream. For example, a source may supply packets of length 128 bytes while a destination may prefer to receive packets no longer than 64 bytes. To allow for such variations, the network must be free to renumber packets for delivery. These considerations have two consequences.

1) X.25 packet sequence numbers cannot be relied on for end-to-end signaling, though they could be so used if requisite information is known about the intermediate transit networks.

2) Packets must be delivered in sequence when passing to or from gateways and hosts on X.25 networks.

The second conclusion may be modified slightly. It is at least essential that packets be delivered in relative sequence on each virtual circuit. By maintaining independent sequence numbering on each virtual circuit, it is possible for hosts and gateways to refuse traffic on one virtual circuit while accepting traffic on another. There are two penalties for this. First, a gateway must keep track of which virtual circuits are passing through it. Second, dynamic alternate routing of packets belonging to the same virtual circuit through alternate gateways is not possible without resetting or clearing the virtual circuit. This last point is simply the consequence of not defining an end-to-end sequence numbering scheme, but instead relying on sequencing of the packets of a virtual circuit on entry to and exit from each intermediate network.

Some networks implement X.25 level acknowledgments (i.e., level 3) that have an end-to-end significance, but others make this purely a host-to-packet switch matter. As a conse-

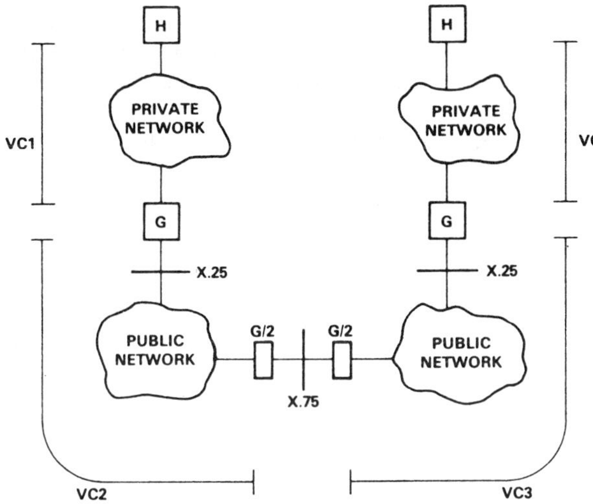

Fig. 14. Use of X.25 for public/private network interconnection.

quence, it is not possible to rely on X.25 packet acknowledgments to determine which, if any, packets were not delivered as a result of the resetting or clearing of a virtual circuit. Furthermore, even if a subnet were to offer an end-to-end acknowledgment between a source host and an X.75 gateway, this could not be assumed to guarantee that the acknowledged packet was delivered to the ultimate X.25 destination in another network.

X.75 is an interface intended for use between public networks. Thus, it is not likely to be used or even allowed as an interface between public networks and private networks. For the case illustrated in Fig. 14, X.25 interfaces could be provided between public and private networks (or other special interfaces) and X.75 interfaces between public networks. Consequently, gateways between public and private networks are likely to appear to be ordinary host computers in the view of the public networks.

The use of X.25 for private/public network interfaces and X.75 for public/public network interfaces leads to the situation shown in Fig. 14 in which an internetwork virtual circuit would have to be made up of several concatenated parts such as virtual circuits 1-2-3-4 (see also [52, Fig. 3.4]). Even if X.25 implementations uniformly permitted an end-to-end interpretation of packet sequence numbers and acknowledgments, there would still be separate virtual circuits required between the source or destination hosts and the gateways into the public networks. However, the concatenation of virtual circuits does not yield a virtual circuit. For instance, a gateway between the public and private net could acknowledge a packet but fail to get it delivered, in which case the subscriber will have been misinformed as to the delivery of the packet. This situation forces the end subscribers of private networks to implement end-to-end procedures on top of any concatenated virtual circuits provided by the public networks.

VIII. Practical Network Connections and Experiments in Progress

A number of networks have been connected successfully over the last few years. Most of these connections have been made in an *ad hoc* manner, using one of the following techniques.

1) One network is a star network with remote RJE and interactive stations. The other is a star or distributed network with clearly defined protocols. A device on the star network provides exactly the functions required by its own network on one side, and those of the other network on the other side.

2) Formal gateways are provided between the two networks, and protocol mapping occurs in the gateway.

3) A computer is a host on two networks. It is arranged that services are provided by accepting input from one network and putting it out on another, possibly after substantial processing.

4) Formal gateways are provided between the two networks. Sufficient agreement is obtained that end-to-end protocols (even high level ones) are common in the two networks. In this case, less activity is required in the gateway.

In the first method, a form of front-end computer is used. It has been adopted in the large airline and banking networks SITA [13] and SWIFT [14]. In each case the standards for the networks have been defined rigidly. SWIFT has even certified officially the devices of three manufacturers to provide interfaces to its network. The other side of the device is then programmed to meet the requirements of the star system being attached. In the two cases cited, only a simple message level of interface needed to be defined.

Other examples of the same technique are the connection of the Rutherford Laboratory (RL) star system [53] and the Livermore CTRNET to ARPANET. In these examples, more serious protocol mapping was required. ARPANET has a well-defined set of HOST-IMP, HOST-HOST, Virtual Terminal, and File Transfer protocols. All these had to be mapped into the appropriate procedures for the other network.

The second method has been applied only experimentally. The UCL interface between ARPANET and the UK Post Office Experimental Packet Switched Service (EPSS, [55]) and the National Physical Laboratory interface between EPSS and the European Informatics Network (EIN, [56]) are examples of this technique; a demonstration has even been made of EIN-EPSS-ARPANET with no extra problems encountered from the three networks being concatenated. Technically there is almost no difference between the first two methods. The second looks at first sight somewhat more general than the first, but almost the same problems have to be overcome. The difficulties come from the fundamental differences in the design choices made in the protocols of the different networks; these differences are in general difficult, and even sometimes impossible, to resolve completely. In the first method, they can sometimes be resolved using a specific facility in the star network; in the second, where two distributed networks are involved, this recourse may no longer be available.

One example of the problem occurs in the connection of EPSS and ARPANET. ARPANET can forward any number of characters at a time, and often uses full duplex remote echoing. EPSS works in a half-duplex mode, forwarding only complete records. A special "Transmit Now" has to be input by the user, and interpreted by the gateway, to ensure that partial records are forwarded. Another example, from the same application, occurs in File Transfer. ARPANET assumes an interactive process is live throughout the file transfer; all completion codes are passed over this live channel. The RL network (and EPSS) assume that file transfer is a batch process; they return network completion codes at a later time, and may delay acting on the commands. With the ARPANET-RL link [53], the file transfer job had to be given a very high priority, so that the completion code usually arrived before a timeout occurred; because of the nature of the way the computer was used for large real-time jobs, this did not always ensure that the job was run in a reasonable time.

There are several examples of the third technique. A DEC PDP 10 machine used on the Stanford University SUMEX project is a host both on ARPANET and on TYMNET; several machines at Bolt, Beranek and Newman are both on ARPANET and TELENET. Because the TENEX operating system has good facilities for linking between programs, it would be possible for interactive streams to come in one network and go out on another. File transfer problems would be simple in this configuration, because the hosts obey all the conventions, in any case, of each network. Of course, this mode of operation may require that files in transit between networks may have to be stored temporarily in their entirety in the host serving as the gateway between the networks.

The fourth technique is newer, and has many variations. As a result of agreement on the X.25, and partial agreement on the X.75, protocols, PTT networks are able to interconnect in a reasonably straightforward manner. The connections between DATAPAC and both TELENET and TYMNET have been done in this way. In each case, there has not been any agreement on higher level protocols, so the problems of host-host communication across concatenated networks is not resolved by these linkups of the subnets.

The ARPA-sponsored INTERNET project has tried to standardize to a higher level. A host-host protocol has been defined (TCP, [25]), and is being implemented on a number of different networks including Packet Radio [20], [21], ETHERNET [18], LCSNET [64] and the SATNET [22], in addition to ARPANET. This protocol is defined for use across networks; thus each packet includes an "Internet Header" which is kept invariant as the packet crosses the different networks. One aspect of the INTERNET program is to develop gateways which can interpret this header appropriately.

By late 1976, the ARPA project had connected together the Packet Radio Network, the ARPANET, and the Atlantic Packet Satellite Network using two gateways between the Packet Radio Network and the ARPANET and three gateways between the ARPANET and Packet Satellite Network. It is routinely possible to access ARPANET computing resources via either of the other nets and to artificially route traffic through multiple nets to test the impact on performance. In one such test, a user in a mobile van in the San Francisco area accessed a DEC PDP-10 TENEX system at the University of Southern California's Information Sciences Institute over the following path:

1) from van to the first gateway into ARPANET via the Packet Radio Network;
2) across the ARPANET to a second gateway in London, using a satellite link internal to the ARPANET;
3) across the Atlantic Satellite Network to a third gateway in Boston;
4) across the ARPANET again to USC-ISI.

The user and server were 400 geographical miles apart, but the communication path was 50000 miles long and passed through three gateways and four networks. Except for a slightly increased round-trip delay time, service was equivalent to a direct path through the ARPANET. Since the Packet Radio Network is potentially lossy, can duplicate packets, and can deliver packets out of order, the end/end TCP protocol was used to exercise flow and error control on an end-to-end basis. The availability of a common set of host-level protocols substantially aided the ease with which this test could be conducted.

The ARPA project also has high-level standard protocols already in existence to support file transfer and virtual terminals (the FTP and TELNET protocols [40]), and these are being retrofitted above the internet TCP protocol to provide a standard high-level internetwork protocol hierarchy.

IX. Regulatory Issues

The regulatory issues in the interconnection of packet networks takes a different form in North America than elsewhere. It is hard in a paper of this type to more than touch on some of the problems involved. The discussion here is simplistic in the extreme, and no attempt is made to put the issues in the legalistic language they really require.

In almost all countries the provision of long distance communication transmission and switching is provided by a regulated carrier. In most countries outside North America, this carrier is a single national entity—called the "PTT". In some countries (e.g., Italy) there are different carriers for different services—e.g., telegraph, telephone, intercity, international telephone, etc. In North America there are many carriers. Usually only one in each geographical area has a monopoly on public switched voice traffic. Also the so-called "Record Carriers" have some sort of monopoly on "record traffic," which is message traffic. In a "Value Added Network" (VAN), the operators rent transmission equipment from the carriers, and then add their own switching equipment. These VAN's are themselves regulated in what they may do, what traffic they may carry, and what rates they may charge. Between North America and Europe, specific "International Record Carriers" (IRC) have monopoly rights on data and message transmission —in collaboration with the appropriate European PTT's. The regulations take into account who owns the hosts and terminals, who owns the switches, who rents the transmission lines, what types of traffic is carried, what is the geographic extent of the network, and what is the technology of long distance transmission.

In Fig. 15, a single network N is sketched. It consists of switches S and transmission lines L; these together are called the data network, DN. It consists also of terminals T and hosts H; the exact difference between a terminal and a host is not very clear; we believe it is assumed that terminals mainly enter and retrieve data without processing; while a host transforms the information by processing. This definition probably does not meet the picture of modern "intelligent terminals," but it is always hard for the regulations to keep up with the technology. If the total network is all localized in one site, so that no communication lines cross public rights of way, then it can usually be considered from a regulatory viewpoint, as a single host in more complex network connections. The hosts and the terminals can be connected to the switches, and the switches to each other, either by leased lines, or by the Public Switched Telephone Network; the first type of connection is called a *leased* connection, the second *switched*. In the subsequent discussion of this section, the term "host" will include localized networks. In general we will assume the connections between the switches are via leased lines; if that is not the case, the regulations are much eased in general (though in some countries, like Brazil, no data transmission is permitted at all via switched telephone lines).

If all the hosts and switches are owned by one organization P, which also leases the lines, then P is said to own and operate the network, and it is called a "Private Network." There are

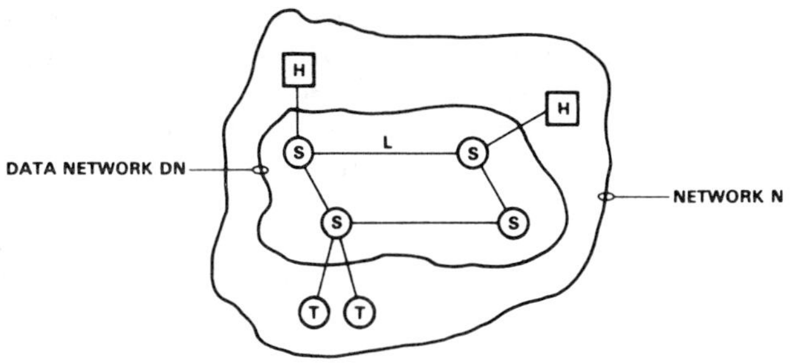

Fig. 15. Schematic of one network.

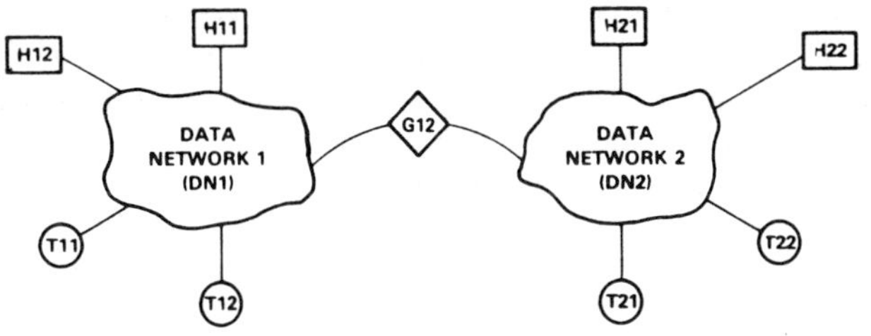

Fig. 16. Schematic of two connected networks.

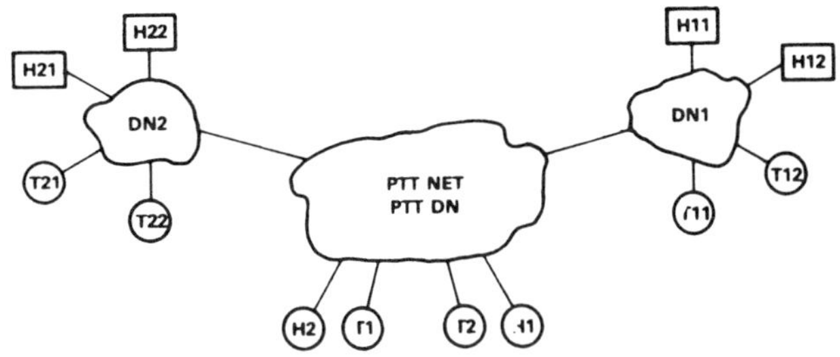

Fig. 17. Schematic of PTT model.

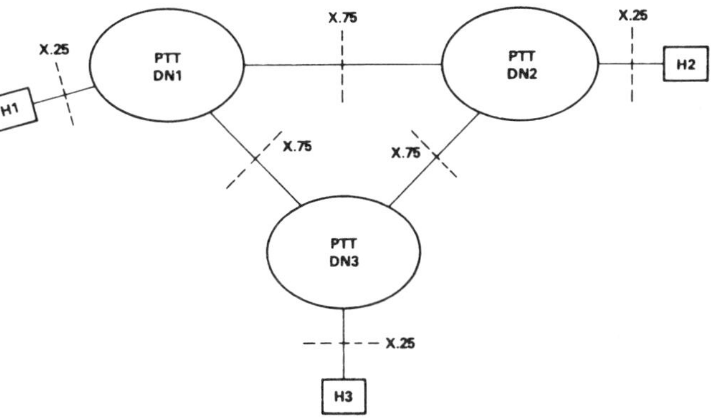

Fig. 18. Multiple PTT network interconnection.

minimal restrictions on such networks—though in West Germany, for example, higher tariffs are charged for the leased lines if any terminals or hosts are connected via the PSTN. In most countries such a network may not be used for the transfer of messages between terminals belonging to organizations other than *P*.

If the data network belongs to one organization, and the hosts to others, the data network is a VAN. Stringent regulations apply to VAN's, in most countries. With rare exceptions, in most European countries, VAN's can be operated only by the PTT's. In the U.S., they can be operated by other organizations, but only if approved as regulated Value Added Carriers (VAC's) by the Federal Communications Commission (FCC). One regulation imposed by the U.S. is that an organization operating as a VAC may not also operate a host for outside sale of services. For this reason, the companies TYMSHARE and ITT have had to spin off their VAC's into separate subsidiaries, TYMNET and ITT Data Services.

In the past, a few VAN's have been permitted to operate internationally for specific interest groups. Two such VAN's are SITA [14], for the airlines, and SWIFT [14] for the banking community. Here the regulations can be stringent. SWIFT has to pay specially high tariffs for its leased lines; its license to operate may be revoked when the PTT's can offer a comparable international service.

As soon as two networks, owned by different organizations, are interconnected, there are regulatory difficulties. This situation is illustrated schematically in Fig. 16. Even if one network is an internal one, so that it can be treated as a single host, its connection to other network immediately changes the latter's status. Thus in Fig. 16, the connection of *DN*1 to *DN*2 immediately changes *DN*2 to a VAN. In Europe it has been decreed that such private networks may not connect directly to each other, but only through a PTT network. Thus the most general configuration permitted by the European PTT's is illustrated in Fig. 17. Moreover, the PTT's have also agreed that only the X.25 interface will be provided to customers, though that interface was defined for the configuration of Fig. 15 rather than 17. The different PTT networks will themselves connect to each other by the different interface X.75 as illustrated in Fig. 18. This does not change, however, the interface seen by the private networks. Further work is needed to assess the suitability of X.25 in this role.

In the U.S., the regulations are not quite so stringent. Connections such as Fig. 15 are permitted even where one host belongs to a different organization than the network operator *P*—provided such connection is only limited and for the purposes of using the facilities of that network. This type of relaxation is really necessary, because of the difficulty of distinguishing between a "host" and a "terminal". In practice, in most countries, the line is drawn between leased line and PSTN connections. The former are usually not permitted without change of status of the network; the latter seem to downgrade the connection to that of a terminal.

The discussion above has treated the types of connections which can be made. In addition, the PTT's, and the FCC in the U.S., usually regulate the purposes for which the network can be used. In particular, there is a ban on such networks being used for message or voice transmission between organizations. How such measures are to be policed, gets us into another regulatory problem. For example the UK PO [57] has claimed a right to inspect the contents of any data message sent across lines leased from it; this right would be at variance with the privacy laws being enacted in many countries [58], [59]. This subject is a large one in its own right, and it is clearly beyond the scope of this paper.

Two other service problems will arise in international connections. First the impact and form of the privacy and transnational data flow regulations in different countries are different. Thus in the interconnection of international networks, a particular set of problems may arise, even when the appropriate regulations are obeyed in each network separately. Thus both Network 1 in country *A* and Network 2 in country *B* may obey their own national regulations. However when the networks A and B are connected, Network 1's practices may break country B's regulations, and yet be accessible from country B. It is this class of problems which delayed seriously the permission by the Swedish Data Inspectorate Board for Swedish banks to connect their networks to SWIFT.

Secondly, some of the functions of networks or gateways legal in one country may be illegal in another. Thus U.S. carriers are not permitted to do data processing in their data networks; no such considerations apply in most European countries. Some of the protocol translation activities, some of the message processing activities, and some of the high-level services (e.g. the provision of multiaddress links) may well be classed as "Data Processing," and hence be illegal in the U.S. In interconnected networks, this raises the possibility that functions can be carried out outside the jurisdiction of the country in which the operator initiating the activity is sited, and yet which is illegal in that country. This subject is treated rather fully elsewhere [60]. A clear example of this is the use of message services operated by TYMSHARE and CCA on TELENET and TYMNET. While these services are legal in the U.S., their use by UK persons connected to TYMNET by the official International Packet Switched Service is clearly technically illegal; this use would contravene the UK Post Office Monopoly.

X. Unresolved Research Questions

There are many unresolved research questions; on some of them even the present authors do not agree with each other! Primarily these questions have a technical, policy, administrative, economic, regulatory, or operational aspect, or a combination of these.

One example of this is the question of the procedures to be used for internet routing. Here there are technical questions on what is feasible in view of the technologies used in the subnets; there are policy questions on when third country routing might be allowed; there are economic considerations on how much it would cost to do the necessary protocol translation to route through third countries, and on what charges the connecting transit network might make; there may be regulatory questions on which classes of data may flow through specific countries (related to the transnational data flow regulations); and there may be operational questions on whether in the event of failure in dynamic rerouting, reestablishment could take place with sufficient rapidity.

Among the outstanding research questions are, in alphabetic order, the following.

Access Control: What are the requirements and methods of implementation of access control? How should they affect internetwork routing?

Addressing: How should the International Numbering Plan, which goes to the level of known subscribers of public networks, be extended? Should this extension be in the numbering plan itself, or should additional user and network information be supplied? Should there be local, or only physical, addressing? Should there be internetwork source routing implied by the addressing?

Broadcast Facilities: What is the role of broadcast communication facilities in the provision of internet services? Should facilities using it be offered? Should technologies supporting it use it, particularly at gateways? What are the implications on protocols, especially with respect to duplicate and error detection?

Datagram versus Virtual Call Facilities: How should datagram and virtual call facilities be interconnected? How can one compare the relative performance and costs of the implementations? What criteria should be used in any comparison? When might datagram, or alternatively virtual calls, be desirable or essential between networks?

Data Protection: What are the effects of end-to-end data encryption on protocol translation?

Flow and Congestion Control: To what extent should one adopt congestion and flow control between gateways and their feeding networks, between gateways directly, or between gateways and the source? What are the relative effects of just discarding packets in gateways, and relying on the end-to-end protocol to detect and compensate for this? How is charging for discarded packets arranged?

High Level Protocols: There are still many questions on what should be standardized, and how rigid the standards should be. To what extent should the individual networks support common standards, and to what extent should protocol translation be feasible technically or attractive economically? What are the costs of maintaining standards or the economic advantages of standard hardware and software? How does the technology of individual networks and the proportion of internetwork traffic affect the decisions?

Internetwork Diagnosis: There are many technical problems in isolating faults in concatenated networks. There are also organizational and economic problems on who should be responsible for their repair, and how costs for service failures should be allocated.

Performance: How do choices of design parameters, and network services, affect the costs of the individual networks? How do the individual network performances and costs scale to large networks? How do the choices affect the feasibility, costs and performance of the gateways? How do the variations in technology or choice of parameters affect the performance in interconnected networks?

Routing Policies: To what extent and when should adaptive routing be used between networks? How can one recover from the partitioning of a single network, when there are still routes existing by going through other networks? How should administrative considerations affect routing policies between networks (privacy regulations, economic considerations of internet payments, desire to provide for high availability, etc.)? When is a hierarchical organization more efficient that a direct route search?

Services: What services are needed on an internetwork level? Clearly interactive and bulk transport services must be supported. What else is needed? Should the internetwork facilities be able to support voice, telemetry, and teleconferencing? What is the cost of supporting these latter services, and what is their effect on other facilities?

X.25 and X.75 and Related Recommendations: Is X.25 suitable for transaction processing? Are the present datagram proposals adequate? How should X.25 be extended for internet addressing? How should X.25/X.75 be modified to allow the connection of private to public networks, or private networks to each other? Do the X.3, X.28, X.29 pad concepts extend well to the internet environment, or should they be modified?

XI. Conclusions

In view of all the unresolved questions discussed in Section X, most of the conclusions which can be drawn in this paper must be tentative. From the early part of the paper, we have shown that it is essential that techniques be developed for connecting computer networks. Moreover, no single set of techniques will fit all applications.

The services which will normally have to be supported are terminal access, bulk transfer, remote job entry, and transaction processing. The quality and facilities of the services required will be very dependent on the applications.

The connections between networks can be made at the level of the packet switches or of hosts, and can be on a datagram or virtual call basis. Connection at the packet-switch level requires broadly similar network access procedures, or complex protocol transformation at the gateways between the networks. If the network protocols are different, interconnection can be most easily achieved if done at the host level. The higher levels of service can be mapped at service centers, which need not be colocated with the gateways—but very different philosophies of network services can be very difficult to map. Alternatively, subscribers can implement common higher level protocols if these can be agreed upon.

The principal problems in connecting networks are much the same as those in the design of the individual networks of heterogeneous systems—but the lack of a single controlling authority can make the multinet design problem more difficult to solve. It is essential to resolve the usual problems of flow control, congestion control, routing, addressing, fault recovery, flexibility, protocol standards, and economy. The public carriers have attempted to resolve many of these problems; particularly in the areas of flexibility, addressing, and economy we feel their solutions are not yet adequate. At the higher levels of protocol, much more standardization is required before we have really satisfactory long term solutions.

The advent of international computer networks, private networks which must communicate with other private networks (even if via public ones), and the new applications of computer networks, raise regulatory and legal issues which are far from resolution.

Many technical solutions to the problems of the connection of networks are discussed in this paper. Their applicability in view of the different technical, economic, and policy constraints imposed in different countries must still be assessed.

References

[1] L. G. Roberts, "Telenet: Principles and practice," in *Proc. Eur. Computing Conf. Communication Networks,* London, England, pp. 315-329, 1975.

[2] W. W. Clipsham, F. E. Glave, and M. L. Narraway, "Datapac network overview," in *Proc. Third Int. Conf. Computer Communication,* Toronto, Canada, pp. 131-136, 1976.

[3] J. Rinde, "TYMNET: An alternative to packet switching technology," in *Proc. Third Int. Conf. Computer Communication,* Toronto, Canada, pp. 268-273, 1976.

[4] R. E. Millstein, "The national software works: a distributed processing system," in *Proc. ACM Nat. Conf.*, Seattle, WA. 1977.

[5] A. Danet, R. Despres, A. Le Rest, G. Pichon, and S. Ritzenthaler, "The French public packet switching service, The TRANSPAC network," in *Proc. Third Int. Conf. Computer Communication,* Toronto, Canada, pp. 251-269, 1976.

[6] G. W. P. Davies, "EURONET project," in *Proc. Third Int. Conf. Computer Communication,* Toronto, Canada, pp. 229-239, 1976.

[7] R. Nakamura, F. Ishino, M. Sasaoka, and M. Nakamura, "Some design aspects of a public switched network," in *Proc. Third Int. Conf. Computer Communication,* Toronto, Canada, pp. 317-322, 1976.

[8] F. A. Helsel and A. J. Spadafora, "Siemens system EDS–A new stored program controlled switching system for telex and data networks," in *Proc. Third Int. Computer Communications Conf.*, Toronto, Canada, pp. 51-55, 1976.

[9] T. Larsson, "A public data network in the nordic countries," in *Proc. Third Int. Computer Communications Conf.*, Toronto, Canada, pp. 246-250, 1976.

[10] P. T. Kirstein, "Planned new public data networks," *Comput. Networks*, vol. 1, no. 2, pp. 79-94, 1976.

[11] P. T. F. Kelly, "An overview of recent developments in common user data communications networks," in *Proc. Third Int. Computer Communications Conf.*, Toronto, Canada, pp. 5-10, 1976.

[12] ——, "Public packet switched data networks," this issue, pp. 1539-1549.

[13] P. Hirsch, "SITA rating a packet-switched network," *Datamation*, vol. 20, pp. 60-63, 1974.

[14] G. Lapidus, "SWIFT network," *Data Communications*, vol. 5, no. 5, pp. 20-24, 1976.

[15] L. G. Roberts and B. D. Wessler, "The ARPA network," in *Computer-Communications Networks*, N. Abramson and F. Kuo, Eds. Englewood Cliffs, NJ: Prentice-Hall, 1973, pp. 485-500.

[16] P. M. Karp, "Origin, development, and current status of the ARPANET," in *Proc. COMPCON73*, San Francisco, CA, Feb.-Mar. 1973, pp. 49-52.

[17] L. Pouzin, "Presentation and major design aspects of the CYCLADES computer network," in *Proc. Third Data Communications Symp.*, Tampa, FL, Nov. 1973, pp. 80-85.

[18] R. M. Metcalfe and D. R. Boggs, "ETHERNET: Distributed packet switching for local computer networks," *Commun. ACM*, vol. 19, no. 7, pp. 395-404, July 1976.

[19] A. S. Fraser, "SPYDER–A data communications experiment," *Comput. Sci. Tech. Report*, no. 23, Bell Laboratories, Dec. 1974.

[20] R. E. Kahn, "The organization of computer resources in a packet radio network," in *Proc. Nat. Computer Conf.*, AFIPS Press, pp. 177-186, May 1975.

[21] R. E. Kahn, S. A. Gronemeyer, J. Burchfiel, and R. C. Kunzelman, "Advances in packet radio technology," this issue, pp. 1468-1496.

[22] I. M. Jacobs, R. Binder, and E. V. Hoversten, "General purpose satellite networks," this issue, pp. 1448-1467.

[23] D. Lloyd and P. T. Kirstein, "Alternate approaches to the connection of computer networks," in *Proc. Eur. Computing Conf. Communication Networks*, London, England, ONLINE, pp. 499-504, 1975.

[24] L. Pouzin, "A proposal for interconnecting packet switching networks," IFIP Working Group 6.1, General Note no. 60, Mar. 1974.

[25] V. G. Cerf and R. E. Kahn, "A protocol for packet network interconnection," *IEEE Trans. Commun. Technol.*, vol. COM-22, pp. 637-641, 1974.

[26] C. Sunshine, "Interconnection of computer networks," *Comput. Networks*, vol. 1, 1977, pp. 175-195.

[27] CCITT, "Recommendation X.3: International user facilities in public data networks," *Public Data Networks, Orange Book*, vol. viii.2, Sixth Plenary Assembly, Int. Telecommunications Union, Geneva, Switzerland, pp. 21-23, 1977.

[28] CCITT, "Recommendation X.25: Interface between data terminal equipment (DTE) and data circuit-terminating equipment (DEC) for terminals operating in the packet mode on public data networks," *Public Data Networks, Orange Book*, vol. VIII.2, Sixth Plenary Assembly, Int. Telecommunications Union, Geneva, Switzerland, pp. 70-108, 1977.

[29] CCITT, "Provisional recommendations X.3, X.25, X.28 and X.29 on packet-switched data transmission services," Int. Telecommunications Union, Geneva, Switzerland, 1977.

[30] CCITT, "Recommendation X.121–Int. numbering plan for public data networks," Study Group VII, Temporary Document 76-E, Int. Telecommunications Union, Geneva, Switzerland, April 25, 1978.

[31] L. Pouzin, "Virtual circuits vs. datagrams–Technical and political problems," in *Proc. Nat. Computer Conf.*, AFIPS Press, pp. 483-494, 1976.

[32] L. G. Roberts, "International connection of public packet networks," in *Proc. Third Int. Conf. Computer Communications*, Toronto, Canada, pp. 239-245, 1976.

[33] CCITT, "Recommendation X.75–Terminal and transit call control procedures and data transfer system on international circuits between packet-switched data networks," Study Group VII, Temporary Document 132-E, Int. Telecommunications Union, Geneva, Switzerland, Apr. 25, 1978.

[34] D. J. Farber and L. C. Larson, "The structure of a distributed computing system–The communication system," in *Proc. Symp. Computer Communications Networks and Traffic*, Polytechnic Institute of Brooklyn, pp. 21-27, Apr. 1972.

[35] P. Baran, "Broad-band interactive communication services to the home: Part II–Impasse," *IEEE Trans. Communications*, p. 178, Jan. 1975.

[36] R. E. Schantz and R. Thomas, "Operating systems for computer networks," *Computer*, Jan. 1978.

[37] L. Pouzin and H. Zimmermann, "A tutorial on protocols," this issue, pp. 1346-1370.

[38] F. E. Heart, R. E. Kahn, S. M. Ornstein, W. R. Crowther, and D. C. Walden, "The interface message processor for the ARPA computer network," in *Proc. Spring Joint Computer Conf.*, vol. 36, AFIPS Press, pp. 551-567, 1970.

[39] S. Carr, S. D. Crocker and V. G. Cerf, "Host-Host communication protocol in the ARPA network," in *Proc. Spring Joint Computer Conf.*, vol. 36. Atlantic City, NJ: AFIPS Press, Montvale, NJ, pp. 589-598, 1970.

[40] E. Feinler and J. B. Postel (Eds.), *ARPANET Protocol Handbook*. Network Information Center, SRI International, for the Defense Communication Agency, Jan. 1978.

[41] R. F. Sproull and R. D. Cohen, "High-level protocols," this issue, pp. 1371-1386.

[42] S. D. Crocker, J. F. Heafner, R. M. Metcalfe, and J. B. Postel, "Function-oriented protocols for the ARPA computer network," in *Proc. Spring Joint Computer Conf.*, vol. 40. Atlantic City, NJ: AFIPS Press, Montvale, NJ, pp. 271-279, 1972.

[43] S. M. Ornstein, F. E. Heart, W. R. Crowther, H. K. Rising, S. B. Russel, and A. Michel, "The terminal IMP for the ARPA computer network," in *Proc. Spring Joint Computer Conf.*, vol. 40, Atlantic City, NJ: AFIPS Press, Montvale, NJ, pp. 243-254, 1972.

[44] CCITT, "Recommendation X.21: General purpose interface between data terminal equipment (DTE) and data-circuit terminating equipment (DCE) for synchronous operation on public data networks," *Public Data Networks*, Orange Book, vol. VIII.2, Sixth Plenary Assembly, Int. Telecommunications Union, Geneva, Switzerland, pp. 38-56, 1977.

[45] CCITT, "Recommendation X.21-bis: Use on public data networks of data terminal equipments (DTE's) which are designed for interfacing to V-series modems," *Public Data Networks, Orange Book*, vol. viii.2, Sixth Plenary Assembly, Int. Telecommunications Union, Geneva, Switzerland, pp. 38-56, 1977.

[46] ISO, "High level data link control (HDLC)," *DIS 3309.2 and DIS 4335*, Int. Standards Org.

[47] V. Cerf, A. McKenzie, R. Scantlebury, and H. Zimmermann, "Proposal for an international end-to-end protocol," *Computer Communication Review*, ACM Special Interest Group on Data Communication, vol. 6, no. 1, Jan. 1976, pp. 63-89.

[48] A. S. Chandler, "Network independent high level protocols," in *Proc. Eur. Computing Conf. Communication Networks*, London, England, ONLINE, pp. 583-602, 1975.

[49] —, "A network independent file transfer protocol," EPSS High Level Protocol Group, 1977.

[50] R. E. Kahn and W. R. Crowther, "Flow control in resource sharing computer networks," *IEEE Trans. Commun.*, vol. COM-20, pp. 539-546, 1972.

[51] L. Pouzin, "Flow control in data networks—Methods and tools," in *Proc. Third Int. Conf. Computer Communication*, Toronto, Canada, pp. 467-474, Aug. 1976.

[52] G. V. Bochmann and P. Goyer, "Datagrams as a public packet-switched data transmission service," Universite de Montreal, *Departement D'Informatique Report*, Mar. 1977.

[53] P. L. Higginson, "The problems of linking several networks with a gateway computer," in *Proc. Eur. Computing Conf. Communication Networks*, London, England, ONLINE, pp. 453-465, 1975.

[54] J. Shoch, *private communication*.

[55] P. L. Higginson and Z. Z. Fischer, "Experience with the initial EPSS service," in *Proc. Eur. Computing Conf. Communication Networks*, London, England, ONLINE, pp. 581-600, 1978.

[56] D. L. A. Barber, "A European informatics network: Achievements and prospects," in *Proc. Third Int. Conf. Computer Communication*, Toronto, Canada, pp. 44-50, 1976.

[57] B. Cross, "General license for message conveying computers," *London Gazette*, pp. 7662-7663, May 28, 1976.

[58] J. Freese, "The Swedish data act," in *Proc. Conf. Transnational Data Regulation*, Brussels, Belgium, ONLINE, pp. 197-208, 1978.

[59] R. Turn, "Implementation of privacy and security requirements in transnational data processing systems," in *Proc. Conf. Transnational Data Regulations*, Brussels, Belgium, ONLINE, pp. 113-132, 1978.

[60] A. R. D. Norman, "Project goldfish," in *Proc. Conf. Transnational Data Regulations*, Brussels, Belgium, ONLINE, pp. 67-94, 1978.

[61] E. Raubold and J. Haenle, "A method of deadlock-free resource allocation and flow control in packet networks," in *Proc. Third Int. Conf. Computer Communication*, Toronto, Canada, pp. 485-487, Aug. 1976.

[62] J. McQuillan, "The evolution of message processing techniques in the ARPA network," *Network Systems and Software*, Infotech State of the Art Report 24, Infotech Information Limited, Nicholson House, Maidenhead, Berkshire, England, 1975.

[63] P. Curran, "Design of a gateway to interconnect the DATAPAC and TRANSPAC packet switching networks," *Computer Communication Networks Group*, E-Report E-67, University of Waterloo, Canada, Sept. 1977 (ISSN 384-5702).

[64] D. D. Clark, K. T. Pogran, and D. P. Reed, "An introduction to local area networks," this issue, pp. 1497-1517.

Packet Fragmentation in Inter-Network Protocols

John F. Shoch

Xerox Palo Alto Research Center, Palo Alto, California 94304, USA

Individual computer networks may impose very different upper limits on the size of packets which they can accept and transport. As networks are inter-connected, the successful design of general *inter-network protocols* must include a mechanism to cope with these differences; this is often accomplished by breaking up oversize *packets* into smaller *fragments* for transport through some networks, a process usually known as *fragmentation*. A gateway into a network may choose 1) some form of *intra-network fragmentation*, providing reassembly of fragments before entering the next network, or 2) some form of *inter-network fragmentation*, producing smaller inter-network packets which can propagate through subsequent networks. Either approach is acceptable, and there has already been some experience with intra-network fragmentation; several more general inter-network schemes have been proposed, but none of them yet seems to be in regular use.

Keywords: Fragmentation, packet switching, protocols, inter-networking, computer communication.

John F. Shoch joined the research staff of the Xerox Palo Alto Research Center in 1971. Recent research interests have included the development of local networks (such as the Ethernet), communication protocols, internetworking, and packet radio, as well as the integration of communications facilities into programming language systems. Undergraduate and graduate work were done at Stanford University; he has taught in the Computer Science department there, has worked for the Department of Health, Education, and Welfare, and is a member of the ACM and the IEEE.

A portion of this material was presented at the Third Berkeley Workshop on Distributed Data Management and Computer Networks, San Francisco, California, August 1978.

Computer Networks 3 (1979) 3–8

1. Introduction

The evolution of individual packet switched computer networks naturally led to the selection of different maximum packet sizes in each of the various systems. There are many distinct criteria which led to such design decisions, including, for example:

– absolute hardware constraints, such as a TDM time slot;
– protocol limitations, perhaps a small number of bits allocated to specify a length field;
– software limits;
– storage allocation problems, affecting buffer lengths;
– minimizing store and forward delay;
– error control, since higher error rates make it more difficult to send large packets successfully;
– fairness, to enforce equal utilization of a channel;
– performance; or,
– conformity with relevant standards.

The actual maximum packet sizes selected in particular environments have ranged over several orders of magnitude, as the partial list of Table 1 suggests. These differences in maximum packet size become much more important as efforts continue to interconnect heterogeneous computer networks. The

Table 1
Typical limits on packet size

BiSynch	unspecified, but effectively limited by error characteristics
SDLC/HDLC frames	unspecified, but described as a "system parameter"
Spider network	TDM slots, with 256 bits of user data per slot
Arpanet	8159 bits per message, 1008 bits per packet
Alohanet	640 bits, one 80-character line
Ethernet	no explicit hardware limits, usually governed by buffer size
Packet Radio Net	127 16-bit words = 2032 bits
Chaosnet	1024 bits in an external, hardware buffer
X.25	set at subscription time, default max. = 128 octets = 1024 bits; optionally 16–1024 octets = 128–8192 bits

problem is simple: some systems in the inter-network environment are prepared to generate packets which may be larger than the maximum packet size of a subsequent network; in the design of *inter-network protocols,* this is the problem now known as *fragmentation.*

One very straightforward solution to the problem would be to adopt the smallest maximum packet size as the system-wide maximum, and thus render the fragmentation issue moot; this is certainly not a very desirable, nor flexible, approach. Instead, the inter-network protocols must incorporate a way to break up large *packets* into smaller *fragments.*

The fragmentation alternatives affect the source and destination processes, and particularly impact the inter-network gateways which may lie between differing networks. Implementation of a fragmentation mechanism must reflect both the *tactical* choices available at individual gateways, and the *strategic* choices available as the system is designed.

In any case, fragmentation need not be made part of a single, monolithic inter-network protocol, but can be viewed as a separate layer in the hierarchy of inter-network protocols.

2. Tactics: the fragmentation alternatives available to a gateway

The critical decision about fragmenting a large packet would usually take place at an internetwork gateway: it might be necessary to forward the packet to the next gateway, through a network which could not directly handle a packet of that size. There are three possible alternatives available to the designer of a gateway process:

2.1. Discard the packet

The gateway could find itself completely unable to forward the packet, and merely discard it. In our model of gateway processes it is acceptable – but certainly not desirable – for a gateway to take such an action. One would hope that this information might propagate back through the inter-network, so that subsequent packets would be routed away from this black hole.

2.2. Intra-network fragmentation (or network-specific fragmentation)

The *entrance gateway* can choose to do some sort of network-specific fragmentation, breaking up the oversize packet into smaller pieces, and allowing the *exit gateway* at the other end of this network to do the reassembly. This might utilize a network-specific protocol, such as the Arpanet host-to-host protocol or the Packet Radio Network's SPP protocol.

Advantages:

- This form of fragmentation is essentially performed by the network-specific driver, and is invisible to any higher level process in the gateway.
- The network can select a locally efficient protocol for transporting the fragments, and need not, for example, replicate the inter-network header on every fragment.
- If there is only one network in the path which necessitates fragmentation, all of the small pieces are brought together at the exit from that net, and the many pieces need not individually cascade through the rest of the path.
- If the destination host was within this "small packet" network, that host could also use the network-specific protocol to reassemble an oversize inter-network packet.

Disadvantages:

- This is, of course, more complicated than throwing the packet on the floor: there is some processing to be done, and the exit gateway must try to accumulate the fragments and perform reassembly.
- One could not take advantage of alternate gateways out of the intermediate network, since all of the fragments must reach the same exit gateway for reassembly.
- If there are many subsequent nets in the path which also require fragmentation, then there may be a fair amount of duplication as the same large packet is repeatedly fragmented and reassembled within each network.

It is important to note that this kind of fragmentation is *always* an acceptable decision by the gateway, since it remains transparent to other inter-network processes. We should already be familiar with circumstances where it might take place:

- Oversize "messages" are fragmented into smaller "packets" by the Arpanet IMPs.
- In a low-bandwidth telephone link between two gateways, it may be desirable to fragment a large data packet in order to 1) minimize the probability of an error which would corrupt the whole unit, and 2) allow smaller packets (characters) to be interleaved with the fragments, and not be held up for several seconds behind a lengthy data block.

2.3. Inter-network fragmentation

In this case the gateway may instead divide the packet into smaller pieces which are themselves inter-network packets, or fragments. These fragments remain addressed to the ultimate destination, and must be reassembled there. The gateway uses a suitable means for identifying the related pieces: sequence numbers, hierarchical subdivision, etc.

Advantages:
– There is no necessity for the next gateway to do reassembly.
– If an entrance gateway fragments into inter-network fragments, they need not all depart the net through the same exit gateway. (Provided, of course, that the inter-network routing process in the gateway has enough information to sensibly decide how to apportion the outgoing pieces.)

Disadvantages:
– The gateway must be able to suitably divide up the original inter-network packet into pieces that the destination – any destination – can properly reassemble; it cannot merely use a network-specific technique.
– If not designed with care, the gateway might need to know some intimate details about the internals of an inter-network packet.
– The inter-network header must be replicated in all of the outgoing fragments.
– The destination now has to perform the reassembly task.

3. Strategy: the selection of a system-wide technique

With these tactical alternatives, what kinds of strategies can one build for handling over-size packets within the framework of an inter-network environment?

3.1. Discard packets

The simplest strategy is to just use the simplest tactic: if one tries to route a packet out over a network for which it is too large, just drop it. Certainly not an acceptable approach.

3.2. Avoid small networks

If a source process can specify details of the inter-network route, and can obtain good information about the topology and size constraints in specific nets, then the source routing mechanism could merely dispatch "large" packets in such a way that they did not encounter any networks where they would not fit.

This strategy means that the gateways need only implement the simplest of the tactics: discard a packet if it wanders into the wrong gateway. But the preconditions are severe: if we are using some form of dynamic routing, we must be able to propagate the size parameter back through intervening networks to each source – a non-trivial task. If, on the other hand, we are limited to fixed source routing where the size limitations can also be known in advance, then this may become an attractive strategy [15–17].

3.3. Use intra-network fragmentation

Here we permit gateways to use either of the first two tactics: discard a packet, or fragment it in a network-specific fashion, but don't try to create inter-network fragments.

Such a strategy is usually accompanied with the specification of a maximum size for inter-network packets, implying that any network which wishes to join the inter-net must have a driver that is able (by some means) to forward a packet of this size to the next gateway [18].

As a corollary, a process can then be assured that any packet up to this size can be transmitted through any inter-network gateway. Furthermore, the destination process need not provide any kind of reassembly mechanism.

3.4. Use inter-network fragmentation

Finally, one could endorse the use of all three tactics by the gateways. Note that the gateway process would still have the choice of using some form of intra-network fragmentation, if there were some information available which made that the preferred choice.

Now, however, the destination process would be required to perform reasembly.

It is worth noting that this approach still specifies a packet size which all networks must be able to handle: an inter-network header plus (presumably) one unit of data.

4. Choosing a strategy

We have very little empirical evidence upon which to base the choice of any particular strategy – there is no analytical work, for example, describing the error probabilities or efficiency associated with fragmenting a packet into ten small ones which cascade through subsequent networks. (See [16] for a good introduction to the problem of computing the "cost" of a fragmentation scheme.)

Most of our decisions have been based on instinct, some experience, and a desire to minimize the "complexity coefficient". While the inter-net fragmentation strategy may provide the greatest generality, endorsing only intra-network fragmentation seems perfectly adequate; it also obviates the need for simple destination processes to perform reassembly.

This latter point is important: we should be able to layer our protocols in such a way that a destination process is able to specify if it is willing to do reassembly of inter-network packets, in return for possible benefits (e.g., simpler code).

In any case, however, the selection of a fragmentation strategy should be an inter-net issue, but not necessarily integrated with a particular higher level end-to-end protocol.

5. More on inter-network fragmentation

If one chooses to implement a full inter-network fragmentation scheme, the fragmentation and identification of fragments can be done in several ways:
- Have a sequence number for each byte, allowing individual fragments to be identified by the sequence number of the first data byte in that fragment [6]. An "End of Segment" control bit is set on the last fragment of the original inter-network segment. (In TCP-3, this evolved into a pair of bits: "Beginning of Segment" and "End of Segment" [7].)
- Fragment on the basis of some larger unit, with each fragment indicating which set of these units (one or more) it currently contains [1,10].
- Split fragments in some hierarchical manner, perhaps identifying each of two descendents with a binary encoding of their place in the family tree of this fragmented packet [9].

All three of these methods allow repeated application of the fragmentation procedure, should a fragment produced at one gateway later encounter a network with an even smaller maximum packet size.

A general inter-net strategy, perhaps using one of these techniques for identifying fragments, should still allow a resource-limited process to decline the use of the more complex inter-net fragmentation; thus, the strategy may be embellished with these capabilities:
- We could include in the inter-network header a bit which indicates if the destination process is willing to reassemble inter-network fragments.
- When a gateway receives a packet which must then be fragmented, this bit is checked. If it is off, then the gateway is not permitted to generate inter-net fragments, and must either use a network-specific method to reach the next gateway, or discard the packet. If the bit is on, the gateway has the option of doing inter-network fragmentation.

Thus, a minimal gateway need not even implement any inter-network fragmentation scheme. Alternatively, if a gateway has no intra-net method available, but the destination refuses to reassemble inter-net fragments, then the packet can only be discarded (although it would be nice if some sort of error message were returned to the source). If this turned out to be a common situation, it might be a good argument for adaptive source routing.

This strategy would even support the co-resident use of different inter-network fragmentation systems: an optional field in the internet header could indicate the type of fragmentation to be done on the way to this destination (based on byte sequence numbers, larger blocks, hierarchical, etc.).

In the process of establishing a connection, a destination could indicate to the source of packets what kind of reassembly it could perform, thus providing the information needed to appropriately mark packets which will then flow to that destination. The packets exchanged while setting up the connection would have to indicate that they themselves could not be fragmented.

By splitting out the fragmentation strategy, as outlined here, it would now be possible for different higher-level protocols to share this mechanism, or decline to use it if it were deemed unnecessary.

6. Three specific proposals for inter-network fragmentation

Several general approaches to inter-network fragmentation were suggested above, incorporating different schemes for identifying the fragments derived from a packet: sequence numbering every byte, a hierarchical indication of the place of this fragment in the original packet, or dividing the packet into a number of fixed-sized blocks. Most recent proposals have chosen this last approach, using a field in the inter-network header to indicate which blocks are included in a particular fragment.

6.1. The Transmission Control Program (TCP)

The initial designs of the Inter-network Transmission Control Program (TCP) attacked this problem by integrating a full inter-network fragmentation scheme into the higher-level protocol ([6], TCP version 2 [3], and TCP version 3 [7]).

That proposal was the subject of comment, and criticism, from various researchers: it depended upon TCP-specific functions (the byte sequence numbers), required the gateway process to look not only at the inter-net header, but also to have knowledge of the TCP header (FIN, SYN, etc.), did not provide a clear layering of protocols, and more. Version 3 warned that "...fragmentation...may in the future be removed from TCP's concern...."

In early 1978, further discussions of these issues took place among researchers examining TCP and inter-networking [14]; those collective efforts have led to proposals for major change to the TCP fragmentation strategy:

- The entire fragmentation facility will be removed from the TCP, and a distinct inter-net level of protocol will be responsible for this function. Thus, end-to-end protocols other than TCP will be able to co-exist, taking advantage of the fragmentation facility provided by this "lower" level in the protocol hierarchy [11]. Fields will be reserved in the inter-net header for use by fragmentation processes in gateways.
- The fragmentation units will not be based upon the TCP-specific byte sequence numbers, but instead will use a larger block of data as the fragmentation unit; a field in the inter-net header is provided to identify the fragment. Early proposals used a 512 bit fragmentation unit, an 8 bit *fragment offset*, and a *not-end-of-segment* flag [12]. Selection of a large block size reduces the number of bits required for the fragment offset field, but a large size can also lead to inefficient use of communications facilities [4,5]; more recent proposals use a 64 bit fragmentation unit and 13 bits for the fragment offset, with the flag renamed *more fragments* [12].
- A "Don't Fragment" bit is proposed for the inter-net header, indicating that no fragmentation should take place, since the destination will not perform reassembly of inter-network fragments (although, of course, network-specific fragmentation may still occur).

This revised TCP fragmentation proposal is now very similar to the scheme included with the proposal to add datagram service to the X.25 international standard, described below [1,13]. These proposed changes should represent significant improvements in the TCP fragmentation strategy.

6.2. The INWG 96 End-to-End Protocol

The International Network Working Group (IFIP Working Group 6.1, or INWG) has also developed a proposed inter-network protocol, generally known by its report number, INWG 96 [8]; it also includes a mechanism for providing inter-network fragmentation as part of the end-to-end protocol:

- Individual *letters* submitted to the network may be broken up into *fragments,* to be reassembled by the receiver.
- Each fragment will carry an inter-network header derived from the original letter, and 216 octets of data (1728 bits); the last fragment created from a letter may contain less data.
- The inter-network header includes an 8-bit field, combining a 7-bit *fragment number* and an *End of Letter* flag to be set on the last fragment of a letter.
- As an option, multiple fragments may be initially combined into a single transport frame with one inter-network header; the fragment number identifies the first fragment in the frame, and the length of the frame can be used to infer the number of frames included. In "large packet" networks this option eliminates the need to carry multiple headers, but still allows subsequent fragmentation at a later gateway. The protocol does not suggest that intermediate gateways attempt to recombine any fragments along the way.

This proposal is unusual in that is specifies a rather large fragment size, larger than some networks now in use could directly transmit (and thus necessitating some form of network specific fragmentation in order to carry an INWG 96 fragment). The use of large fragments, however, makes it reasonable to have a very modest fragment number field – only 7 bits – thus minimizing the overhead carried in all inter-network packets.

6.3. Proposal to add Datagrams to X.25

Recent proposals to integrate a datagram service into the X.25 standard have also included provisions for fragmenting oversize packets (primarily undertaken by the ANSI X3S37 group). Some of the early versions of the datagram proposal had serious flaws in the fragmentation proposal (e.g., requiring the length of all data fields to be a precise multiple of 4 octets) ([1], section 8.1.2), the current proposal is quite straightforward [2]:

- Individual packets submitted to the network may be broken up into fragments.
- Each fragment will carry an inter-network header including the source, destination, and Datagram Identifier of the original packet.
- Each fragment contains some number of consecutive 16-octet (128 bit) blocks, or *parts,* from the original packet, the last part (carried in the last fragment) need not contain the full 128 bits. The N parts in a packet are numbered from 0 to N-1.
- Unlike regular X.25/virtual circuit data packets which do not carry a *facilities* field, X.25/datagram data packets always include a *Facility Length* field and may, optionally, carry facilities information. By including an appropriate *Facility Code,* the facilities field is used to carry two octets of fragmentation information: "the part number of the first 16 octet part contained in the fragment" and "the count of parts contained in the fragment".
- The *More Data* flag in the inter-network header is set on each fragment, except the last.
- Fragments carrying multiple parts may be further broken up in subsequent gateways.

7. Conclusions

Any successful inter-network protocol must include some means for utilizing networks with different maximum packet sizes, and thus must confront the fragmentation problem. There are two basic strategies: using intra-network fragmentation when needed to carry packets within each net, or providing a more general inter-network fragmentation technique (which does not, though, preclude the use of network-specific fragmentation within some networks). There has already been some experience with the use of intra-network fragmentation, and several substantial proposals for inter-network algorithms; as far as we know, however, none of those proposals is yet in regular use.

Acknowledgements

The material in this paper has evolved from many conversations with David Boggs, Ed Taft, Bob Metcalfe, Yogen Dalal, and Vint Cerf; as always, Jon Postel's very careful and thoughtful work has been invaluable in following the development of the TCP.

References

[1] ANSI X3S37, DTE/DCE Datagram Interface Standard, draft proposal, X3S37-77-80/3, 1977.

[2] ANSI X3S37, Proposal for the DATAGRAM Interface, submission to CCITT, X3S37-77-115, December 1977.

[3] Vinton G. Cerf, Specification of Internetwork Transmission Control Program – TCP (Version 2), March 1977.

[4] Vinton G. Cerf, A proposed new internet header format, Internet Experiment Note no. 26, February 14, 1978.

[5] Vinton G. Cerf, A proposal for TCP version 3.1 header format, Internet Experiment Note no. 27, February 14, 1978.

[6] Vinton G. Cerf and Robert E. Kahn, A protocol for packet network intercommunication, IEEE Trans. Communications, COM-22, 1974.

[7] Vinton G. Cerf and Jonathan B. Postel, Specification of Internetwork Transmission Control Program: TCP Version 3, January 1978, ISI.

[8] International Network Working Group (IFIP Working Group 6.1), Proposal for an Internetwork End-to-End Protocol, INWG General Note #96.1, February 1978.

[9] G. LeMoli, A Proposal for Fragmenting Packets in Internetworking, INWG Protocol Note #21, April 1975.

[10] A.M. McKenzie, Internetwork host-to-host protocol, INWG General Note #74, December 1974.

[11] Jonathan B. Postel, Draft Internetwork Protocol Specification, Version 2, ISI, February 1978.

[12] Jonathan B. Postel, Draft Internetwork Protocol Specification, Version 4, ISI, June 1978.

[13] Peter J. Sevcik, Why the datagram is needed – and how it will operate, Data Communications, March 1978.

[14] John F. Shoch, Inter-network Fragmentation and the TCP, Third Berkeley Workshop on Distributed Data Management and Computer Networks, San Francisco, August 1978. (Originally prepared as Internet Experiment Note #20, January 1978.)

[15] John F. Shoch, Inter-network Naming, Addressing, and Routing, IEEE Computer Society COMPCON, Fall 1978, Washington DC. (Originally prepared as Internet Experiment Note #19, January 1978.)

[16] Carl A. Sunshine, Interconnection of Computer Networks, Computer Networks, 1977.

[17] Carl A. Sunshine, Source Routing in Computer Networks, Computer Communication Review (ACM SigComm), January, 1977.

[18] Hubert Zimmermann and Michele Elie, Proposed Standard Host-Host Protocol for Heterogeneous Computer Networks: Transport Protocol, INWG General Note #43, December 1973. (Also IRIA Project Cyclades report SCM 519.)

Inter-Network Naming, Addressing, and Routing

John F. Shoch

Xerox Palo Alto Research Center
Palo Alto, California 94304

Summary

As work continues to interconnect computer networks, it becomes increasingly important to clarify the differences between *names*, *addresses* and *routes* -- while closely related, these are three distinct functions in any communications system. A clear appreciation for some of the more subtle aspects of their use can help in understanding such traditional models as the switched telephone system, as well as more recent designs for bringing together heterogeneous computer systems.

Introduction

Taxonomies and terminology will not, by themselves, solve some of the difficult problems associated with the interconnection of computer networks; but carefully choosing our words can help us to avoid misunderstanding and refine our perceptions of the task.

In *Through the Looking Glass*, the White Knight tries to elucidate (for an imprecise Alice) the important differences between what a song is, what it is called, what it is named, and what the name is called; we need to be equally vigilant with our use of the words *name*, *address*, and *route*.

Here we outline one scheme which has proven useful in analyzing this domain, and which has been of great use in constructing complex computer communications systems. The primary assertion is that *names*, *addresses*, and *routes* are all different entities. [Even one of the best papers in this area merges two of these characteristics: "The question of addressing, or how to name all the participants in an interconnected communication system...."]

The General Model

We can first construct an extremely general definition:

> The *name* of a resource indicates what we seek,
>
> an *address* indicates where it is, and
>
> a *route* tells us how to get there.

Some further detail to flesh this out:

I. A *name* is a symbol -- usually a human-readable string -- identifying some resource, or set of resources.

> The strings need not be meaningful to all users, and need not be drawn from a uniform name space.
>
> The strings can identify processes, places, people, machines, functions, or anything else the user chooses.
>
> To be useful, however, there will probably be some mechanism available to the user that will map names into addresses.
>
> The name (what we seek) need not be bound to the address (where it is) until this mapping takes place; the address (or addresses) associated with a particular name may change over time.

II. An *address*, however, is the data structure whose format can be recognized by all elements in the domain, and which defines the fundamental addressable object.

> Addresses must, therefore, be meaningful throughout the domain, and must be drawn from some uniform address space.
>
> This address space may be a "flat" one which spans the entire domain (such as Social Security numbers), or it may be a hierarchical address space (such as telephone numbers).
>
> If a name has produced several different addresses for a particular resource, some form of *a priori* information may prove useful in selecting a preferred address.
>
> At the time one wishes to communicate with a particular address, there will be some mechanism that will map an address into an appropriate route.
>
> The address (where something is) need not be bound to the route (how to get there) until this mapping takes place; the choice of an "appropriate" route may change over time.

Reprinted from *The Proceedings of COMPCON F78*, 1978, pages 72-79.

III. A *route* is the specific information needed to forward a piece of information to its specified address.

The routing action may only require one step to reach a destination (a direct route), or it may require a series of steps in order to forward the information on its way.

Where there is merely one hop in a simple topology, the routing decision is usually straightforward.

When the path to an address requires several steps (as in a store and forward system), the route defines a path through intermediate switching points.

In categorizing such routing mechanisms, one dimension is the *place* at which each intermediate routing decision is specified:

a. The source may specificy all of the intermediate routing decisions, and include this information along with the data being sent (*source routing*). The source must have fairly comprehensive information about the environment, but the switching points need not maintain routing tables.

b. Alternatively, the source may only specify the destination address, and the intermediate switching points choose the next portion of the route (*hop-by-hop routing*, sometimes called *intermediate routing* or *incremental routing*). In this case, the source only needs enough information to reach the next switching point, but each of these points must then have a routing table of some sort.

c. There may be a *hybrid routing* mechanism combining these two, in which the source specifies certain major intermediate points, but allows the underlying system to choose routes between those points.

A second dimension of the routing mechanims is the *time constant* of the information upon which the routing decisions are based -- when is that information specified, and how frequently is it modified:

a. Routing tables may be set once, left unchanged for relatively long periods of time, and only changed to reflect major modifications to the system (*fixed routing*, or *deterministic routing*).

b. Alternatively, routing tables may be updated relatively frequently, reflecting shorter term changes in the environment (*dynamic routing*, or *adaptive routing*). [This measure is, in some sense, relative to the time constants of the communication system itself.]

If there is a dynamic routing system providing periodic updates of appropriate information, a third dimension of the routing process is the *control* mechanism:

a. Individual switching points may try to update their information in an *isolated* manner, perhaps by periodically trying various routes and observing performance.

b. Changes in the environment, connectivity, or performance may all be reported back to one *centralized* point, which is then responsible for promulgating this information to the sources (if we use source routing) or to the switches (if we use hop-by-hop routing).

c. Alternatively, control of the dynamic update process may be *distributed* among all of the sources or switches, which individualy obtain information about the state of the system.

It is meaningful to talk about possible combinations of these dimensions: *fixed source routing* may be quite simple to implement, while *dynamic source routing* may be beneficial if the source can learn about changes occurring throughout the system. *Fixed hop-by-hop routing* requires setting the routing tables at the switching points, while *dynamic hop-by-hop routing* then requires updates to these routing tables. *Distributed, dynamic, hop-by-hop routing* might obtain these periodic updates from neighboring switches, while a *centralized, dynamic, hop-by-hop* system would depend on some form of network control center to provide new information.

Thus, a *name* may be used to derive an *address*, which may then be used to derive a *route*.

[There is an interesting similarity between this structure and mechanisms used in other areas of computing:
---compiling and loading a program, as symbols are mapped from the original name space of the program into successive address spaces [see, for example, Graham, 1975, pp. 294-295, or Habermann, 1976, pp. 201-203];
---executing a program, as a value is bound to a variable;

---virtual memory, which temporarily binds a real address to a virtual address; or,

---operating systems, where one must link a particular piece of code into a module.

In all these cases, there is a certain amount of added flexibility gained by deferring the binding process as long as possible: MULTICS defers the binding of pieces of code until run-time so that new instantiations of code will be used automatically, while the Arpanet tries to defer routing decisions as long as possible, in order to make the most informed choice.]

If one fails to deliver a piece of information to the resource originally specified, an error recovery procedure can systematically try to undo each of these binding decisions: first try an *alternate route*, then an *alternate address*, then an *alternate name*.

Example #1: Naming/Addressing/Routing in the Telephone System

Before attempting to apply this scheme to a connected set of computer networks, let's see how well it serves to understand the workings of another domain: placing a telephone call. [The telephone system, of course, uses circuit switching, and dedicates resources for the lifetime of a call. We are here discussing the naming, addressing, and routing which take place during call set-up.]

I. We can look up a *name* in the phone book.

The name may be a specific person ("D. B. Cooper"), an institution ("Stanford University"), the local representative of a nation-wide service ("the nearest TWA office"), or a generic function ("Get me the police!", or the time server).

The names of different individuals may yield the same phone number.

One name may yield several phone numbers, if there are two telephones in one home or if a business provides multiple incoming lines. In addition, a considerate business might provide several incoming lines with different area codes.

Should a name yield more than one number, the caller may use some additional information to aid in the choice of which to dial: is one number less likely to be in use, or is one address in our own area code, and thus cheaper.

There can be a two-level name-to-address mapping process: look up the name "Information" in the phone book, get that number (411), place a call, and then present a new name to be looked-up by the information operator.

II. The *address* which we eventually find is just the telephone number.

The phone system did not have to understand the subscribers' names, but it certainly must be able to understand their addresses (numbers).

Addressing in the phone network is based on a hierarchical structure -- the major contribution of area codes, as specified in the North American Numbering Plan [AT&T 1975].

There are certain conventions for defaulting parts of the address when it is found: if the area code is not listed, we generally assume it is the same as our own.

Every resource (person) accessible through the phone system is actually represented by a telephone instrument, which we can address. Actual signals are intended for the person, but they are always sent via the instrument.

III. When we dial the number (in fact, each time we dial the number) the phone network attempts to build an appropriate route to the destination, reflecting current conditions.

Two successive calls to the same number need not be routed through the same path, and the telephone plant provides alternate routes if a trunk is busy. The distributed, adaptive nature of this routing is one of the major factors which contributes to the reliability of the phone system.

Now consider the error recovery procedure if we are not able to reach the person we seek: we move back through the hierarchy, trying alternate routes, alternate addresses, and alternate names.

1. If we get a busy trunk indication, we know that the route chosen by the network turned out to be inadequate. We can, in effect, ask the system to try picking a route again, by re-dialing (re-transmitting). If we are particularly concerned, we can ask an operator to override some of the automatic routing decisions, and attempt an alternate route.

2. If all of the routes to this address are inadequte, or if the address is unavailable (perhaps busy, or broken), we must fall back and find an alternate address: perhaps there were two phone numbers listed, and we can try the second. (How many of us know people who have second phones for a data terminal, which we call in on when the regular line is busy?) This will lead to the selection of a completely new route.

3. If the alternate address fails, we can fall back one more step, and try to find an alternate name: perhaps the phone is listed in the name of one's spouse, or maybe we should look up the name of the organization where one works.

The Implications of Hierarchical vs. Flat Address Spaces

It should be apparent that the structure of the address space is of central importance: it is the major element of commonality in such an environment, and can have a profound influence on the naming mechanism "above" and the routing mechanism "below."

An address space can be partitioned in a hierarchical manner, or left as a single uniform space. Use of a flat address space implies that:

1. The address given to any resource must be unique over the whole domain; and,
2. There is no structure to the address which might aid the routing process; instead, the routing mechanism must be able to handle all addresses, without segmenting them into parts (in the telephone example, there would be a 10-digit number, but no indication of a separate area code).

There are some advantages to this approach: it is logically simple, and has the potential to optimize the particular route between any two resources. But there are certain kinds of costs: upon adding a new set of resources to an existing system, one must ensure that none of the new addresses conflict with those already used, and the routing process must now be able to directly recognize all of the legal addresses (in the phone system, 10^{10}).

Thus, there are two different -- but often interacting -- reasons to adopt a hierarchical address structure (as has been done with area codes): to simplify the creation of unique addresses, or to aid in routing.

Partitioning of the address space allows autonomous addressing authorities the freedom to create and assign new addresses, within their portion of the hierarchy. If a new area is added to the system, it can be incorporated into the hierarchy without changing any of the network-specific addresses already assigned. Local addresses can then be changed within areas, but need not be coordinated with all of the other parts.

Yet the choice of hierarchical addressing can have important ramifications for the levels "below."

We would certainly not want to allow a strictly hierarchical address scheme to serve as the justification for a strictly hierarchical physical topology: that would allow only one path to each resource, and severely diminish reliability.

> [This is, however, the approach taken in some designs: IBM's System Network Architecture (SNA) has been modified to support multiple hosts, and uses a two-part address space -- subarea address and element number. The subarea associated with the address is used as the basis for routing, and "only one active path can exist between any two subareas in the network." [IBM 1976]]

In general, the underlying communications should provide alternate paths to a destination.

Furthermore, the routing mechanism must now be flexible enough to take advantage of the alternate paths available -- it would make litle sense to lay a strictly hierarchical static routing algorithm on top of a richly-connected network. Given a hierarchical address, this form of area routing should be able to pick out an appropriate field from the address, and route the data towards that area, through one of the available paths, but be able to identify an alternate path when necessary.

Though the hierarchical address space is often viewed as preferable, there is a cost here too: if the routing decision does in fact use the hierarchical structure of the address and route to an area, then some information has been lost: the ability to specify precise routes between two resources. This can lead to several kinds of difficulties:

1. Two resources may be geographically close, but on distant branches of the hierarchical tree. If the routing strictly parallels the addressing hierarchy, it may require many hops to reach a nearby node.

   The telephone system provides a routing hierarchy which matches the addressing scheme, but then provides additional routes (high usage trunks) across the tree, as warranted by the traffic; switching centers then have the choice of routing through the specially allocated trunk, or back up the regular hierarchy, which then becomes the alternate route.

   This means, however, that some central offices within an area code are reachable through direct lines, while other less-heavily used offices must be reached through the standard hierarchy. To make that routing decision, the foreign switch must be provided with additional information about the internal structure of the system within the destination area code -- i.e., which central office prefixes are reachable through a "short-cut".

   To take advantage of a direct high-usage trunk from downtown New York to a central office in downtown San Francisco, without going through the California area code hierarchy, the switch in New York must be able to perform what is called "6-digit translation" on the phone number, examining both the area code and the central office prefix [AT&T 1975].

2. If a sub-area (network) is unintentionally partitioned so that half of its internal addresses are now unreachable, a distant routing process won't be able to recognize that, given only the sub-area number.

3. Should there be alternate paths into the partitioned sub-area, now making those lost nodes reachable, the distant routing process will not be able to make an informed choice about the proper route into the sub-area.

4. Two resources may be in the same sub-area, but perhaps connected by an inefficient route (many hops or poor quality). Provided there are two paths into the sub-area, it may make more sense for a resource to route its traffic out of the area and back in through the other path, but area routing will indicate that the source is already in the area of the destination, and may not allow a route going outside of that area.

In these unusual circumstances, we see that there are clear weaknesses at the routing level which evolve from the choice of a hierarchical address space; but in the most common cases this approach will work well.

This choice of hierarchical addresses may also impact the naming mechanism, although that ought not be necessary. The name-to-address mapping can be supplied by a process which is external to the system itself, and there is no reason to enforce hierarchical names. A user may offer a name from which one can directly derive the address, but it should also be acceptable to provide a symbolic name, independent of the address format. An example may show the different kinds of names which might be converted into adresses (telephone numbers):

1. The syntax of the string "(415) 767-2676" explicitly indicates the three fields of the address, and their values.

2. The string "(SanFrancisco) Pop-Corn" has the syntactic structure of a proper hierarchical address, but will require a symbolic look-up of the component parts in order to get the address of this resource (the time recording).

3. Yet the string "GetMeTheTimeLady" -- when looked-up in the context of my name dictionary -- should produce this same address.

The virtue of the third approach is that the names may remain the same, even if the resource is moved to a different address, or if I should move to a different area; only the name-lookup process must be made aware of the change.

Example #2: Interconnected Computer Networks

It seems that this model of naming/addressing/routing provides a useful framework for discussing the phone system, and that system can serve as a basis for comparison with the domain of computer networks.

I. A name is merely a human-readable string meant to denote some resource: "BBN-TenexA" (a host), "SAIL" and "SU-AI" (two names for the same host), "the SRI mobile van", "a time server", "the Telnet server at ISI", "the Telnet server on any Tenex", "the nearest FORTRAN compiler", "the error-logging process in IMP32", "the inter-network routing process in Gateway21"..... Note that these names may identify resources outside of the communications system, or processes within it.

Virtually any object can have a name. In practice, of course, any such resource is usually represented by some sort of process which can act on its behalf.

> The Arpanet system for handling text messages describes a slightly different kind of name, in the form "User@Host," but that would not really resolve down to a proper inter-network address. Instead, the "host" name is used to derive an address for the mail server process, and the "user" name is sent along as data, to be interpreted by a higher-level protocol (the mail server) at the destination.

A suitable process (either local or part of some distant resource) may offer to convert names into appropriate addesses, although a single name may yield many addresses. The name-lookup process may know about the precise address of certain well-known servers, and may provide certain default conventions if some portions of the address are not fully specified.

> We have not yet mentioned the notion of names and addresses for multi-destination pieces of information. The name "Internet-Working-Group" could produce a whole set of names, which in turn could be transformed into individual addressess, and individual copies of the information could be sent to each place. Most communications subsystems do not yet have protocols which would provide more congenial support for multi-destination packets [Dalal 1977].

If a single name does yield many addresses, one of them may be chosen on the basis of some other information: bandwidth and delay characteristics, cost, etc.

II. An address, in this context, really means an inter-network address: a collection of bits in a standard format, recognizable by any object cognizant of the inter-network protocols.

Many inter-network efforts have suggested a hierarchical address space, usually partitioned into <net, host, socket> tuples.

> Note that this model is not quite adequate to describe the dynamic naming and addessing conventions originally planned for the Distributed Computing System (DCS) at UC Irvine.
>
> In the actual implementation, individual processes are assigned to specific processors; part of the process address includes the machine number, or a special indicator used to broadcast to multiple instances of the same generic server.
>
> In contrast, some of the original work had proposed that processes not be bound to particular machines, but would be free to migrate around the ring; 16-bit process ID's on each packet would be dynamically checked in each host, and the packet given to the appropriate process, if it happened to be in that host. The actual address of a destination process would remain hidden from the sending program.
>
> Therefore, the 16-bit process ID (although not human-readable) might have been more accurately called a process *name*, since it may be used to describe a generic resource without specifying a particular address. Thus, this mechanism pushes "down" and distributes the task of mapping from names to addresses, thereby deferring the binding until even later.
>
> The mechanism would have depended heavily on two aspects of the DCS ring:
> ---the ability of the communications subsystem to broadcast a packet to all nodes on the ring, and,
> ---the ability of each interface to quickly look up a process name in a content addressable memory (associative memory) used to identify those processes resident in the node. (In the original proposal, this memory could hold the names of 16 resident processes.)
>
> In a different communications environment -- or if there were more than 16 processes in one host -- this mechanism would not function properly. In those cases, however, one can provide the same effect (allowing users to communicate with resources strictly by name, without specifying an address) merely by providing an extra layer of protocol. The different naming/addressing conventions in DCS are perhaps more of a difference in style, rather than a difference in substance.

We often think of these components of an address as corresponding to physical objects -- networks and machines -- but they are really only logical groupings used to form the address. In a particular environment, for example, the "host" might be a front-end processor, and the "sockets" might be specialized processors, performing the function which the user sought at that address.

If a machine has only one network interface, processes in that machine will all have the same <net, host> address, although from many other addresses there may be multiple paths to this address.

If a machine has two network interfaces, to the same network or to two different networks, it will have two alternate inter-network addresses for each process resident there. Another process seeking to communicate might select either address.

An important example of a hierarchical addressing scheme for use in inter-networking is the proposed "International numbering plan for public data networks" prepared within Study Group VII of CCITT [CCITT 1977, 1978a].

Derived from an original proposal from Canada, some of the important characteristics are:

---Each network is identified by a 4-digit *data network identification code* (DNIC), including a 3-digit "country code" plus a network digit (in practice, there may be more than one "country code" assigned to a specific country or geographic area). The format of this basic network component of an address "should be the same for all countries."
---A data terminal connected to such a network would have a *national data number* (address) which would be unique within that network; these numbers could be assigned independently by each network, and "it should not be mandatory to integrate the numbering plans of the various networks."
---A network address (DNIC) concatenated with a national data number yields an "international data number, which should also be unique on a worldwide basis."
---A form of area routing is suggested, in which the originating station uses the 3-digit country code for routing. It is also feasible to examine all 4 digits of the DNIC in order to identify a specific network, to aid in routing or billing.
---Inter-network gateways would also use these 3 or 4 digits for routing through transit networks.

While still only a draft recommendation, this proposed numbering plan has been embraced by several agencies as their addressing scheme for inter-network communication. Canada, for example, has been assigned the country code of 302; thus, the Datapac network (Trans Canada Telephone System) has been given DNIC 3020, and the Infoswitch network (Canadian National/Canadian Pacific Telecommunications) has been given DNIC 3029 [CCITT 1978b].

III. The underlying communications system provides the means for routing packets to their destination.

Individual networks use different routing strategies for forwarding their internal traffic: the DCS ring has a simple topology with no alternate routes, while the Alohanet and the Etherent use a broadcast communications media, requiring no routing [Metcalfe and Boggs 1975]. The Arpanet uses dynamic hop-by-hop routing, while the Packet Radionet uses dynamic source routing.

Inter-network packets, however, may travel through various networks, routed among inter-network gateways. The gateway routing processes make use of the information specified in the inter-network address, and can route to the areas specified. Upon arrival at a gateway entering the destination network, the network-specific routing mechanism can be used to route it to the specified "host."

The gateway processes may implement a form of dynamic hop-by-hop routing, using complete networks as the communications channel to "adjacent" gateways. These gateways can exchange routing tables and perform dynamic hop-by-hop routing, or one could simplify the gateway by requiring users to perform source routing.

In one sense, these two methods can be combined: while the gateways normally do hop-by-hop routing, there could be a special process resident in the gateway which would take incoming packets, examine the data field, extract the next address indicated there, and forward the packet to that destination. (Danny Cohen has called this process a "forwarder," and Steve Crocker once called it an "oasis." [Cohen 1978]) The effect is to provide source routing to the user, by simply incorporating the list of intermediate addresses in the data field of a packet, rather than in the header.

Alternatively, the inter-network header can be designed to include a partial or complete list of intermediate addresses, and thus support this form of hybrid routing. Most recently, this proposal has been called "optional high level source routing" [Clark and Cohen, 1978].

We have spoken earlier of the reasons why area routing using hierarchical addresses cannot properly identify resources which may have been stuck in different parts of a partitioned network -- it requires some additional information to guide the selection of an appropriate route. If we are using some form of source routing, and if some information about the internal structure of the destination net can propogate back to the source, it may be possible to then choose an alternate route which will lead into one part of a partitioned network.

In addition, a source routing or hybrid scheme which allows a user to specify certain intermediate addresses allows a process to force traffic over a particular network, perhaps in response to political, economic, or performance considerations: "take any reasonable path across the country, but I must use the Packet Satellite system across the Atlantic." More difficult, however, is selectively eliminating some paths from the routing decision: "take me to Europe, but don't ever go through these networks...."

Naming/Addressing/Routing and Inter-network Gateways

The gateway function is, in general, performed in a machine which is connected to at least two networks, and which therefore has at least two addresses. Incoming packets which need to be forwarded may enter on any attached net, using any of the legal addresses.

Yet there is a single gateway process which handles all of this traffic, and which is responsible for maintaining relevant routing tables.

It has been suggested that a gateway might be viewed as two completely separate "halves" actually residing on different machines, connected by a "thin wire" communications channel. We do not find this abstraction particularly useful, since it does not easily account for the shared gateway processes which actually perform the routing function.

In this model, the gateway processes maintain routing tables to reach network areas through other gateways, but they do not attempt to maintain any other state about networks, hosts, or connections. Thus, these intermediate gateways -- using dynamic hop-by-hop routing -- will not be able to deal with partitioned networks.

Acknowledgements

The material in this paper has evolved from many conversations with David Boggs, Ed Taft, Bob Metcalfe, and Yogen Dalal; any clarity which has emerged is due to their willingness to struggle with the semantic demons. An earlier version of this work, [Shoch 1978a] and [Shoch 1978b], served as the basis for fruitful discussion with the Internet Planning Group. Recent conversations with Danny Cohen have been particularly useful in understanding his proposal for hybrid routing schemes (where the source routing process specifies only some of the intermediate stops), and the manner in which area routing may obscure a preferred off-net route. Much of the commentary on routing has evolved from [McQuillan 1974] and [Sunshine 1977]; the latter paper is a particularly useful one, touching on many of the issues raised here, although we tend to differ on some of the fine points. In addition, Jack Wheeler provided some valuable suggestions regarding the proposed international numbering plan.

Bibliography

[AT&T 1975]
AT&T, *Notes on Distance Dialing*, 1975.

[CCITT 1977]
CCITT Study Group VII, *Draft recommendation, International numbering plan for public data networks*, COM VII-No. 101, Annex 10, Appendix 2, April 1977.

[CCITT 1978a]
CCITT Study Group VII, Contribution No. 159 (from Canada), *Numbering Plan for Public Data Networks*, COM VII-No. 159, January 1978.

[CCITT 1978b]
CCITT Study Group VII, Contribution No. 161 (from Canada), *Interim Adoption of Codes for a Numbering Plan for Public Data Networks*, COM VII-No. 161, January 1978.

[Clark and Cohen 1978]
David Clark and Danny Cohen, *A Proposal for Internetwork Addressing*, forthcoming.

[Cohen 1978]
Danny Cohen, *On Names, Addresses and Routings*, Internet Experiment Note, January 1978.

[Dalal 1977]
Yogen K. Dalal, *Broadcast Protocols in Packet Switched Computer Networks*, Technical Report No. 128, Digital System Laboratory, Stanford University, Stanford, California, April 1977.

[Graham 1975]
Robert M. Graham, *Principles of Systems Programming*, John Wiley, 1975.

[Habermann 1976]
A. N. Habermann, *Introduction to Operating System Design*, SRA, 1976.

[IBM 1976]
IBM, *Introduction to Advanced Communications Function, Multiple System Data Communication Networks*, Report GC30-3033-0, 1976.

[McQuillan 1974]
J. M. McQuillan, *Adaptive routing algorithms for distributed computer networks*, BBN Report No. 2831, May 1974; AD-781 467.

[Metcalfe and Boggs 1975]
Robert M. Metcalfe and David R. Boggs, *Ethernet: Distributed Packet Switching for Local Computer Networks*, Report CSL-75-7, Xerox Palo Alto Research Center, November 1975; CACM, vol. 19 no. 7, July 1976.

[Shoch 1978a]
John F. Shoch, *A Note on Inter-Network Fragmentation and the TCP*, Internet Experiment Note #20, January 1978.

[Shoch 1978b]
John F. Shoch, *A Note on Inter-Network Naming, Addressing, and Routing*, Internet Experiment Note #19, January 1978.

[Sunshine 1977]
Carl A. Sunshine, *Interconnection of computer networks*, Computer Networks, 1977.

The ARPA Internet Protocol

Jonathan B. Postel, Carl A. Sunshine and Danny Cohen

Information Sciences Institute, University of Southern California, 4676 Admiralty Way, Marina del Rey, California 90291, USA

A variety of computer networks are interconnected by gateway computers in the ARPA internetwork system. Processes on different networks may exchange messages with each other by means of an Internet Protocol which must be implemented in each subscriber (host) computer and in the gateways. The Internet Protocol is a relatively simple protocol that provides for the delivery of individual messages (datagrams) with high but not perfect reliability. This Internet Protocol does not replace the existing protocol in any network, but is used by processes to extend the range of communications. Messages in Internet Protocol are transmitted through any individual network by encapsulating them in that network's protocol. This paper presents an overview of the Internet Protocol and the operation of the gateway computers in the ARPA internet system.

Keywords: Protocol, ARPA Net, Internetwork, Datagram, Gateway.

Jonathan Postel received his B.S. and M.S. degrees in Engineering and his Ph.D. in Computer Science from the University of California, Los Angeles. Dr. Postel has worked for the MITRE Corporation in McLean, Virginia and SRI International in Menlo Park, California. He is currently a Computer Scientist at the University of Southern California Information Sciences Institute in Marina del Rey, California. At UCLA he was involved in the development of the ARPANET Network Measurement Center and the installation of the first host on the ARPANET. Since that time, he has participated in the development of many of the higher level protocols used in the ARPANET. His current research focuses on the interconnection of computer networks.

This research is supported by the Advanced Research Projects Agency under Contract No. DAHC15 72C 0308, Arpa Order No. 2223. The views and conclusions in this study are the authors' and should not be interpreted as representing the official opinion or policy of ARPA, the U.S. Government or any other person or agency connected with them.

North-Holland Publishing Company
Computer Networks 5 (1981) 261–271

1. Introduction

The family of computer networks developed for the United States Defense Advanced Research Projects Agency (DARPA) represents one of the largest and most diverse internetwork systems currently in operation. The basic approach to interconnecting this variety of networks was developed over several years, and has resulted in the definition of an Internet Protocol (IP) [1]. This paper is intended primarily to document the details of the IP in the open literature, and secondarily to provide a brief discussion of the major design tradeoffs which caused the IP to take its current form.

Section 2 presents an overview of the DARPA approach to interconnection and the operation of IP. Section 3 details IP's main features, while some additional options are treated in section 4. Section 5 summarizes the IP and other functions performed in the *gateways* which interconnect networks. Section 6 discusses the major design choices in developing IP. Section 7 outlines several questions and extensions requiring further work.

Carl Sunshine is with the University of Southern California Information Sciences Institute where he is engaged in research on computer networks and their protocols. He is particularly interested in protocol modeling, and analysis, and network interconnection. Sunshine received a PhD in computer science from Stanford University in 1975, and worked at the Rand Corporation from 1975 to 1979. He is active in IFIP TC6.1 (the Internetwork Working Group) and ISO SC16, is Secretary/Treasurer of ACM SIGCOMM, and serves on the editorial board of Computer Networks journal.

Dan Cohen was born in Haifa, Israel, in 1937. He received the B.Sc. degree in mathematics from the Technion-Israel Institute of Technology in 1963, and the Ph.D. degree in computer science from Harvard University, Cambridge, MA, in 1969.

Since 1969, he has been on the faculty of Harvard University, Technion-Israel Institute of Technology, and the California Institute of Technology, Pasadena. In 1973, he joined the Information Sciences Institute of the University of Southern California, Los Angeles, here he leads several computer network-related projects. His research interests include interactive realtime systems, graphics voice communication, networking and computer architecture.

2. Overview

Since the development of the ARPANET in the early 1970's, a variety of new packet switching network technologies and operational networks have been developed under DARPA sponsorship, including satellite, packet radio, and local networks. In order to allow processes on different networks to communicate with each other, a means for interconnecting networks has been developed without requiring changes to the internal operation of any network.

The method chosen for interconnecting networks makes minimal demands on individual networks. To facilitate inclusion of a wide variety of networks, each net is required to provide only a minimal *datagram* level of service (i.e. to deliver individual packets of moderate length between its users with high but not perfect reliability). Networks are inter-connected by gateway computers that appear to be local subscribers on two or more nets. The gateways are responsible for routing traffic across multiple networks, and for forwarding messages across each net using the packet transmission protocol in each network. The gateways provide a point-to-point internet datagram service by concatenating the datagram services available on each individual net. Such a system of interconnected networks has been called a *Catenet* [2].

This approach allows the interconnection of networks that have significantly different internal protocols and performance. The networks in the ARPA-Catenet were originally designed as independent entities. In the Catenet approach no changes are required in the internal functions of any network.

Gateways provide an internet service by means of an Internet Protocol (IP) that defines the format of internet packets and the rules for performing internet protocol functions based on the control information (internet header) in these packets. IP must be implemented in host computers (subscribers) engaged in internet communication as well as in the gateways. Gateways also use a gateway-to-gateway protocol to exchange routing and control information.

IP provides for transmitting datagrams from an internet source to an internet destination, potentially in another net. IP also provides for *fragmentation* and *reassembly* of long datagrams, if necessary, for transmission through networks with small packet size limits.

IP is purposely limited in scope to provide only the function necessary to deliver datagrams over an interconnected system of networks. The functions of flow control, sequencing, additional data reliability, or other services commonly found in host-to-host protocols, and multidestination delivery capability or other services are purposely left for higher level protocols to provide as necessary. This allows the higher levels to be tailored to specific applications, and allows a simple and efficient implementation of IP.

2.1. Place in Protocol Hierarchy

As described above, IP functions on top of, or uses, the packet transmission protocol in each individual network. IP is used by higher level end-to-end protocols such as a reliable transport protocol, e.g., Transmission Control Protocol (TCP) [3] in the ARPA-Catenet or a "real time" protocol, e.g., for packet speech.

As shown in Figure 1, IP is the only level in the protocol hierarchy where a single common protocol is used. By locating this point of convergence at the internet datagram level, the Catenet approach preserves the flexibility to incorporate a variety of individual networks and protocols providing packet transmission below IP, while remaining general and efficient enough to serve as a common basis for a variety of higher level protocols. With this approach,

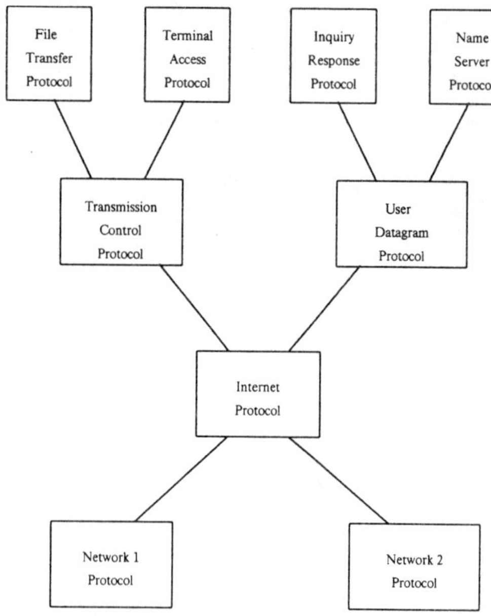

Fig. 1. Protocol Hierarchy.

gateways need only provide datagram service, and remain relatively simple, inexpensive, and efficient.

2.2. Model of Operation

The Internet Protocol provides two major functions: routing a datagram across successive networks to its internet destination address, and fragmentation/reassembly of large packets when needed to cross nets with small packet size limits. To accomplish this, an IP module must reside in each host engaged in internet communication and in each gateway that interconnects networks. The following scenario describes the progress of a datagram from source to destination (assuming one intermediate gateway is involved-see Figure 2).

The basic notion is *encapsulation.* The data to be transmitted must pass through a variety of network environments. To do this the data is encapsulated in an internet datagram. to send the datagram through an individual network, it is in turn encapsulated in a local network packet, and extracted at the other side of that network where it is decapsulated from the first network protocol and is encapsulated in the second network protocol. Thus the model is a series of encapsulation/extractions, not translations. This encapsulation is an information preserving transformation, all the information is preserved even if the individual network cannot make use of it.

The sending internet user (typically a higher level protocol module such as TCP) prepares its data and calls on its local IP module to send the data as a datagram, passing the destination address and other parameters as arguments of the call.

The IP module encapsulates the data in a datagram and fills in the datagram header. The IP module examines the internet destination address. If it is on the same network as this host, it sends the datagram directly to the destination. If the datagram is not on the same network then the IP module sends the datagram to a gateway for forwarding. The selection of which gateway to send the datagram to is an internet routing decision.

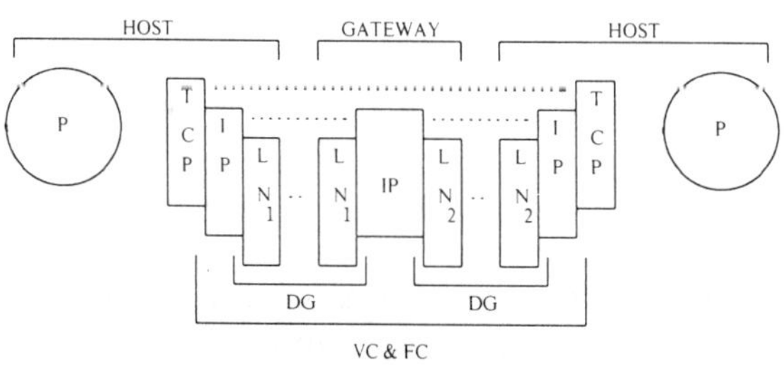

Fig. 2. ARPA Model Transmission Path.

The local network interface (note that from the IP point of view, all actual networks are "local" even if they span across the world) creates a local network packet with its own header, and encapsulates the datagram (complete with internet header) in it, then sends the result via the local network.

The datagram arrives at a gateway host encapsulated in the local network packet. The local network interface extracts the IP datagram and turns it over to the IP module.

The IP module determines from the internet destination address that the datagram should be forwarded to another host in a second network. The IP module uses the local portion of the destination address to determine the local net address for the destination host. It calls on the local network interface for the second network to send the datagram to that address.

If the datagram is too large to be sent through the second network, the IP module fragments it into several smaller datagrams and passes each one to the local net interface.

The local network interface creates a local network packet and encapsulates the datagram, sending the result to the destination host. At the destination host, the datagram is extracted from the local net packet and passed to the IP module.

The IP module determines that the datagram is for an internet user in this host. If the datagram is a fragment, the IP module collects all fragments of a particular datagram and reassembles the complete original datagram. It then passes the data to the user along with the internet source address and other information from the internet header.

2.3. Additional Mechanisms

In addition to the basic addressing and fragmentation functions described above, IP uses four key mechanisms in providing its service: *Type of Service, Time to Live, Options,* and *Header Checksum.* Each of these is summarized here and fully described in Sections 2 and 3.

The Type of Service (TOS) is used to indicate the quality of the service desired – this may be thought of as selecting among Interactive, Bulk, or Real Time, for example. The type of service is an abstract or generalized set of parameters which characterize the service choices provided in the networks that make up the Catenet. This type of service information is used by gateways to select the actual parameters for transmission through each individual network.

The Time to Live (TTL) is an indication of the lifetime of a datagram. Datagrams must not be allowed to persist in the ARPA-Catenet indefinitely. This is because reliable end-to-end protocols depend on there being an upper bound on datagram lifetime, especially old duplicates due to retransmissions. The time to live can be thought of as a self-destruct time limit.

The Options provide for control functions useful in some situations but unnecessary for the most common communications. The options include provisions for timestamps, error reports, and special routing.

The Header Checksum provides a verification that the information used in processing the datagram has been transmitted correctly. However, the data is not covered by the checksum, and may contain errors (see Section 2.6). If the header checksum fails, the internet datagram is discarded by the entity which detects the error.

2.4. Relation to Other Work

The current ARPA Internet Protocol evolved from ideas suggested by Cerf and Kahn [4], and from contemporaneous proposals within the International Federation for Information Processing (IFIP) Technical Committee 6.1 (also known as the International Network Working Group or INWG), in which internet functions and reliable transport functions were combined in a single protocol. Subsequent development of other high level protocols (such as packet speech) that needed internet services led to splitting internet functions and reliable transport functions into separate protocols (the current IP and TCP).

The Internet Protocol used in the ARPA-Catenet is quite similar in philosophy to the PUP protocol [5] developed by the Xerox Corporation. The PUP protocol does not include fragmentation (leaving this to each local net to perform if necessary), but does include a third level of addressing (Ports within hosts) in the internet packet header. IP and PUP share the important principle of having a single common internet datagram protocol as a point of convergence in their protocol hierarchies. Both the PUP and IP systems use the encapsulation technique, and a scheme for "mutual encapsulation" has been worked out [6]. PUP and IP both trace their roots to a joint XEROX-DARPA project at Stanford University. The network interconnection approach used by the European Informatics Network [7] is also quite similar.

Public packet switching networks, on the other hand, have chosen to use virtual circuit (VC) level of service as the level of interconnection, providing end-to-end service as a concatenation of VCs through each network. Since gateways must participate at the VC level, they are more complex and costly, and the end-to-end service may be less efficient and less robust. They are also unable to accommodate "transaction" type users without setting up a VC, although the CCITT is currently considering adding a datagram type of service. For further comparison of CCITT and Catenet approaches see [8–12].

In summary, the ARPA Internet Protocol supports delivery of datagrams from an internet source to a single internet destination. IP treats each datagram as an independent entity unrelated to any other datagram. There are not connections or logical circuits (virtual or otherwise). There are no acknowledgements either end-to-end or hop-by-hop. There is no error control for data, only a header checksum. There are no retransmissions. There is minimal flow control. For flexibility, it is explicitly left to higher level protocols to provide these functions.

3. Main Features

The following paragraphs describe in some detail the mechanisms of the IP. A summary of the contents of the IP header is shown in Figure 3. Further information may be found in the current specification [1].

3.1. Addressing

The IP provides a two level addressing hierarchy. The upper level of the hierarchy is the *network number* (8 bits), and the lower level is an address within that network (24 bits), and is commonly called the *host*. This second level of the hierarchical address is sometimes called the *local address*. The details of the local address are dependent on the particular network.

The local address should allow a single physical host to act as several logically distinct internet hosts. That is, there should be mapping between internet

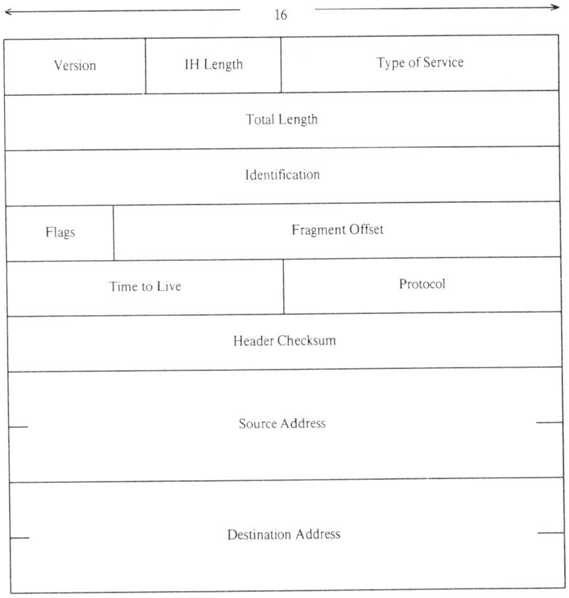

Fig. 3. INTERNET Protocol Header.

host addresses and network/host interfaces that allows several internet addresses to correspond to one physical interface. It should also be possible for several interfaces to accept or emit datagrams for the same internet address.

3.2. Protocol Number

The *Protocol Number* indicates the next level protocol used in the data portion of the datagram. This allows the internet module to demultiplex the incoming datagrams to higher level protocol modules for further processing. Hence, the protocol number indicates the format for parsing the rest of the datagram. Note that there is only one protocol number rather than a source protocol and a destination protocol because, higher level protocol modules exchange datagrams with each other using the same protocol. For example, two TCP modules exchange TCP segments via datagrams marked "TCP" in the protocol number.

One particular protocol number designates a multiplexing protocol which allows several independent data blocks from possibly different higher level protocol modules to be aggregrated together into one datagram for transmission [13].

3.3. Fragmentation and Reassembly

The IP provides information to allow datagrams to be fragmented for passage through networks with small packet size limits and to be reassembled at the destination. The necessary information includes an identification of the fragments that belong to the same datagram and the position of each fragment within the datagram.

The *Identification* (ID) field is used together with the source and destination address, and the protocol number, to identify datagram fragments to be assembled together. The *More Fragments* flag (MF) is set if the datagram is not the last fragment. The *Fragment Offset* (FO) identifies the fragment location, relative to the beginning of the original unfragmented datagram. These offsets are counted in units of 8 octets. Hence, if a datagram is fragmented, its data portion must be broken on 8 octet boundaries. This convention is designed so than an unfragmented datagram has all zero fragmentation information (MF = 0, FO = 0).

If the *Don't Fragment* flag (DF) is set, then internet fragmentation of this datagram is not permitted, although this may force it to be discarded at a gateway to a small packet network. DF can be used to prohibit fragmentation in cases where the receiving host does not wish to reassemble internet fragments. It is also possible that a small packet network could use network specific fragmentation and reassembly without the knowledge or involvement of the IP modules [14].

If a datagram is too large to be forwarded through any net, the entrance gateway breaks it into as many fragments as are necessary to fit within that net's packet size limit. Figure 4 shows a large datagram of 452 octets being fragmented into two smaller fragments (only the header fields relevant to fragmentation are given). Subsequent gateways may break the fragments into even smaller fragments if necessary using the same procedure.

Datagrams arriving at the destination IP are easily recognizable as fragments if either MF or FO is nonzero. Fragments from the same original datagram are identified by having identical ID fields (for a particular source, destination, and protocol number). Fragments are queued until the original datagram can be fully reassembled. Reassembly may be accomplished by placing the data from each fragment in a buffer at the position indicated by FO. Using the header information from the first fragment, the reas-

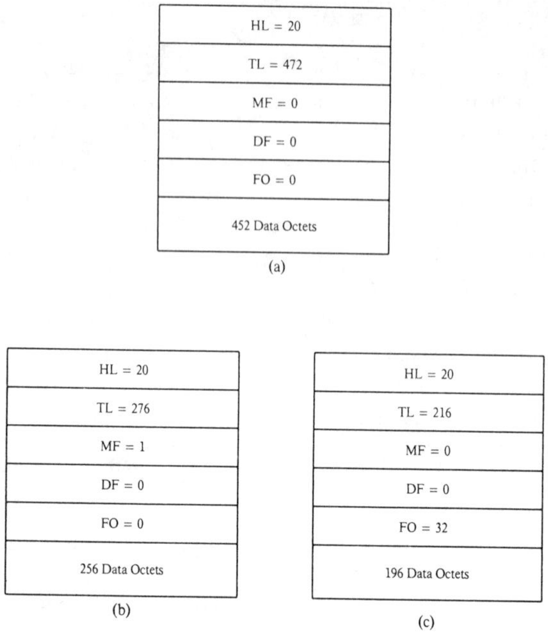

Fig. 4. Fragmentation Example.

sembled datagram is processed further just as if it had been received intact. If the time to live on any fragment expires during reassembly, the partially assembled datagram is discarded, and an error datagram is sent to the source.

A convention has been established in the current ARPA-Catenet that no datagrams larger that 576 octets will be sent, and that all receivers will be prepared to receive a reassemble datagrams up to this length (unless specifically arranged otherwise). This number is chosen to allow a data block of 512 octets and a reasonable number of header octets for several protocol levels to be transmitted in one datagram. Note that the IP header is repeated in each fragment. Hence, the minimum maximum packet size for any network in the Catenet is 20 header octets plus 8 data octets or 28 octets total.

The internet fragmentation procedure allows the fragments to be treated as independent datagrams the rest of the way to their destination (even taking different routes), with reassembly occurring only at the destination.

There is a need to uniquely identify the fragments of a particular datagram. Hence the sender must choose the identification field to be unique for each source/destination pair and protocol number for the time the datagram (or any fragment of it) could exist in the internet. Since the ID field allows 65,536 different values, some host may be able to simply use unique identifiers independent of destination.

It is beneficial for some higher level protocols to choose the identification field. For example, TCP protocol modules may retransmit an identical TCP segment, and the probability for correct reception would be enhanced if the retransmission carried the same identifier as the original transmission since fragments of either datagram could be used to construct a correct TCP segment. Note that a retransmission might be routed via a different set of networks and gateways and also may be fragmented into a different number of different sized fragments. The fragmentation information permits reassembly from fragments from either copy of the datagram.

3.4. Type of Service

The Type of Service (TOS) provides a network independent indication of the quality of service desired. These parameters are to be used to guide the selection of the actual service parameters when transmitting a datagram through a particular network. Some networks offer several piecedence levels of service. Another choice involves a low-delay vs. high-reliability trade off. Typically networks invoke more complex (and delay producing) mechanisms as the need for reliability increases. A few networks offer a stream service, whereby one can achieve a "smoother" service at some cost. Typically this involves the reservation of resources within the network.

The abstract service quality parameters provided by IP are:

Precedence: Indicates the importance of this datagram.

Stream or Datagram: Indicates if there will be other datagrams from this source to this destination at regular frequent intervals justifying the maintenance of stream processing information.

Reliability: A measure of the level of effort desired to ensure delivery of this datagram.

Speed: A measure of the importance of prompt delivery of this datagram.

Speed over Reliability: Indicates the relative importance of speed and reliability when a conflict arises in achieving both.

3.5. Time to Live

The Time to Live (TTL) indicates the maximum time the datagram is allowed to exist in the Catenet.

As a datagram moves through the Catenet the TTL is decremented. If the TTL reaches zero the datagram should be discarded. The intention is to cause long delayed or undeliverable datagrams to be discarded. Guaranteeing a maximum lifetime for datagrams is important for the correct functioning of some higher level protocols such as TCP, and to protect the Catenet resources.

This field should be decreased at each point that the internet header is processed to reflect the time spent processing the datagram. Even if no information is available on the time actually spent, the field should be decremented by 1. The time is measured in units of seconds, and the maximum TTL is 255 seconds.

3.6. Checksum

The IP provides a checksum on the header only. Since some header fields may change (e.g., TTL, MF, FO), this is recomputed and verified at each point that the internet header is processed. This is a hop-by-hop checksum.

This checksum at the internet level is intended to protect the internet header fields from transmission errors. If the internet header contained undetected errors, misrouting and other unanticipated behavior could result. There may be applications in which it is desirable to receive data even though there are a few bit errors. If the IP enforced a data checksum and discarded datagrams with data checksum failures such applications would be restricted unnecessarily.

The checksum is computed as the 16 bit one's complement of the one's complement sum of all 16 bit words in the header. For purposes of computing the checksum, the value of the checksum field is zero. This checksum is simple to compute and has been adequately reliable for usage to date, but it is provisional and may be replaced by a CRC procedure, depending on further experience.

3.7. Header Format

In addition to the main features discussed above, the IP includes the following items in the datagram header:

A *Version Number* (VER) which indicates the version of the IP in use, and hence the format of the internet header.

The *Internet Header Length* (IHL) is the length of the internet header and thus points to the beginning of the data.

The *Total Length* (TL) is the length of the datagram, including internet header and data. There are several protocol options, some of which are discussed in the next section.

4. Additional Features

The following optional mechanisms are available in the IP for use when needed.

4.1. Source Routing

The *Source Route* option provides a means for the source of a datagram to supply routing information to be used by the gateways in forwarding the datagram to the destination.

As described above, routing at each gateway is based on the internet address in the destination field of the datagram header. If the source routing option is used, a series of additional internet addresses will be present in the option field. When the address in the destination field has been reached and the source route is not empty, the next address from the source route becomes the new destination (and is deleted from the source route list).

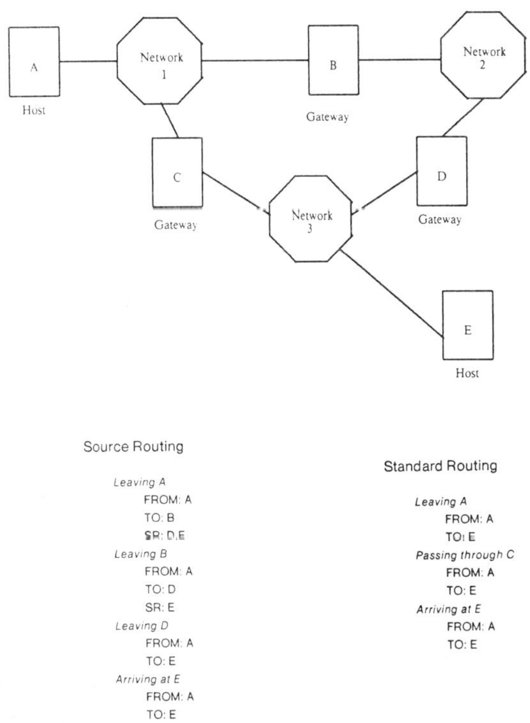

Fig. 5. Source Routing Example.

Thus, the source specifies a series of points the datagram must pass through on the way to its final destination. Normal internet routing is used to reach each of these points in turn, and the datagram may pass through a number of intermediate points between the specified addresses. Source routing may be used to specify routes to networks that are not known to the full internet system.

In Figure 5 an example of source routing is shown. Here host A is sending a datagram to host E. The normal routing would most likely be through the gateway C. We assume the user at host A would prefer in this case to have this datagram routed through gateways B and D. The Figure shows the address information at each step along the route.

4.2. Return (or Record) Route

The *Return Route* option provides a means to record the route taken by a datagram. A return route is composed of a series of internet addresses. When an IP module routes a datagram and the return route option is present, the gateway inserts its own internet address (in the environment of the next destination) into the return route option data.

4.3. Error Report

The *Error Report* option is used to report an error detected in processing a datagram to the source. A code indicates the type of error detected, and the ID is copied from the datagram in error, and additional octets of error information may be present depending on the error code. If a datagram consisting only of an error report option is found to be in error or must be discarded, no error report is sent.

Error codes are defined to report the following conditions: (0) No reason given, (1) Not Accepted – no program at the destination will accept the datagram, (2) Fragmentation Problem – the datagram cannot be delivered without fragmenting and the DF flag is set, (3) Reassembly Problem – the datagram cannot be reassembled because there are missing fragments and the time to live has expired, and (4) Gateway Congestion – the datagram was discarded to relieve congestion.

5. Gateway Functions

This section summarizes the tasks performed by a gateway; which are, interfacing to the local networks, and performing the IP functions.

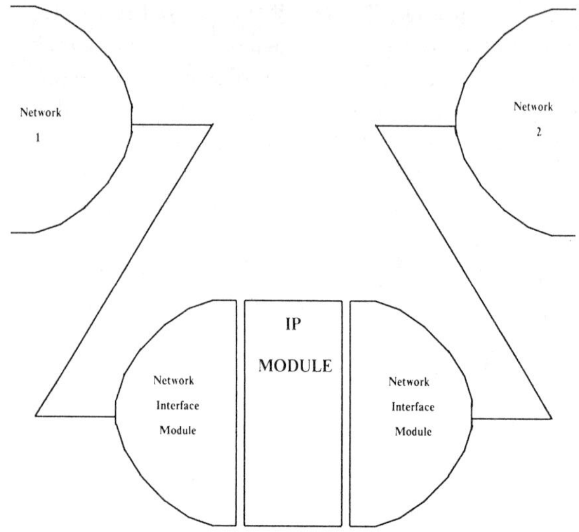

Fig. 6. Gateway.

The actual interconnection of networks is performed by gateways which are computers connected as hosts on several networks (see Figure 6). Messages are communicated across networks by using the protocols and conventions of the individual networks. While traversing each network the IP datagram is encapsulated within the local network protocols. At the gateway the IP datagram is decapsulated and examined by the gateway to determine how to route this datagram, and what local network options to use, if any. The gateway handles issues of routing, fragmentation (if the local network cannot handle regular size datagrams), error reporting and control, and interfacing to local networks.

The essential purpose of a gateway is to forward each datagram toward its destination. The key decision a gateway must make is the routing decision. When a gateway receives a datagram it must use the destination address in the IP header along with routing information stored in the gateway to determine where to send the datagram.

The routing information stored in the gateway may be relatively static (changed only by manual intervention) or dynamic (changed automatically). Both cases are allowed in the ARPA-Catenet system. The discussion of the techniques for dynamically updating the routing information are described by Strazisar [15].

Another important task of a gateway is to encapsulate datagrams for transmission through the next network, using that network's existing message transfer protocol. This involves adding an appropriate message header (and perhaps trailer), to the datagram. The gateway must interpret the type of service field of the IP header to select the appropriate service in the next network.

The gateway decreases the TTL to account for the time elapsed since the TTL was last adjusted. This is an estimate of the time spent in transmission and processing. If this reduces the TTL to zero the gateway discards the datagram.

If the datagram is larger than the maximum packet size of the next network, the gateway may fragment it into pieces that will be sent separately.

If the gateway must discard a datagram due to congestion or errors in processing the datagram (such as an unknown or currently unreachable address), it sends an error report datagram to the source of the discarded datagram.

Of course, the gateway verifies the IP header checksum on every datagram it receives before processing it. If the check fails the datagram is discarded with no notification to the source or adjacent gateway. Since some of the IP header information is changed during gateway processing (e.g. TTL), the gateway computes a new IP header checksum before sending it on.

Each datagram can be processed completely independently of other datagrams. The provision of error recovery, sequencing, or flow control functions are left for end-to-end protocols, and the gateway does not maintain any status information or dedicate any resources for individual virtual circuits. Indeed, the gateway is unaware of any details of the higher protocol levels.

6. Design Decisions

The key decision in the design of the ARPA Internet Protocol is the choice of a datagram basis rather than a virtual circuit basis. Using datagrams as the basis of communication in the Catenet permits the use of simpler gateways since they are not required to maintain state information about the individual virtual circuits, and allows the end-to-end communication to continue via alternate routing if a gateway fails.

Using datagrams as the basic communication service allows the construction of virtual circuit style end-to-end services (e.g., TCP), and other services. In the DARPA research program there are needs for other styles of communication service. For example, the packet speech requires a service which provides minimal delay even at the cost of a few dropped messages. Such a service can be built on a datagram base, but not on a virtual circuit base. For more detail on the tradeoff between a datagram base and a virtual circuit base for communications see references [8–12].

This choice of a datagram base for the operation of the Catenet results in the separation of the internet protocol from the end-to-end protocols in general and TCP in particular. The early proposals for TCP did not focus clearly on the responsibilities of the gateways and did not allow for alternate styles of communication service. Once these needs were apparent the protocol functions were separated into distinct layers.

The decision to use the encapsulation/decapsulation technique to send the IP datagrams through local nets was made to maximize individual networks' autonomy, and to avoid the need for modifications of individual networks (particularly in the area of routing) to support internet traffic [10].

The decision to fragment datagrams in gateways as they pass from a large packet network into a small packet network, but not reassemble the fragments until they reach the destination host, allows simpler gateways and minimizes the delay in the Catenet. The alternate approach of reassembly in the next gateway is explored in reference [14].

Perhaps the most difficult design decision was the choice of the address size and structure. The size of the address field is a compromise that allows enough addresses for the anticipated growth of the Catenet yet is not an excessive overhead burden. The structuring of the address into network and host fields allows the gateways to process datagrams destined for distant networks on the basis of just the network field. This field separation also reflects an administrative delegation of the address assignment function.

In addition to the address, IP carries additional address or multiplexing information in the protocol field. This indicates which next level protocol should be used to interpret this datagram. Most of the higher level protocols have further multiplexing information called *ports* in their headers. The IP approach to addressing may be characterized as hierarchical [10].

An option in IP supports the concept of source routing. This means a source may specify a series of addresses which are used in turn until the ultimate destination is reached [10]. The decision to include this feature was motivated by the realization that many small networks may be interconnected to the Catenet via ad hoc arrangements, and destinations in such networks (or such networks themselves) may be unknown to gateways in the general Catenet.

IP uses a Time To Live which is decremented by each gateway by at least one unit (more if the datagram is delayed in the gateway for a substantial time). Other protocols use a hop count which is incremented by each gateway [5]. The practical difference is small, though the time to live approach remains effective as the size of the network changes, and allows the source to specify a maximum life for the datagram.

7. Research Issues

7.1. Multiple Addresses

There are several issues related to more flexible addressing that the current IP does not deal with. One case is a host with two (or more) internet addresses, either on one network or even on different networks. Sometimes this serves to distinguish between logically separate hosts, but in other cases it is desirable to consider both addresses as the "same place" as far as higher level protocols are concerned. It is not clear how a gateway could know when or how to route messages sent to one address to another address (e.g. if the first address was unreachable). A particularly difficult example of this problem is a mobile packet radio which moves from one network to another while trying to maintain unbroken communication.

7.2. Local Networks

A second issue is the addressing of local networks. There will soon be a large number of local networks (e.g., networks within one building or on a campus) wishing to use the ARPA-Catenet for long distance interconnection. It seems unreasonable that every one of these should have the same status as a nationwide network, with all gateways responsible for maintaining routing information about them. It may be preferable to introduce another level in the addressing hierarchy, or to combine a gateway plus internal address for such nets in the local address field of IP addresses [16].

7.3. Multiple Destinations

Another addressing issue is provision of a capability to send datagrams to a number of destinations at once. Broadcast to all is, of course, the ultimate multi-destination, but "to all" is easier to handle then "to some." This capability is inherent in the technology of some networks (e.g. satellite, ring, and Ethernets) but there is no provision in the current IP for such multidestination addressing. These is work underway in the ARPA community on an internetwork digital packet speech conferencing experiment. A protocol called ST developed for that experiment does contain a multidestination capability [17].

7.4. Naming/Addressing/Routing

The mapping of character string names that are convenient for people into internet addresses is often a problem. This can be eased by the provision of a "directory assistance" service or name server [18]. A name server is a service with a table of name/address correspondences. When the name server is sent a query about a name it responds with the name and corresponding address(es). Directory services can be provided in a centralized and/or distributed fashion. For a further discussion of the roles of names, addresses, and routes see [19].

7.5. Congestion Control

Congestion control is a problem for any network. The gateways may be viewed as nodes of the Catenet, much as IMPs are the nodes of the ARPANET. As internet traffic increases, gateways may become overloaded, even while the individual networks connecting them are enforcing their own congestion controls. Thus there may be a need for an internet congestion control mechanism which is effective with the datagram mode of operation in the Catenet. Several methods such as isarithmic control, buffer categories, and "choke" packets [20] have been proposed for such environments. The ARPA gateways implement a simple strategy of notifying the source when a packet must be discarded due to congestion.

7.6. Monitoring and Adminstrative Control

Accounting is another basic internetworking requirement. Traffic statistics are useful for monitoring and control purposes, and are easily collected by the gateways either on a net-to-net basis, or with more detail by internet source/destination pairs. Volume of packets and/or bits can be collected by a set of counters, and periodically dumped to a Catenet monitoring and accounting center. A gateway monitoring and control center is now operating to coordinate the collection of these statistics [21].

8. Conclusions

The ARPA Internet Protocol provides a common base for supporting higher level protocols in a network independent multi-network environment. The datagram basis of the internet protocol has allowed the flexible evolution of a variety of application specific higher level protocols while allowing simple gateways to interconnect networks. The principle of encapsulation for transmission through individual networks is essential for the provision of internet service over a variety of networks without requiring changes to each networks' internal operation.

As of August 1980, IP is implemented in 12 gateways interconnecting 10 networks, including packet radio, satellite, local nets, and the original ARPANET. Gateways are typically PDP 11/40 or 11/03 processors with limited memory. High level protocols including TCP, terminal access (Telnet), and file transfer (FTP) are in use above IP. Transaction oriented services such as directory assistance (Name Server) are also in use. Other applications are under development.

Acknowledgments

IP has developed in the context of a multicontractor research effort. It is not possible to list all the contributors that have participated in the DARPA Internet Program, however special mention should be made of the coordinating effort and technical contributions of Dr. Vinton G. Cerf of DARPA.

References

[1] Postel, J., "DOD Standard Internet Protocol," IEN 128, RFC 760, USC/Information Sciences Institute, NTIS document number ADA079730, January 1980.

[2] Cerf, V., "The Catenet Model for Internetworking," IEN 48, Defense Advanced Research Projects Agency, July 1978.

[3] Postel, J., "DOD Standard Transmission Control Protocol," IEN 129, RFC 761, USC/Information Sciences Institute, NTIS document number ADA082609, January 1980.

[4] Cerf, V. and R. Kahn, "A Protocol for Packet Network Intercommunication," IEEE Transactions on Communications, vol. COM-22, no. 5, May 1974.

[5] Boggs, D.R., et al., 'Pup: An Internetwork Architecture," IEEE Transactions on Communications, vol. COM-28, no. 4, April 1980.

[6] Shoch, J., D. Cohen, and E. Taft, "Mutual Encapsulation of Internet Protocols," Trends and Applications 1980: Computer Network Protocols, National Bureau of Standards, Gaithersbug, Maryland, May 1980.

[7] Deparis, M., et. al., "The Implementation of an End-to-End Protocol by EIN Centers: A Survey and Comparison," Proceedings International Conference on Computer Communication, Toronto, Canada, August 1976.

[8] Grossman, G.R., A. Hinchley, and C.A. Sunshine, "Issues in International Public Data Networking," Computer Networks, vol. 3, no. 4, August 1979.

[9] DiCiccio, V., et. al., "Alternatives for Interconnection of Public Packet Switching Networks," Proceedings. Sixth Data Communication Symposium, ACM/IEEE, November 1979.

[10] Sunshine, C., "Interconnection of Computer Networks," Computer Networks vol. 1, no. 3, pp. 175–195, January 1977.

[11] Cerf, V. and P. Kirstein, "Issues in Packet-Network Interconnection," Proceedings of the IEEE, vol. 66, no. 11, November 1978.

[12] Postel, J., "Internetwork Protocol Approaches," IEEE Transactions on Communications, vol. COM-28, no. 4, April 1980.

[13] Cohen, D. and J. Postel, "On Protocol Multiplexing," Sixth Data Communication Symposium, ACM/IEEE, November 1979.

[14] Shoch, J., "Packet Fragmentation in Internetwork Protocols," Computer Networks, vol. 3, no. 1, February 1979.

[15] Strazisar, V., "How to Build a Gateway," IEN 109, Bolt, Beranek, and Newman, August 1979.

[16] Cohen, D., "On Addressing and Related Issues (Or Fuel for a Discussion)," IEN 122, USC/Information Sciences Institute, October 1979.

[17] Forgie, J., "ST – A Proposed Internet Stream Protocol," IEN 119, M.I.T. Lincoln Laboratory, September 1979.

[18] Pickens, J., E. Feinler, and J. Mathis, "The NIC Name Server – A Datagram Based Information Utility," Proceedings of the Fourth Berkeley Conference on Distributed Data Management and Computer Networks, August 1979.

[19] Shoch, J., "Inter-Network Naming, Addressing, and Routing," COMPCON Fall 78 Proceedings, (IEEE Catalog Number 78CH-1388-8C), Washington, D.C., September 1978.

[20] Grange, J., and M. Gien, eds., Flow Control in Computer Networks, North Holland, February 1979.

[21] Flood Page, D., "ARPA Catenet Monitoring and Control," IEN 105, Bolt, Beranek, and Newman, May 1979.

Reprinted from *The Seventh Data Communications Symposium*, 1981, pages 232-239. Copyright © by The Institute of Electrical and Electronics Engineers, Inc.

X.75 INTERNETWORKING OF DATAPAC AND TELENET

by

Mehmet S. Unsoy and Theresa A. Shanahan

TransCanada Telephone System
Ottawa, Canada

GTE Telenet Communications Corporation
Vienna, Virginia

Abstract - In 1980, agreement was reached by CCITT defining a standard for the interconnection of public data networks. As a result, networks have been able to proceed with the establishment of international services using CCITT Recommendation X.75. This paper discusses the methodology used and the operating experience gained by the introduction of an X.75 interface between the GTE Telenet and Datapac public packet switching networks.

1 INTRODUCTION

Several public packet switching networks have been operational around the world such as Telenet in the United States and Datapac in Canada. Other packet switching networks are currently being developed in a large number of countries.

By interconnecting these public packet switching networks, international data services are offered to network users. Before any standards were reached for internetworking, interim gateways were installed to interconnect public networks (Ref. 1), thus achieving early introduction of international packet switching services.

Recently, CCITT (International Telegraph and Telephone Consultative Committee) has agreed upon the Recommendation X.75 which is an internetwork signalling procedure for the interconnection of public packet switching data networks (Ref. 2).

Both Datapac and Telenet have implemented the CCITT X.75 procedures to interconnect with each other as well as with other public data networks (PDNs) (Ref. 3, 4). This paper discusses the introduction of an X.75 interface between Datapac and Telenet.

In the rest of this section, a brief description of Telenet and Datapac will be given. Also, the interim connections and the characteristics of the data traffic between the two networks will be discussed.

Section 2 provides a brief description of the internetwork signalling procedures as outlined in CCITT Recommendation X.75. Section 3 explains those characteristics of the X.75 interface that have been bilaterally agreed upon between Telenet and Datapac. The operating experience in establishing the X.75 interface between the networks is the topic of Section 4.

1.1 Datapac Network

Datapac is a public packet switching data communication network operated by the Computer Communications Group (CCG) of the TransCanada Telephone System (TCTS). The basic service offering is the ability to set up a virtual circuit between a pair of network access points. The network topology presently consists of 16 packet switching nodes interconnected in a mesh of 56 Kbps digital transmission facilities and providing service to 60 Datapac Serving Areas across Canada. Each node consists of the SL-10 packet switch developed by Bell Northern Research and manufactured by Northern Telecom Canada. The SL-10 is a multi-microprocessor configured on a common bus; it can be modularly extended to support the required number of access lines and mix of software-based access services (Ref. 5).

1.2 Telenet Network

Commercially operational since August 1975, Telenet is a public packet switching data communications network operated by the GTE Telenet Communications Corporation (Ref. 6). The network is virtual circuit based (Ref. 4) and currently consists of twelve packet switching exchanges. These twelve exchanges are made up of 153 switches and 141 concentrators which provide nationwide access in over 300 cities. The Telenet switches (TP 4000s) have a multi-microprocessor architecture and are interconnected with 56 Kbps digital trunks.

1.3 Interim Connection Between Telenet and Datapac

The commmercial international service between Datapac and Telenet was started on May 3, 1978, using interim gateways developed by the Computer Communications Group of TransCanada Telephone System. These gateways were implemented on minicomputers, connected to both networks via an X.25 interface (Ref. 1).

The configuration of the interconnection of Datapac and Telenet through these interim gateways is shown in Figure 1.

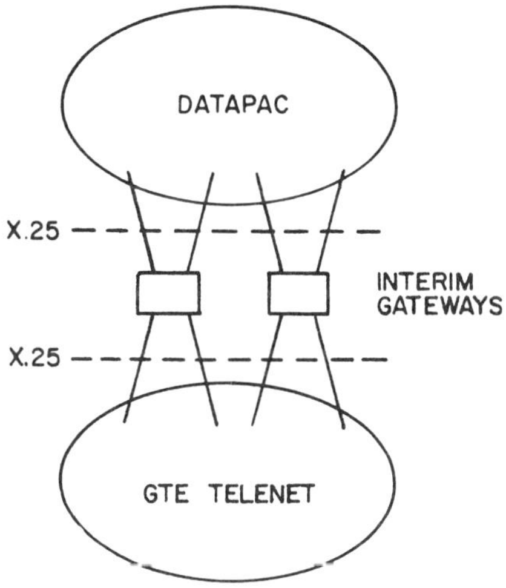

FIGURE I
DATAPAC-GTE TELENET INTERIM INTERCONNECTIONS

The interim gateways not only provided international service between the two networks, but supplied traffic information which facilitated planning for the X.75 interconnection of the networks. Most of the Datapac/Telenet traffic is terminal-to-host traffic. A balance exists between Telenet and Datapac originated calls. The duration of the calls as well as the number of packets sent per call are important traffic engineering parameters. Traffic studies showed that the average call duration for Datapac/Telenet calls is 17 minutes, while the average number of packets sent per call is approximately 200. The distribution of the call duration is not uniform; for example, the duration of 70 percent of the calls is less than 10 minutes while 6 percent are longer than 60 minutes (Ref. 7).

2 X.75 INTERNETWORKING

CCITT Study Group VII defined a group of protocol recommendations during the 1976-1980 Study Period. To accomplish the interconnection of Public Data Networks, X.75 was defined in 1978 based upon Recommendation X.25. A revised version of X.75 was approved in February 1980 (Ref. 2).

2.1 CCITT Recommendation X.75

X.75 procedures are defined at the interface between two Signalling Terminal Equipments (STEs) (Figure 2). Like X.25 (Ref. 8), X.75 specifies procedures at three distinct levels: Physical, Link, and Packet.

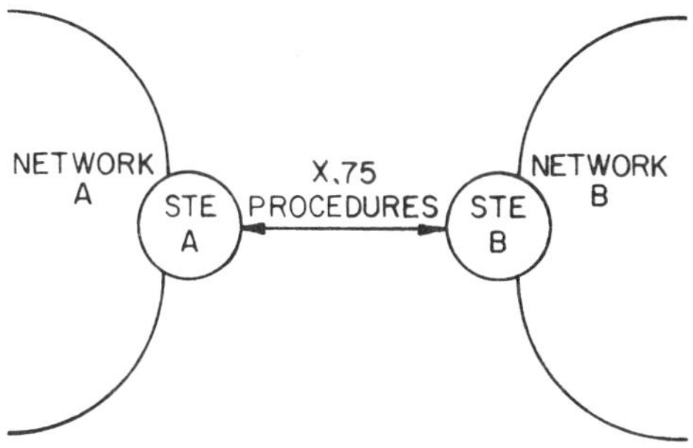

FIGURE 2
X.75 INTERCONNECTION

The Physical level defines the electrical and functional characterstics of the interface between two STEs. The transmission link is one or several full duplex, high speed, synchronous circuits.

The Link level specifies the use of the data link control procedure LAPB which is compatible with the High-Level Data Link Control (HDLC) procedures specified by the International Organization for Standarization (ISO). The Link level procedures guarantee the correct exchange of information across the international link. X.75 defines the use of modulo 8 or modulo 128 frame sequence numbering allowing for the efficient use of satellite circuits between countries.

At the Link level, X.75 defines both a Single Link Procedure (SLP) and a Multilink Procedure which allows the interface to operate over multiple lines and achieve greater reliability and throughput.

The Packet level defines procedures by which switched virtual calls are established, maintained and cleared across the X.75 interface. A single interface may support up to 4095 simultaneous virtual calls. Compatibility exists between X.25 and X.75 procedures and packet formats in order to maintain the semantics of X.25. However, the X.75 Call Request, Clear Request and Call Connected packets contain an additional field for utilities which are used for signalling network information between the STEs. These utilities are discussed in Section 2.3.

2.2 X.75 Call Establishment

The Packet level of X.75 defines procedures for the establishment of switched virtual calls. An STE initiates a call by transmitting a Call Request packet across the X.75 interface. See Figure 3.

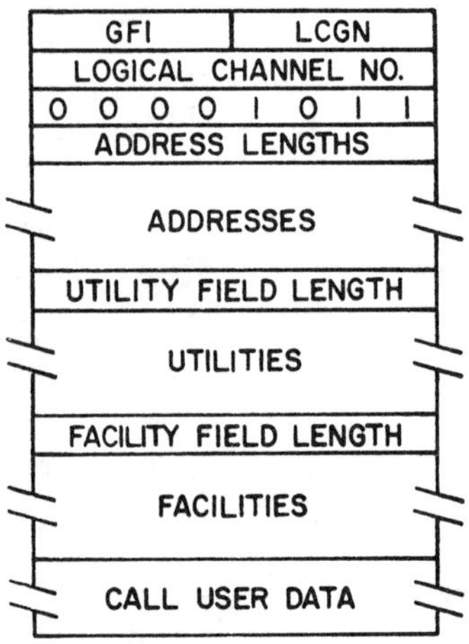

FIGURE 3
X.75 CALL REQUEST PACKET

The Call Request packet contains a Logical Channel Number chosen by the STE which will identify all packets associated with the call. The Call Request includes the calling and called DTE addresses or international data numbers as defined in Recommendation X.121 (Ref. 9). The utility, facility and call user data fields follow. The facility field may only be used for national facilities since currently international facilities have not been defined. Call user data may be a maximum of 16 octets in length or 128 octets if the Fast Select utility is requested.

The calling STE will receive a Call Connected packet if the called STE accepts the call. Similar to the Call Request, the Call Connected packet contains an address field, network utility field, facility field, and user data (only in response to a Fast Select call). When a switched virtual call cannot be established, the called STE will transmit a Clear Request packet which contains the appropriate cause and diagnostic codes.

2.3 X.75 Utilities

Twelve network utilities are defined in order that network administrative information may be signalled in the Call Request, Call Connected and Clear Request packets:

- Transit Network Identification
- Call Identifier
- Throughput Class Indication
- Window Size Indication
- Packet Size Indication
- Fast Select Indication
- Closed User Group Indication
- Closed User Group with Outgoing Access Indication
- Reverse Charging Indication
- Traffic Class Indication
- Estimated Transit Delay
- Tariff

The utilities pertinent to the Telenet/Datapac interconnection are discussed here.

The Call Identifier Utility is used to uniquely identify the call by all of the networks involved for accounting, auditing, and trouble reporting purposes.

The Throughput Class Indication Utility is used by the STE for negotiating the throughput classes applying to the call. A throughput class is an indication of the maximum throughput, in bits per second, requested for a given virtual circuit in each direction of transmission.

The Window Size Indication Utility is used by the STE for negotiating the window sizes for both directions of transmission over the X.75 interface for a given virtual circuit. The standard value to be supported by all PDNs is 2.

The Packet Size Indication Utility is used by the STE for negotiating the maximum data field length of Data packets for a given virtual circuit and for each direction of transmission. The standard value to be supported by all PDNs is 128 octets.

The Reverse Charging Indication Utility allows for the establishment of international virtual calls in which the calling terminal has reversed the applicable charges. Its use is subject to agreement between PDN administrations.

The Tariff Utility may be used to indicate the individual network's tariff requirements on a per call basis. The definition and coding of this utility is currently designated for further study by CCITT.

2.4 International Addressing

One of the basic elements of international network connections is an international numbering plan. CCITT Recommendation X.121 defines the international numbering plan for identifying public network addresses.

Each public packet switching network is assigned a Data Network Identification Code (DNIC). A DNIC is a four digit number; the first three digits identify the country and the fourth identifies a particular public packet switching network in that country. Telenet's DNIC is 3110 while Datapac's DNIC is 3020.

Following the DNIC, an international address contains a Network Terminal Number (NTN) which specifies the address of the terminal within the PDN. The NTN is a 1-10 digit number and is assigned to a particular terminal by the PDN administration.

Generally, the routing of calls between PDN's is based upon DNICs, while the routing of calls within a PDN is based upon NTNs.

3 CHARACTERISTICS OF TELENET - DATAPAC X.75 INTERFACE

CCITT Recommendations X.75 and X.121 do not cover all aspects of public packet switching network interworking. Several interworking issues require bilateral agreements between the networks involved. The value of various parameters defined in X.75 must be negotiated and agreed upon by the two networks. This section describes the bilaterally agreed interworking procedures and parameters between Datapac and Telenet.

3.1 Link Level

Telenet and Datapac utilize the Single Link Procedure (SLP) only. The Multilink Procedure (MLP) will not be supported at this time. Both administrations also agreed to use modulo 8 numbering at the Link level. The extended modulo 128 numbering will not be supported.

The SLP in CCITT Recommendation X.75 is based upon the Link Access Procedure LAPB described in Section 2 of CCITT Recommendation X.25 (Ref. 8). Currently, LAPB procedures are under development in Datapac and to achieve early introduction of the X.75 interface, it was agreed to use the Link Access Procedures LAP as described in Recommendation X.25 (Ref. 8). When tested and available on Datapac, LAPB will be used at the Link level.

3.2 Packet Level

In order to reduce the occurrence of call collisions, the STEs assign logical channel numbers in a reverse order. The Telenet STE assigns the logical channels in an ascending order, starting with the lowest numbered available channel. The Datapac STE assigns logical channels in a descending order, starting with the highest numbered available channel.

Both networks agree to use modulo 8 numbering at the Packet level. Also, at this time, it is agreed not to support the optional Fast Select utility.

To ensure the availability of the X.75 interface, the Datapac STE periodically sends a Clear Request packet, as an idle line probe, to the Telenet STE on an available logical channel. If a Clear Confirmation packet is not received within the specified time (e.g., 3 minutes), a major failure has occurred; the Datapac STE declares the interface down and the appropriate Datapac alarm is generated.

It is agreed to provide multiple X.75 gateways between Datapac and Telenet, thus supporting higher traffic volume and insuring the availability of the X.75 interconnection. The routing procedures for the outgoing international calls, implemented in both networks, select the closest and the least congested gateway during call establishment.

Both the Telenet and the Datapac STEs check and verify the DNICs of all addresses on incoming/outgoing Call Request and Call Connected packets. By specifying the authorized DNICs in the STEs, both networks can enforce any policy bilaterally agreed upon, with regard to incoming, outgoing and transit calls.

It is agreed between the networks that collect calls over the X.75 gateways are accepted and thus reverse charging is allowed. The reverse charging requests and confirmations are exchanged between the networks using the Reverse Charging Indication Utility.

Telenet supports full 14 digit calling and called addresses. This includes a 4 digit DNIC and a 10 digit Network Terminal Number (NTN). The Datapac network currently supports a NTN of 8 digits as a national address, in addition to the 4 digit DNIC. It was therefore agreed that Telenet insure that Datapac called or calling addresses are limited to 12 digits before transmittal to the Datapac STE.

The network access services that are allowed to establish international calls via X.75 between Datapac and Telenet are limited to X.25 and X.28 asynchronous terminal access on both networks. These are the access services that were being supported through the interim gateways. In the near future, other international services, such as synchronous terminal support, may be offered.

3.3 Bilaterally Agreed Parameters

The following is the list of parameters and their initial values bilaterally agreed upon for the X.75 interface.

- Frame retransmission timer, T1 = 3 seconds
- Maximum number of frame retransmissions, N2 = 10
- Maximum number of outstanding I Frames, k = 7
- Range of logical channel numbers = 1 to 64
- Maximum Data packet length = 128 octets (default)
- Packet level window size = 2 (default)
- Restart Request timer, T30 = 180 seconds
- Call Request timer, T31 = 180 seconds
- Reset Request timer, T32 = 180 seconds
- Clear Request timer, T33 = 180 seconds

4 TESTING OF THE X.75 INTERFACE

The X.75 interface between two public packet switching networks must be tested thoroughly before it is introduced into commercial service. In this section, the testing conducted by Telenet and Datapac for their interconnection is described.

4.1 Testing Stages

The Recommendation X.75 specifies the signalling procedures between two STEs. However, the X.75 interface is only a portion of the end-to-end (DTE-to-DTE) connection. Thus, the testing of the X.75 interconnection involved two stages:

- X.75 interface testing, and
- end-to-end testing.

The purpose of the X.75 interface testing was to verify that the implementation on each network's STE conformed to the procedures specified by CCITT recommendations as well as other interface requirements. Datapac employed a test plan which included over 500 individual tests to verify the functional correctness of the Datapac STE implementation. Telenet carried out a similar test plan to verify its STE.

Using these test plans and the test tools described in Section 4.2, both Datapac and Telenet conducted X.75 interface testing internally. During this stage, the testing system of Figure 4(a) simulated both a foreign network's STE and a local X.25 DTE.

The purpose of the second stage of testing (i.e., end-to-end testing) was two-fold. First, it was to verify that the X.75 implementations and the interface parameters of both networks were compatible. The second purpose was to verify and demonstrate that international virtual circuits from DTE to DTE could be established, maintained and cleared as expected. This stage of testing required the full cooperation of both networks involved.

Telenet and Datapac conducted this stage of testing jointly, using the test configuration shown in Figure 4(b). An end-to-end test plan was prepared and executed. The description and results of this testing are given in section 4.3.

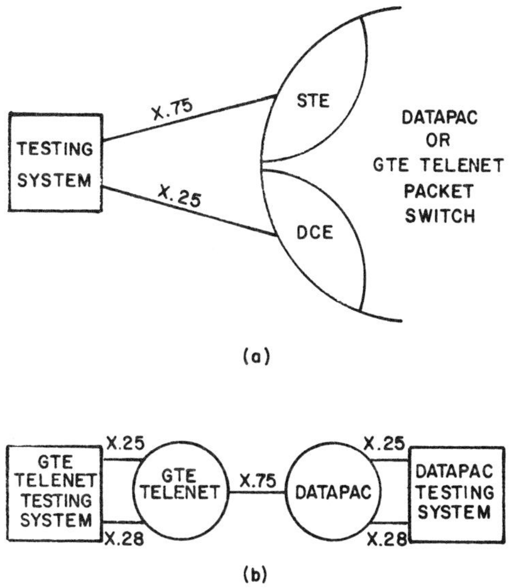

FIGURE 4
X.75 TESTING CONFIGURATIONS

4.2 Test Tools

To perform thorough functional and performance testing of network interfaces such as X.25, X.75, X.28 and X.29, automatic testing tools were developed by Datapac and Telenet.

4.2.1 GTE Telenet

Telenet designed and developed a testing system to perform both functional and stress testing of its hardware and software products. The testing system is composed of a specially modified TP 4000 packet switch which is used in conjunction with a simulation system, known as SIMSYS.

SIMSYS is a high level computer language that runs on a Tandem computer, providing the capability to easily define test programs or scripts that cause SIMSYS to establish, control and clear any number of virtual calls. SIMSYS automatically generates a transcript file which serves as an audit trail of each testing session and contains statistics and timing information on various aspects of the test script executions. During internal testing, SIMSYS performed the simulation of a Telenet X.25 DTE, asynchronous terminal, X.75 Telenet STE, X.25 DCE as well as a Datapac X.75 STE. During Datapac/Telenet testing, SIMSYS performed as an X.25 DTE or asynchronous terminal.

In those instances where complete control of individual bit fields within the frame or packet formats is necessary, SIMSYS is linked to a modified TP 4000. This allows for the introduction of forced error conditions that would normally be prevented by the SIMSYS Tandem host computer, for example, the generation of illegal packet sequence numbers.

With this combination of tools, the generation of standardized tests are possible that can force a protocol procedure through its entire range of operation, including unusual error conditions. Also, it provides the capability to stress or flood test a product while automatically obtaining valuable performance analysis data.

4.2.2 Datapac

The following is a brief description of test tools that are currently used by Datapac for various purposes. Several other test tools are under development.

- o ANTS (Automated Network Testing System) is a software package originally implemented under the UNIX operating system on a PDP-11, to allow automated protocol tests of X.25 and X.75 interfaces. ANTS is written in the C language and currently runs under the RSX-11M operating system of PDP-11.
- o BILGE (Bell Interactive Load Generation Environment) is a software package, written in the C language, implemented under RSX-11M, to allow automated load generation and performance measurements of an X.25 interface and virtual circuits.
- o Interactive Terminal Interface (ITI) Tester is a software package implemented under RSX-11M to allow automated protocol tests on ITI protocols (i.e. X.3, X.28 and X.29). It is written partly in the C language and partly in the Macro-11 language of PDP-11.

During Telenet/Datapac testing, these testing tools were successfully used in conjunction to insure that the semantics of international virtual circuits were maintained on an end-to-end basis.

4.3 End-to-End Testing Experience

The X.75 interconnection between Datapac and Telenet supports virtual circuits between X.25 DTEs and/or ITI terminals on both networks. The end-to-end tests conducted were classified into four groups:

- Datapac X.25 DTE to Telenet X.25 DTE,
- Datapac X.25 DTE to Telenet asynchronous terminal,
- Telenet X.25 DTE to Datapac asynchronous terminal,
- Telenet asynchronous terminal to Datapac asynchronous terminal.

Each category included a series of tests for call setup, data transfer, call reset, and call clearing, in both Telenet to Datapac and Datapac to Telenet directions. These tests were performed to check every possible end-to-end situation in different phases of a virtual call. For example, the Data transfer phase was tested by sending data packets with/without M-bit, with/without Q-bit, with different data field lengths, and by sending Interrupt packets under various conditions, for example, in flow-control blocked state.

Discussed below are the problems found during testing and their resolution:

Immediately following the initialization of the X.75 link between Datapac and Telenet, it was found that X.75 logical channel ranges did not match. Even though 64 logical channels were agreed upon, Telenet implements 64 logical channels from 0 to 63, while Datapac implements them from 1 to 64. This problem was corrected by increasing the Telenet's logical channel range by one.

The next problem encountered was an incompatibility in the X.75 Call Connected packet format. The format used by the Datapac STE was based upon the version of CCITT X.75 provisionally approved in 1978. However, Telenet's STE uses the format specified in the 1980 version of X.75. The problem was resolved by Datapac modifying the Call Connected packet format in accordance to the 1980 version of X.75.

Another problem at the call setup phase was related to a bilaterally agreed utility field, the Tariff Class Utility. This field was missing in the Call Connected packets sent by Telenet's STE while it was expected by Datapac's STE. The problem was resolved by modifying Telenet's STE to include the Tariff Class Utility in the Call Connected packets.

No problems or incompatibilities were encountered during the data transfer, call reset and call clearing phases.

The last problem which surfaced during testing was the incompatibility in the use of the Protocol Identifier Field of Call Request packets generated by the asynchronous Packet Assemblers/ Disassemblers (PADs). According to CCITT Recommendation X.29 (Ref. 10), the four octet field should be specified as X"01000000". Datapac aysnchronous PADs expect the protocol identifier field to contain this value. However, Telenet uses the 2nd and 3rd octets of this field to specify the type and speed of the terminal which caused call clearing by the Datapac PAD. Telenet agreed to provide the protocol identifier field as specified by X.29.

As a result of this thorough testing of the Telenet/Datapac X.75 interconnection, incompatibilities were identified and resolved. It was proven that the interface provided a stable and reliable interconnection. The parameters on both sides of the interface were made compatible and were also fine-tuned to the specific requirements of the interface.

4.4 Customer Trials

After the completion of end-to-end testing, a group of network users were asked to participate in a customer trial where other end-to-end aspects of the X.75 internetworking could be tested. Among the purposes of this trial were testing the acceptability of X.75 interconnections, X.121 addressing, and end-to-end performance. The customers for this trial were carefully selected so that a variety of end-to-end connections and traffic profiles could be tested. They included customers with X.25 hosts on Datapac and with ITI terminals on Telenet, customers with X.25 hosts on Telenet and ITI terminals on Datapac, as well as customers with X.25 hosts on both networks.

Before the trial started, these customers were informed and advised about the procedures for establishing international calls between Datapac and Telenet via the X.75 gateways. During the trial, Telenet and Datapac maintained close support with those customers involved in the trial. Problem reports and other types of information from the customers are being used to improve various aspects of the interconnection.

5 CONCLUSIONS

By interconnecting public packet switching data networks, international data services are offered to network users. The interconnection of Telenet and Datapac networks has been provided through interim gateways since May 1978. However, after the CCITT standards for interconnection were firmly established, both networks implemented the necessary procedures for direct interconnections (i.e. X.75 and X.121).

Before the X.75 interconnection between the two networks was introduced, the network administrations conducted discussions and negotiations to agree on bilateral issues and aspects which are not covered by X.75 and X.121. This was followed by extensive testing of the X.75 interface as well as the end-to-end connections. All the incompatibilities were identified and resolved. Harmonious operation of the X.75 interface was demonstrated. Finally, a customer trial was held to verify the acceptability of the X.75 interconnection by the network users.

As a result of these tests and trials, X.75 interfaces between Datapac and Telenet are being put into commercial service, thus eliminating the need for interim gateways and enhancing the quality and scope of the international services offered to network users.

6 ACKNOWLEDGEMENTS

The development, implementation, and testing of the X.75 interface on both the GTE Telenet and Datapac networks were the result of team efforts. Essential roles were played by many individuals in the GTE Telenet Product Development Group, Computer Communications Group of the TransCanada Telephone System and Bell Northern Research. Their considerable efforts are gratefully acknowledged. Special acknowledgement is extended to Veronica Wright of GTE Telenet for testing and supervising the Telenet X.75 interface during the customer trial.

REFERENCES

1. A.M. Rybczynski, D.F. Weir and I.M. Cunningham, "Datapac Internetworking for International Services", ICCC '78, Kyoto, Japan, Sept. 1978.

2. CCITT Revised Recommendation X.75, "Terminal and Transit Control Procedures and Data Transfer System on International Circuits between Packet Switched Data Networks". COM VII - No 441 as amended and approved by Study Group VII, Feb. 1980.

3. A.M. Rybczynksi, J.D. Palframan and A. Thomas, "Design of the Datapac X.75 Internetworking Capability, ICCC '80, Atlanta, October 1980.

4. D.F. Weir, J.B. Holmblad and A.C. Rothberg, "An X.75 Based Network Architecture", ICCC '80, Atlanta, October 1980.

5. C.I. McGibbon, et al., "DATAPAC - Initial Experience with a Commercial Packet Network", ICCC '78, Kyoto, Japan, Sept. 1978.

6. Lawrence G. Roberts, "The Evolution of Packet Switching", Proceedings of the IEEE, Vol. 66, No. 11, Nov. 1978.

7. M.S. Unsoy, A.M. Rybczynski, and D. Rhynas, "Datapac International Packet Switching Services", ELECTRO '81, New York, April 1981.

8. CCITT Revised Recommendation X.25, "Interface between Data Terminal Equipment (DTE) and Data Circuit-Terminating Equipment (DCE) for Terminals Operating in the Packet Mode on Public Data Networks", as amended and approved by Study Group VII, Feb. 1980.

9. CCITT Revised Recommendation X.121, "International Numbering Plan for Public Data Networks", CCITT Grey Book, as amended and approved by Study Group VII, Feb. 1980.

10. CCITT Provisional Recommendation X.29, "Procedures for the Exchange of Control Information and User Data between a Packet Mode DTE and a PAD Facility", 1978.

A Protocol for Packet Network Intercommunication

VINTON G. CERF AND ROBERT E. KAHN, MEMBER, IEEE

***Abstract*—A protocol that supports the sharing of resources that exist in different packet switching networks is presented. The protocol provides for variation in individual network packet sizes, transmission failures, sequencing, flow control, end-to-end error checking, and the creation and destruction of logical process-to-process connections. Some implementation issues are considered, and problems such as internetwork routing, accounting, and timeouts are exposed.**

INTRODUCTION

IN THE LAST few years considerable effort has been expended on the design and implementation of packet switching networks [1]-[7],[14],[17]. A principle reason for developing such networks has been to facilitate the sharing of computer resources. A packet communication network includes a transportation mechanism for delivering data between computers or between computers and terminals. To make the data meaningful, computers and terminals share a common protocol (i.e., a set of agreed upon conventions). Several protocols have already been developed for this purpose [8]-[12],[16]. However, these protocols have addressed only the problem of communication on the same network. In this paper we present a protocol design and philosophy that supports the sharing of resources that exist in different packet switching networks.

After a brief introduction to internetwork protocol issues, we describe the function of a GATEWAY as an interface between networks and discuss its role in the protocol. We then consider the various details of the protocol, including addressing, formatting, buffering, sequencing, flow control, error control, and so forth. We close with a description of an interprocess communication mechanism and show how it can be supported by the internetwork protocol.

Even though many different and complex problems must be solved in the design of an individual packet switching network, these problems are manifestly compounded when dissimilar networks are interconnected. Issues arise which may have no direct counterpart in an individual network and which strongly influence the way in which internetwork communication can take place.

A typical packet switching network is composed of a set of computer resources called HOSTS, a set of one or more *packet switches*, and a collection of communication media that interconnect the packet switches. Within each HOST, we assume that there exist *processes* which must communicate with processes in their own or other HOSTS. Any current definition of a process will be adequate for our purposes [13]. These processes are generally the ultimate source and destination of data in the network. Typically, within an individual network, there exists a protocol for communication between any source and destination process. Only the source and destination processes require knowledge of this convention for communication to take place. Processes in two distinct networks would ordinarily use different protocols for this purpose. The ensemble of packet switches and communication media is called the *packet switching subnet*. Fig. 1 illustrates these ideas.

In a typical packet switching subnet, data of a fixed maximum size are accepted from a source HOST, together with a formatted destination address which is used to route the data in a store and forward fashion. The transmit time for this data is usually dependent upon internal network parameters such as communication media data rates, buffering and signaling strategies, routing, propagation delays, etc. In addition, some mechanism is generally present for error handling and determination of status of the networks components.

Individual packet switching networks may differ in their implementations as follows.

1) Each network may have distinct ways of addressing the receiver, thus requiring that a uniform addressing scheme be created which can be understood by each individual network.

2) Each network may accept data of different maximum size, thus requiring networks to deal in units of the smallest maximum size (which may be impractically small) or requiring procedures which allow data crossing a network boundary to be reformatted into smaller pieces.

3) The success or failure of a transmission and its performance in each network is governed by different time delays in accepting, delivering, and transporting the data. This requires careful development of internetwork timing procedures to insure that data can be successfully delivered through the various networks.

4) Within each network, communication may be disrupted due to unrecoverable mutation of the data or missing data. End-to-end restoration procedures are desirable to allow complete recovery from these conditions.

Paper approved by the Associate Editor for Data Communications of the IEEE Communications Society for publication without oral presentation. Manuscript received November 5, 1973. The research reported in this paper was supported in part by the Advanced Research Projects Agency of the Department of Defense under Contract DAHC 15-73-C-0370.

V. G. Cerf is with the Department of Computer Science and Electrical Engineering, Stanford University, Stanford, Calif.

R. E. Kahn is with the Information Processing Technology Office, Advanced Research Projects Agency, Department of Defense, Arlington, Va.

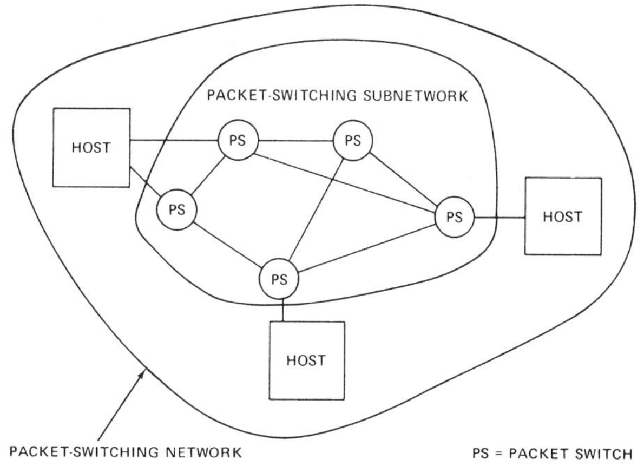

Fig. 1. Typical packet switching network.

5) Status information, routing, fault detection, and isolation are typically different in each network. Thus, to obtain verification of certain conditions, such as an inaccessible or dead destination, various kinds of coordination must be invoked between the communicating networks.

It would be extremely convenient if all the differences between networks could be economically resolved by suitable interfacing at the network boundaries. For many of the differences, this objective can be achieved. However, both economic and technical considerations lead us to prefer that the interface be as simple and reliable as possible and deal primarily with passing data between networks that use different packet switching strategies.

The question now arises as to whether the interface ought to account for differences in HOST or process level protocols by transforming the source conventions into the corresponding destination conventions. We obviously want to allow conversion between packet switching strategies at the interface, to permit interconnection of existing and planned networks. However, the complexity and dissimilarity of the HOST or process level protocols makes it desirable to avoid having to transform between them at the interface, even if this transformation were always possible. Rather, compatible HOST and process level protocols must be developed to achieve effective internetwork resource sharing. The unacceptable alternative is for every HOST or process to implement every protocol (a potentially unbounded number) that may be needed to communicate with other networks. We therefore assume that a common protocol is to be used between HOST's or processes in different networks and that the interface between networks should take as small a role as possible in this protocol.

To allow networks under different ownership to interconnect, some accounting will undoubtedly be needed for traffic that passes across the interface. In its simplest terms, this involves an accounting of packets handled by each net for which charges are passed from net to net until the buck finally stops at the user or his representative. Furthermore, the interconnection must preserve intact the internal operation of each individual network. This is easily achieved if two networks interconnect as if each were a HOST to the other network, but without utilizing or indeed incorporating any elaborate HOST protocol transformations.

It is thus apparent that the interface between networks must play a central role in the development of any network interconnection strategy. We give a special name to this interface that performs these functions and call it a GATEWAY.

THE GATEWAY NOTION

In Fig. 2 we illustrate three individual networks labeled A, B, and C which are joined by GATEWAYS M and N. GATEWAY M interfaces network A with network B, and GATEWAY N interfaces network B to network C. We assume that an individual network may have more than one GATEWAY (e.g., network B) and that there may be more than one GATEWAY path to use in going between a pair of networks. The responsibility for properly routing data resides in the GATEWAY.

In practice, a GATEWAY between two networks may be composed of two halves, each associated with its own network. It is possible to implement each half of a GATEWAY so it need only embed internetwork packets in local packet format or extract them. We propose that the GATEWAYS handle internetwork packets in a standard format, but we are not proposing any particular transmission procedure between GATEWAY halves.

Let us now trace the flow of data through the interconnected networks. We assume a packet of data from process X enters network A destined for process Y in network C. The address of Y is initially specified by process X and the address of GATEWAY M is derived from the address of process Y. We make no attempt to specify whether the choice of GATEWAY is made by process X, its HOST, or one of the packet switches in network A. The packet traverses network A until it reaches GATEWAY M. At the GATEWAY, the packet is reformatted to meet the requirements of network B, account is taken of this unit of flow between A and B, and the GATEWAY delivers the packet to network B. Again the derivation of the next GATEWAY address is accomplished based on the address of the destination Y. In this case, GATEWAY N is the next one. The packet traverses network B until it finally reaches GATEWAY N where it is formatted to meet the requirements of network C. Account is again taken of this unit of flow between networks B and C. Upon entering network C, the packet is routed to the HOST in which process Y resides and there it is delivered to its ultimate destination.

Since the GATEWAY must understand the address of the source and destination HOSTS, this information must be available in a standard format in every packet which arrives at the GATEWAY. This information is contained in an *internetwork header* prefixed to the packet by the source HOST. The packet format, including the internet-

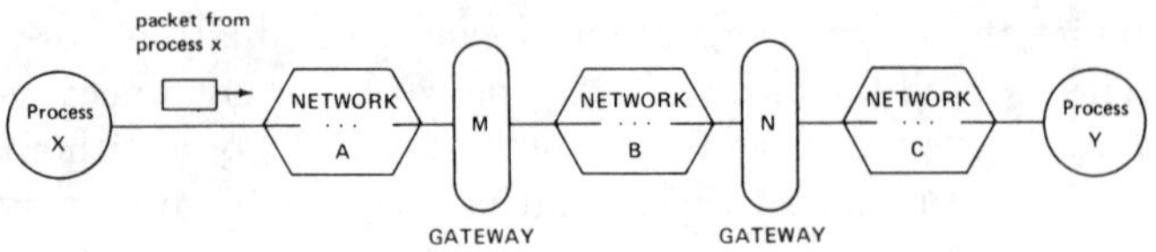

Fig. 2. Three networks interconnected by two GATEWAYS.

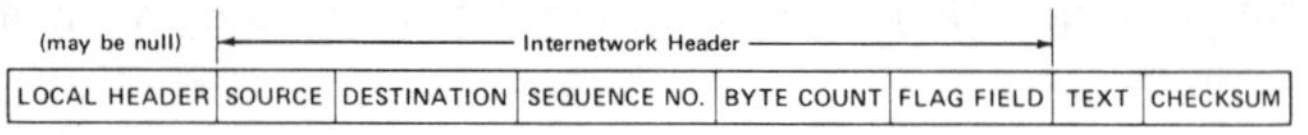

Fig. 3. Internetwork packet format (fields not shown to scale).

work header, is illustrated in Fig. 3. The source and destination entries uniformly and uniquely identify the address of every HOST in the composite network. Addressing is a subject of considerable complexity which is discussed in greater detail in the next section. The next two entries in the header provide a sequence number and a byte count that may be used to properly sequence the packets upon delivery to the destination and may also enable the GATEWAYS to detect fault conditions affecting the packet. The flag field is used to convey specific control information and is discussed in the section on retransmission and duplicate detection later. The remainder of the packet consists of text for delivery to the destination and a trailing check sum used for end-to-end software verification. The GATEWAY does *not* modify the text and merely forwards the check sum along without computing or recomputing it.

Each network may need to augment the packet format before it can pass through the individual network. We have indicated a *local header* in the figure which is prefixed to the beginning of the packet. This local header is introduced merely to illustrate the concept of embedding an internetwork packet in the format of the individual network through which the packet must pass. It will obviously vary in its exact form from network to network and may even be unnecessary in some cases. Although not explicitly indicated in the figure, it is also possible that a local trailer may be appended to the end of the packet.

Unless all transmitted packets are legislatively restricted to be small enough to be accepted by every individual network, the GATEWAY may be forced to split a packet into two or more smaller packets. This action is called fragmentation and must be done in such a way that the destination is able to piece together the fragmented packet. It is clear that the internetwork header format imposes a minimum packet size which all networks must carry (obviously all networks will want to carry packets larger than this minimum). We believe the long range growth and development of internetwork communication would be seriously inhibited by specifying how much larger than the minimum a packet size can be, for the following reasons.

1) If a maximum permitted packet size is specified then it becomes impossible to completely isolate the internal packet size parameters of one network from the internal packet size parameters of all other networks.

2) It would be very difficult to increase the maximum permitted packet size in response to new technology (e.g., large memory systems, higher data rate communication facilities, etc.) since this would require the agreement and then implementation by all participating networks.

3) Associative addressing and packet encryption may require the size of a particular packet to expand during transit for incorporation of new information.

Provision for fragmentation (regardless of where it is performed) permits packet size variations to be handled on an individual network basis without global administration and also permits HOSTS and processes to be insulated from changes in the packet sizes permitted in any networks through which their data must pass.

If fragmentation must be done, it appears best to do it upon entering the next network at the GATEWAY since only this GATEWAY (and not the other networks) must be aware of the internal packet size parameters which made the fragmentation necessary.

If a GATEWAY fragments an incoming packet into two or more packets, they must eventually be passed along to the destination HOST as fragments or reassembled for the HOST. It is conceivable that one might desire the GATEWAY to perform the reassembly to simplify the task of the destination HOST (or process) and/or to take advantage of a larger packet size. We take the position that GATEWAYS should not perform this function since GATEWAY reassembly can lead to serious buffering problems, potential deadlocks, the necessity for all fragments of a packet to pass through the same GATEWAY, and increased delay in transmission. Furthermore, it is not sufficient for the GATEWAYS to provide this function since the final GATEWAY may also have to fragment a packet for transmission. Thus the destination HOST must be prepared to do this task.

Let us now turn briefly to the somewhat unusual accounting effect which arises when a packet may be fragmented by one or more GATEWAYS. We assume, for simplicity, that each network initially charges a fixed rate per packet transmitted, regardless of distance, and if one network can handle a larger packet size than another, it charges a proportionally larger price per packet. We also assume that a subsequent increase in any network's packet size does not result in additional cost per packet to its users. The charge to a user thus remains basically constant through any net which must fragment a packet. The unusual effect occurs when a packet is fragmented into smaller packets which must individually pass through a subsequent network with a larger packet size than the original unfragmented packet. We expect that most networks will naturally select packet sizes close to one another, but in any case, an increase in packet size in one net, even when it causes fragmentation, will not increase the cost of transmission and may actually decrease it. In the event that any other packet charging policies (than the one we suggest) are adopted, differences in cost can be used as an economic lever toward optimization of individual network performance.

PROCESS LEVEL COMMUNICATION

We suppose that processes wish to communicate in full duplex with their correspondents using unbounded but finite length messages. A single character might constitute the text of a message from a process to a terminal or vice versa. An entire page of characters might constitute the text of a message from a file to a process. A data stream (e.g., a continuously generated bit string) can be represented as a sequence of finite length messages.

Within a HOST we assume the existence of a transmission control program (TCP) which handles the transmission and acceptance of messages on behalf of the processes it serves. The TCP is in turn served by one or more packet switches connected to the HOST in which the TCP resides. Processes that want to communicate present messages to the TCP for transmission, and TCP's deliver incoming messages to the appropriate destination processes. We allow the TCP to break up messages into segments because the destination may restrict the amount of data that may arrive, because the local network may limit the maximum transmission size, or because the TCP may need to share its resources among many processes concurrently. Furthermore, we constrain the length of a segment to an integral number of 8-bit bytes. This uniformity is most helpful in simplifying the software needed with HOST machines of different natural word lengths. Provision at the process level can be made for padding a message that is not an integral number of bytes and for identifying which of the arriving bytes of text contain information of interest to the receiving process.

Multiplexing and demultiplexing of segments among processes are fundamental tasks of the TCP. On transmission, a TCP must multiplex together segments from different source processes and produce internetwork packets for delivery to one of its serving packet switches. On reception, a TCP will accept a sequence of packets from its serving packet switch(es). From this sequence of arriving packets (generally from different HOSTS), the TCP must be able to reconstruct and deliver messages to the proper destination processes.

We assume that every segment is augmented with additional information that allows transmitting and receiving TCP's to identify destination and source processes, respectively. At this point, we must face a major issue. How should the source TCP format segments destined for the same destination TCP? We consider two cases.

Case 1): If we take the position that segment boundaries are immaterial and that a byte stream can be formed of segments destined for the same TCP, then we may gain improved transmission efficiency and resource sharing by arbitrarily parceling the stream into packets, permitting many segments to share a single internetwork packet header. However, this position results in the need to reconstruct exactly, and in order, the stream of text bytes produced by the source TCP. At the destination, this stream must first be parsed into segments and these in turn must be used to reconstruct messages for delivery to the appropriate processes.

There are fundamental problems associated with this strategy due to the possible arrival of packets out of order at the destination. The most critical problem appears to be the amount of interference that processes sharing the same TCP–TCP byte stream may cause among themselves. This is especially so at the receiving end. First, the TCP may be put to some trouble to parse the stream back into segments and then distribute them to buffers where messages are reassembled. If it is not readily apparent that all of a segment has arrived (remember, it may come as several packets), the receiving TCP may have to suspend parsing temporarily until more packets have arrived. Second, if a packet is missing, it may not be clear whether succeeding segments, even if they are identifiable, can be passed on to the receiving process, unless the TCP has knowledge of some process level sequencing scheme. Such knowledge would permit the TCP to decide whether a succeeding segment could be delivered to its waiting process. Finding the beginning of a segment when there are gaps in the byte stream may also be hard.

Case 2): Alternatively, we might take the position that the destination TCP should be able to determine, upon its arrival and without additional information, for which process or processes a received packet is intended, and if so, whether it should be delivered then.

If the TCP is to determine for which process an arriving packet is intended, every packet must contain a *process header* (distinct from the internetwork header) that completely identifies the destination process. For simplicity, we assume that each packet contains text from a single process which is destined for a single process. Thus each packet need contain only one process header. To decide whether the arriving data is deliverable to the destination process, the TCP must be able to determine whether the data is in the proper sequence (we can make provision for the destination process to instruct its TCP to ignore sequencing, but this is considered a special case). With the assumption that each arriving packet contains a process header, the necessary sequencing and destination process identification is immediately available to the destination TCP.

Both Cases 1) and 2) provide for the demultiplexing and delivery of segments to destination processes, but only Case 2) does so without the introduction of potential interprocess interference. Furthermore, Case 1) introduces extra machinery to handle flow control on a HOST-to-HOST basis, since there must also be some provision for process level control, and this machinery is little used since the probability is small that within a given HOST, two processes will be coincidentally scheduled to send messages to the same destination HOST. For this reason, we select the method of Case 2) as a part of the *internetwork transmission protocol.*

ADDRESS FORMATS

The selection of address formats is a problem between networks because the local network addresses of TCP's may vary substantially in format and size. A uniform internetwork TCP address space, understood by each GATEWAY and TCP, is essential to routing and delivery of internetwork packets.

Similar troubles are encountered when we deal with process addressing and, more generally, port addressing. We introduce the notion of *ports* in order to permit a process to distinguish between multiple message streams. The port is simply a designator of one such message stream associated with a process. The means for identifying a port are generally different in different operating systems, and therefore, to obtain uniform addressing, a standard port address format is also required. A port address designates a full duplex message stream.

TCP ADDRESSING

TCP addressing is intimately bound up in routing issues, since a HOST or GATEWAY must choose a suitable destination HOST or GATEWAY for an outgoing internetwork packet. Let us postulate the following address format for the TCP address (Fig. 4). The choice for network identification (8 bits) allows up to 256 distinct networks. This size seems sufficient for the forseeable future. Similarly, the TCP identifier field permits up to 65 536 distinct TCP's to be addressed, which seems more than sufficient for any given network.

As each packet passes through a GATEWAY, the GATEWAY observes the destination network ID to determine how to route the packet. If the destination network is connected to the GATEWAY, the lower 16 bits of the TCP address are used to produce a local TCP address in the destination network. If the destination network is not connected to the GATEWAY, the upper 8 bits are used to select a subsequent GATEWAY. We make no effort to specify how each individual network shall associate the internetwork TCP identifier with its local TCP address. We also do not rule out the possibility that the local network understands the internetwork addressing scheme and thus alleviates the GATEWAY of the routing responsibility.

PORT ADDRESSING

A receiving TCP is faced with the task of demultiplexing the stream of internetwork packets it receives and reconstructing the original messages for each destination process. Each operating system has its own internal means of identifying processes and ports. We assume that 16 bits are sufficient to serve as internetwork port identifiers. A sending process need not know how the destination port identification will be used. The destination TCP will be able to parse this number appropriately to find the proper buffer into which it will place arriving packets. We permit a large port number field to support processes which want to distinguish between many different messages streams concurrently. In reality, we do not care how the 16 bits are sliced up by the TCP's involved.

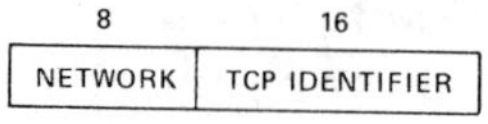

Fig. 4. TCP address.

Even though the transmitted port name field is large, it is still a compact external name for the internal representation of the port. The use of short names for port identifiers is often desirable to reduce transmission overhead and possibly reduce packet processing time at the destination TCP. Assigning short names to each port, however, requires an initial negotiation between source and destination to agree on a suitable short name assignment, the subsequent maintenance of conversion tables at both the source and the destination, and a final transaction to release the short name. For dynamic assignment of port names, this negotiation is generally necessary in any case.

SEGMENT AND PACKET FORMATS

As shown in Fig. 5, messages are broken by the TCP into segments whose format is shown in more detail in Fig. 6. The field lengths illustrated are merely suggestive. The first two fields (source port and destination port in the figure) have already been discussed in the preceding section on addressing. The uses of the third and fourth fields (window and acknowledgment in the figure) will be discussed later in the section on retransmission and duplicate detection.

We recall from Fig. 3 that an internetwork header contains both a sequence number and a byte count, as well as a flag field and a check sum. The uses of these fields are explained in the following section.

REASSEMBLY AND SEQUENCING

The reconstruction of a message at the receiving TCP clearly requires[1] that each internetwork packet carry a sequence number which is unique to its particular destination port message stream. The sequence numbers must be monotonic increasing (or decreasing) since they are used to reorder and reassemble arriving packets into a message. If the space of sequence numbers were infinite, we could simply assign the next one to each new packet. Clearly, this space cannot be infinite, and we will consider what problems a finite sequence number space will cause when we discuss retransmission and duplicate detection in the next section. We propose the following scheme for performing the sequencing of packets and hence the reconstruction of messages by the destination TCP.

A pair of ports will exchange one or more messages over a period of time. We could view the sequence of messages produced by one port as if it were embedded in an infinitely long stream of bytes. Each byte of the message has a unique sequence number which we take to be its byte location relative to the beginning of the stream. When a

[1] In the case of encrypted packets, a preliminary stage of reassembly may be required prior to decryption.

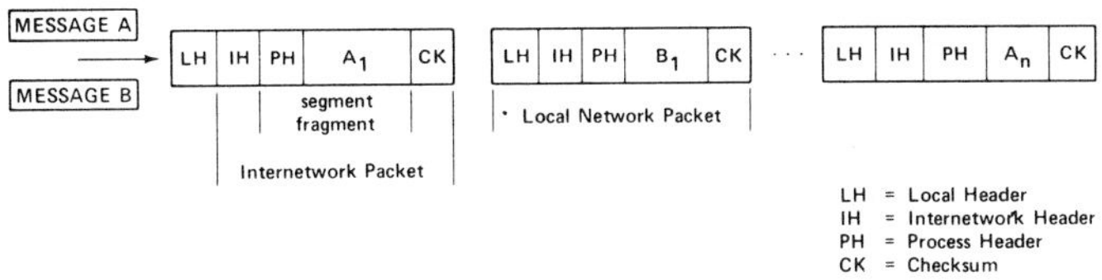

Fig. 5. Creation of segments and packets from messages.

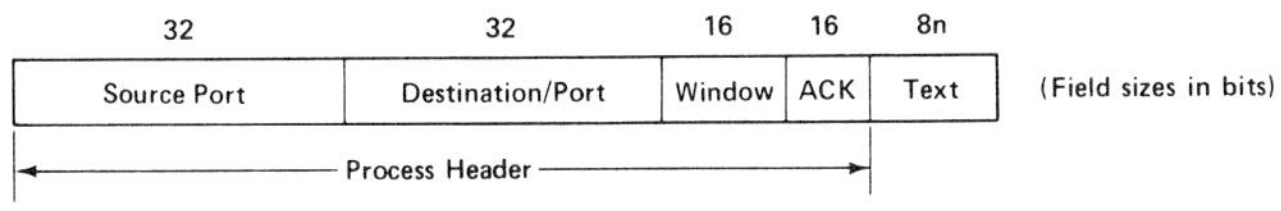

Fig. 6. Segment format (process header and text).

segment is extracted from the message by the source TCP and formatted for internetwork transmission, the relative location of the first byte of segment text is used as the sequence number for the packet. The byte count field in the internetwork header accounts for all the text in the segment (but does not include the check-sum bytes or the bytes in either internetwork or process header). We emphasize that the sequence number associated with a given packet is unique only to the pair of ports that are communicating (see Fig. 7). Arriving packets are examined to determine for which port they are intended. The sequence numbers on each arriving packet are then used to determine the relative location of the packet text in the messages under reconstruction. We note that this allows the exact position of the data in the reconstructed message to be determined even when pieces are still missing.

Every segment produced by a source TCP is packaged in a single internetwork packet and a check sum is computed over the text and process header associated with the segment.

The splitting of messages into segments by the TCP and the potential splitting of segments into smaller pieces by GATEWAYS creates the necessity for indicating to the destination TCP when the end of a segment (ES) has arrived and when the end of a message (EM) has arrived. The flag field of the internetwork header is used for this purpose (see Fig. 8).

The ES flag is set by the source TCP each time it prepares a segment for transmission. If it should happen that the message is completely contained in the segment, then the EM flag would also be set. The EM flag is also set on the last segment of a message, if the message could not be contained in one segment. These two flags are used by the destination TCP, respectively, to discover the presence of a check sum for a given segment and to discover that a complete message has arrived.

The ES and EM flags in the internetwork header are known to the GATEWAY and are of special importance when packets must be split apart for propagation through the next local network. We illustrate their use with an example in Fig. 9.

The original message A in Fig. 9 is shown split into two segments A_1 and A_2 and formatted by the TCP into a pair

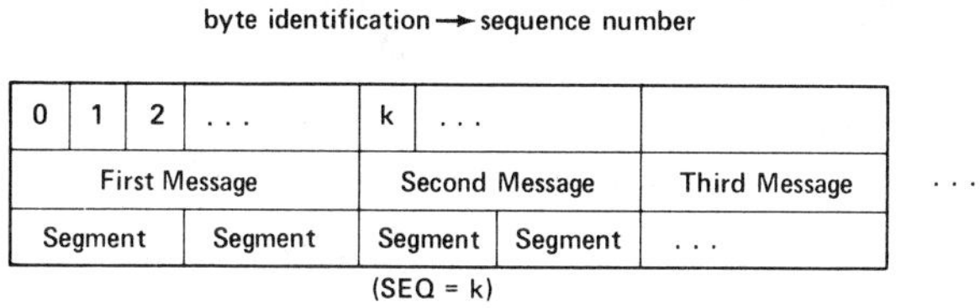

Fig. 7. Assignment of sequence numbers.

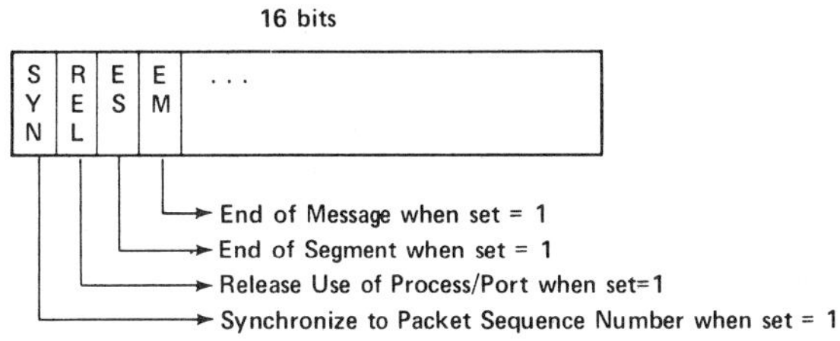

Fig. 8. Internetwork header flag field.

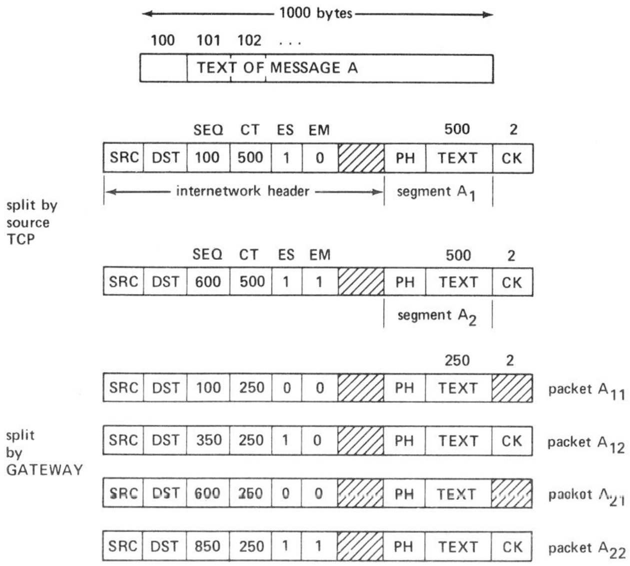

Fig. 9. Message splitting and packet splitting.

of internetwork packets. Packets A_1 and A_2 have their ES bits set, and A_2 has its EM bit set as well. When packet A_1 passes through the GATEWAY, it is split into two pieces: packet A_{11} for which neither EM nor ES bits are set, and packet A_{12} whose ES bit is set. Similarly, packet A_2 is split such that the first piece, packet A_{21}, has neither bit set, but packet A_{22} has both bits set. The sequence number field (SEQ) and the byte count field (CT) of each packet is modified by the GATEWAY to properly identify the text bytes of each packet. The GATEWAY need only examine the internetwork header to do fragmentation.

The destination TCP, upon reassembling segment A_1, will detect the ES flag and will verify the check sum it knows is contained in packet A_{12}. Upon receipt of packet A_{22}, assuming all other packets have arrived, the destination TCP detects that it has reassembled a complete message and can now advise the destination process of its receipt.

RETRANSMISSION AND DUPLICATE DETECTION

No transmission can be 100 percent reliable. We propose a timeout and positive acknowledgment mechanism which will allow TCP's to recover from packet losses from one HOST to another. A TCP transmits packets and waits for replies (acknowledgements) that are carried in the reverse packet stream. If no acknowledgment for a particular packet is received, the TCP will retransmit. It is our expectation that the HOST level retransmission mechanism, which is described in the following paragraphs, will not be called upon very often in practice. Evidence already exists[2] that individual networks can be effectively constructed without this feature. However, the inclusion of a HOST retransmission capability makes it possible to recover from occasional network problems and allows a wide range of HOST protocol strategies to be incorporated. We envision it will occasionally be invoked to allow HOST accommodation to infrequent overdemands for limited buffer resources, and otherwise not used much.

Any retransmission policy requires some means by which the receiver can detect duplicate arrivals. Even if an infinite number of distinct packet sequence numbers were available, the receiver would still have the problem of knowing how long to remember previously received packets in order to detect duplicates. Matters are complicated by the fact that only a finite number of distinct sequence numbers are in fact available, and if they are reused, the receiver must be able to distinguish between new transmissions and retransmissions.

A *window* strategy, similar to that used by the French CYCLADES system (voie virtuelle transmission mode [8]) and the ARPANET very distant HOST connection [18], is proposed here (see Fig. 10).

Suppose that the sequence number field in the internetwork header permits sequence numbers to range from 0 to $n - 1$. We assume that the sender will not transmit more than w bytes without receiving an acknowledgment. The w bytes serve as the window (see Fig. 11). Clearly, w must be less than n. The rules for sender and receiver are as follows.

Sender: Let L be the sequence number associated with the left window edge.

1) The sender transmits bytes from segments whose text lies between L and up to $L + w - 1$.

2) On timeout (duration unspecified), the sender retransmits unacknowledged bytes.

3) On receipt of acknowledgment consisting of the receiver's current left window edge, the sender's left window edge is advanced over the acknowledged bytes (advancing the right window edge implicitly).

Receiver:

1) Arriving packets whose sequence numbers coincide with the receiver's current left window edge are acknowledged by sending to the source the next sequence number expected. This effectively acknowledges bytes in between. The left window edge is advanced to the next sequence number expected.

2) Packets arriving with a sequence number to the left of the window edge (or, in fact, outside of the window) are discarded, and the current left window edge is returned as acknowledgment.

3) Packets whose sequence numbers lie within the receiver's window but do not coincide with the receiver's left window edge are optionally kept or discarded, but are not acknowledged. This is the case when packets arrive out of order.

We make some observations on this strategy. First, all computations with sequence numbers and window edges must be made modulo n (e.g., byte 0 follows byte $n - 1$). Second, w must be less than $n/2$[3]; otherwise a retransmission may appear to the receiver to be a new transmission in the case that the receiver has accepted a window's worth of incoming packets, but all acknowledgments have been lost. Third, the receiver can either save or discard arriving packets whose sequence numbers do not coincide with the receiver's left window. Thus, in the simplest implementation, the receiver need not buffer more than one packet per message stream if space is critical. Fourth, multiple packets can be acknowledged simultaneously. Fifth, the receiver is able to deliver messages to processes in their proper order as a natural result of the reassembly mechanism. Sixth, when duplicates are detected, the acknowledgment method used naturally works to resynchronize sender and receiver. Furthermore, if the receiver accepts packets whose sequence numbers lie within the current window but

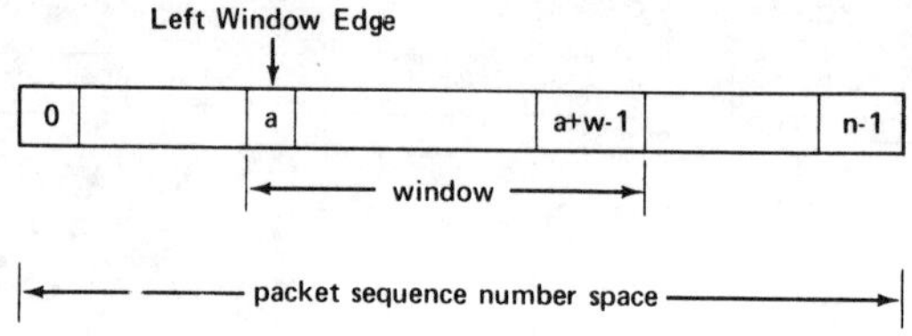

Fig. 10. The window concept.

1	Source Address	
2	Destination Address	
3	Next Packet Seq.	
4	Current Buffer Size	
5	Next Write Position	
6	Next Read Position	
7	End Read Position	
8	No. Retrans.	Max Retrans.
9	Timeout	Flags
10	Curr. Ack	Window

Fig. 11. Conceptual TCB format.

[2] The ARPANET is one such example.

[3] Actually $n/2$ is merely a convenient number to use; it is only required that a retransmission not appear to be a new transmission.

which are not coincident with the left window edge, an acknowledgment consisting of the current left window edge would act as a stimulus to cause retransmission of the unacknowledged bytes. Finally, we mention an overlap problem which results from retransmission, packet splitting, and alternate routing of packets through different GATEWAYS.

A 600-byte packet might pass through one GATEWAY and be broken into two 300-byte packets. On retransmission, the same packet might be broken into three 200-byte packets going through a different GATEWAY. Since each byte has a sequence number, there is no confusion at the receiving TCP. We leave for later the issue of initially synchronizing the sender and receiver left window edges and the window size.

FLOW CONTROL

Every segment that arrives at the destination TCP is ultimately acknowledged by returning the sequence number of the next segment which must be passed to the process (it may not yet have arrived).

Earlier we described the use of a sequence number space and window to aid in duplicate detection. Acknowledgments are carried in the process header (see Fig. 6) and along with them there is provision for a "suggested window" which the receiver can use to control the flow of data from the sender. This is intended to be the main component of the process flow control mechanism. The receiver is free to vary the window size according to any algorithm it desires so long as the window size never exceeds half the sequence number space.[3]

This flow control mechanism is exceedingly powerful and flexible and does not suffer from synchronization troubles that may be encountered by incremental buffer allocation schemes [9],[10]. However, it relies heavily on an effective retransmission strategy. The receiver can reduce the window even while packets are en route from the sender whose window is presently larger. The net effect of this reduction will be that the receiver may discard incoming packets (they may be outside the window) and reiterate the current window size along with a current window edge as acknowledgment. By the same token, the sender can, upon occasion, choose to send more than a window's worth of data on the possibility that the receiver will expand the window to accept it (of course, the sender must not send more than half the sequence number space at any time). Normally, we would expect the sender to abide by the window limitation. Expansion of the window by the receiver merely allows more data to be accepted. For the receiving HOST with a small amount of buffer space, a strategy of discarding all packets whose sequence numbers do not coincide with the current left edge of the window is probably necessary, but it will incur the expense of extra delay and overhead for retransmission.

TCP INPUT/OUTPUT HANDLING

The TCP has a component which handles input/output (I/O) to and from the network.[4] When a packet has arrived, it validates the addresses and places the packet on a queue. A pool of buffers can be set up to handle arrivals, and if all available buffers are used up, succeeding arrivals can be discarded since unacknowledged packets will be retransmitted.

On output, a smaller amount of buffering is needed, since process buffers can hold the data to be transmitted. Perhaps double buffering will be adequate. We make no attempt to specify how the buffering should be done, except to require that it be able to service the network with as little overhead as possible. Packet sized buffers, one or more ring buffers, or any other combination are possible candidates.

When a packet arrives at the destination TCP, it is placed on a queue which the TCP services frequently. For example, the TCP could be interrupted when a queue placement occurs. The TCP then attempts to place the packet text into the proper place in the appropriate process receive buffer. If the packet terminates a segment, then it can be checksummed and acknowledged. Placement may fail for several reasons.

1) The destination process may not be prepared to receive from the stated source, or the destination port ID may not exist.

2) There may be insufficient buffer space for the text.

3) The beginning sequence number of the text may not coincide with the next sequence number to be delivered to the process (e.g., the packet has arrived out of order).

In the first case, the TCP should simply discard the packet (thus far, no provision has been made for error acknowledgments). In the second and third cases, the packet sequence number can be inspected to determine whether the packet text lies within the legitimate window for reception. If it does, the TCP may optionally keep the packet queued for later processing. If not, the TCP can discard the packet. In either case the TCP can optionally acknowledge with the current left window edge.

It may happen that the process receive buffer is not present in the active memory of the HOST, but is stored on secondary storage. If this is the case, the TCP can prompt the scheduler to bring in the appropriate buffer and the packet can be queued for later processing.

If there are no more input buffers available to the TCP for temporary queueing of incoming packets, and if the TCP cannot quickly use the arriving data (e.g., a TCP to TCP message), then the packet is discarded. Assuming a sensibly functioning system, no other processes than the one for which the packet was intended should be affected by this discarding. If the delayed processing queue grows

[4] This component can serve to handle other protocols whose associated control programs are designated by internetwork destination address.

excessively long, any packets in it can be safely discarded since none of them have yet been acknowledged. Congestion at the TCP level is flexibly handled owing to the robust retransmission and duplicate detection strategy.

TCP/PROCESS COMMUNICATION

In order to send a message, a process sets up its text in a buffer region in its own address space, inserts the requisite control information (described in the following list) in a transmit control block (TCB) and passes control to the TCP. The exact form of a TCB is not specified here, but it might take the form of a passed pointer, a pseudointerrupt, or various other forms. To receive a message in its address space, a process sets up a receive buffer, inserts the requisite control information in a receive control block (RCB) and again passes control to the TCP.

In some simple systems, the buffer space may in fact be provided by the TCP. For simplicity we assume that a ring buffer is used by each process, but other structures (e.g., buffer chaining) are not ruled out.

A possible format for the TCB is shown in Fig. 11. The TCB contains information necessary to allow the TCP to extract and send the process data. Some of the information might be implicitly known, but we are not concerned with that level of detail. The various fields in the TCB are described as follows.

1) *Source Address*: This is the full net/HOST/TCP/port address of the transmitter.

2) *Destination Address*: This is the full net/HOST/TCP/port of the receiver.

3) *Next Packet Sequence Number*: This is the sequence number to be used for the next packet the TCP will transmit from this port.

4) *Current Buffer Size*: This is the present size of the process transmit buffer.

5) *Next Write Position*: This is the address of the next position in the buffer at which the process can place new data for transmission.

6) *Next Read Position*: This is the address at which the TCP should begin reading to build the next segment for output.

7) *End Read Position*: This is the address at which the TCP should halt transmission. Initially 6) and 7) bound the message which the process wishes to transmit.

8) *Number of Retransmissions/Maximum Retransmissions*: These fields enable the TCP to keep track of the number of times it has retransmitted the data and could be omitted if the TCP is not to give up.

9) *Timeout/Flags*: The timeout field specifies the delay after which unacknowledged data should be retransmitted. The flag field is used for semaphores and other TCP/process synchronization, status reporting, etc.

10) *Current Acknowledgment/Window*: The current acknowledgment field identifies the first byte of data still unacknowledged by the destination TCP.

The read and write positions move circularly around the transmit buffer, with the write position always to the left (module the buffer size) of the read position.

The next packet sequence number should be constrained to be less than or equal to the sum of the current acknowledgment and the window fields. In any event, the next sequence number should not exceed the sum of the current acknowledgment and half of the maximum possible sequence number (to avoid confusing the receiver's duplicate detection algorithm). A possible buffer layout is shown in Fig. 12.

The RCB is substantially the same, except that the end read field is replaced by a partial segment check-sum register which permits the receiving TCP to compute and remember partial check sums in the event that a segment arrives in several packets. When the final packet of the segment arrives, the TCP can verify the check sum and if successful, acknowledge the segment.

CONNECTIONS AND ASSOCIATIONS

Much of the thinking about process-to-process communication in packet switched networks has been influenced by the ubiquitous telephone system. The HOST–HOST protocol for the ARPANET deals explicitly with the opening and closing of simplex connections between processes [9],[10]. Evidence has been presented that message-based "connection-free" protocols can be constructed [12], and this leads us to carefully examine the notion of a connection.

The term *connection* has a wide variety of meanings. It can refer to a physical or logical path between two entities, it can refer to the flow over the path, it can inferentially refer to an action associated with the setting up of a path, or it can refer to an association between two or more entities, with or without regard to any path between them. In this paper, we do not explicitly reject the term connection, since it is in such widespread use, and does connote a meaningful relation, but consider it exclusively in the sense of an association between two or more entities without regard to a path. To be more precise about our intent, we shall define the relationship between two or more ports that are in communication, or are prepared to communicate to be an *association*. Ports that are associated with each other are called *associates*.

It is clear that for any communication to take place between two processes, one must be able to address the other. The two important cases here are that the destination port may have a global and unchanging address or that it may be globally unique but dynamically reassigned. While in either case the sender may have to learn the destination address, given the destination name, only in the second instance is there a requirement for learning the address from the destination (or its representative) each time an association is desired. Only after the source has learned how to address the destination can an association be said to have occurred. But this is not yet sufficient. If

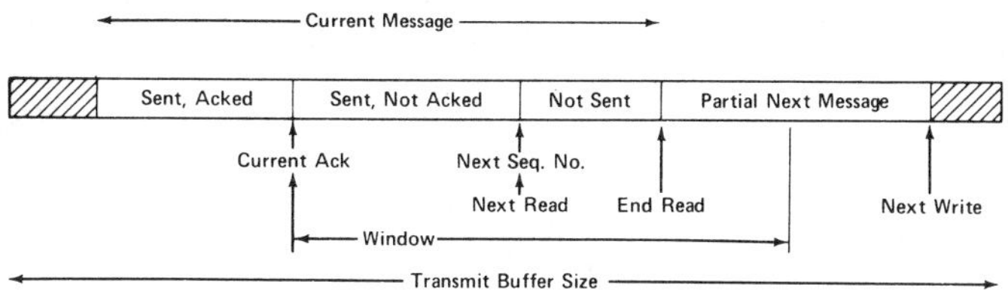

Fig. 12. Transmit buffer layout.

ordering of delivered messages is also desired, both TCP's must maintain sufficient information to allow proper sequencing. When this information is also present at both ends, then an association is said to have occurred.

Note that we have not said anything about a path, nor anything which implies that either end be aware of the condition of the other. Only when both partners are prepared to communicate with each other has an association occurred, and it is possible that neither partner may be able to verify that an association exists until some data flows between them.

CONNECTION-FREE PROTOCOLS WITH ASSOCIATIONS

In the ARPANET, the interface message processors (IMP's) do not have to open and close connections from source to destination. The reason for this is that connections are, in effect, always open, since the address of every source and destination is never[5] reassigned. When the name and the place are static and unchanging, it is only necessary to label a packet with source and destination to transmit it through the network. In our parlance, every source and destination forms an association.

In the case of processes, however, we find that port addresses are continually being used and reused. Some ever-present processes could be assigned fixed addresses which do not change (e.g., the logger process). If we supposed, however, that every TCP had an infinite supply of port addresses so that no old address would ever be reused, then any dynamically created port would be assigned the next unused address. In such an environment, there could never be any confusion by source and destination TCP as to the intended recipient or implied source of each message, and all ports would be associates.

Unfortunately, TCP's (or more properly, operating systems) tend not to have an infinite supply of internal port addresses. These internal addresses are reassigned after the demise of each port. Walden [12] suggests that a set of unique uniform external port addresses could be supplied by a central registry. A newly created port could apply to the central registry for an address which the central registry would guarantee to be unused by any HOST system in the network. Each TCP could maintain tables matching external names with internal ones, and use the external ones for communication with other processes. This idea violates the premise that interprocess communication should not require centralized control. One would have to extend the central registry service to include all HOST's in all the interconnected networks to apply this idea to our situation, and we therefore do not attempt to adopt it.

Let us consider the situation from the standpoint of the TCP. In order to send or receive data for a given port, the TCP needs to set up a TCB and RCB and initialize the window size and left window edge for both. On the receive side, this task might even be delayed until the first packet destined for a given port arrives. By convention, the first packet should be marked so that the receiver will synchronize to the received sequence number.

On the send side, the first request to transmit could cause a TCB to be set up with some initial sequence number (say, zero) and an assumed window size. The receiving TCP can reject the packet if it wishes and notify the sending TCP of the correct window size via the acknowledgment mechanism, but only if either

1) we insist that the first packet be a complete segment;
2) an acknowledgment can be sent for the first packet (even if not a segment, as long as the acknowledgment specifies the next sequence number such that the source also understands that no bytes have been accepted).

It is apparent, therefore, that the synchronizing of window size and left window edge can be accomplished without what would ordinarily be called a connection setup.

The first packet referencing a newly created RCB sent from one associate to another can be marked with a bit which requests that the receiver synchronize his left window edge with the sequence number of the arriving packet (see SYN bit in Fig. 8). The TCP can examine the source and destination port addresses in the packet and in the RCB to decide whether to accept or ignore the request.

Provision should be made for a destination process to specify that it is willing to LISTEN to a specific port or "any" port. This last idea permits processes such as the logger process to accept data arriving from unspecified sources. This is purely a HOST matter, however.

The initial packet may contain data which can be stored or discarded by the destination, depending on the availability of destination buffer space at the time. In the other direction, acknowledgment is returned for receipt of data which also specifies the receiver's window size.

If the receiving TCP should want to reject the synchronization request, it merely transmits an acknowledgment carrying a release (REL) bit (see Fig. 8) indicating that the destination port address is unknown or inaccessible. The sending HOST waits for the acknowledgment (after accepting or rejecting the synchronization request) before sending the next message or segment. This rejection is quite different from a negative data acknowledgment. We do not have explicit negative acknowledgments. If no acknowledgment is returned, the sending HOST may

[5] Unless the IMP is physically moved to another site, or the HOST is connected to a different IMP.

retransmit without introducing confusion if, for example, the left window edge is not changed on the retransmission.

Because messages may be broken up into many packets for transmission or during transmission, it will be necessary to ignore the REL flag except in the case that the EM flag is also set. This could be accomplished either by the TCP or by the GATEWAY which could reset the flag on all but the packet containing the set EM flag (see Fig. 9).

At the end of an association, the TCP sends a packet with ES, EM, and REL flags set. The packet sequence number scheme will alert the receiving TCP if there are still outstanding packets in transit which have not yet arrived, so a premature dissociation cannot occur.

To assure that both TCP's are aware that the association has ended, we insist that the receiving TCP respond to the REL by sending a REL acknowledgment of its own.

Suppose now that a process sends a single message to an associate including an REL along with the data. Assuming an RCB has been prepared for the receiving TCP to accept the data, the TCP will accumulate the incoming packets until the one marked ES, EM, REL arrives, at which point a REL is returned to the sender. The association is thereby terminated and the appropriate TCB and RCB are destroyed. If the first packet of a message contains a SYN request bit and the last packet contains ES, EM, and REL bits, then data will flow "one message at a time." This mode is very similar to the scheme described by Walden [12], since each succeeding message can only be accepted at the receiver after a new LISTEN (like Walden's RECEIVE) command is issued by the receiving process to its serving TCP. Note that only if the acknowledgment is received by the sender can the association be terminated properly. It has been pointed out[6] that the receiver may erroneously accept duplicate transmissions if the sender does not receive the acknowledgment. This may happen if the sender transmits a duplicate message with the SYN and REL bits set and the destination has already destroyed any record of the previous transmission. One way of preventing this problem is to destroy the record of the association at the destination only after some known and suitably chosen timeout. However, this implies that a new association with the same source and destination port identifiers could not be established until this timeout had expired. This problem can occur even with sequences of messages whose SYN and REL bits are separated into different internetwork packets. We recognize that this problem must be solved, but do not go into further detail here.

Alternatively, both processes can send one message, causing the respective TCP's to allocate RCB/TCB pairs at both ends which rendezvous with the exchanged data and then disappear. If the overhead of creating and destroying RCB's and TCB's is small, such a protocol might be adequate for most low-bandwidth uses. This idea might also form the basis for a relatively secure transmission system. If the communicating processes agree to change their external port addresses in some way known only to each other (i.e., pseudorandom), then each message will appear to the outside world as if it is part of a different association message stream. Even if the data is intercepted by a third party, he will have no way of knowing that the data should in fact be considered part of a sequence of messages.

We have described the way in which processes develop associations with each other, thereby becoming associates for possible exchange of data. These associations need not involve the transmission of data prior to their formation and indeed two associates need not be able to determine that they are associates until they attempt to communicate.

[6] S. Crocker of ARPA/IPT.

CONCLUSIONS

We have discussed some fundamental issues related to the interconnection of packet switching networks. In particular, we have described a simple but very powerful and flexible protocol which provides for variation in individual network packet sizes, transmission failures, sequencing, flow control, and the creation and destruction of process-to-process associations. We have considered some of the implementation issues that arise and found that the proposed protocol is implementable by HOST's of widely varying capacity.

The next important step is to produce a detailed specification of the protocol so that some initial experiments with it can be performed. These experiments are needed to determine some of the operational parameters (e.g., how often and how far out of order do packets actually arrive; what sort of delay is there between segment acknowledgments; what should be retransmission timeouts be?) of the proposed protocol.

ACKNOWLEDGMENT

The authors wish to thank a number of colleagues for helpful comments during early discussions of international network protocols, especially R. Metcalfe, R. Scantlebury, D. Walden, and H. Zimmerman; D. Davies and L. Pouzin who constructively commented on the fragmentation and accounting issues; and S. Crocker who commented on the creation and destruction of associations.

REFERENCES

[1] L. Roberts and B. Wessler, "Computer network development to achieve resource sharing," in *1970 Spring Joint Computer Conf., AFIPS Conf. Proc.*, vol. 36. Montvale, N. J.: AFIPS Press, 1970, pp. 543–549.

[2] L. Pouzin, "Presentation and major design aspects of the CYCLADES computer network," in *Proc. 3rd Data Communications Symp.*, 1973.

[3] F. R. E. Dell, "Features of a proposed synchronous data network," in *Proc. 2nd Symp. Problems in the Optimization of Data Communications Systems*, 1971, pp. 50–57.

[4] R. A. Scantlebury and P. T. Wilkinson, "The design of a switching system to allow remote access to computer services by other computers and terminal devices," in *Proc. 2nd Symp. Problems in the Optimization of Data Communications Systems*, 1971, pp. 160–167.
[5] D. L. A. Barber, "The European computer network project," in *Computer Communications: Impacts and Implications*, S. Winkler, Ed. Washington, D. C., 1972, pp. 192–200.
[6] R. Despres, "A packet switching network with graceful saturated operation," in *Computer Communications: Impacts and Implications*, S. Winkler, Ed. Washington, D. C., 1972, pp. 345–351.
[7] R. E. Kahn and W. R. Crowther, "Flow control in a resource-sharing computer network," *IEEE Trans. Commun.*, vol. COM-20, pp. 539–546, June 1972.
[8] J. F. Chambon, M. Elie, J. Le Bihan, G. LeLann, and H. Zimmerman, "Functional specification of transmission station in the CYCLADES network. ST-ST protocol" (in French), I.R.I.A. Tech. Rep. SCH502.3, May 1973.
[9] S. Carr, S. Crocker, and V. Cerf, "HOST-HOST Communication Protocol In the ARPA Network," in *Spring Joint Computer Conf., AFIPS Conf. Proc.*, vol. 36. Montvale, N. J.: AFIPS Press, 1970, pp. 589–597.
[10] A. McKenzie, "HOST/HOST protocol for the ARPA network," in *Current Network Protocols*, Network Information Cen., Menlo Park, Calif., NIC 8246, Jan. 1972.
[11] L. Pouzin, "Address format in Mitranet," NIC 14497, INWG 20, Jan. 1973.
[12] D. Walden, "A system for interprocess communication in a resource sharing computer network," *Commun. Ass. Comput. Mach.*, vol. 15, pp. 221–230, Apr. 1972.
[13] B. Lampson, "A scheduling philosophy for multiprocessing systems," *Commun. Ass. Comput. Mach.*, vol. 11, pp. 347–360, May 1968.
[14] F. E. Heart, R. E. Kahn, S. Ornstein, W. Crowther, and D. Walden, "The interface message processor for the ARPA computer network," in *Proc. Spring Joint Computer Conf., AFIPS Conf. Proc.*, vol. 36. Montvale, N. J.: AFIPS Press, 1970, pp. 551–567.
[15] N. G. Anslow and J. Hanscoff, "Implementation of international data exchange networks," in *Computer Communications: Impacts and Implications*, S. Winkler, Ed. Washington, D. C., 1972, pp. 181–184
[16] A. McKenzie, "HOST/HOST protocol design considerations," INWG Note 16, NIC 13879, Jan. 1973.
[17] R. E. Kahn, "Resource-sharing computer communication networks," *Proc. IEEE*, vol. 60, pp. 1397–1407, Nov. 1972.
[18] Bolt, Beranek, and Newman, "Specification for the interconnection of a host and an IMP," Bolt Beranek and Newman, Inc., Cambridge, Mass., BBN Rep. 1822 (revised), Apr. 1973.

Vinton G. Cerf was born in New Haven, Conn., in 1943. He did undergraduate work in mathematics at Stanford University, Stanford, Calif., and received the Ph.D. degree in computer science from the University of California at Los Angeles, Los Angeles, Calif., in 1972.

He was with IBM in Los Angeles from 1965 through 1967 and consulted and/or worked part time at UCLA from 1967 through 1972. Currently he is Assistant Professor of Computer Science and Electrical Engineering at Stanford University, and consultant to Cabledata Associates. Most of his current research is supported by the Defense Advanced Research Projects Agency and by the National Science Foundation on the technology and economics of computer networking. He is Chairman of IFIP TC6.1, an international network working group which is studying the problem of packet network interconnection.

★

Robert E. Kahn (M'65) was born in Brooklyn, N. Y., on December 23, 1938. He received the B.E.E. degree from the City College of New York, New York, in 1960, and the M.A. and Ph.D. degrees from Princeton University, Princeton, N. J., in 1962 and 1964, respectively.

From 1960 to 1962 he was a Member of the Technical Staff of Bell Telephone Laboratories, Murray Hill, N. J., engaged in traffic and communication studies. From 1964 to 1966 he was a Ford Postdoctoral Fellow and an Assistant Professor of Electrical Engineering at the Massachusetts Institute of Technology, Cambridge, where he worked on communications and information theory. From 1966 to 1972 he was a Senior Scientist at Bolt Beranek and Newman, Inc., Cambridge, Mass., where he worked on computer communications network design and techniques for distributed computation. Since 1972 he has been with the Advanced Research Projects Agency, Department of Defense, Arlington, Va.

Dr. Kahn is a member of Tau Beta Pi, Sigma Xi, Eta Kappa Nu, the Institute of Mathematical Statistics, and the Mathematical Association of America. He was selected to serve as a National Lecturer for the Association for Computing Machinery in 1972.

Reprinted from *The Proceedings of the Fifth Data Communications Symposium*, 1977, pages 4-58—4-65. Copyright © 1977 by The Institute of Electrical and Electronics Engineers, Inc.

RELIABLE HOST-TO-HOST PROTOCOLS: PROBLEMS AND TECHNIQUES

Lawrence L. Garlick and Raphael Rom
SRI International
Menlo Park, California 94025

Jonathan B. Postel
University of Southern California
Information Sciences Institute
Marina Del Ray, California 90291

Abstract

Host-to-host protocols capable of supporting internetworking and reliable transmission have been under development for several years. This paper discusses problems and techniques related to one type of reliable protocol, which features end-to-end positive acknowledgement, retransmission, internetwork addressing capabilities, and ordered delivery.

The issues of interest are protocol correctness and completeness, protocol efficiency, and complexity of implementation. These will be discussed in a framework of three problem areas, flow control, sequence number space management, and reliable transmission of controls.

Flow control heuristics using windowing techniques are explored. Flow control information is augmented to allow fair apportionment of bandwidth, better bandwidth utilization through optimistic credits, flow control credits matched to the type of traffic, and increased performance for high precedence connections.

Alternatives for selecting the startup sequence number for a connection are presented. Techniques and problems of several sequence number space management strategies are presented. These include delayed startup, incarnation numbers, and resynchronization.

The transmission of controls are discussed, with emphasis on whether or not to share a logical transmission channel between controls and data. The effect of data flow control on the delivery of out-of-band signals is an important consideration.

The findings are presented both to further the understanding of and to encourage intelligent implementations of reliable protocols.

Introduction

Computer networking has emerged as a significant segment of the growing data communications field. At the forefront of computer networking technology is packet-switching. Packet-switching networks are being used or implemented for research, military, and commercial applications. An important part of the progress in packet-switching technology has been the development of distributed protocols.

Tremendous development has been done in the area of host-to-host protocols since the first major packet-switching network, the ARPA (Advanced Research Projects Agency) network, was designed. In fact, the ARPA host-to-host protocol has been the reference point for process-to-process protocols for several years.

As users have gained experience with networking, new applications, new topologies, new network access methods, and new higher level protocols have emerged. The ARPA network host-to-host protocol is not suitable for meeting the demands associated with these new developments. For instance it does not support some important features like end-to-end acknowledgement, internetworking, and high throughput flow control techniques.

In the last few years, several efforts have been made to design new host-to-host protocols. The most notable of these has been TCP, the Transmission Control Program, which was initially designed to be a reliable internetwork host-to-host protocol [1], as well as a solution to many of the problems of the ARPA network protocol. Among its reliability features are positive acknowledgement, retransmission, and sequencing of data and controls. It guarantees the error free delivery of each message for which it claims successful delivery. Other improvements include duplex connections and the ability to use the same network address (socket) in several connections.

Even while implementation of TCP proceeds, there are still some unresolved important issues to be discussed, solutions to be found. The paper is organized around three of the more important issues--a discussion of flow control techniques, strategies for the management of connection sequence number space, and the need for a mechanism to reliably deliver controls. Reference will be made to TCP, since it is representative of a reliable host-to-host protocol; however, the problems and techniques discussed in this paper are general in nature and are representative of those encountered in any such protocol.

It is assumed that the reader is somewhat familiar with ARPA network and TCP-like protocols [1], [2], [6]. To assist the reader with recall of the basic characteristics of these protocols, a brief summary of TCP features is presented. A glossary of abbreviations and terms, and appendices that magnify a few of the more involved issues can be found at the end of the paper.

TCP: A Reliable Transmission Protocol

Network Characteristics

TCP does not depend on the transmission medium for its reliability, i.e., it is assumed that the subnetwork may be unreliable. The subnet need not ensure the orderly or errorless delivery of subnet packets, or account for lost packets. TCP functions correctly in the face of large packet lifetimes, and the opening and closing of connections in quick succession.

Connections

Logical connections are established for process-to-process (user-to-user) communication. TCP connections are full-duplex channels established between source and destination sockets (network-wide process names). A socket may be a party to more than one connection, but only one connection can exist between any pair of sockets.
TCP provides the means by which a connection between the processes is established, controlled during the transfer of data, and terminated at the completion of the session. Connection management requires the exchange of controls between TCP's. There are controls for connection synchronization, out-of-band signalling (interrupt), data flushing, resynchronization, and connection closing. As described below, controls accompany data whenever possible to avoid the overhead of separate control packets.

Packaging and Headers

TCP packages user letters (messages) into packets suitable for transmission over a subnetwork. Each letter or partial letter is prefixed by a TCP header, which includes fields for addressing, sequencing, acknowledgements, flow control, controls, and error checking. The header is optionally followed by a block of data. The smallest unit of data transfer and the unit of sequencing is the 8-bit byte (octet).

Sequencing

Sequence numbers are used as acknowledgement identifiers and as an ordering mechanism. They are assigned to each octet of data and to those controls that need synchronization with the data stream. The data and controls sent on a connection may be assigned sequence numbers from the same sequence number space, representing one transmission channel, or they may be tagged separately, representing two logical transmission channels. Since only one sequence number is sent per logical channel, the packet length and control fields are used to determine the highest sequence number consumed by the packet.
Reuse of sequence numbers is allowed only for duplicate retransmissions. The sequence number space is managed cooperatively by the sender and the receiver.

Acknowledgement and Retransmission

A TCP acknowledgement represents the successful delivery of some number of octets to the receiving process's buffer or to the remote TCP (controls). It is sent to the transmitting TCP in the acknowledgement field of a subsequent TCP header. The sequence number placed in this field is the highest sequence number acknowledged by the receiver and implies acknowledgement of all previous octets. If packets arrive out of order, an acknowledgement cannot be sent for octets with sequence numbers higher than the missing octets, since that would implicitly acknowledge the missing data.
Packets can be retransmitted at will until they are acknowledged; however, bandwidth may be underutilized if improper retransmission policies are followed. Duplicates naturally arise from retransmissions that occur prior to the receipt of an acknowledgment and are detected and handled as described below.

Packet Acceptance Checking

The receiving TCP is responsible for the detection of packets with improper sequence numbers. These may have sequence numbers that are either old duplicates (from previous connections) or illegal because they are not within an acceptable flow control range.
To determine the action to be taken for a newly received packet, acceptability ranges are defined. The following three ranges are mutually exclusive and collectively exhaustive of the sequence number space.

Acknowledge-deliver range (ADR). The packet has arrived in-order and does not exceed the receiving process's buffer space. Data will be placed in the buffer and an acknowledgement will be generated to indicate successful delivery.

Acknowledge-only range (AOR). A duplicate packet has arrived, as a result of retransmission. It will be acknowledged, but not delivered, since delivery has already occurred.

Discard range (DR). An illegal packet has arrived. It may be an old duplicate or a packet that cannot be delivered due to flow control.

Appendix A provides more details of the packet acceptance policy.

Flow Control Techniques

Introduction

Flow control is basically a mechanism to prevent the sender of data from overflowing the receiver's buffers. Flow control may exist at each level of protocol as well as between levels of protocols, though the latter tends to be somewhat implementation dependent.
The techniques to be considered here assume that flow control information is passed from the receiver to the sender. Flow control information typically reflects the receiver's ability to buffer data. The information often represents a count of some resource, such as a unit of buffering or a message queue element.
A good flow control scheme must handle a whole spectrum of problems that result from preventing buffer overflow in the receiver. This section first discusses general flow control goals and methods, and then specific techniques that could significantly improve protocol performance.
The goals and methods of an ambitious flow control scheme include the following:

End-to-End Flow Control. Flow control for a particular level of protocol should be exerted at the point closest to the final destination. For a host-to-host protocol, this means that flow control information is passed between the hosts supporting the communicating processes.

Receiver's Allocation. Any flow control strategy should consider the buffer space offered by a receiving user, since this represents a depository for incoming messages and relieves the protocol module of resource allocation problems.

Congestion Prevention. The flow control strategy should prevent queueing of messages in the protocol module, so that module resources can be used to handle those messages that have a high probability of being delivered immediately. Congestion in the subnet can be caused by a positive-acknowledgement, retransmission protocol, since each unacknowledged packet is retransmitted. The flow control scheme should make it easy to slow or stop transmission from the sender.

Deadlock Prevention. When congestion does occur, resources must be available to handle traffic-clearing messages. Controls and flow control information must be delivered and interpreted even when data is queued.

Fair Apportionment and Utilization of Bandwidth. It is important to be able to fairly allocate the available host-to-host bandwidth to users, based on a variety of criteria. One criterion may be precedence of the user or the connection. Another may be the mode of traffic, e.g., interactive traffic may get preference over bulk traffic. In addition, to fully utilize the available bandwidth, different flow control strategies may be appropriate for different modes of traffic.

Interplay With Subnet Flow Control. Often the interfaces between modules representing levels of protocol can cause flow control problems [8]. For instance, the subnet flow control of the ARPANET is adversely affected whenever a host does not readily accept incoming data from the packet switch (IMP). Retransmission protocols are especially flexible in this regard, because they can absorb congested traffic from the subnet and discard it if necessary.

Exchanging Flow Control Information

A windowing scheme to convey flow control information has been used for many different types of protocols. It is an efficient technique that is useful whenever positive acknowledgement and retransmission are used for reliable transmission.

A flow control window is a dynamic range in the sequence number space that defines the current flow control credit. The window edges, the range of the window, are defined by the last received acknowledgement sequence number (the window's left edge) and the window size. Flow control is exerted by the receiver by issuing credits, which represent the receiving process's willingness to buffer data. The window's left edge plus the window size give the highest sequence number that can be transmitted with some assurance that it will be acknowledged without retransmission.

A nonzero window size gives permission to send up to a certain sequence number, the right edge of the flow control window. It is an "oversend" to send messages with sequence numbers that exceed the window right edge. Oversends will occur occasionally, since the flow control information is always slightly out of date and it is possible for the receiver to withdraw flow control credits. Oversends are not a problem in a retransmission protocol, because the receiver can always discard incoming data without sending acknowledgements (knowing that the data will be retransmitted later).

Flow Control Between Processes

A host-to-host protocol provides a reliable transmission medium for communicating processes. Consider the case in which no flow control is used. If the sending process knows the buffer sizes used in the receiving process then it can send messages of the right size. It will not attempt to send a message larger than the receiver can buffer nor will it break up a large message unnecessarily. If the sender is unfamiliar with the receiver, it might send messages that are too large, resulting in lost data, or send messages that are too short, resulting in inefficiencies. The addition of flow control in the transmission medium cannot guarantee that a sender will always send the optimum sized message. It is still ideal for the sender to know the receiver's buffer size. However, for unfamiliar processes the protocol can repackage messages from the sender into messages that the receiver can buffer. It cannot solve the problem of the sender sending buffers that are unnecessarily small, resulting in inefficient handling in the receiver.

Determining the Window Size

As the distance increases between the modules that support a particular protocol, so does the age of the flow control information. For subnetwork packet sending, where the delay to the next packet switch node is minimal, the flow control information is current enough to be useful. For host-to-host protocols that support internetworking, the round-trip delay is so large that the flow control information is bound to be inaccurate.

The positive-acknowledgement and retransmission protocol allows flexibility in determining the correct flow control window size. The window size should indicate the willingness of the receiving process to provide buffer space. The window size could represent exactly the available buffer space that the user has offered for letter receiving (the conservative strategy), or it could reflect some expected buffer space, based on previous allocations (the optimistic strategy).

Conservative (Guaranteed) Allocation. The conservative approach to window size setting gives the receiving process almost full control over the flow control mechanism. By assuring the sender that there will be space for a particular number of octets, the policy reduces discards thus reducing the number of retransmissions. (Some messages may still be discarded if they arrive out of order and sufficient reassembly space is not available.)

There are some disadvantages to the conservative strategy of window size setting. Flow control information is always slightly out of date when it is finally received. The receiving process could have drastically increased or decreased its allocation, making the information useless. Unless a process provides for double buffering, the window very likely will go from a fixed size (whatever the user's buffer is) to zero, each time a message is passed on to the receiving process. Depending on the scheduling algorithm in the host, this could result in windows of size zero, totally inhibiting message flow. Before messages can flow again, a packet with flow control information must arrive at the source. Thus, a round trip delay is experienced between messages and there is an increase of dataless packets in the network.

Another related problem is that large single buffers may be used to receive small messages that require immediate delivery to the receiving process. If a window of say size k is advertised and a packet of size << k arrives that indicates immediate delivery, then the destination buffer is returned to the receiving process. The previous flow control credit, which was large, is withdrawn and the window becomes zero. In the interim, the sender may have sent several small messages tagged for immediate delivery, thinking the receiver has the buffers to accept them. The receiving protocol module, knowing that the receiving process has no available buffer space, will advertise a zero window. By the time the window information arrives at the sending protocol module, it likely will be an inaccurate report and cause further delays.

Optimistic Credits. The alternative to the conservative approach is to send flow control information that is a good estimate of the expected

receiver's available space [3],[7]. Thus, the window size should be a function of previous window sizes as well as the current available space. The window size should be an average, weighted very heavily toward the current time, so that a process that is truly rejecting data will soon reflect a very small window.
This method could even be mixed with heuristics to force the window to zero after a fixed period without receiving.
Optimistic allocation can do much to help solve the problem of drastic window size changes experienced with the conservative scheme. In granting permission to transmit messages before the user has allocated buffer space, it fills the pipe and allows a smoother flow. It is still reliable, because any message can be discarded in the receiver since it will be retransmitted later.
The disadvantages of the method are its instability when faced with very irregular receiving patterns. A poorly behaving receiver can still sabotage this policy, but not as easily as with conservative technique. As will be shown below, an optimistic strategy may be quite dynamic with respect to recent receiving patterns, connection precedence, and the fair sharing of the available bandwidth.
It may be possible to determine the semantics associated with the window size by exchanging transmission mode or topological information. When a connection is opened, the transmission mode (e.g., interactive, bulk) and the topology (e.g., satellite link) could be exchanged. This would be used to determine the weighting of previous window sizes in calculating the current window.
To demonstrate the idea of an optimistic flow control policy, a method for setting the receive window size is given in Appendix B.

Zero Flow Control Windows

It may be necessary to stop the flow on a connection, i.e., stop all new transmissions and unnecessary retransmissions. A zero receive window, sent in packets to the sender, indicates an unwillingless to receive data. The protocol module must perform special functions with regard to sending packets into a zero window. If necessary, new data from the sending process must be rejected, and old unacknowledged data must be queued.
Opening a window of size zero also presents some special problems [6]. Since a window size can accompany each packet, it seems that the normal data packet and acknowledgement transmissions should be sufficient to vary the size of the windows. However, when both protocol modules are showing a zero receive window, a deadlock can arise. A data packet cannot be sent because the closed window indicates that only controls should be retransmitted; moreover, there may be no data to send. If ACKs are used and they arrive out of order, it may be impossible to tell if the window is opening or closing.
One method of handling the problem of opening a window of size zero is by using a pair of controls, one sent by the local protocol module that is making its window size nonzero (WOPEN) and one that is sent by the foreign protocol module to acknowledge the opening (WACK). These are special controls that must be handled immediately, without regard for flow control restrictions. If controls can be blocked by data, as in the present TCP, then the WOPEN must be tagged with, but must not consume a sequence number.

Sequence Number Space Management

The second problem area that needs attention is that of the reliable handling of the sequence number space. Two difficulties associated with sequence numbers are how to select the startup number and how to reliably exchange the selected number with the remote protocol module. The exchange of sequence numbers is accomplished by using a "three-way handshake" method [2], [4], [5]. This method provides positive acknowledgement of the exchanged sequence numbers and is sufficient to handle the problem of simultaneous connection establishment attempts. The rest of this section will deal with the techniques to select startup sequence numbers.
In a packet-switching network with alternative routing schemes, a packet can have a relatively long lifetime, especially if the topology of the network includes satellite links. Due to misrouting, a packet can arrive at its destination minutes or even hours late, depending on the topology. A reliable protocol must be able to determine if such a packet is deliverable, acknowledgeable, or if it must be discarded without acknowledgement. If during the packet's transit time the connection is closed or broken due to a crash with loss of memory, then the packet is no longer valid. If the connection is reestablished, using the same source and destination addresses, then the arrival of the old packet can cause confusion in the receiving protocol module. A reliable mechanism must exist to guarantee that the receiving protocol module can distinguish packets of the current connection from packets of an old connection.
The key issue is the maximum packet lifetime, the time a misrouted packet can stay in the network(s). For small self-contained networks with no internetwork connections, this time is probably less than a second. For large, interconnected networks, this time could be much longer. Below is a discussion of several techniques for sequence number space management. They are ordered by size of network and simplicity of implementation. Ultimately, methods for handling the internetworking protocol are given.

Delayed Startup

For small networks, problems arising from packets belonging to old connections can be solved by waiting the maximum packet lifetime before opening connections, either at host startup or following the closing of a connection with the same source and destination addresses. Each connection can start with sequence number equal to zero since no old packets from an old connection exist anywhere in the network.
If the maximum packet lifetime exceeds a second, it may not be appropriate to wait a second before opening every connection. A solution would be to use delayed startup only after a crash and use some kind of connection table to remember the sequence number for a recently closed connection. Entries in this table need be remembered only for a maximum packet lifetime.

Incarnation Numbers

If packet lifetimes are too large to use delayed startup, an incarnation number approach may be suitable. An incarnation number is a unique name for an instance of the protocol module.
The name (or incarnation number) is sent in each packet and is used by the receiver to filter out packets from old connections caused by a crash and restart. The incarnation number is used in conjunction with the sequence numbers to uniquely

identify an octet of data or control. The uniqueness of the incarnation number allows the resetting of the sequence number space to zero at initialization of each new path (first connection between two users).

The incarnation number may be generated in several ways. The most reliable is from nonvolatile storage using error detecting and correcting encodings. The old incarnation number is read, incremented, and rewritten each time the host restarts. When a new connection is opened the current incarnation number is read. The disadvantage of this scheme is that nonvolatile storage has been too expensive for small hosts, especially those acting as network access devices. It is expected, however, that new technology, such as bubble memories, will overcome this disadvantage.

A second method is to determine the incarnation number from a clock. The appropriate clock resolution and wraparound period is a factor of the maximum packet lifetime for the network or interconnected networks. Let us assume that the clock has a resolution of one minute and a wraparound period of 256 minutes. The resulting incarnation number is 8 bits long, and is used to assure the receiver that any message received with this incarnation number is from the active connection and not an old one.

The clock method has a slight drawback. If the incarnation number clock and the sequence number space both wraparound at the same time, and the host crashes just prior to this time, then there is a chance that illegal packets will be in the network when a new incarnation number (equal to the old one due to wraparound) and a new sequence number (0) are chosen at startup. The probability that the sequence number space does wraparound is extremely small, especially if a sequence number space of 2**32 octets is used, as in TCP. The combined probability that the incarnation number clock also wraps around is even smaller.

No matter which method is used to generate the incarnation number, there must be a mechanism to remember the last sequence number used on a connection between a specific source and destination pair. When a connection is closed, the protocol module must save the last sequence number used. It must retain the number for the maximum packet lifetime. Saving the sequence number, the destination, the destination incarnation number, and the time of a closed connection solves the problem of the repeated opening and closing of the same connection (source and destination). It does not solve the problem created by host computer crashes; the incarnation number handles that.

When connection establishment is requested, the list of old connections must be searched by <source, destination> pair. If a match is found, the sequence number plus one is the first sequence number used when the connection is opened. If there is no match, then numbering can start at zero. Management of the old connection list entails removal of outdated items. This can be handled, for the most part, during normal searching. When list storage becomes scarce, a simple garbage collection routine can be invoked.

There are two problems with the method using incarnation numbers. First, there is some concern about the size of the old connection list. It would not be surprising to see 1000 connections per hour for an average host. Allowing a socket to be party to many connections will lead to fewer source and destination pairs; thus, many connections will be reused. (This is in contrast to the ARPA network, where restrictions in socket usage result in contact connections being used to spawn direct, dynamically named service connections.) Another factor that alleviates concern about the space required for the old connection list is the recent progress in inexpensive memories.

The second problem is how to keep the incarnation number small enough to be sent in each header and still keep the name space large enough to ensure uniqueness. It is felt that an incarnation number field greater than 8 bits is excessive header overhead. To accommodate this with the clock method, the resolution of the clock is constrained, which leads to the following restriction applied at host startup time. When a host comes up after a crash, it must delay at least (maximum packet lifetime) / 2**8 before any connections are opened, so that a unique incarnation number is always chosen. A startup delay of one minute is probably sufficient for the internetting case since it implies a maximum packet lifetime of 256 minutes.

Resynchronization

Resynchronization, suggested by Tomlinson [4], [5], is another sequence number space management mechanism. Resynchronization is used in this paper to denote the mechanism itself, rather than the stage of the mechanism when the actual resetting of the sequence numbers is done. The scheme is based on selecting initial sequence numbers (ISN's) from a curve in the sequence-number/time plane derived from a clock. When a new connection is opened, its first sequence number is taken from the ISN curve. If the consumption of sequence numbers is satisfactory, i.e., similar in slope to the ISN curve, resynchronization of sequence numbers need not occur. However, if the rate of consumption is too slow, resynchronization may be required to avoid colliding with the ISN curve. The ISN curve has a parallel boundary (defining a "forbidden zone") that indicates that no new sequence numbers may be assigned and that resynchronization must take place immediately. If this is not done and if a crash occurs, sequence numbers assigned in the forbidden zone could conflict with the ISN chosen for the new connection. See [4], [5], [6] for further details of the resynchronization mechanism.

A few of the problems related to implementing resynchronization are discussed below.

Understanding and Documenting the Problem. Even though the resynchronization method is a workable one, it is not at all straightforward. It takes numerous pages and illustrations just to document the concept [4], [5], [6]. As has been pointed out in the past by weathered ARPANET protocol implementers, a protocol must be reasonably easy to understand and easy to document. After all, if the network is heterogeneous, it will be implemented on numerous kinds of hardware by system programmers with various degrees of skill.

Testing for the Need to Resynchronize. The protocol requires that if a connection is broken due to a system crash, the sequence number chosen at startup must be one that cannot be confused with any sequence number still in the network for the old instance of that connection. To satisfy this requirement, periodic runtime checking must be done to determine if the sequence number consumption rate is satisfactory, i.e., if it is not approaching the forbidden zone. This check must be done at fixed time intervals, not just when sequence numbers are being assigned. The check may result in the need to resynchronize even (and especially) if the connection is idle.

Resynchronization and Flow Control. The need to resynchronize may occur at any time, and the resynchronization must proceed in a timely manner if normal activity is to continue. However, since resynchronization means changing from the old sequence numbers to new sequence numbers and since the resynchronization control must be acknowledged (marked with an "old" sequence number), all data marked with the "old" numbers must be acknowledged before the resynchronization control is acknowledged. If data is not being accepted because the user is not receiving, then resynchronization cannot proceed. If resynchronization cannot proceed, then neither new controls nor new data may be sent.

The Loss of a Truly Out-Of-Band Signal. Due to the flow control problem mentioned above, all controls can be blocked during a resynchronization process. This includes the interrupt, which is supposed to be an out-of-band signal. Losing the out-of-band capability, even in rare instances, is an unfortunate deficiency. Higher-level protocols that rely on an out-of-band signal could be severely crippled by the inability to interrupt a "runaway" process. In fact, it is the runaway process, by not accepting data, that will soon force resynchronization and will not be interruptable.

Reliable Transmission Of Controls

Introduction

Controls are special commands that are sent between two protocol modules to coordinate connection management. Opening and closing of connections, and providing an out-of-band signalling mechanism are all part of connection management. If synchronizing sequence numbers or a flushing feature are required, then maintenance of the medium might be considered connection management. Thus, a list of controls for a particular protocol might look something like the following: OPEN, CLOSE, INTERRUPT, FLUSH, SYNCH.

To reliably transmit controls, it is necessary to acknowledge their receipt. This means different things for different controls; for the case of an OPEN, it could mean the establishment of a connection table entry at the receiver. For the INTERRUPT it could mean that the receiving process is signalled, via the operating system signalling mechanism.

As with sending data, the sequence number used for ordering can be used as the acknowledgement identifier for controls. The main question is whether to use the same sequence number space for both data and controls. Using the same sequence number space is equivalent to having one logical channel for both data and controls. If a separate sequence number space were to be used for controls, then a new logical channel would be necessary.

Before discussing the tradeoffs involved in one logical channel versus two, some background information concerning out-of-band signals will be presented [10]. An out-of-band signal should be provided that satisfies the following criteria:

The interrupt should be delivered reliably, i.e., for each one sent, one and only one is delivered to the receiving process. Ordering is not crucial.

The interrupt should be independent of the data flow control mechanism. An interrupt must be delivered whether or not there are buffers provided for data, whether or not controls are being handled. The interrupt should not interfere with the reliable delivery of other data and controls.

The interrupt is delivered to the receiving process via an operating system signalling mechanism. Once so delivered, no other semantics are associated with the interrupt.

The interrupt serves several purposes. For terminal users, it could be the only method of getting the attention of a runaway process. For higher-level protocols, it can be used in conjunction with a mark in the data stream to synchronize the sender and receiver. Of course, for process-to-process communication it can be used to simply signal the receiver that some event has occurred.

A Single Logical Channel

Combining data and controls on the same channel has several advantages. There is savings in packet overhead, since data and control piggybacking can occur by sending a single sequence number and packet length. Savings are also realized in the maintenance of a single sequence number space. As was discussed earlier in this paper, this is a significant maintenance problem.

Two disadvantages of the single sequence number space scheme have been discovered recently: reassembly of data mixed with controls is costly when packets arrive out of order, and a true out-of-band signal is not being provided. The first problem is an efficiency matter that has plagued early implementers [9]. User buffer space cannot be used for the reassembly of out of order packets because there is no way to know if the unarrived packets contain only data or if controls are intermixed with the data.

The essence of the second problem is that the acknowledgement scheme requires that acknowledgement of a sequence number is implicit acknowledgement of all preceding sequence numbers. Since interrupts must be acknowledged for reliability, the transmission of an interrupt can be blocked by data flow control in the receiver. This was noticed early by the TCP group [2] and an attempt was made to rectify the matter by giving the interrupt extra semantics--that it always flushes unacknowledged data. This solution is probably sufficient unless resynchronization methods are used for sequence number selection.

As mentioned earlier, delivery of an interrupt should not disturb the reliable delivery of data and controls. What does an interrupt that results in the flushing of data and controls imply? Flushing of data implies extra semantics on the delivery of an interrupt; however, it is acceptable for the known applications. Flushing of certain controls is impossible. When the resynchronization method for sequence number selection is used, an interrupt cannot be sent when a resynchronizing control has just been sent. The resynchronizing control can be blocked by data flow control but it cannot be flushed. In this situation, an interrupt cannot flush and thus cannot be sent. This could result in an uninterruptable runaway process.

A Control Subchannel

To provide a solution to the reassembly problem and to allow the most general implementation of out-of-band signals, a second channel for controls can be used. The method that will be discussed is a control subchannel, a concept that reduces the cost of sequence number space management for the control channel.

The control sequence number is the composite of the data channel sequence number (DCSN) and the subchannel sequence number (SCSN). This serves the dual purpose of synchronizing the two streams and using the resynchronization mechanism of the data channel for all subchannels. A subchannel allows reliable transmission even when the data channel is inactive, without flushing data.

From the SCSN, the number of control fields, and the last SCSN received, the receiver can determine if subchannel traffic is coming in order and thus, whether it can be acknowledged.

The field size holding the SCSN determines the wraparound point in the SCSN space. The SCSN space is initialized to zero when the DCSN is synchronized. It IS NOT reset with each DCSN change.

There is no flow control information passed for the subchannel. Discarding controls (without acknowledgement) is the flow control mechanism. The subchannel sequence number space is small; thus, the protocol module must keep track of the DCSN to which the first SCSN was assigned. If wraparound of the SCSN space occurs, in the rare event that many controls are sent while the data channel is blocked, then the control channel becomes blocked. This is very unlikely since a long series of controls must contain interrupts, and successfully delivered interrupts will usually cause the receiving process to unblock the data channel.

Acceptability Test for Subchannel Traffic

The acceptability test of items on the subchannel is a composite test of both sequence numbers. First the DCSN is checked to see if it would be acknowledged if it were an octet received on the data channel. Only if it would have been discarded will the item on the subchannel be discarded. Having passed the DCSN test, the SCSN is checked to see if the item is deliverable and acknowledgeable with respect to the SCSN sequence number space. The SCSN test is less involved than the DCSN test because there is no flow control range. To be believable, the SCSN must fall in the range of SCSN's sent and SCSN's for which acknowledgements have been received. This is a check for everything except the existence of old duplicates from old instances of the connection, which is made by checking the DCSN.

Summary

Several problems, solutions, and techniques have been presented. The discussions relate to improved efficiency, simplification of implementation, and protocol functionality. The motivation for the discussions is more than to improve a specific protocol. It is also to focus attention on a set of issues that are common to all reliable host-to-host protocols.

Flow control ideas have been discussed, with attention to implementation ideas that satisfy fairly ambitious goals. Window management techniques have been suggested that could improve efficiency. A window setting method was presented that features optimistic credits that are a function of past credits, congestion, and available buffer space. Several techniques for sequence number space management have been given. Methods have been presented that are suitable for small networks, with short packet lifetimes. Two methods suitable for internetworking have been proposed and compared--incarnation numbers and resynchronization.

Finally, the alternatives for the reliable transmission of controls were set forth. A single channel for data and controls was contrasted with a control subchannel. Correct handling of out-of-band signals was emphasized.

There are interdependencies involved; that is, some of the stated problems become less severe when others are solved. For example, if resynchronization is abandoned, then the argument for separate channels is motivated only by the need for the efficient reassembly of out-of-order packets.

The discussion of flow control indicated areas that should gain attention as more experience with protocols is gained. This should be an area for significant measurement, under many different transmission modes.

References

[1] Cerf, V. and R. Kahn, "A Protocol for Packet Network Intercommunication," IEEE Transactions on Communication, Vol COM-20, No. 5, May 1974.

[2] Cerf, V., Y. Dalal, C. Sunshine, "Specification of Internet Transmission Control Program," INWG General Note #72, December 1974 (Revised).

[3] Sunshine, C., "Interprocess Communication Protocols for Computer Networks," Digital Systems Laboratory Technical Note #105, December 1975.

[4] Tomlinson, R., "Selecting Sequence Numbers," INWG Protocol Note #2, September 1974.

[5] Dalal, Y., "More on Selecting Sequence Numbers," INWG Protocol Note #4, October 1974.

[6] Postel, J., L. Garlick, R. Rom, "Transmission Control Protocol Specification (AUTODIN II)," SRI-ARC Catalog #35938 & #35939, July 1976.

[7] Sunshine, C., "Factors In Interprocess Communication Protocol Efficiency For Computer Networks," Proc. National Computer Conf., 1976, AFIPS Press, pp 571-576.

[8] Herrmann, Jeff, "Flow Control in the ARPA Network," Networks, Vol 1, Number 1, June 1976.

[9] Burchfiel, J., W. Plummer, R. Tomlinson, "Proposed Revisions to the TCP," INWG Protocol Note #44, September 1976.

[10] Garlick, L., "Out-of-Band Control Signals in a Host-to-Host Protocol," RFC 721, NIC Catalog #36636, September 1976.

Glossary

control -- commands passed between protocol modules that are used to coordinate connection management.

DCSN -- data channel sequence number.

host -- a computer that is connected to the network and that executes programs on behalf of its users. A host may provide services to other computers on the network.

ISN -- Initial sequence number; the first sequence number used when a connection is synchronized or resynchronized.

MPL -- maximum packet lifetime.

octet -- eight bits.

SCSN -- subchannel sequence number; control channel sequence number.

socket -- an entity defining one end of a connection; the internetwork-wide name of a process port.

subnetwork- the network of computers that provides a communication medium for network hosts. The nodes of a subnetwork may function as host interface points as well as store and forward computers.

TCP -- Transmission Control Program and the protocol it implements.

window -- a dynamic range in the sequence number space used in flow control management.

Appendix A: Packet Acceptance

This appendix provides details of a packet acceptance testing scheme. It should clarify the possible actions the receiving protocol module may take when it receives an arbitrary packet. Remember, the receiver is responsible for the detection of packets with improper sequence numbers from either old connections or ill-behaving senders. For notation, let

- ADR = acknowledge and deliver range
- AOR = acknowledge only range
- DR = discard range
- S = size of sequence number space
- x = sequence number to be tested
- FCLE = flow control left window edge
- ADRE = (FCLE+ADR) mod S = Ack-deliver right edge (Discard left edge - 1)
- AOLE = the first sequence number received for this connection
- MPL = maximum packet lifetime (in sec)
- TB = Total protocol bandwidth (in octets/sec)

For any sequence number, x, and packet text length, l, if

(AOLE <= x <= ADRE) mod S and
(AOLE <= x+l-1 <= ADRE) mod S

then the packet should be acknowledged.
If x and l satisfy

(FCLE <= x <= ADRE) mod S and
(FCLE <= x+l-1 <= ADRE) mod S

then x can also be delivered to the user; however, ordered delivery requires that x = FCLE.
A packet is not in a range only if all of it lies outside a range. When a packet falls in more than one range, precedence is ADR, then AOR, then DR.
When a packet falls in the AOR then an ACK should be sent, even if a packet has to be created. The ACK will specify the current left window edge. This assures acknowledgment of all duplicates.
ADRE is exactly the maximum sequence number ever "advertised" through the flow control window, plus one. This allows for controls to be accepted even though permission for them may never have been explicitly given. Of course, each time a control with a sequence number equal to the ADRE is sent, the ADRE must be incremented by one.

Appendix B: Window Size Setting

To demonstrate the idea of an optimistic policy for window size setting, a method for setting the receive window size is given [6]. The scheme satisfies the flow control goals discussed earlier. Several parameters have been vaguely unspecified since they can be determined only after considerable testing and measurement of a specific implementation.
First, some notation:

- B -- Total bandwidth of the protocol, given unlimited user resources
- N -- The number of connections
- RTD -- Round trip delay between hosts
- CONGEST-- A congestion factor which reflects available protocol module resources (CONGEST =< 1)
- WLT -- The long term window
- W -- The current window
- AVWT -- Weighting coefficient for available buffer space
- OLDWT -- Weighting coefficient for old window (OLDWT = 1 - AVWT)
- Tot -- Total user buffer space
- Avail -- The unfilled part of Tot

The long term window might look like:

WLT = B/N * RTD * CONGEST.

The algorithm used to update the current window is the following. Upon the processing of a user's receive request (buffer offering), the local receive window is set so that:

W = MINIMUM(WLT, Tot).

Each time a packet is sent for this connection, the local protocol module sets the receive window and the packet header window size field so that

W = (AVWT * Avail/Tot) * WLT + (OLDWT * W)
(for nonzero Tot)
and
W = OLDWT * W
(for Tot = 0).

It is important to note that a user's receive buffer is returned when an End-of-Letter is received. Thus, a small letter sent to a large buffer can cause the Avail and Tot to vary abruptly, even though there may be a smooth flow of letters.
This window size setting scheme meets the goals mentioned in section 3 in the following ways:

WLT is dependent upon the number of the connections, thereby administering fairness among connections. It also considers the level of congestion in the receiving protocol module, assuming some measure of resource availability can be provided.

The window size will never exceed the bandwidth allocated to the connection. The algorithm may sometimes give credit to a "well behaving" process by setting his window to greater than the actual buffer available. This window will be reduced if the process does not supply new receive buffers promptly.

The current window size is dependent upon previous window sizes and upon the rate at which the process makes letter space available. If a process fails to make such space available, its receive window will be reduced by OLDWT every time a packet is sent. (A threshold mechanism, by which a window is set to zero when it is reduced below the threshold, may be appropriate.)

The algorithm can be modified slightly to support high throughput for high precedence connections. Parameter WLT can be made dependent on some criterion for the high priority traffic. Categories of priority can be used with some guaranteed service (part of the bandwidth) given the highest priority categories.

Connection Management in Transport Protocols

Carl A. Sunshine

Information Sciences Department, The Rand Corporation, 1700 Main Street, Santa Monica, California 90406, USA

Yogen K. Dalal

Xerox Systems Development Department, 3408 Hillview Avenue, Palo Alto, California 94304, USA

Transport protocols are designed to provide fully reliable communication between processes which must communicate over a less reliable medium such as a packet switching network (which may damage, lose, or duplicate packets, or deliver them out of order). This is typically accomplished by assigning a sequence number and checksum to each packet transmitted, and retransmitting any packets not positively acknowledged by the other side. The use of such mechanisms requires the maintenance of state information describing the progress of data exchange. The initialization and maintenance of this state information constitutes a *connection* between the two processes, provided by the transport protocol programs on each side of the connection. Since a connection requires significant resources, it is desirable to maintain a connection only while processes are communicating. This requires mechanisms for *opening* a connection when needed, and for *closing* a connection after ensuring that all user data have been properly exchanged. These connection management procedures form the main subject of this paper. Mechanisms for establishing connections, terminating connections, recovering from *crashes* or failures of either side, and for resynchronizing a connection are presented. Connection management functions are intimately involved in protocol reliability, and if not designed properly may result in deadlocks or old data being erroneously delivered in place of current data. Some protocol modeling techniques useful in analyzing connection management are discussed, using verification of connection establishment as an example. The paper is based on experience with the Transmission Control Protocol (TCP), and examples throughout the paper are taken from TCP.

Keywords: Computer network, host-to-host protocol, transport protocols, interprocess communication, connections, connection management, reliability, synchronization, 3 way handshake, resynchronization, correctness, verification.

Computer Networks 2 (1978) 454–473

1. Introduction

Distributed computing systems, consisting of computers connected to one another by a communication network, require processes to interact by means of explicit interprocess communication protocols. These protocols are often composed of several layers, with higher layers making use of the functions performed by lower layers. A typical protocol architecture consists of a partially reliable "best effort" communication service at the lowest level, followed by a general purpose fully reliable transport protocol, and finally various higher level protocols that provide specialized services such as file transfer, remote job entry, interactive terminal support, graphics, and resource coordination. Each protocol layer provides an augmented service by using appropriate mechanisms on top of the lower level protocol.

This paper focuses on transport protocols (TP) for use on packet switching networks which may damage, duplicate, lose, and delay packets, or deliver them in a different sequence than submitted. The basic technique used by transport protocols to achieve reliable

Carl Sunshine received a PhD in computer science from Stanford University in 1975 where he worked on analysis, design, and implementation of communication protocols for computer networks. Since 1975 he has been with the Rand Corporation, where he is involved in research on computer network protocols, network interconnection network planning, distributed systems, and operating systems. Dr. Sunshine is active in IFIP TC6.1, the Internetwork Working Group.

Yogen K. Dalal received his BTech degree in Electrical Engineering from the Indian Institute of Technology, Bombay, in 1972, and his MS and PhD degrees in Electrical Engineering from Stanford University in 1973 and 1977 respectively. He is currently with the Xerox Systems Development Department in Palo Alto working on the design, analysis and implementation of computer communication protocols, and the interconnection of computer networks. His research interests also include local networks, distributed systems architecture, packet switching, broadcast protocols and operating systems. Dr. Dalal is a member of the ACM and IEEE.

communication over such an unreliable transmission medium is to assign a sequence number and checksum to each packet transmitted, to verify the checksum and positively acknowledge successfully received packets, and to retransmit packets that remain unacknowledged beyond a timeout period. Further discussion on the motivation for and use of these techniques in transport protocols may be found in refs. [4,17,22]. Transport protocols can also perform a multiplexing function to allow many processes in a host to share the network access path.

The salient point for this paper is that the use of these mechanisms requires the maintenance of state information describing the progress of data exchange. The initialization and maintenance of this state information constitutes a *connection* between the two processes, provided by the protocol *machines* on each side of the connection. Connection oriented protocols typically include an initialization phase during which necessary parameters (e.g. sequence numbers) are synchronized at each end, a data transfer phase, and a termination phase. Such connection oriented or virtual circuit protocols are in contrast to message oriented interprocess communication protocols [25] which are inherently unreliable.

Although a connection potentially exists between every pair of processes, only some processes will need to converse at any given time. Since a connection requires significant resources, it is desirable to maintain a connection only while processes are communicating, and then to terminate the connection and free the resources when the processes are done. This leads to mechanisms for *opening* a connection when needed, and for *closing* a connection after insuring that all user data have been properly exchanged.

In opening and then closing a connection, it is convenient to describe the protocol machines as going through a number of *states.* Each machine starts in the *NotActive* state in which no connection exists. On command from the user process, a machine may actively initiate connection establishment (*Opening* state), or passively wait for connection establishment to be initiated from the remote end (*Listening* state). Once the connection is established (*Established* state), either user may terminate it, placing the protocol machine in a *Closing* state. Once the connection has been closed, the protocol machine is in the NotActive state again. Figure 1 illustrates the life-cycle of a connection as it passes from one state to another. The Opening and Closing states may in reality consist of several substates depending on the protocol used for accomplishing the desired effects.

These connection management procedures form the main subject of this paper. They include procedures for dealing with *crashes* or failures of either side of a connection as well as opening and closing connections under normal circumstances. This paper does not discuss the multiplexing function of

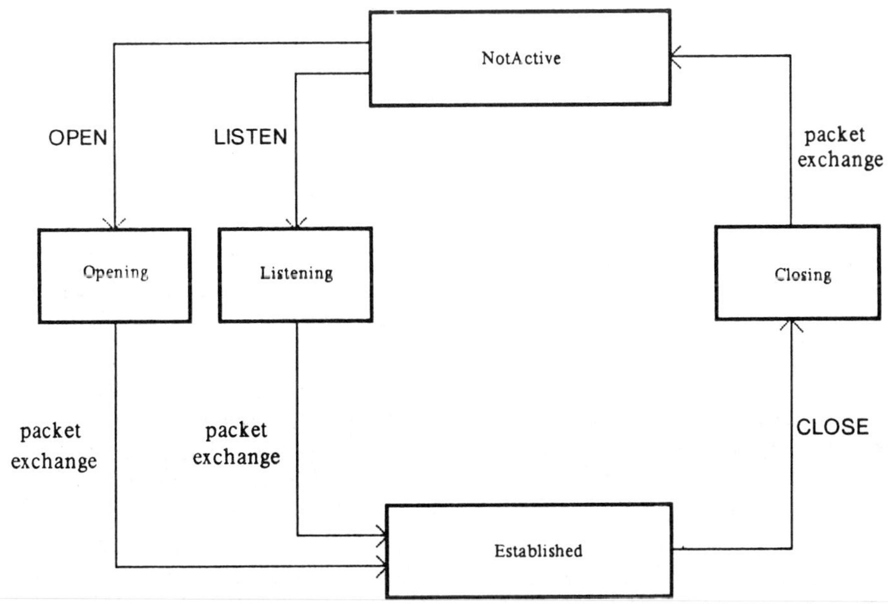

Fig. 1. Connection life-cycle.

transport protocols which is independent of connection management functions for individual connections. Connection management functions are intimately involved in protocol reliability, and if not designed properly may result in deadlocks or old data being erroneously accepted in place of current data.

This paper is based on our experience with the Transmission Control Program (TCP) [5,7,8]. Our efforts in designing TCP have resulted in continuing changes to the original Internetwork Protocol described by Cerf and Kahn [4]. We will use TCP to designate the class of transport protocols based on the Internetwork Protocol. Lessons are drawn from various stages of TCP development throughout the paper, so the reader is cautioned that some examples do not reflect the current TCP. In particular, the formal analysis in Section 6 is based on an early version of TCP. We will use TP and TCP to stand for both the protocol and the program that implements it.

TCP was designed with strong "worst case" assumptions about the underlying transmission medium. In particular it was assumed that packets could be damaged, lost, duplicated, and delivered out of order, with a widely varying delay. All of these events are known to occur through various "natural" causes in packet switching networks. However, TCP was not designed to solve the additional problems imposed by "malicious intruders" [15] which require procedures involving encryption. In considering connection management mechanisms within a TP, it will be helpful to use examples of the dialogue between two TPs. All of our examples will be drawn from TCP, but similar scenarios exist in other transport protocols. These dialogues consist of the exchange of packets between TCPs A and B and will be illustrated as follows:

Each packet contains a sequence number, some optional control information, an optional acknowledgement, and some optional data, represented in the following notation:

⟨Seq #⟩⟨Control⟩⟨Ack #⟩⟨data⟩.

Each line of the dialogue consists of a packet label in parentheses followed by the activity at A where "<- -" signifies the packet being received at A, "- ->" signifies the packet being transmitted at A, "....." signifies that A is unaware of the packet at that time, and "|" indicates no activity. Next appears a description of the packet in the notation described earlier. Lastly, the activity at process B is described, where "- ->" signifies that the packet is received at B, "<- -" signifies that the packet is transmitted at B, and "....." signifies that B is unaware of the packet at this particular time. Comments appear on the extreme right. The vertical direction towards the bottom of the page represents the time axis.

The label of a packet is simply a reference for purposes of discussion. When a packet is duplicated or retransmitted, it is given the same label, the superscript after the closing parenthesis indicating the number of the copy. For brevity, the original copy of the packet does not contain the superscript 1. Packets that are damaged or lost by the communication system will have their label superscripted with an asterisk. When the dealy between transmission and reception of a packet is unimportant, the packet will be shown to be transmitted and received on the same line. This notation is a modification of the notation introduced by Tomlinson [24]. When a packet arrives at a TP it may cause a state change at that TP, and in addition may cause the TP to perform some actions. In examples of dialogues between two TPs we will use a small font to represent the state of the TP and a normal font to describe actions a TP may perform. User process commands to the TP will be shown USING THIS FONT. Figure 2 illustrates these conventions.

2.Connection establishment

Since transport protocols use sequence numbers to validate arriving packets (check for duplicates and correct order), one of the main function of connection establishment is to properly initialize sequence number parameters used by the protocol. Each TP has a Next Sequence Number (NSN) that it will assign to the next (new) packet transmitted, and an Expected Sequence Number (ESN) which it expects to see on the next arriving packet. NSN must be initialized to some Initial Sequence Number (ISN) when a connection is started, and ESN in the opposite TP must be set equal to ISN. Sequence numbers may be assigned to various size units of information from a full packet to a bit. In TCP, each octet is assigned a sequence number, and each packet carries the sequence number of the first octet contained and a count of the number of octets in the packet. This facilitates fragmentation of packets at an intermediate point and their later reassembly at their destination as described in [4].

Many transport protocols employ the simple

	A		B	
	OPEN		LISTEN	
	Opening		Listening	
(1)	- ->	⟨Seq 0⟩⟨data ABC⟩	- ->	
	|		accept	
(2)	<- -	⟨Seq 0⟩⟨Ack 3⟩	<- -	
(3)	- ->	⟨Seq 3⟩⟨data DE⟩	.....	*delayed*
$(3)^2$	- ->	⟨Seq 3⟩⟨data DE⟩	- ->	*retransmission*
(4)	<- -	⟨Seq 0⟩⟨Ack 5⟩	<- -	*terminate connection*
	CLOSE		CLOSE	
	Not active		Not active	
	|		|	
	|		|	
	|		|	
	OPEN		LISTEN	*start new connection*
	Opening		Listening	
(5)	- ->	⟨Seq 0⟩⟨data GHI⟩	- ->	
			accept	
(6)	<- -	⟨Seq 0⟩⟨Ack 3⟩	<- -	
(7)	- ->	⟨Seq 3⟩⟨data JK⟩	.....	*new data delayed*
$(3)^2$	.....	⟨Seq 3⟩⟨data DE⟩	- ->	*old duplicate arrives*
(8)	<- -	⟨Seq 0⟩⟨Ack 5⟩	<- -	
	|		old data accepted	

Fig. 2. Old data delivered instead of current data.

approach of using a fixed number (zero) for ISN (and ESN) whenever a connection is eatablished. This is satisfactory for opening a single instance of a connection, but if the connection is opened and closed in rapid succession then such a strategy may lead to errors as shown in figure 2 when packets are retransmitted or duplicates are generated inside the transmission medium.

If the duplicate packet is delayed in the network until another connection has started between the processes, it may look like a valid new data packet and be accepted, causing the data to be delivered twice. Solutions to this problem revolve around a more careful selection of ISN for new connections.

2.1. ISN selection

The fundamental problem shown in fig. 2 stems from two causes: (1) the possibility for the network to delay and subsequently deliver duplicate packets out of order., and (2) the inability of the TP to differentiate packets on an old connection from packets on a current connection between the same pair of processes. Accordingly, there are two avenues for solution: (1) Prevent packets from old connections from arriving during later connections, or (2) make sure that old packets can be distinguished from new packets.

Solutions of the first type require that a packet may not be stored in the transmission medium beyond a *maximum packet lifetime* L. This may be enforced by using "self-destructing" packets [12], or by the physical characteristics of the medium. If no connection is opened before time L after its last closing, all old packets will be gone, and any ISN may be used to initialize the connection.

This solution requires TPs to remember for time L that a connection was closed, and hence runs counter to the goal of minimizing state information maintained for inactive connections. Furthermore, if a TP fails and forgets which connections were recently closed, it must prevent opening connections for all its processes for time L since any of them might have recently closed connections. The cost of this type of solution is then storage of status information, and delay in reestablishing connections after failures. When L is large, as in multinetwork systems, these costs may be high.

Ways to achieve the second type of solution require a careful selection of ISN or some other identifier to unambiguously distinguish packets of different connections. The other identifier may be an *incarnation number* [13,22] which is derived from some global counter. If the counter has cycle time greater than *L*, no confusion is possible. However, another field on every packet sent is required, increasing overhead. The address field may also serve as a unique identifier if a new *port* address is used by a process each time it opens a connection [4,19]. Some port addresses may be reused to facilitate addressing "well-known" services, but two reusable ports can never be connected, guaranteeing that the pair of port addresses will be unique for every connection.

If the ISN is used to distinguish packets from different connections, it must be carefully selected based on memory of previous connection sequence numbers, or based on a clock. In the memory approach, the ISN is set to the last sequence number used in the previous connection, plus one. This requires maintaining state information for inactive connections because the last sequence number used must be remembered for time *L* on every connection. Once time *L* has passed, any value for ISN may be used. In the clock approach, the ISN is set from a single clock for all connections at a host. The clock value is the only state information that must be preserved through inactive connections and host crashes. However, use of a cyclic clock requires resetting the sequence number if the clock is about to "catch up" with the sequence number as described in Section 3. The process of resetting the sequence number is called *resynchronization*. An additional cost of this mechanism is testing to see if it is time to resynchronize the connection.

In general, all solutions of the second type may fail if the state information which distinguished connections is lost. In this case the TP must resort to a solution of the first type and wait time *L* before initiating new connections. To reduce the likelihood of failure, the state information can be reduced to a minimum and maintained by some specially reliable mechanism like an independent clock or counter.

A combination of mechanisms is also possible. For example, Garlick et. al. [13] propose remembering sequence numbers for a time *L* after closing connections, plus a clock-based incarnation number that is changed only after crashes and thus avoids the need to wait before restarting.

2.2. Validation of connection requests

The techniques for ISN selection described above define procedures for the sending portion of TP that will allow the receiving modules to correctly reject old packets. Once a connection is established, the ESN, in combination with the incarnation number or unique port address pair if they are used, allow the receiver to tell old packets from new ones. The major function of connection establishment is to set ESN and any additional connection identifiers in the receiving modules to match ISN values used by the sending modules on the other side of the connection.

To accomplish this, each TP may try to maintain enough state information about closed connections to set its own ESN and recognize old packets. This would require remembering sequence numbers and/or

```
        A                                                   B

        OPEN                                                LISTEN
        Opening                                             Listening
        pick ISN = x                                        |
(1)     -->            <Seq x><SYN>                         -->
        |                                                   set ESN = x + 1
(2)     <--               <Ack x + 1>                       <--
        |                                                   pick ISN = y
(3)     <--               <Seq y><SYN>                      <--
        set ESN = y + 1                                     |
(4)     -->            <Seq x + 1><Ack y + 1><data AB>      -->
        Established                                         Established
```

Fig. 3. Simple connection establishment using SYN control packet.

incarnation numbers for every connection for a time L [12], and may again impose an unacceptable burden. In the vent of failure with loss of memory, no connections may be accepted for time L.

Alternatively, the sending modules responsible for selecting ISN may also inform the remote TP of the ISN they will use for each new connection. The sending modules transmit a Synchronization control packet (SYN) containing the ISN value as the first packet on the connection (Figure 3). The SYN packet is assigned a sequence number and must be acknowledged just as a data packet to ensure its reliable transmission. The receiving module can set ESN to this value without maintianing any state information about the connection. The receiving TP returns a SYN giving its own ISN, or can reject any SYN that arrives when the protocol machine is in an inappropriate state. Inappropriately timed arrivals are either old retransmissions, protocol errors, or attempts to establish a conversation with an unwilling partner.

Unfortunately, this simple system of a credulous TP is inadequate when packets may arrive out-of-order. Once the connection is established, sequence numbers serve to validate incoming packets. But there is no mechanism for validating an arriving SYN control packet. Suppose a SYN packet is delayed in the network and retransmitted by A. It may arrive at B just at the moment when B is ready to establish a new connection (Figure 4). B will accept the SYN as a new connection request, reply with its own SYN, and consider the connection established. A will receive the replying SYN and interpret it as a new connection request. A's attempt to reply will be discarded by B who thinks the connection is already established, and a deadlock will occur which prevents successful data transfer.

2.3 Three way handshake

To avoid this problem, a more reliable means of transmitting the current ISN to a remote TP must be used. Tomlinson [24] has presented such a scheme called the *3 way handshake* which is used in TCP. Instead of simply accepting an arriving SYN, the receiving TP must ask the sending TP to verify the SYN as current. The receiving TP returns a SYN-ACK control packet to the sending TP which refers to the ISN from the SYN (Figure 5). If the SYN was a current packet, the sender returns a positive acknowledgement, and only then does the receiver accept the SYN and set ESN. This synchronization must occur in both directions, with the SYN-ACK also carrying ISN of the receiver in the other direction. Any packet of the 3 way handshake may also carry data which will be processed after the connection is established, but this is omitted from the figures for simplicity.

If B receives an old SYN packet, it returns a SYN-ACK referencing the ISN in the old packet (Figure 6). A returns a negative acknowledgement (Reset packet) since it is not trying to initiate a connection. Upon receiving the Reset (RST), B knows that the original SYN was an old packet, so B returns to the Opening

```
      A                                            B
      Listening                                    Listening
(1)   .....            ⟨Seq z⟩⟨SYN⟩                -->               old connection request
      |                                            set ESN = z + 1
(2)   <--                ⟨Ack z + 1⟩               <--
      discard                                      |
      |                                            pick ISN = y
(3)   <--                ⟨Seq y⟩⟨SYN⟩              <--
      set ESN = y + 1                              |
(4)   -->              ⟨Ack y + 1⟩                 -->
      |                                            Established
      pick ISN = x                                 |
(5)   -->              ⟨Seq x⟩⟨SYN⟩                -->
      |                                            discard
(6)   <--                ⟨Seq y + 1⟩⟨Ack z + 1⟩    <--
      discard                                      |
```

Fig. 4. Deadlock with simple establishment.

	A		B	
	OPEN Opening pick ISN = x		LISTEN Listening |	
(1)	--> | |	⟨Seq 0⟩⟨SYN⟩	--> remember x pick ISN = y	
(2)	<-- set ESN = y + 1 Established |	⟨Seq y⟩⟨SYN⟩⟨Ack x + 1⟩	<-- | |	*wait for verification*
(3)	--> | |	⟨Seq x + 1⟩⟨Ack y + 1⟩	--> set ESN = x + 1 Established	

Fig. 5. Three way handshake connection establishment.

or Listening state. A similar scenario takes care of old SYN-ACK packets. The use of RST packets is described in greater detail in section 5 on recovering from crashes.

The basic *3 way handshake* mechanism for establishing connections is inherently asymmetric, with one side initiating the attempt by sending a SYN, and the other side waiting to respond to a SYN from the active side. Occasionally a pair of processes may simultaneously attempt to initate a connection to each other, in which case a "collision" is said to occur. Early versions of TCP simply gave up and retried after a random delay to resolve such collisions. More recent versions of TCP will accept a SYN packet after having sent their own SYN by replying with an ACK to successfully establish the connection. However, if two different SYN packets (one an old duplicate) arrive while a connection is being established, the approach of retrying after a delay may still have to be used.

The 3 way handshake mechanism is adequate to reliably establish connections under the worst case assumptions of packet switching network transmission characteristics without requiring any memory of previous connections to set ESN. It also accommodates failure recovery as discussed in Section 5. Techniques for verifying these mechanisms more rigorously than the informal discussion in this section has allowed are presented in Section 6.

Incarnation numbers are essentially equivalent to sequence numbers for purposes of connection establishment, and the 3 way handshake may also be used to reliably exchange incarnation numbers [13]. Other mechanisms requiring memory of previous activity by the receiving modules [12], or use of unique port addresses [19] may provide the required reliability without a 3 way handshake. If end-to-end encryption is incorporated into the transport protocol, then the initialization of a new encryption key for each connection serves a similar role to the 3 way hand-

	A		B	
	Not active		Listening	
(1)	..... | |	⟨Seq z⟩⟨SYN⟩	--> remember z pick ISN = y	*old connection request*
(2)	<-- invalid	⟨Seq y⟩⟨SYN⟩⟨Ack z + 1⟩	<-- |	*wait for verification*
(3)	--> | Not active	⟨Seq z + 1⟩⟨RST⟩⟨Ack y + 1⟩	--> reject SYN Listening	

Fig. 6. Rejections of old SYN packet with 3 way handshake.

shake in guaranteeing that old packets will be rejected [15].

3. Clock driven ISN and resynchronization

A basic goal of the ISN selection mechanism is to prevent packets from being emitted with sequence numbers which duplicate those that are atill in the multinetwork. This should be assured even when TPs crash and lose all knowledge of the sequence numbers they have been using. In TCP, when new connections are created, an ISN generator is employed which selects a new 32 bit ISN. The generator is bound to a (possibly fictitious) clock that is assumed to keep running even if the TCP or its supporting host crashes. We now describe the implementation of such a clock driven scheme, and the necessary relationships between the clock tick, the maximum packet lifetime L, the size of the sequence number, the transmission rate, and the notion of resynchronization [6,9].

Refer to Fig. 7 for a pictorial representation of the analysis to follow. Let D = duration of the clock tick in seconds, C = period of the clock in seconds, L = maximum lifetime of packets in the multinetwork in seconds, R = time in seconds until resynchronization is necessary under average bandwidth b, b = average bandwidth of transmission in octets/sec, B = maximum average bandwidth in octets/sec, S = length of sequence numbers in bits, p = length of clock time in bits ($p < S$), $q = S - p$.

The figure illustrates a curve, the *ISN curve,* representing a clock ticking every D units of time, and wrapping around in a time C. The *ISN + 1 curve* is a curve similar to the ISN curve, but displaced by D, and the *forbidden zone boundary* is another curve similar to the ISN curve, but displaced from it by a time $L + D$. Sequence numbers are S bits long. (This theory and analysis holds for any radix system, we have chosen binary only for convenience.) When a connection is to be established, a unique ISN is picked, and from then on sequence numbers are incremented as and when data is transmitted. In the proposed scheme [24], when a connection is to be established, the clock is allowed to tick at least once, and then the ISN is a number which has the current value of the clock in the high order p bits and zeros in the low order q bits of S (i.e. the ISN is picked from the ISN curve). The actual rate b at which data is transmitted, and sequence numbers assigned are illustrated by the curve marked *actual transmission rate.* The connection must be *resynchronized* when the actual transmission rate curve touches the forbidden zone boundary. Otherwise should a connection be closed and reopened within the forbidden zone, then old duplicate packets might be accepted by the receiver, as follows (Figure 8).

Suppose that at time t_b, sequence numbers s_a

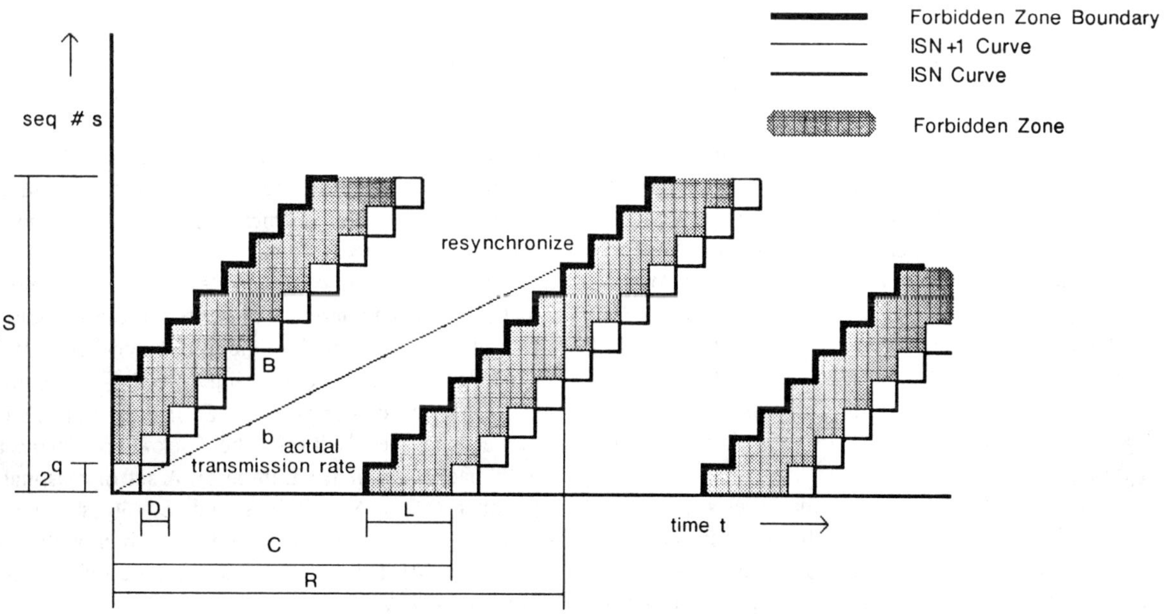

Fig. 7. The forbidden zone and ISN curve.

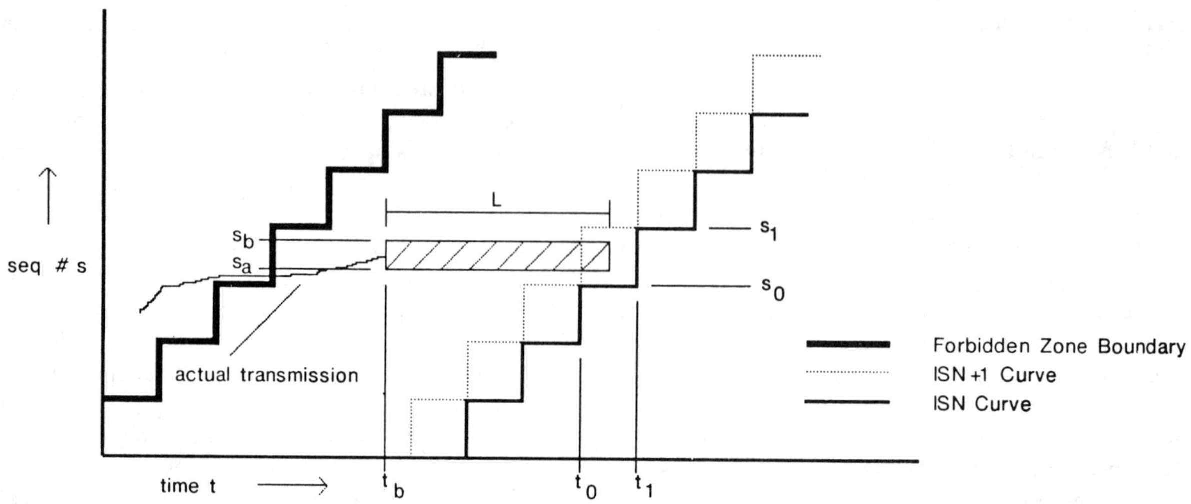

Fig. 8. The need to resynchronize.

through s_b have been used, at which point the connection is closed. A new connection is started at time t_0 using ISN s_0 derived from the clock. But packets carrying sequence numbers s_a through s_b can persist in the net for L seconds, and the new connection can use sequence numbers s_0 through s_1 during time t_0 to t_1. Since this includes s_a to s_b, the old duplicates can be confused with new packets. The same arguments hold for the case where the transmitting TCP crashed while generating packets with sequence numbers in the forbidden zone, and then immediately restarted.

This example shows that the TCP must not be allowed to generate packets with sequence numbers in the forbidden zone. This can happen (1) if the clock catches up with the TCP, thus causing entry into the forbidden zone from the left, or (2) if the TCP transmits too fast and enters the forbidden zone from the bottom. Therefore two tests are required:

1) Is the sequence number of the packet about to be transmitted (NSN) in the forbidden zone to the right?

2) Will the sequence numbers assigned to the data in the entire packet lie outside the forbidden zone? (i.e. Will any of the sequence numbers used exceed the maximum given by the ISN + 1 curve at this instant?)

If the first condition is true, then the NSN at the transmitting TCP must be resynchronized in order to permit continued transmission without assigning sequence numbers in the forbidden zone. A protocol by which this can be achieved can be found in [7]. Since the protocol involves the exchange of control packets the forbidden zone boundary is made wider to allow the exchange to be completed before the real forbidden zone is entered. If the second condition is true, then the TCP must either delay transmitting the packet, or must transmit less data in the packet. If both conditions are false then the packet may be transmitted.

The test for resynchronization need only be made when a packet is to be transmitted. Hence, if a process does not transmit anything while the forbidden zone moves past its NSN then no resynchronization is necessary. However, if a sender is inactive for a period of time and then tries to transmit while in the forbidden zone, the sender must be prohibited from sending until the forbidden zone had been crossed. Hence, some implementations may decide to periodically check the need to resynchronize connections, or to perform resynchronization at fixed intervals such as $C/2$ to avoid such difficulties.

An exact formulation of rules (1) and (2) in terms of the clock parameters is presented in the Appendix. It is also shown that the time until resynchronization is needed on a connection ranges from $C–L$ for small b, to infinity as b approaches B (if data transmission proceeds at the clock rate, the clock *never* catches up with packet sequence numbers). A set of reasonable parameters for $S = 32$ bits and $L = 30$ seconds is presented, allowing a maximum bandwidth of MBits/sec with resynchronization required at most every 4.5 hours.

4. Connection termination

Once a connection between two communicating processes has become established, reliable communication can take place over it. Eventually one or both of the processes will decide that the connection should be *closed* because there is no more to say. There are a number of different ways by which an established connection may be closed.

4.1. Using a higher level protocol

The simplest way to close a connection is for both processes to have decided, using a higher level protocol, that they are going to stop communicating and then to inform their local TP that the present connection should no longer exist by giving the *Abort* command. The TP would then simply remove knowledge of that connection from its local tables.

4.2. Using TP supplied mechanisms

Alternatively, the connection management aspect of the TP could provide a mechanism by which one of the processes can inform the other that communication over the connection is to cease. A special control packet indicating that that conversation is finished (FIN) is used achieve this. A FIN is assigned a sequence number for reliability, and travels in a packet with no accompanying data, or control. There are three cases of connection closing as seen by a TP:

1) A user process initiates connection termination by telling its TP to close the connection.
2) The remote TP initiates termination (on request from the remote process) by sending a FIN packet.
3) Both users initiate termination simultaneously by telling their respective TPs to close the connection.

There are a number of different protocols by which FIN packets may be exchanged. These protocols must accommodate all three cases described above. We now describe some possible protocols and indicate their suitability for various purposes.

4.3. Simple FIN exchange

In the simplest case, the user would like to terminate communication immediately without caring about the state of previously transmitted data which may as yet be unacknowledged, or data as yet not received. Instead of just aborting the connection, the TPs could conclude that the connection has closed when each has transmitted and received a FIN command. The reason for requiring receipt of a FIN in addition to transmitting one, is that the receipt of the FIN indicates that the other end has noticed that the connection should be terminated and will proceed to do so. The initiator of the termination has assurance that the remote end will not continue computing and/or charging the user as in a timesharing system. If a FIN is not received in response to one sent within a timeout, then the connection is closed none the less.

When one of the user processes decides that the connection should be closed it tells its local TP to close the connection. The TP sends a FIN to the other TP with the usual next sequence number and current acknowledgement. Upon receipt of an unsolicited FIN packet with an acceptable sequence number, the TP informs its local user that the connection is closing and replies with a FIN packet of its own (Figure 9). A TP that has both transmitted and received a FIN packet may destroy all knowledge of the connection. If both TPs transmit a FIN simultaneously, then they will interpret the other's as a response to their own.

This simple scheme is not very reliable. The data transmitted prior to the transmission of FINs is not guranteed to be delivered (data in packet 1 of Figure

	A		B	
(1)	Established		Established	
	.....	⟨Seq 78⟩⟨Ack 29⟩⟨data HI⟩	<- -	*data in transit*
	CLOSE		|	
	Closing		|	
(2)	- ->	⟨Seq 29⟩⟨FIN⟩⟨Ack 78⟩	- ->	*A requests termination*
	|		Closing	
(3)	<- -	⟨Seq 80⟩⟨FIN⟩⟨Ack 30⟩	<- -	*B complies*
	Not active		Not active	

Fig. 9. Connection termination using simple FIN exchange.

9). If full delivery is important, the high level protocol must wait to close the connection until all data has been successfully transmitted. More seriously, if the initiating TP times out it can not be certain whether the other side has received the FIN and the reply 'was lost, or whether the other side never received the FIN and is still open.

4.4. Acknowledged FIN exchange

To guarantee that the connection will be closed on both sides (without necessarily guaranteeing delivery of data in transit), a protocol requiring acknowledgement of FINs may be used. Each TP transmits a FIN packet and waits for it to be acknowledged by the other end, in addition to waiting for a FIN from the other end. This scheme is very much like the 3 way handshake used to exchange SYNs reliably.

In the first of the three cases mentioned earlier, when the user process closes the connection, the TP transmits a FIN packet and will not accept any more data from the user process. All packets preceeding and including the FIN will be retransmitted until acknowledged. When the remote TP has both acknowledged the FIN and sent a FIN of its own, the first TCP can acknowledge the remote FIN and delete knowledge of this connection from its state tables.

In the second case, a TP receives an unsolicited FIN from the remote TP. The receiving TP then acknowledges the FIN and sends back one of its own even if intervening data have not been received. (Data packet 1 in Figure 10 is never delivered.). It also informs its user of the remote close request, and does not accept any more data to send. The TP waits for an acknowledgement of its FIN packet before it can delete knowledge of the connection (Figure 10). If an acknowledgement is not forthcoming, after a timeout the connection is deleted none the less.

In the third case, a simultaneous close by both processes will cause FIN packets to be exchanged. Each TP acknowledges the FIN it received. Both TPs upon receiving these eacknowledgements can delete the connection (Figure 11). In the event that the acknowledgements are lost, one or both TPs will continue retransmitting the FIN until they timeout.

By requiring FINs to be acknowledged, both sides can be sure that the connection will close, once the initiating FIN has been received. In particular, if the replying TP times out it may be that the replying FIN never reached the initiating TP, or that the final acknowledgement was lost as in Figure 12. In the first case, both TPs will timeout, and in the second, the initiating TP closes normally and the replying TP times out. In either case both sides will close the connection.

4.5. Graceful acknowledged FIN exchange

Users may in addition desire that the data in the pipe during connection termination be reliably delivered. Close is an operation meaning *I have no more data to send.* The notion of closing a full duplex connection is subject to ambiguous interpretation, since it may not be obvious how to treat the receiving side to the connection. The TP interprets close in a half duplex fashion. The user who closes may continue to receive data until it is told that the other end has closed too. The TP will reliably deliver all data sent prior to closing the connection, so a user that expects no data in return need only wait to hear that the connection was closed successfully to know that all its data was received at the destination end. This is often been termed a *graceful* termination. The algorithms by which this is achieved are very similar to those described for the acknowledged FIN exchange. The receiver of a FIN does not acknow-

	A		**B**	
	Established		Established	
(1)	- ->	⟨Seq 29⟩⟨Ack 78⟩⟨data HIJKL⟩	.....	*data in transit*
	CLOSE			
	Closing			
(2)	- ->	⟨Seq 34⟩⟨FIN⟩⟨Ack 78⟩	- ->	*A requests termination*
			Closing	
(3)	<- -	⟨Seq 78⟩⟨FIN⟩⟨Ack 35⟩	<- -	*B complies*
(4)	- ->	⟨Seq 35⟩⟨Ack 79⟩	- ->	
	Not active		Not active	

Fig. 10. Connection termination using acknowledged FIN exchange.

	A		B
	Established, CLOSE		Established, CLOSE
(1)	-->	〈Seq 29〉〈FIN〉〈Ack 78〉	.....
(2)	.....	〈Seq 78〉〈FIN〉〈Ack 29〉	<--
	Closing		Closing
(2)	<--	〈Seq 78〉〈FIN〉〈Ack 29〉	|
(1)	|	〈Seq 29〉〈FIN〉〈Ack 78〉	-->
(3)	-->	〈Seq 30〉〈Ack 79〉	-->
(4)	<--	〈Seq 79〉〈Ack 30〉	<--
	Not active		Not active

Fig. 11. Simultaneous exchange of confirming FINs.

ledge the FIN until all data transmitted before the FIN has been successfully received. In addition, a FIN is not returned until the local user indicates that it too wants the connection closed. On receipt of a FIN the TCP informs its local user so that the user may request that the connection be closed from its end as well.

5. Failure recovery

The protocal mechanisms described so far adequately manage connections as long as the protocol machines on each side continue to function normally. Unfortunately, hosts and their TPs occasionally crash with loss of state information. When a host fails and subsequently restarts, all knowledge of TP connections is lost. Connections which were established become *half open* with the failed side thinking they are not active, while the other side believes the connection is still established. Half open connections may also result from protocol design flaws without requiring crashes.

Under these circumstances a TP cannot guarantee whether data in transit during the crash was delivered or not [1,22] and higher level error recovery must be invoked.

Since the established side is consuming resources, it is desirable to reset half open connections promptly. One way to close half open connections is to have a timer in each TP that goes off if an established connection has not actively received any correct packets for some time, or if a retransmission timeout exceeds some predefined value. The occurrence of such a timeout will prompt the TP to remove knowledge of the half open connection once the user process owning the connection agrees. This mechanism was used to terminate connections owing to timeouts in Section 4.

Alternatively, a control packet indicating that the connection should be Reset (RST), can be used. An example of this was illustrated in Figure 6. The

	A		B
	Established		Established
(1)	-->	〈Seq 29〉〈Ack 78〉〈data ABCDE〉	.....
	CLOSE		|
	Closing		|
(2)	-->	〈Seq 34〉〈FIN〉〈Ack 78〉	-->
	|		Closing
(3)	<--	〈Seq 78〉〈FIN〉〈Ack 35〉	<--
(4)	-->	〈Seq 35〉〈Ack 79〉	.....
	Not active		|
(3)[1]	.....	〈Seq 78〉〈FIN〉〈Ack 35〉	<--
	|		Timeout
	|		Not active

Fig. 12. Acknowledged FIN exchange terminated by timeout.

```
        A                                                   B
        |                                                   |
        crash                                               NSN = 300, ESN = 100
        OPEN                                                Established
        Opening                                             |
(1)     -->          ⟨Seq 6⟩⟨SYN⟩                           -->
(2)     <--              ⟨Seq 300⟩⟨Ack 100⟩                 <--
        rejected                                            |
(3)     -->          ⟨Seq 100⟩⟨RST⟩⟨Ack 300⟩                -->
        |                                                   believable
        |                                                   Not active
(1)²    -->          ⟨Seq 6⟩⟨SYN⟩                           .....
```

Fig. 13. Half-open connection discovery and reset.

general use of this command is now described.

Assume that two TPs A and B are communicating with one another when a crash occurs causing loss of memory to A. When A is up again it is likely to restart from the beginning, or continue from some recovery point. As a result the user process at A will probably try to open the connection again or try to send on the connection it believes is established. In the latter case it receives the error message *connection not open* from its TP. In an attempt to establish the connection, A will send a packet containing SYN. When the SYN arrives, B being in the Established state ignores the SYN, but responds with an acknowledgement indicating what sequence it next expects to hear. A sees that this packet does not acknowledge anything it sent and, being unsynchronized, sends a RST because it has detected a half open connection. B can believe the RST since it refers to its ESN and NSN and aborts the connection, notifying the user. This scenario is illustrated in Figure 13. If the acknowledgement packet was instead an old duplicate, the RST referring to it would not be acceptable at B. A will continue to retransmit its SYN and if the user at B reopens the connection, it will eventually be established.

The case when A crashes and B tries to send data on what it thinks is an established connection is illustrated in Figure 14. The data arriving at A from B is unacceptable because no connection exists. So A sends back a RST. The RST is acceptable and B processes it and aborts the connection.

A variety of other cases are possible, all of which are accounted for, by the following rules for RST generation and processing:

1) If the connection is not yet Established (or does not exist), a RST should be formed and sent for any packet that does not acknowledge something the receiver sent earlier. The RST should take its sequence number field from the acknowledgement field of the offending packet (if it has one) and its acknowledgement field should acknowledge all data and control in the offending packet.

2) If the connection has been Established, any unacceptable packet should elicit only an empty acknowledgement packet containing the current NSN and an acknowledgement indicating the ESN.

```
        A                                                   B
        |                                                   |
        crash                                               NSN = 300, ESN = 100
        Not active                                          Established
(1)     <--          ⟨Seq 300⟩⟨Ack 100⟩⟨data AB⟩            <--
        rejected                                            |
(2)     -->          ⟨Seq 100⟩⟨RST⟩⟨Ack 302⟩                -->
        |                                                   believable,
        Not active                                          Not active
```

Fig. 14. Half-open connection discovery and reset.

3) All RST packets are validated by first checking their sequence field as for other packets, then if the RST acknowledges something the receiver sent (but has not yet received acknowledgement for), the RST must be valid. After validating the RST, the TCP changes state. If the connection was not Established it returns to the Opeing, of Listening state. If the connection was Established, it is aborted, placed in the NotActive state, and the local user process is notified.

6. Modeling and analysis techniques

Since overall protocol reliability depends heavily on the operation of connection management mechanisms, it is particularly important to verify that they function correctly. Most often this has been done by the sort of informal case studies performed in Section 3 to 5. In this form of analysis, the designer tries to identify all situations of interest, and to verify that the protocol "does the right thing" in each case. These narrative analyses are very valuable to provide motivation for and intuitive understanding of protocol mechanisms, and have successfully uncovered a number of design flaws. In the case of TCP, the problems associated with the credulous connection opening mechanism described in Section 2 were found this way, leading to the development of the 3 way handshake.

More rigorous analysis techniques must be used to verify the reliability of transport protocols with greater certainty. This requires a precise model of the protocol whose detailed operation can be analyzed. This model typically consists of a pair of protocol machines connected by a transmission medium. The machines receive commands from their respective users, and messages from each other via the transmission medium. The transmission medium is itself a simple kind of machine that may introduce errors, delays, and other perturbations between its input and its output.

This model may be approached from two viewpoints, local and global [14]. The local viewpoint focuses on an individual protocol machine and is most useful for specification and implementation purposes. The global viewpoint considers the entire system as a black box with inputs and outputs to each user. The global view is most useful for verification which must show that the outputs to each user are as desired in all cases.

Protocol verification techniques fall into two main classes, program proofs and state models [23]. In the former, each machine is specified algorithmically, and assertions which reflect the desired reliability goals must be formulated and proved. This approach has been effectively applied to verifying the data transfer features of transport protocols where large or infinite numbers of interaction sequences are possible due to large sequence number spaces and retransmissions [2,21].

State models have been developed using such formalisms as Petri nets, state diagrams, state transition matrixes, flow charts, and programs to define the protocol machines [14,16,18,20]. Some form of reachability analysis is typically performed to generate all possible interactions of the system, followed by a check for undesirable states. This approach has been successful in verifying data transfer features where simplifying assumptions are made to keep the number of states tractable, but is most applicable to connection management where the number of states is inherently small. Several *mixed* systems have also been developed in which state models are used for the *basic states* of the protocol machine, augmented by *context variables* which are not part of the basic state. [3,11].

A comprehensive treatment of these alternative techniques is beyond the scope of this paper. As an illustration, we present a brief description of the technique used to formally verify portions of the TCP connection management procedures in [22]. This technique falls into the state model class, and takes a global view.

Each protocol machine is modeled as a classic state machine with an input set, an output set, a set of internal states, and functions giving the next state and output for each combination of input and current state. Inputs consist of user commands, messages from the other protocol machine (or the network), and internally generated events such as timeouts. The two machines operate independently, with synchronization achieved by one machine waiting for a particular type of packet from the other machine.

We define the composite state of the system as the state of the protocol machine on each side of the connection, plus any *relevant* packets in the transmission medium between them. Transitions from one composite state to another are derived from the state transitions of the individual protocol machines by including all possible transitions of either protocol machine, given the state of the transmission medium.

The number of composite states is then the number of protocol machine states squared times the number of different states of the transmission medium. In a straightforward approach, every packet (including retransmissions) since the time the composite system was created would have to included in the state, making the state space unworkably large. This potential state explosion may be limited in two ways: by reducing the number of protocol machine states, and by treating as equivalent different sets of packets in transit as described below.

In order to verify connection management functions, the protocol machine is defined with basic states for connection establishment and termination functions only. These include a NotActive state, an Established state, and several intermediate states for going from one to the other as connections are opened and colsed. All data transfer takes place in the Established state, and is therefore not modeled by the basic protocol machine. Information about sequence numbers is part of the context information maintained outside the basic states of the protocol. This context information is used along with the basic state to determine the processing of inputs.

To limit the number of transmission medium states, all packets in the transmission medium can be classified as either *current* or *old* by considering the protocol's use of sequence numbers. Packets are current if either

1) The packet is pending (waiting for retransmission) at the sender. Normally this condition holds until the sender receives some form of acknowledgement. For packets which are not retransmitted (ACK, RST) it does not hold.

2) The packet refers to a current packet traveling in the opposite direction (e.g. ACK), RST of another packet). When the opposite packet is no longer current, both packets are removed from the composite state.

Since we are primarily interested in worst case analysis, we assume that duplicate packets from previous connections may be held in the transmission medium and emerge during or after establishment of the current connection (subject to packet lifetime constraints). We group all old packets into a single class for each packet type (since their processing will be equivalent), and implicitly attach this set of old packet types to the transmission medium state. This means that we allow all old packet arrival events to occur in every state, which is a more rigorous but simpler to represent test for the protocol than any real transmission medium. Hence only current packets must be explicitly represented as part of the composite state which determines which packets can

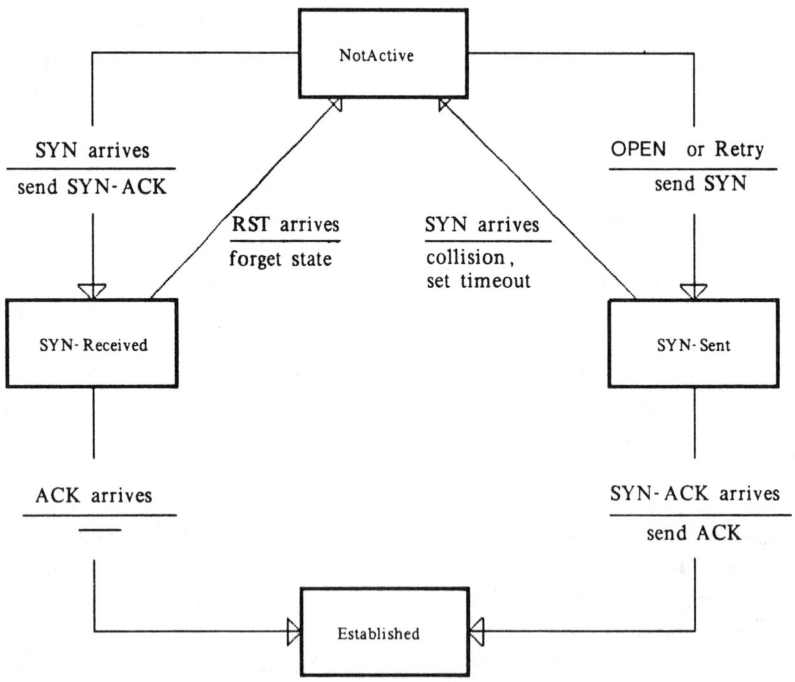

Fig. 15. Three way handshake protocol machine.

arrive, since all old packets are implicitly part of the state.

ONce a packet is generated by a protocol transition, it remains in the composite state until it is no longer current, despite the assumption that the transmission medium can lose or damage packets. Since every current packet is either being retransmitted, or is a response to a packet being retransmitted, we can assume that current packets are always available to cause transitions. In reality, packets may temporarily disappear from the composite state if lost or damaged, but will always reappear due to retransmissions.

By taking advantage of these reductions, a relatively compact model of connection establishment in TCP may be developed. Figure 15 shows the basic protocol machine states and state transitions in opening a connection. Each transition is marked by the input causing the transition, and the output (if any) accompanying it. Four states are needed to represent a simple 3 way handshake protocol which retries on collision. The figure shows only normal events for clarity. The set of operations {detect event, take appropriate action, move to new state} are assumed to be atomic or uninterruptable so that no confusion can result from nearly simultaneous events.

For a complete model, the processing of all possible input events in each state must be specified. As an example, the table for the SYN-Received state is shown in Figure 16. The set of input events consists of packets (SYN, SYN-ACK, Data, ACK, RST), user commands (OPEN), and internal timeouts (Retransmit, Quit, Retry-after-collision). Note that the same input event results in different outcomes depending on the context information.

Fig. 17 shows the composite state diagram resulting from the connection establishment protocol of Figure 15. Each composite state is represented by a pair of process states and a list of current packets. Some context is represented along with the basic state of each process. This consists of the sequence number for outgoing packets in the SYN-Sent, SYN-Received, and Established states, and also the sequence number for incoming packets in the Established state. This allows us to determine whether the protocol has correctly initialized sequence numbers when the Established state is reached.

Current packets are represented by their packet types, with a subscript giving their own sequence number if relevant, followed by the sequence number

Event	Next State	Action and Context
SYN	self	Send ACK if SYN is duplicate for current connection.
SYN	self	Send RST if SYN is not from current connection.
SYN-ACK	self	Send RST referencing SYN-ACK.
Data	self	Discard as out of order (or hold).
ACK	ES	If ACK refers to transmitted SYN-ACK. (Third part of 3 way handshake).
RST	NA	If RST refers to transmitted SYN-ACK. (SYN previously received was an old duplicate.)
ACK, RST	self	Ignore if does not refer to transmitted SYN-ACK.
OPEN	self	Ignore since already in progress.
Retrans	self	Retransmit SYN-ACK.
Quit	self	Notify local process.
Retry	self	Ignore since other side has already started.

ES = Established NA = Not Active

Fig. 16. State transition table for SYN-received state.

of another packet they may refer to (in parentheses). An arrow above the packet shows its direction of travel. Thus $\overrightarrow{\text{SYN-ACK}}_y(x)$ represents a SYN-ACK packet with sequence number y, referring to another packet with sequence number x, and traveling from left to right.

Symmetric states (identical except for switching process identities and packet directions) have been eliminated to simplify the figure. Transitions to the same state such as retransmissions are not shown. Composite transitions resulting from simultaneous transitions of both protocol machines are perfectly legal, but are shown as sequential individial transitions to reduce the number of arrows.

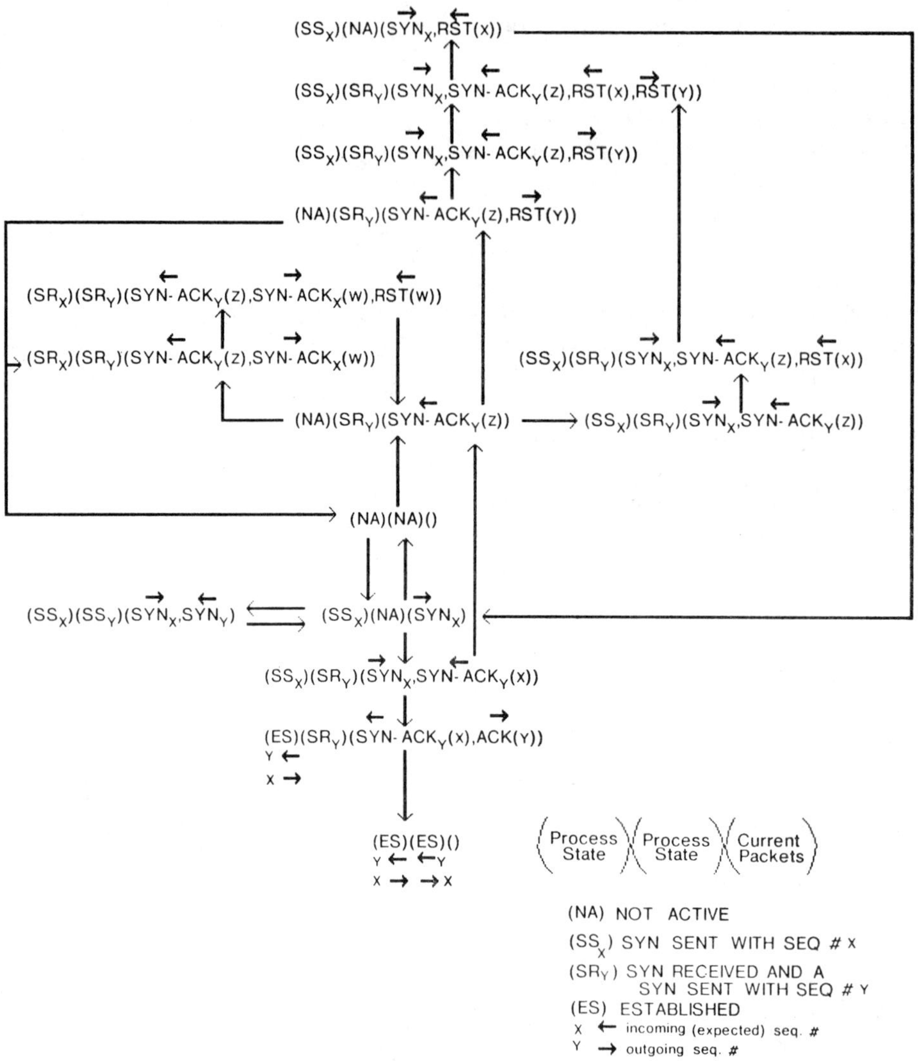

Fig. 17. Composite state diagram for "three way handshake".

This composite state model demonstrates several aspects of protocol correctness for the normal case where both protocol machines start in the NotActive state and function according to their definition (no failures). This includes safety considerations (absence of deadlocks, correctness of outcome), and liveness considerations (progress and eventual termination) as follows.

There are no terminal states with one machine Established and the other not Established. The only terminal states have both processes NotActive (if a connection was rejected) or both processes Established. Furthermore, when both processes are Established, sequence numbers for both directions are properly initialized. Hence there is no deadlock in the procedure for connection establishment.

All paths leading back to the NotActive state for either process are caused by collisions (simultaneous open requests) which will cause a later retry to establish the connection. Assuming that perpetual collisions are avoided by the random retry interval, and that the transmission medium provides a nonzero probability of delivering any packet, the protocol will eventually succeed in establishing a connection (unless the attempt is rejected).

These results show the sufficiency of the connection establishment mechanisms embodied in the 3 way handshake. The inadequacy of simpler technique (given worst case transmission medium behavior) was demonstrated informally in the discussion accompanying Figure 2, and is shown formally using the above techniques in [22]. The mechanisms for recovering from protocol failures described in Section 5 can also be incorporated into the model by adding corresponding transitions to the protocol machine. These introduce transitions out of the half closed composite state which lead to reestablishing the connection [22].

7. Conclusions

Connection management functions are intimately involved in transport protocol reliability and require careful design if errors are to be avoided under unusual but possible circumstances. Special care must be taken to avoid the possibility of confusing packets from different connections between the same pair of processes since old packets may persist in the network and be delivered during later connections. This requires a unique identifier for each new connection, or careful selection of the initial sequence number (ISN) to be used. A clock may be used to reliably determine the ISN even after protocol failures, but clock-based schemes require resynchronization of the connection at certain points. The 3 way handshake provides a means for reliably synchronizing the two sides of the protocol to establish a connection while minimizing the amount of state information that must be maintained for inactive connections. This involves the exchange of special synchronization control packets (SYN) at the start of a connection.

Control packets (FIN) may also be used to terminate a connection. In a *graceful* closing, the protocol guarantees that all data sent before the close command is issued will be delivered. In an immediate closing, data in transit may or may not be delivered, but both sides know that the connection has terminated. A unilateral closing or *abort* does not guarantee that resources on the other side of the connection have been released. *Half open* connections resulting from failure of on side of the protocol can also be terminated by an exchange of control packets.

While informal analysis of scenarios is a very useful tool for designing connection management mechanisms, it is not adequate for a fully reliable analysis. More precise models defining the detailed operation of the protocol *machines* on each side of the connection must be developed for this purpose. One such model specifying the machines as finite automata augmented by *context* information is presented and was successfully used to verify connection establishment in TCP.

Acknowledgements

The development of the Transmission Control Protocol which provided the basis for this work was carried out while the authors were at the Stanford University Digital Systems Laboratory, supported in part by the Defense Advanced Research Projects Agency (under contract number MDA903-76C-0093) and by the National Science Foundation Graduate Fellowship Program. Vint Cerf and Robert Kahn provided many of the original ideas behind TCP and Vint Cerf has been a constant participant in discussions on improvements. The Cyclades research group under Louis Pouzin also contributed many early ideas through discussions in IFIP TC 6.1. Ray Tomlinson suggested several important modifications including the 3 way handshake. Bill Plummer, Dick Karp, Jim Mathis, and Bob Metcalfe also contributed significantly to the work. The continuing support of TCP development by ARPA has made this work possible.

Appendix

The following relationships between the clock parameters presented in section 5 are useful in analyzing resynchronization.

$$S = 32 \text{ bits} \tag{1}$$

D – This is a design parameter which is chosen primarily on the basis of the time the TCP is willing to wait before the same processes can communicate again. Since it affects some of the other parameters too, it should not be chosen completely arbitrarily.

$$B = (2^q)/D \text{ octets/sec} \tag{2}$$

$$C = 2^p D \text{ sec} \tag{3}$$

$2^S > 2BL$ – The maximum rate at which sequence numbers are used is related to L and S [4]. This prevents packet sequence numbers from cycling and hence being reused while old packets with identical sequence numbers may still be in the network.

Time until clock resynchronization

The connection must be resynchronized when packet sequence numbers about to be assigned lie in the forbidden zone to the right. We now show how the resynchronization time R, since the connection was synchronized or last resynchronized, depends on the actual average bandwidth b being achieved.

Assume that the step curves in Figure 7 have been linearized, and have the same average slope. s is the sequence number at any time t. The equation of the line giving the (linearized) forbidden zone boundary is

$$s = B(t - (C - L)),$$

because the line is displaced in time from the origin by $(C - L)$, and has a slope B.

The equation of the line giving the actual use of sequence

numbers is

$s = bt$.

Hence the point of intersection gives $t = R$.

$$bR = B(R - C + L)$$

$$\begin{aligned} R &= (C - L)/(1 - b/B) \\ &= \infty \text{ when } b \doteq B \\ &= C - L \text{ when } b = 0 \end{aligned} \quad (4)$$

The end conditions are intuitively correct, because if $b = B$ then the clock never catches up with the actual rate of transmission and therefore resynchronization never has to be performed, or if $b = 0$ then resynchronization has to be performed at a time corresponding to the potential assignment of a sequence number that lies within the forbidden zone.

Forbidden zone tests

We now describe the two tests for determining whether sequence numbers assigned to data will lie in the forbidden zone or not, in terms of the clock parameters. Let x be this current sequence number and n be the current value of the clock. In order to determine whether x is in the forbidden zone to the right, the TCP tests if x lies within the range [forbidden zone boundary, ISN + 1 curve] i.e. $[(2^q(n + 1 + \ulcorner L/D\urcorner - 1), 2^q(n + 1)]$ [9].

Therefore, if

$$(\{2^q(n + 1 + \ulcorner L/D\urcorner) - 1 - x\} \bmod 2^S) < 2^q\ulcorner L/D\urcorner, \quad (5)$$

then the connection must be resynchronized.

In order to determine whether sequence number assignment will enter the forbidden zone from the bottom, the TCP tests whether any of the sequence numbers assigned to data in the packet lie in the range [ISN + 1 curve, forbidden zone boundary].

Let d be the length of the data in the packet in octets and define

$$y = (x + d - 1) \bmod 2^S.$$

The test can be reformulated as whether the ISN + 1 curve lies within the range $[x,y]$.

Therefore, if

$$(\{y - 2^q(n + 1)\} \bmod 2^S) < d \quad (6)$$

then only the portion between x and $2^q(n + 1) - 1$ can be transmitted in this packet. Note that this test can be omitted with if it can be *guaranteed* that sequence number assignement will never enter the borbidden zone from the bottom. This is possible if B is larger than the bandwidth attainable through the network.

Assuming that both tests must be performed, each packet must be tested as follows before it can be transmitted:
IF eqn (5) is true THEN resynchronize the connection
ELSE IF eqn (6) is true THEN transmit partial packet or wait for the clock to tick
ELSE transmit entire packet.

We assume a zero time for putting a packet on the transmit queue, and take into account the maximum packet length and finite time to transmit by increasing the effective forbidden zone. We also assume that resynchronization occurs before entry into the *real* forbidden zone.

Example parameters

A suitable choice of the various parameters is

p = 14 bits, q = 18 bits,

D = 1 sec, $L \approx 30$ secs.

This gives $B \approx 2$ Mbits/sec and $C \approx 4.5$ hours and permits opening new connecxtions every 1 second.

References

[1] D. Belsnes, Single Message Communication, *IEEE Trans. on Communication,* Vol 24, No 2, February 1976, pp. 190–194.

[2] G.V. Bochman, Logical Verification and Implementation of Protocols, *Proc. Fourth Data Communications Symp.,* Quebec, Canada, October 1975, pp. 7.15–7.20. IEEE 75CH1001–7DATA)

[3] G.V. Bochmann and J. Gecsei, A Unified Method for the Specification and Verification of Protocols, *Proc, IFIP Congress,* Toronto, Canada, August 1977, pp. 229–234.

[4] V.G. Cerf, and Robert E. Kahn, A Protocol for Packet Network Intercommunication, *IEEE Trans. on Communication,* COM-22, May 1974, pp. 673–648.

[5] V.G. Cerf, Y.K. Dalal, and C.A. Sunshine, Specificiation of Internet Transmission Control Program, INWG Note 72, revised December 1974.

[6] V.G. Cerf, TCP Resynchronization, Digital Systems Lab Technical Note Number 79, Stanford University, January 1976.

[7] V.G. Cerf, Specificiation of Internet Transmission Control Program, TCP (Version 2), March 1977, (available from DARPA/IPTO).

[8] V.G. Cerf and J.B. Postel, Specificiation of Internet Transmission Control Program, TCP (Version 3), January 1978, (available from USC/ISI).

[9] Y.K. Dalal, More on Selecting Sequence Numbers, *Proc. ACM SIGCOMM/SIGOPS Interprocess Communications Workshop,* Santa Monica, March 1975, pp. 25–36. (*ACM Operating Systems Review,* 9, 3, July 1975). Also INWG Protocol Note 4, October 1974.

[10] Y.K. Dalal, Estabishing a Connection, INWG Protocol Note 14, March 1975.

[11] A. Danthine and J. Bremer, Modeling and Verification of End-to-End Transport Protocol, *Proc. Symp. on Computer Network Protocols,* Liege, Belgium, February 1978.

[12] J.G. Fletcher and R.W. Watson, Mechanisms for a Reliable Timer-Based Protocol, *Proc. Symp. on Computer Network Protocols,* Liege, Belgium, February 1978.

[13] L.L. Garlick and R. Rom, Reliable Host-to-Host Protocols: Problems and Techniques, *Proc. Fifth Data Communications Symp.,* Snowbird, Utah, September 1977, pp. 4.58–4.65. (IEEE 77CH1260–9C).

[14] M.G. Gouda and E.G. Manning, On the Modelling, Analysis, and Design of Protocols – A Special Class of Software Structures, *Proc. Int. Conf. on Software Engineering,* October 1976, pp. 256–262.

[15] S.T. Kent, Encryption Based Protection for Interactive User/Computer Communication, *Proc. Fifth Data Communications Symp.,* Snowbird, Utah, September 1977, pp. 5.7–5.13.

[16] P.M. Merlin and D.J. Farber, Recoverability of Communication Protocols – Implications of a Theoretical Study, *IEEE Trans. Communications,* September 1976, pp. 1036–1043.

[17] R.M. Metcalfe, Packet Communication, MIT Project MAC Report TR-114, December 1973. (PhD Thesis, Harvard Univ.)

[18] J.B. Postel and D.J. Farber, Graph Modeling of Computer Communications Protocols, *Proc. Fifth Texas Conf. on Computing Systems,* Austin, Texas, October 1976, pp. 66–77.

[19] D.P. Reed, The Initial Connection Mechanism in DSP, MIT Lab for Computer Science LNN 10, August 1977.

[20] H. Rudin, C.H. West, and P. Zafiropulo, Automated Protocol Validation: One Chain of Development, *Proc. Symp. on Computer Network Protocols,* Liege, Belgium, February 1978.

[21] N.V. Stenning, A Data Transfer Protocol, *Computer Networks,* 1, 2, September 1976, pp. 99–110.

[22] C.A. Sunshine, Interprocess Communication Protocols for Computer Networks, Digital Systems Lab Technical Report No. 105, Stanford Univ., December 1975. (PhD Thesis).

[23] C.A. Sunshine, Survey of Communication Protocol Verification Techniques, *Proc. Symp. on Computer Networks: Trends and Applications,* Gaithersburg, Maryland, November 1976, pp. 24–26. (IEEE 76CH1143–7C).

[24] R.S. Tomlinson, Selecting Sequence Numbers, *Proc. ACM SIGCOM/SIGOPS Interprocess Communications Workshop,* Santa Monica, California, March 1975, pp. 11–23. (*ACM Operating Systems Review,* Vol. 9, No. 3, July 1975) Also INWG Protocol Note No. 2, August 1974.

[25] D.C. Walden, A System for Interprocess Communication in a Resource Sharing Computer Network, *Comm. ACM* 15, 4, April 1972, pp. 221–230.

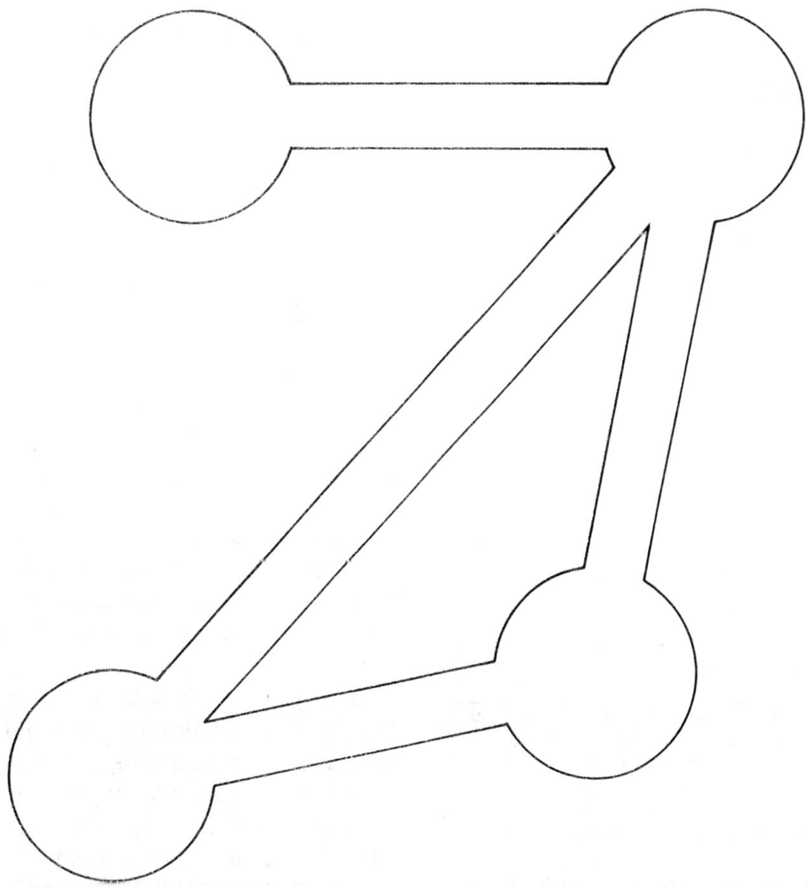

"Using Encryption for Authentication in Large Networks of Computers" by R.M. Needham and M.D. Schroeder from *Communications of the ACM*, Volume 21, Number 12, December 1978, pages 993-999. Copyright 1978, Association for Computing Machinery, Inc., reprinted by permission.

Operating Systems

R. Stockton Gaines Editor

Using Encryption for Authentication in Large Networks of Computers

Roger M. Needham and Michael D. Schroeder
Xerox Palo Alto Research Center

Use of encryption to achieve authenticated communication in computer networks is discussed. Example protocols are presented for the establishment of authenticated connections, for the management of authenticated mail, and for signature verification and document integrity guarantee. Both conventional and public-key encryption algorithms are considered as the basis for protocols.

Key Words and Phrases: encryption, security, authentication, networks, protocols, public-key cryptosystems, data encryption standard

CR Categories: 3.81, 4.31, 4.35

Introduction

In the context of secure computer communications, authentication means verifying the identity of the communicating principals to one another. A network in which a large number of computers communicate may have no central machine or system that contains authoritative descriptions of the connected computers, of the purposes for which they are used, or of the individuals who use them. We present protocols for decentralized authentication in such a network that are integrated with the allied subject of naming. There is minimal reliance on network-wide services; in particular there is no reliance on a single network clock or a single network name management authority.

Three functions are discussed:

(1) Establishment of authenticated interactive communication between two principals on different machines. By interactive communication we mean a series of messages in either direction, typically each in response to a previous one.

(2) Authenticated one-way communication, such as is found in mail systems, where it is impossible to require protocol exchanges between the sender and the recipient while sending an item, since there can be no guarantee that sender and recipient are simultaneously available.

(3) Signed communication, in which the origin of a communication and the integrity of the content can be authenticated to a third party.

Secure communication in physically vulnerable networks depends upon encryption of material passed between machines. We assume that it is feasible for each computer in the network to encrypt and decrypt material efficiently with arbitrary keys, and that these keys are not readily discoverable by exhaustive search or cryptanalysis. We consider both conventional encryption algorithms and public-key encryption algorithms as a basis for the protocols presented.

We assume that an intruder can interpose a computer in all communication paths, and thus can alter or copy parts of messages, replay messages, or emit false material. While this may seem an extreme view, it is the only safe one when designing authentication protocols.

We also assume that each principal has a secure environment in which to compute, such as is provided by a personal computer or would be by a secure shared operating system. Our viewpoint throughout is to provide authentication services to principals that choose to communicate securely. We have not considered the extra problems encountered when trying to force all communication to be performed in a secure fashion or when trying to prevent communication between particular principals in order to enforce restrictions on information flow.

Our protocols should be regarded as examples that expose the authentication issues in large networks rather than as fully engineered solutions to the overall security problems of a particular application. While providing an adequate solution to the authentication problems specified and meeting most common security objectives, our protocols would need elaboration to meet other security goals such as preventing traffic analysis, withholding all matching cleartext-ciphertext pairs from an eavesdrop-

Authors' present addresses: R.M. Needham, University of Cambridge Computer Laboratory, Corn Exchange Street, Cambridge, England; M.D. Schroeder, Xerox Palo Alto Research Center, 3333 Coyote Hill Road, Palo Alto, California 94304.

per, and ensuring instantaneous detection of tampering, and also to maximize efficiency in particular networks. It is possible to devise other protocols similar to those presented that also meet the stated objectives.

There is a modest amount of literature on our subject, and methods have been proposed for several of the individual functions we describe [1, 3, 5, 6], although no work is reported that integrates these techniques and applies them in a decentralized environment, or that provides functionally equivalent protocols based on both conventional and public-key encryption.

1. Encryption Algorithms

The important difference between conventional and public-key encryption algorithms is the way keys are used. With a conventional encryption algorithm, such as the NBS Data Encryption Standard [7], the same key is used for both encryption and decryption. Authentication depends upon the two participants in a conversation being the only two principals (apart possibly from trusted servers) who know the key that is being used to encrypt the transmitted material. With a public-key encryption algorithm, a concept originated by Diffie and Hellman [3], two keys are necessary: one that is used in the conversion of cleartext to ciphertext, and another that is used in the conversion of ciphertext to cleartext. Furthermore, knowledge of one key gives no help in finding the other, and the two keys will act as inverses for each other. Elegant systems may be devised in which each principal has one public key and one secret key. Anyone may encrypt a communication for A using his public key, but only A can decrypt the result using his secret key. Likewise, only A can encrypt messages that will decrypt sensibly with A's public key. The first example of a public-key encryption algorithm was devised by Rivest et al. [9], and others are sure to follow.

2. Authentication Servers

With both kinds of encryption the basis of authenticated communication is a secret key belonging to each principal using the network, and there is need for an authoritative source of information about these keys. We use the term *authentication server* for a server that can deliver identifying information computed from a requested principal's secret key.

Since the main database of an authentication server is indexed by name, the management of authentication servers is related to the management of names. In an extended network it is inexpedient to have a single central name registration authority, so we suppose that there are multiple naming authorities, each of which assigns and cancels names as it wishes. With this organization, principals have names of the form "NamingAuthority.SimpleName." Associated with each naming authority are one or more name lookup servers and one or more authentication servers.[1]

A name lookup server is prepared to provide various network addresses associated with a given SimpleName, for example, the address of that principal's mail system buffer. One or more instances of a master name lookup server will provide the network addresses of appropriate name lookup and authentication servers when given a naming authority's name. Authentication servers perform strikingly similar functions for the two classes of encryption algorithms; the differences will be brought out as they arise.

3. Means of Encryption

One significant issue in this area of study is where the encryption and decryption are done. Branstad [2] suggests that these actions take place in the network interface of a computer. It is a requirement of some of our protocols that the encryption be done elsewhere, because it is necessary to prepare an encrypted message without actually sending it yet or to receive an encrypted message without knowing at the network interface what the key is. Accordingly we have assumed that any hardware encryption aid is located so one can say

```
X := encrypt(Y, Key)
```

and still have X in hand, or say

```
if (X := decrypt(Y, Key1)) = nonsense
then X := decrypt(Y, Key2) fi
```

4. Protocols for Establishing Interactive Connections

Protocol 1. With Conventional Algorithms

If a conventional algorithm is used then each principal has a secret key that is known only to itself and to its authentication server, the contents of which are accordingly secret. The essential step in setting up secure communication between A and B is for the initiator, say A, to generate a message with two properties:

(a) It must be comprehensible only to B, i.e. allow only B to use its contents to identify himself to A.

(b) It must be evident to B that it originated with A.

The use of encryption to achieve these properties was first described by Feistel [4] and applied to a network context by Branstad [1].

[1] Naming authorities are independent of network topology; they need have nothing to do with subnetworks or with particular computers on the network. Multiple identical name lookup servers and authentication servers for a single naming authority may be used to make sure that these services are topologically "close" to those needing to use them, and to enhance reliability. Our multiple authentication servers must be carefully distinguished from those proposed by Diffie and Hellman [3], which perform the quite different function of checking one another. In that case every user is registered with every authenticator, the aim being to defend against corruption of particular authenticators.

Assuming for the moment that A and B are in the purview of the same authentication server AS, we now outline a protocol. The notation used will be followed throughout: encryption is indicated by braces that are superscripted with the key used.

The protocol opens with A communicating in clear to AS his own claimed identity and the identity of the desired correspondent, B, together with A's nonce identifier for this transaction, I_{A1}. ("Nonce" means "used only once.") Here the nonce identifier must be different than others used by A in previous messages of the same type. The first message of the protocol is:

$$A \rightarrow AS: \quad A, B, I_{A1} \tag{1.1}$$

Upon receiving message (1.1), AS looks up the secret, identifying keys of both parties and also computes a new key CK that will be the key for the conversation if all goes well.[2] The next transaction is a rather complicated message from AS to A:

$$AS \rightarrow A: \quad \{I_{A1}, B, CK, \{CK, A\}^{KB}\}^{KA} \tag{1.2}$$

where KA and KB are A's and B's secret, identifying keys. Because (1.2) is encrypted with A's secret key, only A can decrypt it and discover the conversation key CK. Following decryption, A checks for the presence of the intended recipient's name, B, and the correct identifier, I_{A1}, in order to verify that the message really is a reply by AS to the current enquiry. Both the name of the intended recipient and the transaction identifier must appear in message (1.2). If the recipient's name is left out, then an intruder could change that name in message (1.1), say to X, before AS receives it, with the subsequent result that A would unknowingly communicate with X instead of B. If the identifier is left out, then an intruder could substitute a previously recorded message (1.2) (from AS to A about B) and force A to reuse a previous conversation key.[3] A remembers CK and sends the part encrypted with KB to B:

$$A \rightarrow B: \quad \{CK, A\}^{KB} \tag{1.3}$$

The real B, but no other, will be able to decrypt message (1.3) and emerge with the conversation key CK, the same as A has. B also knows the identity of the intending correspondent, as authenticated by AS.

It is worth reviewing at this point the state of knowledge of the two parties. A now knows that any communication he receives encrypted with CK must have originated with B, and also that any communication he emits with CK encryption will be understood only by B. Both are known because the only messages containing CK that have ever been sent are tied to A's and B's secret keys. B is in a similar state, mutatis mutandis. It is important, however, to be sure that no part of the protocol exchange or ensuing conversation is being replayed by an intruder from a recording of a previous conversation between A and B. In relationship to this question the positions of A and B differ. A is aware that he has not used the key CK before and therefore has no reason to fear that material encrypted with it is other than the legitimate responses from B. B's position is not so good; unless he remembers indefinitely keys previously used by A in order to check that CK is new, he is unclear that the message (1.3) and the subsequent messages supposedly from A are not being replayed. To guard against this possibility, B generates a nonce identifier for the transaction, I_B, and sends it to A under CK:

$$B \rightarrow A: \quad \{I_B\}^{CK} \tag{1.4}$$

expecting a related reply, say one less:

$$A \rightarrow B: \quad \{I_B - 1\}^{CK} \tag{1.5}$$

If this reply is satisfactorily received, then the mutual confidence is sufficient to enable substantive communication, encrypted with CK, to begin.

There are five messages in protocol 1. The number may be reduced to three by A's keeping, for regular interaction partners, a cache of items of the form B: CK, $\{CK, A\}^{KB}$ derived from message (1.2), thus eliminating messages (1.1) and (1.2). Note however that, if such authenticators are cached, changes are needed to the protocol. With caching, the same CK is being used again and again, so the conversation identifier handshakes need to be two-way, for example, by replacing steps (1.3) and (1.4) with:

$$A \rightarrow B: \quad \{CK, A\}^{KB}, \{I_{A2}\}^{CK} \tag{1.3'}$$

$$B \rightarrow A: \quad \{I_{A2} - 1, I_B\}^{CK} \tag{1.4'}$$

The change does not increase the number of protocol messages but does alter the content slightly. In practice, messages (1.3)–(1.5) would be used to start a two-way seriation in order to ensure the integrity of the subsequent conversation. Methods for ensuring integrity following initial contact have been studied by Kent [5].

Protocol 2. With Public-Key Algorithms

We use key labels such as PKA for A's public key and SKA for his secret one. The exchange opens with A consulting the authentication server in the clear to find B's public key.

$$A \rightarrow AS: \quad A, B \tag{2.1}$$

AS responds with:

$$AS \rightarrow A: \quad \{PKB, B\}^{SKAS} \tag{2.2}$$

where $SKAS$ is the authentication server's secret key. A is presumed to know the AS's public key, $PKAS$, which is used to decrypt the message. A must obtain and store $PKAS$ in a reliable way, so he is sure it is correct. If an

[2] The new key must be unpredictable and should never have been used before.

[3] Also note that messages (1.1) and (1.2) together, and others in our protocols, make available known plaintext encrypted with a principal's identifying key. If there is concern about cryptanalytic attack based on known plaintext being used to expose an identifying key, then an additional temporary key TK may be used where appropriate throughout, so that $\{X\}^{KA}$ becomes $\{TK\}^{KA}\{X\}^{TK}$.

intruder somehow could provide an arbitrary value that A thinks is $PKAS$, then that intruder could impersonate AS.

The importance of the reciprocity between the public and secret keys is shown here. Encryption of message (2.2) is required not to ensure the *privacy* of the information but to ensure its *integrity*. It is important that A should be sure that he is getting PKB rather than the public key of some miscreant. A knows that the name of the intended recipient, B, was correctly communicated to AS because that name is returned in message (2.2).

The next step is for the communication with B to be initiated:

$$A \rightarrow B: \quad \{I_A, A\}^{PKB} \tag{2.3}$$

This message, which can only be understood by B, indicates that someone purporting to be A wishes to establish communication, and secretly communicates a nonce identifier, I_A, generated by A. B decrypts the message with his secret key and then finds PKA with steps similar to (2.1) and (2.2):

$$B \rightarrow AS: \quad B, A \tag{2.4}$$

$$AS \rightarrow B: \quad \{PKA, A\}^{SKAS} \tag{2.5}$$

Message (2.5) is encrypted for integrity, as was (2.2), not for secrecy. At this point a double handshake is needed to authenticate A and B to one another and to establish the time integrity of the conversation. The handshake is completed as steps (2.6) and (2.7):

$$B \rightarrow A: \quad \{I_A, I_B\}^{PKA} \tag{2.6}$$

$$A \rightarrow B: \quad \{I_B\}^{PKB} \tag{2.7}$$

There are thus seven steps in this protocol as against five with protocol 1, but four of them (2.1, 2.2, 2.4, and 2.5) can be done away with by A and B both having local caches of commonly used public keys. The resulting three protocol steps have very similar purposes to the three remaining after caching in protocol 1.

Observe that, because public keys are not secret, double encryption, i.e. $\{\{message\}^{SKA}\}^{PKB}$, or some equivalent is required during the course of the ensuing interaction. If the data were simply encrypted with the public key of the recipient, then anyone else could inject material into the stream. An equivalent safeguard is to use an arbitrary number from a large space as the base for seriation of encryption blocks. This number may be initialized as I_A or I_B according to direction. An intruder would have no way of knowing what was the correct serial to insert in a forged packet, even if he had counted previous packets, since he could not know the correct base. The more bits that are devoted to this redundant seriation the fewer good data bits we get per unit decryption effort.

5. Multiple Authentication Servers

In the protocols just given we assumed that A and B were clients of the same authentication server. This restriction is not necessary, and we now remove it. When extending the protocols we must bear in mind that, while an authentication server must be regarded as the final authority for its clients, it must be able to have no effect for good or ill on communication between clients of other authentication servers. Then our system will not be upset completely by the conduct of a shoddy authenticator. Of course, outsiders will show circumspection on a human level in their dealings with a shoddy authenticator's clients.

The effects on the protocols of multiple authentication servers differ somewhat between the two encryption techniques. Consider first the case of conventional encryption. The requirement is still to produce an item of the form $\{CK, A\}^{KB}$ for A to use when making his first approach to B (see step (1.3)). To produce this quantity both authentication servers (which will be called AS_A and AS_B) are involved, since only AS_B can produce items encrypted with KB and only AS_A can produce items encrypted with KA. We find two more steps between (1.1) and (1.2), which constitute an interchange between the two servers. We suppose that separate measures have been taken to ensure secure communication between the servers—for example, their secret keys are held by a master server, and the regular servers establish secure links (by protocol 1 already given) whenever they come into operation. We also presume that names are, where necessary, always full "NamingAuthority.SimpleName" names, so that the correct authentication server can be located. As explained above, the knowledge of a naming authority's name leads to the network address of the associated authentication server.

$$AS_A \rightarrow AS_B: \quad CK, B, A, I_{A1} \tag{1.11}$$

$$AS_B \rightarrow AS_A: \quad \{CK, A\}^{KB}, I_{A1}, A \tag{1.12}$$

(I_{A1} is transmitted to avoid retention of state in AS_A between messages (1.11) and (1.12).) Following (1.12) AS_A is in a position to complete the protocol.

In the public-key case, since no secret keys are moved around, it is possible for A to approach AS_B directly if A knows that server's public key. We assume that A already has this knowledge, though in a strict case of total ignorance there would be key lookup steps, for example, correspondence with a master authentication server, before (2.1). With the knowledge of $PKAS_B$, A corresponds directly with AS_B in steps (2.1) and (2.2). Likewise, with knowledge of $PKAS_A$, B corresponds directly with AS_A in (2.4) and (2.5).

In both cases caching can be expected to reduce the number of protocol messages to three.

6. Implementing Authentication Servers

There are differences in the implementation of authentication servers for the two varieties of encryption. In the conventional case the content of the database, items of the form $A{:}KA$, must be kept secret (which could be done by encrypting it with the secret, identifying key of the server). A secure transaction takes place every time the server is used: at step (1.2) the keys of both customers must be extracted in order to construct the message contents. By contrast, in the public-key case the content of the database need not be secret, and no secure transaction need take place when the server is used if the server's database is set up to contain items of the form A: $\{PKA, A\}^{SKAS}$ as required at step (2.2). (If the server contained the public keys directly, there would still be a secure operation at each use, for the reasons mentioned in the discussion of step (2.2).) With the public-key authentication server there still is a requirement for a secure computation, creating $\{PKA, A\}^{SKAS}$, but only when a new public key is registered, and this operation may be done outside the authentication server and the result added to the database in a nonsecure way. In practice, however, we suspect that the implementation of authentication servers would not differ as much as we have indicated, for reasons such as the need to prevent corruption of the public-key authentication server's data, which could prevent communication even though it will not lead to faulty authentication.

Note that with both encryption techniques the communications with servers can be done without the formalities of establishing what is usually called a "connection." The servers need never retain information about an ongoing transaction from one message to the next, so that repetition or loss of protocol packets does not matter. Only at step (1.11) does anything special have to be done to ensure lack of connection state. If this simplicity were lost, then the total cost of protocol exchanges would become higher.

7. One-Way Communication

In a computerized mail system it is impossible to depend upon interaction between the sender and the receiver in the course of each delivery. The mail is put into the hands of a transport mechanism and may be delivered later when the sender is no longer available. On the other hand, two-way authentication of sender and receiver is as desirable for mail as it is for interactive communication. Good design of a mail system would suggest that the mail transport mechanism not be part of the security system, and the proposals here meet that goal.

With Conventional Algorithms

Consider a message used in a previous protocol:

$$A \rightarrow B: \quad \{CK, A\}^{KB} \tag{1.3}$$

This message has the property that if it be put at the head of mail encrypted with CK, then the whole is self-authenticating both as to recipient and originator even though B played no part at all in the setting-up protocol. We assume that the subsequent individual blocks of the mail are securely seriated in, for example, the manner of Kent. The very fact of delay, however, causes special steps to be needed to ensure the time integrity of mail, i.e. that it has not been recorded by an intruder from an earlier transmission and repeated. We have avoided proposing the use of time-stamps elsewhere, because it presupposes a network-wide reliable source of time. Here there seems little alternative to the use of time-stamps; but it is possible to use them here without requiring a universal clock. A suitable technique is as follows. Each message has in its body a time-stamp indicating the time of sending. (Such a time-stamp is a normal part of most mail anyway.) The resolution needs to be fine enough that no two messages from the same source will have the same stamp. Any recipient, say B, maintains a register in which an entry of the form {*source, time-stamp*} is stored for each mail item received. A time interval T is associated with B. T is taken as an upper bound on clock asynchrony in the network and the interval between the time the mail was sent and the time of its arrival within B's security control, after which time the mail cannot be diverted. A mail item is rejected if either its {*source, time-stamp*} is on the register or its time-stamp predates the current time by more than T. The register is kept small by discarding entries older than T. T may vary dependent on B's activity if a message may only arrive in his security control when he is present.

With Public-Key Algorithms

The means of ensuring time integrity are identical in this case and will not be repeated. We have two alternative courses. With the first a header is sent that identifies A to B without using a handshake:

$$A \rightarrow B: \quad \{A, I, \{B\}^{SKA}\}^{PKB}$$

Here A denotes the sender and $\{B\}^{SKA}$ enables authentication by B of the identity of the sender using protocol transactions as at (2.4) and (2.5) (which may of course be short-cut by caching). I is a nonce identifier that is used to connect the header with the ensuing message text sent under the protection of PKB, with a time-stamp as above and with a secure seriation as discussed earlier. The connection between header and message provided explicitly by I in this protocol is provided implicitly by CK in the case of a conventional encryption algorithm.

The other way to handle mail using the public-key system achieves the additional function of signature and is described in the next section.

8. Digital Signatures

The previous protocols are designed to authenticate each communicant to the other. It is sometimes necessary to provide evidence to a third party that a particular communication is exactly as received from a particular sender. This requirement is met by signatures on paper documents. A common example is instructions from a superior to do something; the recipient needs to retain them as evidence that his actions were proper. To produce the analog of signed documents with messages, it is necessary that the recipient could not alter a signed text undetected and that the sender cannot credibly disclaim it. The ability to provide digital signatures depends upon there being something the originator can do which the recipient cannot.

Protocol 3. Signatures with Conventional Encryption and a Little Help.

One method uses a *characteristic function* of the cleartext message that is to be signed. The characteristic function must have the property that, given the cleartext message, the function, and the resulting characteristic value, it is hard to find another sensible cleartext message that produces the same characteristic value. It also is useful if the characteristic value is noticeably smaller than the cleartext message. Hard-to-invert transformations of the sort used to protect passwords [8] is a class of functions with the required properties.

While sending the text, say using the interactive or mail protocols described earlier, A computes the characteristic value CS. He then requests a *signature block* from the authentication server:

$$A \rightarrow AS: \quad A, \{CS\}^{KA} \tag{3.1}$$

which the server supplies:

$$AS \rightarrow A: \quad \{A, CS\}^{KAS} \tag{3.2}$$

Message 3.2 is encrypted with AS's key and therefore is accessible only to AS. Note that A cannot validate the message, but if it has been interfered with, then B subsequently will be unable to validate the signature, which he likely will do anyway before acting on the message if it contains instructions worthy of signature. A sends the signature block to B following the text to be signed.

On receipt B first decrypts the text and computes its characteristic value, CSC. B then communicates the signature block to the authentication server for decryption:

$$B \rightarrow AS: \quad B, \{A, CS\}^{KAS} \tag{3.3}$$

The server decrypts the signature block and returns its contents to B:

$$AS \rightarrow B: \quad \{A, CS\}^{KB} \tag{3.4}$$

If the returned CS matches CSC, then the principal named in (3.4) is the sender of the signed text. CSC not matching CS could mean that any of the steps (3.1)–(3.3), or the association of the signature block with the signed text, has been interfered with. Earlier detection of certain types of interference is possible by using nonce identifiers in transactions (3.1)–(3.2) and (3.3)–(3.4). If B wishes to retain the text as evidence, all he has to do is to retain the signature block and the text itself. In response to a challenge B would produce the text and the signature block for an arbiter who would go through the communication of steps (3.3) and (3.4).

The extension of protocol 3 to the case of multiple authentication servers is straightforward.

Signatures with Public-Key Encryption

It is possible to provide signed text with a public-key system using a characteristic function as above. The public key system, however, provides another, more elegant, method that was first described by Diffie and Hellman. The first steps are for A to find out B's public key from cache or server, as before. The successive blocks of text, seriated for time integrity, are doubly encrypted:

$$A \rightarrow B: \quad \{\{\textit{text-block}\}^{SKA}\}^{PKB}$$

B can carry out the first decryption because of knowing SKB, and the second because of being able to find out PKA by protocol exchange or from a cache. There is a need for header information to convey securely the identity of the originator so that PKA can be correctly sought. B is in no position to alter the content, since SKA is not available to him. When challenged, B simply performs the outer decryption on the whole text and passes the result to the arbiter who can use PKA to finish the job. Note that the ability of an arbiter to perform his function seems to depend on A not changing his key pair. Since such changes must be allowed as the only response to a key being compromised, it is necessary for the authentication server to retain a record of the old public keys of its principals and the time of the change, and for signed texts to contain the time that they were signed. An advantage of the signature protocol for conventional encryption algorithms is that an authentication server only need retain a record of changes to its own key to guarantee correct future arbitration.

9. Commentary

We conclude from this study that protocols using public-key cryptosystems and using conventional encryption algorithms are strikingly similar. The number of protocol messages exchanged is very comparable, the public-key system having a noticeable advantage only in the case of signed communications. As in many network applications of computers, caching is important to reduce transactions with lookup servers; this is particularly so with the public-key system. In that system we noticed also that there was a requirement for encryption of public data (the authentication server's database) in order to ensure its integrity. A consequence of the similarity of protocols is that any helpful tricks for the conventional system have analogs in the public-key system, though they may not be needed. Because of this, there may be scope for hybrid systems in which a public-key method may be used to establish an authenticated connection to be used conventionally. The intrinsic security requirements of a public-key authentication server are easier to meet than those of a conventional one, but a complete evaluation of the system problems in implementing such a server in a real system, and the need to retain a secure record of old public keys to guarantee future correct arbitration of old signatures may minimize this advantage. We conclude that the choice of technique should be based on the economy and cryptographic strength of the encryption techniques themselves, rather than for their effects on protocol complexity.

Finally, protocols such as those developed here are prone to extremely subtle errors that are unlikely to be detected in normal operation. The need for techniques to verify the correctness of such protocols is great, and we encourage those interested in such problems to consider this area.

Acknowledgments. We are indebted to a number of people who have read drafts of this paper and made careful and helpful comments, notably: Peter Denning, Stockton Gaines, Jim Gray, Steve Kent, Gerry Popek, Ron Rivest, Jerry Saltzer, and Robin Walker.

Received September 1977; revised April 1978; final revision May 1978

References

1. Branstad, D. Security aspects of computer networks, Proc. AIAA Comptr. Network Syst. Conf., April 1973, paper 73-427.

2. Branstad, D. Encryption protection in computer data communications. Proc. Fourth Data Communications Symp., Oct. 1975, pp. 8.1–8.7 (available from ACM, New York).

3. Diffie, W., and Hellman, M. Multiuser Cryptographic Techniques, Proc AFIPS 1976 NCC, AFIPS Press, Montvale, N.J., pp. 109–112.

4. Feistel, H. Cryptographic coding for data bank privacy. Res. Rep. RC2827, IBM T.J. Watson Res. Ctr., Yorktown Heights, N.Y., March 1970.

5. Kent, S. Encryption-based protection protocols for interactive user-computer communication, M.S. Th., EECS Dept., M.I.T., 1976; also available as Tech. Rep. 162, Lab. for Comptr. Sci., M.I.T., Cambridge, Mass., 1976.

6. Kent, S. Encryption-based protection for interactive user/computer communication. Proc. Fifth Data Communication Symp., Sept. 1977, pp. 5–7–5–13 (available from ACM, New York).

7. National Bureau of Standards. Data Encryption Standard. Fed. Inform. Processing Standards Pub. 46, NBS Washington, D.C., Jan. 1977.

8. Pohlig, S. Algebraic and combinatoric aspects of cryptography. Tech. Rep. No. 6602-1, Stanford Electron. Labs., Stanford, Calif., Oct. 1977.

9. Rivest, R.L., et al. A method for obtaining digital signatures and public-key cryptosystems. *Comm. ACM 21*, 2 (Feb. 1978), 120–126.

Chapter 7
Formal Methods for Protocol Verification and Construction

7.1. OVERVIEW OF MODELS AND METHODS

Numerous formal models and verification methods have been proposed and applied to the verification and construction of protocols. Excellent survey articles were written by Bochmann and Sunshine [BOCH 80] and Sunshine [SUNS 79]. ([SUNS 79] is reprinted below.) We mention a few of the models and methods below.

Stenning was one of the first to apply program verification techniques to the study of protocols. He proved some safety properties for a one-way data transfer protocol. His protocol gives a very good illustration of the window mechanism for error and sequence control and was specified using Pascal-like code. He formulated invariant safety assertions and proved them by induction [STEN 76].

Communicating finite state machines provide a different formalism for specifying protocols. With such a formalism, some realistic protocols have been shown to have certain desirable logical properties (e.g. freedom from deadlocks and unspecified receptions). The reader is referred to the articles in [WEST 78, ZAFI 80, RAZO 80]. In each case verification is carried out by a state-space exploration performed automatically by a program.

There were various attempts at protocol verification in a semi-automatic fashion. Brand and Joyner [BRAN 78] employed a program that can perform symbolic execution. DiVito [DIVI 83] employed automatic theorem provers.

To prove liveness properties of protocols, Hailpern and Owicki proposed the use of temporal logic [HAIL 80].

Instead of verifying that a given protocol has certain desirable properties, several researchers investigated methods to construct protocols that are guaranteed to have certain logical properties [ZAFI 80, MERL 83, GOUD 83b, CHOW 83].

7.2. STATE-SPACE REDUCTION METHODS

The concept of a layered architecture helps to delineate a network's functions into different layers and to organize the layers into a hierarchy. It is a step in the right direction toward a systematic approach for constructing software for a high-performance and reliable computer network. It is, however, a relatively small step toward that goal from the following observation. Each protocol layer in a typical layered architecture (ISO, SNA, ARPANET, etc.) when implemented would still be a highly complex set of parallel programs. Here, "complexity" is measured in terms of the current state of the art in the design of parallel programs whose logical behavior can be analyzed rigorously. In simpler terms, a protocol layer is complex because it typically has several functions (tasks) to perform. For example, the software for a basic data link layer in most architectures would have to implement at least three functions: connection management and two one-way data transfers in opposite directions.

A systematic approach does not exist for the construction of correct and efficient protocol systems comparable in complexity to that of a protocol layer. Typically, different abstractions of a protocol system are used for independently analyzing the behavior of different mechanisms in the system, that implement various protocol functions. As a result, logical correctness properties

EHO216-2/84/0000/0463$01.00

verified for "toy protocols," that are abstractions of a multifunction protocol system, may in fact be *invalid* for the protocol system itself if the abstractions have not been constructed to account for interactions between different mechanisms in the system.

The theory of projections was developed to reduce the analysis of a complex multifunction protocol to that of simpler single-function "image protocols" [LAM 82a, LAM 82b, LAM 82c]. Each image protocol is an abstraction of the given protocol but it is specified just like a real protocol. Each image protocol is of the same complexity as that of toy protocols that have been analyzed in the literature. The construction method guarantees that each image protocol is faithful in the sense that any logical correctness property, a safety or liveness property, that is valid for the image protocol must also be valid for the original protocol. ([LAM 82c] is reprinted below.) An application of the method of projections to verify a version of the HDLC protocol is presented in [SHAN 83].

In general, to reduce the problem of directly constructing a multifunction protocol to that of composing it from several single-function protocols is very difficult. However many real-life protocols can be observed to go through different phases, one at a time, performing a distinct function in each phase. A multiphase model for such protocols was developed in [CHOW 83, CHOW 84]. A phase is formally defined to be a network of communicating finite state machines with certain desirable correctness properties; these include proper termination and freedom from deadlocks and unspecified receptions. A multifunction protocol is constructed by first constructing separate phases to perform its different functions. Chow et al. presented a method to connect these phases together to implement the multifunction protocol such that the resulting network of communicating finite state machines is also a phase (i.e., it possesses the desirable properties defined for phases). We reprint [CHOW 84] below.

The method of closed covers presented by Gouda [GOUD 83a] is another state-space reduction approach. This method can provide finite representations of some protocols whose reachable states are unbounded. This approach was also used to formulate algorithms for detecting livelocks in networks of communicating finite state machines [GOUD 84].

7.3. MODELING OF TIME-DEPENDENT PROTOCOLS

Time-dependent systems are those whose correct functioning depends upon certain time relationships between system event occurrences [SHAN 82]. Most real-life communication protocols are time-dependent systems. Time relationships are widely used in protocol systems to provide concurrency control and to guarantee the ordering of certain remote events [ESWA 81, FRAT 83]. When used properly, they can simplify a protocol and make it more efficient by reducing the amount of handshaking required in reaching an agreement [WATS 81].

A model for representing time-dependent systems is presented in [SHAN 84] together with inference rules for proving safety and progress properties. [SHAN 84], reprinted below, is written specially for this tutorial text.

References

[BOCH 80] Bochmann, G. V. and C. A. Sunshine, "Formal Methods in Communication Protocol Design," *IEEE Trans. on Commun.*, April, 1980.

[BRAN 78] Brand, D. and W. H. Joyner, "Verification of Protocols using Symbolic Execution," *Computer Networks*, September/October, 1978.

[CHOW 83] Chow, C. H., M. G. Gouda and

S. S. Lam, "A Discipline for Constructing Multi-Phase Communication Protocols," Dept. of Computer Sciences, University of Texas at Austin, Tech. Rep. TR-233, June 1983 (revised October 1983).

*[CHOW 84] Chow, C. H., M. G. Gouda and S. S. Lam, "An Exercise in Constructing Multi-phase Communication Protocols," *Proc. ACM SIGCOMM '84*, Montreal, June 1984.

[DIVI 83] DiVito, B. L., "Mechanical Verification of a Data Transport Protocol," *Proc. ACM SIGCOMM '83 Symp.*, University of Texas at Austin, March 1983, pp. 30-37.

[ESWA 81] Eswaran, K. P., G. S. Shedler, and U. C. Hamacher, "Collision-Free Access Control for Computer Communication Bus Networks," *IEEE Trans. on Software Eng.*, November 1981.

[FRAT 83] Fratta, L., "An Improved Access Protocol for Data Communication Bus Networks with Control Wire," *Proc. ACM SIGCOMM '83* Symposium, Univ. of Texas at Austin, March 1983, pp. 219-225.

[GOUD 83a] Gouda, M. G., "Closed Covers: To Verify Progress for Communicating Finite State Machines," TR-191, Dept. of Computer Sciences, Univ. of Texas at Austin, January 1982. Revised January 1983. To appear in *IEEE Trans. on Software* Engineering.

[GOUD 83b] Gouda, M. G. and Y. T. Yu, "Synthesis of Communicating Machines with Guaranteed Progress," TR-179, Dept. of Computer Sciences, Univ. of Texas at Austin, June 1981. Revised January 1983. Revised October 1983. To appear in *IEEE Trans. on Commun.*

[GOUD 84] Gouda, M. G., C. H. Chow and S. S. Lam, "Livelock Detection in Networks of Communicating Finite State Machines," Dept. of Computer Sciences, University of Texas at Austin, Tech. Rep. TR-84-10, March 1984.

[HAIL 80] Hailpern, B. T. and S. S. Owicki, "Verifying Network Protocols using Temporal Logic," Technical Report 192, Computer Systems Laboratories, Stanford Univ., June, 1980.

[LAM 82a] Lam, S. S. and A. U. Shankar, "Verification of Communication Protocols via Protocol Projections," *Proc. INFOCOM '82*, IEEE Computer Society Press, April 1982, Las Vegas.

[LAM 82b] Lam, S. S. and A. U. Shankar, "An Illustration of Protocol Projections," *Proc. 2nd Int. Workshop on Protocol Specification, Testing and Verification*, Idyllwild, Calif., North-Holland Publishing Co., Amsterdam, 1982.

*[LAM 84] Lam, S. S. and A. U. Shankar, "Protocol Verification via Projections," *IEEE Trans. on Software Engineering*, Vol. SE-10, No. 4, July 1984, pp. 325-342.

[MERL 83] Merlin, P. M. and G. V. Bochmann, "On the Construction of Submodule Specifications and Communication Protocols," *ACM TOPLAS*, Vol. 5, No. 1, January 1983, pp. 1-25.

[RAZO 80] Razouk, R. and G. Estrin, "Modeling and Verification of Communication Protocols in SARA: The X.21 Interface," *IEEE Trans. on Comput.*, December 1980.

[SHAN 82] Shankar, A. U. and S. S. Lam, "On

Time-Dependent Communication Protocols and their Projections," *Proc. 2nd Int. Workshop on Protocol Specification, Testing and Verification*, Idyllwild, Calif., North-Holland Publishing Co., Amsterdam, 1982.

[SHAN 83] Shankar, A. U. and S. S. Lam, "An HDLC Protocol Specification and its Verification using Image Protocols," *ACM Trans. on Computer* Systems, November 1983.

*[SHAN 84] Shankar, A. U. and S. S. Lam, "Time-Dependent Communication Protocols," Technical Report TR-84-26, Department of Computer Sciences, the University of Texas at Austin, 1984.

[STEN 76] Stenning, N. V., "A Data Transfer Protocol," *Computer networks*, September, 1976.

*[SUNS 79] Sunshine, C., "Formal Techniques for Protocol Specification and Verification," *Computer*, Vol. 12, No. 9, IEEE, September 1979, pp. 20-27.

[WATS 81] Watson, R. W., "Timer-Based Mechanisms in Reliable Transport Protocol Connection," *Computer Networks*, Vol. 5, No. 1, February 1981, pp. 47-56.

[WEST 78] West, C. H. and P. Zafiropulo, "Automated Validation of a Communications Protocol: The CCITT X.21 Recommendation," *IBM Journal of Res. and Develop.*, January, 1978.

[ZAFI 80] Zafiropulo, P., "Towards Analyzing and Synthesizing Protocols," *IEEE Trans. on Commun.*, Vol. COM-28, April 1980, pp. 651-661.

(* article reprinted below.)

Reprinted from *Computer*, September 1979, pages 20-26. Copyright © 1979 by The Institute of Electrical and Electronics Institute, Inc.

Certain formal approaches, such as transition techniques and reachability analysis, show promising results when applied to protocol specification and verification.

Formal Techniques for Protocol Specification and Verification

Carl Sunshine
The Rand Corporation

Communication protocols play an important role in computer networks and distributed systems. The increasing variety and complexity of such protocols demand more powerful techniques to produce successful systems. This article describes some of the more formal techniques which have been brought to bear on this requirement. We focus on two key problem areas—protocol specification and verification of logical correctness. Methods for analyzing the efficiency of protocols have been discussed elsewhere.[1-4]

As protocols are developed, designers must provide descriptions of them for many purposes. Initial descriptions provide a central frame of reference allowing cooperation among designers of different parts of a protocol system. Descriptions also play a role in the verification process. The design must be checked for logical correctness. Then the protocol must be implemented, and if it is in wide use, many different implementations may have to be checked for compliance with a standard. Although narrative descriptions and informal walk-throughs are invaluable elements of this process, painful experience has shown that by themselves they are inadequate to handle all but the simplest protocols.

A great deal of confusion surrounds the words "specification" and "verification" as they apply to computer communication protocols. Hence our first goal will be the definition of these concepts in the context of a layered model of protocols. Next, an overview of various approaches emphasizes the use of more formal specification and verification techniques. We conclude by reviewing some recent applications of these techniques, and suggesting some directions for future work.

A protocol system model

From the user's point of view, a protocol provides a certain set of services allowing interaction of various sorts with other users. (We will restrict our consideration to interactions between a pair of users, although most of the concepts are applicable to multi-user protocols.) Different protocols provide different services, such as general data transfer or terminal support. The user is concerned with the nature of the service, but not with how the protocol manages to provide it. Hence we may view the protocol as a "black box" (Figure 1) whose service is fully described by the allowable sequences of inputs from and outputs to each user.

This description of the protocol (as the input/output behavior of a "protocol machine") constitutes a *service specification* of the protocol. It should be "abstract" in the sense that it describes the types of commands and their effects but leaves open the exact format and means for conveying them (e.g., procedure calls, system calls, interrupts, etc.) A particular implementation of the service specification which does bind all these decisions may be called an *interface specification.*

Although the protocol machine's internal structure is irrelevant to the user, the protocol designer must be concerned with it. In a network environment with physically separated users, the protocol machine must be implemented in a distributed fashion, with *stations* local to each user communicating among themselves via a *transmission machine* (Figure 2). The interaction among stations constitutes the actual *protocol.* We can immediately recognize a recur-

EHO216-2/84/0000/0467$01.00 © 1979 IEEE

sive situation in which the stations use the transmission machine just as the users use the protocol machine.

In general, there may be multiple protocol layers, each using the layer underlying itself until a lowest layer (which is actually implemented as a single machine) is reached. Considering a general layer N, we have an *N-service specification* describing the abstract service provided to layer $N+1$ users. Within layer N, the service is provided by the interaction of layer N stations (entities) distributed among different systems, according to an *N-protocol*. The layer N entities use the services provided by layer $N-1$ to support their interactions. Within each system, the specific means for invoking layer N services may differ, and is described by an *N-interface specification* derived from the N-service specification.

This model (and its terminology) is similar to earlier models of protocol hierarchies; it is consistent with the model for open systems interconnection being developed within ISO.[5] It clarifies the concepts of specification and verification.

Specification

In the broadest sense, specification refers to any information that helps describe an object. However, its proper engineering usage is much narrower, involving the key concept of abstraction. A specification should state all the requirements that an object must satisfy, *and no more*. To be abstract, it must separate the essential from the inessential, covering the former and omitting the latter. Hence a program, even in a "high-level language," is usually not a satisfactory specification because it is impossible to separate the essential features of the program's functions from the particular way chosen to accomplish those functions.[6]

In the model described above, there are three required specifications in each layer N of a protocol hierarchy:

- The *N-service specification* describes what services the layer N protocol machine provides for its layer $N+1$ users. It is abstract primarily in the sense that it does not describe how this service is accomplished (i.e., the interactions among the N-entities), and secondarily in the sense that it defines only the generic form of the interaction with $N+1$ users.
- The *N-interface specification* is derived from the N-service specification, and eliminates its secondary aspect of abstraction by defining the particular form of interaction between $N+1$ users and the N-protocol machine within a given system.
- The *N-protocol specification* describes the interaction of the N-entities comprising the N-protocol machine. It is abstract primarily in the sense that it only describes the required interactions of N-entities and not how an N-entity works internally (i.e., the program for a protocol module). It does define the exact types and formats for the interactions. It is abstract secondarily in the sense that it defines the interactions of N-entities in terms of the abstract services provided to layer $N+1$ users and the services available from layer $N-1$, rather than in terms of particular interfaces.

Verification

Having defined specification and having identified the objects requiring specification at each layer, we can now discuss the various aspects of verification. In general, verification is a demonstration that an object or system has certain properties or behaves in a certain way. This requires a clear statement of the properties or behavior to be verified—in short, a specification. Verification is simply a demonstration that an object meets its specifications. Because a specification is abstract, there are many ways in which we can design an object to meet its specification.

Applying this to the protocol model, we see that it is meaningless to talk about "verifying" a service specification. Rather, the service specification is the standard against which we are to verify the entities

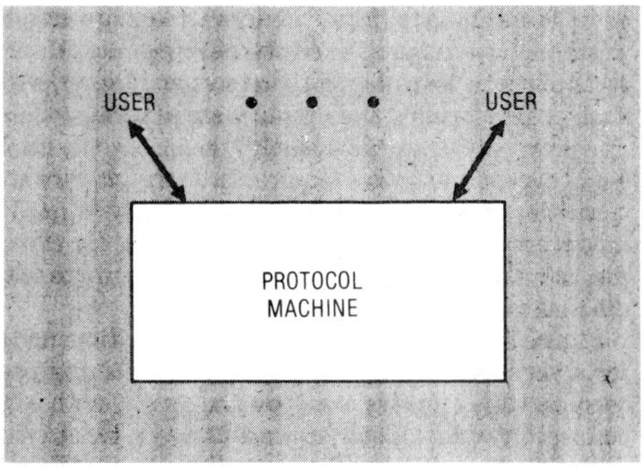

Figure 1. User view of protocol.

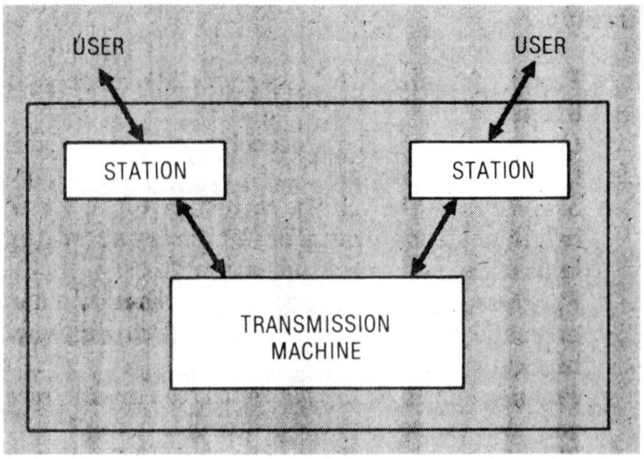

Figure 2. Internal structure of protocol machine.

providing the service. Nevertheless, we have the intuitive idea that the service specification should reflect the users' "real" needs and desires, and should provide an adequate basis for the higher-level protocols using it. Unfortunately, techniques for determining whether specifications properly capture human intentions are still poorly understood. Some checks of service specifications for syntax, consistency, or feasibility are possible.[7]

Most of the work on formal specification of protocols has focused on the protocol itself and not on the service it provides.

Protocol verification is a demonstration that the interactions of distributed protocol modules, according to the protocol specification, do indeed satisfy the service specification. This constitutes a determination that the protocol is "logically" correct. In other words, the logical *design* of the protocol, as given in the (abstract) protocol specification, is correct in the sense that it meets the service specification. It does *not* mean that a particular implementation of the protocol specification (e.g., a program for a transport station) is correct. (We shall return to this problem.)

It is important to note that protocol verification also depends on the properties of the lower-layer protocol. The N-protocol specification is only a partial specification in that it leaves some actions undefined, namely those given by the layer $N-1$ service specification. In verifying that a layer N protocol meets its service specification, it will be necessary to assume the properties of the layer $N-1$ service. Hence verification of the N-protocol rests on the ($N-1$)-protocol meeting its service specification. If an N-protocol is shown not to meet its service specification, the problem may rest either in the protocol itself or in the service provided by the lower layer.

Several authors have noted that protocol verification (as described above) has two aspects. First, there are a number of "general" properties, applicable to all or nearly all protocols, that may be considered to form implicit parts of all service specifications. These include:

- Freedom from *deadlock* (or the related concept of liveness).[8]
- *Completeness* of the protocol to handle all conditions that may arise.[9]
- *Stability*, or the ability to return to "normal" behavior after an initial or temporary aberration (also called self-synchronization).[8]
- *Progress*, or the absence of cyclic behavior where no useful activity takes place[8] (also called tempo blocking.[10]
- *Freedom* from *overflow* (with too many messages) of the service the protocol is using.[9]
- *Termination* or arrival at the desired final situation.[10]

Because these properties are general, it is possible to "verify" a protocol with respect to these properties without having any particular specification of what services the protocol is supposed to provide. This subproblem of the overall verification problem has been termed "validation," and has been compared to the syntax checks or run-time checks performed by compilers.[9] This aspect of verification has proved more amenable to automation, since it is based on a straightforward reachability exploration of the protocol's behavior (see below).

To fully verify a protocol, it is necessary to have a complete service specification of what it is supposed to do. We can regard this as verifying the protocol's "semantics"—generally a difficult task.

Another problem involves determining whether a particular protocol implementation complies with the (abstract) protocol specification. This is a valid verification problem since there is a definite protocol specification against which to check the implementation. We shall call this *implementation verification* as opposed to the *design verification* described above. While the design need only be verified once, every implementation must be verified against the design.

Current approaches to specification

Since we can view protocols simply as a particular type of program, much software engineering work is relevant.[7] Indeed, much of the viewpoint here is taken from that domain. Unfortunately, comprehensive software development techniques are just beginning to be applied to protocols.

Most of the work on formal specification of protocols has focused on the protocol itself and not on the service it provides. A number of formalisms have been used, including flow charts, programming languages, state diagrams, state transition matrices, L-systems, formal grammars, colloquies, Petri nets, and "structured English." Bochmann[11] provides examples of several of these techniques. Generally, they may be classified as either transition techniques or programming language techniques.

Transition techniques grew out of the observation that protocols consist largely of relatively simple processing activities in response to numerous "events" such as commands (from the user), message arrival (from the lower layer), and internal timeouts. Hence state machine formalisms of one sort or another, with such events forming their inputs, are natural models. For protocols of any complexity, however, the number of events and states required in a straightforward transition formalism becomes unworkably large. To model a protocol using sequence numbers, for example, there must be different states and events to handle each possible sequence number.

Figure 3 illustrates a typical state transition model for a very simple pair of sending and receiving protocol modules. States are shown as ovals, with arcs connecting them. Each arc represents a transition, with the event causing the transition shown above a line and the resulting output (if any) below.

Programming language techniques arose out of the observation that protocols are simply one type of algorithm, and that high-level programming languages provide a clear and relatively concise means of describing algorithms. This approach to specification may be quite near to an implementation of the protocol, depending on how high level and abstract a language is. As noted earlier, such nearness is a mixed blessing, since programs often combine unessential features with the essential algorithm. This approach's major advantage over pure state machine techniques is the ease it provides in handling variables and parameters—they may take on a large number of values, e.g., sequence numbers and timers.

A number of hybrid techniques which attempt to combine the advantages of state models and programs have been proposed.[12-14] These typically employ a small state model to capture only the main features of the protocol, e.g., connection establishment, resets, interrupts. This state model is then augmented with additional "context" variables and processing routines for each state. In such hybrid systems, the actions to be taken are determined by using parameters from the inputs and values of the context variables, according to the processing routine for each major state. For example, the sequence number of an arriving message may be compared with a variable giving the next expected sequence number; this determines whether the message should be accepted and what the next state should be. Bochmann[14] has demonstrated the potential for trading off the complexity of the state model with the amount of context information for a given protocol.

Common to all techniques is the problem of handling the complexity of real protocols so they may be understood, analyzed, and implemented. As in other areas, the divide and conquer strategy is frequently used. The division of protocol systems into layers serves this purpose. Further divisions within a layer—either lateral or vertical—may also be possible. An example of the former might be separate modules for handling user commands and incoming messages, or for sending and receiving. An example of vertical or hierarchical decomposition might be a module for bit stuffing within a module forming checksums within the frame-sending module of HDLC.

Current approaches to verification

Approaches to protocol verification have followed the two main paths of formal specification—reachability analysis for transistion models and program proofs for program models. This article's scope allows us only to outline these two approaches. The references cited in "Results to date" (below) provide more details about particular techniques, while others[11,15-17] provide a wider survey.

Reachability analysis involves the exhaustive exploration of all the possible interactions of two (or more) protocol machines. A composite or global system state is defined as a combination of the states of both the cooperating protocol machines and the transmission media connecting them. From a given initial state, all possible transitions (user commands, timeouts, message arrivals) are generated, leading to a number of new global states. This process is repeated for each of the newly generated states until no new states are generated (some transitions lead back to already generated states). Figure 4 shows such a global state reachability graph for the simple protocol of Figure 3, assuming a perfect transmission medium. For a given initial state and set of assumptions about the underlying protocol (the type of service it offers), this type of analysis determines all the possible outcomes the protocol may achieve.

Reachability analysis is well-suited to checking the general "correctness" properties described earlier because these properties are a direct consequence of the structure of the reachability graph. Global states

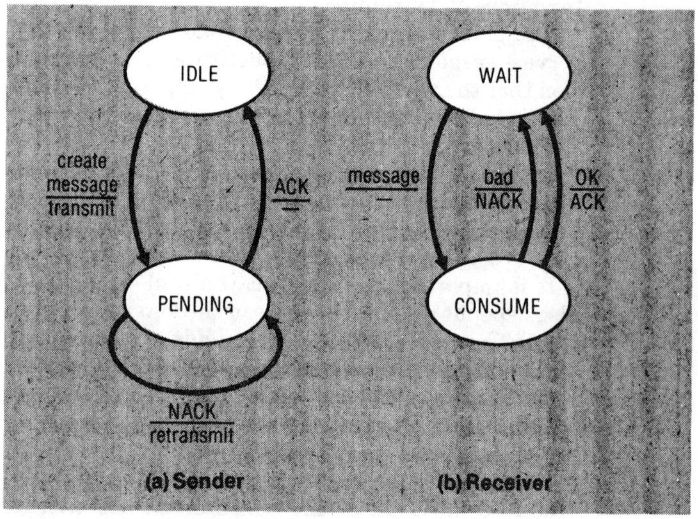

Figure 3. State transition model of simple protocol.

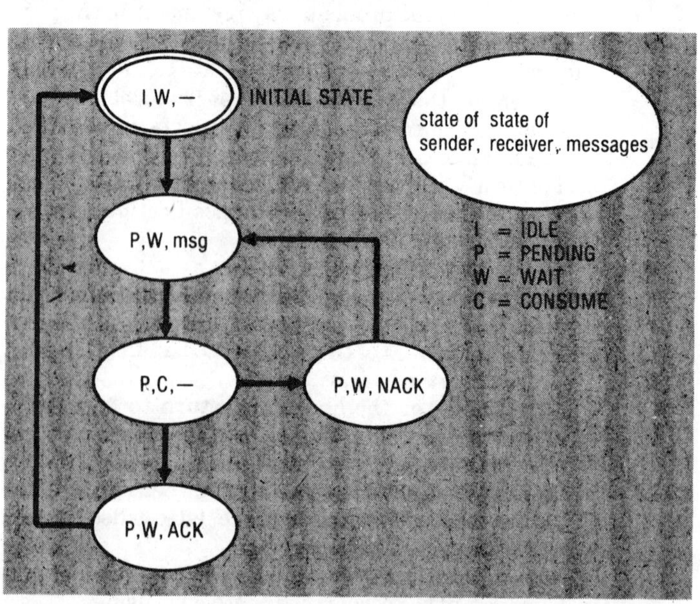

Figure 4. Composite state model for protocol of Figure 3.

with no exits are either deadlocks or desired termination states. Similarly, situations in which the processing for a received message is not defined or in which the transmission medium capacity is exceeded are easily detected. Global state space generation is easily automated and several computer-aided systems for this purpose have been developed.[9,10,13,18] The major difficulty of this technique is "state explosion"—the size of the reachability graph typically grows rapidly with protocol complexity, making it impossible to generate and check all reachable states in reasonable time or storage.

We can view symbolic execution[19] as a form of reachability analysis that attempts to reduce state explosion. It does so by creating a reachability graph with symbolic states that may represent large classes of explicit situations. For example, instead of explicitly treating all possible values of a sequence counter variable as different states, it may be possible to consider only the three conditions in which the variable is "less than," "equal to," or "greater than" some symbolic value. The reachability graph is smaller, but the symbolic interpretation of the interacting protocol machines needed to derive it is more difficult.

The program proving approach involves the usual formulation of assertions reflecting the desired correctness properties. Ideally, these would be supplied by the service specification, but as noted above, services have not been rigorously defined in most protocol work; the verifier must therefore formulate appropriate assertions on his own. The basic task is then to show (prove) that the protocol program satisfies the high-level assertions. This often requires formulation of additional low-level assertions at appropriate places in the program.[20,21]

A major strength of this approach is its ability to deal with the full range of protocol properties to be verified rather than only general properties. Ideally, any property for which an appropriate assertion can be formulated can be verified, but formulation and proof often require a great deal of ingenuity. Only modest progress has been made to date in the automation of this process.

While a large body of work on general program proof exists, several characteristics of protocols pose special difficulties for protocol proofs. These include concurrency of multiple protocol modules and physical separation of modules, the latter preventing the use of shared variables. A further complication is that message exchange between modules may be unreliable. A few early applications of general program proof work to protocols are cited in "Results" (below).

As with specification, a hybrid approach promises to combine the advantages of both techniques. By using a state model for the major states of the protocol, the state space is kept small and the general properties can be checked by an automated analysis. Other properties, for which a state model would be awkward (e.g., sequenced delivery), can be handled by assertion proofs for the variables and procedures accompanying the state model. Such combined techniques are described in the literature.[13,14]

Two other techniques used as forms of protocol verification are simulation and testing. In simulation the protocol design is exercised much as in state exploration, with the key difference that the exploration is incomplete and only some of the possible interactions are explored.[1,2] In testing, an actual implementation of the protocol is exercised with selected sequences of inputs, usually for purposes of comparing its behavior with the desired behavior specified in a test procedure.[22,23] Running two protocol implementations against each other is another common form of testing, but responsibility for any unexpected behavior must be traced to one (or both) of the implementations. Both simulation and testing may find important flaws, but they cannot guarantee that all errors have been eliminated.

When an error is found by some verification technique, the cause must still be determined. The cause may be transitions or program statements removed when an error is found—for example, the acceptance of a duplicate packet at the receiver may be caused by the too rapid reuse of a sequence number at the sender. In some cases the protocol may be incorrectly modeled or the correctness conditions may be incorrectly formulated. In other cases, undesirable behavior may be due to transmission medium properties not accounted for when the protocol was designed (e.g., reordering of messages in transit). Even when an automated verification system is available, considerable human ingenuity is required to understand and repair any errors that are discovered.

Results to date

Despite some of the limitations discussed above, considerable progress has been made in using formal techniques on real world protocols of significant complexity. A number of applications of these techniques to the specification, verification, and implementation of such protocols are noteworthy.

Protocol specification. The HDLC link protocol has been specified with a regular grammar model[24] incorporating an indexing technique to accommodate sequence numbering. The same protocol has also been specified with a hybrid model combining state transitions with context variables and procedures.[25] The latter technique employs decomposition to partition the protocol into seven separate components.

IBM's SNA has been specified with a hybrid model using state machines augmented by context information and processing routines.[26,27] The model uses hierarchical decomposition to create a large number of more manageable modules.

The transport protocol for the French Cyclades network has been specified with a hybrid model using state machines augmented by context information and processing routines.[28]

Protocol verification. Call establishment in the CCITT X.21 protocol has been modeled with a state transition model and analyzed with a form of reachability analysis.[29] The analysis checked for the general correctness properties of completeness and deadlock, and uncovered a number of completeness errors, (i.e., a protocol module received a message for which no processing was defined).

Virtual circuit establishment in the CCITT X.25 protocol has been modeled with a state transition model and analyzed with a manual reachability analysis.[8] The analysis showed that the CCITT specification was ambiguous, and that several cycles with no useful progress could persist if the protocol once entered certain unsynchronized states.

Connection establishment in the transport protocol for the Arpanet (TCP[30]) has been partially modeled with a hybrid state transition model and validated with a manual reachability analysis.[12] An automated reachability analysis[10] was also used on a simplified model and revealed both an error in sequence number handling and incorrect modeling of the transmission medium.[31]

A general-purpose data transfer protocol has been modeled with a high-level program language and verified using manual program proving techniques.[20,21] (However, Hajek[10] has identified several flaws in the verification in Bochmann.[21]) The protocol included window-based flow control and a large but finite sequence number space.

A simple data transfer protocol has been analyzed with a transition model augmeted with time constraints.[32] This model shows that proper data transfer requires certain time constraints to be maintained between retransmission, propagation, and processing times.

A simplified version of the Arpanet communications subsystem has been modeled with a high-level progamming language and verified using partially automated program proving techniques.[7,33] Program modules can be either comprehensively verified in advance or checked against their specifications at run time for the particular inputs which occur. A complete software engineering system called Gypsy supports the design process from specification to implementation.

Connection establishment between a requester and a shared server process (the Arpanet Initial Connection Protocol) has been modeled with a state transition model and analyzed with an automated reachability analysis.[18] The analysis showed that one of a pair of simultaneous requests for service might be rejected. A revised version of the protocol was shown to eliminate this error. The same analysis technique was also used to validate a simple data transfer protocol.

Protocol implementation. A basic data transfer protocol has been specified using a formal language model, BNF, to describe both the syntax of interactions between protocol modules and the detailed structure of individual messages.[34] This specification may be directly used to drive a "recognizer" for the language (protocol). Additional processing routines to perform the "semantics" of the protocol must be added to the grammar-driven recognizer.

A simple link protocol has been specified with a specialized flow chart type model. This model also provides a means for automatically converting the flowcharts to equivalent data and control networks directly realizable in hardware.[35]

The Gypsy system[7] mentioned above provides a unified language for expressing both specifications and programs; high-level design specifications can therefore be progressively refined into detailed programs. A management system maintains the implementation and verification status of all system components under development.

Both the link and packet level of X.25 have been specified with a hybrid model like that described in Bochmann and Chung.[25] An approach for manually converting such protocol specifications into an implementation in Concurrent Pascal has been developed.[36]

Protocol specification requires a clear definition of both the services to be provided by a given protocol layer and the modules within the layer that cooperate to provide the service. Design verification consists of showing that the interaction of protocol modules is indeed adequate to provide the specified services. Implementation verification consists of showing that the protocol modules satisfy their (abstract) protocol specifications. A useful subset of design verification may be described as verification of "general properties" such as deadlock, looping, and completeness. For most protocols, these properties may be checked without requiring any particular service specification.

Although protocol specifications may take various forms to serve various purposes, verification and implementation require rigorous or formal techniques in order to be fully successful. There has been considerable progress in this area using combinations of two main approaches—state transition models with reachability analysis and high-level programming language models with program proofs. Automation of reachability analysis is well underway, while program proofs still require much manual work.

Unfortunately, the need for complete and independent service specifications has not been widely understood; this has limited most verification efforts to validation of general properties (in the case of state models) or to incomplete correctness assertions developed by ad hoc procedures (in the case of program proofs). Means for specifying and analyzing the performance of protocols are also poorly understood and poorly integrated with correctness concerns. In the area of implementation, both state and program models have moved toward mechanzing the production of hardware or software from formal protocol specifications, but more work is needed. A promising avenue is the application of software engineering systems such as Gypsy to the problem of protocol development. ■

References

1. G. LeLann and H. LeGoff, "Verification and Evalua-

tion of Communication Protocols," *Computer Networks,* Vol. 2, No. 1, Feb. 1978, pp. 50-69.

2. J. E. Donnelley and J. W. Yeh, "Interaction Between Protocol Levels in a Prioritized CSMA Broadcast Network," *Proc. 3rd Berkeley Workshop on Distributed Data Management and Computer Networks,* Aug. 1978, pp. 123-143. Also in *Computer Networks,* Vol. 3, No. 1, Feb. 1979, pp. 9-23.
3. C. A Sunshine, "Efficiency of Interprocess Communication Protocols for Computer Networks," *IEEE Trans. on Communications,* Vol. COM-25, No.2, Feb. 1977, pp. 287-293.
4. J. L. Grange and M. Gien, eds., *Proc. Int'l Symposium on Flow Control in Computer Networks,* Versailles, France, Feb. 1979 (North-Holland Pub. Co.).
5. *Reference Model of Open Systems Architecture* (Version 3), TC9/SC16 N117, International Organization for Standardization, Nov. 1978.
6. D. L. Parnas, "The Use of Precise Specifications in the Development of Software," *Proc. IFIP Congress 1977,* Toronto, pp. 861-867.
7. D. I. Good, "Constructing Verified and Reliable Communications Processing Systems," *Software Engineering Notes* (ACM SIGSOFT bulletin), Vol. 2, No. 5, Oct. 1977, pp. 8-13.
8. G. V. Bochmann, "Finite State Description of Communication Protocols," *Computer Networks,* Vol. 2, No. 4/5, Oct. 1978, pp. 361-372.
9. H. Rudin, C. H. West, and P. Zafiropulo, "Automated Protocol Validation: One Chain of Development," *Computer Networks,* Vol. 2, No. 4/5, Oct. 1978, pp. 373-380.
10. J. Hajek, "Automatically Verified Data Transfer Protocols," *Proc. 4th Int'l Computer Communications Conf.,* Kyoto, Sept. 1978, pp. 749-756. Also see progress reports in *Computer Communications Review,* (ACM SIGCOMM bulletin), Jan. 1978 and Jan. 1979.
11. G. V. Bochmann, "Specification and Verification of Computer Communication Protocols," to appear in *Computer Networks.*
12. C. A. Sunshine and Y. K. Dalal, "Connection Management in Transport Protocols," *Computer Networks,* Vol. 2, No. 6, Dec. 1978, pp. 454-473.
13. A. Danthine and J. Bremer, "Modelling and Verification of End-to-End Transport Protocols," *Computer Networks,* Vol. 2, No. 4/5, Oct. 1978, pp. 381-395.
14. G. V. Bochmann and J. Gecsei, "A Unified Model for the Specification and Verification of Protocols," *Proc. IFIP Congress 1977,* Toronto, pp. 229-234.
15. C. A. Sunshine, "Survey of Communication Protocol Verification Techniques," *Trends and Applications 1976: Computer Networks* (Proceedings of the IEEE-CS/NBS Computer Network Symposium), Gaithersburg, Maryland, Nov. 1976, pp. 24-26.
16. C. A. Sunshine, "Survey of Protocol Definition and Verification Techniques," *Computer Networks,* Vol. 2, No. 4/5, Oct. 1978, pp. 346-350.
17. P. M. Merlin, "Specification and Validation of Protocols," to appear in *IEEE Trans. on Communications.*
18. J. B. Postel, *A Graph Model Analysis of Computer Communications Protocols,* UCLA-ENG-7410, Computer Science Dept., UCLA, 1974 (PhD thesis).
19. D. Brand and W. H. Joyner, Jr., "Verification of Protocols Using Symbolic Execution," *Computer Networks,* Vol. 2, No. 4/5, Oct. 1978, pp. 351-360.
20. N. V. Stenning, "A Data-Transfer Protocol," *Computer Networks,* Vol. 1, No. 2, Sept. 1976, pp. 99-110.
21. G. V. Bochmann, "Logical Verification and Implementation of Protocols," *Network Structures in an Evolving Operational Environment—Fourth Data Communications Symposium,* (Proceedings), Quebec, Oct. 1975, pp. 8-15 to 8-20.
22. N. P. Fong, "NTS—A Protocol Test and Development System," *Proc. Computer Networking Symposium,* Gaithersburg, Maryland, Dec. 1978, pp. 124-128.
23. D. F. Weir and W. E. Prater, "X.25 Test Facilities on DATAPAC," *Proc. 4th Int'l Computer Communications Conf.,* Kyoto, Sept. 1978, pp. 273-279.
24. J. Harangozo, "Protocol Definition with Formal Grammars," *Proc. Computer Network Protocols Symposium,* University of Liege, Feb. 1978, paper F6.
25. G. V. Bochmann and R. J. Chung, "A Formalized Specification of HDLC Classes of Procedures," *Proc. Nat'l Telecommunications Conf.,* Los Angeles, Dec. 1977, paper 3A.2.
26. R. J. Sundstrom, "Formal Definition of IBM's Systems Network Architecture," *Proc. Nat'l Telecommunications Conf.,* Los Angeles, Dec. 1977, paper 3A.1.
27. *SNA Format and Protocol Reference Manual: Architecture Logic,* SC30-3112-01, IBM Corp., June 1978.
28. A. S. Danthine and J. Bremer, "An Axiomatic Description of the Transport Protocol of Cyclades," *Rechnernetze and Datenfernverarbeitung,* Springer-Verlag, Aachen, Germany, 1976, pp. 259-273.
29. C. H. West and P. Zafiropulo, "Automated Validation of a Communications Protocol: The CCITT X.21 Recommendations," *IBM Journal of Research and Development,* Vol. 22, No. 1, Jan. 1978, pp. 60-71.
30. J. B. Postel, ed., *Transmission Control Protocol* (Version 4), Feb. 1979 (available from Defense Documentation Center).
31. C. A. Sunshine and J. Hajek, private communication, 1978.
32. P. M. Merlin and D. J. Farber, "Recoverability of Communication Protocols—Implications of a Theoretical Study," *IEEE Trans. on Communications,* Vol. COM-24, No. 9, Sept. 1976, pp. 1036-1043.
33. D. I. Good, ed., *Constructing Verifiably Reliable and Secure Communications Processing Systems,* ICSCA-CPM-6, Univ. of Texas at Austin, 1977.
34. A. Y. Teng and M. T. Liu, "A Formal Model for Automatic Implementation and Logical Validation of Network Communication Protocols," *Proc. Computer Networking Symposium,* Gaithersburg, Maryland, Dec. 1978, pp. 114-123.
35. M. G. Gouda and E. G. Manning, "Protocol Machines: A Concise Formal Model and its Automatic Implementation," *Proc. 3rd Int'l Computer Communications Conf.,* Toronto, 1976, pp. 346-350.
36. G. V. Bochmann and T. Joachim, "Development and Structure of an X.25 Implementation," to appear in *IEEE Trans. on Software Engineering.*

Carl Sunshine is with the Rand Corporation, where he is involved in research on computer network protocols, network interconnection, network planning, distributed systems, and operating systems. He received a PhD in computer science from Stanford University in 1975, where he worked on the analysis, design, and implementation of communication protocols for computer networks. Sunshine is active in IFIP TC6.1, the Internetwork Working Group.

Protocol Verification via Projections

SIMON S. LAM, SENIOR MEMBER, IEEE, AND A. UDAYA SHANKAR, SENIOR MEMBER, IEEE

Abstract—The method of projections is a new approach to reduce the complexity of analyzing nontrivial communication protocols. A protocol system consists of a network of protocol entities and communication channels. Protocol entities interact by exchanging messages through channels; messages in transit may be lost, duplicated as well as reordered. Our method is intended for protocols with several distinguishable functions. We show how to construct image protocols for each function. An image protocol is specified just like a real protocol. An image protocol system is said to be faithful if it preserves all safety and liveness properties of the original protocol system concerning the projected function. An image protocol is smaller than the original protocol and can typically be more easily analyzed. Two protocol examples are employed herein to illustrate our method. An application of this method to verify a version of the high-level data link control (HDLC) protocol is described in a companion paper.

Index Terms—Communicating processes, communication protocols, distributed systems, image protocols, message-passing networks, method of projections, protocol analysis, verification.

I. Introduction

MOST real-life communication protocols are very complex because they typically have to perform several distinct functions. For example, the high-level data link control (HDLC) protocol has at least three functions: connection management and one-way data transfers in two directions [10], [15], [20]. To reduce the complexity of analyzing such a multifunction protocol, an approach that appears attractive is to decompose each protocol entity into modules for handling the different functions of the protocol. For example, each protocol entity in HDLC may be decomposed into three functional modules such as shown in Fig. 1. Each module communicates with a corresponding module in the other protocol entity to accomplish one of the three functions [1]. However, the decomposition approach does not seem to facilitate an analysis of the protocol. The main difficulty is that significant interaction exists among the modules. We identify two types of dependencies. First, modules interact through *shared variables* within an entity. Second, they also interact because data and control messages sent by different modules in one entity to their respective modules in the other entity are typically encoded in the same protocol message (*shared messages*).

Most communication protocols that have been rigorously

Manuscript received October 6, 1982; revised July 20, 1983. This work was supported by the National Science Foundation under Grants ECS-78-01803 and ECS-83-04734.

S. S. Lam is with the Department of Computer Sciences, University of Texas, Austin, TX 78712.

A. U. Shankar was with the Department of Computer Sciences, University of Texas, Austin, TX 78712. He is now with the Department of Computer Science, University of Maryland, College Park, MD 20742.

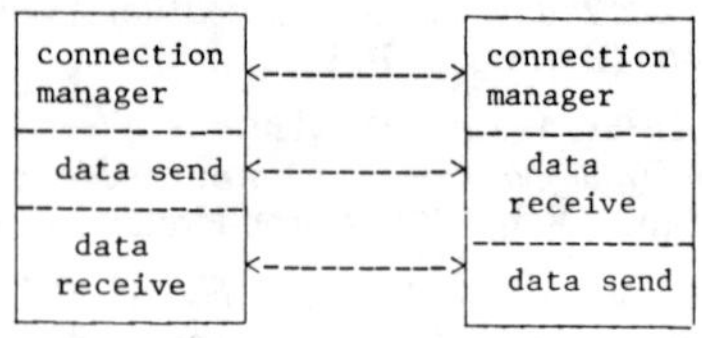

Fig. 1. The three functions of an HDLC protocol.

analyzed and presented in the literature are concerned with a single function: either a connection management function [2], [11], [16] or a one-way data transfer function [6], [9], [23]. A one-way data transfer protocol, for example, corresponds to the interaction of a data send module and a data receive module in isolation (see Fig. 1). Interactions between these modules and other modules are not accounted for. As such, it is a single-function abstraction of a multifunction real-life protocol. The following question arises. Are the safety and liveness properties that are proved for a single-function abstraction still valid when it is implemented as part of a multifunction protocol with the two types of dependencies mentioned above?

The method of projections provides an approach to transforming the analysis of a multifunction protocol into analyses of smaller single-function protocols, called image protocols. It is different from the straightforward approach of decomposing protocol entities into functional modules.

A. The Abstract Model

The underlying abstract model for the development of our theory uses states to encode meaning [3], [17]. Our results are applicable to two widely used protocol specification formalisms: state machines [24] and programming language descriptions [1], [8], [20]. (We illustrate below their application to each formalism with examples.)

A protocol system consists of a network of protocol entities and channels. At any time, the *global state* of the system is specified by a joint description of the states of the entities and channels. Let G denote the set of all global states of the protocol system. The states of entities and channels (and hence the global state) may change due to the occurrence of certain events: entities sending messages, entities receiving messages, timeouts, channel errors, etc. These global state transitions define a directed graph on G. Given any initial global state g_0, the portion of the graph that is reachable from g_0 is referred to as the *reachability graph R*. R contains all available information on the logical properties of the protocol system.

Specifically, assertions of liveness properties are predicates

EHO216-2/84/0000/0474$01.00 © 1984 IEEE

Reprinted from *IEEE Transactions on Software Engineering*, Volume SE-10, Number 4, July 1984, pages 325-342. Copyright © 1984 by The Institute of Electrical and Electronics Engineers, Inc.

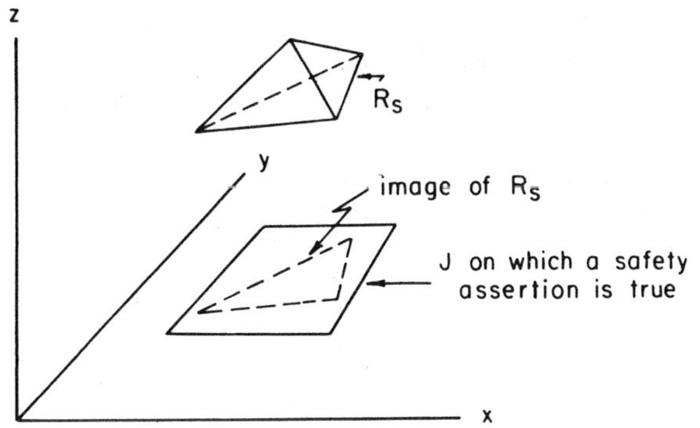

Fig. 2. An illustration of the projection idea.

on the set of paths in G. A liveness assertion is valid if it is satisfied by paths in R. Assertions of safety properties are predicates on G. Let R_s denote the set of states reachable from g_0. A safety assertion is valid if it is satisfied by states in R_s.

Verification of these properties may be carried out by a brute-force state exploration (in the case of a small finite R), or by proof techniques for parallel programs. The method of projections can be used in conjunction with either verification approach.

B. The Projection Approach

Consider a protocol with several distinguishable functions. We would like to ask questions regarding the logical behavior of the protocol system concerning these functions. Instead of asking such questions all at the same time, we may ask them with respect to one function of the protocol at a time. The projection idea can be illustrated by the picture in Fig. 2. Consider a protocol system with the state description (x, y, z) and the set R_s of reachable states. Suppose that we are interested in a safety assertion that involves only the variables x and y. To determine whether the assertion is true, it is sufficient to know the image of R_s on the (x, y) plane. Obviously, if R_s is known, its image on the (x, y) plane is readily available. However, the complexity of R (and thus R_s) is the basic source of difficulty in any protocol analysis.

Our analysis approach avoids a characterization of R. Instead, we construct from the given protocol an image protocol for each of the functions that are of interest to us (to be referred to as the *projected functions*). An *image protocol* is specified just like any real protocol. The states, messages, and events of entities in an image protocol are obtained by aggregating groups of states, messages, and events of the corresponding entities in the original protocol. Definitions needed for the construction of an image protocol are presented in Section III.

Given an image protocol, suppose that a second image protocol is obtained by aggregating some of the entity states, messages and events of the first one. We say that the second image protocol has a lower *resolution* than the first image protocol. The original protocol can be thought of as an image protocol of itself, and obviously it has the highest resolution available.

An image protocol, obtained by aggregations, is smaller than the original protocol and is typically easier to analyze. However, the reachability graph of an image protocol captures only part of the logical behavior of the original protocol. The following useful properties of image protocols are proved in Section IV.

First, any safety property that holds for an image protocol must also hold for the original protocol. Second, if an image protocol is constructed with sufficient resolution so that its events satisfy a well-formed property, then it is *faithful:* any logical property, safety or liveness, that can be stated for the image protocol holds in the image protocol *if and only if* it holds in the original protocol. The well-formedness of an image protocol is determined by checking protocol entities *individually*. The well-formed property is the weakest sufficient condition for faithfulness that can be stated without any knowledge of R.

Given a protocol and an assertion A_0 stating the desired logical behavior of the protocol for the function being projected, our objective is to construct the smallest image protocol that is of sufficient resolution to verify A_0. Towards this goal, we construct a sequence of image protocols of increasing resolution by a stepwise refinement procedure. The initial image protocol can be determined by the resolution needed to *describe* A_0. The stepwise refinement is terminated when an image protocol with sufficient resolution to *verify* A_0 is constructed. Two stepwise refinement methods are presented in Section V with termination conditions based upon the two image protocol properties mentioned above.

Given a multifunction protocol, a faithful image protocol can always be obtained for each function by adjusting its resolution. However, the successful construction of faithful image protocols that are much smaller than the original protocol depends upon whether the protocol has a good structure. Thus, one can think of a multifunction protocol as being *well-structured* if it possesses small faithful image protocols for its functions.

Our protocol system model is described in Section II. Several extensions to this model can be accommodated by our theory (e.g., broadcast channels, message priority classes). To streamline our presentation below, we postpone these extensions to Appendix I. Proofs of lemmas, theorems, and corollaries are given in Appendix II.

Two examples are employed throughout Sections II–V for illustration. In the first example, the protocol entities are specified using a finite state machine description. The second example is a full-duplex data transfer protocol. Its entities are specified using a programming language description.

C. Related Work

The idea of projection is similar to various notions of abstraction in the design and analysis of software systems and programming languages. Within the communication protocols literature, the term "protocol projection" has been used by Bochmann and Merlin to describe an operation in their method for protocol synthesis [4]. Their basic idea of "projection onto the relevant action" is similar to ours herein, but the development and application of the idea in their work and ours are different. The idea of projection as applied to various special cases of our protocol system model has been previously explored in [12]-[14], [18], [19]. Extension of our results to a more structured model of protocol entities is presented in [21]. Efficient rules for constructing image protocols as well as the modeling of timing relationships in protocol systems are also addressed therein. An application of the method of projections to verify a version of the HDLC protocol is presented in [20].

II. The Protocol System Model

Let there be I protocol entities $P_1, P_2, \cdots, P_I$ and K channels $C_1, C_2, \cdots, C_K$. Let S_i be the set of states of P_i, and M_{ik} be the set of messages that P_i can send into C_k. For notational convenience, we shall assume that the message sets M_{ik}, for all i and k, are mutually exclusive. (In practice, this is achieved by encoding each entity's unique address in its messages.)

Each protocol entity can send messages into a subset of channels, called its *outgoing set* of channels. Each protocol entity can receive messages from a subset of channels, called its *incoming set* of channels. We do not require the outgoing and incoming channel sets of a protocol entity to be mutually exclusive. We consider channels that have a single destination protocol entity, although the number of protocol entities that can send into a channel can be more than one. (An extension of the model to include multidestination or broadcast channels is given in Appendix I.)

A channel can be real or logical. In any case, all buffers and communication media between two entities connected by a channel are considered to be part of the channel. Hence, channels may have large storage capacities for messages in transit. At any time, a channel contains a (possibly empty) sequence of messages. We further distinguish channels into the following categories.)

1) *Infinite-Buffer Channels:* Most communication protocols have some measure of flow control. As a result, their buffer requirements for messages in transit between two entities are bounded. Hence the assumption of an infinite buffering capacity is equivalent to being able to satisfy these buffer requirements.

2) *Finite-Buffer Blocking Channels:* With a blocking channel, protocol entities are not permittted to send into the channel whenever the channel is full.

3) *Finite-Buffer Loss Channels:* With a loss channel, the sending of a message into a full channel results in the instantaneous *bumping* (deletion) of a message. The message bumped may be the new message or a message already in the channel.

Bumping Rule: Whenever bumping is necessary, the selection of a message to delete may be specified by any rule that depends only upon the channel positions of messages.

Define the set of messages that can be in channel C_k to be

$$M_k = \bigcup_{i=1}^{I} M_{ik}.$$

The set of all possible sequences in C_k is a subset of

$$\boldsymbol{M}_k = \left(\bigcup_{j=1}^{J} M_k^j\right) \cup \{<>\}$$

where $<>$ denotes the null sequence, M_k^j is the Cartesian product of M_k with itself j times, and J is the maximum number (possibly infinite) of messages that C_k can accommodate. If we think of C_k as having J buffers, then any message sequence of length j in C_k occupies the first j buffers.

The global state space of the protocol system is

$$G = (S_1 \times S_2 \times \cdots \times S_I) \times (\boldsymbol{M}_1 \times \boldsymbol{M}_2 \times \cdots \times \boldsymbol{M}_K).$$

Each global state in G is an $(I + K)$-tuple

$$(s_1, s_2, \cdots, s_I; \boldsymbol{m}_1, \boldsymbol{m}_2, \cdots, \boldsymbol{m}_K)$$

where $s_i \in S_i$ for each i and $\boldsymbol{m}_k \in \boldsymbol{M}_k$ for each k.

The dynamics of protocol entities and channels are described by events. Each event is specified by its enabling condition and its action. The *enabling condition* of an event is a predicate in the components of the global state of the protocol system. The action of an event specifies an update to the components of the global state. An event can occur only if the protocol system is in a state where the enabling predicate of the event is true. Its occurrence, consisting of the execution of its action, is treated as an indivisible transition from one global state to another. Thus, each event corresponds to a set of transitions in the global state space G. The union of these sets of transitions over all events specified for the protocol system will be denoted by τ. We make the assumption that the simultaneous occurrence of multiple events in the protocol system can be treated as occurrences of the same events in some arbitrary order. We will next describe the types of events in our (abstract) protocol system model.

A. Entity Events

There are three types of entity events. The events of entity P_i are specified as follows.

1) Send Events: Let $(s, r, -m)$ denote the event of P_i sending message m into channel C_k where $m \in M_{ik}$ and C_k is in the outgoing channel set of P_i. This send event is enabled when P_i is in state s. With a finite-buffer blocking channel, it is also required that the channel is not full. After the event occurrence, P_i is in state r and m has been appended to the end of the message sequence in C_k. If C_k is a finite-buffer loss channel and is already full, then a message is bumped instantaneously according to the bumping rule of C_k. The set of such send events that can be specified is a subset of $S_i \times S_i \times M_{ik}$.

2) Receive Events: Let $(s, r, +m)$ denote the event of P_i receiving message m from channel C_k where $m \in M_k$ and C_k is in the incoming channel set of P_i. This receive event is enabled when P_i is in state s and m is the first message in channel C_k. After the event occurrence, P_i is in state r and m is deleted from the channel. The set of such receive events that can be specified is a subset of $S_i \times S_i \times M_k$.

3) Internal Events: Let (s, r, α) denote an internal event of P_i where α is a special symbol indicating the absence of a message. This internal event is enabled when P_i is in state s. After the event occurrence, P_i is in state r. Internal events model timeout occurrences internal to P_i, as well as interactions between the entity and its local user. (The latter can be treated as internal events if message exchanges between P_i and its local user are not explicitly modeled.) The set of internal events that can be specified is a subset of $S_i \times S_i \times \{\alpha\}$.

Note that each send or receive event may alter the states of the entity and channel involved in the event. Internal entity events do not affect the state of any channel. We shall use T_i to denote the set of events specified for P_i, $i = 1, 2, \cdots, I$. Note that the behavior of P_i may be nondeterministic. For example, we may specify T_i to contain both $(s, r, +m)$ and $(s, u, +m)$ where $r \neq u$.

B. Channel Events

Let E_k denote the set of channel events specified for channel C_k. The occurrence of a channel event in E_k depends on and changes only the state of C_k; no other channel or protocol entity is involved. We use such channel events to model various types of channel errors.

The following three types of channel error events are considered: loss events, duplication events, and reordering events. Each event is defined for a position or pair of positions in C_k. Let the sequence of messages in C_k be $\boldsymbol{m}_k$. A loss event for the ith position of C_k is enabled if $\boldsymbol{m}_k$ has a message in that position; its occurrence deletes that message from $\boldsymbol{m}_k$. A duplication event for the ith position of C_k is enabled if $\boldsymbol{m}_k$ has a message in that position; its occurrence inserts a duplicate of that message immediately behind it in $\boldsymbol{m}_k$. A reordering event from the ith to the jth position of C_k is enabled if $\boldsymbol{m}_k$ has messages in both these positions; its occurrence moves the message in the ith position to immediately behind the message in the jth position.

E_k can be specified to contain any collection of events of each type.

For consistency, we require that all duplication events are inhibited if C_k is a finite-buffer blocking channel and it is full. If C_k is a finite-buffer loss channel, the bumping rule applies when a duplication event results in a message sequence whose length exceeds the buffering capacity of the channel.

C. Paths in the Global State Space

The protocol system is completely specified by the following:

$$S_i, M_{ik}, T_i, E_k, g_0 \quad \text{for} \quad i = 1, 2, \cdots, I, \quad k = 1, 2, \cdots, K \tag{1}$$

where g_0 denotes the initial global state of the protocol system. Define

$$E = \left(\bigcup_{i=1}^{I} T_i \right) \cup \left(\bigcup_{k=1}^{K} E_k \right).$$

Given event $e \in E$ and global states g and h (not necessarily distinct) we say that e *can take* the protocol system from g to h, if e is enabled when the protocol system is at state g and its occurrence results in the protocol system entering state h.

Recall that τ denotes the set of global state transitions due to the events in E. The pair (G, τ) defines a directed graph whose nodes are elements of G and whose arcs are elements of τ. We now formally define a *path in* (G, τ) to be a sequence of global states $f_0, f_1, \cdots, f_n$ in G, such that there exist events $e_1, e_2, \cdots, e_n$ in E and e_i can take the protocol system from f_{i-1} to f_i for $i = 1, 2, \cdots, n$. Since R denotes that portion of the graph (G, τ) that is reachable from the initial global state g_0, a *path in* R is a path in (G, τ) that starts from the initial state g_0. The *length of a path* is defined to be the number of elements (global states) in it. For notational convenience, we consider any global state $g \in G$ as a path of length 1 in (G, τ). Thus, g_0 is the only path of length 1 in R.

Given two sequences $x = f_0, f_1, \cdots, f_n$ and $y = g_0, g_1, \cdots, g_m$, we denote by x, y the sequence $f_0, f_1, \cdots, f_n, g_0, g_1, \cdots, g_m$ obtained by concatenating x and y. A path x is *extendable* by sequence y to $z = x, y$ if z is also a path.

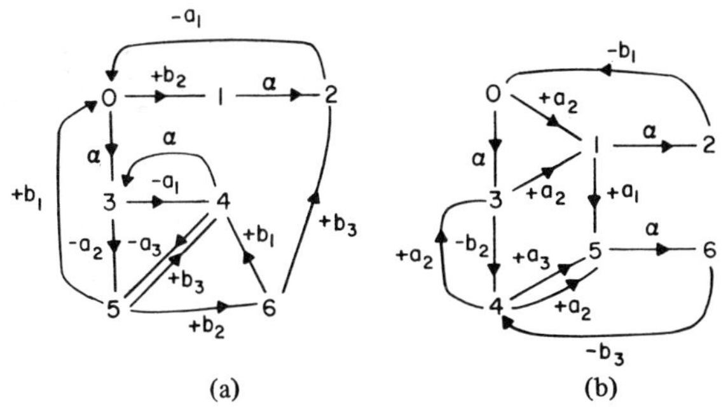

Fig. 3. Two communicating finite-state machines.

D. Two Protocol Examples

Finite State Machines Example: We first illustrate the specification of protocol entities with an example of two interacting finite state machines. (See Fig. 3.) Let C_1 and C_2 be two channels connecting P_1 to P_2, and P_2 to P_1, respectively. Protocol entity P_1 has state space $S_1 = \{0, 1, 2, 3, 4, 5, 6\}$ and sends messages into channel C_1 from $M_1 = \{a_1, a_2, a_3\}$. P_1 receives messages from C_2. Protocol entity P_2 has state space $S_2 = \{0, 1, 2, 3, 4, 5, 6\}$ and sends messages into channel C_2 from $M_2 = \{b_1, b_2, b_3\}$. P_2 receives messages from C_1. The events of entity P_1 are shown in Fig. 3(a). An arc from node i to node j with a label x specifies event (i, j, x), where x is α for an internal event, x is $-a_i$ for sending message a_i, and x is $+b_i$ for receiving message b_i. The events of entity P_2 are similarly shown in Fig. 3(b).

Note that from state 4 in S_2, the reception of a_2 can cause a transition to either state 3 or 5. This nondeterministic behavior is allowed, and is useful for representing certain features in real protocol systems.

We have not given meaning to the protocol entity states and messages. The example in Fig. 3 will be used expressly to illustrate definitions for the construction of image protocols to be presented in Sections III and IV.

Full-Duplex Data Transfer Example: We next illustrate the specification of protocol entities using a programming language model. A full-duplex data transfer protocol is considered.

Let C_1 and C_2 be infinite-buffer channels connecting P_1 to P_2, and P_2 to P_1, respectively. Let variables CHANNEL1 and CHANNEL2 denote the sequences of messages in C_1 and C_2, respectively.

Let DATASET denote the set of data blocks that can be sent

TABLE I
EVENTS OF ENTITY P_1 IN THE FULL—DUPLEX DATA TRANSFER PROTOCOL

Event Name	Enabling Condition	Action
1. SEND_DATA	not BUSY and not D_OUT	SDATA := SOURCE[VS]; put(CHANNEL1, (DATA,SDATA)); VS := VS + 1; D_OUT := true
2. SEND_DATA&ACK	not BUSY and not D_OUT and ACK_DUE	SDATA := SOURCE[VS]; put(CHANNEL1, (DATA&ACK,SDATA)); VS := VS + 1; D_OUT := true; ACK_DUE := false
3. SEND_ACK	not BUSY and ACK_DUE	put(CHANNEL1, (ACK)); ACK_DUE := false
4. START_BUSY	not BUSY	BUSY := true
5. STOP_BUSY	BUSY	BUSY := false
6. REC_DATA	first(CHANNEL2) = DATA	get(CHANNEL2, (DATA,RDATA)); SINK[VR] := RDATA; VR := VR + 1; ACK_DUE := true
7. REC_DATA&ACK	first(CHANNEL2) = DATA&ACK	get(CHANNEL2, (DATA&ACK,RDATA)); SINK[VR] := RDATA; VR := VR + 1; ACK_DUE := true; D_OUT := false
8. REC_ACK	first(CHANNEL2) = ACK	get(CHANNEL2, (ACK)); D_OUT := false

in this protocol. Consider protocol entity P_1. P_1 has an infinite array of data blocks, SOURCE[i] for $i = 0, 1, 2, \cdots$, destined for P_2, and an infinite array, SINK[i] for $i = 0, 1, 2, \cdots$, to store data blocks received from P_2. SINK is initially empty. (SOURCE and SINK should be interpreted as history variables that are not actually implemented.) Additionally, the following variables are used in P_1: VS and VR which are nonnegative integers, and D_OUT, ACK_DUE, and BUSY which are Boolean variables. VS points to the data block in SOURCE to be sent next. VR points to the position in SINK to be next filled. D_OUT is true if (and only if) a data block has been sent but not yet acknowledged. ACK_DUE is true if (and only if) a received data block has to be acknowledged. BUSY can be viewed as an externally operated switch indicating that P_1 is given access to send into channel C_1.

The state of P_1, at any time, is given by the value of the 7-tuple <VS, D_OUT, SOURCE, VR, ACK_DUE, SINK, BUSY> of P_1. Let S_1 denote the state space of P_1. Entity P_2 has a similar set of variables. For convenience, we have omitted qualifiers (1 or 2) for these variables and we shall omit them as long as it is clear whether we are referring to P_1 or P_2. In both entities, the initial state is given by VS and VR equal to 0, D_OUT and ACK_DUE equal to false, SINK equal to empty, and SOURCE equal to some infinite array of data blocks. (In both entities, SOURCE does not change its value during the protocol interaction.)

Each message in the protocol is a tuple with one or more components. The first component is used to identify the message types, and it can take the (character string) values DATA, ACK, and DATA&ACK, corresponding to three different message types. A DATA message is a 2-tuple (DATA, d) where d is a data block from DATASET. There are as many DATA messages as data blocks in DATASET. An ACK message is the 1-tuple (ACK), signifying a positive acknowledgment for a received data block. Unlike DATA messages, there is only one ACK message. A DATA&ACK message is a 2-tuple (DATA&ACK, d) where d is a data block from DATASET.

The set of messages that can be sent by P_1 is given by

$$M_1 = \{(\text{ACK})\} \bigcup \{(\text{DATA}, d) : d \in \text{DATASET}\} \bigcup \{(\text{DATA\&ACK}, d) : d \in \text{DATASET}\}$$

The message set M_2 for P_2 is the same as M_1; each message has a sender identity field which will not be explicitly indicated whenever there is no ambiguity.

The set of entity events for P_1 is presented in Table I. (Note that each event in Table I corresponds to a collection of events as defined in Section II-A.) Events 1-3 are send events for the three message types of M_1. Events 6-8 are receive events for the three message types of M_2. Events 4 and 5 are internal events caused by an agent locally connected to P_1 but which is not explicitly modeled (e.g., a channel controller). The enabling condition of an event defines the entity states and channel states at which the event may take place. The action of each event causes the system to enter a new state.

SDATA and RDATA are variables taking values from DATASET. SDATA and RDATA can be thought of as temporary buffers for transmission and reception (respectively) of data blocks. In Table I, the operation put(CHANNEL1, (DATA,SDATA)) sends a DATA message with the value of SDATA as its data block into CHANNEL1 (i.e., appends the DATA message to the end of the sequence of messages in CHANNEL1). The operation put(CHANNEL1, (DATA&ACK,SDATA)) sends into CHANNEL1 a DATA&ACK message with the value of SDATA as its data block. The operation put(CHANNEL1, (ACK)) sends an ACK message into CHANNEL1.

The function first(CHANNEL2) indicates the type of the message that is at the head of CHANNEL2 and has arrived at P_1. When a DATA message is at the head of CHANNEL2, the operation get(CHANNEL2, (DATA,RDATA)) removes the message from CHANNEL2 and assigns the data block in the message to RDATA. When a DATA&ACK message is at the head of CHANNEL2, the operation get(CHANNEL2, (DATA&ACK,RDATA)) removes the message from CHANNEL2, and assigns the data block in the message to RDATA. When an ACK message is at the head of CHANNEL2, the operation get(CHANNEL2, (ACK)) removes the message from CHANNEL2.

We will come back to both of the above examples when we use them to illustrate the construction of image protocols in the following section.

III. Constructing an Image Protocol System

An image protocol system is constructed by first partitioning each of the sets

$$S_i, M_{ik}, T_i, E_k, \quad \text{for all } i \text{ and } k$$

in the original protocol system specification. Protocol quantities (entity states, messages, or events) in each partition subset are *treated as equivalent* and are *aggregated* to form a single quantity, called their *image*, in the image protocol system. Since partition subsets are mutually exclusive and collectively exhaustive, quantities that are treated as equivalent have the same image; quantities not treated as equivalent have different images.

For a protocol quantity x, we use x' to denote its image. The same notation x' will also be used to refer to the set of protocol quantities in the original protocol system that have the x' image. For a set A of protocol quantities in the original system specification, we use A' to denote the set of image quantities derived from A, i.e., $A' = \{x' : x \in A\}$. Note that an image protocol system, defined by

$$S_i', M_{ik}', T_i', E_k', g_0' \quad \text{for} \quad i = 1, 2, \cdots, I$$
$$k = 1, 2, \cdots, K \tag{2}$$

is specified just like any real protocol system. We cannot tell from inspecting (2) that it is an image of another protocol system.

Since an image protocol is obtained from the original protocol by aggregations, it captures only part of the logical behavior of the original protocol system. First, global states of the image protocol system correspond to aggregations of global states of the original protocol system. Second, in the global state space of the image protocol system, the observable effect of different events in the original protocol system may be identical (these events will become the same image event) or nil (these will be eliminated).

Section III is devoted to the definitions needed for the construction of an image protocol for a given partitioning of the entity state spaces of the original protocol. Stepwise refinement methods for obtaining an image protocol of sufficient resolution to verify some logical assertion are presented in Section V. Properties of image properties are presented in Section IV.

A. Aggregation of Entity States

We start with a given partitioning of the state space S_i of protocol entity P_i, for all i. All entity states in a partition subset are aggregated to the same image. Let S_i' denote the set of images of states in S_i, i.e., $S_i' = \{s' : s \in S_i\}$. S_i' is said to be the image state space of P_i. Elements of S_i' are also referred to as *image entity states*.

Note that if a protocol entity does not participate in the projected function, then the entire state space of that protocol entity may be aggregated to a single degenerate image state.

Finite State Machines Example (Continued): Consider the example in Fig. 3. Suppose that the partition $\{\{0, 1, 2, 3, 4\}, \{5, 6\}\}$ of S_1 has been chosen; see Fig. 4(a). Let image state $0'$ denote the image of states 0, 1, 2, 3, and 4 in S_1. Let image state $5'$ denote the image of states 5 and 6 in S_1. The image state space of P_1 is $S_i' = \{0', 5'\}$.

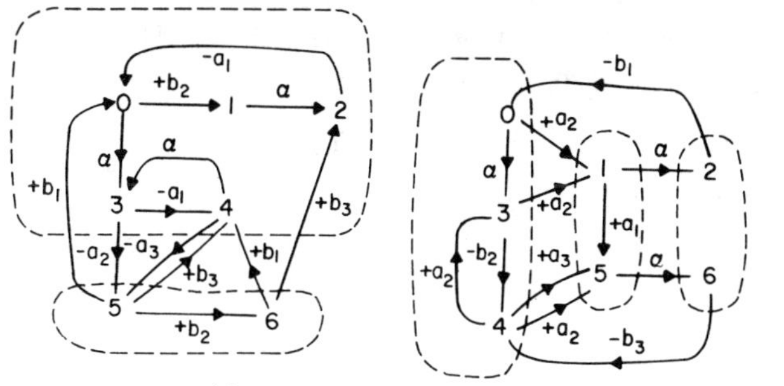

(a) (b)

Fig. 4. A partitioning of the entity state spaces.

For the same image protocol, suppose that the partition $\{\{0, 3, 4\}, \{1, 5\}, \{2, 6\}\}$ of S_2 has been chosen; see Fig. 4(b). Let image states $0'$, $1'$, and $2'$, respectively, denote the images of the states in the partition subsets $\{0, 3, 4\}$, $\{1, 5\}$, and $\{2, 6\}$. Then, the image state space of P_2 is $S_2' = \{0', 1', 2'\}$.

Full-Duplex Data Transfer Example (Continued): This example protocol has two functions corresponding to data transfers in the two directions. The protocol is extremely simple but it embodies both types of dependencies that are encountered when one attempts to decompose protocol entities into functional modules. First, the variable BUSY is shared by both functions of the protocol. Second, messages of type DATA&ACK are also shared. Such dependencies present difficulties for protocol analysis using a decomposition approach, but not when using a projection approach.

Consider the function of one-way data transfer from P_1 to P_2. Two desirable properties of the protocol with respect to this function may be stated as follows:

$$\text{DP1}: \text{SINK}_2[i] = \text{SOURCE}_1[i] \quad \text{for} \quad 0 \leq i < \text{VR}_2$$

$$\text{DP2}: \text{VS}_1 \geq \text{VR}_2 \geq \text{VS}_1 - 1$$

where the subscripts indicate which entity the variables belong to. This assertion can be described using just the variables SOURCE and VS in P_1 and the variables SINK and VR in P_2. However, image protocol entities specified using only these variables do not have sufficient resolution to verify the above assertion. The necessary resolution is obtained by a stepwise refinement procedure (see Section V). For now, suppose that we retain the following variables in the image protocol: VS, D_OUT and SOURCE in P_1, and VR, ACK_DUE, and SINK in P_2.

At any time, the image state of P_1 is given by the value of <VS, D_OUT, SOURCE>. Let S_1' denote the image state space of P_1. Thus, two states s and r in S_1 are equivalent if they differ only in the values of VR, ACK_DUE, SINK, and BUSY.

At any time, the image state of P_2 is given by the value of <VR, ACK_DUE, SINK>. Let S_2' denote the image state space of P_2. Thus, two states s and r in S_2 are equivalent if they differ only in the values of VS, D_OUT, SOURCE, and BUSY.

B. Aggregation of Messages

The partitioning and aggregation of messages in the message set M_{ik} depend upon the partitioning of the entity state spaces. Two messages m and n may be treated as equivalent only if their receptions cause identical state changes in the image state space of the receiver of C_k. This equivalence relation partitions M_{ik} and messages within the same partition subset may be aggregated to form an *image message* m'. The image message sets are given by

$$M'_{ik} = \{m' : m \in M_{ik}\} \qquad \text{for all } i \text{ and } k.$$

In particular, messages in M_{ik} whose receptions do not cause any state change in the image state space of the receiver are said to have a *null image*. The null image message in M'_{ik} is denoted by β. Define

$$M'_k = \bigcup_{i=1}^{I} M'_{ik}.$$

The null image messages from different M'_{ik} are all denoted by β and not distinguished in M'_k.

Sometimes it is desirable to have a finer partitioning of a message set. A higher resolution may be needed to describe and/or verify the behavior of the protocol system. For example, a stronger criterion for treating messages as equivalent is to require also that their send events cause identical state changes in the image state space of their sender.

We shall deal with a null image message β in two different ways depending upon whether C_k is a finite-buffer channel or an infinite-buffer channel. With a finite-buffer channel, β is included in M'_k, as described above. If C_k is an infinite-buffer channel, it is possible to ignore β because even though β occupies a buffer in C_k, it can never cause C_k to be full. Specifically, β may be excluded from M'_k if C_k is an infinite-buffer channel which is also characterized by the following *uniform error model.*

1) Either E_k contains no loss events, or the only loss event in E_k is for the first position in C_k, or E_k contains a loss event for every position in C_k.

2) Either E_k contains no duplication events, or E_k contains a duplication event for every position in C_k.

3) Either E_k contains no reordering events, or E_k contains a reordering event for every pair of positions in C_k.

The uniform error model is a realistic characterization of most conventional physical and logical communication channels. Henceforth in this paper, an infinite-buffer channel C_k will be considered to be characterized by the uniform error model and β will be deleted from M'_k.

If E_k does not satisfy the uniform error model then C_k is said to be characterized by a nonuniform error model.

Finite State Machines Example (Continued): In Fig. 4(a) and (b), if we relabel each state by its image and collapse all identically labeled states, without deleting any events, then we obtain Fig. 5(a) and (b). In these figures we can observe the state changes in S'_1 and S'_2 caused by the messages in M_1 and M_2. Assume that C_1 and C_2 have adequate buffers (infinite-buffer channels).

We will first examine the message set M_1. The state transitions caused by message a_1 are $(0', 0')$ in S'_1, and $(1', 1')$ in S'_2. Hence, a_1 has a null image. Both messages a_2 and a_3 cause the state transition $(0', 5')$ in S'_1 and the state transition $(0', 1')$ in S'_2. However, a_2 is not treated as equivalent to a_3 because a_2 causes state transition $(0', 0')$ in S'_2 while a_3 does not. Thus, we partition M_1 to be $\{\{a_1\}, \{a_2\}, \{a_3\}\}$. The image of a_1 is null. Let the image messages a'_2 and a'_3 denote

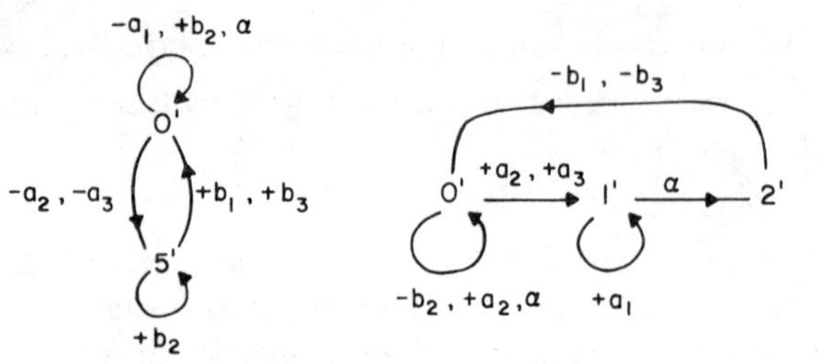

(a) (b)

Fig. 5. Transitions in image state spaces.

the images of a_2 and a_3, respectively. The image message set M'_1 is $\{a'_2, a'_3\}$.

We will now examine the message set M_2. The state changes caused by message b_1 are $(5', 0')$ in S'_1 and $(2', 0')$ in S'_2. The state changes caused by message b_3 are $(5', 0')$ in S'_1 and $(2', 0')$ in S'_2. We will treat b_1 as equivalent to b_3. The state changes caused by message b_2 are $(0', 0')$, $(5', 5')$ in S'_1, and $(0', 0')$ in S_2. Hence, b_2 has a null image. Hence, we partition M_2 to be $\{\{b_1, b_3\}, \{b_2\}\}$. The image of b_2 is null. Let image message b'_1 denote the image of messages b_1 and b_3. The image message set M'_2 is $\{b'_1\}$.

Full-Duplex Data Transfer Example (Continued): By examining the state changes in the image spaces S'_1 and S'_2 due to send and receive events, the following can be shown about messages in M_1. The message (ACK) has a null image. The messages (DATA, d) and (DATA&ACK, d) may be treated as equivalent; let their image be denoted by (DATA$'$,d). Thus $M'_1 = \{(\text{DATA}', d) : d \in \text{DATASET}\}$.

Similarly, the following can be shown about messages in M_2. All (DATA,d) messages have the null image. All (DATA&ACK,d) messages may be treated as equivalent to the ACK message; denote their image by (ACK$'$). Thus $M'_2 = \{(\text{ACK}')\}$.

C. Images of Channel States

The preceding equivalence relation defined for messages is now extended to channel states. The image $\boldsymbol{m}'_k$ of channel state $\boldsymbol{m}_k$ is obtained by taking the image of each message in $\boldsymbol{m}_k$. For infinite-buffer channels, messages with a null image are deleted from $\boldsymbol{m}_k$ to form $\boldsymbol{m}'_k$. All channel states with the same image are treated as equivalent. Let $\boldsymbol{M}'_k$ denote the set of images of channel states in $\boldsymbol{M}_k$. Then

$$\boldsymbol{M}'_k = \left(\bigcup_{j=1}^{J} M'^{j}_k\right) \cup \{\langle\rangle\}$$

where M'^{j}_k denotes the Cartesian product of M'_k with itself j times, and J is the number of buffers in C_k (possibly infinite). The image of a channel state is also referred to as an *image channel state*. $\boldsymbol{M}'_k$ is said to be the image state space of C_k.

D. Images of Global States

The above equivalence relations defined for entity states and channel states are now extended to global states. The image of global state $g = (s_1, s_2, \cdots, s_I; \boldsymbol{m}_1, \boldsymbol{m}_2, \cdots, \boldsymbol{m}_K)$ is defined to be $g' = (s'_1, s'_2, \cdots, s'_I; \boldsymbol{m}'_1, \boldsymbol{m}'_2, \cdots, \boldsymbol{m}'_K)$. All global states with the same image are treated as equivalent. Let G' denote the set of images of global states in G. Thus, we have

TABLE II
EVENTS OF P_1 IN THE IMAGE PROTOCOL FOR ONE-WAY DATA TRANSFER

Event Name	Enabling Condition	Action
1. SEND_DATA'	not D_OUT	SDATA := SOURCE[VS]; put(CHANNEL1, (DATA', SDATA)); VS := VS + 1; D_OUT := true
2. REC_ACK'	first(CHANNEL2) = ACK'	get(CHANNEL2, (ACK')); D_OUT := false

TABLE III
EVENTS OF P_2 IN THE IMAGE PROTOCOL FOR ONE-WAY DATA TRANSFER

Event Name	Enabling Condition	Action
1. REC_DATA'	first(CHANNEL1) = DATA'	get(CHANNEL1, (DATA', RDATA)); SINK[VR] := RDATA; VR := VR + 1; ACK_DUE := true
2. SEND_ACK'	ACK_DUE	put(CHANNEL1, (ACK')); ACK_DUE := false

$$G' = (S_1' \times S_2' \times \cdots \times S_I') \times (M_1' \times M_2' \times \cdots \times M_K').$$

The image of a global state is also referred to as an *image global state*. G' is said to be the image global state space of the protocol system.

E. Image of a Sequence of Global States

The preceding equivalence relation defined for global states is now extended to sequences of global states in G. Given w, a sequence of global states in G, its image w' is obtained as follows: first, take the image of each global state in w; second, any consecutive occurrences of the same image state in the sequence are replaced by a single occurrence of the image state. All sequences having the same image are treated as equivalent. Recall that paths in (G, τ) are sequences of global states in G. Thus, the image of a path in (G, τ) is defined as above for sequences.

F. Aggregation of Entity Events

The above equivalence relations defined for entity states and messages are now extended to entity events. Entity events that have the same observable effect in the image global state space are aggregated to the same *image entity event*. The images of the three types of entity events $(s, r, +m)$, $(s, r, -m)$ and (s, r, α) are $(s', r', +m')$, $(s', r', -m')$, and (s', r', α), respectively.

An image event whose occurrence does not have any observable effect in the image global state space is said to be a *null image event*. An image internal event (s', r', α) is a null image event if $s' = r'$. Image send events involving null image messages and infinite-buffer channels are treated as image internal events in T_i'; in this case the image event $(s', r', -\beta)$ is represented as (s', r', α), and it is a null image event if $s' = r'$. Finally, image receive events involving null image messages must have $s' = r'$ by definition; hence such receive events are null image events if the channel involved is an infinite-buffer channel.

The set of image entity events for P_i is defined by

$$T_i' = \{(s', r', x') : (s, r, x) \in T_i, \quad \text{where } x = +m, -m, \text{or } \alpha, \text{ and the image of } (s, r, x) \text{ is not a null image event}\}.$$

Finite State Machines Example (Continued): Recall that messages a_1 and b_2 have null images. From Figs. 4(a) and 5(a), the events in P_1 having null images are $(0, 1, +b_2)$, $(1, 2, \alpha)$, $(2, 0, -a_1)$, $(0, 3, \alpha)$, $(3, 4, -a_1)$, $(4, 3, \alpha)$, and $(5, 6, +b_2)$. Event $(3, 5, -a_2)$ has the image $(0', 5', -a_2')$. Event $(4, 5, -a_3)$ has the image $(0', 5', -a_3')$. Events $(5, 0, +b_1)$, $(5, 4, +b_3)$, $(6, 4, +b_1)$, and $(6, 2, +b_3)$ are treated as equivalent and have the image $(5', 0', +b_1')$. Hence,

$$T_i' = \{(0', 5', -a_2'), (0', 5', -a_3'), (5', 0', +b_1')\}.$$

From Figs. 4(b) and 5(b), the events in P_2 having null images are $(0, 3, \alpha)$, $(3, 4, -b_2)$, and $(1, 5, +a_1)$. The image of $(4, 3, +a_2)$ is $(0', 0', +a_2')$. Events $(0, 1, +a_2)$, $(3, 1, +a_2)$, and $(4, 5, +a_2)$ are treated as equivalent and have the image $(0', 1', +a_2')$. Event $(4, 5, +a_3)$ has the image $(0', 1', +a_3')$. Events $(1, 2, \alpha)$ and $(5, 6, \alpha)$ have the image $(1', 2', \alpha)$. Events $(2, 0, -b_1)$ and $(6, 4, -b_3)$ have the image $(2', 0', -b_1')$. Therefore,

$$T_2' = \{(0', 0', +a_2'), (0', 1', +a_2'), (0', 1', +a_3'), (1', 2', \alpha), (2', 0', -b_1')\}.$$

Full-Duplex Data Transfer Example (Continued): The entity events of the image protocol for the projected function of one-way data transfer from P_1 to P_2 are shown in Tables II and III. They can be derived using the above definition as illustrated in [14], [21]. In Table II, for example, SEND_DATA' is the image of events SEND_DATA and SEND_DATA&ACK of P_1; REC_ACK' is the image of REC_ACK and REC_DATA&ACK. The events SEND_ACK, START_BUSY, STOP_BUSY, and REC_DATA of P_1 have null images.

G. Channel Events

The image of a channel event should describe the effect of the event that can be observed in the image channel state space. We now show that for every channel event e in E_k, we need to specify an image channel event e' in E_k' which is identical to e. Hence, we do not aggregate events in E_k. We need to consider two possible cases.

First, C_k is a finite-buffer channel (null image messages are included in M_k'). Let $\boldsymbol{m}_k$ be a sequence of messages in C_k. The observable effect in the image channel state space of an error event occurring to $\boldsymbol{m}_k$ is identical to the effect observable in the original channel state space. Hence, for a finite-buffer channel, E_k' must be identical to E_k.

Second, C_k is an infinite-buffer channel (null image messages

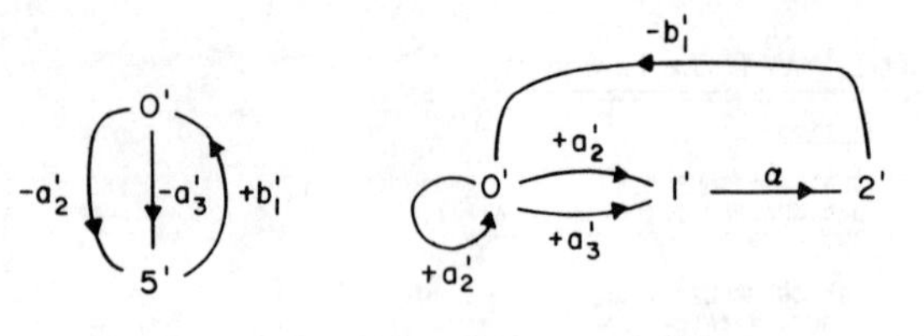

(a) (b)

Fig. 6. An image protocol of the communicating finite-state machines.

are deleted from M_k'). Now, the effect of an error event occurring to $\boldsymbol{m}_k$ observed in the image channel state space, is either nil or in the form of an error event of the same type occurring to $\boldsymbol{m}_k'$. Suppose that the error event is not a loss of the first message in $\boldsymbol{m}_k'$. The uniform error model requires that E_k' contains error events of this type specified for all positions or pairs of positions of C_k. On the other hand, if the first message in $\boldsymbol{m}_k$ is lost, the observable effect in the image channel state space is either nil or that of an identically defined event. Hence, for an infinite-buffer channel also, E_k' must be identical to E_k.

H. An Image Protocol System

The specification

$$S_i', M_{ik}', T_i', E_k', g_0' \quad \text{for} \quad i = 1, 2, \cdots, I, \quad k = 1, 2, \cdots, K$$

defines an image protocol system. Here, g_0', the image of g_0, is the initial state of the image protocol. Due to aggregations, an image protocol system is always smaller than the original protocol system.

Finite State Machines Example (Continued): We have already obtained the image state spaces $S_1' = \{0', 5'\}$ and $S_2' = \{0', 1', 2'\}$, the image message sets $M_1' = \{a_2', a_3'\}$ and $M_2' = \{b_1'\}$, and the image event sets $T_1' = \{(0', 5', -a_2'), (0', 5', -a_3'), (5', 0', +b_1')\}$ and $T_2' = \{(0', 0', +a_2'), (0', 1', +a_2'), (0', 1', +a_3'), (1', 2', \alpha), (2', 0', -b_1')\}$. These quantities define the image protocol system which is shown in Fig. 6(a) and (b). The channels C_1 and C_2 in the image protocol system have the same characterization as in the original protocol system. (We have not yet specified the event sets E_1 and E_2 for these channels.)

Full-Duplex Data Transfer Example (Continued): For P_1 and P_2, we have already obtained their image state spaces to be defined by the state vectors <VS, D_OUT, SOURCE> and <VR, ACK_DUE, SINK>, respectively, their image message types to be (DATA$'$,d) and (ACK$'$), respectively, and their image events shown in Tables II and III. These quantities define the image protocol system. The channels C_1 and C_2 in the image protocol system have the same characterization as in the original protocol system.

IV. Properties of Image Protocols

For the original protocol system with global state space G and initial state g_0, assertions of its safety properties are predicates on G, while assertions of its liveness properties are predicates on the set of paths in G. The validity of such assertions can be decided by examining the reachability graph R.

Recall that an image protocol is specified just like any real protocol. It has the following set of events:

$$E' = \left(\bigcup_{i=1}^{I} T_i'\right) \cup \left(\bigcup_{k=1}^{K} E_k'\right).$$

E' gives rise to a set of transitions τ' in the global state space G'. The transition system (G', τ') governs the logical behavior of the image protocol system. Let R' denote the reachability graph from g_0'. Let R_s' denote the set of global states reachable from g_0'. Informally, an image protocol system is faithful if any logical property, safety or liveness, that can be stated for the image protocol system holds in the image protocol system if and only if it holds in the original protocol system.

When an assertion stated for the image protocol system is considered in the context of the original protocol system, an image protocol quantity x' (entity state, message, or event) in the assertion denotes any protocol quantity in the original system whose image is x'.

An image protocol system as defined in Section III is in general not faithful. However, we show in Section IV-A that image protocols have the following nice property: any safety property that holds in the image protocol system also holds in the original protocol system. Given a safety assertion to verify for a protocol function, this property of image protocols can be used as a termination condition for the stepwise refinement process to find an image protocol with adequate resolution. In Section IV-B, we formally define faithfulness for an image protocol system. This definition involves the reachability graphs R and R'. In Section IV-C, we give sufficient conditions for an image protocol system to be faithful. These conditions can be checked by examining individually the entity and channel events of a protocol system. These conditions are the weakest sufficient conditions that can be stated without any knowledge of R and R'.

A. Safety Properties of Image Protocols

The results below apply to any image protocol system obtained according to the definitions in Section III. Let the original protocol system be characterized by (G, τ), and the image protocol system by (G', τ').

Lemma 1: Given a protocol system and channel states $\boldsymbol{m}$ and $\boldsymbol{n}$ in $\boldsymbol{M}_k$, for any k, if a channel event in E_k can take C_k from $\boldsymbol{m}$ to $\boldsymbol{n}$, then in an image protocol system, either $\boldsymbol{m}' = \boldsymbol{n}'$ or a channel event in E_k' can take C_k from $\boldsymbol{m}'$ to $\boldsymbol{n}'$. (A proof of Lemma 1 is given in Appendix II.)

Lemma 2: For any two global states g and h of the original protocol system, if g is extendable to g, h, then in an image protocol system, either $g' = h'$ or g' is extendable to g', h'. (A proof of Lemma 2 is given in Appendix II.)

Theorem 1: The image of every path in (G, τ) is a path in (G', τ').

Corollary 1: Given any initial global state g_0, the image of every path in R is a path in R'.

Corollary 2: $\{g' : g \in R_s\} \subseteq R_s'$.

The above theorem and corollaries follow readily from Lemma 2 (proofs are given in Appendix II).

Observation: Suppose that a safety assertion has been found to be invariant in an image protocol system. Note that a safety assertion is invariant if it is true on a superset of R_s' in G'. By Corollary 2, the safety assertion must also hold invariantly in the original protocol system.

Finite State Machines Example (Continued): Given the initial state $(0', 0'; \langle\rangle, \langle\rangle)$ for this image protocol system, and assuming channels C_1 and C_2 to be error-free (E_1 and E_2 are empty sets), it is easy to verify that the following assertion holds for the image protocol system.

P_1 is in state $5' \Rightarrow$ exactly one of the following holds:

a) message a_2' or a_3' is in C_1, or
b) P_2 is in state $1'$ or $2'$, or
c) message b_1' is in C_2, or
d) P_2 is in state $0'$ and channels C_1 and C_2 are empty (deadlock situation).

Note that P_1 in state $5'$ means that in the original protocol P_1 is in any state whose image is $5'$. Similarly, message b_1' is in C_2 means that in the original protocol any message whose image is b_1' is in C_2.

We can verify whether this assertion is valid for the original protocol by examining the reachability graph of the original protocol system in Fig. 3. However, by Corollary 2, we know that the above assertion is valid for the original protocol system.

The assumption of error-free channels is necessary for the above assertion to hold in both the original and image protocol systems. This assumption is not required in order for the nice property of image protocols stated in Corollary 2 to hold.

Full-Duplex Data Transfer Example (Continued): Assuming C_1 and C_2 to be error-free channels, the following safety assertion has been found to hold for the one-way data transfer image protocol constructed in Section III-H:

1) SINK[i] = SOURCE[i] for $0 \leqslant i < $ VR.
2) VS $\geqslant$ VR $\geqslant$ VS-1.
3) (DATA$'$,d) in CHANNEL1 $\Rightarrow$ (D_OUT)
   and (d = SOURCE[VS-1])
   and (exactly one DATA$'$ message in CHANNEL1)
   and (not ACK_DUE) and (VS = VR + 1)
   and (no ACK$'$ message in CHANNEL2).
4) ACK_DUE $\Rightarrow$ (D_OUT)
   and (no DATA$'$ message in CHANNEL1)
   and (VS = VR) and (no ACK$'$ message in CHANNEL2).
5) ACK$'$ in CHANNEL2 $\Rightarrow$ (D_OUT)
   and (no DATA$'$ message in CHANNEL1) and (VS = VR)
   and (not ACK_DUE)
   and (exactly one ACK$'$ message in CHANNEL2).
6) not D_OUT $\Rightarrow$ VS = VR.

By Corollary 2, the above assertion holds in the original full-duplex data transfer protocol.

Again, the assumption of error-free channels is needed for the above assertion to hold because the protocol is relatively simple and is not designed to handle errors. Without this assumption, no meaningful assertion can be stated. For larger protocol examples involving error-prone channels, the reader is referred to [19], [20].

B. Conditions for Faithfulness

Liveness properties of a protocol system are concerned with the future behavior of paths in the reachability graph R. Consider an image protocol system with reachability graph R'. Our definition of faithfulness is formally stated as follows.

Definition (Faithful Image Protocol): For every path w in R and every path u' in R' such that $w' = u'$, the following two conditions hold.

($F1$) If w can be extended to a path x in R then u' can be extended to a path v' in R' such that $x' = v'$.

($F2$) If u' can be extended to a path v' in R' then w can be extended to a path x in R such that $v' = x'$.

The above two conditions guarantee *faithfulness of the image protocol's safety properties* as a result of the following implications:

$$(F1) \Rightarrow R_s' \supseteq \{g' : g \in R_s\}$$

$$(F2) \Rightarrow R_s' \subseteq \{g' : g \in R_s\}$$

where R_s' is the set of reachable states of the image protocol system, and $\{g' : g \in R_s\}$ is the set of images of reachable global states of the original protocol system.

To be able to characterize the liveness properties of R given the liveness properties of R', we assume that the original protocol system satisfies the following *fairness assumption:* no event will be indefinitely delayed if it is enabled infinitely often. Given the fairness assumption, conditions ($F1$) and ($F2$) guarantee *faithfulness of the image protocol's liveness properties.*

We have proved that all image protocols as constructed in Section III satisfy condition ($F1$). However, an image protocol system satisfies condition ($F2$) only if it has adequate resolution. To check if ($F2$) holds requires an examination of R and R'. However, the complexity of R is to be avoided unless it has a special structure that facilitates the checking of ($F2$). We give in Section IV-C sufficient conditions for an image protocol to satisfy ($F2$). These conditions can be checked by examining individually the entity and channel events of the original protocol system, without any knowledge of R or R'.

C. Sufficient Conditions Without Knowledge of R or R'

To satisfy condition ($F2$) above, we require that channels in the original protocol system satisfy a finite lifetime assumption, and each event in the image protocol system is well-formed. These requirements are now explained below.

1) Assumption About the Original Protocol System:

Finite Lifetime Assumption: The first message residing in a channel will be deleted in finite time.

The finite lifetime assumption is satisfied by protocol systems in several ways. First, this assumption is satisfied by protocol systems which have been carefully designed to completely avoid "unspecified receptions" [24]. In any reachable state of such a system, if m is the first message in channel C_k whose receiver P_i is in state s, there exists a receive event $(s, r, +m)$ in T_i for some r.

We shall refer to such protocol systems as having a *complete* set of receive events.

If we do not know whether the original protocol system has a complete set of receive events, then unspecified receptions can be avoided by augmenting each entity event set T_i with a receive event set L_i containing receive events of the form $(s, s, +m)$. Two cases are of interest.

Case 1: Exhaustive specification

$L_i = \{(s, s, +m): s \in S_i, m \in M_k$ for all C_k in the incoming set of $P_i\}$.

Case 2: Complementary specification

$L_i = \{(s, s, +m): s \in S_i, m \in M_k$ for all C_k in the incoming set of P_i, such that $(s, r, +m)$ is not in T_i for some $r\}$.

Since occurrences of events in L_i do not change the state of P_i, they can be interpreted not as entity receive events but as events that enforce a finite lifetime for messages in a channel. Specifically, a message residing at the head of a channel will be deleted by some "channel controller" within a finite time. Finite lifetimes for messages are highly realistic. First, messages propagating within a physical channel have a small transit time. Second, if a channel is logical and messages are actually travelling within a store-and-forward communication network, they are often subject to mechanisms that enforce bounds on their lifetimes [22].

Whether we assume Case 1 or 2 above depends upon the magnitude of message lifetimes compared to the magnitude of a receiving entity's reaction time to handle receive events. If a receiving protocol entity can always execute an enabled receive event for a message prior to the expiration of the message's lifetime, then the complementary specification of L_i is realistic; otherwise, the exhaustive specification should be assumed.

Observation: An exhaustive L_i is logically equivalent to a set of loss events specified for the first position of channel C_k for every channel in the incoming set of P_i. The finite lifetime assumption is automatically satisfied if such loss events are already specified in the channel event sets.

In summary, the original protocol system can satisfy the finite lifetime assumption in one of three ways. First, it has completely specified receive events; in this case, the L_i sets are null. Second, it is augmented by a complementary specification of receive events in $\{L_i\}$. Third, it is augmented by an exhaustive specification of receive events in $\{L_i\}$. It should be clear that in an actual system, the $\{L_i\}$ sets do not have to be explicitly specified and stored.

Lastly, images of events in L_i are defined in the same way as image receive events in Section III-F.

2) The Well-Formed Property:

The well-formed property of events in an image protocol system is next defined. The image events in T_i' for entity P_i are first considered.

Definition: For a and b in S_i, b is *internally reachable* from a if $a' = b'$ (they have the same image) and there is a sequence of internal events in T_i causing state changes inside a' that will take P_i from a to b.

A send event involving P_i and C_k for some k, can be regarded as an internal event for the above definition if C_k is an infinite-buffer channel and the message being sent has a null image. Under these conditions, the send event $(a, b, -m) \in T_i$ can be treated as an internal event $(a, b, \alpha) \in T_i$.

Definition: An *image internal event* of P_i, $(s', r', \alpha) \in T_i'$ where $s' \neq r'$, is well-formed if for every a whose image is s', there is some $b \in S_i$ that is internally reachable from a and $(b, c, \alpha) \in T_i$ for some $c \in r'$.

Again, in the above definition, a send event $(b, c, -m) \in T_i$ where $m \in M_{ik}$ for some k, can be used instead of (b, c, α) if m has a null image and C_k is an infinite-buffer channel.

Definition: An *image send event* of P_i, $(s', r', -n') \in T_i'$, is *well-formed* if for every a whose image is s', there is some $b \in S_i$ that is internally reachable from a and $(b, c, -y) \in T_i$ for some $c \in r'$ and some y whose image is n'.

Definition: An *image receive event* of P_i, $(s', r', +n') \in T_i'$, is *well-formed* if for every a whose image is s', the following holds: for *every* y whose image is n' there is some $b \in S_i$ that is internally reachable from a, and $(b, c, +y) \in T_i$ for some $c \in r'$.

If in any of the above definitions of well-formed events, the length of the internal path is 0 (i.e., $b = a$), then we say that the image event is *strongly well-formed*.

Note from the construction of T_i' that for every $e' \in T_i'$, there is an event $e \in T_i$ whose image is e'.

Finite State Machines Example (Continued): We will now show that the image events in T_i' are well-formed. (Refer to Figs. 4 and 5.) First, consider event $(0', 5', -a_2') \in T_1'$. Because of the paths $1 \xrightarrow{\alpha} 2 \xrightarrow{-a_1} 0 \xrightarrow{\alpha} 3$ and $4 \xrightarrow{\alpha} 3$, state 3 is internally reachable from states 1, 2, 0, and 4. From state 3, the event $(3, 5, -a_2)$ can be executed. Hence, $(0', 5', -a_2')$ is well-formed.

Because of event $(3, 4, -a_1)$, where a_1 has a null image, state 4 is internally reachable from state 3, and hence from states 0, 1 and 2 also. From 4, event $(4, 5, -a_3) \in T_1$ can be executed. Thus, event $(0', 5', -a_3') \in T_i'$ is well-formed.

Because of the events $(5, 0, +b_1)$, $(5, 4, +b_3)$, $(6, 4, +b_1)$, and $(6, 2, +b_3)$ in T_1, image event $(5', 0', +b_1') \in T_1'$ is strongly well-formed.

Next, we will show that the image events in T_2' are well-formed. Consider image event $(0', 0', +a_2') \in T_2'$. Because of events $(0, 3, \alpha)$ and $(3, 4, -b_2)$ in T_2, state 4 is internally reachable from 0 and 3. These and the event $(4, 3, +a_2) \in T_2$ make image event $(0', 0', +a_2')$ well-formed.

Image event $(0', 1', +a_2') \in T_2'$ is strongly well-formed because of events $(0, 1, +a_2)$, $(3, 1, +a_2)$, and $(4, 5, +a_2)$ in T_2.

Image event $(0', 1', +a_3') \in T_2'$ is well-formed because of event $(4, 5, +a_3)$ in T_2, and because 4 is internally reachable from 0 and 3.

Image event $(1', 2', \alpha) \in T_2'$ is strongly well-formed because of events $(1, 2, \alpha)$ and $(5, 6, \alpha)$ in T_2.

Image event $(2', 0', -b_1') \in T_2'$ is strongly well-formed because of events $(2, 0, -b_1)$ and $(6, 4, -b_3)$ in T_2.

We conclude that all entity events of the image protocol shown in Fig. 6 are well-formed.

We next consider image events in E_k' for channel C_k. Note that the occurrence of a channel event affects only the state of the channel. Thus, channel events are analogous to internal events of entities; the well-formed property of channel events is defined similarly.

Definition: An *image channel event* $e' \in E_k'$ is *well-formed* if given any two distinct message sequences $\mathbf{m}'$ and $\mathbf{n}'$ in $\mathbf{M}_k'$ such that e' can take C_k from $\mathbf{m}'$ to $\mathbf{n}'$, the following holds: for every message sequence $\boldsymbol{p} \in \boldsymbol{M}_k$ whose image is $\boldsymbol{m}'$, there is a sequence of channel events in E_k that can take C_k from $\boldsymbol{p}$, via states each with image $\boldsymbol{m}'$, to some message sequence $\boldsymbol{q}$ whose image is $\boldsymbol{n}'$.

In the above definition, if the sequence of channel events consists of only one event, then e' is said to be *strongly well-formed.*

The channel event sets defined in Section II-B have two properties. Firstly, we have shown that for any channel C_k, the image event set E_k' remains the same as E_k. Secondly, we have the following result.

Lemma 3: Each event in E_k' is well-formed. (A proof of Lemma 3 is given in Appendix II.)

(A channel event set E_k, that is more general than those defined in Section II-B, can be specified as an arbitary subset of $\boldsymbol{M}_k \times \boldsymbol{M}_k$. In this case, the above definition for well-formed image channel events must be applied to check each image event in E_k' to see if it is well-formed.)

Lemma 4: Given two distinct global states g' and h' of an image protocol system with well-formed events, if g' is extendable to g', h', then for any global state f in G such that $f' = g'$, f is extendable to a path w such that $w' = g', h'$. (A proof of Lemma 4 is given in Appendix II.)

Consider a protocol system characterized by (G, τ) and an image protocol system characterized by (G', τ'), the following theorem implies that condition $(F2)$ needed for faithfulness is satisfied if all events of the image protocol in T_i', L_i', E_k' for all i and k are well-formed. Note that events in E_k' are well-formed by virtue of Lemma 3. Events in L_i' are well-formed if L_i is given by the exhaustive specification (or is null).

Theorem 2: Given an image protocol system with well-formed events, for any path w in (G, τ) and u' in (G', τ') such that $w' = u'$, if u' is extendable to a path v', then w is extendable to a path x such that $x' = v'$.

Corollary 3: Given any initial global state $g_0 \in G$ and the corresponding image global state $g_0' \in G'$, for any path w in R and u' in R' such that $w' = u'$, if u' is extendable to a path v' in R', then w is extendable to a path x in R such that $x' = v'$.

Corollary 4: $R_s' \subseteq \{g' : g \in R_s\}$.

Theorem 2 follows readily from Lemma 4. Proofs of the preceding theorem and corollaries are given in Appendix II.

Theorem 3: An image protocol system with well-formed events is faithful.

Theorem 3 is an immediate consequence of Corollaries 1-4 and the definition of faithfulness. The original protocol system is assumed to satisfy the fairness and finite lifetime assumptions.

Full-Duplex Data Transfer Example (Continued): The image entity events in Tables II and III can be shown to be well-formed (see [14], [21] for details). Let C_1 and C_2 be error-free channels. Then, in addition to the safety assertions stated earlier for the image protocol system, it can also be easily shown that the variable VR in P_2 grows without bound. Thus, the following liveness property is established:

For any integer $n \geqslant 0$ the image protocol will eventually satisfy:

$$\text{SOURCE}[i] = \text{SINK}[i] \qquad \text{for } 0 \leqslant i \leqslant n.$$

From Table I, we see that the receive events of the original protocol system are complete. Assuming that the scheduling of events in P_1 and P_2 satisfies the fairness assumption, the one-way image protocol constructed is faithful and the above liveness property holds for the original full-duplex protocol as well.

V. Stepwise Refinement Methods

Given an assertion A_0 describing the desired logical behavior of a given protocol system, our objective is to find the smallest image protocol with sufficient resolution to verify whether A_0 holds in the original protocol system.

We start with an image protocol with sufficient resolution to describe A_0. A sequence of image protocols with increasing resolution is then constructed by stepwise refinement. Each successive protocol in the sequence is obtained by a finer partitioning of the original protocol's entity state spaces and/or message sets. Thus, each protocol in the sequence is actually an image protocol of all succeeding protocols constructed. (This property facilitates the verification of safety assertions in Section V-B.)

Two stepwise refinement algorithms with different termination conditions are presented in the next two subsections. The choice of a termination condition depends upon whether A_0 is a liveness or a safety assertion. Assuming that A_0 is a decidable property of the original protocol system, the following algorithms always terminate. In the worst case, they terminate with the original protocol as their output.

A. Termination Based Upon the Well-Formed Property

Algorithm 1: To find an image protocol for verifying a liveness or safety assertion A_0.

1) "Initial step"
   partition the entity state spaces so that image entity states in $\{S_i'\}$ have enough resolution for describing A_0;
2) "Image protocol construction"
   obtain the image message sets $\{M_{ik}'\}$ based upon $\{S_i'\}$; obtain the image entity events based upon $\{S_i'\}$ and $\{M_{ik}'\}$;
3) check each event for well-formedness;
4) **if** all events are well-formed **then** terminate algorithm
   "We have a faithful image protocol for verifying A_0"
5) **else** "Refinement step"
   the point(s) of failure in events that are not well-formed indicate refinements necessary in the partitioning of $\{S_i\}$; update $\{S_i'\}$; go to step 2.

(End of Algorithm 1)

By using the well-formedness of image entity events as the termination condition, Algorithm 1 does not involve any characterization of the reachability graph of each intermediate image protocol constructed.

In step 2, the image message sets $\{M_{ik}'\}$ are derived from the entity state space partitions $\{S_i'\}$ as defined in Section III-B. We have assumed that the resolution of these image message sets is adequate to describe A_0. As discussed in Section III-B, given $\{S_i'\}$ the resolution of an image protocol can also be increased by increasing the resolution of the image message sets. This provides an extra degree of freedom which may be utilized in steps 1, 2, and 5 of the above algorithm.

TABLE IV
EVENTS OF P_1 IN THE INITIAL IMAGE PROTOCOL

Event Name	Enabling Condition	Action
1. SEND_DATA'		SDATA := SOURCE[VS]; put(CHANNEL1, (DATA', SDATA)); VS := VS + 1

TABLE V
EVENTS OF P_2 IN THE INITIAL IMAGE PROTOCOL

Event Name	Enabling Condition	Action
1. REC_DATA'	first(CHANNEL1) = DATA'	get(CHANNEL1, (DATA', RDATA)); SINK[VR] := RDATA; VR := VR + 1

Full-Duplex Data Transfer Example (Continued): We will use this example protocol to illustrate Algorithm 1. We wanted to verify that the original protocol satisfies:

$$DP_1 : \text{SINK}_2[i] = \text{SOURCE}_1[i] \quad \text{for } 0 \leqslant i < \text{VR}2$$

$$DP_2 : \text{VS}_1 \geqslant \text{VR}_2 \geqslant \text{VS}_1 - 1.$$

In step 1), the initial resolution of the entity state spaces is defined by the variables SOURCE and VS in P_1 and SINK and VR in P_2.

Next in step 2, we construct an image protocol. The image states of P_1 and P_2 are given by the values of <VS, SOURCE> and <VR, SINK>, respectively. By examining the state changes in the image entity state spaces, we obtain the following image message sets. In M_1, (ACK) has a null image, and (DATA,d) and (DATA&ACK,d) have the same image (DATA$'$,d). All the messages in M_2 have the null image. Thus $M_1' = \{(\text{DATA}',d): d \in \text{DATASET}\}$ and M_2' is empty. The events of this initial image protocol are shown in Tables IV and V. In P_1, SEND_DATA and SEND_DATA&ACK have the image SEND_DATA$'$. In P_2, REC_DATA and REC_DATA&ACK have the image REC_DATA$'$. The remaining entity events have a null image.

Having obtained the above initial image protocol, we determine in step 3 whether all its events are well-formed. Consider the event SEND_DATA$'$. From the events of P_1 in the original protocol, we see that SEND_DATA and SEND_DATA&ACK can occur only when BUSY = D_OUT = False. If BUSY = True, then internal event STOP_BUSY can set BUSY = False. However if D_OUT = True, there is no sequence of null image send or internal events of P_1 that will set D_OUT to False. Hence SEND_DATA$'$ is not well-formed and we go to step 5.

The point of failure is the absence in the image protocol of the variable D_OUT of P_1. Hence, we update the entity state space of P_1 to be defined by <VS, D_OUT, SOURCE>, and go back to step 2 and repeat the procedure. Note that there has been no attempt at verification of the image protocol.

In the next iteration we would include ACK_DUE of P_2. In the iteration following that, we would obtain the well-formed image protocol shown in Section III-H (and Tables II and III), and terminate the algorithm.

B. Termination Based Upon Safety Properties of Image Protocols

Given a safety assertion A_0, we present another algorithm to find an image protocol with sufficient resolution to verify A_0. Unlike Algorithm 1, A_0 is verified for each image protocol constructed. This verification of A_0 is aided by the fact that a safety property that holds for an intermediate image protocol also holds for all succeeding image protocols. The termination condition for this algorithm is based upon Corollary 1.

In what follows, we use A_0 to denote the set of states in G on which the safety assertion is true. We use B to represent safety properties that have been found to hold for the image protocols already constructed. B can be thought of as a superset of R_s' of the current image protocol.

Algorithm 2: To find an image protocol for verifying a safety assertion A_0.

1) "Initial step"
   partition the entity state spaces so that image entity states in $\{S_i'\}$ have enough resolution for describing A_0; let B be G' "Nothing is known initially";
2) "Image protocol construction"
   obtain the image message sets $\{M_{ik}'\}$ based upon $\{S_i'\}$; obtain the image entity events based upon $\{S_i'\}$ and $\{M_{ik}'\}$;
3) verify A_0 given B for this image protocol;
4) **if** A_0 holds **then** terminate algorithm
   "A_0 also holds in the original protocol system"
5) **else** "We have found a sequence of image events e_1', $e_2', \cdots, e_n'$, referred to as a *test sequence*, that takes the image protocol system from g_0' to some $g' \notin A_0$" consider those event sequences $e_1, e_2, \cdots, e_m$ where $m \geqslant n$, whose image equals the test sequence;
   5.1) **if** any of these event sequences can occur in the original protocol system **then** terminate algorithm
   "A_0 does not hold in the original protocol system"
   5.2) **else** "Refinement step"
   by observing how the test sequence is prevented from occurring in the original protocol system, refinements necessary in the partitioning of $\{S_i\}$ are obtained; update $\{S_i'\}$; if it is observed that the image protocol satisfies some safety property B' then update B to be $B \cap B'$; go to step 2.

(End of Algorithm 2)

In practice, since image protocols are relatively small, many safety properties can often be observed by inspection. Once a safety property has been proved, it is accumulated into B and it will hold for all succeeding image protocols. We note that the smaller B is, the easier it is to verify A_0. Methods to verify A_0 (given B) are described in Section V-C.

As in the case of Algorithm 1, the resolution of the $\{M_{ik}'\}$ obtained from $\{S_i'\}$ in step 2 can be increased further if needed to describe A_0 in step 1 or in the refinement step.

Full-Duplex Data Transfer Example (Continued): We will use this example protocol to illustrate Algorithm 2. The initial resolution of the entity state spaces in step 1 and the initial image protocol in step 2 are the same as in Algorithm 1 (see Tables IV and V).

In step 3, assuming that channels C_1 and C_2 are error-free, we can easily verify that this initial image protocol satisfies DP_1. However, this image protocol does not satisfy DP_2. For instance, from the initial state the image protocol can execute SEND_DATA′ twice in succession. The image protocol would then be in a state with VS=2, VR=0, and CHANNEL1=(DATA′, SOURCE[1]), (DATA′,SOURCE[0]). This state clearly violates DP_2.

Next, in step 5, we have to determine whether the test sequence SEND_DATA′, SEND_DATA′ can occur in the original protocol. From the initial state we observe that once P_1 executes a SEND-DATA′ (either SEND_DATA or SEND_DATA&ACK), D_OUT is set to True, and another SEND_DATA′ cannot occur. Further D_OUT is reset to False only in REC_ACK or REC_DATA&ACK. But for either of these to occur, P_2 must execute either SEND_ACK or SEND_DATA&ACK. For that to occur P_2 must have ACK_DUE=True. But ACK_DUE is set to True only when REC_DATA or REC_DATA&ACK occurs at P_2. Neither of these events has a null image. Hence we conclude that the original protocol cannot execute an event sequence whose image equals the test sequence SEND_DATA′, SEND_DATA′.

This brings us to step 5.2. The test sequence is prevented from occurring due to the variable D_OUT of P_1. Hence, we update the image entity state spaces of P_1 and P_2 to be <VS,D_OUT,SOURCE> and <VR,SINK>, respectively. Also, B can now be set to DP_1, which has already been established. We now go to step 2 and repeat the iterative step.

In the next iteration we would include ACK_DUE of P_2. In the iteration following that, we would have DP_2 holding for the image protocol in Tables II and III. Note that property DP_1 needs not be verified again for any of the future image protocols that we obtain, since it has been shown to hold for the initial image protocol considered above.

C. Verification Methods

Whether we use Algorithm 1 or Algorithm 2, we need to verify A_0 for an image protocol system. With Algorithm 1, this verification is done for the well-formed image protocol obtained. With Algorithm 2, we need to verify A_0 (given B) for each image protocol considered in step 3.

One way to verify A_0 for an image protocol system is by generating the reachable set R_s' of states starting from g_0'. This can be done by brute force (assuming that R_s' is a small finite set) or by symbolic execution [5]. Either A_0 holds at each state in R_s' or a test sequence is obtained.

Another way to verify A_0 is to use the method of weakest preconditions [7]. The objective here is to find an inductively complete set that is a subset of $A_0 \cap B$. We expand on this method here.

For a protocol system with global state space G' and initial state g_0', A is an *inductively complete set* if the following conditions hold:

1) $g_0' \in A$, and
2) $\forall g' \in A, \forall e' \in E'$, if e' is enabled at g', then $e'(g') \in A$

where $e'(g')$ denotes a state that e' can take the protocol system to from g'. The class of inductively complete sets is closed under intersection i.e., if A and B are inductively complete sets, so is $A \cap B$. It should be obvious that R_s' is the smallest inductively complete set of the protocol system.

Algorithm 3: Verify A_0 given B for a protocol system.

1) "Initial step"
   $C := A_0 \cap B$;
   $i := 1$;
2) "Find weakest preconditions"
   $A_i := \{g' \in C : \forall e' \in E'$ if e' is enabled at g' then $e'(g') \in C\}$;
3) **if** $g_0' \notin A_i$ **then**
   "A_0 does not hold for the protocol system"
   obtain a test sequence by examining $A_{i-1}, A_{i-2}, \cdots, A_0$; terminate algorithm
4) **else if** ($g_0' \in A_i$ and $A_i = C$) **then** terminate algorithm
   "$A_i \subseteq A_0$ is inductively complete and A_0 holds"
5) **else** $C := A_i; i := i + 1$; go to step 2).

(End of Algorithm 3)

If it is observed that the protocol system satisfies some safety property B' then C is updated to $A_i \cap B'$ in step 5 of the above algorithm. Such observations will speed up the algorithm's search.

VI. Conclusions

The method of projections is intended to reduce the complexity of analyzing multifunction protocols. We show how to construct image protocols for individual protocol functions. Image protocols are specified like any real protocol. Each image protocol is obtained by aggregating entity states, messages and events of the original protocol system. As a result, an image protocol is smaller (never larger) than the original protocol, and can typically be more easily analyzed. Our method effectively breaks up a protocol analysis problem into smaller problems. Unlike the straightforward approach of decomposing protocol entities into functional modules, our method is not handicapped by dependencies that exist between functional modules due to shared variables and shared messages.

Given an assertion A_0 stating the desired logical behavior of a protocol system with respect to a particular protocol function, we have presented two stepwise refinement algorithms for finding an image protocol with sufficient resolution to verify A_0. Algorithm termination assumes that A_0 is a decidable property of the original protocol system. Termination of these algorithms makes use of either one of the following two important properties of image protocols.

First, any safety property that holds for an image protocol system also holds for the original protocol system. Second, given that the original protocol system satisfies a fairness assumption in its event scheduling and its channels satisfy a finite lifetime assumption, an image protocol system with well-formed events is faithful in all its safety and liveness properties to the original protocol system. A faithful image protocol can always be constructed by increasing the resolution of its entity state spaces and message sets. We propose that a multifunction protocol may be considered as well-structured if it possesses small faithful image protocols for its individual functions.

In this paper a protocol system is specified by sets of entity states, messages, and events. A set-theoretic notation is used for stating the definitions and properties of image protocols. These results are very general since sets have no internal structure. However, application of these definitions and properties requires operations on sets. Such application is straightforward for protocol entities specified by a finite state machines formalism, but rather cumbersome for protocol entities specified by a programming language formalism. A more structured specification of protocol entities and messages is presented in [21]; specialization to such a model leads to some efficient rules for image protocol construction. In addition, time variables and time events useful for modeling global timing relations in a protocol system are developed therein. An application of the method of projections to verify a version of the HDLC protocol is presented in [20]. This serves as a rigorous exercise to illustrate the applicability of the method of projections to the analysis of real-life protocols.

Appendix I
Extensions to the Protocol System Model

Many extensions to the protocol system model are possible without affecting the properties of image protocols presented in Section IV. Almost all such extensions are concerned with generalizing the model of channel behavior.

The channel model described in Section II-B is already quite general. However, in some real systems, additional features in the channel model are desirable. For example, control messages in the BSC protocol are not protected by error detection [15]. If a BSC control message has bit errors, it may be received and mistaken by the receiving entity as some other control message. Such behavior can be modeled as a new type of error event. In general, channel events can be specified as a subset of $\boldsymbol{M}_k \times \boldsymbol{M}_k$. In this case, Lemma 3 no longer applies and all image channel events must individually satisfy the well-formed property.

The method of projections allows very general channel behavior because its objective is limited to defining image protocols that preserve specific logical properties of a given protocol system. We must keep in mind that if channels have many different types of error events, communication protocols have to be extremely complex in order to possess desirable logical properties. Thus for protocols with limited capabilities, such as the full-duplex data transfer example in this article, we must assume that the channels are well-behaved in order for them to possess desirable properties. The assumption of error-free channels in our examples is due to the simplicity of our example protocols and not required by the method of projections.

Multidestination Channels: A channel can be in the incoming channel set of more than one protocol entity. It is a broadcast channel if it is in the incoming set of every protocol entity. When one of these protocol entities executes a receive event, the message being received is not deleted from the channel after the event occurrence. For a multidestination channel, we assume that the message at the head of the channel has a finite lifetime which is enforced by some "channel controller." (See [20], [21] for discussions on the modeling of real-time and global timing relationships in a system.)

We shall refer to protocol entities that can receive messages from channel C_k as its eligible receivers. The equivalence relation used in the definition of image messages is modified as follows: two messages m and n in M_{ik} are treated as equivalent only if their receptions cause identical state changes in the image state spaces of *all eligible receivers* of C_k. Also, messages in M_{ik} have a null image if (and only if) their receptions do not cause any state change in the image state space of each of the eligible receivers of C_k.

Lastly for a multidestination channel, any image receive event $(s', r', +m')$ where $s' = r'$ is a null image event since m is not deleted from the channel by receive events.

The proofs in Appendix II are given with this extension incorporated into the protocol system model.

Channel Insertions/Deletions: For the sake of clarity, we have specified that a send event appends a message to the end of a channel's message sequence, and only the first message in the channel is eligible for reception. This requirement is necessary only when null image messages are deleted from the image message set of a channel (i.e., infinite-buffer channel). If null image messages are included in the image message set of C_k, a send event can insert anywhere into the message sequence in C_k, and any message in C_k can be made eligible for reception. The proofs in Appendix II can be trivially extended to accommodate this generalization. Note also that relaxing the assumption that only the first message in the channel is eligible for reception will also allow us to relax the finite lifetime assumption in Section IV-C-1.

Message Priority Classes: Messages in the message sets M_{ik} of C_k may be specified as belonging to different priority classes. Two types of behavior may depend upon a message's priority class. First, error events of a channel C_k can be defined for each position of C_k as well as the priority class of the message residing in that position. Messages in some classes can be made invulnerable to a particular type of error. For example, the following specification can be made: a loss event for the ith position of C_k is enabled if $\boldsymbol{m}_k$ has a message in that position *and* it belongs to a class that is vulnerable to a loss.

Second, the bumping rule in Section II can be generalized to the following: the selection of a message to delete may be specified by any rule that depends upon the positions and priority classes of the messages in the channel.

In the construction of an image protocol, messages in M_{ik} can be aggregated to form the same image message only if they have the same priority class and invulnerability to errors. Note that if M_k' includes null image messages, we have to define different β's, one for each combination of priority class and invulnerability.

The proofs in Appendix II are given with this extension incorporated into the protocol system model.

Initial State of the Protocol System: For notational simplicity, we have assumed that the initial state g_0 of the protocol system is uniquely specified and R is the reachability graph from g_0. Note that all lemmas and theorems in this article do not depend upon an initial state g_0. Thus, instead of specifying a single initial state, a set G_0 of possible initial states can be specified. Redefine R to be the reachability graph from G_0 and R' to be the reachability graph from $G_0' = \{g' : g \in G_0\}$. Proofs of the four corollaries can be trivially extended to accommodate this generalization.

Appendix II
Proofs

The proofs are given with some of the extensions in Appendix I incorporated into the protocol system model.

Proof of Lemma 1: For message sequences $\boldsymbol{m}$ and $\boldsymbol{n}$ in M_k, suppose that a loss event in E_k can take $\boldsymbol{m}$ to $\boldsymbol{n}$. Then, $\boldsymbol{n}$ is obtained by deleting a message y from $\boldsymbol{m}$. If C_k is a finite-buffer channel, then the corresponding image message y' is in $\boldsymbol{m}'$, and the same loss event in E_k' can delete y' and take the channel to state $\boldsymbol{n}'$. If C_k is an infinite-buffer channel, then null images are not included in $\boldsymbol{m}'$. If y has a null image, then $\boldsymbol{m}' = \boldsymbol{n}'$; otherwise, y' is in $\boldsymbol{m}'$ and there is a loss event in E_k' that can delete y' and take the channel to state $\boldsymbol{n}'$.

Similar arguments can be used for duplication and reordering events.

(End of proof of Lemma 1)

Proof of Lemma 2: Since g is extendable to g, h, there is an event e in E that takes the protocol system from g to h. The event e can be either a channel event or an entity event. If e is a channel event, then the statement in Lemma 2 is implied by Lemma 1, since a channel event changes the state of the channel only. We next consider the three types of entity events. In the rest of this proof, let $g = (s_1, s_2, \cdots, s_I; \boldsymbol{m}_1, \boldsymbol{m}_2, \cdots, \boldsymbol{m}_K)$ with the image $g' = (s_1', s_2', \cdots, s_I'; \boldsymbol{m}_1', \boldsymbol{m}_2', \cdots, \boldsymbol{m}_K')$.

Case 1: e is an internal event of P_i. Since e is enabled at g, $e = (s_i, r_i, \alpha)$ for some $r_i \in S_i$. h is obtained from g by replacing s_i with r_i. Now, consider the image state g' and the image event $e' = (s_i', r_i', \alpha)$. If $s_i' = r_i'$, then $g' = h'$. If $s_i' \neq r_i'$, then e' is not null and belongs to T_i'. e' is enabled at g' and takes the image protocol system to a state f', where f' is obtained from g' by replacing s_i' with r_i'. It is easy to see that f' is the same as the image of h.

Case 2: e is a send event involving P_i and C_k. Since e is enabled at g, $e = (s_i, r_i, -n)$ for some $r_i \in S_i$ and some $n \in M_{ik}$. Then, h is obtained from g by replacing s_i with r_i and appending n to the tail of $\boldsymbol{m}_k$. (Assume no bumping for now.) Consider the image state g' and the image event $e' = (s_i', r_i', -n')$. If e' is a null image event, we have $g' = h'$. Otherwise, e' belongs to T_i'. e' is enabled at g' and takes the image protocol system to the image global state f' which is obtained from g' by replacing s_i' with r_i' and appending n' to the tail of $\boldsymbol{m}_k'$. (For an infinite-buffer channel, if n' is a null image message, its insertion has no effect on the channel state. The image channel state of C_k in f' remains the same as $\boldsymbol{m}_k'$.) It is easy to see that f' is the same as h', the image of h.

Now suppose that bumping occurred. Let the message bumped be y; y is either the message sent or a message in $\boldsymbol{m}_k$. Consider the image message y, corresponding to y. Note that each message in $\boldsymbol{m}_k$ and its image in $\boldsymbol{m}_k'$ must have the same priority class and occupy the same position in C_k. Hence y' can be bumped in the image protocol system. Again, it is easy to see that f' is the same as h'.

Case 3: e is a receive event involving P_i and C_k. Since e is enabled at g, the following two conditions hold. First, $\boldsymbol{m}_k$ is not empty; let $n \in M_k$ be the first message in $\boldsymbol{m}_k$. Second, $e = (s_i, r_i, +n)$ for some $r_i \in S_i$. Then, h is obtained from g by replacing s_i with r_i and removing n from $\boldsymbol{m}_k$. (Let C_k be a single-destination channel.) Consider the image state g' and the image event $e' = (s_i', r_i', +n')$. If e' is a null image event, then $g' = h'$. Otherwise, e' belongs to T_i'. (If C_k is an infinite-buffer channel, we also know that n' is not a null image message.) e' is enabled at g' and takes the image protocol system to the image global state f', which is obtained from g' by replacing s_i' with r_i' and removing n' from the head of $\boldsymbol{m}_k'$. It is easy to see that f' is the same as h', the image of h. Lastly, if C_k is a multidestination channel, the occurrence of e does not remove n from $\boldsymbol{m}_k$ and the occurrence of e' does not remove n' from $\boldsymbol{m}_k'$. f' is still equal to h'.

(End of proof of Lemma 2)

Proof of Theorem 1: The proof is by induction on path length. A unit-length path in (G, τ) corresponds to a global state g in G. The image of g is g', which is a unit length path in (G', τ').

For some positive integer n, assume that the image of every path in (G, τ) of length n is a path in (G', τ'). We will show that the image of any path of length $n + 1$ is a path in (G', τ'). Let $w = u, f_n$ be a path of length $n + 1$ in (G, τ), where $u = f_0, f_1, \cdots, f_{n-1}$. Obviously, u is a path of length n in (G, τ). From the above hypothesis, u' is a path in (G', τ') and the last state in u' is f_{n-1}'. If $f_n' = f_{n-1}'$, then $w' = u'$ and the image of w is a path in (G', τ'). If $f_n' \neq f_{n-1}'$, then by Lemma 2, f_{n-1}' is extendable to f_{n-1}', f_n'. Hence u' is extendable to u', f_n' which is w', and the image of w is a path in (G', τ').

(End of proof of Theorem 1)

Proof of Corollary 1: The first element of any path w in R is g_0. Let the image of w be w'. From Theorem 1, w' is a path in (G', τ'). The first element of w' is g_0'. Hence, w' is a path in R'.

(End of proof of Corollary 1)

Proof of Corollary 2: For any reachable state $g \in R_s$, there is a path w leading from g_0 to g. From Corollary 1, w' is a path in R'. The last element of w' is g'. Hence, g' is in R_s'.

(End of proof of Corollary 2)

Proof of Lemma 3: Consider message sequences $\boldsymbol{m}'$ and $\boldsymbol{n}'$ in M_k' and an error event in E_k' that can take $\boldsymbol{m}'$ to $\boldsymbol{n}'$. Suppose that null image messages are included in M_k', so that each element y' in $\boldsymbol{m}'$ has a corresponding element y at the same position in any $\boldsymbol{p}$ whose image is $\boldsymbol{m}'$. Also all messages with the same image have by definition identical priority and invulnerability to errors. Thus, the same error event in E_k can take any $\boldsymbol{p}$ whose image is $\boldsymbol{m}'$ to some $\boldsymbol{q}$ whose image is $\boldsymbol{n}'$. Each event in E_k' is strongly well-formed.

Let C_k be an infinite-buffer channel and E_k specified by the uniform error model. Suppose that E_k' (same as E_k) contains the loss event is specified for the first position of C_k. Consider a message sequence $\boldsymbol{m}'$ with y' as its first element. Any message sequence $\boldsymbol{p}$ whose image is $\boldsymbol{m}'$ must contain a corresponding element y that is preceded by null image messages (if any).

The same loss event in E_k can delete the null image messages one by one and then delete y in $\boldsymbol{p}$. Hence, this loss event is well-formed (but not strongly well-formed). Other error events (loss, duplication or reordering) in E_k, when present, are specified for all positions of C_k for each type of event. Consider message sequences $\boldsymbol{m}'$ and $\boldsymbol{n}'$ in M_k' and an error event in E_k that can take $\boldsymbol{m}'$ to $\boldsymbol{n}'$. Each element y' in $\boldsymbol{m}'$ has a corresponding element y in any $\boldsymbol{p}$ whose image is $\boldsymbol{m}'$. The position of y in $\boldsymbol{p}$ may be different from that of y' in $\boldsymbol{m}'$. Since the uniform error model specifies this type of error event for all positions of C_k, an error event of the same type exists that can take $\boldsymbol{p}$ to some $\boldsymbol{q}$ whose image is $\boldsymbol{n}'$. Such error events are strongly well-formed.

With duplication events, remember that all messages with the same image must have the same priority class when applying the bumping rule.

(End of proof of Lemma 3)

Proof of Lemma 4: Since g' is extendable to g', h', there is an event $e' \in E'$ that takes the image protocol system from g' to h'. Let $g' = (s_1', s_2', \cdots, s_I'; \boldsymbol{m}_1', \boldsymbol{m}_2', \cdots, \boldsymbol{m}_K')$. e' can be either a channel event or an entity event. If e' is a channel event in E_k, then h' is the same as g' except for the state of channel C_k. Let $\boldsymbol{n}_k'$ be the state of channel C_k in h'. From Lemma 3, we note that the same channel event will take any $\boldsymbol{p}$ whose image is $\boldsymbol{m}_k'$ to some $\boldsymbol{q}$ whose image is $\boldsymbol{n}_k'$. Hence, it will take any f_1 whose image is g' to some f_2 whose image is h'. We next consider e' to be an image entity event of P_i'. Three cases are considered for the three types of entity events. Since the image protocol system has well-formed events, e' is well-formed in each case. Let $f_1 = (a_1, a_2, \cdots, a_I; \boldsymbol{p}_1, \boldsymbol{p}_2, \cdots, \boldsymbol{p}_K)$ be any global state whose image is g'.

Case 1: e' is an image internal event of P_i'. Since e' is enabled at g', T_i' contains $e' = (s_i', r_i', \alpha)$ for some $r_i' \in S_i'$. h' is the same as g' except for the state of P_i'. Since e' is well-formed, we know that there exists some $b \in S_i$ that is internally reachable from a_i, and event (b, c, α) exists in T_i such that $b' = s_i'$ and $c' = r_i'$. The sequence of events that makes b internally reachable from a_i will extend f_1 to some global state f_n; the image of each element in the extension is g'. In the global state f_n, the state of P_i is b and (b, c, α) in T_i will take f_n to some f_{n+1} whose image is h'.

Case 2: e' is an image send event involving P_i and C_k. Since e' is enabled at g', T_i' contains $e' = (s_i', r_i', -n')$ for some $r_i' \in S_i'$ and $n' \in M_{ik}'$. h' is obtained from g' by replacing s_i' with r_i' and appending n' to the tail of $\boldsymbol{m}_k'$. (Assume no bumping for now.) Since e' is well-formed, we know that there exists some $b \in S_i$ that is internally reachable from a_i, and event $(b, c, -y)$ exists in T_i for some c and some y such that $b' = s_i', c' = r_i'$, and $y' = n'$. The sequence of events that makes b internally reachable from a_i will extend f_1 to a global state f_n; the image of each element in the extension is g'. In the global state f_n, the state of P_i is b and $(b, c, -y)$ in T_i will take f_n to some f_{n+1} whose image is h'.

Now assume that bumping occurred. Let z' be the message bumped; z' is either the message n' that was sent or a message in $\boldsymbol{m}_k'$. Consider the message z corresponding to z'. Since the bumping rule depends only on positions in C_k and message priority classes, both of which are preserved when aggregating messages, z can be bumped in the original protocol system. Again, f_{n+1} has the image h'.

Case 3: e' is an image receive event involving P_i and C_k. Since e' is enabled at g', T_i' contains $e' = (s_i', r_i', +n')$ for some $r_i' \in S_i'$ and $n' \in M_k'$. h' is obtained from g' by replacing s_i' with r_i' and removing n' from the head of $\boldsymbol{m}_k'$. (If C_k is a multi-destination channel, n' is not removed from $\boldsymbol{m}_k'$.) Consider the state of channel C_k in any global state f_1 whose image is g'. If null image messages are included in $\boldsymbol{M}_k'$, then the first element in the channel state $\boldsymbol{p}_k$ has the image n'. If null image messages are deleted from M_k' (i.e., C_k is an infinite-buffer channel), then the message y in $\boldsymbol{p}_k$ corresponding to the image message n' may be preceded by messages with a null image. By the finite life-time assumption of the original protocol system, these messages having a null image will be deleted in finite time (each message deletion is an event that affects only the state of the channel). Suppose now that the first element in channel C_k is y with the image n'. Since e' is well-formed, we know that there exists some b in S_i that is internally reachable from a_i, and event $(b, c, +y)$ exists in T_i for some c such that $b' = s_i'$ and $c' = r_i'$. The sequence of events that makes b internally reachable (as well as those events that delete null image messages in front of y in an infinite-buffer channel) will extend f_1 to some global state f_n; the image of each element in the extension is g'. In the global state f_n, the state of P_i is b and $(b, c, +y)$ in T_i will take f_n to some f_{n+1} whose image is h'.

(End of proof of Lemma 4)

Proof of Theorem 2: Let the last element in u' be $g' \in G'$ and the last element in w be $f \in G$. Since $w' = u'$, we must have $f' = g'$. To prove Theorem 2, it suffices to show the following: if g' is extendable to a path y' in (G', τ'), then f is extendable to a path z in (G, τ) such that $z' = y'$. This can be easily shown using Lemma 4 and applying induction.

(End of proof of Theorem 2)

Proof of Corollary 3: The corollary follows immediately from Thoerem 2.

(End of proof of Corollary 3)

Proof of Corollary 4: Any g' in R_s' lies on a path u' from g_0' to g'. Since g_0 is in R, from Corollary 3, g_0 can be extended to a path w such that $w' = u'$. Let the last element in w be f. We must have $f \in R_s$ and $f' = g'$.

(End of proof of Corollary 4)

REFERENCES

[1] G. V. Bochmann and R. J. Chung, "A formalized specification of HDLC classes of procedures," in *Conf. Rec. Nat. Telecommun. Conf.*, Los Angeles, CA, Dec. 1977, pp. 3A: 2-1-2-11.

[2] G. V. Bochmann, "Finite state description of communication protocols," *Comput. Networks*, vol. 2, pp. 361-372, Oct. 1978.

[3] G. V. Bochmann and C. A. Sunshine, "Formal methods in communication protocol design," *IEEE Trans. Commun.*, vol. COM-28, pp. 624-631, Apr. 1980.

[4] G. V. Bochmann and P. Merlin, "On the construction of communication protocols," in *Proc. 5th ICCC*, Atlanta, GA, Oct. 1980.

[5] D. Brand and W. H. Joyner, "Verification of protocols using symbolic execution," *Comput. Networks*, vol. 2, pp. 351-360, Sept. 1978.

[6] ——, "Verification of HDLC," *IEEE Trans. Commun.*, vol. COM-30, pp. 1136-1142, May 1982.

[7] E. W. Dijkstra, *A Discipline of Programming.* Englewood Cliffs, NJ: Prentice-Hall, 1976, pp. 15-23, ch. 3.
[8] B. L. DiVito, "Verification of communication protocols and abstract process models," Ph.D. dissertation, Dep. Comput. Sci., Univ. Texas, Austin, 1982.
[9] B. T. Hailpern and S. S. Owicki, "Verifying network protocols using temporal logic," Comput. Syst. Lab., Stanford Univ., Tech. Rep. 192, June 1980.
[10] Int. Standards Org., "Data communications–HDLC procedures–Elements of procedures," Ref. ISO 4335, 1979.
[11] J. Kurose, "The specification and verification of a connection establishment protocol using temporal logic," in *Proc. 2nd Int. Workshop Protocol Specification, Testing and Verification*, Idyllwild, CA, May 1982, pp. 43-62.
[12] S. S. Lam and A. U. Shankar, "Protocol projections: A method for analyzing communication protocols," in *Conf. Rec. Nat. Telecommun. Conf.*, New Orleans, LA, Nov. 1981.
[13] —, "Verification of communication protocols via protocol projections," in *Proc. INFOCOM'82*, Las Vegas, NV, Apr. 1982, pp. 229-240.
[14] —, "An illustration of protocol projections," in *Proc. 2nd Int. Workshop Protocol Specification, Testing and Verification*, Idyllwild, CA, May 1982 (original version).
[15] S. S. Lam, "Data link control procedures," in *Computer Communications–Vol. I: Principles*, W. Chou, Ed. Englewood Cliffs, NJ: Prentice-Hall, 1983, ch. 3.
[16] R. Razouk, "Modeling X.25 using the graph model of behavior," in *Proc. 2nd Int. Workshop Protocol Specification, Testing and Verification*, Idyllwild, CA, May 1982, pp. 197-214.
[17] R. L. Schwartz and P. M. Melliar-Smith, "From state machines to temporal logic: Specification methods for protocol standards," *IEEE Trans. Commun.*, vol. COM-30, pp. 2486-2496, Dec. 1982.
[18] A. U. Shankar and S. S. Lam, "On time-dependent communication protocols and their projections," in *Proc. 2nd Int. Workshop Protocol Specification, Testing and Verification*, Idyllwild, CA, May 1982, pp. 215-236.
[19] A. U. Shankar, "Analysis of communication protocols via protocol projections," Ph.D. dissertation, Dep. Elec. Eng., Univ. Texas, Austin, Dec. 1982.
[20] A. U. Shankar and S. S. Lam, "An HDLC protocol specification and its verification using image protocols," *ACM Trans. Comput. Syst.*, vol. 4, pp. 331-368, Nov. 1983.
[21] —, "*Specification and verification of communication networks, Part 1: Safety, liveness and real time properties, Part 2: Method of projections*," Dep. Comput. Sci., Univ. Texas, Austin, Tech. Reps., 1984, in preparation.
[22] L. Sloan, "Mechanisms that enforce bounds on packet lifetimes," *ACM Trans. Comput. Syst.*, vol. 1, Nov. 1983.
[23] N. V. Stenning, "A data transfer protocol," *Comput. Networks*, vol. 1, pp. 99-110, Sept. 1976.
[24] P. Zafiropulo *et al.*, "Towards analyzing and synthesizing protocols," *IEEE Trans. Commun.*, vol. COM-28, pp. 651-660, Apr. 1980.

Simon S. Lam (S'69-M'74-SM'80) was born in Macao on July 31, 1947. He received the B.S.E.E. degree (with distinction) from Washington State University, Pullman, in 1969, and the M.S. and Ph.D. degrees in engineering from the University of California, Los Angeles, in 1970 and 1974, respectively.

From 1972 to 1974, he was with the ARPA Network project at UCLA and did research on satellite packet communication. From 1974 to 1977, he was a research staff member with the IBM Thomas J. Watson Research Center, Yorktown Heights, NY, where he worked on performance analysis problems of packet switching networks, SNA, and satellite networks. Since September 1977, he has been with the University of Texas at Austin where he is now a Professor of Computer Sciences. His current research interests include: specification and verification of communication protocols, modeling and design of computer networks and distributed systems, and queueing theory.

Dr. Lam is a member of Tau Beta Pi, Sigma Tau, Phi Kappa Psi, Pi Mu Epsilon, and the Association for Computing Machinery. At the University of California, Los Angeles, he held a Phi Kappa Phi Fellowship from 1969 to 1970, and a Chancellor's Teaching Fellowship from 1969 to 1973. He received the 1975 Leonard G. Abraham Award for the best paper in the field of communications systems published in IEEE TRANSACTIONS IN COMMUNICATIONS. He was Program Chairman of the first ACM SIGCOMM Symposium on Communications Architectures and Protocols in 1983. He serves on the Board of Editors of the international journal *Performance Evaluation* and is Associate Editor for Network Protocols of the IEEE TRANSACTIONS ON COMMUNICATIONS and the IEEE JOURNAL ON SELECTED AREAS IN COMMUNICATIONS.

A. Udaya Shankar (SM'82-M'83) received the B. Tech degree in electrical engineering from the Indian Institute of Technology, Kanpur, India, in 1976, the M.S. degree in computer engineering from Syracuse University, Syracuse, NY, in 1978, and the Ph.D. degree in electrical engineering from the University of Texas, Austin, in 1982.

Since January 1983, he has been with the University of Maryland, College Park, where he is an Assistant Professor of Computer Science. His current research interests include modeling and analysis of computer networks, communication protocols, and distributed operating systems.

"An Exercise in Constructing Multi-Phase Communication Protocols" by C.H. Chow, M.G. Gouda, and S.S. Lam from *The Proceedings of the ACM SIGCOMM'84 Conference,* June 1984. Copyright 1984, Association for Computing Machinery, Inc., reprinted by permission.

AN EXERCISE IN CONSTRUCTING MULTI-PHASE COMMUNICATION PROTOCOLS

C. H. Chow†, M. G. Gouda and S. S. Lam†

Department of Computer Sciences
University of Texas at Austin

ABSTRACT

Many real-life protocols can be observed to go through different phases performing a distinct function in each phase. We present a multi-phase model for such protocols. A phase is formally defined to be a network of communicating finite state machines with certain desirable correctness properties; these include proper termination, and freedom from deadlocks and unspecified receptions. A multi-function protocol is constructed by first constructing separate phases to perform its different functions. We discuss how to connect these phases together to implement the multi-function protocol such that the resulting network of communicating finite state machines is also a phase (i.e. it possesses the desirable properties defined for phases). A high-level session control protocol modeled after one in IBM's Systems Network Architecture is discussed, and constructed as a multi-phase protocol.

†Work supported in part by National Science Foundation Grants No. ECS78-01803 and No. ECS83-04734, and in part by a research grant from IBM Corporation.

1. Introduction

A layered communications architecture facilitates the construction of networking software in a modular fashion. Nevertheless each protocol layer is a set of complex parallel programs. Several distinct functions can usually be identified among the tasks designated for a protocol layer to perform. Of interest to us are methods for reducing the analysis/construction of a multi-function protocol to the analyses/construction of smaller single-function protocols. Given a multi-function protocol, its analysis can be reduced to the analyses of several smaller single-function protocols, called image protocols, using the method of projections [LAM 81, LAM 82, SHAN 83].

This paper is concerned with the construction of a multi-function protocol from a composition of single-function protocols. In general, this is a difficult problem. However, many real-life protocols can be observed to go through different phases of behavior. In particular, these protocols go through their phases one at a time with a distinct function performed in each phase. For protocols characterized by this model of multi-phase behavior, the following three-step methodology for constructing a multi-function protocol is proposed:

i. Divide the protocol's functionality into separate functions.

ii. For each function, construct and verify a phase to perform this function. A phase is a network of communicating finite state machines that satisfies certain desirable general properties (including proper termination, and freedom from deadlocks and unspecified receptions) to be defined.

iii. Connect individual phases together to form the required protocol. The resulting protocol should satisfy the same general properties of proper termination, and freedom from deadlocks and unspecified receptions as the individual phases.

Step i of the above methodology is straightforward; the protocol's functions can often be divided quite naturally. For example, a half-duplex data link control protocol such as IBM's BSC protocol can be divided into three functions [IBM 70, LAM 83]: a call setup function, a data transfer function, and a call clear function.

For step ii of the methodology, there are two basic approaches. In the first approach, each phase is constructed based on the designer's knowledge and experience. It is then verified using available verification techniques, e.g. efficient reachability analysis [BOCH 78, RUBI 82, YU 82, YU 83, GOUD 82c], program proving methods [GOOD 77, HAIL 80, MISR 81, MISR 82], or symbolic execution [BRAN 78]. If an error is found in a phase, the phase is modified and the verification repeated, and so on until a provably correct phase is obtained. In the second approach, each phase is constructed using some constructive design rules that automatically result in correct phases. See for example [BOCH 80, ZAFI 80, MERL 83, GOUD 81].

Step iii of the methodology has received little attention so far, although it is agreed in [RAZO 80, WEST 78] that many errors in a protocol are caused by improper connections between different phases of the protocol.

In this paper, we formally characterize the concept of a phase, and present a methodology to connect the different phases of a protocol to yield a protocol that satisfies the general correctness properties of proper termination, freedom from deadlocks and unspecified receptions, and also boundedness. We demonstrate how one realistic protocol can be constructed (and understood) in this fashion. Details of our theory and two other examples can be found in [CHOW 83].

This paper is organized as follows. In Section 2, the model of communicating finite state machines is presented. The concept of phases is formally defined in Section 3. The construction of a protocol by connecting phases together is discussed in Section 4; the construction method guarantees that the resulting multi-phase protocol terminates properly and is free from deadlocks and unspecified receptions. In Section 5, we present a multi-phase protocol example, namely a high-level session control protocol modeled after IBM's SNA specification for LU-LU session management [CYPS 78]. Concluding remarks are in Section 6.

2. Networks of Communicating Finite State Machines

For the sake of conciseness, we present our theory (Sections 2, 3 and 4) using networks of two communicating finite state machines. However, our results can be extended in a straightforward manner to networks of n communicating finite state machines [CHOW 83].

A *communicating finite state machine* M is a directed labelled graph with two types of edges, namely *sending* and *receiving edges*. A sending (or receiving) edge is labelled -g (or +g, respectively) for some *message* g in a finite set G of messages. A node in M whose outgoing edges are all sending (or all receiving) edges is called a *sending* (or *receiving*, respectively) *node*. A node in M whose outgoing edges include both sending and receiving edges is called a *mixed node*, and a node in M that has no outgoing edges is called a *final node*. One of the nodes in M is identified as its *initial node*, and each node in M is reachable by a directed path from the initial node.

Let M and N be two communicating finite state machines with the same set G of messages; the pair (M,N) is called a *network* of M and N.

A *state* of network (M,N) is a four-tuple [v,w,x,y], where v and w are two nodes in M and N respectively, and x and y are two strings over the messages in G. Informally, a state [v,w,x,y] means that the executions of M and N have reached nodes v and w respectively, while the input channels of M and N store the strings x and y respectively.

The *initial state* of network (M,N) is $[v_0, w_0, E, E]$ where v_0 and w_0 are the initial nodes in M and N respectively, and E is the empty string.

Let s=[v,w,x,y] be a state of network (M,N); and let e be an outgoing edge of node v or w. A state s' is said to *follow s over e* iff one of the following four conditions is satisfied:

i. e is a sending edge, labelled -g, from v to v' in M, and s'=[v',w,x,y.g], where "." is the concatenation operator.

ii. e is a sending edge, labelled -g, form w to w' in N, and s'=[v,w',x.g,y].

iii. e is a receiving edge, labelled +g, from v to v' in M, and s'=[v',w,x',y], where x=g.x'.

iv. e is a receiving edge, labelled +g, from w to w' in N, and s'=[v,w',x,y'], where y=g.y'.

Let s and s' be two states of network (M,N), s' *follows* s iff there is a directed edge e in M or N such that s' follows s over e.

Let s and s' be two states of (M,N), s' is *reachable from* s iff s=s' or there exist states $s_1,...,s_r$ such that $s=s_1$, $s'=s_r$ and s_{i+1} follows s_i for i=1,...,r-1.

A state s of network (M,N) is said to be *reachable* iff it is reachable from the initial state of (M,N). Next, we use the concept of reachable states to define what it means for the communication of a network (M,N) to terminate properly and to be free from deadlocks and unspecified receptions, and to be bounded.

The communication of a network (M,N) is said to *terminate properly* iff the following two conditions are satisfied:

i. For any reachable state [v,w,x,y] of (M,N), if v is a final node of M, then x must be the empty string and there must be a directed path of all receiving edges from node w to a final node w' in N, where the string y is received.

ii. For any reachable state [v,w,x,y] of (M,N), if w is a final node of N, then y must be the empty string and there must be a directed path of all receiving edges from node v to a final node v' in M, where the string x is received.

A reachable state [v,w,E,E] of (M,N) is called a *proper terminating state* iff both nodes v and w are final nodes.

A reachable state [v,w,x,y] of a network (M,N) is a *deadlock state* iff (i) both v and w are receiving nodes, and (ii) x=y=E (the empty string). If no reachable state of network (M,N) is a deadlock state, then the communication of (M,N) is said to be *deadlock-free*.

A reachable state [v,w,x,y] of a network (M,N) is an *unspecified reception state* iff one of the following two conditions is satisfied:

i. $x=g_1 \cdot g_2 \cdot \ldots \cdot g_k$ $(k \geq 1)$, and v is a receiving node and none of its outgoing edges is labelled $+g_1$.

ii. $y=g_1 \cdot g_2 \cdot \ldots \cdot g_k$ $(k \geq 1)$, and w is a receiving node and none of its outgoing edges is labelled $+g_1$.

If no reachable state of (M,N) is an unspecified reception state, then the communication of (M,N) is said to be *free from unspecified receptions*.

The communication of a network (M,N) is said to be *bounded by* K, where K is a nonnegative integer, iff for every reachable state [v,w,x,y] of (M,N), $|x| \leq K$ and $|y| \leq K$ where |x| is the number of messages in string x. The communication is said to be *bounded* iff it is bounded by some nonnegative integer K; otherwise it is *unbounded*.

3. Phases

Let M and N be two communicating finite state machines. The network (M,N) is called *safe* iff its communication terminates properly and is free from deadlocks and unspecified receptions.

Let (M,N) be a safe network, and let v and w be two final nodes in machines M and N respectively. The node pair (v,w) is called an *exit node pair* of (M,N) iff the state [v,w,E,E] of (M,N) is reachable.

The *exit set* of a safe network (M,N) is the set of all exit node pairs of (M,N).

A safe network (M,N) is called a *phase* iff every final node in M or N appears in exactly one exit node pair in the exit set of (M,N).

Consider the following problem. Is it decidable whether an arbitrary network is a phase? In general, this problem is undecidable as discussed in [BRAN 83, GOUD 82b]. However, the problem can be decided in some special cases: For instance, if the communication of the given network (M,N) is bounded, then the problem can be decided by generating and checking all the reachable states of (M,N). In [CHOW 83], we discuss a technique, based on the concept of closed covers in [GOUD 82a], to verify that a given network is a phase even if the number of its reachable states is infinite.

4. Constructing Multi-Phase Networks

In this section we discuss a discipline to connect a number of phases together to construct a multi-phase network that is also a phase (thus guaranteeing that its communication terminates properly and is free from deadlocks and unspecified receptions). Phases are connected by joining the exit node pairs of one phase to the initial node pair of another phase, or the same phase. The technique is discussed in detail next.

Let $p_1=(M_1,N_1)$ and $p_2=(M_2,N_2)$ be two phases, with exit sets S_1 and S_2 respectively, and let C be a subset of of S_1. We define a *composite network* of p_1, C, and p_2, denoted by $<p_1,C,p_2>$, to be the network (M,N) where

i. M is the communicating finite state machine constructed (from M_1, C, and M_2) by joining all the final nodes of M_1 in C to the initial node of M_2. The initial node of M_1 becomes the initial node of M.

ii. N is the communicating finite state machine constructed (from N_1, C, and N_2) by joining all the final nodes of N_1 in C to the initial node of N_2. The initial node of N_1 becomes the initial node of N.

The two phases $p_1=(M_1,N_1)$ and $p_2=(M_2,N_2)$ are called the *constituent phases* of the composite network $<p_1,C,p_2>$. In this case, machines M_1 and M_2 are called the *constituent machines* of M, and machines N_1 and N_2 are called the *constituent machines* of N. It is proved in [CHOW 83] that the composite network $<p_1,C,p_2>$ is also a phase whose exit set is $(S_1 \cup S_2) - C$.

As an example, Figure 1a shows two phases $p_1=(M_1,N_1)$ and $p_2=(M_2,N_2)$. In phase p_1, the node pair (1,1) is its initial node pair and {(2,2),(3,3)} is its exit set. In phase p_2 the node pair (4,4) is its initial node pair and {(5,5)} is its exit set. By joining the exit node pair (2,2) of p_1 to the initial node pair (4,4), we have the composite network $p_{1,2}=<p_1,\{(2,2)\},p_2>$ shown in Figure 1b.

So far we have discussed how to connect one phase to another. Next, we discuss how to connect a phase to itself.

Let $p_1=(M_1,N_1)$ be a phase whose exit set is S_1, and let C be a subset of S_1. The *composite network* of p_1 and C, denoted $<p_1,C>$, is a network (M,N) where

i. M is the communicating finite state machine constructed (from M_1 and C) by joining all the final nodes of M_1 in C to the initial node of M_1. The initial node of M_1 becomes the initial node of M.

ii. N is the communicating finite state machine constructed (from N_1 and C) by joining all the final nodes of N_1 in C to the initial node of N_1. The initial node of N_1 becomes the initial node of N.

Phase $p_1=(M_1,N_1)$ is called the *constituent phase* of the composite network $<p_1,C>=(M,N)$. In this case, machines M_1 and N_1 are called the *constituent machines* of M and N respectively. It is proved in [CHOW 83] that the composite network $<p_1,C>$ is also a phase whose exit set is $S_1 - C$.

For example, consider phase $p_{1,2}$ in Figure 1b, if we join the exit node pair (5,5) of $p_{1,2}$ to its initial node pair, then we get the composite network $<p_{1,2},\{(5,5)\}>$ shown in Figure 1c.

The construction process of the multi-phase network p^* in Figure 1c from the two phases p_1 and p_2 in Figure 1a can be represented by the following sequence of equations:

$$\begin{aligned} p_1 &= (M_1,N_1) \\ p_2 &= (M_2,N_2) \\ p_{1,2} &= <p_1,\{(2,2)\},p_2> \\ p^* &= <p_{1,2},\{(5,5)\}> \end{aligned}$$

This equation sequence clearly provides all the information needed to construct p^* from p_1 and p_2; moreover it is a more concise notation than the graphical representations in Figures 1b and 1c.

5. A Session Protocol Example

The concept of phases can be extended in a straightforward manner to networks with r $(r\geq 2)$ communicating finite state machines. As an example, we construct in this section a high-level session control protocol modeled after IBM's SNA specification for LU-LU session management [CYPS 78]. It is a multi-phase network of three communicating finite state machines. We discuss next how to extend earlier definitions to the case of networks with three communicating machines.

Consider a network of three communicating finite state machines. Each machine in the network can communicate with each of the other machines by exchanging messages over two, one-directional unbounded FIFO channels. In order to uniquely specify which machine is intended by each sending (receiving) operation, a sending (receiving) edge is now labelled -g/M (+g/M), where M is the machine to (from) which the message g is sent (received).

Let M_1, M_2 and M_3 be three communicating finite state machines with the same set G of messages; the triple (M_1,M_2,M_3) is called a *network* of the three machines. A *state* of the network (M_1,M_2,M_3) is a 3x3 matrix s_{ij}, where the component s_{ii} is a node in M_i,i=1,2,3, and the component s_{ij} $(i\neq j)$ is a string over the messages in G representing the contents of the channel from machine M_i to M_j. The definitions of reachable state, proper termination, freedom from deadlocks and unspecified receptions, boundedness and phases can now be extended in a straightforward manner to networks with three communicating finite state machines.

Next, we discuss the basic phases of the session protocol, where each phase is a network of three machines. Later, we discuss how to connect these phases to construct the protocol.

Session Establishment Phase

Consider the three communicating finite state machines L_1,M_1 and N_1 in Figure 2; they model the IBM LU-LU session establishment procedure in a single domain [CYPS 78]: L_1 models the primary logical unit, M_1 models the session controller, and N_1 models the secondary logical unit. The exchanged messages have the following meanings:

INIT   denotes a "request to set up a session"

message.
RSP denotes a "positive response" message.
NRSP denotes a "negative response" message.
CINIT denotes a "control initiate" message.
BIND denotes a "bind session" message.
BINDF denotes a "bind failure" message.
SST denotes a "session started" message.
SDT denotes a "start data traffic" message.

Starting from node 1, if L_1 (or N_1) wants to setup a session with N_1 (or L_1), it sends an INIT message to the controller M_1. M_1 may reject the request by sending back an NRSP message, that contains the rejection reasons. If M_1 accepts the request, it sends back an RSP message to the sender (L_1 or N_1), then sends a CINIT message to the primary L_1. On receiving CINIT, the primary L_1 may reject the controller's request by sending an NRSP message back to M_1. Or it may accept the request by sending an RSP message back to M_1 followed by a BIND message, that contains the proposed session parameters, to machine N_1. There are two possibilities:

i. *Machine N_1 accepts the session parameters proposed by L_1:* In this case, N_1 sends an RSP message to L_1. L_1 then notifies M_1 about the success of the session setup by sending an SST message. After L_1 gets an RSP message from M_1, L_1 sends an SDT message to N_1. When N_1 is ready for the data transfer, it sends an RSP message back to L_1 and the data transfer between L_1 and N_1 begins without the intervening of M_1.

ii. *Machine N_1 does not accept the session parameters proposed by L_1:* In this case, N_1 sends an NRSP message to L_1. L_1 then notifies M_1 about the failure of the session setup by sending a BINDF message, and L_1, M_1 and N_1 return to their initial nodes.

Using state exploration, it can be shown that network (L_1,M_1,N_1) is a phase whose exit set is {(14,13,7)}.

Data Transfer Phase

Consider the three communicating finite state machines L_2, M_2, and N_2 in Figure 3; they model a simplified half-duplex flip-flop data transfer procedure in the IBM session protocol: L_2 models the primary logical unit, M_2 models the session controller, and N_2 models the secondary logical unit. The exchanged messages have the following meanings:

D denotes a data message.
RSP denotes a "positive response" message.
SHUT denotes a "shutdown" message.
SHUTC denotes a "shutdown complete" message.

Since machine M_2 is not involved in the data transfer procedure, it is modeled as a single node without any outgoing edges, as shown in Figure 3.

Starting from their initial nodes, L_2 and N_2 take turns to send data and wait for a response. When the primary L_2 wants to terminate the data transfer, it can send at node 1 a SHUT message to N_2. In this case N_2 completes its session processing, then sends a SHUTC message to L_2 and each of L_2 and N_2 reaches its final node. It is straightforward to show that (L_2,M_2,N_2) is a phase whose exit set is {(6,1,6)}.

Session Termination Phase

Consider the three communicating finite state machines L_3, M_3 and N_3 in Figure 4; they model a simplified version of the session termination procedure: L_3 models the primary logical unit, M_3 models the session controller, and N_3 models the secondary logical unit. The exchanged messages have the following meanings:

TERM denotes a "request to terminate a session" message.
RSP denotes a "positive response" message.
CTERM denotes a "control terminate" message.
UNBIND denotes a "unbind session" message.
SE denotes a "session ended" message.

Starting from its initial node, if L_1 (or N_1)

wants to terminate the current session, it sends a TERM message to M_3. When M_3 receives the TERM message, it first responds with an RSP message, and then sends a CTERM message to the primary logical unit L_3. L_3 responds with an RSP message and then sends an UNBIND message to notify N_3 to end the session. On receiving the response to the UNBIND message from N_3, L_3 sends an SE message to notify the controller M_3 that the session between L_3 and N_3 has been ended . M_3 replies with an RSP message and the session termination procedure is then complete.

Note that the three small loops at nodes 4, 8 and 9 of M_3 are dealing with the message collision situations where both L_3 and N_3 concurrently send TERM messages to M_3.

It is straightforward to show that (L_3,M_3,N_3) is a phase whose exit set is $\{(11,12,5)\}$.

Constructing a Multi-Phase Session Protocol

The following equation sequence represents a multi-phase session protocol that consists of the three phases defined earlier (namely, one session establishment phase, one data transfer phase and one session termination phase).

$$
\begin{aligned}
p_1 &= (L_1,M_1,N_1) \\
p_2 &= (L_2,M_2,N_2) \\
p_3 &= (L_3,M_3,N_3) \\
p_{1,2} &= \langle p_1,C_1,p_2 \rangle \\
p_{1,2,3} &= \langle p_{1,2},C_2,p_3 \rangle \\
p &= \langle p_{1,2,3},C_3 \rangle
\end{aligned}
$$

where L_1, M_1 and N_1 are defined in Figure 2
L_2, M_2 and N_2 are defined in Figure 3
L_3, M_3 and N_3 are defined in Figure 4
$C_1=\{(14,13,7) \text{ in } p_1\}$
$C_2=\{(6,1,6) \text{ in } p_2\}$
$C_3=\{(11,12,5) \text{ in } p_3\}$
where (i,j,k) in p_l= the node triple (i,j,k) in phase p_l.

The above multi-phase protocol is guaranteed to terminate properly and be free from deadlocks and unspecified receptions.

6. Concluding Remarks

We have proposed a construction methodology for large multi-phase communication protocols, and demonstrated that this methodology can be used to construct (and explain) some realistic protocols. The resulting protocols are guaranteed to terminate properly and be free from deadlocks and unspecified receptions. More results and examples about the construction of multi-phase protocols can be found in [CHOW 83].

Although the phase concept and the proposed methodology are discussed using communicating finite state machines, it is straightforward to extend the results to facilitate protocol construction using other models such as the extended state transition model of Bochmann et al [BOCH 82].

REFERENCES

[BOCH 78] Bochmann, G. V. "Finite state description of communication protocols," *Computer Networks,* Vol. 2, 1978, pp. 361-371.

[BOCH 80] Bochmann, G. V. and C. Sunshine, "Formal methods in communication protocol design," *IEEE Trans. on Commun.*, April 1980, pp.624-631.

[BOCH 82] Bochmann, G. V. et al, "Experience with formal specifications using an extended state transition model," *IEEE Trans. on Commun.*, Dec. 1982, pp. 2506-2513.

[BRAN 78] Brand, D. and W. H. Joyner, Jr., "Verification of protocols using symbolic execution," *Comput. Networks,* vol. 2, Oct. 1978, pp.351-360.

[BRAN 83] Brand, D. and P. Zafiropulo, "On communicating finite-state machines," *JACM,* Vol. 30, No. 2, April 1983, pp. 323-342.

[CHOW 83] C. H. Chow, M. G. Gouda, and S. S.

Lam, "A discipline for constructing multiphase communication protocols," TR-233, Dept. of Computer Sciences, Univ. of Texas at Austin, June 1983. Revised Oct. 1983. Submitted for publication.

[CYPS 78] Cypser, R. J., "Communications architecture for distributed systems," Reading, Mass., Addison-Wesley, 1978.

[GOOD 77] Good, D. I., "Constructing verified and reliable communications processing systems," *ACM Software Eng. Notes*, vol. 2, Oct. 1977, pp.8-13.

[GOUD 81] Gouda, M. G. and Y. T. Yu, "Synthesis of communicating machines with guaranteed progress", *TR-179*, Dept. of Computer Sciences, Univ. of Texas at Austin, June 1981. Revised Jan. 1983, Oct. 1983. To appear in *IEEE Trans. on Commun.*

[GOUD 82a] Gouda, M. G., "Closed covers: to verify progress for communicating finite state machines," *TR-191*, Dept. of Computer Sciences, Univ. of Texas at Austin, Jan. 1982. Revised Jan. 1983. To appear in *IEEE Trans. on Software Engineering.*

[GOUD 82b] Gouda, M. G., E. G. Manning, and Y. T. Yu, "On the progress of communication between two finite state machines," *TR-200*, Dept. of Computer Sciences, Univ. of Texas at Austin, May 1982. Revised Oct. 1983.

[GOUD 82c] Gouda, M. G. and Y. T. Yu, "Protocol validation by maximal progress state exploration", *TR-211*, Dept. of Computer Sciences, Univ. of Texas at Austin, July 1982. To appear in *IEEE Trans. on Commun.* Jan. 1984.

[GOUD 83] Gouda, M. G., "An example for constructing communicating machines by stepwise refinement," *Proc. 3rd IFIP Workshop on Protocol Specification, Testing, and Verification,* edited by H. Rudin and C. H. West, North-Holland, 1983, pp. 63-74.

[HAIL 80] Hailpern, B. T. and S. S. Owicki, "Verifying network protocols using temporal logic," In *Proceedings Trends and Applications 1980: Computer Network Protocols,* IEEE Computer Society, 1980, pp. 18-28.

[IBM 70] IBM Corp., "General Information--Binary Synchronous Communications," *Manual No. GA27-3004-2, 3rd. ed.*, Oct. 1970.

[LAM 81] Lam, S. S. and A. U. Shankar, "Protocol projections: a method for analyzing communication protocols," *Conf. Rec. National Telecommunications Conference,* Nov. 1981, New Orleans.

[LAM 82] Lam, S. S. and A. U. Shankar, "Protocol verification via projections," *TR-207,* Dept. of Computer Sciences, Univ. of Texas at Austin, August, 1982. To appear in *IEEE Trans. on Software Engineering.*

[LAM 83] Lam, S. S., "Data link control procedures," in *Computer Communications,* Vol. 1, ed. W. Chou, Prentice-Hall, Englewood Cliffs, 1983, pp. 81-113.

[MERL 83] Merlin, P. M. and G. V. Bochmann, "On the construction of submodule specifications and communication protocols," *ACM TOPLAS,* Vol. 5, No. 1, Jan. 1983, pp. 1- 25.

[MISR 81] Misra, J. and K. M. Chandy, "Proof of networks of processes," *IEEE Tran. on Software Eng.*, Vol. SE-7, No. 4, July 1981.

[MISR 82] Misra, J., K. M. Chandy and T. Smith, "Proving safety and liveness of communicating processes with examples," *Proc ACM SIGACT-SIGOPS Symposium on Principles of Distributed Computing,* Aug. 1982, pp. 18-20.

[RAZO 80] Razouk, R. R. and G. Estrin, "Modeling and verification of communication protocols in SARA: The X.21 interface," *IEEE Trans. on Comput.*, vol. C-29, No. 12, Dec. 1980, pp. 1038-1052.

[RUBI 82] Rubin, J. and C. H. West, "An improved protocol validation technique," *Com-*

puter Networks, April 1982.

[SHAN 83] Shankar, A. U. and S. S. Lam, "An HDLC protocol specification and its verification using image protocols," *ACM Trans. on Computer Systems*, Vol. 1, No. 4, November 1983, pp. 331-368.

[WEST 78] West, C. H. and P. Zafiropulo, "Automated validation of a communications protocol: The CCITT X.21 recommendations," *IBM J. Res. Develop.*, vol. 22, Jan. 1978, pp. 60-71.

[YU 82] Yu, Y. T. and M. G. Gouda, "Deadlock detection for a class of communicating finite state machines," *IEEE Trans. on Commun.*, Dec. 1982, pp. 2514-2519.

[YU 83] Yu, Y. T. and M. G. Gouda, "Unboundedness detection for a class of communicating finite-state machines," *Information Processing Letters*, Vol. 17, Dec. 1983, pp. 235-240.

[ZAFI 80] Zafiropulo, P. et al, "Towards analyzing and synthesizing protocols," *IEEE Trans. on Commun.*, vol. COM-28, No. 4, April 1980, pp. 651-661.

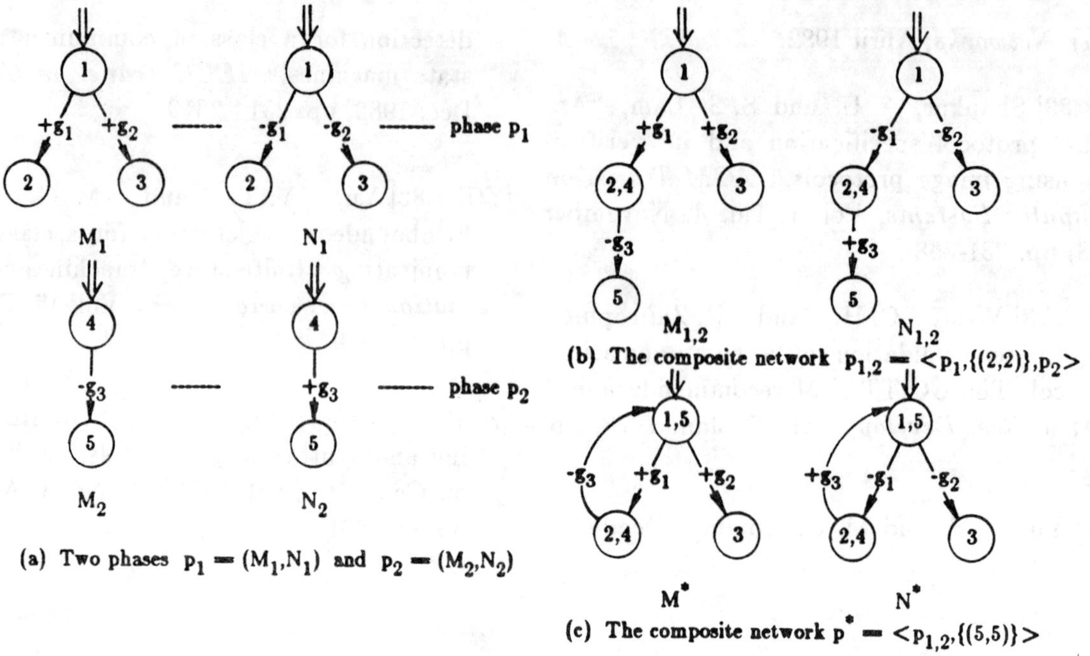

Figure 1. An example for constructing multi-phase networks.

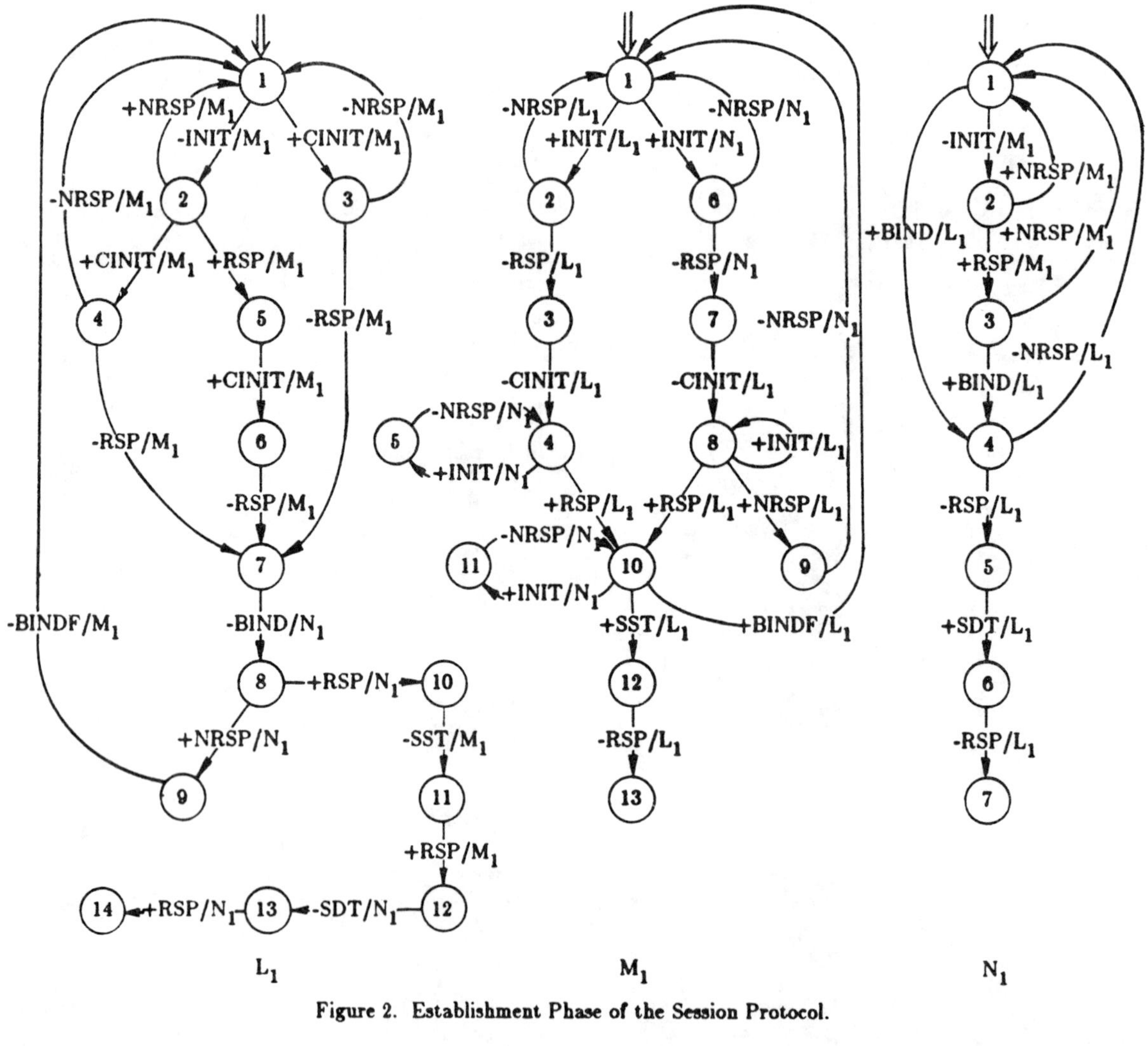

Figure 2. Establishment Phase of the Session Protocol.

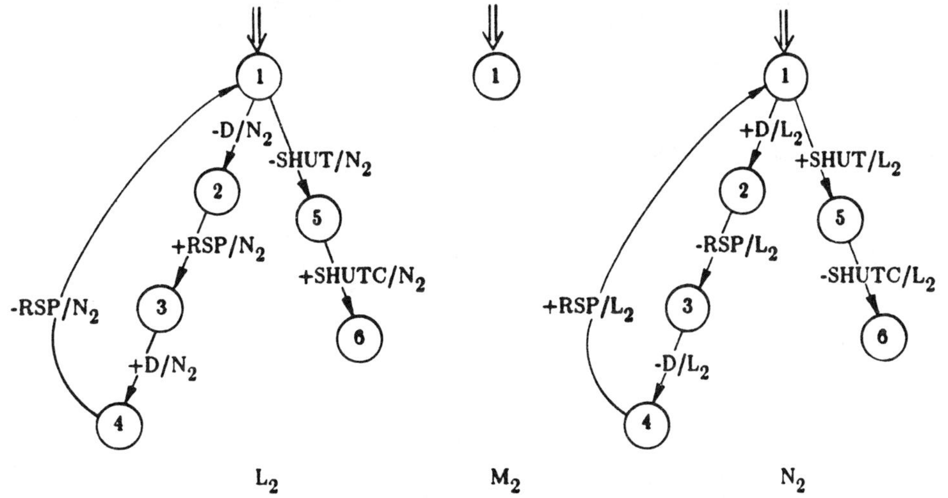

Figure 3. Data Transfer Phase of the Session Protocol.

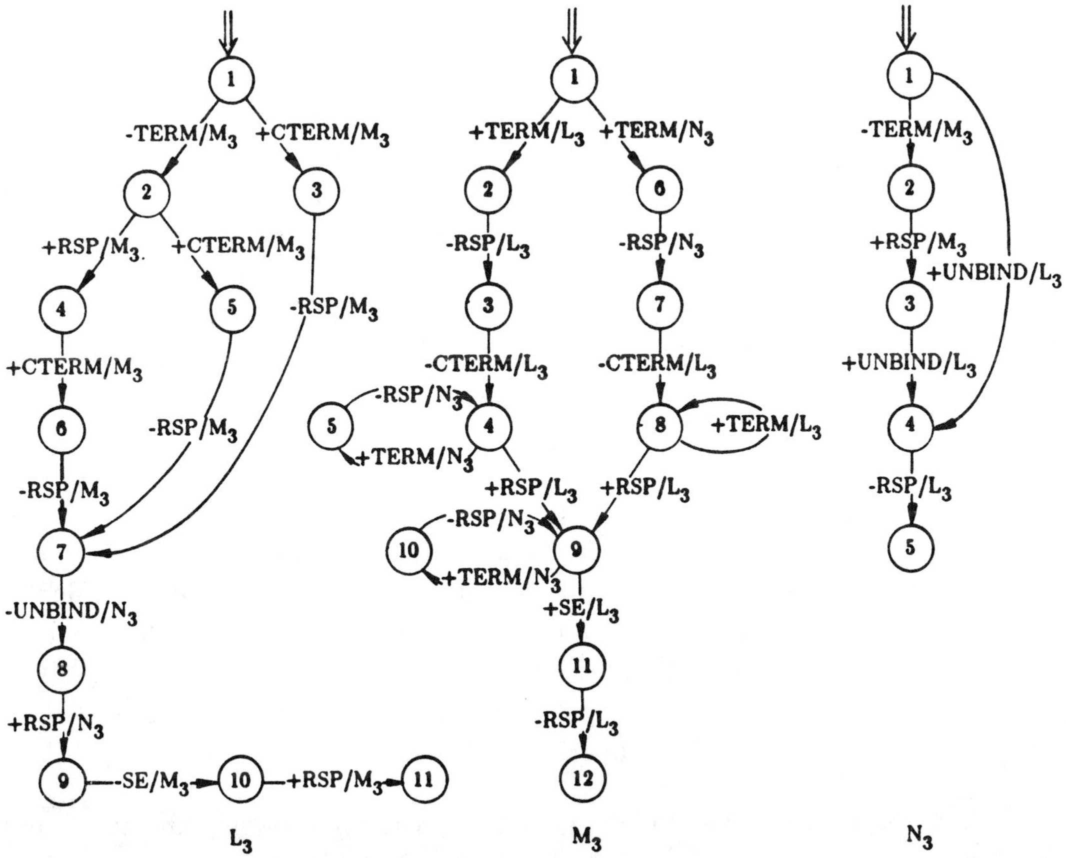

Figure 4. Termination Phase of the Session Protocol.

TIME-DEPENDENT COMMUNICATION PROTOCOLS

A. Udaya Shankar
Department of Computer Science
University of Maryland
College Park, Maryland 20742

Simon S. Lam
Department of Computer Sciences
University of Texas at Austin
Austin, Texas 78712

Abstract

Most real-life communication protocol systems utilize timers and clocks to implement real-time constraints between system event occurrences. Such protocol systems are said to be *time-dependent* if these real-time constraints are crucial to the correct functioning of the systems. We present a model for specifying and verifying time-dependent systems. Specifically, we consider networks of processes that communicate with one another by message-passing. In the context of communication network protocols, each process is either a communication channel or a protocol entity.

A process in our model is specified by a set of state variables and a set of events. An event is described by a predicate that relates the values of the system state variables immediately before to their values immediately after the event occurrence. The predicate embodies specifications of both the event's enabling condition and action. Measures of time are explicitly included in our model. Furthermore, clocks are not coupled and they can tick at any rate within some specified error bounds. Inference rules for both safety and liveness properties are presented. Liveness properties are expressed in the form of inductive properties of bounded-length paths in a system's reachability space. Real-time properties are expressed as safety properties.

We have applied our methodology to the verification of several large communication protocols including a version of the High-level Data Link Control (HDLC) protocol. For the sake of brevity, a relatively small data transfer protocol is modeled herein for illustration. This protocol can reliably transfer data over bounded-delay channels that can lose, reorder and duplicate messages in transit. The protocol's safety, liveness and real-time properties are presented.

1. INTRODUCTION

We consider real-time systems that employ clocks and timers to enforce time constraints between system event occurrences. We refer to a system as *time-dependent* when it contains time constraints that are essential to the correct functioning of the system. Our work has been motivated primarily by real-life communication network protocols which are invariably time-dependent systems [1-4].

Time-dependent behavior arises naturally in communication networks because errors and failures that occur in a network component are usually not communicated explicitly to other network components that may be affected by these errors and failures. In such situations, only by the use of timeouts can a component infer that a failure (or an error) has occurred and initiate recovery action. Because such recovery mechanisms are themselves subject to the same kinds of failures or errors, the real-time behavior can be very complex.

We present in Sections 2, 3 and 5 an event-driven process model for specifying and verifying distributed systems, both time-dependent and time-independent. We have applied this model to the analysis of several nontrivial protocol examples, including a version of the High-level Data Link Control (HDLC) protocol [5]. To illustrate our model, we present below a transport-level protocol for reliable data transfer over bounded-delay channels that can lose, reorder and duplicate messages in transit. The protocol employs cyclic sequence numbers, timers and timeouts.

Review of protocol verification

The aim of protocol verification is to establish that certain desired logical correctness properties of a protocol system are guaranteed by its specifications. For distributed systems in general, such logical correctness properties are generaly categorized into safety properties and liveness properties. Informally, a *safety property* states that certain relations always hold between a set of system variables irrespective of whether the system progresses or not (e.g., if data blocks are delivered to a remote user, then they are delivered in the same order as the order in which they were submitted by the local user). A *liveness property* states that the system will indeed progress in a certain manner (e.g., a data block that is submitted by the local user will *eventually* be delivered to the remote user).

However, in the case of communication network protocols, it is often desirable to describe progress in terms of real-time properties. Typically, if a protocol does not achieve progress (transfer of data, establishment of a connection, etc.) within a bounded time duration T, then the protocol resets or aborts. Hence, a liveness assertion stating progress within a finite but *unbounded* time duration is not realistic. More appropriate is a real-time assertion such as "if within a time duration T the data block is not transferred, then at least n retransmissions of the data block have occurred, all of which failed." In our model, such real-time assertions can usually be stated as safety assertions.

Protocol verification consists of proving, in some deductive inference system, that the correctness properties of a protocol system follow from the system specifications. An inference system consists of a syntax for expressing statements, as well as a collection of axioms and inference rules. An axiom is a statement whose truth is taken for granted. An inference rule specifies how a new statement can be derived from other statements. A proof of a statement A_0 in such a system is a sequence of statements (with A_0 at the end) where each statement is either an axiom or is derived from previous statements by an application of an inference rule. First-order predicate logic is an example of a deductive inference system. An inference system for protocol verification can be obtained by extending first-order predicate logic with additional inference rules for proving safety and liveness properties. These additional inference rules define the semantics of constructs that are used in protocol specification.

Some features of our model

We model distributed systems as networks of processes that communicate with one another by message-passing. For communication network protocols in particular, each process in a network is either a communication channel or a protocol entity. Each process has a set of *state variables* and a set of *events*. An event is described by a predicate that relates the values of the system state variables immediately before the event occurrence to their values immediately after the event occurrence. The predicate embodies specifications of both the event's enabling condition and action. There is no algorithmic code in our model.

What we have is a compromise that incorporates both implementation-dependent features (the state variables) and implementation-independent features (the use of predicates to specify events). Such a combination has several advantages. First, it allows for very simple inference rules for safety and liveness properties. In particular, we do not need any special notation (such as temporal logic [6]) to express liveness properties of *unbounded-length* paths in a system's reachability graph. Instead, we describe such liveness properties in the form of inductive properties of bounded-length paths. Second, because the events are specified by predicates, their specifications can be directly substituted into proofs in predicate logic. Third, the use of state variables simplifies the modeling of time measures.

We use discrete-valued time variables to measure the elapse of time, and define time events to age these time variables. By imposing certain conditions, referred to as *accuracy axioms*, on the time events, we are able to model clocks realistically: our clocks are uncoupled and can tick at any rate within specified error bounds of a given rate. Additional conditions on the time events, referred to as *time axioms*, allow us to model many types of time constraints between system events.

Related work

In addition to time-dependent behavior, another characteristic of real-life communication protocols is that each protocol typically performs multiple distinct functions, such as connection management, one-way data transfers, etc. The method of projections provides an approach to transform the analysis of a multi-function protocol into analyses of smaller single-function protocols, called image protocols [7].

The theory of projections was originally developed in [7] using a set-theoretic notation. In Part 2 of [8], we specialize the theory to the time-dependent protocol system model herein. The use of state variables and predicates (to specify events) greatly facilitates the construction of image protocols.

2. MODELING MEASURES OF TIME

Protocol system components have devices, such as crystal oscillators, that issue "ticks" at (almost) regular time intervals (e.g., once every microsecond). We refer to such devices as *local tickers*. In order to measure intervals of time larger than that between consecutive ticks, the system components typically employ counters to accumulate the number of elapsed ticks generated by a local ticker since the occurrence of some system event. These counters are the clocks and timers used in the protocol system. We refer to such counters as *time variables*.

The tickers in protocol systems have several properties that should not be ignored in any realistic modeling. First, the interval between successive ticks is not infinitesimally small. Second, tickers in different components are not coupled: the ticks of one ticker do not coincide in time with the ticks of another ticker. Third, the rate at which a ticker ticks is not constant but may vary within certain error bounds of a constant rate. We account for each one of these features in our model.

The time variables in our model are discrete-valued variables. Without loss of generality, we consider them to take values from the set of non-negative integers. For each local ticker i, there is a *local time event* (corresponding to a tick) whose occurrence ages (increments) all time variables driven by the ticker. Since no other ticker is affected, this ticker is effectively decoupled from other tickers. All the time variables driven by a local ticker must necessarily lie within a single component of the protocol system. In addition to being aged, a time variable can be *reset* to some value by an event of its component. Thus, a time variable can be used to measure the time elapsed (in number of ticks of its local ticker) since an event occurrence.

At this point in the modeling, the tickers are entirely decoupled. There is nothing to prevent different local tickers from ticking at vastly different rates. To complete the modeling of real-time measures, we must keep local tickers within specified drifts. To do this we include in our model a hypothetical ticker, referred to as the *global ticker*, that is assumed to tick at an absolutely constant rate. Each local ticker will be allowed to drift within a specified bound of the global ticker. For each local ticker i, let η_i denote the number of ticks issued since system initialization, and let ϵ_i denote the maximum error in the tick rate. Let η denote the number of global ticks since initialization. The η's are (auxiliary) time variables that do not correspond to actually implemented clocks or timers, and can never be reset by any system event. Neither the local time event for ticker i nor the global time event is allowed to occur if such an occurrence will violate the following *accuracy axiom* of local ticker i (below, the notation $\eta(a)$ refers to the value of η at instant a, while η refers to the current value of the time variable η):

AccuracyAxiom$_i(\eta_i,\eta)$: For any earlier instant a,

$$|(\eta_i - \eta_i(a)) - (\eta - \eta(a))| \leq \max(1,\epsilon_i(\eta-\eta(a))).$$

The above accuracy axiom states that over any time span since initialization, the number of ticks of local ticker i differs from the number of global ticks by at most ϵ_i times the number of global ticks. (The minimum upper bound of 1 is necessary since the tickers are integer-valued.) This accuracy axiom is a discrete version of the following drift condition for continuous clocks

$$\left| 1 - \frac{d\eta_i}{d\eta} \right| \leq \epsilon_i$$

usually found in the literature [9].

Recall that time variables are used to measure the time elapsed since a system event occurrence. Thus, by including time variables in the enabling condition of a system event e, we can model time constraints of the form "event e *will not occur unless* certain time intervals have elapsed." To model time constraints of the form "event e *will occur within* certain elapsed time intervals," we impose conditions, referred to as *time axioms* on the allowed values of time variables. As a result, in addition to the constraints imposed by accuracy axioms, time events will not be allowed to occur if their occurrence will violate any time axioms. This modeling of real-time behavior is valid provided that the time events do not get deadlocked because of the accuracy and time axioms. We have shown that the tickers will continue to accumulate ticks if the time axioms correspond to *feasible constraints*; i.e., constraints that can be realistically met by the protocol entities [8]. A precise notation for specifying the time events is presented with the protocol example in Section 4.

We shall refer to time variables driven by local tickers as *local time variables.* We also allow time variables to be driven by the global ticker. These time variables are referred to as *global time variables*; they do not correspond to clocks and timers that are implemented in the system. Rather they are used to record the exact (i.e., global) time elapsed between system events. Such measurements may be needed in stating assertions of time-dependent behavior.

In particular, for a local time variable v, we often find it convenient to specify a global time variable v* such that any system event that resets v also resets v* to the same value. v* is referred to as the global time variable associated with v. Clearly, if v is driven by η_i, then AccuracyAxiom$_i$(v,v*) holds between all instants after the last reset.

3. DISTRIBUTED SYSTEM MODEL

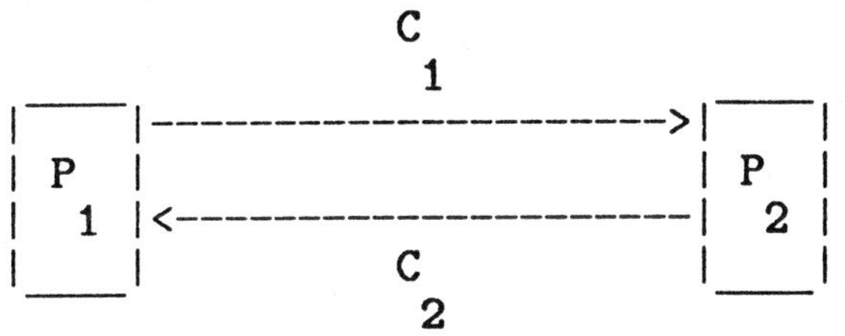

Fig. 1. Network configuration of protocol example in Section 4.

In this section, we specify the messages, state variables and events of the protocol system model. Instead of describing the model for communication networks in general, we present the model for the special configuration and channel behavior of the protocol example in Section 4. (See Fig. 1.) P_1 and P_2 are two protocol entities connected by bounded-delay channels C_1 and C_2. For i=1 and 2, any message attempting to stay in channel C_i for longer than a specified time MaxDelay_i is lost (e.g., removed by some intermediate network node [3, 10]). (For a general network configuration with various types of channels, the reader is referred to [8].)

Messages and state variables

For i=1 and 2, the messages sent by P_i are categorized into *message types*. Each message type q specifies multi-field messages of the form $(q, f_1,...,f_n)$ where $n \geq 0$. The first component indicates the name of the message type, while each of the other components f_i is a parameter ranging over a specified set of values. The vector notation $(q,\mathbf{f})$ is used to refer to the message type q. We note that multi-field messages are characteristic of most real-life communication protocols.

Let $\mathbf{v}_i$ be the set of state variables of P_i. Every variable in $\mathbf{v}_i$ takes values from a specified domain of values. In order to model timing constraints of P_i, $\mathbf{v}_i$ can include time variables (which may be constrained by time axioms). Assume that all time variables in $\mathbf{v}_i$ (if any) are driven by a local ticker with count η_i and maximum error ϵ_i. $\mathbf{v}_i$ can also have auxiliary variables used for verification purposes. An auxiliary variable is used only to record the behavior of the entity over time (e.g., sequence of data blocks delivered to a user); its value never affects the behavior of the entity.

For each message in channel C_i, we associate with the message a time variable *age* that indicates the age of the message (time spent in the channel). Let $\mathbf{z}_i$ be the sequence of (message, age) pairs in C_i. We let the *age* time variable be driven by the global ticker. The channel's bounded-delay behavior is modeled by the *time axiom*

$\text{TimeAxiom}_i(\mathbf{z}_i)$: For every (m,t) in $\mathbf{z}_i$, $t \leq \text{MaxDelay}_i$.

The global state vector is defined as $\mathbf{v} = (\mathbf{v}_1,\mathbf{v}_2,\mathbf{z}_1,\mathbf{z}_2)$. The initial conditions of the protocol system are given by a predicate named $\text{Initial}(\mathbf{v})$.

Events

Before we describe how events are specified, we first introduce our use of predicates to specify relations between sets of input and output parameter values. Let **x** and **y** be sets of parameters that can take values from domains **X** and **Y** respectively. Assume that **x** and **y** have no parameters in common.

Consider a predicate with parameters from **x** and **y**. For example, the expression $(x_1=y+1)$ **or** $(x_2=y)$ is a predicate. For every value pair in **X**×**Y**, a predicate evaluates to either True or False. The predicate specifies a set of value pairs in **X**×**Y**, namely those where the predicate evaluates to True. The predicate is said to be *enabled* for any value of **x** if there is a value of **y** such that the predicate is True for that value pair.

Instead of using algorithmic code, we use predicates to specify input-output relations. For example, given integers x and y, an algorithm that assigns to y the value $x+1$, can be modeled by the predicate $(y=x+1)$. It can also be modeled by the predicate $(y-x=1)$. A nondeterministic algorithm that assigns to y either the value $x+1$ or the value $x-2$ provided that y is positive, can be modeled by the predicate ($y>0$ **and** ($y=x+1$ **or** $y=x+2$)). (We use **and** and **or** to denote logical conjunction and disjunction respectively.) Note that within a predicate there is no distinction between the input and output parameters because there are no assignment statements as found in algorithmic code.

We now introduce some notation. We use e(**x**;**y**) to denote a predicate named e with parameters from **x** and **y**. Note that the input parameters are listed before the semicolon. The output parameters are listed after the semicolon. For any given values of **x** and **y**, we shall also use e(**x**;**y**) to denote the value of the predicate.

We now describe how to use predicates to specify events. Since a system event may cause certain changes to the values of the system state variables, it corresponds to a collection of input-output value pairs where the input and output parameters are the values of the system variables before and after the event occurrence. Applying the above notation, we specify a system event e by a predicate e(**v**; **v"**), where the parameter **v** denotes the value of the global state vector immediately before the event occurrence and the parameter **v"** denotes the value of the global state vector immediately after the event occurrence.

The events of a distributed system usually have structure that we wish to explicitly indicate. First, an event e typically affects only a few components of the global state vector. When specifying such an event e, we will include only these components in its parameter list, and adopt the convention that the missing components are not affected by the event. Second, though an entity can affect the value of a channel state variable, it can do so only in certain ways: namely, sending a message (appending it to the tail of the channel state variable) and receiving a message (removing it from the head of the channel state variable). To incorporate these constraints in the model, we define send and receive *service primitives* for the channels, and allow entity events to access the channel state variables only through these primitives.

For channel C_i, the send service primitive is $\text{Send}_i(m,\mathbf{z}_i;\mathbf{z}_i")$ which denotes the predicate $(\mathbf{z}_i" = ((m,0),\mathbf{z}_i))$ i.e., append m with an age of 0 to the tail of $\mathbf{z}_i$. Similarly, the receive service primitive is $\text{Rec}_i(\mathbf{z}_i;m,\mathbf{z}_i")$ which denotes the predicate $((\mathbf{z}_i",(m,t))=\mathbf{z}_i)$ i.e., if $\mathbf{z}_i$ has m at its head, then irrespective of m's age, remove it and pass it out. When these service primitives are included in the predicates of the entity events, the formal message parameter m is replaced by the actual message sent or received.

Thus the events of entity P_i have the structures indicated below:

(1) for each message type $(q,\mathbf{f})$ sent by P_i,
$\text{Send}\_q\ (\mathbf{v}_i,\mathbf{z}_i;\mathbf{v}_i",\mathbf{z}_i") \equiv e_{sq}(\mathbf{v}_i;\mathbf{v}_i",\mathbf{f})$ **and** $\text{Send}_i((q,\mathbf{f}),\mathbf{z}_i;\mathbf{z}_i")$;

(2) for each message type $(q,\mathbf{f})$ received by P_i from Channel C_j,
$\text{Rec}\_q(\mathbf{v}_i,\mathbf{z}_j;\mathbf{v}_i",\mathbf{z}_j") \equiv e_{rq}(\mathbf{v}_i,\mathbf{f};\mathbf{v}_i")$ **and** $\text{Rec}_j(\mathbf{z}_j;(q,\mathbf{f}),\mathbf{z}_j")$;

(3) internal events of the form $e_{int}(\mathbf{v}_i;\mathbf{v}_i")$ used to model timeouts, etc.

where the predicates e_{sq}, e_{rq} and e_{int} are to be specified for a particular protocol system.

For each channel C_i, the channel behavior (loss, reordering, etc.) is specified by a predicate called $\text{ChannelError}(\mathbf{z}_i;\mathbf{z}_i")$.

The time events are completely specified by the accuracy and time axioms in a straightforward manner. (See Part 1 of [8] and see the protocol example in Section 4 for an illustration.)

4. A TIME-DEPENDENT DATA TRANSFER PROTOCOL

We now present a data transfer protocol that reliably transfers data blocks from entity P_1 to P_2 using channels C_1 and C_2 (see Fig. 1), where we allow the bounded-delay channels to lose, duplicate and reorder messages in transit.

Let DataSet be the set of data blocks that can be sent in this protocol. P_1 sends messages of type (D,data,ns) where D identifies the name of the message type, data is a data block from DataSet, and ns is a send sequence number. P_2 sends messages of type (ACK,nr) where nr is a receive sequence number. In this protocol, ns and nr are restricted to the values of 0 and 1. When P_2 receives a (D,data,ns) message, if ns equals the next expected sequence number then the data block is passed on to the destination, else it is ignored. In either case, P_2 sends an (ACK,nr).

In order that the data transfer be reliable in spite of the channel errors, P_1 must ensure before sending a *new* data block that MaxDelay_1 time has elapsed since the last data block was sent, and MaxDelay_2 time has elapsed since receiving the last acknowledgement to a previously unacknowledged data block. P_1 will repeatedly transmit this data block until it is acknowledged. However, neither of the time constraints apply to the retransmission of a previously sent but unacknowledged data block. The time to wait before a retransmission should be chosen on the basis of performance goals and the probability distributions of channel delays, channel loss, etc. Here we see a system with two different types of time constraints: one necessary for logical correctness and one concerned only with performance. In other protocols, the separation is not always so clear.

We now list the state variables and events of the entities. (Below, $\text{MDelay}_i = (1 + \epsilon_1) \times \text{MaxDelay}_i$ for i=1 and 2.)

Variables of P_1

Source: array[0..∞] of DataSet; {auxiliary history variable initialized to the sequence of data blocks to be sent to P_2}

s: 0..∞; {Source[s] is the data block in the next D message to be sent; an auxiliary variable}

vs: 0..1; {sequence number to be used in the next D message to be sent}

ws: 0..1; {sequence number used in the last D message sent}

DTimer,DTimerG: (0,1,2,..); {time elapsed since the last D message sent; DTimer is a local time variable and DTimerG is the global time variable associated with DTimer}

ACKTimer,ACKTimerG: (0,1,2,..); {time elapsed since reception of the last ACK message that caused progress; ACKTimerG is the global time variable associated with ACKTimer}

Let $\mathbf{v}_1$ denote a list of the above variables. The initial condition of P_1 is given by the following predicate.

$\text{Initial}_1(\mathbf{v}_1)$ ≡ (s=vs=0 **and** ws=1 **and** DTimer > MDelay1 **and** ACKTimer > MDelay2 **and** DTimerG = DTimer **and** ACKTimerG = ACKTimer)

Events of P_1

P_1 has two events, one for sending messages of type D and the other for receiving messages of type ACK. These events are specified below.

1. Send_D $(\mathbf{v}_1,\mathbf{z}_1;\mathbf{v}_1",\mathbf{z}_1")$
   ≡ ((ws=vs) {Retransmit old data}
   or (ws≠vs **and** Dtimer > MDelay1 **and** ACKTimer > MDelay2)) {Transmit new data}
   and Send_1((D,Source[s],vs),$\mathbf{z}_1;\mathbf{z}_1"$) {Send message}

and s"=s **and** vs"=vs **and** ws"=vs {Update state vector}
and DTimer"=0 **and** ACKTimer"=ACKTimer **and** Source"=Source
and DTimerG"=0 **and** ACKTimerG"=ACKTimerG

2. Rec_ACK($\mathbf{v}_1$,$\mathbf{z}_2$;$\mathbf{v}_1$",$\mathbf{z}_2$")
≡ Rec_2 ($\mathbf{z}_2$; (ACK,nr), $\mathbf{z}_2$") {Receive nr}
and ((nr=vs ⊕ 1 **and** vs=ws {Outstanding data acknowledged}
and s"=s+1 **and** vs"=nr **and** ACKTimer"=0 **and** ACKTimerG"=0)
or (nr=vs **and** s"=s **and** vs"=vs {Old acknowledgement}
and ACKTimer"=ACKTimer
and ACKTimerG" = ACKTimerG))
and ws"=ws **and** DTimer"=DTimer **and** Source"=Source
and DTimerG" = DTimerG

In the above, ⊕ denotes addition modulo 2.

Variables of P_2

Sink: array [0..∞] of DataSet; {auxiliary history variable that records the sequence of data blocks passed on to the destination}

r: 0..∞; {the next data block received in sequence will be saved in Sink[r]; an auxiliary variable}

vr: 0..1; {sequence number of next expected data block}

SendACK: Boolean; {True iff a received D message has not been acknowledged}

Let $\mathbf{v}_2$ denote a list of the above variables. The initial condition of P_2 is given by the following predicate.

$\text{Initial}_2(\mathbf{v}_2)$ ≡ (r=vr=0 **and** SendACK = False)

Events of P_2

1. Send_ACK ($\mathbf{v}_2$,$\mathbf{z}_2$;$\mathbf{v}_2$",$\mathbf{z}_2$")
≡ (SendACK = True) **and** Send_2 ((ACK,vr), $\mathbf{z}_2$;$\mathbf{z}_2$")
and Sink"=Sink **and** r"=r **and** vr"=vr **and** SendACK"=False

2. Rec_D ($\mathbf{v}_2$,$\mathbf{z}_1$;$\mathbf{v}_2$",$\mathbf{z}_1$")
≡ Rec_1 ($\mathbf{z}_1$;(D,data,ns), $\mathbf{z}_1$")
and ((ns=vr **and** Sink"[r]=data **and** r"=r+1 **and** vr"=vr ⊕ 1) {in-sequence data}
or (ns ≠ vr **and** Sink"=Sink **and** r"=r **and** vr"=vr)) {out-of-sequence data}
and SendACK" = True

Other events

The channel events of C_i are specified by the predicate ChannelError($\mathbf{z}_i$,$\mathbf{z}_i$") that allows all possible losses, duplications and reorderings of messages in the channel.

The *local time event* for the local ticker at P_1 is specified by

$$\text{AccuracyAxiom}_1(\eta_1+1,\eta) \quad \{\text{if local tick will not violate accuracy axiom}\}$$
$$\textbf{and } \eta_1" = \eta_1+1 \textbf{ and } \text{DTimer}" = \text{DTimer}+1 \textbf{ and } \text{ACKTimer}" = \text{ACKTimer}+1$$
$$\{\text{then age } \eta_1 \text{ and all time variables driven by local ticker}\}$$

The *global time event* is specified by

$$\text{AccuracyAxiom}_1(\eta_1,\eta+1) \textbf{ and } \text{TimeAxiom}_1(\text{next}(\mathbf{z}_1)) \textbf{ and } \text{TimeAxiom}_2(\text{next}(\mathbf{z}_2))$$
$$\textbf{and } \eta" = \eta+1 \textbf{ and } \mathbf{z}_1" = \text{next}(\mathbf{z}_1) \textbf{ and } \mathbf{z}_2" = \text{next}(\mathbf{z}_2)$$
$$\textbf{and } \text{DTimerG}" = \text{DTimerG} + 1 \textbf{ and } \text{ACKTimerG}" = \text{ACKTimerG} + 1$$

where next($\mathbf{z}_i$) is $\mathbf{z}_i$ with all ages in it incremented by 1.

System initial condition

The initial condition of the system is given by the following predicate

$\text{Initial}(\mathbf{v}) \equiv \text{Initial}_1(\mathbf{v}_1)$ **and** $\text{Initial}_2(\mathbf{v}_2)$ **and** $\mathbf{z}_1$ is empty **and** $\mathbf{z}_2$ is empty.

5. PROVING SAFETY AND LIVENESS PROPERTIES

The set of all possible value assignments to the system state variables define the global state space of the protocol system. Those global states that satisfy Initial($\mathbf{v}$) are referred to as *initial global states.* Each event specifies a set of transitions between global states; each transition is from a global state where the event is enabled to a global state that can result from changes to the state variable values. A global state that can be reached from an initial state via a sequence of event transitions is referred to as a *reachable global state.* The graph whose nodes are the reachable global states and whose arcs are the event transitions is referred to as the *reachability graph* of the system. A realization of the protocol system behavior is represented by some path in the reachability graph starting from an initial state.

Safety properties

A safety property of the protocol system states relationships between values of the system state variables. It can be represented by a predicate in the variables of the global state vector $\mathbf{v}$. An example of a safety property involving two integer state variables x and y is $(x \le y \le x + 1)$. A safety property A($\mathbf{v}$) holds for the system if it holds at every reachable state. Such a property is said to be *invariant.* We now present the inference rule to prove the invariance of a predicate A($\mathbf{v}$).

Inference rule for safety. If $B(\mathbf{v})$ is invariant and $A(\mathbf{v})$ satisfies

(i) $((\text{Initial}(\mathbf{v}) \Rightarrow A(\mathbf{v}))$ **and**

(ii) $(\forall\, e(\mathbf{v};\mathbf{v}'') : B(\mathbf{v})$ **and** $A(\mathbf{v})$ **and** $e(\mathbf{v};\mathbf{v}'') \Rightarrow A(\mathbf{v}''))$ **and**

(iii) $(A(\mathbf{v}) \Rightarrow A_0(\mathbf{v})))$,

then $A_0(\mathbf{v})$ is invariant.

The validity of the rule is obvious from the following. From (ii) we know that at every global state g where $A(g) = B(g) =$ True, every enabled event e takes the protocol system to a state h where $A(h) =$ True. Because $B(\mathbf{v})$ is invariant, $B(h) =$ True. Hence, once the protocol is in a state where $A(\mathbf{v})$ and $B(\mathbf{v})$ hold, all future states also satisfy the two predicates. From (i), we know that any initial state satisfies $A(\mathbf{v})$ (and $B(\mathbf{v})$ because of its invariance). Hence all reachable states satisfy $A(\mathbf{v})$. Because $A_0(\mathbf{v})$ is implied by $A(\mathbf{v})$ (from (iii)), we know that all reachable states also satisfy $A_0(\mathbf{v})$.

Note that the inference rule is quite simple because of our use of predicates to define events. Typically, we are given $A_0(\mathbf{v})$ as a service requirement, and are asked to verify that it is invariant. The above rule does not explain how to obtain $A(\mathbf{v})$ once we are given $A_0(\mathbf{v})$ and $B(\mathbf{v})$. It just states sufficient conditions that an $A(\mathbf{v})$ must satisfy in order for us to conclude that $A_0(\mathbf{v})$ is invariant. Generating $A(\mathbf{v})$ given $A_0(\mathbf{v})$ and $B(\mathbf{v})$ can be done using the method of weakest preconditions [11] or symbolic execution. (In general, this is a nontrivial task analogous to generating loop invariants in program verification.)

If in the above rule, $B(\mathbf{v})=$ True, then $A(\mathbf{v})$ is said to be *inductively complete.* The time events have been defined so that each of the time and accuracy axioms is inductively complete (and hence invariant) [8].

Liveness properties

A liveness property of the protocol system states relationships that values of the system variables eventually satisfy. An example of a liveness property involving integer state variables x and y is as follows: during the course of the protocol operation, if x does not increase without bounds then y will increase without bounds. Note that a liveness property is not a property of each reachable state (and cannot be stated as a predicate in the variables of $\mathbf{v}$). Rather it is a property of the paths in the reachability graph.

Our method of stating liveness properties is based on specifying inductive properties of *bounded-length* paths in the reachability graph. First, we assume that any implementation of the protocol system is *fair*, by which we mean the following: any event that is enabled infinitely often will eventually occur. Next, we have the following definition.

Given predicates A($\mathbf{v}$) and B($\mathbf{v}$), we say that A($\mathbf{v}$) *leads-next-to* B($\mathbf{v}$) if for every reachable global state g where A(g) = True, the following holds: for every event enabled in state g, its occurrence takes the system to a state h where either A(h) = True or B(h) = True, and there is at least one event enabled in state g whose occurrence can take the system to a state h where B(h) = True.

In any system implementation that is fair, if A($\mathbf{v}$) leads-next-to B($\mathbf{v}$) then on any outgoing path from a reachable state g where A(g) = True, the system will eventually reach a state h where B(h) = True. We now present the inference rule used to establish the leads-next-to property.

Inference rule for liveness. If I($\mathbf{v}$) is invariant, and A($\mathbf{v}$) and B($\mathbf{v}$) satisfy

(i) ($\forall$ e($\mathbf{v}$;$\mathbf{v}$"): (I($\mathbf{v}$) **and** A($\mathbf{v}$) **and** e($\mathbf{v}$;$\mathbf{v}$")) $\Rightarrow$ B($\mathbf{v}$") **or** A($\mathbf{v}$")) **and**

(ii) ((A($\mathbf{v}$) **and** I($\mathbf{v}$)) $\Rightarrow$ $\exists$ e($\mathbf{v}$;$\mathbf{v}$"): (e($\mathbf{v}$;$\mathbf{v}$") = True
and (I($\mathbf{v}$) **and** A($\mathbf{v}$) **and** e($\mathbf{v}$;$\mathbf{v}$")) $\Rightarrow$ B($\mathbf{v}$"))),

then A($\mathbf{v}$) leads-next-to B($\mathbf{v}$).

This inference rule is very similar to the definition of *leads-next-to*, except that it allows us to utilize any safety property I($\mathbf{v}$) that is known. Next, we extend the leads-next-to definition.

Given assertions A($\mathbf{v}$) and B($\mathbf{v}$), we say that A($\mathbf{v}$) *leads-to* B($\mathbf{v}$) if for some specified integer $n \geq 1$ the following holds: (A($\mathbf{v}$) leads-next-to (B($\mathbf{v}$) **or** C_1($\mathbf{v}$))) **and** (C_1($\mathbf{v}$) leads-next-to (B($\mathbf{v}$) **or** C_2($\mathbf{v}$))) **and** ... **and** (C_{n-1}($\mathbf{v}$) leads-next-to (B($\mathbf{v}$) **or** C_n($\mathbf{v}$))) **and** (C_n($\mathbf{v}$) leads-next-to B($\mathbf{v}$)).

Using the leads-to construct, the liveness property example above can be specified by the inductive statement ($\forall$ n,m: ($x = n$ **and** $y = m$) leads-to ($x > n$ **or** $y > m$)). There are other ways to specify liveness properties. For example, one could state liveness properties as predicates on the set of paths in the reachability graph, but that would be too cumbersome. Temporal logic offers another way to specify liveness properties. The liveness property example would be specified in temporal logic by (**not**($\forall n$: $\diamond$ $x > n$) $\Rightarrow$ ($\forall m$: $\diamond$ $y > m$)), where the operator $\diamond$ is to be read as "eventually." It has been our experience that to prove temporal logic statements, it is often necessary to rephrase them into inductive statements of the leads-to type. Hence, by stating our liveness properties directly using the leads-to construct, we avoid some unneccessary overhead.

6. SAFETY, LIVENESS AND REAL-TIME PROPERTIES OF PROTOCOL EXAMPLE

Safety specification and verification

For the protocol in Section 4, we would like to prove that the following safety property is invariant:

A1. (a) $\text{Source}[i] = \text{Sink}[i]$ for $0 \leq i < r$;
(b) $0 \leq s \leq r \leq s + 1$.

A1(a) states that the sequence of data blocks placed in Sink is a prefix of the data blocks in Source. A1(b) states that at most one data block is outstanding (i.e., sent but not acknowledged).

A1 is invariant because A1 **and** A2 **and** A3 **and** A4 **and** A5 is inductively complete (this can be checked easily by applying the inference rule for safety).

A2. (vs = s mod 2) **and** (vr = r mod 2)

A3. ($\forall$(m,t) in $\mathbf{z}_1$: m = (D,Source[s],vs) **and** vs=ws **and** (r=s **or** r=s+1) **and** t $\geq$ DTimerG)
or ($\forall$(m,t) in $\mathbf{z}_1$: m = (D,Source[s-1],vs $\oslash$ 1) **and** vs=ws $\oslash$ 1 **and** r=s **and** t $\geq$ DTimerG)

A4. SendAck = True $\Rightarrow$ r=s **or** (vs=ws **and** r=s+1)

A5. $\forall$(m,t) in $\mathbf{z}_2$: (m=(ACK,vr) **and** (r=s **or** (vs=ws **and** r=s+1)))
or (m=(ACK,vr $\oslash$ 1) **and** ((r=s **and** t $\geq$ ACKTimerG **and** vs $\neq$ ws)
or (r=s+1 **and** vs=ws)))

where $\oslash$ denotes subtraction modulo 2. The above can be shown to be inductively complete by a straightforward application of the inference rule for safety. (See Part 1 of [8].)

Liveness specification and verification

For this protocol, we would like to prove the following: if the channels do not continually lose messages, then s and r will grow without bound.

To specify and verify this formally in our model, we define the auxiliary variables LCount1 and LCount2. LCount1 counts the number of times that a (D,Source[n],n mod 2) message in C_1 has been lost since the previous reception of such a message at P_2. Formally, LCount1=0 initially; whenever a loss event of C_1 deletes a (D,Source[n],n mod 2) message in C_1, LCount1 is incremented by 1; whenever a (D,Source[n],n mod 2) message is received at P_2, LCount1 is reset to 0. LCount2 is similarly specified, except that (D,Source[n],n mod 2), C_1 and P_2 are replaced by (ACK, (n+1) mod 2), C_2 and P_1 respectively.

The desired liveness property is then stated as follows: For any non-negative integer n

L1. (s=r=n **and** LCount1=m1) leads-to ((s=n **and** r=n+1)
or (s=r=n **and** LCount1 > m1))

L2. (s=n **and** r=n+1 **and** LCount1=m1 **and** LCount2=m2) leads-to
((s=r=n+1) **or** ((s=n **and** r=n+1) **and**
((LCount2 > m2) **or** (LCount2 ≥ m2 **and** LCount1 > m1)))).

L1 assures us that from any state where s=r=n, we will get to a state where s=n and r=n+1, provided that LCount1 does not grow without bound. L2 assures us that the system will then get to a state where s=r=n+1, provided that neither LCount1 nor LCount2 grows without bound. Thus, assuming the desired channel behavior, L1 and L2 allow us to say that s and r will grow without bound.

The above liveness (leads-to) property has been verified for the data transfer protocol in Section 4. The verification is very short and may be found in Part 1 of [8].

Real-time specification and verification

To make our data transfer protocol more realistic, we include the following real-time behavior into its model.

First, entity P_2 will send an ACK message within a specified time interval (MaxResponseTime) of receiving a D message. Second, entity P_1 will retransmit a given data block Source[n] at most MaxRetryCount times. Let MRoundTripDelay = MDelay1 + MDelay2 + MaxResponseTime $\times$ $(1+\epsilon_1+\epsilon_2)$. If after sending Source[n] for MaxRetryCount times, P_1 does not receive an (ACK, (n+1) mod 2) within MRoundTripDelay of the last send, it assumes that the channels C_1 and C_2 are bad and aborts the connection (enters a state called RESET).

For this more realistic model, we would like to prove that if P_1 has reset, then indeed over a time period T (=MRoundTripDelay $\times$ MaxRetryCount), more than MaxRetryCount messages sent by P_1 and P_2 have been lost by C_1 and C_2 collectively.

To formally state this real-time specification, define the following auxiliary variables:

MessagesSent1: sequence of (m,t) pairs where m is a message sent by P_1 and t denotes the time at which m was sent; updated whenever P_1 does a send.

MessagesSent2: as above but for P_2.

SCount1: Number of times (D,Source[n], n mod 2) was sent into C_1 but did not get received at P_2 within MaxDelay1 of sending. SCount1 is incremented by 1 whenever a global tick occurs and ((D,Source[n], n mod 2), t) is in MessagesSent1 and r=n and η = t + MaxDelay1. (Recall that η is the global ticker's count.) SCount1 is set to 0 whenever P_1 gets an ACK that causes progress.

SCount2: Same as SCount1, except that (D,Source[n], n mod 2), C_1 and P_2 are replaced by (ACK, n+1 mod 2), C_2 and P_1.

ReferenceTime: Value of η when P_1 last got an ACK that caused progress.

ResetTime: Value of η when P_1 last reset.

With all these auxiliary variables, the real-time specification can be stated as

$$P_1 \text{ at RESET} \Rightarrow (\text{ResetTime - ReferenceTime}) \leq T \\ \quad \textbf{and } \text{SCount1} + \text{SCount2} \geq \text{MaxRetryCount}.$$

Notice that this real-time specification is a safety assertion and not a liveness assertion requiring the leads-to operator. Its verification can be found in Part 1 of [8].

Acknowledgement

The work reported in this article was supported by a grant from the National Science Foundation (Grant No. ECS 83-04734).

REFERENCES

[1] International Standards' Organization, "Data Communication--High-level Data Link Control Procedures--Frame Structure," Ref. No. ISO 3309, Second Edition, 1979. "Data Communications--HDLC Procedures--Elements of Procedures," Ref. No. ISO 4335, First Edition, 1979. International Standards Organization, Geneva, Switzerland.

[2] IEEE Project 802 Local Area Network Standards, "CSMA/CD Access Method and Physical Layer Specifications," Draft IEEE Standard 802.3, Revision D, December 1982.

[3] Postel, J. (ed.), "DOD Standard Transmission Control Protocol," Defense Advanced Research Projects Agency, Information Processing Techniques Office, RFC 761, IEN 129, January 1980; in *ACM Computer Communication Review*, Vol. 10, No. 4, October 1980, pp. 52-132.

[4] Clark, D. D., "Protocol Implementation: Practical Considerations," ACM SIGCOMM'83 Tutorial, University of Texas at Austin, March 7, 1983.

[5] Shankar, A. U. and S. S. Lam, "An HDLC Protocol Specification and its Verification Using Image Protocols," *ACM Trans. on Computer Systems*, Vol. 1, No. 4, November 1983, pp. 331-368.

[6] Owicki, S. and L. Lamport, "Proving Liveness Properties of Concurrent Programs," *ACM TOPLAS*, Vol. 4, No. 3, July 1982, pp. 455-495.

[7] Lam, S. S. and A. U. Shankar, "Protocol Verification via Projections," *IEEE Trans. on Software Eng.,* Vol. SE-10, No. 4, July 1984, pp. 325-342.

[8] Shankar, A. U. and S. S. Lam, "Specification and Verification of Communication Networks, Part 1: Safety, Liveness and Real-time Properties; Part 2: Method of Projections," Tech. Rep. in preparation, Dept. of Computer Sciences, Univ. of Texas at Austin, 1984.

[9] Lamport, L, "Time, Clocks, and the Ordering of Events in a Distributed System," *Comm. ACM,* Vol. 21, No. 7, July 1978, pp. 558-565.

[10] Sloan, L., "Mechanisms that Enforce Bounds on Packet Lifetimes," *ACM Trans. Comput. Syst.*, Vol. 1, No. 4, Nov. 1983, pp. 311-330.

[11] Dijkstra, E. W., *A Discipline of Programming,* Prentice-Hall, Englewood Cliffs, N.J., 1976.